RoboHELP® 2000 Bible

RoboHELP® 2000 Bible

John Hedtke and Elisabeth Knottingham

IDG Books Worldwide, Inc.
An International Data Group Company

Foster City, CA ✦ Chicago, IL ✦ Indianapolis, IN ✦ New York, NY

RoboHELP® 2000 Bible

Published by
IDG Books Worldwide, Inc.
An International Data Group Company
919 E. Hillsdale Blvd., Suite 400
Foster City, CA 94404
www.idgbooks.com (IDG Books Worldwide Web site)

ISBN: 0-7645-4644-9

Printed in the United States of America

10 9 8 7 6 5 4 3 2 1

1B/QT/QY/QQ/FC

Distributed in the United States by IDG Books Worldwide, Inc.

Distributed by CDG Books Canada Inc. for Canada; by Transworld Publishers Limited in the United Kingdom; by IDG Norge Books for Norway; by IDG Sweden Books for Sweden; by IDG Books Australia Publishing Corporation Pty. Ltd. for Australia and New Zealand; by TransQuest Publishers Pte Ltd. for Singapore, Malaysia, Thailand, Indonesia, and Hong Kong; by Gotop Information Inc. for Taiwan; by ICG Muse, Inc. for Japan; by Intersoft for South Africa; by Eyrolles for France; by International Thomson Publishing for Germany, Austria, and Switzerland; by Distribuidora Cuspide for Argentina; by LR International for Brazil; by Galileo Libros for Chile; by Ediciones ZETA S.C.R. Ltda. for Peru; by WS Computer Publishing Corporation, Inc., for the Philippines; by Contemporanea de Ediciones for Venezuela; by Express Computer Distributors for the Caribbean and West Indies; by Micronesia Media Distributor, Inc. for Micronesia; by Chips Computadoras S.A. de C.V. for Mexico; by Editorial Norma de Panama S.A. for Panama; by American Bookshops for Finland.

For general information on IDG Books Worldwide's books in the U.S., please call our Consumer Customer Service department at 800-762-2974. For reseller information, including discounts and premium sales, please call our Reseller Customer Service department at 800-434-3422.

For information on where to purchase IDG Books Worldwide's books outside the U.S., please contact our International Sales department at 317-596-5530 or fax 317-572-4002.

For consumer information on foreign language translations, please contact our Customer Service department at 800-434-3422, fax 317-572-4002, or e-mail rights@idgbooks.com.

For information on licensing foreign or domestic rights, please phone +1-650-653-7098.

For sales inquiries and special prices for bulk quantities, please contact our Order Services department at 800-434-3422 or write to the address above.

For information on using IDG Books Worldwide's books in the classroom or for ordering examination copies, please contact our Educational Sales department at 800-434-2086 or fax 317-572-4005.

For press review copies, author interviews, or other publicity information, please contact our Public Relations department at 650-653-7000 or fax 650-653-7500.

For authorization to photocopy items for corporate, personal, or educational use, please contact Copyright Clearance Center, 222 Rosewood Drive, Danvers, MA 01923, or fax 978-750-4470.

Library of Congress Cataloging-in-Publication Data

Hedtke, John V.
RoboHelp 2000 Bible / John Hedtke and Elisabeth Knottingham.
p. cm.
ISBN 0-7645-4644-9 (alk. paper)
1. RoboHELP (Computer file) I. Knottingham, Elisabeth, 1973- II. Title.
QA76.76.I59 H54 2000
005.3--dc21 00-031971
CIP

ABOUT IDG BOOKS WORLDWIDE

Welcome to the world of IDG Books Worldwide.

IDG Books Worldwide, Inc., is a subsidiary of International Data Group, the world's largest publisher of computer-related information and the leading global provider of information services on information technology. IDG was founded more than 30 years ago by Patrick J. McGovern and now employs more than 9,000 people worldwide. IDG publishes more than 290 computer publications in over 75 countries. More than 90 million people read one or more IDG publications each month.

Launched in 1990, IDG Books Worldwide is today the #1 publisher of best-selling computer books in the United States. We are proud to have received eight awards from the Computer Press Association in recognition of editorial excellence and three from Computer Currents' First Annual Readers' Choice Awards. Our best-selling *...For Dummies®* series has more than 50 million copies in print with translations in 31 languages. IDG Books Worldwide, through a joint venture with IDG's Hi-Tech Beijing, became the first U.S. publisher to publish a computer book in the People's Republic of China. In record time, IDG Books Worldwide has become the first choice for millions of readers around the world who want to learn how to better manage their businesses.

Our mission is simple: Every one of our books is designed to bring extra value and skill-building instructions to the reader. Our books are written by experts who understand and care about our readers. The knowledge base of our editorial staff comes from years of experience in publishing, education, and journalism — experience we use to produce books to carry us into the new millennium. In short, we care about books, so we attract the best people. We devote special attention to details such as audience, interior design, use of icons, and illustrations. And because we use an efficient process of authoring, editing, and desktop publishing our books electronically, we can spend more time ensuring superior content and less time on the technicalities of making books.

You can count on our commitment to deliver high-quality books at competitive prices on topics you want to read about. At IDG Books Worldwide, we continue in the IDG tradition of delivering quality for more than 30 years. You'll find no better book on a subject than one from IDG Books Worldwide.

John Kilcullen
Chairman and CEO
IDG Books Worldwide, Inc.

Eighth Annual Computer Press Awards 1992

Ninth Annual Computer Press Awards 1993

X
WINNER

Tenth Annual Computer Press Awards 1994

Eleventh Annual Computer Press Awards 1995

IDG is the world's leading IT media, research and exposition company. Founded in 1964, IDG had 1997 revenues of $2.05 billion and has more than 9,000 employees worldwide. IDG offers the widest range of media options that reach IT buyers in 75 countries representing 95% of worldwide IT spending. IDG's diverse product and services portfolio spans six key areas including print publishing, online publishing, expositions and conferences, market research, education and training, and global marketing services. More than 90 million people read one or more of IDG's 290 magazines and newspapers, including IDG's leading global brands — Computerworld, PC World, Network World, Macworld and the Channel World family of publications. IDG Books Worldwide is one of the fastest-growing computer book publishers in the world, with more than 700 titles in 36 languages. The "...For Dummies®" series alone has more than 50 million copies in print. IDG offers online users the largest network of technology-specific Web sites around the world through IDG.net (http://www.idg.net), which comprises more than 225 targeted Web sites in 55 countries worldwide. International Data Corporation (IDC) is the world's largest provider of information technology data, analysis and consulting, with research centers in over 41 countries and more than 400 research analysts worldwide. IDG World Expo is a leading producer of more than 168 globally branded conferences and expositions in 35 countries including E3 (Electronic Entertainment Expo), Macworld Expo, ComNet, Windows World Expo, ICE (Internet Commerce Expo), Agenda, DEMO, and Spotlight. IDG's training subsidiary, ExecuTrain, is the world's largest computer training company, with more than 230 locations worldwide and 785 training courses. IDG Marketing Services helps industry-leading IT companies build international brand recognition by developing global integrated marketing programs via IDG's print, online and exposition products worldwide. Further information about the company can be found at www.idg.com.

1/26/00

Credits

Acquisitions Editors
John Osborn
Sherri Morningstar

Project Editor
Eric Newman

Technical Editors
Lori J. McDermeit
Brenda P. Huettner

Copy Editors
Mildred Sanchez
Luann Rouff

Proof Editor
Neil Romanosky

Project Coordinators
Joe Shines
Danette Nurse

Media Development Manager
Laura Carpenter

Graphics and Production Specialists
Robert Bihlmayer
Jude Levinson
Michael Lewis
Victor Pérez-Varela
Ramses Ramirez

Quality Control Technician
Dina F Quan

Book Designer
Drew R. Moore

Illustrators
Mary Jo Weis
Karl Brandt
Gabriele McCann

Proofreading and Indexing
York Production Services

Cover Illustrator
Larry S. Wilson

About the Authors

John Hedtke is an international award-winning author with over two decades in the software business, including five years as a programmer/analyst and seven years in technical publications management. He has done 21 books on a wide variety of topics, including two books on MP3 files and how to create and use them and two books on assorted Windows shareware programs. John has also written more than 60 software manuals and online help systems and has published dozens of articles in magazines such as *Windows*, *Publish!*, *PC Magazine*, and *Accounting Technology*. He has won 19 regional and international writing awards to date. John does frequent speaking appearances and occasionally consults on how to set up Technical Publications departments. John is also very active in the Society of Technical Communication, of which he is a senior member and Past President of the Puget Sound chapter.

John attended Reed College in Portland, Oregon, in the early 1970s. When not otherwise engaged at the computer, John cooks, plays the banjo, sings with The Washingtonians, and travels to other countries. John lives in Seattle with two large cats, pictures of which, along with a complete bibliography of books, articles, and awards, can be found at his Web site, `http://www.hedtke.com`.

Elisabeth Knottingham has a bachelor's degree in Physics and English from the University of Washington in Seattle. She was a contributing author on *Peachtree Complete Business Toolkit*, in which she described in detail how to design and maintain a Web site from the viewpoint of a novice Web user and designer. Elisabeth has also done HTML consulting and training seminars for several companies and organizations and has conducted seminars in basic, intermediate, and advanced HTML, Java, and CGI for technical communications specialists. Her most recent book is the best-selling *Visio 2000: The Official Guide*.

Elisabeth lives in Seattle with her husband, Lonnie Foster. They have two cats, who are larger and smarter than John's cats.

To Constance. . .

. . . without whom I would still be impossible. —John

. . . because you told me I could, and you were right. —Elisabeth

Foreword

Welcome to the world of RoboHELP Office 2000 — the industry standard for developing electronic Help and user assistance. RoboHELP Office speeds and enhances the development of integrated Help systems that improve the usability of desktop software and Web-based applications.

For virtually the past decade, RoboHELP has led the industry as the best-selling tool for creating online Help and user assistance. Today, RoboHELP is used for far more than just authoring traditional Windows-based Help systems — RoboHELP is now the tool of choice for a variety of other projects, including the creation of Web-based user assistance, cross-platform and cross-browser Help, informational Web site user assistance, electronic performance support systems, and other highly effective intranet manuals and documentation.

You should not underestimate the value that RoboHELP will provide to your organization. In addition to making the job of a technical writer much easier, the proactive "self-help" systems created with RoboHELP can raise end-user satisfaction levels, decrease support costs, and increase overall profitability. This is of critical importance in today's highly competitive and cost-conscious business environment.

RoboHELP 2000 Bible is the most comprehensive book written about RoboHELP Office to date. Whether you have used a previous version of RoboHELP and now want to get up to speed on version 2000, or you are completely new to RoboHELP and the process of developing user assistance, *RoboHELP 2000 Bible* will be a valuable reference guide.

Take advantage of *RoboHELP 2000 Bible* as a companion to the award-winning online Help, tutorials, and documentation that are included with RoboHELP Office. eHelp Corporation also provides many other valuable resources to help you get the most out of your investment in RoboHELP Office, including the free online RoboHELP Community (`http://www.ehelp.com/helpcommunity`), the RoboHELP Training Solutions Program, and much more.

If you would like more information about RoboHELP or any of these support programs, please call us from within the U.S. at 800-459-2356 or from outside the U.S. at +1-858-459-6365. You can also visit our Web site at `http://www.ehelp.com`.

eHelp Corporation is committed to providing the industry's most innovative and powerful solutions for all your online Help, user assistance, and electronic documentation needs. We look forward to working with you for many years to come.

Christopher P. Calisi
Chief Executive Officer
eHelp Corporation (formerly Blue Sky Software)

Preface

RoboHELP Office 2000 is is the best-selling help development tool for creating and maintaining WinHelp, WinHelp 2000, HTML Help, WebHelp, JavaHelp, and Netscape NetHelp. While it's possible to develop WinHelp and HTML Help using the basic WinHelp and HTML Help tools and compiler, RoboHELP automates and simplifies almost all of the phases of the help development process. RoboHELP Office 2000 has many improvements over previous versions of the product, including:

- **Microsoft Word 2000 support.** RoboHELP Office 2000 integrates fully with Microsoft Word 2000 to take advantage of its new features. You can also use Microsoft Word 2000 to edit WinHelp and HTML-based projects. RoboHELP Office 2000 also still supports Word 95 and Word 97.
- **New WinHelp features.** RoboHELP Office 2000 has many new features for you to use when creating WinHelp projects, including the following:
  - Ceating HTML topics within WinHelp projects
  - Adding jumps from WinHelp systems to individual HTML files and compiled HTML Help projects
  - Improved importing of Word documents
  - New Online Book templates for application help, policies and procedures documents, and textbook online help
- **New WinHelp 2000 features.** WinHelp 2000 is a split-screen view for WinHelp that displays the table of contents or index at all times. There are extensive navigational features, including a Smart See Also button that automatically detects topics related to the current topic. The new version of WinHelp 2000 can also display secondary windows.
- **New HTML Help features.** RoboHELP Office 2000 provides complete support for all major features in HTML Help v1.21, including the following:
  - Full-text search to look for words or phrases not already indexed
  - A Favorites tab for accessing important topics that you access frequently
  - Support for browse sequences in HTML Help projects
  - Spell checking for an entire HTML Help project
  - Improved hotspot graphic features — you can change a graphic without disturbing the existing hotspots associated with the graphic

- New expanding and drop-down text features that let you add stepwise procedures, glossaries, and other features
- Better conversions from WinHelp—you can quickly and cleanly convert an existing WinHelp project to a complete HTML Help project that includes styles, browse sequences, and context-sensitive links
- Glossary support—you can add glossary items manually or with the RoboHELP Glossary Wizard
- Build tag support for conditional compilations

✦ **New HTML Help tools and utilities.** RoboHELP Office 2000 has expanded its tools and utilities to include HTML Help Studio and HTML Help Finder. HTML Help Studio is a utility that can create the source and project files from compiled HTML Help projects, a boon if you need to re-create lost or damaged source files. HTML Help Finder looks for HTML Help (CHM) files and displays information about them. You can also use the HTML Help Finder to move or delete individual HTML Help files. In addition, RoboHELP Office 2000 contains HTML Help BugHunter, a testing and debugging tool for context-sensitive HTML Help, and Find HTML Help Components, a search tool that lets you find and display information about HTML Help project components such as dynamic link libraries, executable programs, and ActiveX controls.

✦ **Dynamic HTML support.** Dynamic HTML is a powerful new feature for HTML Help supported in RoboHELP Office 2000. You can use Dynamic HTML to add extensive multimedia effects to your HTML Help projects. With Dynamic HTML, you can create many different special visual effects, including zooms, fade-ins, fade-outs, elastic screens, fly-ins, fly-outs, expanding and contracting, glows, spirals, changes triggered by mouse location such as color or object size, drop shadows, and page slides. RoboHELP Office 2000 also lets you create self-sizing popups in HTML Help.

✦ **WebHelp 3.** RoboHELP Office 2000 lets you create and maintain WebHelp 3, the most up-to-date version of eHelp's HTML-based online help that is both browser independent and works across many different platforms. The new features include a table of contents, index, full-text search, and See Also topics. You can use WebHelp on Windows 3.1/95/98/NT/2000, Unix, and Macintosh computers with any browser that supports Dynamic HTML or Java.

✦ **The RoboHELP online community.** eHelp has extended its service and support to include an online community that can be accessed directly via the Web through any online help system you create with RoboHELP. This lets you discuss new ways for creating online help with other help developers around the world.

✦ **Better image handling.** RoboHELP Office 2000 now lets you create composite images. You can also insert a new graphic image into a SHED (hotspot) graphic while maintaining the location and features of the existing hotspots. The Image Workshop has also been improved and expanded to allow you to paste images directly from the Windows Explorer.

✦ **JavaHelp development.** In addition to creating WinHelp, HTML Help, and other forms of online help, you can use RoboHELP Office 2000 to create and maintain JavaHelp. Furthermore, you can quickly translate a WinHelp or HTML Help online help project into a complete JavaHelp system, compile it, and run it.

Why You Should Read This Book

This book and CD-ROM combination is the complete compendium of how to use every aspect of RoboHELP. It provides the beginning user of RoboHELP Office 2000 with an introduction to the product and shows how to create WinHelp and HTML Help files. It also shows intermediate and advanced users how to get the most out of RoboHELP Office 2000 and the ancillary tools. Appendixes provide additional information on internal details and a collection of extended resources.

How This Book Is Organized

RoboHELP 2000 Bible has 28 chapters in five parts, seven appendixes, and a glossary. This section describes what you'll find in each part of this book.

Part I: Getting Started

Part I, "Getting Started," introduces you to RoboHELP Office 2000. There are chapters on installing and configuring RoboHELP Office 2000 and a description of the types of online help you can create with it.

Part II: Creating WinHelp

Part II, "Creating WinHelp," shows you how to create a WinHelp project. This part contains chapters on starting a WinHelp project and on adding topics, jumps, and popups, formatting and special effects, and static and hotspot graphics. You also see how to add tables of contents, indexes, and A-Links, and use multiple windows and browse sequences in a WinHelp file.

Part III: Creating Advanced WinHelp Systems

Part III, "Creating Advanced WinHelp Systems," continues with an in-depth discussion of the advanced features of WinHelp systems. In this part, you learn how to create WinHelp macros, work with context-sensitive help, and extend your reach with the Internet and the RoboHELP online community. You'll also see how to add multimedia to your WinHelp file, create What's This? help, use master tables of contents, and manage large WinHelp projects.

Part IV: Creating HTML Help

Part IV, "Creating HTML Help," introduces you to HTML Help. You learn the basics of HTML Help, including how to start an HTML Help project in RoboHELP Office 2000, create topics, add jumps, create graphics, add windows and popups, use styles, use dynamic HTML, and create a table of contents and index.

Part V: Creating Advanced HTML Help

Part V, "Creating Advanced HTML Help," shows you the advanced features of HTML Help systems. In this part, you learn how to print the RoboHELP HTML Help reports, create context-sensitive HTML Help, use forms and frames, and create WebHelp, JavaHelp, and Netscape NetHelp.

Appendixes and Glossary

The book concludes with a number of useful appendixes. Appendix A, "The WinHelp HPJ File," lists the sections and options found in the HPJ file. Appendix B, "Footnote Symbols," is a quick reference for the footnote symbols used in WinHelp files. Appendix C, "Reports," is a list of all the reports in RoboHELP Office 2000 and a brief description of each one. Appendix D, "Resources," contains a variety of online and printed resources for help developers. Appendix E, "Installing RoboHELP 2000," is a quick reference guide to installing the product. Appendix F, "HTML Quick Guide," is a brief guide to HTML. Appendix G, "What's on the CD-ROM?" describes the contents of the accompanying CD-ROM and tells how to make use of them.

Conventions

This book uses some special conventions that make the material easier to follow and understand:

- Key combinations such as Ctrl+Alt+Delete are joined by plus signs.
- Menu choices use a notation like File ⇨ Edit, which means to choose File from the menu bar, and then choose Edit.
- *Italic text* indicates new terms or placeholders and is also sometimes used for emphasis.
- `Monospaced text` indicates code, on-screen text, or an Internet address.

A Caution icon indicates a procedure that could potentially cause difficulty or even data loss.

Cross-Reference icons point to additional information about a topic, which you can find in other sections of the book.

A Note icon contains a noteworthy piece of information aside from the text.

An On the CD-ROM icon points to information available on the CD-ROM that accompanies this book.

A Tip icon provides useful techniques and helpful hints.

What Is a Sidebar?

Topics in sidebars provide additional information.

Contacting the Authors

This book is perfect. Really. Okay, well, maybe not. . . . We've made every attempt to make sure that this book is complete and correct, but despite our concerted efforts, it's possible that we've left something out or that there's something that isn't right. Should you find an error, please email us at `john@hedtke.com` or `efk@oz.net` and let us know what we need to correct. We're also interested in collecting ideas for ways to improve the book for the next edition. Be sure to check out the WinHelp and HTML Help resources at `www.hedtke.com` as well.

Acknowledgments

This is the largest book either of us has ever done. It was an enormous undertaking that, like any other book, required a network of people making contributions to the finished product. We couldn't have done this without the help of the following people:

- To Lonnie Foster, Elisabeth's partner, who put up with both of us through yet another book.
- To David Rogelberg, Sherry Rogelberg, and Neil Salkind, brilliant and wonderful people all, at Studio B, for really great representation. Thanks, folks — your advice and guidance have made this process much easier.
- To John Osborn, acquisitions editor, who said "Yes" to this book, and to Sherri Morningstar, acquisitions editor, who took over the book after John's departure and brought it to completion.
- To Eric Newman, development editor, who did dazzling editing and project coordination.
- To Lori J. McDermeit of TrainWRITE and to Brenda Huettner, for first-rate technical editing.
- To Mildred Sanchez, copy editor, for amazing copyediting.
- To Neil Romanosky, who was invaluable for his contributions to the artwork on this book and also performed above and beyond the call of duty.
- To the folks who handled the art and production: Linda Marousek, Danette Nurse, Gabriele McCann, Ronald Terry, and Joe Shines.
- To Drew Plastridge, for the chapter on programming for HTML Help and for compiling Appendixes A, B, C, and E.
- To Dave Versdahl, for the chapter on WebHelp, JavaHelp, and Netscape NetHelp.
- To Grant Thornley, for the chapter on HTML Help frames and forms.
- To Suzanne Hardy, for writing the chapter on HTML Help tables of contents and indexes.
- To Kevin Murray, for compiling the glossary.
- To Shannon Shepherd, who did technical reviews on the WinHelp half of the book.

- To Brian Chinn, resident hardware guru, without whom John's computers would doubtless fall apart at the seams.
- To the many wonderful people at eHelp:
  - Christopher P. Calisi, Chief Executive Officer of eHelp.
  - Jorgen Lien, Chairman of the Board of eHelp.
  - Kim Himstreet, Public Relations Specialist, who has been supportive and generous with her time and information. Thank you, Kim—you're *such* a gem to work with.
  - Michael I. Jacobs, Drew Plastridge, Stephen Rossell, Matthew Brown, Jack George, the noble tech support staff led by the brilliant and dynamic Julia Haas, for advice and problem resolution.
  - Keri York, Meggan Kring, Jay Dixit, Jerry McCorkle, Suzanne Hardy, Teri Browne, Maria Banting, David Beck, Phil Branum, Mike Cribier, Jason Eberwein, Vartouhi Galpchian, Robert Hollinger, Michael McLain, Anthony Nelson, Raul Ramos, and a list of other great tech support and development staff too numerous to mention.
- To Jim Lane, for information on Irish music.
- To Lonnie Foster, for the graphics and for the ducks.
- To Zen, for keeping Elisabeth sane.
- To Cara Arnold and David Truman, for contributing great ideas on ways to use RoboHELP.
- To Guy and Rebecca Champ, co-founders of Foggan Drizzle.
- To Sandy Bradley, for being herself, dazzlingly.
- To Paul Magid for being a brilliant entertainer and for creating Magid's Law: "It doesn't matter how you get there if you don't know where you're going."

The following people and companies have also been very supportive and are greatly deserving of recognition:

- Patricia Roché of IMSI, for information on Hijaak Pro.
- Paul Daniel of JASC, Inc., and Ted Mills of Shandwick International, for information about Paint Shop Pro and other fine JASC products.
- Nancy Rosenberg of Inner Media, for information about Collage Complete.
- Diane Bush, Marti Lucich, and Luana Hancock, of Waggener Edstrom, for information about Microsoft Office 2000.
- Bob Berry of Canyon State Systems and Software, for information about CompuShow 32.

Finally, to Azymuth, B.C., Puck, and Willow, for reminding us that we had to get up on schedule if for no other reason than they needed to be fed.

To all these people we've mentioned and to any we may have inadvertently omitted, our deep and continuing thanks for your help and support.

Contents at a Glance

Contents

Getting Started

P A R T

I

✦ ✦ ✦ ✦

In This Part

✦ ✦ ✦ ✦

Installing and Configuring RoboHELP Office 2000

✦ ✦ ✦ ✦

In This Chapter

Introducing RoboHELP Office 2000

Checking system requirements

Installing RoboHELP Office 2000

Exploring the parts of RoboHELP Office 2000

Learning what's new in RoboHELP Office 2000

Getting more information

✦ ✦ ✦ ✦

This chapter tells you how to install RoboHELP Office 2000 and introduces you to the various parts of the product. It also shows you what's new in RoboHELP Office 2000 (that is, what's changed since the previous version) and how to get more information about RoboHELP and creating and maintaining online help.

Introducing RoboHELP Office 2000

RoboHELP Office 2000 is the latest release of eHelp Corporation's (formerly Blue Sky Software) help development suite. RoboHELP Office 2000 makes it easy to create various online help files, including WinHelp and HTML Help for Windows 3.*x*, Windows 95, Windows 98, and Windows 2000; cross-platform WebHelp for Windows, Unix, Macintosh, and intranet and Internet sites; and the new JavaHelp format from Sun Microsystems.

Although you can create WinHelp and HTML Help using Word for Windows and the standard Microsoft WinHelp and HTML Help compilers, RoboHELP Office 2000 automates many of the tedious tasks of the help creation process. Creating basic online help is relatively simple, but many of the tasks are fairly mechanical and can be automated.

The heart of RoboHELP Office 2000 is a suite of macros and templates that are loaded into Microsoft Word for Windows. RoboHELP Office 2000 also comes with external programs such as the RoboHELP Explorer, a program for managing help projects and help project information, and a number of utilities that assist you by converting help projects from one format to another, importing information, and debugging and enhancing your help projects. These macros, templates, and programs eliminate almost all of the mechanical parts of the help creation process, leaving you free to design, write, and polish the help project without having to do jobs the computer can do for you.

System Requirements

You don't need a lot of computer to install RoboHELP Office 2000. To install RoboHELP Office 2000, you must have the following minimum hardware and software:

- 486 processor or faster (Pentium or better is recommended)
- 16 MB of RAM (24 MB or more is recommended)
- Any version of Microsoft Windows 95, Windows 98, Windows NT 4.*x*, or Windows 2000
- Microsoft Word for Windows 95, 97, or 2000
- 45 MB of disk space for the installed RoboHELP Office 2000 files

Microsoft Word requires at least 64 MB of free disk space for its own temporary disk storage when you're editing files.

Generally speaking, if you're already running any version of Windows 9*x* or NT with Word for Windows 97 or Word 2000, you should be able to install RoboHELP Office 2000 with no problems.

Installing RoboHELP Office 2000

Installing RoboHELP Office 2000 is a simple, automated process. You need to make a few choices to identify the options to install and then let RoboHELP Office 2000 install itself.

Although you don't have to have Word for Windows present on your system before you install RoboHELP Office 2000, you'll need to install it before you can start using RoboHELP Office 2000.

To install RoboHELP Office 2000 on your system, do the following:

1. Insert the RoboHELP Office 2000 CD in your CD-ROM drive.

   If your computer has Autorun enabled, the RoboHELP Office 2000 Setup program will start. Otherwise, perform steps 2 and 3.

2. From the Windows Taskbar, select Start ➪ Run.
3. Select Setup.exe on the RoboHELP Office 2000 CD.
4. Follow the instructions on the screen for installing the RoboHELP Office 2000 software.

   You'll need to enter the serial number on the CD envelope as part of the registration process.

If you haven't already purchased RoboHELP Office 2000, you can install the demo version from the CD accompanying this book.

Even if you have a fast CD-ROM drive, the installation process will take a while. There's a lot of material to install.

If you plan to work with HTML Help and you haven't already installed Internet Explorer 4.0 or 5.0 on your computer, you can elect to install Internet Explorer 5.0 as part of the RoboHELP Office 2000 installation process. If Internet Explorer 5.0 is installed already on your system (as part of Windows 98 or Windows 2000), you don't need to install it again.

Taking Your First Look at RoboHELP Office 2000

As part of the installation process, RoboHELP Office 2000 creates the desktop icons shown in Table 1-1. Each of these starts a different portion of RoboHELP.

Table 1-1
The RoboHELP Desktop Icons

Toolbar Item	*Description*
	Starts RoboHELP (also known as "RoboHELP Classic"). Use this icon if you want to create a new WinHelp project or open an existing one.
	Starts RoboHELP HTML Edition. Use this icon if you want to create a new HTML Help project or open an existing one.

Continued

Table 1-1 (continued)

Toolbar Item	Description
	Starts RoboHELP Office. Use this if you want to access a tool without having to open a WinHelp or HTML Help project. (You can create or open projects from the RoboHELP Office windows, but you'll probably find it easier to access a project through the RoboHELP Classic or RoboHELP HTML Edition icons.)

The next section shows you how to start RoboHELP Classic, RoboHELP HTML Edition, and RoboHELP Office.

Starting RoboHELP Classic

To start RoboHELP Classic and take a look around, do the following:

1. Double-click the RoboHELP icon (see the first icon in Table 1-1) that the installation placed on the desktop. As an alternative, you can go to the Windows Taskbar and select Start ➪ Programs ➪ RoboHELP Office ➪ RoboHELP.

   The Open a Help Project dialog box appears, as shown in Figure 1-1.

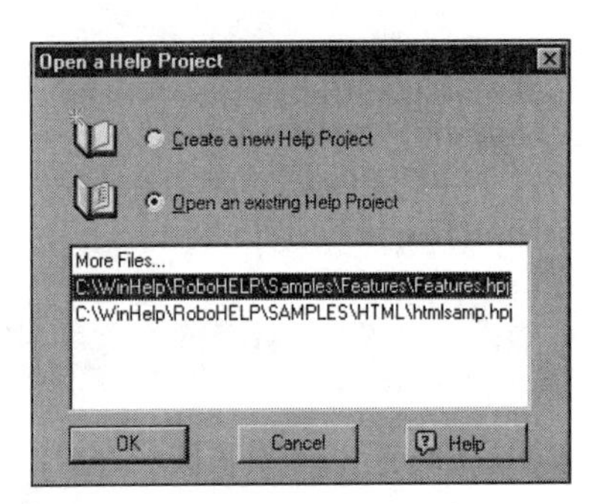

Figure 1-1: The Open a Help Project dialog box

2. From the Open a Help Project dialog box, you can open an existing help project or create a new one. For now, select the Features.hpj project (selected in Figure 1-1) to start RoboHELP and examine the various features and toolbars.

   After you click OK to open this sample file, RoboHELP Office 2000 starts the RoboHELP Explorer (shown in Figure 1-2) and Word for Windows.

If you have the RoboHELP Tip Wizard turned on, you'll see a sample tip for making the most of RoboHELP Office 2000 when you start up. You can turn the Tip Wizard off by clicking Turn Off Tips on the Tip Wizard's button bar.

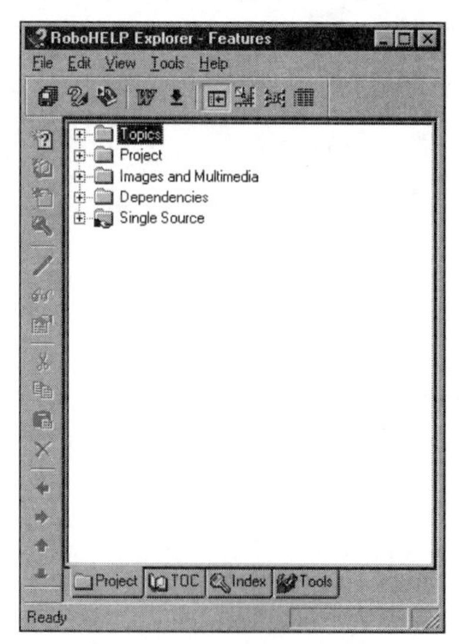

Figure 1-2: The RoboHELP Explorer

The RoboHELP Explorer helps you manage your help project's various source files, pictures, and other elements. There are a number of tools for testing, debugging, and modifying your help projects. You can also use the RoboHELP Explorer to access most of RoboHELP's other utilities and features.

There are four tabs located at the bottom of the RoboHELP Explorer that you will use to manage your help files:

✦ **The Project Manager.** The Project Manager (selected in Figure 1-2) is the default option for the RoboHELP Explorer and the one that you'll use the most. The Project Manager lets you manage the specific elements of your help files using a standard folder style. You can display information about any specific project element by clicking the plus sign to the left of the folder icon and thus expanding the folder contents. You'll see how to use and apply these features in the Project Manager window in Part II, "Creating WinHelp."

✦ **The TOC Composer.** The TOC Composer (see Figure 1-3) shows the table of contents (TOC). You can use the TOC Composer to reorganize your help project, create new entries in your TOC, and create new topic headers in the help project. The TOC Composer is also useful for creating a TOC for your help file if it doesn't already have one.

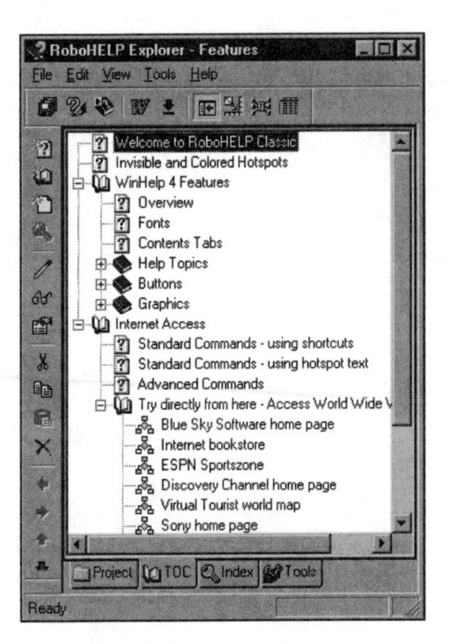

Figure 1-3: The RoboHELP Explorer showing the TOC window

The features in the TOC Composer are described in Chapter 8, "Using Tables of Contents and Indexes."

✦ **The Index Designer.** The Index Designer (Figure 1-4) is a very helpful tool for managing one of the more confusing parts of help project creation and maintenance: indexing and keywords. You can use the Index Designer to add keywords to your help project or to change or delete them. The Index Designer shows you the current index at all times.

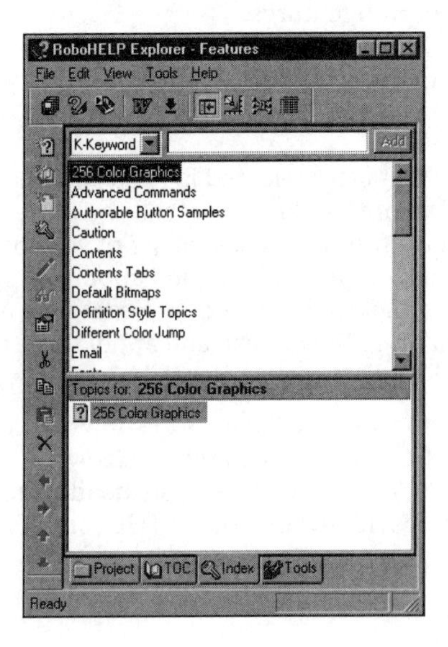

Figure 1-4: The RoboHELP Explorer showing the Index Designer window

✦ **Tools.** RoboHELP also comes with a variety of tools for creating and maintaining your help projects. The tools are covered throughout this book. You can also right-click in the Tools window (Figure 1-5) to add icons for some of your favorite programs and files.

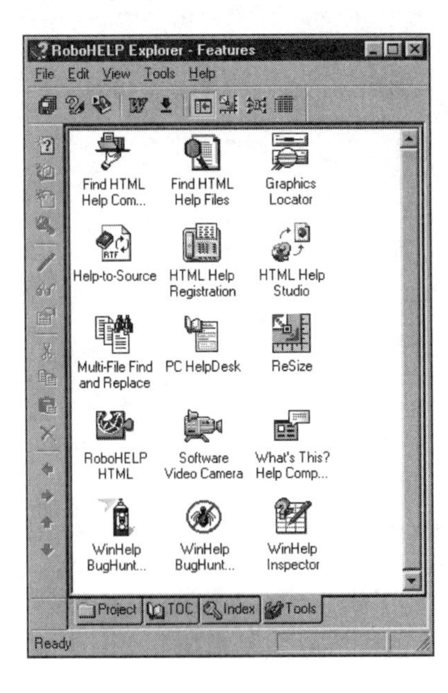

Figure 1-5: The RoboHELP Explorer showing the Tools window

The RoboHELP Explorer has right-pane tabs appearing to the right of the pane that you've already seen that display additional information about the help project. You display the right pane by selecting View ⇨ Hide Right Pane. Figure 1-6 shows the RoboHELP Explorer with the right pane showing topics in the sample help project opened earlier. As you can see, it has an interface similar to that of the Windows Explorer.

The right pane of the RoboHELP Explorer also has multiple options that you can select by clicking the following tabs:

✦ **Topic List.** The Topic List (shown in Figure 1-6) is the default option for the right pane. The Topic List shows each topic and its related information in the help project. You can also use the Topic List to make changes to several topics at once.

Chapter 4, "Adding Jumps and Popups," demonstrates how you will most frequently use the Topics window.

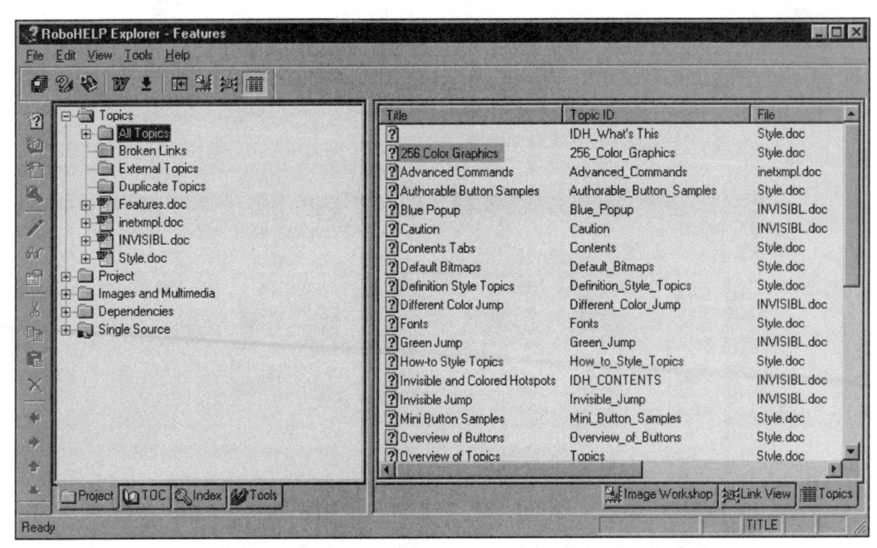

Figure 1-6: The RoboHELP Explorer showing both panes displayed

✦ **Image Workshop.** The Image Workshop (shown in Figure 1-7) is a built-in image manager and simple graphics editor. You can view images, crop them, create hotspot graphics (images with embedded hyperlinks), and so on. The Image Workshop also lets you convert graphics from one format to another.

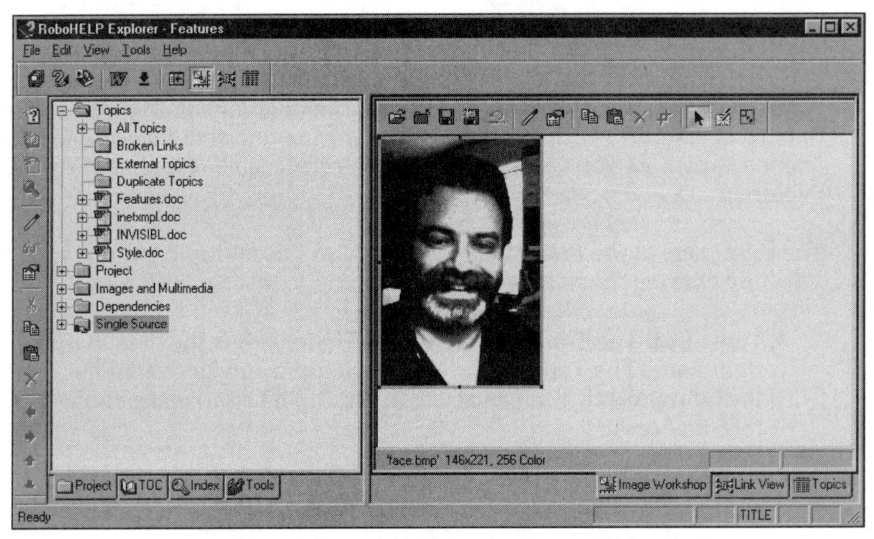

Figure 1-7: The Image Workshop with a sample picture file loaded

You'll see how to use the Image Workshop in Chapter 6, "Adding Simple Graphics," and Chapter 7, "Getting Fancy with Graphics."

✦ **Link View.** The Link View (shown in Figure 1-8) is a graphic display of how topics are linked to other topics. With this, you can follow links between topics, identify and fix broken links, change links and topics, and check complete browse sequences. (Browse sequences let the user page through sections of a help file.)

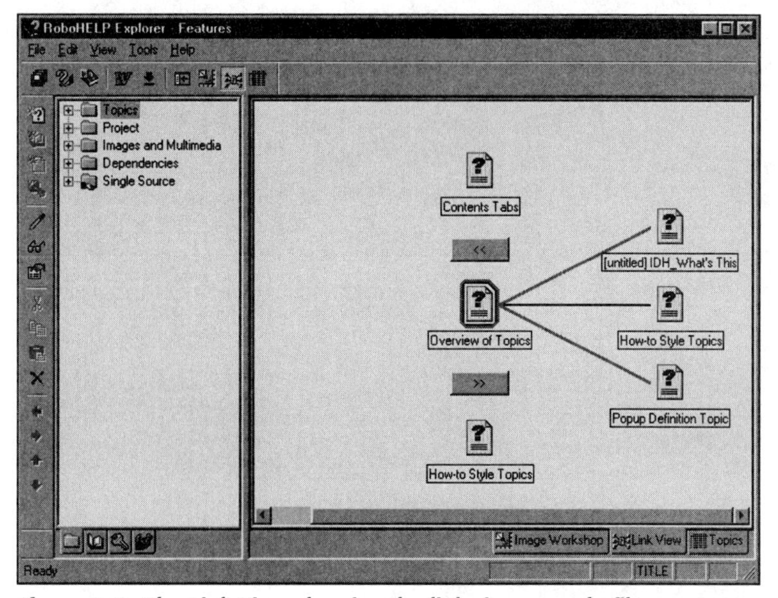

Figure 1-8: The Link View showing the links in a sample file

The Link View is covered in Chapter 8, "Using Tables of Contents and Indexes," and Chapter 9, "Using Help Windows and Browse Sequences."

The core of RoboHELP is that it makes use of the extensive features that let you customize and automate Word's features for creating online help.

Starting RoboHELP HTML Edition

Whereas the RoboHELP Classic icon is the way you create and maintain WinHelp projects, RoboHELP HTML Edition is the way you create a new HTML Help project or open an existing one. You'll see how to use RoboHELP HTML Edition in Part IV, "Creating HTML Help."

To start RoboHELP HTML Edition, do the following:

✦ Double-click the RoboHELP HTML Edition icon (see the second icon in Table 1-1). As an alternative, you can also go to the Windows Taskbar and select Start ➪ Programs ➪ RoboHELP Office ➪ RoboHELP HTML Edition.

The RoboHELP HTML Edition screen appears, as shown in Figure 1-9.

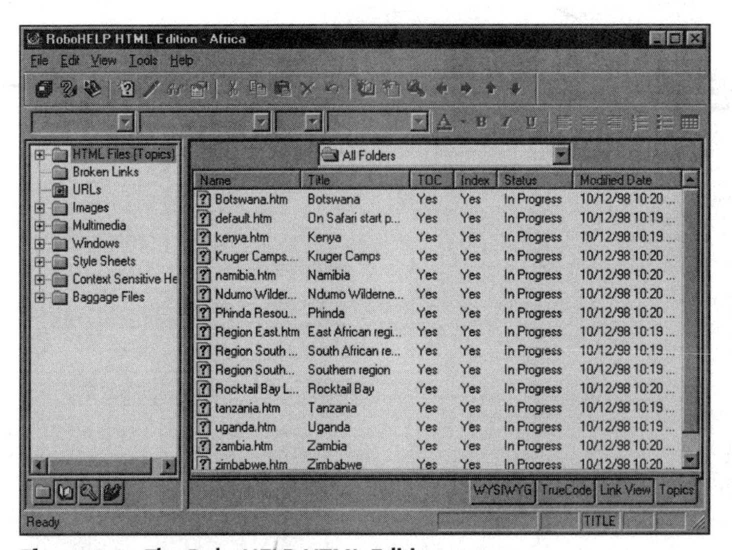

Figure 1-9: The RoboHELP HTML Edition screen

Starting RoboHELP Office

RoboHELP Office provides you with a front end to the entire RoboHELP Office 2000 system. From RoboHELP Office, you can create new WinHelp and HTML Help projects or open existing ones and access RoboHELP tools.

RoboHELP Office is primarily of use if you want to use a RoboHELP tool (such as a decompiler) without having to open a help project. Most help authors tend to use the RoboHELP Classic or RoboHELP HTML Edition icons if they're working with a specific project.

To start RoboHELP Office, do the following:

✦ Double-click the RoboHELP Office icon (see the third icon in Table 1-1). As an alternative, you can also go to the Windows Taskbar and select Start ➪ Programs ➪ RoboHELP Office ➪ RoboHELP Office.

The RoboHELP Office screen appears, as shown in Figure 1-10.

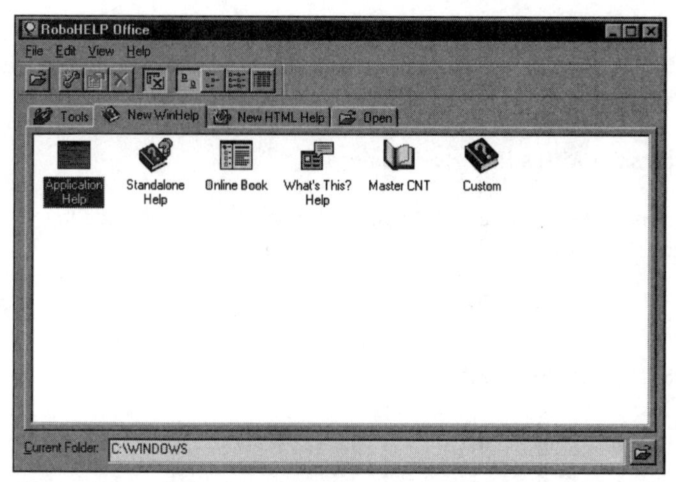

Figure 1-10: The RoboHELP Office screen with the New WinHelp tab displayed

You can use the options on the screen to create a new WinHelp or HTML Help project, open an existing WinHelp or HTML Help project, or access any of the RoboHELP tools (described briefly in the following section).

Using the RoboHELP Office QuickBar

In addition to the desktop icons described in the previous section, RoboHELP Office 2000 has an optional QuickBar that automatically appears as part of your system startup. You can install the QuickBar by doing a Custom rather than a Typical install of RoboHELP Office 2000. In the Custom setup screen, highlight the WinHelp Toolkit option and click Change, then select the RoboHELP Office QuickBar and click OK to install the QuickBar with the rest of RoboHELP Office 2000. Table 1-2 shows you the various icons that appear on the Quick Office Bar and what they do.

Table 1-2
The RoboHELP Office 2000 Quick Office Bar

Toolbar Item	*Description*
	Starts RoboHELP Office
	Starts RoboHELP Classic

Continued

Table 1-2 (continued)

Toolbar Item	Description
	Starts the What's This? Help Composer
	Starts Getting Started with RoboHELP Office, the online guide to RoboHELP Office
	Starts the WinHelp Graphic Locators
	Starts the PC HelpDesk
	Starts ReSize, the RoboHELP image resizing tool
	Starts WinHelp Inspector, a tool for obtaining and reporting information about WinHelp files
	Starts the WinHelp BugHunter, a tool for identifying and fixing bugs
	Starts Software Video Camera, a tool for creating video files of screen activities
	Starts the Video Wizard, which lets you play video and sound files from within WinHelp files
	Starts the WinHelp Compatibility Wizard, a tool for retrofitting Windows 95 help features to a Windows 3.x WinHelp file while letting you continue to run the WinHelp file on Windows 3.x systems
	Starts the WinHelp Hyperviewer Wizard, a tool for adding Hyperviewer and Find+ buttons to a help project
	Starts Help-to-Source, a tool that extracts source files from compiled WinHelp files
	Starts Help-to-Word, a tool for creating formatted Word files from compiled WinHelp files
	Starts Help-to-HTML, a tool for creating HTML Help, Windows CE Help, Netscape NetHelp, web pages, or RoboHELP's WebHelp from a compiled WinHelp file

What's New and Improved in RoboHELP Office 2000?

RoboHELP Office 2000 has many substantial new and enhanced features over previous editions of RoboHELP.

- **eHelp.** eHelp lets the help users click the eHelp button in online help files. eHelp then does a search on the Web for answers to specific questions. eHelp automatically detects the product the help user is using, so the Web search can be targeted to specific products. You can also use eHelp to encourage your help users to interact with online communities and product knowledge bases, and even chat with other product users. There is a new tool called the eHelp Injector, which adds eHelp to help projects that are already compiled. eHelp works with WinHelp, HTML Help, and WebHelp.
- **JavaHelp.** RoboHELP Office 2000 supports JavaHelp 1.0 in its native format. It also provides extensions to JavaHelp in the form of Java- and HTML-compliant browse sequences and "See Also" capability. RoboHELP Office 2000 lets you create JavaHelp optimized for Sun's JavaHelp viewer.

Chapter 28, "Examining WebHelp, JavaHelp, and other Help Systems," introduces you to the basics of creating JavaHelp with RoboHELP Office 2000.

- **Support for Microsoft Office 2000.** RoboHELP Office 2000 provides extended support for the features of Microsoft Office 2000, particularly the HTML publishing features. Word 2000 lets users create and maintain Word DOC and RTF formats, as well as HTML formats, which you can use to create WinHelp, HTML Help, JavaHelp, and WebHelp. (RoboHELP Office 2000 supports the Microsoft Office 95 and Office 97 product suites as well.)
- **Direct conversion of HTML Help from WinHelp.** RoboHELP Office 2000 has a new program for converting WinHelp projects seamlessly into HTML Help projects. The converted HTML Help projects will contain the content, formatting, and style information in the original WinHelp project. In addition, the HTML Help project will have the WinHelp project's browse sequences and even context-sensitive information. RoboHELP Office 2000 also supports self-sizing pop-up windows, a first for HTML Help authoring systems. All this lets you create help systems in WinHelp and convert them to HTML Help or even WebHelp systems with minimum effort.

✦ **New WebHelp features.** RoboHELP Office 2000 has a new version of WebHelp, WebHelp 3, that uses Dynamic HTML. WebHelp 3's primary advantages are that it loads faster and is much more robust than previous versions of WebHelp. WebHelp 3 also supports full-text searches and searches using Boolean operators (such as AND, OR, and NOT) for advanced access to the information in the help project. WebHelp 3 is an excellent solution for cross-platform and intranet online help systems. WebHelp 3 projects also can be converted from Dynamic HTML to straight HTML to accommodate older browsers.

✦ **Image Workshop.** Several image and graphics management utilities from previous versions of RoboHELP Office 2000 were combined into the Image Workshop. The Image Workshop lets you view, edit, and manipulate graphic images. Files in graphics formats that are not directly supported by WinHelp or HTML Help can be converted easily. You can also use the Image Workshop to add, change, or delete hotspots in graphics images. The most significant change in Image Workshop is the ability to paste a new underlying picture in an image or a SHED image.

✦ **Reporting.** Good reports are essential to testing, debugging, and help project source control. RoboHELP Office 2000 comes with 30 reports that you can view or print to help you identify problems, optimize results, and track changes. The new reports are an Images report for RoboHELP Classic and Map IDs and Duplicate Map IDs reports for RoboHELP HTML.

✦ **Supporting utilities.** RoboHELP Office 2000 has a suite of 16 supporting utilities to make it even easier to create first-class WinHelp and HTML Help. Several of these are new or have been updated for this release, including the following:

- Find HTML Help Files, which searches your computer for compiled HTML Help files (CHM files)
- Find HTML Help Components, a new tool (similar to Find HTML Help Files) that searches for HTML Help project components such as dynamic link libraries (DLL files), programs (EXE files), and some ActiveX controls (OCX files)
- HTML Help Registration, another new tool for finding, registering, unregistering and replacing compiled HTML Help files on your computer
- HTML Help Studio, a new tool for creating and maintaining HTML Help
- HTML Help Bug Hunter, a new tool for debugging context-sensitive HTML Help projects

✦ **New Import features in RoboHELP Classic.** Help authors who used previous versions of RoboHELP will appreciate the changes to the import and conversion features. The conversion interface is much simpler and the conversions themselves are smoother and more accurate than in previous versions of the RoboHELP software.

✦ **Support for WinHelp 2000 format.** WinHelp 2000 lets you use a split-screen format for the WinHelp files you create. The users can display secondary windows along with the split screen (or "tri-pane") window, with the TOC on the left side of the screen and the help topic on the right side. RoboHELP Office 2000 offers support for creating and maintaining WinHelp 2000 help projects, particularly in the area of automatically creating "See Also" buttons for related topics, making your finished WinHelp 2000 projects much more effective by adding more cross-references.

✦ **Creation and access of HTML topics from WinHelp files.** RoboHELP Office 2000 lets you create jumps from WinHelp projects to individual HTML files (HTML Help files or local Web page files) and include content from compiled HTML Help files in WinHelp files.

✦ **Quick HTML topics.** RoboHELP Office 2000 supports the quick creation of new HTML topics in HTML Help projects. And, in addition to index keywords, HTML Help also has topic file keywords that let you do searches for specific keywords in topics.

✦ **New WinHelp templates.** RoboHELP templates are useful for starting a new help project and establishing a consistent style for a project from the beginning. There are three new project templates in RoboHELP Office 2000 for creating WinHelp online books: Application Help, Policies & Procedures Guide, and Textbook or Reference Manual.

✦ **Creation master HTML Help projects.** You can combine several smaller HTML Help projects into a single master project, letting you create modular HTML Help systems. This feature is also very useful if you have a team of writers creating a suite of HTML Help. The individual HTML Help projects can be maintained separately, but the tables of contents and indexes are combined when the master project is run, making them appear to be seamless parts of the whole.

✦ **Improved printing of HTML Help projects.** RoboHELP Office 2000 has improved features for printing HTML Help projects, including support for tables of contents and indexing and page references. You can also customize your templates for fancier printed output.

✦ **Self-sizing popups for Dynamic HTML.** RoboHELP Office 2000 supports a new feature for creating attractive, self-sizing Dynamic HTML pop-up windows that do not need to use ActiveX or Java controls. These popups are in addition to the standard HTML Help text-only pop-up windows.

✦ **Glossary support.** Now you can manage glossaries that span multiple HTML Help projects. You can use these glossaries to create glossary terms and definitions in your topic content. The resulting glossary definitions will then be displayed in a Glossary tab in the HTML Help project.

✦ **Advanced HTML Help support.** RoboHELP Office 2000 supports all the advanced features in Microsoft HTML Help 1.2, including a Favorites tab for quick navigation to previous or frequently referenced help topics, comprehensive full-text search features, and associative and keyword links for effective cross-references.

✦ **Build tag support.** WinHelp authors have been able to use build tags for selective compilations. RoboHELP Office 2000 supports build tags for HTML Help projects as well, allowing you greater flexibility for creating and customizing HTML Help files without having to recreate the source files or maintain multiple versions of the help project's source files tailored for each compiled version.

Build tags are discussed in Chapter 24, "Using Reports and Compiling."

✦ **Enhanced Dynamic HTML support.** RoboHELP Office 2000 offers increased support for creating and maintaining Dynamic HTML features and effects.

✦ **Enhanced expanding and drop-down text support.** RoboHELP Office 2000 has more support for drop-down and expanding text. Drop-down text is useful and attractive for displaying sequence steps, additional levels of detail, and so on. You can use dynamic expanding text for a variety of applications, either manually or automatically.

✦ **Spell checking for HTML Help projects.** RoboHELP Office 2000 does global spell check and corrections throughout an HTML Help project, eliminating the need to check each HTML Help help topic separately. As with most other spell checking programs, you can customize the dictionary by adding words.

Getting More Information about RoboHELP

There are many resources for getting more information about RoboHELP Office 2000.

Online Help

RoboHELP Office 2000 has a complete suite of online help about the various products. You can access online help about any specific product or tool by pressing F1. Figure 1-11 shows the main screen for the online help for RoboHELP Classic.

You can also go to the Windows Taskbar and select Start ⇨ Programs ⇨ RoboHELP Office ⇨ Getting Started with RoboHELP Office. Figure 1-12 shows the online help for the RoboHELP Office suite. This provides more of an overview than specific technical information, but it is very helpful if you are new to RoboHELP and would like to get more information about the various products and tools.

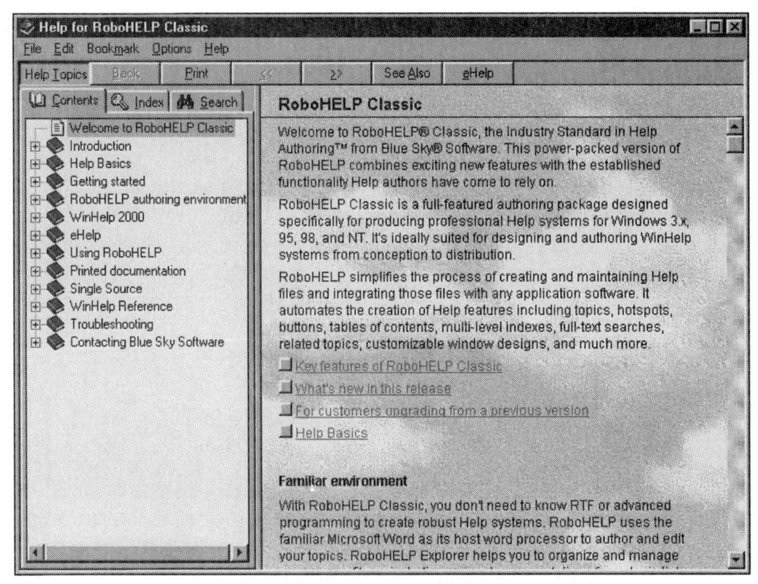

Figure 1-11: The RoboHELP Classic online help

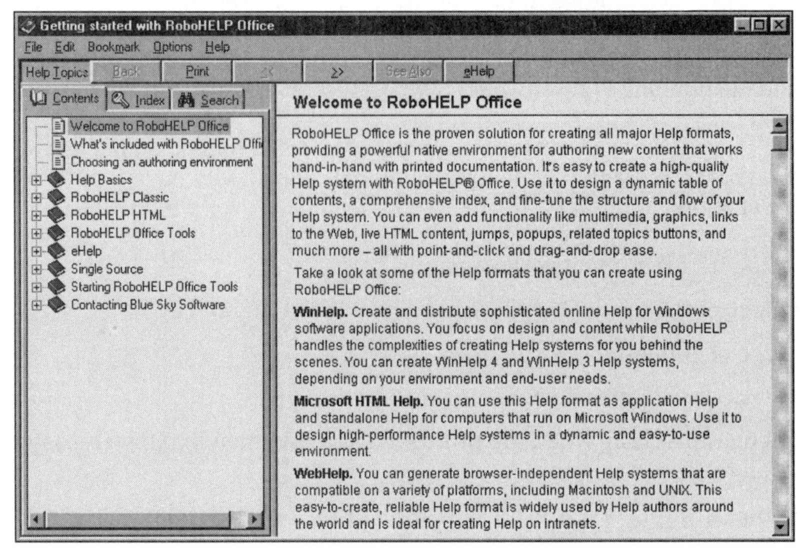

Figure 1-12: The Getting Started with RoboHELP Office online help

Contacting eHelp Corporation

You can contact eHelp Corporation, makers of RoboHELP, for additional information on RoboHELP and online help.

The main mailing address and phone numbers are:

eHelp Corporation
7777 Fay Avenue
La Jolla, CA USA 92037

Voice: 858-551-2485 (M-F from 6:00 A.M. to 5:00 P.M. Pacific time)

Fax: 858-551-2486

The eHelp Corporation Web site is `www.ehelp.com`.

You can also e-mail Technical Support with questions at `support@ehelp.com`. Be sure to include your product's serial number in your e-mail message. (You must be a registered RoboHELP user to use eHelp Corporation technical support. Extended and premium help is also available; check the eHelp Web site for terms.)

There's also a very active RoboHELP Web site at `www.ehelp.com/helpcommunity`. You can access the RoboHELP knowledge base, talk to support technicians and other RoboHELP users, and take part in online forums aimed at specific topics on creating and maintaining WinHelp and HTML Help with RoboHELP Office 2000.

You can call eHelp Corporation technical support at 858-551-5680 on M-F between 8:30 A.M. and 5:00 P.M. Pacific Time. When you call, you should have the following information at hand:

- Your RoboHELP product serial number
- The name of the product and the product version number
- The type of computer you are using
- The version of Windows you are using
- What you were doing when the problem occurred, including the steps up to that point
- The exact wording of any error messages or dialog boxes that appear on the screen
- What you've already tried to solve the problem and the results of your efforts

Other Resources

There are many other resources for getting help and advice on creating and maintaining online help. This section contains a variety of resources you should examine.

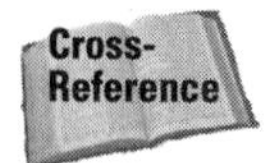

For a more extensive list of books, Web sites, and newsgroups, see Appendix D, "Resources."

Books

For a brief overview of some of RoboHELP's features, you may want to consider the following:

RoboHELP 7 for Dummies, by Jim Meade (IDG Books, 1999). A basic book that will introduce you to the previous version of RoboHELP.

Managing Your Documentation Projects by JoAnn T. Hackos (Wiley & Sons, 1994). An excellent book on how to plan, start, and manage documentation projects.

Designing Online Help for Windows 95 by Scott Boggan, Dave Farkas, and Joe Welinske (Solutions, 1999). The basics of WinHelp 4 using the Microsoft Help Compiler Workshop. Available directly from the Solutions online bookstore at `http://www.sol-sems.com`.

Designing and Writing Online Documentation (2nd Edition) by William Horton (Wiley & Sons, 1994). A guide to designing and creating good online help. Also check out Horton's *Designing Web-Based Training* (Wiley & Sons, 2000).

Web Sites

There are an enormous number of Web sites devoted to RoboHELP support, WinHelp, and HTML Help, as well as professional organizations for technical communicators, including the following:

`http://winwriters.com`: The WinWriters Web site. WinWriters is the premier organization for online help developers. They sponsor the WinWriters Online Help Conferences, publish salary surveys for help developers, and have an enormous variety of resources online. You should make a point of looking at the WinWriters' Online Help Journal at `http://www.ohj.com`.

`http://www.keyworks.net`: The KeyWorks Software Web site. There's a variety of software add-ons and standalone tools that are essential for help developers.

`http://www.helpmaster.com`: Josef Becker's first-rate web site for help developers. The motto, "More stuff than you can find in an hour of searching," is a serious understatement.

`http://www.stc.org` and `http://www.stc-va.org`: The Society for Technical Communication Web sites. An international professional organization for technical communicators of all kinds.

Newsgroups and listservs

There are a number of newsgroups and listservs worth considering. (A listserv is an email-based mailing list/chat with a specific subject or focus.)

The `bit.listserv.techwr-l` newsgroup is aimed at technical writers and editors. You must subscribe to the group to post to it, but you can read messages without becoming a member of the newsgroup.

The WinHelp listserv is a listserv for WinHelp questions and issues. You can subscribe by sending an email message to `listserv@admin.humberc.on.ca` with "subscribe winhlp-l" in the body.

Summary

In this chapter, you learned how to install RoboHELP Office 2000 on your computer. You were introduced to the various sections of RoboHELP — RoboHELP Classic, RoboHELP HTML Edition, and RoboHELP Office — and what you use them for. You also saw the RoboHELP Explorer and were introduced to many of the tools and features you will be using as you create and maintain help projects.

✦ ✦ ✦

What Makes Help 'Help'?

✦ ✦ ✦ ✦

In This Chapter

What is online help?

Reasons to use online help for your documentation

Reasons not to use online help for your documentation

Things you can use online help for

Determining the type of online help to create

Planning an online help system

✦ ✦ ✦ ✦

This chapter shows you the types of online help you can create with RoboHELP 2000 and gives you some ways to evaluate what documentation you should put online and what you shouldn't put online. It then tells you some of the applications for which online help is particularly well suited. The chapter concludes with information on how to create a documentation plan for your online help system so you know what you're going to do and how you're going to do it.

What Is Online Help?

Online help is more than just throwing blocks of text online. Online help combines the following elements into a complete integrated system:

✦ **Topics.** Topics are the blocks of text that constitute the written content in a help system. Each topic is displayed on a single screen.

✦ **Links.** Links (also known as *hyperlinks*) connect topics and let the user navigate the online help in a nonlinear fashion from topic to topic.

✦ **Table of contents and index.** The table of contents provides a hierarchical or outline view of the topics in the online help. The index, or *keywords*, is very much like the index of a book. The user can look up a word or phrase in the index and find all the related topics in the online help.

✦ **Formatting.** You can use a wide range of formatting options to enhance the information in the online help, including fonts, styles, colors, and even window location and attributes. The size and shape of the windows that content is displayed in is an important part of communicating information in online help. By displaying types of information (such as tips or glossary items) in a specific window, you can cue the users on how to use the information being displayed.

In addition, most forms of online help offer full-text search features that let you look for words or phrases that are not specifically included in the index.

Online help is usually compiled from a collection of source files that are run through a help compiler and combined into a single file. The compiled file is then viewed with a help viewer or Internet browser. Compiled help runs quicker because the content, formatting, and other information is already optimized. Some types of online help file are not compiled, which makes them easier to edit—you don't have to compile them each time you make a change to the online help—but uncompiled online help runs a little bit slower.

Online help is usually associated with a program or a suite of programs, though you can have standalone online help about a general topic (such as a file that introduces the reader to the basics of using the Internet).

Why You Should Use Online Help

Publishing documentation in an online format has many advantages over printing documentation, such as the following:

✦ **Online help is faster to use.** Rather than having to page through a printed manual, the users can search for a specific topic or keyword to get exactly the help they need. Effective use of navigational aids such as browse sequences, keywords, and See Also jumps can assist the users in finding information.

✦ **Online help is easier to use.** Printed documentation is fairly linear: the users go from one point to the next. Flipping from topic to topic is possible, but difficult. Online help lets the users choose their own path through the file with navigational aids such as keywords, browse sequences, tables of contents, and See Also jumps. More sophisticated help files can interact directly with the users through prompts and dialog boxes that can identify the types of information to present and the order in which to present it. As a result, the users can get exactly the information they want or need with minimum effort.

✦ **Online help provides more options for communicating.** Although the information on a printed page is static and unchanging, online help lets you add a plethora of effects, including pictures, sounds, multimedia presentations, context-sensitive program links, buttons, browse sequences, jumps, and popups. Perhaps one of the greatest and simplest advantages of using online help is that you can use multiple colors to emphasize your message—something that is prohibitively expensive in most printed manuals. In addition, users can copy sample macros, code, commands, and other information from the online help to paste into their own documents and files.

✦ **Online help communicates more effectively.** When you tell or show someone something, the average retention rate for new material is 10 to 20 percent three days later. However, when you combine showing and telling (such as with a multimedia presentation), the average retention rate for new material goes up to 65 percent three days later. By creating online help that steps the users through a procedure as if you were standing by the computer and saying, "Now click this button," you can dramatically increase the users' understanding and retention of new concepts and techniques.

✦ **Online help is faster to create.** Printed documentation typically requires at least two to three weeks to be printed. Given the typical software development cycle—with material changes frequently happening up to the last minute—this means that the manuals are rarely completely accurate. The product must ship with a README file on the disks or CD to describe the changes to the product after the manual was sent out for printing. Online help lets you develop the help in parallel with the software development cycle. The last three weeks of product development required for printing can be used for final testing against the product as it approaches release. Any changes or additions to the software at the last minute can be reflected accurately in the online help.

✦ **Online help is cheaper to create.** The single biggest cost when releasing a software product is almost always the printed manual. In fact, the cost of the printed manual is frequently greater than or equal to the cost of all the other elements in the box combined. By reducing the size of the printed manual to a basic installation and tip guide and shifting the documentation to an online help format, for example, you can substantially reduce the cost of goods and the cost of shipping. (There have been popular software products that weighed as much as 35 pounds, 30 of which were the manuals.) Product updates are cheaper, too, as you don't have to print and ship a large manual.

✦ **Online help is easier to maintain.** Online help is very easy to change. If you have a new option on a command or a new feature, you can update the help files frequently in as little as five minutes, and then recompile the file and release it to production. By comparison, updating a printed manual would require making the change, possible repagination (and re-indexing), and printing and distributing a new edition of the manual or an update sheet.

- **Online help is easier to customize.** Because your files are electronic, you can customize your online help for large or OEM (Original Equipment Manufacturer) customers. You can change phrases, add logos and copyright information, eliminate topics or features, or change the look and feel of the entire help system. You can also create modular online help systems by combining individual modules into an integrated suite of online help.

- **Online help is easier to distribute.** Depending on the product and the users, you can update your users' online help electronically via the Internet or your company's intranet. The users can check your company's web site for updates to the online help whenever they like. Some companies go one step further and provide an automatic update service that tells users when to check for updates to the online help and product.

- **Online help reaches a larger audience.** Many companies that buy site licenses for products do not pay for a manual for everyone, with the result that there may be only a single printed manual per department. This can result in lost productivity by users' spending time looking for the one copy of the manual or by their simply not understanding how to use product features that could save them time and effort. By distributing your documentation in an online help format, you guarantee that each user of the product will have a complete copy of the documentation.

- **Online help is better integrated with the product.** Online help can be linked directly to the program it documents through context-sensitive links, interactive help wizards, and What's This? help. You can even create a "knowledge-based" help system that anticipates the users' questions based on the screen or field the users are in when they open help. This will lead to lower support costs, as the users will have the answers they need when they need them.

To summarize, online help can reduce your development, product, and support costs, help your customers become proficient in the product faster, and improve their overall satisfaction with the product.

Why You Shouldn't Use Online Help

Just because online help has a number of advantages over printed documentation doesn't mean that you should automatically consider putting everything online. Here are some of the reasons you may not want to use online help for your documentation:

- **Online help can't be used away from the computer.** Printed documentation can be read anywhere: on a bus, while watching TV, in the bathroom. To use online help, you must have a computer handy. If your documentation is providing background or general information that your users might want to read when they're away from the computer, you may want to consider printing parts of the documentation.

✦ **Online help can't be used before the product is installed.** Generally speaking, online help is installed as part of the product installation process, which makes the online help useless for gathering any necessary preinstallation requirements or configuration information. In addition, it's usually a good idea to write down specific configuration information (such as the IP address and user ID for a particular workstation) for future reference. A simple booklet on installing the product is usually much better for presenting this kind of documentation.

✦ **Online help takes additional skills to create.** Being a good writer isn't enough to create online help; you must also know how to use the help tools as well. You must also be more involved in the creation of the product itself; online help requires you to work with the developers to add context-sensitive links and identify areas where the online help can best support the users.

✦ **Online help looks different from printed documentation.** The amount of information you can put onto a standard 7" × 10" printed manual page is about two and a half times as much as you can put on a typical online help screen. Because online help usually works best when the information for a topic is available at a glance without scrolling (similar to keeping the information on a topic presented in a printed form limited to two pages, that which can be seen at a glance), the amount of information per topic is substantially reduced. Your online help must also be designed with the lowest common denominator for screen resolutions in mind: 640 × 480 or 800 × 600 work very well. However, you may not be able to take full advantage of the features offered by higher resolution monitors because not all your users have them.

✦ **Online help is used differently from printed documentation.** When you pick up a manual and want to find something, the first thing you usually do is thumb through the manual, skimming for topics that may catch your eye. Depending on what you're looking for, you might thumb through the manual several times, flipping pages slower and slower until you spot the thing you're looking for. No matter how well the online help is indexed or referenced, you can't really thumb it: The topics and modules aren't necessarily in any particular order and, even with online navigational aids like browse sequences, it's difficult to flip through pages with the same speed and flexibility that thumbing a printed manual allows.

✦ **Online help is harder to read than printed documentation.** The resolution for text and pictures displayed on a screen isn't nearly as good as for the printed page: although the resolution for printed text can be as much as 2400 dpi, monitors display at much lower resolutions. In addition, you must sit in one position when reading online help, as opposed to being able to shift positions or move around when carrying a manual or book. Furthermore, because the information is frequently "chunked" differently (broken up into small topic-sized units of information that are smaller than page-sized units of information), it is easy for the online help to feel more fragmented, which can also contribute to making it harder to read than printed documentation.

✦ **Online help requires additional disk space.** Although the need to conserve disk space is not nearly as great as it was a few years ago, online help can take up several megabytes easily. Also, if you included multimedia presentations, it can take up as much as 20 megabytes of disk space, which could impede distributing and installing the software.

To summarize, although online help is very cool, it is not a perfect solution for everything. It lacks some of the flexibility of printed documentation, it is harder to read than printed documentation, and it is used differently.

The best solution for your products will likely involve some combination of online help and printed documentation. What you choose depends on the type of product you are documenting and the specific needs of your users. "Planning Your Help System," which appears later in this chapter, will show you how to identify your requirements and make an effective plan for creating and maintaining your help files.

What Can You Use Online Help For?

There are many ways in which you can use online help. Most common is program-related online help. Programs come with built-in online help (and increasingly without printed manuals) that provides users with tutorial and reference information. This type of help is usually context sensitive, letting the user get specific help about a screen, field, or feature.

Related to this is the increasingly common practice of putting internal documents online, such as manuals, handbooks, and reference materials. Although there may be some disadvantages to doing so as mentioned earlier in this chapter, this practice can be very cost effective. Updates do not waste paper, nor is there any lead time for printing manuals. If your users are accessing the information through a company intranet, you can be sure that they will always have access to the very latest information. If you're providing reference documentation that's being used by field personnel, online help may increase the quality of service. Many service organizations have gone to an online help format for their service manuals, letting service personnel carry a complete set of manuals for every product they service on a laptop instead of having to carry as many as 200 pounds of manuals around in the back of their car.

Online help may provide your company's salespeople with better tools for making sales. Although almost every sales pitch these days seems to have a PowerPoint presentation in the middle of it, you can create sales materials with online help that can be left with the prospective clients. These materials can have product and service information, multimedia demonstrations, contact information, and hot links to your company's web site or the salesperson's e-mail address. Additional sales support can be provided in the form of online price lists and product catalogs, which can be quickly loaded into a salesperson's laptop or palmtop and referred to quickly and easily during a sales call or, alternately, left with clients for them to look at on their own.

For the marketing department in your company, you can use online help to create online newsletters, catalogs, company profiles, and brochures, as well as other marketing and press materials. These can be posted on a web site to provide quick access to extended information about the company and its products and services.

Many technical support departments give each tech support person a complete copy of the product manuals in online help rather than in a printed format. This reduces operating costs — printed manuals cost money and can represent a substantial overhead item for each new product release — and increases the speed of service to the customers who call in for support: finding information in online manuals is frequently quicker than looking it up in a printed manual.

For your users, you can use online help to create extensive tutorials and computer-based training (CBT) programs. The advantages of online tutorials are that they are available to your users constantly, they can be updated and distributed quickly and easily, and they do not require an external trainer. Online tutorials also allow users to move at their own pace through material, to repeat sections they find difficult, and to refer to the course materials at a later date to refresh their memories. It is also possible to make online tutorials interactive, making the training more effective than a series of canned slides by allowing the users to experiment and choose or enter answers. Multimedia can even be added to enliven presentations of complex material.

Another possible use for online help is to publish books in an online format. Although online help lends itself to publishing technical information with many opportunities for hyperlinking (such as cookbooks or do-it-yourself books), there's no reason you can't put other kinds of nonfiction and even fiction into online help and distribute it without paper. Consider a gardening guide in an online format: You could insert color pictures of the plants and flowers you're discussing. Or even better, what about a guide to birds in the region? Online help would let you see pictures and hear embedded sound clips of the birds' calls. A do-it-yourself guide could include a short video clip showing how to change the chain on a mountain bike or how to remove the oil pan on a VW Beetle without barking your knuckles.

Because online help provides information on demand with almost negligible costs of distribution, it is an effective solution to a wide variety of publishing problems.

What Kind of Online Help Should You Create?

Before you begin writing online help, it's important to consider the type(s) of online help you want to create. RoboHELP lets you create help in one format and then convert it to another relatively easily. However, it's easiest to create the type of online help you want from the start so you can take advantage of the full features of that help and also so that you don't have to worry about converting later on.

WinHelp

WinHelp is the "classic" (the best-known) version of online help. WinHelp was first released to the public as part of the Windows 3.0 Software Development Kit (SDK), a suite of tools and documentation released to developers of Windows products. It has evolved considerably since then, going from a simple hypertext system to a complete help environment capable of running sound, video, and multimedia applications, linking to other help systems and programs, and interacting directly with the user.

When you press F1 in most Windows programs to get online help, WinHelp is usually what you see. Figure 2-1 shows a typical WinHelp file.

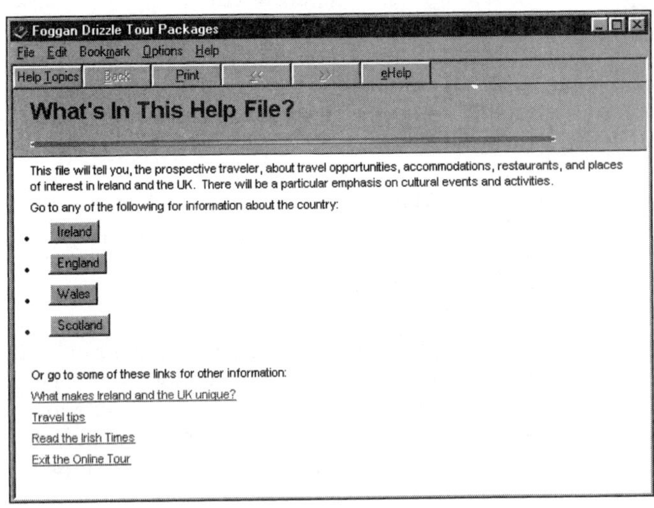

Figure 2-1: A typical WinHelp screen

WinHelp is the most common and most widely recognized format for online help. (WinHelp is the first compiled help format.) WinHelp works exclusively on Windows systems without any additional software (the WinHelp viewing program is part of every version of Windows from 3.1 on), but you can't run WinHelp under any other operating system. You will probably want to use WinHelp for developing Windows-only help with the widest range of available features for online help. (There are several types of HTML-based online help, such as WebHelp, that can be used on a variety of platforms. WebHelp and other cross-platform online help formats are discussed later in this chapter.)

HTML Help

HTML Help is another type of compiled online help from Microsoft. Designed for Windows 98, Microsoft introduced the Microsoft HTML Help format in August 1997. This is Microsoft's standard help format for all its operating systems and applications starting with Windows 98.

HTML Help has many features similar to those of WinHelp, but it is written using standard HTML (HyperText Markup Language) to format the information, like a web page. HTML Help must be displayed using Microsoft Internet Explorer version 4.0 or later running on a Windows system. HTML Help looks more like web pages than the classic WinHelp. Figure 2-2 shows a typical HTML Help screen.

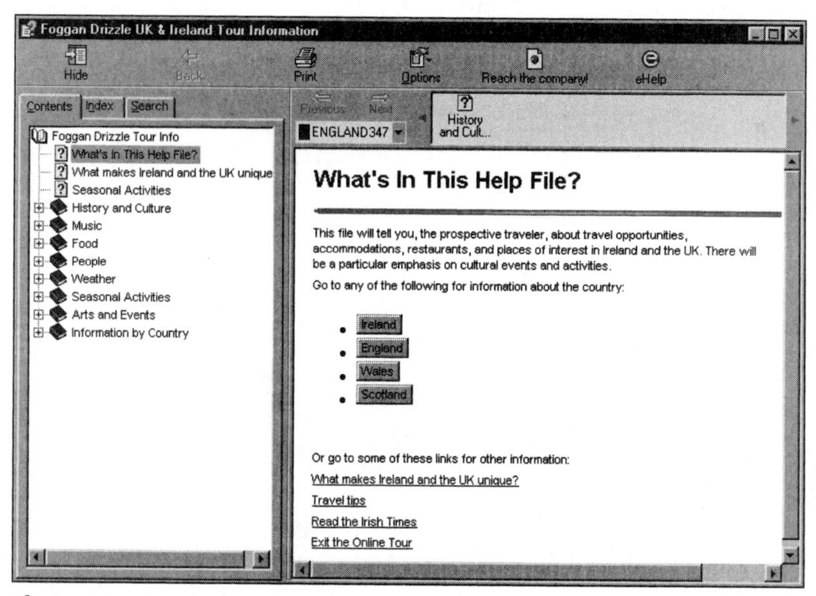

Figure 2-2: A typical HTML Help screen

One of the big advantages of HTML Help is that you can create online help that can be distributed easily on a company intranet that uses Windows and Internet Explorer.

WebHelp

WebHelp, developed by Blue Sky, is a variation on HTML Help. It has the same general internal format and looks about the same as HTML Help on the screen. WebHelp's big advantage is that it runs on a variety of browsers and operating systems, unlike HTML Help (which runs only on Internet Explorer and Windows). With WebHelp, you can create HTML-based help that your users can view with different browsers on Windows (3.*x*, 95, 98, 2000, or NT), Macintosh, Linux, Sun Solaris, and several other Unix platforms.

WebHelp is an exceptional solution for providing online help for products or systems that run on Windows, Unix, and/or Macintosh. Consider using WebHelp anytime you need HTML-based help that isn't restricted to Windows systems or to systems with Internet Explorer.

What's This? Help

What's This? help was first introduced as a usable feature in Windows 95. (It was possible to create What's This? help in Windows 3.1, but it required a lot of work by the developers and was hard to maintain.) A sample of What's This? help appears in Figure 2-3.

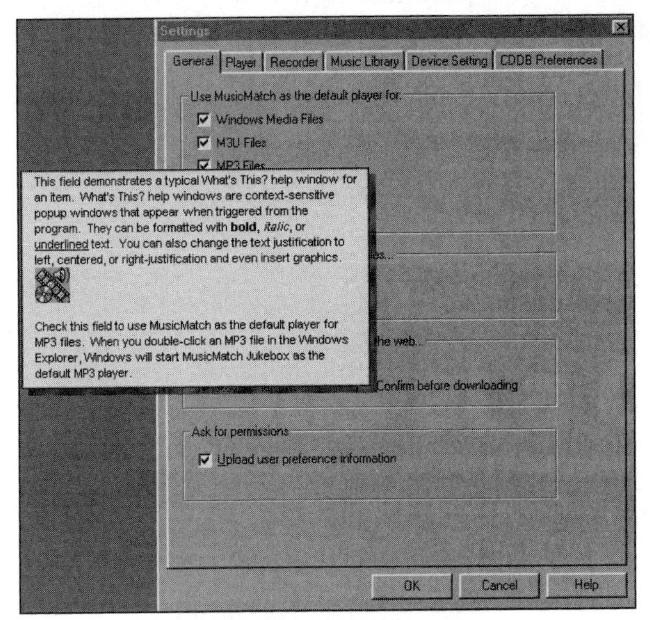

Figure 2-3: A typical What's This? help prompt

What's This? help is designed to provide you with quick information about a program, an element of a dialog box, and other information. What's This? help is context-sensitive popup help for individual elements of dialog boxes. What's This? help is related to the standard WinHelp (and can be used in conjunction with it) but it can also be used as a standalone help system for programs. You can use the What's This? Help Composer (a tool in RoboHELP for creating and maintaining What's This? help) to create quick help for an application on the fly.

You can use What's This? help with any Windows application to provide additional information on a program's features. It can be used in conjunction with WinHelp or HTML Help.

JavaHelp

JavaHelp is a new help format developed by Sun Microsystems that works with Java applications. Java applications and JavaHelp work on a broad range of platforms and browsers. JavaHelp looks similar to HTML Help. Like WebHelp, JavaHelp can be run on a variety of browsers and operating systems. JavaHelp is compiled from HTML generated in RoboHELP.

RoboHELP 2000 provides extensive support for JavaHelp 1.0 with Java- and HTML-based features such as HTML content, hyperlinks, GIF files, Java applets, tables of contents, full-text search, dynamic index, navigation controls, popup windows, browse sequencing, and See Also features. You can also compile and compress your JavaHelp files for easy distribution of your JavaHelp systems. A sample of JavaHelp appears in Figure 2-4.

JavaHelp is still being developed. It is not as feature-rich as other online help formats. Moreover, you can't print topics from the JavaHelp Help viewer in this release. If you are not developing help for a Java application but you need to run on different browsers and operating systems, you should use WebHelp.

Windows CE Help

Windows CE Help is an abbreviated version of HTML Help that runs on products using Windows CE. (Windows CE is a version of Windows designed to run on handheld and palmtop computers, pagers, cell phones, and home electronic gear.) A sample of Windows CE Help appears in Figure 2-5.

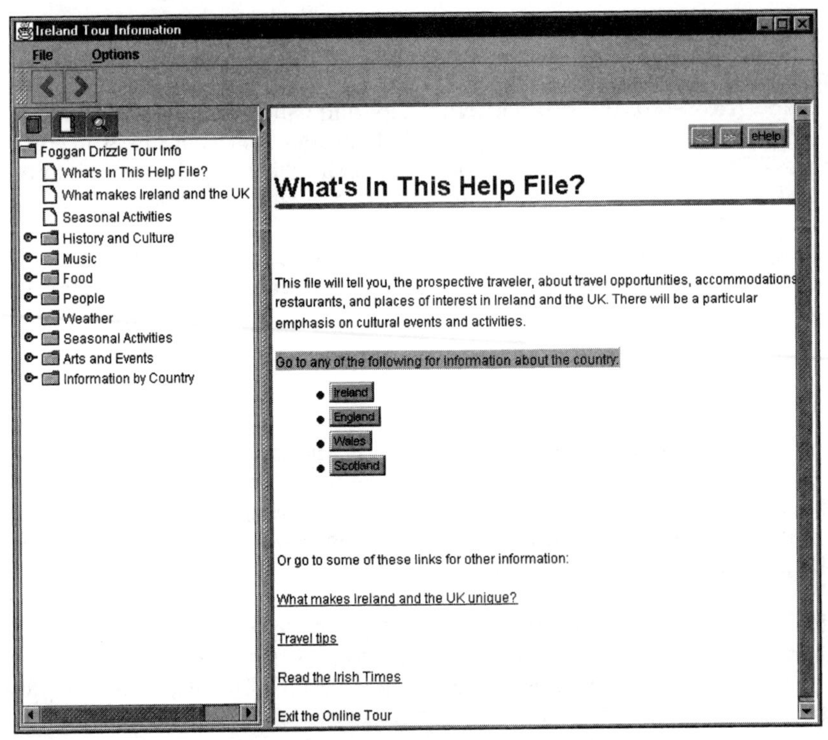

Figure 2-4: A typical JavaHelp prompt

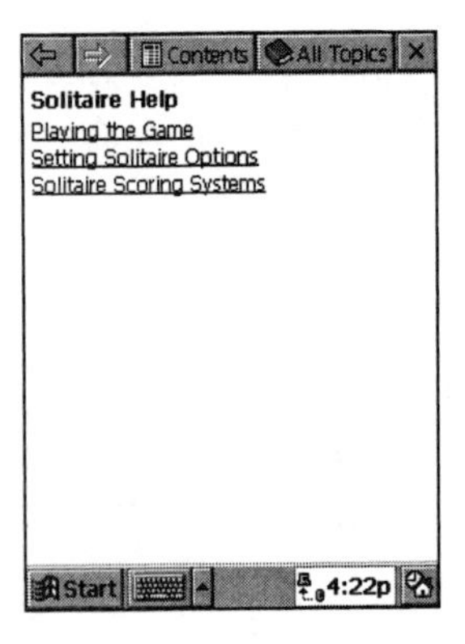

Figure 2-5: A typical Windows CE Help screen

Unlike HTML Help, Windows CE Help doesn't have a table of contents or an index. Because it's designed for small, simple units that usually use flat liquid-crystal displays, Windows CE Help is monochromatic: Text appears in black and white and any embedded graphics images are converted to black-and-white bitmaps.

Windows CE Help files must be small, as the devices they are used in usually have a limited amount of memory and storage. As a result, it's usually best to create a simple (usually less than a dozen topics) WinHelp system using RoboHELP and then convert it to Windows CE Help. For more information about Windows CE Help, check out the Microsoft web sites `http://microsoft.com/products/prodref/120_ov.htm` and `http://msdn.microsoft.com/cetools/`.

Netscape NetHelp

Netscape NetHelp is an uncompiled HTML-based help format that runs on Netscape Communicator and on any operating system that you can run Netscape Communicator on, including Windows, Unix, and Macintosh. There are two versions of Netscape NetHelp: NetHelp1 and NetHelp2. Netscape NetHelp1 is for earlier versions of Netscape. A sample Netscape NetHelp1 screen appears in Figure 2-6.

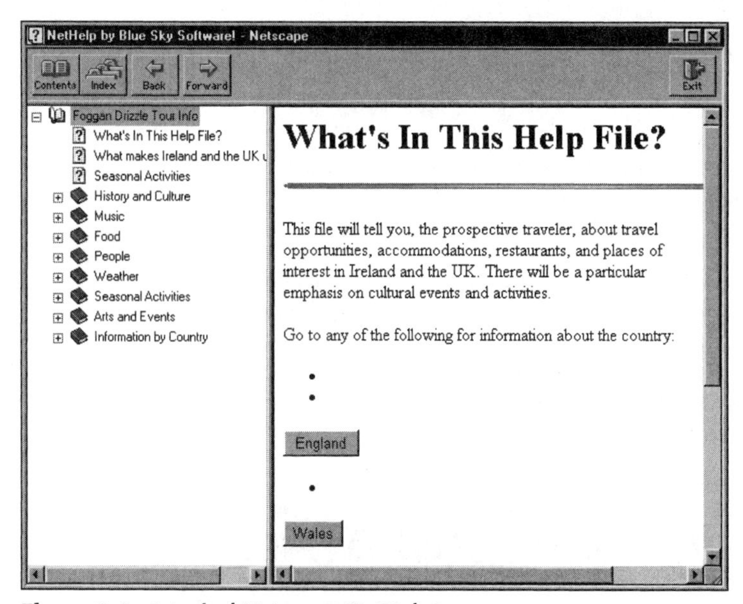

Figure 2-6: A typical Netscape NetHelp1 screen

Netscape NetHelp2 is for the current versions (4.0 and later) of Netscape. Figure 2-7 shows a sample of the same help shown in Figure 2-6 in NetHelp2 format.

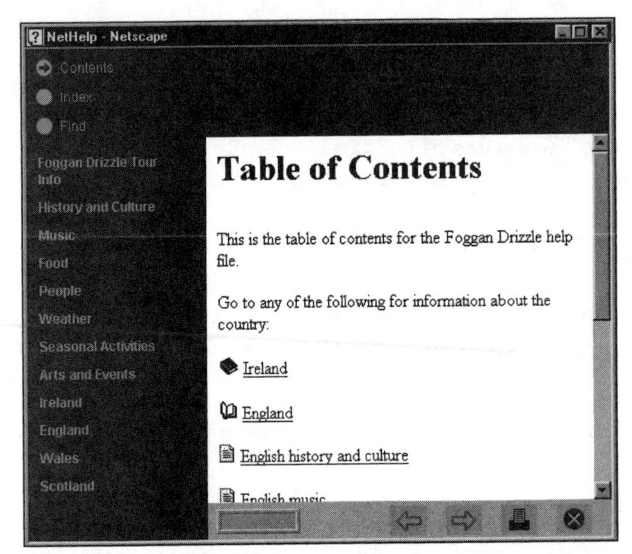

Figure 2-7: A typical Netscape NetHelp2 screen

Specific information about the current version of NetHelp (NetHelp2) can be found through the Netscape web site `http://home.netscape.com/eng/help/home/home.htm`.

As you consider what type of online help format to use, remember that it is possible to release online help in several different formats without having to develop in more than one. For example, you might develop online help in a WinHelp format but want to distribute Windows CE help as well. In cases such as this, you should determine what the primary help format will be and develop in that, and then use RoboHELP's features to convert the help to any other online help formats you need.

Planning Your Online Help System

Although the urge to leap into creating a help system can be overpowering, it's a good idea to spend some time planning what you want to accomplish. For any help system (or a technical document of any kind, for that matter), you should evaluate a number of issues such as the following:

- ✦ What do you want to write?
- ✦ Whom do you want to write it for?
- ✦ Why do you want to write it?
- ✦ How do you want to write it?
- ✦ Where will the document be written and produced?

✦ Who will do the work?

✦ When will they do it?

The most effective way to identify these and other issues it to create a documentation plan.

Why Build a Documentation Plan?

There are a number of reasons to build a documentation plan. First, and most important, a documentation plan identifies what you're going to do and how you're going to do it before you begin. Without this information, you can't make accurate estimates of resources and a schedule, nor can you have any way of making sure that what you're doing is practical or the best method to use.

Another important reason to build a documentation plan is credibility. By creating a detailed and comprehensive plan of what you intend to accomplish, you are showing that you are a professional. Furthermore, it is a rare software development effort that has specs of any kind, which makes your own spec look all the better.

Very few online help files are written unilaterally for the exclusive use of one person or group. Most online help files are written for use throughout a company or for use with a product by the company's customers. As a result, you must have some buy-in and cooperation from the other departments that will be developing and maintaining the finished product. A documentation plan gives you a tool for identifying and delineating areas of responsibility.

An additional reason to build a documentation plan is that it gives you a measure of political protection, particularly if you have gotten sign-offs on the plan from the various department and group managers. By writing down your goals, assumptions, and the method of execution, you can use the documentation plan as a basis for renegotiating the schedule when the inevitable product or scope changes occur. In other words, the documentation plan is a contract for what you are going to do and how you're going to do it. If the terms of the contract are changed, you have some latitude for changing your resource requirements and the size and shape of the delivered product.

Building a Documentation Plan

There are five basic sections of a typical documentation plan:

✦ The **overview**, which covers the basic description of the project: the scope and purpose of the online help, the audience definition, the goals, and additional comments

✦ The **production information** section, which describes the format, the look and feel, and the production requirements for the online help

✦ The **staffing** section, which identifies the writers, reviewers, and individuals with sign-off authority

✦ The **schedule**, which gives the schedule benchmarks and the assumptions upon which the schedule is based

✦ The **outline**, which provides a detailed look at the topics in the online help

You'll obtain most of the information for creating the documentation plan by interviewing a number of the subject-matter experts (SMEs) and key players on the project, such as the product development managers and leads, testing leads, product managers, and other marketing folks. You should also talk to as many of the individual developers who will be creating the product as you can; the opinions of the people actually doing the product development can be markedly different from those of the product development managers and are frequently more accurate.

As you assemble the information for the documentation plan, also make note of who seems to have the clearest idea of what the product is and what they want the documentation to be.

The overview

The overview of a documentation plan answers questions about what the online help will be and whom it's being written for, and what they'll get out of it. The overview of your documentation plan should answer the following questions:

✦ **What will this online help be called?** The project title identifies the project. If you're working on several closely related projects that are being described in one documentation plan, list each one. It's important to determine the name of the project up front, as this will help crystallize the direction of the project. Be sure to get input on this from the project development lead and marketing: Although deciding the name of the online help project may seem trivial, it can actually be a major political football between departments and managers.

Whenever you mention the online help project name in the documentation plan, it's a good idea to list it in *italics*.

✦ **What type of online help is this?** Identify the type of documentation for this online help project. Will it be a tutorial, a reference, a general user's guide, or a combination of all three? Will the online help be a standalone file or will it tie into the program and provide context-sensitive help and information?

✦ **What is the online help's scope?** Describe the scope of the online help. Tell what it will cover and to what depth. Be sure also to identify what the online help won't cover. For example, the scope statement for a drawing product might be something like this: "This online help is a complete online compendium for how to use every aspect of the product. The online help starts with a tutorial introduction to the basic product features and identifies the various tools for the product. The online help then shows you how to navigate the screens and options to create a drawing from scratch, how to add features, and how to enhance the drawing with text. The online help will continue with more advanced topics such as preparing a drawing for color printing using separations. The online help will have a comprehensive reference of commands and features and a glossary. Note that this online help will not cover the details of using the product in conjunction with the high-end version of the same product; this will be covered in the online help for that product."

✦ **What is the online help's purpose?** Describe the purpose of the online help and tell why someone should use this online help. What is the overall goal for the online help? For example, the purpose for the online help for a drawing product might be something like this: "This online help provides the beginning user with an introduction to using this product through an online tutorial and by providing a vocabulary of concepts. The online help continues with information for the intermediate user about commands and how to use the various features, tools, and templates to create complex drawings. The online help concludes with information about the advanced features used by a small percentage of the users."

✦ **Who is the online help aimed at?** Describe the target audience. Who is this online help being written for: beginning, intermediate, or advanced users, specialists in the product, professionals, students, the home market? A typical statement of an online help file's audience is: "The primary audience for this online help is the beginning or intermediate business user who has little or no previous experience with an online drawing product."

Note

There may be more than one class of members in the primary audience, such as accountants and small businesses who are using accounting software. There may also be a primary and a secondary audience, such as musicians who want to experiment with music software and professional musicians who need an online composition tool. Marketing frequently will have an idea of who the audience is, but you should also talk to technical support for an understanding of the audience and the audience's needs based on the kinds of questions they ask.

✦ **What is the average user's background?** Identify the minimum level of knowledge that the user must have to make use of this online help. What skills and knowledge does the average user possess? For example, a statement of the user's background might be: "The user is expected to know simple computer concepts, how to use their computer, simple Windows 95/98/NT concepts, how to use a mouse, and simple word processing concepts. In addition, the users may also know intermediate word processing concepts and simple online drawing concepts, but this is not required. The users are not expected to know anything about advanced word processing or drawing concepts. In addition, although it's likely that the users will know some basic Internet concepts, it's not certain that they will."

✦ **What will the user get out of this online help?** Make a list of the specific topics and concepts that the users can learn about. What are the specific goals for users of this online help? A typical set of goals would look like this:

The online help should help the user with the following specific tasks:

- determining which version of the product they need
- installing and configuring the product
- setting up personal information on the product
- understanding the product's working environment
- creating a basic diagram or drawing
- adding colors and textures to the drawing
- creating and selecting drawing templates
- including a drawing created in the product in a Microsoft Office product
- dynamically linking a drawing to an Office product
- dynamically linking a drawing to the user's network
- creating a hyperlink in a drawing
- saving a diagram as an Internet-ready file
- creating a project timeline in the product
- assigning attributes to shapes in a drawing
- generating reports about drawings

✦ **What's the competition like?** Marketing information about the competition will give you an idea of what the market expects and will highlight much of what your online help must accomplish in order to be competitive. Moreover, if the product you are documenting is the market leader, competitive analysis will show you where you need to move ahead in order to stay competitive.

✦ **Are there related projects?** Describe the relationship to any other documentation projects and other software projects. Will the online help be based on previous versions of the online help and/or on other documents? Are there any additional documents planned for this release, such as marketing collateral, installation cards, or CD inserts? Are there online help projects that will dovetail neatly with this project? Most often, an online help project will be tied to a printed manual, but an increasing number of products are shipping with minimal printed documentation and relying on the online help to provide the bulk of the documentation for the product. You should also identify any subsequent uses of the online help; for example, you might be creating online help that will be used subsequently as the basis for custom help for large OEM or VAR (Value-Added Reseller) clients, for localization, or for cut-down or modular versions of the product. If you have a suite of products, you may also have simultaneous development of several different but related online help projects, which will require coordination of effort so the finished projects look the same (yet another reason for effective planning at the start of a project).

✦ **What are the general assumptions for the project?** Identify the assumptions for the project and the project plan. This is a typical set of assumptions in a documentation plan:

The estimates and proposed outline presented in this plan are based on the following assumptions:

- all the information in the Overview section of this plan is complete and correct
- the first and second drafts will each be reviewed once, with buyoff occurring with delivery of the third draft
- any proposed changes to the format and contents will not add significantly to the writing and editing time

The biggest value of the assumptions is usually as protection: If there are sudden changes to the scope that will require a lot more work, you can point to the assumptions and say, "We'll have to change the plan to accommodate these changes."

Production information

The production information section answers questions about what the finished online help should look like. It will answer questions such as these:

✦ **What are the writing and editing standards for the online help?** Identify the style guide(s) you will follow. For example, "This online help will follow the standards stated in the company style guide and the 14th edition of the *Chicago Manual of Style*."

✦ **What format(s) will this online help be available in?** It's important to identify what format or formats the online help will be available in, as the format will have an effect on the development process.

The section "What Kind of Help Should You Create?" discussed earlier in this chapter provides some guidelines for choosing the right kind of help for your project.

- **What style will be used for the online help?** "Style" here refers to the way the online help looks: how the topics appear, what colors you'll use for links, popups, headings, what font(s) will appear in the text, how windows are used, and so on. Because online help is a visual medium with many options, it's a good idea to create a sample help file as an online style guide that shows what each of the features looks like.
- **How will the online help be distributed?** The online help probably will probably be distributed on CD to your company's customers, but it may also be distributed on diskettes or online. The distribution method may provide some limitations on how big the online help files can be.
- **Are there any special art requirements?** Describe the art requirements. Art requirements are usually of two types: screen shots and conceptual art. *Screen shots* are any forms of artwork directly captured from the product itself, such as screens, buttons, toolbars, or on-screen reports and displays. RoboHELP has several excellent utilities for capturing and editing screen shots. *Conceptual art* is artwork such as block diagrams, process flows, and the like. Screen shots are quick and easy to create, but conceptual art will require that someone draws and edits the picture using a drawing or painting program. For purposes of planning, estimate the type and approximate quantity of illustrations the online help will have.
- **Are there other materials?** This is similar to the "Are there related projects" question in the Overview section. Mention any additional materials that will be included with the product and any relevant production or packaging information.

Staffing

The staffing section discusses who will be writing, editing, indexing, testing, and reviewing. (At the beginning of a project, many of these are likely to be unknown or unassigned.) It will answer questions such as these:

- **Who's in charge?** This may be one of the writers or it may be someone who's in a purely management role, but you must identify who is authorized to make decisions as the project unfolds.
- **Who will write this?** Identify the writer or writers who will be responsible for creating the online help file. If you have multiple writers, briefly identify the tasks or sections of the online help for which each writer will be responsible.
- **Who will edit this?** Identify the editor who will edit the online help. Also identify if there's going to be any editing to bring the online help in line with other similar online help projects.

✦ **Who will do the indexing and compilation of keywords?** Although the writer(s) will usually do this, indexing the document is a task that can be delegated easily. If you have a staff indexer or someone who specializes in creating keywords for online help files, you may want to have that person, rather than the writers who wrote the file, perform this task.

✦ **Who will review and test the online help?** Testing is an essential part of making sure that the online help file works. The writers will be responsible for doing initial testing on the online help file, but people in development, product testing, and marketing will be responsible for testing and reviewing the file for content. You should have reviewers look at the help for overall content and style, technical accuracy, and compliance with standards and formatting. Each of these categories will have a separate list of reviewers. Some names may appear on all three lists whereas others appear on only one. An effective way to get qualified reviewers is to enlist the aid of the technical support department. They are the frequently qualified to judge if online help will be complete and appropriate for the audience. Technical support also has the most to gain or lose on the quality of the finished online help, so they're likely to be motivated to work with writers to make sure the online help is good.

Note

Always list the names of the reviewers alphabetically and say that you're doing so. You'll avoid a lot of bruised feelings this way.

✦ **Who will approve the online help?** You can and should have as many informed reviewers as you can find, but you should have only one person approving each aspect — content and style, technical accuracy, and standards and formatting — of the online help. If you have multiple people in the approval loop, you may find that your approval will be held up in committee.

Schedule

The schedule lists the proposed schedule together with the assumptions upon which the schedule is based. Be sure to make allowances in the schedule for holidays, vacations, sick time, and any other requirements. The schedule should identify the following benchmarks:

✦ **Project start.** The project start date is the date when you actually begin working on the project or project plan.

✦ **Handoff of the documentation plan for review.** This is the date to hand off the first draft of the documentation plan. Most of the information should be in the draft, including the outline. If you have a sample for the online help style, include this with the documentation plan (or refer to it) so that the people can review this for style and presentation as well.

✦ **Approval of documentation plan.** When all the comments have been incorporated, route a copy of the documentation plan with a sign-off sheet to the various managers and leads involved in the project. As a rule of thumb, you should get signatures from the department heads of Product Development, Product Testing, Technical Support, your boss, and the product manager. If the project is large, you may also want to have group leads within the product development team sign off. Who gets to approve the documentation plan is largely a political decision. It's a good idea if you're not sure to discuss the question of signoffs with your boss. Carefully save the signed-off copy; this can be valuable if there are sudden surprising shifts in the project that require you to renegotiate your deadlines.

✦ **Handoff of online help for first draft review.** The first draft of the online help should have 50–70 percent of the rough content and 60–80 percent of the topics. Reviewers should be able to navigate much of the online help, but there will definitely be pieces that need more writing and polishing. Context-sensitive hooks to the program may or may not work at this time. There will be little or no formatting for finished style, and the content will be largely unedited. In this review, the reviewers should focus exclusively on reviewing and developing the content and topics.

Note

It's very common to submit portions of online help for first draft review in modules as they become complete. This can speed up the process and isn't as likely to overwhelm the reviewers with a large quantity of work all at once.

✦ **Return of first draft review comments.** You will likely have to pursue several of your reviewers to make sure they get their comments back to you; however, for your key reviewers and source material experts, don't accept silence as a sign of acquiescence.

✦ **Handoff of online help for second draft review.** The second draft of the online help will have the review comments from the first review as well as additional material that has been generated in the interim. The second draft should contain 70–85 percent of the content and 90 percent of the topics. All sections of the online help should be navigable, with sections that are known to be incomplete clearly flagged as such. Some formatting for the finished style should be visible in this document, but not all features of the style (such as the See Also links and a comprehensive keyword list) will be present in this review. Most of the context-sensitive hooks to the program should work at this point. Reviewers should focus on filling in the holes in the content and topic list and checking all content to make sure that it's complete and correct. Depending on the development cycle, this version of the help is likely to ship with the first product beta.

Coordinating the context-sensitive help hooks during the development cycle can be difficult, as many developers will frequently change the program several times before its release. Chapter 11, "Creating Context-Sensitive Help," discusses strategies for nailing down the context-sensitive help information early in the development process.

- **Return of second draft review comments.** If the reviews are going smoothly, the second draft review comments will have less to do with overall content than with fine-tuning what is in the online help file. However, don't be too surprised if a missing subject area is identified and requested by a reviewer at this stage. Many reviewers aren't able to envision what something looks like until they actually see it. In addition, looking at the presentation of a topic list may trigger an idea for how to do something better. Allow for this possibility in your schedule and resource assignments.
- **Handoff of online help for final review.** The final review should be nominally complete, with 95–98 percent of the content and 99 percent of the topics in place. All of the context-sensitive hooks should work. The online help should be fully navigable and should be formatted in accordance with the final style (such as screen colors, fonts, windows, and so on). Keywords, See Also links, and other features should be 80–100 percent complete. The text should be edited, though final editing and proofreading will not have been done yet. Reviewers should check for online help features, usability of the context-sensitive and search features, and presentation of material in the format. This version of the online help should work with a late beta release of the software. The product testing group should also be able to start doing test builds of the finished product with this version of the online help.
- **Return of final review comments.** Review comments for the final review should not involve anything major but should instead focus on small changes ("The help says that the blah blah command has three options but it really has four, including this one...."). There should not be any significant changes to the online help at this stage.
- **Handoff of "gold master" candidate for online help.** The online help should be completely finished and ready for approval. All features, content, and context-sensitive hooks will be present in the product, and any comments to reviewers or internal guides should have been removed. Product testing and the reviewers should perform final acceptance tests on the online help with the gold master candidates. With the approval of the file, the online help is ready for release to production. (This is usually referred to as the "gold master" version.)
- **Project completion.** All source files are checked into the source control system as part of the source code for this release of the product. All e-mail, project documentation, plans, and other materials are archived in preparation for the next release.

You should also have a boilerplate comment about the assumptions to create the schedule in this section, such as: "In general, these estimates assume that the scope, purpose, and outline in this proposal are complete and correct, and that no time will be lost because of sickness or other delays. Any changes to these assumptions will result in a comparable, day-for-day extension of the schedule."

Estimating Schedules

Setting the schedule is one of the hardest parts of planning a project. You need to evaluate such factors as the size and depth of the online help, the technical complexity required, the quantity of finished output of the writer(s) assigned to the task, the number of illustrations and screen shots, the relative difficulty of getting meaningful information and reviews, and the likelihood of scope changes. The ability to consistently make a good estimate that accurately hits the actual time and resources necessary to complete a project within 10 percent is the mark of a seasoned professional.

The basic metric for planning written projects is 4 hours of time for each new page of documentation. However, the individual topics in an online help file can be anywhere from a couple of sentences to a couple of pages long, which makes it hard to estimate the amount of time it will take based solely on the number of topics in an online help file. As an initial strategy, budget an average of two hours of time per topic, which should cover anything you're likely to encounter. As you progress in a project, you should evaluate your actual time spent versus your projected time and refine your estimates accordingly.

This assumption statement is one more opportunity to avoid being held accountable for delays in the development cycle and on-the-fly changes to the product (both of which are so common as to be inevitable). By stating that you will be writing online help for the stated scope and purpose, you have some room to renegotiate the schedule if the product changes substantially in the middle of the development effort.

The outline

The last section in the documentation plan is the outline, which presents an in-depth outline of the online help. A detailed outline is a requirement for a good online help system! Even though online help is not as linear as a printed manual is, you can identify large sections of material that can be arranged in a reasonably hierarchical order.

The outline should contain 1-, 2-, and 3-level headings with comments about what each heading will cover. If this is a revision or expansion of a previous online help system, you can use the preceding version of the online help as the basis for the new outline and add comments where new or revised headings appear. (This technique can also give you very accurate information for measuring your productivity.)

As you gain experience with creating online help, you may find it helpful to create an outline based on the proposed table of contents, which may reflect the way concepts are grouped more accurately than a standard outline. For more information on creating tables of contents, see Chapter 8, "Using Tables of Contents and Indexes."

Using and Maintaining the Documentation Plan

At the start of a project, the documentation plan provides you with detailed information about the scope, purpose, and depth of the project so you can make effective decisions when assigning resources. Furthermore, the documentation plan clarifies everyone's perception of what the finished product should actually look like. Writing down your understanding of what you need to produce and when, and getting this approved can spare you vast quantities of time redoing work because you or someone else didn't understand what was being described.

After you have completed the documentation plan and had the various participants sign off on it, distribute a copy of the completed plan to everyone involved. It will let everyone know what you're doing, when they should expect to receive first and second draft reviews from you, and when their review comments are due. This kind of advance planning and scheduling gives you professional credibility and also encourages other groups to proffer the same kind of information.

There are political advantages to creating a documentation plan, too. And, apart from the basic advantage of eliminating the friction of misunderstandings about what is being requested, a documentation plan is an agreement between you and the other participants in a project as to what you're doing. If there are subsequent changes to the scope, purpose, or schedule, the documentation plan gives you a tool to renegotiate the resources necessary.

With the schedule and outline information, you can also use the documentation plan as a tool for delegating sections of a project to subcontractors or other authors on the book.

As work on the online help progresses, a documentation plan is useful as a tool for tracking progress against the project schedule. Checking the progress of each writer or contributor against the sections assigned to them and the estimated hours can help avoid writing crunches near the end of a project. Should you need to bring additional writers into the project, you can also use the documentation plan as a tool for identifying the sections and responsibilities of each new contributor.

Be sure that you update the documentation plan whenever necessary. Identify changes in the personnel writing and editing the document, the reviewers, the schedule, or (most important) the outline. Also amend the documentation plan to include changes to the overview, particularly the scope and purpose. Keep a running change log at the front of the documentation plan, so that whenever you make a change, you make a dated entry on the change log. Also be sure to route a new copy to the participants when you make a change. (If you're working at a company with a network or intranet, you simply may want to post a copy of the documentation plan online. You also should send everyone e-mail saying that there has been a change of such-and-such type to the plan and that the revised plan is available at some location on the network.)

Because of the need to update information frequently and to distribute the revised documentation plan, a documentation plan is a perfect candidate for being distributed in an online help format. Consider creating an online help version of your documentation plan and then post it on the network for the interested parties to download whenever they need the latest version.

At the end of a project, the documentation plan is an essential tool for doing a post mortem analysis of the project to identify problems and to determine what could have been done better. Check your original assumptions and thoughts about the project against the finished product and see where they changed and why. Identify the final hours worked measured against the number of topics and the number of words in the online help file. This information will prove invaluable for building an accurate metric for productivity when creating the next online help project.

Creating a clear documentation plan is absolutely invaluable for creating good online help. It serves as a reminder of the scope, purpose, and goals for a project and is a standard against which you can check your work. As Paul Magid of the Flying Karamazovs said, "It doesn't matter how you get there if you don't know where you're going."

Project planning is an entire field of study unto itself. There are many excellent books and resources if you'd like to find out more about how to plan and manage projects, such as "Managing Your Documentation Projects" by JoAnn Hackos (Wiley & Sons, 1994) and "Standards for Online Communication" by JoAnn Hackos and Dawn Stevens (Wiley & Sons, 1997).

Summary

In this chapter, you were introduced to the types of online help you can create with RoboHELP 2000. You learned many of the reasons for and against using online help for a document, as well as some of the ways you can use online help. You also learned how to plan an online help system to minimize your effort and to give you a clear picture of what you wanted to accomplish.

✦ ✦ ✦

Creating WinHelp

P A R T

✦ ✦ ✦ ✦

In This Part

✦ ✦ ✦ ✦

Creating Your First WinHelp Project

In This Chapter

Learning the basics of how WinHelp files work

Understanding how to develop a WinHelp project

Starting a new WinHelp project

Adding, modifying, and deleting topics in a WinHelp file

Compiling a WinHelp file

Adding keywords to create an index

Learning about topics and footnote codes

Learning about RoboHELP reports

This chapter introduces you to the basics of creating a WinHelp file of your own. You'll first learn about the component files in WinHelp projects and how they interact. You'll then see how to start a new WinHelp project using the RoboHELP Explorer and how to add, modify, and delete topics using RoboHELP features. You'll next learn how to compile your first WinHelp file and view your results. The chapter continues with information on adding keywords to the help file's index. Finally, you'll learn about the mechanics of WinHelp (how to use footnotes to add and modify topics and keywords directly) and how to generate reports on the project and the topics.

This section deals exclusively with WinHelp projects. If you want to create an HTML Help project, go to Part IV, "Creating HTML Help."

The Components of WinHelp Files

Before you create a WinHelp file of your own, you need a brief understanding of how WinHelp files are created and to learn about the files that are used to create a compiled WinHelp file.

As you've read in previous chapters, WinHelp is a compiled online help format. This means that one or more *source files* (files containing the content that will appear in the compiled WinHelp file) and one or more *instruction files* (files containing instructions about how to compile the WinHelp file) are run through the WinHelp 4 compiler (distributed by Microsoft free of charge) and turned into a single compiled file. If you think of running ingredients into a sausage grinder, you're about right. (In fact, the icon for the WinHelp 4 compiler is a little sausage grinder.)

Typical WinHelp source files used by the WinHelp compiler include:

- ✦ The RTF (Rich Text Format) file or files containing the actual topics that will appear in the online help
- ✦ Graphics files
- ✦ Sound, video, and multimedia files
- ✦ Tables of contents files

Typical WinHelp instruction files used by the WinHelp compiler include:

- ✦ An HPJ (Help Project File) file that contains the basic instructions for what to compile and how to compile it, as well as information on how the online help system looks and acts (including the help windows used to display topics)
- ✦ Map (HH) files that contain context-sensitive information for linking the WinHelp to its associated program

In its simplest form, you need only one RTF file and an HPJ file for a WinHelp project, which you run through the Microsoft WinHelp compiler to create a WinHelp file. Depending on the online help project, you could also have additional source files, such as graphics files or additional RTF files, and additional map files. (An online help file will have only one HPJ file.)

A number of types files are created and used during the help development process for creating and maintaining information in a WinHelp project. Table 3-1 shows the file types that you may encounter while working with RoboHELP projects and a description of each one.

Table 3-1
WinHelp Project Files

File extension	*Description*
AKW	This is an internal file created and maintained by RoboHELP. It contains information on "See Also" keywords that aren't currently used in the WinHelp project. (For more information on See Also keywords, see Chapter 8, "Using Tables of Contents and Indexes.")
BMP	These files are BMP (bitmap) graphics files. (For more information on using BMP files, see Chapter 6, "Adding Simple Graphics.")

File extension	*Description*
CNT	This file contains the online help project's table of contents information. When you compile the online help project in WinHelp 4, this information appears on the Contents tab. (You must have the CNT file with the HLP file for this information to appear.) RoboHELP has a Compatibility Wizard that lets you create a Contents tab for online help that runs on Windows 3.1 systems. See Chapter 8, "Using Tables of Contents and Indexes," for more information.
DOC	This file is a standard Word for Windows DOC file. The DOC file contains the online help topics, text, and hyperlinks that appear in the compiled WinHelp file. (You can also embed graphics and other files in the RTF file itself or keep them as separate files.) You can have multiple DOC files that constitute the content of the finished WinHelp file. You'll see how to use multiple DOC files later in this chapter. RoboHELP DOC files are automatically assigned a Word template called ROBOHELP.DOT, which contains standard RoboHELP styles and macros, which tell Word that this is a RoboHELP file and enable the RoboHELP features.
GHC	This file is a map file for creating context-sensitive help with a Visual Basic application. (For more information on using map files and creating context-sensitive help, see Chapter 11, "Creating Context-Sensitive Help.")
GID	This hidden file is created by the WinHelp viewer when you run a WinHelp file for the first time or when you update the file—for example, when you change the position of a WinHelp window or generate the keywords for a full-text search. If you delete this file, WinHelp will create a new GID file when the WinHelp file is opened the next time.
HH	These files contain map IDs, which are used to create context-sensitive links between your WinHelp file and the associated application. (For more information on creating context-sensitive help, see Chapter 11, "Creating Context-Sensitive Help.")
HLP	This file is the compiled WinHelp file. It is viewed with the standard WinHelp viewer included with Windows (either WINHELP.EXE for Windows 3.*x* or WINHLP32.EXE for Windows 95/98/NT/2000).
HPJ	This file is the Help Project File. The HPJ file is a set of instructions in an ASCII text file that describe how to compile the online help project and what source files to use. The Project tab in the RoboHELP Explorer and the RoboHELP ⇨ Project Settings in Word let you examine and maintain the various options in the HPJ file. You can also use the Windows Notepad (or any text editor) to view and edit the raw information in the HPJ file. (For more information on the specifics of the HPJ file, see Appendix A, "The WinHelp HPJ file.")

Continued

Table 3-1 *(continued)*

File extension	*Description*
HPT	This is an internal file created and maintained by RoboHELP. It contains a list of the topics in the DOC files and is used to identify topics for hyperlinks.
INC	This is a file created and maintained by RoboHELP. It is a map file that is distributed to programmers for creating context-sensitive help with a Turbo Pascal Include application. (For more information on using map files and creating context-sensitive help, see Chapter 11, "Creating Context-Sensitive Help.")
KKW	This is an internal file created and maintained by RoboHELP. It contains information on index keywords ("K-Keywords") that aren't currently used in the WinHelp project. (For more information on See Also keywords, see Chapter 8, "Using Tables of Contents and Indexes.")
MRB	These files are MRB (multiresolution bitmap format) graphics files. (For more information on using MRB files, see Chapter 7, "Getting Fancy with Graphics.")
PAS	This is a file created and maintained by RoboHELP. It is a map file that is distributed to programmers for creating context-sensitive help with a Delphi application. (For more information on using map files and creating context-sensitive help, see Chapter 11, "Creating Context-Sensitive Help.")
RTF	This file is the RTF (rich text format) version of the DOC file containing the content. RTF is a document exchange format that is recognized by many different word processors and applications. The WinHelp compiler uses the content in an RTF format rather than in the standard Word DOC file format.
RBH	This is an internal file created and maintained by RoboHELP for tracking information about the DOC and RTF files used in a project.
SHG	These files are SHG (segmented hypergraphic format) graphics files. (For more information on using SHG files, see Chapter 7, "Getting Fancy with Graphics.")
WMF	These files are WMF (Windows Metafile format) graphics files. (For more information on using WMF files, see Chapter 6, "Adding Simple Graphics.")

When you start a new WinHelp project in RoboHELP, it creates an HPJ file and a Word DOC file for the project along with the internal files used by RoboHELP to manage the project. The following section shows you how to start a WinHelp project and create your first WinHelp file.

Understanding the WinHelp Development Process

The overall process for creating a WinHelp project in RoboHELP is fairly straightforward. To create a WinHelp file, you can follow these steps in roughly sequential order:

1. **Create a new help project in RoboHELP.** This creates the basic source and instruction files, sets properties and options for the project, and identifies the online help project to RoboHELP so that it can manage the files.
2. **Create the topics in the document.** Enter the topics, the text, graphics, multimedia, and so on in the DOC file that will communicate the information to the users. Format the topics.
3. **Add hyperlinks.** Insert jumps, popups, and other hyperlinks to link the topics and provide navigation methods between topics in the WinHelp file.
4. **Create the table of contents.** The table of contents is a powerful navigational tool that provides a fast way for users to find information. The table of contents also provides an effective hierarchical order to the information in the WinHelp file.
5. **Create the index.** You'll generate many of the basic keywords when you create the topics, but you'll need to index the document when the topics have been written and organized to add index words and phrases.
6. **Compile the WinHelp file.** Check any warnings and errors that may be reported and correct them, and then recompile. Repeat this step as necessary.
7. **Test the compiled WinHelp file.** Evaluate the style for the headings, the formatting, fonts, and colors for the topic text, and the overall content and organization. Also make sure that any context-sensitive links in the WinHelp file work correctly with the associated program. When you find errors or make changes, correct them, recompile, and then test again.
8. **Hand off the completed WinHelp file.** Distribute the WinHelp file as appropriate. Archive all the source files that went into creating this version of the WinHelp file.

Starting a WinHelp Project

Once you've created a project plan as described in Chapter 2, "What Makes Help 'Help'?" you're ready to start a new WinHelp project. The sample help project you'll see in the screen shots is a standalone help project for Foggan Drizzle Tours, a travel agency specializing in travel to the United Kingdom. This online help will be distributed initially through the agency's Web site, but in later chapters, you'll see how to connect this online help project to a do-it-yourself trip planning program that Foggan Drizzle Tours is selling.

To start a new project help project, do the following:

1. Double-click the RoboHELP icon, shown in Figure 3-1. (As an alternative, you can also go to the Windows Taskbar and select Start ➪ Programs ➪ RoboHELP Office ➪ RoboHELP.)

Figure 3-1: The RoboHELP icon

RoboHELP Explorer starts and the Open a Help Project dialog box appears, as shown in Figure 3-2.

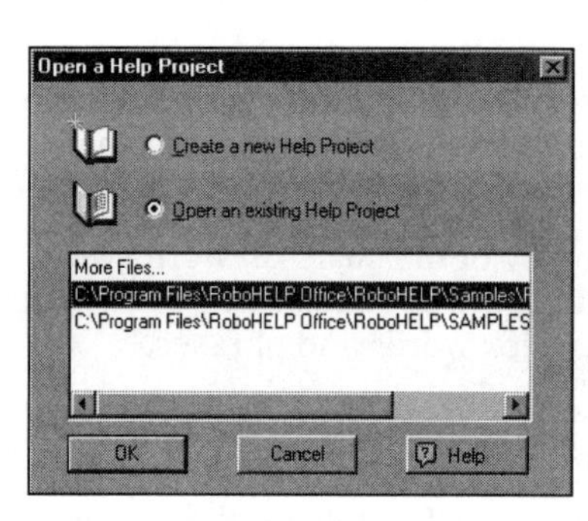

Figure 3-2: The Open a Help Project dialog box

2. Select the Create a new Help project radio button in the Open a Help Project dialog box (as shown in Figure 3-2) to start the RoboHELP Explorer and then click OK. The New Project dialog box appears (shown in Figure 3-3).

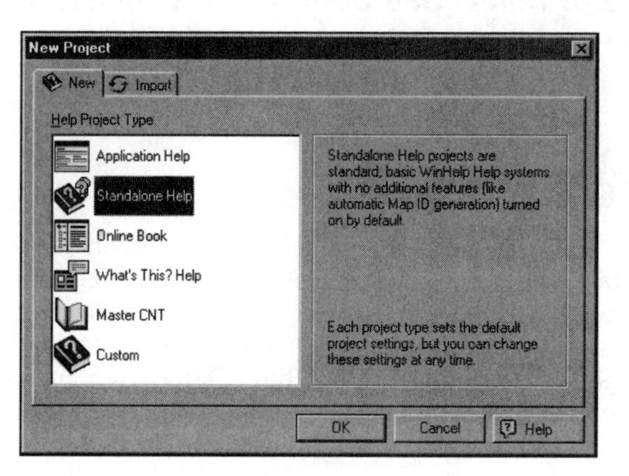

Figure 3-3: The New Project dialog box

3. The New Project dialog box lets you select the type of online help you want to create. The various options in this dialog box are described in Table 3-2.

Table 3-2
The New Project Help Options

Selection	*Description*
Application Help	Use this option for an online help project that will provide context-sensitive help specific to a development environment (such as C++ or Visual Basic) for a program. If you are creating online help that will be used with a program but you don't know or aren't sure of the development environment, use the Standalone Help option.
Standalone Help	Use this option to create a vanilla online help project. You can link a help file created with this option to a program, but you must manually turn on a few options that are set automatically with the Application Help option.
Online Book	Use this option to create an online book. Help created with this option automatically includes Contents, Index, and Search tabs on the Help window. This format is useful for standalone help files of policies, general information, procedures, field service manuals, and so on. You should also use this format for creating online help versions of fiction. You can create this help only for Windows 9*x*/NT or later. (For more information on creating online books, see Chapter 15, "Managing Large Projects.")
What's This? Help	Use this option to create What's This? help using What's This? Help Composer. You can create this help only for Windows 9*x*/NT or later. (For more information on creating What's This? help, see Chapter 13, "Creating What's This? and Training Card Help.")
Master CNT	Use this option to join several separate online help files into a single online help system using a contents (CNT) file. This option is very useful if you're creating customized online help systems that are modular. (For more information on creating files using the Master CNT option, see Chapter 15, "Managing Large Projects.")
Custom	Use this option to create online help using a custom project template. If you choose this option, you'll then select a custom template to apply to the help project. This option is helpful if you want to customize RoboHELP to create a custom standard for the look and feel of your online help projects. (For more information on creating custom help, see Chapter 15, "Managing Large Projects.")

The options in the New Project dialog box tell RoboHELP which defaults to set for automating the online help creation process. If you're not sure which option to select, you can always use the Standalone help option to create a basic online help project without any of the automatic settings and then turn on the RoboHELP features you want as you need them.

4. To create the sample file, select the Standalone Help option and click OK. (You'll see later how to change some of the defaults to make this an Application Help file.) The second New Project screen appears (shown in Figure 3-4).

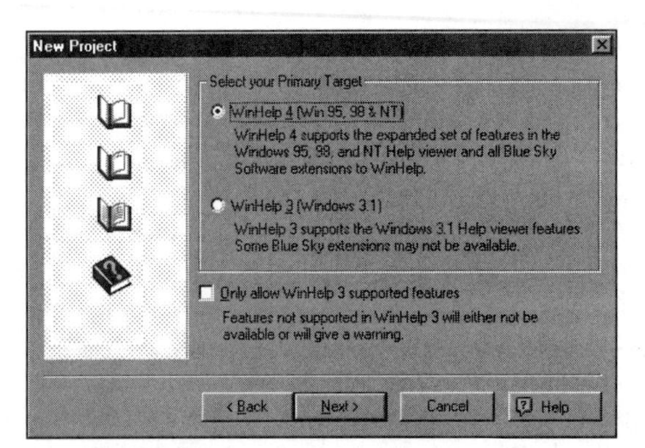

Figure 3-4: The second New Project screen

5. Select the primary target in the second New Project screen. The primary target tells RoboHELP which WinHelp compiler to use and what options should be supported. The type of Windows system(s) on which you're going to be running determines the primary target. Make your choices as follows:

   - **WinHelp 4 (Win 9*x*/NT/2000):** This is the default option for creating new WinHelp. It tells RoboHELP to use the WinHelp 4 compiler. This gives you all the features of WinHelp for Windows 9*x*/NT/2000 as well as the full range of add-ons and extensions of WinHelp from eHelp.

   - **WinHelp 3 (Windows 3.1):** Select this option if you are creating WinHelp 3 files (WinHelp that can be run on Windows 3.*x* using the Windows 3.*x* help engine). RoboHELP will use the Windows 3.*x* help compiler. Some of the add-ons and extensions of WinHelp from eHelp will not be available when you create WinHelp 3 files.

   - **Only allow WinHelp 3 supported features:** Check this box if you want to restrict the WinHelp you are creating to WinHelp 3 features. This option is helpful if you're creating WinHelp that will be used primarily on WinHelp 4 systems (Windows 9*x*/NT/2000) but that will be usable on Windows 3.*x* computers as well. Any features that aren't available in WinHelp 3 will not be available in RoboHELP or will trigger a warning message when you compile. Many of the WinHelp 4 features and the eHelp add-ons and extensions will not be available.

You can change the primary target for the help file at any time. RoboHELP will back up the HPJ file and create a new file with the appropriate features. If you change the primary target from WinHelp 4 to an earlier version, RoboHELP won't automatically identify any incompatibilities between current WinHelp 4 features you may be using and the WinHelp 3 restrictions, although any new features or options you add will be flagged as usual.

When you're satisfied with your entries, click Next. The third New Project screen appears (shown in Figure 3-5 with sample entries).

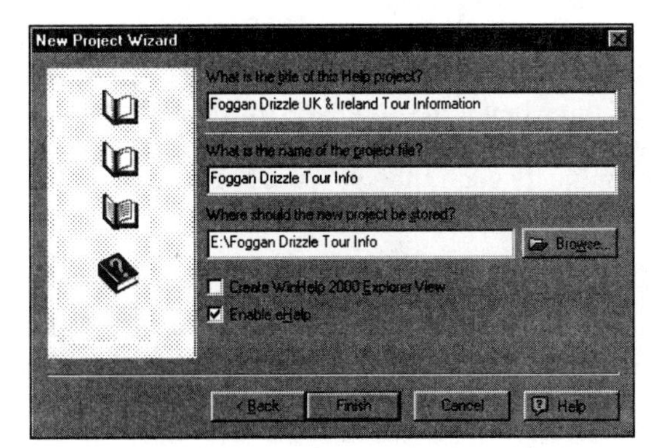

Figure 3-5: The third New Project screen

Unless you are creating online help that must run on a Windows 3.1 computer, select the WinHelp 4 option. This lets you take advantage of all the latest features in RoboHELP and WinHelp.

6. Enter information in the third New Project screen as follows:

   - **What is the title of this Help project?:** Enter the title for the online help project in this field. The title appears in the title bar of the compiled help file. While the title can be up to 127 characters long, you'll probably want to keep the title down to fewer than 60 characters so that the entire title will be visible to the users when they display the online help. Make your titles descriptive — say "Foggan Drizzle UK & Ireland Tour Information" instead of "FD Tour Info."
   - **What is the name of the project file?:** Enter the file name for your help file. Keep this reasonably short. You use this name when you open the project file. (If you are creating an online help for use with Windows 3.*x*, keep the file name to eight characters.)
   - **Where should the new project be stored?:** Enter the path name for the folder in which to store the project. You can browse to a folder using the Browse button. If you enter a folder that doesn't exist, RoboHELP creates it for you.

- **Create WinHelp 2000 Explorer View Help:** Check this box if you want the compiled help to look like standard Windows 98 HTML Help. Leaving this option unchecked generates a standard WinHelp 4 file. (This option isn't available if you're using a WinHelp 3 help compiler.)
- **Enable eHelp:** Check this box if you want to include eHelp, a RoboHELP feature that lets users find additional information on the Web. eHelp also lets your users connect with other users in online communities. (This option isn't available if you're using a WinHelp 3 help compiler.) For more information on eHelp, see Chapter 12, "Linking to the Internet and Adding Multimedia."

When you're satisfied with your entries, click Finish. RoboHELP creates the help files and opens Word with the new DOC file open. The right side of Figure 3-6 shows the new DOC file when it first appears in Word. (Depending on your settings, you may also see the RoboHELP Tip Wizard, which displays helpful tips about a variety of subjects each time you start or open a project.)

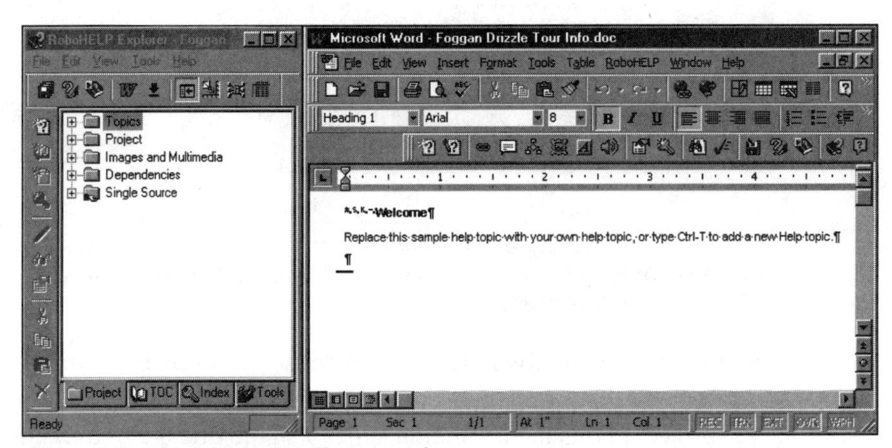

Figure 3-6: The initial DOC file in Word

When you have a RoboHELP project open in Word, RoboHELP adds RoboHELP commands to the Word menus and also creates a new Word menu, "RoboHELP." In addition to starting a help project from the RoboHELP Explorer, you can start a new online help project from the New WinHelp tab in RoboHELP Office or by selecting File ⇨ New RoboHELP Project in Word when you have a RoboHELP project open.

When you open a file in Word that has the ROBOHELP.DOT template attached to it, Word adds a number of menus, commands, and options to Word. As you can see in Figure 3-6, there is a RoboHELP menu in the Word menu bar, which contains a number of commands specific to RoboHELP. As you will see in this and subsequent chapters, a number of RoboHELP commands have been added to the standard Word menus.

In addition to the RoboHELP menu, a RoboHELP toolbar is displayed along with the standard Word toolbars. The icons on the toolbar are shortcuts for a number of RoboHELP commands. The icons and their descriptions appear in Table 3-3.

Table 3-3
RoboHELP Toolbar Icons

Icon	*Description*
	Insert a new topic. This is the same as the Insert ➪ Help Topic command.
	View and modify the topic properties. This is the same as the Edit ➪ Topic Properties command.
	Insert a new jump. This is the same as the Insert ➪ Help Jump command.
	Insert a new popup. This is the same as the Insert ➪ Help Popup command.
	Insert a new macro hotspot. This is the same as the Insert ➪ Other Hotspots ➪ New Macro Hotspot command.
	Insert a new help image. This is the same as the Insert ➪ Help Image command.
	Insert a new help button. This is the same as the Insert ➪ Help Button command.
	Insert a new multimedia file. This is the same as the Insert ➪ Help Multimedia command.
	View and modify the properties. This is the same as the Edit ➪ Properties command.
	Add the highlighted word(s) to the index as a K-Keyword. This is the same as the Edit ➪ Add to Index (K-Keyword) command.
	Finds a help topic or the destination topic of a hotspot. This is the same as the Edit ➪ Find Help Topic command.
	Perform an Active Test on the help file. This is the same as the RoboHELP ➪ Active Test command.
	Save the current document as an RTF file, then save the DOC file. This is the same as the File ➪ Save as RTF command.
	Compile the help project. If any of the DOC files for the help project are open and need to be saved before compiling, this command saves them first, and then continues with the compilation. This is the same as the RoboHELP ➪ Compile command.

Continued

Table 3-3 *(continued)*

Icon	*Description*
	Run the compiled help file. This is the same as the RoboHELP ➪ Run Help File command.
	Display the RoboHELP Explorer. If necessary, RoboHELP also resizes Word so that it and the RoboHELP Explorer are displayed side by side. This is the same as the RoboHELP ➪ RoboHELP Explorer command.
	Display the contents and index for RoboHELP's online help. This is the same as the Help ➪ RoboHELP Contents and Index command.

If you're running a Word antiviral template, such as MVK.DOT, you must disable it before you can use RoboHELP. The RoboHELP templates rely on template macros to perform many of the help creation and maintenance tasks. Antiviral templates frequently block these macros, which interfere with normal operation of RoboHELP.

Adding Topics

When RoboHELP starts a new project, it enters a default Welcome topic with a line of default text. (This topic is shown in Figure 3-7.) The default topic and text are simply a placeholder to get you started with the file.

Adding a New Topic

The first thing to try in your new help project is adding a topic. RoboHELP automates the topic-creation process by letting you fill in information on a dialog box, and then it makes the appropriate entries to create the topic. Here's how to add a topic:

1. Position the insertion point where you want the new topic to start — in this case, at the end of the default topic shown in Figure 3-6.
2. Select Insert ➪ Help Topic. (Alternately, you can press Ctrl+T or click the Help New Topic icon on the RoboHELP toolbar.) The New Topic screen appears (shown in Figure 3-7 with sample topic information).
3. Enter information in the fields on the General tab as follows:
   - **Topic Title:** Enter the topic title. The topic title is the information the users see when they display the topic. For example, in the default topic displayed in Figure 3-6, the topic title is Welcome. The topic title can contain numbers, spaces, special characters, and punctuation.

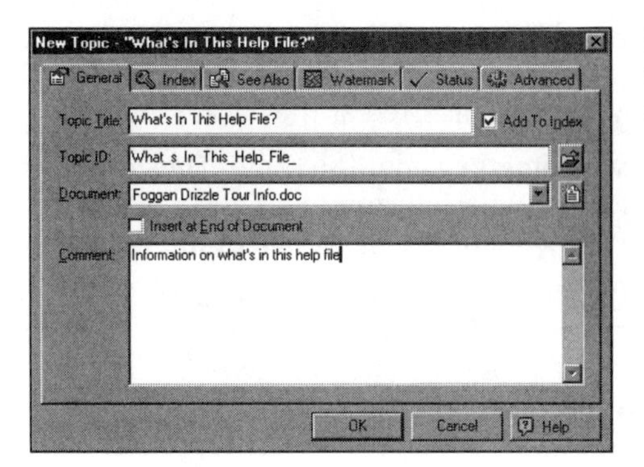

Figure 3-7: The New Topic screen with information added to the General tab

The topic title appears in the index, in See Also help displays, and other navigational aids. The topic heading is the actual text that appears in the DOC file at the start of the topic. These should always be the same to make the WinHelp file easier to use, but they are separate items in the WinHelp file. Whenever you modify one, modify the other.

- **Add to Index:** Check this box if you want to add the topic title as a keyword to the index. (RoboHELP checks to make sure that this isn't a duplicate keyword entry.)
- **Topic ID:** Enter the topic ID. The topic ID is used to identify each topic in the DOC file uniquely. You use topic IDs when doing such things as creating hyperlinks and context-sensitive links. The topic ID is not visible to the users. As you enter the topic title in the Topic Title field, RoboHELP automatically creates a default topic ID in this field. Topic IDs can't have embedded spaces, many special characters, or punctuation except for the underscore, the hyphen, and a few other characters. If you enter a space, a special character, or punctuation that isn't allowed in a topic ID, RoboHELP automatically changes the character to an underscore. As you can see in Figure 3-7, the spaces in the topic title "What's In This Help File?" have been changed so that it now reads "What_s In_This_Help_File_ " in the Topic ID field. You can keep this default topic ID or you can enter a different one if you wish.

If you're creating context-sensitive help, you can click the folder icon to the right of the Topic ID field to create a new topic based on an unused map ID or on a missing topic ID. See Chapter 11, "Creating Context-Sensitive Help," for more information.

- **Document:** Enter the DOC file in which you want to insert this topic. The default is the DOC file you are currently working with, but you can select a document in the open project from the drop-down list, or you can start a new DOC file by clicking the new document icon to the right of this field. When you enter a file name, RoboHELP creates a new, empty DOC file in the project directory and inserts the new topic in it.

- **Insert at End of Document:** Check this box if you want RoboHELP to insert the new topic at the end of the selected DOC file. If this box is not checked, the new topic is inserted at the cursor location.
- **Comment:** Enter any comments about the topic. These comments are optional and are solely for your information. They appear in this folder and in the Comments column of the Topic List in the RoboHELP Explorer.

4. There are several other options and properties you can set for the topic using the various tabs in this screen, but for now, simply click OK to create the new topic with the default settings. (You can always update and modify the topic properties later.) You can add body text and other content below the new topic title. The Foggan Drizzle DOC file with the new topic and body text is shown in Figure 3-8.

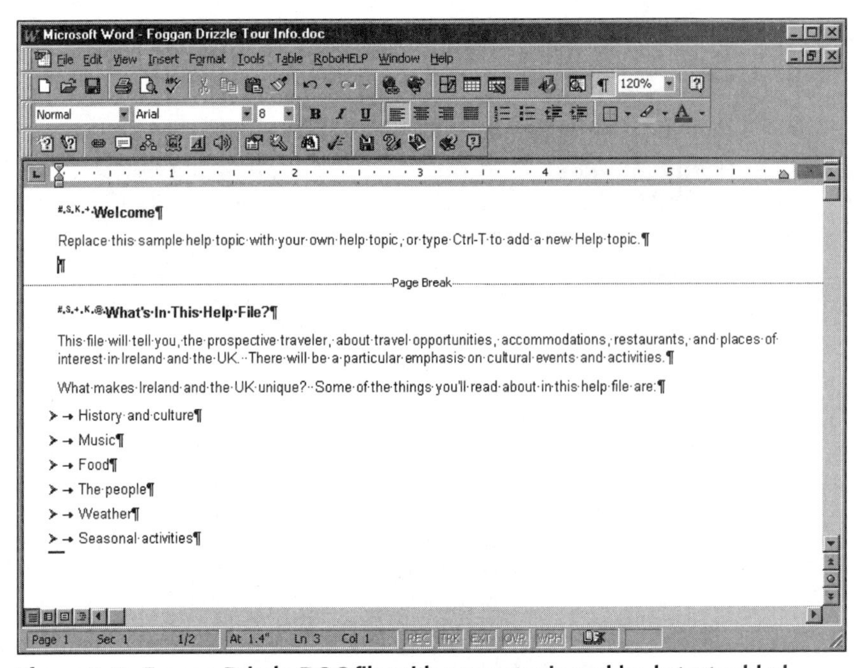

Figure 3-8: Foggan Drizzle DOC file with a new topic and body text added

RoboHELP uses the Heading 1 style in the ROBOHELP.DOT template for the topic headers. By default, this is 8-point bold Arial type. You can change the ROBOHELP.DOT template like any other Word template to reflect your company's preferred styles. Be sure to make a copy of the original template in case you want to revert to the original.

Tips for Creating Good Topics

There are a number of general tips for creating effective topics. Like many writing rules, these are guidelines, not hard rules.

✦ Topics should be chunked effectively. *Chunking* is presenting the optimal number of concepts for the user in a section, usually seven concepts, plus or minus two, depending on the complexity and depth of the material. If you present too many concepts in a section, you may overload your users' ability to absorb and retain material. Similarly, procedures should be kept reasonably short—no more than seven steps, plus or minus two.

✦ Try to break topics up to minimize the amount of scrolling that the users must do. The best design has most of the topics completely visible on a single screen without the need to scroll up or down. However, you must balance this with minimizing the amount of clicking the users must do to get to a topic. The users should be able to reach any topic from the main screen in no more than three or four clicks of the mouse. One way to do this is to break out material into large sections; for example, tutorial, procedures, and reference materials for a product can each go into separate sections.

Depending on the scope of the online help and the depth and complexity of the material being covered, it may be impossible to balance these two goals. Careful planning and an understanding of exactly what your users want most will help you produce the best online help for your users.

✦ As with printed documentation, the old rule of "tell 'em three times" applies. You should have an overview for each section that cues the users as to what is being presented, followed by specific information, and then a summary. Take advantage of hyperlinks to create a menu on each overview that lets the users jump directly to a topic within the section.

✦ Use gerunds for your topic headers.

✦ Don't feel you're limited to a specific number of topics. An online help file can contain as many topics as you'd like.

Creating a Quick Topic

Suppose you already have a block of text you want to use to create a new topic, such as if you want to break an existing topic into several smaller topics. RoboHELP makes this process quick and easy with the *quick topic* feature, as follows.

Highlight the text you want to turn into a separate topic, and then select the Insert ⇨ Special Help Topics ⇨ Quick Topic command (you can also press Ctrl+Q to create a quick topic).

RoboHELP creates a topic from the highlighted information. The insertion point for the new topic is at the start of the highlighted text and the first line of the highlighted text becomes the topic header. Figure 3-9 shows some of the body text from the new topic you added earlier turned into a separate topic.

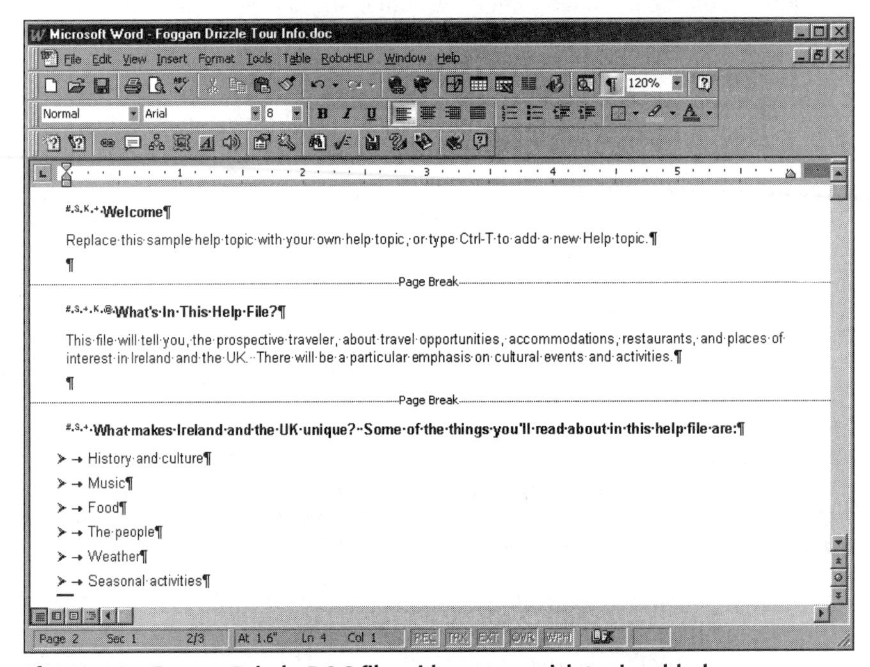

Figure 3-9: Foggan Drizzle DOC file with a new quick topic added

Modifying Topic Properties

As you can see in Figure 3-9, the topic header is a little long to be really practical. You could modify the topic header like any other text string, but doing so wouldn't affect the topic title or the other topic information. You can modify the topic header, topic title, and topic ID together, as follows:

1. Place the cursor within the topic (it doesn't matter where), and then select the Edit ➪ Topic Properties command (you can also just press Ctrl+E to create a quick topic). The Topic Properties screen appears with the topic information in the fields, as shown in Figure 3-10.
2. As you can see, the topic title and the topic ID have been created from the text that appears in the topic header. Modify both the topic title and the topic ID by eliminating the sentence starting "Some of…" When you're satisfied with your entries, click OK.

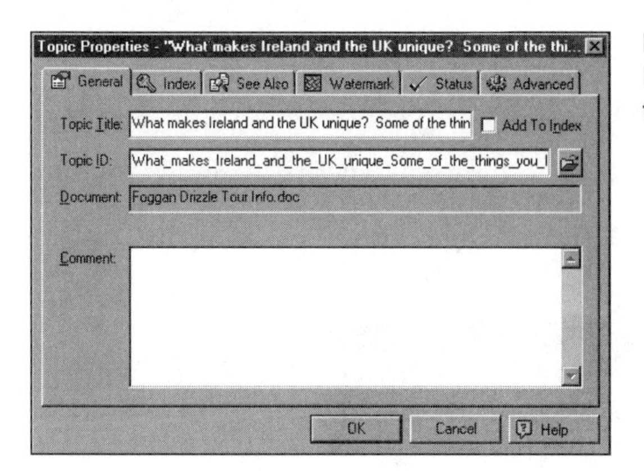

Figure 3-10: The Topic Properties screen featuring the quick topic information

3. Because you've modified the topic title, RoboHELP asks if you would like to update the topic heading as well. You'll usually want to say Yes to this question. RoboHELP will make the topic header match the entry in the modified topic title. You can then make any other changes to the body text for the topic. Figure 3-11 shows the modified quick topic.

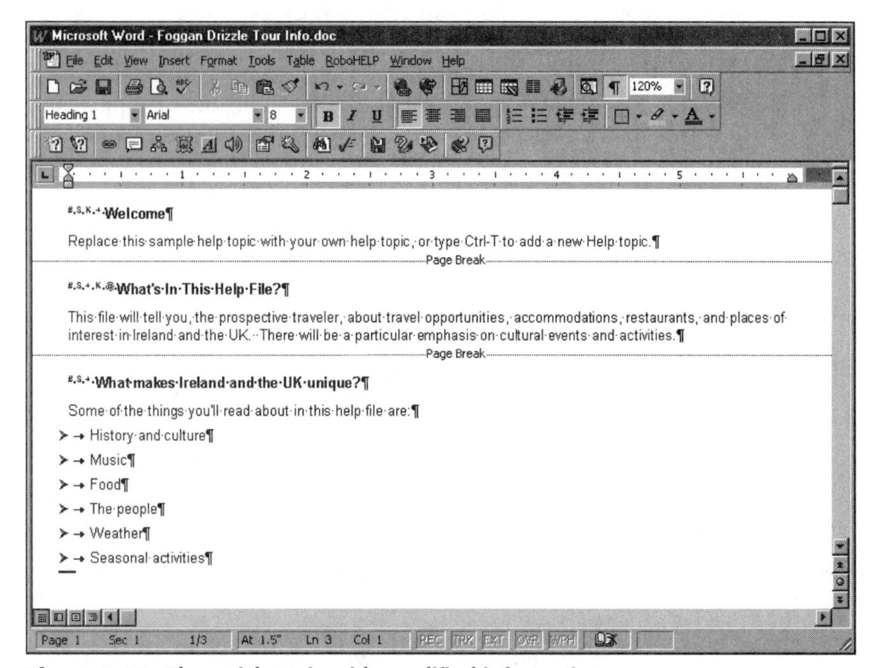

Figure 3-11: The quick topic with modified information

Deleting a Topic

You can delete a topic easily:

1. Place the cursor in the topic you want to delete (it doesn't matter where) and select the Edit ➪ Delete ➪ Topic command. The Delete Topic screen appears (shown in Figure 3-12).

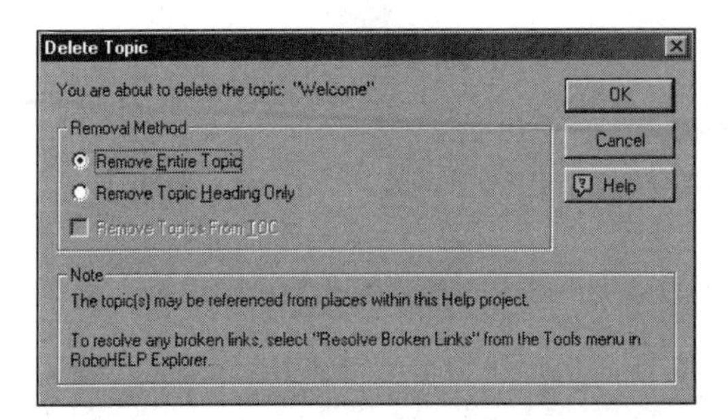

Figure 3-12: The Delete Topic screen

2. Select Remove Entire Topic (the default) to delete the topic and click OK. RoboHELP deletes the topic and eliminates all references to the topic in the internal RoboHELP files.

If you want to combine a topic's content with the preceding topic, select Remove Topic Heading Only. RoboHELP deletes the page break, the topic footnotes, and the topic header and runs the body of the topic into the preceding topic's body text.

Although you can delete the topic itself from the DOC file simply by selecting the page break, the topic footnotes, topic header, and the body of the topic and deleting them, using this method won't remove the information stored internally in the RoboHELP project files. If you have deleted a topic this way, you need to use the Tools ➪ Resolve Broken Links command in the RoboHELP Explorer to make sure there aren't any unresolved references to the deleted topic in existing jumps or popups. (See Chapter 4, "Adding Jumps and Popups," for more information.).

Compiling Your WinHelp File

With a couple of topics in the help file, you're ready to try compiling your WinHelp file for the first time.

Compiling lets you see the WinHelp file as your users would see it. You can use the compiled file to examine a new color scheme, review the look of a new topic on the screen, test hyperlinks and keywords, and check context-sensitive links.

You can compile the WinHelp file whenever you like and as frequently as you like. You'll probably compile your help file at least several times a day as you're creating it. If you're in testing and debugging mode, you'll likely compile several times an hour: make a fix to a bug, recompile, test the fix, and go on to the next bug. Compiling frequently also lets you monitor the progression of your work and allows you to identify potential problems with the content, layout, colors, or format when they're still easy to fix.

To compile the Foggan Drizzle help file, do the following:

Select the RoboHELP ⇨ Compile command (you can also press Ctrl+M or click the Compile icon in the RoboHELP toolbar, which is shown in Figure 3-13). When the compiler starts, RoboHELP displays the Result screen. As the help file is compiled, the compiler displays information in this screen. When the file has been compiled, you can click Run to see what the finished help file looks like. Figure 3-14 shows the Result screen after the help file has been successfully compiled.

Figure 3-13: The Compile icon

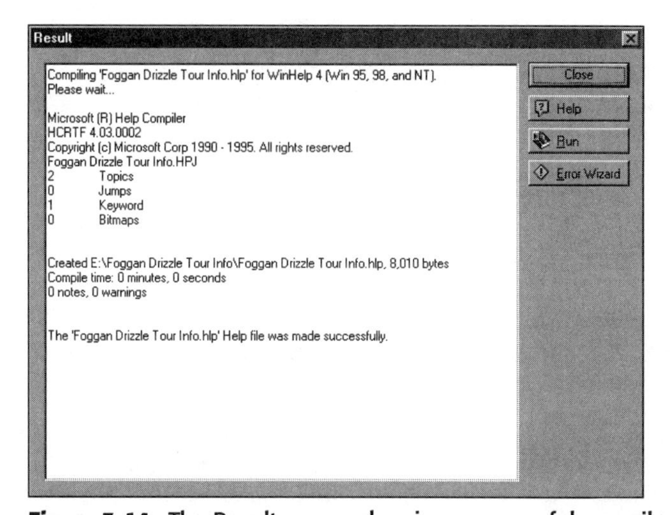

Figure 3-14: The Result screen showing a successful compile

If you have one or more DOC files open in Word that will be used to create this help file and that have unsaved changes, RoboHELP will save the files before continuing.

As you can see from Figure 3-14, the Result screen shows information about the following:

✦ The type of compiler and the specific version being used

✦ The HPJ file being used

✦ The number of topics, jumps, keywords, and bitmaps in the help file

✦ The name and size of the compiled help file

✦ The amount of time it took to compile the file

✦ The number of notes and warnings

Any notes or warnings generated during the compile would have been displayed on the Result screen as well.

The newly compiled WinHelp file will have an extension of HLP. If there's a file of the same name in the target directory, the WinHelp compiler will replace the existing file. You can run the help file right away by clicking Run on the right side of the Result screen. Figure 3-15 shows a topic in the compiled help file.

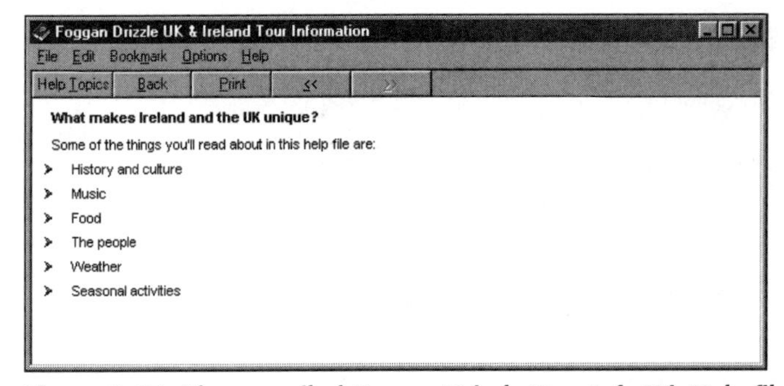

Figure 3-15: The compiled Foggan Drizzle Tour Info WinHelp file

The compiled file looks like any other simple help file. You can navigate this file using the previous and next buttons in the button bar (shown in Figures 3-16 and 3-17), but using just this method to go from one topic to another would be cumbersome and not very helpful to the users. The next section shows you how to add keywords to your help file to create an index.

Figure 3-16: The previous button in the Winhelp button bar

Figure 3-17: The next button in the Winhelp button bar

Adding Index Keywords

Index keywords (also known as K-Keywords or simply keywords) give the users an important way to navigate the WinHelp file. As with a printed index, the index contains words and phrases that help you find topics in the WinHelp file.

The users usually access the index from the button bar through the Help Topics button. As Figure 3-18 shows, there is only one keyword entry for the Foggan Drizzle help file. Because the Add to Index field in the New Topics screen was checked when you created this topic, RoboHELP created the keyword automatically. There isn't a keyword entry yet for the second topic because it was created with the Quick Topic feature.

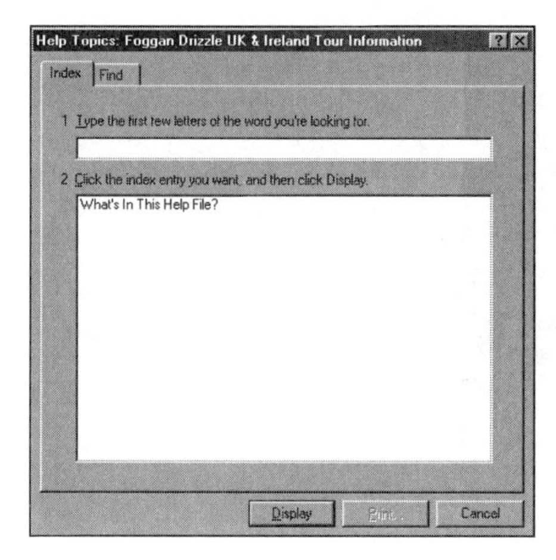

Figure 3-18: The index for the Foggan Drizzle help file

The first thing to do to expand the list of keywords is to add keywords for the second topic so that it appears in the list, as follows:

1. Place the cursor within the topic you want to add keywords to (it doesn't matter where) and then select the Edit ➪ Topic Properties command (you can also press Ctrl+E to create a quick topic). The Topic Properties screen appears with the topic information in the fields, as shown in Figure 3-19.
2. Select the Index tab. The Index tab for the topic appears, as shown in Figure 3-20.
3. To add a keyword, click New on the right of the Index tab. A new keyword placeholder appears. Type the word or phrase to add to the keyword list. Start by adding the topic title to the list. When you're satisfied with your entry for the keyword, press Enter. You can add another keyword by clicking New and entering the next word or phrase. You can add as many keywords as you like. Click OK when you're done. (By the way, it's a good idea to save your changes after you make a lot of changes and additions by selecting the File ➪ Save command.) Figure 3-21 shows a list of keywords added to this topic.

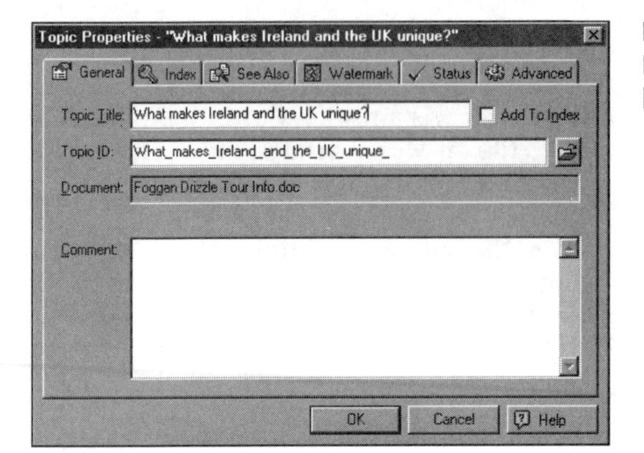

Figure 3-19: The Topic Properties screen showing basic topic information

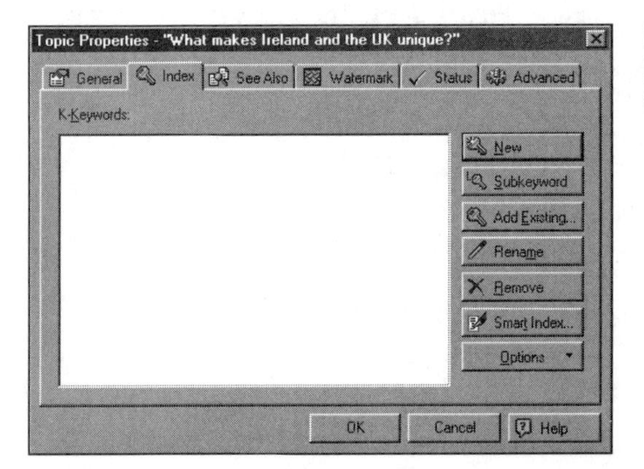

Figure 3-20: The Topic Properties screen showing the Index tab

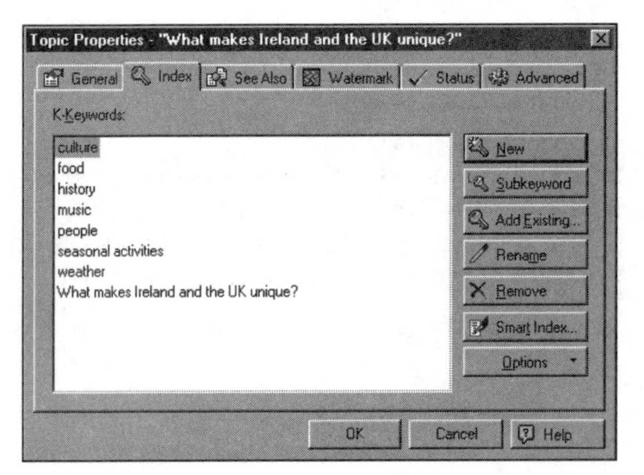

Figure 3-21: Keywords added to the topic

Tips for entering keywords are as follows:

✦ Keywords don't have to be entered in alphabetical order. RoboHELP sorts your entries for you when they're displayed in the help file.

✦ Don't capitalize keyword entries unless they're proper nouns.

✦ Use simple gerunds to describe actions, such as "adding," "changing," "printing," and so on.

✦ Generally speaking, the more comprehensive the keyword list, the more useful the index will be to your users. However, avoid keywords that duplicate entries, such as "changing" and "modifying" or "adding" and "entering."

You can add keywords to a topic at any time using the Topic Properties screen. You can also add keywords to a topic using the Index tab on the New Topic screen when you're creating the topic. However, as with creating any index, you probably won't have all the keywords you want to use when you're setting up the topic. Most RoboHELP help authors tend to make basic keyword entries on the Index tab when they set up the topic and then add more keywords later as part of an indexing phase when the online help file is largely complete.

If you just want to add one or two keywords to a topic, you might try the following:

1. Highlight the word or phrase you want to add as a keyword.
2. From the RoboHELP right-click menu (which appears when you right-click in the topic), select the Add to Index (K-Keyword) command. You can simply select the Edit ➪ Add to Index (K-Keyword) command if you prefer.

RoboHELP adds the highlighted word or phrase as a keyword to this topic exactly as it appears, including capitalization. (You may need to edit the keyword after you've created it.)

When you compile the Foggan Drizzle file again, you'll see an increase in the number of keywords listed in the Result screen. The revised index appears in Figure 3-22.

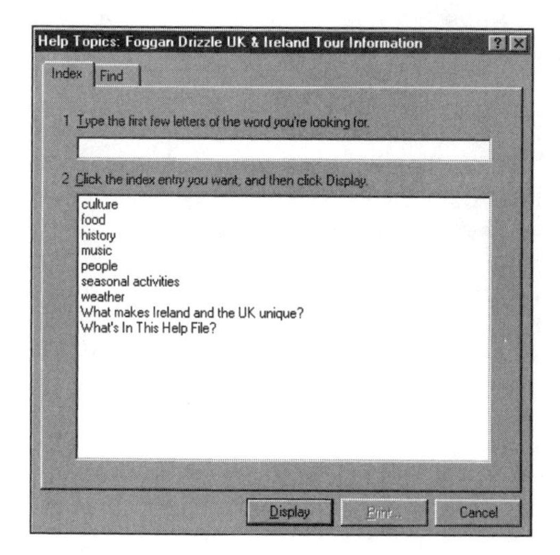

Figure 3-22: The revised index showing the added keywords

Adding Subkeywords

In addition to the keywords you see in Figure 3-22, you can add multiple levels of keywords known as *subkeywords*. These appear in the index as indented items beneath the associated keyword.

To add subkeywords, do the following:

1. Display the Topic Properties screen and go to the Index tab as you did before. Highlight the keyword you want to add subkeywords to and click the Subkeyword button on the right of the Index tab. A new subkeyword entry appears below the keyword, as shown in Figure 3-23.
2. As before when you added a keyword, type the word or phrase for the subkeyword and press Enter. You can add another subkeyword by highlighting the word you want to add the subkeyword to (in this example, "history"), and clicking Subkeyword, then entering the next subkeyword word or phrase. Click OK when you're done. Figure 3-24 shows several subkeywords added to the "history" keyword.

You can have only two levels of keywords in WinHelp files.

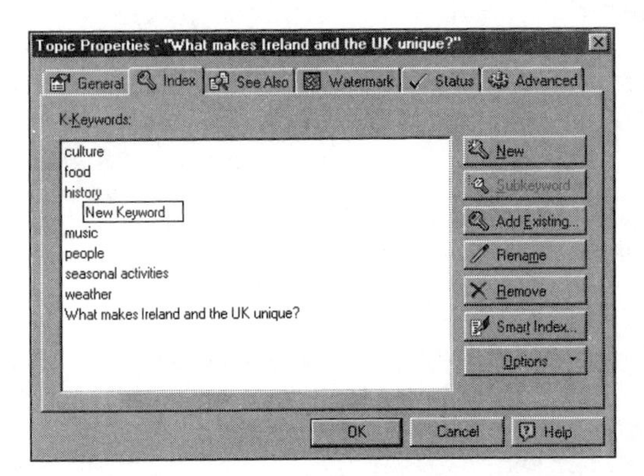

Figure 3-23: Adding a subkeyword to a keyword

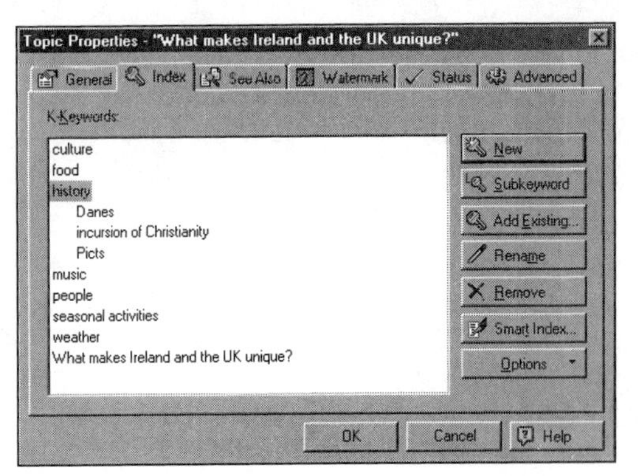

Figure 3-24: Subkeywords added to the keyword list

Adding Keywords from Existing Topics

Most of the time when you're adding keywords, you have a group of related topics, all of which should have the same keywords. Adding keywords with the method you've seen in the previous section would be tedious and also would run the risk of there being slight differences between keywords. A much more efficient way of copying keywords from one topic to several others is to use the Add Existing Keyword option, as follows:

1. Place the cursor within the topic you want to copy keywords to, display the Topic Properties screen, and select the Index tab. Click Add Existing on the right of the Index tab. The Add Existing Keyword screen appears (shown in Figure 3-25).

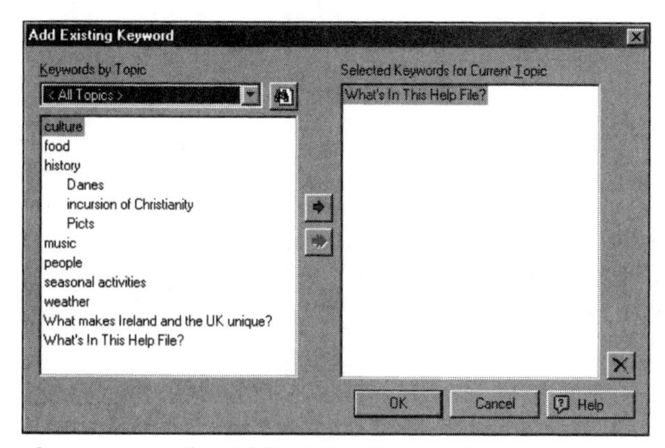

Figure 3-25: The Add Existing Keyword screen

2. Select a keyword from the list on the left and click the single arrow to copy the keyword to the topic. The Keywords by Topic field lets you select from all the keywords in the DOC file (the default) or from a specific topic, which you can select from the drop-down list. (If you're not sure which topic to use, you can click the Find button to the right of the Keywords by Topic field to search for a specific topic title, topic ID, or text item.) You can copy all the keywords in the list by clicking the double arrow. When you're satisfied with your keyword entries, click OK to return to the Index tab, then click OK once more to exit the Topic Properties screen and save your changes.

If you decide you don't want a keyword in the list for the topic (including keywords that were already there), you can highlight the keyword and click the large X on the Add Existing Keywords screen.

You can use this technique to copy keywords quickly from one or more topics to the selected topic. If you have a lot of topics that have the same keywords, you might want to build a dummy topic to hold the selected list of keywords and then use the double arrow to copy all the keywords to one topic after another. After you've added all the keywords, you can delete the dummy topic.

For more information on creating and maintaining keywords and indexes, see Chapter 8, "Using Tables of Contents and Indexes."

Understanding Topic Elements

Every topic in a RoboHELP DOC file has the following traits:

- ✦ The topic begins with a hard page break (or the start of the DOC file), which signifies to the compiler that a new topic is starting. (You get a warning when you compile if you have embedded page breaks that are just to break up pages.)
- ✦ Immediately following the page break are one or more footnotes using specific characters that identify such things to the help compiler as the topic title, the unique topic identifier, keywords, and so on. For example, when the compiler sees the $ footnote code before a topic header in the DOC file, it uses the information in that footnote for the topic title. Similarly, the information in the # footnote is the topic ID. (You'll have a chance to examine the basic footnote codes later in this section.)
- ✦ Following the footnote codes is a line of text that appears as the topic header (also known as the topic caption) when you display the topic.
- ✦ After the topic header is the body of the topic, which can be topic text, hyperlinks, graphics, or other material.
- ✦ The topic ends with a paragraph mark.

As you have seen, when you add the two topics to the DOC file, RoboHELP handles most of the formatting necessary to create a topic.

Understanding Topic Footnotes

If you've ever had to add footnotes to a Word document, you'll know what a nuisance it would be to have to add several footnotes to each topic in your DOC file, particularly if you had several hundred topics. Fortunately, RoboHELP adds the footnotes for you automatically when you create a topic and provides you with an easy-to-use interface for maintaining the topic and its footnotes.

Although you won't usually have to add footnotes to a topic yourself, it's a good idea to know what they are. This is frequently helpful when you want to make a quick change and don't want to use RoboHELP (for example, when you're adding a keyword or correcting a duplicate entry).

The three most common types of footnotes are the #, $, and K footnotes:

- ✦ The first and most important footnote is the # footnote. The # (pound) character denotes the topic ID. The topic ID uniquely identifies the topic to the help system. The WinHelp viewer uses this information internally to display the topic. You also use this information to identify a topic so you can create a hyperlink. Each topic must have a # footnote, although it doesn't need any other footnote.
- ✦ The next footnote is the $ (dollar sign) footnote, which is used to specify the topic title. The information entered in this footnote appears in the WinHelp viewer when the user searches an associated index keyword. Although most topics have a $ footnote, you can omit this if you don't want to display a topic title—for example, if you are creating a topic that appears only in a popup window.
- ✦ The third most common footnote is the K footnote. The K footnote is used to list the index keywords for a topic. These keywords appear on the Index tab when the users are searching the WinHelp file. Adding keywords is optional, but usually desirable (a good index is an invaluable navigational tool for the completed WinHelp file).

Each topic must have at least one footnote (the # footnote for the topic ID). You can use as many of the footnote codes as appropriate, however. Most topics have from three to six footnote codes.

The next section shows you how to use these footnotes later directly with Word. Other types of footnotes also can appear in the topic headers. These will be discussed later in this book.

A complete list of footnotes appears in Appendix B, "Footnote Symbols."

Adding and Modifying Topics and Keywords Manually

Like many parts of the help development process, RoboHELP simply automates tasks that you could do manually (but would prefer not to), such as inserting footnote codes. Most of the time, you'll want to let RoboHELP do the work for you, but occasionally, you'll want to add or modify a topic directly in Word. (It may help to think of this as peeking under the hood to see how everything works.)

Figure 3-26 shows you the footnotes for a topic in the Foggan Drizzle help file. (To open the footnotes window in Word, select the View ➪ Footnotes command.) As you can see, the topic ID in the # footnote appears first, followed by the topic title ($). The browse sequence, denoted by a +, appears next. (The + is a footnote you haven't seen yet. Browse sequences are discussed in Chapter 9, "Using Help Windows and Browse Sequences.") Finally, the list of keywords for the topic appears in the K footnote.

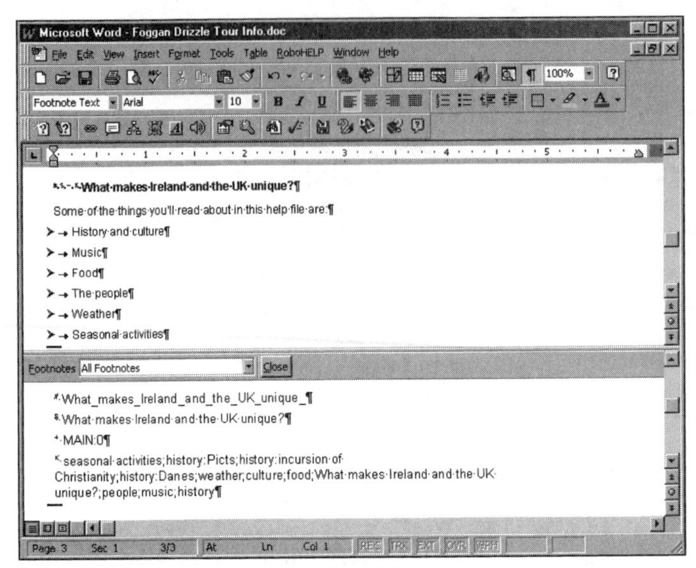

Figure 3-26: A topic and its related footnotes

Adding and modifying topics manually

Adding and modifying topics manually is not difficult, but you should keep a few things in mind:

✦ Place the footnotes at the start of the topic header using the Insert ⇨ Footnote command in Word. (A common mistake is to simply type in the character for the footnote rather than use the Insert ⇨ Footnote command in Word.) Enter the appropriate information for each footnote in the View Footnotes window.

✦ You can copy an entire topic from the page break to the last paragraph mark before the following topic's page break and then paste it in a new location. Be sure to change the information in the footnotes as appropriate—particularly the topic ID.

✦ There should never be a paragraph mark or text between the page break and the footnote symbols, nor should there be a paragraph mark between the footnote symbols and the topic header.

✦ You can use Word search and edit features in the View Footnotes window if you need to find or replace specific words or phrases. Remember that if your cursor is in the View Footnotes window, you won't find information in the document window. (You can switch back and forth between these two windows easily by pressing Shift+F6.)

✦ Adding or modifying topic information manually shortcuts many of the processes that RoboHELP has for tracking changes. The new topic will not show up in the internal list of topics until the next time you save and compile the project, the topic ID could be a duplicate of another topic ID that's already in the project, and so on.

Adding and modifying keywords manually

You may want to add keywords manually in cases where there is a large block of keywords already in the topic and you want to quickly replace it with another block of keywords using Word cut and paste features. You might also want to do this if you are making a global change from one word or phrase to another that could be accomplished quickly with a search-and-replace operation.

To change keywords manually, open the View Footnote window. As you can see in Figure 3-26, each keyword is separated by a semicolon. Subkeywords have the primary keyword, a colon, and then the subkeyword itself. For example, the three subkeywords in the topic featured in Figure 3-26 — Dane, incursion of Christianity, and Picts — are all preceded by "history:" to show that they are subkeywords of the "history" keyword.

Keywords don't have to be entered in alphabetical order. If you're adding a keyword to a footnote, it's okay to put it at the end of the list. RoboHELP sorts your entries for you when they're displayed in the help file.

You can have a maximum of 1,023 characters in the K footnote for a topic and only one K footnote for each topic. Characters beyond this limit will be ignored when the file is compiled. You probably won't bump into this limit unless you're aggressively indexing the document.

Printing the Topic Properties Report

RoboHELP comes with a number of reports that can help you track topic information as well as most other elements of your WinHelp projects. Most of these reports are customizable so that you can report on a specific range of information or group of items. All of these reports are accessible through the RoboHELP Explorer.

The Topic Properties report provides you with information about your help topics and their properties. You can optionally display information about such things as topic jumps and popups, TOC references, Index entries, See Also keywords, and aliases.

To generate a Topic Properties report, do the following:

From RoboHELP Explorer, select the Tools ➪ Reports ➪ Topic Properties command. The Topic Properties report is displayed on the screen, as shown in Figure 3-27. The help topics appear on the report in order by topic title or topic ID, depending on whether you have selected the View ➪ By Topic Title or the View ➪ By Topic ID command in RoboHELP Explorer.

You can filter the information on the Topic Properties report in several ways. You can show the topics created by each author, all authors, or those that aren't assigned to specific authors, depending on your selection in the drop-down list in the Author field. You can also look at the topics in all the documents in the project or in individual documents with the drop-down list in the Document field.

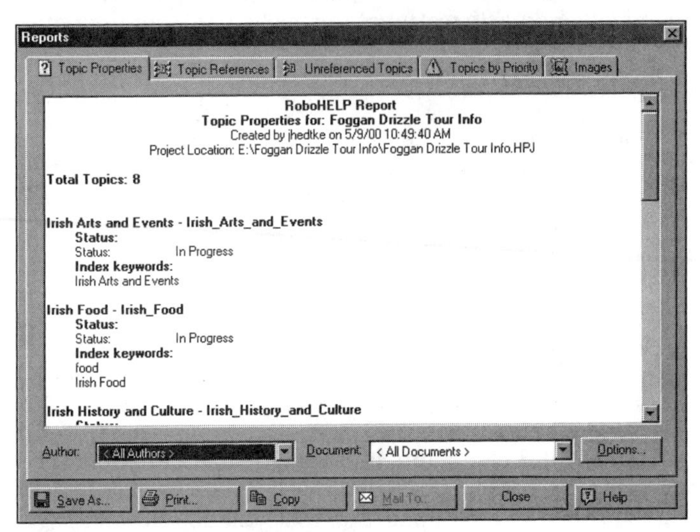

Figure 3-27: The Topic Properties report

In addition, RoboHELP lets you specify what information to display on the report, as follows:

1. Click Options on the lower-right corner of the Topic Properties report. The Topic Report Options screen appears (shown in Figure 3-28).

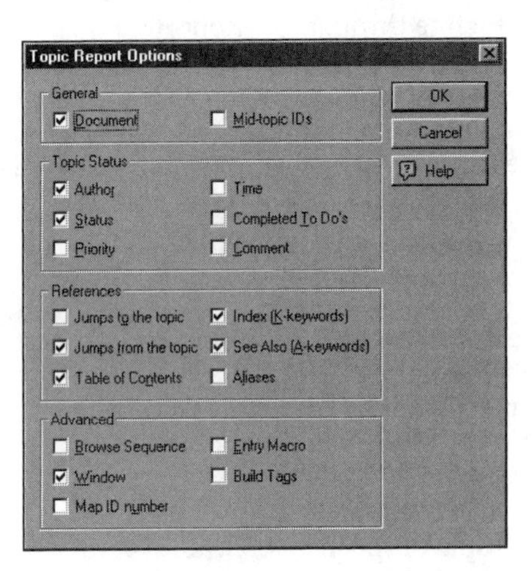

Figure 3-28: The Topic Report Options screen

2. Select the information you want to display on the report as follows:
   - **Document:** Displays the document in which each help topic appears. (This is very useful when reporting on a project with several DOC files.)
   - **Mid-topic IDs:** Displays all the mid-topics IDs for the topics in the report.

Cross-Reference

For more information on mid-topic IDs, see Chapter 4, "Adding Jumps and Popups."

   - **Author:** Displays the author who's assigned to each topic that appears in the report.
   - **Status:** Displays the current status of each topic that appears in the report.
   - **Priority:** Displays the priority of each topic that appears in the report.
   - **Time:** Displays the estimated hours per topic of each topic that appears in the report.
   - **Completed To Do's:** Displays the to-do status of each topic that appears in the report.

Cross-Reference

For more information on assigning authors and setting status, priority, time estimates, and to-do items, see Chapter 15, "Managing Large Projects."

   - **Comment:** Displays the topic comment of each topic that appears in the report.
   - **Jumps to the Topic:** Displays the jumps and popups to the topics that appear in the report.
   - **Jumps from the Topic:** Displays the jumps and popups from the topics that appear in the report to other topics (whether those topics appear in the report or not).

Cross-Reference

For more information on jumps and popups, see Chapter 4, "Adding Jumps and Popups."

   - **Table of Contents:** Displays the page references to the TOC for the project.
   - **Index (K-Keywords):** Displays the index entries of each topic that appears in the report.

Cross-Reference

For more information on the TOC and index, see Chapter 8, "Using Tables of Contents and Indexes."

   - **See Also (A-Keywords):** Displays the See Also entries (A-Keywords) of each topic that appears in the report.

Cross-Reference

For more information on See Also entries, see Chapter 8, "Using Tables of Contents and Indexes."

- **Aliases:** Displays the aliases for the map ID of each topic that appears in the report.

For more information on aliases, see Chapter 11, "Creating Context-Sensitive Help."

- **Browse Sequence:** Displays the browse sequence of each topic that appears in the report.

For more information on browse sequences, see Chapter 9, "Using Help Windows and Browse Sequences."

- **Window:** Displays the default help window used for each topic that appears in the report.

For more information on help windows, see Chapter 9, "Using Help Windows and Browse Sequences."

- **Map ID number:** Displays the map ID of each topic that appears in the report.

For more information on map IDs, see Chapter 11, "Creating Context-Sensitive Help."

- **Entry Macro:** Displays the entry macro of each topic that appears in the report.

For more information on entry macros, see Chapter 10, "Understanding Macros."

- **Build Tags:** Displays the build tags of each topic that appears in the report.

For more information on build tags, see Chapter 15, "Managing Large Projects."

3. When you're satisfied with your entries, click OK. RoboHELP will generate the report with the new options that you've selected.

There are several standard output and distribution options for all RoboHELP reports. You can save the report as an RTF or TXT file by clicking Save As, print the report by clicking Print, copy the report to the Windows clipboard by clicking Copy, or mail the report to someone by clicking Mail to. To close the report window, click Close.

You can run the Topic Properties report (or any of the RoboHELP reports) at any time.

Summary

In this chapter, you were introduced to the concepts of creating WinHelp. You saw the typical flow for creating a WinHelp project. Next, you learned how to create a new WinHelp project in RoboHELP and how to add topics to it, as well as modify and delete them. You then saw how to compile the file and run the resulting WinHelp file. You next learned how to add keywords to the index to make navigation easier. You saw some of the technical aspects of creating and maintaining topics and learned how to add and modify topics and keywords without using RoboHELP. Finally, you saw how to print the Topic Properties report to examine information about topics in your WinHelp project.

In the next chapter, you'll learn how to create hyperlinks: jumps and popups. You'll see ways to use jumps to create menus and popups for quick reference and glossary items.

✦ ✦ ✦

Adding Jumps and Popups

In This Chapter

Learning about hyperlinks

Adding and using different kinds of jumps

Adding and using popups

Testing jumps and popups

Maintaining jumps and popups

Creating jumps and popups automatically

Viewing topic references

Using the Link View to see references

Printing reports on local and internal topic references

This chapter introduces you to creating hyperlinks: jumps and popups. You'll learn about the basic concepts of hyperlinks and how they're used in online help. You'll be introduced to a wide range of jumps and see ways you can use them to add navigation options to your help files. Next, the chapter shows you how to add popups and provides some examples of the more common ways to use them. The chapter continues with information on testing and maintaining the jumps and popups you've added and shows you how to create them automatically. Finally, you'll learn several ways to examine topic references.

Understanding Hyperlinks

Hyperlinks (known in RoboHELP as *hotspots*) are a method of moving directly from one topic to another. The most common types of hotspots are jumps and popups. When you click a jump, you "jump" from one topic to the next. Popups display a WinHelp topic temporarily (useful for displaying tidbits of information such as a glossary entry or a note). You use hotspots in your WinHelp file to link topics to other topics, terms, reference materials, and even topics in other WinHelp files or Internet sites.

Hotspots are one of the strengths of online help — they are one of the key features that distinguish online help from simple pages of text online. By providing hotspots that link information in a topic to related information elsewhere in the online help file, the users can click the hotspots to follow a specific "thread" of information from subject to subject through the online help, a process known as navigating. Hotspots make it possible for the help users to access the specific information they need or want without having to work through the material in a linear or hierarchical fashion from chapter to chapter. By providing additional paths for viewing information, the online help file becomes increasingly useful to the help users.

Both jumps and popups are identifiable by their formatting. Hotspots are typically green and have a solid or a dotted underline to show that they are items or areas you can click (although if you prefer, you can format them so that they have a different color or no color at all and/or no underlining). Regardless of how they're formatted, however, the help users can always identify a hotspot by moving the cursor over it: the pointer changes to a pointing hand, signifying that you can click to activate the hotspot.

This chapter and the subsequent chapters in this part of the book will show you a variety of ways in which you can format hotspots. Make sure that you use hotspot formatting consistently so as not to confuse the help users.

There are six types of WinHelp hotspots in RoboHELP, which perform different types of actions when clicked (see Table 4-1).

Table 4-1
Types of Hotspots

Type of Hotspot	*Description*
Jump	When clicked, a jump hotspot takes you to the specified topic (also known as the *destination topic* or the *target topic*) within the current WinHelp file. Jumps are used for navigating from topic to topic.
Popup	When clicked, a pop-up hotspot displays the specified topic in a small, self-sizing window that disappears when you click a mouse button or press a key. Popups are usually used for quick reference material or glossary definitions.
External topic jump	When clicked, an external topic jump hotspot takes you to a specified topic in another WinHelp file.
HTML hotspot	When clicked, an HTML hotspot takes you to intranet sites, Internet web sites, or topics in HTML Help files.
Macro hotspot	When clicked, a macro hotspot starts a macro. You can use macro hotspots to run programs or perform complex tasks. (Macros are covered in Chapter 10, "Understanding Macros.")
See Also hotspots	When clicked, a See Also hotspot (also known as a Related Topics link) checks for See Also keywords (A-keywords) and displays them in a dialog box that lists the related topics. (For more information on creating and using See Also links and keywords, see Chapter 8, "Using Tables of Contents and Indexes.")

Adding Jumps

Adding a jump is as simple as adding a topic. Start by opening the help project you created in Chapter 3 as follows:

1. Start RoboHELP Explorer by double-clicking the RoboHELP icon as you did when you started the help project. (You can also go to the Windows Taskbar and select Programs ⇨ RoboHELP Office ⇨ RoboHELP.) RoboHELP Explorer starts and the Open a Help Project dialog box appears, as shown in Figure 4-1.

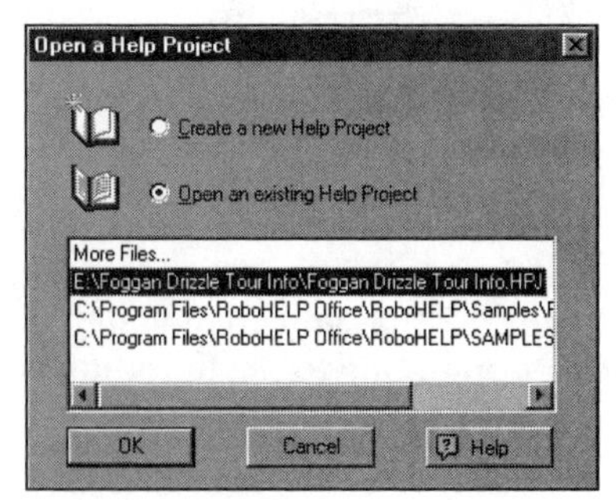

Figure 4-1: The Open a Help Project dialog box

2. As you can see, the help project you created now appears on the list of projects in the box. Select the Foggan Drizzle project and click OK, or simply double-click the Foggan Drizzle project entry. RoboHELP Explorer starts Word with the Foggan Drizzle doc file.

Now that the file is open, add a jump to go from the first topic in the file to the next topic, as follows:

3. Position the cursor in the topic where you'd like to place the jump. (You may need to insert a paragraph mark if you want the jump to start on a new line.) Select the Insert ⇨ Help Jump command. (Alternately, you can press Ctrl+J or you can click the New Jump button on the RoboHELP toolbar, shown in Figure 4-2.) The Insert Help Hotspot screen appears, as shown in Figure 4-3.

Figure 4-2: The New Jump button

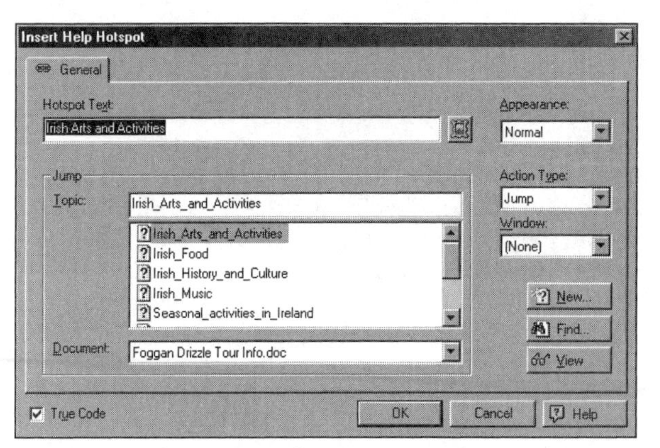

Figure 4-3: The Insert Help Hotspot screen

4. In the Topic field, select the topic ID of the topic you want to create a jump to (the destination topic). This tells RoboHELP that you are going to link from the topic you selected in the previous step to this topic. Enter information in the other fields in the Insert Help Hotspot screen as follows:

   - **Hotspot Text:** This is the text that will appear to the user as the text to click in the help file. It defaults to the topic title for the topic you select in the Topic field, but you can change this to anything you like.

   - **Appearance:** Select an appearance for the jump from the drop-down list. Normal means that the jump will appear to the users as the standard green, bold and underlined text. Hidden creates a jump that has no special color or underlining, but the cursor will still turn to a pointing hand as it slides over the hotspot. (This type of jump is often referred as an invisible hotspot.) No Color creates a jump that is underlined in the help file, but it uses the normal text color instead of the bold green text that is used for the Normal jumps.

   - **Action Type:** You can select any of the hotspots from the drop-down list. To enter a jump, leave this at the default entry in this field, Jump. (You'll see how to use several of the other options later in this chapter.)

   - **Topic:** Click to select the topic ID for the destination topic from the list. RoboHELP will automatically update the Hotspot Text field with the topic title associated with the selected topic ID.

   - **Document:** Select the document for which you want to display the list of topics. The default is the document you are currently working with, but you can select any document associated with this WinHelp project. You can also select (All) in the drop-down list to display all the topic IDs for all the documents associated with this WinHelp project, regardless of the DOC file they appear in.

   - **Window:** Select the help window in which you want to display the target topic. You can select any of the defined help windows from the drop-down list, or simply leave this field at (None) to select the default help window.

You'll see how to create and use different help windows in Chapter 9, "Using Help Windows and Browse Sequences."

- **New:** Click this button to create a new topic using the New Topic screen.
- **Find:** Click this button to display the Find Topic screen (described later in this chapter) to search for a topic.
- **View:** Click this button to view the topic as it appears in the last compiled version of the WinHelp project. (If this is a new topic or you have not compiled the help file, you won't be able to see the topic.)
- **TrueCode:** Select this option to see everything as TrueCode. TrueCode lets you see the underlying commands for placing graphics and many other objects. (People who have been working with RoboHELP for a long time or who have created WinHelp files directly without RoboHELP will be familiar with this format.) Leave this box unchecked to see images and other objects in the file as your users will see them (this RoboHELP mode is known as Dynamic WYSIWYG).

When you're satisfied with your entries, click OK. RoboHELP inserts the jump at the cursor position, as shown in Figure 4-4.

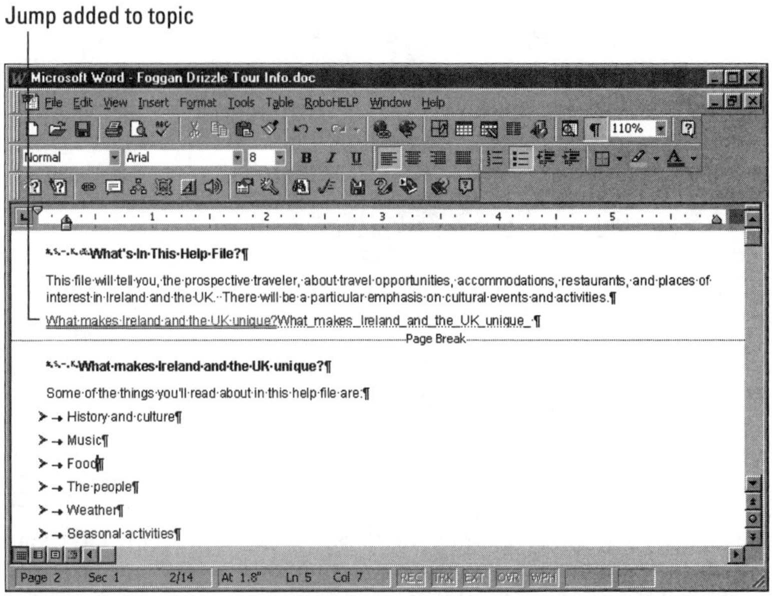

Jump added to topic

Figure 4-4: The Foggan Drizzle file with a jump added to the first topic

Tip

If you don't want to change any of the entries in the field, you can create a jump quickly by opening the Insert Help Hotspot screen and double-clicking the topic ID of the destination topic.

As you can see, the jump instruction has two parts in the DOC file, telling what to click and where to go. The first part of the jump is the hotspot text itself. This is the information that the users actually see and will click to jump to the destination topic. The hotspot text for a jump is double-underlined in the DOC file. The second part of the jump is the topic ID of the destination topic. The topic ID is formatted as hidden text immediately following the hotspot text. There should be no intervening characters between the hotspot and the topic ID of the destination topic.

Tip

When you're working on RoboHELP files, it's frequently a good idea to display all hidden text and nonprinting characters. You can click the Show/Hide button on the Standard toolbar in Word to display hidden text. To display all non-printing characters, select the Tools ➪ Options command in Word, and then check All on the View tab.

When you compile the file, the WinHelp compiler sees the double-underlined text for the hotspot text, which is changed to single-underlined text (that's simply the way it works) and flagged as a hotspot associated with the specified topic ID that follows the double-underlined hotspot text.

When you compile the WinHelp file, the jump looks like Figure 4-5.

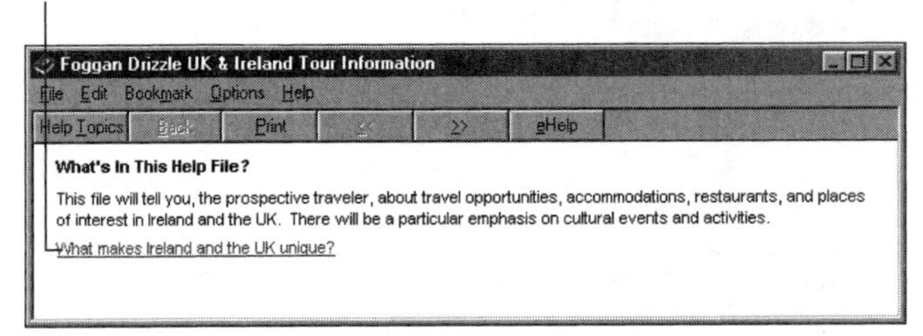

Figure 4-5: The compiled Foggan Drizzle file showing the new jump

You can also select text to use for the hotspot text. For example, you could highlight a word or phrase that you want to use as the hotspot text for a jump, and then select the Insert ➪ Help Jump command. The text you've highlighted will appear in the Hotspot Text field of the Insert Help Hotspot screen.

Finding a Topic

As your help project grows, you may start having trouble finding the topic ID of the topic you want to create a hotspot to. You can take advantage of the Find Topic feature while you're creating a jump or popup to identify the topic you want to use, as follows.

1. In the Insert Help Hotspot screen, click Find (on the lower right corner of the screen). The Find Topic screen appears. Figure 4-6 shows a sample WinHelp file with a number of topics added.

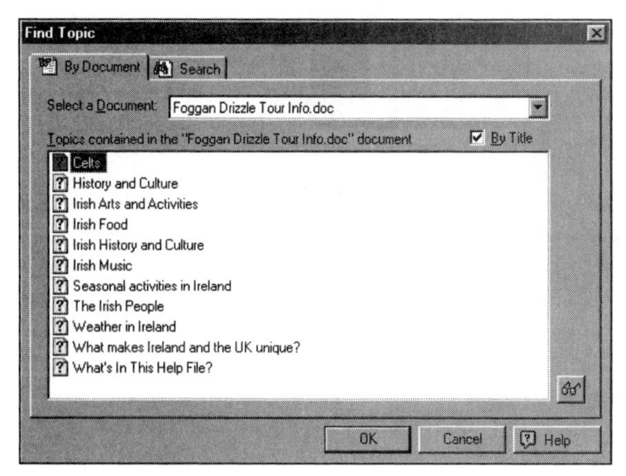

Figure 4-6: The Find Topic screen

2. You can look through topics by topic title (the default) or by topic ID; when you uncheck the By Title box, the topics are listed by topic ID. You can also check for topics in other documents than the current DOC file by selecting a document from the drop-down list in the Select a Document field. To display the highlighted topic as the users see it, click the View icon on the lower right corner of the screen. (Remember, the View option is only available if the WinHelp file has been compiled.)

   You can also search for a specific topic through the Search tab of the Find Topic screen. Figure 4-7 shows a search in a sample WinHelp file.

3. Enter a word or phrase to search for in the Topic Title Includes field. Robo HELP displays all the topics in the document(s) specified in the By Document tab that contain the word or phrase you entered. If you prefer, you can search by topic ID by unchecking the By Title box. As with the preceding tab, you can display the highlighted topic as the users see it by clicking the View icon on the lower right corner of the screen. When you've found the topic you want to jump to, you can double-click the topic title or the topic ID. RoboHELP displays the information for the topic in the Insert Help Hotspot screen so you can complete creating the jump.

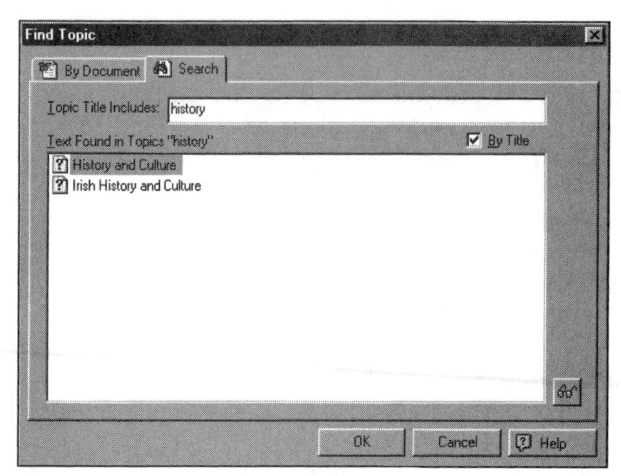

Figure 4-7: The Find Topic screen showing the Search tab

You can display the Find Topic screen independently by selecting the Edit ➪ Find Help Topic command, pressing Ctrl+O, or by clicking the Find Topic icon (see Figure 4-8) in the RoboHELP toolbar.

Figure 4-8: The Find Topic icon

Creating a Jump and a New Topic at the Same Time

You'll frequently discover as you're adding jumps that you want to jump to a topic that isn't there yet. Rather than stop and create a new topic, and then return to the process of creating a jump, RoboHELP enables you to create a jump and a new topic in a single operation.

1. As before when creating a jump, position the cursor in the topic where you'd like to place the jump. (You can also highlight text for the jump hotspot if you like.)
2. Select the Insert ➪ Help Jump command to display the Insert Help Hotspot screen.
3. Make the appropriate entries in the fields for the jump. When you're satisfied with your entries, click New. The New Topic screen appears.

For information on creating a new topic, see Chapter 3, "Creating Your First WinHelp Project."

4. Enter the information on the New Topic screen to create a new topic. When you're satisfied with your entries, click OK. When you return to the Insert Help Hotspot screen, the new topic information will appear in the Hotspot, Topic, and Document fields as appropriate.
5. Click OK to create the new topic and the jump to it.

You can then enter content in the topic as usual.

Creating Mid-Topic Jumps

Although it's usually a good idea to keep topics short, you may have a topic that goes on for three or four screen pages; for example, you may have a list of commands for a program that doesn't break up easily into smaller pages. With a long page, you may want to create a jump that goes from the top of the page to a designated location somewhere in the middle of the topic, such as jumping to a subordinate heading for a group of commands. To jump to the middle of a topic, you must first create a mid-topic ID, as follows:

1. Position the cursor in the topic where you'd like to create the mid-topic ID.

Be sure to position the cursor before the text in the topic where the mid-topic ID should appear.

2. Select the Insert ➪ Special Help Topics ➪ Mid-Topic ID command. The New Mid-Topic ID screen appears (shown in Figure 4-9 with a sample mid-topic ID entered).

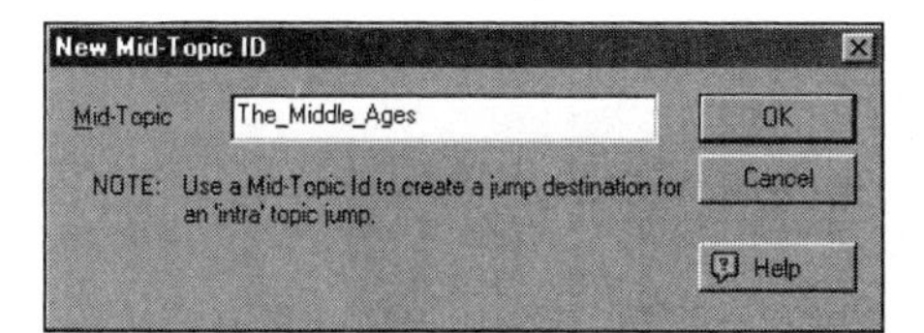

Figure 4-9: The New Mid-Topic ID screen

3. Enter the mid-topic ID to use. RoboHELP automatically changes spaces and punctuation to underscore characters as you type. When you're satisfied with your entries, click OK.

RoboHELP inserts a single topic ID footnote character (#) at the cursor. Figure 4-10 shows a mid-topic ID ("#The Middle Ages") inserted before a heading within a topic.

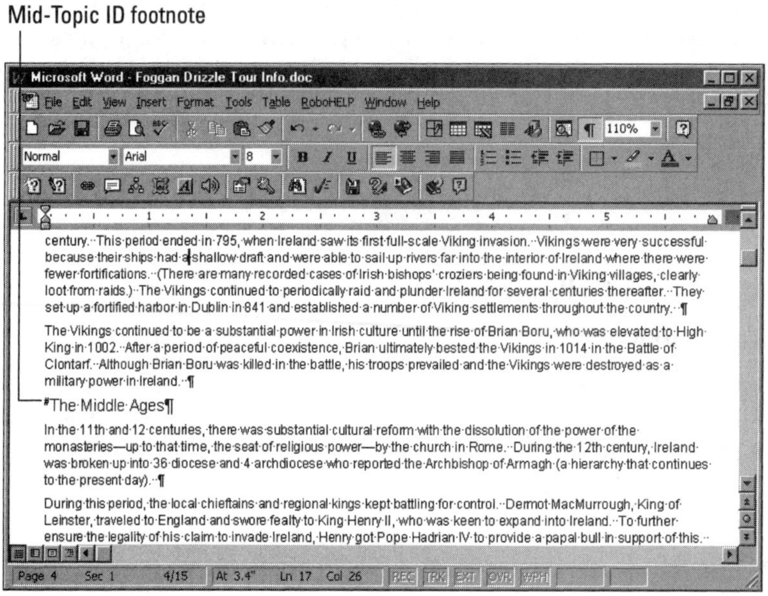

Mid-Topic ID footnote

Figure 4-10: The mid-topic ID inserted in the topic

After you've created the mid-topic ID, you can create a jump to it:

1. Position the cursor in the topic where you'd like to place the jump and select the Insert ➪ Help Jump command. The Insert Help Hotspot screen appears, as shown in Figure 4-11.

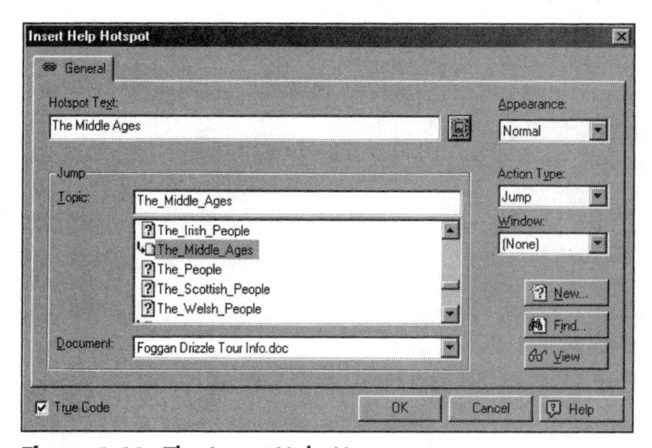

Figure 4-11: The Insert Help Hotspot screen

2. Enter the information for the jump to the mid-topic ID as you did earlier to create a regular jump. However, you'll see that the mid-topic ID has a different icon to identify that it's a mid-topic ID. When you're satisfied with your entries, click OK. The jump appears in the online help file as it did earlier. These jumps are identical to the jumps you created earlier; the only difference is in the destination topic.

Creating Jumps to Topics in Other Help Files

If you are creating a suite of related online help files (for example, if you have a large online help system that you're documenting that has several discreet components), you will want to create a jump from one online help file to a topic in another online help file. This type of jump is known as an external jump, because it jumps to a topic that's not in the current help project.

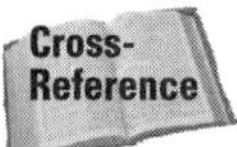

For more information on having multiple connected WinHelp files, see Chapter 15, "Managing Large Projects."

1. Position the cursor in the topic where you'd like to place the jump and select the Insert ➪ Other Hotspots ➪ External Topic Hotspot command. The Insert Help Hotspot screen appears with a list of the external topics.

You could also select the Insert ➪ Help Jump command and then select External Topic in the Action Type field of the Insert Help Hotspot screen.

2. Select the WinHelp project containing the topic to which you want to create a jump. RoboHELP will display the list of topics in the Topic field.

You must have the project already set up as a RoboHELP project to see the topic IDs in the Topic field. RoboHELP looks for the help project's HPT file in the directory containing the HLP file. The HPT file is created automatically when you save a help project in RoboHELP.

3. Select the topic ID as usual. When you're satisfied with your entries, click OK. RoboHELP creates the jump to the external topic. As you can see in Figure 4-12, the external jump is a little different from the regular jump. The hidden text includes the JumpID macro, a canned instruction that WinHelp uses to specify jumps to topics in other help files.

For more information on macros and how to use them, see Chapter 10, "Understanding Macros."

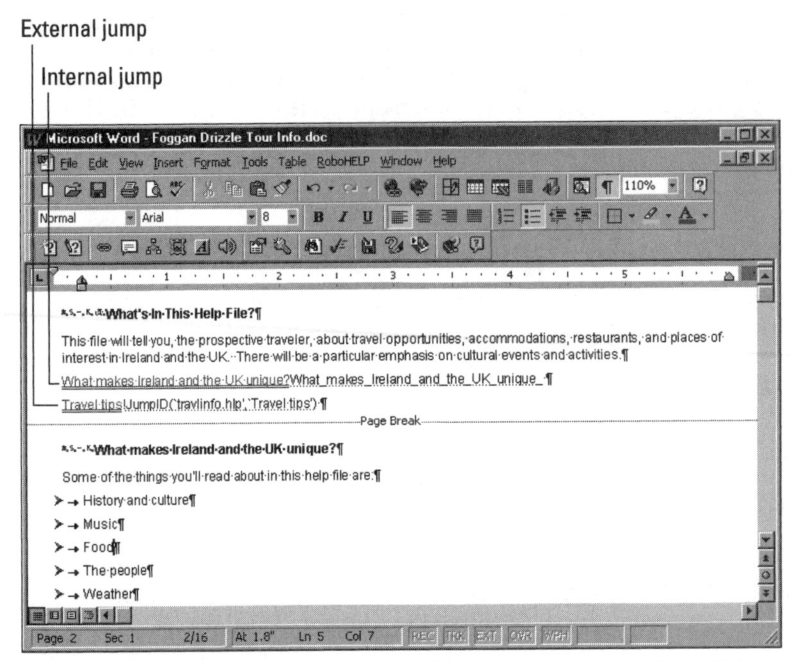

Figure 4-12: A sample external jump added to the Foggan Drizzle file

Creating Jumps to HTML Topics

In addition to the other types of jumps you've seen, you can create jumps to HTML topics, web pages, and HTML files. There are many advantages to creating jumps to HTML topics:

- ✦ Jumping to an HTML topic in an HTML Help file is helpful if you are producing a help suite that uses both WinHelp and HTML Help.
- ✦ Jumping to a web page is an excellent way of linking users of a help file with external resources, such as a company web site.
- ✦ Jumping to an HTML file lets you interface with HTML files, such as for a company intranet.

Creating a jump to an HTML topic is similar to creating an external jump.

1. Position the cursor in the topic where you'd like to place the jump and select the Insert ➪ Other Hotspots ➪ HTML Hotspot command. The Insert Help Hotspot screen appears as shown in Figure 4-13. (You could also select the Insert ➪ Help Jump command and then select HTML Jump in the Action Type field of the Insert Help Hotspot screen.)
2. Enter the hotspot text in the Hotspot Text field.

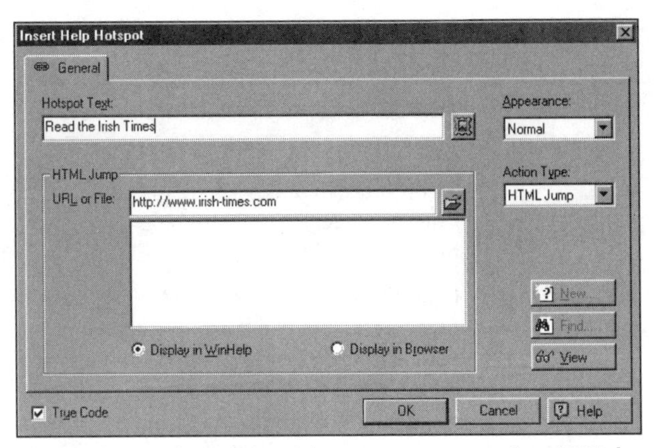

Figure 4-13: The Insert Help Hotspot screen for HTML jumps

If you are creating a hotspot using text that's already in the topic, you can highlight the hotspot text before selecting the Insert ⇨ Help Jump command to display the selected text in the Hotspot Text field automatically.

3. In the URL or File field, enter information as described in Table 4-2.

Table 4-2
Options for the URL or File Field

What you want to do	*What to enter in the URL or File field*
Create a link to a web page.	Enter a URL, such as `http://home.iol.ie` or `http://www.irish-times.com`. (Technically, the http:// isn't required; if you leave it off, RoboHELP will still recognize it as a URL.) When the users click this hotspot, the HTML file is displayed in WinHelp or in the default browser.
Create a link to a file for downloading.	Enter a URL, such as `http://www.abcdefgh.com/info.doc`. When the users click this hotspot, the file is downloaded from the URL and opened or saved to your computer's hard disk.
Create a link to an FTP site to open it as a folder.	Enter the FTP address, such as `ftp://ftp.cdrom.com`. When the users click this hotspot, the FTP site is accessed and the directory folder is opened.

Continued

Table 4-2 (continued)

What you want to do	***What to enter in the URL or File field***
Create a link to an FTP site to download a specific file.	Enter the FTP address with the name of the file you want to download, such as `ftp://ftp.cdrom.com/catalog.txt`. When the users click this hotspot, the file is downloaded from the FTP site.
Create a link to an HTML file stored locally or on your network.	Enter the path and name of the file, such as `index.html`. (You can use the browse button to the right of the URL or File field to find a specific file.) When the users click this hotspot, the HTML file is displayed in WinHelp or in the default browser. You can also select a .CHM file and an HTML topic inside that .CHM file using this technique, although it's eaiser to use the External Topic link.

You can also use a macro to add a link for sending an e-mail message. Jumping to an e-mail address lets you build in an e-mail response option; for example, you can have the users e-mail a sales person or customer support representative for more information. For information on how to add an e-mail link, see Chapter 10, "Understanding Macros."

4. Select Display in WinHelp to display the web page or file directly within the WinHelp window or Display in Browser to have WinHelp display the web page or file in your default browser. (Figure 4-14 shows a sample page for the *Irish Times* dispayed in WinHelp rather than in a browser.)

The help users must have Internet Explorer 4.0 or higher installed on their computers to view Web pages. It's not necessary for them to use Internet Explorer as their default browser, but RoboHELP Office 2000 needs some of the drivers in order to display Web pages properly. You must also ship the RoboEx32.dll file with the compiled WinHelp file that has HTML jumps of any kind. The RoboEx32.dll file is a redistributable RoboHELP file that contains macros and routines for accessing the Internet and displaying HTML information.

Displaying a URL or file from within WinHelp will not give your users as much control over the display of the web page, but it will control their access to the Internet. The users will be able to access only the options and features that appear in controls on the web pages. This may be particularly convenient if you're linking to an intranet web site on your local network and want the users to step through the materials you're presenting without branching out on their own. In addition, displaying a web page from within WinHelp will mask the fact that the users are looking at a web page — the connection to the Internet is fairly seamless.

Figure 4-14: Sample web page displayed from within WinHelp

5. Make any other entries on the screen as desired and click OK to create the jump. Figure 4-15 shows an HTML jump to the *Irish Times* web site added to the list of jumps. (Hidden text is displayed in this figure to show the mechanics of the jump syntax.)

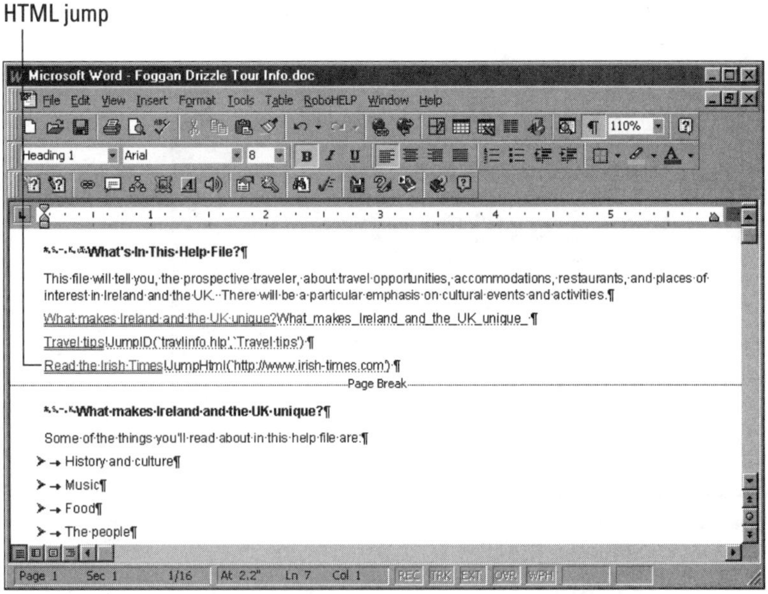

HTML jump

Figure 4-15: An HTML jump to a web site

The HTML jump looks like any other jump when you compile it, but the instructions in the hidden text of the jump are different. You'll notice the JumpHTML macro at the start of the hidden text. The JumpHTML macro is similar to the JumpID macro, except that you tell the macro to go to a specified URL rather than a help topic and a help file.

For more information on macros and how to use them, see Chapter 10, "Understanding Macros."

When you use the *Inet* macro, you need to ship the following files with your compiled Help file to ensure that the Inet macro functions properly. You can find these files on your PC in the \WinHelp\RoboHELP\Internet\Distrib folder. Install the appropriate DLL in the user's \Windows\system folder (\WinNT\system for Windows NT users), and install the Setbrowse.exe file in the same folder as the Help file.

Setbrowse.exe	May be included to allow users to specify the browse path for an Internet browser or navigator other than the default.
Inetwh16.dll	Adds Internet access capabilities to Windows 3.1 Help systems using the Hc31.exe or hcp.exe Help Compiler.
Inetwh32.dll	Adds Internet access functionality to Windows 95, 98 and NT Help systems using the Hcw.exe Help Compiler.

Using Jumps to Create Menus

In addition to providing text jumps from within the body of a topic, you can create lists of jumps to a group of topics. For example, Figure 4-16 shows the opening topic in the Foggan Drizzle help file. When you click any of the jumps shown, you're taken to the appropriate topic.

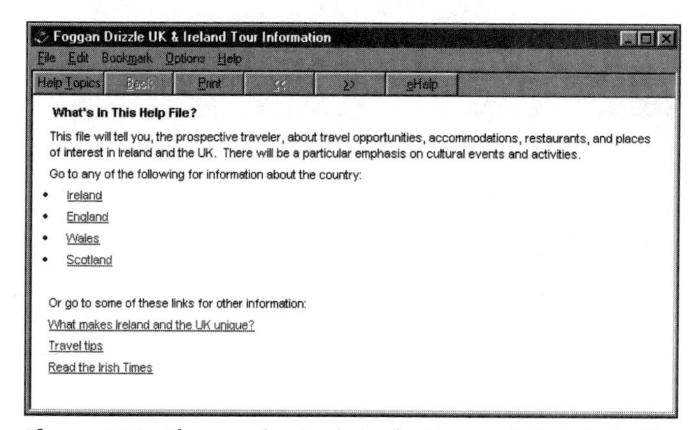

Figure 4-16: The opening topic in the Foggan Drizzle help file, showing a simple menu

You can use this technique to create menus throughout your help file. This is particularly effective where you have hierarchically organized information that can be stacked well. Providing a menu from the main topic in a group of topics to each of the topics below it lets the users know what they can expect to find and makes it easy for them to reach the right topic.

You should limit your menus to the standard *chunking* metric (discussed in Chapter 2, "What Makes Help 'Help'?") of seven items, plus or minus two. If you have more than the limit, you may want to consider breaking the hierarchy into several pieces or subsections.

Adding Popups

The previous section showed you how to create a several types of jumps to various destinations. This section describes how to create popups. Where jumps take you from one topic to a destination topic or file, a popup displays information in a temporary window that disappears as soon as you type something on the keyboard or click the mouse. Popups are useful for notes, tips, glossary items, quick references, and sidebar information.

Here are a few tips for adding and creating popups:

- Popups should be short. You can't scroll down in a popup because the first mouse-click will make the popup window disappear.
- For the same reason, you can't have links or macros in a popup. Clicking a link makes the popup disappear.
- You can't create popups to HTML topics and web pages.
- The topics you display in popups can't contain a nonscrolling region (a way to display the topic heading). If the destination topic has a nonscrolling region, the topic heading is the only thing you see in the popup window.

For more information on nonscrolling regions, see Chapter 5, "Adding Color, Formatting, and Special Effects."

Creating a New Popup Topic

Creating a popup is very similar to the process for creating a standard WinHelp jump. To create a new popup topic and a popup jump, do the following:

1. Position the cursor in the topic where you'd like to place the popup. (You may need to insert a paragraph mark if you want the popup to start on a new line.) Select the Insert ⇨ Help Popup command. (Alternately, you can press Ctrl+P or you can click the Help New Popup button on the RoboHELP toolbar, as shown in Figure 4-17.) The Insert Popup screen appears, as shown in Figure 4-18.

Figure 4-17: The Help New Popup button

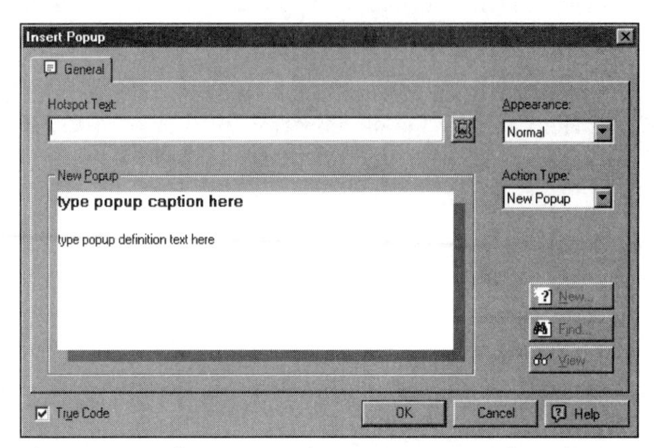

Figure 4-18: The Insert Help Hotspot screen for popups

When you select the Insert ➪ Help Popup command, the Insert Popup screen appears. This screen has the same appearance as if you had selected the Insert ➪ Help Jump command and then selected New Popup in the Action Type field.

2. Enter the information to appear in the caption and body of the popup as shown in the screen. Figure 4-19 shows a sample popup for a word in the Foggan Drizzle file.

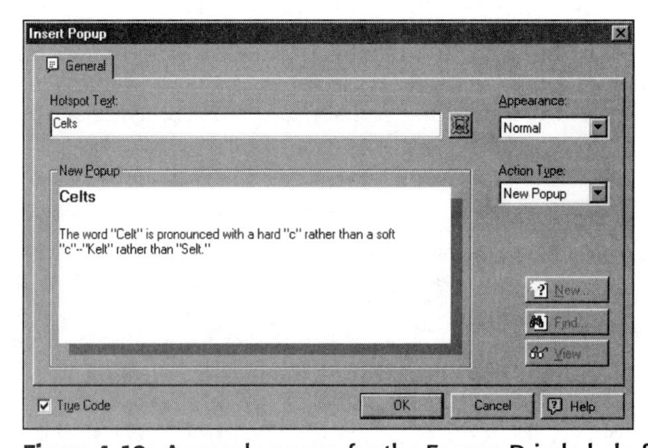

Figure 4-19: A sample popup for the Foggan Drizzle help file

3. When you're satisfied with your entries, click OK. The popup code appears in the DOC file, as shown in Figure 4-20. In addition, the text you entered is added as a new popup topic at the end of the current DOC file. This topic has only a topic ID and a topic title (the # and $ footnotes).

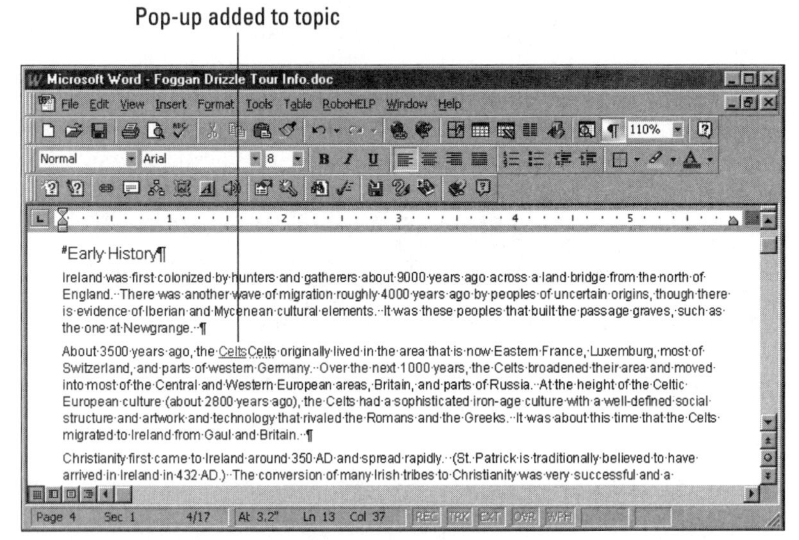

Figure 4-20: The popup inserted in the DOC file

As you can see, the hotspot text for the popup is identified with a single underline rather than a double underline. It's important to note that this is the only difference between a hotspot that will popup to a topic and one that will jump to a topic. The compiler identifies the type of hotspot you are creating by the single- or double-underlining of the hotspot text.

When you compile the file, the popup is identified by a dotted underline. When you click the popup, the popup window appears on top of the WinHelp file (see Figure 4-21).

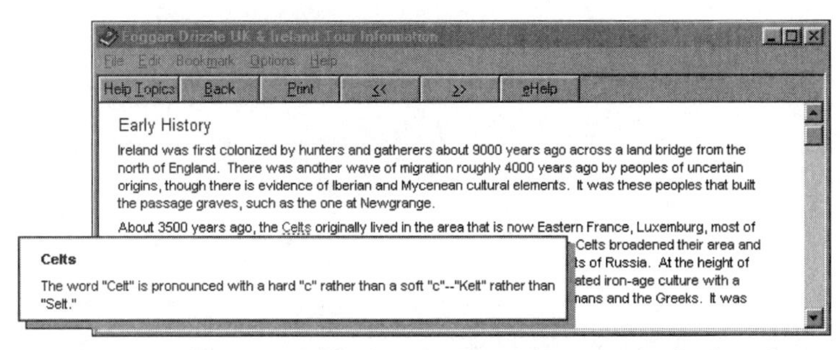

Figure 4-21: The compiled WinHelp file with a popup displayed

Creating a Popup for an Existing Topic

The preceding procedure creates a new popup topic on the fly, similar to when you saw earlier in this chapter how to create a jump and new topic simultaneously. However, you may already have a list of popups you want to use — such as a glossary of definitions — and you simply want to create a link to an existing pop-up topic. This is a process similar to adding a jump hotspot, as follows:

1. Position the cursor in the topic where you'd like to place the popup and select either the Insert ➪ Help Jump or the Insert ➪ Help Popup command.
2. On the Insert Help Hotspot screen, select Popup in the Action Type field. (This is different from selecting the Insert ➪ Help Popup command, which requires you to create a popup topic as well as the popup link.)
3. Select the topic ID for the topic you want to access as a popup. Make any other entries as appropriate in the screen. When you're satisfied with your entries, click OK. RoboHELP will insert the information for the popup at the cursor position.

You can use the Find option to search for a topic as shown earlier in this chapter.

Creating Glossaries

One of the handy uses of popups is creating a self-contained glossary. Create a topic with a level-1 heading of "Glossary," then add lists of popup definitions to this topic, as shown in the following figure. Each of the glossary entries is defined as a separate popup. By keeping the definitions as popups, you can avoid taking up any room with the definitions, making it easier for the users to find the topic for which they want a definition. (You can add formatting to break the glossary into groups or tables using Word if you prefer.)

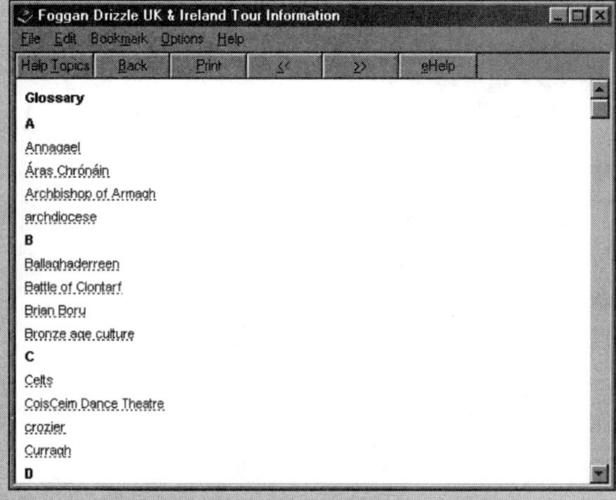

Sample glossary in a compiled WinHelp file.

If you have many definitions in your glossary, you may want to create submenus for each letter of the alphabet that then takes you to a topic listing all the definitions starting with "A." As an alternative, you can create mid-topic IDs and then a series of jumps at the start of the topic (as shown in the following sample figure). This will let the users scroll to the section of the glossary they want or jump directly to it by clicking on the appropriate letter at the top of the screen.

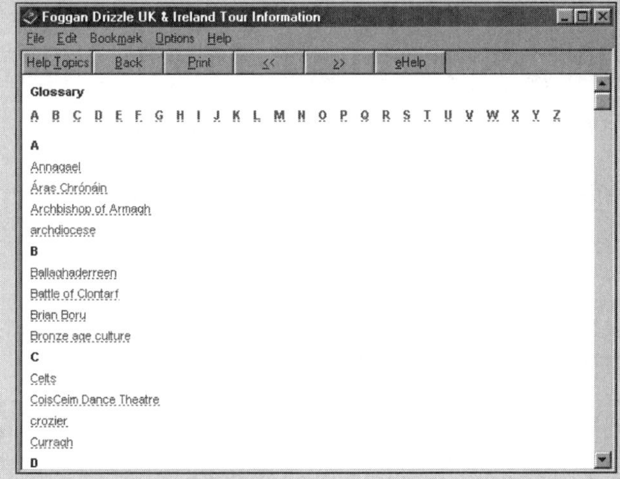

Sample glossary with mid-topic IDs for quick access.

For a snappier look for this kind of mid-topic ID jump, you can create hotspot buttons for letters and numbers. For more information on creating hotspot buttons, see Chapter 7, "Getting Fancy with Graphics."

Testing Your Hotspots

After you've created hotspots, test them to make sure they work correctly. The typical method for testing hotspots is to compile the project, and then go through the topics, clicking hotspots, and verifying that they go to the correct destination topic.

However, it may be impractical to recompile the WinHelp project just to test a single topic. Here's how t test a topic without compiling the WinHelp project:

1. Click inside the hotspot you want to test. (Nothing will happen when you do except that RoboHELP will highlight the link.)

2. Select the Edit ➪ Find Help Topic command. (You can also right-click on the topic and select the Find Help Topic command from the right-click menu.) RoboHELP uses the information in the highlighted hotspot and displays the designated topic.

You can use this technique only if the destination topic is in the current WinHelp project. You can't use this for HTML topics.

Changing and Deleting Hotspots

You can change and delete hotspots of any kind fairly simply. As you saw with changing and deleting topics, you should use the RoboHELP commands to change and delete hotspots so you can keep the internal RoboHELP files up-to-date.

To change a hotspot, do the following:

1. Right-click the hotspot, then select Properties from the right-click menu. (You can also click inside the hotspot, then select the Insert ➪ Help Jump command.) The Help Hotspot Properties screen (identical to the Insert Help Hotspot screen) appears.
2. Make any changes to the hotspot. When you're satisfied with your entries, click OK.

To delete a hotspot, do the following:

1. Place the cursor in the hotspot you want to delete (it doesn't matter where) and select the Edit ➪ Delete ➪ Hotspot command. The Delete Hotspot screen (shown in Figure 4-22) appears.

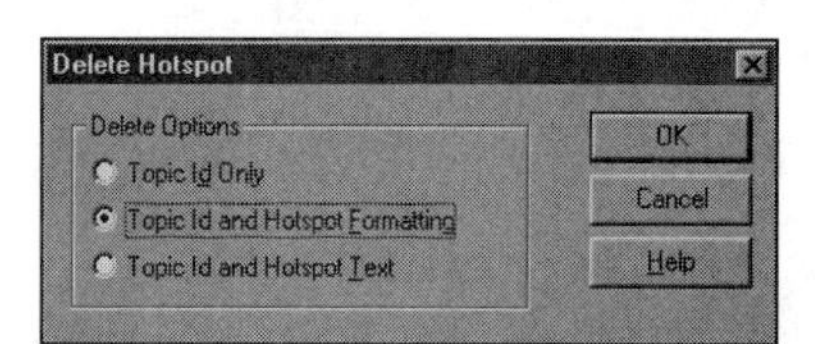

Figure 4-22: The Delete Hotspot screen

2. Select Topic Id and Hotspot Text to delete the hotspot and click OK. Robo HELP deletes the hotspot. You can also select the default, "Topic Id and Hotspot Formatting," which deletes the hotspot information in hidden text and turn the hotspot text back into regular text. Selecting "Topic Id Only" deletes the hidden hotspot information but doesn't reformat the associated hotspot text.

Creating Hotspots Automatically

So far in this chapter, you've seen how to create jumps and popups manually by selecting the location of the hotspot, optionally selecting the text to use for the hotspot, and then making entries on the Insert Help Hotspot screen. This is very effective, but it could be tedious if you have to create dozens or even hundreds of links throughout a help file to the same topic. Fortunately, RoboHELP has a slick feature called Find & Link for adding numerous hotspots.

Find & Link is an interesting combination of the standard find-and-replace feature in Word with the Insert Help Hotspot screen you've seen earlier in this chapter. You can search for a specific word or phrase through a single document or the entire WinHelp project and then automatically insert a hotspot at each location, as follows:

1. Select the Edit ⇨ RoboHELP Find & Link command. The RoboHELP Find & Link screen (shown in Figure 4-23) appears.

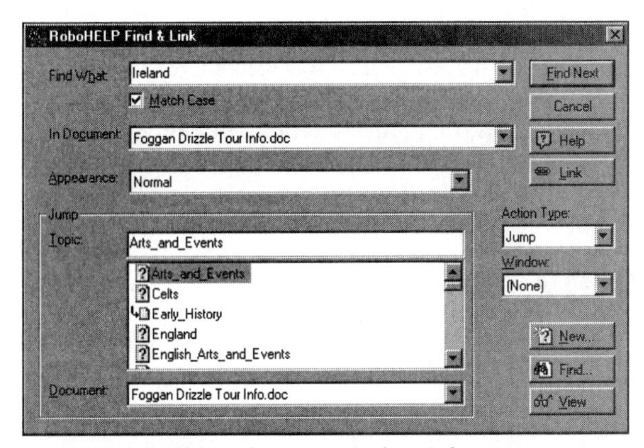

Figure 4-23: The RoboHELP Find & Link screen

2. Enter information in the fields of the RoboHELP Find & Link screen as follows:
   - **Find What:** Enter the word or phrase to search for.
   - **Match Case:** Check this box to match the case of the word or phrase you're looking for (such as in the word "PCs"). If you leave this box unchecked, RoboHELP will find all occurrences of the word or phrase, regardless of the case.
   - **In Document:** Select the document in which you want to search for the word or phrase.

- **Appearance:** Select an appearance for the jump from the drop-down list. Normal means that the jump will appear to the users as the standard green, bold and underlined text. Hidden creates a jump that has no special color or underlining, but the cursor will still turn to a pointing hand as it slides over the hotspot. No Color creates a jump that is underlined in the help file but it uses the normal text color instead of the bold green text that is used for the Normal jumps.

As you can see in Figure 4-23, the lower portion of the RoboHELP Find & Link screen is the same as the Insert Help Hotspot screen shown earlier in Figure 4-3. As with the Insert Help Hotspot screen, when you select a different Action Type, the lower portion of the RoboHELP Find & Link screen changes accordingly.

3. When you're satisfied with your entries, click Find Next. RoboHELP finds the first occurrence of the word or phrase in the specified file. If you want to insert a hotspot here, click Link. RoboHELP inserts a hotspot and automatically finds the next occurrence of the search item. If you want to skip this occurrence, you can click Find Next.
4. When all occurrences of the search term are found, you see a small dialog box that says "RoboHELP has finished searching." Click OK. RoboHELP positions the cursor at the start of the file. You can then search a different document, enter another search term in the Find What field and enter more hotspots in the file, or click Cancel to close the RoboHELP Find & Link screen.

Tracking Hotspots

This section shows you several ways to examine the links from and to an individual topic or for all the topics in a DOC file or WinHelp project.

Viewing Topic References

As you add more jumps and popups to your topics, you need to be increasingly careful about how you change and delete topics, as you may invalidate a number of jumps or popups that refer to this topic as their destination.

The first way to examine the links (or *references*) for a topic is to use the Show Topic References feature in RoboHELP Explorer, as follows:

1. In the RoboHELP Explorer, open the right pane of the RoboHELP Explorer by selecting the View ⇨ Hide Right Pane command. (You can also click the Hide Right Pane icon, shown in Figure 4-24.) The right pane of the RoboHELP Explorer screen appears (shown in Figure 4-25 with the Topic List displayed).

RoboHELP displays whatever was last selected — the Topic List, Image Workshop, or Link View — in the right pane.

Figure 4-24: The Hide Right Pane icon

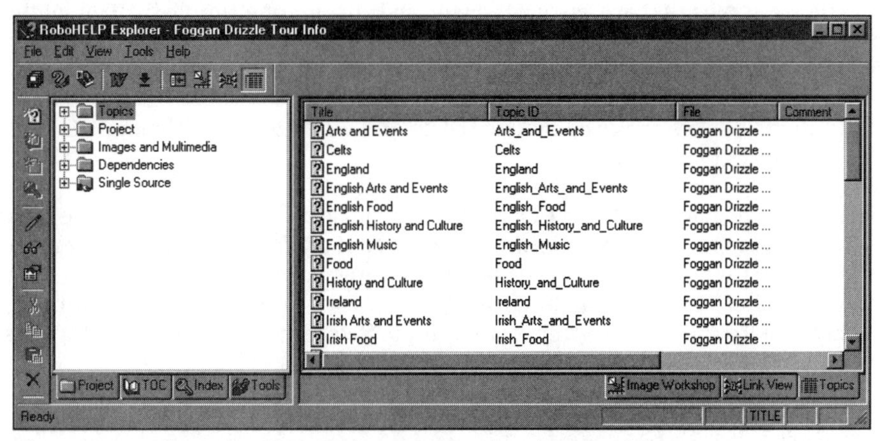

Figure 4-25: The RoboHELP Explorer screen showing the right pane

As you can see, the topics in the DOC file are displayed in the right pane. (If you don't see the topics, you may need to click the Topics tab at the bottom right corner of the right pane.)

2. Highlight the topic you want to examine, and then select the Tools ➪ Show Topic References command in the RoboHELP Explorer. Figure 4-26 shows the Topic References screen.

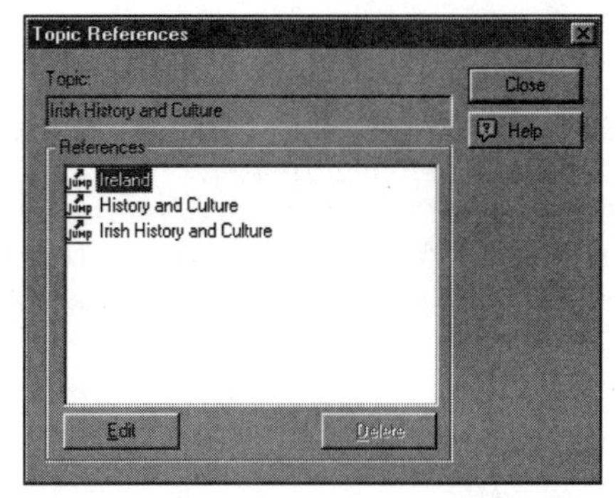

Figure 4-26: The Topic References screen

The references to the topic appear in the References field. The icons next to the topics in Figure 4-26 show that each reference is a jump. The small green square on the last item in the list shows that this is a mid-topic jump. (The references will also show TOC references, aliases, and SHED (hotspot) graphics. You'll see how to create and use each of these features later in this book.)

The value of showing the topic references in the Topic References screen is that you can edit the topics that are associated with the current one simply by highlighting the topic and clicking Edit at the bottom of the screen. RoboHELP will find the topic in the DOC file and display it in Word so that you can edit it.

You can't delete topics by clicking Delete; this works only for deleting TOC references or aliases.

You can also display the Topic References in a single step by positioning the cursor in the topic and selecting the RoboHELP ⇨ Show Topic References command in Word. (As an alternative, you can also right-click the topic you want and then select the Show Topic References command from the right-click RoboHELP menu.) RoboHELP displays the RoboHELP Explorer and the Topic References screen for the topic as before.

Using the Link View

Although the Show Topic References option is helpful for identifying the links to a specific topic, it doesn't do a good job of showing you how a topic connects with other topics in the help file. To do this, RoboHELP Explorer includes the Link View, a very useful interactive tool for displaying links in a graphic format.

To see how a topic links to other topics in the help file, do the following:

1. In the RoboHELP Explorer, open the right pane of the RoboHELP Explorer by selecting the View ⇨ Pane ⇨ Topics command or by clicking the Hide Right Pane icon, as shown earlier. The right pane of the RoboHELP Explorer screen appears with the Topics List.
2. Highlight a topic in the right pane, and then select the Tools ⇨ Show Topic Links command in RoboHELP Explorer. The highlighted topic and its links are displayed in the Link View window, shown in Figure 4-27. (You can also display the links by right-clicking the topic in the Project Manager on the left side of the RoboHELP Explorer, then selecting Show Topic References from the right-click menu.)

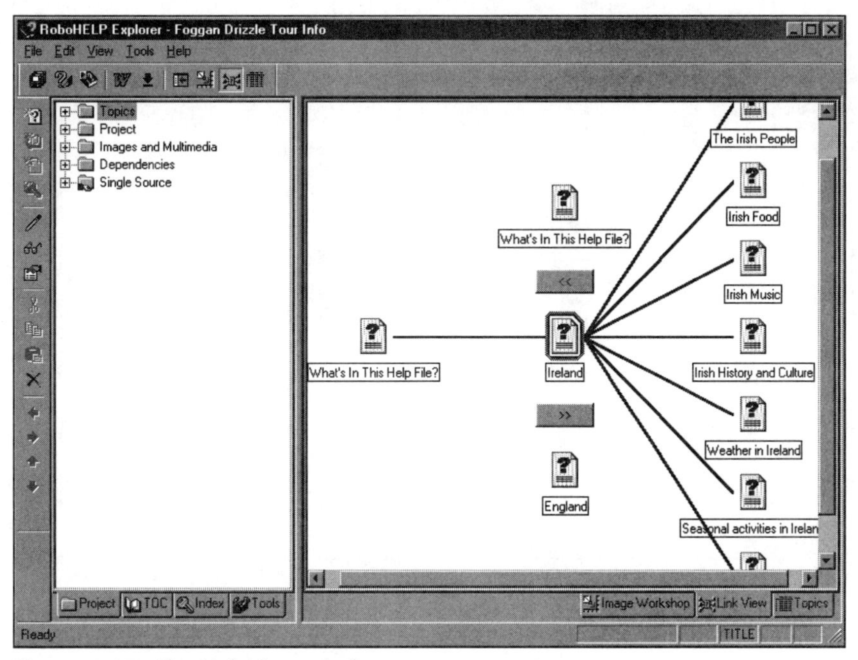

Figure 4-27: The Link View window

The Link View window shows a great deal of information about the links to and from a topic. By default, the topic being examined appears in the center of the display (in this example, History and Culture). The topic or topics that you can jump to or popup from appear to the left of the display, whereas the topics you can navigate to from this topic appear to the right of the display. The topics above and below are the topics you can browse to using the previous and next buttons (also shown on the display in Figure 4-27).

What makes the Link View window so useful is that you can navigate the links of your help file by clicking a topic or a browse button. For example, double-clicking one of the destination topics shown in Figure 4-27 takes you to that topic, as shown in Figure 4-28. You can also examine specific topics by dragging and dropping them into the Link View window from any of the topic lists in the Project Manager, TOC Composer, and Index Designer (appearing in the RoboHELP Explorer's left window).

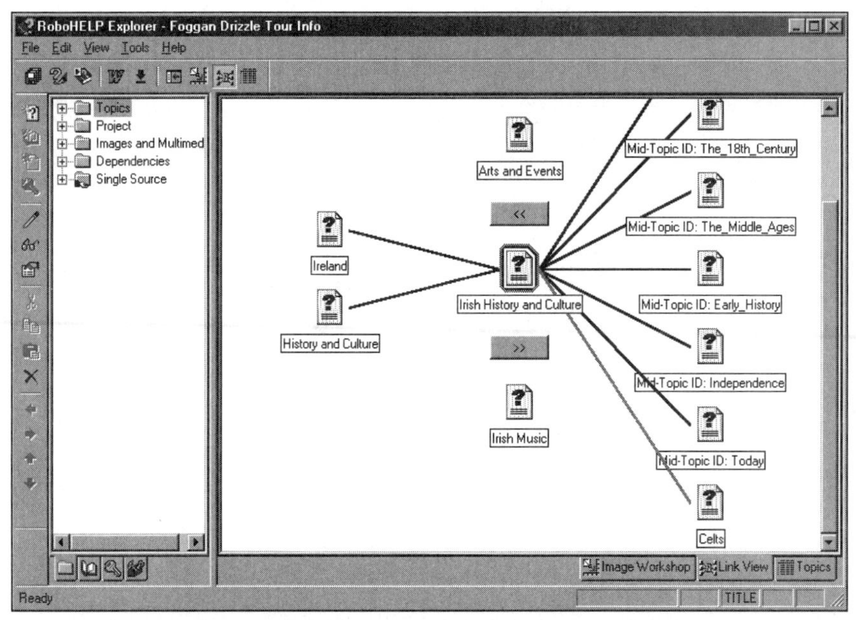

Figure 4-28: Displaying a linked topic in the Link View window

As you can see from Figure 4-28, the topic formerly at the center of the display has moved to the left. The topic being examined is in the center of the display. One difference on the screen is that the link to the Celts topic is displayed in green rather than blue to show that the link to the topic is a popup rather than a jump. Table 4-3 shows the link colors and what they mean.

Table 4-3
Link Colors in the Link View Window

Color of link	***What type of link it represents***
Blue	A jump to a topic in this or another WinHelp project
Green	A popup to a topic in this or another WinHelp project
Yellow	A link to a SHED graphic (SHED graphics are discussed in Chapter 7, "Getting Fancy with Graphics.")
Pink	A See Also link, an HTML jump, or a link to a macro or an external topic
Red	A broken link (usually caused by manually creating a hotspot or changing or deleting a topic rather than using the RoboHELP commands)

The type of topic is also displayed in the Link View window. For example, all the topics on the screen shown in Figure 4-28 are local to the Foggan Drizzle project and consequently have blue question marks in the icon. External topics have a small brown book in the icon. Missing topics (that is, broken links of any kind) have a red question mark in the icon.

When you move the mouse pointer over a topic, RoboHELP will highlight the topic's border. If you right-click directly over a topic, a right-click menu appears that lets you edit the topic in the DOC file, view the topic in the compiled help file, delete the topic, find a topic, make the highlighted topic the center of the Link View window (if it isn't already), add See Also references, view and edit the topic references, set RoboHELP Explorer options, set topic properties, and get help. When you right-click over a blank section of the Link View window, you can only find a topic, set RoboHELP Explorer options, and get help.

There are only a few choices for the Link View window options, all of which are aimed at providing effective display options for topics with large numbers of links. First, you can change the size of the topic icons from large (the default size) to small icons. This is handy for displaying topics that have many links that would otherwise be hard to see without excessive scrolling in the Link View window. You can also choose to keep the selected topic centered when you scroll, another handy feature if you're examining topics that have many links. Finally, you can choose to display only the first 50 links to a topic. If you are looking at a topic with several hundred links (for example, the main page of an online glossary), you can save time and computer memory by displaying only the first 50 links. Figure 4-29 shows the screen shown in Figure 4-28 with the mini-icons option selected. Now you can see all the links without having to scroll the Link View window.

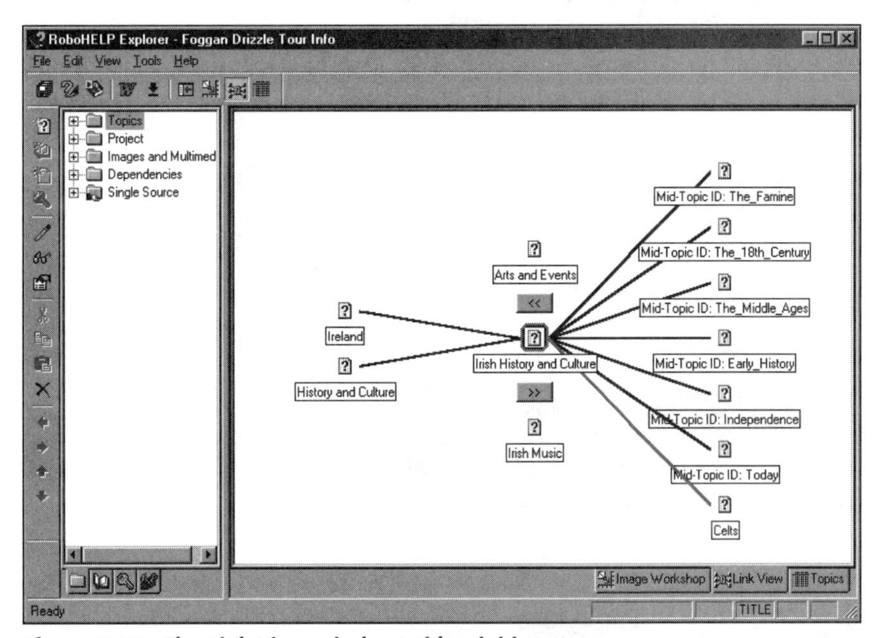

Figure 4-29: The Link View window with mini-icons

If you're only interested in exploring the help file's links, you can open the Topic List window by clicking the Topics tab at the bottom right of the right pane in RoboHELP Explorer. This takes you to the main topic, from which you then navigate your way through the help project in the Link View window.

Printing Topic Reference Reports

There are two reports that can help you track information about your hotspots: the Topic References report and the External Topic References report. This section shows you how to use each of these reports.

Printing the Topic References report

The Topic References report shows the links, TOC and index (K-keywords) entries, graphics, and macro references for each topic in the report.

To generate a Topic References report, do the following:

From RoboHELP Explorer, select the Tools ➪ Reports ➪ Topic References command. The Topic References report is displayed on the screen, as shown in Figure 4-30. The help topics appear on the report in order by topic title or topic ID, depending on whether you have selected the View ➪ By Topic Title or the View ➪ By Topic ID command in RoboHELP Explorer.

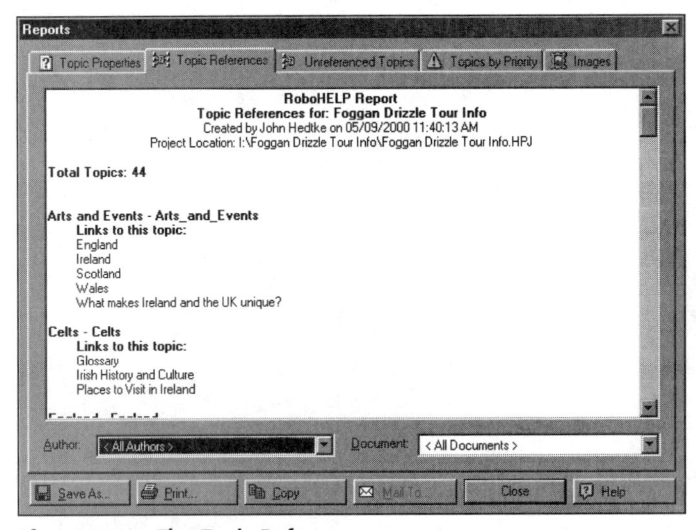

Figure 4-30: The Topic References report

You can show the topics created by each author, all authors, or those that aren't assigned to specific authors, depending on your selection in the drop-down list in the Author field. You can also look at the topics in all the documents in the project or in individual documents with the drop-down list in the Document field.

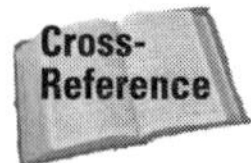

For more information on assigning authors and setting status, priority, time estimates, and to-do items, see Chapter 15, "Managing Large Projects."

There are no filtering options to select on the Topic Reference report.

Printing the External Topic References report

The External Topic References report shows the external links in your project's topics, TOC, and index (K-keywords) entries. The report lists the total number of external topics in the WinHelp project and the specific external topics referenced. These are listed alphabetically.

To generate an External Topic References report, do the following:

From RoboHELP Explorer, select the Tools ➪ Reports ➪ External Topic References command. The Topic References report is displayed on the screen, as shown in Figure 4-31.

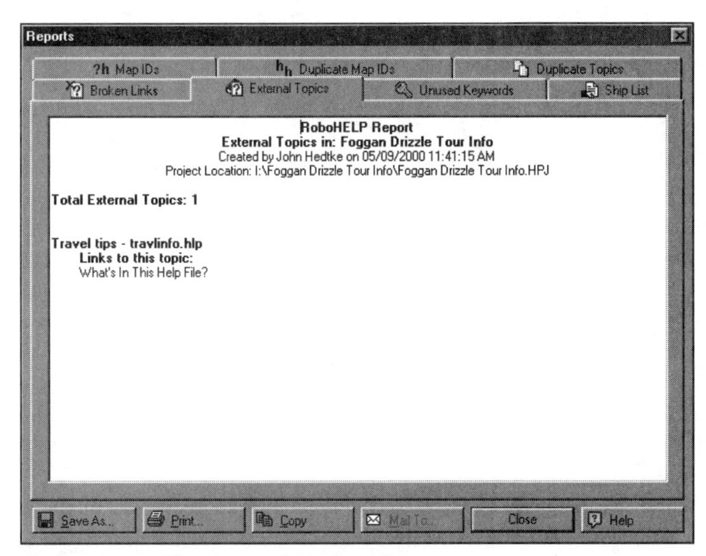

Figure 4-31: The External Topic References report

There are no options to select on the External Topic Reference report.

There are several other reports that may be useful when working with links, including the Topic Properties report described in Chapter 3, "Creating Your First WinHelp Project" and the Broken Links and Unreferenced Topics reports described in Chapter 15, "Managing Large Projects."

Summary

This chapter showed you how to add jumps and popups to your help files. You learned about the underlying concepts of hotspots. You then saw how to add jumps to local and external jumps, how to add mid-topic ID jumps, and how to use jumps to create simple menus. You also were shown how to use popups to provide quick reference information and how to create a glossary using popups. After that, the chapter discussed ways to test and maintain hotspots. You also learned a number of different ways to view topic references, using the Show Topic References screen, the Link View window, and RoboHELP's topic reference reports.

✦ ✦ ✦

Adding Color, Formatting, and Special Effects

✦ ✦ ✦ ✦

In This Chapter

Formatting fonts and font attributes

Formatting paragraphs

Adding and formatting bulleted and numbered lists

Adding and formatting tables

Inserting symbols and special characters in your help files

Using color to add interest

Using and customizing the RoboHELP styles

Creating WinHelp 2000 and using watermarks

✦ ✦ ✦ ✦

In this chapter, you'll see how to enhance the message of your help file by using formatting and color in your compiled WinHelp files. You'll start by seeing how to change fonts and their attributes, how to format paragraphs, and how to use bulleted and numbered lists. You'll also see how to create and format tables in your WinHelp files and to insert symbols and special characters so that they appear correctly. Next, this chapter will show you how to use color throughout your online help files to communicate more clearly and consistently. After that, you'll see how to use styles in the standard RoboHELP template to automate many formatting tasks and also how to customize the templates to precisely the format you want. Finally, this chapter introduces you to the WinHelp 2000 format and shows you how to add watermarks.

Using Fonts

When you compile WinHelp files from your DOC files, the formatting in the DOC files is also included in the compiled file. This lets you take advantage of the many text-formatting features in Word.

Some of the things you can do in Word to change the formatting of your files are:

- ✦ Change fonts
- ✦ Change font sizes, colors, and characteristics (bold, italic, and so on)
- ✦ Change paragraph margins, alignment, and leading

✦ Set indents and tabs

✦ Add bulleted and numbered lists

✦ Add tables

WinHelp files don't support all of Word's formatting features, but there's enough of a range that you can dramatically improve the impact your help files have. Many of the techniques for adding formatting discussed in this chapter will be designed to work around some of the limitations in WinHelp.

Tip

For more information on making Word work more effectively for you, check out *Word 97 Annoyances* (O'Reilly & Associates, 1997) or *Word 2000 Annoyances* (O'Reilly & Associates, 2000) for a plethora of tips on how to avoid or disable Word's most annoying problems and features (including turning off the paperclip for good).

You can change your fonts and their characteristics at any time using Word's Format ➪ Font command exactly as you would for the fonts in any other file. For example, Figure 5-1 shows the first topic in the Foggan Drizzle file with portions of the body text changed to 8-, 10-, 11-, and 12-point text (the first paragraph, the text preceding the bulleted list, and the text following the bulleted list, respectively).

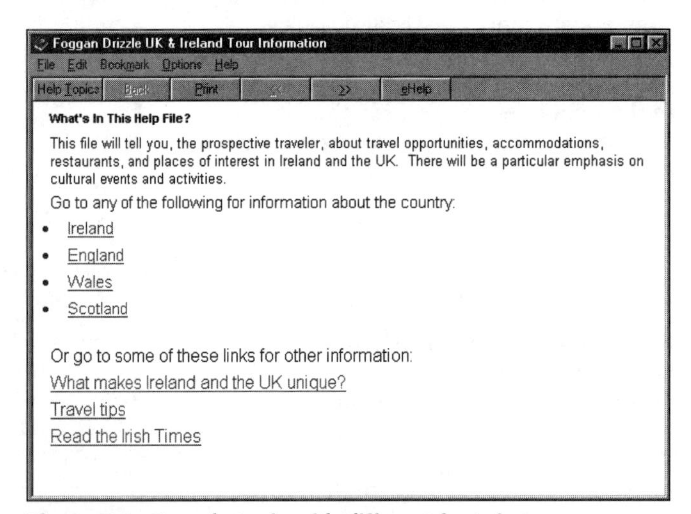

Figure 5-1: Sample topic with different font sizes

Tip

Pressing Ctrl+D has the same effect as selecting the Format ➪ Font command in Word and is a lot faster when you're making a lot of font changes.

You can also change the font characteristics with the Format ➪ Font command. In Figure 5-2, the font characteristics were changed in some of the body text in the Foggan Drizzle topic file.

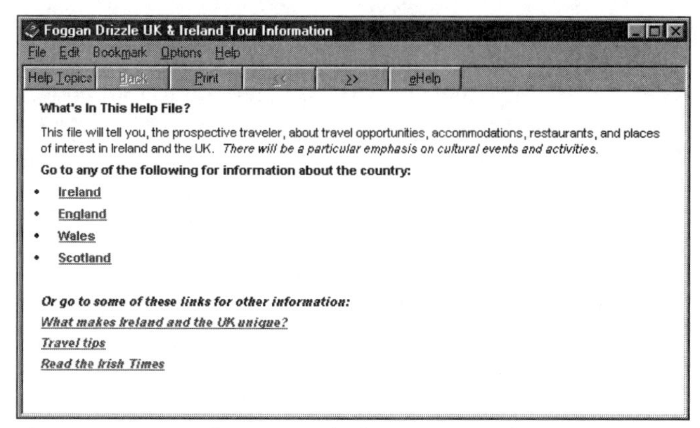

Figure 5-2: Sample topic with different font characteristics

Although you can format text in the file with underlining for emphasis using the Format ➪ Font command, the users may interpret such text as a non-working jump.

In addition to changing font sizes and attributes, you can also change the fonts themselves. Figure 5-3 shows several different fonts used in a topic. The first paragraph is set in Times New Roman, the text preceding the bulleted list is Book Antiqua, and the text preceding the hyperlinks at the bottom is in Arial.

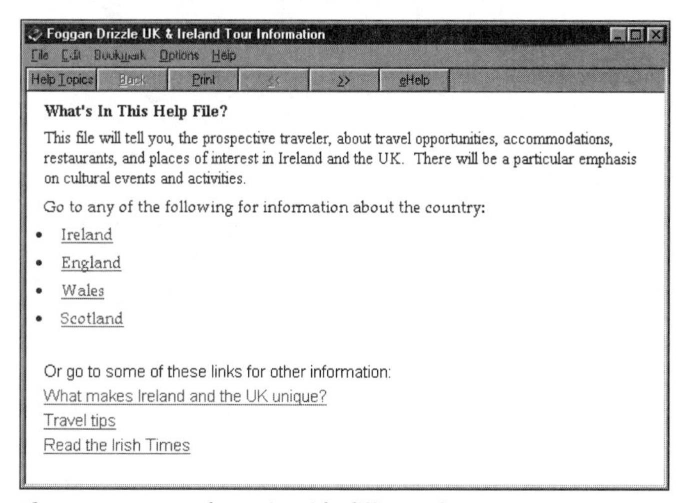

Figure 5-3: Sample topic with different fonts

It's worth noting that each font in Figure 5-3 is 11-point, but because of differences in the basic font size, they appear different. Be careful to adjust your font size appropriately to match the fonts you select.

Although there's no rule against it, some people choose to avoid serif fonts such as Times New Roman for your body text and stick with san serif fonts such as Arial. Because of the poorer resolution of screen displays versus printed text, serif fonts can be slightly harder to read. Regardless of what you prefer to use for body text, serif fonts can be used very effectively in topic headings because of the larger font sizes usually used in topic headings.

Some of the rules you've gotten used to when creating well-formatted documents in Word transfer directly to formatting WinHelp files. For example, you shouldn't mix too many fonts in a page or a document. Having multiple fonts in different sizes and characteristics makes it harder to read the topic and looks amateurish. Instead, you should choose a few fonts — one for 1-level headings, possibly a second for all other headings, one for body text, and one for embedded code/macro/other samples — and vary their sizes, characteristics, and colors to communicate your message.

Something else you should know about fonts: if you use a font in the WinHelp file that isn't installed on the user's computer, WinHelp will guess what font to use when it displays the topic. (The Word Tools ➪ Options ➪ Compatibility tab lets you select "Substitute fonts based on font size" as well as click Font Substitution to change the fonts in the document.) Depending on the type of font you've specified and the fonts available on the user's computer, WinHelp may be able to find something appropriate . . . or it may find something wildly different. If there is nothing at all like the required font on the computer, WinHelp will default to using Courier 10 point: sturdy, unattractive, and monospaced. It's therefore a good reason to stick to relatively standard fonts that you know will be available on the users' computers (such as the standard Windows fonts). If you have a requirement for a font that may not be in your users' computers, you may want to include this as part of your distribution package with instructions on how to add a font or a setup procedure that does it for them. (Be sure you have the rights to distribute the font with your online help.)

Formatting Paragraphs

You can use Word's Format ➪ Paragraph command to change the appearance of text in a topic. Figure 5-4 shows a sample topic with paragraphs formatted left-justified (top), centered (middle), and right-justified (bottom), and with single, 1.5-line, and double spacing.

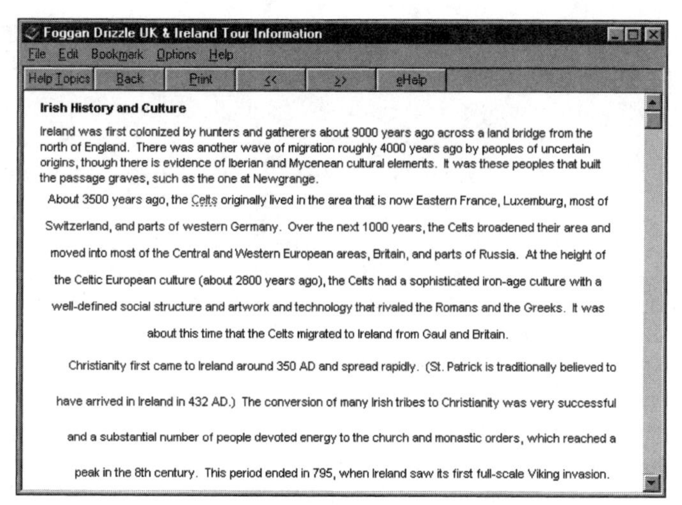

Figure 5-4: Changing paragraph justification and leading in a topic

It's also possible to set different indents for paragraphs. Figure 5-5 shows sample indents for the paragraphs in a topic — from the top, left-indented, right-indented, left and right indented, and hanging indent.

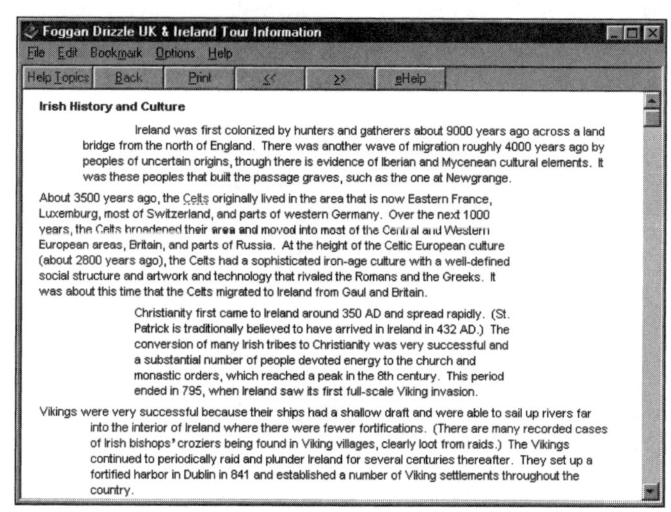

Figure 5-5: Changing paragraph indents

Using Shortcuts in Word to Save Time

Pressing F4 in Word repeats the last editing action: typing text, changing a font, setting paragraph formats, deleting text, and so on. You can perform one editing action, such as changing the indentation for a paragraph, and then move the cursor to another paragraph you'd like to indent and press F4 to repeat the action. Be careful not to type or undo anything, or else you'll have to repeat the action to reset the F4 key.

You can combine this shortcut with the shortcut key for Find Next, which is Shift+F4. Search for an item and make an editing change. Then press Shift+F4 to find the next item. When you want to apply the edit change, press F4. This combination of shortcuts can make it quick and easy to skim through a file and apply changes to selected items.

You can even use the F4 shortcut to copy a font or paragraph format quickly. Highlight the text or paragraph you want to copy the formatting of, and then select the Format ➪ Font or Format ➪ Paragraph command and click OK without making any changes. Highlight the text you want to change or (if you're copying paragraph formats) simply insert the cursor in the paragraph. Press F4 to apply the changes. (Because F4 copies only the last change, you can't use this technique to simultaneously apply a font and a paragraph formatting change.)

When you adjust the size of the help window, the paragraph text is adjusted to maintain the formatting. For example, if a user resizes the window to be tall and thin, the paragraphs still have the same indents and justification. Figure 5-6 shows the help topic from Figure 5-5 with the display window resized. As you can see, the left and right indents are still displayed correctly, even though the line wrapping was automatically adjusted when the window became smaller.

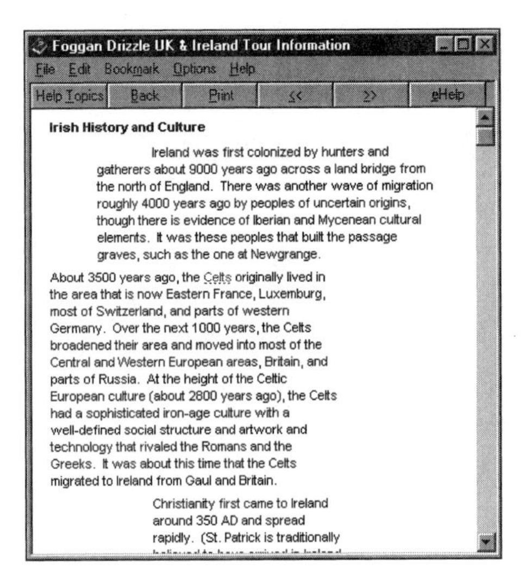

Figure 5-6: Displaying paragraph indents in a resized window

You can't use the Keep with Next paragraph option in the topic text, as this tells the WinHelp compiler that the paragraph is part of a non-scrolling region and will cause a compiler warning for the topic. Non-scrolling regions are described later in this chapter.

Using Bulleted and Numbered Lists

Bulleted and numbered lists are vital tools when formatting information in your online help files. Creating bulleted and numbered lists in Word can be done quickly and easily with the Format ⇨ Bullets and Numbering command (or the appropriate toolbar buttons), but this will cause some unexpected side-effects when the lists are compiled. Here are some tips and techniques to avoid some of the problems in Word and the WinHelp compiler.

If you're using Word 97, make sure that you have the latest service release installed before doing anything else. To find out which version of Word you have, select the Help ⇨ About Microsoft Word command. The top line should show that you're using Word 97 version SR-2 or later. If you don't have the latest version or if you're using Word 2000, you can download the latest service releases for your version of Word from the Microsoft web site, `http://www.microsoft.com`.

Several problems with bulleted and numbered lists are caused by Word's being overly helpful with its formatting. If the AutoFormat features are on, Word automatically copies the list formatting to the paragraph following the list and attempts to automatically renumber numbered lists. In addition, the WinHelp 4 compiler doesn't support lists created with automatic numbering, which can result in numbered lists' being numbered out of sequence.

You can disable the offending AutoFormat and AutoCorrect features as follows:

1. Select the Tools ⇨ AutoCorrect command in Word. When the AutoCorrect screen appears, select the AutoFormat As You Type tab and make sure that the following options are not selected:
    - Automatic bulleted lists
    - Automatic numbered lists
    - Format beginning of list item like the one before it
    - Define styles based on your formatting
2. Next, go to the AutoFormat tab and make sure that the Lists and Automatic bulleted lists option isn't selected. When you're satisfied with your entries, click OK.

One of the most common formatting problems with bulleted and numbered lists is for the bullets and numbers to take on the formatting of the hotspots (usually green text). This usually happens when you have a list that has the first word as part of a hotspot. (An example of this problem is shown in Figure 5-7.)

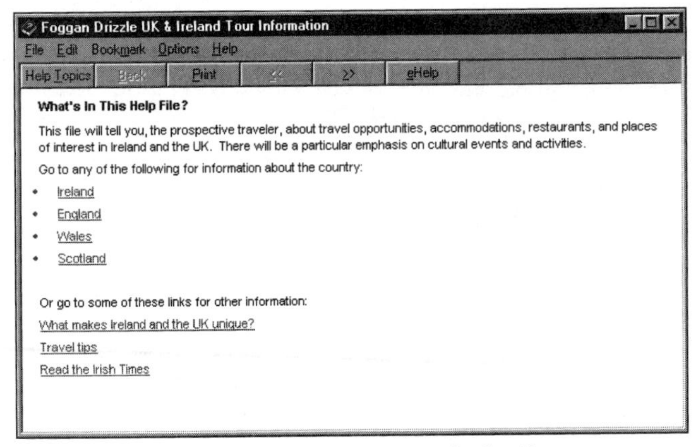

Figure 5-7: Green bullet characters in a bullet list

A known bug in the WinHelp compiler causes this problem, but you can usually correct it as follows:

1. Select either the Tools ➪ Options command in RoboHELP Explorer or the RoboHELP ➪ Options command in Word.
2. Click the Compile tab and select Remove Hotspot color from Bullets at the bottom of the screen. Click OK.
3. Click Yes when RoboHELP asks you if you want to save all documents now to apply this feature to your help project. (Be aware that this may take a while if you've got a lot of DOC files in the project.)

Now when you compile the WinHelp project, the bullets or numbers will appear in the appropriate color, as shown in Figure 5-8.

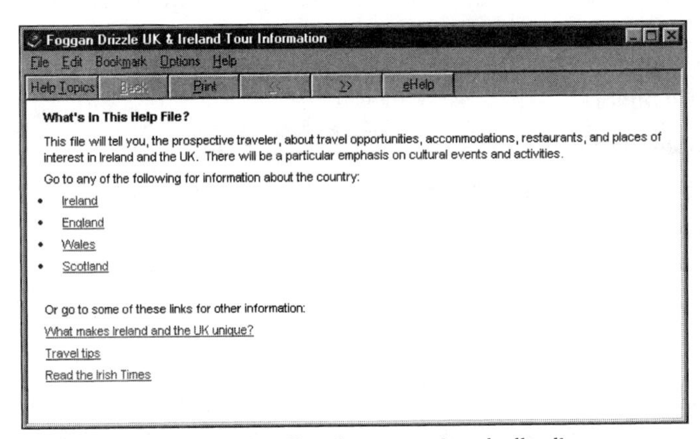

Figure 5-8: Corrected bullet characters in a bullet list

Another common problem is when lists change their formatting or lose their bullets or numbers when you open an existing WinHelp project. Usually, this is caused by your using the Format ➪ Bullets and Numbering command in Word (or the shortcuts on the Word toolbar that apply numbered or bulleted list formatting to the selected paragraphs) rather than a style and then changing the Normal style (or the default bullet or number style) in the document's template. You can fix this by applying a bullet or a number style to the list. You can also use Word's Insert ➪ Symbol command to insert a bullet character and then manually format the items in the bullet list.

While Wingdings and Webdings have neat characters for bullets, many PCs can't display them, particularly if they're using WinNT. For that reason, it's best to use bullet characters just from the standard Windows Symbol font.

You may also have problems with lists changing their formatting if you have two different bullet or list styles in the DOC file and the template. You can usually solve this by copying the appropriate bullet or number style from the ROBOHELP.DOT template to the template you're using. (The Topic Text Numbered style in ROBOHELP.DOT doesn't use automatic numbering.) As an alternative, try selecting the Tools ➪ Templates and Add-Ins command in Word and checking the Automatically update document styles box on the Templates and Add-Ins screen.

Applying a style can also solve problems if the hanging indent in the bulleted and numbered lists isn't indented correctly. This is most often caused by your having created the list using Word's Format ➪ Bullets and Numbering command rather than with a style. If you then remove the bullets or numbers or apply other formatting, Word loses the hanging indent information. This problem can generally be corrected by assigning the appropriate bullet or number style from ROBOHELP.DOT to the items in the list. As an alternative, try inserting a left tab stop to the location of the hanging indent to override the hanging indent and then recompile the WinHelp project.

Using Tables

Tables are another great tool for presenting large quantities of related information. Word supports much larger and more complex tables than the WinHelp compiler is capable of rendering. In particular, you can't use some of the standard Word table formatting techniques such as table borders and background shading.

If your table is too complex or has features unsupported by the WinHelp compiler, you'll receive an error message when you compile the WinHelp project.

Fortunately, there are several ways to circumvent the limitations of the WinHelp compiler. The first of these is to use tabs rather than Word tables to create organized columns of information on the screen. Figure 5-9 shows the glossary topic organized into a simple two-column table using tab stops. The compiled two-column topic is shown in Figure 5-10.

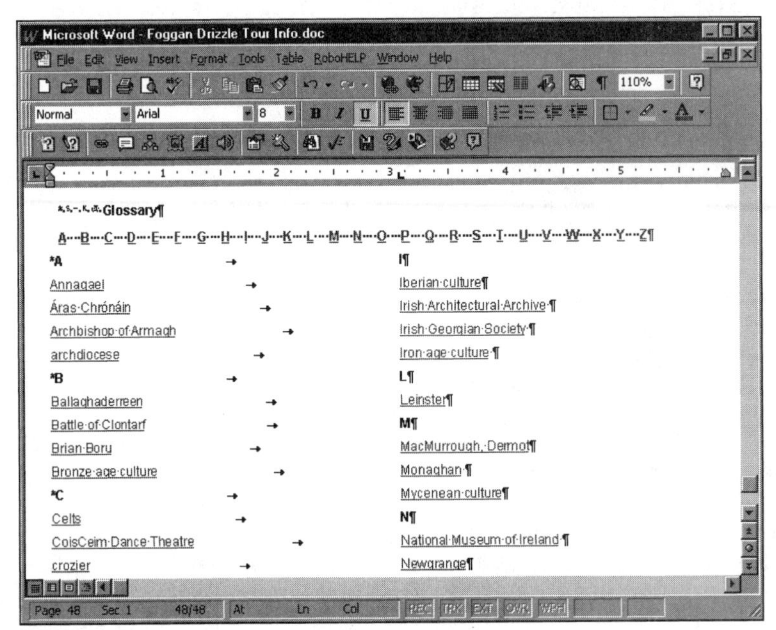

Figure 5-9: Formatting a two-column list with tab stops

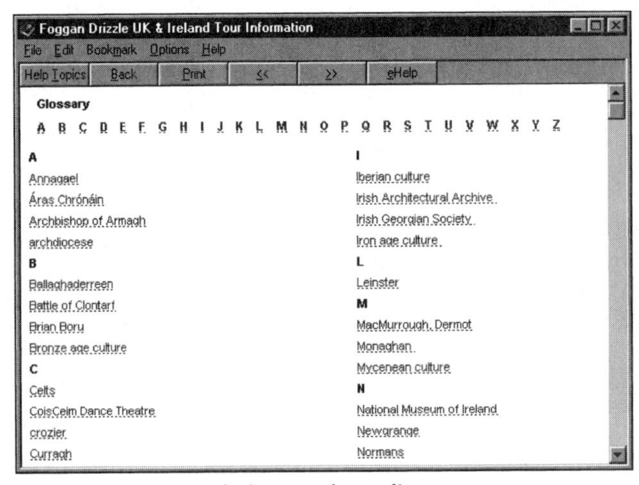

Figure 5-10: Compiled two-column list

Tab stops are very effective when working with two-column lists that don't have more than one line of text for each item. If you have several lines of text in an item, however, you'll have problems getting your vertical alignment correct and the table will become more of an effort than it's worth to maintain. In addition, your table may not align correctly if the user shrinks the window too much, as the text in the columns will wrap incorrectly. An alternative way to structure a table with multiple lines of information in the item in the right column is to use hanging indents, as follows:

1. Enter the information in your columns, separating the columns by tabs.
2. Select the Format ➪ Paragraph command to set a hanging indent for the lines of text. The hanging indent should be the left margin of the rightmost column of information. If necessary, use the Format ➪ Tabs command to adjust the tab stops of your columns. Figure 5-11 shows a list created using this technique.

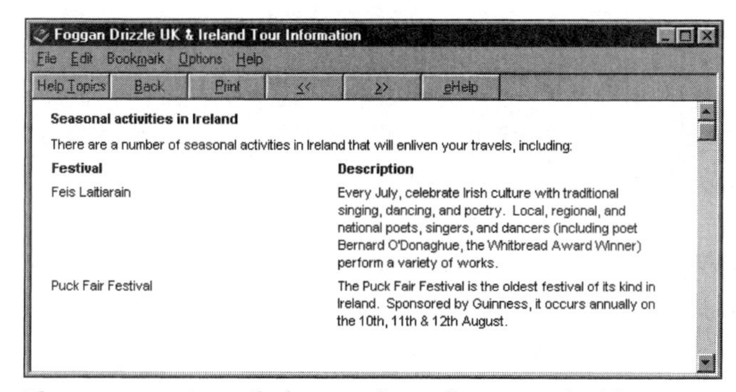

Figure 5-11: Compiled two-column list created with hanging indents

The third way to create a table in a WinHelp file is to use the table features in Word. Although this is the easiest way to do it, you can't use table borders, shading, and other table formatting. With the table borders and shading removed, the only indication in the Word file that this is a table is the table cell mark appearing at the far right of each row. In addition, you should be aware that you might have problems with Word tables' displaying or resizing incorrectly in WinHelp. Figure 5-12 shows the glossary formatted with a standard Word table.

It's not a bad idea to keep the tables sized so that they're narrower than the typical help window so the users don't have to scroll horizontally to see all of the table. You can minimize the amount of scrolling your users will need to do by setting *scroll limits* for the tables, as follows:

1. Create the table in the DOC file and enter and format all the text.
2. Change the size of each of the columns so that they are as narrow as practical without sacrificing the readability of the text.

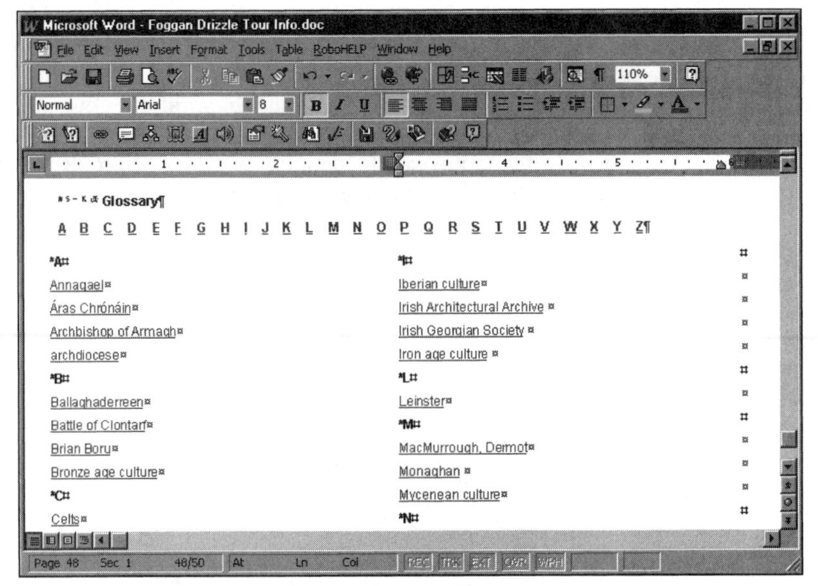

Figure 5-12: Table in Foggan Drizzle DOC file

3. Highlight the entire table in the DOC file (use the Table ➪ Select Table command), and then select the Table ➪ Cell Height and Width command.
4. On the Row tab of Cell Height and Width screen (not shown), select Center for the Alignment, and then click OK.

Word centers the table information in the DOC file. Now, when you compile the WinHelp project, the table will be more resizable when the users change the size of the display window.

If you have a complex table that simply must have fancy borders, shading, and formatting, you can create the table in Word, and then capture the screen using a capturing program and insert the image of the table in the DOC file using the RoboHELP Paste as Help Image command. This lets you keep all the formatting in the table you want. You can also create a table in Microsoft Excel formatted as you prefer and then use the Insert ➪ Object command to insert the contents of the file as an OLE object. The disadvantages to including a table in these ways are that the inserted table won't resize (being an embedded graphic) and the text in the table won't appear in the full-text search. Embedding a large graphic may also swell the help file size substantially, depending on the size of the graphic file. However, if you have a table of information that requires complex formatting that's not supported by the WinHelp compiler, this can be the most effective option.

For more information on adding graphics to your help files, see Chapter 6, "Adding Simple Graphics."

Using Symbols and Special Characters

Many online help files contain symbols and special characters, such as the copyright symbol (©), the trademark and registered trademark symbols (™ and ®), and currency symbols (₤, ¥, and €). The conventional procedure for adding symbols and special characters is to use Word's Insert ⇨ Symbol command and then select the symbol from the chart in the Symbol screen. However, this can cause problems, as characters inserted this way appear as a solid block (▮) in the compiled WinHelp file. An alternative that causes fewer problems is to insert the symbols and special characters using the Windows Character Map utility (Charmap.exe in the \Windows directory).

1. From the Windows Start button, select Programs ⇨ Accessories ⇨ Character Map. (It may also appear at Programs ⇨ Accessories ⇨ System Tools ⇨ Character Map, depending on your installation.) The Character Map screen (shown in Figure 5-13) appears.

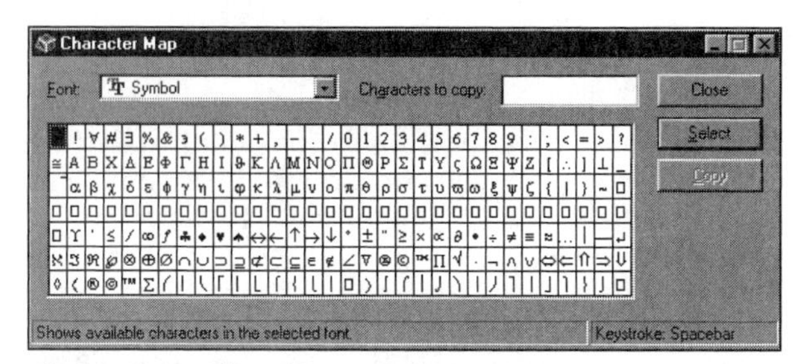

Figure 5-13: The Character Map screen

You may not have Character Map installed on your system. If not, you can add it with Add/Remove Programs option on the Windows CD.

2. Select the font you want from the drop-down list in the Font field. (Remember, it's a good idea to use the Symbol font or a TrueType font that's readily available to your users.)

3. Double-click the symbol you want to use. It appears in the Characters to copy field. Continue selecting symbols as necessary. When you're satisfied with your entries, click Copy to copy the character(s) to the Windows Clipboard.

4. Position the cursor and paste the symbols into the DOC file using Word's Edit ⇨ Paste command.

Adding Color

Up until now, the body text and headings in your online help files have been in one color, with color reserved for jumps and popups. Using different colors is one of the most effective tools (after changing fonts and font sizes) for conveying your message and providing visual cues to your users on how to find and interpret information.

There are many places to use color as an effective design element for your text and headings, such as these:

✦ **Headings:** You can combine color with different font sizes and characteristics to show different levels of headings. One common pattern is to use blue or dark blue for heading 1 items, dark red for heading 2 items, and dark green for heading 3 items.

✦ **Submenus:** Color can cue the users to a submenu or a set of hotspot references. For example, you can start each submenu with the line "For more information, see the following topics:" and color this dark red or teal. The important thing is to be consistent.

✦ **Hotspots:** The default color for hotspots is green, but you can create the hotspot with an attribute of hidden or no color and then set the color to anything you like. Using this technique, you can identify popups for new terms as violet, jumps to reference topics as green, and links to external help systems or Internet locations as dark red.

As you design your color schemes, it's important to consider how the colors are going to appear to the users. The colors you choose should communicate your message effectively and consistently. As with other font characteristics, you should avoid using too many colors in a single topic to avoid the circus poster effect. It's a good idea to keep the maximum colors in a topic to between three and seven.

Most users will probably have their computers set to use one of the Windows default desktop settings, but they may not. If you're creating online help to accompany a software application, keep in mind how your color choices will interact with the color choices for the program.

It's also important to consider the minimum hardware configuration and Windows settings of your users. Windows maintains a list of available colors called a *palette*, a collection of the colors Windows can display at the time. Although it's a fair assumption that your users will have video cards that are capable of displaying over 16.7 million colors with default display settings of 800 × 600 and 16-bit (High Color) colors, many corporate environments still have users running at 800 × 600 and 256 colors. Windows can't display more than 256 different colors at a time on these machines without shifting its palette. Moreover, the wallpaper and desktop settings can take as many as 100 of the available colors, leaving the true available palette for other colors at 150 or so.

Color Blindness

As you are designing your color combinations, it's important to remember that between 12 percent and 17 percent of the male population and between 0.25 percent and 0.5 percent of the female population has some form of color deficiency (color blindness). The most common form of this is red-green deficiency (an inability to distinguish red from green), although there are other types of color deficiencies such as blue-yellow. The least common form is total color blindness (no color vision at all), which affects only a very small percentage of those with color deficiencies.

As part of your testing procedure, you may want to find people in the office who have some form of color deficiency and ask them to evaluate the color combinations for your online help. (There are many versions of the standard Ishihara color-blindness tests online if you want to test yourself.) A workaround for this potential problem is to choose colors with a high contrast, which will enable users with moderate or severe color deficiencies to differentiate text from background.

When you display a topic in a WinHelp file that requires colors not currently on the Windows palette, the users will see a *palette shift*, a flash on the screen and a change in the colors that are being displayed. Palette shifts are rather distracting and can scare novice users. If you don't know for sure the type of computers on which the WinHelp file is going to be used, be conservative in your choices and keep your layout and your colors designed for an 800 × 600 × 256 computer.

Finally, keep in mind that it's not possible to predict all of the possible yucky color combinations your users may have set their computers to display. The color choices for the title bars, default text font and color, active window color, and so on are determined by the users' personal taste or lack thereof. However, if you keep your WinHelp file consistent and conservatively formatted (even a little boring), you will be much more likely to fit the needs of your users than if you try for something more elaborate and garish. Some of the best WinHelp files have used nothing more than white, yellow, gray, and black throughout.

Changing Font Colors

As with fonts and font characteristics, you can use the Format ➪ Font command in Word to change the color of selected text, as follows:

1. Highlight the text whose color you want to change.
2. Select the Format ➪ Font command, and then select the color you want in the Color field. (A sample of the text in the selected color appears at the bottom of the Font screen.) Click OK.

Your color choices should be high-contrast, easy to read, and pleasing to the eye. Some effective color combinations are shown in Table 5-1.

Table 5-1
Color Combinations to Use

Background color	*Text color*
White	Black, blue or dark blue, red or dark red
Black	White, yellow, bright green, turquoise (cyan)
Turquoise (cyan)	Black, dark green
Dark blue	White, yellow, turquoise (cyan)
Dark red	White, yellow
Dark gray	White, yellow, turquoise (cyan)
Light gray	Black, dark green, dark blue, dark red

There are some color combinations you should avoid (either as background or as text) because they're too garish or they don't provide enough contrast to be read easily:

✦ light or dark blue with red, green, or black

✦ red and green

✦ black with red, magenta, dark gray, dark or light blue, or dark green

✦ white and yellow, turquoise (cyan), or light green

The default color for text in Word is Auto, which means that the text will be displayed in the default text color on the computer. In most cases, this is black, but it's possible that your users will have changed this for some reason. It's a good idea when using colors to set all text from auto to black to make sure that it shows up the way you intended.

Changing Background Colors

The techniques you've seen so far are effective for changing your fonts — the information in the foreground. You can also change the background colors through the Windows Properties screen, as follows:

1. From the Project Manager in RoboHELP Explorer, expand the Project folder, and then expand the Windows folder, as shown in Figure 5-14.

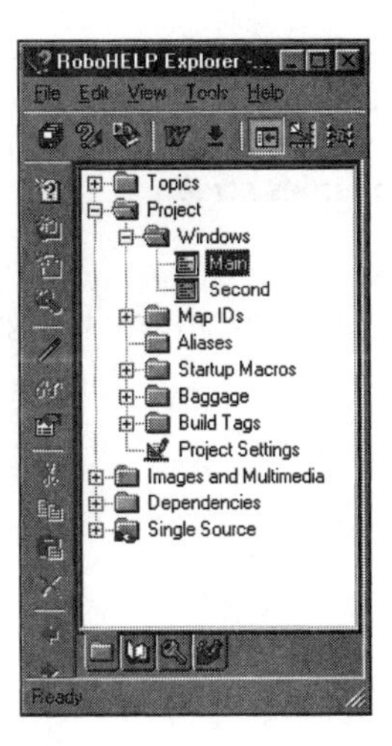

Figure 5-14: RoboHELP Explorer showing the Windows folder expanded

2. Double-click the Main icon to display the Windows Properties screen, shown in Figure 5-15. (You can also go directly to the Windows Properties screen by selecting the RoboHELP Explorer Edit ⇨ Windows command.) The Windows Properties screen lets you change the size, location, and colors for your display windows. Right now, you're going to see how to change the colors; later on in Chapter 9, "Using Help Windows and Browse Sequences," you'll see how to change other properties for your display windows.

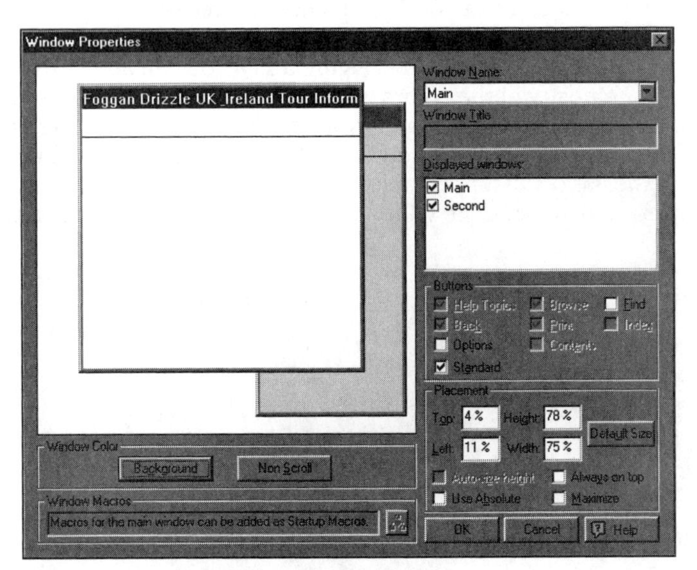

Figure 5-15: The Windows Properties screen

You can also reach the Windows Properties screen by selecting the RoboHELP ➪ Project Settings command or the File ➪ Project Settings command in RoboHELP Explorer, and then selecting the Windows tab in the Project Settings and double-clicking the Main icon to display the Windows Properties screen.

3. To change the background color of the window, click Background. The Microsoft standard color selection window appears, as shown in Figure 5-16.

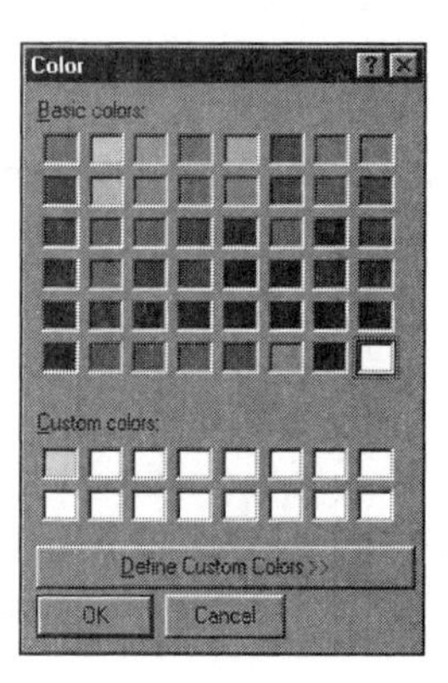

Figure 5-16: The Color screen

4. Select a color from the predefined color list. If you don't like any of the colors on the list of basic colors, you can create a custom color by clicking Define Custom Colors at the bottom of the screen. (Be judicious when adding custom colors, as they can cause a palette shift.) The Color screen expands to show the custom color options (shown in Figure 5-17). You can adjust the hue, saturation, and luminosity of the colors with the color selection area and the luminosity slider bar. When you're happy with the color you've selected (displayed in the Color | Solid field), click Add to Custom Colors. The custom color appears in the list of custom colors. You can then select the custom color to color objects and areas in the WinHelp project like any of the basic colors.

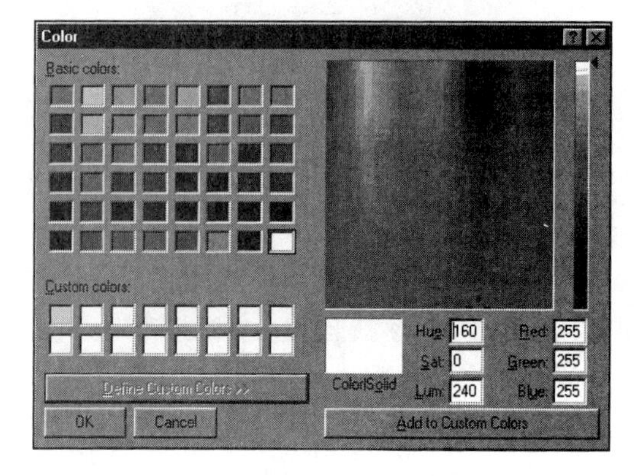

Figure 5-17: The Color screen showing the custom color palette

5. When you're satisfied with your color selection, click OK. RoboHELP applies the color to the background area of the window, as shown in Figure 5-18.

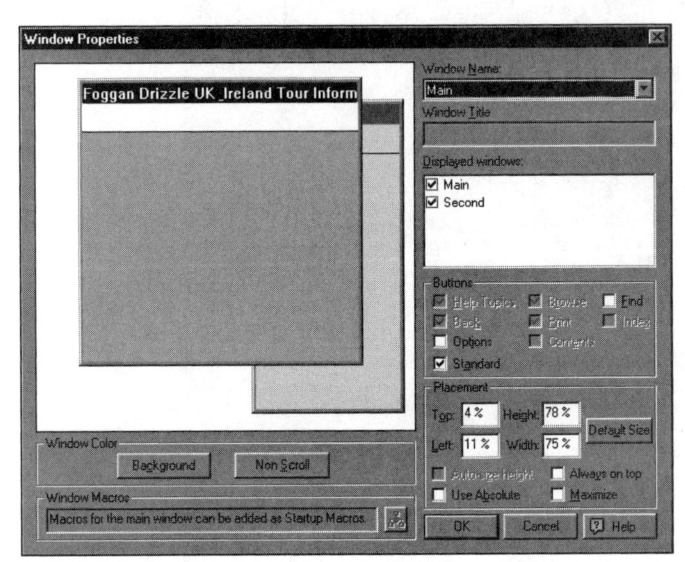

Figure 5-18: Applying a color to the background area

If you reached the Windows Properties screen by selecting the RoboHELP⇨ Project Settings command or the File⇨Project Settings command in RoboHELP Explorer, click OK on the Project Settings screen to apply the new background color to the WinHelp project.

RoboHELP stores the information for the background color. When you compile the project, RoboHELP uses the background color you've selected. An example of how this looks appears in Figure 5-19.

If you don't like the background color you've selected, you can select another one using the same technique. You can return to the default background color by right-clicking the background window in the Windows Properties screen and selecting Default from the right-click menu. You can have only one background color for each display window in a WinHelp project.

At this point, you're only using the main window to display your online help. You'll see how to use different display windows in Chapter 9, "Using Help Windows and Browse Sequences."

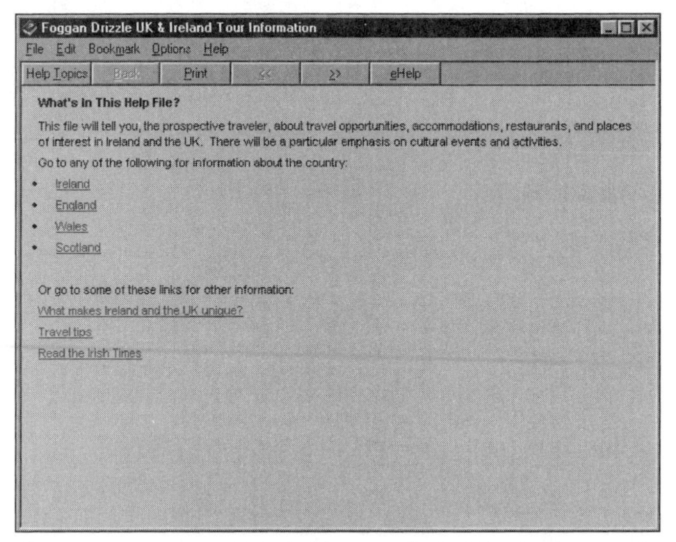

Figure 5-19: Foggan Drizzle file compiled with a background color

Be sure to experiment with the color choices for your background and text to make sure they look good. You should also try them out on other computers and with other display settings to make sure that they look good on a range of systems. (If the colors appear different from what you selected, you may need to select a color from the 16-color palette, rather than the 256-color palette, and recompile the WinHelp project.)

Using Non-Scrolling Regions

When you saw how to select background color in the Windows Properties screen (shown earlier in Figure 5-17), you may have noticed the area at the top of the window that didn't change color. This is the *non-scrolling region*, which contains the topic title at the top of the topic window. The non-scrolling region works like this: if there's a topic longer than a single screen and the users scroll down to read more information, the topic title scrolls off the top of the screen with the rest of the text. However, if you set the topic heading to be a non-scrolling region when you compile the WinHelp project, the topic title will stay at the top of the screen and the topic text will appear to scroll underneath it. This lets the users see which topic they're viewing and looks a little sharper than simply scrolling the heading off the top of the screen. (An example of how this looks appears in Figure 5-20.)

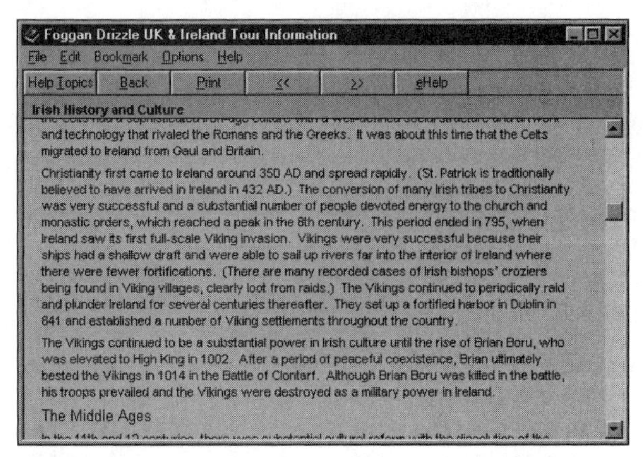

Figure 5-20: Sample non-scrolling region with text scrolled under it

To set a topic title to non-scrolling, do the following:

1. Select the text of the topic heading you want to change and select the Format ➪ Paragraph command in Word.
2. Go to the Line and Page Breaks tab.
3. Select the Keep with next option and click OK.

That's all there is to it! The Keep with next option is flagged in the document by a small black square that appears to the left of the formatted paragraph. If there's a manual page break after the preceding paragraph mark — as there is for the topic headings — the square will actually appear above the page break. When the DOC file is compiled, the WinHelp compiler looks for this paragraph attribute and sets the paragraph to be part of a non-scrolling region.

You can add a non-scrolling region with a handy RoboHELP feature:

1. Position the cursor in the topic heading you want to change. Select the RoboHELP ➪ Set Non-Scrolling Region command. The Set Non-Scrolling Region screen appears (shown in Figure 5-21).

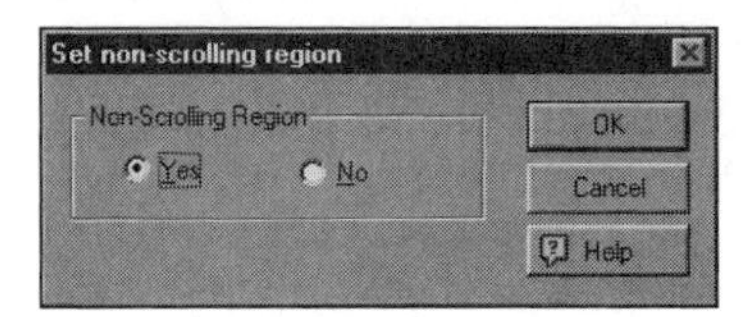

Figure 5-21: The Set Non-Scrolling Region screen

2. Select Yes and click OK. RoboHELP sets the topic heading to Keep with next.

This method of creating a non-scrolling region is preferable, as it minimizes the chance of non-scrolling region compiler warnings that can occur when you select and format the non-scrolling region manually.

You can have only one non-scrolling region in a topic. The non-scrolling region must appear at the start of the topic and can't be preceded by a scrolling region. If you have stray paragraphs that have the Keep with next paragraph option, the WinHelp compiler will give you an error message. (An advantage of using the RoboHELP ➪ Set Non-Scrolling Region command is that RoboHELP sets the Keep with next option only for the topic heading.)

It's a good formatting technique to set the standard topic headings to be non-scrolling. You'll see how to modify the styles in the RoboHELP templates later in this chapter in "Customizing RoboHELP Templates."

Setting the color for the non-scrolling region is similar to the process for setting the background color you saw earlier:

1. From the Project Manager in RoboHELP Explorer, expand the Project folder, expand the Windows folder, and then double-click the Main icon to display the Windows Properties screen (shown earlier in Figure 5-15).
2. Click Non Scroll at the bottom of the Window Properties screen to change the color of the non-scrolling region. The standard color selection window appears (shown earlier in Figure 5-16).
3. Select a color from the predefined color list or create a custom color by clicking Define Custom Colors at the bottom of the screen. When you're satisfied with your color selection, click OK. RoboHELP applies the color to the non-scrolling region area of the window, as shown in Figure 5-22.

When you compile the project, RoboHELP uses the color you've selected for the non-scrolling region. An example of how this looks appears in Figure 5-23. Adding color to non-scrolling regions is a good idea even if the topics are rarely going to be scrolled, as the color makes the heading stand out and provides visual cues to the users.

As with background colors, you can always change the color for the non-scrolling region at any time using this technique. You can also return to the default non-scrolling region color by right-clicking the non-scrolling region in the Window Properties screen and selecting Default from the right-click menu. You can have only one color for the non-scrolling regions in each display window in a WinHelp project.

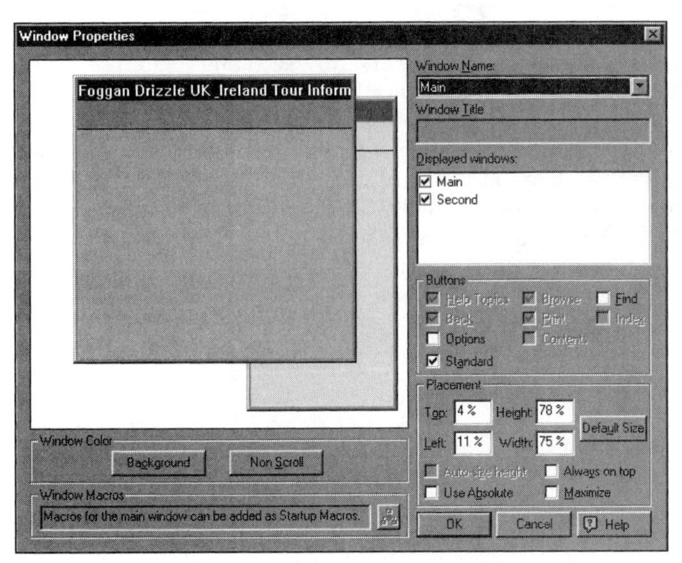

Figure 5-22: Applying a color to the non-scrolling region

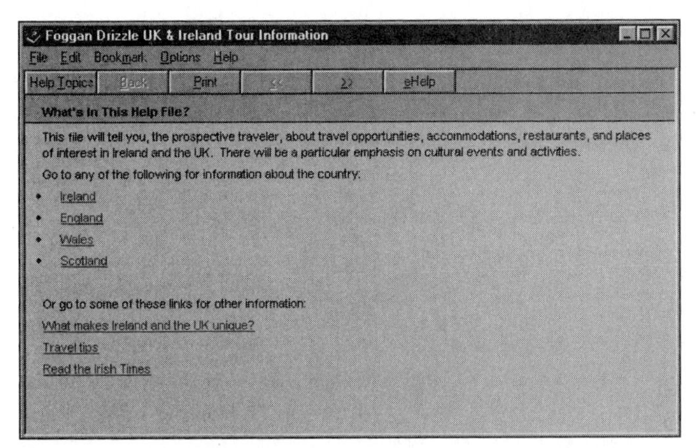

Figure 5-23: Foggan Drizzle file compiled with a color in the non-scrolling region

For more information on using different display windows, see Chapter 9, "Using Help Windows and Browse Sequences."

It's generally accepted practice to have the non-scrolling region to be of a color saturation and luminosity equal to or greater than that of the background color for the topic. For example, you could have light gray or dark gray for the non-scrolling region and white, yellow, or turquoise (cyan) for the background color. Light gray and dark gray are both excellent choices for the non-scrolling region, as they're neutral and go well with any background color.

Experiment with the color combinations for your non-scrolling regions and backgrounds and the text that appears in each area. Because the topic headings tend to be larger than the typical body text (typically, 12–24 points for heading text versus 8–12 points for body text), you can choose brighter colors than you might for body text. For example, you could use dark gray for the non-scrolling region, bright green for the topic heading, light yellow for the topic background, and black or dark blue for the body text. Normally, it would be difficult to use bright green for text, but against a dark gray background and in a larger font, it's perfectly readable without being tiring.

Try to use colors and headings in non-scrolling regions as you would when designing the headings in a manual or book. Let the colors and other font characteristics make the help file more accessible for the users by showing the hierarchy of topics and concepts.

Here are some general tips for adding non-scrolling regions to your topics:

✦ Non-scrolling regions can contain several lines of text. Figure 5-24 shows a non-scrolling region for the topic shown in Figure 5-23 with the Keep with next attribute set for the following paragraph. As long as there are no intervening paragraphs that don't have this attribute set, the WinHelp compiler will add the paragraphs to the non-scrolling region.

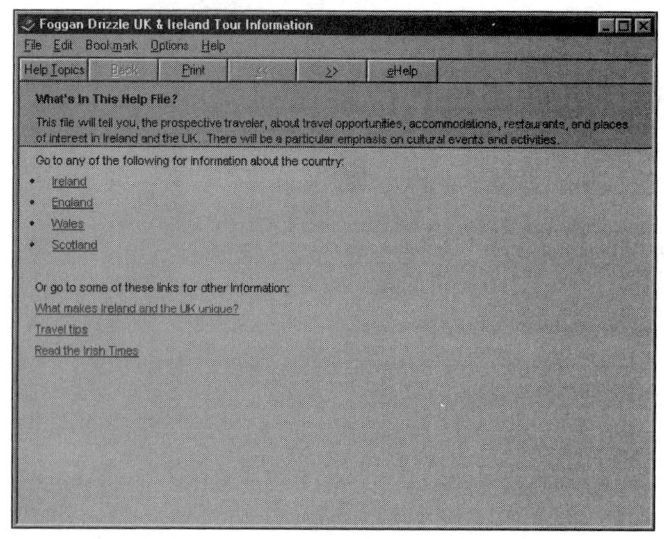

Figure 5-24: A non-scrolling region with several lines of text

✦ Under no circumstances should you have a non-scrolling region that crosses a page break from one topic to another. This will confuse the WinHelp compiler and result in an error message when you compile the project.

✦ Popup topics can't have non-scrolling regions because only the topic heading will appear when you select the topic, as you can see in the popup displayed in Figure 5-25.

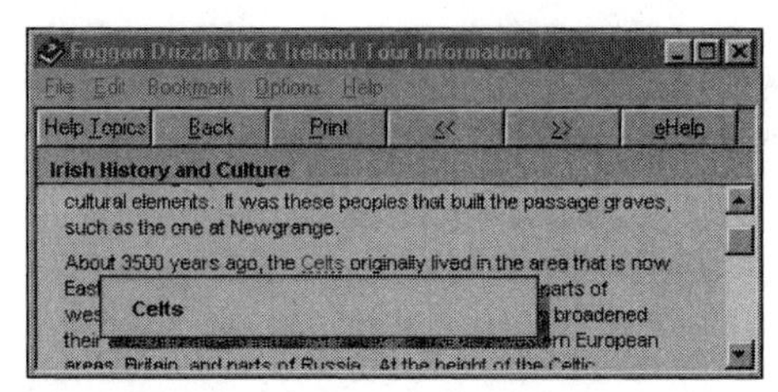

Figure 5-25: A popup formatted with a non-scrolling region

If you haven't set the Keep with next attribute for a topic, it won't have a non-scrolling region. You can check for this by scrolling through the topics one at a time, but there's a faster way to check to see if your topics have the non-scrolling region set:

1. Display the topic list in the right pane of the RoboHELP Explorer.
2. Select the Tools ➪ Options command. In the Options screen, display the Topic List tab (shown in Figure 5-26).

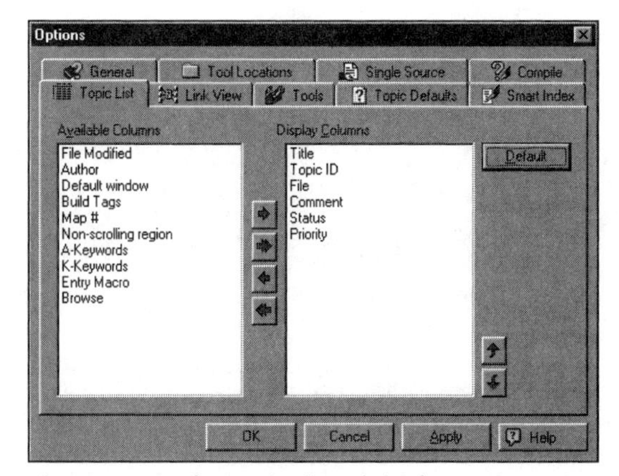

Figure 5-26: The Topic List tab in the Options screen

This tab identifies what topic attributes are displayed in the topic list. The list of default attributes appears in the Display Columns field on the right. You can display additional topic attributes by highlighting the attribute(s) in the Available Columns field you want to display, and then clicking the right arrow between the two lists, or simply double-clicking the attribute. RoboHELP adds the attribute to the bottom of the list. You can move all attributes to the Display Columns field by clicking the right double arrow.

You can also remove topics from the list by highlighting the attribute(s) in the Display Columns field, and then clicking the left arrow between the two lists, or simply double-clicking the attribute. RoboHELP removes the attribute from the display list. You can remove all attributes from the list by clicking the left double arrow.

You can change the order in which attributes are displayed by highlighting an attribute in the Display columns field and then clicking the up or down arrows at the bottom right of the Topic List tab until the attribute is positioned appropriately in the list. Clicking Default restores the default attribute list and order in the Display Columns field. To display the nonscrolling region information, do the following:

1. Double-click Non-scrolling region in the Available Columns field. For convenience, move the non-scrolling region attribute up to the third position, right after topic ID, and then click OK. The Topic List now displays the non-scrolling region information, as shown in Figure 5-27.

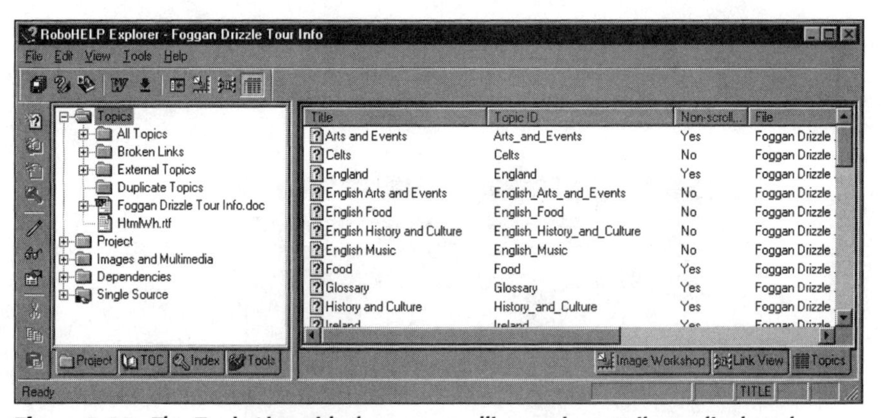

Figure 5-27: The Topic List with the non-scrolling region attribute displayed

2. From the list, you can see that the Celts popup does not have a non-scrolling region — appropriate for a popup topic — but that some of the topics for England are also not defined with non-scrolling regions. If you have a lot of topics, you can sort the topics by non-scrolling region by clicking on the Non-scrolling region heading, as shown in Figure 5-28.

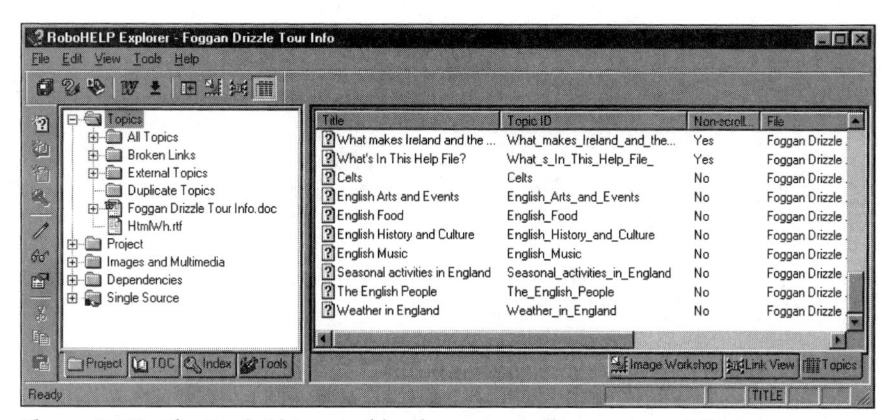

Figure 5-28: The Topic List sorted by the non-scrolling region attribute

You can't store your settings for the background and non-scrolling region colors from project to project.

Customizing RoboHELP Templates

So far in this chapter, you have seen how to set specific font and paragraph attributes manually using Word's Format ➪ Font and Format ➪ Paragraph commands. However, this requires you to apply extensive, finicky changes to your documents that cannot be undone easily. In such cases, it's a good idea to take advantage of Word's template and style features to format the elements of your document automatically. This section shows you how you can customize the RoboHELP templates to reflect the preferred font and paragraph settings for your WinHelp project.

The following section assumes that you're already familiar with basic template and style concepts in Microsoft Word. If you aren't, you may want to take a few moments to review the information on how templates and styles work in the Word documentation.

When you use a style in a template, Word automatically applies the font, paragraph, and other attributes to the selected paragraph. Using styles also lets you change attributes quickly and easily for specific elements such as headings or body text by changing the style in the style sheet for that element.

RoboHELP applies the ROBOHELP.DOT template to the DOC files for the WinHelp projects. This template contains the RoboHELP styles, commands, and toolbars. You can modify the styles in ROBOHELP.DOT to customize the appearance of your WinHelp projects as follows:

1. Close any RoboHELP documents you have open and open ROBOHELP.DOT in Word.

Before you make any changes to ROBOHELP.DOT, *always* make a backup copy!

If you have an antiviral template running in Word that prevents macros from loading, you will need to disable the template while you're working on the ROBOHELP.DOT template.

2. Select the Format ➪ Style command in Word. The standard Style screen appears, as shown in Figure 5-29.

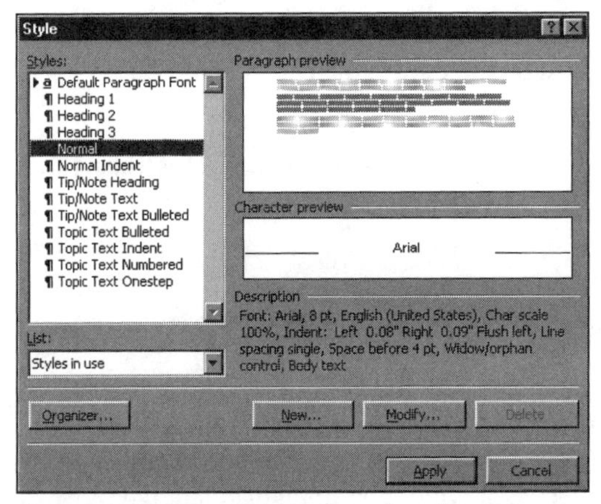

Figure 5-29: The Style screen showing the ROBOHELP.DOT styles

3. Make changes to the styles as appropriate. (Refer to the Word documentation for detailed information on how to change styles.)

Be sure that you select Add to template on the Modify Style screen so that the updated style is available to any new WinHelp projects.

4. When you are satisfied with your changes, click OK.
5. Close ROBOHELP.DOT and save the changes.

If the Automatically update document styles option is selected on the Templates and Add-Ins screen in Word, the new ROBOHELP.DOT template styles will also apply to older projects when they're subsequently opened in RoboHELP. However, if you don't select this option, the new styles won't be applied when the project is re-opened. If you're not sure that you want to automatically apply an updated style to an existing document, you should probably leave the Automatically update document styles unselected and then reapply the styles when and where appropriate.

When you open the WinHelp project again, the updated styles will be applied to the headings and body text. Figure 5-30 shows the Foggan Drizzle file compiled with changes to the Heading 1 style and the body text. (Contrast the font sizes in the heading and body with those in Figure 5-23.)

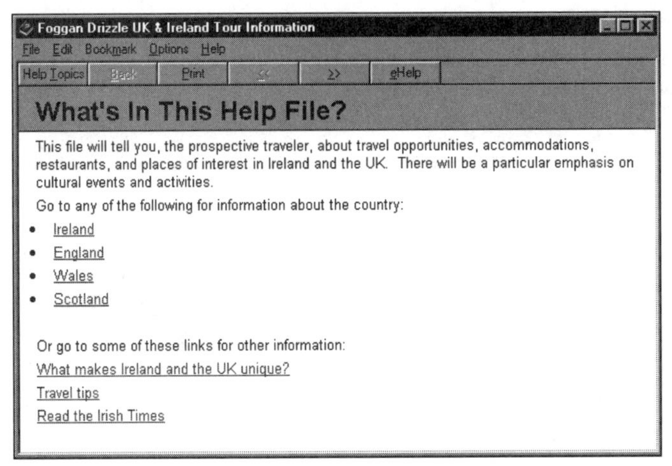

Figure 5-30: The Foggan Drizzle file with changed heading and body styles

Here are some tips for modifying ROBOHELP.DOT:

✦ One of the most common customizations to ROBOHELP.DOT is to set the Heading 1 style to include the Keep with next attribute so that the topics have a non-scrolling region.

✦ If you have styles in another template you'd like to add to ROBOHELP.DOT, you can use copy them to ROBOHELP.DOT (if you'd like them to be available for all WinHelp projects) or to the current DOC file (if you'd like them to be available for the current DOC file only).

✦ RoboHELP 2000 has several other templates for projects created with older versions of RoboHELP: ROBORTF.DOT, ROBOHP31.DOT, and ROBORTF31.DOT. If you open a WinHelp project that was created with RoboHELP v4 or earlier, RoboHELP 2000 uses these templates. There is also a ROBODOCS.DOT template that lets you create well-formatted documents for printing. You can modify this template in the same fashion as you did ROBOHELP.DOT.

Changing the styles in ROBOHELP.DOT will affect all WinHelp projects. If you want to change the styles in this particular DOC file only, you can use the Format ➪ Style command to change styles locally without affecting the ROBOHELP.DOT template. However, you may want to have groups of documents that have the same styles — for example, if you have generally preferred styles for your topic text but you want to vary heading styles and indents. The easiest thing to do is to create individual templates, like this:

1. Make a backup copy of ROBOHELP.DOT.
2. Make any basic changes to ROBOHELP.DOT that you want to propagate through your templates.
3. In the Windows Explorer, make as many copies of the template as you want. It's a good idea to give them related names such as PROJECT1.DOT, PROJECT2.DOT, and so on.
4. Open each template in Word and make the specific changes to the styles. Save each template.

With the customized templates set up, you're ready to create new WinHelp projects. When you create or open a WinHelp project, RoboHELP uses the ROBOHELP.DOT template. To use the customized template, you'll need to use the customized template in place of the standard ROBOHELP.DOT template, as follows:

1. In the Windows Explorer, rename ROBOHELP.DOT to ROBOHELP.SAV.
2. Rename the customized template to ROBOHELP.DOT.

When you're done working with the file and that template, do the following:

1. In the Windows Explorer, delete ROBOHELP.DOT (the copy of the customized project template).
2. Rename ROBOHELP.SAV back to ROBOHELP.DOT.

When you create a new topic in a WinHelp file, RoboHELP uses Heading 1 as the default style for the topic heading. Although this will do for regular topics, you may want to change this for popup and other topics. If you've set up your Heading 1 style to format with the Keep with next attribute so that topics automatically have a non-scrolling region (something that's a very typical customization for the Heading 1 style), you won't want to use this heading for the popup topics as you saw earlier in Figure 5-25. Rather than having to manually assigning a new style to the popup headings, you can have RoboHELP use a different style for the headings, as follows:

1. Select the RoboHELP ⇨ Advanced Settings command. The Advanced Settings screen appears. As you can see in Figure 5-31, the default style for all headings is Heading 1.
2. Select from the drop-down list the new heading style you want to apply as the default heading style. (For popup topics, you may want to create a Popup Heading style that's identical to your default Heading 1 style but doesn't have the Keep with next attribute set.) When you are satisfied with your changes, click OK.

Now when you create topics, RoboHELP will use the styles you've specified for the topic headers.

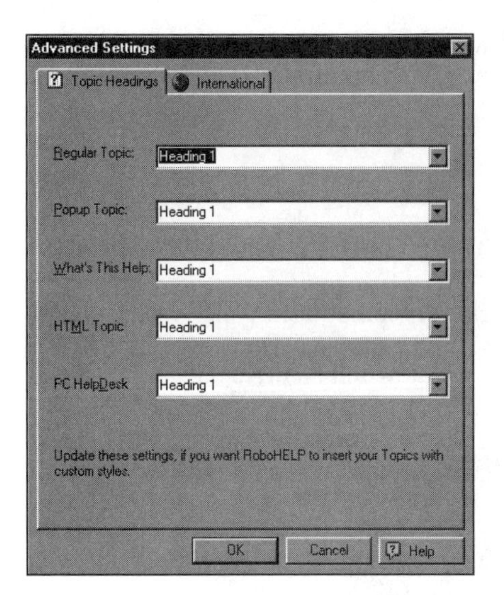

Figure 5-31: The Advanced Settings screen

Using WinHelp 2000

So far in the examples in this book, when you compile the WinHelp files, they appear as standard WinHelp files. RoboHELP also lets you compile your WinHelp into a different format known as WinHelp 2000. WinHelp 2000 gives you an expanded view of your WinHelp file in a new format. Figure 5-32 shows the Foggan Drizzle help file compiled into WinHelp 2000.

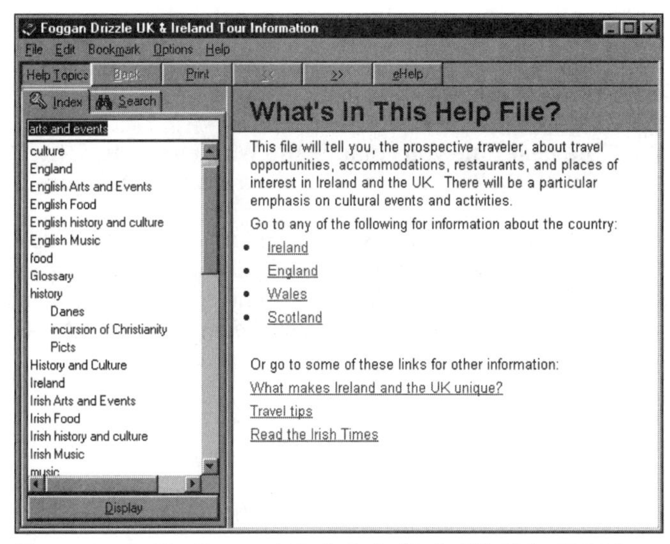

Figure 5-32: The Foggan Drizzle help file in WinHelp 2000 format

WinHelp 2000 always displays the TOC, index, and search windows to the left of the help topic, which makes navigation easier. (The new look of WinHelp 2000 is also known as *Explorer View Help*.)

Compiling WinHelp 2000

Compiling WinHelp 2000 is very simple:

1. Select the RoboHELP ➪ Project Settings command (in Word) or the File ➪ Project Settings command (in RoboHELP Explorer). On the Project Settings screen, go to the WinHelp 2000 tab, as shown in Figure 5-33.

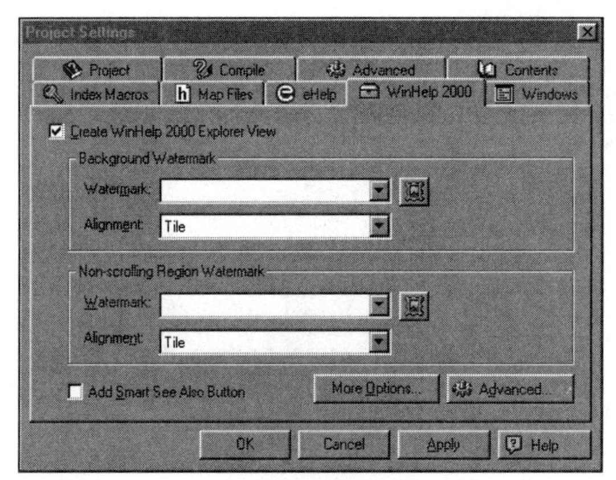

Figure 5-33: The WinHelp 2000 tab of the Project Settings screen

2. Select Create WinHelp 2000 Explorer View and click OK.

That's all you need to do! The next time you compile the WinHelp project, the resulting help file will be in WinHelp 2000 format, as you saw earlier in Figure 5-33.

WinHelp 2000 uses routines in the RoboEx32.DLL file to display the help file in WinHelp 2000 format. When you ship the compiled help file to your users, you must also include RoboEx32.DLL.The specific requirements for the redistributable RoboHELP files you need to ship with your online help file are detailed in the Ship List Report, described in Chapter 15, "Managing Large Projects."

Adding Watermarks in WinHelp 2000

One of the great formatting features you can take advantage of with WinHelp 2000 files is adding *watermarks*. Watermarks are graphics that appear as formatting for the topic background and the non-scrolling region. For example, the RoboHELP 2000 online help uses a cloud graphic as a watermark for the topic text. Where you can change the color of the help background area and non-scrolling region, you can use watermarks to add colors, textures, pictures, or logos to your online help file.

To add a watermark to a WinHelp 2000 file:

1. Select the RoboHELP ➪ Project Settings command or the File ➪ Project Settings command to display the WinHelp 2000 tab on the Project Settings screen.
2. To set a background watermark, select a graphic from the drop-down list in the Watermark field. The graphic appears on the right side of the screen so you can see what it looks like. You can also click the image button to the immediate right of the Watermark field and browse and select graphics through the Select Image screen, shown in Figure 5-34.

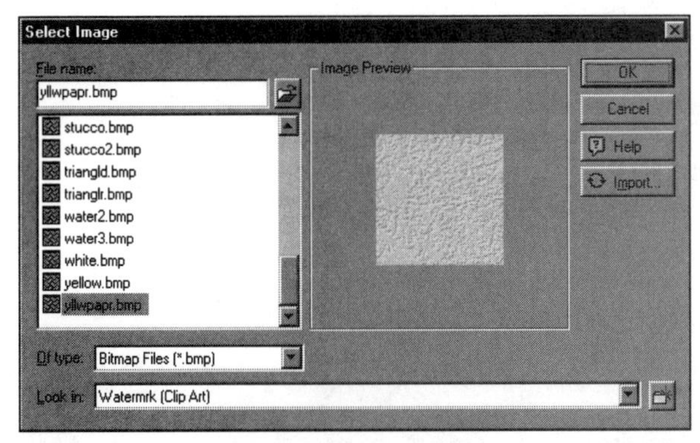

Figure 5-34: The Select Image screen

3. When you've selected the watermark to use, you need to select the alignment from the drop-down list in the associated Alignment field. You can tile the watermark, stretch or center it, or position the watermark in a variety of locations on the topic screen.
4. If you wish, you can also add a watermark and alignment for the non-scrolling region. Figure 5-35 shows watermarks selected for the background and the non-scrolling region. When you are satisfied with your changes, click OK.

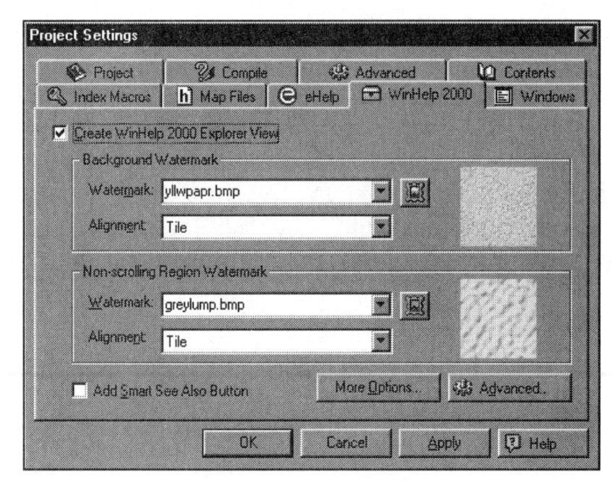

Figure 5-35: Watermarks selected in the WinHelp 2000 tab of the Project Settings screen

When you compile the project, the watermarks appear on the topic display as shown in Figure 5-36.

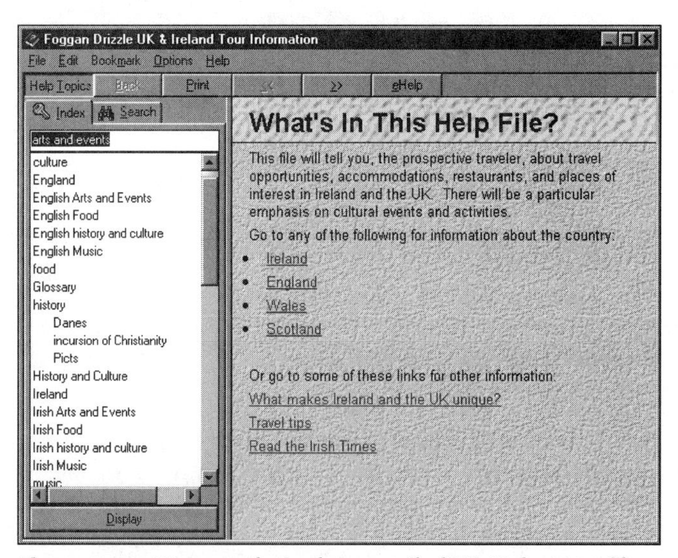

Figure 5-36: Watermarks in the compiled WinHelp 2000 file

You may also want to add a watermark to the background and/or non-scrolling region for a specific topic. Topic watermarks will override any general watermarks you've set for the project on the WinHelp 2000 tab.

1. Place the cursor within the topic, then select the Edit ➪ Topic Properties command. When the Topic Properties screen appears, select the Watermark tab, shown in Figure 5-37.

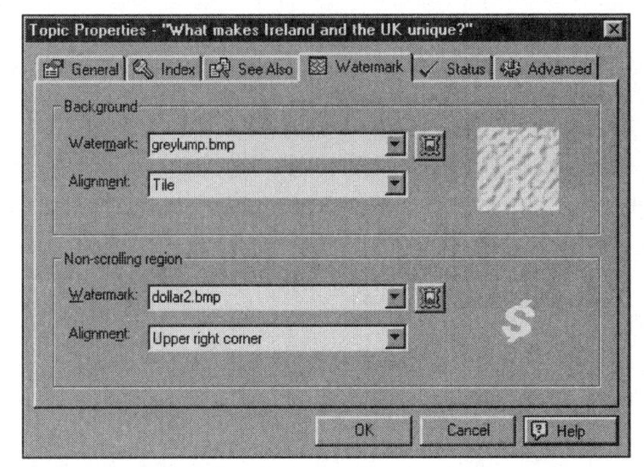

Figure 5-37: The Watermark tab in the Topic Properties screen

2. Select background and non-scrolling region watermark graphics and their alignments as you did before. When you are satisfied with your changes, click OK.

Here are some tips for using watermarks:

- ✦ The graphic files for watermarks must be in 16-color or 256-color BMP format, but you can click Import on the Select Image screen to search for and import graphic files in several other formats. You can import graphic files in GIF, JPG, WMF, high-res BMP, and PCX formats. You can also import files in the WinHelp graphics formats MRB and SHG, which are discussed in Chapter 7, "Getting Fancy with Graphics."
- ✦ When using watermarks, particularly 256-color watermarks, be careful that the colors in the watermark bitmap don't cause a palette shift when the topic is displayed.

Summary

This chapter showed you how to communicate more effectively by adding formatting and color to elements of your online help files. You saw how to change fonts, font characteristics, and font attributes, how to format paragraphs, and how to use bulleted and numbered lists. You also saw how to create and format tables in your

WinHelp files and how to work around some of the limitations of the WinHelp compiler, and how to insert symbols and special characters so that they appear correctly when compiled. The chapter also introduced you to many of the ways you can use color for your text, background areas, and non-scrolling regions. You also learned ways to automate many formatting tasks by using the RoboHELP template and how to customize the template to fit your specific formatting needs. Last, you saw how to create WinHelp 2000 files and how to add watermarks for increased impact and color.

The next chapter will introduce you to basic graphics. You'll see how to add graphics to your help files and how to use some of the RoboHELP graphics tools and utilities.

✦ ✦ ✦

Adding Simple Graphics

✦ ✦ ✦ ✦

In This Chapter

Learning about graphic files

Adding graphics to a WinHelp file

Adding transparent graphics to a WinHelp file

Editing graphics with Microsoft Paint and the Image Workshop

Changing the default editing program

Capturing graphics from the screen

Importing graphics from other formats

Organizing graphics with the Project Manager

Adding folders of graphic files to the Project Manager

Finding missing graphics and graphic folders

Printing the Images report

✦ ✦ ✦ ✦

This chapter introduces you to the basics of adding graphics to your WinHelp projects. It starts by discussing how graphics are stored. You then learn how to add a graphic to your WinHelp project. Next, you learn how to make transparent graphics in a topic. You then see ways you can edit the properties of graphic files and the images themselves with Microsoft Paint (Windows' default graphics program) and RoboHELP's Image Workshop. You also see how to use different graphic editing programs. After that, the chapter continues with information about capturing screen images and importing graphics in other formats. You'll then learn to organize and track graphics using the Project Manager in RoboHELP Explorer and find missing graphics and graphic folders. Finally, you'll learn how to print the Images report.

Understanding Graphic File Formats

Before you add graphics to your WinHelp file, it's helpful for you to understand a little information about the types and formats of graphic files.

Information is displayed on your computer's screen in individual dots called *pixels*. Your computer's video card and the settings thereof determine the number of pixels and colors you can display. Typical video settings are 640 × 480, 800 × 600, 1,024 × 768, and 1,280 × 1,024. These settings identify how many pixels appear horizontally (640) and vertically (480). The number of colors you can display is based on the number of bits assigned for the color for each pixel. The more color bits for each pixel, the greater the range (or *depth*) of colors you can display. Table 6-1 shows the standard color settings.

Table 6-1
Color Settings

Number of bits	*Description*
1	Monochrome (black-and-white) graphics. Monochrome graphics are black and white, with no shading or color. Because they use only one color bit, monochrome graphics are very small. They are generally used when one has line drawings or other black-and-white artwork and the WinHelp file must be as small as possible.
4	16-color graphics. Most WinHelp file graphics are in 16 colors. Virtually all computers can support 16-color graphics. In addition, by using the standard 16-color palette in Windows, you are guaranteed that the graphics will appear exactly as you see them. 16-color graphics are also fully supported for WinHelp systems that must be backward compatible with older software running on Windows 3.*x*.
8	256-color graphics. WinHelp 4 can support 256-color graphics. 256-color graphics can take substantially more space than 16-color graphics. In addition, you may have problems with palette shifts if you use a nonstandard 256-color palette.
16, 24	High-color (16-bit) and true-color (24-bit) graphics. High-color and true-color graphics (commonly found in GIF and JPG files) aren't supported by the WinHelp compiler. However, they can be used in HTML Help or other Web-based help systems such as WebHelp or JavaHelp.

Settings for the number of pixels and colors in the screen resolution can be found by right-clicking on the Windows desktop. Select the Active Desktop ⇨ Customize My Desktop command, and then select the Settings tab of the Display Properties screen (shown in Figure 6-1).

The greater the depth of color in a graphic file, the larger the file and the longer it will take to display. In addition, if the graphic is displayed on a system that doesn't support all the colors (such as a high-color graphic displayed on a 256-color system), Windows will substitute the closest color from the standard 16-color palette.

You can use monochrome, 16-color, and 256-color graphics in your WinHelp files. WinHelp can compile graphic files in several different graphic formats, as shown in Table 6-2.

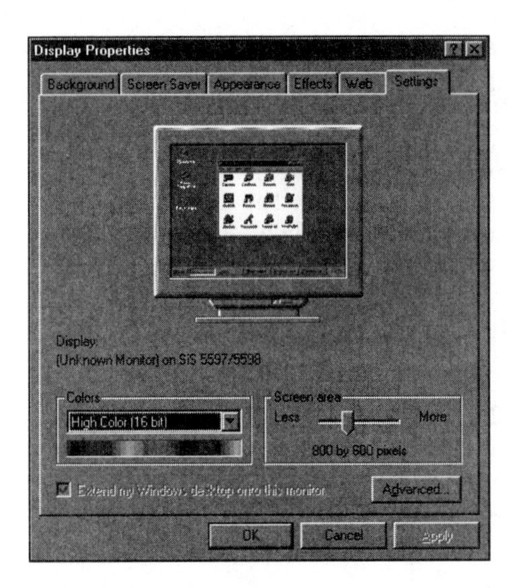

Figure 6-1: The Settings tab of the Display Properties screen

Table 6-2
Supported Graphic File Formats

File Extension	*Description*
BMP	These files are BMP (bitmap) graphic files. Bitmaps store graphics in pixels. Virtually every program that uses graphics recognizes bitmaps.
MRB	These files are MRB (Multi-Resolution Bitmap format) graphic files. (For more information on using MRB files, see Chapter 7, "Getting Fancy with Graphics.") MRB files are used exclusively with WinHelp and almost always with WinHelp 3 files.
SHG	These files are SHG (Segmented Hypergraphic format) graphic files, which contain both a graphic image and hotspot areas that can be linked to jumps, popups, and other hotspots. (For more information on using SHG files, see Chapter 7, "Getting Fancy with Graphics.") SHG files are used exclusively with WinHelp files.
WMF	These files are WMF (Windows Metafile format) graphic files. Windows metafiles store data differently than bitmaps and are usually smaller than bitmaps of the same image, but not as many graphics editing tools can work with Windows metafiles.

There are many other graphic file formats, such as GIF, JPG, EPS, and TIF. You can't use these formats in WinHelp files, but you can convert them using the RoboHELP Image Workshop, as described later in this chapter.

When you are planning how to use graphics in your online help files, it's a good idea to be conservative and use fewer, simpler graphics. Too many graphics can expand the size of the WinHelp file excessively, and make it hard to understand by cluttering the screen with distracting images.

As with other design elements, it also helps to be consistent. You can save time creating your online help files if you use the same graphic elements in a predictable manner in accordance with an editorial style sheet. Be sure also to check out the Clip Art Gallery that comes with RoboHELP to see if there are existing graphics you can use; you may be able to save time and money with one of the supplied graphics, rather than create your own. As you add graphics to the online help files, test them on as many different computer configurations as you can to make sure that they will display correctly on your users' computers.

Adding Graphics to Your WinHelp Files

In the preceding chapters, you've seen how to start a help project, add help topics, compile the project, create navigation options with jumps and popups, and format the online help file to enhance your message. These skills constitute the majority of your activities when you work on a WinHelp project. You can create an effective WinHelp file with these skills alone, as many WinHelp files for Windows 3.*x* attest.

The next step in expanding your online help files is to add graphics. Graphics can add substantial color and focus to your online help, presenting an idea quickly and easily. Some things, such as goatees and spiral staircases, are relatively difficult to describe in text but are instantly understandable when you see pictures of them. Graphics can also make your online help more appealing by adding color and formatting in the form of buttons, lines, dividers, and other features.

You can use graphics for a wide variety of things, including the following:

- ✦ Program screens and dialog boxes
- ✦ Screen buttons
- ✦ Sample reports
- ✦ Circuit diagrams
- ✦ Maps
- ✦ Office layouts
- ✦ Company logos in topic headings

✦ Mechanical assembly instructions

✦ Birds native to a specific area

✦ Wiring plans

You can also use graphics to add formatting and color to topic screens; for example, you could insert a horizontal line graphic as a separator between blocks of text. Another use of graphics is highlighting topic headings by adding logos or other images.

Adding a Graphic

It's very easy to add a graphic to a help file:

1. Select the Insert ⇨ Help Image command in Word. The Insert Help Image screen (shown in Figure 6-2 with a sample graphic selected) appears. (Alternately, you can press Ctrl+G or you can click the New Help Image icon on the RoboHELP toolbar.)

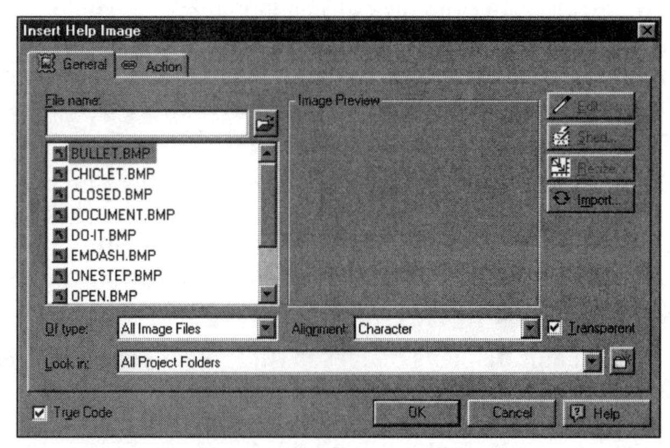

Figure 6-2: The Insert Help Image screen

2. Select the graphic you want to display by filling in the Insert Help Image screen as follows:

   - **File name:** Select a file name from the list or click the folder to browse for a graphic file. The list in the window below this field defaults to the files in the \RoboHELP\ClipArt\Special folder and any graphics in the project folders. You can change this with your selections in the Of type and Look in fields.

   - **Image Preview:** When you select a graphic file in the file list, RoboHELP displays it in the Image Preview field.

- **Edit:** Click this to edit the graphic with the default image editor. (You can set the default editor with the Tools ➪ Options ➪ Tool Locations command in the RoboHELP Explorer.) Editing graphics is discussed later in this chapter.
- **Shed:** Click this to edit or create the graphic in the Image Workshop. If the graphic isn't already a segmented hypergraphic (a SHG file), you can create a SHG file from the graphic.

For information on creating SHG (segmented hypergraphic) files, see Chapter 7, "Getting Fancy with Graphics."

- **Resize:** Click this to resize the graphic in the Image Workshop. (Resizing graphics is discussed later in this chapter.)
- **Import:** Click this to locate or convert graphics from formats that aren't supported by the WinHelp compiler to BMP files. (Importing graphics is discussed later in this chapter.)
- **Of type:** The default displays all graphic files, but you can choose to display BMP, MRB, SHG, or WMF files exclusively.
- **Alignment:** Specify from the drop-down list where you want the graphic to appear. Character (the default) inserts the graphic at the cursor position. Left left-justifies the graphic, and Right right-justifies the graphic. Depending on which option you select, the text flows around or to the side of the graphic.
- **Transparent:** Check this box if you want the graphic to be *transparent*. When you display a topic containing a transparent graphic, WinHelp replaces the white pixels in the graphic with the background color of the window so that the graphic blends smoothly into the surrounding topic. The graphic must be at least a 16-color bitmap to use this option.
- **Look in:** The default displays images in All Project Folders — the project folder plus all image folders associated with the project plus graphic file in the \RoboHELP\ClipArt\Special folder — but you can select folders of types of clip art included with RoboHELP. The various Clip Art folders located in the RoboHELP\Clip Art folder and what they contain are described in Table 6-3. You can also add a different folder by clicking the folder icon to the right of the field.
- **True Code:** Check this box to insert the reference to the graphic as a command statement. Uncheck the box if you want to see the graphic inserted in the file using RoboHELP's Dynamic WYSIWYG. Inserting the command statement is useful for advanced WinHelp users and allows you to edit graphic information using Word's Find and Replace features. (You'll see how to do this a little later in the chapter.) Inserting the graphic lets you view the topic with the graphic as it will appear to your users, but including lots of graphics can make the DOC file much larger and slower to save.

Table 6-3
RoboHELP Clip Art Folders

Folder	*What It Contains*
Balls	Two-dimensional and three-dimensional balls in various colors
Bookpage	Books, pages, and related icons
Bullets	Checkmarks, squares, diamonds, and other bullet symbols
Buttons	Assorted graphics for buttons and topic images
Computer	Graphics of computers, disks, printers, and accessories
Icons	Assorted icons such as posted notes, ending symbols, and folders
Letter	Letters of the alphabet on small buttons. (These are very useful for creating navigational tools for glossaries, as you'll see later in this chapter.)
Lines	Horizontal dividing lines and some colored balls
Misc	Miscellaneous graphics of all kinds
Special	Shortcut buttons
Starbrst	"New," "Special," and "Hot" buttons of various kinds
Watermrk	Watermark graphics (for use with WinHelp 2000 files)

3. When you are satisfied with your changes, click OK. Depending on your setting in the True Code field, you'll see the graphic inserted in the DOC file at the cursor location or a command. Figure 6-3 shows two insertions of a map of Ireland, the first using True Code to show the command, and the second using Dynamic WYSIWYG to show the graphic in the file.

Take a look at the True Code command shown in Figure 6-3. The curly braces (`{}`) indicate that this is a RoboHELP command. The first part of the command shows that this is a graphic (`bm`) that will be inserted left justified (`l`), followed by the name of the graphic (`irishmap.bmp`). A command to insert a right-justified graphic called LOGO.BMP would look like this: `{bmr logo.bmp}`. Similarly, a command to insert a graphic called FD.BMP at the character insertion point would look like this: `{bmc fd.bmp}`.

Figure 6-4 shows the compiled help topic from Figure 6-3. The topic text wraps around the graphic. As you can see, it doesn't matter whether you use True Code or display the graphic in the DOC file. They both compile the same in the WinHelp file.

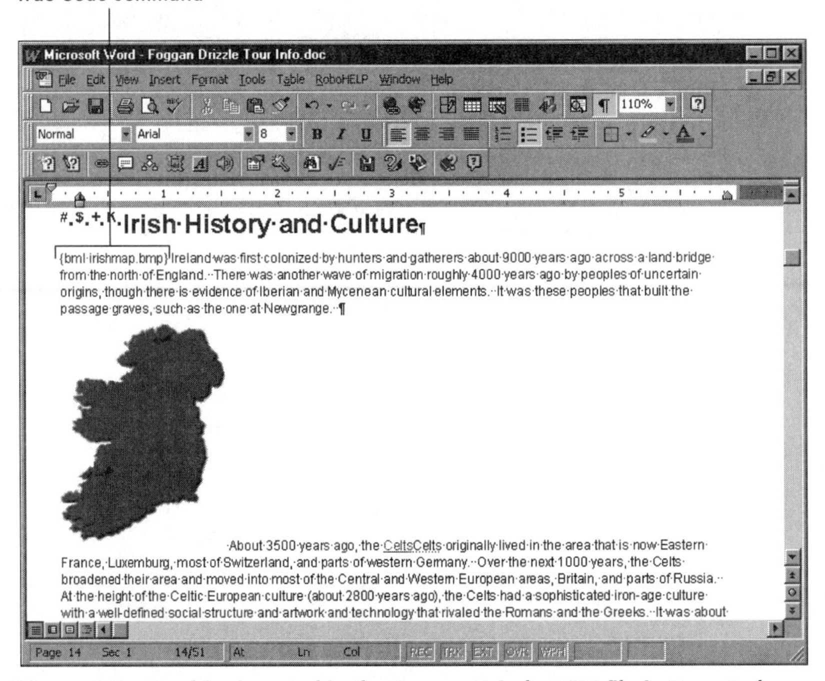

Figure 6-3: Graphics inserted in the Foggan Drizzle DOC file in True Code and Dynamic WYSIWYG

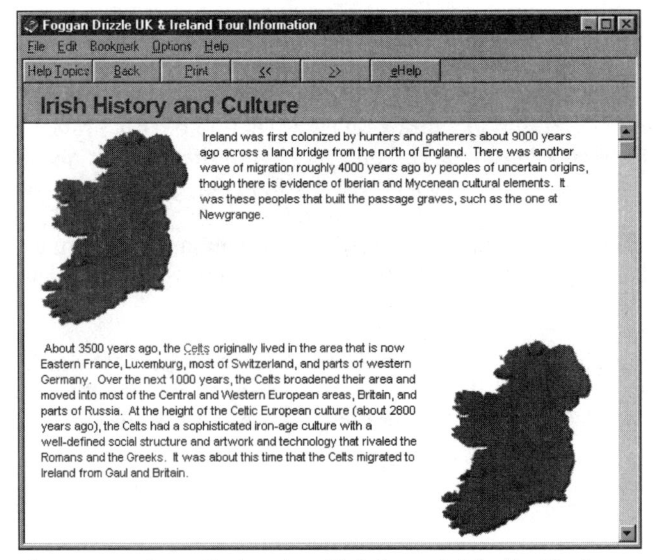

Figure 6-4: Compiled topic with left- and right-justified graphics

To Embed or Not To Embed?

Which method of inserting graphics should you choose, adding graphics by reference with the True Code and Dynamic WYSIWYG features or embedding a graphic file directly into the document? True Code and Dynamic WYSIWYG let you see the graphic in the DOC file either as a line of code referencing the external graphic file or as the actual graphic. Inserting a graphic in the DOC file embeds the actual graphic in the file, eliminating the need for an external file. There are several advantages to using True Code and Dynamic WYSIWYG.

First, when you use True Code and Dynamic WYSIWYG references, you can see more of the DOC file on the screen, so navigating the DOC file may be easier if you don't have to wait for Word to display graphics as you page down. However, if you have graphics embedded in the DOC file, you can speed up navigation in Word by selecting the Tools ⇨ Options command in Word and unchecking the Picture placeholders option on the View tab to display an outline showing the graphic's location.

The second advantage is that right-justified graphics (such as the graphic at the start of the second paragraph in Figure 6-3) don't appear as such in the Word file, even though they compile correctly. Using True Code and Dynamic WYSIWYG would show that the graphic was a right-justified graphic, by the `bmr` code in the command.

Another reason to use True Code and Dynamic WYSIWYG is because DOC files are smaller (having only a text reference as opposed to an inserted graphic file), and the compiled WinHelp files are smaller, as they have only a single link to the graphic file, which is then copied wherever the graphic appears in the WinHelp file. Graphics inserted in the DOC file are compiled and added to the WinHelp file as they appear, so half a dozen occurrences of the same graphic could add a substantial amount to the size of the file.

Finally, when you use references to a graphic with True Code and Dynamic WYSIWYG, you can modify the graphic and recompile easily without having to re-insert and resize the graphic at each location in the file. (And even if the graphic's name has changed, you can use Word's search and replace features to change the references.)

Following are a few common problems when adding graphics:

- ✦ If the graphic appears in strange colors or there's a palette shift when you display a topic, make sure that the graphics in the topic are using the same colors and that they're within the standard Windows color palette. (Many graphics packages have palette analyzers.)
- ✦ If the topic text doesn't flow around the graphic, make sure that you've selected left or right alignment. (Text won't flow around a graphic placed with character alignment.)
- ✦ If the graphic appears to be misaligned in the text, check the graphic's alignment. Also make sure that the paragraph settings in Word are correct; for example, make sure that the paragraph isn't centered when it should be left justified.

You should not use the Insert ➪ Picture ➪ Clip Art or Insert ➪ Picture ➪ File commands in Word to add a graphic to the online help file because the default option for the commands inserts the graphic as a floating graphic with an anchor rather than directly in the file. As a result, the graphic's location can float from place to place in the topic. If you want to use a Word clip art graphic, use the Insert ➪ Help Image command and then browse to the Word clip art folder and select the graphic you want to add.

Adding a Transparent Graphic

If your WinHelp file has a colored background, you can set your graphics to be transparent. Any white pixels in the graphic will then take on the color of the topic background. Displaying a graphic as transparent removes the white space around the graphic, letting the graphic blend smoothly into the background. (You won't see any difference if you're using a white background.)

Black-and-white bitmaps are always transparent, regardless of the setting in the Transparent field. Only 16-color bitmaps can be set as transparent. Some 256-color images can be transparent but the results are unpredictable.

Setting the graphic to display in transparent mode requires nothing more than checking the Transparent option in the Insert Help Image screen. Figure 6-5 shows the topic from Figure 6-4 with a background color added to the topic and transparent and nontransparent graphics.

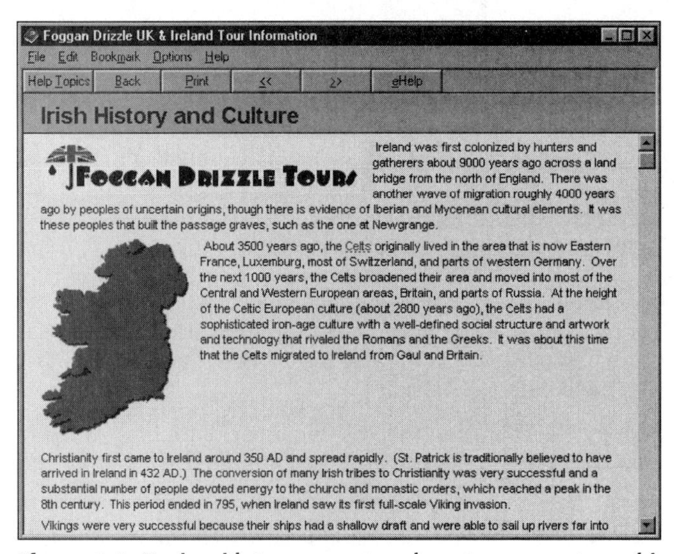

Figure 6-5: Topic with transparent and nontransparent graphics

When you resize the WinHelp screen, the text wraps around the graphics formatted with left justification or right justification, regardless of whether they're transparent or not, as shown in Figure 6-6. (Text won't wrap around graphics inserted with character-alignment.)

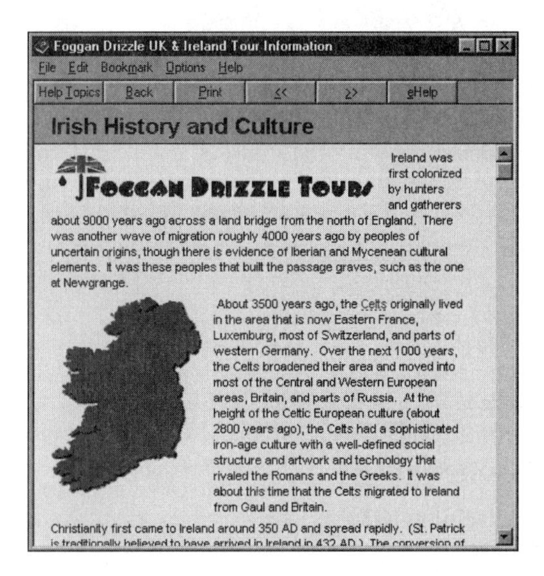

Figure 6-6: Resized topic with transparent and nontransparent graphics

You can make good use of graphics to enhance the non-scrolling regions in topics, too. Figure 6-7 shows a topic with a thin bar from the RoboHELP Lines clip art inserted in the heading. You could also insert a logo or other graphic element.

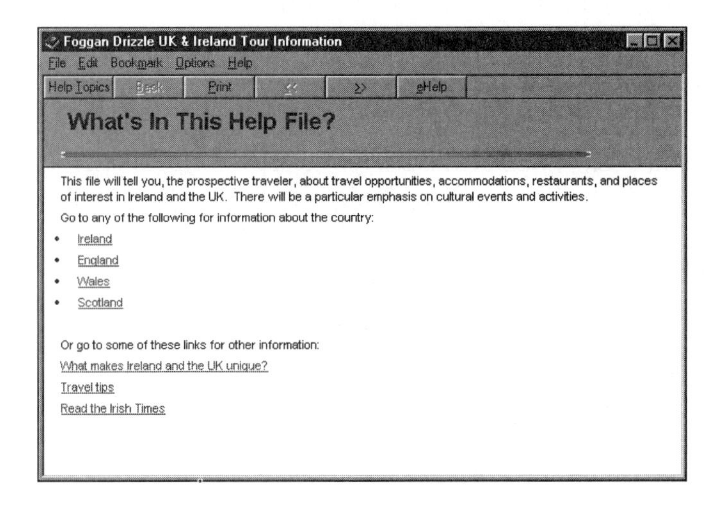

Figure 6-7: Topic with graphic added to the non-scrolling region

When you add a graphic to a topic—if the graphic file doesn't already exist in the project folder or in any of the image folders added to the project—RoboHELP adds the graphic file to the help project's directory so that the WinHelp compiler can locate the graphic file when the project is compiled.

Here are a few tips for creating and using transparent graphics:

✦ Not all graphics can be made transparent. The transparent graphic must be 16 colors and in bitmap (BMP) format.

✦ You can encounter some problems displaying transparent graphics. If the background color isn't one found in the standard 16-color palette in Windows, WinHelp will use the closest solid color. This can make the graphic look like it's surmounted on the background. The light yellow color commonly used on popup windows is not a standard color, so WinHelp uses the closest solid color, which is white.

✦ You can't display a graphic in the WinHelp file in both transparent and non-transparent modes. (If you try to include the file with both settings, you'll get an error message from the WinHelp compiler to the effect that the graphic has already been used as a nontransparent or a transparent bitmap, depending on what version of the graphic the WinHelp compiler encounters.) WinHelp stores only one copy of each bitmap in the compiled file, with the transparency setting of the first occurrence. WinHelp then displays the bitmap with that transparency assignment each time the bitmap appears in a topic. If you need to have the same graphic appear in a WinHelp file in both transparent and non-transparent forms, make a copy of the bitmap with a similar name and use one for the transparent displays and the other for the nontransparent displays.

✦ Because of a WinHelp compiler bug, transparent graphics displayed in the non-scrolling region take on the color of the background area. If the non-scrolling region is gray and the background color is yellow, the graphic will appear in the non-scrolling region with the white pixels replaced by yellow. You can solve this problem by making a copy of the bitmap and changing the background color to the same color as that of the non-scrolling region.

✦ If you display transparent graphics with True Code, a t is appended to the command to signify that the graphic is transparent, such as {bmlt irishmap.bmp}.

Editing Graphics

You can edit graphic properties—changing transparency, justification, view mode (True Code or Dynamic WYSIWYG), or even the graphic itself—by right-clicking the graphic or inside the True Code reference and selecting Properties from the right-click menu. RoboHELP displays the Help Image Properties screen shown in Figure 6-8. (The Help Image Properties screen is identical to the Insert Help Image screen shown in Figure 6-2.) Make whatever changes to the graphic you desire and click OK.

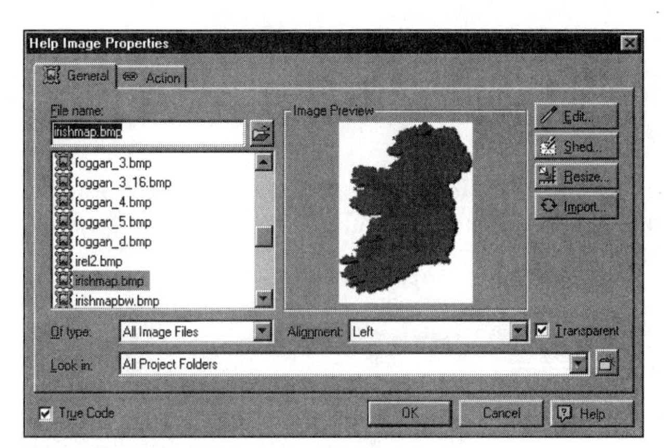

Figure 6-8: The Help Image Properties screen

Unlike deleting a topic or a hotspot, deleting an inserted graphic is simply a matter of selecting the graphic or True Code command and deleting it.

You can edit a graphic itself by displaying the graphic in the Insert Help Image screen (shown in Figure 6-2) and then clicking Edit. This starts the graphics-editing program. The default graphics editor is Windows Paint. (You can change the default editor with the Tools ➪ Options ➪ Tool Locations command in the RoboHELP Explorer and associate the appropriate file extension with the graphics editor of your choice.) You can then make changes to the graphic as appropriate. (You'll see how to use other programs later in this chapter.)

Using the Image Workshop

As easy as Windows Paint is, it's rather limited. RoboHELP comes with a program for viewing and editing graphics called Image Workshop, which you can use for many different graphics operations.

To open a graphic in the DOC file using the Image Workshop, do the following:

1. In the RoboHELP Explorer Project Manager window, expand the Images and Multimedia folder by clicking the plus sign to the left of the folder. Expand the Images folder the same way. The graphics in the file are listed below the Images folder. You can also open the Image Workshop directly from Word by selecting RoboHELP ➪ RoboHELP Explorer ➪ Image Workshop. The Image Workshop window will appear in the right pane of the RoboHELP Explorer, but a graphic file will not be open. You can then use the Open command in the Image Workshop to open a graphic file.

The Images folders display only the graphics already used in the online help project, not all the images associated with or accessible in the project. To open an image you haven't already used in a topic, you must use the Open command from inside Image Workshop.

2. Double-click the graphic you want to load. RoboHELP Explorer automatically expands the right page of the RoboHELP Explorer and loads the graphic into the Image Workshop, as shown in Figure 6-9.

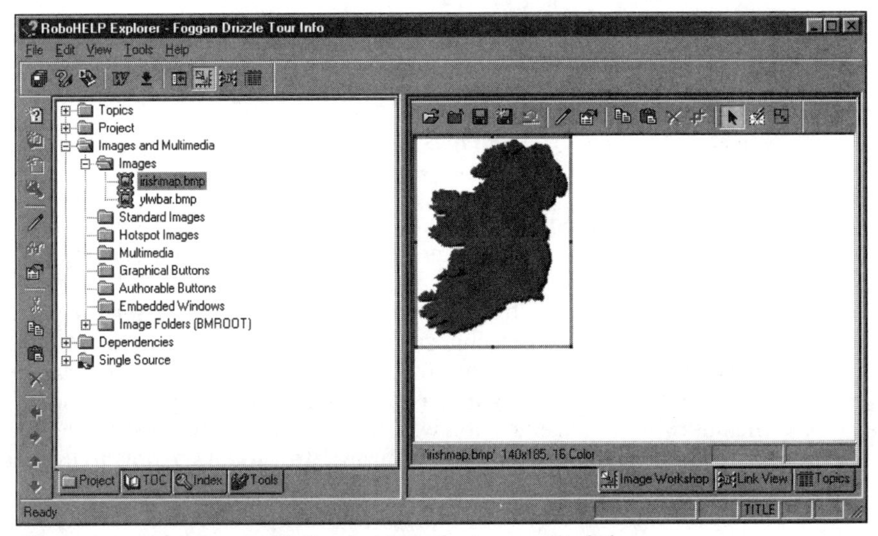

Figure 6-9: Sample graphic loaded into the Image Workshop

The graphic file appears in the Image Workshop work area. (You can have only one graphic open at a time in the Image Workshop.) Information about the graphic appears in the status bar at the bottom of the work area. A border shows the actual size of the graphic. Table 6-4 describes the buttons on the Image Workshop toolbar.

Table 6-4
Image Workshop Toolbar Buttons

Toolbar Button	*Description*
	Opens the graphic file (through the Open Image from Project screen)
	Closes the graphic file and clears the Image Workshop tab

Toolbar Button	*Description*
	Saves the graphic file
	Saves the graphic file with a different file name or in a different location, in a different format, or at a different color depth
	Restores the graphic to the last saved version
	Opens the default graphics editor
	Displays the properties for the graphic file currently open
	Copies the selection from the graphic file to the Windows clipboard. (If you haven't selected anything, RoboHELP copies the entire image to the clipboard.)
	Pastes the contents of the Windows clipboard into the Image Workshop
	Deletes the selected hotspot area. (This is used when creating SHED graphics, which are described in Chapter 7, "Getting Fancy with Graphics.")
	Crops the graphic file with respect to the selected area
	Selects an area in the graphic file
	Creates a new SHED graphic from the graphic file or, if the graphic is already a SHED graphic, lets you create and edit hotspot areas
	Resizes the graphic

One of the first things you can do with the Image Workshop is view and modify the color depth and size of the open graphic, as follows:

1. Click the Properties button on the toolbar, or right-click the graphic and then select the Properties command from the right-click menu. The Properties screen (shown in Figure 6-10) appears.

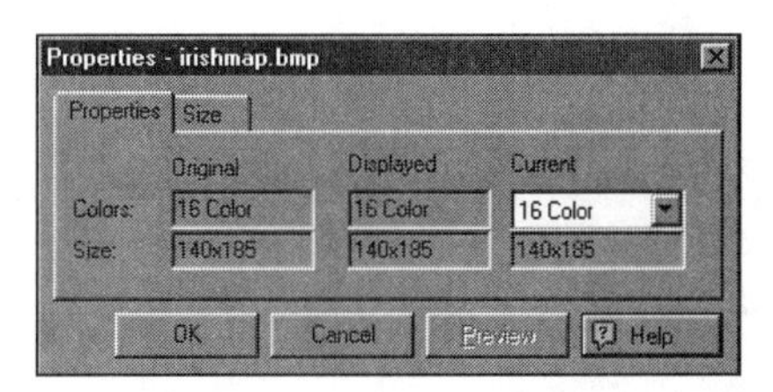

Figure 6-10: The Properties screen

The Properties screen shows the color depth and the size of the graphic. The Original column shows the original properties of the graphic. The Displayed column shows the properties for the graphic being displayed (you can change these from the original properties). The Current column shows the settings that will be applied to the graphic when you click OK.

You may want to change the color depth of a graphic if it has too many colors and isn't supported by WinHelp. You might also want to change a monochrome graphic to a 16-color graphic so that the graphic isn't automatically transparent. Sixteen-color graphics are the most popular choice for WinHelp graphics.

2. To alter the color depth, select a standard color depth from the drop-down list in the Current column: monochrome (1-bit), 16-color (4-bit), 256-color (8-bit), 16-bit, 24-bit, or 32-bit. You can preview this setting by clicking Preview. The graphic's properties are updated in the Image Workshop area and the Displayed column.
3. When you are satisfied with your changes, click OK. Any changes you made on the Properties screen will be applied to the graphic displayed in the Image Workshop area. Be sure to save your changes to the graphic by clicking Save on the toolbar. You can click Reload at any time to clear your changes and start again.

You'll frequently need to change the size of a graphic to better fit your topic format. To change the size of a graphic in the Image Workshop, do the following:

1. Click Resize on the Image Workshop toolbar. Resizing icons appear on the border, as shown in Figure 6-11.

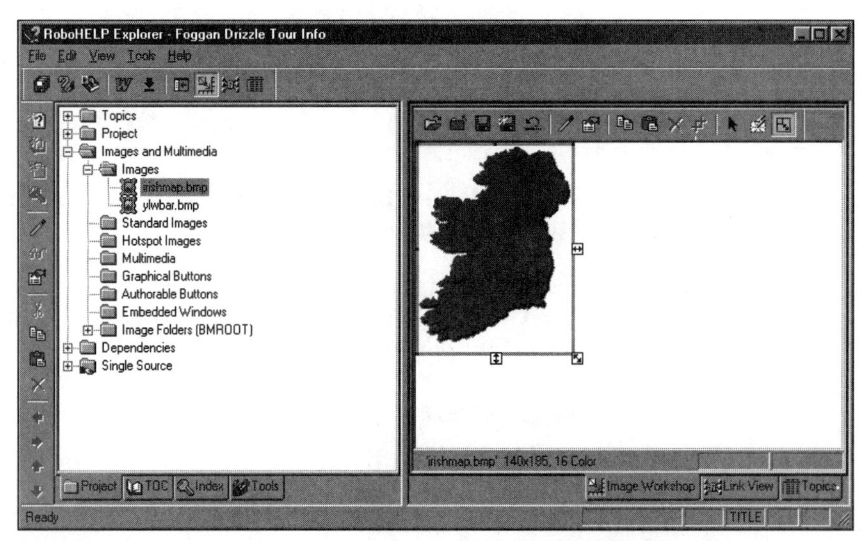

Figure 6-11: It's easy to resize a graphic in the Image Workshop.

The ReSize tool is part of the RoboHELP Office 2000 suite of tools. If you're using one of the individual RoboHELP 2000 modules, you'll need to use another graphics program to resize graphics.

2. Resize the graphic by clicking and dragging one of the resizing icons. Resizing with the horizontal or vertical icon expands or contracts the graphic in that dimension but doesn't maintain the original aspect ratio (the proportional horizontal and vertical size of the graphic). To expand or contract a graphic and keep the aspect ratio the same, use the diagonal icon. As you resize the graphic, the new dimensions appear in the lower right corner of the Image Workshop area. You can size the graphic to specific proportions by watching this indicator as you resize the graphic until you get to the size you want. You can click Reload at any time to clear your changes and start again.

If you prefer, you can right-click the graphic in the Image Workshop and select Properties from the right-click menu to display the Properties screen (not shown). You can use this screen to adjust the size of the graphic by percentage or by pixels. This can be helpful if you need to resize a group of graphics to a consistent size or size ratio.

3. When you are satisfied with your changes, click Save to save the graphic.

Changing the Default Editing Program

As you saw earlier, you can edit the graphic in the Insert Help Image screen or the Image Workshop with the default editor, Windows Paint. You can change this default editor to a different editing program, as follows:

1. Select the RoboHELP ⇨ Options command in Word or the Tools ⇨ Options command in RoboHELP Explorer, and then select the Tool Locations tab.
2. Click the BMP entry from the list of extensions. RoboHELP displays the program associated with BMP files. The default (shown in Figure 6-12) is Windows Paint, pbrush.exe.

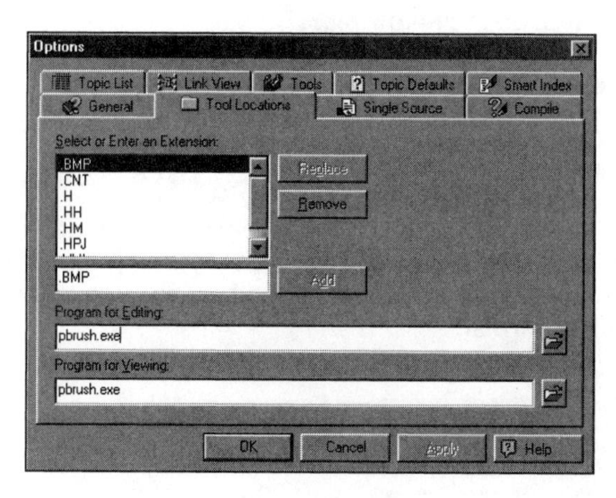

Figure 6-12: The Tool Locations tab of the Project Settings screen

3. Change the program name for the program you wish to use to edit graphics. (If you like, you can specify a different default program to view graphics as well.) When you are satisfied with your changes, click OK. Bear in mind that this change will affect the default image editor for all help projects.

Capturing Graphics from the Screen

Many online help files are written about software and, as a result, use pictures of the screens, windows, dialog boxes, and buttons of the software. Getting screen images in a usable picture format is relatively simple:

1. Display the screen or graphic that you want to capture.
2. Press the Print Screen key. Windows copies whatever is on the screen to the Windows clipboard.

Pressing Print Screen captures the entire screen. To capture a screen with the menu displayed, you need to display the screen you want to capture and then, while pressing and holding the CTRL key, select the menu you want to capture with the mouse. Press Print Screen to capture the entire screen with the menu displayed. You can also capture just the active window by pressing Alt + Print Screen.

3. Start the Image Workshop. (You don't need to open a graphic to start the Image Workshop; you can just select the RoboHELP ⇨ RoboHELP Explorer ⇨ Image Workshop command in Word.)
4. Paste the contents of the Windows clipboard into the Image Workshop area by either clicking Paste on the toolbar or right-clicking in the Image Workshop area and selecting Paste from the right-click menu. The graphic appears in the Image Workshop area. Save the image.

Once the graphic has been pasted into the Image Workshop, you can *crop,* or trim, extraneous images. Cropping is also a handy technique for capturing specific screen elements such as toolbar buttons, icons, and other graphics. To crop a graphic in the Image Workshop, do the following:

1. In the Image Workshop, select the Pointer tool.
2. Select the area you want to crop. Figure 6-13 shows the RoboHELP Explorer screen with the Image Workshop button selected for cropping.
3. Select Crop from the toolbar. (You can also right-click in the Image Workshop area and select Crop from the right-click menu.) Everything that is not in the selected area is removed, leaving only the cropped graphic. You can then edit and save this graphic as normal.

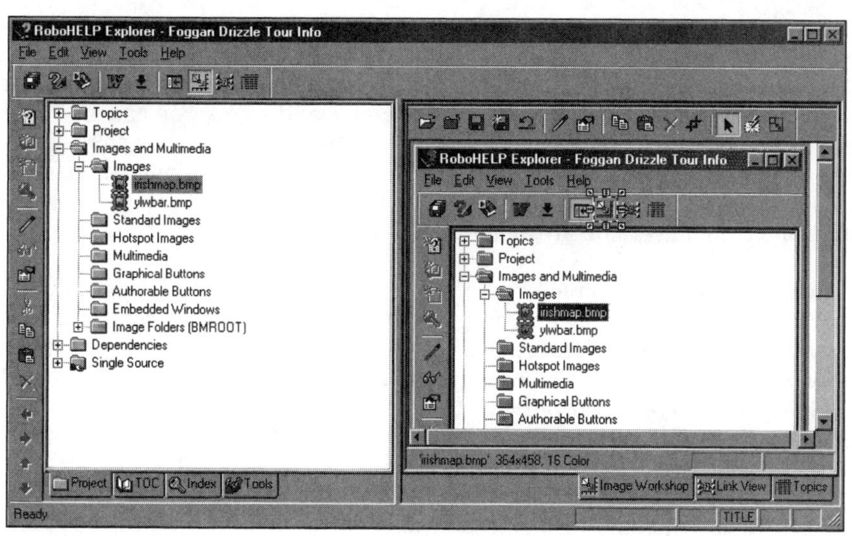

Figure 6-13: Button selected for cropping in the Image Workshop

Capturing screens with the built-in Windows screen capture feature works, but it's rather clumsy and can require that you do a fair amount of subsequent cropping and editing. Also, it will not capture the mouse pointer, which may be a problem. If you need to capture any substantial number of screens or graphics, you should seriously consider acquiring a real screen capture program.

Inbit, Inc., sells a screen capture product called FullShot that lets you do things such as select a specific area or screen element, automatically save the screen on capture, automatically increment file names, and optionally include the mouse pointer. You use FullShot by starting the program and then running whatever application you want to capture screens from. A set of five FullShot buttons automatically appears on the program's titlebar. Click a button to capture the screen, a specific region, or other elements. (The buttons don't show up on the captured graphic.) The captured graphic is placed in the FullShot work area, where you can further select and edit the graphic before saving it.

FullShot also lets you select the key or key combination to start the capture with. If you are doing different types of screen captures — full screen, active window, button, and so on — you can set up different hotkeys for each type of screen capture, making the capture process very fast. FullShot has many appealing features. For more information about FullShot, including a demo version, check the Inbit web site at `http://www.inbit.com`.

Another capture program worth looking at is Collage Capture from Inner Media, Inc. As with FullShot, Collage Capture lets you capture the screen graphic, preview it, and then automatically select the screen element that you are interested in: the active window, active menu bar, the whole screen, and so on. You can also set Collage Capture to automatically increment your file names so that you capture a series of files that are named for you. A corresponding Image Manager lets you edit graphic files. Collage Capture is fast, easy to use, and uncomplicated. Product information and a demo version are available from `http://www.innermedia.com`.

Yet another program for screen capturing is Hijaak Pro from IMSI. Hijaak Pro does an adequate job of capturing and cropping screens, but its real strength is in its extensive graphic conversion capabilities (translating a graphic from one file format to another). Hijaak Pro can also extract graphics from Web sites: give it the URL and it will load the Web page, strip the HTML code, and save the graphics. Product information is available through `http://www.imsisoft.com`.

PaintShop Pro from JASC, Inc., is one of the best editing tools available. You can capture a screen and then perform extensive manipulation on the graphic. PaintShop Pro has long been a top-rated shareware product. Product information and the shareware version of the product are available from `http://www.jasc.com`.

Regardless of the screen capture and editing program you're using, you should also have CompuShow 32 on your system for handy viewing and sorting of your graphics. CompuShow 32, from Canyon State Systems and Software, has extensive viewing capabilities, including the ability to position, flip, and rotate graphics as well as to create albums of *thumbnails,* small images of graphics for quick reference. CompuShow 32 is shareware available from `http://members.aol.com/bobberry`.

Importing Graphics

Many graphics are not stored in a WinHelp-compatible file format. For example, most graphics on Web sites are GIF or JPG format, which are not supported by the WinHelp compiler. To use these graphics, you will need to import them into bitmap format, as follows:

1. Use the Insert ⇨ Help Image command to open the Insert Help Image screen. Click Import on the right side of the screen. The WinHelp Graphics Converter screen appears (shown in Figure 6-14 with a sample file selected). (Alternatively, from the Image Workshop, click Open to display the Open Image from Project screen and click Import.)
2. Enter information in the fields as follows:
    - **File:** Enter the file format(s) you want to search for. The default is to search for all GIF and JPG files. You can select other common file formats from the drop-down list.

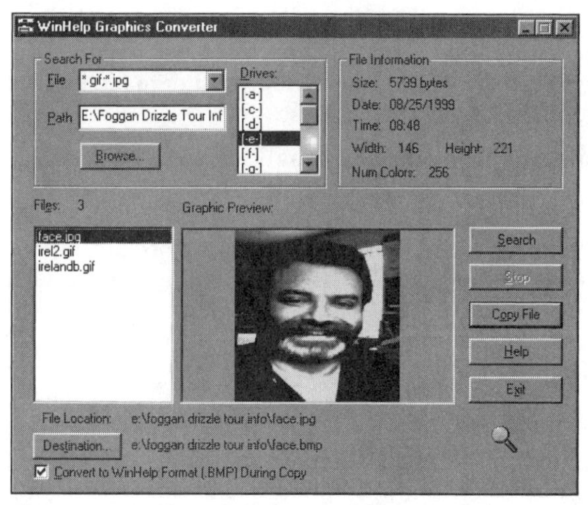

Figure 6-14: The WinHelp Graphics Converter screen

- **Path:** Enter the path for the drive and directory you want to start searching in. The default is the WinHelp project's directory. Click Browse if you'd like to browse for the path. RoboHELP will search for files in this directory and all directories beneath it.
- **Drives:** Select additional drives on which to search for graphics. (When you click a drive letter, the drive is selected, in addition to any other drives already selected.)
- **Files:** The list of files matching the criteria in the path.
- **Graphic Preview:** A preview of the selected file.
- **Search:** Click this button to search for files based on the search criteria.
- **Stop:** Click this button to stop searching for files (for example, if you're finding too many files and want to stop to refine your search criteria). WinHelp Graphics Converter displays all files found to that point.
- **Copy Now:** Copies the file to the destination directory, which is listed next to the Destination button.
- **File Location:** Identifies the fully qualified file name of the file being displayed.
- **Destination:** Displays the target file name and directory. Click the button to change the destination.
- **Convert to WinHelp Format (.BMP) During Copy:** Check this box to automatically convert the file to bitmap format when you copy it. (This isn't necessary if the image is already in a compatible WinHelp format, such as BMP.)

3. When you've entered your search criteria, click Search. RoboHELP finds all files matching the criteria and lists the file names. Click a file to display the graphic in the Graphic Preview window. When you find a file you want to convert or import, click Copy Now.

4. You can convert another file or click Exit to return to the Insert Help Image screen.

The WinHelp Graphic Converter is good for many common formats, but it doesn't handle everything (such as TIF files). It's also useful for finding and importing existing BMP images from other directories if you don't want to add the folder to the Image Folders BMROOT. There are several other ways you can convert graphics into bitmap format for use with WinHelp. Possibly the simplest is to drag and drop a graphic file from the Windows Explorer into the Image Workshop area and then click Save As. You can also open a graphic in one of the editing programs mentioned earlier and convert it to a bitmap. If the graphic comes from a Web page, try right-clicking the graphic in the browser and copying it to the Windows clipboard, and then pasting it into the Image Workshop area and saving it.

Using the Project Manager to Organize Graphic Files

When you add graphics to a WinHelp project, the RoboHELP Explorer Project Manager sorts the graphic files into several different folders for easier access. Figure 6-15 shows the Project Manager with some different graphics folders displayed.

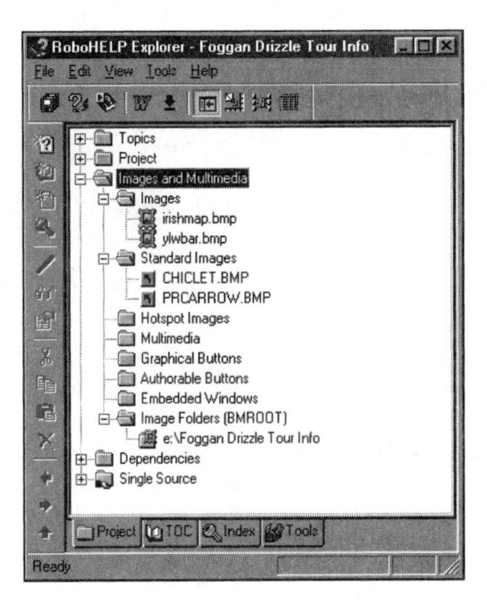

Figure 6-15: The Project Manager, with the graphics folders displayed

When you add a graphic and save the DOC file, RoboHELP updates the graphics in the list. Each of the folders identifies the type of graphic. Remember that the images in the folders are only the images that are actually used in the topics in the project, not a list of all the images in the project, image, or clip art folders.

✦ The Images folder lists the graphics in the WinHelp project (other than those in other folders).

✦ The Standard Images folder lists the graphics in the WinHelp project that come from the Special folder of clip art graphics. (These graphics are automatically displayed in the Insert Help Image screen for selection.)

✦ The Hotspot Images folder lists SHED (hotspot) graphics in the WinHelp project.

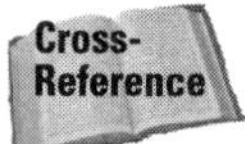

For more information on using SHED files, see Chapter 7, "Getting Fancy with Graphics."

✦ The Multimedia folder lists the sound and video files in the WinHelp project.

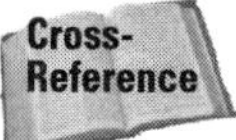

For more information on using sound and video in WinHelp files, see Chapter 12, "Linking to the Internet and Adding Multimedia."

✦ The Graphical Buttons folder lists the *graphical buttons* (custom buttons that have bitmaps) used in the topics in the WinHelp project.

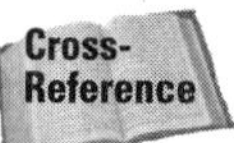

For more information on creating and using graphical buttons, see Chapter 7, "Getting Fancy with Graphics."

✦ The Authorable Buttons folder lists the *authorable buttons* (custom three-dimensional push buttons) used in the topics in the WinHelp project.

✦ The Embedded Windows folder lists the embedded windows used in the topics in the WinHelp project.

For more information on creating and using embedded windows, see Chapter 9, "Using Help Windows and Browse Sequences."

✦ The Image Folders folder lists additional image folders added to the project. These folders are listed in the order WinHelp will search them.

You can get information about a specific graphic by right-clicking on the graphic file's entry in the Project Manager list and selecting Properties on the right-click menu. The Image Properties screen (shown in Figure 6-16) appears with the file name and the graphic.

You can track which topics the graphic appears in by selecting the Used In tab, as shown in Figure 6-17.

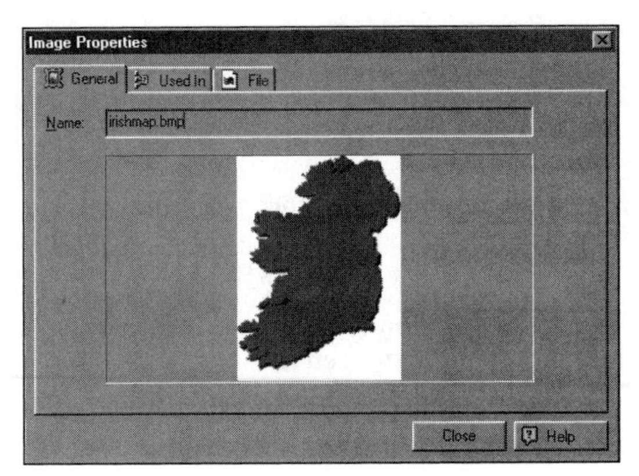

Figure 6-16: The Image Properties screen

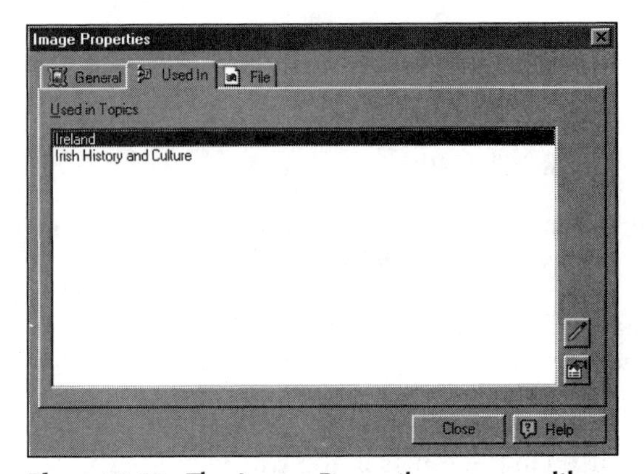

Figure 6-17: The Image Properties screen with the Used In tab displayed

You can view and edit a topic by highlighting the topic and clicking the pencil icon at the lower right of the Used In tab. You can also display the Topic Properties screen for the highlighted topic by clicking the document icon.

The graphic's file information — the file name and directory, file size, and creation and last modified dates — is displayed on the File tab (not shown).

Adding Folders of Graphic Files

The WinHelp compiler needs to know where the graphic files added by reference are stored. The default location for graphics is in the WinHelp project directory. If the WinHelp compiler doesn't find a graphic file there, it will look in the file directories specified in the project's HPJ file in the [BMROOT] section. You can always add graphic files or folders containing the images used in the project.

For more information on the specifics of the HPJ file, see Appendix A, "The WinHelp HPJ file."

Fortunately, you don't need to work directly with the HPJ file to add folders. Instead, you can add folders through the RoboHELP Explorer Project Manager, as follows:

1. Right-click the Image Folders (BMROOT) icon in the Project Manager. The New Image Folder screen appears (shown in Figure 6-18 with a sample directory selected).

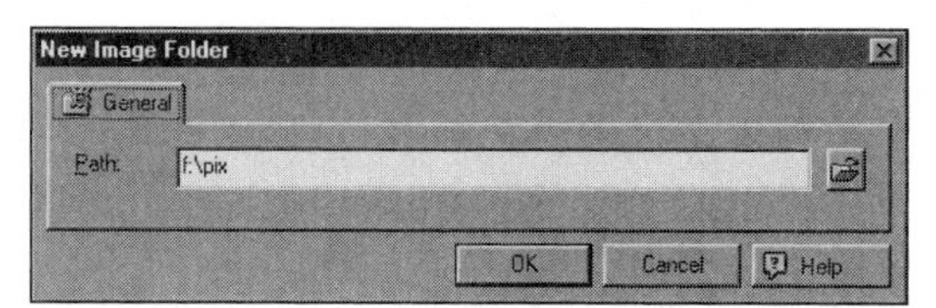

Figure 6-18: The New Image Folder screen

You can specify a new folder to add to the list. This will be added to the list of folders for the WinHelp compiler to search when it compiles the WinHelp project. Figure 6-19 shows the Image Folders after adding a new folder.

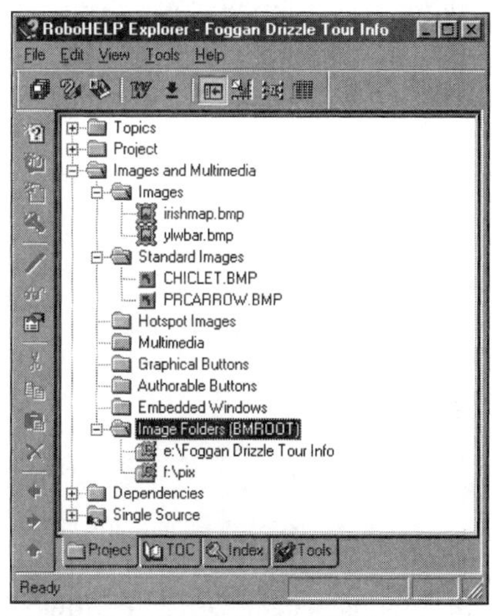

Figure 6-19: The Image Folders (BMROOT) folder with a new graphics folder added

You can use this feature in several ways. First, you can create libraries of standard graphics for your WinHelp projects. For example, if your company has a set of standard logos and icons for online help, you can create a folder of standard logos to be used throughout your online help files. (This is particularly handy if you are sharing graphics with other writers.) This technique guarantees that you'll always have the proper logo in all your files. Furthermore, if the company updates a logo, you can replace the file in the directory and then recompile to effect the change in each WinHelp file.

Another way you can use this technique is to change the look and feel of your WinHelp project. By using a folder of different graphics with the same file names as those referenced in your WinHelp project, you can recompile the online help and view the results.

A variation on this idea is to switch the order of the folders. The WinHelp compiler looks in each of the folders in order for a file and uses the first one it finds. If you had two different versions of the IRISHMAP.BMP file in the two folders listed in Figure 6-19, the WinHelp compiler would use the one in the first folder.

For example, suppose you have U.S. and UK versions of a program, with different screens for each. You could use a generic name for the graphics of the screen captures (MAINSCREEN.BMP, FILEMENU.BMP, and so on) and then keep versions of the bitmaps in separate folders. By switching the order of the folders in this list, you can make WinHelp use one set or another.

You can change the order of the folders by right-clicking a graphics folder and then selecting Set Order from the right-click menu. (Alternately, you can select the Tools ➪ Set Image Folders Order command in RoboHELP Explorer.) The Image Folders Order screen appears (shown in Figure 6-20).

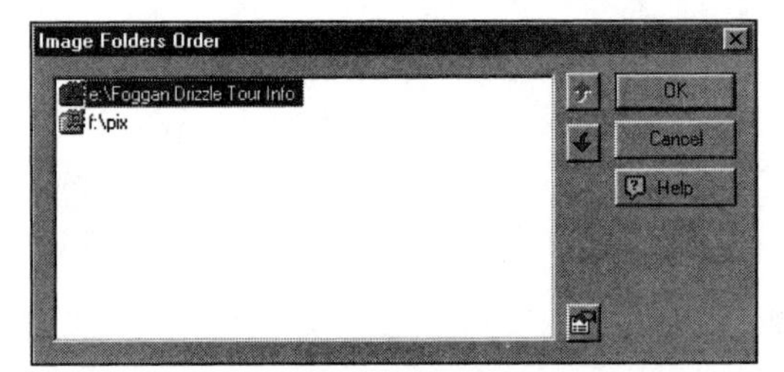

Figure 6-20: The Image Folders Order screen

You can use the up and down arrows on the screen to shift the positions of the folders in the list. When you are satisfied with your changes, click OK. The order of the files will be updated appropriately in the RoboHELP Explorer Project Manager and in the project's HPJ file.

For more information on ways to use folders, see Chapter 15, "Managing Large Projects."

Finding Missing Graphics and Graphic Folders

One of the few disadvantages of inserting external graphics is that you can have missing graphics if they're misreferenced, renamed, or they're no longer residing in the original image folder or the project folder. When you compile the WinHelp project, the WinHelp compiler may fail completely or simply place a bitmap to show that there's a missing graphic in the topic (a sample of this appears in Figure 6-21).

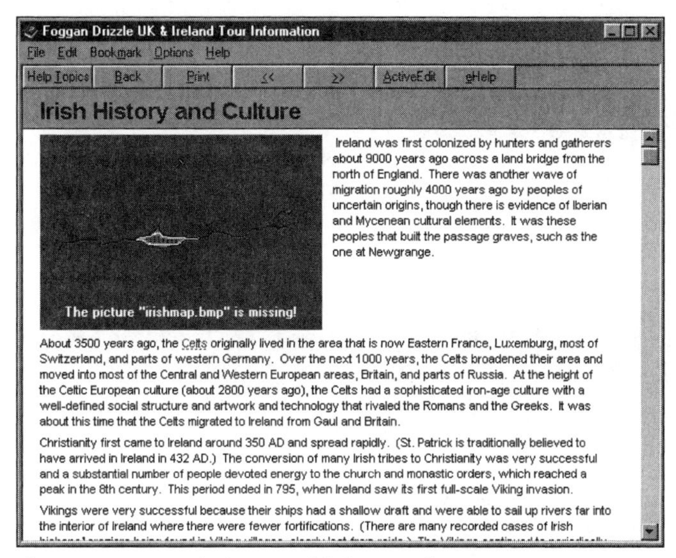

Figure 6-21: A missing graphic in a topic

To find a missing graphic, do the following:

1. Open the RoboHELP Explorer Project Manager and locate the missing graphic. Figure 6-22 shows a missing graphic listing. As you can see, the missing graphic is identified with an "x,"which will appear in red on your monitor.

2. Right-click on the missing graphic. The Locate File screen appears. (The Locate File screen is the same as the standard Open File screen.)

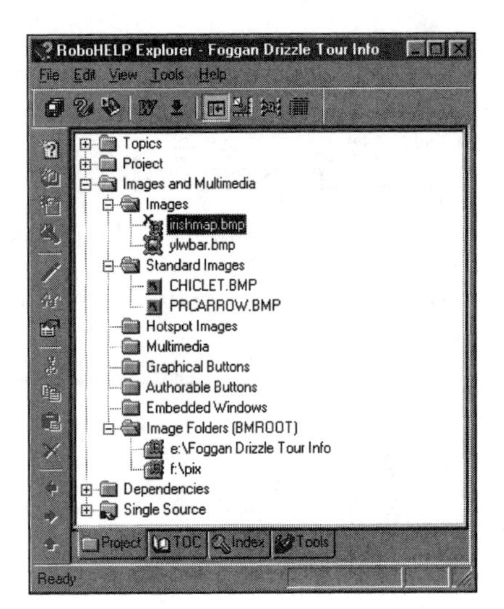

Figure 6-22: The RoboHELP Explorer Project Manager showing a missing graphic

3. Select the graphic and click Open. The Image Found screen appears (shown in Figure 6-23).

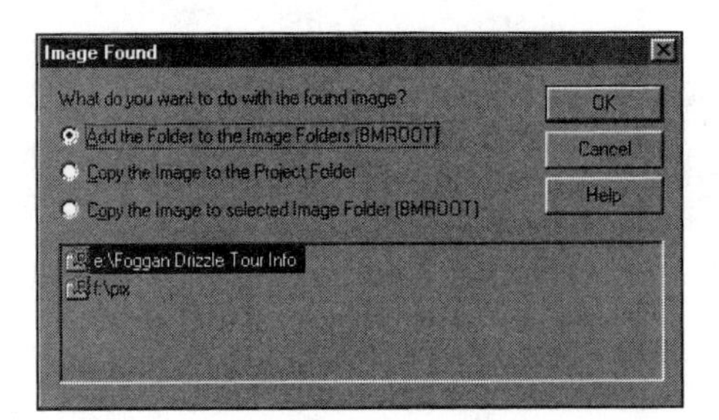

Figure 6-23: The Image Found screen

3. Select one of the options:

   - **Add the Folder to the Image Folders (BMROOT):** Select this option to add the entire folder the graphic file was in to the list of Image Folders. This will make all the graphics in the folder available for use by the WinHelp compiler when it compiles the project.
   - **Copy the Image to the Project Folder:** Select this option to copy the graphic file to the current WinHelp project directory.
   - **Copy the Image to selected Image Folder (BMROOT):** Select this option to copy the graphic file to the selected folder in the list.

When you are satisfied with your changes, click OK.

You can also use the Graphics Locator tool in the Tools window of the RoboHELP Explorer to find missing graphics. This tool works the same as the WinHelp Graphics Converter, shown in Figure 6-15, except that you aren't given the option to convert files when you copy them.

You're most likely to have missing graphics folders if you've renamed a folder on your local drive or if you're using a folder on a network drive that's been reassigned to a different drive letter. Here's how you can locate missing graphics folders:

1. Open the RoboHELP Explorer Project Manager and locate the missing graphic folder. As with missing graphics, missing graphics folders are identified with a red "x."
2. Right-click on the missing graphics folder. The Open screen appears, as shown in Figure 6-24.

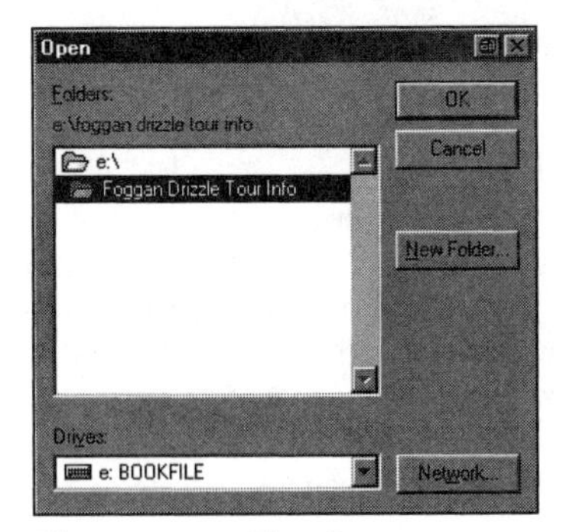

Figure 6-24: The Open screen

3. Browse the folders until you find the graphics folder. You can create a new folder on the fly by clicking New Folder. You can map a network drive on the fly by clicking Network. When you are satisfied with your changes, click OK.

Printing the Images Report

The Images report provides you with information about the graphics used in the topics.

To generate an Images report, do the following:

1. From RoboHELP Explorer, select the Tools ➪ Reports ➪ Images command. The Images report is displayed on the screen, as shown in Figure 6-25. The graphics appear on the report in order by graphic or by topic, depending on your selection in the Sort By field on the lower right corner of the screen.

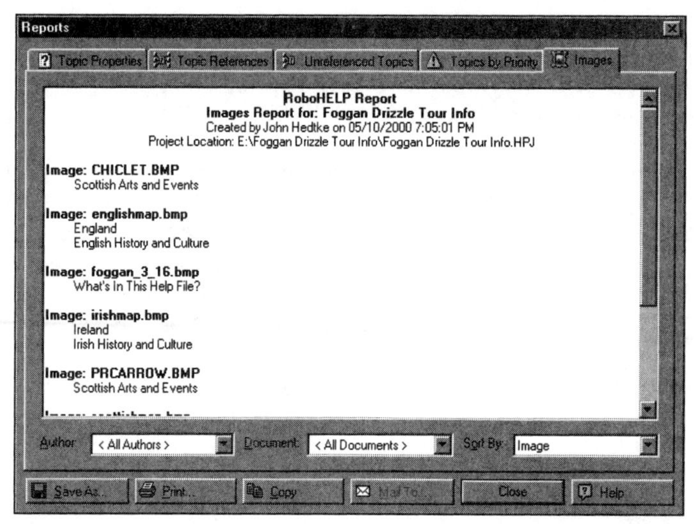

Figure 6-25: The Images report

You can filter the information on the Images report in several ways. You can show the graphics created by each author or all authors, or those graphics that aren't assigned to specific authors, depending on your selection in the drop-down list in the Author field. You can also look at the graphics in all the documents in the project or in individual documents, with the drop-down list in the Document field.

For more information on assigning authors, see Chapter 15, "Managing Large Projects."

You can run the Topic Properties report (or any of the RoboHELP reports) at any time.

You may also want to run the Diagnostics report with the option to report on missing images and missing image folders. The Diagnostics report is described in Chapter 15, "Managing Large Projects."

Summary

This chapter showed you how to add graphics to your WinHelp projects. You first learned the basics of graphic formats and how graphics are stored in files. Next, you saw how to add a simple graphic to your DOC file. You then learned how to create transparent graphics. After that, the chapter introduced you to ways to edit graphic file properties and images with Microsoft Paint and RoboHELP's Image Workshop, as well as how to use other graphic editing programs. You next learned how to capture screen images and how to import graphics saved in other formats. The chapter continued with information on organizing and tracking graphics using the RoboHELP Explorer Project Manager. You also saw ways to locate missing graphics and graphics folders. The chapter concluded with information on how to print the Images report.

The next chapter will continue with information about how to combine graphics and hotspots. You'll see how to use SHED graphics and buttons in WinHelp projects.

✦ ✦ ✦

Getting Fancy with Graphics

In This Chapter

Using graphics in jumps and popups

Creating and adding SHED (hotspot) graphics

Changing the resolution of SHED graphic

Resizing SHED graphics

Replacing the base image in a SHED graphic

Using the Microsoft SHED editor

Adding authorable buttons

Adding mini buttons

Adding shortcut buttons

Adding graphical buttons

Tracking graphics in the Project Manager

Switching between graphical display modes

This chapter continues the discussion from the preceding chapter by first showing you how to include simple graphics in hotspots such as jumps and popups. Next, you see how to create SHED (segmented hypergraphics) graphics using the Image Workshop. The chapter presents techniques for changing the display resolution for and resizing SHED graphics, replacing the image on which a SHED graphic's hotspots are placed, and how to use the Microsoft SHED editor to do certain types of edits. After that, the chapter introduces you to creating help buttons of several kinds: authorable buttons, mini buttons, shortcut buttons, and graphical buttons. The chapter concludes with techniques for using the Project Manager to track graphics in the WinHelp project and to switch between graphic display modes.

Using Graphics in Hotspots

In the preceding chapter, you saw how to insert graphics to add color and interest to your help topics. All these graphics were *static* graphics; that is, they don't do anything when you click them. In this chapter, you'll learn how to use various kinds of hotspot graphics that do something when you click them.

The simplest way to use graphics as part of hotspots is to define them as a jump or popup using the techniques you learned earlier in Chapter 4, "Adding Jumps and Popups." As you saw, you can define text as a hotspot that performs a jump, popup, or other action when you click it. You can also use a graphic as part of the hotspot or even as the entire hotspot. For example, suppose you want to add a "Return to main topic" jump that uses the Foggan Drizzle logo. The easiest way to do this is as follows:

1. Position the cursor where you want to insert the graphic link and select the Insert ➪ Help Jump command. (Alternately, you can press Ctrl+J or you can click the Help New Jump button on the RoboHELP toolbar.) The Insert Help Hotspot screen appears as usual.
2. Click the small picture icon immediately to the right of the Hotspot Text field. RoboHELP displays the Select Image screen (shown in Figure 7-1 with a Foggan Drizzle logo selected). The Select Image screen is very similar to the Insert Help Image screen you saw in Chapter 6.

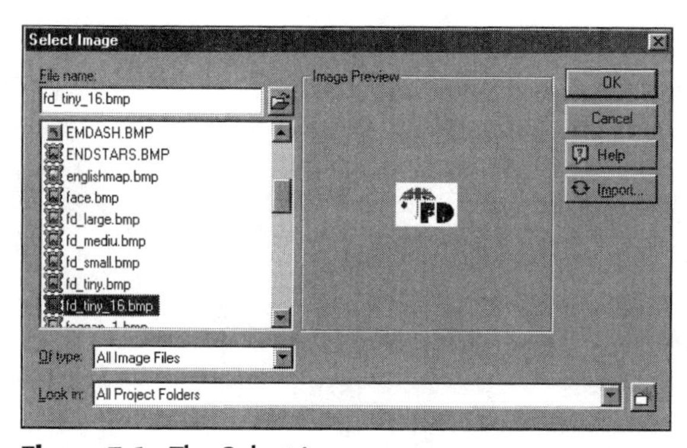

Figure 7-1: The Select Image screen

3. Select the graphic you want to include in the hotspot. When you are satisfied with your changes, click OK. RoboHELP returns to the Insert Help Hotspot screen. The True Code for the graphic appears in the Hotspot Text field. You can leave this as is, or you can add text, as is demonstrated in Figure 7-2.

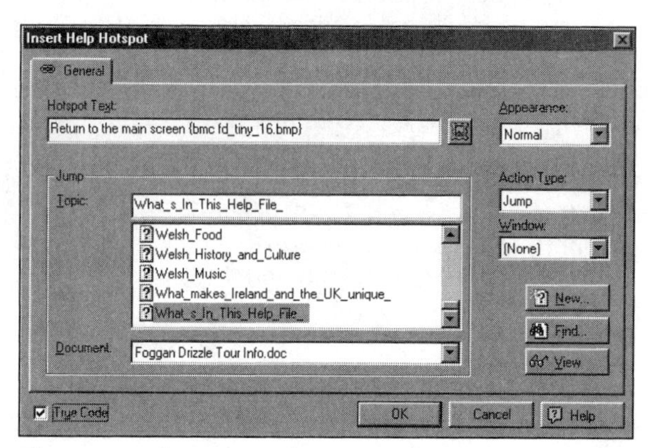

Figure 7-2: The Insert Help Hotspot screen with a graphic in the hotspot text

4. Select the hotspot topic ID and enter other hotspot information as usual.

For more information on adding hotspots, see Chapter 4, "Adding Jumps and Popups."

5. When you are satisfied with your changes, click OK. RoboHELP inserts a hotspot that includes the graphic in the DOC file, as shown in Figure 7-3.

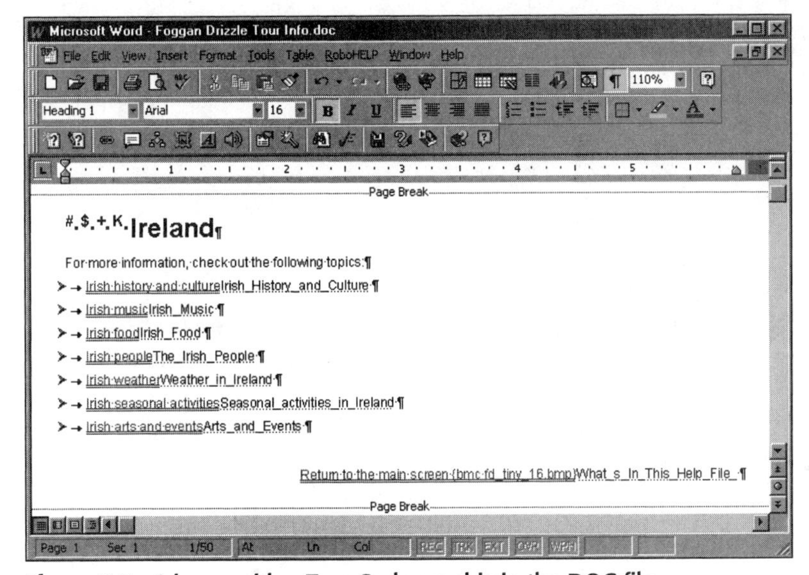

Figure 7-3: A jump with a True Code graphic in the DOC file

It's not necessary for the graphic to be in True Code format; if you deselect the True Code box on the Insert Help Hotspot screen, you can display the graphic in Dynamic WYSIWYG in the DOC file, as shown in Figure 7-4.

When you compile either of these versions of the DOC file, the resulting topic will look like Figure 7-5.

When the mouse pointer moves over the graphic, it will change to a pointing hand just like any other hotspot. Clicking the graphic will jump the user to the main topic ("What's in This Help File?"). Depending on the consistency of your design, you could even eliminate the text in the jump and simply show the graphic in the bottom right corner of the topic as a navigational tool.

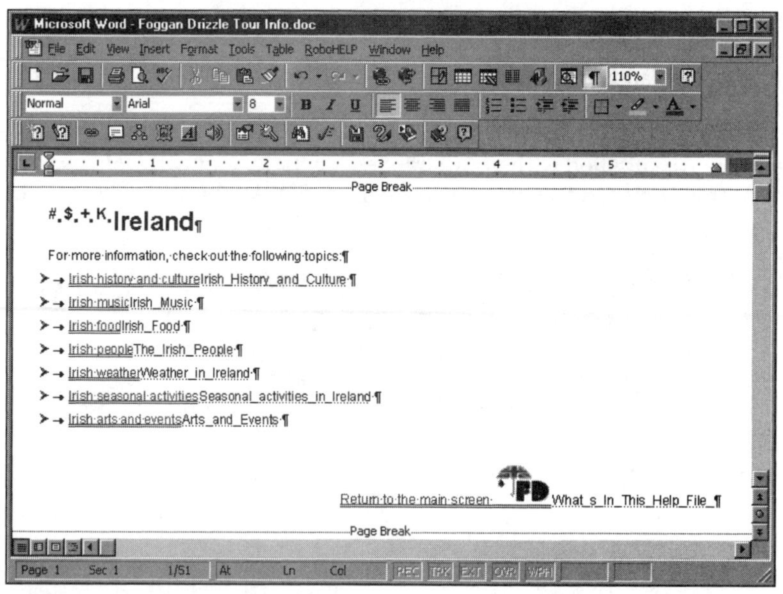

Figure 7-4: A jump with an embedded graphic displayed in Dynamic WYSIWYG in the DOC file

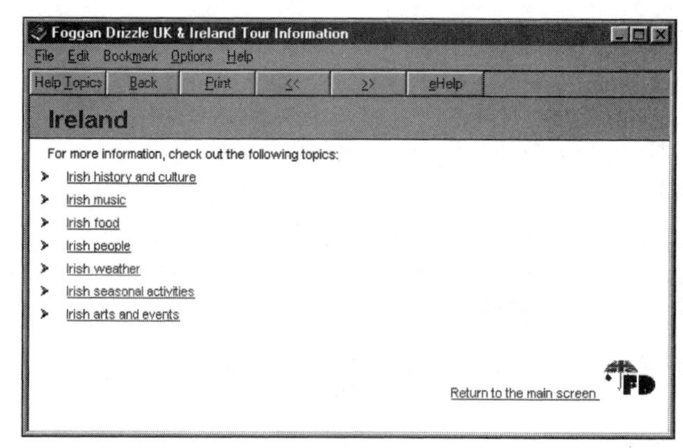

Figure 7-5: Compiled topic with a graphic in the hotspot

You can also use graphics for jumps in the non-scrolling region. Figure 7-6 shows the same graphic (with the white in the graphic background changed in an image editor to light gray to match the non-scrolling region color) inserted in the non-scrolling region. When a user clicks this graphic, the WinHelp file jumps to the main topic.

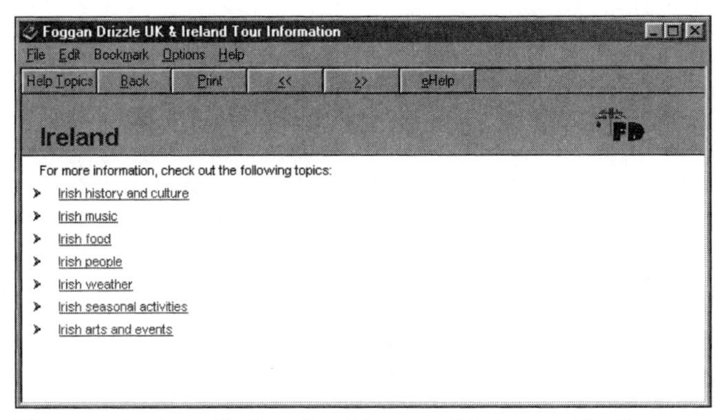

Figure 7-6: Compiled topic with a graphic hotspot in the non-scrolling region

If you're only interested in adding a graphic hotspot without text, you can use the Action tab on the Insert Help Image screen to assign a hotspot action when you insert the graphic:

1. Select the Insert ➪ Help Image command in Word. The Insert Help Image screen appears as usual. (Alternately, you can press Ctrl+G or you can click the New Help Image icon on the RoboHELP toolbar.)
2. Select the graphic you want to add. Make any other entries on this screen as appropriate, and then click the Action tab. Figure 7-7 shows the Insert Help Image screen with the Action tab displayed.

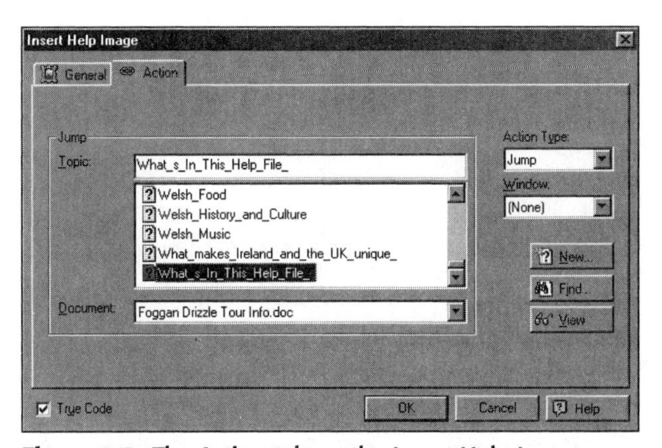

Figure 7-7: The Action tab on the Insert Help Image screen

3. Select an action from the Action Type field and enter the information for the hotspot as you do on the Insert Help Hotspot screen. When you are satisfied with your changes, click OK. RoboHELP inserts the graphic and the jump, popup, or other hotspot action.

You can use this technique to add a hotspot to an existing graphic by right-clicking the graphic or the True Code reference and selecting the Properties command from the right-click menu, and then make entries on the Action tab of the screen as described previously.

Many of the graphics in RoboHELP's clip art galleries can be used as hotspot graphics. For example, the graphics in the Button folder are useful for hotspot graphics. You can assign a jump or a popup to the button and icon graphics. Perhaps the most useful clip art graphics are the A to Z buttons in the Letters folder. You can create an array of quick reference buttons for large, alphabetized lists such as glossaries. Figure 7-8 shows one common way to use these buttons.

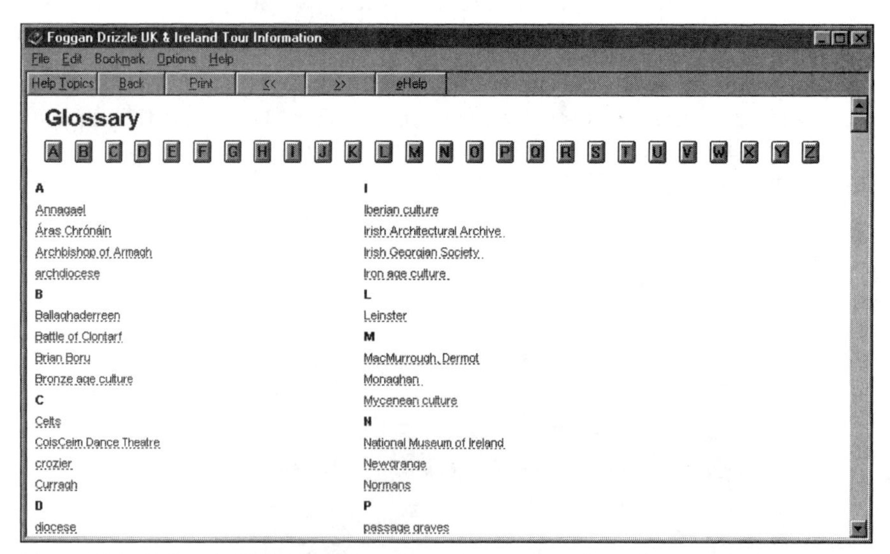

Figure 7-8: Using RoboHELP letter clip art to create quick reference buttons

Using SHED Graphics

Using the technique described in the previous section, you can insert graphics as part of a hotspot exactly like any text string. However, you can insert only one hotspot per graphic; you can't divide a graphic into pieces that do different things using this method.

Segmented hypergraphics (known as .SHG files from the file extension or as SHED graphics from the Segmented Hypergraphic Editor used to create them) give you the opportunity to assign specific actions to different parts of a graphic. A common application of this is to create hotspots for each section of a program's screen.

There are several ways to create SHED graphics. Probably the easiest is through the Image Workshop, as follows:

1. Open a bitmap graphic in the Image Workshop.

SHED graphics can be created only from files in BMP format. If you have a file in another format that you'd like to turn into a SHED graphic, you must first convert it to a bitmap, as described in Chapter 6, "Adding Simple Graphics."

2. Click the SHED graphic icon on the Image Workshop toolbar (Figure 7-9). The Create SHED File screen (shown in Figure 7-10) appears.

Figure 7-9: The SHED graphic icon

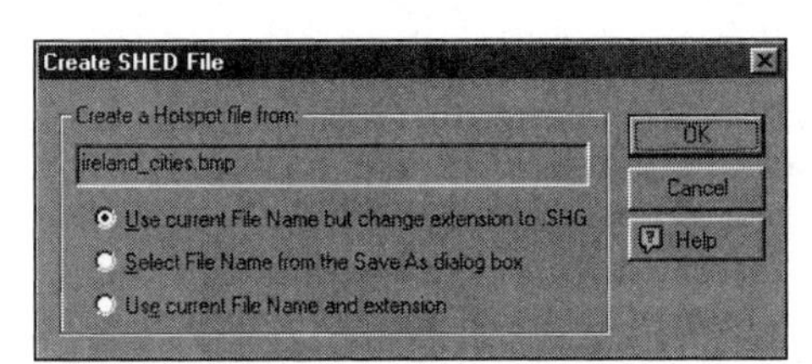

Figure 7-10: The Create SHED File screen

3. Select one of the options on this screen. All of the options will convert the bitmap into a SHED graphic, but you have a choice of how to name the resulting file, as follows:

   - **Use current File Name but change extension to .SHG:** Select this option to save the new graphic file with the same filename and a file extension of .SHG.
   - **Select File Name from the Save As dialog box:** Select this option to save the new graphic file with a different file name using the standard Save As dialog box. Note that the file will still have the standard SHG extension.
   - **Use current File Name and extension:** Select this option to save the new graphic file by overwriting the original file without changing the filename. (This is especially useful if you're updating a bitmap file.)

   Click OK to save the file as a SHED graphic named according to the choices you've made.

RoboHELP lets you create and edit SHED graphics by clicking the SHED button from several of the other graphics screens, including the Insert Help Image, Help Image Properties, and Select Image screens.

Now you can start adding hotspots to the SHED graphic, as follows:

1. With the .SHG file opened in Image Workshop, click and drag to create a hotspot area around a portion of the screen. When you release the mouse button, Insert Hotspot screen (shown in Figure 7-11) appears.

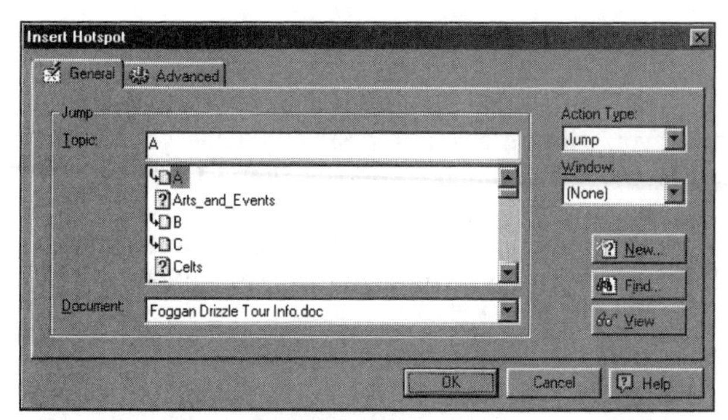

Figure 7-11: The Insert Hotspot screen

2. Select the topic you want to create a link to. As with the Insert Help Hotspot screen, you can create a new topic on the fly by clicking New. When you are satisfied with your changes, click Advanced. The Advanced tab of the Insert Hotspot screen appears, as shown in Figure 7-12.

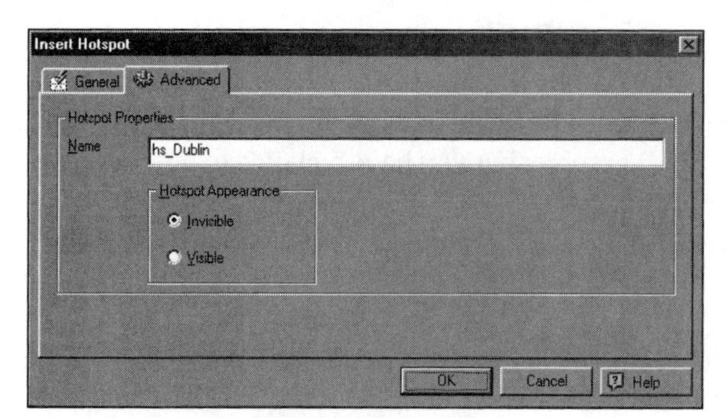

Figure 7-12: The Advanced tab of the Insert Hotspot screen

3. Enter a name for the hotspot. The hotspot name is optional—you only need to name your hotspots if you need to refer to your hotspots in a macro.

For more information on macros, see Chapter 10, "Understanding Macros."

You should also select Invisible or Visible for the hotspot border. If you select invisible (the default), the only indication that there's a hotspot is that the mouse pointer changes to a pointing hand when it's moved over the hotspot area. Selecting Visible leaves a thin black border around the hotspot area. Most SHED graphics use invisible borders.

4. When you are satisfied with your changes, click OK. The hotspot appears on the graphic with resizing handles (as shown in Figure 7-13). You can resize the hotspot by manipulating the resizing handles or move the entire hotspot by clicking in the middle of the hotspot and dragging it to the new location.

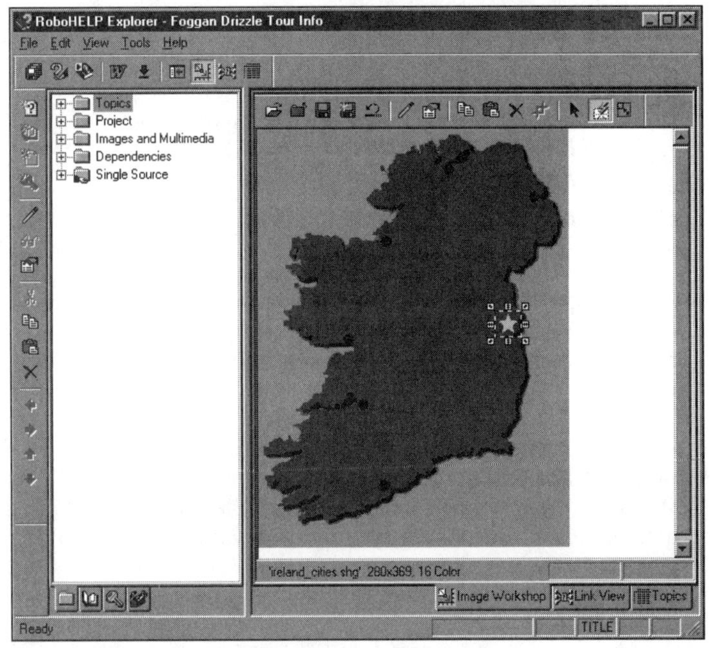

Figure 7-13: SHED graphic with a hotspot added

5. You can continue adding more hotspots to the SHED graphic. Figure 7-14 shows the graphic from Figure 7-13 with visible and invisible hotspots. Visible hotspots are denoted by a solid black line in the editor, whereas invisible hotspots have a black-and-white border in the editor.

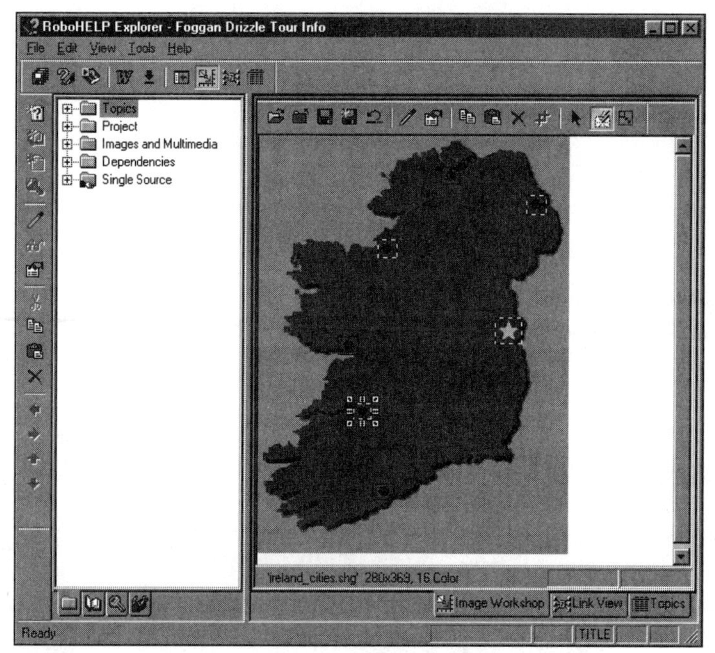

Figure 7-14: SHED graphic with several hotspots added

You can adjust the properties of a hotspot after you've created it by right-clicking the hotspot and then selecting Properties from the right-click menu to display the Hotspot Properties screen (identical to the Insert Hotspot screen). Make your changes to the hotspot properties and click OK to save your changes.

When you insert the SHED graphic in a topic and compile the WinHelp file, the SHED graphic appears like any other graphic file (shown in Figure 7-15) except that visible hotspots appear with a border and that the mouse point changes to a pointing hand when it moves over any hotspot, visible or invisible.

Here are some tips for creating hotspots in a SHED graphic:

- ✦ You can have as many hotspots in a SHED graphic as you like.
- ✦ Make the hotspots as small as possible but as large as necessary. For example, if you have a hotspot defined for a city on a map, keeping the hotspot small and focused on the city will give a more professional appearance to the finished product.
- ✦ Don't overlap hotspot areas.

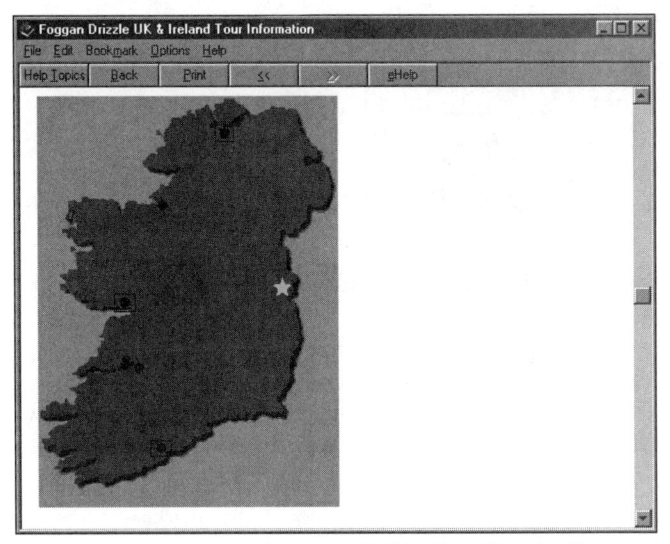

Figure 7-15: SHED graphic compiled in the WinHelp file

- If you have multiple hotspots for similarly shaped areas (such as buttons on a toolbar), make sure that the hotspots are identical in shape and are consistent in placement and alignment. Also make sure that there are no unexpected gaps between button hotspots. When the mouse pointer is dragged over the toolbar, any gaps in hotspot areas will be visible when the pointing hand changes back to a mouse pointer in the gap.
- You can use visible and invisible hotspots in the same SHED file (although this isn't commonly done).

Setting SHED Graphic Resolution

SHED graphics don't always display as smoothly as bitmaps. When the SHED graphic is displayed on the screen, WinHelp changes the number of pixels for the graphic so that it occupies the same screen size. This can cause the graphic to be distorted when the graphic is displayed on monitors with different resolutions. If the users you're writing the online help for have a specific type of monitor and resolution, you can optimize the SHED graphic for a specific display and resolution as follows:

1. Right-click the SHED graphic in the Image Workshop and select the Shed tab on the Properties screen (shown in Figure 7-16).

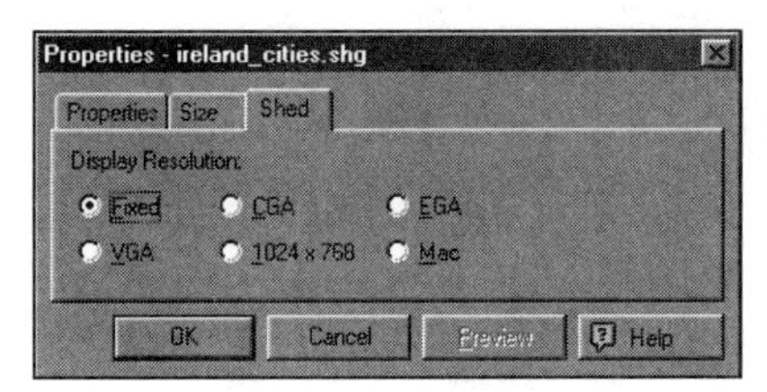

Figure 7-16: The Shed tab on the Properties screen

2. Select a graphic resolution for the SHED graphic:
   - **Fixed:** This is the default option. Fixed size prevents WinHelp from resizing the SHED graphic based on the resolution of the computer that is displaying it. This is the best option where your users don't have the same type of monitor as you do or you don't know what type of monitors they have.
   - **CGA:** Select this option for CGA monitors that display a maximum of 4 colors at 200 × 320. (This option is usually used only when retrofitting an online help file for Windows 3.0 computers.)
   - **EGA:** Select this option for EGA monitors that display up to 16 colors at 640 × 350.
   - **VGA:** Select this option for VGA monitors that display up to 256 colors at 640 × 480.
   - **1024 × 768:** Select this option for SVGA monitors that can display from 256 colors or more and have a resolution of at least 800 × 600. (You will most likely use this and the VGA resolution when not using Fixed.)
   - **Mac:** Select this option if you're creating graphics for small (12" or 13") monitors that run at 640 × 480. (This is the type of monitor typically used with many Macintosh computers.)

You can see how your choice will affect the SHED graphic by clicking Preview. When you are satisfied with your changes, click OK.

If you want to minimize the size of your compiled WinHelp file, you can convert your bitmaps to SHED graphics without creating hotspots. This will reduce the size of the individual graphics. You can also use the graphic resolution options to set the display resolution for a specific monitor and display resolution.

Resizing SHED Graphics

You can resize a SHED graphic in the same way that you can resize another graphic in the Image Workshop:

1. Click Resize on the Image Workshop Toolbar. Resizing handles appear on the border of the graphic.

The graphic resizing feature works only in RoboHELP Office 2000. If you're using one of the individual RoboHELP 2000 modules, you'll need to use another graphics program to resize graphics.

2. Resize the graphic by clicking and dragging one of the handles. Resizing with the horizontal or vertical icon expands or contracts the graphic in the respective dimension but doesn't maintain the original aspect ratio (the proportional horizontal and vertical size of the graphic). To expand or contract a graphic and keep the aspect ratio the same, use the diagonal icon. As you resize the graphic, the new dimensions appear in the lower right corner of the Image Workshop area. You can size the graphic to specific proportions by watching this indicator as you resize the graphic until you get to the size you want. You can click Reload at any time to clear your changes and start again.
3. When you are satisfied with your changes, click Save to save the graphic, or Save As, to keep the original SHG graphic and create a new, resized version.

You can also use the Resize tool in the Tools window of the RoboHELP Explorer to resize graphics. This tool works the same as the Image Workshop.

You can also use the Size tab of the Properties screen to resize a SHED graphic, as follows:

1. Right-click the SHED graphic in the Image Workshop and select the Size tab on the Properties screen (shown in Figure 7-17).

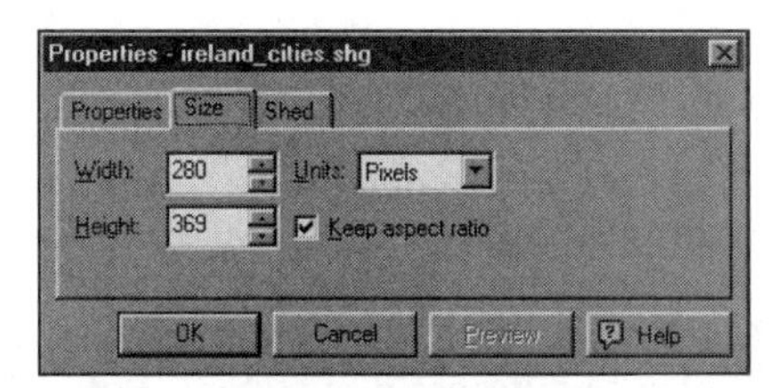

Figure 7-17: The Size tab on the Properties screen

2. Select the width and height for the graphic. You can change the graphic size by adjusting the width and height as described in Chapter 6, "Adding Simple Graphics." You can click Preview to see how the resizing will look. When you are satisfied with your changes, click OK.

Unless you have a specific reason not to, you should always make sure that Keep aspect ratio is checked so that the graphic keeps the width and height ratio when you're resizing it.

Replacing the Image in a SHED Graphic

Creating good SHED graphics can take a fair amount of work. For example, a SHED graphic that has hotspots for each of a program screen's features can take several hours to build and test. The program screen itself may change (frequently during development) and you'll have to replace the image that the hotspots are placed on. Fortunately, you can slip in a new image to a SHED graphic, much like pulling the tablecloth out from under a set of dishes and then slipping another one in its place, as follows:

1. In the Image Workshop, open the SHED graphic you want to modify.
2. In the Windows Explorer, right-click on the graphic file that contains the new bitmap. Select Copy from the right-click menu to copy the bitmap to the Windows clipboard.
3. Paste the image from the Windows clipboard into the Image Workshop by clicking the Paste icon on the toolbar or by right-clicking in the Image Workshop area and then selecting Paste from the right-click menu. The Paste Image screen (shown in Figure 7-18) appears.

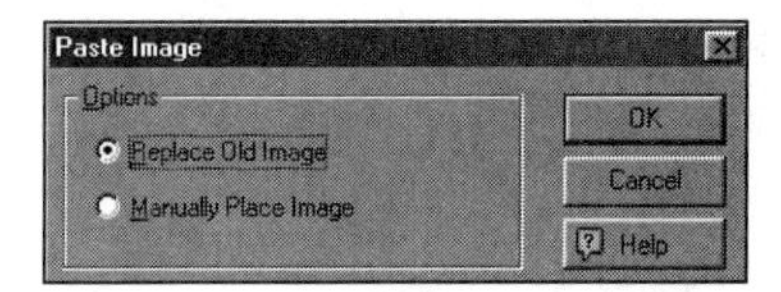

Figure 7-18: The Paste Image screen

4. Select one of the two options on the Paste Image screen and click OK:
   - **Replace Old Image:** Select this option (the default) to replace the existing bitmap image in the SHED graphic with the new bitmap from the Windows clipboard. If the new bitmap is the same size as or larger than the bitmap in the SHED graphic, RoboHELP will keep the hotspots in the same positions. If the new image is smaller or different dimensions, RoboHELP will move any hotspots that fall outside the new area up and/or to the left. RoboHELP will also shrink the hotspots to fit the new bitmap. Use this option if you are replacing one screen shot with another similar screen shot that has a few new or moved features.
   - **Manually Place Image:** Select this option to overlay the new bitmap on the existing SHED graphic. You can position the new bitmap on top of the old bitmap and resize it. You can also move the hotspots from the old bitmap to the new bitmap. Crop the resulting image and save it with an extension of .SHG. (If you save the file without cropping, you'll end up with the new bitmap image surmounting the old bitmap image. This can actually be useful if you want to quickly add a graphic element, such as a logo, to a graphic.)

Any hotspots that are outside the cropped area will be lost.

5. Position the hotspots on the new image as necessary. You may need to resize or even delete some hotspots. When you are satisfied with your changes, save the new SHED graphic. The next time you compile the WinHelp project, the revised SHED graphic will appear in the online help file.

Using the Microsoft SHED Editor

The Image Workshop does many things, but there are a couple of things that you may actually want to use a different (and free) SHED editor that comes from Microsoft as part of the downloadable Help Compiler Workshop.

The advantage of using the Microsoft SHED editor, SHED.EXE, is that you can copy and paste hotspots. For example, suppose you have a program screen with a toolbar that has a series of buttons or icons that you want to add hotspots for. In the Image Workshop, you would need to create and size each hotspot individually, but SHED.EXE lets you copy and paste hotspots. You can also open several SHED graphics simultaneously in SHED.EXE, making it easy to see what you did in one SHED file.

The Microsoft SHED editor is included with RoboHELP and with the Microsoft Help Compiler Workshop. The various components of the Microsoft Help Compiler Workshop appear in the \RoboHELP Office\RoboHELP\hlpcomp directory. You can also download HCWSETUP.EXE from the Microsoft web site, `http://www.microsoft.com` and install it. You may want to create a shortcut to SHED.EXE in your RoboHELP group or on your desktop.

You can also add SHED.EXE as a new tool to the Tools tab of the RoboHELP Explorer. For more information, see Chapter 14, "Using RoboHELP Tools."

After you've installed the Microsoft Help Compiler Workshop, do the following to create and copy hotspots using the Microsoft SHED editor:

1. In the Windows Explorer, double-click SHED.EXE to start the Microsoft SHED editor.
2. Select the File ⇨ Open command to open a bitmap or a SHED graphic in the editor. (SHED.EXE doesn't recognize long filenames or support drag-and-drop features.) Figure 7-19 shows a bitmap opened in SHED.EXE.
3. Create a hotspot by clicking and dragging on the bitmap, and then right-click the hotspot to set the attributes. The Attributes screen appears, as shown in Figure 7-20.
4. Enter hotspot attributes as follows:
   - **Context String:** Enter the context string that uniquely identifies the topic you are creating a jump or popup to. You must enter this manually; there is no link to the WinHelp project.
   - **Type:** Select the type of hotspot — either Jump or Popup — from the drop-down list.

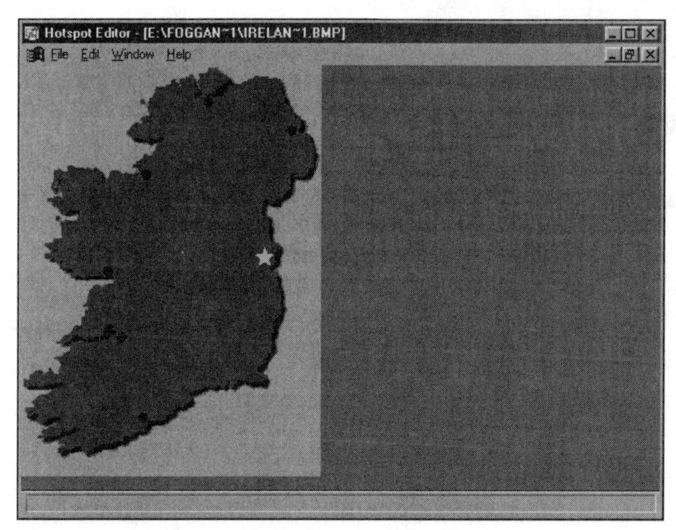

Figure 7-19: Sample bitmap opened in SHED.EXE

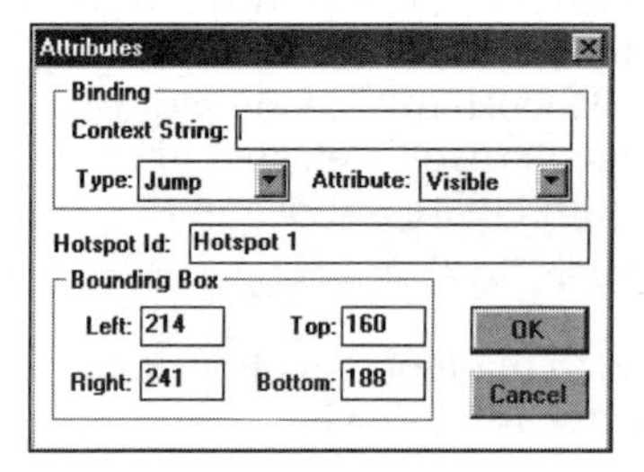

Figure 7-20: The Attributes screen in SHED.EXE

- **Attribute:** Select Visible or Invisible from the drop-down list.
- **Hotspot ID:** Enter a hotspot ID. (This corresponds to the Name field on the Advanced tab of the Insert Hotspot screen shown in Figure 7-12.) This is optional but it's a good idea to give a unique and descriptive name to each hotspot.
- **Bounding Box:** You can set the dimensions and locations of the hotspot by altering these coordinates (expressed as a number of pixels from the upper left corner of the graphic).

5. When you are satisfied with your changes, click OK. The hotspot appears on the screen as usual.

You can now copy and paste the hotspot, as follows:

1. With the hotspot selected (look for the handles on the border of the hotspot), select the Edit ➪ Copy command, and then select the Edit ➪ Paste command. The copy of the hotspot appears in the upper left corner of the graphic, as shown in Figure 7-21.

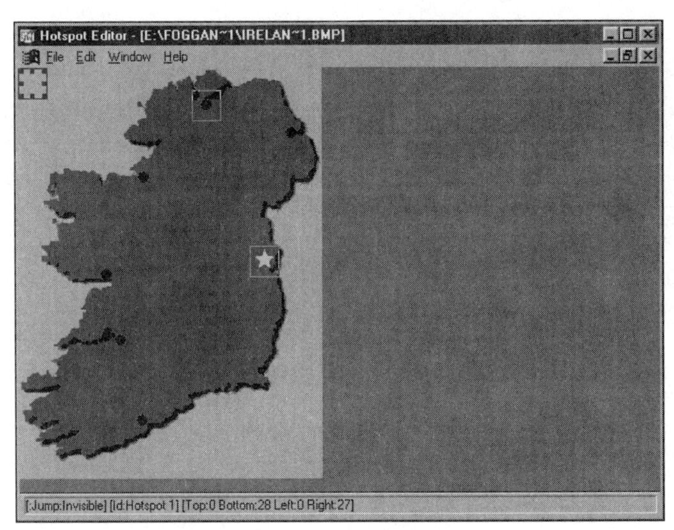

Figure 7-21: Pasted hotspot in SHED.EXE

2. Drag and drop the pasted hotspot to the desired location, and then right-click the hotspot to adjust the attributes. All the attributes of the original hotspot appear in the new hotspot.
3. Continue adding hotspots to the SHED graphic as necessary. When you're done, use the File ➪ Save or File ➪ Save As command to save the file.

You can also use this technique with multiple SHED graphics: you can open one SHED graphic, copy a hotspot, and then paste it into another SHED graphic.

SHED graphics created with the Microsoft SHED editor are fully compatible with the Image Workshop. You can create a SHED graphic in the Image Workshop, modify it with SHED.EXE, and then work with it further in Image Workshop.

The advantages to using the Microsoft SHED editor are that you can copy and paste hotspots quickly and easily. You can also open multiple bitmaps and SHED graphics and even copy and paste hotspots from one .SHG file to another. The disadvantages are that the interface for the Microsoft SHED editor has not changed substantially for several years and long filenames aren't supported. In addition, the .SHG files aren't linked to a specific project, so there is no easy way to select topics to create links to.

You should use the RoboHELP Image Workshop for most features of creating SHED graphics and use the Microsoft SHED editor when you need to copy and paste hotspots or view multiple SHED graphics simultaneously.

Using Multiple Resolution Graphics

Multiple resolution bitmaps are an older way of improving graphics resolution by giving WinHelp several different versions of the same bitmap to display, each one optimized for different resolutions. You generate bitmaps at different resolutions and then bind them together into a single format using the Multiple Resolution Bitmap Compiler (MRBC.EXE).

MRBC.EXE is a DOS program that is included with both RoboHELP and the Microsoft Help Compiler Workshop, HCWSETUP.EXE. MRBC.EXE can combine CGA, EGA, VGA, and 8514 bitmaps into a single MRB bitmap. Because most computers use VGA or better graphics these days, there is very little use for multiple resolution bitmaps in WinHelp files any more, but they may be useful occasionally if you are creating WinHelp files for Windows 3.*x* systems. Complete documentation for using MRBC.EXE to create multiple resolution bitmaps appears in the HCW.HLP file accompanying the Help Compiler Workshop. A copy of the HCW.HLP file can be found in the \RoboHELP Office\RoboHELP\hlpcomp directory.

Using Help Buttons

In addition to the hotspot graphics you've seen how to create so far, you can also create a variety of hotspot buttons within topics. There are four types of buttons: authorable buttons, mini buttons, shortcut buttons, and graphical buttons.

Adding Authorable Buttons

Authorable buttons are gray buttons to which you can add your own custom text. To perform the specified action for the hotspot, the user must click and release the authorable button. When you click an authorable button, you see the button go down, but if you don't release the mouse and drag the pointer off the button, the hotspot action won't be performed.

To add an authorable button, do the following:

1. Select the Insert ➪ Help Button command. The Insert Help Button screen appears (shown in Figure 7-22 with sample text entered for the authorable button).
2. Enter the text for the authorable button in the Button Label field. RoboHELP automatically sizes the button to fit the text you enter, so it's a good idea to keep your button text short.

If you don't enter text, the resulting button is 12 × 12 pixels with no text, the same size as a mini button.

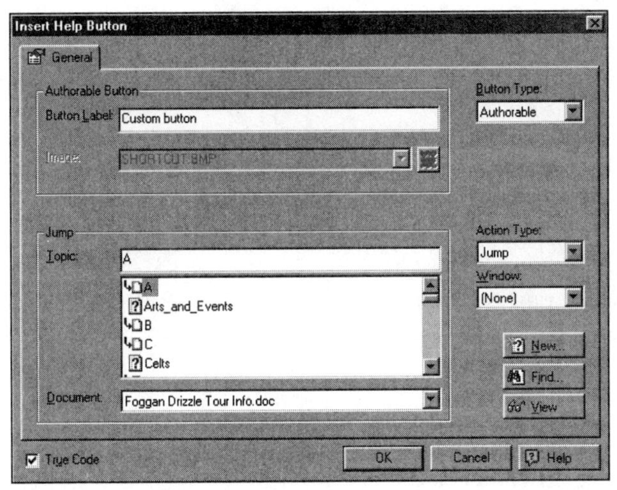

Figure 7-22: The Insert Help Button screen for authorable buttons

3. Select an action type and a topic on the lower portion, the same as when you create any other hotspot. When you are satisfied with your changes, click OK. RoboHELP inserts the entry for the authorable button in the DOC file. When you compile the file, the button appears at the location it was inserted. Figure 7-23 shows the jumps in the bulleted list on the Foggan Drizzle main screen replaced with authorable buttons.

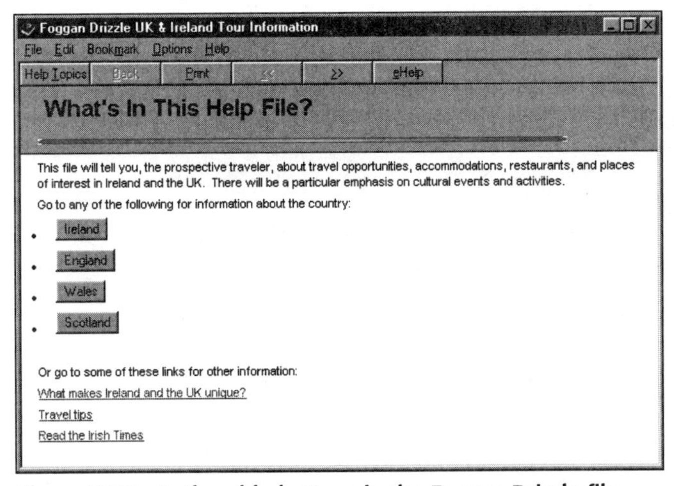

Figure 7-23: Authorable buttons in the Foggan Drizzle file

You can modify an authorable button by right-clicking the button or the True Code and then selecting Properties from the right-click menu. To delete an authorable button, simply highlight the authorable button's graphic or the True Code reference and press Delete.

Adding Mini Buttons

Mini buttons are small gray 12 pixel × 12 pixel buttons that have no text on them. If you created an authorable button with no text, it would look like a mini button. However, unlike authorable buttons, you can also enter text that will appear next to the button and will be formatted with the same hotspot characteristics as the mini button.

When you click a mini button, you see the button go down, but if you don't release the mouse and drag the pointer off the button, the hotspot action won't be performed. However, if you click the hotspot text associated with the mini button, the action is performed immediately.

To add a mini button, do the following:

1. Select the Insert ⇨ Help Button command. When the Insert Help Button screen appears, select Mini Button from the drop-down list in the Button Type field. Figure 7-24 shows the Insert Help Button screen with sample text entered for the mini button.

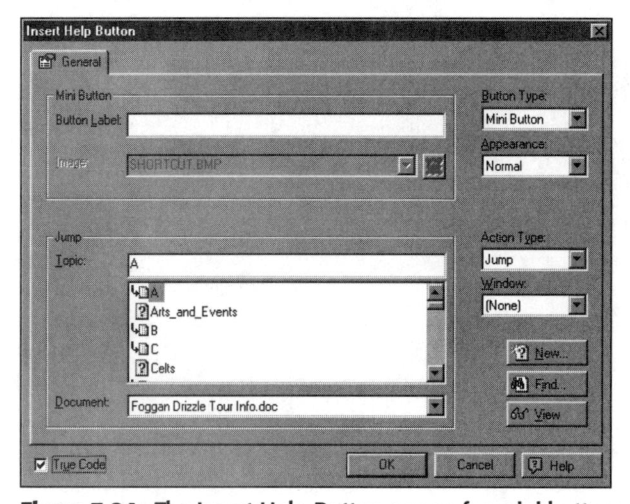

Figure 7-24: The Insert Help Button screen for mini buttons

2. Enter the text for the mini button in the Button Label field. This text will appear in the compiled WinHelp file as a hotspot immediately to the right of the mini button.
3. Select the appearance for the hotspot text from the drop-down list in the Appearance field. You can choose Normal, Hidden, or No Color, as you can with other hotspots.
4. Select an action type and a topic on the lower portion of the screen, the same as when you create any other hotspot. When you are satisfied with your changes, click OK. RoboHELP inserts the entry for the mini button in the DOC file. When you compile the file, the button appears at the location where it was inserted followed by the text you entered. Figure 7-25 shows the jumps in a bulleted list on the Foggan Drizzle main screen replaced with mini buttons with the hotspot text set to Normal, Hidden, and No Color. The fourth button in the list is an authorable button for comparison.

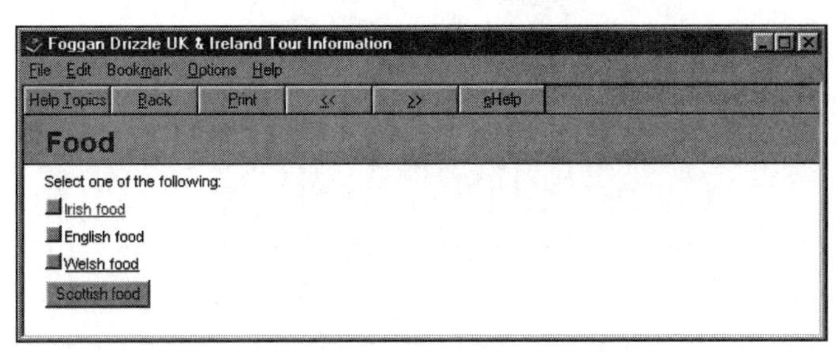

Figure 7-25: Mini buttons in the Foggan Drizzle file

You can modify a mini button by right-clicking the button or the True Code and then selecting Properties from the right-click menu. To delete a mini button, simply highlight the mini button's graphic and hotspot text (or the True Code reference and hotspot text) and press Delete.

Adding Shortcut Buttons

Shortcut buttons are not true buttons. Authorable buttons and mini buttons are actually created with the button macro (visible in the DOC file if you use the True Code option). Shortcut buttons are actually graphics that have been formatted as hotspots (very much like what you learned to do with graphics at the start of this chapter). The advantage of adding shortcut buttons with the Insert Help Button screen is that you can also add optional hotspot text (like a mini button).

For more information on macros, see Chapter 10, "Understanding Macros."

You can use any graphic you wish for the shortcut button. The button will be the size of the graphic you use.

To add a shortcut button, do the following:

1. Select the Insert ➪ Help Button command. When the Insert Help Button screen appears, select Shortcut Button from the drop-down list in the Button Type field. Figure 7-26 shows the Insert Help Button screen with sample text entered for the shortcut button.

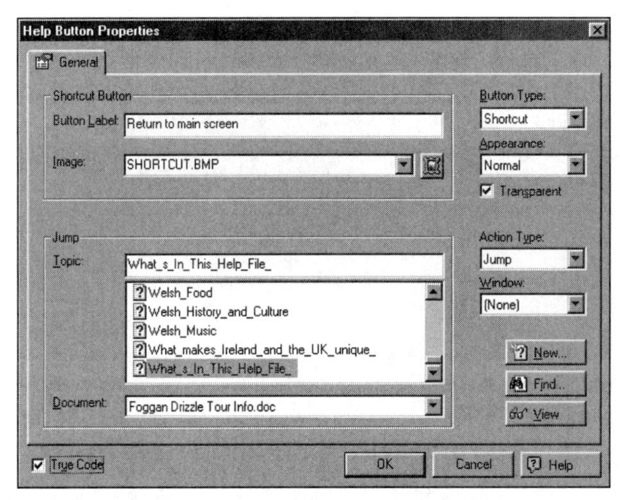

Figure 7-26: The Help Button Properties screen for shortcut buttons

2. Enter the text for the shortcut button in the Button Label field. This text will appear in the compiled WinHelp file as a hotspot immediately to the right of the shortcut button.

3. Select the appearance for the hotspot text from the drop-down list in the Appearance field. You can choose Normal, Hidden, or No Color, as you can with other hotspots. You can also select to display the button as transparent as you can with any other graphic you're inserting.

4. Select the graphic to use from the Image field. This defaults to the Special folder in the RoboHELP directory, but you can click the image button to the right of the Image field and browse for a specific graphic.

5. Select an action type and a topic on the lower portion the same as when you create any other hotspot. When you are satisfied with your changes, click OK. RoboHELP inserts the entry for the shortcut button in the DOC file. When you compile the file, the button appears at the location where it was inserted followed by the text you entered. Figure 7-27 shows a shortcut button using the SHORTCUT.BMP graphic added to the bottom of a list in a Foggan Drizzle menu screen.

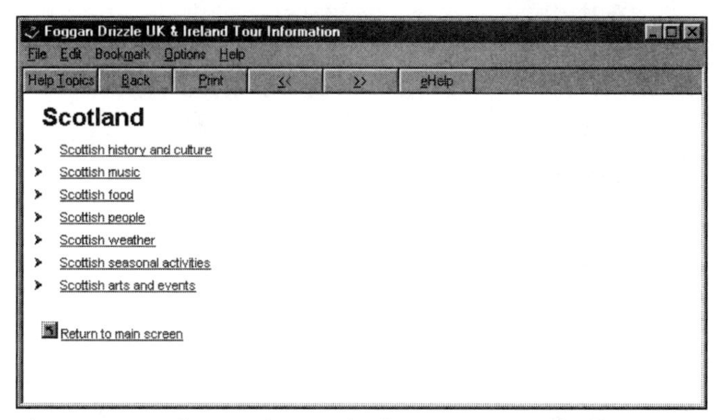

Figure 7-27: Shortcut button in the Foggan Drizzle file

You can modify a shortcut button by right-clicking the button or the True Code and then selecting Properties from the right-click menu. To delete a shortcut button, simply highlight the shortcut button's graphic and hotspot text (or the True Code reference and hotspot text) and press Delete.

Adding Graphical Buttons

Graphical buttons are a combination of several types of buttons. They are true buttons that use a macro, but they also use graphics like a shortcut button. What is special about graphical buttons is that they can have two different graphics: one for when the button is up and another for when the button is down. The size of the button is determined by the graphic used when the button is up (the button's face).

To add a graphical button, do the following:

1. Select the Insert ➪ Help Button command. When the Insert Help Button screen appears, select Graphical Button from the drop-down list in the Button Type field. Figure 7-28 shows the Insert Help Button screen with sample text entered for the graphical button.

The size of a graphical button is determined by the size of the graphic files you use. For example, if your graphic files are 3" × 3", the graphical button will be 3" × 3".

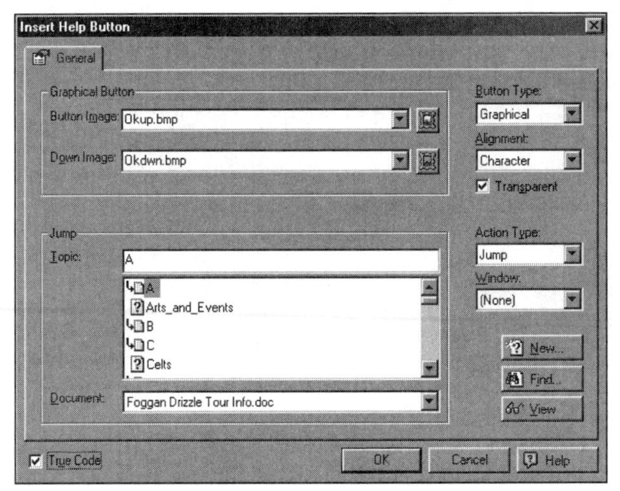

Figure 7-28: The Insert Help Button screen for graphical buttons

2. Select the graphics to use for the up (unpressed) button image and the down (pressed) button image. The drop-down list defaults to the Buttons folder in the RoboHELP directory, but you can click the image button to the right of the two image fields and browse for specific graphics. Table 7-1 shows some sample button combinations you can use from this folder.

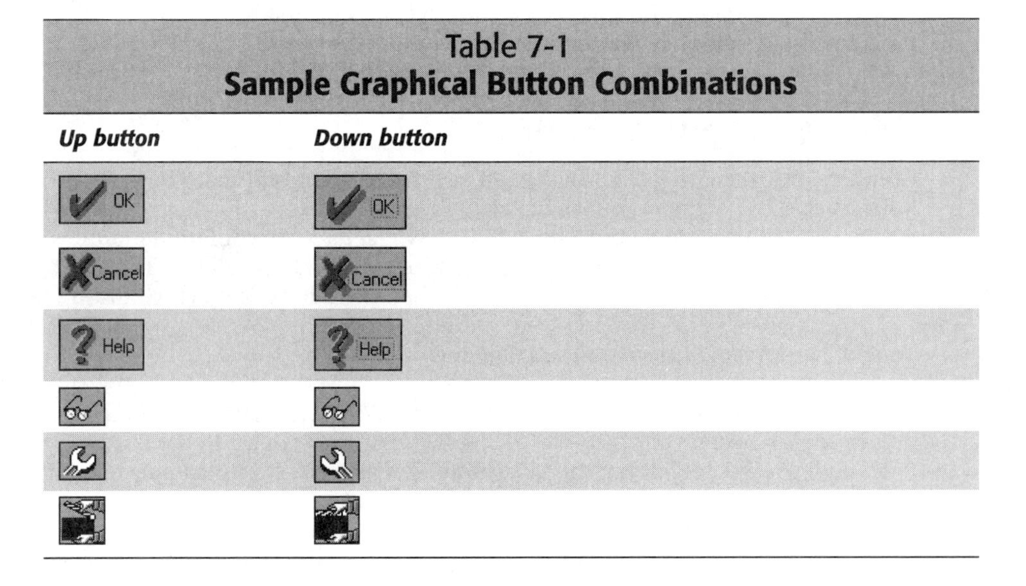

Table 7-1
Sample Graphical Button Combinations

Up button	*Down button*
OK	OK
Cancel	Cancel
Help	Help

You can create your own custom image pairs for graphical buttons. You'll usually want these two images to be identical except for the part that changes to achieve the animation effect. The best way to do this is to create the first button image and then make the second button starting with a Save As of the first button.

3. Specify a graphic alignment and whether or not you want the button graphics to be transparent.
4. Select an action type and a topic on the lower portion, the same as when you create any other hotspot. When you are satisfied with your changes, click OK. RoboHELP inserts the entry for the graphical button in the DOC file. When you compile the file, the button appears at the location it was inserted. When you click the button, the graphic specified in the Down Image field appears on the button face. WinHelp performs the designated hotspot action when you release the button.

In order for graphical buttons to work in the WinHelp file, the users must install one of the redistributable RoboHELP files in the same directory with the compiled WinHelp project, either RGHBTN32.DLL for WinHelp 4 files or RGHBTN16.DLL for WinHelp 3 files. For more information on the files that must accompany the finished WinHelp file, see the section on the Ship List report in Chapter 15, "Managing Large Projects."

You can modify a graphical button by right-clicking the button or the True Code and then selecting Properties from the right-click menu. To delete a graphical button, simply highlight the graphical button's graphic (or the True Code reference) and press Delete.

Using the Project Manager with Graphics

As you saw earlier in Chapter 6, when you add graphics to the DOC file, RoboHELP lists them in the appropriate category. Figure 7-29 shows the Project Manager listings for the 0graphics added throughout this chapter.

You can display the properties for any of these buttons by right-clicking the name of the graphic or button and selecting Properties from the right-click menu. You can also edit standard images and hotspot graphics (SHED graphics) by selecting Edit from the right-click menu. You can also view the two graphics used in graphical buttons through the Project Manager.

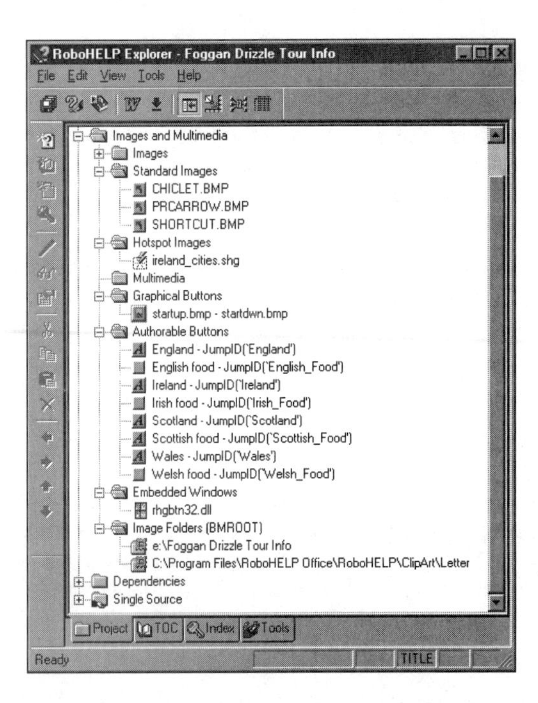

Figure 7-29: The Project Manager showing graphics added to the Foggan Drizzle DOC file

Switching the Graphic Display Mode

Although True Code is useful for heavy editing and development — you don't have to wait for Word to display a lot of graphics if you're scrolling back and forth in a document — there are times when it's convenient to see the actual graphics. Alternatively, you may want to switch from graphics to True Code, such as when you are maintaining a WinHelp project created by someone else.

RoboHELP has an option that lets you switch between True Code and Dynamic WYSIWYG display in your DOC file quickly and easily, as follows:

1. Select the RoboHELP ➪ Dynamic WYSIWYG/TrueCode command. The RoboHELP - WYSIWYG screen (shown in Figure 7-30) appears.

Figure 7-30: The RoboHELP - WYSIWYG screen

2. Select Convert to Dynamic WYSIWYG or Convert to True Code and click OK. RoboHELP will convert all the graphics in the DOC file, which can take a minute or two even for a small DOC file.

It's a good idea to save any changes to the DOC file and make a backup copy before you start this operation, particularly if the DOC file is large or has many graphics.

Summary

In this chapter, you learned how to create a variety of interactive graphics. You first saw how to add graphics to jumps, popups, and other hotspots. After that, you learned how to create and use SHED graphics using the Image Workshop, including ways to change the SHED graphics resolution, resize SHED graphics, replace the base image in a SHED graphic, and use the Microsoft SHED editor for some types of editing. The chapter next showed you how to add and use buttons in your WinHelp projects, including authorable buttons, mini buttons, shortcut buttons, and graphical buttons. Finally, the chapter showed you how to track graphics with the Images and Multimedia folder of the RoboHELP Explorer's Project Manager and how to use a RoboHELP option to change the graphics in your DOC file to True Code or Dynamic WYSIWYG.

The next chapter will show you how to add and maintain tables of contents and indexes. You'll also learn how to use See Also references.

✦ ✦ ✦

Using Tables of Contents and Indexes

✦ ✦ ✦ ✦

In This Chapter

Creating table of contents screens

Creating tables of contents manually, automatically, and using the CNT file

Creating Master Contents files

Adding external CNT files to tables of contents

Testing and fixing your tables of contents

Printing a Table of Contents report

Creating indexes with the Index Designer

Creating indexes with the Smart Index Wizard

Testing and fixing your indexes

Printing the Index (K-Keywords) report

Adding See Also keywords and links

Using the Smart See Also button

Printing the See Also (A-Keywords) and Unused Index and See Also Keywords Reports

✦ ✦ ✦ ✦

This chapter shows you how to add tables of contents and expand your indexes. The chapter starts with information about adding a table of contents screen within the WinHelp file. Next, you are introduced to creating a table of contents with the TOC Composer in the RoboHELP Explorer using drag-and-drop. You are then shown how to create a table of contents using the Auto-Create TOC feature and how to edit the CNT file. After that, you see how to create Master Contents files and add external CNT file to a table of contents. Finally, you see how to troubleshoot the tables of contents you create and how to print a Table of Contents report. In the second part of the chapter, you learn how to use the RoboHELP Explorer to expand and enhance your indexes. You first learn how to use the Index Designer to create and maintain keywords. Next, the chapter discusses the Smart Index Wizard and how to use it to automatically create and maintain comprehensive indexes. As with the Table of Contents section, the Index section concludes with a discussion of ways to test your indexes and work around a WinHelp bug, and print an Index (K-Keywords) report. The final section in this chapter shows you how to add See Also links (A-Links) and print the See Also reports.

Building Tables of Contents

Tables of contents are the first point of contact your users will usually have with your online help system. You can have a table of contents appear that gives an outline, or hierarchical, view of the contents of the WinHelp file. The table of contents shows your users the general structure and focus of the WinHelp file and also provides a reference point for finding more information.

Like the table of contents in a book, a good table of contents is a good reference point for the users. The users can skim the sections of the WinHelp file to find the area they're interested in, and then expand a section to look for specific topics of interest. When they double-click on a topic in the table of contents, the corresponding topic is displayed.

Creating a Table of Contents Screen

There are two ways to build and display tables of contents. The first way is to build a table of contents that appears on the main screen of the WinHelp file, similar to the list of jumps that you've seen in the main topic of the Foggan Drizzle help file in earlier chapters. Figure 8-1 shows a sample table of contents (using shortcut buttons) for the Foggan Drizzle help file.

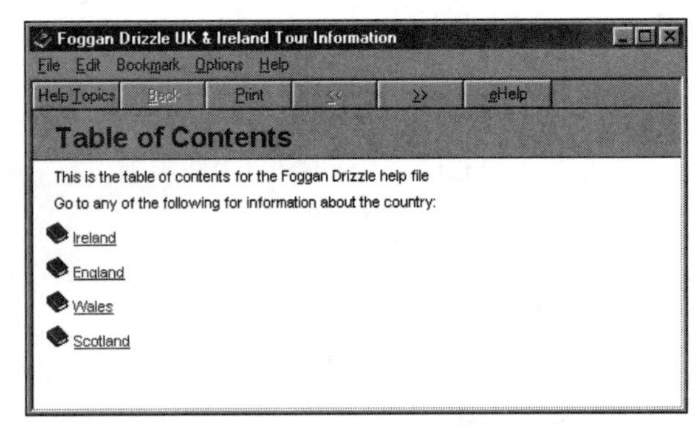

Figure 8-1: Sample table of contents in the Foggan Drizzle help file

You can also add indents and some of the standard book and page icons to the jumps to provide visual cues to hierarchy, as shown in Figure 8-2.

As you can see, including the details can rapidly expand the table of contents to the point where it's hard to find the thing you want. You can create a series of table of contents screens that show a single category expanded, similar to the sample shown in Figure 8-3.

The trick with this technique is that clicking on a closed book jump, such as "England," takes the user to an identical topic screen with a topic ID such as Contents_England that has that particular topic expanded. If the other screen elements and format are unchanged, it appears to the user that clicking on the table of contents entry for England suddenly expanded the selections under the book header. Using the open book bitmap for that topic gives the users an additional cue that this is the topic being opened.

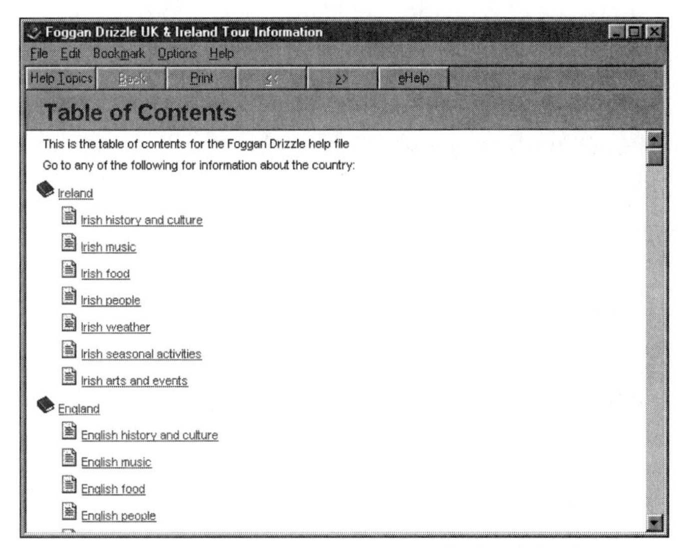

Figure 8-2: Sample table of contents with details in the Foggan Drizzle help file

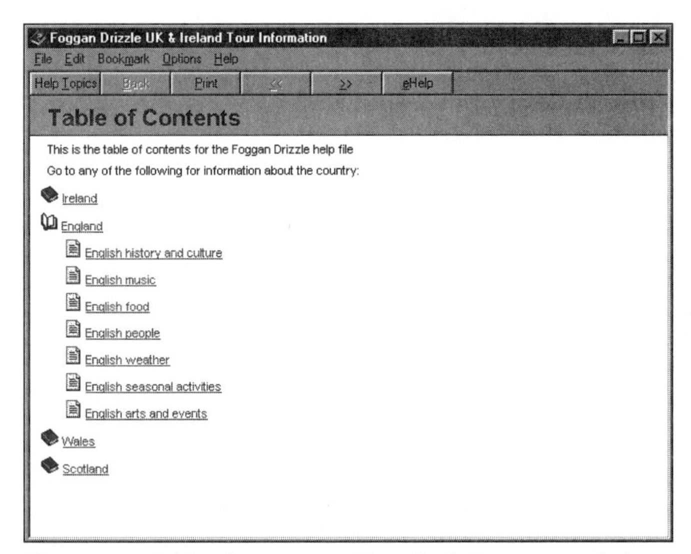

Figure 8-3: Table of contents with a single item expanded

Creating Tables of Contents

The method for creating a table of contents described in the previous section was used widely for WinHelp 3 systems to create extensive and rather effective tables of contents for complex WinHelp systems. The problem with this method is that it's labor-intensive: each item must be entered manually in all relevant contents screens. Furthermore, any changes to a topic name or ID must be reflected in the tables of contents as well.

WinHelp 4 has a built-in Contents feature that is reasonably easy to maintain and very easy to use. As you've seen in earlier chapters, it's also part of the WinHelp 2000 screen. Most WinHelp files use this feature. Figure 8-4 shows a typical table of contents in the Contents tab.

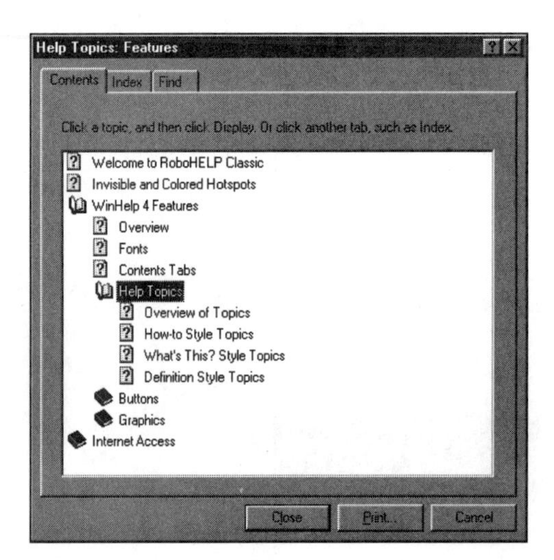

Figure 8-4: Sample table of contents in the Contents tab

As you can see from Figure 8-4, the table of contents is organized hierarchically, like an outline. There are two kinds of entries in the table of contents: books and pages. Books are heading entries that let you group the various topics and subheadings (also shown as books) into a logical order. You can have up to eight levels of books, each of which will have a different group of topics and books. When you click a book, the book "opens" (an example of this is visible in Figure 8-4), and the next level of books and topics appears. You can have multiple levels of books open simultaneously.

Books in WinHelp files aren't connected to a specific topic; they're purely for organizational purposes. (This contrasts with HTML Help files, where the books can be connected to specific topics.) Pages are the entries for specific topics (such as Overview and Fonts in Figure 8-4). When you click a page, the associated topic is displayed.

There are several ways to create tables of contents:

✦ Using drag-and-drop to add each book and page to the table of contents in the RoboHELP Explorer's TOC Composer and modifying or creating new entries as necessary.

- ✦ Using the Auto Create TOC function in the RoboHELP Explorer to create a table of contents automatically from the WinHelp project.
- ✦ Manually creating the CNT (contents) file in a text editor for inclusion with the WinHelp project. (This is the way WinHelp 3 tables of contents were created.)

The following sections tell you how to create a table of contents using each of these techniques.

Each of these techniques for creating and maintaining tables of contents has specific advantages. Try all of them to see which technique to use when.

Creating a table of contents using drag-and-drop

When you create a table of contents using drag-and-drop, you select the topics you want to add to your table of contents from the Topic List in the RoboHELP Explorer. You can select which topics to add and in which order. You can also add individual books or pages in the table of contents and even create a new topic in the WinHelp file when you enter a new page in the table of contents.

To create a table of contents using drag-and-drop, do the following:

1. Select the TOC Composer (the TOC tab) in the RoboHELP Explorer. Select the View ➪ Pane ➪ Topics command to display the right pane and select the Topic List (as shown in Figure 8-5).

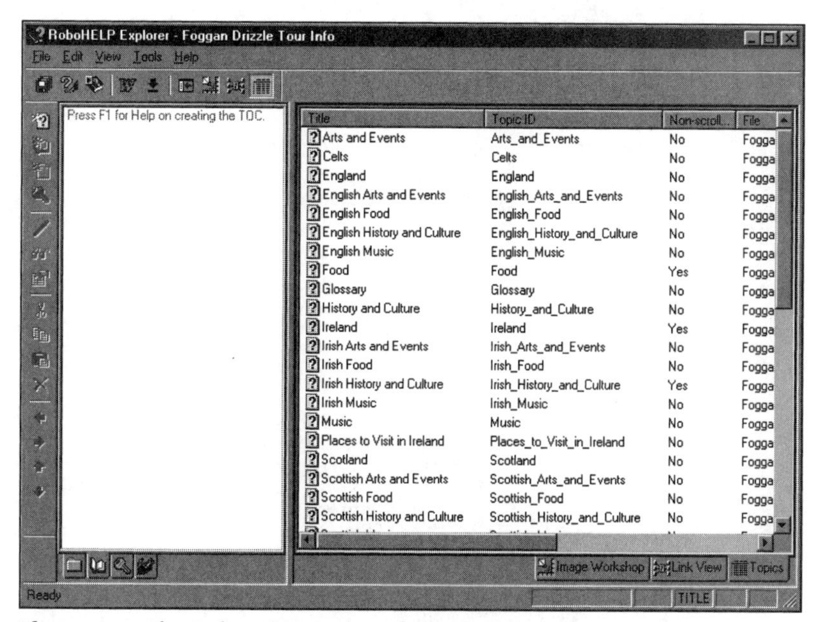

Figure 8-5: The RoboHELP Explorer before adding TOC items

2. Create the first book in the table of contents by clicking in the TOC tab of the RoboHELP Explorer and then clicking the open book icon on the Edit toolbar (the left margin) of the RoboHELP Explorer. You can also just right-click in the TOC tab of the RoboHELP Explorer and then select the New ➪ Book command from the right-click menu. The New Book screen appears, as shown in Figure 8-6 (with sample information added).

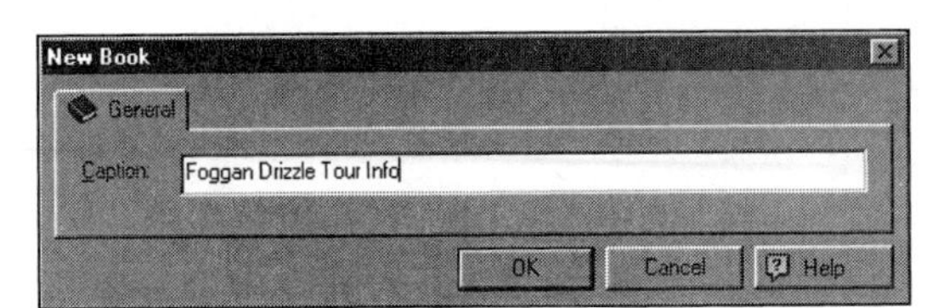

Figure 8-6: The New Book screen

3. Enter the name of the first book in the Caption field and click OK. Remember that books are for organization (something like a chapter title or a section title in a book), but they don't link directly to topics in the WinHelp file. RoboHELP adds the book entry to the table of contents in the left pane, as shown in Figure 8-7.

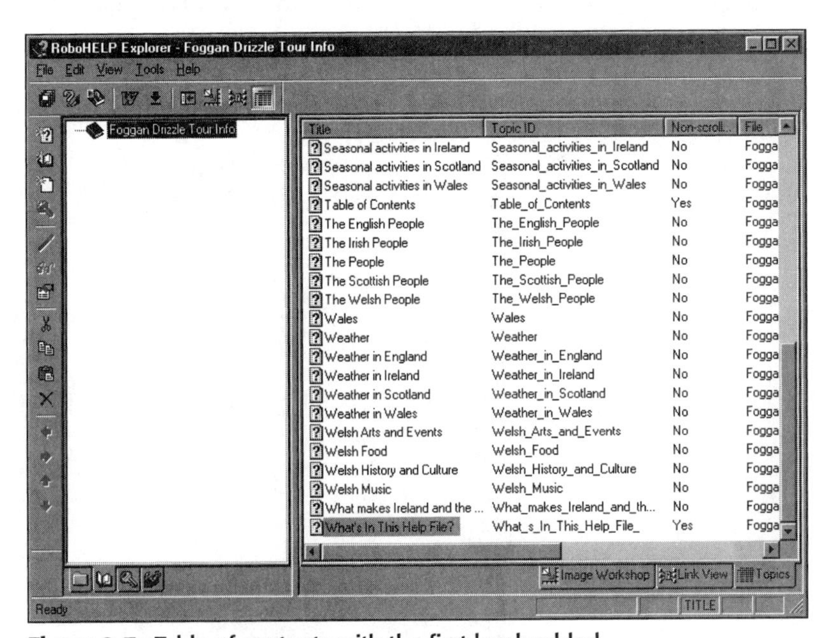

Figure 8-7: Table of contents with the first book added

4. Now add the first page in the table of contents by dragging "What's In This Help File?" from the Topic List and dropping it below the book. As you do so, you'll notice a large yellow arrow that appears in the left pane of the RoboHELP Explorer. This shows where the entry will appear when you drop it. When you have multiple entries in the table of contents, you can shift the insertion point by moving the mouse pointer. When you drop the entry beneath the book you just created, RoboHELP creates a page for the topic, as shown in Figure 8-8.

You can also add pages by dragging topics from the Link View.

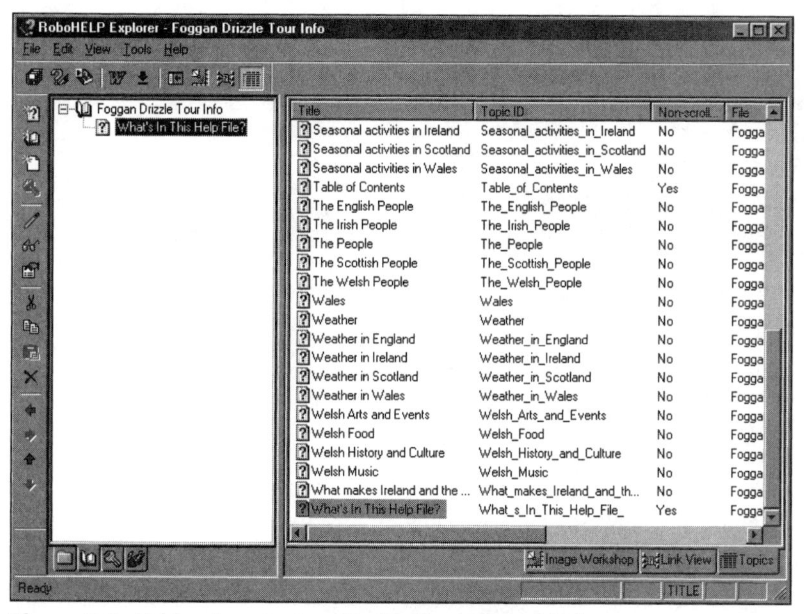

Figure 8-8: Table of contents with the first page added

5. Now you need to add some books as subheadings for each of the countries served by Foggan Drizzle. The topics for Ireland, England, Wales, and Scotland in the Foggan Drizzle help file are nothing more than topics with a submenu, so you can create books with these names and not link to the topics here. You can then add pages under each of these books to parallel the structure of the Foggan Drizzle help file. Figure 8-9 shows several of the countries' topics added to the table of contents.

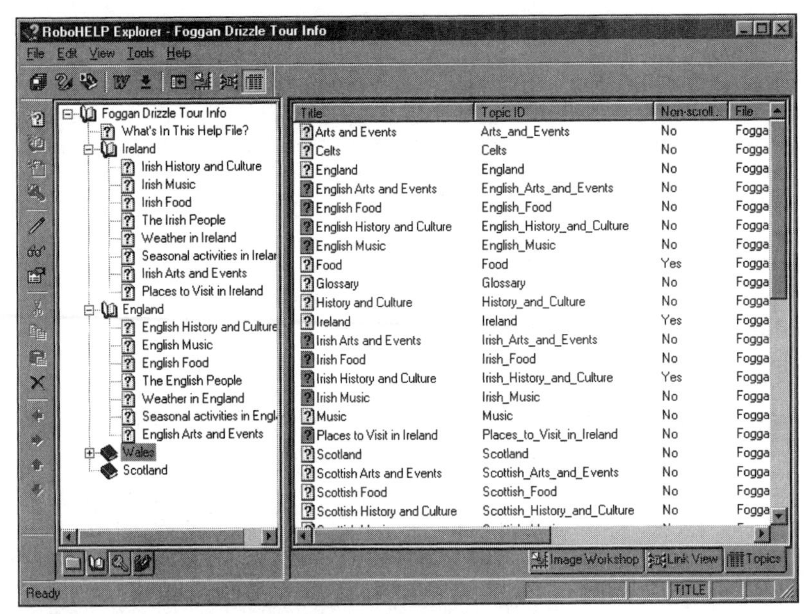

Figure 8-9: Table of contents with multiple entries

As you can see from Figure 8-9, when you drag-and-drop a topic from the Topic List, RoboHELP changes the color of the page icon in the Topic List. This is helpful for making sure you've added all the topics to the table of contents.

You can drag a topic to the table of contents more than once if you wish. RoboHELP adds a page each time you do this. This is helpful if you're creating a table of contents with several different groups that point to overlapping topics, but be careful that you don't inadvertently add a duplicate page for a topic.

6. Continue adding the books and pages to the table of contents. As you build up the books and pages in your table of contents, you can expand and collapse books to make it easier to work on a specific section by clicking on the + and – signs next to the books. (You can also use the View ➪ Expand All and View ➪ Collapse All commands in the RoboHELP Explorer to expand or collapse all the headings at once.) You can select multiple topics in the Topic List by holding down the Ctrl key and clicking each of the topics, then dragging them to the table of contents as a group. Figure 8-10 shows the completed table of contents. When you are satisfied with your entries, select the File ➪ Save TOC or File ➪ Save All command.

Remember that you can provide different books that each point to an overlapping group of topics. For example, the Foggan Drizzle has topics grouped by country and also by interests, such as food, music, weather, and so on. Your table of contents can be structured similarly, although you should remember that a table of contents is linear, like an outline. The interconnectedness of hypertext is lost in the table of contents, but the users gain the advantage of being able to see more groups of topics.

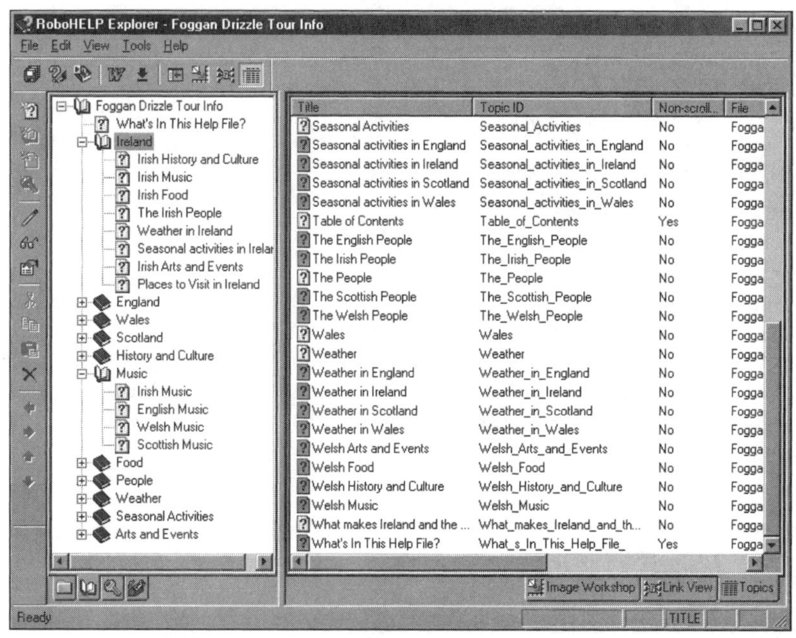

Figure 8-10: Completed table of contents

7. Once you've saved your table of contents, RoboHELP will update the WinHelp project to use the table of contents file. (The table of contents information is stored in a CNT file that doesn't have to be compiled, but it is used when the WinHelp file is run. Information on how the CNT file works is described later in this chapter.) After compiling, when you run the Foggan Drizzle help file, you see the Contents tab rather than the first screen of the help file itself, as shown in Figure 8-11.

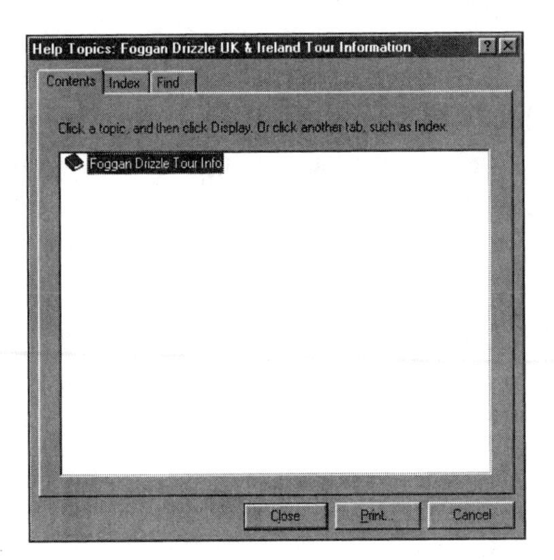

Figure 8-11: Contents tab for the Foggan Drizzle help file.

The users can expand the table of contents in the Contents tab by double-clicking books. The books and pages appear in the table of contents in the same order as they appear in the table of contents as it was assembled in the RoboHELP Explorer. (Figure 8-12 shows the table of contents with several of the books expanded.) As with any other table of contents, the user clicks the appropriate page to go to the associated topic.

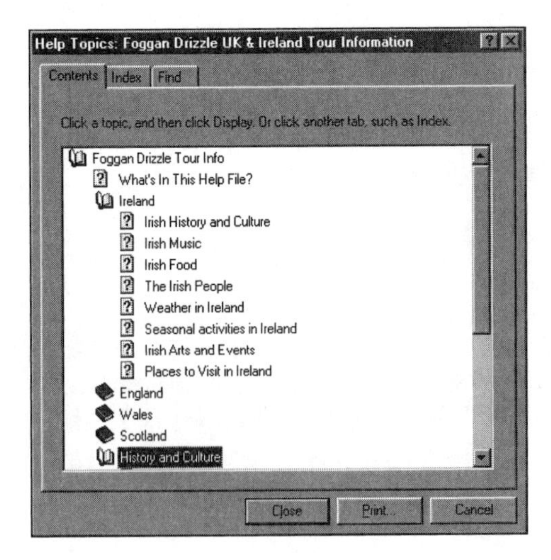

Figure 8-12: Contents tab for the Foggan Drizzle help file with several books expanded

After you've created the initial table of contents, you'll probably want to edit it to change the location of books and pages. You can move books or pages to other locations in the table of contents by clicking and dragging the page or book you want to move. RoboHELP also lets you cut, copy, and paste pages and books in the table of contents: right-click on the page or book and select the appropriate command from the right-click menu. In addition, you can change the indentation of a book or page by right-clicking the item and then selecting Move from the right-click menu. You're then given options for moving the item left, right, up, or down. You can also click the arrow icons on the Edit toolbar on the left margin of the RoboHELP Explorer to move table of contents items.

The right-click menu also has some other features that are handy when creating or maintaining a table of contents. You can delete a book or page with the Delete command, rename a book or page with the Rename command, and find a topic using the Find Topic screen (described in Chapter 4).

You can quickly create a new page by selecting the New ➪ Page command from the right-click menu, or by clicking the page icon on the Edit Toolbar on the left margin of the RoboHELP Explorer. The New Page screen will appear. (This screen is about the same as the Insert Help Hotspot screen described earlier in Chapter 4.) Pages, like jumps in the WinHelp file, can also have jumps to macros, other help files, and even Web sites. You can specify a jump (the standard operation for a page in the table of contents), a macro, an external topic (to another WinHelp file or to a topic in a compiled HTML Help file), or an HTML jump (to a URL). The external topic option is particularly useful, as you can build tables of contents that span multiple help files as a result.

Note The typical way to span multiple help files is to combine the CNT files into a Master CNT file or a Master Help Project, as described later in this chapter.

When the users double-click a page in the TOC Composer in the RoboHELP Explorer, RoboHELP displays the associated topic in the DOC file for viewing or editing. (Remember that editing the topic heading or topic ID will not be reflected automatically in the table of contents.) You can also create a new topic by clicking the New Topic icon on the Edit toolbar on the left margin of the RoboHELP Explorer to display the standard New Topic screen (described in Chapter 3, "Creating Your First WinHelp Project"). You can then add the topic information as normal. When you have added the new topic, RoboHELP automatically adds a corresponding page to the table of contents as well.

You can check how a page will appear to your users by right-clicking the page in the table of contents and then selecting View from the right-click menu. RoboHELP will display the associated topic from the WinHelp file. (The topic must have been compiled already in the online help file for this viewing option to work. If the topic hasn't yet been compiled into the online help file, RoboHELP will display an error message that says, "The topic does not exist.") You can modify the page information by right-clicking the entry and selecting Properties from the right-click menu. If the topic is incorrect, you can use the Find Topic command on the right-click menu to locate a topic and assign it to the page.

Whenever you use a table of contents, it's a good idea to set a default topic for your WinHelp file. The default topic will appear if there is no CNT file or if WinHelp can't find the CNT file. If you don't set a default topic, WinHelp will use the first topic in the WinHelp file.

To set the default topic for your WinHelp project, do the following:

1. Select the File ➪ Project Settings command and click the Project tab.
2. Enter the topic ID for the default topic, or select the topic from the drop-down list, and click OK. (The default topic is set in the Default Topic field of the Project tab on the RoboHELP Project Settings screen.)

Here are some general tips for creating effective tables of contents:

✦ Be consistent! As with your topic headings, your table of contents books and pages should be labeled consistently. Topics should also be structured in groups in a consistent fashion.

✦ Create a meaningful organization of topics. You can organize topics in the table of contents any way you like, although it's a good idea to have the topic connected both logically and by browse sequences. (Browse sequences are discussed in Chapter 9, "Using Help Windows and Browse Sequences.") You should try out several different organizations of topics and possibly even do some hands-on user testing to determine what's most effective.

✦ Make sure that the topics are not buried too deeply in the table of contents because you don't want to force your users to open too many books to find the topic they need. (This is similar to the balancing act you learned about earlier in Chapter 3, "Creating Your First WinHelp Project," when making topics accessible while avoiding making your users click more than three times.)

✦ You can use the Edit ➪ Undo command to undo individual changes. You can undo an unlimited number of actions one at a time this way, but if you prefer, you can use the File ➪ Revert to Saved TOC command to revert to the table of contents as it was the last time you saved it.

✦ Keep the names of books and pages in the table of contents as short as possible to make it easy for your users to find the desired topic without scrolling back and forth horizontally on the Contents tab.

✦ Because of a problem with WinHelp, titles for books and pages must be 92 characters long or less.

✦ To create a table of contents for a WinHelp 3 project, create a table of contents as normal, and then use the WinHelp Compatibility Wizard included with RoboHELP Office to display the table of contents in a Contents tab for Windows 3.1. You can also use the RoboHELP Office Hyperviewer Wizard to provide a book and page layout for your WinHelp 3 files. (Both of these techniques require you to distribute some RoboHELP DLL files with the completed WinHelp file.)

For more information on the WinHelp Compatibility Wizard and the Hyperviewer Wizard, see Chapter 14, "Using RoboHELP Tools."

Creating a table of contents using Auto Create TOC

The previous section showed you how to create and modify a table of contents using drag-and-drop and other manual techniques. Although these techniques are valuable when maintaining your table of contents, you can see that creating a table of contents from scratch this way could be time-consuming and tedious. Fortunately, RoboHELP has a simple feature for creating tables of contents automatically, as follows:

1. Select the TOC tab in the RoboHELP Explorer. (You don't need to have the right pane displayed.)
2. Select the Tools ➪ Auto Create TOC command. RoboHELP creates a quick table of contents by creating a single top-level book for each of the documents in the WinHelp project and then makes pages for each of the topics in the documents in the order they appear in the documents, as shown in Figure 8-13. (The Foggan Drizzle file in this example has only one help document. If you have multiple help documents, creating a quick table of contents will list the topics in the order they appear in each of the help documents. The help documents themselves will be listed in the order they appear in the RoboHELP Explorer Project Manager.)

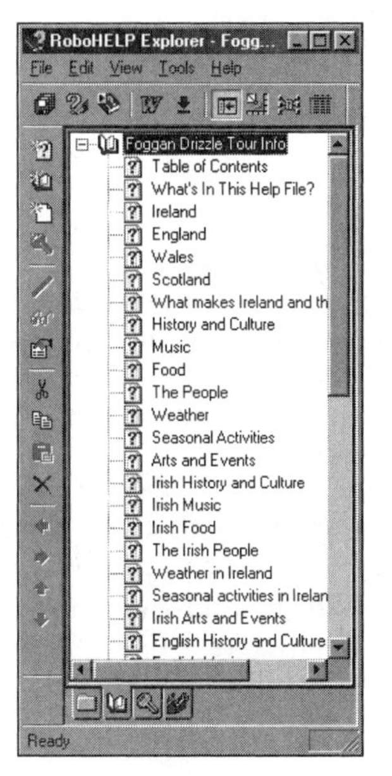

Figure 8-13: Table of contents created with Auto Create TOC

Once you have the entries in the table of contents, you can then use the techniques you learned in the previous section to modify, delete, and reorganize entries in the table of contents.

Creating a table of contents with the Contents (CNT) file

The information for the tables of contents is stored in a text file with an extension of CNT. You can view and edit this file directly if you wish. Although you won't need to do this normally, it can be helpful for debugging and also for making global changes using the search and replace functions in a word processor or text editor. Figure 8-14 shows the CNT for the table of contents displayed earlier in Figure 8-10.

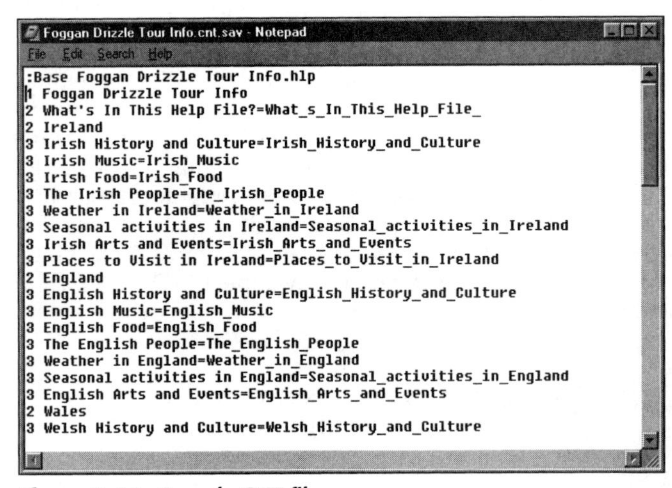

Figure 8-14: Sample CNT file

The phrase "Base:" followed by a help file name in the first line in the CNT file identifies the compiled WinHelp file with which this table of contents is associated. The number at the start of each subsequent line identifies the indentation level for the entry. Entries for books and pages are easy to identify: books have no associated topic. The CNT file should be in the same directory as the HLP file. When the users open the WinHelp file, WinHelp looks for the matching CNT file.

One of the advantages of working directly on the CNT file is that you can edit the entries in the table of contents using search-and-replace techniques. For example, suppose that you have changed a group of your topic IDs to be prefaced with FD_ so that you can identify the topics specifically in the Foggan Drizzle help file. You could open the CNT file, search and replace to change the equals sign to =FD_, and the entries are all updated in one operation.

In addition to the :Base command, there are several commands that are part of the CNT file that tell WinHelp such things as the title of the WinHelp project to display on the Help Topics screen and the names of other WinHelp files for which you want include keywords and text. For the most part, RoboHELP will maintain these for you, but you can modify them directly in the CNT file with a text editor or word processor if you prefer.

You can open the CNT file in Notepad quickly by selecting the using the File⇨Open File from Project command in RoboHELP Explorer. When the Open File from Project screen (not shown) appears, select the Table of Contents (*.CNT) option in the Files of Type field to display the CNT file(s) in the online help project, and then double-click the file you want to open.

The commands that can appear in the CNT file are:

✦ **:Base.** The :Base command identifies the default compiled WinHelp file to use with this CNT file. (Specific pages can refer to topics in different WinHelp files.) If you've included an external CNT file that has a :Base command, WinHelp uses the WinHelp file referred to for the topics in that specific file. (External CNT files are discussed later in this chapter.)

✦ **:Title.** The :Title command adds a title to the Help Topic screen. The title can be entered through RoboHELP on the Contents tab of the Project Settings screen. The title you enter there will override the title on the Project tab of the Project Settings screen.

For more information on secondary windows, see Chapter 9, "Using Help Windows and Browse Sequences."

✦ **:Include.** The :Include command identifies an external CNT file to add to a table of contents. For example, when you add the CNT file for Fasttour.hlp, an ":Include fasttour.cnt" line is added to your CNT file. When you run the WinHelp file, WinHelp opens each file identified by an :Include command and adds the books and pages in the table of contents where the :Include command appears. If WinHelp can't find a referenced CNT file, there is no error message but the books and pages for that CNT file won't appear in the table of contents. The information for the Include command is set automatically when you use the File⇨New⇨External CNT File command in RoboHELP Explorer. (This feature is used as part of creating Master Contents files, described in the next section.)

✦ **:Tab.** The :Tab command adds a custom tab to the Help Topics screen. This is set through RoboHELP using the Custom Tabs field on the Contents tab of the Project Settings screen.

✦ **:Nofind.** The :Nofind command eliminates the standard Find tab on the Help Topics screen. (This command must be added to the CNT file with a text editor or word processor; there is no corresponding field in RoboHELP to set this option.)

✦ **:Index.** The `:Index` command adds a WinHelp file that you want to display the keywords for on the Index and Find tabs of the Help Topics screen. This is set through RoboHELP using the Files Included in Index field on the Contents tab of the Project Settings screen.

✦ **:Link.** The `:Link` command identifies a WinHelp file to search using the ALink and KLink macros. This is set through RoboHELP using the Files Included in Index field on the Contents tab of the Project Settings screen.

Creating See Also links is discussed later in this chapter. For more information on the ALink and KLink macros, see Chapter 10, "Understanding Macros."

These commands are not case-sensitive. Many of these fields can be modified through RoboHELP's Contents tab in the Project Settings screen, described in the next section.

Creating Master Contents Files

The examples in the previous sections have dealt with setting up the table of contents for a single help file, but in fact, your tables of contents can span multiple help files. For example, suppose you have several different WinHelp files: one for the basic features of the product, another for the advanced features specific to this version of the product, a third for the programmer's reference, and so on. Using a Master Contents file, you can integrate these pieces into one seamless whole: when the users click on a topic in the table of contents, they see the associated topic regardless of the WinHelp file it's in.

Master Contents files are helpful when managing large WinHelp projects that have multiple authors. Each WinHelp author can work on her or his own part of the file, and then the separate pieces can be integrated with a Master Contents file. Changes to an individual piece don't require changes to the entire WinHelp project and the concomitant regression testing that may be required.

By breaking up WinHelp files into smaller modules, you can create customized help quickly and easily. One application of this type is for software products with multiple optional modules. If the users don't install a certain module, the installation procedure won't install the CNT and WinHelp files for the product. When the users run WinHelp, any CNT files that aren't installed are simply not displayed (and no error message appears). In other words, WinHelp can dynamically adjust what the users see in the Help Topics screen based on which CNT and WinHelp files it finds.

Creating a Master Contents file uses all the techniques for creating tables of contents you have seen so far. You must first create tables of contents for all the individual WinHelp projects you want to include. You can create tables of contents using any of the techniques shown earlier in this chapter.

Next, you need to prepare the contents files of the individual WinHelp files as external CNT files. The external CNT file must have the WinHelp file (and, if secondary windows have been used for displaying topics, the type of window in which to display the topic) specified as part of the topic information in each page entry in the external CNT file. (This provides a workaround for a problem in WinHelp, in which WinHelp has trouble knowing how to display the information for a page in an external CNT file included in the Master Contents file. If you don't do this and you're using secondary windows, you may receive a "Help topic doesn't exist" message when you select a topic from a Master Contents file.)

To prepare an external CNT file for inclusion in a Master CNT file, do the following:

1. Open the RoboHELP project containing one of the CNT files you want to include in the Master CNT file.
2. Select the File ➪ Project Settings command and click Contents. Figure 8-15 shows the Project Settings screen with the Contents tab displayed.

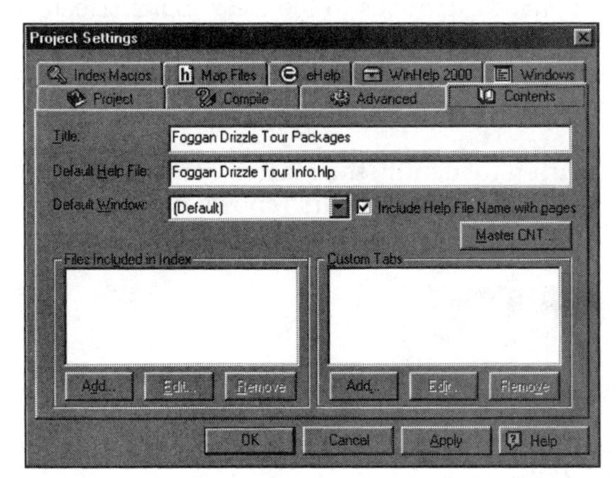

Figure 8-15: The Project Settings screen with the Contents tab displayed

3. Enter information in the fields as follows:
   - **Title:** Enter the title that will appear in the title bar of the WinHelp file. If you leave this field blank, WinHelp will use the title that appears on the Project tab of the Project Settings screen for the WinHelp file. (This creates a `:Title` command in the CNT file.)
   - **Default Help File:** Enter the default help file name. This will be used to create the path information in the pages.
   - **Default Window:** Select the default window from the drop-down list for topics to be displayed in.

For more information on using windows, see Chapter 9, "Using Help Windows and Browse Sequences."

- **Include Help File Name with Pages:** Check this box to add the appropriate information to the CNT file so that it can be used as part of a Master Contents file. RoboHELP will specifically identify topics as being part of the WinHelp file specified in the Default Help File field.

This is the only field necessary for preparing an external CNT file. The other fields are used for setting other options for the CNT file.

- **Files Included in Index:** Enter the names of other WinHelp files for which you want to add indexes and/or See Also links to this WinHelp project. (This creates an `:Index` command in the CNT file.)
- **Custom Tabs:** Enter the names of any Custom Tabs you want to display as part of the Help Topics screen. (This creates a `:Tab` command in the CNT file.)

Custom Tabs are programmatic extensions to the Help Topics screen. You must use a DLL (dynamic link library) to create a Custom Tab. You will need to have your development team create a DLL for your WinHelp project. Check the eHelp Web site for the current information on creating and attaching a Custom Tab DLL.

4. Click the Master CNT button to identify the Master Contents file to this WinHelp file. The Master CNT screen appears (shown in Figure 8-16).

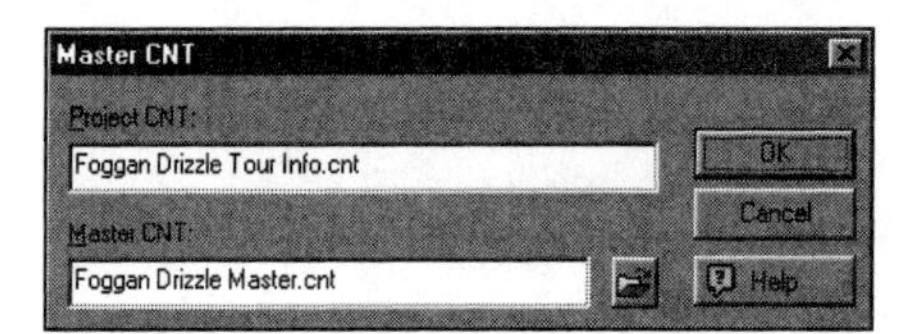

Figure 8-16: The Master CNT screen

5. In the Master Contents field, enter the name of the Master CNT file. (You haven't created this file yet; for now, select an appropriate file name that reflects the name of the online help project such as "Foggan Drizzle Master.CNT" and enter it.) The Project CNT field in the Master CNT screen defaults to the CNT file for the project you have open and doesn't need to be changed. When you click OK, RoboHELP saves information in the `[OPTIONS]` section of the WinHelp project's HPJ file that tells WinHelp to look for the Master Contents file you specified rather than the default WinHelp project CNT file.
6. When you are satisfied with your entries on the Contents tab of the Project Settings screen, click OK and then select File ➪ Save TOC. RoboHELP saves the changes to the CNT file. When you compile the WinHelp project and run the resulting WinHelp file, the changes in the CNT file will be visible in the Contents tab.

Repeat this process with each of the WinHelp projects you want to include in your Master Contents file. Be sure to use the same name for the Master Contents file in the Master CNT screen for all the WinHelp projects.

When you've prepared all the individual external CNT files, you're ready to create the Master Contents file, as follows:

1. Open a text editor or word processor.
2. Enter a title for the Master Contents file and then add an `:Index`, `:Link`, and `:Include` command for each WinHelp file you want to add. For example, if you are combining four help files — IRELAND.HLP, ENGLAND.HLP, WALES.HLP, and SCOTLAND.HLP — to create a Master Contents file entitled "Foggan Drizzle UK Info," you enter commands like this:

```
:Title Foggan Drizzle UK Info
:Include IRELAND.HLP
:Include ENGLAND.HLP
:Include WALES.HLP
:Include SCOTLAND.HLP
:Index Ireland=IRELAND.HLP
:Index England=ENGLAND.HLP
:Index Wales=WALES.HLP
:Index Scotland=SCOTLAND.HLP
:Link IRELAND.HLP
:Link ENGLAND.HLP
:Link WALES.HLP
:Link SCOTLAND.HLP
```

   The `:Include` commands tell WinHelp to use the CNT files for the various WinHelp files specified in the order that they appear. The `:Index` commands and the `:Link` commands, although not strictly necessary for creating a Master Contents file, allow the users to search for keywords and text in the Index and Find tabs (`:Index`) and to take advantage of ALink and KLink macros in the component WinHelp files (`:Link`).
3. Save the file in text-only format in the same directory as the other WinHelp files. The file should have a file name that identifies it as a Master Contents file, such as Foggan Drizzle Master.CNT. This file name must be the same as the file name you entered earlier for the individual WinHelp projects in the Master CNT field of the Master CNT screen.

Now, when you run any of the individual WinHelp files, they will look for the Master Contents file and display the information from that file in the Contents tab of the Help Topics screen rather than the individual CNT files. Remember, when you distribute the Master Contents file, be sure to include the CNT files and the HLP files for all the components. Also make sure the installation procedure puts the Master Contents file and the component WinHelp files into the same directory so that WinHelp can locate WinHelp files and their topics.

Adding External CNT Files to a Table of Contents

You occasionally may want to create a quick customized version of a WinHelp file. This is slightly different from creating a Master Contents file, as the changes are made directly to the CNT file for an actual WinHelp project rather than to a Master Contents file that is pointed to by the component WinHelp files.

You can add external CNT files to a table of contents as follows:

1. Open the WinHelp project you want to modify.
2. Right-click in the TOC Composer where you'd like to insert the external CNT file for one of the other WinHelp projects. Select the New ➪ External CNT File command. The New External CNT File screen appears (shown in Figure 8-17).

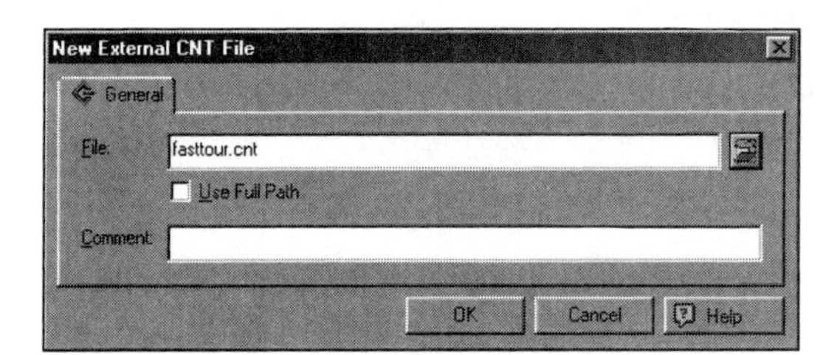

Figure 8-17: The New External CNT File screen

3. Enter the name of the external CNT file you want to add, or click the folder to the right of the File field to browse. In addition, you can optionally enter an internal comment for change maintenance in the Comment field for tracking. When you are satisfied with your entries, click OK. The external CNT file appears in the table of contents, as shown in Figure 8-18.

You need to have prepared the external CNT file as described earlier when creating Master Contents files.

4. You can move or edit the external CNT in the table of contents as you do with other table of contents entries. When you compile and run the WinHelp project, the table of contents will show each of the included tables of contents as a seamless part of the whole.

Figure 8-18: Table of contents with an external CNT file added

Troubleshooting Tables of Contents

There are a few problems you may encounter when you are creating and maintaining tables of contents. Most of them are caused by a missing or damaged CNT file. These problems can usually be corrected by making sure the CNT file (or the Master Contents file) is in the same directory as the WinHelp file and that the CNT file hasn't been saved in a format other than text.

✦ If an individual topic appears in the wrong display window when the users select the page in the table of contents, you will need to change the properties for the page. The Table of Contents Detailed Report (described in the next section) lists the windows for each page in the table of contents.

This problem can be fixed if the topic has an assigned Default Window (in the Advanced tab of the Topic Properties screen) before it's added to the table of contents. The default window at the topic property level becomes the default window for all hotspots and TOC pages.

✦ If many or all of the topics appear in the wrong display window, set a default window for the CNT file in the Contents tab of the Project Settings screen (shown earlier in Figure 8-15).

✦ If the Contents tab doesn't appear in the Help Topics screen, it usually means that WinHelp can't locate the associated CNT file. (In rare cases, it also means that WinHelp can't read the CNT file; for example, if you are editing the CNT file in Word and accidentally save it as Word format rather than text format.) If the CNT file is not in the same directory as the WinHelp file, copy it to the directory, delete the associated GID file from the directory to reset the settings for that WinHelp file, and then open the WinHelp file again. (The GID file is a hidden file created by the WinHelp viewer when you run a WinHelp file for the first time or when you update the file, for example, when you change the position of a WinHelp window or generate the keywords for a full-text search. If you delete this file, WinHelp will create a new GID file when the WinHelp file is opened the next time.)

✦ If the Contents tab is blank (no table of contents is displayed), it may mean that the CNT file is missing or damaged, or the CNT file is included in a Master Contents file, which is not located in the same directory as the WinHelp file. Make sure that the CNT file or Master Contents file is in the same directory as the WinHelp file and that it is complete and in text format.

✦ If WinHelp displays a topic instead of the Contents tab of the Help Topics screen, it means that the CNT file is missing or damaged and that WinHelp is displaying either the default topic you've set for the WinHelp file or the first topic in the WinHelp file.

✦ If part of the table of contents is missing, it usually means that there are missing external CNT files or WinHelp files from the directory. Add the missing CNT files and WinHelp files to the directory and run the WinHelp file again.

Printing the Table of Contents Report

The Table of Contents report provides you with information about the table of contents for your WinHelp project. You can use this report for checking the topic titles and WinHelp file names against the entries in the table of contents. You can also use this report as an easy way to edit the table of contents entries for spelling, grammar, and consistency.

To generate a Table of Contents report, do the following:

1. From RoboHELP Explorer, select the Tools ➪ Reports ➪ Table of Contents command. The Table of Contents report is displayed on the screen, as shown in Figure 8-19. The table of contents entries appear on the report in the order they appear in the table of contents.

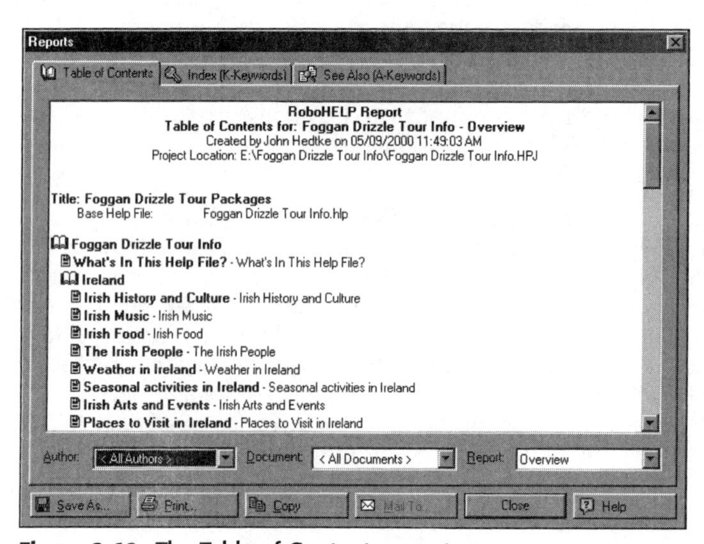

Figure 8-19: The Table of Contents report

As with many of the other reports you've seen in previous chapters, you can filter the information on the Table of Contents report in several ways. You can show the table of contents entries created by each author, all authors, or those that aren't assigned to specific authors, depending on your selection in the drop-down list in the Author field. You can also look at the table of contents entries in all the documents in the project or in individual documents with the drop-down list in the Document field. As with other reports in earlier chapters, you can switch the topic display between Topic Title and Topic ID by selecting View ➪ By Topic Title or View ➪ By Topic ID in the RoboHELP Explorer.

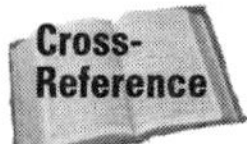

For more information on assigning authors, see Chapter 15, "Managing Large Projects."

The sample Table of Contents report shown in Figure 8-19 is an overview report, displaying book and page titles and the related topics. Selecting the Detailed option in the Report field in the lower right corner of the screen adds information about the documents containing the topics used by the individual page entries, the windows used to display the topics, and the names of any external WinHelp files.

If the TOC tab in RoboHELP Explorer is selected, you can print this report quickly by selecting the File ➪ Print TOC command in the RoboHELP Explorer.

As with other RoboHELP reports, you can run the Table of Contents report at any time.

Building Indexes with the RoboHELP Explorer

In Chapter 3, "Creating Your First WinHelp Project," you have seen how to create keywords and basic indexes using the Topic Properties screen. This is very useful for creating basic indexes and adding keywords and subkeywords for specific topics. However, you'll want to use more powerful techniques for creating indexes for an entire WinHelp project. This section will show you ways to use the Index Designer and the Smart Index Wizard in the RoboHELP Explorer to automate the indexing process.

Before you do extensive indexing of your WinHelp project, you should make some style and formatting decisions so that the finished product is consistent and reflects the preferred style of your company. Consider the following style issues:

- ✦ Do you want keywords to be lowercase (except for proper nouns and abbreviations and acronyms) or do you want all keywords to have initial caps?
- ✦ Do you prefer keywords for general concepts to be plural ("printing reports") but specific keywords to be singular ("Accounts Receivable report")?

- Will the index have more than one level? What words or phrases are acceptable as subkeywords?
- Will there be special words or phrases that should either be included or excluded? (This is particularly important for words or phrases that contain numbers or punctuation.) Also, does the WinHelp project use nonstandard words or acronyms? Are there trademarked or product-specific words or phrases that should be included or excluded?
- Do you want keywords to include phrases? If so, do you want to include verb phrases such as "printing a report"? Can keyword phrases be broken up into component keywords, such as "printing" and "report"?

Making corrections for style throughout a large WinHelp project can be tedious. Determining the style in advance can save you a great deal of time and effort.

Using the Index Designer

The Index Designer in the RoboHELP Explorer is similar to the TOC Composer. It provides you with an easy-to-use, effective interface for creating indexes in WinHelp files.

To enter a new keyword using the Index Designer, do the following:

1. Select the Index Designer (the Index tab) in the RoboHELP Explorer (shown in Figure 8-20).

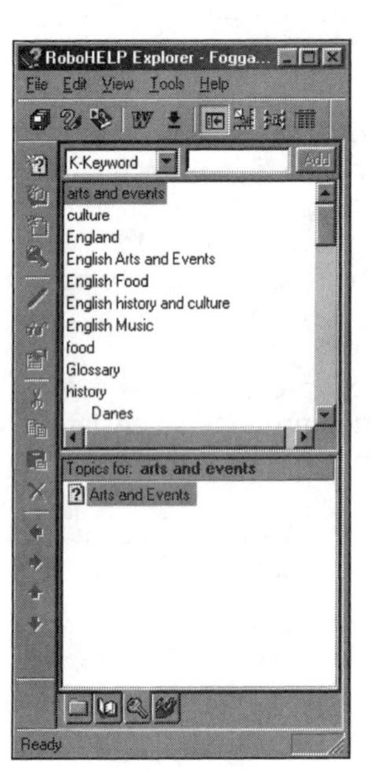

Figure 8-20: The RoboHELP Explorer showing the Index Designer

As you can see from Figure 8-20, the keywords that are already entered in the WinHelp file using the techniques described in Chapter 3, "Creating Your First WinHelp Project," appear in alphabetical order in the Index Designer display. The topic or topics associated with the highlighted keyword appear in the lower half of the Index Designer.

The Index Designer can be used to add standard keywords (also known as K-Keywords) and See Also keywords (also known as A-Keywords). See Also keywords are discussed later in this chapter.

2. Type the keyword you want to add in the Keyword text box in the upper right corner of the Index Designer. If you wish, you can add several keywords at once by typing the keywords and separating them with semicolons (but no spaces), such as "Ireland;England;Wales;Scotland;tours;lodging." When you are satisfied with your entries, click Add. RoboHELP adds the new keyword or keywords to the list. As you can see from Figure 8-21, the new keyword is displayed in bold, showing that there are no topics associated with the keyword yet.

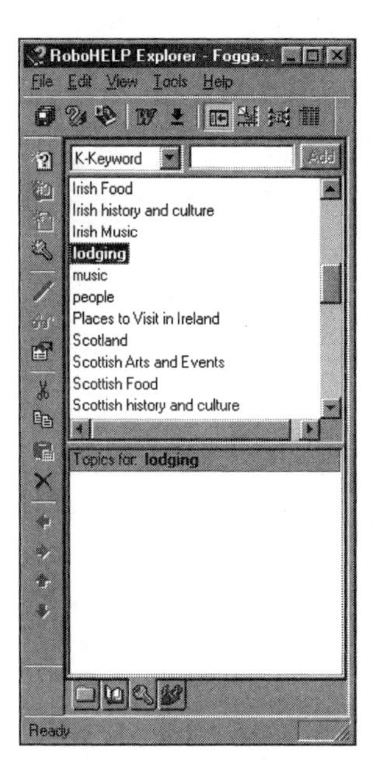

Figure 8-21: Index Designer showing new keyword

With the new keyword added to the list, you now need to associate topics with the keyword, as follows:

1. Right-click the new keyword and select Properties from the right-click menu. (If you prefer, you can just double-click the new keyword.) The Keyword Properties screen appears, shown in Figure 8-22 with some topic selections already associated with this keyword.

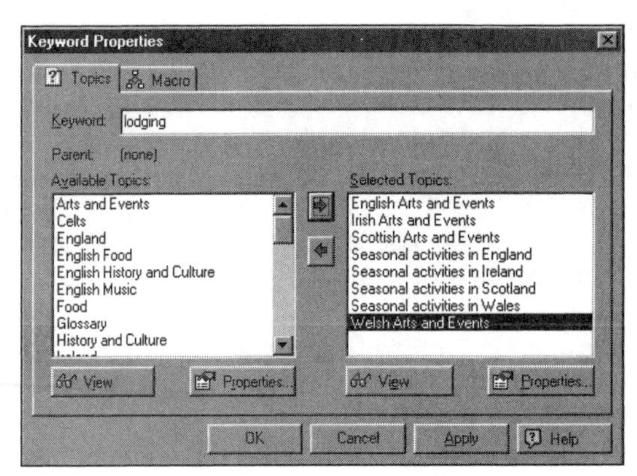

Figure 8-22: The Keyword Properties screen

2. Select a topic from the Available Topics list and click the arrow to move it to the Included in Topics field to associate the keyword and the topic. You can view the highlighted topic in the compiled WinHelp file by clicking View. Click Properties to display the Topic Properties screen for the highlighted topic. When you are satisfied with your entries, click OK. RoboHELP will associate the topics to the keyword (this may take a moment if you've selected a large number of topics). When the association is complete, the associated topics appear in the lower half of the Index Designer, as shown in Figure 8-23.

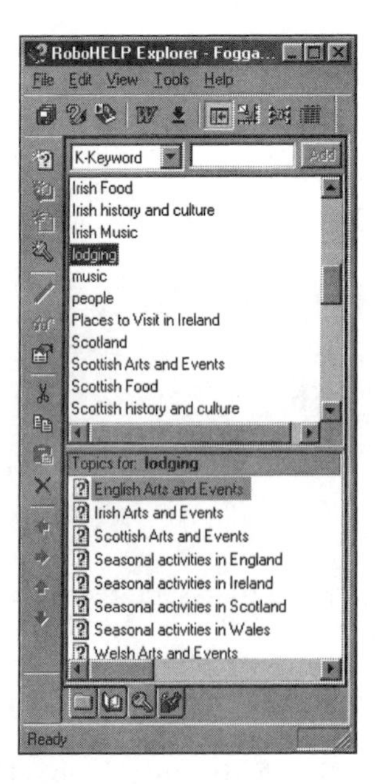

Figure 8-23: Topics associated with a new keyword in the Index Designer

If you prefer, you can add topics to a keyword by dragging and dropping topics from the Topic List in the right pane of the RoboHELP Explorer to the Topics for list in the lower half of the Index Designer. (This is very similar to dragging and dropping items in the TOC Composer, as described in the first part of this chapter.) Topics that are referenced in the Topics list are color-coded blue, making it easy to spot topics that still need to have keywords added.

You can add subkeywords to a keyword by right-clicking the keyword and then selecting the New ➪ Subkeyword command from the right-click menu. RoboHELP positions the subkeyword immediately below the highlighted index entry. You can move subkeywords to the left (this is known as "promoting" a subkeyword) using the Move Left command on the right-click menu or the left arrow on the Edit toolbar on the left margin of the RoboHELP Explorer.

The right-click menu also has some other features that are handy when creating or maintaining keywords. You can create a new keyword with the New ➪ Keyword command, delete a keyword with the Delete command, rename a keyword with the Rename command, and find a topic using the Find Topic screen (described in Chapter 4, "Adding Jumps and Popups").

As with pages in the table of contents, you can associate macros with an index entry. Macros are discussed in Chapter 10, "Understanding Macros."

Using the Smart Index Wizard

The Smart Index Wizard is a tool in RoboHELP Explorer used for automating the creation and maintenance of indexes and keywords. It searches the topics in your WinHelp project based on criteria that you enter to assign keywords. In addition, the Smart Index Wizard can suggest new and existing keywords based on the content of topics. It also lets you copy keywords from one topic to another to speed up the indexing process and to make your indexes more consistent.

To create an index with the Smart Index Wizard, do the following:

1. Select the Tools ➪ Smart Index Wizard command in the RoboHELP Explorer. (If necessary, RoboHELP will prompt you to save any documents that have changed since the last save or compile.) The Smart Index Wizard main screen appears, as shown in Figure 8-24.

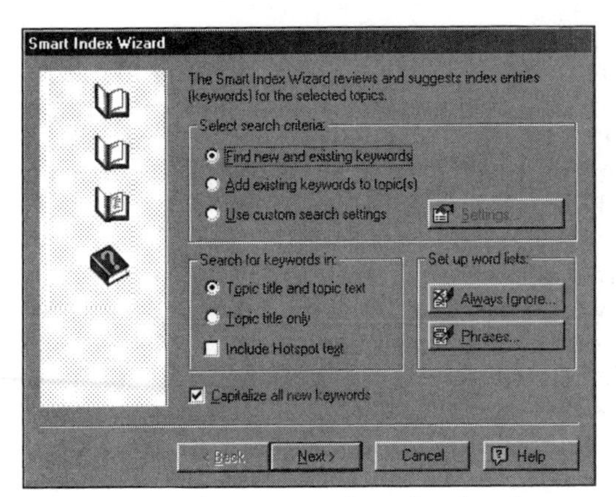

Figure 8-24: The Smart Index Wizard main screen

2. Enter information on the screen as follows:

   - **Find new and existing keywords:** Select this option to add keywords based on the content of the topics using the search criteria you specify. Use this option to create a new index or expand an existing index to add entries for new topics.
   - **Add existing keywords to topic(s):** Select this option to search the topics for existing keywords. When the Smart Index Wizard finds one of the keywords in a topic, it adds the topic to that keyword. Use this option to index a collection of new or expanded topics on a subject that has already been indexed, or to make sure that all existing topics have been indexed completely.
   - **Use custom search settings:** Select this option to create an index using the search criteria you specify through the Smart Index Settings screen.
   - **Search for keywords in:** Select "Topic title and topic text" to have Smart Index Wizard search for keywords in topic titles and topic content, or select "Topic title only" if you want Smart Index Wizard to look only in topic titles.
   - **Include Hotspot text:** Check this to have Smart Index Wizard search for keywords in hotspot text as well as in general body text.
   - **Capitalize all new keywords:** Check this to capitalize the initial letter of any keywords or phrases created by Smart Index Wizard. (This is usually a style decision.)

3. If you wish to search for keywords based on custom settings, click Use custom search settings on the Smart Index Wizard main screen, and then click Settings to display the Smart Index Settings screen, shown in Figure 8-25.

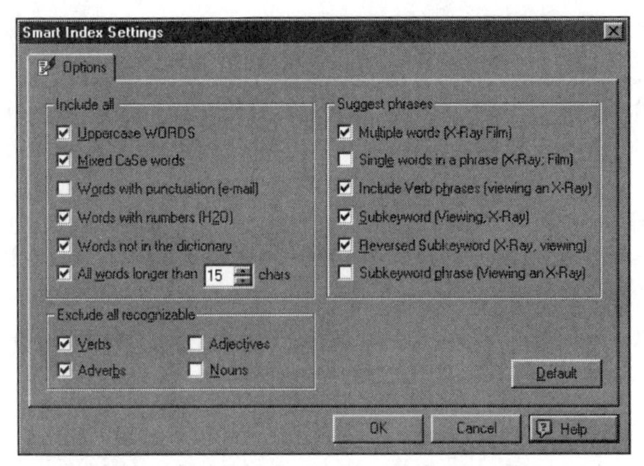

Figure 8-25: The Smart Index Settings screen

4. Select the criteria on the Smart Index Screen to tell Smart Index Wizard what potential keywords and keyword phrases to include and exclude. In general, if an option is not checked, the Smart Index Wizard will not look for that keyword or phrase.

   - **Uppercase WORDS:** Check this to include words in capitals, such as IRELAND.
   - **Mixed CaSe WORDS:** Check this to include mixed case words, such as BritRail. (Words with initial capital letters are not mixed case.)
   - **Words with punctuation:** Check this to include words containing punctuation, such as periods (foggandrizzletours.com), hyphens (Newcastle-on-Tyne), the @ symbol (info@foggandrizzletours.com), slashes (and/or), and so on.
   - **Words not in the dictionary:** Check this to include words that may not be found in a standard dictionary. Smart Index Wizard uses a dictionary program installed as part of RoboHELP Office 2000.
   - **All words longer than _ chars:** Check this to include all words longer than a certain number of characters you set in the associated field.
   - **Exclude all recognizable:** Check the parts of speech you want Smart Index Wizard to ignore: verbs, adverbs, adjectives, and/or nouns.
   - **Multiple words:** Check this to have Smart Index Wizard suggest phrases, such as illuminated manuscript.
   - **Single words in a phrase:** Check this to have Smart Index Wizard suggest the words used in identifiable phrases separately, such as suggesting both illuminated and manuscript from the phrase illuminated manuscript.

- **Include Verb phrases:** Check this to have Smart Index Wizard suggest verb phrases, such as examining an illuminated manuscript.
- **Subkeyword:** Check this to have Smart Index Wizard create subkeywords where there's a relationship between words, such as *illuminated, manuscript.*
- **Reversed Subkeyword:** Check this to have Smart Index Wizard create subkeywords where there's a relationship between words, such as *manuscript, illuminated.*
- **Subkeyword phrase:** Check this to have Smart Index Wizard create a subkeyword from a phrase, such as illuminating a manuscript.

Clicking the Default button will clear any selections and restore the default selections. When you are satisfied with your selections, click OK.

5. To set up an optional list of words and phrases to ignore, click Always Ignore. During indexing, Smart Index Wizard looks in the Always Ignore list for words or phrases that don't need to be indexed. The word or phrase must be an exact match; depending on the indexing criteria you specify, some phrases may be suggested containing words that, by themselves, are ignored. The second Smart Index Settings screen appears with the "Always Ignore" Words tab displayed, as shown in Figure 8-26.

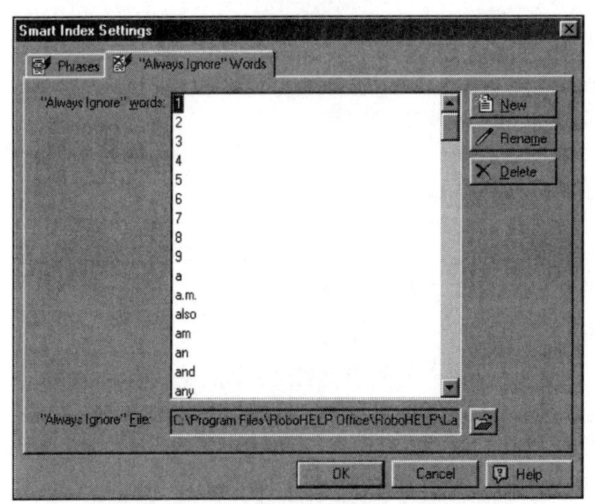

Figure 8-26: The second Smart Index Settings screen showing the "Always Ignore" Words tab

6. Edit the list of words or phrases to ignore. (RoboHELP ships with a standard list of words and phrases that are commonly ignored during indexing.) When you are satisfied with your changes, click OK.

The information for the Always Ignore list is stored in a text file named ALWYSIGN.WLF. Although you'll usually use the "Always Ignore" Words tab to edit the word list, you can edit this file directly with a text editor or word processor and also share the file with other WinHelp authors. You can use a different Always Ignore file by entering the drive and directory in the Phrase File field at the bottom of the screen or browse for it by clicking Browse. (The new Always Ignore file must have the same name and extension as the file it's replacing.)

7. To set up an optional list of specific phrases to search for, click Phrases. The second Smart Index Settings screen appears with the Phrases tab displayed, as shown in Figure 8-27. Phrases entered in lowercase letters are not case-sensitive, but mixed-case or all uppercase entries in the phrase list are case sensitive.

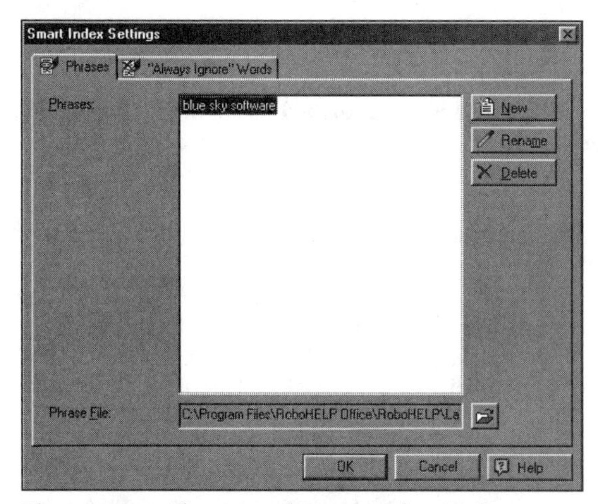

Figure 8-27: The second Smart Index Settings screen showing the Phrases tab

8. Edit the list of phrases to search for. (RoboHELP ships with the phrase "blue sky software" in the list.) When you are satisfied with your changes, click OK.

The information for the phrase list is stored in a text file named PHRASE.WLF. As with the Always Ignore list, you can edit this file directly with a text editor or word processor and also share the file with other WinHelp authors. You can use a different phrase file by entering the drive and directory in the Phrase File field at the bottom of the screen or browse for it by clicking Browse.(The new Phrases file must have the same name and extension as the file it's replacing.)

9. Click Next to continue with the indexing process. The second Smart Index Wizard, shown in Figure 8-28, appears.

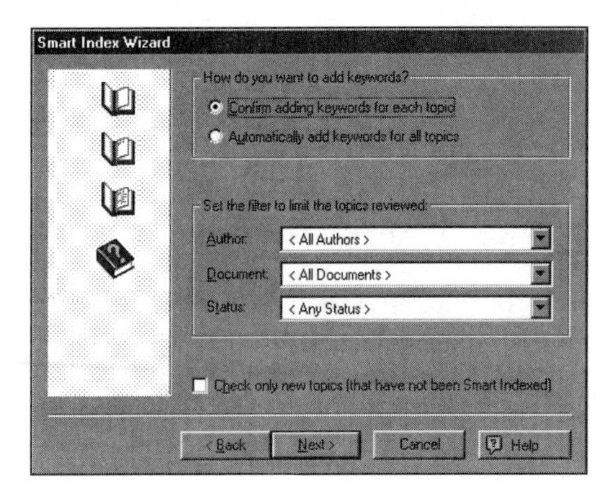

Figure 8-28: The second Smart Index Wizard screen

10. Enter information on the screen as follows:

    - **How do you want to add keywords?:** You can select to confirm the addition of each keyword or to have Smart Index Wizard add keywords automatically.

You may want to confirm keywords the first few times you use the Smart Index Wizard.

    - **Set the filter to limit the topics reviewed:** As with many other screens and reports, you can filter the topics to be indexed based on a specific author, document, or project status. Select the options from the drop-down lists.

For more information on assigning authors and setting status, priority, time estimates, and to-do items, see Chapter 15, "Managing Large Projects."

    - **Check only new topics (that have not been Smart Indexed):** Leave this unchecked to search for keywords in all topics, or check this to search for keywords in topics that haven't already been indexed by the Smart Index Wizard. (When Smart Index Wizard searches a topic, it updates the topic status, in the To Do list on the Status tab of the Topic Properties screen, by checking the Ran Smart Index check box. If you want to exclude a topic manually, you can check Ran Smart Index box.)

11. When you are satisfied with your entries, click Next to start the indexing process. Smart Index Wizard starts working through the DOC files in the WinHelp project checking for keywords. If you choose to have Smart Index Wizard automatically add keywords, you will see a status bar and the name of the topic being indexed. (This process can take some time if you have a large WinHelp project.) If you choose to confirm each entry, you'll see a display for each topic, something like the Smart Index Wizard — Topic screen shown in Figure 8-29.

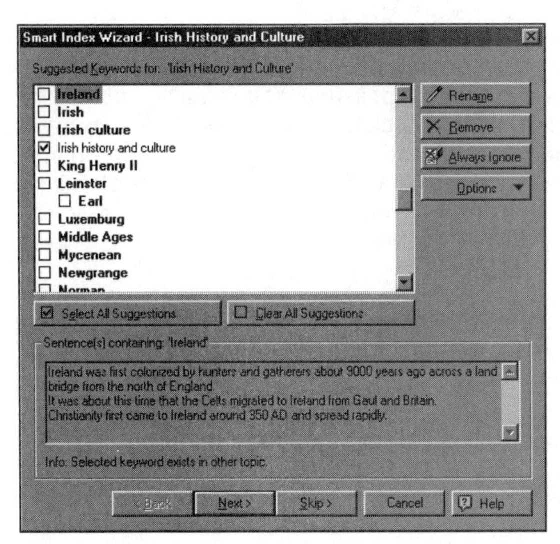

Figure 8-29: The Smart Index Wizard - Topic screen

12. Check the boxes for any of the keywords you want to include for the topic. Any keywords that are already associated with this topic will be checked. Existing keywords appear on the list in normal type; keywords that have not been added appear in bold. When you highlight the keyword, the sentences containing the keyword appear in the lower portion of the screen. To select all the suggested keywords, click Select All Suggestions. Click Next to associate the topic with the keywords you've selected, or click Skip to skip this topic and continue processing the next topic.

There are several helpful indexing options on the Smart Index Wizard - Topic screen. You can rename a keyword by selecting the keyword and then clicking Rename. To remove the highlighted keyword from the list, click Remove. (This won't remove the keyword from any other topics or from the index. To delete a keyword completely, you must delete it in the Index Designer.) You can dynamically add a keyword or phrase to the Ignore list by clicking the Always Ignore button.

The Options button provides you with a variety of options for adding and selecting keywords and suggestions, as follows:

✦ **New Keyword:** Enters a new keyword in the topic list.

✦ **New Subkeyword:** Enters a new subkeyword in the topic list.

✦ **Add Existing Keyword:** Displays the Add Existing Keyword screen (described in Chapter 3, "Creating Your First WinHelp Project") so you can add a keyword to the list that already exists in the index.

✦ **View Topic:** Displays the topic in the compiled WinHelp file.

✦ **Synonyms:** Displays the Synonyms screen (shown in Figure 8-30). From this screen you can look up synonyms and antonyms for the word or phrase so your index can be as complete as possible. You can also enter another word or phrase in the Word field and click Look up to check for synonyms or antonyms for additional words and phrases. (To look for antonyms as well as synonyms, check Antonyms.) To add a new word to the topic's keyword list, click Add to Topic. Click Close to return to the Smart Index Wizard - Topic screen.

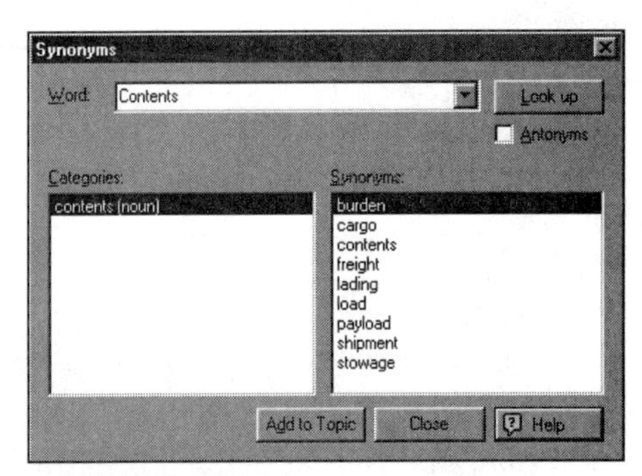

Figure 8-30: The Synonyms screen

✦ **Verbs:** Displays the Add Verb screen. The Add Verbs screen lets you add verbs (usually in the form of gerunds) to the list of common verb subkeywords. As you can see from Figure 8-31, the default list is aimed at software, but you can add other gerunds such as "visiting," "traveling," or "playing" by clicking New and entering a new verb.

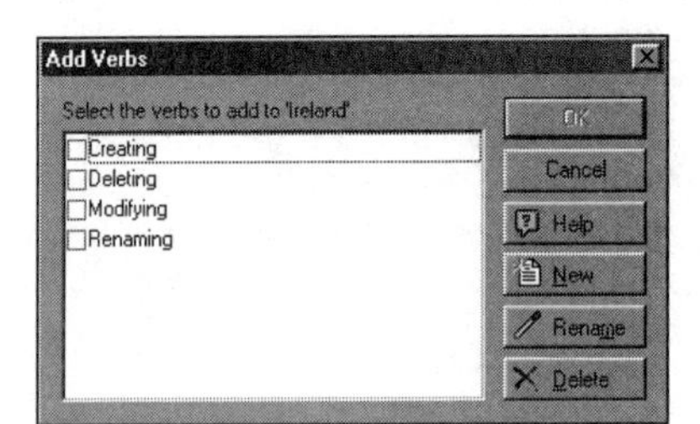

Figure 8-31: The Add Verbs screen

✦ **Auto-Select Suggestions:** Selects all the keyword suggestions automatically, starting with the following topic. This is very useful if you've looked at the first few lists of suggested keywords and are comfortable with automatically selecting the rest quickly. When you display the next topic, all the suggested keywords will be selected. You only need to click Next for each topic to accept all the keywords, but you can stop at any time and edit the lists appropriately. This option will stay in effect until you deselect this option.

✦ **Delete all suggestions:** Deletes all the suggested keywords in the list for this topic.

✦ **Reload suggestions:** Reloads the original list of suggested keywords. This option is useful if you've made a number of changes to the list and want to start over.

✦ **Add Phrase:** Displays the second Smart Index Settings screen showing the Phrases tab, shown earlier in Figure 8-27.

✦ **Add "Always Ignore" Words:** Displays the second Smart Index Settings screen showing the "Always Ignore" Words tab, shown earlier in Figure 8-26.

13. When Smart Index Wizard has completed indexing the WinHelp project, it displays a status screen showing the number of topics reviewed and updated, and the number of keywords that have been added. (This process may take some time, as the properties for each of the affected topics must be updated.) It's a good idea to select the File ➪ Save All command in the RoboHELP Explorer to save the new keywords and topic information, and then compile the WinHelp project and test the index. You can always return to Index Designer or the Smart Index Wizard to re-index some or all of the topics or make other modifications.

Troubleshooting Indexes

Most of the problems you are likely to have with indexes will be easy to fix, such as similar entries that duplicate information, topics associated with the wrong keywords, and so on. You will be able to identify many of these problems using the Index (K-Keywords) report, described in the next section.

There is one problem that will take a little more effort to solve: WinHelp doesn't always display subkeywords correctly. When this happens, the first subkeyword of a multilevel index entry can appear on the same line as the parent (primary) keyword.

This problem is usually caused by having another keyword phrase in the index that begins with the same word as a multilevel entry or by having an unassigned parent keyword. For example, the following entries

```
history
    Danes
    incursion of Christianity
    Picts
history and culture
```

can actually appear like this in the index:

```
history: Danes
    incursion of Christianity
    Picts
history and culture
```

There is a workaround built into RoboHELP, which you can use to fix this bug, as follows:

1. Select the Tools ➪ Fix Subkeywords command from the RoboHELP Explorer. The Fix Subkeywords screen appears (shown in Figure 8-32).

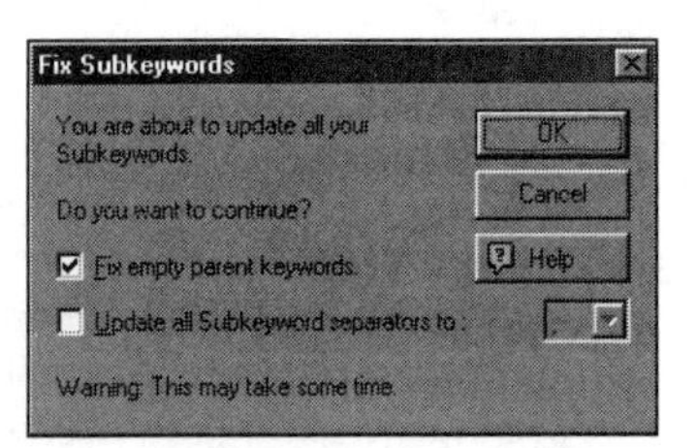

Figure 8-32: The Fix Subkeywords screen

2. Check Fix empty parent keywords to search for and correct parent keywords (keywords at the top level, as opposed to subkeywords) that don't have topics associated with them. You can also update all the keyword separators to either a comma or a semicolon. (You probably won't need to do this unless you're using the RoboHELP Compatibility Wizard to create a WinHelp 3 system.)

For information on the RoboHELP Compatibility Wizard, see Chapter 14, "Using RoboHELP Tools."

3. Click OK to start fixing the subkeywords. RoboHELP examines the K footnotes in each topic. If your WinHelp file is large and there are a lot of multilevel keywords, this may take some time. When the process is completed, RoboHELP will display a message with the number of topics updated.

Printing the Index (K-Keywords) Report

The Index (K-Keywords) report provides you with information about the index keywords for your WinHelp project. You can use this report for checking the keywords and the associated topics. You can also use this report as an easy way to edit the keywords for spelling, grammar, and consistency.

To generate an Index (K-Keywords) report, do the following:

1. From RoboHELP Explorer, select the Tools ➪ Reports ➪ Index (K-Keywords) command. The Index (K-Keywords) report is displayed on the screen, as shown in Figure 8-33. The keywords appear on the report in the order they appear in the index.

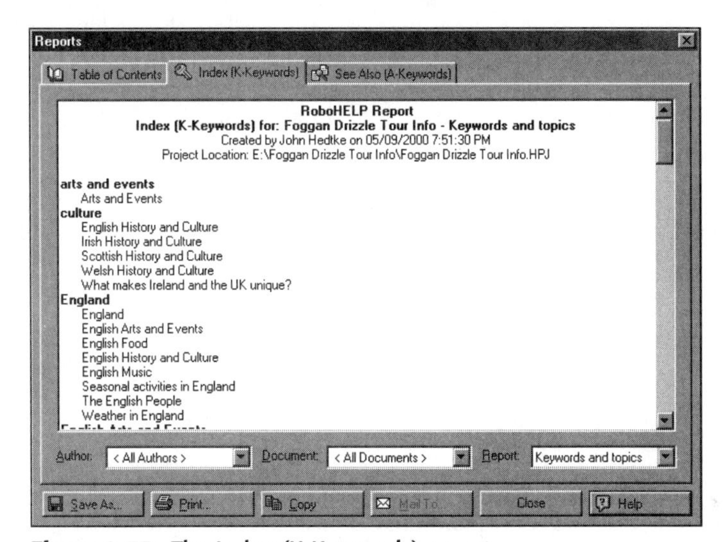

Figure 8-33: The Index (K-Keywords) report

As with many of the other reports you've seen in previous chapters, you can filter the information on the Index (K-Keywords) report in several ways. You can show the keywords created by each author, all authors, or those that aren't assigned to specific authors, depending on your selection in the drop-down list in the Author field. You can also look at the keywords in all the documents in the project or in individual documents with the drop-down list in the Document field. As with other reports, you can switch the topic display between Topic Title and Topic ID by selecting View ➪ By Topic Title or View ➪ By Topic ID in the RoboHELP Explorer.

For more information on assigning authors, see Chapter 15, "Managing Large Projects."

Three different versions of the Index (K-Keywords) report are as follows:

✦ The Keywords report simply lists the keywords and subkeywords in the index. This report is useful for editing your keywords and phrases for spelling, grammar, and consistency.

- The Keywords and Topics report (the version shown in Figure 8-33) lists the keywords in alphabetical order and the topics that are associated with the keywords. This report is useful for identifying keywords that may require additional topics, as well as for spotting keywords that have no topics associated with them.
- The Topics and Keywords report lists the topics in alphabetical order and the keywords that are associated with the topics. This report is useful for comparing similar topics for consistent indexing and for identifying keywords to remove from specific topics.

You can select the report type from the drop-down list in the lower right corner of the screen.

If the Index Designer in RoboHELP Explorer is selected, you can print this report quickly by selecting the File ⇨ Print Index command in the RoboHELP Explorer.

As with other RoboHELP reports, you can run the Index (K-Keywords) report at any time.

Using See Also Links

So far in this chapter, you've seen how to use table of contents entries and index keywords (K-Links) to link topics and provide ways to navigate from topic to topic. This section will introduce you to a third way to find information about related topics: See Also links (also known as A-Links).

The See Also features work in WinHelp 4 only. If you're creating a WinHelp 3 project or a WinHelp 4 project that allows only WinHelp 3 features, you won't be able to create or use See Also keywords or A-Link hotspots or buttons.

See Also links are like cross-references in printed documentation. They point the users to related topics that may be of interest. See Also links are very similar to standard index keywords, except that while K-Keywords are visible in the standard Index screen when you search for a topic, your users never see the actual keywords for the A-Links. You enter A-Link keywords in your topics and then create a See Also hotspot or button that looks for the topics containing those A-Link keywords and displays the topics in a standard Topics Found screen. (A sample of this screen showing topics related to England in the Foggan Drizzle help file appears in Figure 8-34.) From the Topics Found screen, you can select a topic and then jump to it by double-clicking the topic.

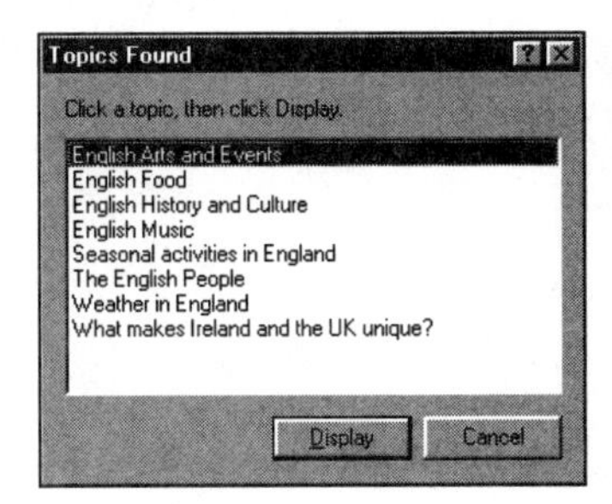

Figure 8-34: A sample Topics Found screen

One of the advantages of using A-Links is that they are dynamically updated when you compile the WinHelp project. If you add See Also keywords to several topics and recompile the project, the new topics will appear in the Topics Found screen for the keywords. This keeps you from having to manually update each hotspot, button, and startup macro that looks for A-Links.

A-Links have several distinct advantages over a direct hyperlink to another topic. First, because the Topic Found screen displays all topics that have the specified See Also keywords, you don't have to guess which topics will be important to your users. For example, if you have a variety of topics that are all broadly related to the concept of entering materials transaction information, you could assign an A-Link keyword of MATERIALS_TRANSACTION to each topic. When you click an A-Link hotspot or button that searches for this A-Link keyword, all the topics will appear in the Topics Found screen.

In addition, although it's possible to add a hard-coded selection of jumps to related topics at the bottom of a topic, this can take up a lot of room on the screen. The Topics Found screen doesn't take up room in the topic screen as a selection of jumps can. Perhaps most important, WinHelp updates the topics to be found so that you don't need to manually update hyperlinks to related topics.

Adding A-Link Keywords

The basic method for adding See Also keywords is similar to adding standard index keywords.

To add See Also keywords, do the following:

1. Place the cursor within the topic (it doesn't matter where), and then select the Edit ➪ Topic Properties command to open the Topic Properties screen. (You can also just press Ctrl+E in Word or right-click the topic in the RoboHELP Explorer Project Manager.) Select the See Also tab in the Topic Properties screen. Figure 8-35 shows the See Also tab with several sample A-Links already added for the Foggan Drizzle help file.

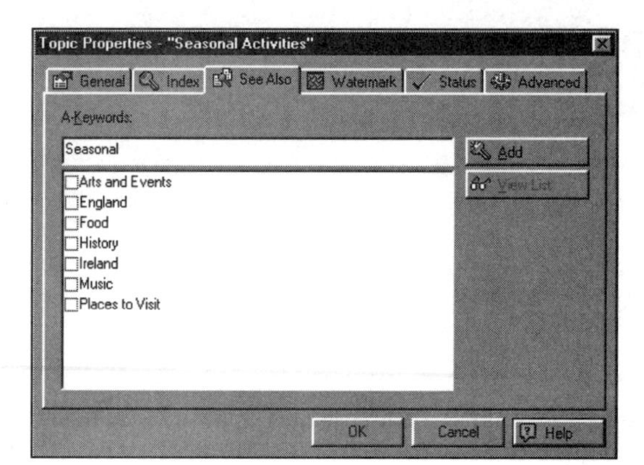

Figure 8-35: The See Also tab in the Topic Properties screen

You can use any words, phrases, or abbreviations as A-Links that you find convenient. A-Links are invisible to the end users of the online help file.

2. Enter a new A-Link keyword in the first field and click Add to add the A-Link keyword to the list. You can also check the boxes for any of the keywords already in the list. Click View List to see the A-Link keywords assigned to the topic already. (An example of this appears in Figure 8-36.) Continue adding new A-Link keywords as necessary.

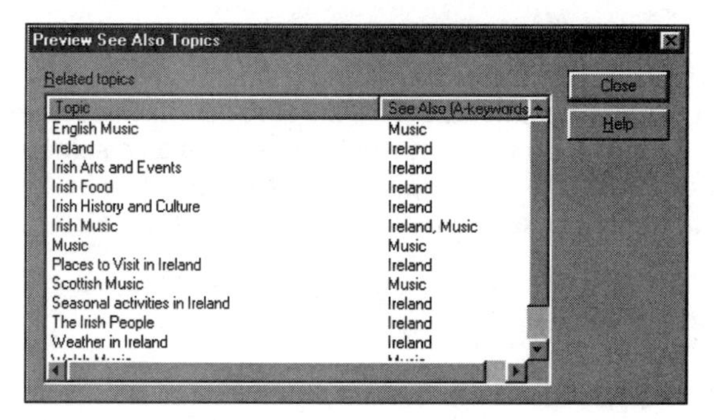

Figure 8-36: A sample list of A-Links

3. When you are satisfied with your entries, click OK. RoboHELP adds the A-Links in an A-Link footnote (with a footnote symbol of "A").

Modifying or removing A-Link keywords for a topic is equally simple: you just open the Insert Help Hotspot screen and check or uncheck the boxes for the appropriate keywords.

Once you have added A-Links to the topics in the online help project, you can add See Also links. The simplest way to add a See Also links is to use the Insert Help

Hotspot screen as you have seen earlier in Chapter 4, "Adding Jumps and Popups," as follows:

1. Position the cursor in the topic where you want to place the jump. Select the Insert ➪ Help Jump command. (Alternately, you can press Ctrl+J or you can click the Help New Jump button on the RoboHELP toolbar.) When the Insert Help Hotspot screen appears, select an action type of See Also. Figure 8-37 shows the Insert Help Hotspot screen with the See Also topics in the online help project displayed.

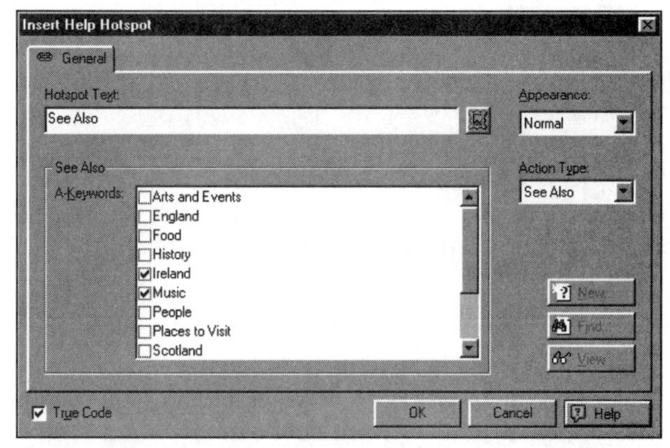

Figure 8-37: The Insert Help Hotspot screen with the See Also links displayed

2. Check the boxes for the A-Links you want to search for. Select the other options you want for the hyperlink.
3. When you are satisfied with your entries, click OK.

When you compile the online help project, the See Also link appears in the topic. When you click the hyperlink, the Topics Found screen appears with all the topics that match the A-Link keywords you specified for the hyperlink. Figure 8-38 shows the Topics Found screen displaying the topics in the Foggan Drizzle help file that have A-Links of Ireland or Music.

You can create A-Link hotspots and buttons the same way you create any other jump. For more information on creating jumps, see Chapter 4, "Adding Jumps and Popups." For more information on creating buttons and hotspot graphics, see Chapter 7, "Getting Fancy with Graphics."

If you use the True Code option, you'll see that RoboHELP is inserting the ALink macro. You can create See Also links directly with the ALink macro, which you can attach to any hotspot, button, or startup macro. Macros are discussed in more detail in Chapter 10, "Understanding Macros."

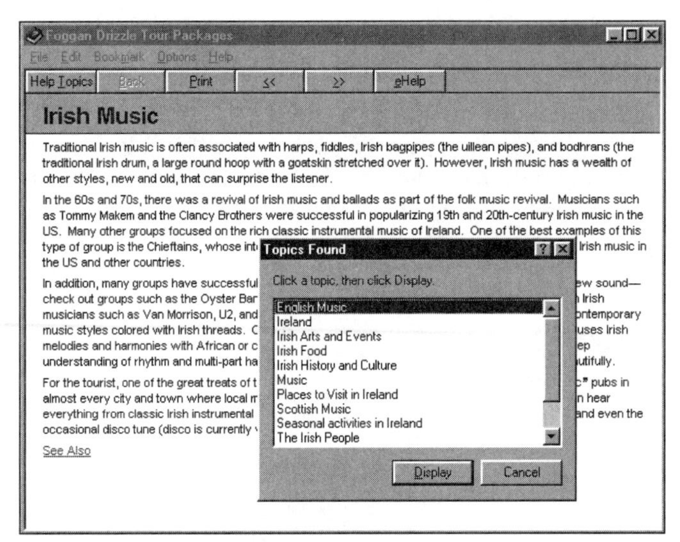

Figure 8-38: A sample Topics Found screen for the Foggan Drizzle help file

If you're using RoboHELP's WinHelp 2000, adding A-Link keywords has an additional effect: whenever the users highlight an entry in the index that has related See Also topics, a small gray box appears that lets you select from the list of related topics. (This is similar to the way the Topics Found screen works.) Figure 8-39 shows the Foggan Drizzle help file in WinHelp 2000 format with the See Also topics for "England" displayed.

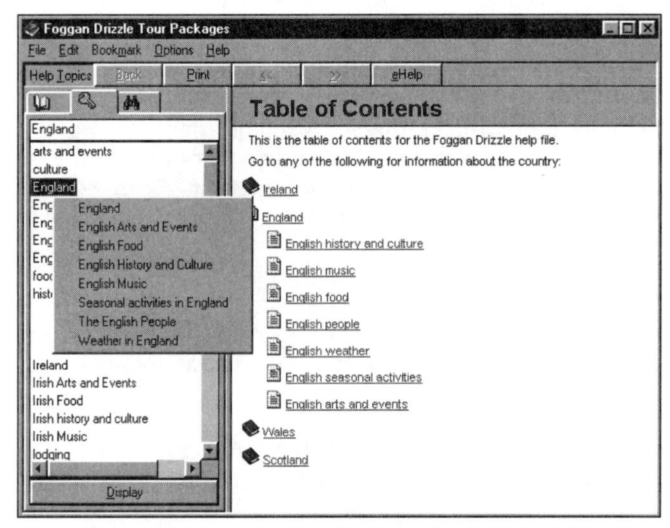

Figure 8-39: The See Also list displayed in the WinHelp 2000 index

Although WinHelp 4 has a limit of not more than 255 A-Link keywords in a single topic, it's unlikely that you will encounter this limit in practice.

Adding A-Link Keywords Using the Index Designer

The previous section showed you how to add A-Link keywords using the standard Topic Properties screen. You can also add A-Link keywords through the RoboHELP Explorer Index Designer, as follows:

1. Select the Index Designer (the Index tab) in the RoboHELP Explorer as shown earlier in Figure 8-20.
2. Select the A-Keyword option from the drop-down list at the top of the screen. The list of A-Link keywords already entered in the file appears in the top window.
3. Enter a new A-Link keyword in the top right field and then click Add (immediately to the right of the field). The new keyword is added to the list, as shown in Figure 8-40.

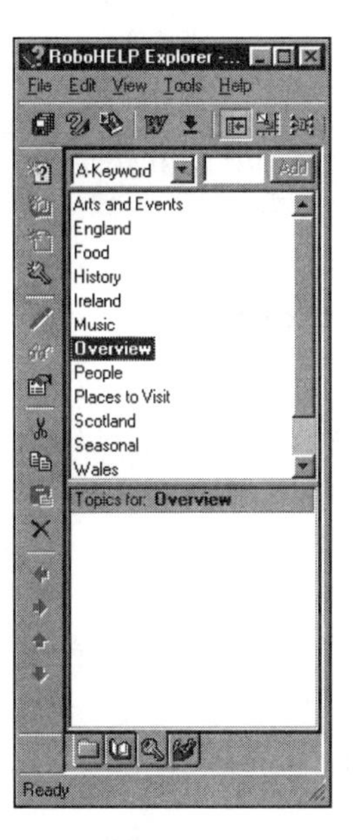

Figure 8-40: The Index Designer with a new A-Link keyword added

Once you've added a new A-Link keyword, you can link topics to it as follows:

1. Right-click the A-Link keyword and select Find Topic from the right-click menu. The Find Topics screen appears (shown in Figure 8-41 with a topic highlighted).

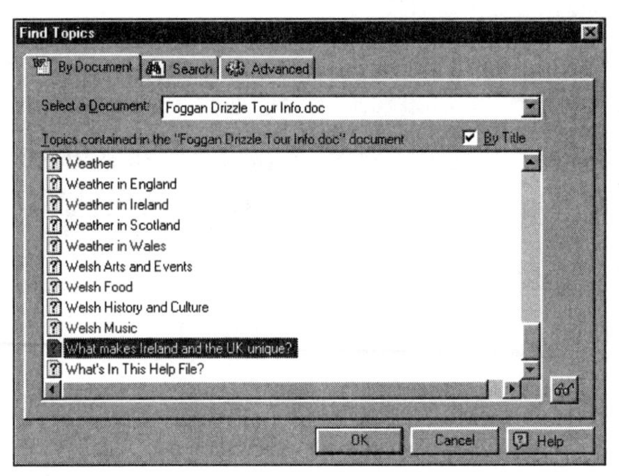

Figure 8-41: The Find Topics screen

2. Select the topic you want to associate with the A-Link keyword and click OK. RoboHELP prompts you to confirm the association. When you click Yes, RoboHELP adds the topic to the topic list at the bottom of the Index Designer. (If you prefer, you can add topics simply by clicking and dragging the topic from the RoboHELP Explorer Link View or the Topic List to the lower window of the Index Designer, similar to adding K-Link keywords as described earlier in this chapter.) Figure 8-42 shows the Index Designer with several topics associated with the new Overview A-Link keyword.

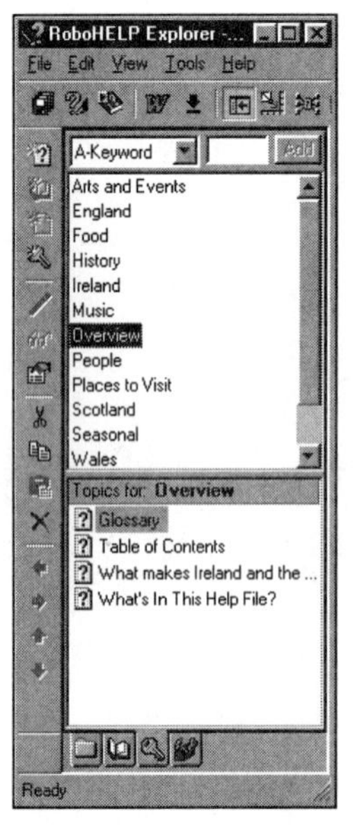

Figure 8-42: The Index Designer with several topics associated with a new A-Link keyword

3. You can continue adding A-Link keywords and associating topics. When you are satisfied with your entries, click OK. Save the file and compile as normal.

You'll need to add the actual See Also hotspots and buttons in the WinHelp file as described in the previous section.

To remove a topic from the list, right-click the topic in the lower window of the Index Designer screen and select Remove from the right-click menu.

You can use the Index Designer to rename an A-Link keyword and automatically update the A-Link keywords in each of the associated topics as follows:

1. Select the Index Designer in the RoboHELP Explorer and select the A-Keyword option from the drop-down list at the top of the screen.
2. Right-click the A-Link keyword you want to rename, and then select Rename from the right-click menu.
3. Enter the new name for the keyword and press Enter. RoboHELP renames the keyword in the Index Designer and then changes that A-Link keyword for each of the associated topics.

If there are a lot of topics and See Also links associated with this A-Link keyword, this may take a little while.

You can also use the Index Designer to delete A-Link keywords, as follows:

1. Select the Index Designer in the RoboHELP Explorer and select the A-Keyword option from the drop-down list at the top of the screen.
2. Right-click the A-Link keyword you want to delete, and then select Delete from the right-click menu. RoboHELP deletes the A-Link keyword from the list and removes the A-Link keywords from the individual topics.

RoboHELP does not ask you to confirm the deletion! Once you select Delete, RoboHELP starts deleting the A-Link keywords from the topics. If you delete the wrong A-Link keyword, you can recover by selecting the Edit⇨Undo Delete Keyword command.

Once you have renamed or deleted A-Link keywords, you must manually change or delete any See Also hotspots, jumps, or startup macros that refer to the changed or deleted keywords. Broken See Also links don't show up in the RoboHELP Explorer Broken Links folder.

Using the Smart See Also Button

The Smart See Also button is a handy feature of WinHelp 2000. When you enable the Smart See Also button, a button appears on the topic button bar that displays related topics.

The main advantage of using the Smart See Also button is that it automatically displays the topics for the A-Link keywords associated with the current topic without your having to specify them. For example, if your topic contains three A-Link keywords and you add a fourth topic, the See Also topic list is automatically updated when you compile the WinHelp project. This means that, unlike See Also hotspots and jumps, you don't need to manually update links when you rename or delete A-Link keywords — everything is updated automatically.

To add the Smart See Also button to your WinHelp project, do the following:

1. Select the File ➪ Project Settings command in the RoboHELP Explorer or select the RoboHELP ➪ Project Settings command in Word. When the Project Settings screen appears, click the WinHelp 2000 tab (as shown in Figure 8-43).

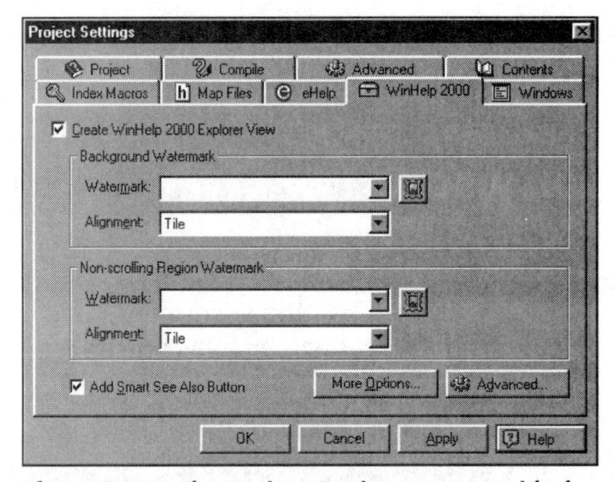

Figure 8-43: The Project Settings screen with the WinHelp 2000 tab displayed

You must be working with a WinHelp 4 project to see the WinHelp 2000 tab.

2. Check Create WinHelp 2000 Explorer View to enable WinHelp 2000. (The Smart See Also button works only in WinHelp 2000.) Also check Add Smart See Also Button at the bottom of the screen.

3. When you are satisfied with your entries, click OK. Recompile the online help project.

Now, when you access a topic that has A-Link keywords, the See Also button appears on the button bar. Figure 8-44 shows the result of clicking this button for the Irish Music topic in the Foggan Drizzle help file. As you can see, the See Also topic list includes all topics that have A-Link keywords of either Ireland or Music.

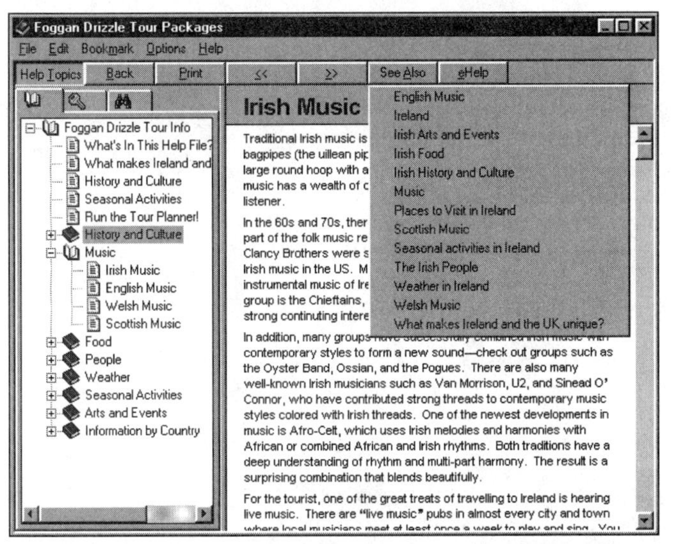

Figure 8-44: The Smart See Also button showing a list of related topics

If the topic doesn't have A-Link keywords, the Smart See Also button will be grayed out on the button bar.

As part of your online help testing, you may want to check with your users to see how effective the Smart See Also button is. Unless they're taught to look for it, the users may miss the Smart See Also button on the button bar. However, it's perfectly acceptable to have a combination of the Smart See Also button and specific See Also links, but remember that you'll need to update the See Also links manually if you rename or delete any of the associated A-Link keywords.

Printing the See Also (A-Keywords) and Unused Index and See Also Keywords Reports

The See Also (A-Keywords) report shows you the A-Link keywords and the topics associated with them. You can use this report to check that all topics appear in the appropriate See Also groups. This report is also helpful if you have a large WinHelp project and you want to combine A-Link keyword groups.

To generate a See Also (A-Keywords) report, do the following:

✦ From RoboHELP Explorer, select the Tools ⇨ Reports ⇨ See Also (A-Keywords) command. The See Also (A-Keywords) report is displayed on the screen, as shown in Figure 8-45. The keywords appear on the report in alphabetical order.

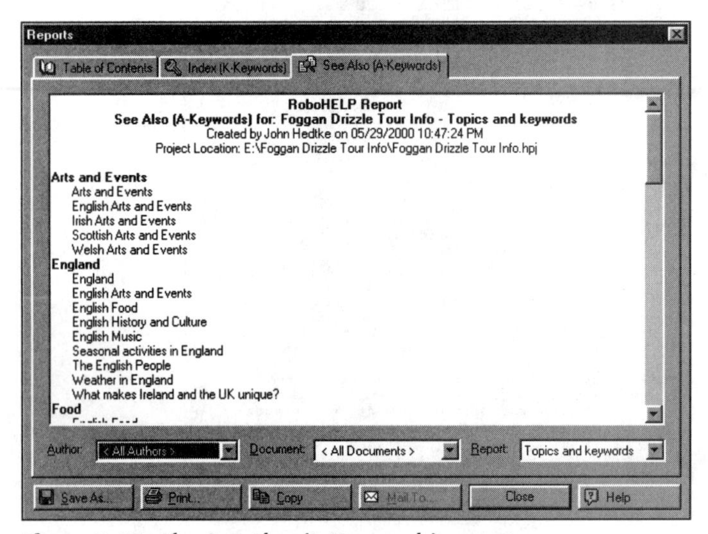

Figure 8-45: The See Also (A-Keywords) report

You can filter the information on the See Also (K-Keywords) report in several ways. As with other reports, you can show the keywords created by each author, those created by all authors, or those that aren't assigned to specific authors, depending on your selection in the drop-down list in the Author field. You can also look at the keywords in all the documents in the project or in individual documents with the drop-down list in the Document field. As with the Index (K-Keywords) report described earlier in this chapter, you can also display A-Link keywords only, show the topics associated with each A-Link keyword, or show the A-Link keywords associated with each topic.

The Unused Index and See Also Keywords report shows you both the index (K-Link) and A-Link keywords that are not currently associated with topics.

For more information on assigning authors, see Chapter 15, "Managing Large Projects."

To generate an Unused Index and See Also Keywords report, do the following:

✦ From RoboHELP Explorer, select the Tools ➪ Reports ➪ Unused Index and See Also Keywords command. The Unused Index and See Also Keywords report is displayed on the screen, as shown in Figure 8-46.

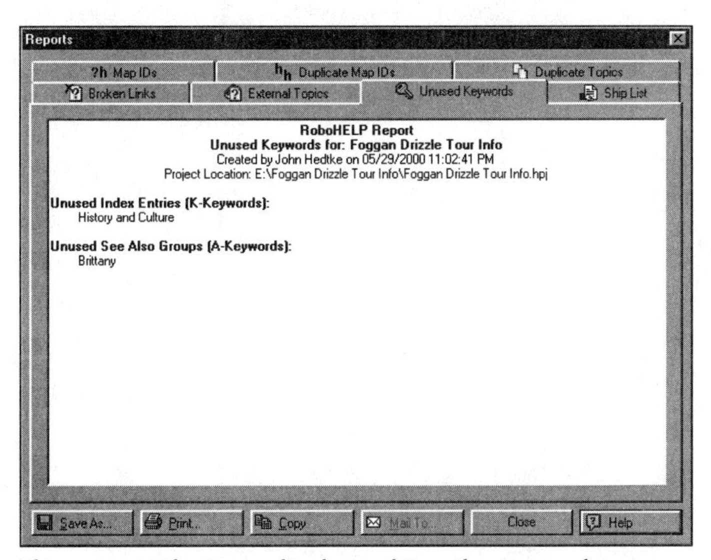

Figure 8-46: The Unused Index and See Also Keywords report

As with other RoboHELP reports, you can run these reports at any time.

Summary

In this chapter, you've learned how to add tables of contents and expand your indexes. You first saw how to add a table of contents screen within the WinHelp file. You next learned how to use drag-and-drop with the TOC Composer to create a table of contents. The chapter continued with information on using the Auto-Create TOC feature to create a table of contents. You also saw how to edit a CNT file using a text editor or word processor. You then were introduced to Master Contents files and how to add external CNT file to a table of contents. The section concluded with information on troubleshooting tables of contents and showed you the Tables of Contents report.

In the second half of the chapter, you saw how to expand and enhance your indexes using indexing tools in the RoboHELP Explorer. The section began with an introduction to the Index Designer to create and maintain keywords using drag-and-drop techniques. You then saw how to use the Smart Index Wizard to automatically create and maintain comprehensive indexes. This section ended with information on troubleshooting indexes, circumventing a known bug in WinHelp, and printing an Index (K-Keywords) report. The chapter concluded with information on adding A-Link keywords and links and printing the See Also reports.

✦ ✦ ✦

Using Help Windows and Browse Sequences

In This Chapter

Understanding the basics of help windows

Displaying topics in help windows

Using help windows with table of contents entries

Setting properties for help windows

Changing the Main window's title

Changing the size and position of help windows

Using help window buttons

Creating new help windows

Understanding browse sequences

Setting the default browse sequence

Creating and maintaining browse sequences manually

Creating and maintaining browse sequences using the Browse Sequence Editor

Linking browse sequences to the table of contents

Troubleshooting browse sequences

This chapter provides you with information on how to display topics in windows and how to create and maintain browse sequences. It starts by describing the basics of help windows and how you can display topics in them. You'll learn to set a default help window for a WinHelp project, identify windows for specific topics, and change the help window used for a topic in a single jump or table of contents. The chapter next discusses how you can change the colors and titles of help windows. You'll also see how to change the size and position of the help windows and use a macro to change the color of the popup window. The first part of the chapter concludes with information on adding buttons to the help window button bars and creating new help windows. The chapter continues with information on browse sequences. You first see how to set the default browse sequence for the WinHelp project. Next, the chapter describes how to create browse sequences manually. The chapter then teaches you how to use the Browse Sequence Editor to simplify the creation and maintenance of browse sequences. After that, you'll learn to create browse sequences that are linked to the table of contents. The chapter concludes with information on how to troubleshoot browse sequences.

Understanding Help Windows

Help windows (also known as display windows or just windows) let you customize the appearance of the topics in your WinHelp files. Up until now, you have seen topics displayed in the default (Main) window, but you can create different types of display windows for different types of topics. In this fashion, you can cue your users as to the type and content of the topic being displayed just from the way the topic appears.

Help windows determine such things as:

✦ Where a topic is displayed on the screen

✦ The background color for the body text and the non-scrolling region

✦ The navigation and feature buttons that appear on the window button bar

There are three basic types of help windows: the Main window, secondary windows, and popup windows. The Main window is the default window. Topics are displayed in the Main window whenever you haven't specified in which window to display a topic. For example, the "Irish History and Culture," "What's In This Help File?", and "Glossary" topics you've already seen in the Foggan Drizzle file have all been displayed in the Main window. You have only one Main window in each WinHelp system.

Secondary windows are other windows that you can use for displaying topics in addition to the Main window. Although you can have one Main window and up to five secondary windows in a WinHelp 3 project and one Main window and up to 255 secondary windows in WinHelp 4 projects, you probably won't use more than two or three secondary windows in all but the largest WinHelp projects. Secondary windows have an important difference from popup windows: they don't vanish when you click the mouse, so you can use them to identify specific types of topics, such as error messages, reference topics, commands, how-to procedures, or company marketing and contact information.

There is a default single predefined secondary window named "Second," but you can rename and modify this window or add more secondary windows as you prefer. Figure 9-1 shows the "What's In This Help File?" topic displayed in the default secondary window. As you can see, the information in the topic is the same, but the display attributes are different: where the Main window has a default color of white and is a medium-large window centered on the screen, the secondary window defaults to a light yellow color and is a smaller, slightly thinner window to the right of the screen.

The size and general appearance of the third type of window, the popup window, is defined automatically by WinHelp. As you saw earlier in Chapter 4, when you click a popup in the WinHelp file, WinHelp displays the topic in a self-sizing window large enough to accommodate the topic title and body text. You can't adjust the size or position of the popup window (as you can with the Main and secondary windows), but you can adjust the background color.

Because popup windows are created as needed by WinHelp, they do not appear in the Window Properties screen with other help windows.

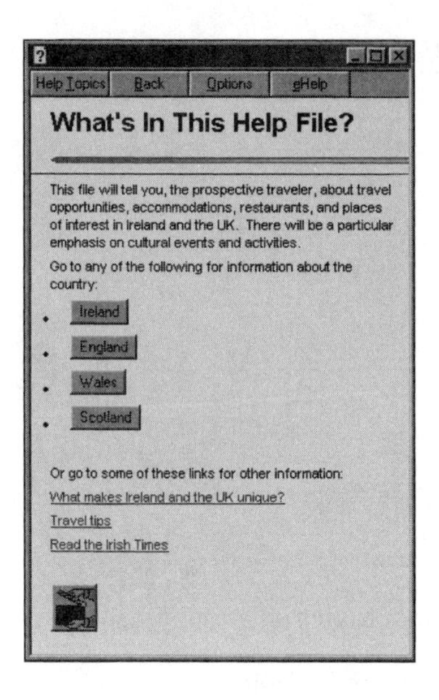

Figure 9-1: Sample topic displayed in the default secondary window

Using Help Windows

Any time you display a topic, you can display it in a specific window. This section shows you how to change the window when you display a topic, when jumping to a topic, and when opening a topic from the table of contents.

Setting a New Default Window

You can set the default window in which to display a topic whenever users access the topic using hotspots, buttons, and the table of contents. (You can subsequently override this default window for specific hotspots, buttons, or tables of contents entries.)

To set a new default window, do the following:

1. Position the cursor in the topic you want to change and select the Edit ⇨ Topic Properties command (or simply press Ctrl+E). Select the Advanced tab (shown in Figure 9-2 with the default secondary window selected).
2. Select the help window from the drop-down list in the Window field and click OK. (All the help windows that have been defined appear in this list.)

Now, whenever the topic is displayed, WinHelp will use the specified help window as the default display window.

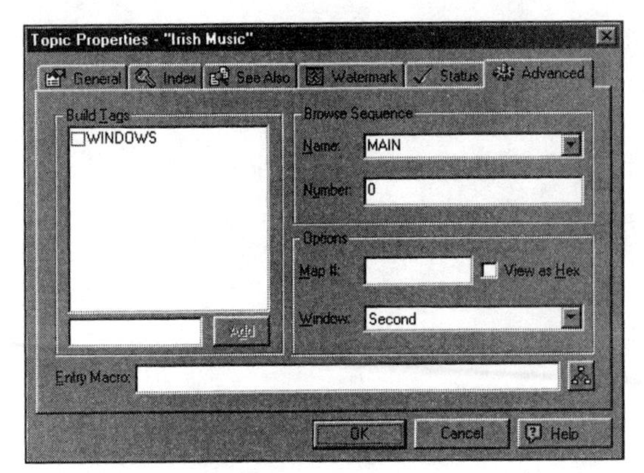

Figure 9-2: The Topic Properties screen showing the Advanced tab

You can also assign a default window to a group of topics all at once, as follows:

1. Select a group of topics in the RoboHELP Explorer Topic List.
2. Right-click the list and select the Default window command from the pop-up menu. The Default Window screen appears (as shown in Figure 9-3).

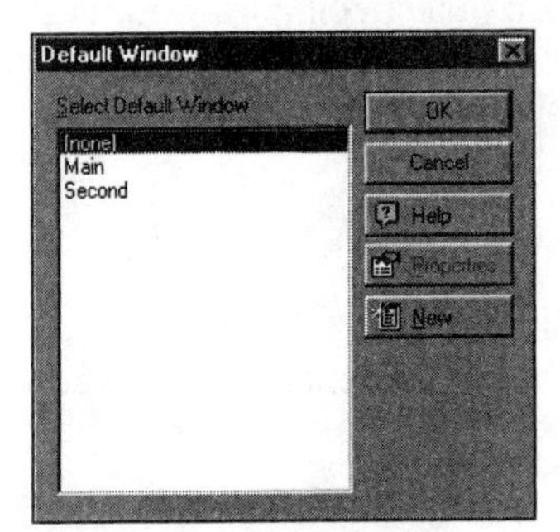

Figure 9-3: The Default Window screen

3. Select the window you want to assign as the default window to the group of topics and click OK. (You can create a new help window by clicking the New button on this screen. You can also edit the Properties for a highlighted window by clicking the Properties button. Creating and editing the properties for help windows are discussed later in this chapter.)

Displaying a Hotspot in a Different Window

You can display a topic in a different window when you open it with a hotspot. This window can be different from the default window set with the Topic Properties screen. To set a specific window for a hotspot, do the following:

1. Position the cursor in the topic and select the Insert ➪ Help Jump command to display the Insert Help Hotspot screen appears (or the Help Hotspot Properties screen if you're modifying an existing hotspot). Figure 9-4 shows a jump with a window assigned to the jump.

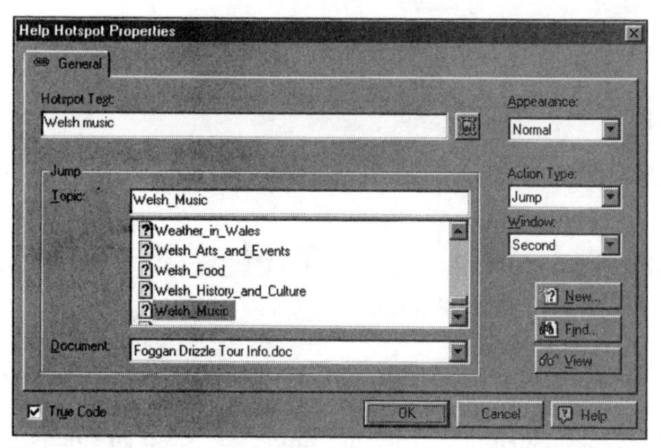

Figure 9-4: The Help Hotspot Properties screen with a help window assigned to the hotspot

2. In the Window field, select the window you want to display the target topic in. You can select any of the defined windows for this help project from the drop-down list, or simply leave this field at (None) to select the default window. Enter information in the other fields in the Insert Help Hotspot screen as usual and click OK.

RoboHELP adds a window to the hidden text for the hotspot. Figure 9-5 shows several jumps in a topic in the Foggan Drizzle file.

As you can see from Figure 9-5, whenever you assign a help window to a hotspot, RoboHELP adds a greater than symbol (>) followed by the name of the window. You could use this technique to manually specify a window type throughout a DOC file using search-and-replace. (Be sure that your changes are formatted as hidden text, also.)

You can use this technique to define help windows for jumps and external topics.

A window assigned to a hotspot will override any default window already set for the topic using the procedure in the previous section.

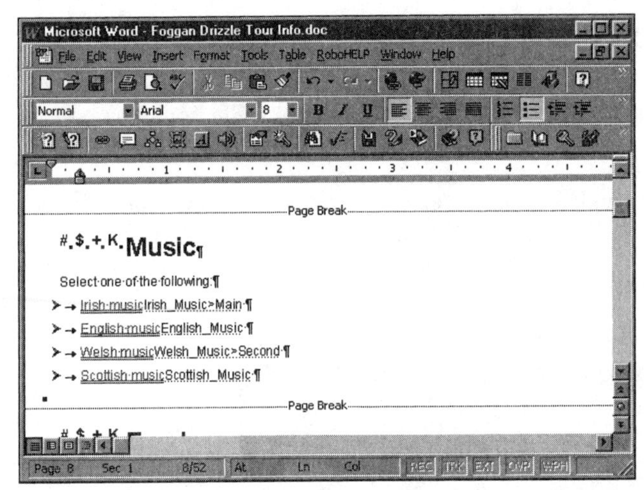

Figure 9-5: Sample jumps with specified help windows

Using Different Windows with Tables of Contents

You can assign a help window to a page in the table of contents, as follows:

1. Start the TOC Composer in the RoboHELP Explorer. Start creating a new page or right-click an existing page you want to change and select Properties from the popup menu, as described earlier in Chapter 8, "Using Tables of Contents and Indexes." Figure 9-6 shows the Page Properties screen with a sample help window assignment.

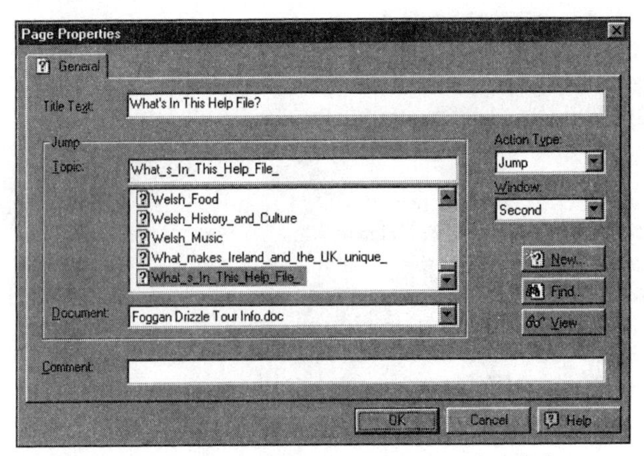

Figure 9-6: The Page Properties screen with a help window assigned

2. In the Window field, select the window you want to display the target topic in. You can select any of the defined windows in this help project from the drop-down list, or simply leave this field at (None) to select the default window. Make entries in the other fields on the Page Properties screen as appropriate and click OK.

If you have not specified a default window at the Topic Properties level, RoboHELP uses the Main window as the default.

When the users now display the topic by clicking on this page in the table of contents, the topic will appear in the help window you've just defined.

You can also set a default TOC window to use for any topics that don't have specific help window assignments, as follows:

1. Select the File ⇨ Project Settings command in the RoboHELP Explorer and select the Contents tab.
2. Select the default help window from the windows defined in this help project from the drop-down list in the Default Window field (as shown in Figure 9-7) and click OK.

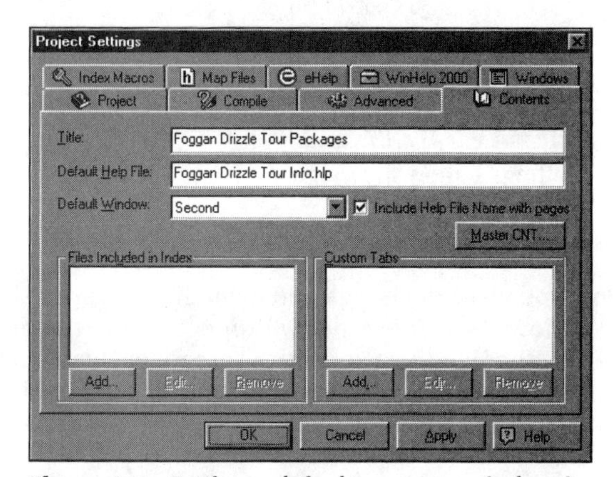

Figure 9-7: Setting a default contents window in the Project Settings screen

WinHelp will use the help window you specify here as the default help window for table of contents entries that don't have a help window specified. (These topics may have a help window selected in the Topic Properties screen or on the Page Properties screen.) Setting a default window at the topic level in the Topic Properties screen will override the default for table of contents entries.

Modifying Help Windows

Each type of help window has a default set of properties. Most of the properties for the Main and secondary windows are set through the Window Properties screen, as follows:

1. Select the RoboHELP ➪ Project Settings command in Word then select the Windows tab in the Project Settings screen. Figure 9-8 shows the Windows tab in the Project Settings screen with the default windows. (You can also select Edit ➪ Windows in the RoboHELP Explorer to go directly to the Windows tab.)

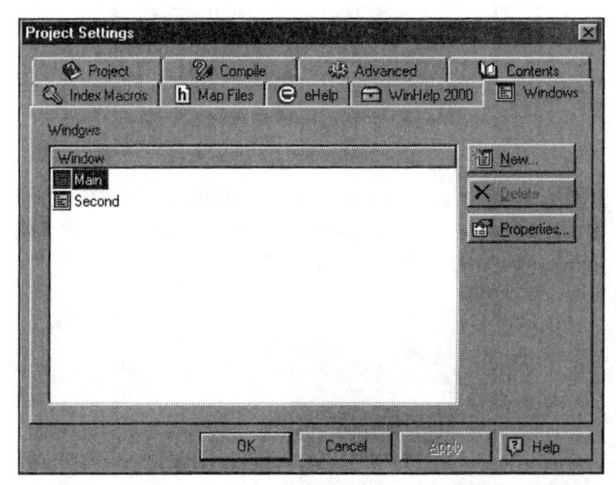

Figure 9-8: The Project Settings screen showing the Windows tab

2. Select the help window you want to change and click the Properties button on the right side of the Windows tab. The Window Properties screen appears, as shown in Figure 9-9. From the Window Properties screen, you can change window colors and titles, adjust the starting window position, and modify the buttons that appear on each window.

The Window Preview section on the left side of the Window Properties screen shows you the way each of the defined windows looks using their current default sizes, positions, and colors. The properties for the current window — the topmost window in the Window Preview section — appear in the various fields on the Window Properties screen. (For example, Figure 9-9 shows the main screen in the Foggan Drizzle file and its current properties.) You can change any of these attributes for any window by selecting the window whose properties you want to change and making the appropriate adjustments.

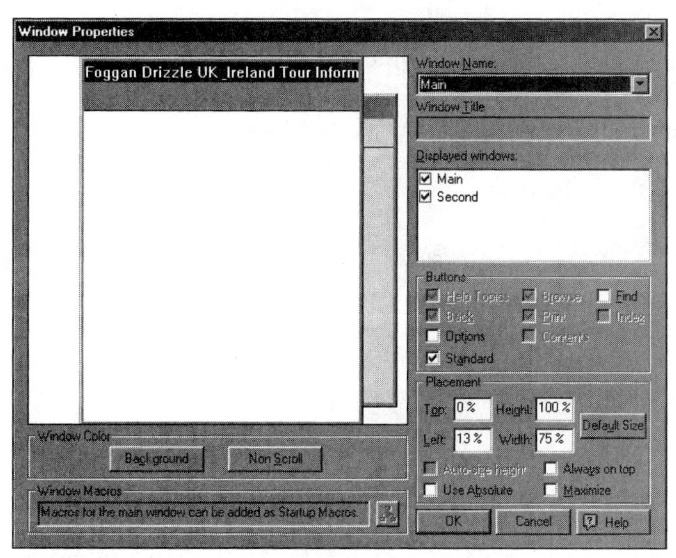

Figure 9-9: The Window Properties screen.

3. Enter information in the fields as follows:

   - **Window Name:** This field displays the name of the selected window. You can select another window either by clicking the window in the Window Preview area or by selecting the window name from the drop-down list in this field. You can't select a window that isn't checked in the Displayed Window field.
   - **Window Title:** Enter the title of the window in this field. (You have already entered a title for the Main window as part of the New Help Project setup procedure described earlier in Chapter 3. You'll see later in this section how to change the title for the Main window.)
   - **Displayed windows:** Check the windows you want to display in the Window Preview area and on the Window Names drop-down list. (This is useful if you have many secondary windows and you only want to view or adjust the properties of a few windows.)
   - **Buttons:** Check the boxes for the buttons you want to appear on the window's button bar. (Buttons and their uses are described later in this section.) You can check "Standard" to select typical sets of buttons for the Main and the secondary windows.
   - **Placement:** Enter the window position in these fields. (Various methods of moving and positioning windows are discussed later in this section.)

- **Window Color:** Click the Background or Non Scroll button to change the color of the selected help window (as described in Chapter 5, "Adding Color, Formatting, and Special Effects").
- **Window Macros:** This field lists the macros associated with this window. You can add, modify, or delete macros by clicking the macro button to the right of the field.

For more information on macros, see Chapter 10, "Understanding Macros."

4. When you are satisfied with your changes, click OK. Details on changing the title of the Main window, changing the default buttons for a window, and changing the opening size and position of a window are described later in this section.

Changing the Title of the Main Window

Although you can change the titles for each of the secondary windows through the Window Properties screen, the title of the Main window is the actual title of the online help project. You change this through the Project Settings screen, as follows:

1. Select the File ➪ Project Settings command and click the Project tab. The Project Settings tab is shown in Figure 9-10.

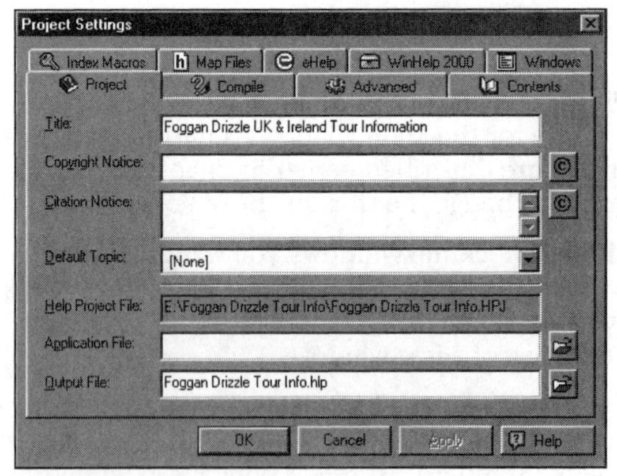

Figure 9-10: The Project tab in the Project Settings screen.

2. Enter the new title for the WinHelp project in the Title field and click OK.

When your users run the WinHelp file, they'll see the new title on topics that appear in the Main window.

Changing Help Window Size and Position

Each window starts with a default size and location, which is shown by the position of the window in the Window Preview section of the Window Properties screen. You can change the size and position of each window in several ways.

The simplest way to change the size of a window is to position it with the cursor (using the same techniques you would for positioning and resizing any other window). In the Window Properties screen, when you move the cursor over the borders of the topmost window, the cursor changes to a double-headed arrow. You can resize the window by clicking and dragging (just like any other window). You can move the entire window by clicking on the title bar of the window in the Window Properties section and dragging the window to its new position. When you release the mouse button after changing the window size or position, the new measurements for the window are reflected in the Top, Left, Height, and Width fields in the lower right corner of the Window Properties screen.

Once you have resized or repositioned the window, click OK. When you recompile the WinHelp project, the resulting WinHelp file will initially display the window with its new size and position. (The users will be able to adjust the windows and positions subsequently as they wish.)

Using the mouse pointer to change the size and position of a window is good for general adjustments, but you may want something more exact; for example, if your WinHelp project runs as part of a suite of programs that appear in specific locations on the screen, you may need the help windows to appear in precise locations. You can enter specific measurements in the Top, Left, Height, and Width fields either as a percentage of the screen measurement or as an absolute measurement, based on the number of pixels.

Entering measurements based on a percentage of the screen is preferable when the WinHelp file will be run on differing screen display resolutions (most commonly, 800 × 600 and 1024 × 768). WinHelp will adjust the help window to fit the screen proportionately.

If you are working with a specific screen resolution, or you want the window to appear in a specific location, you can set window locations using absolute measurements, as follows:

1. In the Window Properties screen (shown in Figure 9-9), check the Use Absolute box in the lower right corner. The measurements in the Top, Left, Height, and Width fields change to pixel measurements.
2. Enter the screen dimensions and location in pixels. (Remember that pixel measurements start at 0,0 in the top left corner of your display.) Again, with either method, you can keep changing properties for this and other windows.

3. When you are satisfied with your changes, click OK to save your measurements. When you compile the WinHelp project, the new window sizes and positions will take effect.

You can always click Default Size to restore the original size and position of any window.

There are a couple other options for help window position you should know about:

✦ If you check Always on Top, topics that are displayed using this help window will always be positioned on top of any other screens currently being displayed on the computer. (The users can subsequently change this option through a window's Options menu.) This option is particularly useful if you have a help window specifically for tips or "how to" procedures and you want to make sure that the users will be able to see it at all times.

✦ If you want the help window to be maximized (occupy the entire screen), check Maximize.

✦ Secondary windows have a special option, Auto-size height, that tells WinHelp to automatically size the height of a secondary windows based on the amount of body text being displayed in the topic. (This option is only available in WinHelp 4.)

Changing the Color of the Popup Window

The only attribute of the popup window that you can change is the background color. The default is for the popup window to use the same color as the background region of the WinHelp file's Main window. There is no straightforward way to change the background color of the popup window, but you can use the SetPopupColor macro to alter the background color.

You can't change the background color for a popup window if you are creating a WinHelp 3 or compatible project. The SetPopupColor macro is only supported with WinHelp 4.

To change the color of the popup window, do the following:

1. Select File ➪ New ➪ Startup Macro from the RoboHELP Explorer. The New Startup Macro screen appears.

2. Enter "SetPopupColor(0,255,255)" in the Macro field, as shown in Figure 9-11. The numbers are the red, green, and blue color components of the color. These tell WinHelp what background color to use. In this example, an RGB value of 0, 255, 255 displays a light blue background. Similarly, an RGB value of 255, 255, 224 displays a light yellow background like the default secondary window color.

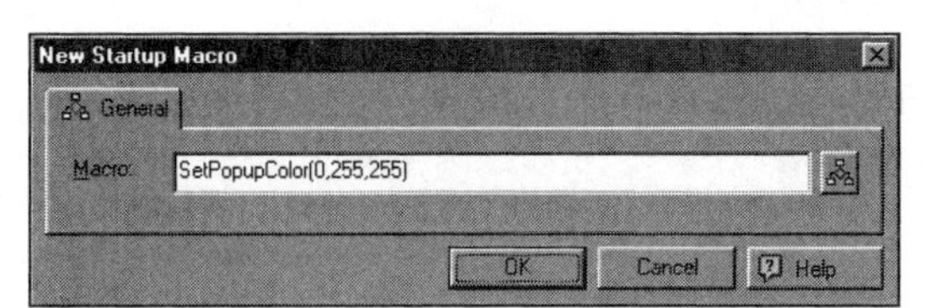

Figure 9-11: The New Startup Macro screen

3. Click OK to save the macro as part of the WinHelp project.
4. When you next compile the WinHelp project, any popup windows will have the new background color. Figure 9-12 shows a topic and the new background color in the popup window.

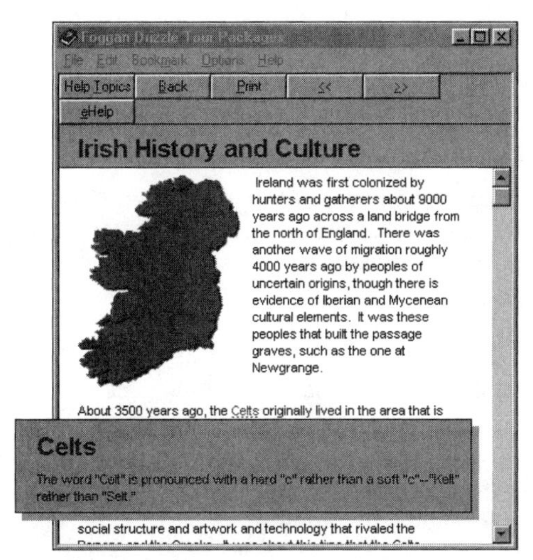

Figure 9-12: Popup window with a new background color

In Chapter 10, "Understanding Macros," you will see how to use the Macro Wizard, which lets you select colors using the standard color selection window rather than having to enter RGB values. The Macro Wizard automates and simplifies the macro creation process.

Adding and Maintaining Buttons

One of the properties you can set for your windows is custom sets of buttons on the button bars. Most of these buttons have already appeared on the button bars of the topic windows you've seen so far in this book.

There are eight buttons that you can select from the Window Properties screen (shown earlier in Figure 9-9), as follows:

- **Help Topics:** This button displays the Help Topics Browser. The default tabs on this screen are the Index and Find tabs. If the WinHelp file has a corresponding CNT file, then the first time you click the button, the Help Topics screen appears with the Contents tab displayed as the default. When you click the button subsequently, the Help Topics screen displays whichever tab was last displayed.
- **Back:** This button takes you to the previous topic.
- **Options:** This button displays the standard help options menu, with the Annotate, Copy, Print Topic, Font, Keep Help on Top, and Use System Colors.
- **Browse:** These buttons let you browse to the previous (<<) and next (>>) topics in the browse sequences.

You must have browse sequences set to use Browse buttons. Browse sequences are discussed later in this chapter.

- **Print:** This button prints the current topic.
- **Contents:** This button displays the Contents tab in the Help Topics screen if the WinHelp file has an associated CNT file. If there is no CNT file for the WinHelp file, clicking the Contents button displays the default topic or the first topic in the WinHelp file.
- **Find:** This button displays the Find tab in the Help Topics screen.
- **Index:** This button displays the Index tab in the Help Topics screen.

The eHelp button is specific to RoboHELP. You turn eHelp on through the eHelp tab of the Project Settings screen. For more information on eHelp, see Chapter 12, "Linking to the Internet and Adding Multimedia."

You can select a standard set of buttons on the Window Properties screen. The standard buttons for a Main window are Help Topics, Back, Browse, and Print. The standard buttons for secondary windows are Help Topics, Back, and Options.

The standard buttons for a WinHelp 3 project Main window are slightly different: Contents, Search, Back, and History. WinHelp 3 secondary windows don't have standard buttons but you can create custom buttons using macros, as described in Chapter 10, "Understanding Macros."

Although WinHelp 4 allows you to have up to 22 buttons on a button bar, you're not likely to want every button on any one window. Buttons, whether standard or custom, should provide your users with a quick way to access the most frequently used features and/or navigation methods. Too many buttons can make it difficult for your users to find what they need. If there isn't room for the buttons on a single line across the window (this happen most frequently when the users resize the help window), WinHelp will stack up rows of buttons as necessary. Figure 9-13 shows you the Main window for the Foggan Drizzle help file with all the buttons selected.

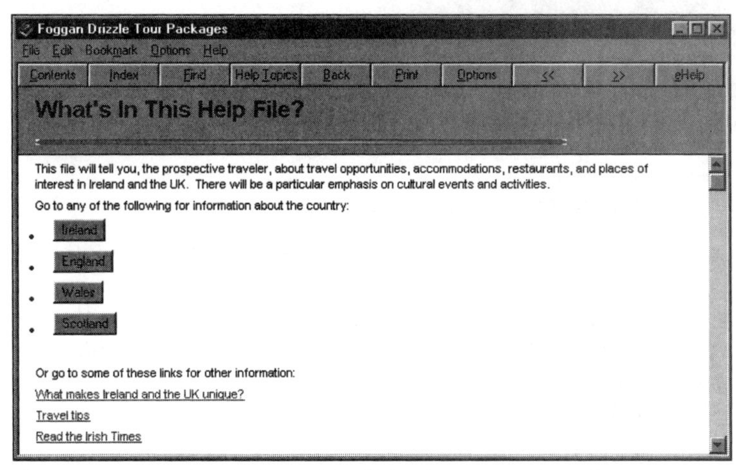

Figure 9-13: Main window with all the buttons selected

In addition to the buttons on the Window Properties screen, you can also create custom buttons using macros. For more information on creating buttons, see Chapter 10, "Understanding Macros."

Creating New Help Windows

RoboHELP comes with two predefined window types, Main and Second, but at some point, you'll probably want to create help windows of your own. You can set up several different secondary windows in a single WinHelp project depending on the types of information you want to display, each of which has separate sizes, shapes, colors, and titles.

Creating a new help window is very simple:

1. From the Windows tab of the Project Settings screen (shown earlier in Figure 9-8), click New. The New Window screen appears (shown in Figure 9-14 with sample information for a new window already entered).

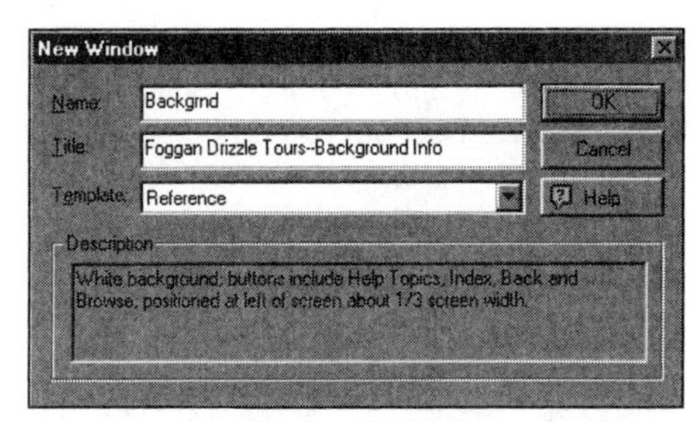

Figure 9-14: The New Window screen

2. Enter information in the fields as follows:

   - **Name:** Enter the name of the new window. This name is limited to eight characters.
   - **Title:** Enter the title of the new window. This is optional, but if you have a single purpose for this help window (such as procedural information), you may want to enter an appropriate title that further identifies the window type, such as the title shown in Figure 9-14.
   - **Template:** Select the template from the drop-down list to use as the model for the new window. RoboHELP has five templates for new help windows, described in Table 9-1. When you select a template, a description of the general appearance and position of the template appears in the Description area of the New Window screen.

If you are creating new help windows in a WinHelp 3 or compatible project, RoboHELP will tailor the window properties to be compatible with WinHelp 3's capabilities. As a result, some help window features listed in Table 9-1 won't be available in the WinHelp 3 versions of the same help windows.

Table 9-1
Window templates

Template	*Description*
Standard Windows 95 Secondary	This window has a pale yellow background. It is set to auto-size height and has the standard buttons for a secondary help window. (The default secondary window in RoboHELP has this format.) The auto-size height feature only appears in WinHelp 4.
Steps	Very similar to the Standard Windows 95 Secondary template, the only difference for this template is that this window has a different width and location. Use this template for procedures and other how-to information.

Template	*Description*
Reference	This window has a white background and has the Help Topics, Index, Back, and Browse buttons in WinHelp 4. (WinHelp 3 uses Contents rather than Help Topics.) The window is positioned at the left of the screen. Use this template for reference or background information such as macros, commands, functions, or other technical data.
Error Message	This window has a white background with no buttons. The window is positioned in the upper right corner of the screen. Use this template for error messages or other brief messages.
Definition	This window has a pale yellow background. It is set to auto-size height and has the just the Back button. The window is positioned in the lower right corner of the screen. Use this window to display definitions, glossary items, and other sidebar information.

3. When you are satisfied with your entries, click OK. RoboHELP creates the new help window and displays the Window Properties screen with the new help window selected, as shown in Figure 9-15.

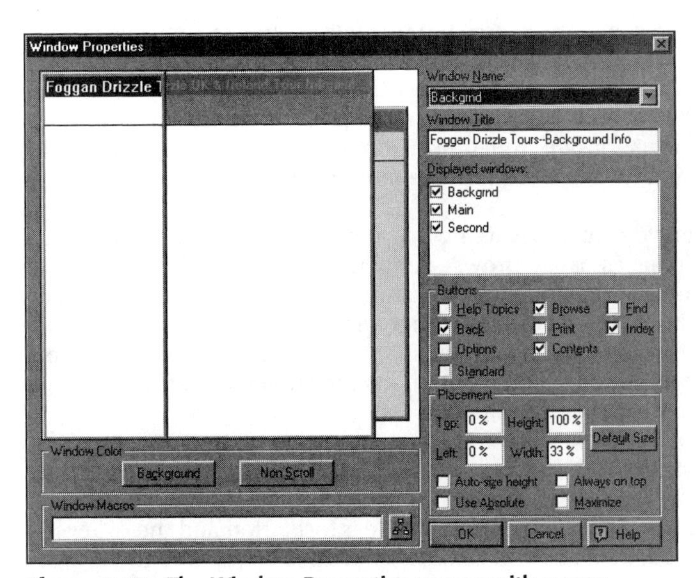

Figure 9-15: The Window Properties screen with a new help window

4. You can modify the properties of the new help window at this point. Click OK in the Window Properties screen, then click OK again in the Project Settings screen when you're ready to save your changes.

To delete a help window, highlight the name of the help window in the Windows tab in the Project Settings screen (shown in Figure 9-8) and click Delete. RoboHELP will ask you to confirm the deletion.

Here are some tips on deleting help windows:

✦ You may find it faster to delete a help window by selecting the window in the Windows folder in the Project folder of the RoboHELP Explorer Project Manager and either clicking Delete or right-clicking and selecting Delete from the right-click menu.

✦ You can only delete a window that's not associated with a topic. If the help window is still associated with a topic, as a default topic window, a default TOC window, or in the hotspot or page properties for a topic, you'll get an error message saying "The window XX is referenced by this Help Project. Referenced windows cannot be removed."

✦ The Main window can't be deleted under any circumstances.

Using Browse Sequences

Browse sequences let your users step through groups of topics very much like paging through a book. You can set up browse sequences that cover a single section of your WinHelp file, such as the topics for the individual fields on a screen or steps in a procedure. You can also set up browse sequences for heading topics at a given level, letting the users skip from one group or another. Figure 9-16 shows you a diagram of the way browse sequences are most commonly created.

In this diagram, you can navigate up and down from the table of contents to the topics using jumps as usual. Browse sequences are useful for navigating from one item to another at a specific level, very much like thumbing through the pages or chapters or a book. In this example, there are browse sequences set up at each of the groups of topics at the bottommost level so you can move from topic to topic. There is also a browse sequence set up for the submenus, so you can quickly browse from one submenu to another.

It's not necessary to add browse sequences to your help files, but they're definitely a good idea. Browse sequences provide one more way to navigate topics. They provide additional cues to the structure of the information and the order in which it should be viewed. Because you can set up browse sequences to let your users page through logically connected groups of topics or menus, they also encourage the users to explore related topics.

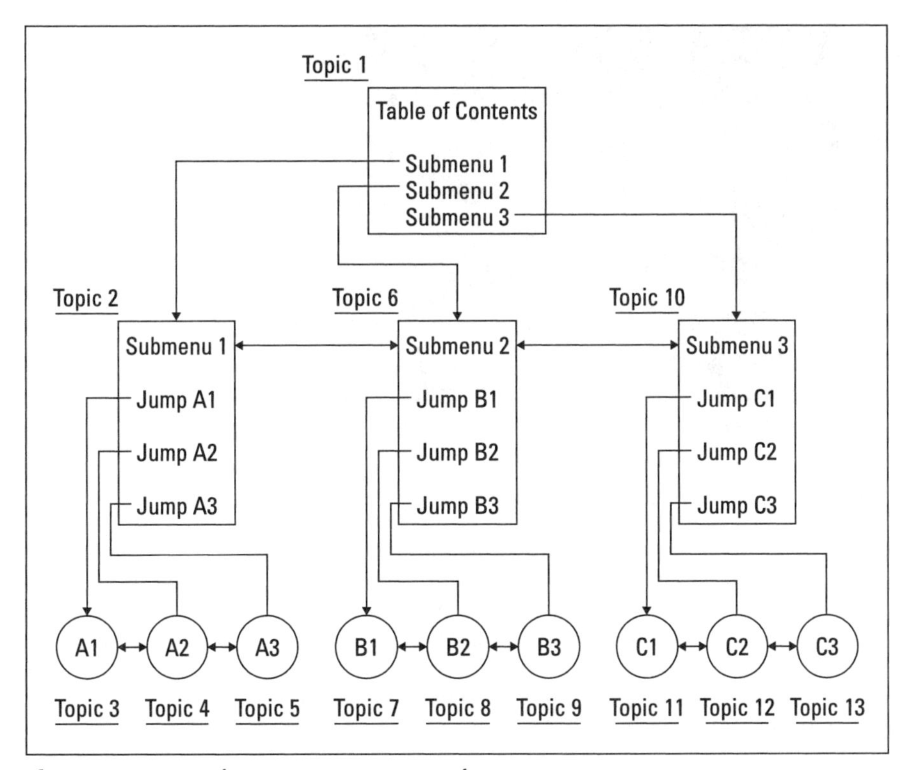

Figure 9-16: How browse sequences work

Setting the Default Browse Sequence

As you saw briefly in Chapter 3, a browse sequence entry in a topic is denoted by a + footnote code. The entry in the browse sequence footnote has a browse sequence string name that uniquely identifies the browse sequence group and a browse number that uniquely identifies the topics order in this browse sequence.

By default, all the topics have a browse sequence string name of `MAIN` and a browse sequence number of 0. (This is because the browse sequence name correlates to the help document: the first document created always has the MAIN browse sequence string name. Subsequent documents take on the browse seqeunce name that matches the document name.) However, you can change the default browse sequence easily, as follows:

1. Select the RoboHELP ➪ Document Properties command in Word. The Document Properties screen (shown in Figure 9-17) appears.

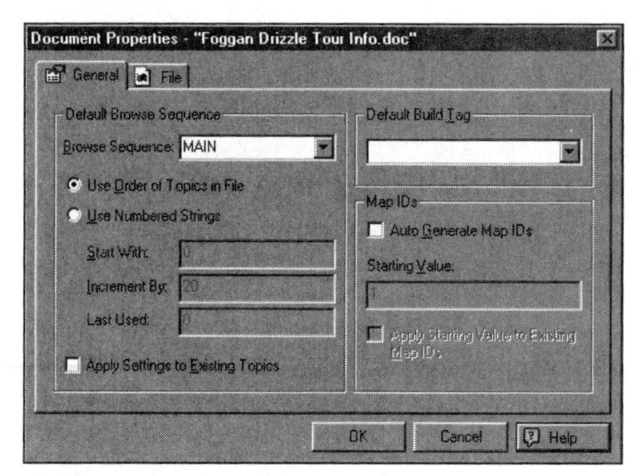

Figure 9-17: The Document Properties screen

2. Enter information on the screen as follows:

   - **Browse Sequence:** Enter the name for the default browse sequence string name. You can also select from one of the existing browse sequence string names in the drop-down list. If you don't want a browse sequence at all, select (No Browse Sequence) from the drop-down list.

If you select the same name for several DOC files, you can browse from topic to topic regardless of the DOC file.

   - **Use Order of Topics in File:** Check this option to use the topics in the order they appear in the WinHelp file. This sets all the topics to the default browse sequence string name and then assigns a number of 0. If you select the same browse string name for more than one DOC file, when you click the browse buttons, you will navigate the topics in the order they appear in the DOC file. If you select this option, the topics will be browsable in whatever order they appear in the DOC file. You can rearrange the topics subsequently without creating conflicts in the browse sequences. For example, if you set up a default browse sequence using the order of the topics in the WinHelp file shown in Figure 9-16, when you clicked the browse buttons, you would move topic 1 (the main menu) to topic 2 (the first submenu) to topics 3 through 5 (A1, A2, and A3), then topic 6 (the second submenu), and so on.

   - **Use Numbered Strings:** Check this option to number the topics in the order they currently appear in the DOC file. (Rearranging the topics subsequently will not affect the browse sequence you have created.) You also need to enter the number to start with and the increment for the browse sequence numbers. The number in the Last Used number shows you the highest number in the browse sequence you've specified.

It's a very good idea to create browse sequence numbers that allow for some growth. For example, instead of numbering topics 1, 2, and 3, you might number them 10, 20, and 30. This way, if you need to add a topic between two of the existing topics, you can do so by numbering the new topic 25. (If you had topics numbered sequentially, you'd need to renumber all the topics to squeeze a new one in.) The default increment is 20.

- **Apply Settings to Existing Topics:** Check this to apply the browse sequence settings you specify to the existing topics. When you click OK, RoboHELP will then renumber all the topics with the browse sequence string name and number you've specified, even if they already had a defined browse sequence. If you leave this blank, RoboHELP will only use the specified options on new topics.

3. When you are satisfied with your entries, click OK.

If you are working on a WinHelp project that already has browse sequences set up, it's a good idea to back up your WinHelp project files before changing the default browse sequence.

Creating Browse Sequences Manually

To create specific browse sequences for a group of topics, you need to enter browse sequence information for the topics. The basic technique for creating browse sequences is to add browse sequence information for each of the topics in the group, as follows:

1. Position the cursor in the first topic in the new browse sequence and select the Edit ⇨ Topic Properties command (or just press Ctrl+E). Select the Advanced tab (shown earlier in Figure 9-2).

2. Enter the browse sequence string name in the Name field. (Once you've entered a name, you'll be able to select the name from the drop-down list when working with subsequent topics.) The name can be up to 50 characters, but it's a good idea to keep the names as short as possible and as long as necessary for easy maintenance and clarity. Don't use the characters !, %, #, +, @, *, =, or > in a browse sequence string name, as they identify other features such as macros, mid-topic jumps, and so on. If WinHelp sees any of these characters in a footnote as part of a browse sequence, it will cause a compiler error and the browse sequence may not work correctly.

3. Enter a number for the browse sequence in the Number field. This number determines where the browse topic appears in the browse sequence. WinHelp displays the topics in order from lowest to highest. When you enter a new browse sequence string name, RoboHELP automatically updates the Number field to `000000`.

WinHelp looks at the browse sequence number and compares it first based on the number of characters and then on the number; for example, topics numbered 8, 44, 310, and 1092, will actually appear in the order 1092, 310, 44, 8, because WinHelp figures out which topic comes next in the browse sequence by comparing the first number in each string followed by the next number and so on. Using leading zeroes so that the numbers appear as 000008, 000044, 000310, and 001092 will ensure that the browse sequences appear in the order you specify.

4. Click OK. RoboHELP enters the browse sequence information for the topic.

You can continue adding browse sequence information to topics using this technique. When you compile the WinHelp project, the browse sequences you have created take effect. When you go to a topic in the browse sequence, the browse buttons are active. (When you're at the first or last topic in a browse sequence, the Previous or Next buttons are grayed out.)

In addition to manually creating browse sequences, you can also use this technique to add an individual topic to an existing browse sequence.

It's also worth noting that when you set a browse sequence for a group of topics, these topics do not appear in the default browse sequence. For example, if you set up a new browse sequence called ENGLAND for topics 7 through 9 in Figure 9-16, the default browse sequence (MAIN) would go from topics 1 through 6, then skip to topic 10 and continue. However, the topics in browse sequences don't need to be in sequential order in the DOC file; you can order the topics anyway you like. For example, in Figure 9-16, you could set up a browse sequence that would go from topic 8 to topic 7 to topic 9, or even topic 12 to topic 6 to topic 2.

Here are some tips for adding browse sequences to your WinHelp project:

- ✦ Each topic can only be included in one browse sequence.
- ✦ When you set up browse sequences, you should plan the groups that will have browse sequences. Make sure that you have include all the items in the group that are relevant. (For example, in the Foggan Drizzle online help, you'd want to have all the topics about Scotland in a single browse sequence, but you probably wouldn't want to include topics on England or Wales.)
- ✦ Make sure that you have Browse buttons enabled on button bars of the help windows you're using to display the topics. There's no point in setting up browse sequences if your users can't access them.
- ✦ Although it's possible to set up browse sequences so that the users can flip from one topic to another through the entire help file, this is probably not the most effective way to provide additional navigation for your users.

✦ If you have set up browse sequences that span multiple DOC files, the order in which topics appear in the default browse sequence will be affected by the order in which the DOC files appear in the WinHelp project. You can rearrange the order of the component DOC files by selecting the Tools ➪ Set Document Order command in the RoboHELP Explorer, and then rearranging the order of the DOC files on the Set Document Order screen (not shown).

✦ Because of the way WinHelp works, if the users browse to a topic by clicking the Browse buttons in the button bar, the topics display in the window of the first topic in the browse sequence. For example, if you displayed a topic that appeared in a secondary window, and then browsed to several other topics, they would all appear in the same secondary window. However, if you then displayed a topic in the Main window and browsed to the same topics, WinHelp would display them in the Main window.

You can examine the browse sequences (without compiling the DOC file) using the Link View. Display the Link View in the RoboHELP Explorer and go to a topic within the browse sequence. The previous and/or next topics in a browse sequence appear above and below the topic currently being examined in the Link View. You can click the previous and next buttons on the Link View to navigate back and forth between the topics. Figure 9-18 shows a sample topic within the Foggan Drizzle file is in the middle of a browse sequence of the Irish topic entries.

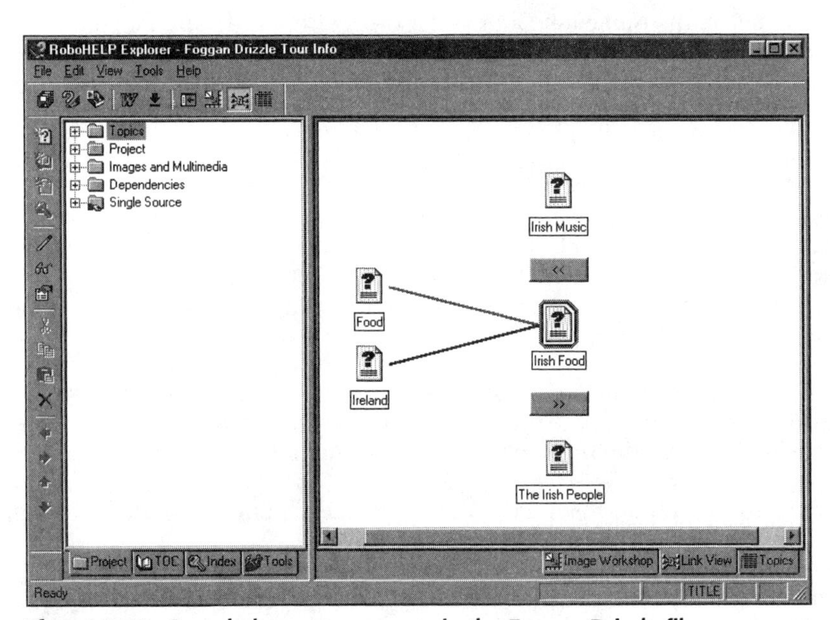

Figure 9-18: Sample browse sequence in the Foggan Drizzle file

For more information on using the Link View, see Chapter 4, "Adding Jumps and Popups."

If you're doing quick maintenance on one or two browse sequence entries, you may just want to edit the browse sequence footnote entries directly in the Word footnote window for the DOC file. The format for the footnote entry is the browse sequence string name followed immediately by a colon, followed by the number. For example, for a browse sequence string name of `WALES` and a sequence number of `001045`, the footnote entry would look like `WALES:001045`. You could also use Word's search and replace feature to change all browse sequence string names; for example, you could search for `WALES:` and change it to `WELSH:` throughout the DOC file.

Making changes to the footnotes directly can be risky, as you are bypassing the normal error-checking features in RoboHELP. You may prefer to edit browse sequence information in the topics Topic Properties screen or using the Browse Sequence Editor, described in the next section.

You remove individual topics from a browse sequence as follows:

1. Position the cursor in the topic you want to remove from the browse sequence and select the Edit ➪ Topic Properties command (or just press Ctrl+E). Select the Advanced tab (shown earlier in Figure 9-2).
2. Right-click in the Name field and select Delete from the popup menu. The information in the Name and Number fields disappears. Click OK, then save the DOC file (the changes aren't final until the file is saved).

Using the Browse Sequence Editor

The previous sections showed you how to create browse sequences and add browse sequence information to individual topics, but this method is relatively slow and cumbersome. RoboHELP has a very useful tool called the Browse Sequence Editor, which can make creating and maintaining browse sequences much easier.

The biggest advantage to using the Browse Sequence Editor is that it lets you design browse sequences in the order that you want them and then the Browse Sequence Editor enters the browse sequence information.

To create a browse sequence with the Browse Sequence Editor, do the following:

1. Select the Tools ➪ Browse Sequence Editor command from the RoboHELP Explorer. The Browse Sequence Editor screen appears. Figure 9-19 shows the Foggan Drizzle without a default browse sequence (MAIN) and with a couple of browse sequences for the individual country topics.

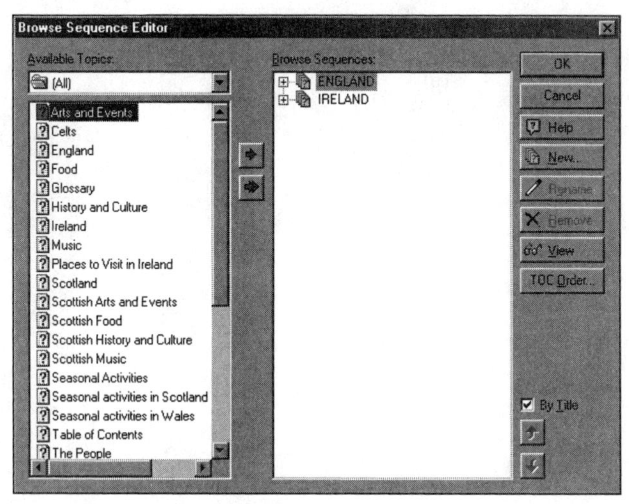

Figure 9-19: The Browse Sequence Editor screen

2. Click New to start a new browse sequence. RoboHELP adds a new browse sequence in the list of browse sequences. Enter a name for the browse sequence.

Now that you've created the new browse sequence using the Browse Sequence Editor, you can add topics to the browse sequence, as follows:

1. From the list of available topics on the left side of the screen, highlight a topic and click the right arrow on the Browse Sequence Editor screen. (You can show all the available topics in the project or the available topics in a specific DOC file by selecting a file from the available topics drop-down list.) RoboHELP moves the topic over to the right side of the screen under the new browse sequence. When you assign a topic to a browse sequence, it is no longer available in the topic list on the left side of the screen.

It's important to remember that the topic is added to whichever browse sequence is highlighted in the Browse Sequences list box. Be sure that you've selected the correct browse sequence before moving the topics.

2. You can continue adding topics to the browse sequence one at a time. Figure 9-20 shows a new browse sequence created called "Menus" that lets the users browse among the individual country menus in the Foggan Drizzle help file. To view a specific topic (to make sure it's the right one), highlight the topic and click View. You can switch from topic titles to topic IDs by deselecting the By Title box in the lower right corner of the screen. If you want to add all the outstanding topics to a browse sequence, click the double arrow. Topics appear at the highlighted insertion point.

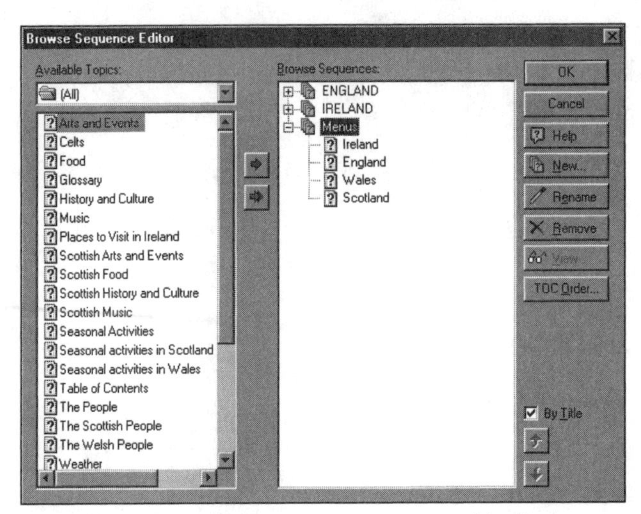

Figure 9-20: New browse sequence created in the Browse Sequence Editor

3. When you are satisfied with your entries, click OK. RoboHELP adds the browse sequence information to each topic. (This may take some time if you have created a large browse sequence.)

Editing browse sequences is straightforward. Move topics by dragging and dropping the topics to their new location in the browse sequence or by highlighting a topic and then using the up and down arrows in the lower right corner of the Browse Sequence Editor screen to move the topic. It's also possible to drag topics from one browse sequence to another—just expand the browse sequences, drag the appropriate topics, and drop them in their new location. If you want to rename an entire browse sequence, highlight the browse sequence name and click Rename, then enter the new browse sequence name.

To delete a topic from a browse sequence, highlight the topic and click Remove. To delete an entire browse sequence, highlight the browse sequence you want to delete and click Remove. (When you delete a topic or an entire browse sequence, the topics reappear on the Available Topics list.)

None of the changes to the browse sequences are implemented in the DOC files until you click OK, so you can continue to make changes or even cancel without affecting the browse sequences in your files.

Creating Browse Sequences Based on the Table of Contents

Regardless of the order of the topics in the DOC files, you can quickly match the browse sequences to an existing table of contents using the Browse Sequence Editor.

Because this procedure will remove all existing browse sequences from your DOC files, it's a good idea to back up your DOC files in case you change your mind about how you want to set up browse sequences.

To create a browse sequence using the table of contents, do the following:

1. From the Browse Sequence Editor screen, click TOC Order. The Auto Create Browse Sequence using TOC screen appears, as shown in Figure 9-21.

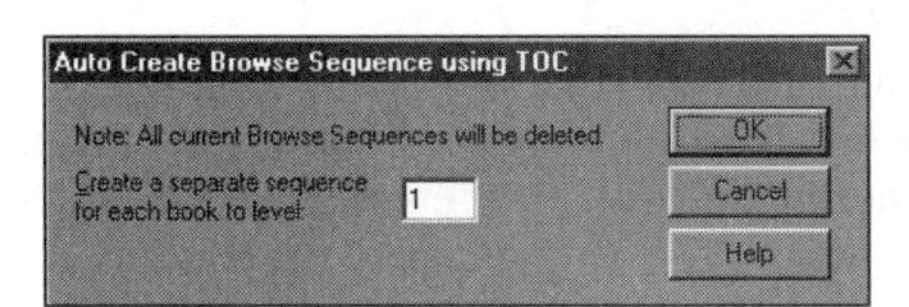

Figure 9-21: The Auto Create Browse Sequence using TOC screen

2. Enter a number (from 0 to 8) of the table of contents level that you want to create the browse sequences for. For example, if you have three levels of books in your table of contents, entering 3 would set up separate browse sequences for the topics in the pages at each level. If you entered 2, however, RoboHELP would create browse sequences only down to the second level of pages in the table of contents. Level 0 is for topics that may be at the first level in the TOC that aren't included in a book.
3. You can make additional changes to the browse sequences as necessary. When you are satisfied with your changes, click OK. RoboHELP will update the browse sequences in the WinHelp project. (Because RoboHELP will need to check each browse sequence number, calculate the next number in sequence, and check that there are no duplicate browse sequence numbers in the file, this may take several minutes.)

If you rearrange the topic order in the table of contents, you will need to make corresponding adjustments to the order of the topics in the browse sequences using the Browse Sequence Editor or manually.

Troubleshooting Browse Sequences

Before you compile your WinHelp project, you can check the order of topics in the browse sequences and make sure that the groups you have defined are complete using the Browse Sequence Editor or the Link View. After you compile the WinHelp project, test the browse sequences by acting like a user: navigate from topic to topic using the Browse buttons. You can make corrections using the Browse Sequence Editor or manually if you prefer.

You can display browse sequence information as part of the Topic References report (described in Chapter 4, "Adding Jumps and Popups") by selecting Browse Sequences as one of the report options. The browse sequence information will be displayed for each topic.

Summary

In this chapter, you learned about help windows and browse sequences. The chapter briefly described help window concepts and how you can display topics in them. Next, you saw how to set a default help window. You then learned to define help windows for specific topics, including defining the help window used for a topic in a jump or table of contents. After that, the chapter continued with information on formatting help windows: how to change the colors, titles, size, and position of help windows. You then learned how to add buttons to the help window button bars and create new help windows. In the second part of the chapter, you learned how to use browse sequence. The section began with information on setting the default browse sequence. Next, you saw how to create browse sequences manually. You subsequently learned to create and maintain browse sequences using the Browse Sequence Editor and to create browse sequences linked to the table of contents. In conclusion, you learned some techniques for troubleshooting browse sequences.

This chapter concludes Part II. You have learned most of the basic skills necessary to create and maintain standalone WinHelp files. In Part III, you will learn about more advanced WinHelp features, such as how to use macros, creating context-sensitive help, embedding multimedia, and creating "What's This?" help.

✦ ✦ ✦

Creating Advanced WinHelp Systems

P A R T

✦ ✦ ✦ ✦

In This Part

✦ ✦ ✦ ✦

CHAPTER 10

Understanding Macros

✦ ✦ ✦ ✦

In This Chapter

✦ ✦ ✦ ✦

This chapter starts Part III, in which you will learn about more advanced WinHelp features, such as using macros, creating context-sensitive help, embedding multimedia, and creating "What's This?" help.

After being introduced to basic macro concepts and how to use the Macro Editor and the Macro Wizard, you will learn how to add startup macros and topic entry macros. You then learn how to add various kinds of hotspot macros, such as macros associated with a specific hotspot, topic button macros, window button macros, table of contents macros, and index macros. You are then introduced to the general process of adding custom macros with DLLs (dynamic link libraries). The chapter concludes with a list of WinHelp macros and a brief description of each one.

What Are Macros?

As you get into the more advanced features of WinHelp, you will want to exercise greater control over its functions and options. One of the best ways to do this is to use macros. Macros are a collection of embedded commands and features that let you create "behind-the-scenes" features and functions, extending the capabilities of your WinHelp files.

You can use macros to customize your WinHelp files in a number of different ways. Some of the things you can do with macros are as follows:

- Search for files on the computer
- Run programs or Control Panel applets from the WinHelp file
- Create, modify, and delete buttons on the help window button bar

- Link to HTML Help, Web pages, or external Web sites
- Add or remove accelerator keys to menu commands
- Embed sound, video, or multimedia files in your WinHelp file

Macros are enormously powerful. In addition to the functions mentioned in this list, you can use macros to register custom dynamic link libraries (DLLs) as part of the WinHelp project. (Registering a DLL tells the computer about the DLL and lets it know where to find the routines that may be used by the online help.) By registering additional routines, you have the ability to add virtually unlimited features and options to the online help files you're developing.

Macros can appear almost anywhere in your WinHelp file. You can set up macros that run at the following times:

- When the WinHelp file starts
- When you display a topic
- When you click a hotspot
- When you click a table of contents entry
- When you click a keyword
- When you click a button on the button bar

There are two parts to every macro: the macro name and the parameter list. The macro name identifies the function to be run, such as `SetPopupColor`, `BrowseButtons`, and `ControlPanel`. The parameter list is a list of parameters (also known as *parms*) that the macro uses. The list of parameters appears in parentheses following the name of the macro. Names, text strings, and some other parameters are usually enclosed in quotation marks, and parameters are separated by commas. For example, the `SetPopupColor` macro takes the red, green, and blue values of the desired background color as parameters, as follows:

```
SetPopupColor(255,255,128)
```

Some macros don't require parameters, though; for example, simply adding the `BrowseButtons` macro to the WinHelp project adds the browse buttons to the window's button bar:

```
BrowseButtons()
```

Even though a macro may not have any parameters, it must still be followed by parentheses.

You can even include a macro as a parameter for another macro. For example, the CreateButton macro creates a button on the help window's button bar. The CreateButton macro in the following example will create a button with the label "Solitaire," which will run the Windows Solitaire program, SOL.EXE, maximized. The first parameter is the button ID, an internal ID that uniquely identifies the button. The second parameter is the text to appear on the button. The third parameter is the macro that runs the Solitaire program when the new Solitaire button is clicked.

```
CreateButton(`Sample_button',`Solitaire',"ExecFile(`sol.exe',`',
SW_SHOWMAXIMIZED,`')")
```

Macro names can be abbreviated; for example, SetPopupColor can be abbreviated as SPC. Macro names aren't case sensitive, either. SetPopupColor, SETPOPUPCOLOR, and setpopupcolor will all work the same. All the following macros will have the same effect, setting the background color of the popup window to a light yellow:

```
setpopupcolor(255,255,128)
SETPOPUPCOLOR(255,255,128)
SPC(255,255,128)
spC(255,255,128)
```

Although macros may look a bit like programming, they're actually pretty simple and easy to understand. Furthermore, RoboHELP makes adding macros very easy by providing two tools to enter macros. The first is the Macro Editor, which is a simple screen for entering macros (shown in Figure 10-1). (You'll learn how to access the Macro Editor later in this chapter.) You can type macros in the Macro field to assign to the hotspot, keyword, or table of contents entry.

If you are entering multiple macros in the Macro Editor, separate the individual macros with semicolons. (The semicolons alert the WinHelp compiler that the one macro has ended and the next one begins.) For example, the following group of macros would set the popup color to a light yellow, toggle the "Help on Top" option, and shift the focus to the Secondary window:

```
setpopupcolor(255,255,128);HelpOnTop();FocusWindow(`Secondary')
```

The buttons at the bottom of the Macro Editor screen let you cut, copy, and paste information, as well as undo and redo entries.

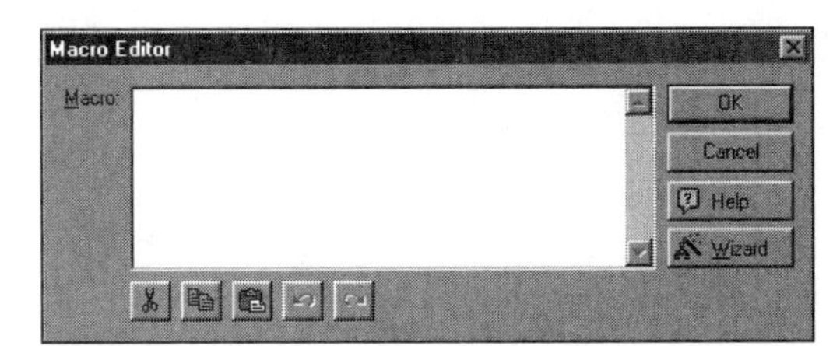

Figure 10-1: The Macro Editor screen

The Macro Editor (which is accessible through a number of places in RoboHELP, including the Insert Help Hotspot screen and the New Macro Hotspot button) is useful for making quick changes to existing macros, for cutting and pasting macros between topics or windows, or for adding macros you're familiar with the syntax of. However, if you're not familiar with a macro or you want the convenience of adding macros through a fill-in-the-blanks interface instead of typing them in by hand, you'll want to use the RoboHELP Macro Wizard (shown in Figure 10-2 with the `ExecFile` macro highlighted).

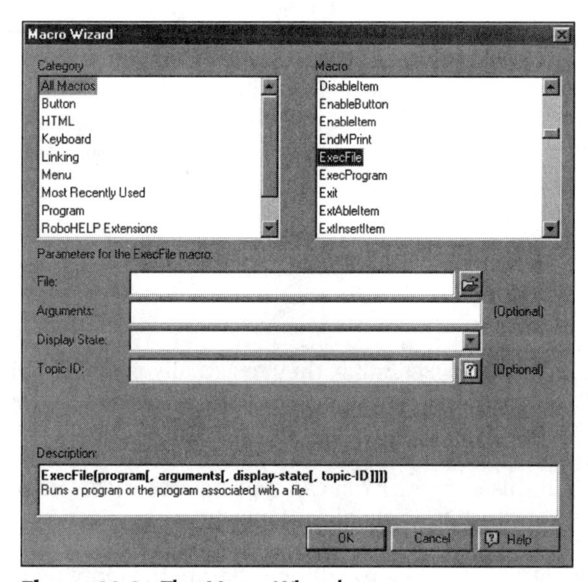

Figure 10-2: The Macro Wizard screen

You can access the Macro Wizard by clicking the Wizard button on the Macro Editor screen. It lets you select the macro you want to add from the Macro list on the upper right of the Macro Wizard screen. You can display all the macros in this list — the default option — or you can select from a group of macros by selecting a category in the Category list on the upper left of the screen. This is helpful if you know that you want to add a specific type of macro, such as a menu macro, and don't want to weed through the entire macro list. You can also use this feature to skim the available macros in a category to see if there's a macro that does what you need. A particularly useful feature is the "Most Recently Used" group in the Category list, which lets you select from the macros that you've used recently in this WinHelp project. (The groups of macros are described later in this chapter.)

The biggest advantage to using the Macro Wizard is that it greatly simplifies the macro creation process. When you highlight a macro in the Macro list, the macro's syntax and a brief description appear in the Description field at the bottom of the screen. The Macro Wizard also displays the fields for each of the parameters. In the example shown in Figure 10-2, there are four fields: the name of the file, the arguments (any information that you must pass to the program you are running such as a user name or file name, or the program start options), the display state (such as hidden, minimized, normal, or maximized), and the topic ID to use. Optional parameters are labeled and you can use drop-down lists or selection screens to choose the appropriate entry for a specific parameter. Most important, you don't have to enter quotes or brackets for the macro (a very common cause of errors when compiling macros). When you use the information you entered in the various fields, the Macro Wizard formats the macro with the correct syntax.

Using Macros

You can create macros that run in three general ways:

✦ **Startup macros:** WinHelp runs startup macros when it opens the WinHelp file. You use startup macros to configure the WinHelp file for optimal operation on a user's computer and to perform specific startup tasks, such as playing music for an opening screen, getting information interactively from the user, or creating and modifying buttons and WinHelp commands based on the programs on a user's computer. Startup macros are also frequently used to register DLLs for use elsewhere in the WinHelp file. Startup macros are listed in the HPJ file and the Startup Macros folder in the RoboHELP Explorer Project tab. As an example, most window macros are startup macros.

✦ **Topic entry macros:** WinHelp runs topic entry macros when the topic is displayed. For example, you could use topic entry macros to add buttons or commands to a specific how-to procedure or to run a multimedia file when users display a topic that provides some sales and marketing information. Topic entry macros are listed in the Topic Properties screen.

✦ **Hotspot macros:** WinHelp runs hotspot macros when users click a hotspot that has an associated macro. This category includes macros associated with hotspots, topic buttons, help window buttons, table of contents entries, and keywords. The macros appear on the appropriate screen for each of these features.

You can link any macro or set of macros to any of these actions. For example, a macro designed to display the topic history or to create a button or run an external program could appear as a startup macro, a topic entry macro, or a hotspot macro, depending on the specific requirements for the WinHelp file.

As you work with macros, you should have a general understanding of how macros and their parameters work, but it's not necessary to memorize lists of macros and exactly how to enter specific parameters. When you need to use a macro, you can look it up in RoboHELP's online help, as well as the Microsoft Help Compiler Workshop online documentation, to get details about how to use it.

Creating Startup Macros

As noted earlier, startup macros are run when the WinHelp file is opened. To add a startup macro to a WinHelp project, do the following:

1. Select the File ⇨ New ⇨ Startup Macro command from the RoboHELP Explorer. The New Startup Macro screen appears (shown in Figure 10-3).

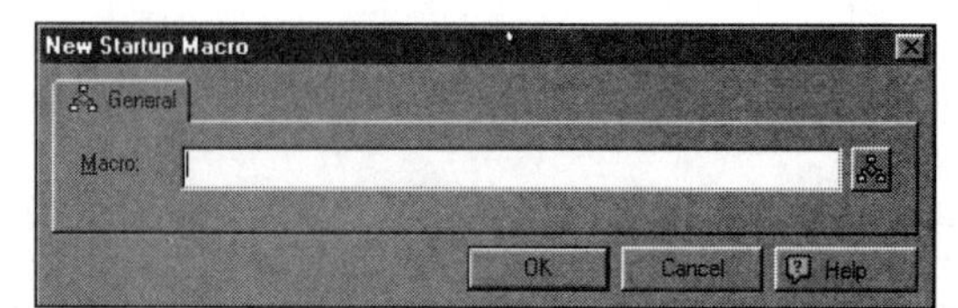

Figure 10-3: The New Startup Macro screen

2. Click the Macro button to the right of the field to display the Macro Editor (shown earlier in Figure 10-1).

If you already know what you want to enter, you can type the macro directly into the Macro field or cut and paste the macro from somewhere else on the New Startup Macro screen.

3. Enter the macro or macros in the Macro field of the Macro Editor. To use the Macro Wizard, click the Wizard button on the right side of the Macro Editor screen. In the Macro Wizard screen (shown earlier in Figure 10-2), select the macro you want to add and enter the information in the various parameter fields. When you are satisfied with your changes, click OK on the various screens you've opened to add the startup macro. The startup macro appears in the Startup Macros folder in the Project tab of the RoboHELP Explorer (as shown in Figure 10-4).

The new macro is added to the end of the list. The list of startup macros in Figure 10-4 shows several registered routines related to accessing and displaying Internet addresses.

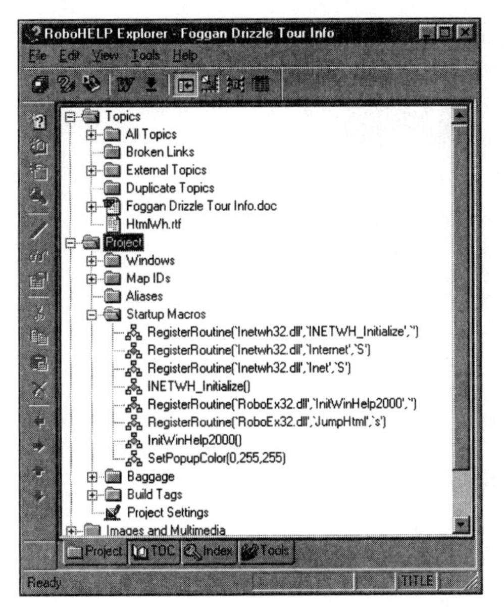

Figure 10-4: The Startup Macros list in the RoboHELP Explorer

You can edit a specific macro in the list as follows:

1. Right-click the macro in the Startup Macros list and select Properties from the right-click menu. (You can also just double-click the macro if you prefer.) The Startup Macro Properties screen appears (identical to the New Startup Macro screen shown in Figure 10-3).
2. You can change the macro's properties (or even change to a different macro) using the Macro Editor and the Macro Wizard as described earlier. When you are satisfied with your changes, click OK.

Deleting a startup macro is simple: Right-click the macro and select Delete from the right-click menu; then confirm the deletion.

Many startup macros are essential for the smooth operation of the WinHelp file. Be aware of what you're doing before you delete a macro and always keep backup copies of the files just in case.

Startup macros are run in the order they appear in the Startup Macros list. Depending on the macros, the order in which they run can dramatically affect the outcome. For example, you might want to register some routines in a specific order because one routine uses another (not uncommon in large WinHelp systems) or because you want to define a custom help window and then shift the focus to this new window. You can change the order of startup macros as follows:

1. Select the Tools ➪ Set Startup Macro Order command in the RoboHELP Explorer. The Startup Macros Order screen appears (shown in Figure 10-5).

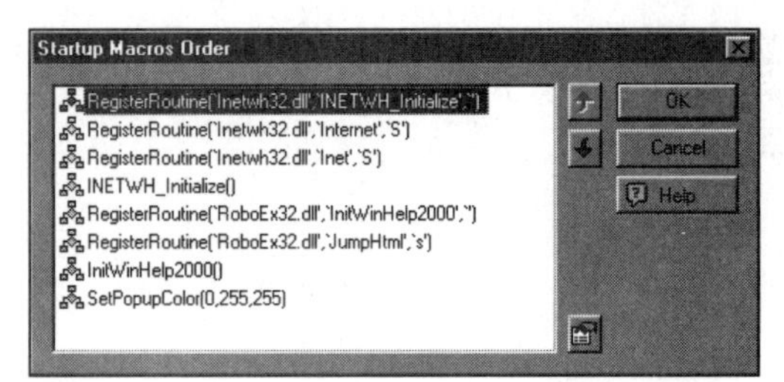

Figure 10-5: The Startup Macros Order screen

2. Highlight the macro whose order you want to change and use the up and down arrows to move the macro to the new location in the list. You can click the properties button in the lower right portion of the screen to edit the macro. When you click the button, the Startup Macro Properties screen appears. When you are satisfied with your changes, click OK.

Startup macros are usually going to affect the entire WinHelp file for such things as registering routines linking to other WinHelp files, and creating custom help windows or custom help buttons and menu options.

Creating Topic Entry Macros

You can create topic entry macros for individual topics. Topic entry macros are run when the topic is displayed. The ! (exclamation mark) footnote is used to indicate a topic entry macro when viewing the topic in Word. Topic entry macros are useful for such things as adding buttons to a specific topic screen or set of screens based on where you've come from in the WinHelp file, starting a multimedia presentation, adding a watermark to the topic, or linking to a file.

You enter topic entry macros to a topic through the Topic Properties screen, as follows:

1. Position the cursor in the topic you want to change and select the Edit ➪ Topic Properties command or just press Ctrl+E. (You can also select the topic in the RoboHELP Explorer, right-click, and select Properties.) Select the Advanced tab (shown in Figure 10-6 with the default secondary window selected).
2. In the Entry Macro field, enter a macro as you did with the Macro field on the New Startup Macro screen earlier. As before, you can click the button to the right of the field to open the Macro Editor and then click the Wizard button to start the Macro Wizard. When you are satisfied with your changes, click OK on the various screens.

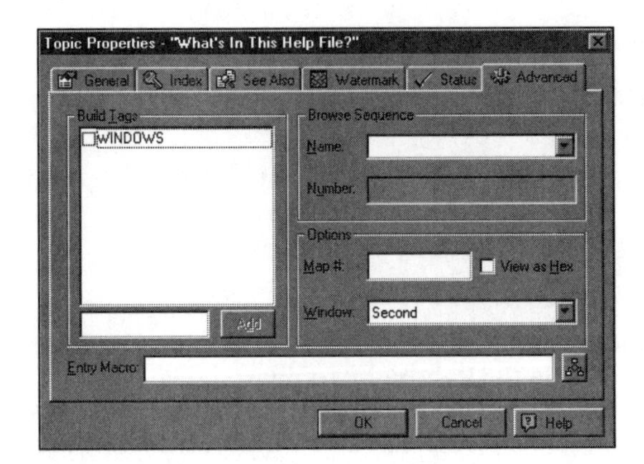

Figure 10-6: The Topic Properties screen showing the Advanced tab

When you recompile the WinHelp project and display this topic, WinHelp will run the macro or macros you have entered for this topic. Some examples of topic entry macros are playing a sound or an AVI file when the topic is opened (such as when doing a product demo), adding a custom button to the window for this topic, or running a program.

To edit the topic entry macros for a topic, display the Advanced tab of the Topic Properties screen as before, and then edit the information in the Entry Macro field. Click the Macro button to the right of the field to open the Macro Editor, and the Wizard button to open the Macro Wizard as needed for the editing process. When you are satisfied with your changes, click OK on the various screens to accept your changes.

To delete a topic entry macro, display the Advanced tab of the Topic Properties screen as before, delete all the text in the Entry Macro field, and then click OK.

Creating Hotspot Macros

The hotspot macro category includes a variety of ways to start macros, including the following:

- ✦ Hotspots
- ✦ Topic buttons
- ✦ Window buttons
- ✦ Table of contents macros
- ✦ Index macros

What all of these have in common is that users must click a hotspot, a button, or an entry to run the macro.

Creating macro hotspots

A macro hotspot is a standard hotspot — text, a graphic, or both — that runs a macro when clicked.

You've already seen a couple of macro hotspots in Chapter 4. The jump to an external topic and the HTML jump both use macros for the jumps.

To create a macro hotspot, do the following:

1. Position the cursor in the topic where you'd like to place the jump and click the New Macro Hotspot button on the RoboHELP toolbar, shown in Figure 10-7. (Alternately, you can select the Insert ➪ Other Hotspots ➪ New Macro Hotspot command.) The Insert Help Hotspot screen appears with the Macro option selected in the Action Type field. Figure 10-8 shows this screen with a macro already entered.

Figure 10-7: The New Macro Hotspot button

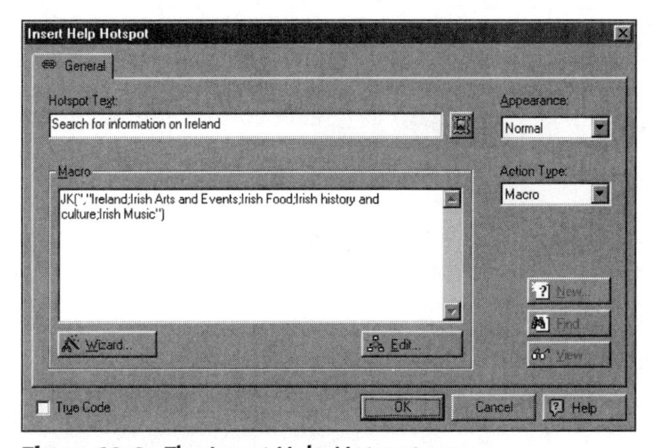

Figure 10-8: The Insert Help Hotspot screen

2. Enter information in the fields as usual when creating a hotspot. Enter the macro or macros in the Macro field of the Insert Help Hotspot screen. If you prefer, you can start the Macro Wizard by clicking the Wizard button or the Macro Editor by clicking the Edit button. When you are satisfied with your entries, click OK on the various screens. Figure 10-9 shows a couple of macro hotspots added to an existing topic in the Foggan Drizzle help file. (The hidden text associated with the hotspots is also displayed in this figure.) The first of these, Travel tips, runs the FDTOURS.AVI file, a multimedia file that is displayed using the default multimedia viewer (usually Microsoft's Media Player). The Exit the Online Tour macro hotspot will exit the online help file.

If the AVI file run by the Travel tips macro hotspot is not available on the users' computers already, it needs to be distributed with the completed WinHelp file. See Chapter 12, "Linking to the Internet and Adding Multimedia," for more information.

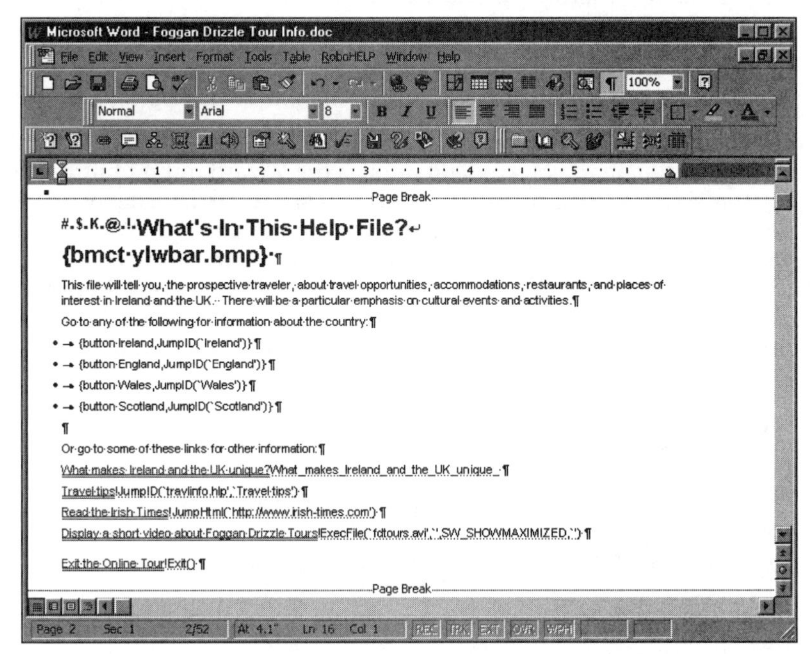

Figure 10-9: Macro hotspot added to the Foggan Drizzle help file

Creating topic button macros

Topic buttons in windows are a specific type of macro hotspot: the `JumpID` macro, which tells WinHelp to jump to a specific topic in the same or a different WinHelp file. In Figure 10-9, the buttons you created in Chapter 7 all use the `JumpID` command to jump to the menu for the various countries in the Foggan Drizzle help file. You could just as easily have the buttons jump to an external topic in a separate file by changing the parameters in the `JumpID` parameter list. For example, if you wanted the first button to jump to a topic called "Ireland_main_topic" in the IRELAND-INFO.HLP file and display the results in the standard secondary window, the information for the button would look like this:

```
{button Ireland,JumpID(`Ireland-info.hlp>Secondary',
`Ireland_main_topic')}
```

Changing the parameters to aim at an external topic is the manual version of using the External Topic action type on the Insert Help Hotspot screen.

Like other macro hotspots, topic button macros don't have to just be jumps. You can add macros to do anything.

To add a topic button macro, do the following:

1. Position the cursor where you'd like the button to appear in the topic and select the Insert ➪ Help Button command. The Insert Help Button screen appears.
2. Select the type of button you want to create — authorable, mini, shortcut, or graphic — and enter the text and other information as appropriate.
3. Select Macro as the action type in the lower portion of the screen. Enter the macro information in the Macro field or click the Wizard or Edit buttons to display the Macro Wizard or Macro Editor. When you are satisfied with your entries, click OK on the various screens to save your changes. When you compile the file, the button appears at the location it was inserted as usual, with the macro or macros you've specified assigned to the topic button. Figure 10-10 shows the Insert Help Button screen for an authorable button, with macro information added for an external topic jump.

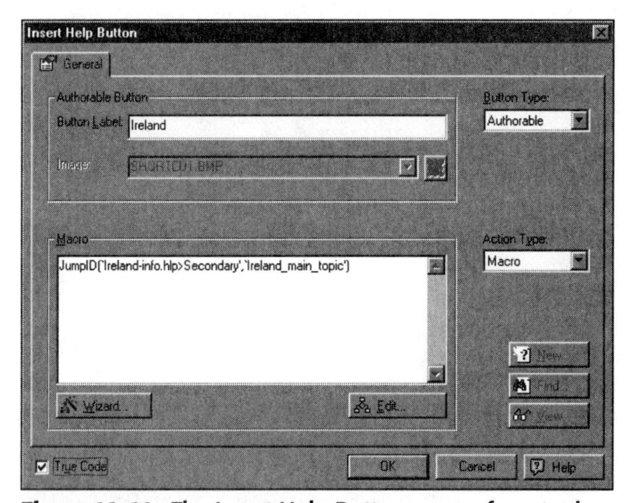

Figure 10-10: The Insert Help Button screen for a topic button macro

For information on creating and maintaining topic buttons, see Chapter 7, "Getting Fancy with Graphics."

Although this example shows how to add an external topic jump macro to a topic button, you can actually assign any macro you like to topic buttons. For example, instead of having a simple text hotspot for the FDTOURS.AVI file shown in Figure 10-9, you would probably want to use a shortcut button with a graphic that cues the users that this is a multimedia file, such as the one shown in Figure 10-11.

Figure 10-11: ACTION.BMP graphic from the RoboHELP clip art folders

Creating custom help window buttons

One of the most popular uses of macros is to customize the help window buttons. You've already seen the effects of one of the simplest macros, `BrowseButtons()` in Chapter 9, "Using Help Windows and Browse Sequences," which adds the Previous and Next browse buttons to the button bar. You can add other buttons using predefined macros, and you can also create entirely new buttons that are customized for your WinHelp project.

Some of the typical buttons you can create with standard macros include the following:

✦ **Contents:** A button using the `Contents()` macro displays the Contents tab of the Help Topics screen or the default topic in the WinHelp file.

✦ **Exit:** A button using the `Exit()` macro exits the WinHelp file. (This is the same as selecting the File ➪ Exit command in the WinHelp file.)

✦ **Find:** A button using the `Find()` macro displays the Find tab of the Help Topics screen.

✦ **History:** A button using the `History()` macro displays the history of the last 31 topics viewed in the WinHelp file.

✦ **Search:** A button using the `Search()` macro displays the Index tab of the Help Topics screen.

To create buttons on a help window's button bar, you use the `CreateButton` macro. Macros for the Main window are added as startup macros (as described earlier), whereas macros for secondary windows are usually added through the Window Macros field of the Window Properties screen.

For more information on the Window Properties screen, see Chapter 9, "Using Help Windows and Browse Sequences."

A typical macro for creating a History button would look like this:

```
CreateButton(`History_btn',`H&istory',"History()")
```

This macro could also use the abbreviation for the macro, CB, as follows:

```
CB(`History_btn',`H&istory',"History()")
```

The first parameter in the list is the internal ID for the button, in this case, `History_btn`. You'd use this internal ID in subsequent macros that alter or delete the button you've created. The second parameter, `H&istory`, is the label for the button. The ampersand (&) in this parameter tells WinHelp where to make the following character in the label an accelerator key (also known as a keyboard shortcut) for the button. (In this example, you'd want to use a character other than the "H" because Alt+H already accesses the Help menu.) The third parameter is the macro that's run when the button is clicked: the `History()` macro.

When you're entering information in the Macro Wizard, you must enter the ampersand as part of the button text in the Button Text field.

When you add this macro to the startup macro list for the Main window and compile the WinHelp project, a History button appears on the button bar. Figure 10-12 shows a window in the Foggan Drizzle help file with an added History button and a sample history window displayed.

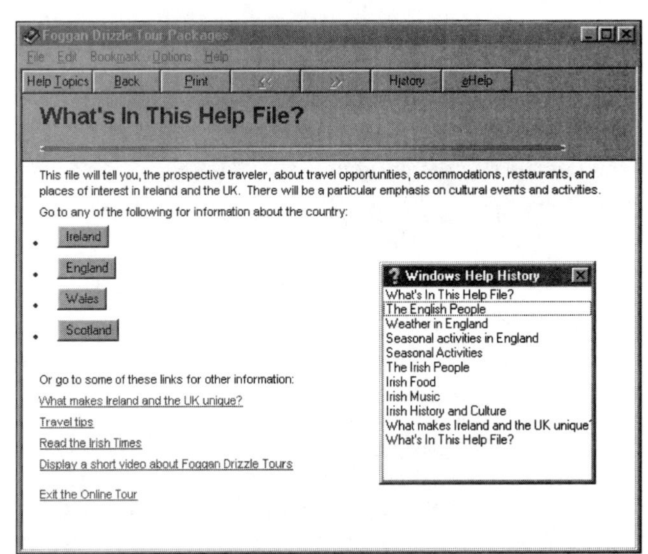

Figure 10-12: The Foggan Drizzle help file with a History button added

Another common button that uses a macro is an `Exit` button:

```
CreateButton(`Exit_btn',`E&xit',"Exit()")
```

This macro creates a button labeled Exit, with the x as the accelerator key. When clicked, it exits the WinHelp file.

If you are entering macros using the Macro Editor, quotation marks must be used correctly in order for the WinHelp compiler to interpret them correctly. A starting single quotation mark is always a slanted quotation mark (the lower character on the key to the left of the 1 key), but the ending quotation mark must be a straight one (such as the quotes enclosing the parameters in the CreateButton macro). Double quotation marks are always straight ones rather than the Word "smart quotes."

Another use of the `CreateButton` macro is to link an external program to a button. You saw earlier in this chapter how to create a button that would start the Windows Solitaire program, SOL.EXE. You could similarly run a travel planning program called FDTOURS.EXE with the following macro:

```
CreateButton(`fdtours_btn',`Foggan
Drizzle',"ExecFile(`fdtours.exe',`',,`')")
```

There are other button macros that allow you to change the macro assigned to a button, disable (gray) a button, or remove a button entirely. These are listed in the section on button macros later in this chapter.

Here are some tips for creating help window buttons:

✦ WinHelp adds custom buttons to the button bar after any standard buttons specified on the Window Properties screen and in the order they're specified. (Use the Tools ⇨ Set Startup Macros Order command in the RoboHELP Explorer to change the order in which the custom button definitions appear in the startup macro list or change the order of the macros in the Window Properties screen if the macros are assigned to a specific window.)

✦ Buttons are automatically sized to fit the button text.

✦ Buttons can have only text in their labels.

If you are creating custom buttons for a WinHelp 3 project, you won't be able to use some of the standard button macros. Check the RoboHELP online help for specific information about which macros are available for use with WinHelp 3 projects.

Creating table of contents macros

You can add macros to pages in the table of contents. These are most commonly used to provide links to multimedia files or external programs such as demos and program wizards.

Perform the following steps to add a page to the table of contents with an associated macro:

1. Select the TOC Composer (the TOC tab) in the RoboHELP Explorer. In the table of contents, right-click the page or book nearest the location you'd like to insert the new page. Select the New ⇨ Page command from the right-click menu. The New Page screen appears.

2. Change the Action Type to Macro. Enter the standard table of contents information as usual. Type a page title in the Title Text field. Enter the macro information in the Macro field or click the Wizard or Edit buttons to display the Macro Wizard or Macro Editor. Figure 10-13 shows the New Page screen with an `ExecFile` macro to run the Foggan Drizzle tour planning program. When you are satisfied with your entries, click OK on the various screens to save your changes.

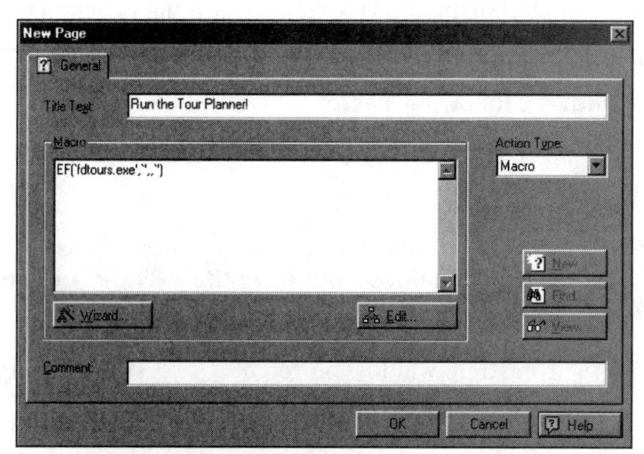

Figure 10-13: The New Page screen with a macro associated with the page entry

RoboHELP adds the page to the table of contents much like when you added other pages to the table of contents (described in Chapter 8, "Using Tables of Contents and Indexes." A macro icon appears to the left of the entry, indicating that this is a table of contents macro (as shown in Figure 10-14). When you compile the project, the table of contents entry appears in the table of contents and looks like any other page.

Because a table of contents macro will do something different than displaying a topic, you should make its title very specific. Use action words such as "run" or "start" to emphasize that clicking this table of contents entry will start a program or display a file.

You can use the standard techniques for modifying and deleting table of contents entries.

For more information on table of contents entries, see Chapter 8, "Using Tables of Contents and Indexes."

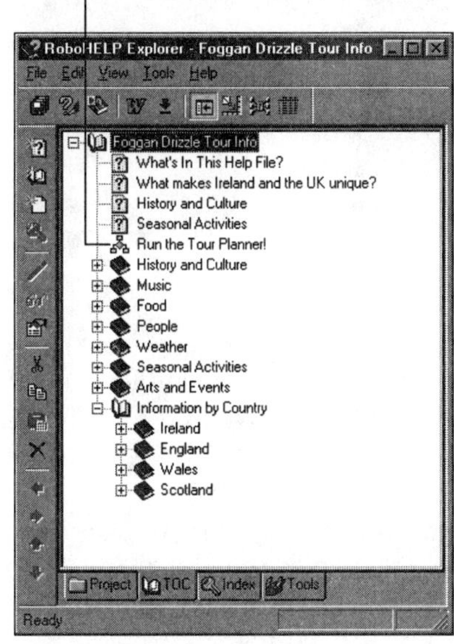

Figure 10-14: A table of contents macro in the TOC Composer

Creating index macros

Index macros have many of the same uses as table of contents macros, although you may also want to include jumps to topics in other help files or to Web sites. Keywords entered through the Topic Properties screen are associated with a specific topic, so you need to use a slightly different procedure from the normal keyword procedure to enter a keyword that has a macro associated with it.

For more information on adding keywords, see Chapter 8, "Using Tables of Contents and Indexes."

To create an index macro, do the following:

1. Select the RoboHELP ⇨ Project Settings command in Word and select the Index Macros tab. (You can reach this directly by selecting the Edit ⇨ Index Macros command in the RoboHELP Explorer.) The Index Macros tab of the Project Settings screen appears.
2. Click Add to add a new index macro. The Index Macro Properties screen appears (shown in Figure 10-15 with sample information added).

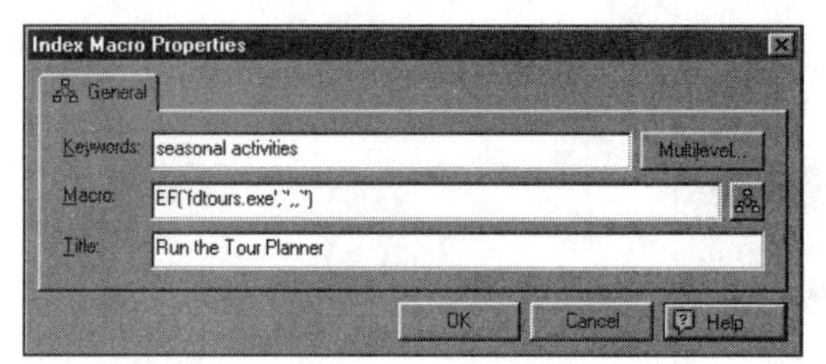

Figure 10-15: The Index Macros Properties screen

3. Enter information in the fields as follows:

   - **Keywords:** Enter the keyword with which the index macro will be associated. You can enter a multilevel keyword by clicking Multilevel and filling in the primary and secondary keyword on the Multilevel Keyword screen (not shown). If you prefer, you can enter multilevel keywords by separating the primary and secondary keywords with a colon.
   - **Macro:** Enter the macro to associate with the keyword, or click the Macro button to the right of the field to display the Macro Editor. To then use the Macro Wizard, click the Wizard button on the right side of the Macro Editor screen as usual.
   - **Title:** Enter the title to appear in the Topics Found list. As with table of contents macros, this should be a distinctive title emphasizing that this keyword will do something different from displaying a topic.

4. When you are satisfied with your changes, click OK on the macro screens. Figure 10-16 shows the Index Macros tab on the Project Settings screen, with an index macro added. Click OK to save the index macro.

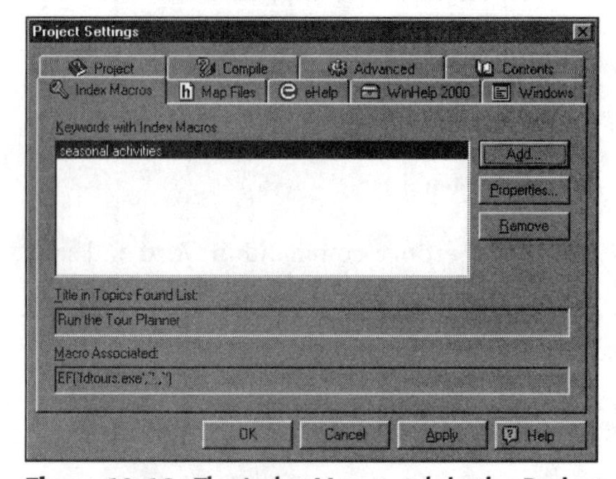

Figure 10-16: The Index Macros tab in the Project Settings screen, showing a new index macro.

When you compile the WinHelp project, the keyword will appear in the index with the other entries. Figure 10-17 shows an index macro that will run the Foggan Drizzle tour planning software, displayed with the other entries in the Topics Found list.

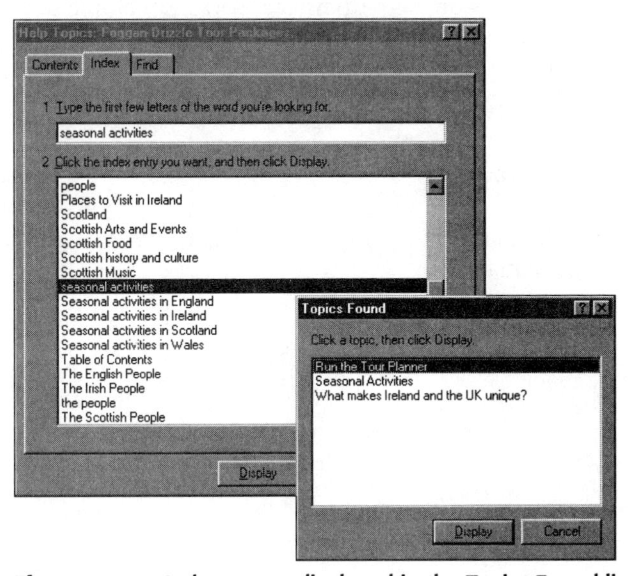

Figure 10-17: Index macro displayed in the Topics Found list

To edit an index macro, highlight the index macro in the Index Macros tab and click Properties. To remove an index macro, highlight the index macro and click Remove, and then confirm the deletion.

Using DLLs to Add Macros

In addition to the macros built into WinHelp and RoboHELP, you can create Dynamic Link Libraries (DLLs) of custom macros. The general procedure is to program a macro in the language of your choice (Visual Basic, C, C++, and so on) and compile it into a DLL. You can then link the macros in the DLL using the `RegisterRoutine` macro, after which you can use them as you would use any other macro. (The RoboHELP extensions are a good example of how you can extend the features available for use in your WinHelp files by adding DLLs.)

Writing DLLs is not a casual enterprise. You will need to work closely with a programmer and also do extensive testing on the macros to make sure that they work correctly before you include them in the final version of the product. You must also ship the DLL with the finished WinHelp files. Detailed information for linking macros in DLLs and programmatically interacting with WinHelp and your WinHelp project appears in the Microsoft Help Compiler Workshop online documentation. (The Microsoft Help Compiler Workshop is automatically installed as part of RoboHELP Office 2000.)

WinHelp Macro Reference

This section contains a list of the macros in WinHelp. The Macro Wizard contains a number of different categories of macros:

- Button macros
- HTML macros
- Keyboard macros
- Linking macros
- Menu macros
- Program macros
- RoboHELP extension macros
- Text-marker macros
- Window macros

However, in addition to the macros in these groups, there are a number of macros not grouped into any categories in the Macro Wizard. These macros are visible only when you select All Macros in the Category list.

This section describes each of the categories, followed by the unclassified macros. For detailed information, as well as for restrictions and suggestions about how to use a specific macro, you are encouraged to look at macro references in RoboHELP's online documentation, and also in the Microsoft Help Compiler Workshop online documentation. (Some macros are documented more completely in the Microsoft Help Compiler Workshop documentation.)

Some macros appear in more than one group.

Button Macros

Button macros (described in Table 10-1) let you create, modify, and delete the buttons that appear on the help window button bars. You can also access the tabs on the Help Topics screen.

Table 10-1
Button Macros

Macro Name	*Description*	*Abbreviation*
`Back`	Displays the previous topic	
`BackFlush`	Clears the list of topics from the history list	
`BrowseButtons`	Adds the Browse buttons to the help window's button bar	
`ChangeButtonBinding`	Assigns a help macro to a custom help button	CBB
`ChangeEnable`	Assigns a macro to a help button and then enables that button. (Using this macro is the same as using the `ChangeButtonBinding` and `EnableButton` macros.)	CE
`Contents`	Displays the Contents tab (if the WinHelp file has an associated CNT file) or the default topic (if it doesn't).	
`CreateButton`	Creates a custom button on the help window's button bar	CB
`DestroyButton`	Removes a button created with the `CreateButton` macro	
`DisableButton`	Grays out (disables) a button created with the `CreateButton` macro	DB
`EnableButton`	Enables a button previously grayed out with the `DisableButton` macro	EB
`Find`	Displays the Find tab in the Help Topics screen	
`Finder`	Displays the Help Topics screen with whatever tab appeared last	FD
`Menu`	Displays a small right-click menu with the standard WinHelp commands (Annotate, Copy, Print Topic, Font, Keep Help On Top, and Use System Colors) for the current help window. (This is the same menu that appears when you right-click in a topic.)	MU

Continued

Table 10-1 *(continued)*

Macro Name	*Description*	*Abbreviation*
`Next`	Displays the next topic in the browse sequence	
`Prev`	Displays the previous topic in the browse sequence	
`Search`	Displays the Index tab in the Help Topics screen	

HTML Macros

HTML macros (described in Table 10-2) let you access URLs on the Internet and jump to an HTML Help topic.

Table 10-2
HTML Macros

Macro Name	*Description*	*Abbreviation*
`Inet`	Jumps to an URL (such as a Web address or an FTP site) or runs other Internet commands (such as `mailto:<address>`). Web sites and FTP sites are displayed in the default Internet browser. `Mailto:` commands are run using the default e-mail client. (This macro requires that you ship the RoboHELP redistributable files SETBROWS.EXE and either INETWH16.DLLor INETWH32.DLL with the compiled WinHelp file.)	
`JumpHtml`	Jumps to a Web site and displays the specified page inside the help window. The default Internet browser must be Internet Explorer 4 or later. (This macro requires that you ship the RoboHELP redistributable file ROBOEX32.DLL with the compiled WinHelp file.)	

Keyboard Macros

Keyboard macros (described in Table 10-3) let you add and remove accelerator keys (also known as keyboard shortcuts) for custom macros.

Table 10-3
Keyboard Macros

Macro Name	*Description*	*Abbreviation*
`AddAccelerator`	Assigns a macro to an accelerator key combination (such as Ctrl+F11).	AA
`RemoveAccelerator`	Removes an accelerator created with the `AddAccelerator` macro	RA

Linking Macros

Linking macros (described in Table 10-4) let you create internal and external jumps, popups, See Also, and keyword links.

Table 10-4
Linking Macros

Macro Name	*Description*	*Abbreviation*
`Alink`	Searches for topics that have See Also keywords (A-Keywords) that match the keyword or keywords specified in the macro	
`Inet`	Jumps to an URL (such as a Web address or an FTP site) or runs other Internet commands (such as `mailto: <address>`). Web sites and FTP sites are displayed in the default Internet browser. `Mailto:` commands are run using the default e-mail client. (This macro requires that you ship the RoboHELP redistributable files SETBROWS.EXE and either INETWH16. DLLor INETWH32.DLL with the compiled WinHelp file.)	
`JumpContents`	Jumps to the default contents topic for a specified WinHelp file	

Continued

Table 10-4 *(continued)*

Macro Name	***Description***	***Abbreviation***
`JumpContext`	Jumps to a topic identified by the specified map number (from the [MAP] section of the HPJ file).	JC
`JumpHash`	Jumps to a topic identified by the specified hash number. (A hash number is a unique number WinHelp creates from the topic ID and uses internally to uniquely refer to a topic.)	JH
`JumpHelpOn`	Jumps to the WinHelp file specified by the `SetHelpOnFile` macro or, if no file has been set, to the contents topic of the standard WINHELP.HLP file, "How to Use Help." (In WinHelp 4, this macro is identical to the `HelpOn` macro.)	
`JumpHtml`	Jumps to a Web site and displays the specified page inside the help window. The default Internet browser must be Internet Explorer 4 or later. (This macro requires that you ship the RoboHELP redistributable file ROBOEX32.DLL with the compiled WinHelp file.)	
`JumpId`	Jumps to the specified topic in the current WinHelp file or a specified WinHelp file	JI
`JumpKeyword`	Opens a WinHelp file, searches the K keywords for the keyword specified in the macro, and then displays the first topic containing the keyword	JK
`KLink`	Searches for matching keywords (K-Keywords) in the current WinHelp file	KL
`PopupContext`	Displays the topic identified by the specified map number (from the [MAP] section of the HPJ file) in a popup window	PC
`PopupHash`	Displays the topic identified by the specified hash number in a popup window. (A hash number is a unique number WinHelp creates from the topic ID and uses internally to uniquely refer to a topic.)	

Macro Name	*Description*	*Abbreviation*
`PopupId`	Displays in a popup window the specified topic in the current WinHelp file or a specified WinHelp file	PI
`UpdateWindow`	Jumps to the specified topic in the current or specified WinHelp file, displays the topic in the specified help window, and then returns the focus to the help window from which the macro was run	JW

Menu Macros

Menu macros (described in Table 10-5) let you create, modify, and delete WinHelp menus; and add, check, change, delete, disable, enable, and uncheck submenus and menu items.

Table 10-5
Menu Macros

Macro Name	*Description*	*Abbreviation*
`AppendItem`	Appends a command to the end of a menu already created with the `InsertMenu` macro	AI
`ChangeItemBinding`	Assigns a macro to an item added to a menu using the `AppendItem` macro	CIB
`CheckItem`	Checks the specified menu item. (Use the `UncheckItem` macro to uncheck a menu item.)	CI
`DeleteItem`	Removes an item added to a menu using the `AppendItem` macro	
`DisableItem`	Grays out (disables) an item created with the `AppendItem` macro	DI
`EnableItem`	Enables an item previously grayed out with the `DisableItem` macro	EI
`ExtAbleItem`	Enables or disables an item created with the `AppendItem`, `ExtInsertItem`, or `InsertItem` macros	

Continued

Table 10-5 *(continued)*

Macro Name	*Description*	*Abbreviation*
`ExtInsertItem`	Inserts a menu item on a menu at the specified position	
`ExtInsertMenu`	Inserts a submenu for an existing command in the specified position on a menu	
`InsertItem`	Inserts a standard or custom menu item in the specified position on a menu	
`InsertMenu`	Inserts a new menu in the specified position on the WinHelp menu bar	
`ResetMenu`	Restores the WinHelp menus and commands to their defaults. All custom menus, items, and settings are removed.	
`UncheckItem`	Unchecks the specified menu item	UI

Program Macros

Program macros (described in Table 10-6) let you access external programs and files.

Table 10-6
Program Macros

Macro Name	*Description*	*Abbreviation*
`ControlPanel`	Opens the specified tab of an applet in the Control Panel	
`ExecFile`	Runs the specified program or opens the specified file with the associated program	EF
`ExecProgram`	Runs the specified program. (The `ExecProgram` macro has been superseded by the `ExecFile` macro in WinHelp 4 systems.)	EP
`FileExist`	Checks for the specified file on the computer	FE
`ShellExecute`	Opens or prints the specified file	SE
`ShortCut`	Runs the specified program	SH

RoboHELP Extension Macros

RoboHELP extension macros (described in Table 10-7) are not part of the standard WinHelp macro set. Instead, they are included as part of the RoboHELP redistributable DLLs. (These are files that may be shipped with your completed WinHelp file.)

Table 10-7
RoboHELP Extension Macros

Macro Name	*Description*	*Abbreviation*
`Inet`	Jumps to an URL (such as a Web address or an FTP site) or runs other Internet commands (such as `mailto: <address>`). Web sites and FTP sites are displayed in the default Internet browser. `Mailto:` commands are run using the default e-mail client. (This macro requires that you ship the RoboHELP redistributable files SETBROWS.EXE and either INETWH16. DLLor INETWH32.DLL with the compiled WinHelp file.)	
`INETWH_`**Initialize**	Enables Internet access for your WinHelp file. This macro is automatically added to the Startup Macros list when you use the `Inet` or `JumpHtml` macros.	
`JumpHtml`	Jumps to a Web site and displays the specified page inside the help window. The default Internet browser must be Internet Explorer 4 or later. (This macro requires that you ship the RoboHELP redistributable file ROBOEX32.DLL with the compiled WinHelp file.)	
`RegisterRoutine`	Registers a function in the specified Dynamic Link Library (DLL) so you can use it in the WinHelp project. `Register Routine` macros are also automatically added to the Startup Macros list when you use any of the RoboHELP extension macros.	

Continued

Table 10-7 (continued)

Macro Name	*Description*	*Abbreviation*
RoboHelpExInitialize	Enables the RoboEx32.DLL features (including the WinHelp 2000 features, watermarks, Smart See Also buttons, and the Jumphtml macro) for your WinHelp file. This macro is automatically added to the Startup Macros list when you use any of these features. (This macro requires that you ship the RoboHELP redistributable file ROBOEX32. DLL with the compiled WinHelp file.)	
RoboHelpExShow SeeAlso	Starts the Smart See Also button on the specified help window. This macro is automatically added to the Startup Macros list when you select the Add Smart See Also Button box on the WinHelp 2000 tab of the Project Settings screen. (This macro requires that you ship the RoboHELP redistributable file ROBOEX32.DLL with the compiled WinHelp file.)	
RoboHelpExShow NavPanep	Provides the WinHelp 2000 Explorer View features. This macro is automatically added to the Startup Macros list when you select the Create WinHelp 2000 Explorer View box on the WinHelp 2000 tab of the Project Settings screen. (This macro requires that you ship the RoboHELP redistributable file ROBOEX32.DLL with the compiled WinHelp file.)	
RoboHelpExWatermark	Adds a watermark to the background region (the body text area) of a topic or an entire WinHelp project. This macro is automatically added to the Startup Macros list when you specify a background watermark in the WinHelp 2000 tab of the Project Settings screen or when you specify a background watermark in the Watermark tab of the Topic Properties screen. (This macro requires that you ship the RoboHELP redistributable file ROBOEX32.DLL with the compiled WinHelp file.)	

Macro Name	Description	Abbreviation
`RoboHelpExWatermarkNonScroll`	Adds a watermark to the non-scrolling region of a topic or an entire WinHelp project. This macro is automatically added to the Startup Macros list when you specify a non-scrolling region watermark in the WinHelp 2000 tab of the Project Settings screen or when you specify a non-scrolling region watermark in the Watermark tab of the Topic Properties screen. (This macro requires that you ship the RoboHELP redistributable file ROBOEX32.DLL with the compiled WinHelp file.)	
`Sound`	Displays the Video/Sound player inside a topic and plays the specified WAV file. (This macro requires that you ship the RoboHELP redistributable file RHMMPLAY.DLL with the compiled WinHelp file.)	
`SoundOnly`	Plays a WAV file but doesn't display the Video/Sound player inside the topic. (This macro requires that you ship the RoboHELP redistributable file RHMMPLAY.DLL with the compiled WinHelp file, as well as the WAV file being played if it's not already available on the end-user's computer.)	
`Video`	Displays the Video/Sound player inside a topic and plays the specified AVI (video) file. (This macro requires that you ship the RoboHELP redistributable file RHMMPLAY.DLL with the compiled WinHelp file, as well as the AVI file being played if it's not already available on the end-user's computer.)	
`VideoCaption`	Changes the caption on the Video/Sound Player's titlebar. (This macro requires that you ship the RoboHELP redistributable file RHMMPLAY.DLL with the compiled WinHelp file.)	
`VideoMenu`	Suppresses or enables the display of the Video/Sound Player when playing an AVI or WAV file. (This macro requires that you ship the RoboHELP redistributable file RHMMPLAY.DLL with the compiled WinHelp file.)	

Continued

Table 10-7 (continued)

Macro Name	*Description*	*Abbreviation*
`VideoPath`	Specifies a directory path for WinHelp to look in for AVI and WAV files. (This macro requires that you ship the RoboHELP redistributable file RHMMPLAY.DLL with the compiled WinHelp file.)	

Text-Marker Macros

Text-marker macros (described in Table 10-8) let you set text markers when a topic is displayed. You can then test for the existence of a topic and perform actions based on this. (For example, you could use this feature to see if a user has displayed a specific topic in the WinHelp file and optionally display a message if they haven't.)

Table 10-8
Text-Marker Macros

Macro Name	*Description*	*Abbreviation*
`DeleteMark`	Deletes the specified text marker created with the `SaveMark` macro	
`GoToMark`	Jumps to the topic associated with the specified text marker created with the `SaveMark` macro	
`IfThen`	Runs the specified macro if a text marker created with the `SaveMark` macro exists	IF
`IfThenElse`	Runs the specified macro if a text marker created with the `SaveMark` macro exists; otherwise, it runs another macro	IE
`IsMark`	Checks to see if a text marker exists. (The text marker must have been set using the SaveMark macro.) If the text marker does, the test returns a nonzero value (a "true" condition); if it doesn't, the test returns a zero (a "false" condition). The result of this test is used by the `IfThen` or `IfThenElse` macros to determine if a condition is true or false.	

Macro Name	*Description*	*Abbreviation*
IsNotMark	Checks to see if a text marker does not exist. (This is the reverse of the IsMark macro. The text marker must have been set using the SaveMark macro.) If the text marker does not exist, the test returns a nonzero value (a "true" condition); if it does, the test returns a zero (a "false" condition). The result of this test is used by the IfThen or IfThenElse macros to determine if a condition is true or false.	NM
Not	Reverses the results of the IsMark and IsNotMark macros: returns zero (FALSE) if the marker text specified by the SaveMark macro exists or nonzero (TRUE) if the marker text does not exist. When used with a macro, the Not macro reverses the results of the macro.	
SaveMark	Assigns a specified text marker to the current topic and WinHelp file	

Window Macros

Window macros (described in Table 10-9) let you close and position windows, set size and position, toggle whether the help is on top of the other windows, and set the background color for the popup window.

Table 10-9
Window Macros

Macro Name	*Description*	*Abbreviation*
CloseSecondarys	Closes all help windows except the current secondary window	CS
CloseWindow	Closes the specified Main window or secondary window	CW
FocusWindow	Switches the focus to the specified Main window or secondary window	
HelpOnTop	Toggles the "On Top" option for the WinHelp file	

Continued

Table 10-9 (continued)

Macro Name	Description	Abbreviation
`PositionWindow`	Sets the size and position of a help window using absolute positioning	PW
`SetPopupColor`	Sets the background color of the popup window	SPC

Other Macros

The remaining macros (described in Table 10-10) are an assortment of macros that appear in the All Macros list of the Macro Wizard, but are not grouped in any of the categories.

Table 10-10
Other Macros

Macro Name	Description	Abbreviation
`About`	Displays the standard Help About box. (Using this macro is the same as selecting the Help➪About command in WinHelp.)	
`Annotate`	Displays the standard Annotate screen. (Using this macro is the same as selecting the Edit➪Annotate command in WinHelp or selecting the Annotate command from the right-click WinHelp menu.)	
`BookmarkDefine`	Displays the standard Bookmark Define screen. (Using this macro is the same as selecting the Bookmark➪Define command in WinHelp.)	
`BookmarkMore`	Displays the additional bookmarks on the Bookmark menu when there are more than nine bookmarks. (Using this macro is the same as selecting the More command from the Bookmark right-click menu in WinHelp.)	
`Compare`	Runs a second instance of WinHelp so you can compare versions of a WinHelp file. (A known WinHelp bug prevents these from being displayed side by side.)	

Macro Name	Description	Abbreviation
CopyDialog	Displays the Edit Copy dialog box. (This macro is only for WinHelp 3 systems; WinHelp 4 systems should use the CopyTopic macro.)	
CopyTopic	Copies the selected text in the topic to the Windows clipboard	CT
EndMPrint	Closes the printing message box and stops the printing of multiple topics started with the MPrintHash or MPrintID macros	
Exit	Exits the WinHelp file. (This is the same as selecting the File ➪ Exit command from the WinHelp menu.)	
FileOpen	Displays the standard File Open screen. (This is the same as selecting the File ➪ Open command from the WinHelp menu.)	FO
FloatingMenu	Displays the WinHelp floating menu at the current cursor position. (This is the same menu that appears when you right-click a topic.)	
Flush	Processes any pending WinHelp messages as well as any previously called macros	FH
Generate	Displays the specified message in the current help window	
HelpOn	Displays the help file for WinHelp. (This is the same as pressing F1 in WinHelp.) In WinHelp 4, this macro is identical to the JumpHelpOn macro.	
History	Displays a list of the last 40 topics that were looked at in the WinHelp file	
InitMPrint	Prepares WinHelp for printing multiple topics	
IsBook	Checks to see if the WinHelp file is running standalone (that is, if it was started by double-clicking the file's icon) or if it is being run from a program.	
MprintHash	Prints a topic identified by the specified hash number. (A hash number is a unique number WinHelp creates from the topic ID and uses internally to uniquely refer to a topic.) This macro is used in the same manner as the InitMPrint and EndMPrint macros.	

Continued

Table 10-10 *(continued)*

Macro Name	***Description***	***Abbreviation***
MprintID	Prints a topic identified by the specified topic ID. This macro is used in the same manner as the InitMPrint and EndMPrint macros.	
NoShow	Suppresses a topic from being displayed if the topic has not already been displayed in this instance of WinHelp	
Print	Prints the current topic	
PrinterSetup	Displays the Printer Setup dialog box. (This macro is only for WinHelp 3 systems; WinHelp 4 systems don't need this macro.)	
SetContents	Sets the specified topic as the default topic for the WinHelp file	
SetHelpOnFile	Identifies a replacement WinHelp file for the standard "How to Use Help" file shipped with WinHelp. (This macro is only for WinHelp 3 systems. The macro is ignored in WinHelp 4 systems.)	
Tcard	Sends a message to the program that is opening the WinHelp file as a training card	
Test	Tests the WinHelp file for any of a variety of conditions as specified by the test criteria you enter	
TestALink	Tests an ALink macro to see if it has a link to at least one topic	
TestKLink	Tests a KLink macro to see if it has a link to at least one topic	

Summary

This chapter introduced you to the use of macros in your WinHelp system. You first learned basic macro concepts. You also saw how to use the Macro Editor and the Macro Wizard, which are used throughout RoboHELP to enter and maintain macros. Next, you learned how to add startup macros and topic entry macros. The chapter continued with information on adding hotspot macros of all kinds and how to link macros to most of the clickable actions in a WinHelp file. You learned the basics of adding custom macros with DLLs to further enhance your WinHelp projects. Finally, the chapter contained tables of the standard categories of WinHelp macros and provided some general descriptions of each one's function.

✦ ✦ ✦

Creating Context-Sensitive Help

In This Chapter

Understanding context-sensitive help

Making a plan for creating context-sensitive help

Adding context-sensitive links manually

Creating context-sensitive links automatically

Adding and maintaining context-sensitive links in the HPJ file

Adding and maintaining context-sensitive links with the RoboHELP Explorer

Understanding and using aliases

Testing and debugging context-sensitive help

Using the WinHelp BugHunter

Printing reports on context-sensitive help files

This chapter tells you how to create context-sensitive help. It starts by describing the basics of context-sensitive help and how applications and WinHelp files interact. Next, the chapter discusses issues to consider with the developers when planning your efforts. You then learn how to add context-sensitive links manually, create them automatically, and add or maintain links in the HPJ file and the RoboHELP Explorer. The chapter continues with information on aliases and how use them. You learn how to test context-sensitive help files using the WinHelp BugHunter and other tools. Last, the chapter introduces you to the Map ID and Duplicate Map ID reports.

What Is Context-Sensitive Help?

You've already learned how to create stand-alone WinHelp files: files that are not linked to a specific program as the associated online documentation. Now you're going to see how to create *context-sensitive help*. Context-sensitive help is help that is directly linked to a program. When you press F1 or click on the help button in a screen or dialog box, the context-sensitive link between the program and the help file identifies the topic to display and then displays it. Figure 11-1 shows a diagram of the interaction between the program and the online help.

As Figure 11-1 shows, when the user requests help for the Tour Destination field in the application, the program looks up the topic number associated with the field in an internal table that is part of the program. (This topic is usually identified by a topic number, also known as *map number, map ID,* or a *help hook,* that you and the developer specify for each topic you want to create context-sensitive help for.) The program then issues a *call*—a request for information or action from one program to another—to the WinHelp viewer to look in the appropriate WinHelp file for the topic associated with the topic number. The WinHelp viewer opens the specified WinHelp file, looks in the WinHelp file's lookup table (entered in the [MAP] section of the HPJ file) for the topic number, and then finds the topic associated with the topic number. The topic is then displayed on the user's screen.

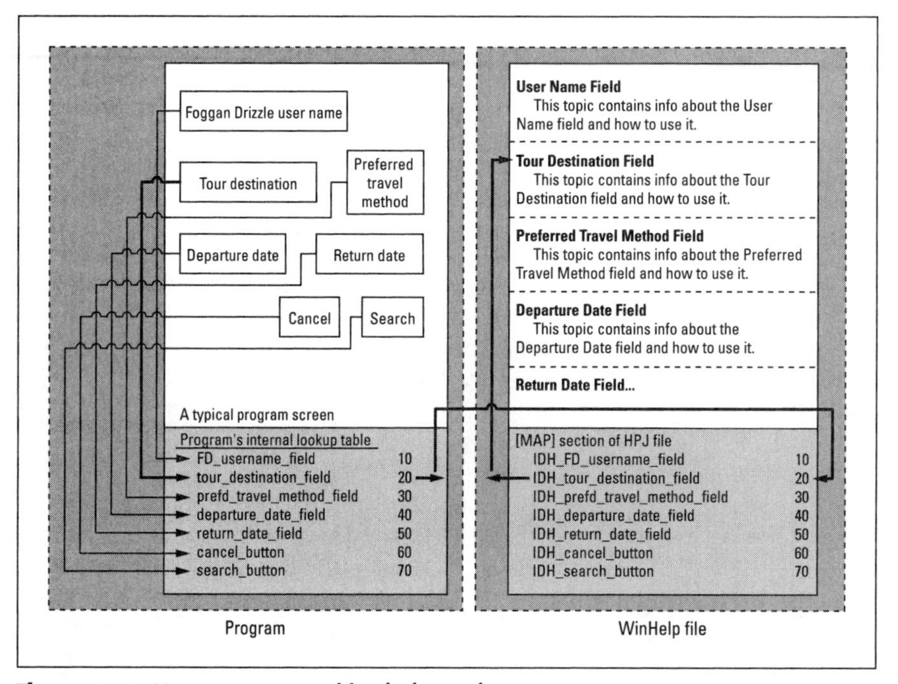

Figure 11-1: How context-sensitive help works

This may sound a little complex, but you won't have to do much once you and the developers have the context-sensitive help numbers set up: most of the mechanisms for context-sensitive help actually work behind the scenes. All the communication between the programs and WinHelp files is done with the WinHelp API (application program interface), which is part of Windows. The developers are in charge of implementing the calls to the WinHelp files using the WinHelp API from within the program. Most of what you and the developer need to do to create context-sensitive help is to agree on the topic numbers for the various topics and link them. It's essential that the writers and developers work together when creating context-sensitive help so that the goals and context-sensitive numbers for the WinHelp files are synchronized.

General documentation on the WinHelp API appears in the Microsoft Help Compiler Workshop help file, which is shipped with RoboHELP 2000. More detailed programming documentation appears in the Microsoft Windows Software Development Kit. You won't have to worry about using the WinHelp API yourself, but understanding the basics of the WinHelp API will be helpful when working with the developers.

Any WinHelp file can be turned into a context-sensitive file. Furthermore, you can run a context-sensitive WinHelp file as a stand-alone file and access topics with keywords, tables of contents, and jumps.

Planning Context-Sensitive Help

Creating context-sensitive help requires that you interact with the software developers. Following are some typical questions to which you should know the answers:

✦ Is this program being designed for a 16-bit or 32-bit operating system? Windows 3.*x* is a 16-bit operating system; later versions of Windows are 32-bit operating systems. Even though you can run 16-bit programs on later versions of Windows, a 16-bit program will limit you to using a 16-bit (WinHelp 3) WinHelp file. This means that you can't take advantage of the extensive features available in WinHelp 4. (WinHelp 4 files for Windows 95/98/NT are 32-bit and can only be used for context-sensitive help with 32-bit programs.)

✦ What programming language is the program being developed in, and are there any restrictions for developing context-sensitive help in the development environment, such as a development system that requires unique map IDs for every screen element or that renumbers the map IDs each time the program is recompiled?

✦ What kinds and levels of context-sensitive help are required? For example, you can create context-sensitive help that provides help at the screen level (also known as the form level or window level) or at the field level. Screen-level help provides a single overarching topic that comes up when the user selects context-sensitive help anywhere on the screen. Field-level help displays individual topics for each of the fields. You can provide context-sensitive help for entire menus or for individual menus and commands.

✦ How will the users access context-sensitive help topics? Some typical options include pressing F1, clicking a button on a screen that says "Help" or shows a question mark, right-clicking the field and selecting a help option from a popup menu, or selecting a Help menu toggle and then clicking on the field or area for which help is required. All of these options will be programmed by the development team, but the choices for accessing WinHelp can affect the phrasing you use in the WinHelp file.

✦ Who will create the link in the WinHelp file? Although this is usually best managed by the WinHelp authors, it is sometimes handled by the development team. Some development environments also dictate the type of help link you use in the WinHelp file.

✦ What are the development schedule benchmarks?

✦ Is there a spec for the project? Will it be followed? What is the process for informing the writers of changes to the user interface? (This will determine when the context-sensitive help topics will be created and which topics will be created at all.)

✦ When will the application's user interface freeze? When will the functions being developed freeze? (The freezes will determine when you can schedule final testing of the WinHelp file against the application.)

✦ What naming conventions are the developers using for the unique names of the program controls? (*Controls* are anything in the program that you can request context-sensitive help for: screens, fields, menus, commands, and so on.) What naming conventions are you using for the topic IDs?

✦ How will you be structuring the WinHelp files? Will there be a single WinHelp file or many help files? What name(s) will you use for the WinHelp file(s)? The name of the WinHelp file needs to be coded into the software.

✦ What windows do you want to display WinHelp topics in? Will you be using multiple window types (such as procedure windows, reference windows, and popup windows) in the online help? This information needs to be coded into the application.

✦ How will the context-sensitive help be tested and who will test it?

✦ How will changes be communicated from the developers to the writers, and vice versa? You may want to distribute a regular report to the developers you are working with to make sure that everyone is kept in the loop.

By answering these questions, you and the developer(s) will have a much better idea of what to expect and what each of you needs to create. You can also set the expectations of the developers and the testers for the tasks related to creating the context-sensitive help that they'll need to schedule. Having a clear understanding of the way in which the developers are creating their context-sensitive help links and how the writers and developers can support one another is an essential part of the context-sensitive help development process.

Working with Developers

Producing great context-sensitive help requires that you be up-to-date regarding the software's features and look and feel, as well as any changes to the software. Developers in many companies are frequently resistant to extensive planning, specs, or information about the changes contained in internal alpha and beta releases, which can make writing the context-sensitive help more challenging than it needs to be. Wherever possible, develop informal lines of communication with the developers to find out what's really happening with a project. For example, many writers get official pronouncements on the schedule and the feature set from the development manager or team lead and then talk to the individual developers and ask them the same questions.

You should also beware of any situation in which the development manager says, "The developers are too busy to talk to the writers," as this is a clear sign that the project has not been planned. (The metric for budgeting time for the developers working on documentation issues is that writers require roughly 10 percent of the developers' time over the course of a project. Good development managers are aware of this.) In such cases, most of your interaction with the developers will be through informal, rather than formal, channels. Plan to take a lot of developers to lunch to get information from them away from the office. It won't be a one-sided relationship; you'll learn a great deal about how your company develops products, and you will be able to anticipate needs and problems much more effectively.

Creating Context-Sensitive Help

The basic steps for creating context-sensitive help are as follows:

1. Work with the developers to identify the screens, fields, commands, and other items in the program for which you want to create context-sensitive help.
2. Create a skeleton of topics for the various controls. (You don't need to have the content written to get the overall structure working, although you may have topics already written for some of the features.)
3. Assign map IDs for each of the topics and the associated controls.
4. Compile and test the online help file with the program to verify that the links work.
5. Develop the content for the topics.
6. Recompile and test the online help file with the program.

The most effective way to identify the items that need to have context-sensitive help topics is to get printouts of the various screens, menus, and objects. If the developers are working for an up-to-date spec, these will be readily available; however, it is more likely that you will have to take screen shots of the latest version of the software to get this information. Highlight all the items that need individual topics.

Developing help for applications that have not frozen (that is, have user interface elements or features that are not yet final) can be tricky, and is frequently one of the most unpleasant parts of the context-sensitive help development process. Identifying the fields, screens, and features in a timely fashion that need to be documented is critical to creating complete and correct context-sensitive help.

If you are adapting an existing online help file to a program, you will probably not need to create many new topics, but when you are creating online help from scratch for a program, it's best to create an online help file with empty topics at first. This will let you test the layout and interaction between the program and the online help file before you spend too much time writing content for the individual topics. (It's a good idea to create topics in the order they appear on the various screens and menus for use when building browse sequences in the online help file.)

Once you have a set of topics ready to be linked, you need to establish the links between the program and the online help file. Much of the work may already be done for you: Depending on the programming language in which the program is being written, the developer may already have a set of topic numbers generated for the various controls. If not, however, you can work with the developer to create a simple system for assigning topic numbers to the controls. Write the topic numbers for each control on the printouts of the screens, fields, and menus. You'll use these for entering topic numbers and for reference when testing the context-sensitive help.

As with browse sequences, it's a good idea to create map IDs with room between them for convenient expansion. For example, all map IDs between 100 and 199 are associated with the program's main screen, all map IDs between 200 and 299 are associated with the next screen in the program, and so on. By grouping the values logically, you can save time when testing and debugging later on. The main contents topic is usually given the value of zero. RoboHELP supports topic numbers from zero to 4,294,967,295 (2^{32}-1), but it's a good idea from a maintenance standpoint to keep the topic numbers in a much smaller range. Most online help writers traditionally use the range from 0 to 32,767 or 0 to 65,535.

With the ranges of topic numbers defined, you're ready to start entering individual topic numbers. Topic numbers are stored in the [MAP] section of the HPJ file, but you don't have to work directly with the HPJ file. RoboHELP lets you enter topic numbers for each topic through the Topic Properties screen.

To enter individual topic numbers, do the following:

1. Position the cursor in the topic you want to add a map ID for and select the Edit ➪ Topic Properties command (or just press Ctrl+E). (As always, you can also select the topic in the RoboHELP Explorer, right-click, and select Properties.) Select the Advanced tab (shown in Figure 11-2 with a map number already entered).

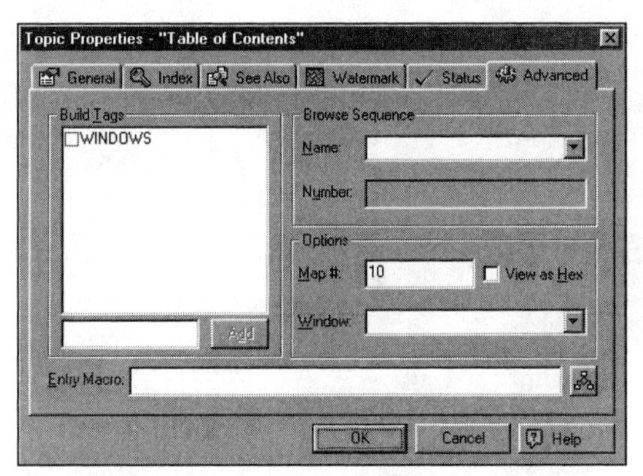

Figure 11-2: The Topic Properties screen showing the Advanced tab

2. In the Map # field, enter the topic number for the topic and click OK.

Depending on the development environment, you may receive the topic numbers from the developers in hexadecimal (base 16), rather than decimal. Hexadecimal numbers are preceded with 0x as an identifier. For example, the hexadecimal equivalent of 10 is 0xa, and the hexadecimal equivalent of 1,000 is 0x3e8. To enter a number as hexadecimal, check the View as Hex box to the right of the Map # field. The format for the number is not important; RoboHELP will accept topic numbers in either format.

Once you've entered the first topic number, you can enter the next one by repeating the process. After you enter all the topic numbers, you can compile the online help as usual and then try it out with the program to see if it works. (Detailed information on testing context-sensitive help appears later in this chapter.)

Generating Topic Numbers Automatically

Entering topic numbers manually is effective, but it can be slow and cumbersome, particularly if you need to enter several hundred or even several thousand context-sensitive entries. Fortunately, RoboHELP offers several ways to make this process faster and easier.

If the development environment doesn't have requirements for the topic numbers for the various controls, you can use RoboHELP's automatic map file generator. A *map file* is simply a file containing entries for the topics and the topic numbers, which is then included by reference in the HPJ file when you compile the WinHelp project.

To automatically generate a map file for the project, do the following:

1. Select the RoboHELP ➪ Project Settings command, and then select the Map Files tab (shown in Figure 11-3).

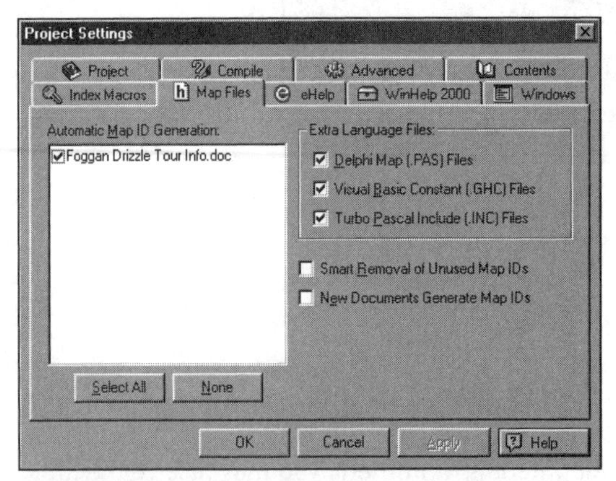

Figure 11-3: The Map Files tab in the Project Settings folder

2. Enter information in the fields as follows:

   - **Automatic Map ID Generation:** Check the source files in the WinHelp project that you want to generate map IDs (topic numbers). You can use the Select All and None buttons to select all the files or to clear all the selections.
   - **Extra Language Files:** Check the boxes for each of the additional files you want to generate. These files are used by the developers to link the map IDs to the program. (Check with the developers to determine the types of additional files they may require.)
   - **Smart Removal of Unused Map IDs:** Check this option if you want Robo HELP to automatically remove the unused map IDs. If you remove unused map IDs, WinHelp won't give you error messages about unused map IDs in the WinHelp project when you compile the file. If you select this option, the system will prompt you with a message explaining that unused IDs will be removed. (You must already have chosen to automatically generate map IDs in order for the smart removal option to work.)
   - **New Documents Generate Map IDs:** Check this option if you want RoboHELP to automatically generate map IDs for any new DOC files you add to this WinHelp project. (This option will already be selected if the WinHelp project was created as an Application Help project that has automatic map ID generation.)

When you start a project as an Application Help project, you can select from a wide variety of development environments. RoboHELP will set the various options for automatic generation of map IDs and the appropriate language files.

3. When you are satisfied with your entries, click OK.

RoboHELP will generate the map file—a text file with the extension HH that contains the map IDs. Figure 11-4 shows a portion of the map file for the Foggan Drizzle help file. As you can see, RoboHELP assigns topic numbers in the order the topics are read in the DOC file. (You can sort or re-organize the entries in the file if you wish; the order in which they appear is not important.)

Foggan Drizzle Tour Info.hh - Notepad

File Edit Search Help

```
#define What_makes_Ireland_and_the_UK_unique_    1
#define History_and_Culture     2
#define Music   3
#define Food    4
#define The_People      5
#define Weather 6
#define Seasonal_Activities     7
#define Arts_and_Events 8
#define Ireland 9
```

Figure 11-4: A portion of a typical map file

The #define that precedes each map ID is a programming language convention that's included in the HH file. This makes it easier to use the map file with a number of common programming languages, but it's not necessary for the entries to have a #define at the start of each one in order for them to work with WinHelp.

RoboHELP also adds to the [MAP] section of the HPJ file an `#include` statement that tells the WinHelp compiler to include the reference file at the location of the `#include` statement. You can have more than one `#include` statement in the HPJ file:

```
[MAP]
#include <Foggan Drizzle Tour Info.hh>
#include <Foggan Drizzle Addon.hh>
#include <Foggan Drizzle Common Elements.hh>
```

As you saw in Figure 11-4, RoboHELP assigns a topic number of 1 to the first topic in the first DOC file and then continues throughout the topics. You can set the starting number for the automatic numbering using the Document Properties screen. (You already used part of the Document Properties screen in Chapter 9, "Using Help Windows and Browse Sequences.")

To change the automatic numbering for map IDs, do the following:

1. In the RoboHELP Explorer, right-click on a document name in the Topics section, and then select Properties from the right-click menu. The Document Properties screen appears (shown in Figure 11-5).

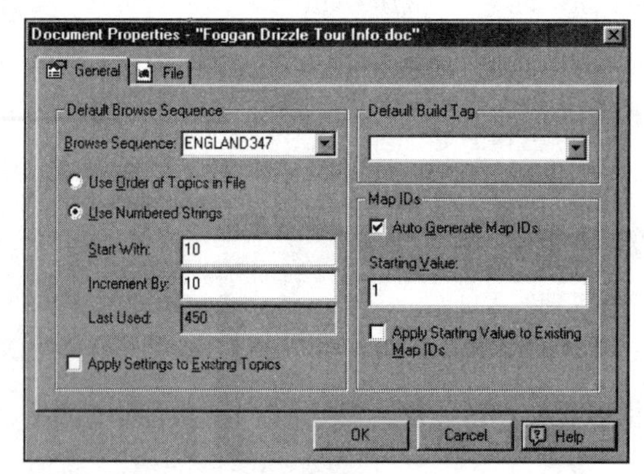

Figure 11-5: The Document Properties screen

2. Enter information in the fields in the Map IDs section as follows:
   - **Auto Generate Map IDs:** Check this box to automatically generate map ID numbers (and any extra language files you may have specified).
   - **Starting Value:** Enter the starting value for the topic numbers. You can enter a number from 0 to 4,294,967,295.
   - **Apply Starting Value to Existing Map IDs:** Check this box to renumber the map IDs for the topics in this document. Renumbering will begin with the number you enter for the starting value.
3. When you are satisfied with your entries, click OK.

Automatic map ID numbering is always incremental by ones, but your choices for topic numbers may be dictated by other factors. For example, some development environments establish the topic numbers used by the various controls automatically. You also might be adding a new or revamped WinHelp system to an existing program that already has numbers for all the controls. Even if the developers have already assigned topic numbers for the controls or you're importing a project into RoboHELP, you can still create a map file to speed up the topic numbering process:

1. Create the map file as described earlier in this section.
2. Open the HH file with an editor such as Notepad or WordPad.
3. Change the topic numbers as appropriate.

If you're using hexadecimal, rather than decimal, numbers, be sure that you're entering numbers in the right format.

4. When you are satisfied with your changes, click OK.

By starting with an automatically generated map file, you can be sure that you'll have all the topic IDs correctly entered in a file. All you need to do is change the topic numbers to fit the program.

You can add comments to the entries in the map file using a semicolon. Figure 11-6 shows a map file with several types of comments entered. Note that you can enter complete lines of comments or add a partial comment at the end of the line as you prefer. The WinHelp compiler ignores everything from the semicolon to the end of the line. (It's a good idea to comment your changes in a fashion similar to that shown in Figure 11-6, with a date and initials.)

Foggan Drizzle Tour Info.hh - Notepad

File Edit Search Help

```
;May 14, 2000: sorted entries alphabetically

#define Arts_and_Events 8
#define Celts    414    ;changed from 411  May 22, 2000 by jds
#define England 17
#define English_Arts_and_Events 24
#define English_Food    20
#define English_History_and_Culture     18
#define English_Music   19
#define Glossary        9001    ;changed from 256  May 22, 2000 by jds
#define Ireland 9
#define Irish_Arts_and_Events   16
```

Figure 11-6: Comments in a map file

Adding Topic Numbers to the HPJ File

You may want to edit the HPJ file manually to add or modify a topic number for a topic. For example, you might want to do this if you are making a quick change to the WinHelp project or you're working on the help files on a computer that doesn't have RoboHELP installed. You might also want to copy and paste some or all of the information from the map file into the [MAP] section of the HPJ file.

To add or change a topic number directly in the HPJ file, do the following:

1. Open the HPJ file in an editor such as Notepad or WordPad. Find the [MAP] section (near the end of the HPJ file).
2. Make entries in the [MAP] section that have the topic ID followed by the topic number (in decimal or hexadecimal format). The topic number should be separated from the topic ID by a tab or spaces.
3. When you are satisfied with your entries, click OK. Compile the WinHelp project as usual.

It's perfectly acceptable to mix `#include` statements and map IDs in the HPJ file like this:

```
[MAP]
#include <Foggan Drizzle Tour Info.hh>
#include <Foggan Drizzle Addon.hh>
#include <Foggan Drizzle Common Elements.hh>
Table_of_Contents    0
What_s_In_This_Help_File_    100
```

If you're using both `#include` statements and map IDs in the HPJ file, be careful not to use the same map IDs in both places.

You can add comments to the entries in the HPJ file using a semicolon in the same way as you did with the map file earlier. (The standard HPJ file generated by Robo HELP has comments embedded in it to describe each of the sections.)

Maintaining Map IDs with the RoboHELP Explorer

As with many other aspects of your WinHelp project, you can use the RoboHELP Explorer to view and maintain map IDs. Figure 11-7 shows the RoboHELP Explorer displaying the map ID sections.

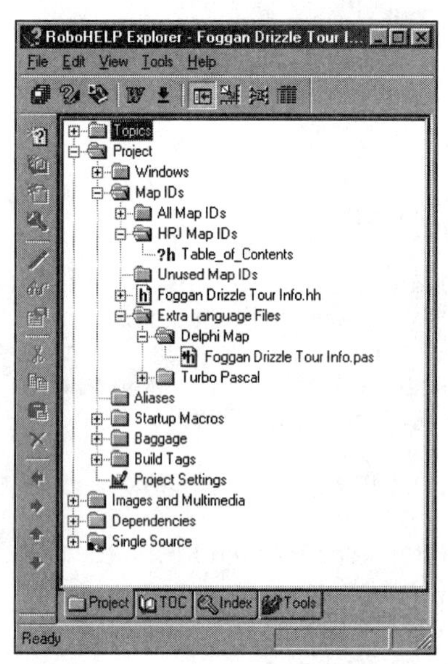

Figure 11-7: The RoboHELP Explorer showing the map ID information

The All Map IDs section lists all the map IDs from every category. The HPJ Map IDs section shows map entries in the HPJ file. The Unused Map IDs section lists map IDs that are otherwise valid but do not have corresponding topics in the file. The map file or files associated with the WinHelp project are preceded with the icon shown in Figure 11-8.

Figure 11-8: The Map File icon

The Extra Language Files section contains entries for any extra language files (created by checking one or more of the boxes in the Extra Language Files section of the Map Files tab on the Project Settings folder. Extra language files are preceded by the icon shown in Figure 11-9, which is similar to the general map files icon.

Figure 11-9: The Extra language File icon

The RoboHELP Explorer offers a number of convenient features for viewing and maintaining map IDs. For example, you can expand and collapse the lists of map IDs in each section by double-clicking the folder or the file name. In Figure 11-10, the All Map IDs section is expanded to show the list of map IDs.

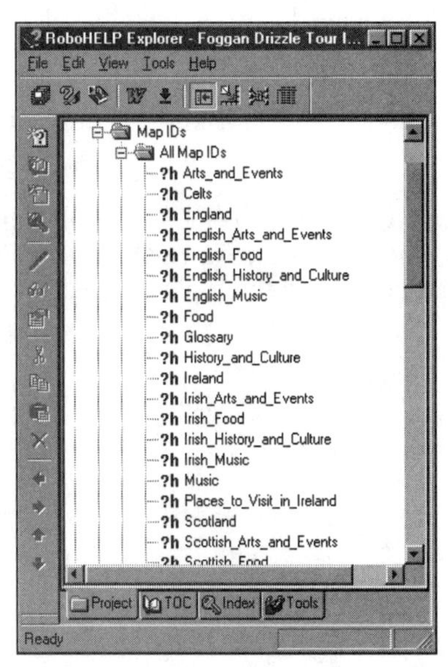

Figure 11-10: The RoboHELP Explorer showing the map IDs

To add a new map ID, do the following:

1. Right-click the folder to which you want to add the new map ID . Map ID folders are found in the Project folder. (If you click the All Map IDs folder, RoboHELP will add the new entry to the HPJ file.) Select the New ➪ Map ID command from the right-click menu. The New Map ID screen appears (shown in Figure 11-11).

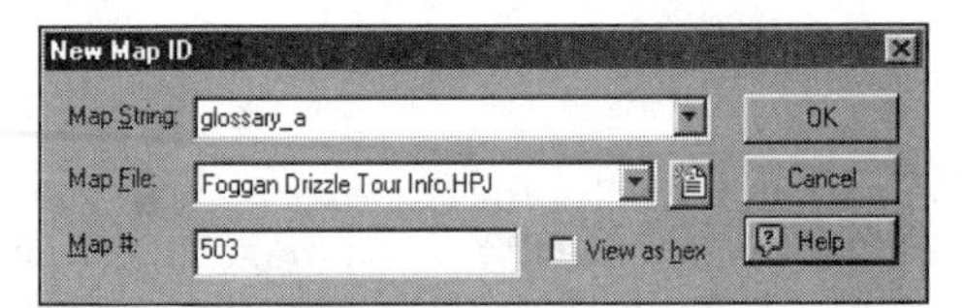

Figure 11-11: The New Map ID screen

2. Enter information in the fields as follows:
   - **Map String:** Enter the name of the topic in this field.
   - **Map File:** Enter the name of the map file to add this entry to. You can select a file from the drop-down list or click the page icon to the right of the field to browse for a file. (The default is the current HPJ file.)
   - **Map #:** Enter the topic number for the map ID. You can view the number as a hexadecimal number by clicking View as Hex.

RoboHELP checks the topic number you're adding to make sure that it isn't already in the project.

3. When you are satisfied with your entries, click OK. RoboHELP will add the map ID to the project.

You can also view and edit the properties for an existing map ID by double-clicking the topic entry to display the Map ID Properties screen (shown in Figure 11-12). From this screen, you can change the topic being referenced and the topic number.

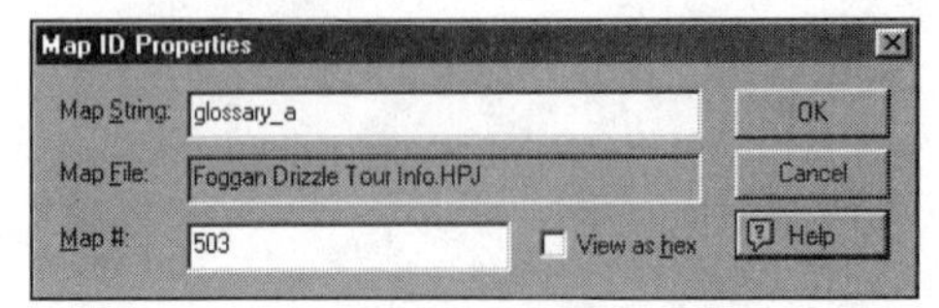

Figure 11-12: The Map ID Properties screen

The RoboHELP Explorer has a handy tool for searching for a specific topic number, as follows:

1. Right-click on a map ID folder in the RoboHELP Explorer (it doesn't matter which one) and select the Find Map ID command from the right-click menu. The Find Map ID screen appears (shown in Figure 11-13).

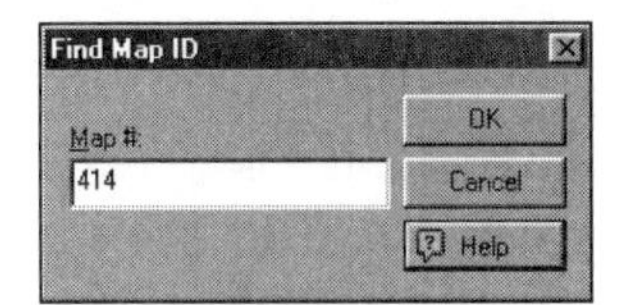

Figure 11-13: The Find Map ID screen

2. Enter the topic number you want to search for in the Map # field and click OK. If the topic number is in the project, RoboHELP will highlight the map ID entry. If the topic number does not appear in the project, RoboHELP will display a "Map ID not found" message.

If you are creating a large number of new map ID entries, you might want to create a new map file and then use that as the location of the new map entries. To create a new map file, do the following:

1. Right-click on a map ID folder in the RoboHELP Explorer (it doesn't matter which one) and select the New ➪ Map File command from the right-click menu. The New Map File screen appears (shown in Figure 11-14).

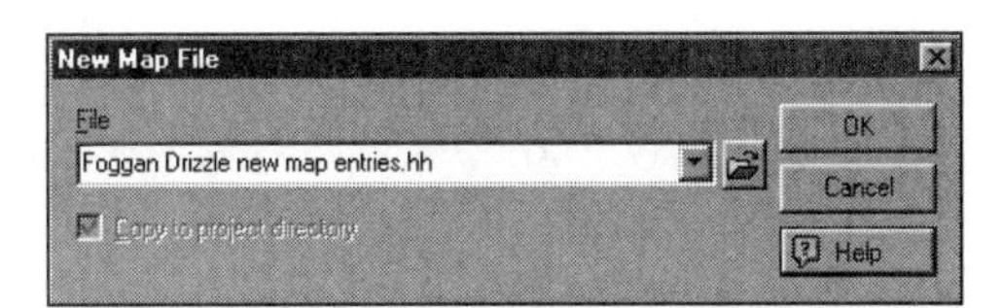

Figure 11-14: The New Map File screen

2. Enter the file name in the File field. If you don't add the HH extension to the file, RoboHELP will add it for you.

3. When you are satisfied with your changes, click OK. RoboHELP will create the file and add the entry to the list of map files in the RoboHELP Explorer.

Once the map file has been created, you can add map entries to it by right-clicking the map file.

Unused map IDs occur most frequently when you have entries for topics that have not yet been created or when the topics referenced have been changed or deleted and the map ID entries have not been updated. To remove unused topic IDs, do the following:

1. Right-click on a map ID folder in the RoboHELP Explorer and select the Remove Unused Map IDs command from the right-click menu. The Remove Unused Map IDs screen appears (shown in Figure 11-15).

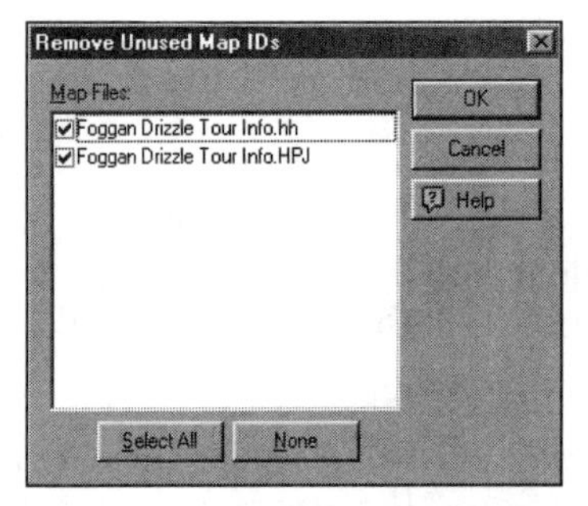

Figure 11-15: The Remove Unused Map IDs screen

2. Select the map files from which you want to remove unused map IDs.
3. When you are satisfied with your changes, click OK. RoboHELP removes all map entries in the selected map and HPJ files that do not correspond to topics in the projects DOC files.

You can delete map IDs by highlighting the entry and right-clicking, and then selecting Delete from the right-click menu. You can also delete individual map IDs by opening a Map ID folder, highlighting the entry, and then selecting Delete from the right-click menu.

Tips for Creating Context-Sensitive Help

Following are some tips for developing context-sensitive help:

✦ If you have context-sensitive help for specific portions of the program, you may want to modularize your context-sensitive help so that the context-sensitive help is in a separate file. This will make testing and maintenance easier. You may also want to break out standard context-sensitive help topics — such as topics on basic buttons, menus, and product functions — into a separate WinHelp file or in separate source documents.

✦ The default context-sensitive help prefix is IDH. The Microsoft Help Compiler 4.0 automatically checks for map numbers for any topics that have this prefix (and displays a warning if there is no corresponding map number). Unless you have a reason to change the prefix, it's best to leave it as is.

✦ What's This? help may be an effective alternative for creating context-sensitive help.

For more information on creating What's This? help and training card help, see Chapter 13, "Creating What's This? and Training Card Help."

✦ Be sure to choose the help development options that are best-suited to the language and development environment for the application and that also fit your needs for effective help maintenance.

Although the techniques and examples in this chapter show you how to use topic numbers and map ID entries to provide links to a WinHelp file, the WinHelp API also allows the developer to call help topics without using map IDs. With the WinHelp API, you can open a WinHelp file and perform the following help actions:

✦ Run a WinHelp macro.

✦ Display the Contents topic (specified in the [OPTIONS] section of the .HPJ file).

✦ Display a topic by its map ID.

✦ Display the Help menu for the window in the program from which you are calling the WinHelp file and then display the specific context-sensitive help topic in a popup window.

✦ Display a topic by its map ID in a popup window.

✦ Display the Help Topics dialog box.

✦ Verify that the WinHelp file currently open is correct.

✦ Display help about using WinHelp (requires that the WINHLP32.HLP file is available on the system).

✦ Display the topic that exactly matches or partially matches the specified keyword. (If the specified keyword has more than one match, the Topics Found list box appears with the matching topics listed.)

✦ Display the topic that matches the keyword in an alternative keyword table (created with an alternative footnote).

✦ Close the WinHelp file.

✦ Set the specified topic as the Contents topic.

✦ Set the popup window position on the screen.

✦ Display the WinHelp window and optionally specify its size and position.

✦ Display a training card.

✦ Display a topic in a popup window.

The ways in which you access the online help are determined by the specific needs of the project and the goals for your users. Discuss this with the developers and the project manager.

Using Aliases

So far in this chapter, you've learned how to create direct links between a single control in a program and a single topic. However, you will frequently need to link several controls to the same topic: For example, you may have several buttons or fields in a section of a screen that are all described in a single topic. Each of the buttons will have a separate topic number, but they all need to go to the same topic. Rather than create multiple identical topics, you can use aliases to aim each of the separate topic numbers at a single topic.

Aliases are stored in the [ALIAS] section of the HPJ file. You use aliases to associate a topic ID with a new topic ID. The [ALIAS] section must precede the [MAP] section in the HPJ file. Alias entries have the following form:

```
old-topic-ID=new-topic-ID
```

As an example of how you might use aliases, suppose that you've made some changes to the way online help is displayed for the Foggan Drizzle program screen described in Figure 11-1. Where there was previously one topic for each control, the screen's fields are now all covered in a single topic, and the buttons are covered in another topic. However, the individual controls still issue the same topic numbers, so you need to set up aliases to tell WinHelp which topic to display.

Figure 11-16 shows the original map entries still in the [MAP] section. When the program calls for a topic number in the online help file, WinHelp gets the topic ID associated with the number. It then checks that topic ID against the entries in the [ALIAS] section of the HPJ file and gets the new topic ID. This is a handy method for quickly patching broken links.

It's worth noting that the original topics (referenced by the topic numbers 10, 20, 30, and so on) don't actually have to exist in the online help file. The topic IDs can be dummy topic IDs that provide the other half of the map entry so that the topic numbers have some place to go. If the original topics have been deleted from the DOC file, it would be just as functional to have topic IDs of Dummy_ID_1, Dummy_ID_2, and so on. (In fact, it's preferable that they don't exist because you'll receive a compiler warning telling you that the topic you've aliased has already been defined in the topic to which you're aliasing it.) All WinHelp needs is to be able to accept an initial topic number from the program. This topic number then resolves through the various map entries and aliases to produce a valid topic ID that can be displayed.

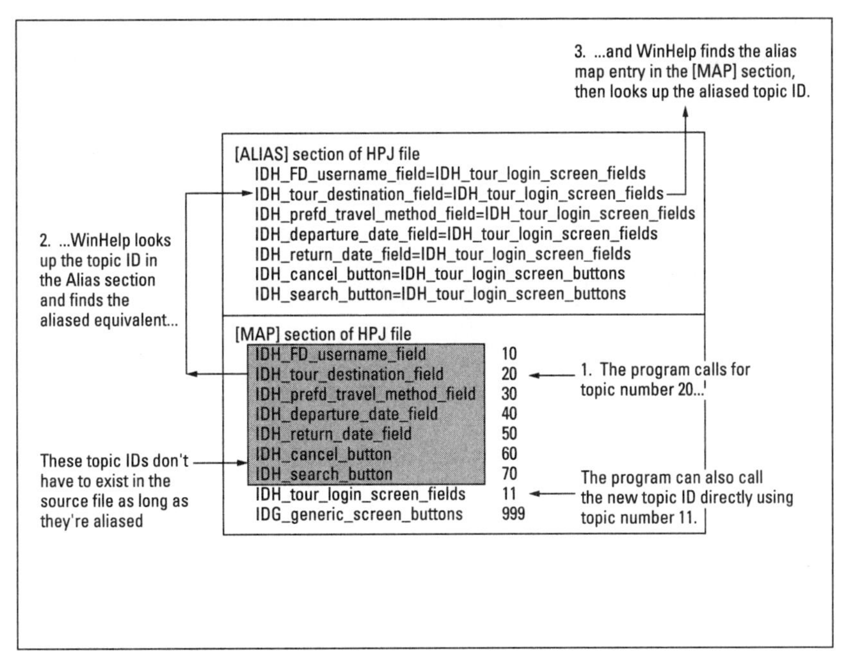

Figure 11-16: Use aliases to associate a topic ID with a new topic ID.

Another example of why you might use aliases is if you decide to use the same help topic for several similar fields, such as departure date and return date. Both buttons will bring up the same help topic, so you'd need to set up aliases to tell WinHelp which topic to display. In such a case, you could alias the map ID for the return date field (50) to the departure date field (40), or you could create a new topic for dates in general and alias both the return and departure date fields to the new field.

Aliases aren't just for external calls from programs. Suppose you have a topic in your WinHelp project that you want replace with another topic. If there were many occurrences of the old topic ID in the DOC files, it may not be practical to change the occurrences and then reverify the entire file. You could set up an alias to aim the old topic to the new topic. At any time the old topic is referenced in the online help file, WinHelp will use the new topic referred to in the alias.

To create an alias for multiple topic numbers, do the following:

1. Create dummy map ID entries for each topic number you want to alias. You can do this through the RoboHELP Explorer or by adding entries directly to the HPJ file as described earlier in this chapter. Be sure to use a name for the dummy topic ID that is easy to remember and clearly not an actual topic ID.

2. In the Map IDs folder of the RoboHELP Explorer's Project Manager, right-click on the first dummy map ID entry you created and select the New ➪ Alias command from the right-click menu. The New Alias screen appears (shown in Figure 11-17).

You can also display the New Alias screen by dragging a single topic from the RoboHELP Explorer Topic List and dropping it on a topic in the Unused Map IDs folder.

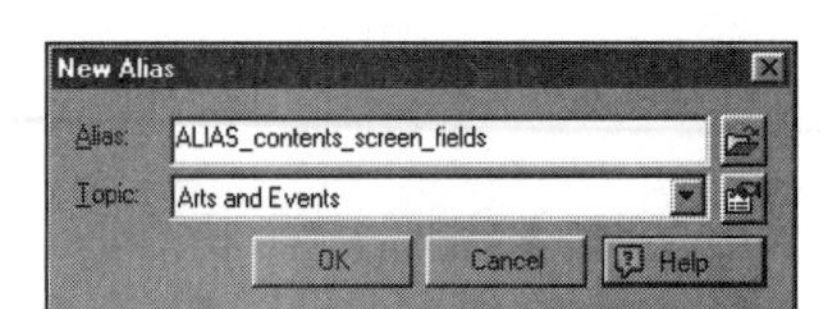

Figure 11-17: The New Alias screen

3. Enter information in the fields as follows:
   - **Alias:** Enter the name of the topic ID to be aliased. (The topic ID you right-clicked appears in this field by default.) Click the folder icon to the right of the field to select from the unused topic IDs.
   - **Topic:** Enter the topic ID that you want to alias to or select from the drop-down list. (Topics are listed in alphabetical order by topic title.) You can click the topic icon to the right of this field to display the Advanced tab of the standard Topic Properties screen if you want to view or change the topic number.
4. When you are satisfied with your entries, click OK. RoboHELP creates the alias, adds it to the HPJ file, and adds an alias entry in the Aliases folder of the RoboHELP Explorer Project Manager, as shown in Figure 11-18. RoboHELP also removes the entry from the Unused Map IDs folder (because the topic ID has now been assigned to something in the online help project).
5. Repeat this process as necessary to add the additional alias entries.

If you haven't already set up dummy map ID entries, you can add an alias by right-clicking the Aliases folder in the RoboHELP Explorer and then making your entries on the New Alias screen. This technique is useful if you are creating an internal alias from one topic to another.

You can delete aliases in the same way as you delete map IDs: by highlighting the entry and right-clicking, and then selecting Delete from the right-click menu.

While there are some legitimate requirements for using aliases when creating online help, a large number of aliases may be a sign that the WinHelp file has been patched repeatedly, rather than actually reworked. Fixing broken links with aliases can lead to multiple levels of aliasing, "ricochets," and links that are very hard to trace and debug. Whenever possible, rework the map IDs so that you need a minimum of aliases.

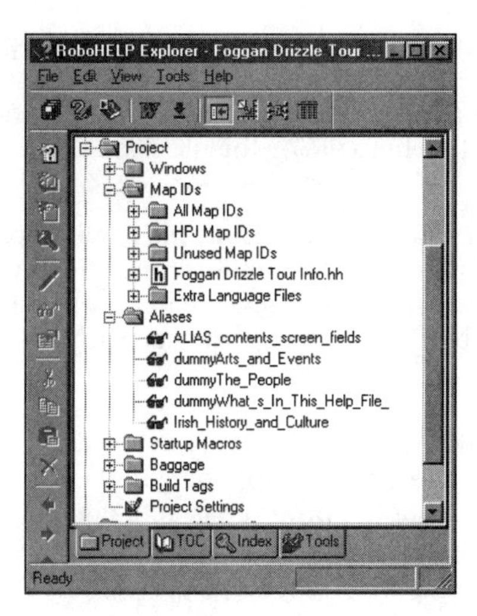

Figure 11-18: The Aliases folder in the RoboHELP Explorer

Testing Context-Sensitive Help

An essential part of creating context-sensitive help is testing the links you've created. The basic testing technique is simply to compile the online help file with the topic numbers and then trigger each context-sensitive link in the program in turn. If the links are correct, you'll see the appropriate topic appear each time. This type of testing can be handled easily by a member of the testing team.

However, it's likely that the testers will find *broken links,* controls requesting context-sensitive help in the program that do not display a topic or that display the wrong topic. These broken links will be reported to you by the testers for identification and resolution. The types of broken link you will generally encounter are as follows:

✦ No topic is found and you see an error message like the one shown in Figure 11-19. In this case, the program is using the wrong topic number. For example, the topic number being called by the program is 2500 but the online help file doesn't have a topic number 2500. You can fix this by changing the online help file and recompiling or by having the developer change the WinHelp call in the program and recompiling.

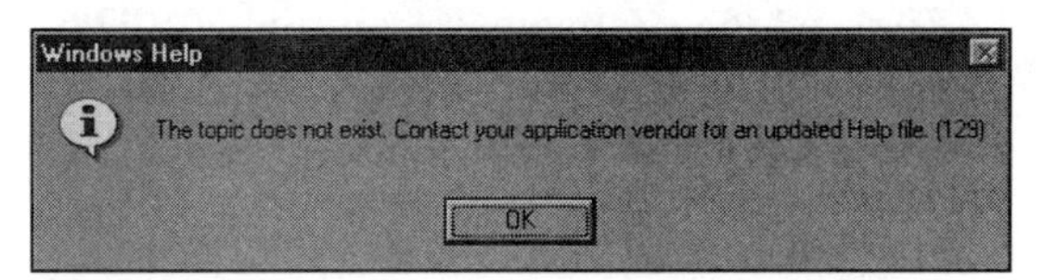

Figure 11-19: Typical context-sensitive help link error message

✦ The wrong topic is displayed. This is similar to the previous error: The topic number the program is calling exists in the online help file but, in this case, the topic number is assigned to the wrong topic. The solution for this is the same: Change the information in the online help file or the program and recompile.

✦ The help file is not found. This is caused by having the wrong file name or path being used by the program, having the online help file in the wrong directory, or otherwise not having the online help file available. Change the name or path of the online help file being called by the program or change the name or location of the compiled online help file.

The challenge when identifying context-sensitive help problems is determining where the error is happening. To determine if the error is happening in the program or in the online help file, you need to find out what the program is actually telling the online help file to display and also to simulate the program's calls for specific topics. To do this, you'll use a handy tool that's part of RoboHELP, the WinHelp BugHunter.

It's a good idea for bugs found in the online help to first be reported to the writers. Although many of them will probably be reassigned to the development team, documentation issues tend to get overlooked by developers when they're fixing bugs; as a result, you may not hear about documentation bugs that are assigned to development until it's too late. In addition, you'll probably be able to quickly identify the specific problem and solution for the developer in charge of fixing it.

Using the WinHelp BugHunter

The WinHelp BugHunter is a diagnostic tool that lets you monitor the behind-the-scenes activities of the program and the online help file when you are testing context-sensitive help. With the WinHelp BugHunter, you can monitor the calls from the program to the online help file to see which file and topic number are being called by the program. You can also use the WinHelp BugHunter as if it were the program to call a topic in a file using a topic number you enter.

To start the WinHelp BugHunter and monitor the interaction of a program and the associated WinHelp file, do the following:

1. From the RoboHELP Explorer, click the Tools tab, and then click the WinHelp BugHunter icon on the Tools window (shown in Figure 11-20). The WinHelp BugHunter screen appears (shown in Figure 11-21).

Figure 11-20: The WinHelp BugHunter (32-bit version) icon

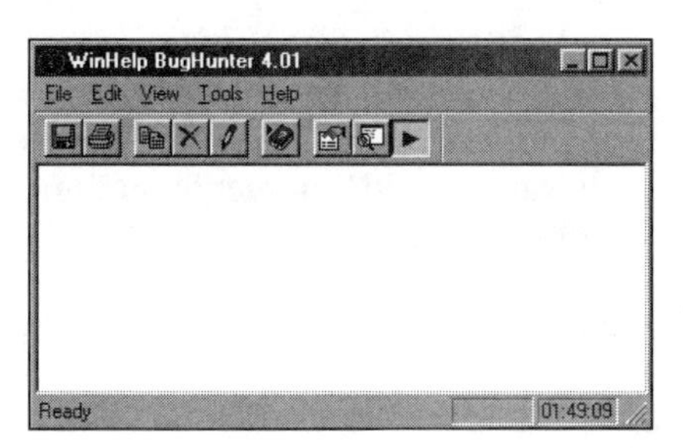

Figure 11-21: The WinHelp BugHunter screen

If you are working with a WinHelp 3 file, you'll want to use the 16-bit version of the WinHelp BugHunter. (The 16-bit WinHelp BugHunter icon appears in Figure 11-22.) The screen shots in this section are all from the 32-bit version of WinHelp BugHunter.

Figure 11-22: The WinHelp BugHunter (16-bit version) icon

2. Start the program. You may need to resize the program and WinHelp BugHunter windows so that you can see both of them simultaneously. (Although you can select "Always on Top" in the WinHelp BugHunter, it's easiest to run the program and the BugHunter side by side.)

3. Trigger context-sensitive help for a control that you want to check. The WinHelp BugHunter will display the calls from the program to the WinHelp file on the screen as well as routines that the WinHelp viewer will process as it opens the file and runs macros. (The information may scroll by quickly, but once it stops, you can scroll through it and examine it section by section.) Figure 11-23 shows typical information from the WinHelp BugHunter window for one of the RoboHELP help files.

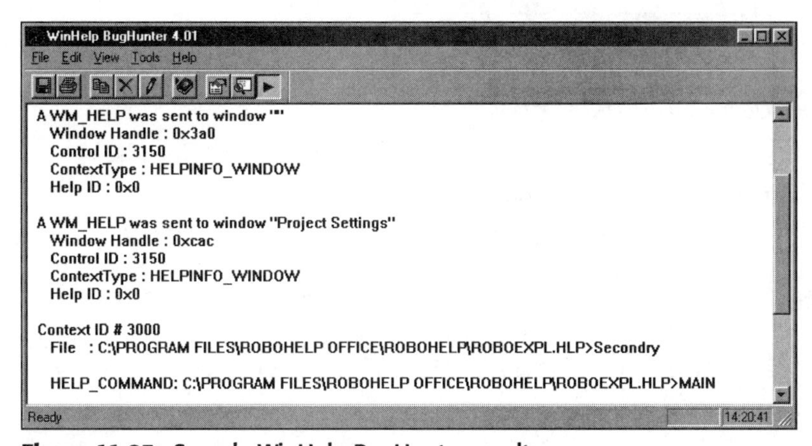

Figure 11-23: Sample WinHelp BugHunter results

4. As you access the WinHelp file from the program or within the WinHelp file itself, the WinHelp BugHunter logs the WinHelp activity. You can save the results in the WinHelp BugHunter window to a text file at any time by selecting the File ➪ Save command. If you want to add comments on the conditions you were testing, position the cursor where you want the text to appear and select the Edit ➪ Annotate command. You can also clear the screen with the Edit ➪ Clear All command.

Any call to a help file by any program will appear in the WinHelp BugHunter. For example, if you're testing a context-sensitive help file and you looked in the Word help file for information, the calls to the Word online help would also appear in the results. You can stop monitoring WinHelp activity by selecting the Tools ➪ Enable WinHelp BugHunter command. Once you're done accessing the other WinHelp file, you can select the command again to start monitoring WinHelp activity once more.

You can also use the WinHelp BugHunter to test a standalone WinHelp file by selecting the File ➪ Launch Help File command and opening the WinHelp file you want to look at. You can then check the various options in the WinHelp file and watch what is happening. This technique is particularly useful for observing macros and their results.

You can set several options in the WinHelp BugHunter, as follows:

1. Select the View ➪ Options command. The WinHelp BugHunter Options screen appears (shown in Figure 11-24).

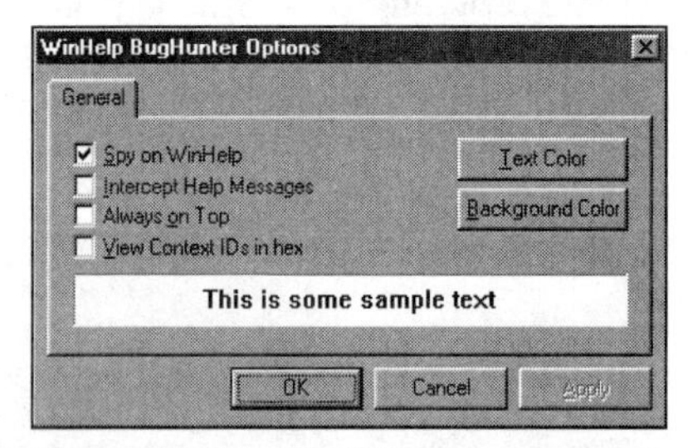

Figure 11-24: The WinHelp BugHunter Options screen

2. Enter information in the fields as follows:

   - **Spy on WinHelp:** Check this box to monitor all WinHelp activity. (This box is checked by default.) If this box is not checked, the WinHelp BugHunter will not report WinHelp activity such as macros.
   - **Intercept Help Messages:** Check this box to display information about WM_HELP and WM_TCARD calls from a program.

If you are using the WinHelp BugHunter to test What's This? help, be sure to have both the Spy on WinHelp and Intercept Help Messages boxes checked.

- **Always on Top:** Check this box to keep the WinHelp BugHunter on top of the open windows.
- **View Context IDs (Map Numbers) in Hex:** Check this box to view topic numbers in hexadecimal, rather than decimal, notation.
- **Text Color:** Click this button to change the text color. RoboHELP displays a standard color selection box.
- **Background Color:** Click this button to change the background color within the WinHelp BugHunter window. RoboHELP displays a standard color selection box.

3. When you are satisfied with your changes, click OK.

When you have become familiar with the WinHelp BugHunter, you may want to compress the results by enabling Expert mode. Expert mode eliminates some blank lines and compresses the macro names to their shorthand equivalents. To turn expert mode on or off, do the following:

✦ Select the View ➪ Expert Mode command (or just press Ctrl+E in the WinHelp BugHunter). The WinHelp BugHunter displays a message that says "Expert Mode is On" or "Expert Mode is Off" in the results.

Possibly the best use of the WinHelp BugHunter is to test specific topic numbers. You can tell the WinHelp BugHunter to open an online help file and search for a specific topic number just as if it were a program calling the topic.

To search for a specific topic number in an online help file, do the following:

1. Select the Tools ➪ Test Context ID command. The Test Context ID screen (shown in Figure 11-25) appears.

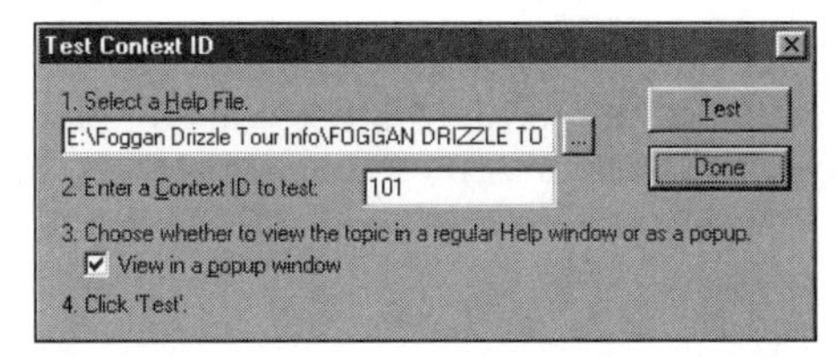

Figure 11-25: The Test Context ID screen

2. Enter information in the fields as follows:
   - **Select a Help File:** Enter the name of the online help file you want to open. Click the button to the right of this field to browse for a help file.
   - **Enter a Context ID to test:** Enter the topic number you want to search for in the file.
   - **View in a popup window:** Check this box if you want to display the topic in a popup window (probably adequate for a quick verification that the topic appears). If the box is unchecked, the topic will appear in its normal window.
3. When you are satisfied with your entries, click Test to display the specified topic.
4. Repeat the process as desired. When you are done testing, click Done to close the screen.

You can also use the `-n` option of the WinHelp viewer to test an individual topic number. For example, suppose you want to open the FDTOUR.HLP file in the C:\foggan directory and look for topic 9001. Do the following:

1. Open the Windows Explorer.
2. Select the Run command from the Start menu.
3. Enter the following command and click OK:

```
winhlp32 -n 9001 c:\foggan\fdtour.hlp
```

Note

If FDTOUR.HLP is a WinHelp 3 file, use *WinHelp,* rather than *WinHlp32,* in the command:

```
winhelp -n 9001 fdtour.hlp
```

4. WinHelp will open the file and search for the topic with the topic number. If it finds the topic, it will display the topic as usual. If it doesn't, you'll see an error message like the one shown earlier in Figure 11-19.

Debugging broken and incorrect links in context-sensitive help can be complex, frustrating, and laborious. By using the WinHelp BugHunter, you can quickly isolate a problem and determine if the program is calling the wrong topic or if the WinHelp file is mismapped.

Printing the Map ID and Duplicate Map ID Reports

The Map ID report provides you with general information about the map IDs. To generate a Map ID report, do the following. From the RoboHELP Explorer, select the Tools ➪ Reports ➪ Map ID command. The Map ID report is displayed on the screen, as shown in Figure 11-26. The map IDs appear on the report in order by topic ID.

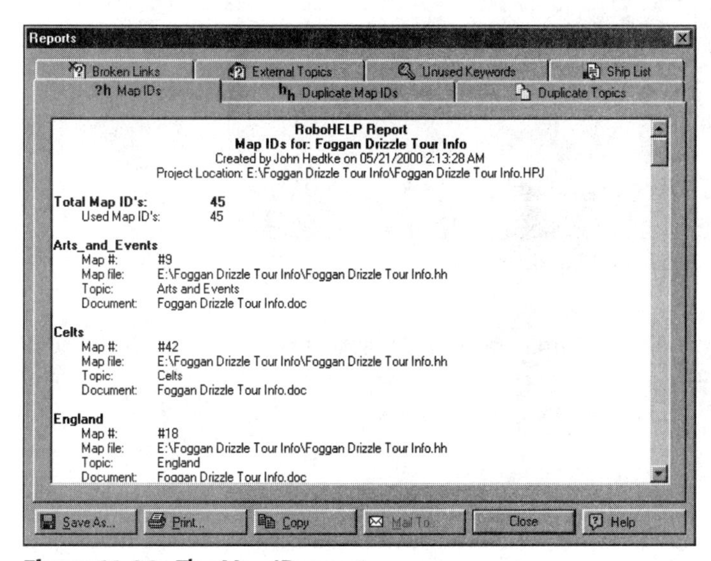

Figure 11-26: The Map ID report

The Duplicate Map ID report is a diagnostic report. It lists all duplicate entries for topic IDs and topic numbers. To generate a Duplicate Map ID report, do the following. From the RoboHELP Explorer, select the Tools ➪ Reports ➪ Duplicate Map ID command. (If you've already displayed the Map IDs report, you can simply click the Duplicate Map IDs report tab.) The Duplicate Map ID report is displayed on the screen, as shown in Figure 11-27.

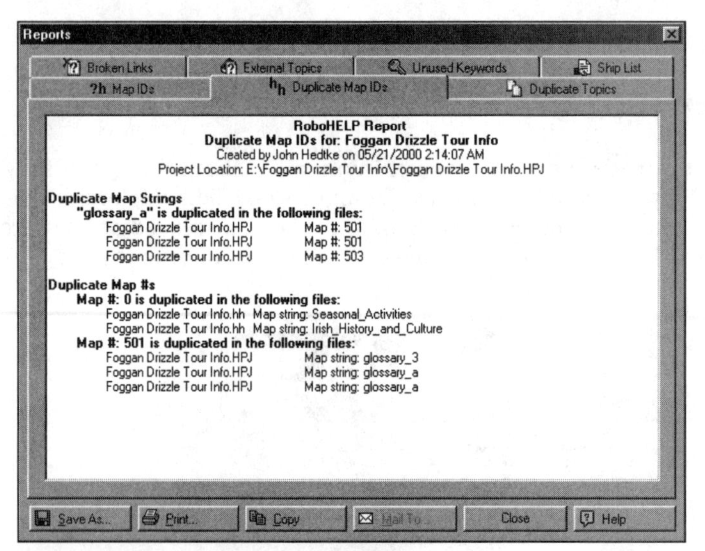

Figure 11-27: The Duplicate Map ID report

You can run the Map ID and Duplicate Map ID reports (or any of the RoboHELP reports) at any time.

Summary

This chapter introduced you to context-sensitive help. You first saw how context-sensitive help works with programs. The chapter then described many of the issues to consider when planning a context-sensitive help project. You next saw how to add context-sensitive links in several ways. You also learned about aliases and how to link multiple controls in a program to a single topic. The chapter continued with information on testing and debugging context-sensitive help files with the WinHelp BugHunter. In conclusion, you saw how to generate the Map ID and Duplicate Map ID reports.

✦ ✦ ✦

CHAPTER 12

Linking to the Internet and Adding Multimedia

✦ ✦ ✦ ✦

In This Chapter

Using eHelp and the RoboHELP Help Community

Adding multimedia with the {mci} command

Adding multimedia with the RHMMPLAY macros

Creating and editing custom WAV files

Creating and editing custom AVI files

✦ ✦ ✦ ✦

This chapter shows you how to link your online help files to the Internet and to add sound and video to WinHelp projects. You are first introduced to eHelp, a new service from eHelp that links your users with search features on the Internet. You'll also see how to use the RoboHELP Help Community to obtain additional information about developing online help files. The chapter continues with information about adding multimedia to your WinHelp files for greater effectiveness, first with the `{mci}` command and then using the RHMMPLAY.DLL macros. The chapter concludes with information about how to create your own WAV files using the Windows Sound Recorder and how to create AVI files using the RoboHELP Office Software Video Camera.

Using eHelp

You've already seen how to access Web sites, FTP sites, and e-mail addresses from WinHelp using jumps in Chapter 4, "Adding Jumps and Popups." This section will show you how to let your users take advantage of a new RoboHELP feature called eHelp.

The eHelp feature is likely to be called "WebSearch" in later releases of RoboHELP Office.

eHelp is a way to provide extended online support for your users. It lets the users locate information automatically on the Web using help keywords, topics, and other information as well as do advanced Web searching for additional information.

Although the eHelp examples in this section use WinHelp files, the procedures are virtually the same for accessing and using eHelp from within an HTML Help file.

Accessing the eHelp Online Search Features

So far in this book, you've seen the eHelp button on the button bar of the sample help files. When you first install RoboHELP 2000, eHelp is automatically enabled—when you compile an online help project, RoboHELP adds the eHelp button and links the external DLL necessary to support the eHelp features.

When the user clicks the eHelp button in your help file, RoboHELP first looks at the keywords in the topic that's currently open. It then opens a connection to the eHelp site, `www.helpcommunity.com`, and searches across the Internet for topics relating to your keywords. (The user must have an Internet connection to use eHelp.) After a moment, the Advanced Web Search screen appears (shown in Figure 12-1).

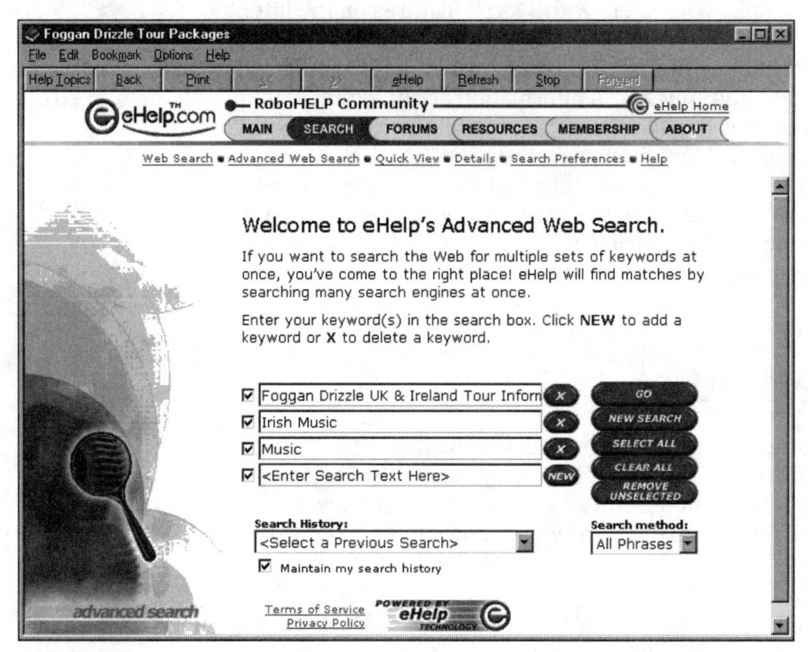

Figure 12-1: The eHelp Advanced Web Search screen

The eHelp features are being updated continually. The screens shown in this chapter may differ slightly from the screens the users see when they use these features.

Take a moment to look at this screen. As you can see, when the users open eHelp, RoboHELP adds three buttons to the button bar—Refresh, Stop, and Forward—and the display in the help screen acts like a standard browser window. These buttons act the same as standard browser buttons. You can reload screens, stop a screen from loading, and, in conjunction with the standard Back button, move backward and forward through the topics.

The default option is for the eHelp button to open eHelp in the online help file window (similar to the way in which Web pages are displayed from a jump) but you can set eHelp's options so that clicking the eHelp button will open your user's browser.

The Advanced Web Search screen uses the topic keywords as search criteria. (You'll see how to change the settings for the default search criteria later in this chapter). Each of the criteria from the search criteria field appears in a separate field. The users can deselect the various criteria by unchecking the box to the left of each field. Clicking X to the right of the field tells eHelp to completely remove the criterion and the field and to display the screen again with that entire line deleted. There is always one additional search criterion field in which the users can enter a new keyword or other search item. To add still more search criteria, click New; eHelp displays the screen with a new empty search criterion field into which the users can enter a new search item.

The buttons on the far right of the Advanced Web Search screen can be used to start a completely new search, select or clear all the fields, or to remove any unselected lines. The users can look for all the items by selecting All Phrases (the default option) in the Search Method drop-down list in the lower right corner. Alternately, the users can tell eHelp to search for any of the criteria by selecting Any Phrase. At any point, the users can click Go to start the search. The search results will be displayed in a screen similar to the one shown in Figure 12-2.

The topics being displayed in the left column are topics found on the Web that match the keywords for the topic. (You can close this window by clicking the Close Quick View button at the top of the list.) The first topic in the list appears in the right side of the screen.

eHelp is a relatively new service. The features and options are expanding continually as the service is revised. Plan on spending a little while exploring the full range of eHelp available features and options to determine what you may choose to offer to your users. If you prefer, you can log on to the Web site directly at `www.helpcommunity.com` and look around instead of working through a help file.

Figure 12-2: Sample search results

Changing eHelp Options

The preceding section showed you how the users can access and use eHelp based on the default eHelp settings in RoboHELP. However, you can change and refine many of the eHelp options, including:

✦ which topics in the WinHelp file offer eHelp

✦ additional search criteria for the help project

✦ preferred domains to search on the Web

✦ how to display eHelp

To set eHelp options, do the following:

1. Select the RoboHELP ➪ Project Settings command in Word and select the eHelp tab. (You can also select the File ➪ Project Settings command in the RoboHELP Explorer.) The eHelp tab of the Project Settings screen appears, as shown in Figure 12-3.

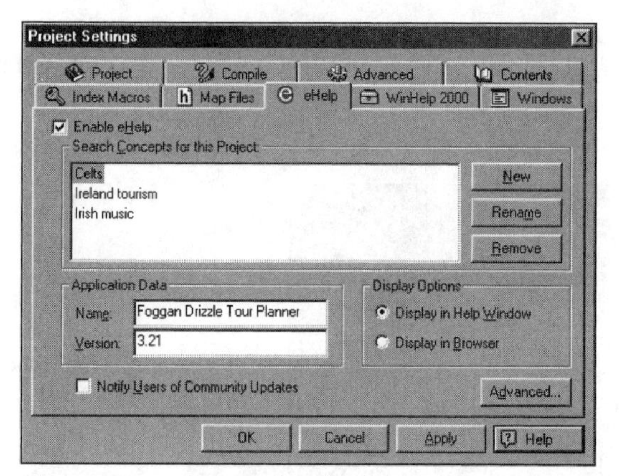

Figure 12-3: The eHelp tab of the Project Settings screen

2. Enter information in the fields as follows:

   - **Enable eHelp:** Check this box to enable eHelp (the default option). If the option is not enabled, the eHelp button will not appear on the online help button bar.

   - **Search Concepts for this Project:** Enter any additional search concepts for the help project, such as words, search phrases, or Web sites. Click New to add a new search concept. (Figure 12-3 shows sample search concepts added in this field.) RoboHELP sorts the search concepts in alphabetical order. You can change an existing search concept by highlighting it and clicking the Rename button. You can also delete a highlighted search concept by clicking the Remove button.

   - **Application Data:** Enter the name and the version number of the program with which the help project is associated. This information will help eHelp search for information more closely related with this version of the program.

   - **Display Options:** Check the appropriate selection for where you want eHelp to appear. The default option is for eHelp to appear in the online help window itself (as shown earlier in this chapter); however, you can select Display in Browser to open the default browser and display eHelp screens there. Displaying information in the browser has the added advantage of showing the URL of the information being displayed.

The default browser that will appear on the user's system is set on the user's system and is not necessarily the default browser set by the help author's system.

   - **Notify Users of Community Updates:** Check this option to enable the users to automatically receive updates when they open the WinHelp project or when they click a help button on one of the associated program screens.

3. When you are satisfied with your changes, click Advanced to set additional options. The General tab of the Advanced screen appears, as shown in Figure 12-4.

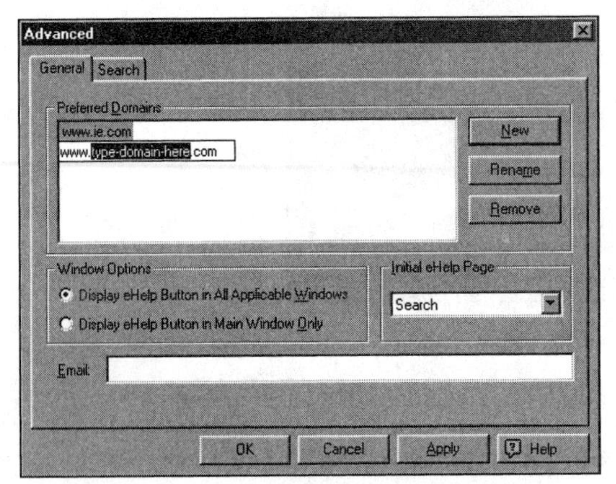

Figure 12-4: The General tab of the Advanced screen

4. Enter information in the fields as follows:

   - **Preferred Domains:** Enter any Web domains that are likely to have relevant information or that you'd like eHelp to search first. When you click New, RoboHELP enters a dummy domain with the center portion selected. Type the domain information. (Figure 12-4 shows a domain added to the field and one in the process of being added.) Highlight a domain and click Rename to change the domain or click Remove to delete it.
   - **Window Options:** Select Display eHelp Button in All Applicable Windows to display the eHelp button in all windows with a button bar (the default option). Select Display eHelp Button in Main Window Only to limit the eHelp button to topics displayed in the Main window.
   - **Initial eHelp Page:** From the drop-down list, select the eHelp screen you first want to display when your users click the eHelp button. You can display the Search screen to enter search criteria, the Results screen to show the results of the search based on the topic search criteria, the Community screen to go to your community, or the Home screen to display all online communities. (The Home screen is helpful if you have users who are not as familiar with using the Internet as others.)
   - **Email:** Enter your e-mail address or the e-mail address of a general information mailbox. RoboHELP will send bulletins to this address with information on how your users are working with the online help and eHelp. (Information gathered in this way is sent only to you; it is not distributed.)

5. When you are satisfied with your changes, click the Search tab. The Search tab appears, as shown in Figure 12-5.

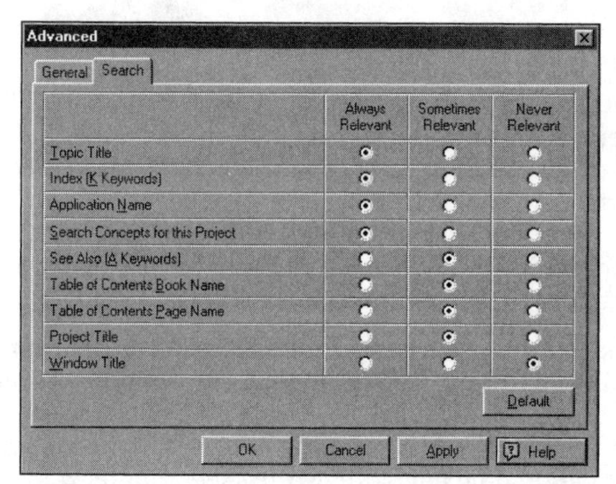

Figure 12-5: The Search tab of the Advanced screen

6. Select the level of relevance for each of the categories by checking the appropriate button as follows:

   - Select Always Relevant for a category if you want eHelp to always select this item as part of the search criteria. For example, one of the defaults is for the topic title to be set as Always Relevant, so eHelp will always use as one of the search criteria the title of the topic the user called eHelp from.
   - Select Sometimes Relevant for a category if you want eHelp to list this item as a possible search criterion on the Search screen, but not to automatically include this criterion when the user performs a search. For example, one of the defaults is for the See Also (A-keywords) to be set as Sometimes Relevant, so eHelp will not use the A-keywords as search criteria but the users will be able to select them on the Search screen.
   - Select Never Relevant for a category if you want eHelp to ignore this when searching and also on the Search screen. For example, the Window Title is set to Never Relevant as a default, so eHelp will not use the window title as a search criterion, nor will it appear automatically as an option on the Search screen.

Note You can reset the fields to their default settings by clicking the Default button on the lower right corner of the screen. The Search tab lets you refine the eHelp search options for this online help project.

7. When you are satisfied with your changes, click OK on each of the screens to save the settings. The options you set in these project settings screens will take effect the next time you compile the online help project.

Here are a few tips when identifying the search criteria for your online help project:

✦ Be cautious about specifying a topic as Always Relevant. If a category is selected as Always Relevant, eHelp will always use that category as part of the search criteria. However, some categories may be overpopulated and consequently make for poor search criteria. For example, having extensive keywords can be a boon for directly searching the online help using the WinHelp index features, but too many keywords can make the results of a Web search too broad. In such a case, you'd probably want to use the Sometimes Relevant option.

✦ An alternative is to have a search criterion set up as Always Relevant that has been designed with an eye toward Web searching. For example, if you are not using A-Keywords extensively in your WinHelp file, you might add A-Keywords designed for Web searching. You'd then set the A-keywords to Always Relevant. (For more information on using A-Keywords, see Chapter 8, "Using Tables of Contents and Indexes.")

Using the RoboHELP Help Community

In addition to the online search features that have been described in this section, there is an extensive online community specifically for RoboHELP users. This had originally been part of the eHelp features but has become a resource and support section of its own at `www.helpcommunity.ehelp.com`. From here, you can access the RoboHELP knowledge base, get technical support, and obtain information on articles, books, product patches, and product trainers.

One of the most valuable features of the RoboHELP Help Community is the ability to interact with other users through the forums. (This feature requires you to log in with a user ID and password. If you haven't already set up a user ID and password, you'll be taken through a simple new user set-up screen.) You can also set eHelp to log you in automatically when you log on from the same computer.

Once you log in, you'll see the main forum screen. Categories of topics appear in the left column. The number of individual messages in the category appears in parentheses to the right of the category title. Clicking the plus sign will expand a topic into the various message threads, as shown in Figure 12-6.

To display an individual message, click on the message header in the left column. The message appears on the right side of the screen, as shown in Figure 12-7. As you can see, the message headers and format are fairly standard. You can post a reply with or without quoting from this message. You can also read the next or previous message in the thread or the next or previous topic. If you click on the name of the person who posted the message, eHelp will display information about the person's account and any basic profile data the person entered.

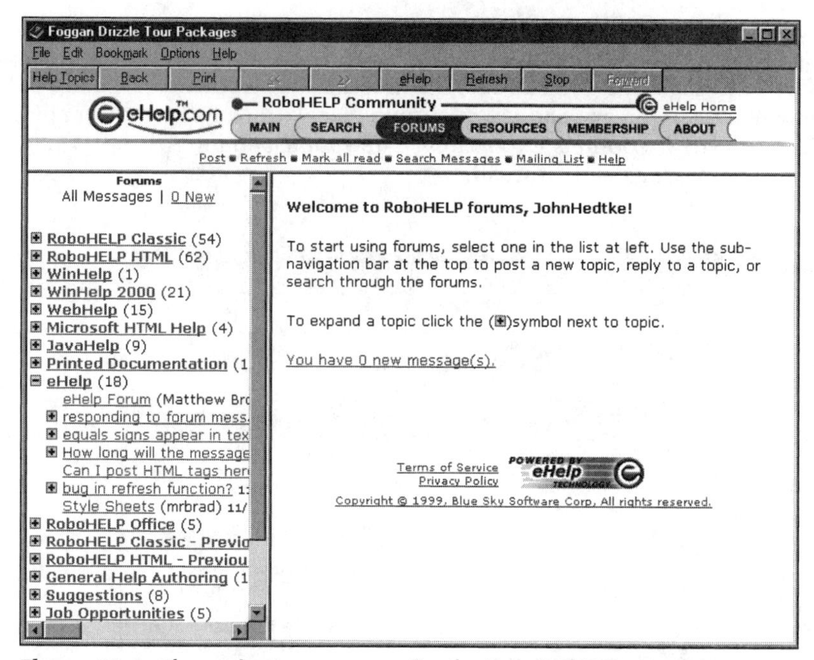

Figure 12-6: The main Forum screen for the RoboHELP Community

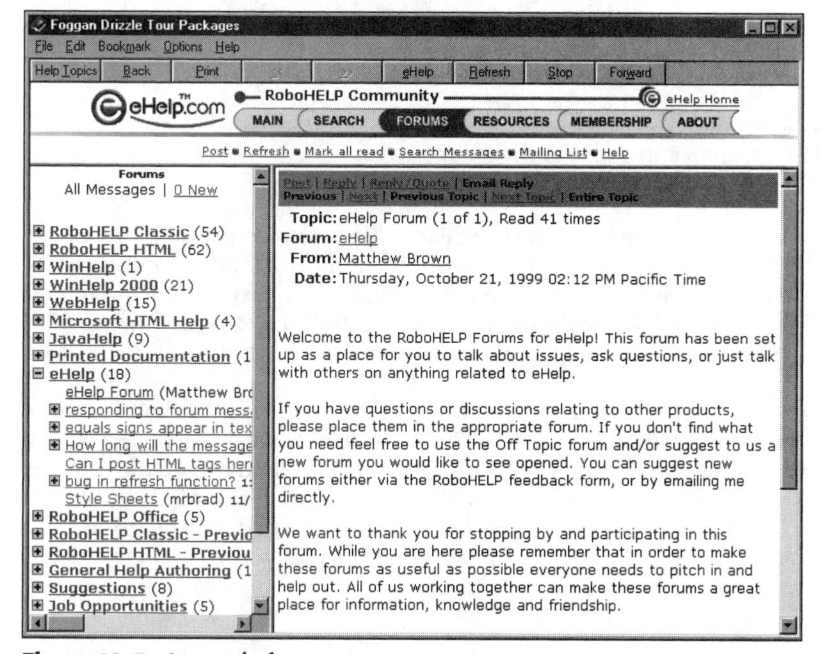

Figure 12-7: A sample forum message

You should also note that all the messages in a thread will appear one after another in the right side of the screen. For example, Figure 12-8 shows the start of a thread that has four messages. As you can see, the first message appears at the top of the list, after which the replies are added in chronological order. At the bottom of the thread (not shown) are options for creating a new topic and for posting a reply to the most recent message in the thread.

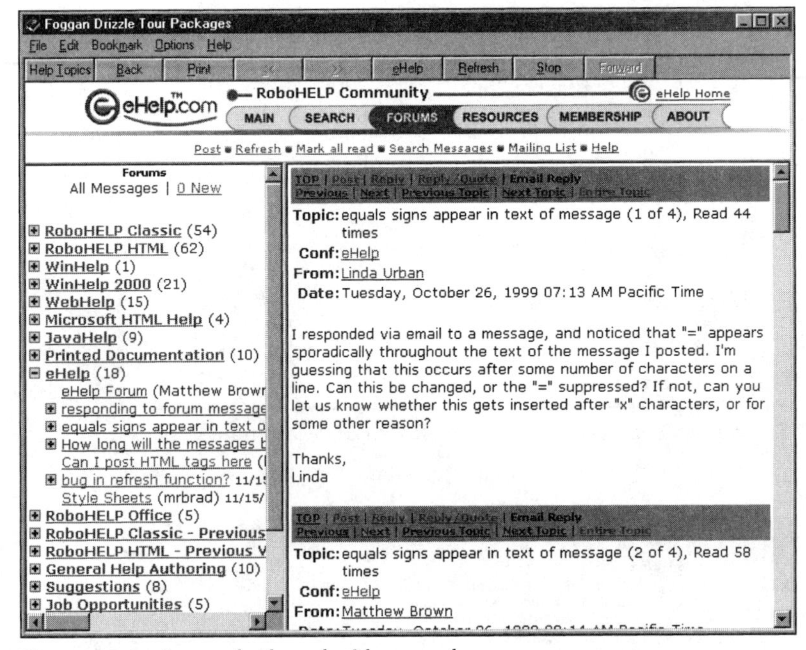

Figure 12-8: A sample thread with several messages

You can search for messages using the Search Messages command. RoboHELP developers will be particularly interested in the RoboHELP Community's Mailing List command. This displays a screen of mailing lists (listservs) that you can subscribe to on such topics as RoboHELP Classic, RoboHELP HTML, WinHelp 2000, Microsoft HTML Help, JavaHelp, and many others.

Many handy features are built into the forum. For example, when you first enter the forums, you'll see a message that says "You have 0 new message(s)." Each time, thereafter, that you enter the forum with this user ID, eHelp will identify how many new messages there are and, when you click on the hyperlink, will highlight the new messages for easy access. In conjunction with this, you can mark all topics in a thread, a category, or the entire forum as "read" so that you can quickly identify any new messages the next time you log in.

You can use the search features to track down additional information on the Web. Figure 12-9 shows the basic search screen (accessed by clicking Search in the menu bar). Note that the Foggan Drizzle help title as well as the topic title and the keywords for the topic (not visible) appear in the search criteria field.

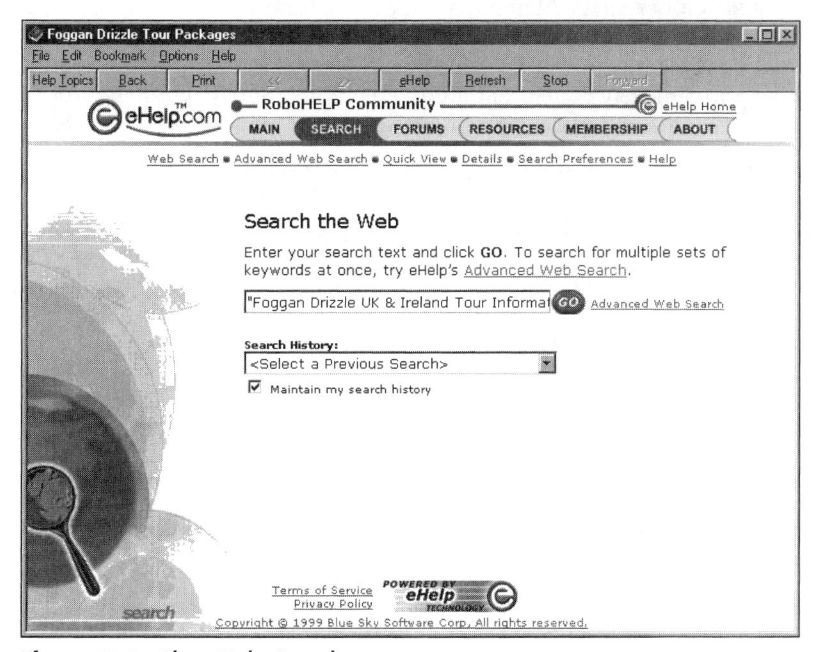

Figure 12-9: The eHelp Search screen

Make any changes to the information in the search criteria field and click Go to start the search. The results appear in the same format as the search results shown earlier in Figure 12-2. If you need more exact search options, you can refine your search by clicking the Advanced Web Search hyperlink.

As with the eHelp features for end users, the features and options offered in the RoboHELP Help Community are continually changing. Take a look at the Help Community Web site for the latest information and options.

What Is Multimedia?

This section of the chapter will show you how to add multimedia to your WinHelp files. *Multimedia* is broadly defined as embedded sounds, video, or combined video and sound. Typical multimedia files include WAV (waveform audio) files and AVI (audio video interleave) files.

The effective use of multimedia can turn a generic online help file into a really snappy one. Adding multimedia to an online help file has many advantages, such as the following:

✦ **Improved comprehension:** Studies have shown that retention rates for material that's simply read is 70 percent after three hours and 10 percent after three days. However, when combined with a demonstration (such as a video presenting the concept or procedure), a study has shown that the retention rate is approximately 85 percent after three hours and 65 percent after three days. Multimedia can make learning new concepts much more effective.

✦ **Better communication of abstract or complex concepts:** Sound and animation can communicate quickly and easily where text alone may not be adequate. For example, you can use animation to show users how to click and drag a block of text much more easily than you can describe the process in text or a video of someone playing a banjo to show proper fingering. As another example, you can include in a help file on the basics of auto mechanics the sounds an engine makes when it's out of tune, has bad rings, or is knocking. You might also have a collection of sounds for different types of birds commonly found in the northeastern United States.

✦ **Greater visual appeal:** As when you added graphics to your online help files, adding video and sound will make the online help files more interesting, more exciting, and more memorable. The multimedia you use can be something as simple as background music when displaying main topics or as complex as a full-screen sound and video tutorial.

✦ **An additional type of information:** Multimedia can be used as another way to provide information on what users should do and how to do it. For example, one software package has two versions of online help for its installation procedure, one text-based and the other multimedia, with an animated figure that describes the information you need to enter in each screen.

While multimedia is very exciting, it's easy to overuse. Use the following questions to evaluate if it's a good idea to add multimedia to your online help files:

✦ **Do your users have the requisite hardware to see and hear multimedia?** Your users must have a sound card and speakers on their computers in order for them to hear sound files. Although this will probably not be an issue for private users — most computers these days have some kind of sound capabilities — but corporate users may not have sound cards or good speakers. Similarly, your users must also have adequate computer power to display video files without bogging down the computer. Be sure to check that your minimum system configuration will support the multimedia features you want to use.

✦ **Is this a WinHelp 3 file?** While multimedia is a built-in feature of WinHelp 4, WinHelp 3 doesn't support it directly. If you are working with WinHelp 3 files, you can use the Video Wizard (described later in this chapter) to add multimedia features to your online help files.

✦ **How much room is available on the users' computers?** Although it's not likely that the help file will take up an appreciable amount of room on a hard disk, including full-sound-and-video files can make an online help file considerably larger. This may have additional consequences for how you ship the online help file or distribute updates.

✦ **What is the environment your users will use the multimedia online help files on?** There are some restrictions on the way in which you can add multimedia files to the WinHelp file. For example, while you can bundle WAV and AVI files as part of the online help file for most Windows systems (you'll see how to do this later in this section), you can't bundle WAV files in WinHelp files that are run on Windows NT. If you try to run the sound file, a bug in Windows NT will crash or freeze help.

✦ **Do you need to create multimedia files for this online help file?** A large number of sound and video files are available on the Internet or on compilation CDs that can be used freely or (occasionally) for a very small licensing fee. However, if you can't find the thing you need, you must create your own sound and/or video files.

The Video Software Kit in RoboHELP Office, described later in this chapter, is a tool for recording and manipulating videos and sound.

✦ **Is it worth the effort of creating multimedia files?** Recording a good voice file may take you an hour or two between writing the text, practicing it, speaking it, and cleaning it up. If you're doing something high-end, you may need to hire voice talent and go into a recording studio, and then edit the resulting files. Even more expensive is creating video files: you must set up cameras and lights, rehearse, get the shots on videotape, and then edit them, all of which can be enormously time consuming. If you're adding sound, you must also edit the sound and match it to the action. By comparison, you may be able to do an adequate job in the same online help file typing a few paragraphs of text to describe a process. On the other hand, some things are much better handled by sound or video files: for example, describing the changes in color, sheen, and sound for pottery fired at various temperatures and durations is much easier to do with a brief animation than with text.

Adding Multimedia to Your WinHelp File

Adding multimedia is actually very simple. In fact, it's very much like including graphics files in an online help file.

Before you start adding multimedia to your WinHelp project, you must make sure that the files are in the right format.

✦ Sound files must be in WAV (waveform audio) format. WAV is the standard file format for sound files in Windows. There are thousands of WAV files on the Internet and on compilation CDs that you can use. You can also create your own WAV files with a microphone and the Windows SNDREC32.EXE program, (which typically appears as Start ➪ Programs ➪ Accessories ➪ Entertainment ➪ Sound Recorder) or other programs that accompany your computer's sound card.

✦ Video files must be in AVI (audio video interleave) format. AVI is the standard file format for video files (with or without sound) in Windows. The AVI video format is playable on most computers with good to excellent full-motion video and audio. Many AVI files can be found on the Internet, but you'll probably have to create your own video files. You can do this by feeding the video from a videotape into your computer through a video capture card or with Software Video Camera utility in RoboHELP Office.

Once you have the sound and video files you want to include in the WinHelp project, you're ready to add them.

To add multimedia to your online help file, do the following:

1. Position the cursor where you want to insert the WAV or AVI file, and then select the Insert ➪ Help Multimedia command, or just click the New Multimedia button on the RoboHELP toolbar as shown in Figure 12-10. The Insert Help Multimedia screen appears (as shown in Figure 12-11).

Figure 12-10: Multimedia button

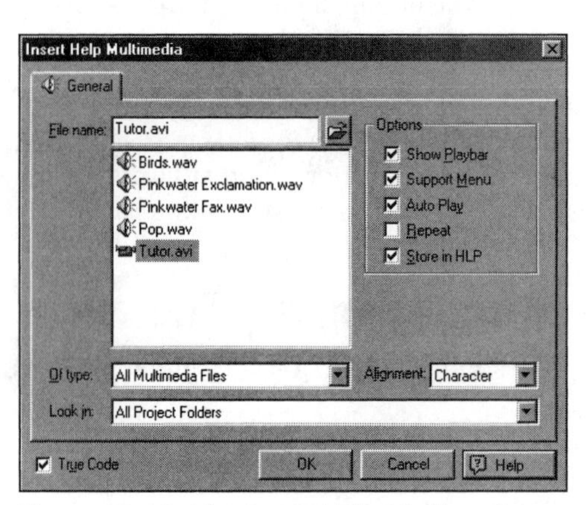

Figure 12-11: The Insert Help Multimedia screen

2. Enter information in the fields as follows:

   - **File name:** Enter the name of the WAV or AVI file you want to include. If you want, you can browse for a specific file by clicking the file folder button to the right of the field.
   - **Show Playbar:** Check this box to display the video playbar so your users can control the playback of the video file. (This box is checked by default.)
   - **Support Menu:** If Show Playbar is checked, checking this box displays the support menu button for additional control of the video file being played. The support menu button lets users change the size of the video window, the volume of the sound, and the speed at which the video file is played. You can also copy the AVI file, configure the video playback properties, and enter an `{mci}` command. If Show Playbar is not checked, the users can right-click on the video to display the Support Menu.

Note

MCI commands let you control multimedia devices. MCI commands are described in documentation accompanying the Microsoft Video for Windows Developers Kit. As an online help developer, you probably won't need to use this feature.

   - **Auto Play:** Check this box to start the file automatically when the help topic is opened. (If you check this option, the Repeat option will be grayed out.) If you select a WAV file, this box is checked by default. If you select an AVI file and you don't check Show Playbar or Support Menu, this box is checked by default.

Note

If you are adding multimedia to a popup window, you must use Auto Play to start the file.

   - **Repeat:** Check this box to loop the video file indefinitely. (The users can stop the file if they wish.) This option is grayed out if you have checked Auto Play.
   - **Store in HLP:** Check this box to store the multimedia file as part of the compiled WinHelp file. RoboHELP will add a reference to the WAV or AVI file to the [BAGGAGE] section of the HPJ file. When you compile the WinHelp project, the files are incorporated in the WinHelp file. Although this means you don't have to ship the multimedia files separately, the compiled WinHelp file can become very large.

If the WinHelp file will be used on Windows NT systems, don't save WAV files inside the WinHelp file. A bug in Windows NT will crash the WinHelp viewer when users try to play a WAV file embedded in a WinHelp file.

   - **Of type:** Select the type of files to display from the drop-down list: all multimedia files, WAV files, or AVI files.

- **Alignment:** Specify where you want the multimedia file to appear from the drop-down list. Character (the default) inserts the multimedia file at the cursor position. Left left-justifies the graphic, and Right right-justifies the multimedia file. Depending on which option you select, the text flows around or to the side of the multimedia file.
- **True Code:** Check this box to insert the reference to the multimedia file as a command statement (True Code). Uncheck the box if you want to see the multimedia file displayed in the file using Dynamic WYSIWYG. Inserting the command statement is useful for advanced WinHelp developers and allows you to edit file information using Word's find-and-replace features. (You'll see how to do this a little later in the chapter.)

3. When you are satisfied with your entries, click OK. RoboHELP inserts the multimedia file as specified.

RoboHELP uses the `{mci}` command as the default for displaying multimedia files. The `{mci}` command is built into the WinHelp 4 compiler. It requires that your users have Microsoft Media Player on their computers to play multimedia files. Microsoft Media Player is a standard feature in Windows 95 and later.

If you select the True Code option, you'll see an entry such as this for an AVI file:

```
{mci play , ireland.avi}
```

If you have not selected the True Code option, the first frame of the AVI file appears in the DOC file, as shown in Figure 12-12. In this figure, you can see both the Playbar and the Support Menu button at the bottom of the AVI.

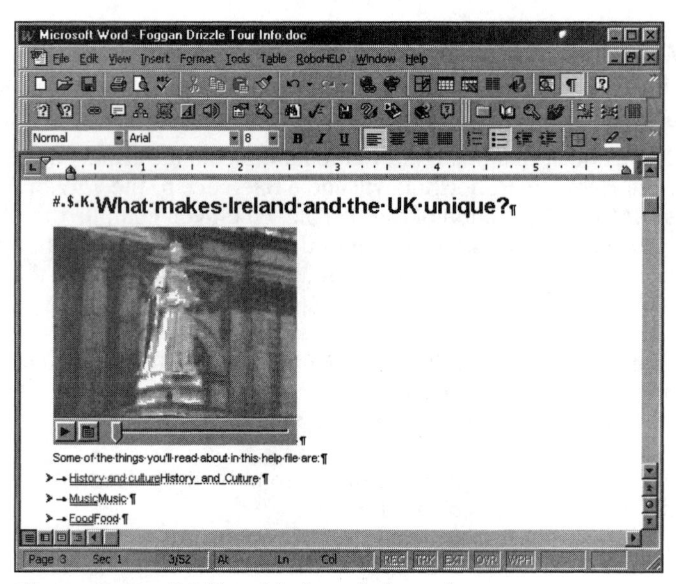

Figure 12-12: AVI file added to a help topic

The True Code for a WAV file looks like this:

```
{mci noplaybar nomenu play , ceilidhe.wav}
```

If you have not selected the True Code option for a WAV file, RoboHELP inserts the New Multimedia button in the file.

When you add multimedia files to the WinHelp project, they appear in the RoboHELP Explorer Project Manager as well:

1. In the RoboHELP Explorer Project Manager, click the Images and Multimedia folder.
2. Open the Multimedia folder. The multimedia files are listed in alphabetical order.

If you are storing the files in the WinHelp file, the multimedia files (and any other files stored in the WinHelp file) are also listed in the Baggage folder within the Project folder.

You can edit the properties for an embedded multimedia file by right-clicking the True Code or the file and selecting Properties from the right-click menu, or by just double-clicking the multimedia file in the DOC file. You can also right-click the file name in the RoboHELP Explorer and select Properties from the right-click menu. Double-clicking the multimedia file name in the RoboHELP Explorer displays the Multimedia Properties screen (not shown), which lets you view the file name, file information, and topics in which the multimedia file is used.

Deleting a multimedia file is simply a matter of selecting the True Code or the Dynamic WYSIWYG file insert and pressing Delete. If you are also storing multimedia files in the [BAGGAGE] section of the HPJ file using the Store in HLP option, you also need to delete the files from the [BAGGAGE] section.

Adding Multimedia Using RHMMPLAY

The `{mci}` command shown in the previous section works exclusively with WinHelp 4. However, you may want to use multimedia in WinHelp 3 files or to play multimedia files from a hotspot, graphic image, or button. In cases such .as these, you need to use RHMMPLAY.DLL, the RoboHELP multimedia extension.

RHMMPLAY.DLL is available only with RoboHELP Office.

Adding multimedia files to your WinHelp file with RHMMPLAY is slightly different from adding them with the `{mci}` command. RHMMPLAY lets you use macros to play multimedia files and to set several multimedia options.

To add a multimedia file to your WinHelp project using the RHMMPLAY macros, do the following:

1. Position the cursor in the topic where you want to add the multimedia file and click the New Macro Hotspot button on the RoboHELP toolbar. The Insert Help Hotspot screen appears as usual with the Macro option selected in the Action Type field.
2. Enter the hotspot text in the Hotspot Text field, and then click the Wizard button at the lower left of the Insert Help Hotspot screen to display the Macro Wizard.
3. Select one of the following macros from the RoboHELP Extensions category and enter the appropriate information on the Wizard screen for the macro (usually the file name to display):
   - **Sound:** Displays the Video/Sound player inside a topic and plays the specified WAV file
   - **SoundOnly:** Plays a WAV file but doesn't display the Video/Sound player inside the topic
   - **Video:** Displays the Video/Sound player inside a topic and plays the specified AVI (video) file
   - **VideoCaption:** Changes the caption on the Video/Sound Player's titlebar
   - **VideoMenu:** Toggles the display of the Video/Sound Player when playing an AVI or WAV file
   - **VideoPath:** Specifies a directory path for WinHelp to look in for AVI and WAV files
4. When you are satisfied with your changes, click OK to return to the Insert Help Hotspot screen. Make any additional changes or entries to the information on this screen, and then click OK. RoboHELP adds the macro and the hotspot text to the topic at the insertion point.

After you've compiled the WinHelp project, you'll have a standard macro hotspot that will play a sound or video file. Figure 12-13 shows a topic with a macro hotspot that plays a sound file using the SOUND macro.

As an alternative to using the RHMMPLAY macros, you can use the generic ExecFile and ShellExecute macros, described in Chapter 10, "Understanding Macros." Playing a multimedia file this way requires that the users have a specific file association set up for WAV and AVI files. You also won't be able to set any player options as you can with some of the RHMMPLAY macros.

You can use the multimedia macros in the same ways as you can use any other macros. For example, to have the multimedia file play when users open a topic, you can set the macro up as a topic entry macro. Similarly, you can play a multimedia file as a startup macro: you might want to have a sound file play music when the users open the file.

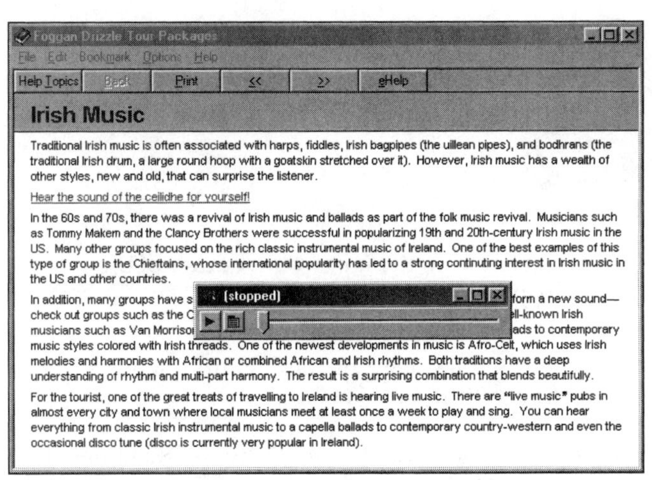

Figure 12-13: Sample macro hotspot to play a sound file

For more information on adding and using macros, see Chapter 10, "Understanding Macros."

If you use any of the RHMMPLAY macros, you will need to ship the RHMMPLAY.DLL file with the finished WinHelp file. This file should be installed in the users' \WINDOWS\SYSTEM32 or \WINDOWS\SYSTEM folder as part of the standard Windows installation process. You'll also need to ship the WAV and AVI files and install them in the same folder as the WinHelp file, or in the file designated by the VideoPath macro. (Multimedia files played with RHMMPLAY macros are not bundled in the WinHelp file or in the [BAGGAGE] section of the HPJ file.)

Creating Your Own Multimedia Files

Although you can find many WAV and AVI files on the Internet, you'll probably have to create at least some of the files you use in your online help. This section will show you how to create and edit your own WAV and AVI files.

Creating Your Own WAV Files

There are several ways to create WAV files. You can speak directly into a microphone connected to your computer's sound card and record the information. Most sound cards come with some kind of WAV recording and editing software, but even if you don't have special software, you can use the standard Windows Sound Recorder, as follows:

1. Start the Windows Sound Recorder (SNDREC32.EXE in the \WINDOWS folder or, typically, Start ➪ Programs ➪ Accessories ➪ Multimedia ➪ Entertainment ➪ Sound Recorder). The Sound Recorder appears, as shown in Figure 12-14.

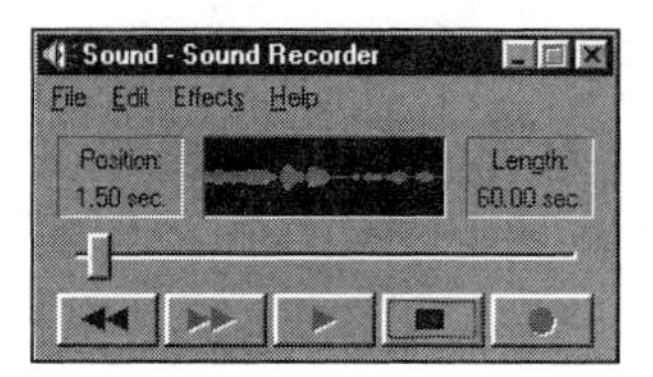

Figure 12-14: The Windows Sound Recorder

2. Click the Rec button (a red circle on the lower right corner of the screen) to start recording. As you record, the display will show the wave forms of the audio input.

3. When you complete your recording, click the Stop button (a black square to the left of the Rec button). Save the WAV file.

You can play the WAV file using the Sound Recorder. The Sound Recorder also lets you do basic edits and add simple special effects such as adding echos and mixing files. For better WAV file editing, you'll want to use a complete WAV-editing program such as Cool Edit Pro from Syntrillium (`www.syntrillium.com`). (A downloadable demo version of this program is available.)

You can also digitize sounds by connecting an audio source, such as a tape deck, into the sound card and digitizing the audio input (this process is known as *ripping*). If your audio source is on an audio CD, note that many inexpensive programs such as AudioGrabber by Jackie Franck (`www.audiograbber.com-us.net`) and AudioCatalyst from Xing Technology (`www.audiocatalyst.com`) allow you to rip audio from CDs directly into WAV format. For additional information on how to digitize audio and music, take a look at *MP3 and the Digital Music Revolution* (Top Floor Publishing, 1999).

When you are digitizing audio for use as a WAV file, you should be aware of copyright issues. Using background music from the latest hit movie may make for a good online help file, but it is also a basic violation of the copyright owner's distribution rights and could cost your company money and reputation. Moreover, the No Electronic Theft (or NET) Act of 1997 makes it a federal crime to digitize music from a CD without the expressed permission of the copyright owners.

Creating Your Own AVI Files

Creating videos of actions that occur on a computer screen has been difficult in the past, requiring video camera/computer setups that are both expensive and a little difficult to use for creating digital AVI files. Fortunately, RoboHELP Office comes with a product called Software Video Camera that creates AVI files of actions that occur on your computer screen. Software Video Camera also lets you add a soundtrack so that you can add narration or comments. You can then incorporate these AVI files into your WinHelp files. Software Video Camera can record the activity on any Windows computer.

You can also use the AVI files from Software Video Camera with your HTML Help files.

Setting up your computer to capture videos

Before you start recording your actions, you need to make sure your computer's display options are set correctly.

The most important limitation to consider is that Software Video Camera will make recordings only in 16 colors or 256 colors. (Display settings higher than this will create AVI files that are too large to be used.) As with adding graphics, you need to consider the type of display your users will have. If your users are still restricted to a 16-color display — almost exclusively older systems, particularly some computers running Windows 3.1 — they won't be able to display 256-color AVI files. (This won't likely be a large problem today; virtually all Windows 9*x* and later computers are set for 256 colors at least.) 256-color AVI files are also substantially larger than 16-color files. Depending on the time length and screen size of the AVIs, you may be able to save a significant amount of size for the completed files if you can capture them in 16-color mode. Keep in mind, however, that most software today uses a 256-color palette that will not reproduce well in 16 colors.

As with other screen capture programs, you must also have the wallpaper and background set appropriately. To set the display options for video capturing with Software Video Camera, do the following:

1. From the Windows Start menu, select Settings ⇨ Control Panel.
2. In the Control Panel, double-click the Display option.
3. On the Background tab, set the wallpaper to None.
4. On the Appearance tab, set the background color to a solid color. (Use one of the standard colors on the default palette rather than a custom color.)
5. On the Settings tab, set the Colors to 16-color or 256-color.
6. Click OK to save your settings. It's possible that you may need to reboot to reset the display options.

Configuring Software Video Camera

Once your display settings are set, you're ready to configure Software Video Camera:

✦ In the RoboHELP Explorer, go to the Tools tab, and then double-click Software Video Camera. (The Software Video Camera icon appears, as shown in Figure 12-15.) The Software Video Camera (shown in Figure 12-16) appears.

Figure 12-15: The Software Video Camera icon

Figure 12-16: The Software Video Camera main screen

The first thing you need to do now is to set up the Software Video Camera options as follows:

1. Click Setup on the Software Video Camera main screen. The Software Video Camera Options screen appears (shown in Figure 12-17).

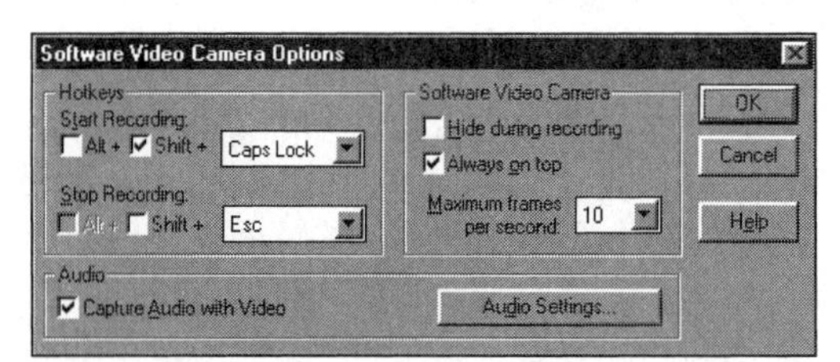

Figure 12-17: The Software Video Camera Options screen

2. Enter information in the fields as follows:

   - **Start Recording:** Set the keys to start recording. Select a key from the drop-down list. You can also check the Alt and/or Shift boxes to add the Alt key and/or the Shift key to the key combination.
   - **Stop Recording:** Set the keys to stop recording. Select a key from the drop-down list. You can also check the Alt and/or Shift boxes to add the Alt key and/or the Shift key to the key combination.
   - **Hide during recording:** Check this box to hide the Software Video Camera screen when you're recording. You'll want to use this option if you are making a full-screen recording.
   - **Always on top:** Check this box to keep the Software Video Camera screen always on top even if it's not the active screen. (This is checked as the default option.)
   - **Maximum frames per second:** Select the maximum number of frames to record for each second of video. The default is 10, but you can select from 1 to 10 from the drop-down list. Remember that the more frames per second you record, the bigger the resulting AVI file will be.
   - **Capture Audio with Video:** Check this box to capture audio when you're capturing video.

You must have a microphone and a sound card configured to record audio to use this feature.

3. If you check Capture Audio with Video, you can also click the Audio Settings button in the lower right corner of the Software Video Camera Options screen. The Sound Selection screen appears (shown in Figure 12-18).

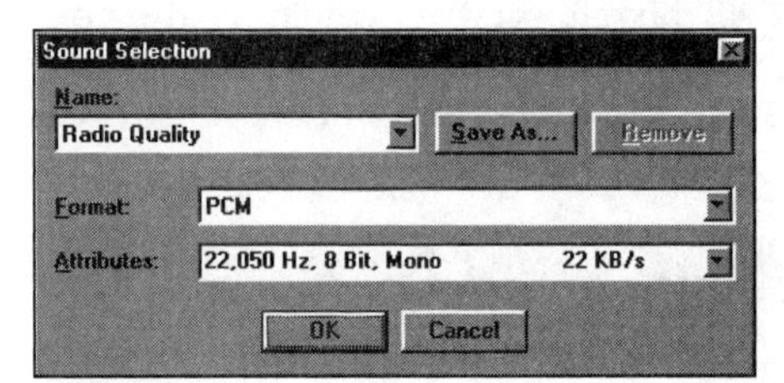

Figure 12-18: The Sound Selection screen

4. Enter information in the fields as follows:
   - **Name:** Select from the drop-down list the name for the recording quality parameters you want to use. (You can choose from several predefined sets of formats and attributes.) You can save a format and attributes under a new or existing name by clicking the Save As button. To remove a format, highlight the name in the drop-down list and click Remove.
   - **Format:** Select the format from the drop-down list. The formats available are dependent on the type of sound card and drivers you have.
   - **Attributes:** Select the recording attributes you want to use. The formats available are dependent on the type of sound card and drivers you have. (Remember that the higher the quality, the more space the finished file will take up on your and your users' hard disks.)

You may want to experiment with recordings in various formats and with various attributes to see which work best for you.

5. When you are satisfied with your entries, click OK to return to the Software Video Camera Options screen and then click OK there to return to the Software Video Camera main screen.

With the Software Video Camera recording options set, you're ready to tell Software Video Camera what part of the screen to record as follows:

1. Start the application you want to record and get it positioned on the screen.
2. Click Area on the Software Video Camera main screen. A red and white box appears on your screen, and the Set Recording Area screen appears (shown in Figure 12-19).

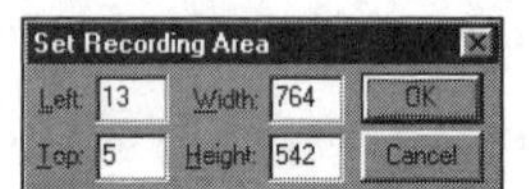

Figure 12-19: The Set Recording Area screen

3. Using your mouse, position the box around the application or area you want to record, as shown in Figure 12-20. Everything within the box (to the outer edges of the red and white border) will be recorded. As you move the box, the coordinates in the Set Recording Area screen will change. If you prefer, you can enter the screen coordinates in the fields on the Set Recording Area screen.

Figure 12-20: Setting the recording area

4. When you are satisfied with the position of the box, click OK.

The Software Video Camera options and record area are now set. You're ready to record video off the computer.

Before you begin recording, step through the sequences you plan to record and rehearse any audio or mouse movements you want to add. (It's also a good idea to write down the audio and mouse movements in a simple script.) This will ensure a smoother recording.

Recording video with Software Video Camera

To record video using Software Video Camera, do the following:

1. Open the application(s) you want to record. It's a good idea to close any extraneous applications when you're recording a video clip.
2. Start Software Video Camera. Click the Rec button or press the key combination you set in the Start Recording field on the Software Video Camera Options screen. Software Video Camera starts recording the screen activity in the record area. Be aware that *any* activity in the recording area — mouse movements, screen popups, and so on — will show up in the final file. If you're also recording sound while displaying video, remember to speak into the microphone.
3. When you're done with the recording, click Stop or press the Stop Recording key combination. Software Video Camera will prompt you to save the AVI file. (The default folder for the file is the WinHelp project folder.)

You can now test the AVI file, edit it if necessary, and include it in your online help as described earlier in the chapter. You can play the AVI file by pressing the Play button on the Software Video Camera main screen and then opening the AVI file you want to play. You can also use the Windows Media Player to play the AVI file if you prefer.

Tip

Editing AVI files requires special software. Probably the best product on the market right now is Premiere from Adobe (`www.adobe.com`), a full-featured product that can produce broadcast-quality audio and video files. Sound Forge from Sonic Foundry (`www.soundforge.com`) is another high-end editor for audio and video files. In addition, there are many inexpensive products available for editing audio and video files, such as Videotrope from Jasc Software (`www.jasc.com`). You can look for a range of shareware and freeware audio and video editing programs on sites such as `www.shareware.com`.

It's worth remembering that, while this section has focused largely on creating AVI files of software displays and screen actions using the RoboHELP tools, there is no reason that you can't include AVI files of any activity of potential interest, such as someone speaking to the user of the help file, demonstrations of a maintenance procedure, or a guided tour of a production facility. This will require you to create the initial video footage and then transfer it to a digital format using a combination of hardware and software for this purpose. If you have video footage that needs to be converted for use in a WinHelp file, you'll likely want to send the footage to a studio or processing center that specializes in conversions.

One final tip when you're creating AVI files: remember that a picture is worth a thousand words, but it may take up a thousand times as much disk space, too. Multimedia files stored in the WinHelp file will require a great deal of space. As you create WAV and AVI files, keep the hard disk requirements for the online help files in mind.

Summary

In this chapter, you've seen how to use eHelp to provide additional resources for your users. You also learned how you can enhance the message of your online help by adding multimedia using both the standard WinHelp `{mci}` command and the RoboHELP extension macros in RHMMPLAY. The chapter also introduced you to tools you can use to create your own WAV and AVI files: the Microsoft Sound Recorder and RoboHELP Office's Software Video Camera.

✦ ✦ ✦

Creating What's This? and Training Card Help

✦ ✦ ✦ ✦

In This Chapter

How What's This? help works

Strengths and weaknesses of What's This? help

Creating and editing a stand-alone What's This? help project

Compiling and testing What's This? help

Maintaining a What's This? help project

Making allowances for special coding conventions

Combining What's This? help with WinHelp

Printing What's This? help reports

Releasing What's This? help for shipping

Using training cards

✦ ✦ ✦ ✦

This chapter shows you how to create What's This? and training card help. You first learn the basics of What's This? help and its advantages and disadvantages. You next are shown how to create and edit a basic What's This? help file using What's This? Help Composer. The chapter continues with information on configuring What's This? Help Composer, compiling What's This? help, and testing the result. After that, you learn how to maintain What's This? help. You then learn about some of the special dialog boxes and controls you may need to work with. Next, the chapter shows you how to use What's This? help and WinHelp together to create and maintain a single help file. Printing What's This? help reports and shipping the completed What's This? help files are discussed. The chapter concludes with an introduction to creating training cards.

Understanding What's This? Help

In Chapter 11, "Creating Context-Sensitive Help," you have seen how to create context-sensitive help for the various controls in a program using the [MAP] section of the HPJ file and the context-sensitive IDs. As you have seen, the process for creating context-sensitive help can be complex.

There's another, faster way to create basic context-sensitive help for many of the controls on your program's dialog boxes. RoboHELP provides What's This? Help Composer to create context-sensitive What's This? help.

What's This? help provides quick popup help for individual options and controls in an application. Figure 13-1 shows a sample of What's This? help for an application.

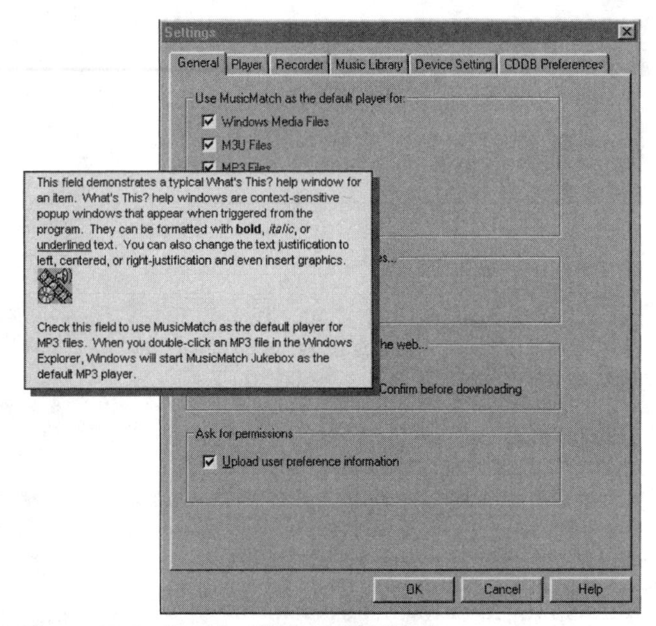

Figure 13-1: Sample of What's This? help

What's This? help can be started in several different ways:

- ✦ The user can click the question mark in the upper right corner of a screen to change the mouse pointer to a question mark pointer, and then click an item on the screen.
- ✦ The user can position the mouse pointer on an item on the screen and press F1 on his or her keyboard.
- ✦ The user can right-click an item on the screen and then select What's This? on the right-click menu.

The options you have for starting What's This? help in a program will depend on the way the program has been designed and which options are enabled. You'll need to talk to the developers to find out what will start What's This? help in the program with which you're working.

How What's This? Help Composer Works

You can use What's This? Help Composer to create help for the following file types:

- ✦ Program files (EXE)
- ✦ Dynamic Link Libraries (DLL)
- ✦ Visual Basic Projects (VBP and FRM)
- ✦ ActiveX Controls (OCX)

What's This? help supports 32-bit applications written for Windows 9*x* and later or Windows NT. It also supports a number of C and C++ compilers, including Borland, Microsoft, Symantec, and Watcom.

When you start a new What's This? help project, What's This? Help ComposerWhat's This? Help Composer examines the program file for dialog box controls and uses this information to generate a database of information, with a topic with suggested text for each control in the dialog boxes. It then creates the RTF file each time you compile the project. You can create What's This? help projects that are stand-alone, with only the What's This? help, or you can link What's This? help to an existing WinHelp project in RoboHELP.

The general process for creating What's This? help is as follows:

1. The developers create a program.
2. The help author checks out the program files and uses What's This? Help ComposerWhat's This? Help Composer to create the initial What's This? help files, and then checks the program files back in so that they can be incorporated. (The developers need to pause working on the files while the What's This? help files are being created.)
3. The help author works on the help files, testing and compiling the What's This? help and refining the text for the various controls.
4. The help author sends the completed help files back to the developers for incorporation into the program.

Working with Developers

As with other types of context-sensitive help, it's important that the help author and the developers work together to create effective What's This? help. The timing for hand offs of files is important; for example, if the developers change the program files while the help author is working on the initial What's This? help before they've been checked back in and incorporated into the program code, any changes to the program will cause What's This? Help Composer to treat the revised program as new, and it will wipe out the changes and start over.

During the program development process, the developers should provide frequent program updates to the help author. (If the developers store the program files on a shared network drive that you also use as the program source for the What's This? help project, then What's This? Help Composer will automatically update the What's This? help project every time you open it.) The developers can also make the What's This? help development process easier by letting you know if the program contains any dynamic dialog boxes, custom class dialog boxes, unused dialog boxes, or dynamic controls in the application and, if so, where they can be found. In addition, the programmers can set a tab order for the controls in the dialog boxes and link controls where appropriate.

Advantages and Disadvantages of What's This? Help

The biggest advantage of using What's This? Help Composer is that it creates online help for you with a minimum of effort: you don't need to worry about matching topic IDs with context-sensitive IDs. The What's This? Help Composer lets you work directly with the program's dialog boxes in a dialog box editor, which makes it unnecessary to print screen shots and write the various IDs on the fields when writing text for the various topics. It also provides a variety of tools for examining the dialog box controls, testing and editing the What's This? help, and printing help status reports. In addition to the advantages to the help author, using What's This? Help Composer can save time for the developers as well. They can call What's This? Help Composer DLL to generate context-sensitive help instead of having to add code for the controls in the dialog box.

However, despite its simplicity, there are a few disadvantages to What's This? help. One of the biggest disadvantages is that, unlike standard online help, What's This? help is usually a brief description of the feature displayed in a popup window. Also, because it is directly linked to controls in the program, you can't have What's This? help topics that are background or descriptive topics. What's This? help topics are also stand-alone; they don't link to other topics. Furthermore, the What's This? help requires a certain amount of standardization on the part of the developers. The program's source code must use any of a wide range of standard dialog box features, as What's This? Help Composer may not be able to see or identify certain types of custom-coded screens.

You can create What's This? help as a stand-alone online help system for quick context-sensitive help for dialog boxes or you can add What's This? help to an existing RoboHELP WinHelp file and use the two forms of online help in conjunction.

Starting a What's This? Help Project

Creating What's This? help is fairly simple. You don't need to have an existing RoboHELP project to create What's This? help for a program, although you can tie What's This? help to an existing RoboHELP project if you wish. (You'll see how to do this later in this chapter.)

To create stand-alone What's This? help, do the following:

1. Start RoboHELP.
2. From the Tools tab in the RoboHELP Explorer, double-click What's This? Help Composer icon, shown in Figure 13-2. The first time you do this, What's This? Help Composer starts a project wizard to set up the new project. (You can also start What's This? Help Composer and select the File ➪ New command to start the project wizard.) The first What's This? Help Composer New Project Wizard screen is shown in Figure 13-3.

Figure 13-2: What's This? Help Composer icon

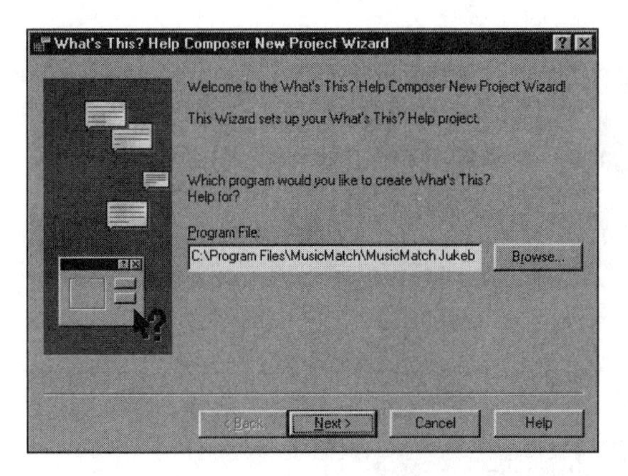

Figure 13-3: The first What's This? Help Composer New Project Wizard screen

3. Enter the name of the program for which you want to create What's This? help. You can browse for a program by clicking the button to the right of the Program File field. When you are satisfied with your entries, click Next. The second What's This? Help Composer New Project Wizard screen appears (as shown in Figure 13-4).

This example demonstrates creating What's This? help for MusicMatch Jukebox, an excellent all-in-one MP3 player and recorder available at `www.musicmatch.com`.

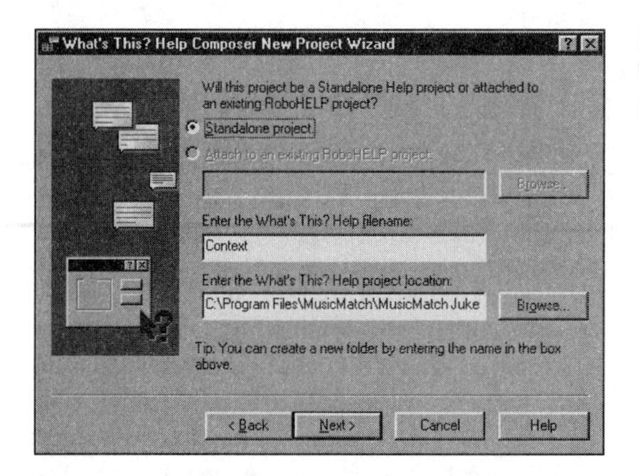

Figure 13-4: The second What's This? Help Composer New Project Wizard screen

4. Enter information in the fields as follows:
   - **Enter the What's This? Help filename:** Enter the file name for the What's This? help file. (The default entry is Context.)
   - **Enter the What's This? Help project location:** Enter the path for the What's This? help project. (The default entry is the same drive and folder as the program for which you're creating What's This? help.)
5. When you are satisfied with your entries, click OK. The third What's This? Help Composer New Project Wizard screen appears (shown in Figure 13-5).

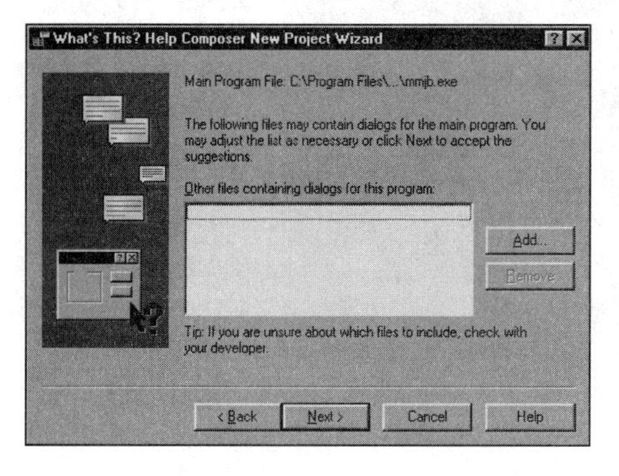

Figure 13-5: The third What's This? Help Composer New Project Wizard screen

6. Add or remove the names of any additional files (subprograms, DLLs, and so on) that contain controls and dialog boxes for the program. When you are satisfied with your entries, click OK. The fourth What's This? Help Composer New Project Wizard screen appears, as shown in Figure 13-6.

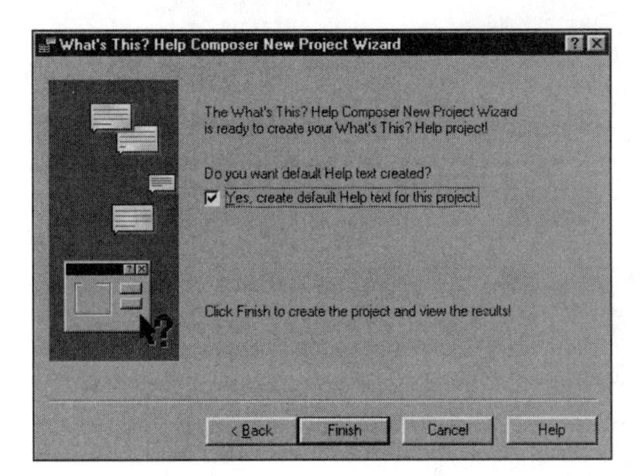

Figure 13-6: The fourth What's This? Help Composer New Project Wizard screen

7. Check the default help box if you want What's This? Help Composer to create default help text for the project. Although the box is not checked as the default option, it's a good idea to check this. Even if you're going to create custom entries for all the controls, this will ensure that every control has a text entry.

If you're working with a Visual Basic application, you'll also have the option of checking Set up Forms for What's This? Help. When you select this option, What's This? Help Composer will add the standard What's This? help question mark to the upper right corner of all forms, as well as set the forms to fixed size. If you're not sure about whether to select this option or not, check with the developer.

8. Click Finish to generate the What's This? help files. Figure 13-7 shows What's This? Help Composer Project Results summary report.

The Project Results summary report lists extensive information about the What's This? help you're creating, including such things as:

✦ The path and name of the project file (.CHJ)

✦ The number of files What's This? Help Composer scanned and did not scan (16-bit files and files with dialog boxes will not be scanned.)

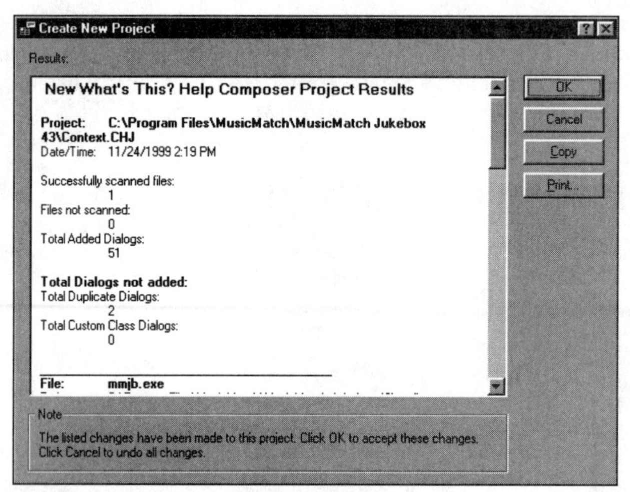

Figure 13-7: The What's This? Help Composer Project Results summary report

✦ The number of dialog boxes that have changed and the number of dialog boxes added to and removed from the What's This? help project

✦ The number of dialog boxes that were not added to the What's This? help project because they are duplicates or because they are coded as a custom class (You'll need to create What's This? help manually for dialog boxes coded with a custom class.)

The report also shows information for each file that you've selected to scan, including the following:

✦ The path and name of the file

✦ The version number of the file (if applicable; this will be encoded by the developer)

✦ The file date and time

✦ Any comments about the file

✦ The dialog boxes that have been added, changed, or removed since the last time you scanned the file

✦ Any dialog boxes that weren't added because they're duplicate or coded as a custom class

The What's This? Help Composer generates a report when you create the What's This? help project and when you update and recompile the files. It's a good idea to print a copy of this report each time it's generated and save it for an audit trail and for subsequent maintenance.

At this point, What's This? Help Composer has created context-sensitive entries for each of the controls in the dialog boxes. The new What's This? help project contents appear in What's This? Help Composer (shown in Figure 13-8).

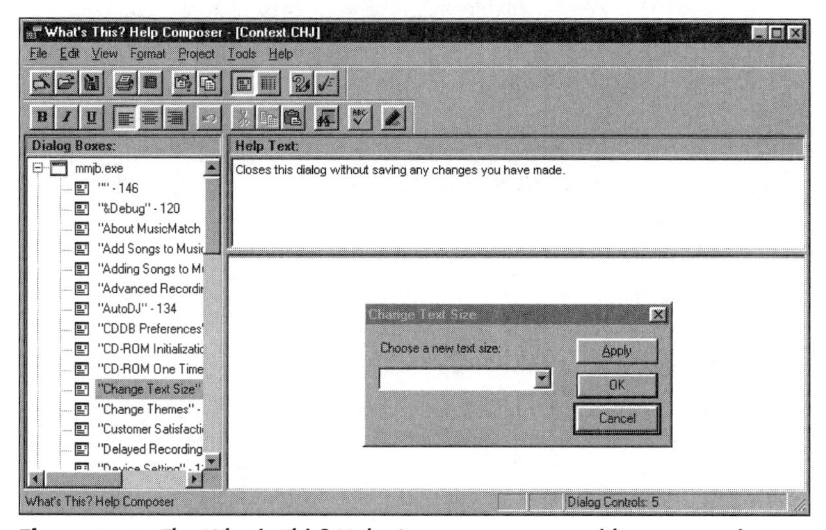

Figure 13-8: The What's This? Help Composer screen with a new project

As you can see from Figure 13-8, What's This? Help Composer lists the program (in this case, MMJB.EXE) and any additional files and all the dialog boxes in the program along with the additional files by their assigned names. In the sample dialog box shown, What's This? Help Composer has identified each of the buttons, fields, and controls on the dialog box and assigned a brief default text description to each of them. The Cancel button highlighted in Figure 13-8 has a default text entry of "Closes this dialog without saving any changes you have made."

You can examine each of the controls and areas on the dialog box by clicking the area on the dialog box in the dialog box editor window. (The display in the status bar shows that there are five controls that What's This? Help Composer has identified.) By highlighting the various areas on the screen, you can see the default text. For example, the OK button has a default text entry of "Closes this dialog and saves any changes you have made" and the Apply button has a default text entry of "Click this button to make your choice." Similarly, when you highlight the field with the drop-down list, the default text is "Choose an item from the list."

When What's This? Help Composer creates a new What's This? help project, it creates a number of project files, as described in Table 13-1.

Table 13-1
What's This? Help Project Files

Extension	*Description*
CDX	One of the What's This? help database indexing files.
CHJ	The What's This? help project file, which contains project settings and other information.
CID	The context-sensitive ID file. This contains the links for the dialog box controls and the topic IDs in the What's This? help file. When you compile the What's This? help project file, it is stored as baggage in the compiled help file.
DBF	The What's This? help database file.
DTO	The default topic information. This information appears in the default topic if you open the What's This? help file as a standard WinHelp file.
FPT	One of the What's This? help database indexing files.
FRM	The Visual Basic form files (which contain the dialog boxes) with additional information added for the What's This? help calls. (Visual Basic projects only)
HH	The What's This? help map file. (The What's This? help HH file is maintained by What's This? Help Composer. It is not the same as a standard WinHelp HH file.)
HLP	The compiled What's This? help file.
HPJ	The What's this? project file (which is very similar to the HPJ for a WinHelp project).
RTF	The source file for the What's This? help. The RTF file is created when you compile the What's This? help project.
VBP	The Visual Basic project file containing the files and resources in the project. (Visual Basic projects only)

Modifying the Default Text Entries

The default text entries in What's This? Help Composer are pretty useful and will fit most of the generic controls for programs. However, if you have specific application requirements, you can modify the default text entries for each category of control through the Windows Registry, as follows:

1. Start the Registry Editor (REGEDIT.EXE).

Editing the Registry can damage your computer to the point where you need to reinstall Windows and your applications. It is strongly advisable to make a backup copy of your Registry before making any changes to the Registry.

2. Go to the \Hkey_Current_User\Software\Blue Sky Software\What's This? Help Composer\1.00\Default Text registry key. Figure 13-9 shows the Registry Editor with the information for this registry key displayed.

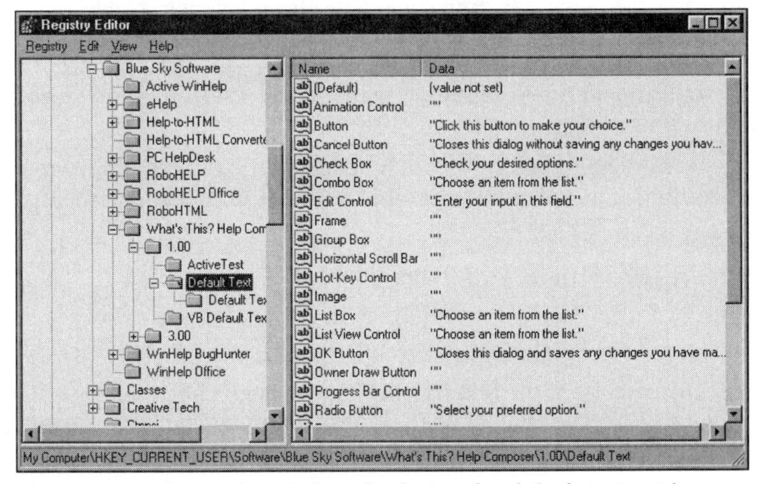

Figure 13-9: The Registry Editor displaying the default text entries

3. Double-click the entry that you want to change. Edit the text for the entry and click OK.

4. Select the Registry ➪ Exit command. The Registry Editor saves your changes. (You may need to restart your computer for the changes to take effect.)

Modifying Individual Text Entries

In many cases, the default text entries for items such as OK and Cancel buttons will be just fine for your program. However, the default entries for individual items that are more complex or specific to the application (such as radio buttons and drop-down lists) will require editing to make them apply to the specific control on the dialog box.

To edit the text for a single context-sensitive help entry, do the following:

1. Select the dialog box you want to edit from the list on the left side of What's This? Help Composer screen.

2. Highlight the control you want to edit in the dialog box editor window on the lower right portion of the screen.
3. Edit the text in the Help Text window. The standard text editing commands are available on the Edit menu. You can also use the buttons on the formatting toolbar to add character attributes such as bold, italic, and underline, text justification, and so on.

You can change the font for all entries in the What's This? help file by selecting the Format ➪ Project Help Text Font command. This is a global change.

4. If the dialog box has a More button or is otherwise expandable, you can display the expanded version of the dialog box by selecting the View ➪ Expand Dialog command.
5. You can optionally add a graphic by clicking the Graphics button (shown in Figure 13-10) and selecting a graphic to insert from a standard graphic screen.

Figure 13-10: Graphics button

6. You can spell check the text by clicking the Spell check button shown in Figure 13-11. The Project Spell Check screen appears (as shown in Figure 13-12). You can check the spelling for this control, all the controls in the dialog box, or throughout the entire What's This? help file (the default selection). Click OK to start spell-checking.

Figure 13-11: Spell check button

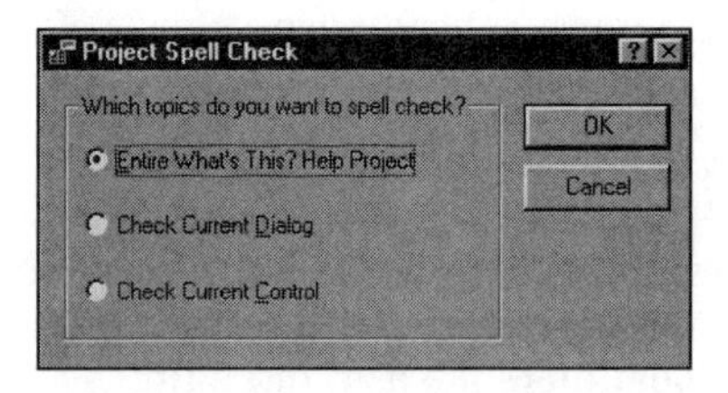

Figure 13-12: The Project Spell Check screen

7. When you are satisfied with your changes, click OK to close the Project Spell Check screen. You can continue making changes to specific What's This? help entries.
8. To save your changes, select the File ➪ Save as RTF command or click the Save as RTF button (shown in Figure 13-13) on the standard toolbar.

Figure 13-13: Save as RTF button

Here are some tips for editing topic text:

✦ You can use the graphic insertion feature to create bulleted lists by inserting a bullet bitmap from the standard RoboHELP Clipart files, as described in Chapter 6, "Adding Simple Graphics."

✦ To create a numbered list, just type the numbers into the list where you want them to appear.

✦ If you delete all the topic text, What's This? Help Composer will delete the topic from the file and will not display a What's This? help topic. (If the users try to display What's This? help, a message will appear that says "No Help topic associated with this item.")

✦ Although you can't put popups into What's This? help topics, you can put jumps into a topic by using the JumpID macro.

See Chapter 10, "Understanding Macros," for more information on using the JumpID macro.

Using Control View

If you're editing several entries, you may prefer to switch from Dialog View (the default display mode) to Control View, as follows:

✦ Select the View ➪ Control View command, or simply click the Control View button (shown in Figure 13-14) on the standard toolbar. Figure 13-15 shows What's This? Help Composer screen shown in Figure 13-8 in Control View.

Figure 13-14: Control View button

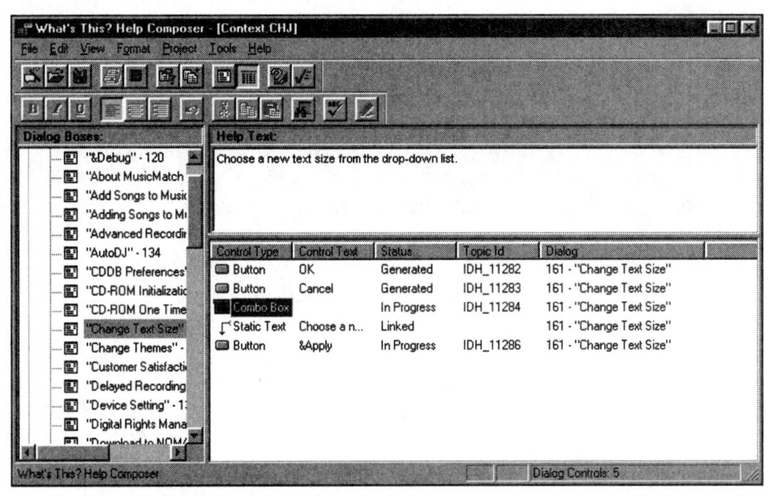

Figure 13-15: The What's This? Help Composer screen displaying Control View

Control View has a number of advantages. You can view all the controls for the dialog box, the topic status, and the topic ID.

The topic status is very useful when tracking changes. When What's This? Help Composer first generates the topic, the default status for topics is "Generated." Once you edit a topic, the status changes to "In Progress." There are two other status conditions that you can set manually: For Review and Complete.

You can change the status of a topic between any of these three conditions as follows:

✦ Highlight the control that you want to change the status of and select the appropriate status option from the Edit menu. You can also press Ctrl+1, Ctrl+2, or Ctrl+3 as keyboard shortcuts for In Progress, For Review, and Complete, respectively. As an alternative, you can right-click the control you want to change the status of and then select the status from the right-click menu.

To change the status for all the topics in a dialog box, do the following:

✦ Right-click the dialog box you want to change and select Set Dialog Status from the right-click menu.

By changing the status to reflect the editing status of the controls, you can track the status of the controls using the What's This? help reports described later in this chapter. As an interim technique, if all the controls in a dialog box have a status of "Completed," the dialog box icon in the Dialog Box list turns blue, making it easy to identify dialog boxes that have not been completely edited.

Linked controls always have a status of Linked. In Figure 13-15, the static information is also coded as a control, and has a status of "Linked." The arrow in the example shows the control to which it is linked. You don't need to write text for linked controls as What's This Help Composer will display the text for the control to which it is linked. (You can suppress the display of linked controls by selecting the View ➪ Linked Controls command.)

Press Ctrl+PgUp and Ctrl+PgDn to navigate to the previous and next controls in the dialog box. When you highlight a control on the Control View, the associated text appears in the Help Text display. You can also press Ctrl+PgUp and Ctrl+PgDn to navigate to the previous and next dialog boxes. To change the sort order for the displayed items, click the column header.

Another thing that's visible in the Control View display is the type of control. Table 13-2 shows the icons for each of the controls and the descriptions. Knowing the type of control can be helpful when testing and debugging What's This? help and also when interacting with the developers.

Table 13-2
Control View Icons

Icon	*Type*	*Description*
	Button	A button is a control that does something when clicked, such as OK and Cancel buttons.
	Check box	A check box lets the users select an option. If there is a group of check boxes, the users can select multiple options.
	Combo box	A combo box is similar to a list box in that it contains a drop-down list of selectable items; however, the users can select from the drop-down list or type in an entry.
ab|	Edit control	An edit control is a box in which the user can enter multiple lines of text (such as a comment). Edit controls will frequently also have scroll bars and other features.
	Frame	A frame is a box that encloses two or more related controls, such as check boxes or radio buttons, to show a relationship. As with group boxes, frames are frequently linked to the first control in the group they contain and, as a consequence, do not need to have their own descriptive text.
XYZ	Group box	A group box contains two or more related controls, such as check boxes or radio buttons. Group boxes are frequently linked to the first control in the group they contain and, as a consequence, do not need to have their own descriptive text.
	Horizontal scroll bar	A horizontal scroll bar is a control that lets the users move the contents of the window horizontally (left and right).
	Image	An image is a type of graphical control that displays a picture.
	List box	A list box contains a drop-down list of selectable items. Items can be selected from the list but the user cannot type a selection.

Continued

Table 13-2 *(continued)*

Icon	*Type*	*Description*
	List view control	A list view control is a display window that displays a list of items the users can select. Items can be selected from the list but the user cannot type a selection.
	Owner draw button	An owner draw button is a type of button that the program creates on the fly when the program runs.
	Progress bar control	A progress bar control is a control in the status bar that shows the progress of an operation.
	Radio button	A radio button is a control that lets the users to select an option to use. If there is a group of radio buttons, the users can select a single option.
	Rectangle	A rectangle is a type of control that specifies an area of a dialog box. Common examples of rectangles are scrolling or formatting areas.
	Slider control	A slider control is a control that is moved left and right or up and down to change the value being controlled. The most common examples of a slider control are the sliders used to change the sound volume on the Window Play Control screen.
	Static text	Static text is descriptive text that appears on the dialog box, usually as a description or label for a field or button. Static text is frequently linked to the control it describes. Static text cannot be changed by the user.
	Tab control	A tab control is a control with two or more tabs. When a tab is selected, the corresponding folder appears.
	Tree view control	A tree view control is a control that lists information in a tree view (such as the list of dialog boxes in What's This? Help Composer).
	Vertical scroll bar	A vertical scroll bar is a control that lets the users move the contents of the window vertically (up and down).

Compiling and Testing What's This? Help

When you have made all your changes, you're ready to compile and test the What's This? help file. Compiling and testing a What's This? help is very similar to compiling and testing a standard WinHelp file.

Configuring What's This? Help Composer

The first time you compile a What's This? help project, you'll need to make sure that your configuration and compiler options are correct, as follows:

1. Select the Project ➪ Configuration command. The Configuration screen appears (shown in Figure 13-16).

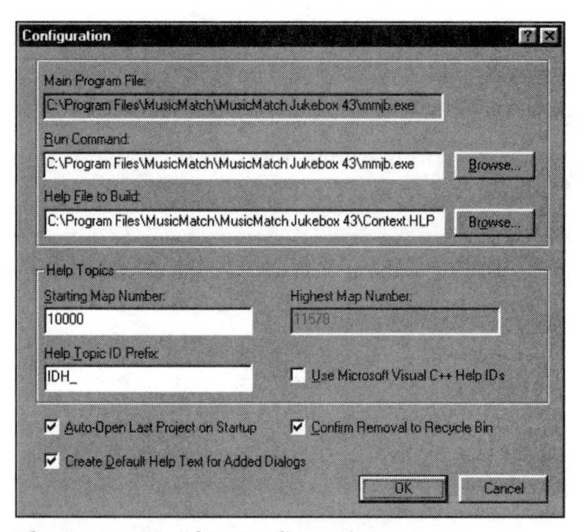

Figure 13-16: The Configuration screen

2. Enter information in the fields as follows:

   - **Main Program File:** This display-only field shows the path and file name for the main program file for which you're creating What's This? help.
   - **Run Command:** Enter the path and file name for the command to run the program file for which you're creating What's This? help. This is usually the same as the entry in Main Program File, but you might also add parameters for specific files or runtime options.
   - **Help File to Build:** Enter the path and file name for the help file you are going to build.

- **Starting Map Number:** If you're creating What's This? help for a C or C++ program, you can enter the starting map number (context-sensitive ID) that What's This? Help Composer assigns to the topics. The map numbers are maintained internally (although you can change them if you need to), so all you have to do is make sure that the map numbers used in What's This? Help Composer don't conflict with the map numbers used when creating context-sensitive help in the main RoboHELP project. The highest map number used appears in the display-only Highest Map Number field to the right of this field.
- **Help Topic ID Prefix:** Enter the help topic prefix for What's This? Help Composer to use when creating help topics. The default is IDH_.
- **Use Microsoft Visual C++ Help IDs:** Check this box to use the existing Microsoft Visual C++ help IDs instead of the map IDs created by What's This Help Composer.

This option may cause duplicate ID errors because the IDs in the Visual C++ help file aren't verified.

- **Auto-Open Last Project on Startup:** Check this box to open the last What's This? help project you were working automatically. (This box is checked by default.)
- **Create Default Help Text for Added Dialogs:** Check this box to have What's This? Help Composer automatically generate default help text when creating or updating the What's This? help project. (This box is checked by default.)
- **Confirm Removal to Recycle Bin:** Check this box to confirm removal of a dialog box or control to What's This? Help Composer recycle bin.

3. When you are satisfied with your entries, click OK.

Setting Compiler Options

In addition to the configuration options in the previous section, there are several compiler options you may want to set or change, as follows:

1. Select the Project ⇨ Compile Settings command. The Compile Settings screen (with the Compiler tab displayed) appears, as shown in Figure 13-17.
2. Enter information in the fields as follows:
   - **Report on Progress:** Check this box to display messages from the compiler when you compile the What's This? help project. (This box is checked by default.)

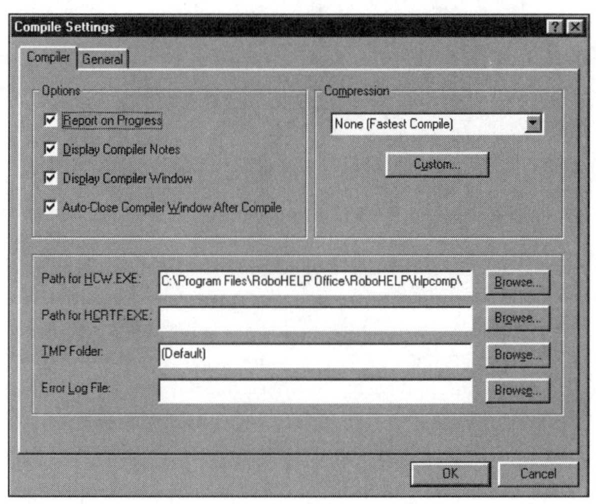

Figure 13-17: The Compile Settings screen with the Compiler tab displayed

- **Display Compiler Notes:** Check this box to display compiler comments when you compile the What's This? help project. Comments are information about the project being compiled and do not include errors. (This box is checked by default.)
- **Display Compiler Window:** Check this box to display the WinHelp compiler window when you compile the What's This? help project. (This box is checked by default.)
- **Auto-Close Compiler Window After Compile:** Check this box to automatically close the WinHelp compiler window and return to What's This? Help Composer when the What's This? help project has been compiled. You must have checked the Display Compiler Window option to select this option. (This box is checked by default.)
- **Compression:** Select the compression option from the drop-down list. You can also choose specific types of compression by clicking Custom to display the Custom Compression Settings screen shown in Figure 13-18. Select one or more compression options as described in Table 13-3 and click OK when you are satisfied with your entries.

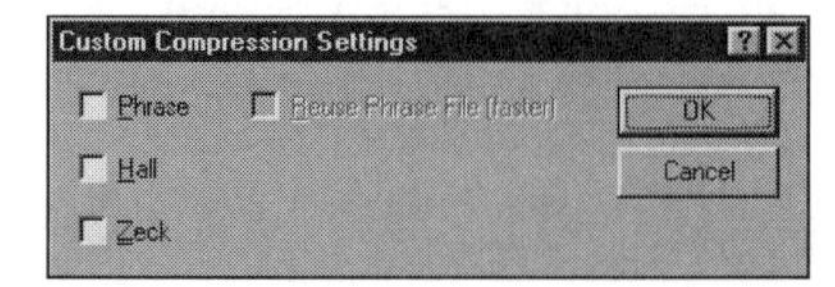

Figure 13-18: The Custom Compression Settings screen

Table 13-3
Custom Compression Options

Compression Option	*When to Select It*
Phrase	Use Phrase compression to compile files that are under 100KB. When you compile with Phrase compression, the WinHelp compiler will create a file of phrases with the extension .PH as part of the compression process. If you have selected Phrase compression, you can optionally select Reuse Phrase File to reuse the phrase file. If you haven't made many changes to the project since the last time you created the phrase file, this will result in a faster compile. You should periodically uncheck this option so that the WinHelp compiler creates a new phrase file for maximum compression.
Hall	Use Hall compression to compile files that are over 100KB. Hall compression usually provides the most effective compression when combined with Zeck compression, but they can be used separately.
Zeck	Use Zeck with Phrase compression for greater compression of files under 100KB. Use Zeck with Hall compression to maximize the compression for files over 100KB.

- **Path for HCW.EXE:** Enter the path for the HCW.EXE help compiler.
- **Path for HCRTF.EXE:** Enter the path for the HCRTF.EXE help compiler. (The HCRTF.EXE program compiles a WinHelp file. The HCW.EXE program calls it automatically when you compile a file. You won't normally have to call this program directly unless you need to use some of the testing options described in the Microsoft Help Compiler Workshop documentation.)
- **TMP Folder:** Enter the path for the temporary folder to use during the compile. The default entry for this field is [Default], which tells What's This? Help Composer to use the Windows system default temporary folder.
- **Error Log File:** Enter the path and name of the log file in which to save error messages generated by the compiler.

3. When you are satisfied with your entries, click the General tab. The General tab appears, as shown in Figure 13-19.

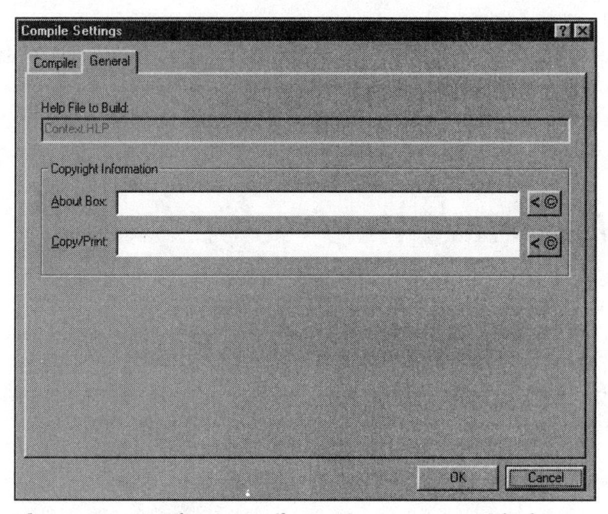

Figure 13-19: The Compile Settings screen with the General tab displayed.

4. Enter information in the fields as follows:
   - **Help File to Build:** This display-only field shows the name of the What's This? help project you're about to create.
   - **About Box:** Enter the copyright statement or the text that appears in the What's This? help project's About box. You can click the button to the right of the field to insert a copyright symbol (©) at the cursor location.
   - **Copy/Print:** Enter the copyright statement or the text that appears when you copy or print a topic. You can click the button to the right of the field to insert a copyright symbol (©) at the cursor location.
5. When you are satisfied with your entries, click OK.

Compiling the What's This? Help Project

Once you've configured What's This? Help Composer and set the compiler options you need for this project, you're ready to compile the What's This? help project.

To compile a stand-alone What's This? help project, do the following:

✦ In What's This? Help Composer, select the Project ⇨ Compile command or simply click the standard compile button on the toolbar. The What's This? Help Composer will generate the source files and then compile the What's This? help.

It's not necessary to save the What's This? help project as you must when you are compiling standard WinHelp projects in RoboHELP. The What's This? Help Composer automatically saves the information as you work on the file in What's This? Help Composer and creates the RTF file each time you compile the What's This? help project.

Testing the What's This? Help Project

One of the advantages of developing What's This? help is that you can test it quickly and easily using the ActiveTest and ActiveEdit features. The ActiveTest feature lets you test the What's This? help against the program before the developers have enabled the What's This? help links and calls in the program. This can speed up the What's This? help development process by letting you refine the text in the What's This? help while the developers are working on the program.

Once you've compiled your What's This? help, you can test it against the program as follows:

1. Select the Project ➪ ActiveTest command or just click the ActiveTest button (shown in Figure 13-20). What's This? Help Composer starts the program specified in the Run Command on the Configuration screen.

Figure 13-20: ActiveTest button

2. To test the What's This? help for a field, button, or other control, right-click on the control. Select What's This? from the right-click menu or click the What's This icon in the upper right corner of the displayed screen. The What's This? help for that control will appear in a small yellow popup window as usual.
3. To edit the What's This? help text or make other changes for a control, right-click on the control and select ActiveEdit from the right-click menu. ActiveEdit displays the text and other information for that control in What's This? Help Composer so you can edit the help easily. When you are satisfied with your changes, recompile the What's This? help project, and then select the Project ➪ ActiveTest command or click the ActiveTest button again. This updates the What's This? help and you can check your changes immediately.

You can't use ActiveEdit with Visual Basic programs.

4. Continue testing the entries for the controls. When you are done testing, close the program as you would normally.

If you are working on a Visual Basic program and you have only the EXE file (not the project files), you must change the extension of the program file from VBP to EXE in the Run Command field on the Configuration screen shown earlier in Figure 13-16.

A technique that may be helpful for tracking topics while you're testing is to turn on Help Author mode. Help Author mode displays the topic number in the topic's title bar. In addition, any jump text is also displayed.

To turn on Help Author mode, do the following:

✦ Select the Project ⇨ WinHelp Mode ⇨ Help Author command. You'll see a check mark by the option to show that Help Author mode is now on.

Note that Help Author mode affects only how topics are displayed in the What's This? help file when it's run directly as a WinHelp file. Topic numbers and information do not appear when the What's This? help project is run in conjunction with the program as What's This? help.

One of the most effective strategies for testing the What's This? help in a file is to work through each of the controls in a dialog box. When you're satisfied with all the controls on a given dialog box, use ActiveEdit to return to What's This? Help Composer, display the dialog box in Control View, and update the status for each of the controls to For Review or Complete, as described earlier in this chapter. Later in this chapter, you'll see how to run status reports that will report on the help topic status and let you quickly identify any controls that haven't been checked yet.

What's This? Help Composer works a little differently for Visual Basic programs than it does for C/C++ programs. One of the differences is that What's This? Help Composer adds information to the Visual Basic FRM and VBP files rather than creating its own project files. Because dialog boxes are stored in FRM files in Visual Basic, you can't see the dialog boxes in Dialog View in What's This? Help Composer (although you can use the Control View). Finally, in order to test What's This? help for a Visual Basic program, you must compile the help project, run the program, and then run the What's This? help project from within the Visual Basic program.

Updating a What's This? Help Project

If you're creating What's This? help for a program that is being developed at the same time, you will periodically need to update the What's This? help to add the new controls and dialog boxes. For example, suppose that you've just received a new copy of the program from the developers. To update the information in the What's This? help project, do the following:

1. Install the new version of the program in the same place on your system and start What's This? Help Composer. (If necessary, open the What's This? help project file.) The What's This? Help Composer examines the program when it loads the What's This? help project's database. When What's This? Help Composer sees changes to the file, it displays the message shown in Figurer 13-21.

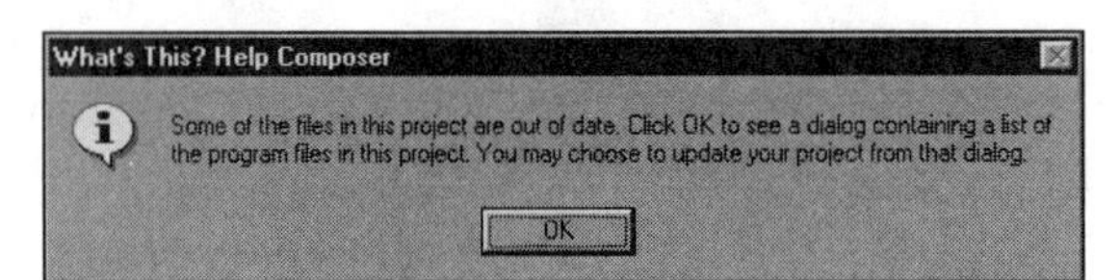

Figure 13-21: Message showing that the program files have changed

2. When you click OK on the message, What's This? Help Composer displays the Update Project screen, shown in Figure 13-22.

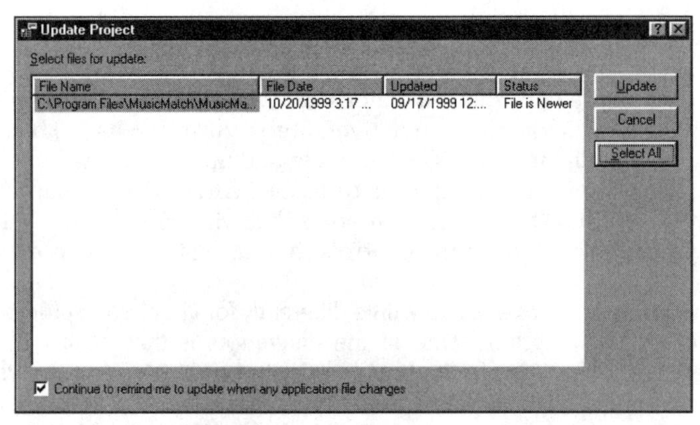

Figure 13-22: The Update Project screen

3. Select the file or files to scan for updated dialog boxes. (You can click Select All on the right side of the screen to select all the files.) When you are satisfied with your entries, click Update to start updating the What's This? help project. The What's This? Help Composer scans the selected files for new or updated dialog boxes and then generates a report of the changes, as shown in Figure 13-23. (Remember that you'll have to write or update text entries for dialog boxes that have changed.)

Unchecking the box at the bottom of the screen will prevent What's This? Help Composer from reminding you to update the What's This? help project for the remainder of the session. (The What's This? Help Composer will reset this option when you start it the next time.)

4. Click OK to accept the changes and incorporate them in your What's This? help project. The What's This? Help Composer will update the database of information for the project. You can now recompile the WinHelp project and test it against the program as described earlier.

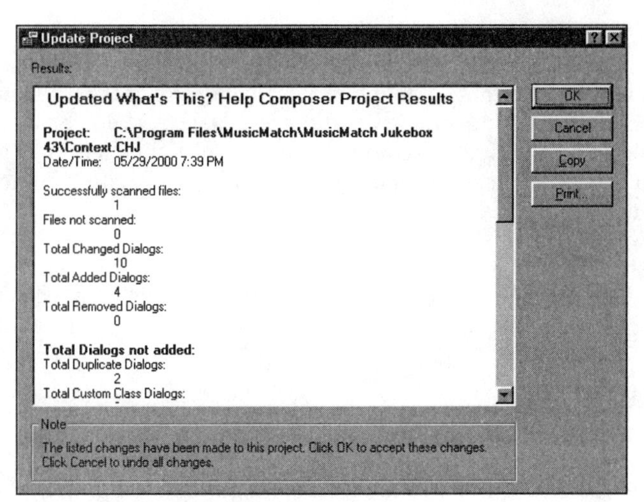

Figure 13-23: The Update Project report

You can also manually update a What's This? help project. This is a good idea if you want to check the entries in the project or if you are using a new program file. To start a manual update, do the following:

✦ Select the Project ⇨ Update Project command, or just click the Update button on the standard toolbar (shown in Figure 13-24).

Figure 13-24: Update button

You can then continue updating the What's This? help project as before.

Removing and Replacing Dialog Boxes

You may need to delete the entry for a control or a dialog box. For example, the program may have several internal dialog boxes that are for debugging or internal program options for use only by the developers. There may also be unused dialog boxes — dialog boxes that are still in the program files but are not used in the program. Documenting dialog boxes such as these is usually unnecessary and may even present security problems if the users are aware of them. Removing extraneous or unused dialog boxes also makes it easier to maintain the active dialog boxes.

To remove a dialog box in the What's This? help, do the following:

1. Highlight the dialog box you want to delete in the Dialog Box list on the left side of What's This? Help Composer screen and press Delete. (You can also right-click the dialog box and select Remove from the right-click menu.) The What's This? Help Composer displays a message asking you to confirm the deletion, as shown in Figure 13-25.

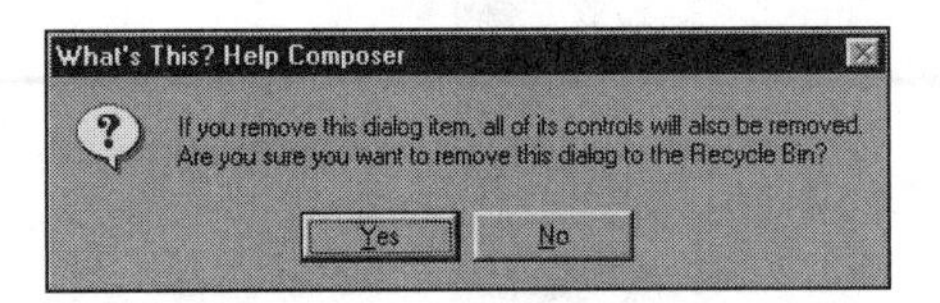

Figure 13-25: Confirming the deletion of a dialog box.

2. Click OK to remove the dialog box to the recycle bin. All deleted dialog boxes appear in the recycle bin at the bottom of the dialog box list.

When you update a What's This? help project and What's This? Help Composer finds a control or dialog box that's no longer used, it automatically removes the entry and puts it into the recycle bin.

As with files deleted but still in the Windows Recycle Bin, you can view the dialog box information by highlighting the entry. You can even "undelete" dialog box entries in the recycle bin, as follows:

✦ Right-click on the dialog box entry you want to restore and select Restore Recycled from the right-click menu. (You can also click and drag the dialog box entry to the active part of the dialog box list.)

If you prefer, you can restore all the entries in the recycle bin by selecting the Edit ➪ Restore Recycled command.

You can delete an entry from the recycle bin by right-clicking and selecting Delete from the right-click menu, and then confirming the deletion. This will remove the dialog box entry completely from the What's This? help project. You can delete all the entries in the recycle bin by selecting the Project ➪ Empty Recycle Bin command.

It's a good idea to keep all the entries in the recycle bin until you're ready to create the final version of the What's This? help project.

Changing, Adding, and Removing Program Files

It's not unusual as part of the development cycle for the program to change its name or for the installation program to add the program to another folder. When this happens, you need to tell the What's This? help project where to look for the program, as follows:

1. Select the File ➪ Relocate Main Program File command. The Locate File screen appears (shown in Figure 13-26).

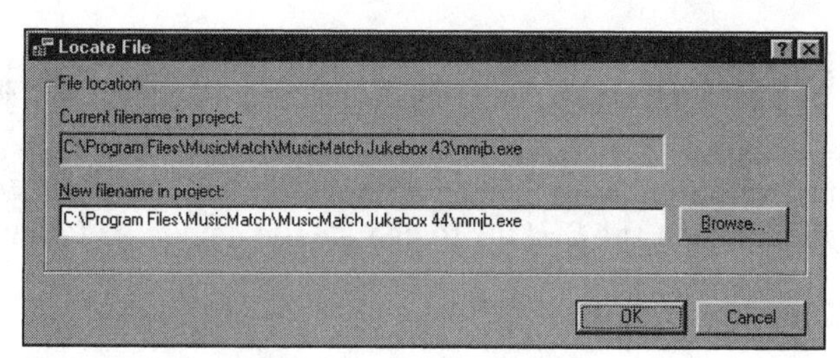

Figure 13-26: The Locate File screen

2. Enter the new path and file name in New filename in project. You can browse for the file using the browse button to the right of the field. When you are satisfied with your entry, click OK. The What's This? Help Composer will then use the new program for the What's This? help project.

Occasionally, you may also need to add program files to a What's This? help project. Normally, any DLL or other program files called by the program from within the program's EXE file will be found and examined automatically by What's This? Help Composer when it does an update. However, you may need to specify an additional file; for example, if the program requires that you use a different DLL file from the one called in the program. To add a program file to the What's This? help project, do the following:

1. Select the Project ➪ Add File command, or just click the Add File button on the standard toolbar, shown in Figure 13-27. A standard Open File screen appears.

Figure 13-27: Add File button

2. Select the program or file you want to add to the project from the list and click OK. The What's This? Help Composer will scan the program or file, add the information for the dialog boxes, and generate the standard update report like the one shown earlier in Figure 13-22.

You can also remove a program or file from a What's This? help project as follows:

✦ Highlight the name of the program or file in the Dialog Box list on the left side of What's This? Help Composer screen and select the Edit ➪ Remove File command. You can also just right-click the file and select Remove from the right-click menu.

When you remove a program or file, What's This? Help Composer puts it in the recycle bin. You can restore a program or file from the recycle bin in the same way as restoring a dialog box.

Renaming a Stand-alone What's This? Help Project

It's possible that you will need to rename a stand-alone What's This? help project after you've created it. Although there is not a command that renames a What's This? help project, you can edit the CHJ file to change the names, as follows:

1. Close What's This? Help Composer.
2. With the Windows Explorer, rename the What's This? help files to the new project name.

Be sure to rename *all* the files in the project. It's a good idea to use the file extensions in Table 13-1 as a checklist. If you miss a file, What's This? Help Composer may update the project with new information and overwrite any edits you've made.

3. Open the project's CHJ file in a text editor such as Notepad.
4. In the `[PROJECT]` section of the CHJ file, change the file names of the HLP, DBF, HPJ, DTO, and HH files. The following code shows a portion of the CHJ file for a program file of FDTOURS.EXE and a What's This? help project named Travel.

```
[PROJECT]
Primary File=fdtours.exe
Help File To Build=travel.HLP
Database File=travel.DBF
Run Command=fdtours.exe
Help Project File=travel.HPJ
DefaultTopicFile=travel.DTO
HelpMapFile=travel.HH
```

5. When you are satisfied with your changes, save your changes and close the CHJ file.
6. Open the project's HPJ file in a text editor.
7. Change the file name on the `HLP=` line and the title in the `[OPTIONS]` section, the file name for the RTF file in the `[FILES]` section, and the file name for the HH file in the `[MAP]` section to the new name of your project Help file. The following code shows the HPJ file for a What's This? help project named Travel.

```
[OPTIONS]
HLP=travel.HLP
```

```
TITLE=Travel
CONTENTS=IDC_DEFAULT_TOPIC
REPORT=YES
[FILES]
travel.RTF
[MAP]
#include <travel.HH>
[BAGGAGE]
DIALOG.CID
```

8. When you are satisfied with your changes, save your changes and close the HPJ file.

After you've renamed the project, the automatic file open option won't know where to find it. Open the project using the File ➪ Open command in What's This? Help Composer the first time after you've renamed it.

Using Special Dialog Boxes and Controls

There are several types of dialog boxes and controls that What's This? Help Composer does not automatically identify when it scans the program and files, including dynamic, custom class, and duplicate dialog boxes and dynamic, custom, and OLE controls. This section describes the various dialog boxes and controls and shows you how to work with them.

Adding Dynamic Dialog Boxes and Controls

Dynamic dialog boxes and controls are created by the program only when it runs. As a result, What's This? Help Composer won't be able to find them when it scans the program. (You can usually identify dynamic dialog boxes because they don't appear in the What's This? help project's dialog box list even though you can see them in the program when it's running. Similarly, dynamic controls don't appear in the control list for a dialog box although they're on the dialog box when the program runs.)

You can add help for dynamic dialog boxes using the ActiveTest and ActiveEdit features, as follows:

1. Compile the What's This? help project and run the program in ActiveTest mode.

2. Display the dialog box you want to add to the What's This? help project, and then right-click to display the right-click menu.
3. Select ActiveEdit. The What's This? Help Composer appears with the dialog box selected and the controls for the dialog box in the control list. (You must use Control View in What's This? Help Composer to see the controls in the dialog box, as there is no dialog box to display.)
4. Edit the help text for each of the controls as usual.

When you add dynamic dialog boxes to the project, they appear in the Dialog Boxes list in uppercase text with "dynamic" in either the dialog box name (the caption as it appears on the dialog box) or the dialog box ID (the ID assigned by the developer to identify the dialog box within the program.)

To add text for a dynamic control, you use a similar process, except that you'll right-click the specific control you want to add What's This Help for and then add text for this control.

Adding Custom Class Dialog Boxes

Custom class dialog boxes are any dialog boxes that have been defined as belonging to a nonstandard class by the programmer. Custom class dialog boxes must be added directly to the WinHelp project in RoboHELP rather than in the What's This? help project. You'll need to work with the programmer to build the links for calls for custom class dialog boxes.

Adding Duplicate Dialog Boxes

Duplicate dialog boxes appear in the program more than once but are coded and look identical. When What's This? Help Composer scans the program, it creates entries only for the first version of the dialog box it encounters.

There are several options for dealing with duplicate dialog boxes in a program:

✦ Have the developer delete the duplicate dialog box. (Frequently, duplicate dialog boxes have simply been overlooked during the coding process.)

✦ The programmer can register the duplicate dialog box using the CSUSER.H function (described in What's This? Help Composer documentation), and then document the dialog box as usual.

✦ Change the duplicate dialog box slightly so it's not an exact duplicate, and then update the What's This? help project.

Adding Custom Controls

Custom controls do not appear on the dialog box in Dialog View, but they are listed in Control View. To add text for custom controls, display the dialog box in Control View and then add text as normal.

Adding OLE Controls

OLE (Object Linking and Embedding) controls can't be used with What's This? help. OLE controls appear as a border when you view the dialog box in Dialog View.

Using What's This? Help and WinHelp Together

So far, this chapter has shown you how to create What's This? help as a stand-alone help system. However, it's likely that any program you're creating What's This? help for will also have WinHelp. You can combine What's This? help with WinHelp from the beginning or by combining existing help systems.

Creating a New What's This? Help Project Inside an Existing RoboHELP Project

Although What's This? help works well as a stand-alone help file, you can bundle it with the WinHelp file you've created in RoboHELP. The What's This? help files are included as part of the `[BAGGAGE]` section of the WinHelp project. This has the advantage of reducing the number of compiled help files you ship with the application.

To create What's This? help inside your WinHelp project, do the following:

1. Open the WinHelp project in RoboHELP.
2. Select the RoboHELP ⇨ What's This? Help Composer Project ⇨ Insert/Edit command in RoboHELP. The What's This? Help Composer starts and displays the first What's This? Help Composer project wizard screen (shown earlier in Figure 13-2).
3. Go through the standard steps for creating a new What's This? help project as described at the beginning of this project.

Once you have added the What's This? help file, you can open it from within RoboHELP by selecting the RoboHELP ⇨ What's This? Help Composer Project ⇨ Insert/Edit command in RoboHELP. The What's This? Help Composer will automatically open the What's This? help project. (You can also open the What's This? help project directly within What's This? Help Composer as usual.)

Combining a What's This? Help Project and a RoboHELP Project

If you've already set up your What's This? help, you can still combine an existing What's This? help project with an existing RoboHELP project. To do this, start by editing the What's This? help project's CHJ file, as follows:

1. Close What's This? Help Composer.
2. Open the What's This? help project's CHJ file in a text editor such as Notepad.
3. In the [PROJECT] section of the CHJ file, change the file names of the HLP and HPJ files to show the HLP and HPJ files for the WinHelp files. The following code shows a portion of the CHJ file for a program file of FDTOURS.EXE, a What's This? help project named Travel, and a WinHelp file name of Foggan Drizzle Tour Info.

```
[PROJECT]
Primary File=fdtours.exe
Help File To Build=Foggan Drizzle Tour Info.HLP
Database File=travel.DBF
Run Command=fdtours.exe
Help Project File=Foggan Drizzle Tour Info.HPJ
DefaultTopicFile=travel.DTO
HelpMapFile=travel.HH
```

4. When you are satisfied with your changes, save your changes and close the CHJ file.

Next, you need to edit the WinHelp project's RBH file so that it knows where to look for the What's This? help.

1. Open the WinHelp project's RBH file in a text editor.
2. In the [PROJECT] section of the RBH file, add a line that says `CHFile=` followed by the name of the What's This? help project's RTF file. The following code shows a portion of the RBH file for a What's This? help project named Travel.

```
[Project]
CHFile=travel.RTF
```

3. When you are satisfied with your changes, save your changes and close the RBH file.

The next step is to modify the WinHelp project's HPJ file to include the What's This? help files and add the What's This? help to the [BAGGAGE] section of the WinHelp project.

1. Open the WinHelp project's HPJ file in a text editor.
2. In the [FILES] section of the HPJ file, add a line with the name of the What's This? help project's RTF file. The following code shows the [FILES] portion of the HPJ file with a line added for a What's This? help project named Travel.

```
[FILES]
Foggan Drizzle Tour Info.rtf
travel.rtf
```

3. In the [BAGGAGE] section of the HPJ file, add a line for DIALOG.CID, as shown in the following code:

```
[BAGGAGE]
DIALOG.CID
```

4. In the [MAP] section of the HPJ file, add a #include line for the What's This? help project's to include the HH file, as shown in the following code:

```
[MAP]
#include <travel.HH>
```

5. When you are satisfied with your changes, save your changes and close the HPJ file.

Renaming a What's This? Help Project Combined with a RoboHELP Project

The process for renaming a What's This? help project that has been combined with a RoboHELP project is similar to the process for renaming a stand-alone What's This? help project.

It's possible that you will need to rename a stand-alone What's This? help project after you've created it. Although there is not a command that renames a What's This? help project, you can edit the CHJ file to change the names, as follows:

1. Close What's This? Help Composer and RoboHELP.
2. With the Windows Explorer, rename the What's This? help files to the new project name.
3. Open the project's CHJ file in a text editor such as Notepad.

4. In the [PROJECT] section of the CHJ file, change the file names of the DBF, DTO, and HH files. The following code shows the CHJ file with the What's This? help name changed to New Travel:

```
[PROJECT]
Primary File=fdtours.exe
Help File To Build=Foggan Drizzle Tour Info.HLP
Database File=new travel.DBF
Run Command=fdtours.exe
Help Project File=Foggan Drizzle Tour Info.HPJ
DefaultTopicFile=new travel.DTO
HelpMapFile=new travel.HH
```

5. When you are satisfied with your changes, save your changes and close the file.

You now must edit the WinHelp project's RBH file so that it knows where to look for the renamed What's This? help.

1. Open the WinHelp project's RBH file in a text editor.
2. In the [PROJECT] section of the RBH file, modify the line that says CHFile= with the new name of the What's This? help project's RTF file. The following code shows a portion of the RBH file for a What's This? help project named New Travel.

```
[Project]
CHFile=new travel.RTF
```

3. When you are satisfied with your changes, save your changes and close the RBH file.

Finally, you need to adjust the WinHelp project's HPJ file, as follows:

1. Open the WinHelp project's HPJ file in a text editor.
2. Change the name of the What's This? help RTF file in the [FILES] section. Also change the name of the HH file in the [MAP] section to the new name of your What's This? help file. The following code shows portions of the HPJ file for a What's This? help project named New Travel.

```
[FILES]
Foggan Drizzle Tour Info.rtf
new travel.rtf

[MAP]
#include <new travel.HH>
```

3. When you are satisfied with your changes, save your changes and close the HPJ file.

Tip

After you've renamed the project, the automatic file open option in What's This? Help Composer won't know where to find the project. Open the project using the File ➪ Open command in What's This? Help Composer the first time after you've renamed it.

Moving a What's This? Help Project Combined with a RoboHELP Project

You may need to move the What's This? help files to a new folder. Although this is very simple when the What's This? help project is stand-alone, you need to make a few adjustments to the files when the What's This? help file is combined with a RoboHELP project, as follows:

1. Close What's This? Help Composer and RoboHELP.
2. Move the What's This? help files to the new folder.
3. Open the WinHelp project's RBH file in a text editor.
4. In the `[PROJECT]` section of the RBH file, modify the line that says `CHFile=` with the new path of the What's This? help project's RTF file.
5. When you are satisfied with your changes, save your changes and close the RBH file.
6. Open the WinHelp project's HPJ file in a text editor.
7. Change the path of the What's This? help RTF file in the `[FILES]` section and the path of the What's This? help project's HH file in the `[MAP]` section. Also be sure to change the path of the DIALOG.CID file in the `[BAGGAGE]` section.
8. When you are satisfied with your changes, save your changes and close the HPJ file.

As when you rename a What's This? help project, you will need to tell What's This? Help Composer where to find the What's This? help project the first time you run What's This? Help Composer after having moved the project.

Removing What's This? Help from a RoboHELP Project

You may choose to remove What's This? help from a RoboHELP project for several reasons. One of the most common is that a large What's This? help file will add substantially to the compile time. Moreover, you may want to break the two types of online help apart so that they can be tested or developed separately and then rejoin them shortly before releasing the finished online help file.

To remove a What's This? help project from a RoboHELP project, do the following:

1. Close What's This? Help Composer and RoboHELP.
2. Open the What's This? help project's CHJ file in a text editor such as Notepad.
3. In the [PROJECT] section of the CHJ file, change the file names of the HLP and HPJ files back to the name of the What's This? help project.
4. When you are satisfied with your changes, save your changes and close the CHJ file.
5. Open the WinHelp project's HPJ file in a text editor.
6. Remove the What's This? help file's RTF file in the [FILES] section and the What's This? help project's HH file in the [MAP] section. Also remove the DIALOG.CID file in the [BAGGAGE] section.
7. When you are satisfied with your changes, save your changes and close the HPJ file.

   You can always re-add the What's This? help file to the RoboHELP file later on.

Editing What's This? Help in RoboHELP

Although you'll normally do all your What's This? help editing in What's This? Help Composer, one of the advantages of combining What's This? help and WinHelp is that you can perform the final edits of the help topics in RoboHELP. This lets you take advantage of the extensive formatting options in Microsoft Word.

The What's This? Help Composer stores the What's This? help information in an internal database and creates the RTF file only when you compile the What's This? help. Any changes you make to the RTF file in RoboHELP are not transferred back to the database in What's This? Help Composer. As a result, you should edit the RTF file in RoboHELP as the absolutely final stage before you ship the files. If you compile the What's This? help in What's This? Help Composer for any reason instead of through the RoboHELP compiler, it will overwrite the changes you've made to the RTF file in RoboHELP.

To edit the What's This? help file in RoboHELP, do the following:

1. Select the RoboHELP ➪ What's This? Help Composer Project ➪ Unlock Document command to unlock the What's This? help RTF file. A warning message appears (shown in Figure 13-28).
2. Click OK in the message box. RoboHELP attaches the standard RoboHELP template to the RTF file. The topics in the RTF file appear sorted in the order of the topic IDs.
3. Edit the RTF file as appropriate.
4. Save the file and compile as usual.

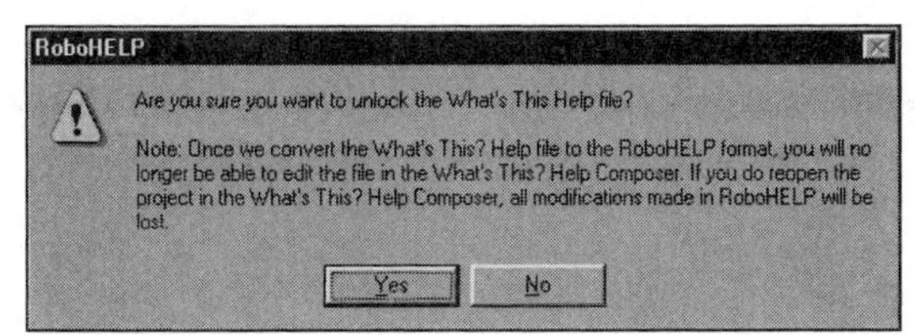

Figure 13-28: Warning message prior to unlocking the What's This? help RTF file

Once the RTF file has been unlocked (regardless of whether or not you've edited it), you can view it in RoboHELP by selecting the RoboHELP ➪ What's This? Help Composer Project ➪ Unlock Document command.

Using Programmer-Generated Topic IDs

The What's This? Help Composer automatically creates your What's This? help topics and topic IDs. However, the programmer may already have generated the topic IDs. In the likely event that you won't be able to get these changed, you'll need to edit the What's This? help to use these topics IDs, as follows:

1. Create a stand-alone What's This? help project for the program. Compile and test the What's This? help.
2. If the program doesn't have an associated WinHelp project in RoboHELP, create a "dummy" WinHelp project. (This project is only for the purpose of importing the What's This? help project into RoboHELP for editing, so it doesn't need anything other than the default topic.)
3. Make sure that the file is set to auto-generate map IDs by selecting the File ➪ Project Settings command, displaying the Map IDs tab, selecting the current map file and checking New Documents Generate Map IDs, and then clicking OK.
4. Add the What's This? help project to the WinHelp project by selecting the File ➪ Import ➪ Document command in the RoboHELP Explorer, and then selecting the What's This Help project's RTF file in the Import Document screen (not shown). Make sure that the"Copy to Project Directory" box is checked and the "Add document as read-only RTF" box is not checked, and then click OK. This doesn't import the external help file itself, but rather imports the RTF file that's created by What's This Help Composer.
5. Edit the generated HH file (use any text editor, such as Notepad), changing the topic IDs to those provided by the programmer. You can also edit topic IDs by opening the Map IDs folder (under the Project folder) in the RoboHELP Explorer Project Manager. Double-click on an entry to display the map ID properties and change as necessary.

As an alternative, you can have the developer create an HH file in the proper format and then import it into the project through the RoboHELP Explorer Project Manager as an external map ID file.

Notes for Programmers

If you are a programmer developing with a C or C++ program, there are some things you need to do to enable What's This? help in the program:

- ✦ You must set the tab order for the controls in each dialog box. The tab order should move the focus logically from one control to the next and from one group of controls to the next. Controls that have an ID of –1 are not included in the tab order and will not have a What's This? help topic. It's a good idea to set static text to –1 and to have the control the static text is describing as the next item in the tab order. For group boxes, use either a unique ID or set the group box to –1 so the next control will have the same What's This? help text as the group box.
- ✦ If you are developing with a C or C++ program, you'll need to use the calls in the CSHUSER.H file. These calls are documented in detail in What's This? Help Composer documentation. The CSH.DEF, CSH.DLL, and CSHUSER.H files appear in the \RoboHELP Office\RoboHELP\WhatsThs\ProgDlls folder along with the LIB files for the various supported C/C++ compilers.
- ✦ If the program is being developed with the C++ AppWizard, enabling the context-sensitive help in the AppWizard will duplicate the What's This? help project's topic information.
- ✦ What's This? help works only for the Cdialog class of dialog boxes in C++ programs.
- ✦ You can use What's This? help with HTML Help for C++ programs.
- ✦ A common mistake when creating What's This? help for Visual Basic programs is for the programmer to give a copy of their program's source files to the help author but they'll also continue to work on the source files. As a result, when the help author gets the next version of the program, What's This? Help Composer will detect changes to the program and overwrite the What's This? help files. The preferred method is for the programmer to check out the source files to the help author and stop working on them. The help author will then create the initial version of the What's This? help and immediately check the source files back in and also hand off the What's This? help files to the programmer. The programmer can then incorporate them in the program's source files. Both the help author and the programmer can then continue working on their respective projects. By doing this, What's This? Help Composer will treat any changes to the program as updates and will just add new dialog boxes to the What's This? help file rather than recreating the entire What's This? help file.

Printing the Help Author and Project Status Reports

There are two reports in What's This? Help Composer: the Help Author report and the Project Status report. The Help Author report is a detail report showing information, notably the editing status, of the controls of your report. The Project Status report is a summary report that shows the number of topics with each status classification.

To generate a Help Author or a Project Status report, do the following:

1. In What's This? Help Composer, select the File ➪ Reports command. The Project Reports screen appears (as shown in Figure 13-29).

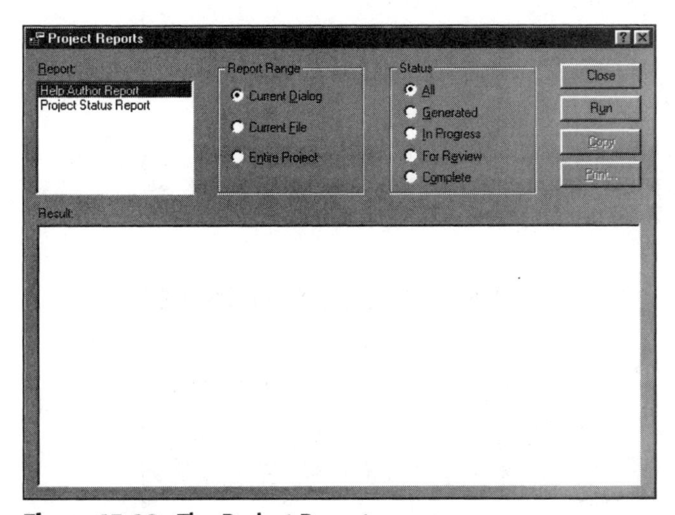

Figure 13-29: The Project Reports screen

2. Enter information in the fields as follows:
   - **Report:** Select Help Author Report or Project Status Report to run the appropriate report.
   - **Report Range:** Select the scope of the report: Current Dialog, Current File, or Entire Project.
   - **Status:** Select the help topic status to report on: All, Generated, In Progress, For Review, Complete. (You can select the help topic status only if you're printing a Help Author report.)

3. When you are satisfied with your entries, click Run. The report appears in the Result field. Figure 13-30 shows a typical Help Author report, whereas Figure 13-31 shows a typical Project Status report. You can scroll up and down to view the reports.

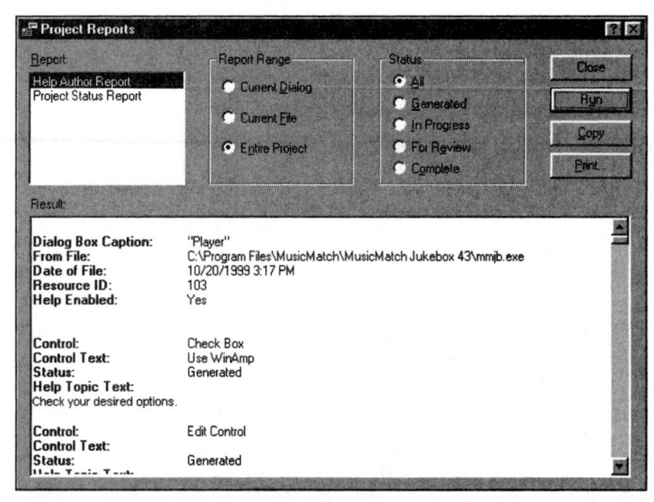

Figure 13-30: A typical Help Author report

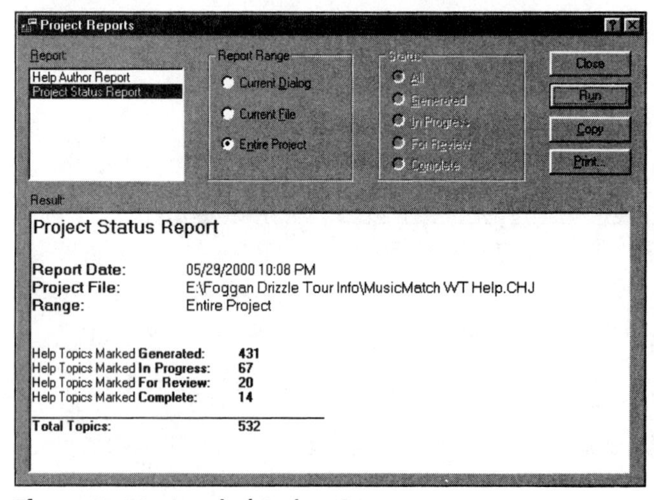

Figure 13-31: A typical Project Status report

4. You can copy the report to the Windows Clipboard by clicking Copy, and then paste it into e-mail or a departmental status report like any other text. To print the report, click Print. Click Close to exit the Project Reports screen.

The total number of topics listed in the Project Status Report may disagree with the total number of controls listed in the lower right corner of What's This? Help Composer. This is because the Project Status report lists all controls that have context help, whereas the status line on What's This? Help Composer lists all the controls in the dialog box. Most frequently, the difference in the count will be because of static text controls in the dialog box.

You can run the Help Author and Project Status reports at any time.

Shipping What's This? Help

As part of the release to shipping, you'll need to do a final verification that the What's This? help code has been added to the program, as follows:

1. Get the final version of the program and any related files from the developer.
2. Update the What's This? help in What's This? Help Composer to make sure that any last changes to the program have been incorporated in the What's This? help.
3. Test the program together with the What's This? help independent of What's This? Help Composer. Verify each of the What's This? help links.

If the What's This? help passes the tests, you can optionally make any final edits to the RTF file as described earlier in this chapter and then ship the What's This? help HLP file (if stand-alone) or the compiled files for the WinHelp project (if combined with WinHelp). If the program is a C/C++ file, you must also provide the CSH.DLL file, which should be installed in the user's \Windows\System folder. This DLL file contains the code the program requires to call the What's This? help.

Understanding Training Cards

Training cards are basically a set of WinHelp topics that appear in secondary windows. (They usually appear either in the main WinHelp project or as a small stand-alone WinHelp file.) What's special about training cards is that you can set them up to directly interact with a program. For example, you can have the program pass a text string or a result from something the user has entered to the training card, and then have information from the training card passed back to the program, such as having different training cards appear based on whether the user clicks on Save or Cancel.

Figure 13-32 shows a sample application and the related training card help. (An example you can try on your own appears in the Microsoft Help Compiler Workshop , HCW.EXE, which is shipped with RoboHELP Office. Start the Microsoft Help Compiler Workshop (in the \RoboHELP Office\RoboHELP\hlpcomp\ folder), and then select the Help ➪ Training Cards ➪ Creating a Project. When you start, only one training card project is available. As you go through the steps of creating a project with this tool, additional training cards become available.

In this example, you enter the sum of the two numbers in the first field. If you enter the correct value, the training card displays a topic that shows that the input was correct. However, if the answer is wrong, the training card steps the users through the addition process.

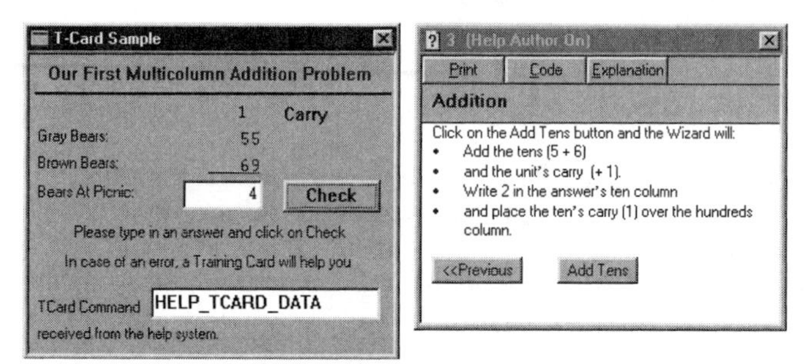

Figure 13-32: Sample application and associated training card

Training cards are most typically used for intensive online tutorials and demonstrating specific procedures on a step-by-step basis. The users can read information and answer a question by making an entry or clicking a multiple-choice button. If they're correct, the nest training card in the series appears; otherwise, you can explain why the answer is incorrect and describe what to do to correct the mistake.

To program training card help, the programmers use the standard WinHelp API to communicate with the WinHelp file. On the WinHelp side, the help author uses the TCard macro to send information back to the program. (This process will require extensive help author/programmer interaction.)

The first step to start the communication between the program and the WinHelp file is for the program to use the WinHelp API with the `HELP_TCARD` parameter to open the help system as a training card. This also sets up the WinHelp file to send information back to the program using the TCard macro. An example of the WinHelp API call to open the WinHelp file TCTRAV.HLP as training card help and to display the topic IDH_First_step in a secondary window named tcard follows.

```
WinHelp(hWnd,"TCTRAV.HLP>tcard",HELP_TCARD|HELP_CONTEXT,IDH_Fir
st_step);
```

For more information on using macros and a brief description of the TCard macro, see Chapter 10, "Understanding Macros." For detailed information on the TCard macro and the WinHelp API, check the online documentation for RoboHELP and also the HCW.HLP file (the Microsoft Help Compiler Workshop help).

If you have a series of steps in training card format, you may want to use an authorable button with both a TCard macro and a Next macro. This lets you communicate with the calling program and then automatically display the next training card.

For more information on using authorable buttons, see Chapter 7, "Getting Fancy with Graphics."

Depending on the results of the training card activity, the TCard macro in the WinHelp file will transmit information back to the calling program. The program will then use the WM_TCARD API to receive a message that will tell the results of training card activity.

Training card help is not used very often simply because it is very time-consuming to plan, create, and test. Prototyping the training card help is an essential part of the project planning process. The help authors and developers must work very closely together to determine the messages you want to pass back and forth and to correctly program the inputs and outputs for each training card. Training card help also requires some familiarity with the TCard macro and the WinHelp and WM_TCARD APIs.

In addition to these requirements, the testing process for training card help will be as time consuming as for any other program. The most likely strategy for success is to have a multidisciplinary help author, who also has some skill at programming and curriculum development, do most of the development of the training card help. But despite the extra effort necessary to create a complete training card help system, the level of interaction with the program and the online help can provide dramatic results for the users.

Summary

This chapter has taught you how to create What's This? and training card help. After being introduced to the basics of What's This? help, you learned how to use What's This? Help Composer to create and edit a basic What's This? help file. Next, you saw how to configure What's This? Help Composer, compile What's This? help, and then test the result. The chapter then discussed how to maintain and update What's This? help. You next learned about special dialog boxes and controls that are not automatically maintained by What's This? Help Composer. After that, the chapter showed you how to create and maintain a single help file by combining What's This? help and WinHelp. You then saw how to print What's This? help reports and release the completed What's This? help files for shipping. The chapter concluded with a discussion of the basics of designing and creating training cards.

✦ ✦ ✦

Using RoboHELP Tools

CHAPTER 14

✦ ✦ ✦ ✦

In This Chapter

Decompiling WinHelp files

Searching and replacing across multiple files

Creating knowledge bases

Creating other kinds of help from WinHelp projects

Adding WinHelp 4 features to WinHelp 3 files

✦ ✦ ✦ ✦

In this chapter, you'll learn how to use some additional RoboHELP tools. You first learn to decompile WinHelp files into source documents you can then modify and recompile. You'll then learn how to use Multi-File Find and Replace to search for and optionally replace information in multiple files. The chapter then discusses how to create standalone knowledge bases using PC HelpDesk. Next, you see how to convert WinHelp 4 projects into a variety of other online help formats such as WinHelp 3, HTML Help, and Windows CE help. The chapter concludes with information on how to retrofit WinHelp 3 files with WinHelp 4 features using the WinHelp Compatibility Wizard, the WinHelp HyperViewer, and the WinHelp Inspector.

Using Help-to-Source

As you've seen in preceding chapters, RoboHELP Office comes with a wide variety of tools for working with graphics and video, and debugging WinHelp files, such as the Graphics Locator, ReSize, the Software Video Camera, the WinHelp BugHunter, and the What's This? Help Composer. You'll now learn about several additional tools and features of RoboHELP that will make you more effective and save you time.

It's always a good idea to keep your skills up by looking at other online help systems to see how they're done. You can learn a lot about how best to organize, format, and present the information in your WinHelp systems by looking at the WinHelp systems for similar or competing products. However, just looking at a compiled WinHelp file won't tell you how a topic was coded or what sequence of macros the author may have used to implement a particularly slick technique. What you need to do in cases like these is to *decompile* the WinHelp file.

RoboHELP provides you with a tool for decompiling WinHelp files called Help-to-Source. Help-to-Source opens a WinHelp file and turns it back into its component source (project) files and graphics (something like putting sausage in a grinder and turning it back into a pig). You can examine the decompiled files to figure out how the author pulled off a fancy technique, or you can extract a specific graphic from the file. Decompiling WinHelp files is also an invaluable technique if the source files for the compiled WinHelp file have been lost or damaged. (This happens occasionally; being able to decompile WinHelp and recover from the problem is very helpful.)

The exact coding or way in which an online help system has been put together may be covered by the company's copyright. Most software licenses also specifically proscribe decompiling WinHelp files. Be prudent when decompiling WinHelp files that are not your own or when using code or techniques taken from decompiled online help files.

The general procedure for decompiling a WinHelp file is very simple:

1. In the RoboHELP Explorer, double-click the Help-to-Source icon in the Tools folder, as shown in Figure 14-1. The first Help-to-Source Wizard screen (shown in Figure 14-2) appears.

Figure 14-1: The Help-to-Source icon

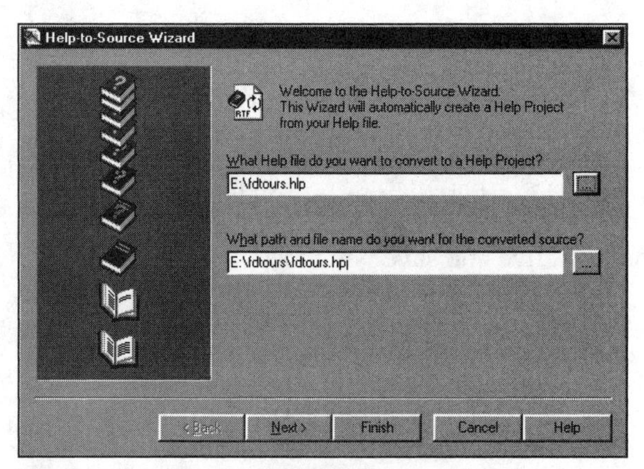

Figure 14-2: The first Help-to-Source Wizard screen

2. Enter information in the fields as follows:

   - **What Help file do you want to convert to a Help Project?:** Enter the name of the WinHelp file you want to decompile. Click the button to the right of this field to browse the files.

- **What path and file name do you want for the converted source?:** Help-to-Source automatically enters a folder name with the same name as the WinHelp file you're decompiling. The associated HPJ file also has the same name as the WinHelp file. Click the button to the right of the field to browse the files.

3. When you are satisfied with your changes, click Next. The second Help-to-Source Wizard screen appears (as shown in Figure 14-3).

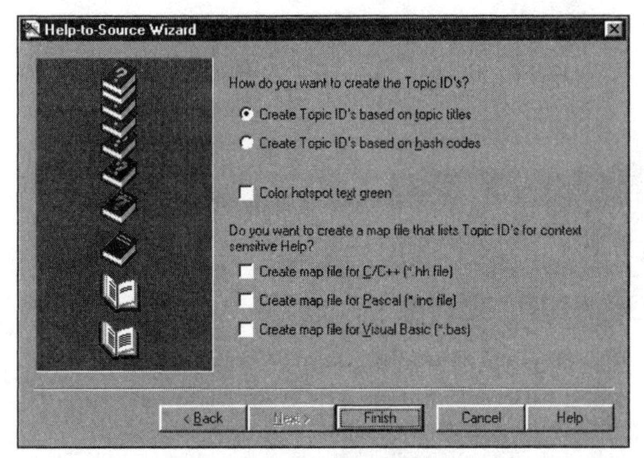

Figure 14-3: The second Help-to-Source Wizard screen

4. Enter information in the fields as follows:

   - **Create Topic ID's based on topic titles:** Select this option to create the topic IDs from the topic titles. (This is the default selection.) This option will produce topic IDs that are more maintainable than those created from hash codes because the topic IDs are easier to understand. You will usually use this option for creating topic IDs; however, using this option require you to correct the topic ID links in any macros in the WinHelp file. (Use the Broken Links folder in the RoboHELP Explorer Project Manager once you have decompiled the WinHelp file and then opened the new WinHelp project in RoboHELP. You can also search for ! (the symbol that appears at the start of each macro) in Word and then correct the macros by hand.

   - **Create Topic ID's based on hash codes:** Select this option to create the topic IDs from the *hash codes*. (Hash codes are internal codes created by the compiler that tell the WinHelp viewer where to find topics in the WinHelp file.) Use this option if the WinHelp file has a lot of macros and is lacking a CNT file. Help-to-Source will create topic IDs from hash codes and update the macros automatically with the appropriate topic IDs. However, the topic IDs will be hexadecimal numbers, which are difficult to maintain.

- **Color hotspot text green:** Check this box to color the hotspot text green. If you don't check this box, the hotspot text will be black.
- **Do you want to create a map file that lists Topic ID's for context sensitive Help?:** Check the appropriate boxes to create map files for the various program types. You may select any or all of these file types. Check with the developer if you aren't sure which file types you'll need.

5. When you are satisfied with your entries, click Finish. Help-to-Source reads the WinHelp file you've specified and decompiles it. You'll see a variety of displays during the process showing the progress (a typical display appears in Figure 14-4). The entire process may take several minutes, particularly if you're working with a large WinHelp file.

Figure 14-4: Decompiling the WinHelp file

6. When the decompiling process is complete, Help-to-Source will display information about the finished file, showing the number of topics and graphics decompiled. (An example of this screen is shown in Figure 14-5.)

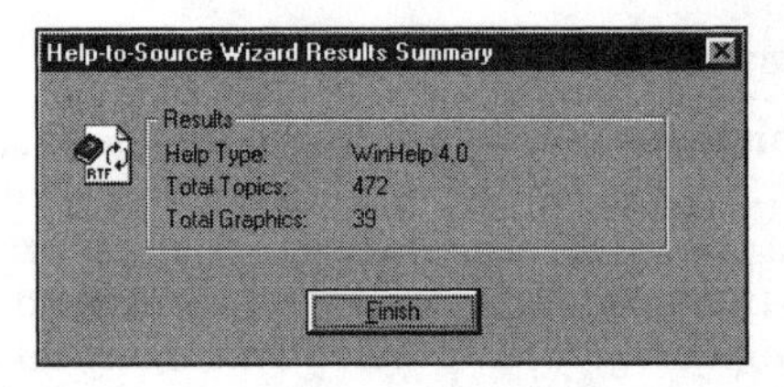

Figure 14-5: Help-to-Source results screen

The component files for the WinHelp project appear in the directory you specified on the first Help-to-Source Wizard screen. Although you could immediately open the WinHelp project and then compile it into the same WinHelp file, there are several important differences between the decompiled files and the original source files:

✦ Graphics will have a name based on the name of the WinHelp file and their order of appearance in the WinHelp file. BMP (bitmap) files, WMF (Windows metafiles) files, and SHG (segmented hypergraphic) files will all be numbered in their order of appearance. For example, the first bitmap graphic in the decompiled FDTOURS.HLP file would have the name FDTO0000.BMP, the second graphic (a SHG file) would have the name FDTO0001.SHG, and so on.

✦ The decompiler doesn't create a DOC file but it does create an RTF file.

✦ If you're using context-sensitive help, the [ALIAS] and [MAP] information in the HPJ file will be generated by Help-to-Source. For example, some of the [ALIAS] entries in the decompiled FDTOURS.HLP file look like this:

```
R5CNGI = Arts_and_Events
A4DAG5E = What_makes_Ireland_and_the_UK_unique?
ARHOJFC = History_and_Culture
V1IIVU = What_makes_Ireland_and_the_UK_unique?
```

✦ Browse sequences will have names assigned by Help-to-Source during the decompiling process. For example, a typical browse sequence in the decompiled FDTOURS.RTF file is Group0001:0002.

✦ When you open the HPJ file, you may see one of several messages, such as a message warning that the help file is not a RoboHELP file, and that once a message has been opened in RoboHELP, you cannot revert to the original files. You also may have to choose whether you want to open the help file in WinHelp 3 or WinHelp 4 depending on what was used to create the original help file.

✦ Depending on how you decompile the WinHelp file, you may need to fix macros to correct topic ID references.

If you are decompiling a WinHelp file to recover lost or damaged source files, you'll need to examine the resulting source files and make appropriate changes to the information so that the files will be more maintainable in the long run. (You won't need to do this if you're decompiling a WinHelp file only to see how it works.)

Using Multi-File Find and Replace

One simple but enormously handy utility that accompanies RoboHELP Office is Multi-File Find and Replace. You can use Multi-File Find and Replace to find and optionally replace text in multiple text or RTF files in a single operation. (Multi-File Find and Replace doesn't work on DOC files because of the proprietary Word file format. Furthermore, the changes to the RTF files are not stored in the DOC files; you'll need to save the changes to the DOC files yourself before continuing.) This is very useful in larger WinHelp projects in whichthere are multiple files requiring the same changes, such as a product name or terminology change.

To find and change text in multiple files, do the following:

1. In the RoboHELP Explorer, double-click the Multi-File Find and Replace icon in the Tools folder, as shown in Figure 14-6. The Multi-File Find and Replace screen (shown in Figure 14-7) appears.

Figure 14-6: The Multi-File Find and Replace icon

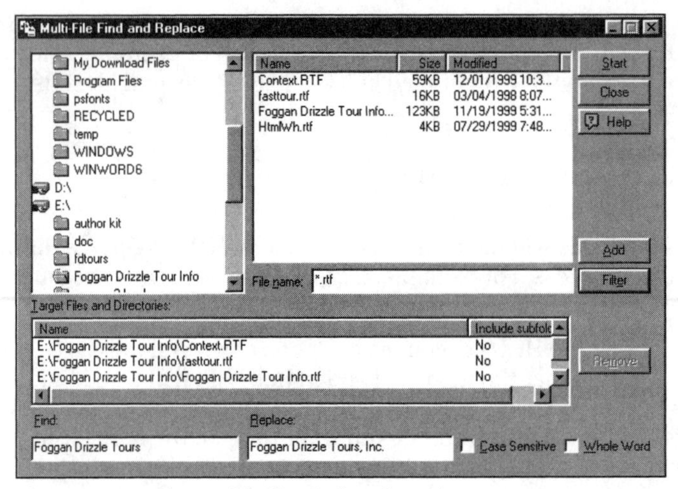

Figure 14-7: The Multi-File Find and Replace screen

2. Select the drive and directory in the field on the left side of the screen. The files in the directory will appear in the file display on the upper right of the screen.

Microsoft Word (DOC) files will appear in the list, and can be selected. However, because it can't read the DOC format, Multi-File Find and Replace will always find 0 instances of any word you try to find in a Word document.

3. To select the files you want to search, hold down the CTRL key and click the files with the mouse. (If you have too many files in the display, you can filter the files by entering a filtering criterion (as shown in Figure 14-7) and clicking Filter.) When you are satisfied with your changes, click Add. The files you've selected will appear in the Target Files and Directories field on the lower portion of the screen.
4. Continue selecting files and directories to search, clicking Add to add your selections. You can remove files and directories from the Target Files and Directories field by highlighting the items and clicking Remove.
5. Enter the text string to search for in the Find field. If you also want to replace this string with something, enter the information in the Replace field. You can optionally check Case Sensitive and Whole Word to search and replace exactly as the text items appear in the fields and to search for the whole word only (as opposed to finding the string as part of a larger string).
6. When you are satisfied with your selections, click Start in the upper right corner of the screen to start searching. The Search Results screen appears with a dialog box showing the number of occurrences of the search string that were found, as shown in Figure 14-8. (If no occurrences are found, it displays a message and does not display the Results screen.)

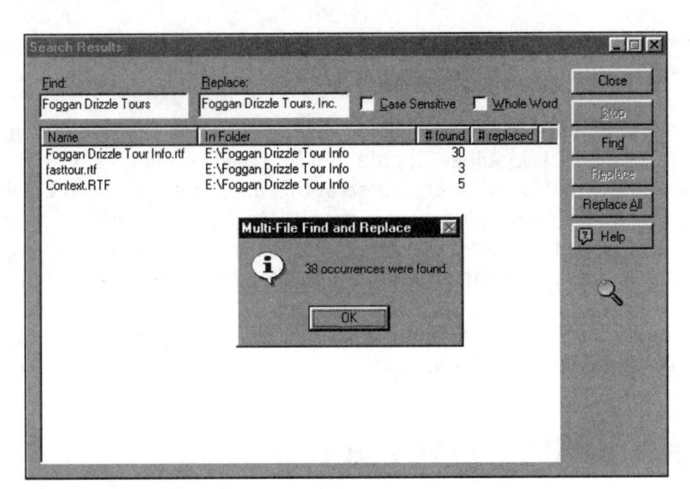

Figure 14-8: The Search Results screen

7. Click OK to close the dialog box.

At this point, Multi-File Find and Replace has simply found the search item. The number of appearances found in each file appears on the display.

To replace the occurrences of the search string that were found, do the following:

✦ Click Replace All to replace all the occurrences in all of the files. The number of replacements for each file is displayed. If you wish, you can replace occurrences in individual files by highlighting the files and then clicking Replace, rather than Replace All. You can stop the replacement by clicking Stop.

You can do another search and replace directly from the Search Results screen by entering the text strings to find and replace in the fields at the top of the screen and clicking Find.

Once you've made changes to the RTF files for a WinHelp project, be sure to delete the corresponding DOC files. This is because RoboHELP opens the DOC file, which will not contain any of the changes you make with Multi-File Find and Replace. Moreover, when you save the DOC file, RoboHELP will overwrite the RTF file with the current DOC file.

Using PC HelpDesk

PC HelpDesk is a tool for creating *knowledge bases*. A knowledge base is a collection of online resources, FAQs, tips, technical support information, bugs, notes, and comments that is used to augment the primary documentation. A good example of a knowledge base created with PC HelpDesk is the eHelp knowledge base available on the eHelp Web site. The default PC HelpDesk is actually an Access database, although you could build your database using other tools.

PC HelpDesk was a first step in providing access over the Internet to help topics and help information. It is still a valuable tool for basic knowledge base functions, but it is not being developed or expanded at this time. If you want to create a live knowledge base with extended access to remote help, discussions with other users, and Web search features, use eHelp. For more information on using eHelp, see Chapter 12, "Linking to the Internet and Adding Multimedia."

One very good use for a PC HelpDesk file is as an internal testing and error-logging tool for creating online help systems.

Creating a New PC HelpDesk File

To create a new PC HelpDesk file, do the following:

1. In the RoboHELP Explorer, double-click the PC HelpDesk icon in the Tools folder, as shown in Figure 14-9. PC HelpDesk displays a screen (not shown) that prompts you to create a new HelpDesk, open an existing HelpDesk, open an ODBC data source, or open a PowerSQL data source. Select the "Create a new HelpDesk" option and click OK. The standard new file screen appears.

Figure 14-9: The PC HelpDesk icon

2. Enter the name of the new PC HelpDesk file in the standard new file screen and click OK.

PC HelpDesk files have an extension of PHD.

3. PC HelpDesk prompts you for a username and password for the database. You can enter any username and password you wish. (If you don't need to use a password with your HelpDesk, you can uncheck the Always require a login option on the PC HelpDesk Options screen, shown later in Figure 14-11.) When you are satisfied with your changes, click OK. The PC HelpDesk screen appears (shown in Figure 14-10 with a new file opened).

Because the PC HelpDesk is designed to provide knowledge base help for a range of products, the screen has a slightly different focus than that of standard WinHelp, although many of the elements are similar. The left side of the screen, known as the Project pane, gives you a tree view of the PC HelpDesk file, showing the products, product areas, and topics. The upper right side, known as the Topic pane, shows the information that will appear in the knowledge base for the topic. The lower right side, known as the Properties pane, shows the properties for the topic.

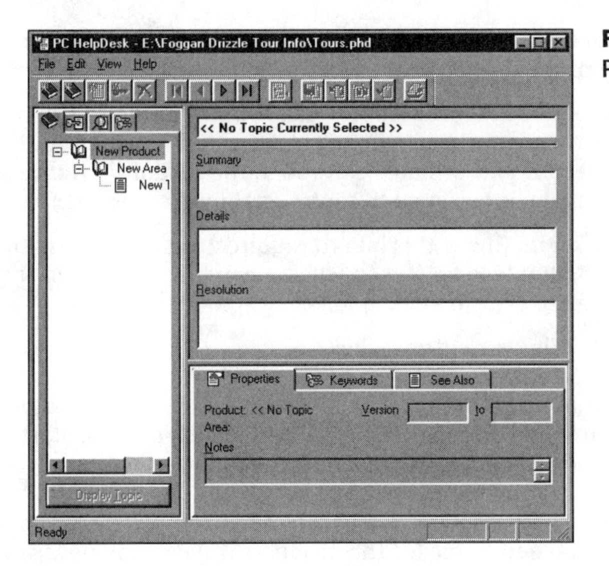

Figure 14-10: The PC HelpDesk screen

When you start PC HelpDesk and start a new PC HelpDesk file, there is a default New Product, New Area, and New Topic entry. You may want to customize PC HelpDesk and the PC HelpDesk file a little before you start entering topics and information.

To customize PC HelpDesk, do the following:

1. Select the View ➪ Options command. The PC HelpDesk Options screen appears (shown in Figure 14-11).

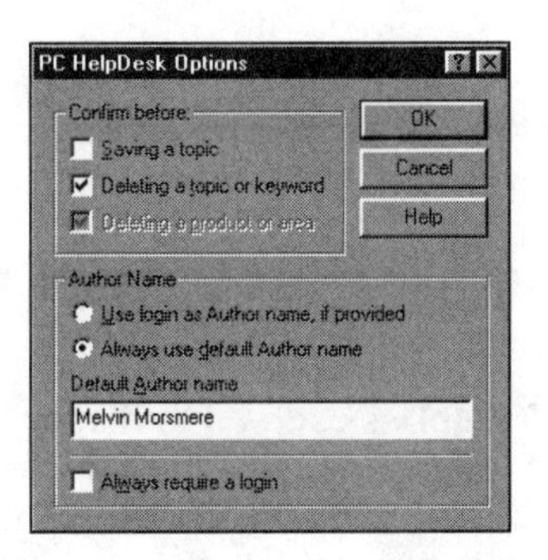

Figure 14-11: The PC HelpDesk Options screen

2. Enter information in the fields as follows:
   - **Saving a topic:** Check this box to have PC HelpDesk confirm before saving a topic.
   - **Deleting a topic or keyword:** Check this box to have PC HelpDesk confirm before deleting a topic or keyword. (This is the default option.)

- **Deleting a product or area:** Check this box to have PC HelpDesk confirm before deleting a product or area.
- **Author Name:** Select Use login as Author name, if prompted to use the login name as the author name, or select Always use default Author name to use the default author name entered in the Default Author name field. (The author name is assigned to topics as they are created.)
- **Always require a login:** Check this box to require a login to access the PC HelpDesk file. A simple login screen will appear when you open the knowledge base again. (This is the default.)

3. When you are satisfied with your entries, click OK.

Before you enter information in the knowledge base, it's a good idea to add and rename products and areas to build a framework for entering information. Start by renaming the default New Product and New Area topics, as follows:

1. Right-click the default New Product entry and select Rename Product from the right-click menu. Enter the new name for the product. You can add new product entries by right-clicking a product entry and selecting New Product from the right-click menu, then entering a name for the product entry.
2. Right-click the default New Area entry and enter the new name for the area. You can add new area entries in the same way as you added new product entries: right-click the product or area, select New Area from the right-click menu, and then enter a name for the area entry.

When you enter new product and area entries, PC HelpDesk sorts them alphabetically in the tree. Figure 14-12 shows a sample PC HelpDesk file with some additional new product and area entries.

You can size the PC HelpDesk screen by clicking and dragging on the border of the screen. You can size the individual panes of the PC HelpDesk by clicking and dragging the borders of the panes.

Once you've set up some product and area entries, you're ready to enter topic information in the PC HelpDesk file, as follows:

1. Expand the tree on the left side of the PC HelpDesk screen to display the first New Topic item and double-click it. The topic heading for the selected topic appears in the Topic Heading field at the top of the fields on the right side of the screen. When you first select a new topic, the default heading, New Topic Title, appears in this field. You can change this by entering a new title in this field. (Changing the information in this field will change the name of the topic in the tree view on the left side of the screen.) The topic heading should be descriptive and concise.

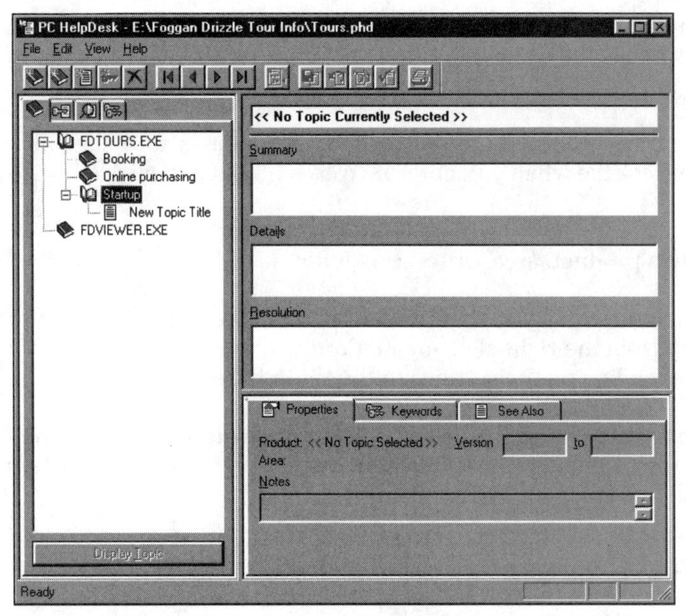

Figure 14-12: Adding and renaming product and area entries in the PC HelpDesk file

You can also change the topic title by right-clicking the topic, selecting Rename Topic from the right-click menu, and then entering the new topic name as usual.

2. Enter information in the Topic fields as follows:

   - **Summary:** Enter the topic summary. The topic summary should be a brief summary description of the problem being described.
   - **Details:** Enter a detailed description of the problem. This should be complete and as long as necessary.
   - **Resolution:** Enter the resolution for the problem defined by the summary and details. (If you don't have a resolution when you enter the problem — frequently the case — leave this field blank.) If the situation you're reporting isn't truly a problem, you can also use this field for comments and follow-up information.

3. Enter the information in the Properties pane as follows:

   - **Version:** Enter the version number(s) that this item applies to. (The product name is taken automatically from the product entry this topic entry appears under.)
   - **Notes:** Enter any notes relevant to the topic, such as auditing information.

4. You can continue by adding new topics and entering information. (Adding new topic entries is the same as adding new product and area entries: right-click a topic and select Add Topic from the right-click menu.)

Unlike in most other RoboHELP operations, information is automatically updated in the PC HelpDesk file when you enter it. You don't have to click OK to log your changes.

You can delete a product, area, or topic as follows:

✦ Right-click the entry you want to delete, then select the Delete command for the entry from the right-click menu. (You may be prompted to confirm deletions, depending on the settings in the PC HelpDesk Options screen.)

If you want to undo a change to a topic before you switch to another topic, you can revert to the changed topic by clicking the Revert to Saved Topic button on the toolbar, shown in Figure 14-13.

Figure 14-13: The Revert to Saved Topic button

Adding Keywords and See Also Links to Topics

You can expand your topic entries by adding keywords and See Also links in the Properties pane. To add keywords, do the following:

1. Select the Keywords folder in the Properties pane and click Add. The Add Keyword to Topic screen appears (shown in Figure 14-14).

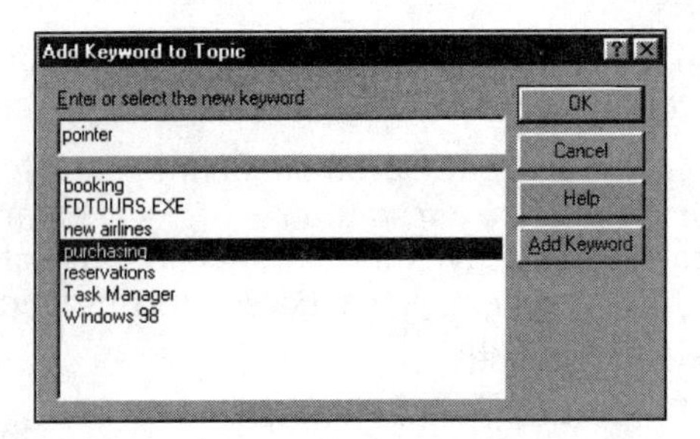

Figure 14-14: The Add Keyword to Topic screen

2. Enter a keyword for the topic and click Add. PC HelpDesk adds the keyword to the list of keywords for the topic. Figure 14-15 shows several keywords added to this entry.

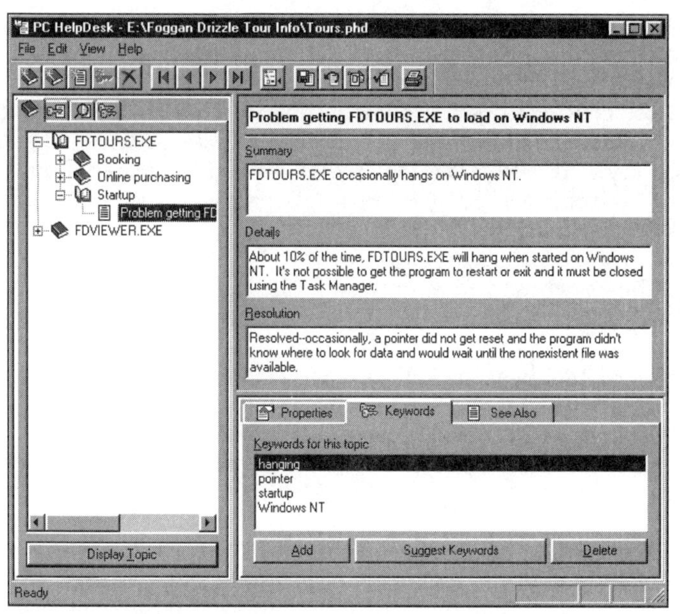

Figure 14-15: Adding keywords to a topic

As you add keywords to the topics, you'll build a list of keywords in the Add Keyword to Topic screen.

Once you've added keywords to several topics, you can have PC HelpDesk suggest keywords to add to a topic, as follows:

1. Click Suggest Keywords at the bottom of the Keywords folder. The Add Suggested Keywords screen (shown in Figure 14-16) appears.

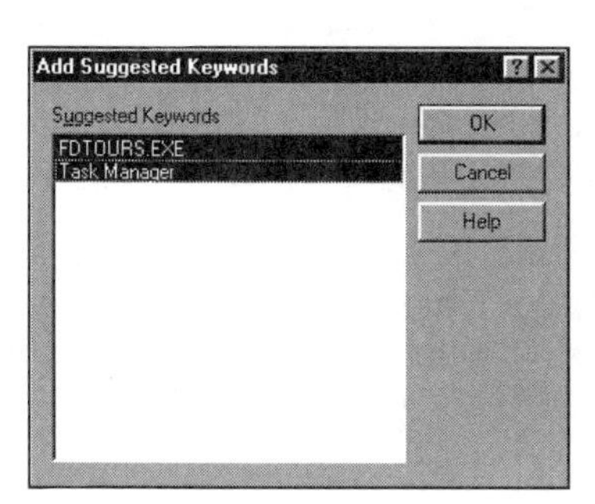

Figure 14-16: The Add Suggested Keywords screen

The Add Suggested Keywords feature works by comparing the words you've already entered as keywords against the text in the current topic. It will not have any suggestions if you have not entered any keywords yet. PC HelpDesk scans the information you've entered in the topic fields for possible matches to existing keywords, and then displays them on the list. The Add Suggested Keywords screen only appears if any of the keywords you've already entered happen to appear in the HelpDesk topic. If no keywords are found, PC HelpDesk displays a message saying that no entered keywords are in that particular topic.

2. Highlight the keywords you want to add. Click OK to add these to the keyword list for the topic.

To delete a keyword, highlight the keyword and click Delete.

If you prefer to start with a list of standard keywords to give PC HelpDesk a glossary of keywords to search for, you can add new keywords directly to the keyword list as follows:

1. Select the Keys folder on the left side of the PC HelpDesk screen, then select the Edit ➪ New ➪ Keyword command or just click the New Keyword button (shown in Figure 14-17) on the main PC HelpDesk toolbar. The New Keywords screen appears, shown in Figure 14-18 with a new keyword entered.

Figure 14-17: The New Keyword button

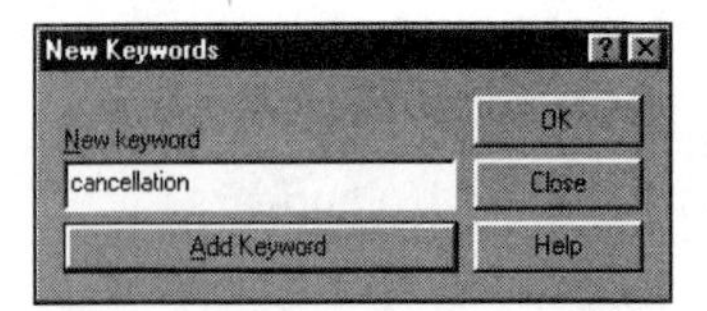

Figure 14-18: The New Keywords screen

2. Enter a keyword in the New Keyword field and click Add Keyword (if you want to add more keywords); or click OK (to add the keyword and exit the New Keywords screen).

The complete list of keywords appears on the Project Keywords folder in the Project pane. Figure 14-19 shows the list of keywords in the PC HelpDesk file. You can view the topics associated with each keyword simply by highlighting it. The topics appear at the bottom of the Project pane.

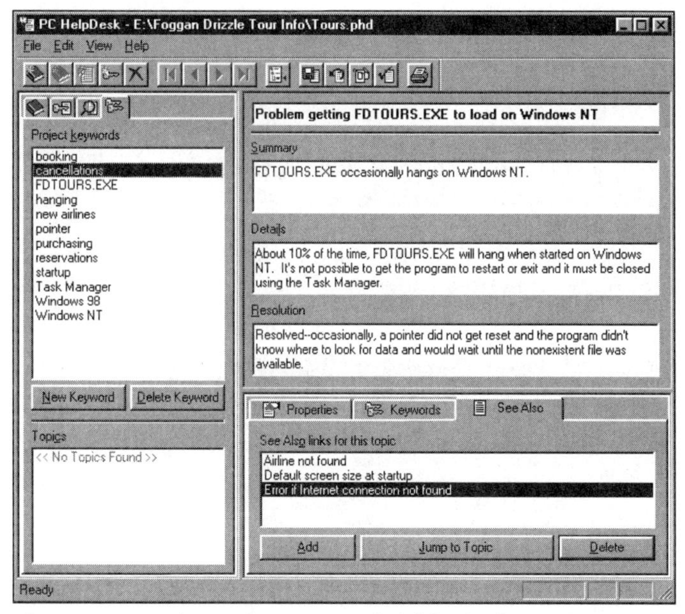

Figure 14-19: The Project Keywords folder in the Project pane

In addition to standard K-Link keywords, you can also add See Also links (A-Links) to PC HelpDesk topics. As with A-Links in standard WinHelp files, you can provide quick links to other relevant topics in the PC HelpDesk file, as follows:

1. Select the See Also folder in the Properties pane and click Add. The Add See Also Links screen appears. As you can see in Figure 14-20, the topics in the PC HelpDesk file are displayed in this screen. The current topic is displayed with a blue icon.

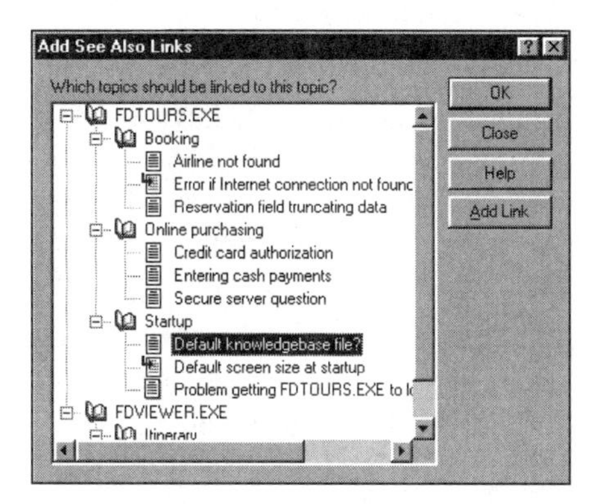

Figure 14-20: The Add See Also Links screen

2. Highlight a topic to add a See Also link and click Add Link, or simply double-click the topic. When you add a See Also link to a topic, a small blue arrow appears in the display to identify the link. (Several examples of this appear in Figure 14-20).

If you are adding only a single See Also entry, click OK, rather than Add Link, to add the link and also close the Add See Also Links screen.

3. When you are satisfied with your entries, click Close. Figure 14-21 shows a topic with several See Also entries added.

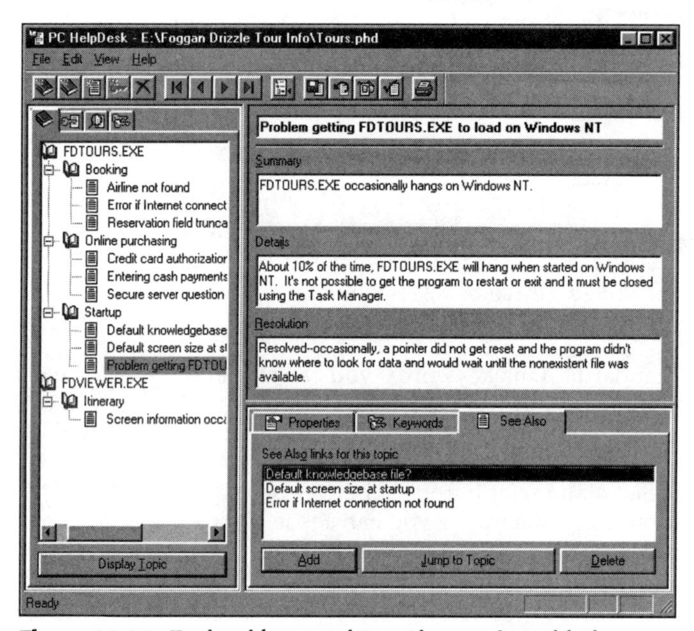

Figure 14-21: Topic with several See Also entries added

You can check your links by highlighting a link and then clicking Jump to Topic to display the topic in the PC HelpDesk screen. When you add a See Also link from one topic to another, PC HelpDesk automatically adds a corresponding link in the second topic back to the first. To delete a See Also link, highlight the link in the See Also field and click Delete.

Although you can use PC HelpDesk with an ODBC or PowerSQL database, you may find PC HelpDesk's features somewhat limited compared to the other tools available for ODBC and PowerSQL database management. If you're alreadying using an ODBC or a PowerSQL database for a knowledgebase, you should experiment with PC HelpDesk to see if it's the right tool for your application.

Checking Spelling in a PC HelpDesk File

PC HelpDesk comes with a built-in spell check. You can spell-check individual topic entries, the entire knowledge base, or product and area names and topic keywords.

To spell-check a single topic, do the following:

1. Display the topic you want to spell-check.
2. Select the Edit ➪ Spelling ➪ Current Topic command or press F7. You can also click the Spell-Check icon (shown in Figure 14-22) on the PC HelpDesk toolbar. PC HelpDesk starts checking the spelling for the topic. If it finds a misspelled or questionable word, the Check Spelling screen appears (shown in Figure 14-23).

Figure 14-22: The Spell-Check icon

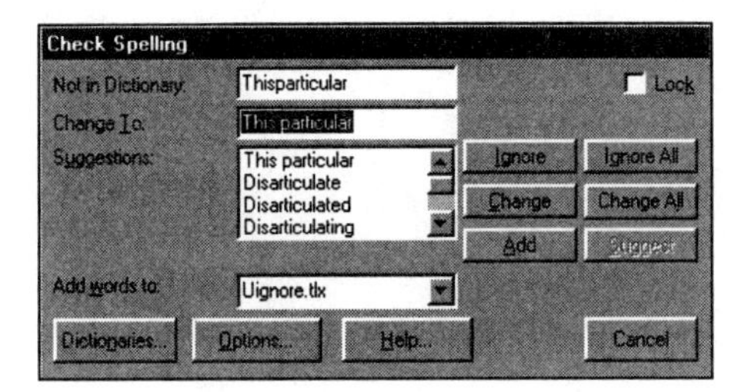

Figure 14-23: The Check Spelling screen

2. As you can see from Figure 14-23, the Check Spelling screen is similar to the spell checker in Word. You can ignore the word in question, change the word, or add the word to the dictionary selected in the Add words to field. When you've selected an action, PC HelpDesk continues spell-checking.
3. When the topic has been spell-checked, PC HelpDesk displays a message box that says the spell-check is complete. Click OK.

You use a similar process to check all the topics in the PC HelpDesk file:

1. Select the Edit ➪ Spelling ➪ All Topics command. PC HelpDesk checks the current topic for spelling errors and then continues throughout the topics in the file, displaying each one in turn as it does so. PC HelpDesk will display the Check Spelling screen (as shown in Figure 14-23) whenever it finds a word that is misspelled or questionable.
2. When the file has been spell-checked, PC HelpDesk displays a message box that says the spell-check is complete. Click OK.

Setting options in the spell checker

The spell check has a few convenient options. By checking the Lock box in the upper right corner, you can lock the Check Spelling screen so that it appears in the same location as the last place it appeared. (Normally, PC HelpDesk will try to position the Check Spelling screen so that it doesn't block the text it is checking.)

You can view and edit the information in the spelling dictionaries, as follows:

✦ Click Dictionaries on the Check Spelling screen to display the Dictionaries screen (shown in Figure 14-24).

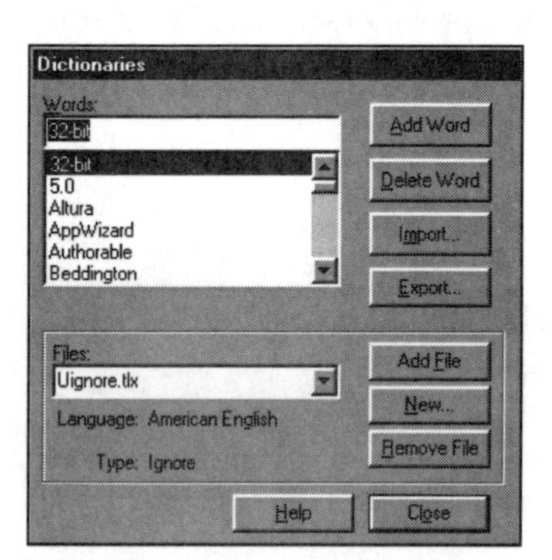

Figure 14-24: The Dictionaries screen

Modifying dictionaries

There are three basic dictionaries in the spell checker, as shown in Table 14-1. You'll typically add new words to the uignore.tlx dictionary, but you may want to add new pairs of words for automatic or conditional correction in the other two dictionaries. You can add a standard list of words or a list of word pairs for correction as follows:

1. Create a file of words in the standard format. (Model this after the existing uignore.tlx dictionary.)
2. Click Import. A standard file open dialog box appears.
3. Open the text file. PC HepDesk adds entries to the list.

If you want to see the format to use for the word lists you want to import, export the existing directories to text files by clicking Export and specifying a file name in the standard dialog box; then make your new entries match the existing file format.

Table 14-1
Dictionary Files

Dictionary File	*Description*
uignore.tlx	This file contains words to ignore when doing the spell-check. Add company names, trademarks, and proper names.
autocorr.tlx	This file contains words to automatically correct – common misspellings (such as "accompanyed" for "accompanied") that can be corrected without approval by PC HelpDesk.
condcorr.tlx	This file contains words to conditionally correct – words that are often mistyped, such as "teh" for "the."

Creating a new dictionary

PC HelpDesk lets you create and add new dictionaries. For example, if you are creating a number of PC HelpDesk knowledge bases, you may have specific technical dictionaries to use.

To create a new dictionary, do the following:

1. Click New on the Dictionaries screen shown in Figure 14-24. The New Dictionary screen appears (shown in Figure 14-25 with a sample dictionary name entered).

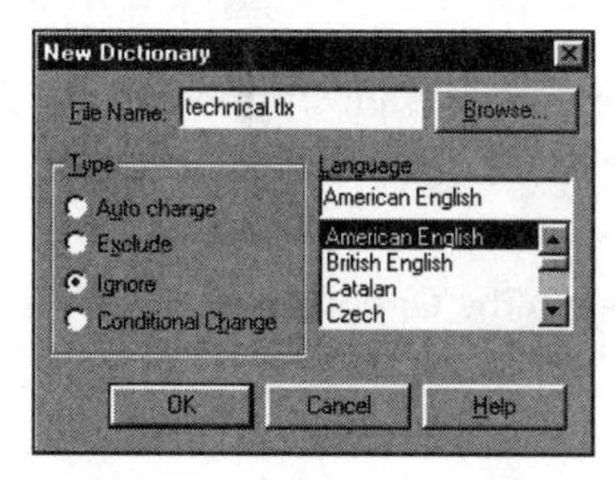

Figure 14-25: The New Dictionary screen

2. Enter information in the fields as follows:

   - **File Name:** Enter the name of the new dictionary. Click Browse to the right of the field to browse for a directory.

- **Type:** Select the type of dictionary to create. Select Auto change to create a dictionary of automatic correction items (like the autocorr.tlx dictionary). Select Exclude to create a dictionary of items to always query on, such as trademarks and technical abbreviations. Select Ignore to create a dictionary of words to ignore during spell-checking (like the uignore.tlx dictionary). Select Conditional Change to create a dictionary of words to flag for conditional correction (like the condcorr.tlx dictionary).
- **Language:** Select the language to use. (You'll have to create your own special language dictionaries to use this feature.)

3. When you are satisfied with your entries, click OK. PC HelpDesk displays the Dictionaries screen again with the new dictionary file loaded. There will be no entries in the word list.

   At this point, you can add words to the new dictionary as before.

To use an auxiliary dictionary, it must be added to the list of dictionaries (PC HelpDesk does this automatically when you first create the dictionary file, and then remembers to use it as part of the list of dictionaries thereafter.) However, you may not always want to use a specific dictionary; for example, a technical or exclude dictionary may unnecessarily flag a number of otherwise correct entries. You can remove a dictionary from the list by highlighting the dictionary and clicking Remove File. The dictionary will be removed from the list, and PC HelpDesk won't use the entries in that dictionary for spell-checking. You can re-add the file for spell-checking by clicking Add File and specifying the dictionary file to use.

Setting other spell-checking options

You can set a number of miscellaneous options for the spell checker, as follows:

1. Select the Edit ➪ Spelling Options command or click Options on the Dictionaries screen. The Options screen appears (as shown in Figure 14-26).

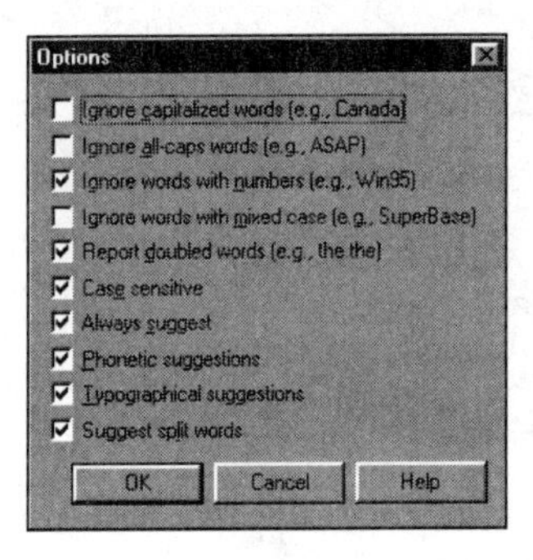

Figure 14-26: The Options screen

2. Check the boxes for the spell-checking options you prefer. (Figure 14-26 shows the default options checked.)
3. When you are satisfied with your entries, click OK.

Using PC HelpDesk Files

Once you have created a PC HelpDesk file, you can use it as a reference tool for information. You can navigate the topics in the file using the topic tree in the Project pane, or you can use the standard First, Previous, Next, and Last topic keys on the toolbar, shown in Figure 14-27.

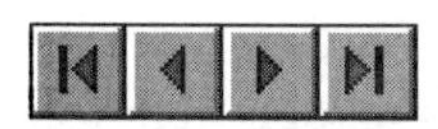

Figure 14-27: Standard toolbar navigation keys

In addition to basic navigation features, PC HelpDesk has index and full-text search features in the Project pane. These let you take advantage of existing keywords as well as text items within the topics.

Searching for topics using keywords

To search for topics using keyword entries, do the following:

1. Select the Index folder (denoted by a single key and a page on the folder tab) in the Project pane. The Index folder appears, as shown in Figure 14-28.

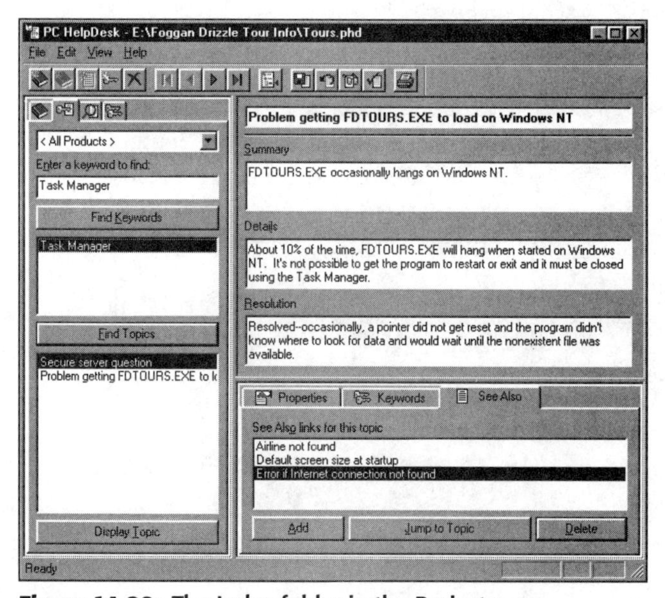

Figure 14-28: The Index folder in the Project pane

2. Select from the drop-down list at the top of the Index folder the product you want to search in. The default is to search through all products in the PC HelpDesk file, but you can select individual products if you prefer.

3. Enter the keyword to search for in the Enter a keyword to find field and click Find Keywords. PC HelpDesk displays all keywords that match the entry. In the example shown in Figure 14-28, the entry is Task Manager, but if you only entered "t" in the field, PC HelpDesk would find all the keywords starting with "t."
4. Select a keyword from the list of keywords and click Find Topic, or simply double-click a keyword. PC HelpDesk displays all the topics with that keyword.
5. Display one of the topics found in the keyword search by highlighting the topic and clicking Display Topic, or by double-clicking the topic in the list of found topics. The topic and properties information appears in the Topic and Properties panes.

Once you have displayed a topic, you can view the information. You can also edit the information by making any changes you want in the various fields. (Again, you don't need to click OK to log your changes in the PC HelpDesk file.)

Searching for topics using full-text search

You can also do a full-text search for information in the knowledge base as follows:

1. Select the Full Text Search folder (denoted by a magnifying glass on the folder tab) in the Project pane. The Full Text Search folder appears, as shown in Figure 14-29.

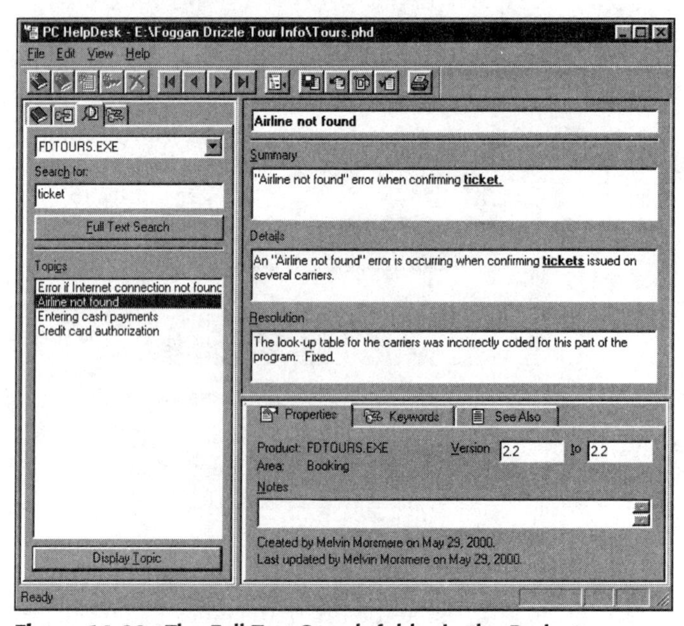

Figure 14-29: The Full Text Search folder in the Project pane

2. Select from the drop-down list at the top of the Full Text Search folder the product you want to search in. The default is to search through all products in the PC HelpDesk file, but you can select individual products if you prefer.
3. Enter the text to search for in the Search for field and click Full Text Search. PC HelpDesk displays all the topics that contain the specified text.
4. Display one of the topics by highlighting the topic and clicking Display Topic, or by double-clicking the topic in the list of found topics. The topic and properties information appears in the Topic and Properties panes. The text string that was found appears in underlined bold type. (An example of this is shown in Figure 14-29.)

As with the keyword search described earlier, you can view the information once you have displayed a topic. You can also edit the information by making any changes you want in the various fields. (Again, you don't need to click OK to log your changes in the PC HelpDesk file.)

Printing Topics

Once you've located the individual topic you're interested in, you can print it or save it to a file.

It's a good idea to preview a topic before printing it, as follows:

1. Select the File ➪ Preview Current Topic command, or click the Preview Current Topic button (shown in Figure 14-30) on the toolbar. The topic is displayed as it will be printed. Figure 14-31 shows a sample topic being previewed.

Figure 14-30: The Preview Current Topic button

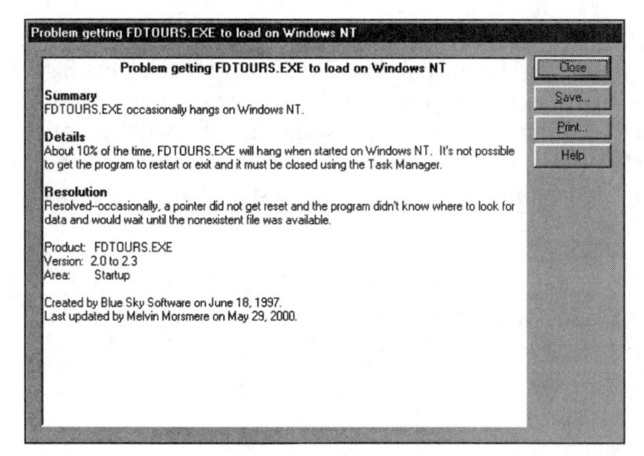

Figure 14-31: Sample topic being previewed

2. To print the topic directly from the Preview screen, click Print. You can also print the topic directly (without previewing) by selecting the File ➪ Print command or by clicking the standard Print icon on the toolbar.

You can also save the topic to an RTF or text file, as follows:

1. Select the File ➪ Export Current Topic command or click Save on the right of the Preview screen. A standard file save dialog box appears.
2. Enter the name of the file you're saving. Select the file type (RTF or text) in the Save as type field.
3. When you are satisfied with your changes, click OK.

Tips on PC HelpDesk

The advantage to using PC HelpDesk is that it lets you create knowledge bases that look like WinHelp files. It's a very good tool for tracking changes for a project within your work group. The basic tools and techniques for adding and modifying topic information and keywords in WinHelp can also be applied to creating PC HelpDesk knowledge bases. Moreover, the PC HelpDesk file is stored in Microsoft Access database format. This means that you can open and use a file created with PC HelpDesk using Microsoft Access or another compatible program to further edit or manage.

However, PC HelpDesk has some substantial disadvantages as well. For one thing, the product is not being updated at this time. No new enhancements or maintenance releases are being planned. This means that any application developed with it will very likely have a short life span. Another disadvantage is that Power SQL, used to connect over the Internet with other applications, is shipped with RoboHELP Office 2000—but only to provide support for legacy systems. It is not documented and may well not be compatible with many newer systems and products. Furthermore, setting ODBC drivers and compatibles can be difficult and are frequently rather fussy to set up and debug.

PC HelpDesk's biggest disadvantage is simply that it has been superseded by other, even better, products. When PC HelpDesk was first introduced, Blue Sky WebHelp had not yet been developed, and eHelp was still some years away. Now, however, you can use WebHelp to provide effective cross-platform knowledge base help on a Web site. In addition, the new eHelp features allow you to provide direct links from existing WinHelp files to an online community of product users, resources, and a product knowledge base.

As a result of these new developments, consider using PC HelpDesk exclusively for creating knowledge bases for standalone use without connecting to the Internet, and using WebHelp and eHelp for Web-based or Internet-ready help.

If you are interested in extending the power of your knowledge base through the Internet, you are strongly encouraged to use eHelp (described in Chapter 12, "Linking to the Internet and Adding Multimedia"). To learn more about creating WebHelp, see Chapter 28, "Examining WebHelp, JavaHelp, and Other Help Systems."

Converting WinHelp to Other Help Formats

One of the really great advantages of using RoboHELP to create and maintain online help is that RoboHELP supports *single-sourcing*—you can do all of your help development in one format and then export it to other online help formats.

You can convert any project in RoboHELP to any other format. The conversion options are:

- ✦ WinHelp 3
- ✦ WinHelp 4
- ✦ Microsoft HTML Help
- ✦ WebHelp 3
- ✦ JavaHelp
- ✦ Windows CE Help
- ✦ Netscape NetHelp 1
- ✦ Netscape NetHelp 2
- ✦ Printed Documentation (Word DOC files for printing)

Almost no conversion will go perfectly. You should always plan on compiling, reviewing, and testing converted projects before releasing them for distribution.

Converting from WinHelp 4 to WinHelp 3

To convert a WinHelp project to WinHelp 3, do the following:

1. Open the project in RoboHELP.
2. From the RoboHELP Explorer, select the File ➪ Generate ➪ WinHelp 3 (Win 3.1) command. RoboHELP will display a message warning you that the file conversion may take a few moments.
3. Click OK to start the conversion.

If you are converting from WinHelp 4 to WinHelp 3, you may have problems with long file names that need to be removed from the source files. You'll also lose a number of features that you're used to using in WinHelp 4, such as Internet access and a number of macros. (You'll see later in this chapter how to retrofit WinHelp 3 files for many of these features.)

Converting from WinHelp 4 to HTML Help

This is possibly the most common conversion from WinHelp 4 you'll be making. By creating WinHelp files and then converting them to HTML Help, you can take advantage of many of Word's text editing capabilities when creating and editing the topics in a project and then convert the project to HTML Help for final editing and polishing.

If you are not already familiar with how to create and use HTML Help, see the chapters in Parts IV and V of this book. Note also that HTML Help requires that you have Internet Explorer v4.x or higher on your computer. (If you need cross-platform HTML-based help that does not require a specific browser, consider using RoboHELP's WebHelp, described in Chapter 28.)

To convert a WinHelp project to HTML Help, do the following:

1. Open the project in RoboHELP.
2. From the RoboHELP Explorer, select the File ➪ Generate ➪ Microsoft HTML Help (Win 98) command. The Generate Microsoft HTML Help screen (shown in Figure 14-32) appears.

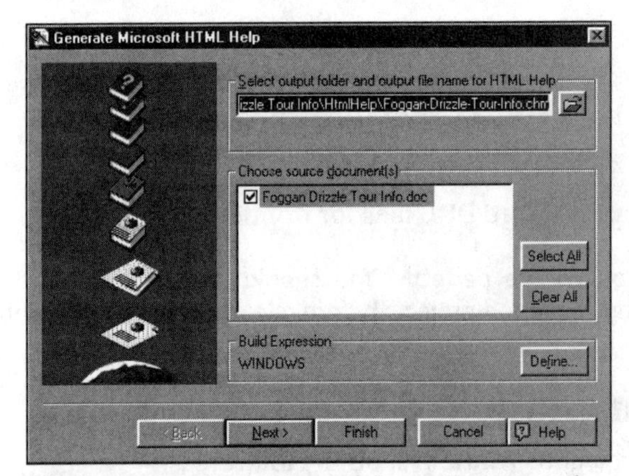

Figure 14-32: The Generate Microsoft HTML Help screen

3. Enter information in the fields as follows:
   - **Select output folder and output file name for HTML Help:** Enter the path and name for the CHM file for the new HTML Help project. Click the button to the right of the field to browse for a file.

- **Choose source document(s):** Check the source documents you want to use. Use the Select All and Clear All buttons to the right of this field for quick selection.
- **Build Expression:** The default build tag appears in this field. Click Add to display the Define Build Tag Expression screen (shown in Figure 14-33). You can select which items to use in the new HTML Help project by selecting the various build tags.

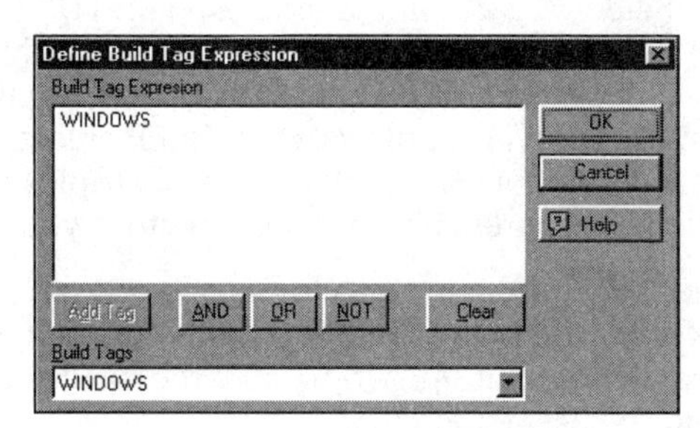

Figure 14-33: The Define Build Tag Expression screen

For more information on build tags, see Chapter 15, "Managing Large Projects."

4. When you are satisfied with your entries, click Next. The Microsoft HTML Help - Folders screen appears, as shown in Figure 14-34.

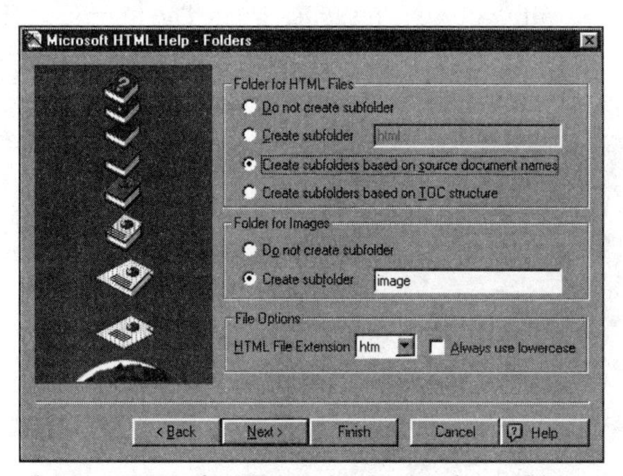

Figure 14-34: The Microsoft HTML Help - Folders screen

5. Enter information in the fields as follows:

   - **Folder for HTML Files:** Select one of the options for the HTML files as follows. Select Do not create subfolder to simply save the HTML topic files in the root directory you specified in the first Generate Microsoft HTML Help screen. Select Create subfolder to save the HTML topic files in the subfolder you specify in the associated field. Select Create subfolders based on source document names (the default option) to create and save HTML topic files grouped into subfolders, which are created based on the names of the DOC files. Select Create subfolders based on TOC structure to create and save HTML topic files grouped into subfolders, which are based on the book titles in the table of contents in the WinHelp file. If the table of contents has multiple levels of books, RoboHELP creates corresponding multiple levels of folders. RoboHELP saves any topics that are not referenced in the table of contents in the root directory you specified.
   - **Folder for Images:** Select one of the options for saving images. Select Do not create subfolder to save the images in the specified root directory. Select Create subfolder (the default option) to save the images in the subfolder you specify in the associated field.
   - **HTML File Extension:** Select from the drop-down list the HTML file extension to use. The default option is htm, but you can select html if you prefer.
   - **Always use lowercase:** Check this box to save all file names using lowercase letters. This is particularly helpful if you are using the HTML Help files on a case-sensitive platform (such as Unix).

6. When you are satisfied with your entries, click Next. The Microsoft HTML Help - Formatting screen appears, as shown in Figure 14-35.

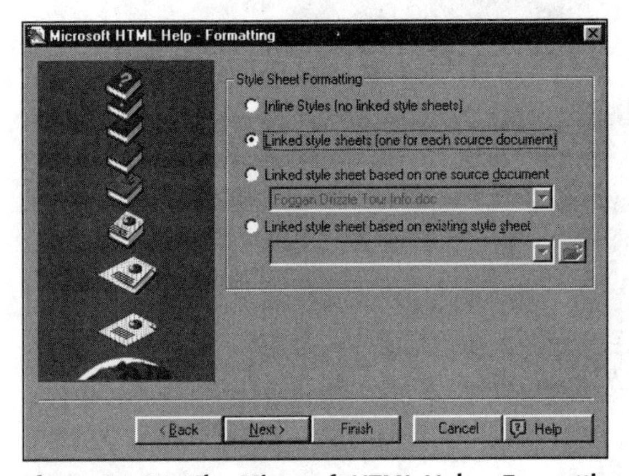

Figure 14-35: The Microsoft HTML Help - Formatting screen

7. Select one of the style sheet formatting options as follows:

   - **Inline Styles (no linked style sheets):** Select this option to convert all document formatting into HTML inline styles, somewhat similar to using manual formatting in Word.
   - **Linked style sheets (one for each source document):** Select this option (the default) to create a style sheet file (CSS) for each DOC file included in the HTML Help project as a source document. If you have multiple DOC files that have unique styles, RoboHELP creates separate CSS files for each DOC file with unique styles.
   - **Linked style sheets based on one source document:** Select this option to create a single CSS file based on the DOC file you specify in the associated field. Formatting for all HTML topics is based on the styles that appear in this style sheet.
   - **Linked style sheets based on existing style sheet:** Select this option to use an existing CSS file for the styles in this project. If you don't have corresponding styles in the style sheets for some of the topics in the project, RoboHELP will apply manual formatting as necessary.

This option is very powerful for creating uniform help files, but it will probably require a certain amount of experimentation and fine-tuning of your help styles.

8. When you are satisfied with your entries, click Next. The Microsoft HTML Help - Features screen appears, as shown in Figure 14-36.

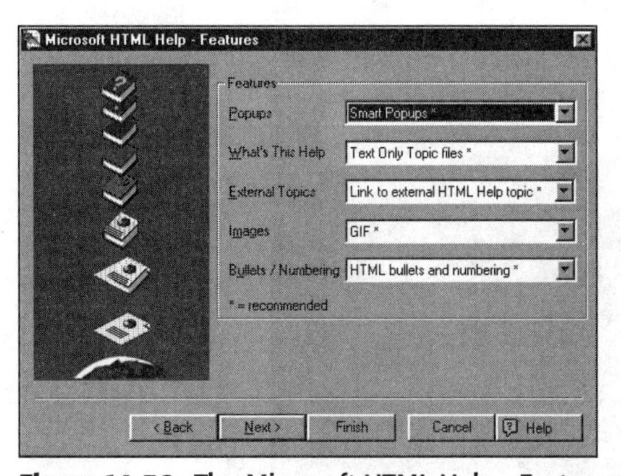

Figure 14-36: The Microsoft HTML Help - Features screen

9. Enter information in the fields as follows:

   - **Popups:** Select Smart Popups or Regular Hyperlinks from the drop-down list. Smart Popups creates links that display destination topics in popup windows that automatically size based on their content. Regular Hyperlinks displays destination topics in the same window as the topic containing the link.

- **What's This? Help:** Select Text Only Topic files, Individual HTML files, or Remove Topics. Text Only Topic files creates and saves What's This? help topics in TXT files. Selecting Individual HTML files creates and saves topics as regular HTML topic files so they can be used as context-sensitive help. Remove Topics removes the What's This? topics from the project you're converting.
- **External Topics:** Select Link to External HTML Help Topic, Retain, or Remove. Link to External HTML Help Topic converts any external WinHelp links to links to HTML files in external CHM files. (This option is very useful if you are creating a single HTML Help project from multiple WinHelp projects.) Retain keeps any external WinHelp topic links in the finished HTML Help project. You can use this to subsequently link HTML topics to WinHelp topics using the WinHelp Topic control. Remove eliminates any links to external WinHelp topics.
- **Images:** Select GIF or JPG as the preferred format to use for converting the bitmap graphics in the WinHelp file.
- **Bullets/Numbering:** Select HTML Bullets and Numbering to convert bulleted and numbered lists into HTML auto-bulleted and auto-numbered lists. Select Formatted Text to convert bulleted and numbered lists into text paragraphs with a symbol character for a bullet and hard-coded text numbers.

10. When you are satisfied with your entries, click Next. The Microsoft HTML Help - Options screen appears, as shown in Figure 14-37.

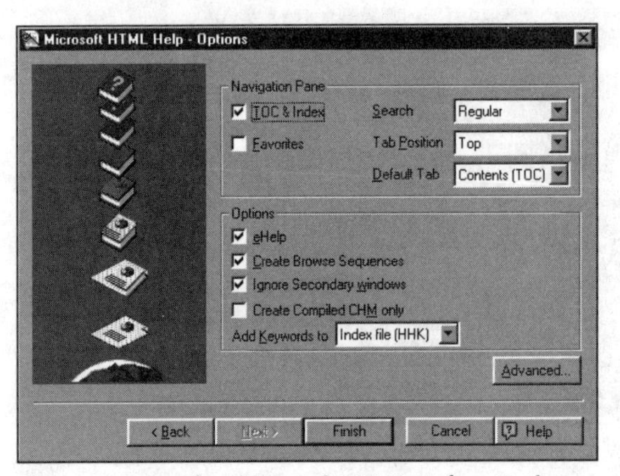

Figure 14-37: The Microsoft HTML Help - Options screen

11. Enter information in the fields as follows:
    - **TOC & Index:** Check this box to include TOC and Index information from the WinHelp project.

- **Favorites:** Check this box to include a Favorites tab, which lets the user bookmark topics by adding them to the Favorites tab.
- **Search:** Select No Search, Regular, or Advanced from the drop-down list. Select No Search to exclude the Search tab. Select Regular for simple searches based on topic titles. Select Advanced for more advanced searches based on topic properties.
- **Tab Position:** Select Top, Left, or Bottom from the drop-down list to specify where the TOC, Index, and Search tabs will appear in the HTML Help viewer or browser.
- **Default Tab:** Select the default tab from the drop-down list.
- **eHelp:** Check this box (the default) to enable the eHelp button on the main button bar in the HTML Help project.
- **Create Browse Sequences:** Check this box (the default) to use the browse sequences in the WinHelp file.
- **Ignore Secondary windows:** Check this box (the default) to ignore secondary windows (which are not supported in HTML Help). If this box is not checked, RoboHELP converts secondary windows in the WinHelp project to popup windows in the HTML Help project.
- **Select Create Compiled CHM:** Check this box if you just want to create a compiled HTML Help file and don't want to generate the associated HTML Help source files.
- **Add Keywords to:** Select the destination for the keywords from the drop-down list: the HHK index file or embedded in each topic file. The HHK file will be created in the same directory as the HTML files. If you add the keywords to the individual topics, you can also use the HTML files in other projects without having to re-index them.

12. If you want to customize display and button options, click Advanced. The Microsoft HTML Help Advanced Settings screen appears with the Tri-Pane tab displayed, as shown in Figure 14-38.

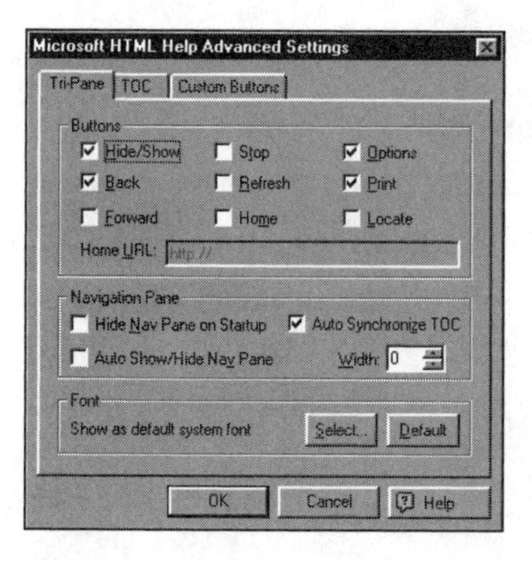

Figure 14-38: The Tri-pane tab in the Microsoft HTML Help Advanced Settings screen.

13. Enter information in the fields as follows:

   - **Buttons:** Check the boxes for the buttons you want to display. If you check Home, you must also enter the URL to associate with the Home button.
   - **Hide Nav Page on Startup:** Check this box to hide the left tab components of the HTML Help viewer.
   - **Auto Show/Hide Nav Pane:** Check this box to automatically hide the navigation pane when the users switch the focus from the HTML Help file to something else.
   - **Auto Synchronize TOC:** Check this box to automatically synchronize the left and right panes of the HTML Help viewer as you navigate the HTML Help file.
   - **Width:** Enter the width of the navigation pane in pixels.
   - **Font:** Click Select to specify the font for HTML Help to use on the TOC and Index tabs. Click Default to change the default font used in HTML Help back to the system default.

14. When you are satisfied with your entries, click the TOC tab to display the TOC options, as shown in Figure 14-39.

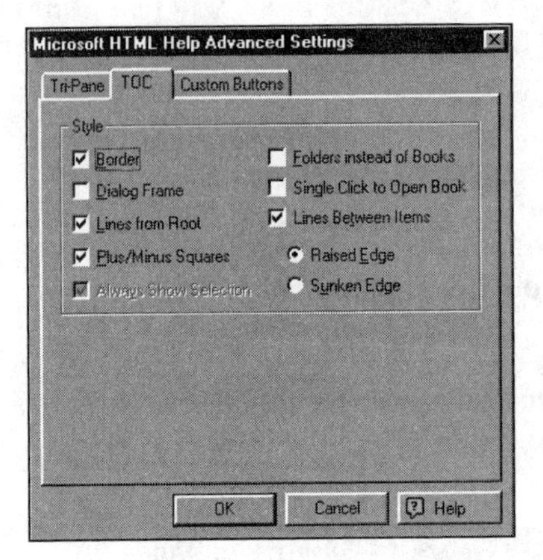

Figure 14-39: The TOC tab in the Microsoft HTML Help Advanced Settings screen

15. Enter information in the fields as follows:

   - **Border:** Check this box (the default) to add a border around the TOC pane.
   - **Dialog Frame:** Check this box to add a frame around the TOC pane.
   - **Lines from Root:** Check this box (the default) to display lines that connect books and pages, starting at the root.

- **Plus/Minus Squares:** Check this box (the default) to display the standard "tree-view" plus and minus squares for opening and closing books. (You must also have checked Lines from Root in order to use this option.)
- **Always Show Selection:** Check this box to show the selected page even if the TOC pane is not the currently selected item. You must also uncheck Auto Synchronize TOC in the Tri-Pane tab (shown in Figure 14-38) in order to use this option.
- **Folders instead of Books:** Check this box to display folder icons in the TOC pane instead of book icons. (This will result in a slightly different appears for the TOC pane from the usual TOC.)
- **Single Click to Open Book:** Check this box to open books with a single click, rather than a double-click.
- **Lines Between Items:** Check this box (the default) to add lines between books and pages.
- **Raised Edge:** Select this option (the default) to add a "raised" 3-D formatting.
- **Sunken Edge:** Select this option (the default) to add a "sunken" 3-D formatting.

16. When you are done, click the Custom Buttons tab to display the Custom Buttons options, shown in Figure 14-40 with a sample custom button selected.

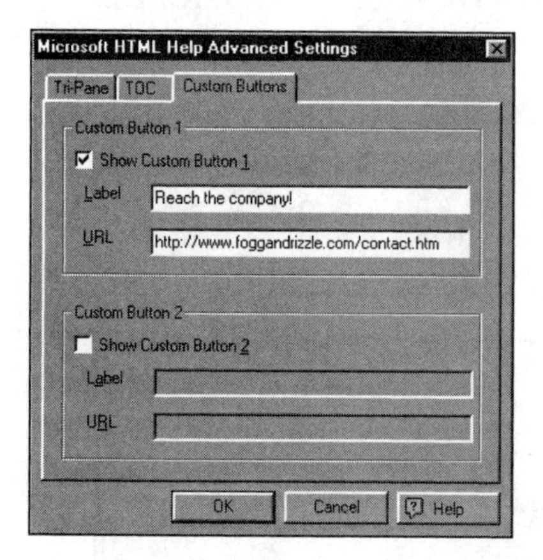

Figure 14-40: The Custom Buttons tab in the Microsoft HTML Help Advanced Settings screen

17. Check Show Custom Button 1 to add a custom button that links to a URL. Add a button label and the URL. (Entries for a sample button appear in Figure 14-40.) Repeat this with Show Custom Button 2 if you want a second custom button. The two custom buttons have predefined icons, shown in Figures 14-41 and 14-42. You choose which button to use: button 1, button 2, or both custom buttons.

Figure 14-41: Custom button 1

Figure 14-42: Custom button 2

18. When you are done, click OK, and then click Finish on the Microsoft HTML Help - Options screen). RoboHELP starts generating the HTML Help project files using the various options you've selected. When the project is completed, RoboHELP displays the Microsoft HTML Help Wizard Result screen shown in Figure 14-43.

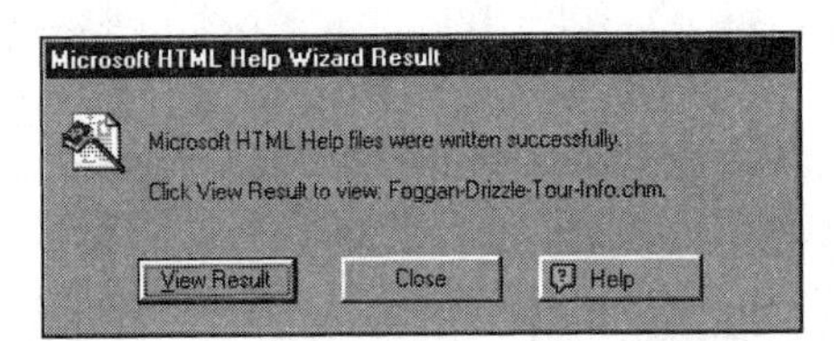

Figure 14-43: The Microsoft HTML Help Wizard Result screen

19. Click Close to simply exit and return to the RoboHELP Explorer. Click View Result to see the HTML Help file as it has been converted. Figure 14-44 shows the Foggan Drizzle WinHelp project converted into HTML Help.

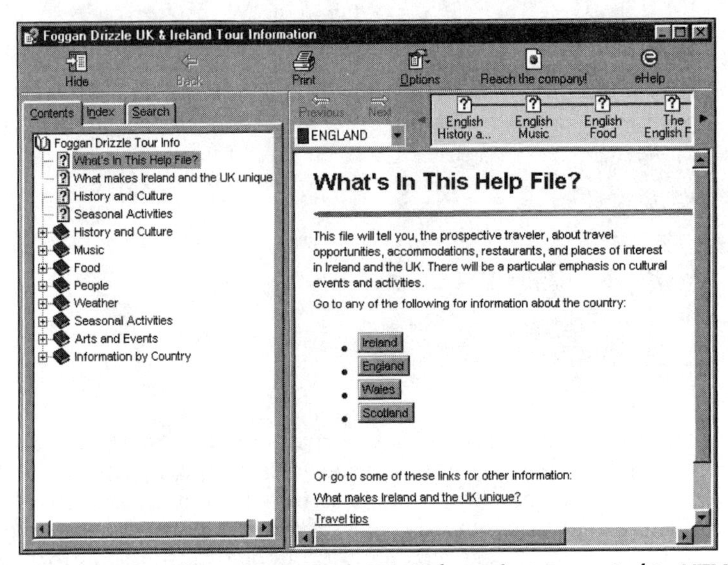

Figure 14-44: The Foggan Drizzle WinHelp project converted to HTML Help

Converting from WinHelp 4 to WebHelp 3

The conversion process from WinHelp 4 to WebHelp 3 is very similar to the process for converting from WinHelp 4 to HTML Help.

If you are not already familiar with WebHelp concepts, see Chapter 28, "Examining WebHelp, JavaHelp, and Other Help Systems."

To convert a WinHelp project to WebHelp, do the following:

1. Open the project in RoboHELP.
2. From the RoboHELP Explorer, select the File ➪ Generate ➪ WebHelp 3 (Cross-Platform Help) command. The Generate WebHelp screen appears.

The screens for generating WebHelp are almost identical to those for creating HTML Help. The significant differences are that you can also specify file and folder names using 8.3 file-naming conventions, specify a minimum font size but not select a font, specify Dynamic HTML or Java applet as the preferred format, and prefix HTML files with the topic name. There are no advanced option screens like those shown in Figures 14-38, 14-39, and 14-40.

3. Step through the various WebHelp conversion screens as you did with the HTML Help conversion screens shown earlier in this chapter. When you have set all the options and are ready to convert the project, click Finish. RoboHELP converts the project as it did for the HTML Help conversion. Figure 14-45 shows the Foggan Drizzle file converted to WebHelp and displayed in Netscape Navigator.

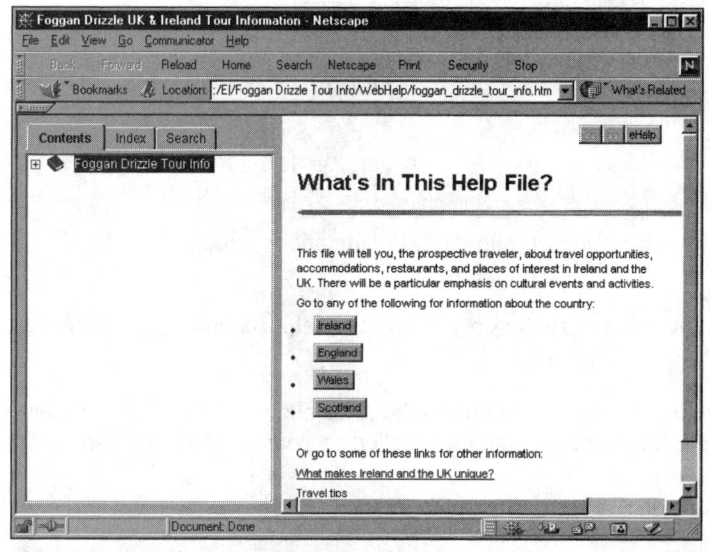

Figure 14-45: The Foggan Drizzle WinHelp project converted to WebHelp

Converting from WinHelp 4 to JavaHelp

The conversion process from WinHelp 4 to JavaHelp is very similar to the processes for converting from WinHelp 4 to HTML Help and to WebHelp.

If you are not already familiar with JavaHelp concepts, see Chapter 28, "Examining WebHelp, JavaHelp, and Other Help Systems."

To convert a WinHelp project to JavaHelp, do the following:

1. Open the project in RoboHELP.
2. From the RoboHELP Explorer, select the File ➪ Generate ➪ JavaHelp command. The Generate JavaHelp screen appears.

The screens for generating JavaHelp are almost identical to those for creating HTML Help and WebHelp. The significant difference is that you can specify the conversion output as compressed JavaHelp with or without source files or as uncompressed JavaHelp with source files.

3. Step through the various JavaHelp conversion screens as you did with the HTML Help conversion screens shown earlier in this chapter. When you have set all the options and are ready to convert the project, click Finish. RoboHELP converts the project as it did for the HTML Help conversion. If your project contains any features not supported in JavaHelp, RoboHELP displays a list of the limitations of JavaHelp, as shown in Figure 14-46.

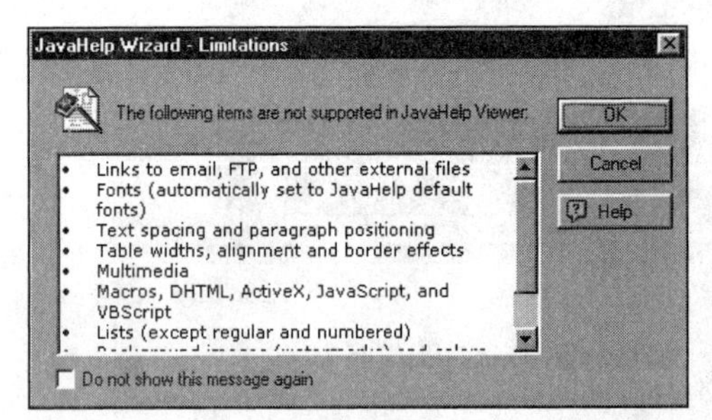

Figure 14-46: The JavaHelp Wizard - Limitations screen

4. Click OK to convert the project to JavaHelp. As before, you can display the resulting JavaHelp file.

Although you can convert projects to JavaHelp with RoboHELP by itself, you must have the Java Development Kit installed on your computer to display it.

Converting from WinHelp 4 to Windows CE Help

Windows CE (also known as "Win CE") help is used on handheld and palmtop devices.

To convert a WinHelp project to Windows CE help, do the following:

1. Open the project in RoboHELP.
2. From the RoboHELP Explorer, select the File ➪ Generate ➪ Windows CE Help command. The Creating Windows CE Help screen appears (shown in Figure 14-47).

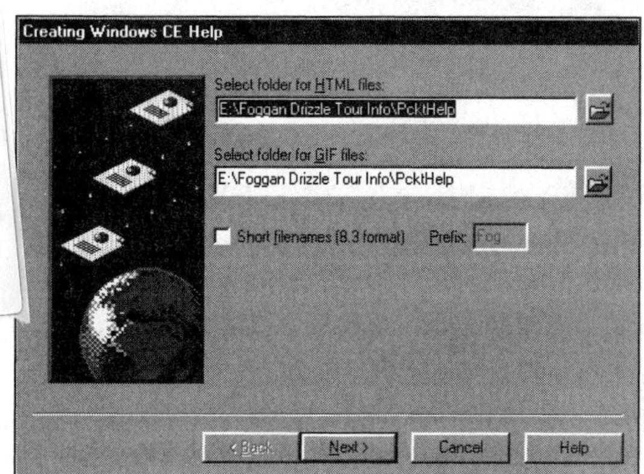

Figure 14-47: The Creating Windows CE Help screen

3. Enter information in the fields as follows:
   - **Select the folder for HTML files:** Enter the drive and directory for the HTML files or click the Browse button to the right of this field.
   - **Select the folder for GIF files:** Enter the drive and directory for the GIF files or click the Browse button to the right of this field.
   - **Short filenames (8.3 format):** Check this box to use standard DOS 8.3 file names instead of the extended filenames.
   - **Prefix:** Enter a three-character prefix to use for Windows CE help files using the short file names.
4. When you are done, click Next. The HTML Conversion Options screen appears, as shown in Figure 14-48.

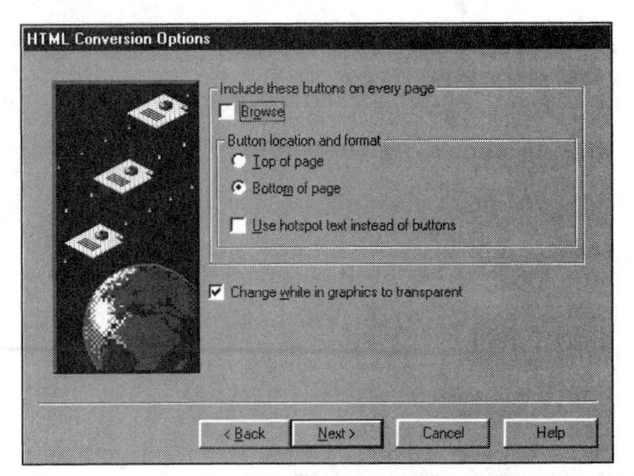

Figure 14-48: The HTML Conversion Options screen

5. Enter information in the fields as follows:
   - **Browse:** Check this box to include a Browse button on every page.
   - **Button location and format:** Select Top of Page or Bottom of Page for the location of the buttons.
   - **Use hotspot text instead of buttons:** Check this box to use text, rather than graphic Browse buttons. (Text buttons display a little faster.)
   - **Change white in graphics to transparent:** Check this box to change the white in any graphics to transparent, allowing the background color to show through.
6. When you are done, click Next. The Windows CE Help Options screen appears, as shown in Figure 14-49.

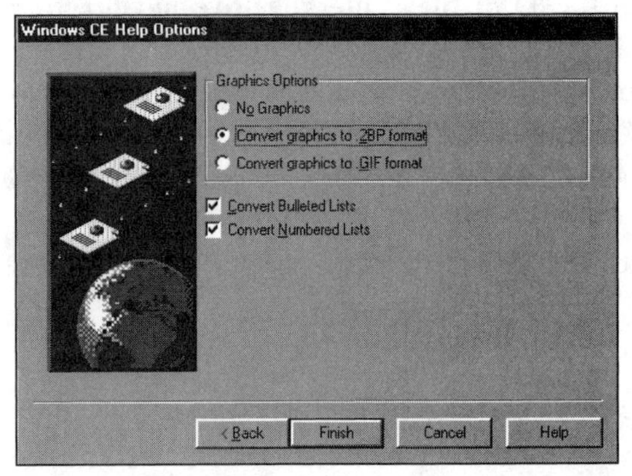

Figure 14-49: The Windows CE Help Options screen

7. Enter information in the fields as follows:

   - **Graphics Options:** Select one of the three options for graphics. Select No Graphics to comment out the graphics references in the Windows CE help file so the graphics don't appear in the Windows CE help. (This option also converts the graphics from the WinHelp file into BMP files.) Select Convert Graphics to .2BP Format (the default option) to convert the graphics into 2BP (black and white) format. This option converts the graphics from the WinHelp file into BMP files (which automatically turn into .2BP files when they're copied to the handheld or palmtop device). RoboHELP changes all the references in the Windows CE help files to .2BP references. Select Convert Graphics to .GIF format to convert the graphics to GIF. Because GIF files are usually too large to display, all the graphics files are converted and appear in the Windows CE help directory, but they don't appear in the Windows CE help file.
   - **Convert Bulleted Lists:** Check this box (the default) to convert standard bulleted lists. Clearing this box will cause your bulleted lists to display as text with no indentation.
   - **Convert Numbered Lists:** Check this box (the default) to convert standard numbered lists. Clearing this box will cause your numbered lists to display as text with no indentation.

8. When you are done, click Finish. RoboHELP starts converting the project into Windows CE help. When the process is complete, it displays the Results screen, shown in Figure 14-50.

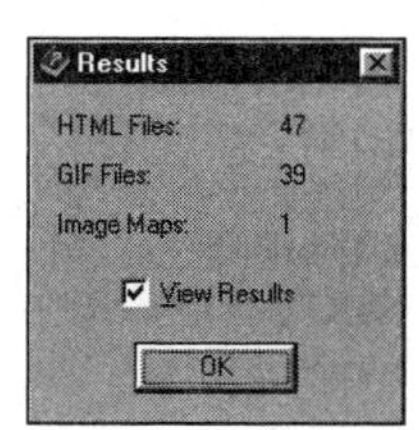

Figure 14-50: The Results screen

9. Click OK to close the screen. You can also check View Results before clicking OK to view the Windows CE help.

The computer you convert the files on will probably not be able to display Windows CE help.

It's a good idea to keep Windows CE help files as small and compact as you can. You should also test regularly to make sure that you don't encounter any limitations of the handheld or palmtop unit you're creating the Windows CE help for.

Converting from WinHelp 4 to Netscape NetHelp

Netscape NetHelp is another type of Web-based help aimed at Netscape Navigator. NetHelp uses HTML files, but (unlike HTML Help) you don't compile NetHelp. Netscape NetHelp 1 is for Netscape Navigator 3 or later; Netscape NetHelp 2 is for Netscape Navigator 4 or later.

Creating Netscape NetHelp 1

Converting from WinHelp 4 to Netscape NetHelp 1 is similar to the process for converting from WinHelp 4 to Windows CE help.

To convert a WinHelp project to Netscape NetHelp 1, do the following:

1. Open the project in RoboHELP.
2. From the RoboHELP Explorer, select the File ➪ Generate ➪ Netscape NetHelp 1 command. The Creating Nethelp 1.0 screen appears, as shown in Figure 14-51.

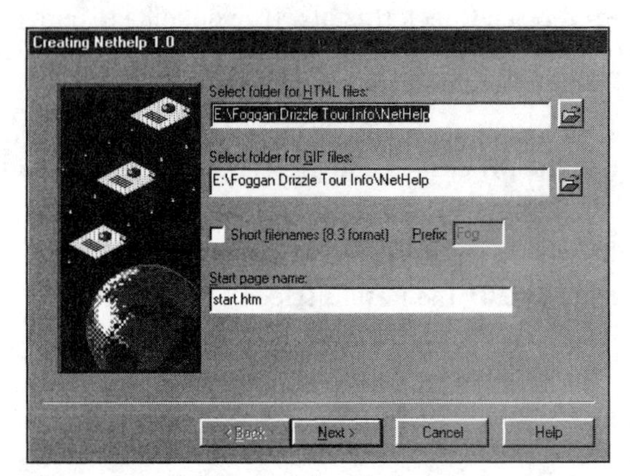

Figure 14-51: The Creating Nethelp 1.0 screen

3. Enter information in the fields as follows:
   - **Select the folder for HTML files:** Enter the drive and directory for the HTML files or click the Browse button to the right of this field.
   - **Select the folder for GIF files:** Enter the drive and directory for the GIF files or click the Browse button to the right of this field.
   - **Short filenames (8.3 format):** Check this box to use standard DOS 8.3 file names.

- **Prefix:** Enter a three-character prefix to use for Windows CE help files using the short file names.
- **Start page name:** Enter the URL for the start page. The default for Netscape NetHelp 1 is START.HTM. If you leave this field blank, Netscape looks for the first topic in the project's CNT file, or the default Contents topic, or the first compiled topic in the Netscape NetHelp1 file.

4. When you are satisfied with your entries, click Next. The Style Options screen appears, as shown in Figure 14-52.

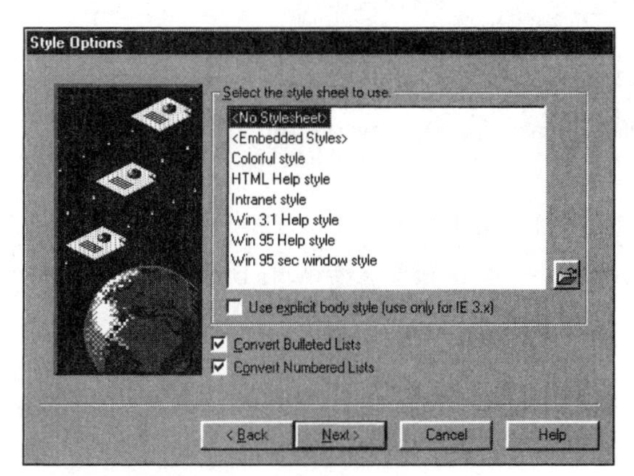

Figure 14-52: The Style Options screen

5. Enter information in the fields as follows:

- **Select the style sheet to use:** Select the style sheet you want to use. You can browse by clicking the icon to the right of the field.
- **Use explicit body style (use only for IE 3.x):** Check this box if you are using the resulting help files on Internet Explorer 3.*x*. It's a good idea to select the Win 95 sec window style sheet with this option.
- **Convert Bulleted Lists:** Check this box (the default) to convert standard bulleted lists. Clearing this box will cause your bulleted lists to display as text with no indentation.
- **Convert Numbered Lists:** Check this box (the default) to convert standard numbered lists. Clearing this box will cause your numbered lists to display as text with no indentation.

6. When you are done, click Next. The HTML Conversion Options screen appears, as shown in Figure 14-53.

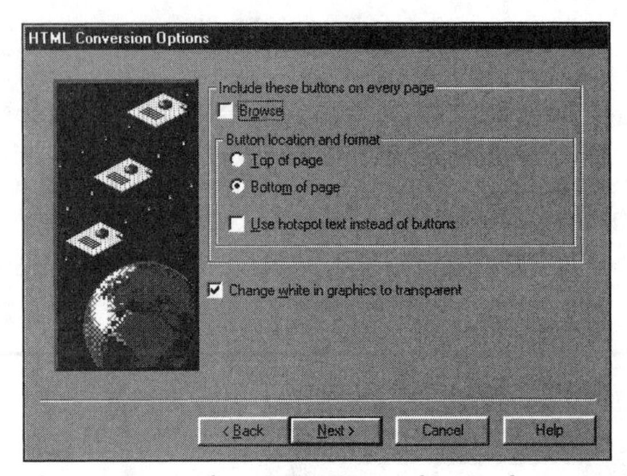

Figure 14-53: The HTML Conversion Options screen

7. Enter information in the fields as follows:
   - **Browse:** Check this box to include a Browse button on every page.
   - **Button location and format:** Select Top of Page or Bottom of Page for the location of the buttons.
   - **Use hotspot text instead of buttons:** Check this box to use text, rather than graphical Browse buttons. (Text buttons display faster.)
   - **Change white in graphics to transparent:** Check this box to change the white in any graphics to transparent, allowing the background color to show through.
8. When you are satisfied with your entries, click Next. The Netscape NetHelp Options screen appears, as shown in Figure 14-54.

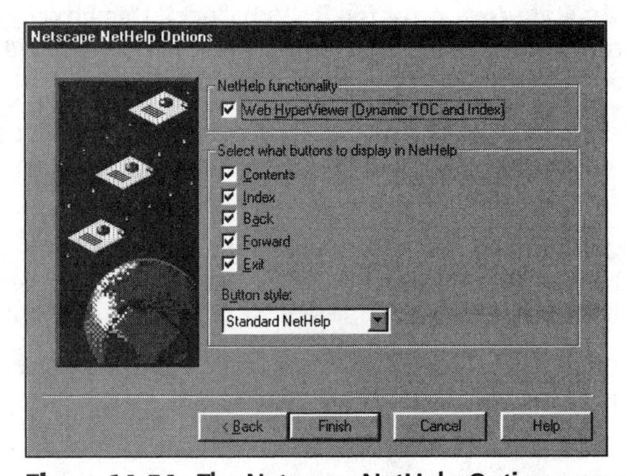

Figure 14-54: The Netscape NetHelp Options screen

9. Enter information in the fields as follows:

   • **NetHelp functionality:** Check this box to display a table of contents and index on the left side of the screen.

You must have the Netscape plug-in (npwsc32.dll) installed with RoboHELP to use the NetHelp functionality features.

   • **Select what buttons to display in NetHelp:** Check the boxes for the buttons you want to appear in the navigation bar at the top of the Netscape NetHelp window. Select the button style for the buttons from the drop-down list.

10. When you are satisfied with your entries, click Finish. RoboHELP starts converting the project into Netscape NetHelp 1 help. When the process is complete, it displays the Results screen (shown earlier in Figure 14-50).

11. Click OK to close the screen. You can also check View Results before clicking OK to view the Netscape NetHelp 1 project. Figure 14-55 shows the Foggan Drizzle file converted to Netscape NetHelp 1.

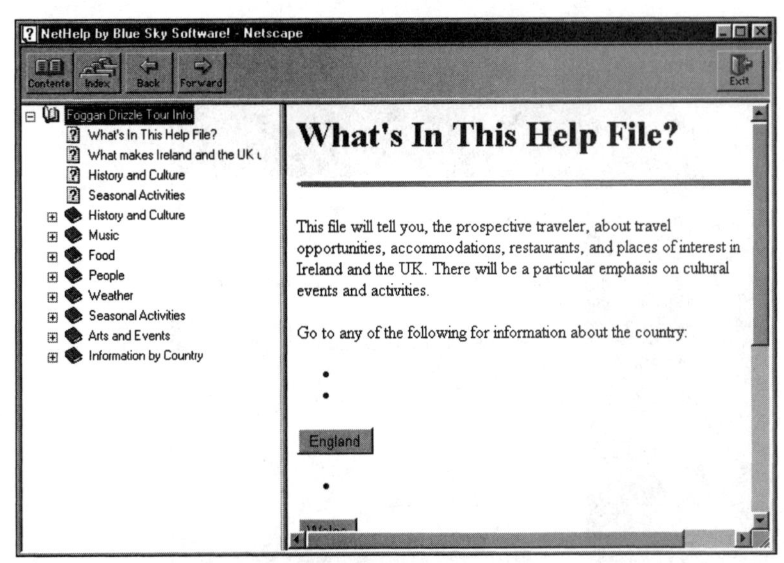

Figure 14-55: The Foggan Drizzle WinHelp project converted to Netscape NetHelp 1

Creating Netscape NetHelp 2

Converting from WinHelp 4 to Netscape NetHelp 2 is similar to the process for converting from WinHelp 4 to Netscape NetHelp 1, but you have fewer screens to fill out as part of the conversion process.

To convert a WinHelp project to Netscape NetHelp 2, do the following:

1. Open the project in RoboHELP.
2. From the RoboHELP Explorer, select the File ➪ Generate ➪ Netscape NetHelp 2 command. The Creating NetHelp 2 screen appears. (This screen is identical to the Style Options screen shown in Figure 14-52.)
3. Enter information in the screen fields as described earlier. When you are satisfied with your entries, click Next. The HTML Conversion Options screen appears, as shown in Figure 14-53.
4. Enter information in the HTML Conversion Options fields as described earlier. When you are satisfied with your entries, click Finish. RoboHELP starts converting the project into Netscape NetHelp 2 help. When the process is complete, it displays the Results screen (shown in Figure 14-50).
5. Click OK to close the screen. You can also check View Results before clicking OK to view the Netscape NetHelp 2 project. Figure 14-56 shows the Foggan Drizzle file converted to Netscape NetHelp 2. As you can see, Netscape NetHelp 2 has a much more distinctive style than that of the preceding version of NetHelp.

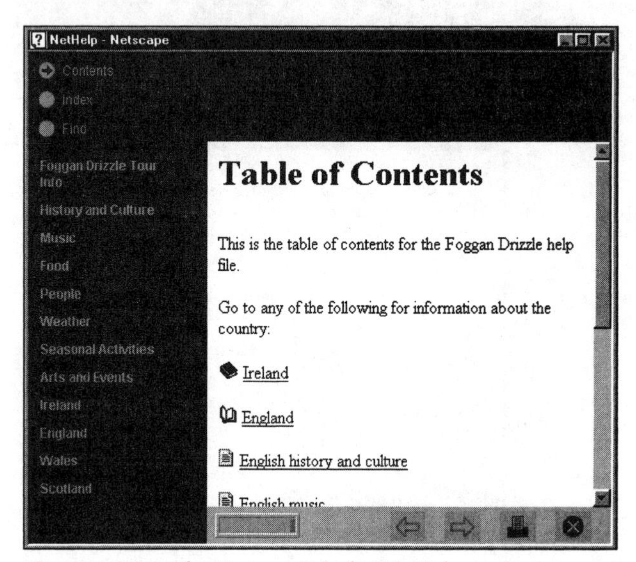

Figure 14-56: The Foggan Drizzle WinHelp project converted to Netscape NetHelp 2

Converting from WinHelp 4 to Printed Documentation

The final conversion option is converting to printed documentation. RoboHELP takes the project files, removes all online help jumps, popups, and embedded information, and saves the source files as Word DOC files.

To convert a WinHelp project to DOC files, do the following:

1. Open the project in RoboHELP.
2. From the RoboHELP Explorer, select the File ➪ Generate ➪ Printed Documentation command. The first Documentation Wizard screen appears, as shown in Figure 14-57.

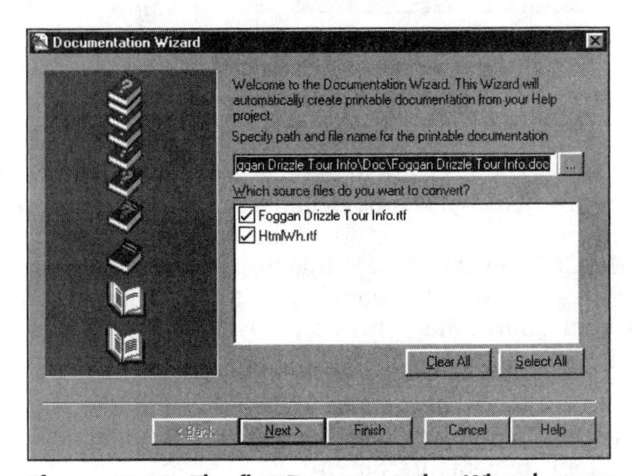

Figure 14-57: The first Documentation Wizard screen

3. Enter information in the fields as follows:
   - **Specify path and file name for the printable documentation:** Enter the path and name for the DOC file or click the Browse button to the right of the field.
   - **Which source files do you want to convert?:** Check the source documents you want to use. Use the Select All and Clear All buttons to the right of this field for quick selection.
4. When you are satisfied with your entries, click Next. The second Documentation Wizard screen appears (shown in Figure 14-58).

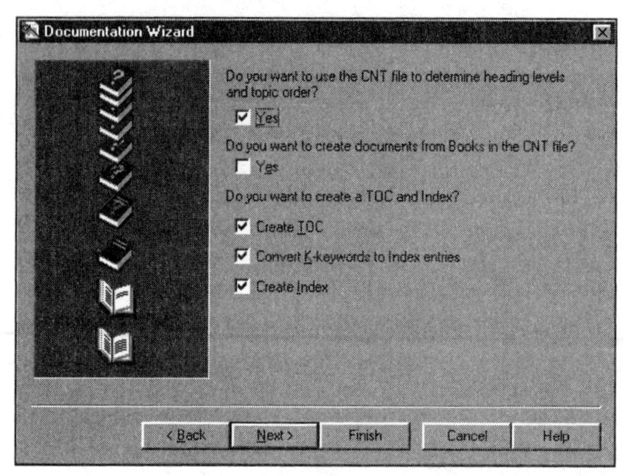

Figure 14-58: The second Documentation Wizard screen

5. Enter information in the fields as follows:

   - **Do you want to use the CNT file to determine heading levels and topic order?:** Check Yes (it's checked by default) to base the document's headings and topic order on the structure of the WinHelp project's table of contents in the CNT file. If you clear this box, RoboHELP creates the DOC file based on the order of the source files in the HPJ file and the order of the topics in each source file. (This option is greyed out if you do not have a CNT file.)

   - **Do you want to create documents from Books in the CNT file?:** Check this box to create separate DOC files for each top-level book in the WinHelp project's table of contents. Subordinate books become headings within the document. Any topics that are not included in the table of contents are saved in the file EXTRATOPICS.DOC. If you leave this box blank, RoboHELP creates a single DOC file from the specified source files.

   - **Create TOC:** Check this box to create a table of contents with the DOC file's heading levels using the standard Word TOC field code, {TOC \O}. If you checked Do you want to create documents from Books in the CNT file?, RoboHELP will create a separate TOC.DOC file that contains the table of contents. Otherwise, the table of contents will appear at the start of the DOC file.

   - **Convert K-keywords to Index entries:** Check this box to add Word index entries using the standard Word index entry field code, {xe "<indexitem>"} from the keyword entries in the WinHelp file.

   - **Create Index:** Check this box to create an index using the standard Word index field code, {INDEX \c "#"}. (The \c in the field code creates an index with multiple columns, and the "#" denotes the number of columns on the page.) If you checked Do you want to create documents from Books in the CNT file?, RoboHELP will create a separate INDEX.DOC file that contains the index. Otherwise, the index will appear at the start of the DOC file.

6. When you are satisfied with your entries, click Next. The third Documentation Wizard screen appears (shown in Figure 14-59).

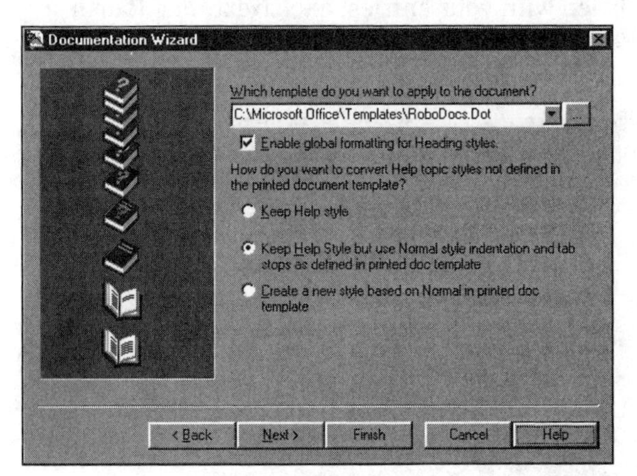

Figure 14-59: The third Documentation Wizard screen

7. Enter information in the fields as follows:

   - **Which template do you want to apply to the document?:** Enter the Word template file (.DOT file) you want to use for formatting the text in the DOC file. The default template is the ROBODOCS.DOT template.
   - **Enable global formatting for Heading styles:** Check this box to preserve the global template formatting for all heading styles. This lets you modify the printed document template for all printed documentation.
   - **How do you want to convert Help topic styles not defined in the printed doc template?:** Select one of the three options. Select Keep Help style to copy any styles (and their attributes) that don't exist in the template from the WinHelp files into the DOC file. Any text that uses this copied style will have the same appearance in the DOC file that it did in the WinHelp files. Select Keep Help Style but use Normal style indentation and tab stops as defined in printed doc template to copy any styles that don't exist in the template from the WinHelp files into the DOC file, but to change the new paragraph formatting to use the Normal style. (The font attributes are unchanged from what they were in the WinHelp files.) Select Create a new style based on Normal style in the printed doc template to copy the names of any styles that don't exist in the template from the WinHelp files into the DOC file, but to use the Normal style's attributes for this style. You can use this selection to tag items with a style name and then make global changes for that style in the printed document template.

Any styles that RoboHELP couldn't find during the conversion are displayed in a dialog box at the end of the conversion process.

8. When you are satisfied with your entries, click Next. The fourth Documentation Wizard screen appears (shown in Figure 14-60).

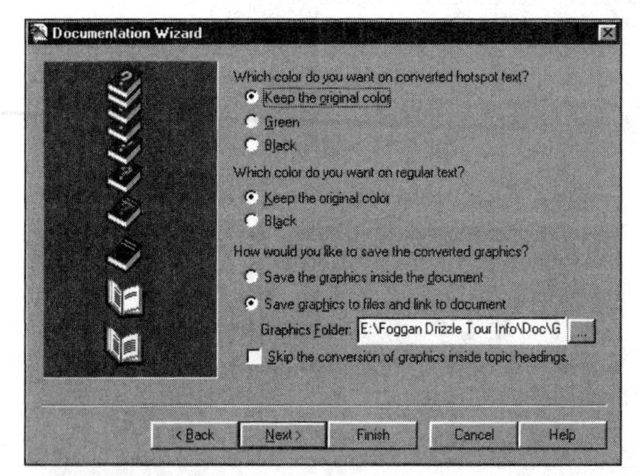

Figure 14-60: The fourth Documentation Wizard screen

9. Enter information in the fields as follows:

   - **Which color do you want on converted hotspot text?:** Select Keep the original color to use the original hotspot color as it appeared in the WinHelp files. Select Green or Black to use green or black for all hotspot text in the DOC file, regardless of the original hotspot color.
   - **Which color do you want on regular text?:** Select Keep the original color to keep the original text color used in the WinHelp files. Select Black to use black as the color for all non-hotspot text in the DOC file.
   - **How would you like to save the converted graphics?:** Select Save the graphics inside the document to embed the graphics in the DOC file. (If your WinHelp file is large and/or has a lot of graphics, it's not a good idea to embed graphics in the document, because of the resulting file size.) Select Save graphics to files and link to document (the default) to save the graphics in the Graphic folder specified in the associated field and then use the standard Word Include Picture field code {INCLUDEPICTURE "path\\filename" * MERGEFORMAT \d.}
   - **Skip the conversion of graphics inside topic titles:** Check this box to eliminate any graphics that are associated with heading styles.

10. When you are satisfied with your entries, click Next. The fifth Documentation Wizard screen (shown in Figure 14-61) appears.

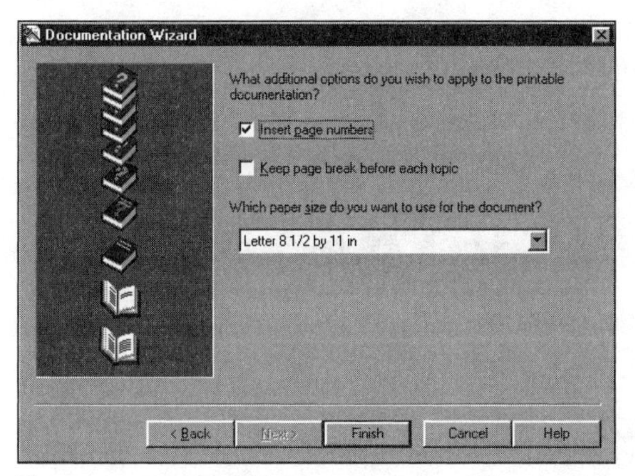

Figure 14-61: The fifth Documentation Wizard screen

11. Enter information in the fields as follows:

    - **Insert page numbers:** Check this box (the default) to insert page numbers in the DOC file.
    - **Keep page break before each topic:** Check this box to retain the page break that appears before a topic in the WinHelp source files. (You may not want to do this, as you can get a lot of very short pages in the resulting DOC files.)
    - **Which paper size do you want to use for the document?:** Select the paper size from the drop-down list. RoboHELP will use this information to set the margins in the DOC file.

12. When you are satisfied with your entries, click Finish. RoboHELP starts converting the project into DOC files. When the process is complete, it displays any styles that weren't found (as shown in Figure 14-62).

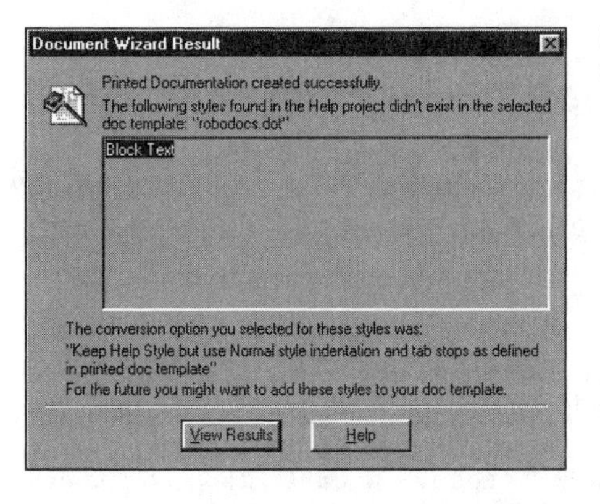

Figure 14-62: The Document Wizard Result screen

13. Click View Results to start Word and display the new DOC file. Figure 14-63 shows the Foggan Drizzle file converted to a DOC file.

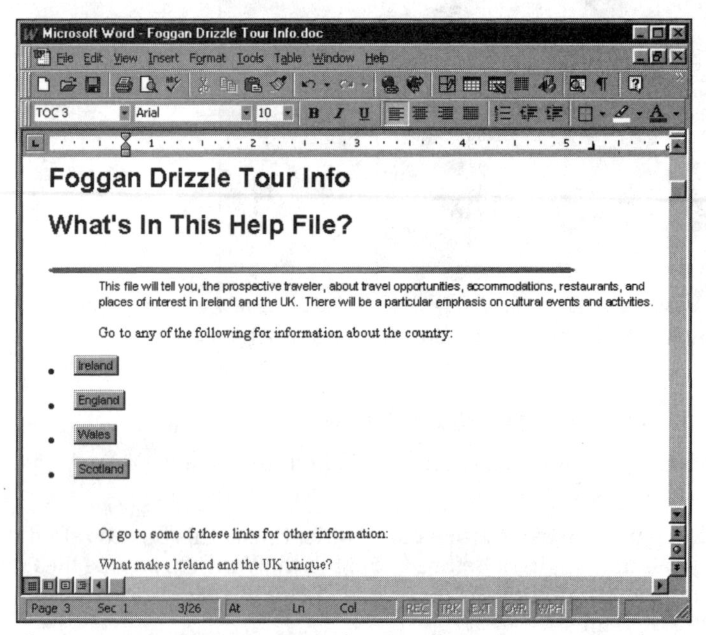

Figure 14-63: The Foggan Drizzle WinHelp project converted to a DOC file

Using WinHelp 3 Tools

In addition to the other WinHelp tools included with RoboHELP, there are several tools used specifically for maintaining WinHelp 3 files: the WinHelp Compatibility Wizard, the WinHelp HyperViewer, and the WinHelp Inspector.

Adding WinHelp 4 Features to WinHelp 3 Files

There are two tools for adding WinHelp 4 features to WinHelp 3 files: WinHelp Compatibility Wizard and WinHelp HyperViewer. The WinHelp Compatibility Wizard is a tool for adding basic WinHelp 4 features — specifically, the standard Contents, Index, and Find tabs — to WinHelp 3 files. The resulting file will still run on Windows 3.1 systems, but will have the WinHelp 4 look and feel.

Note

The WinHelp 3 features that the WinHelp Compatibility Wizard adds are automatically supported by the WinHelp 4 viewer on Windows 98. If the users are opening the WinHelp 3 file on Windows 98, they don't need to add anything to the WinHelp 3 file. However, you will need to use the WinHelp Compatibility Wizard to get WinHelp 4 features if you're running WinHelp 3 files on Windows 3.1 or on Windows NT.

The WinHelp HyperViewer automatically creates a table of contents the users can expand and collapse headings in for the WinHelp 3 file using the links and structure of the help topics in the file. It also adds a button that brings up a full-text search screen, which, while not the same as the standard WinHelp 4 screen, lets you do all the same things.

To add WinHelp 4 features to a WinHelp 3 file, do the following:

1. Open the WinHelp 3 project in RoboHELP.
2. In the RoboHELP Explorer, select the RoboHELP ⇨ Project Settings command. Select the Extensions tab to display the Extensions folder (as shown in Figure 14-64).

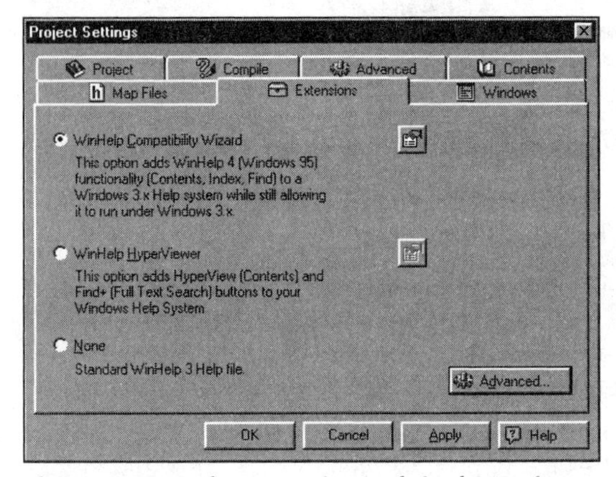

Figure 14-64: The Extensions tab in the Project Settings screen

3. Select WinHelp Compatibility Wizard, and then click the button to the right of the WinHelp Compatibility Wizard option. The Compatibility Wizard screen appears, as shown in Figure 14-65.

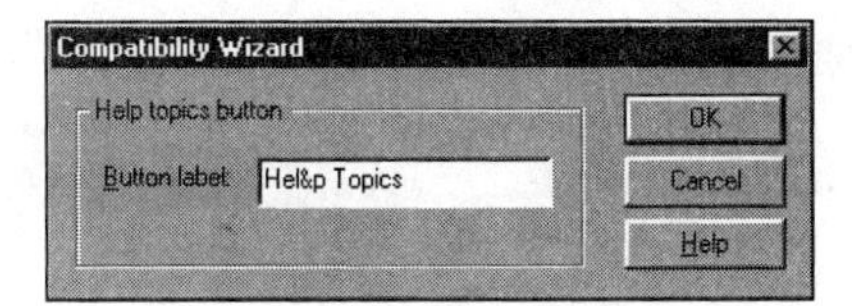

Figure 14-65: The Compatibility Wizard screen

4. Enter information for the button to display in the button bar. The default button is Help Topic, with an accelerator key of "p." You can replace this button label with the button label of your choice. Insert an ampersand (&) before the character you want to use as the accelerator key.

5. Click OK to save the button information and return to the Extensions tab, and then click Apply to apply the settings to the WinHelp 3 file.

Now add the WinHelp HyperViewer features, as follows

1. Select WinHelp HyperViewer in the Extensions folder, and then click the button to the right of the WinHelp HyperViewer option. The WinHelp HyperViewer screen appears (shown in Figure 14-66).

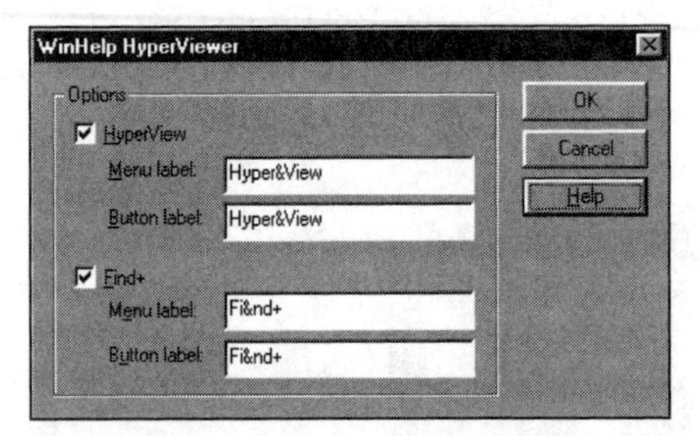

Figure 14-66: The WinHelp HyperViewer screen

2. Enter information in the fields as follows:
   - **Hyperview:** Check this box to add the HyperViewer features. Enter the menu and button labels in the appropriate fields. (The menu label is the command that appears on the WinHelp file's File menu.) The default entry for this item is HyperView, with an accelerator key of "v."
   - **Find+:** Check this box to add the Find+ features. (Find+ provides full-text search capabilities for WinHelp 3 files.) Enter the menu and button labels in the appropriate fields. The default entry for this item is Find+, with an accelerator key of "n."
3. When you are satisfied with your entries, click OK to save the button information and return to the Extensions tab, and then click Apply to apply the settings to the WinHelp 3 file.

The last step is to add the RoboHELP extensions to the WinHelp 3 file, as follows:

1. Click Advanced in the Extensions tab. The Add/Remove RoboHELP Extensions screen appears (shown in Figure 14-67).
2. Enter information in the fields as follows:
   - **Inetwh16.dll extensions:** Check this box to register the Inet macro routines so you can access the Internet from the WinHelp file. Clearing this box will remove the INETWH16.DLL routine from the WinHelp file.

- **Rhmmplay.dll extensions:** Check this box to register the Video and Sound macros so the users can play video and sound files from the WinHelp file. Clearing this box will remove the RHMMPLAY.DLL routine from the WinHelp file.

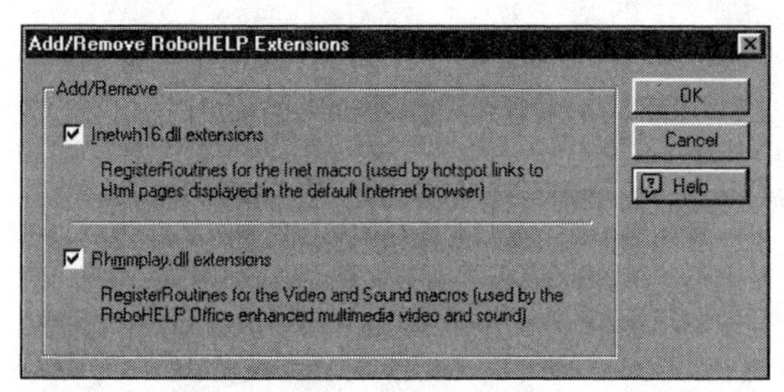

Figure 14-67: The Add/Remove RoboHELP Extensions screen

3. When you are done, click OK, and then click OK to apply the settings to the WinHelp 3 file and return to the RoboHELP Explorer.

Once you have added the various WinHelp extensions, you can compile the WinHelp 3 file as normal. Following are a few tips to keep in mind when working on the compiled WinHelp 3 file with the WinHelp Compatibility Wizard and WinHelp HyperViewer extensions:

✦ When you have a WinHelp 3 project opened in RoboHELP and you run the compiled file, RoboHELP uses the WinHelp 3 viewer. To view the features added with the WinHelp Compatibility Wizard, you need to open the WinHelp 3 file in the Windows Explorer.

✦ If you're using the RHMMPLAY.DLL extensions, be sure to use the 16-bit version of the RHMMPLAY.DLL file. (RoboHELP installs the 32-bit version in your \Windows\System directory.) You can find the 16-bit version of the RHMMPLAY.DLL file in the \Program Files\RoboHELP Office\VideoCam\Redist\16bit folder. Both versions of the file have the same name, but they have different file sizes: the 16-bit version is 10.5K, whereas the 32-bit version is 22K. Copy the 16-bit version of the file to the \Windows\System directory to test your WinHelp 3 project.

Figure 14-68 shows the Foggan Drizzle WinHelp file compiled as WinHelp 3 with the buttons and features added. (Note the WinHelp HyperViewer buttons, Find+ and HyperView, on the button bar.)

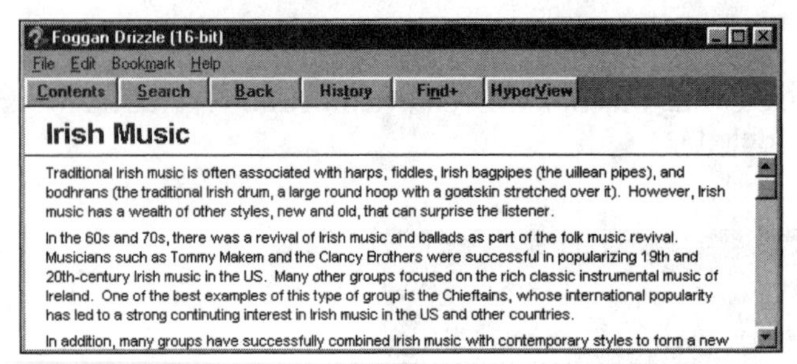

Figure 14-68: A sample WinHelp 3 file with the WinHelp extensions added

Using the extension features is fairly straightforward. You can select the new options from the File menu or click the button on the button bar. Figure 14-69 shows how the Find+ feature looks when finding a sample term in the Foggan Drizzle WinHelp file.

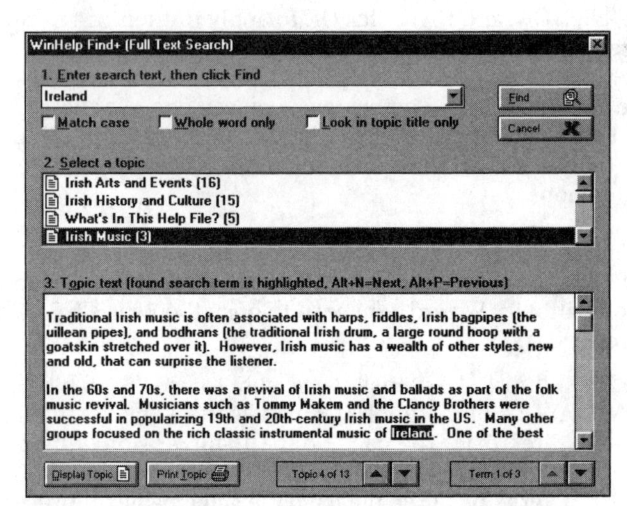

Figure 14-69: The WinHelp Find+ (Full Text Search) screen in the Foggan Drizzle file

When you enter search text in the first field of the WinHelp Find+ (Full Text Search) screen, WinHelp finds the topics that the word or phrase appears in and displays the number of occurrences of the search item in the text. Once you click a topic in the second field, the topic text appears in the third field with the first occurrence of the search item highlighted. From here, you can display the actual topic in the WinHelp file, print the topic, navigate to other topics that contain the search item, and navigate within the topic itself to find the other occurrences of the search item.

The WinHelp HyperViewer generates a table of contents from the topics you're viewing in the WinHelp file. Figure 14-70 shows a sample table of contents in the WinHelp HyperViewer screen. One of the biggest advantages of the WinHelp HyperViewer is that the users can use the WinHelp HyperViewer screen to print multiple topics.

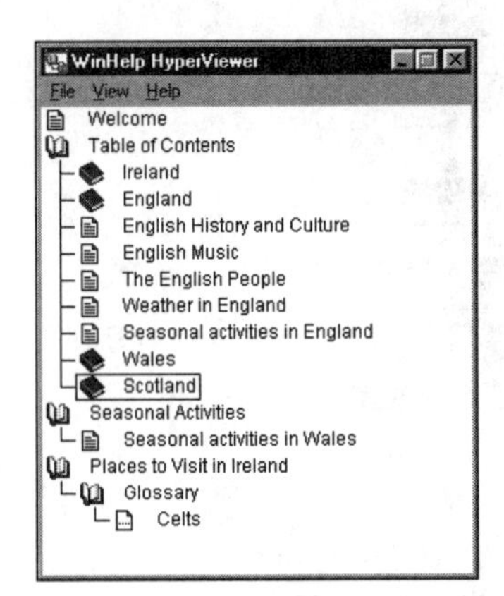

Figure 14-70: The WinHelp HyperViewer screen

Using the WinHelp Inspector

The WinHelp Inspector is an older tool from eHelp for analyzing WinHelp files that are already compiled. It works on WinHelp 3 files and some WinHelp 4 files that are not overly complex.

To open a file in the WinHelp Inspector, do the following:

1. In the RoboHELP Explorer, double-click the WinHelp Inspector icon (shown in Figure 14-71) in the Tools folder. The WinHelp Inspector screen appears (shown in Figure 14-72 with the WinHelp 3 version of the Foggan Drizzle file already opened).

Figure 14-71: The WinHelp Inspector icon

2. Select a WinHelp 3 file in the File Name field. The file information appears in the lower half of the screen.

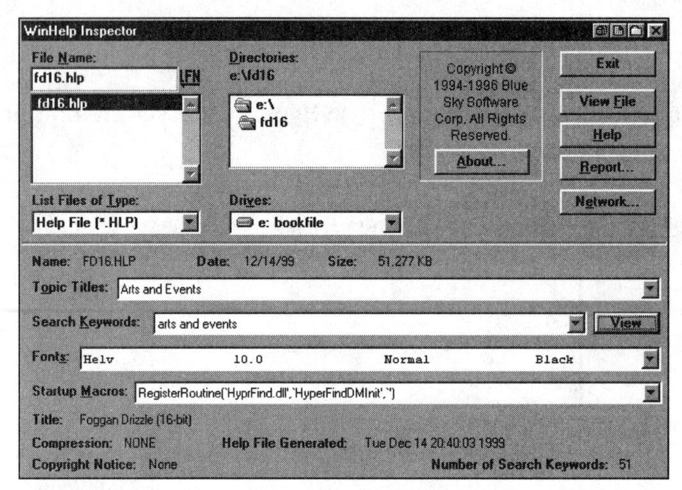

Figure 14-72: The WinHelp Inspector screen

You can examine several different aspects of the WinHelp file in the various fields, including the topic titles, the keywords, the fonts that are used in the WinHelp file, and the startup macros. In addition, the WinHelp Inspector displays general information about the WinHelp file such as when it was compiled, the compression type, and so on. You can open the WinHelp file by clicking the View File button on the right side of the screen. To display and print a report on the WinHelp file's statistics, click the Report button.

The version of WinHelp Inspector currently shipping with RoboHELP Office 2000 cannot print reports under Windows 98, although it does work under Windows NT.

Like PC HelpDesk, the WinHelp Inspector is not currently being updated by eHelp. As an alternative, you can try decompiling with WinHelp file using Help-to-Source (described earlier in this chapter) and examine the file's statistics with the various RoboHELP reports.

Summary

In this chapter, you saw how to use several RoboHELP tools. The chapter started with information about using Help-to-Source to decompile WinHelp files into source documents. You then saw how to search for and optionally replace information in multiple files using Multi-File Find and Replace. Next, you learned how to use PC HelpDesk to create standalone knowledge bases. The chapter continued with extensive information on *single-sourcing,* creating different online help formats from a single WinHelp 4 project. Last, you saw how to add a variety of WinHelp 4 features to WinHelp 3 files.

✦ ✦ ✦

Managing Large Projects

✦ ✦ ✦ ✦

In This Chapter

Backing up files and implementing a source control system

Importing documents, help projects, and map files to your WinHelp project

Creating and using separate style sheets, custom project templates, and online books

Tracking topic status

Printing Project Status, Diagnostics, and Ship List reports

Using build tags for conditional compiles

Finding and repairing broken links and unreferenced topics

Using ActiveEdit and Help Author mode

Preparing WinHelp files for final release

✦ ✦ ✦ ✦

In this final chapter on WinHelp projects, you'll learn how to manage and release your help window projects. The chapter tells you how to manage large projects, including such topics as making effective backups and using source control for tracking your work. Next, the chapter teaches you how to convert and import existing documents and projects into your WinHelp project. You then learn to create and use style sheets and custom project templates (including online books and other RoboHELP templates) to ensure a consistent look and feel to your online help. The chapter continues with information on how to track topic status, priority, work by author, and time estimates. You next see how to use build tags for conditional compilation. In the final section, the chapter presents information on how to prepare WinHelp files for release, including how to print a variety of diagnostic reports, use ActiveEdit and Help Author mode for testing, set compile options and print a Ship List report for a release version, and wrap up your WinHelp project.

Managing Your Projects

Many online help projects are small enough that their creation and maintenance can be managed by one or two people. However, some online help projects require the combined efforts of an entire workgroup.

The single biggest problem with a large online help project is one of coordination. Good coordination of everyone's efforts will minimize the problems and maximize the workgroup's efficiency, all of which requires some careful planning. This section shows you some techniques for structuring and organizing an online help project for the best results.

Backing Up Your Files

The most important thing to do when creating a large online help project is to back up your files regularly. Almost nobody likes to back up; it's annoying and time consuming at best and it usually isn't necessary. But good backups are an essential insurance for avoiding disaster if you have a hard disk crash or a viral infection, or just need to recover a file damaged by a system crash.

If you ever find yourself saying, "We don't have time to back up right now," stop what you're doing and do a full backup immediately.

There are two levels of backups you should consider:

- **Local backups.** Each writer should make a regular backup of the files they're working on. Backups can be done to diskettes, a Zip drive, CD, or to a network drive. Many writers make individual file-level backups every few hours when they're making a lot of changes to a source document and then back up their entire work directories nightly.
- **Network backups.** If you're on a network (usually the case when you're creating a large online help project), do a full backup of all the files for the project at least once a week. This can usually be scheduled with the company's IT department so all your team will have to do is check in all the files to a designated folder or drive by quitting time on a specified day.

A certain percentage of backups should be kept offsite in case of fire, theft, or other form of physical loss. In addition, many companies have a legal requirement to their clients to maintain their source code in an offsite facility as part of an escrow agreement should the company fail. This is likely to be part of your project closure tasks. You should include all source files and as well as copies of the compiled help files, CNT files, and supporting DLLs and programs. You may also want to print hard copies of your source files for final storage; however, keep in mind that large help files can run into thousands of pages of printed output.

When you are creating long-term backups, it's an excellent idea to burn the files onto a CD-R (CD recordable). CDs are currently the most stable storage method available for good permanent storage. In contrast, diskettes, tapes, and other magnetic media are susceptible to heat, moisture, and electromagnetic fields and must be reverified every couple of years. Furthermore, many storage and backup programs are notorious for poor backward compatibility, making it difficult to recover information stored with an earlier version of the program.

If you are drastically restricted by time or space, you can back up only your HLP, CNT, and supporting DLL files. In an emergency, you could then decompile the HLP file with the Help-to-Source utility and re-create your online help project.

Using Source Control

The next step after making sure your files are backed up is to apply some measure of source control. A source control system tracks the component files of a project. With a source control system, you can check files in and out, very much like a software library system. This lets you control who is working on an individual file and will limit the potential for errors caused by two people's working on the same file. A source control system also provides you with historical data by keeping the source for past versions of an online help project. In addition, you can store common files — such as company logos, standard screen shots, and generic help files — in the source control system. The source control system also keeps a copy of the file even if it's checked out, so you can always revert to the previous version of the file.

In a large project, it's almost certain that the developers will already have a source control system set up for tracking and maintaining code versions. You can probably enlist the aid of the development source control person to set up a parallel source control system for your help project. However, if there is not a source control system already set up, you may want to invest in a source control for your group. Two of the most popular source control packages are Visual Source Safe from Microsoft and PVCS from Intersolv, although there are many others.

You don't need to store every file in the online help project, as many of the files are automatically generated by RoboHELP if they're needed. Table 15-1 shows you the file types that are essential in an online help project.

You should also check in versions of DLLs and other supporting programs. In addition, don't forget project documents such as the project plan and any design documents you may have created as part of the project.

The source control system will let you check out files (with full read-write permission so you can change them) or get files (read-only). You don't always need to check out all the files for a project; for example, to add and maintain topics, you'll need to check out the DOC, RTF, and RBH files with read-write access, but you'll need to get only the project's HPJ, CNT, HH, and any additional map files. Conversely, to change project settings, you need to check out the HPJ, CNT, HH, and any additional map files, but you need to get only the DOC, RTF, and RBH files. Compiling the WinHelp project requires only that you check out the HPJ and CNT files; all other project files can be read-only.

Table 15-1
File Types to Save in a Source Control System

File Type	***Description***
DOC	Word for Windows version of the source file for the online help project.
RTF	RTF version of the source file for the online help project.
RHB	An internal file that tracks document properties and other information for a DOC or RTF file.
HPJ	The help project file for the online help project.
HPT	An internal file that contains the help topics in the online help project. When you create external topic jumps, RoboHELP uses this for displaying topic IDs.
CNT	The table of contents file.
BMP, SHG, WMF, MRB	WinHelp-compatible images.
HH	The help hook information for context-sensitive help.
GHC, INC, PAS	Additional map files for Visual Basic, Turbo Pascal, and Pascal.
HLP	The compiled WinHelp file.

The following are some suggestions for using a source control system effectively:

✦ Identify how the source control system will be used for the project. Discuss the the general procedures and guidelines for using the source control system as part of the help creation process. Determine the general layout of working directories, security rights, and access privileges for the team members. Don't be afraid to change the structure if something isn't working — what you design should work for you and the project — but do make sure that the folder structures are always parallel on each writer's computer so that the files can be checked in and out in the same way. (The development leads and IT staff will be able to help you come up with workable policies.)

✦ Appoint one person as project integrator who compiles the project. This may be the project lead or another person who enjoys coordinating and is good at manipulating files and directories. Each writer will hand off the sources for his or her modules to the project integrator, who will then assemble them and compile the project. This will ensure that all the component pieces are integrated and compiled in the same way. When the project is ready to be handed off for testing and integration with the rest of the product, the project integrator will also be responsible for writing any instructions for compiling the project.

✦ The source control system lets you set up ownership—identifying the primary person responsible for the file. The project lead or the project integrator should be listed in the source control system as the owner of the HPJ, CNT, and HLP files in the source control system. The team members will be able to get and use the files, but only the owner will be able to change them. For all files, set the source control system's date options to show the date the files were last modified rather than the date they were checked in and out.

✦ Depending on how often you want to compile the file, you may want to establish a general check-in time so that the team members can check in their files for integration and compiling. (Most development teams use a similar procedure; you'll probably be able to get some advice on how to integrate this with your normal help development process from the program lead.) How often you want to compile is dependent on the size of the project and where you are in the schedule.

✦ If you store the project plans, design documents, and project schedules, be sure to set the access privileges carefully for who can read them and also who can see them.

Depending on the complexity of your WinHelp project, it may not be necessary or desirable to use a full source control system. You can, instead, create an effective manual source control system, as follows:

1. Create a project folder on a shared network drive that contains all the source files, images, DLLs, and other files and documents.

2. Identify an owner for each file. (Ownership in this case is a matter of whom the file is assigned to rather than a file attribute set in the source control system.)

3. Set the default file attributes for the DOC, RTF, and other project files in the project folder to read-only. The project lead should have copies of all the files in the project with read-write access, as should the team members for the files they own. This will allow everyone to read and use the files but to make changes only to the files they own. (RoboHELP can acess read-only files but does not save changes to them.) Check-in of files will be a manual process, wherein the files are copied to the shared network drive.

Only the project lead or the designated project integrator should be allowed to copy files to the shared network drive.

Using RoboHELP in a Workgroup

The previous section discussed some of the general techniques for managing large online help projects. This section will show you how you can take advantage of RoboHELP to standardize your online help and to facilitate the efforts of a workgroup on large online help projects.

One of the first things you should do after creating the help project is to create a library of common topic and graphic elements. You may want to mandate a specific BMROOT folder for graphics as part of the basic help project structure. Also predefine such things as:

✦ The number and attributes of the various help windows and how they're to be used

✦ The colors and formatting for text

✦ When and how to use standard common topics (such as OK and Cancel buttons)

✦ The preferred style in keywords (you may also want to build a list of words for use with RoboHELP's Smart Index feature that are available to all the writers)

If you have developed a set of documentation standards for your online help, most of this work will already have been done. For more information on planning and creating standards, see Chapter 2, "What Makes Help 'Help'?"

It's important that all the team members write as closely as possible to the group's documentation standard. Remember that a documentation standard doesn't stifle creativity; it simply eliminates "cuteness" on the part of the original writers. A consistent writing and presentation style from section to section will make the reader's job that much easier when it comes to navigating the finished product.

Converting and Importing

RoboHELP offers you several ways to simplify the creation of your WinHelp projects. Two of the most popular are converting and importing information. Converting changes information in a Word (DOC or RTF) format to RoboHELP format. Importing converts the information and also adds it to the open RoboHELP project. Importing can also be used with WinHelp projects created by other help development systems and even with compiled WinHelp (HLP) files. Both techniques are valuable for building on existing work when creating a large WinHelp project.

Adding Word Documents to a WinHelp project

Probably the most common scenario is adding the information from a Word document to your RoboHELP project. You'll do this this most commonly when you're changing a chapter of a printed manual or an entire manual into online help. Other applications for this feature are:

✦ Copying blocks of technical text from a printed document

✦ Adding blocks of boilerplate documentation for standardized features

✦ Assembling a custom WinHelp file from a selection of document modules

✦ Adding a DOC or RTF file already converted to WinHelp format

There are a couple of different ways you can do this. The simplest is to import the document, as follows:

1. Open the RoboHELP project to which you want to import the document.

Always have a backup copy of the document in case something goes wrong with the conversion.

2. Select the RoboHELP ➪ Import Document command in Word or the File ➪ Import ➪ Document command in the RoboHELP Explorer. The Import Document screen appears (shown in Figure 15-1).

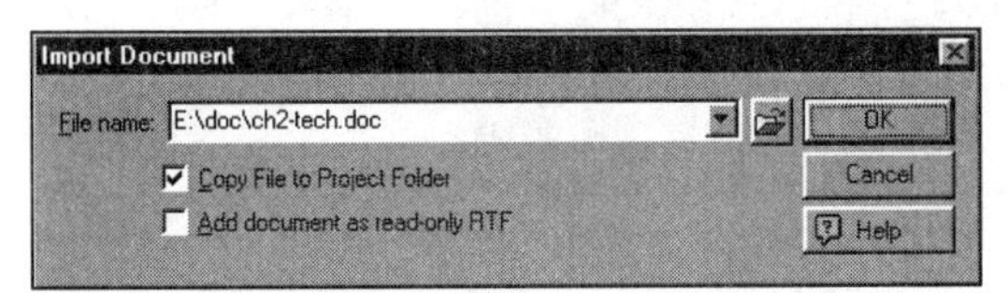

Figure 15-1: The Import Document screen

3. Enter information in the fields as follows:
   - **File name:** Enter the name of the file to import, select a file from the drop-down list, or use the browse button to the right of the field to search for the file. You can import existing WinHelp source files, Word files (DOC or RTF), or FrameMaker documents.
   - **Copy File to Project Folder:** Check this box (the default) to copy the document being imported to the project folder for the online help project. Changes made to the document to add it to the project will be made to the copy and not to the original. You may want to uncheck this if you are importing files that will subsequently be used in other WinHelp projects and you want to convert them to the preferred styles.
   - **Add document as read-only RTF:** Check this box if you want to import the document as a read-only file to the WinHelp project. The file's information will be converted to WinHelp format as necessary and will appear in the compiled WinHelp file, but the file will not be editable in RoboHELP. (You can create jumps and popups for topics in the read-only RTF by manually entering the appropriate topic ID.) This is useful for preset company information, boilerplate topics, or legal descriptions that should not be changed. Documents added as read-only RTF files appear as system documents in the RoboHELP Explorer Project Manager.

4. When you are satisfied with your entries, click OK. RoboHELP prompts you to make a backup of the file, then opens the document to be imported in Word and then displays the Import Options screen (shown in Figure 15-2). The Import Options screen lets you set the various conversion options for this document.

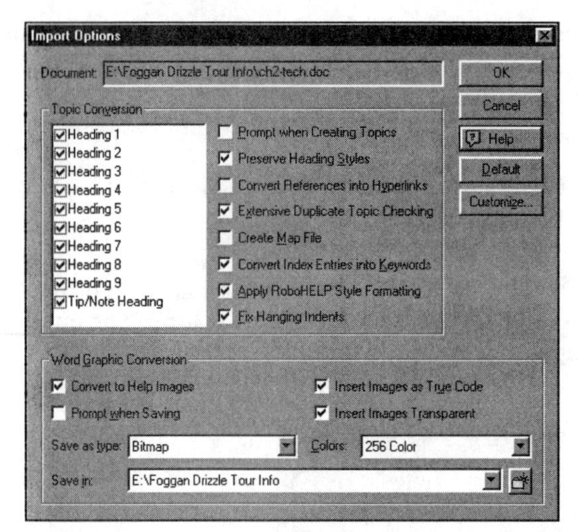

Figure 15-2: The Import Options screen

5. Enter information in the fields as follows:

- **Document:** This display-only field shows the document about to be imported.
- **Styles:** Check the boxes for each heading style that identifies a new topic. The default is for all nine levels of heading and the Tip/Note heading. As RoboHELP converts the document, it will change topics formatted with the selected headings into new topics and apply the appropriate style from the ROBOHELP.DOT template.

The default styles selected in this list can be changed in the Customize Import screen (shown later in this section). You can also add to the list styles that appear in the document you're importing that you want RoboHELP to search for.

- **Prompt when Creating Topics:** Check this box to have RoboHELP prompt you before creating a topic.

Note

The first few times you import documents, check this box so you can see how RoboHELP converts the information.

- **Preserve Heading Styles:** Check this box (the default) to save the style for the various topic headings. For example, when this box is checked, the converted document will have headings with styles Heading 1, Heading 2, Heading 3, and so on. If this box is unchecked, RoboHELP assigns the Heading 1 style to all topic headings regardless of their original style.

- **Convert References into Hyperlinks:** Check this box to convert the cross-references in the Word document into WinHelp jumps and the embedded table of contents entries into pages in the project's table of contents.
- **Extensive Duplicate Topic Checking:** Check this box (the default) to check the topic IDs that are created during the conversion to make sure that they aren't duplicates for any of the existing topics. (This option is useful if you're working in RoboHELP but don't have RoboHELP Explorer open, but it can lengthen the amount of time RoboHELP uses to convert the document.)
- **Create Map File:** Check this box to generate map IDs and create a map file for the document. If the project has an extra language map file designated in the project settings, RoboHELP will create the appropriate extra language map file as well.
- **Convert Index Entries into Keywords:** Check this box (the default) to convert embedded index entries in the Word document to standard WinHelp keywords.
- **Apply RoboHELP Style Formatting:** Check this box (the default) to apply standard RoboHELP styles to the imported text.
- **Fix Hanging Indents:** Check this box (the default) to change hanging indents in the Word document to a standard paragraph format.
- **Convert to Help Images:** Check this box (the default) to convert graphics embedded in the document to help images. Uncheck this box if you don't want to convert embedded graphics to help images. (If you uncheck this box, the topics in the converted document will not contain graphics.)
- **Prompt when Saving:** Check this box to have RoboHELP prompt you for a file name whenever it converts a graphic.
- **Insert Images as True Code:** Check this box (the default) to insert True Code references for images rather than the images themselves. If you uncheck this box, RoboHELP will insert the actual graphic.

Adding the graphics to the document requires more memory and takes longer to convert. If the document is long and it contains a substantial number of graphics, it's a good idea to insert the images as True Code during the conversion and then change them later on.

- **Insert Images Transparent:** Check this box (the default) to insert the images as transparent images.
- **Save as type:** Choose Bitmap or Hotspot Image from the drop-down list as the format RoboHELP should use when saving graphics from the imported document.

- **Colors:** Choose from the drop-down list the color depth — Monochrome, 16 Color, 256 Color, or 24-bit — that RoboHELP should use when saving graphics from the imported document.
- **Save in:** Select the folder in which to save the converted graphics from the imported document. The default entry in this field is the folder for the online help project, but you can specify an existing folder or create a new one on the fly if you wish. You can browse directories by clicking the browse button to the right of the field.
- **Default:** Click this button to update the styles in the Styles list with all the heading styles that appear in the document being imported. RoboHELP looks in the template attached to the document being imported for styles that are identified as heading styles or that have "Heading" in the style name.
- **Customize:** Click this to open the Customize Import screen (shown in Figure 15-3). Check and uncheck the headings and styles for the defaults in the Styles list on the Import Options screen shown earlier in Figure 15-2. You can add styles that you want RoboHELP to search for and create topic headings by selecting the style from the New Style drop-down list and clicking Add. You can remove styles you've added by highlighting them on the list and clicking Remove. When you are satisfied with your changes, click OK to return to the Import Options screen.

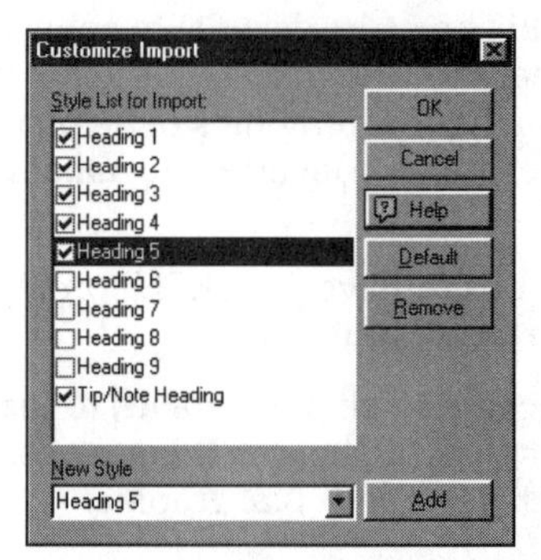

Figure 15-3: The Customize Import screen

If you're working with a file created in FrameMaker, you should add the FrameMaker "Heading1" style and then select it in the Styles list on the Import Options screen.

6. When you are satisfied with your entries, click OK to start the conversion. RoboHELP will process the information in the document being imported. A status bar will be displayed (a sample of this is shown in Figure 15-4) during the process to show you the progress of the conversion.

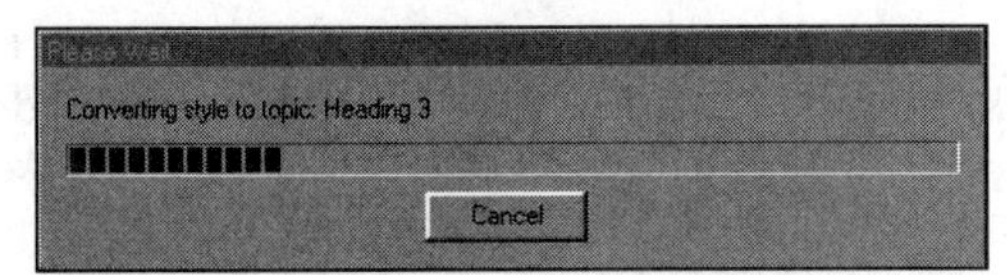

Figure 15-4: The conversion status bar

7. When the conversion is complete, the now-converted file will remain open in Word. RoboHELP will have updated the HPJ file to include the imported document in the [FILES] section and will also have created several supporting RoboHELP files for the imported document. At this point, you can work with the project files as normal.

As with attaching other help source files, the information for the file appears at the end of the compiled WinHelp file in the order the file(s) are listed in the [FILES] section of the HPJ file. Be sure to adjust your browse sequences appropriately in the source files.

Although the import process is good for adding whole documents in separate files, you need to use a slightly different process if you simply want to add a few pages of text to a project. You can cut and paste blocks of text into an open file and then convert it to RoboHELP format as follows:

1. Open a WinHelp project.
2. Cut the text you want to add from the original document and paste it into the project document at the appropriate insertion point.

Be sure that the headings in the text you're pasting are formatted with the appropriate heading styles.

3. Select the RoboHELP ⇨ Convert Document command. The Conversion Options screen (identical to the Import Options screen) appears. The document designated in the Document field will be the project document currently open. Select the appropriate options as you did earlier when you imported a document. When you click OK, RoboHELP will convert the pasted text in the file.

You can perform the conversion process on a document as many times as you want. However, it's not necessary to convert information as soon as you've pasted it; for example, you can add a number of blocks of information and then covert them all at once.

The choice of whether you want to import documents or convert them is dependent on the size and number of text blocks you may want to add to an online help project. It may be more efficient to cut and paste text blocks into a single-project DOC file and then convert them instead of importing a dozen separate files. Having all the information in a single file is usually easier to edit. On the other hand, having individual files can be easier to maintain if your project has been set up as separate modules. Making a change to half a dozen WinHelp files that use information in one of the modules is then just a function of changing the individual file and recompiling the various WinHelp files.

If you want to add information from a DOC or RTF file that's already in WinHelp format, you can use the same import or conversion procedures described in this section. You should be sure that the heading styles are compatible and that any additional styles have been added to the Styles list as necessary.

Opening individual files in a project

It's a good idea when you're importing files to make sure you're importing the right files. Backing out an imported file is not very difficult, but the process can be time consuming. RoboHELP has a feature that lets you open an individual file in a project. (This feature is also useful for opening files such as the HPJ or MAP files in the current project.)

To look at a specific file in an online help project, do the following:

1. In the RoboHELP Explorer, select the File ➪ Open File From Project command. The Open File From Project screen appears (as shown in Figure 15-5).

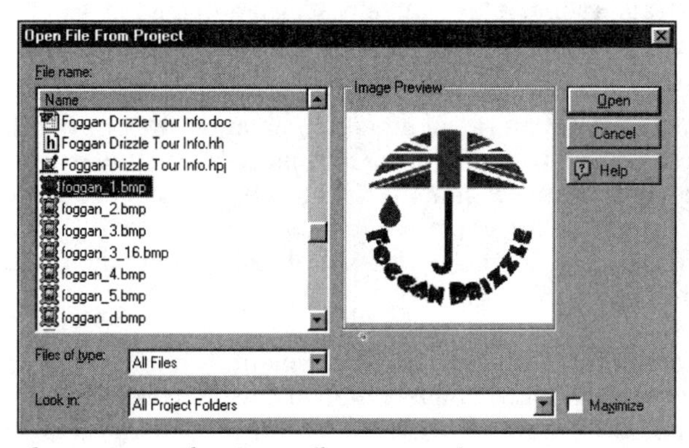

Figure 15-5: The Open File From Project screen

2. Select the file you want to open. Graphics appear in the Image Preview section on the right side of the screen. When you click OK, RoboHELP opens the highlighted file using the appropriate program. For example, DOC and RTF files are opened in Word; HPJ, HH, CNT, and other text files are opened in Notepad; and help images are opened in the RoboHELP Image Workshop.

Importing WinHelp projects

In addition to importing and converting documents, RoboHELP can import an entire WinHelp project. You can use this if you're bringing a WinHelp project into RoboHELP or if you're switching from another WinHelp development system such as Doc-to-Help or ForeHelp and want to use RoboHELP for further help development.

To import a WinHelp project, do the following:

1. Back up the files for the help project you're about to import. The conversion process will permanently change the online help project to RoboHELP format. By keeping a copy, you will maintain an audit trail of the work done on the files. You may also need to use the backup files if the conversion fails for any reason or if you need to use the other help authoring system again.
2. Start the RoboHELP Explorer.
3. Select the File ➪ New ➪ Project command, and then click the Import tab on the New Project screen to display the project import options (shown in Figure 15-6).

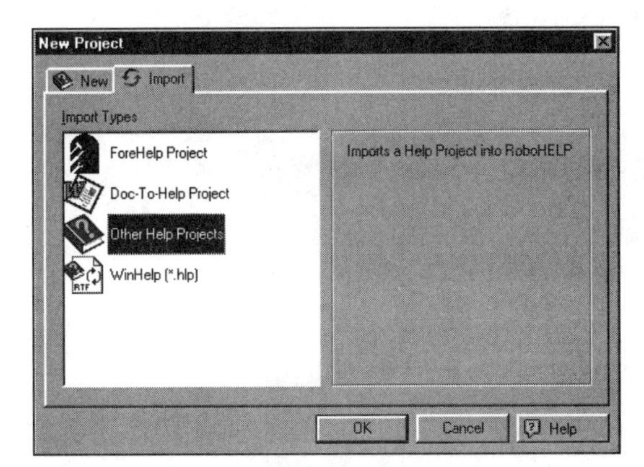

Figure 15-6: The New Project screen with the Import tab displayed

4. Select the appropriate option from the list:
   - If you're importing a ForeHelp or a Doc-to-Help file, use the ForeHelp Project or Doc-to-Help Project options.
   - If you're importing a project created with another help tool (including the Microsoft Help Compiler Workshop), use the Other Help Projects option.

The final option on the list can be used to create a new project from a compiled WinHelp file by running the Help-to-Source utility described in Chapter 14, "Using RoboHELP Tools."

5. Click OK. RoboHELP will convert the project, create the supporting RoboHELP files, and open the project in Word.

You can use the File ➪ Import ➪ External Help File document command to import a compiled WinHelp file to a project for external dependencies. This is different from running Help-to-Source to create a new project in that it links an external WinHelp file to the project so that it's available when you create jumps to external topics. For more information on creating jumps to external topics, see Chapter 4, "Adding Jumps and Popups."

Importing HTML Help projects

You can import an HTML Help project to a WinHelp project by first converting the HTML Help project's files to Word files and then importing the Word files to a WinHelp project.

For additional information on using RoboHELP HTML, see Parts IV and V of this book.

To create Word files files from the HTML Help project, do the following:

1. Open the HTML Help project in RoboHELP HTML.
2. Select the File ➪ Generate ➪ Printed Documentation command. The first Document Wizard screen appears, as shown in Figure 15-7.

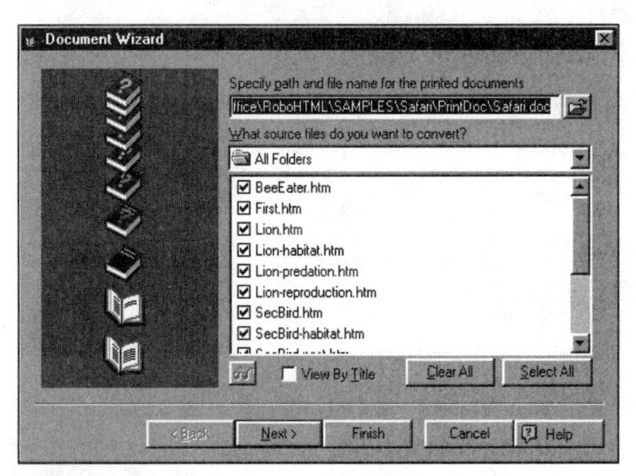

Figure 15-7: The Document Wizard screen

3. Specify the path for the resulting files and select the HTM files you want to convert from the HTML Help project. Click Next to display the Style Sheet screen, shown in Figure 15-8.

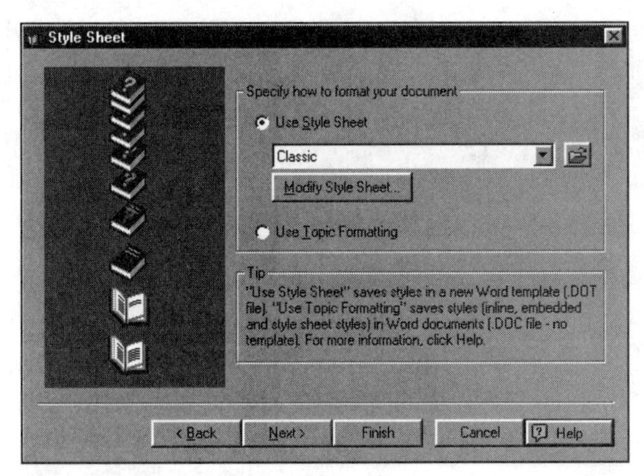

Figure 15-8: The Style Sheet screen

4. Select the style sheet options you want for the output. Set any other options on this screen, and then click Next to display the TOC and Index screen (as shown in Figure 15-9).

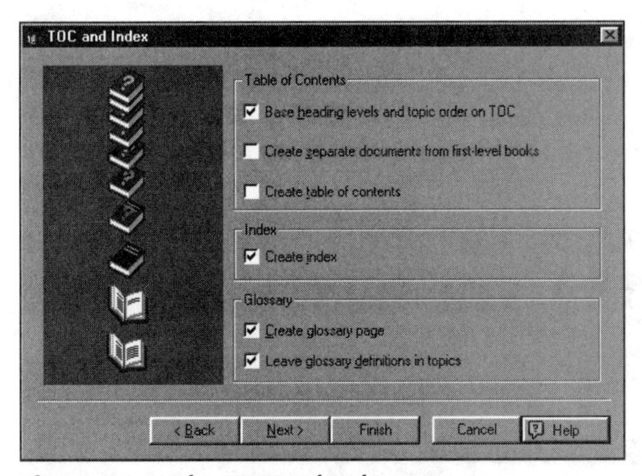

Figure 15-9: The TOC and Index screen

5. Uncheck the Create TOC option (you won't be importing the table of contents for the printed documentation). Make sure that Create Index is checked, as this embeds index entries in the Word documents that are turned into keywords in the second phase of this process. Set any other options on this screen, and then click Next to display the Text Color and Images screen (displayed in Figure 15-10).

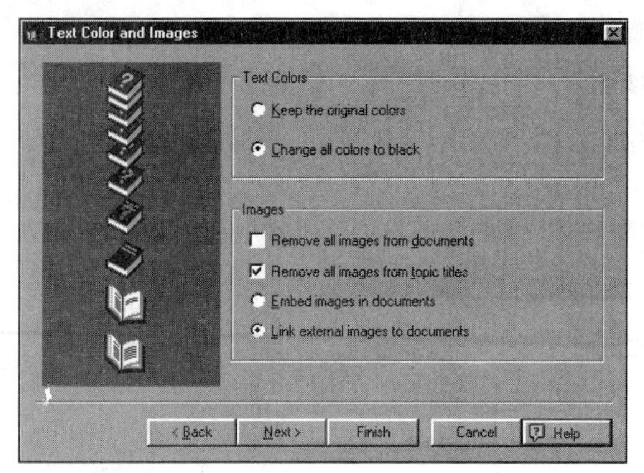

Figure 15-10: The Text Color and Images screen

6. Make sure that you link external images to the documents so that all the figures are linked to the topics. Set any other options on this screen, and then click Next to display the Page Options screen (displayed in Figure 15-11).

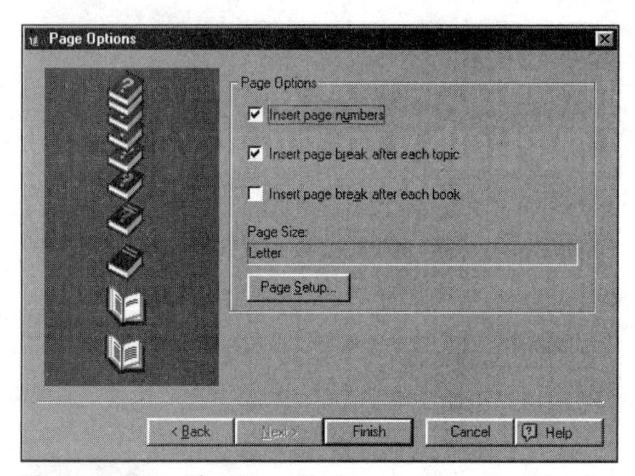

Figure 15-11: The Page Options screen

7. Set any options on this screen, and then click Finish. RoboHELP HTML generates the individual Word files from the HTM files in the HTML Help project.

Once the Word files have been created, you can then import or convert them as described earlier. Be sure that you check Convert References into Hyperlinks, Convert Index Entries into Keywords, and Convert to Help Images on the Import Options screen during the import process.

You'll need to do some manual checking and modification of the imported HTML files to complete the process to adjust the styles. If your HTML Help project uses a custom template for the printed documentation, you can use Word's style features to copy the appropriate styles. You'll also need to create a CNT file for the resulting WinHelp file, as RoboHELP won't convert the HTML table of contents file (HHC) to a CNT file. Once the documents have been imported to a new WinHelp project, you can use the TOC Composer to create a new CNT file.

Importing map files

Although you can attach map files using a `#include` statement in the HPJ file, you may prefer to import an external map file into your WinHelp project.

To import a map file, do the following:

1. In the RoboHELP Explorer, select the File ➪ Import ➪ Map File command. The Import Map File screen appears (shown in Figure 15-12).

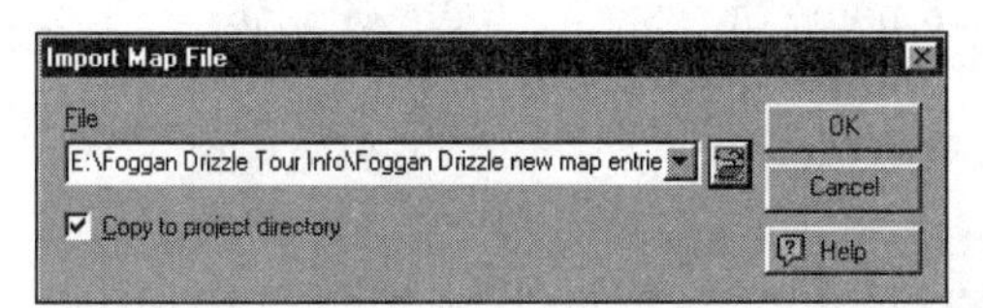

Figure 15-12: The Import Map File screen

2. Enter the name of the map file in the File field. As when you imported a Word document, checking Copy to project directory (the default) copies the map file to the project folder for the online help project. Click OK to import the map file.

Maintaining Separate Style Sheets

Depending on your company's requirements, you will probably want to have several style sheets for different types of online help. For example, the online help for the company's main product line is likely to have a different look and feel from that of tutorial help or online help for marketing purposes.

The ROBOHELP.DOT template contains the styles used by RoboHELP, as well as several internal macros necessary for RoboHELP to work in Word. However, RoboHELP expects to find the ROBOHELP.DOT template by name attached to RoboHELP documents. What you need to do is create multiple copies of ROBOHELP.DOT and then swap them in as you need them.

To create customized versions of ROBOHELP.DOT, do the following:

1. In the Windows Explorer, go to the templates folder in Word and create a new subfolder for each version of ROBOHELP.DOT you want to create. Name the subdirectories appropriately; for example, "Main," "Tutorial," and "Marketing." Also create a subfolder named "Original."
2. Copy ROBOHELP.DOT to each subfolder.
3. Open each copy of ROBOHELP.DOT in Word and modify the styles. Save the files. Don't modify the ROBOHELP.DOT file in the Original subfolder.

Be sure that all macro virus detection features are turned off in Word before you open the ROBOHELP.DOT files. Saving the ROBOHELP.DOT file with macro virus detection turned on will damage the ability of the ROBOHELP.DOT file to work.

Once you've created the versions of the ROBOHELP.DOT files, you can use them to create new WinHelp projects as follows:

1. In the Windows Explorer, rename the existing ROBOHELP.DOT file in the Word template folder to ROBOHELP.DOT.SAV.
2. Copy the new ROBOHELP.DOT file from the appropriate subfolder to the Word template folder.
3. Create the WinHelp project as normal. RoboHELP will use the styles in the new ROBOHELP.DOT file.
4. When you've created the new WinHelp project, delete the ROBOHELP.DOT file you just copied to the Word template folder and then rename the ROBOHELP.DOT.SAV file back to ROBOHELP.DOT.

You should never modify the copy of the ROBOHELP.DOT file in the Original subfolder. It is there for backup purposes in case you accidentally overwrite the primary ROBOHELP.DOT file.

As an alternative to swapping ROBOHELP.DOT files, you may be able to just copy a set of styles to the main ROBOHELP.DOT file with the Style Organizer in Word. You can use the Style Organizer to copy styles from a document or template to another document or template. This is also useful for transferring styles from previous versions of RoboHELP. See the Microsoft Word documentation for information on how to use the Style Organizer.

Using Custom Project Templates

One of the ways in which you can ensure consistency while supporting your group's editing and presentation choices is to use custom project templates. A custom project template is not a DOT file; rather, it is a set of RoboHELP project files used for creating a new WinHelp project. When you start a WinHelp project using a custom project template, RoboHELP uses the options in the custom project templates to ensure that the online help will have a look and feel consistent with that of other help projects.

RoboHELP ships with two custom project templates that you can tailor to your company's specific requirements. You can set up a number of standard elements and project settings for your WinHelp project in a custom project template, including standardized and boilerplate topics and documents, keywords, image libraries, tables of contents, help window definitions, and so on. Because custom project templates are just model WinHelp projects, you can preset any option or feature you set or change in RoboHELP as part of creating a help project.

To modify a custom project template, do the following:

1. In the RoboHELP Explorer, select the File ➪ Open Project command, and then open one of the custom template HPJ files in the RoboHELP Office\RoboHELP\Template\Custom\Custom 1 and RoboHELP Office\RoboHELP\Template\Custom\Custom 2 folders. RoboHELP opens the custom project template like any other WinHelp project.
2. Make any changes to the project you want, just as you would to any other WinHelp project. Add topics, set options and styles, and so on.
3. When you are satisfied with your changes, save and close the project.

Now you need to modify the information that will appear on the screen when you select the custom project template, as follows:

1. In the folder for the custom project template you've just modified, open the TEMPLATE.HPR file in a text editor such as Notepad or WordPad.
2. In the `[NewWizardValues]` section, change `TemplateName` and `TemplateDescription` to reflect the changes you've made to the template. Figure 15-13 shows a sample of how this looks.

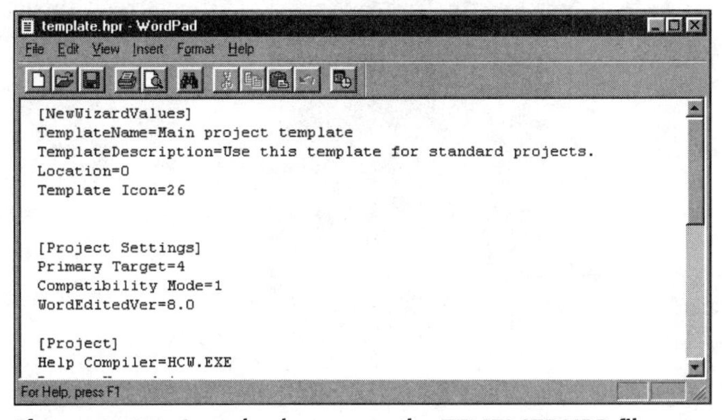

Figure 15-13: Sample changes to the TEMPLATE.HPR file

3. When you are satisfied with your changes, save the TEMPLATE.HPR file and exit the text editor.

It's a good idea to check your work by quickly creating a new project using the modified custom project template as follows:

1. In the RoboHELP Explorer, select the File ➪ New ➪ Project command. The New Project screen appears (shown in Figure 15-14).

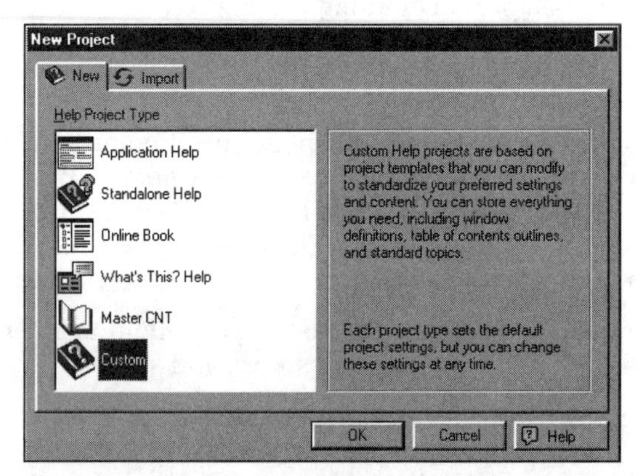

Figure 15-14: The New Project screen

2. Select Custom from the list and click OK. The New Project Wizard screen for the custom templates appears (as shown in Figure 15-15). You can see the changes shown in Figure 15-13 reflected in the first custom project template in this figure.

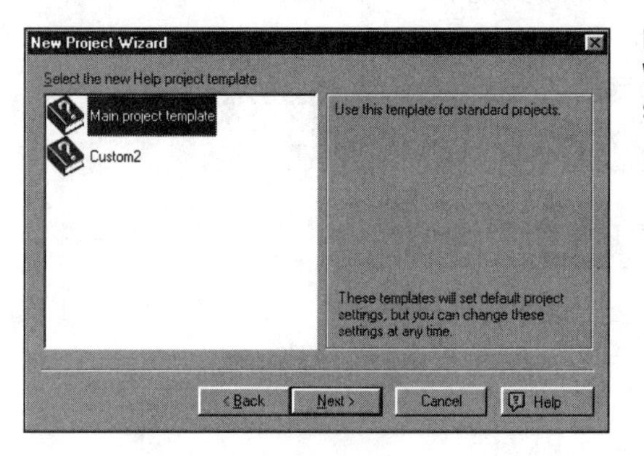

Figure 15-15: The New Project Wizard screen showing the standard custom templates

3. Select a custom template, click Next, and then continue with the new WinHelp project creation process as normal. RoboHELP will create the new project using the defaults in the custom project template you selected.

4. Check the features, topics, and options in the new project. You can always modify the custom project template further to refine and enhance the features in the custom project template.

You can change the order in which the custom project templates appear in the New Project Wizard screen by adjusting the Location option in the TEMPLATE.HPR file. This is the only option, other than `TemplateName` and `TemplateDescription`, that you should change in this file.

Most workgroups will need only one or two custom project templates for their WinHelp projects, but you can always add another, as follows:

1. In the Windows Explorer, copy one of the existing custom project template folders to a new folder (such as Custom3). You can copy one of the default custom project templates or you can copy a custom project template that you have already modified so you can build on the changes already in place.

Custom project templates must be stored within the \Template\Custom folder for RoboHELP to find them when you are creating a new WinHelp project.

2. In the new custom project template, make any changes to the defaults and information that you wish. You should also be sure to change the information in the TEMPLATE.HPR file; otherwise, the new custom project template will have the same name as the custom project template from which you copied it.

When you next start a new WinHelp project using custom project templates, you'll see the new custom project template added to the list, as shown in Figure 15-16.

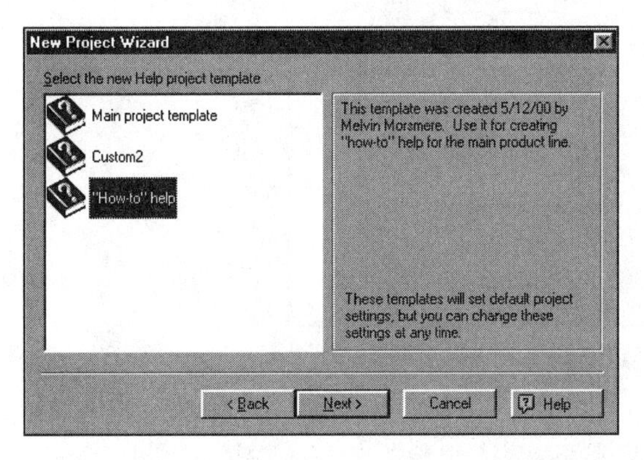

Figure 15-16: New custom project template added to the list

Custom project templates can be distributed to your workgroup by distributing them to each of the members of the team for copying into the \Template\Custom folders on their machines or by sharing the drive with the files across your network.

Creating online books

Online books are a special type of custom project templates offered by RoboHELP. These are templates for creating WinHelp with contents, index, and search tabs displayed in a WinHelp 2000 format. The various online book templates that accompany RoboHELP are:

- **Blank:** Sets up help in an online book format but doesn't add any predefined topics.
- **Application help:** Sets up an online book for application help, including sample topics for introduction to the product, contact information, product tutorial, and troubleshooting information.
- **Policies and Procedures:** Sets up an online book for a policies and procedures manual, including a sample company logo and sample overview topics, HR topics, a list of frequently asked questions, and a company phone list.
- **Textbook or Reference Manual:** Sets up an online book for an online textbook or reference manual, including sample topics for the front matter such as a foreword and information about the author, a chapter, appendixes, and a glossary.

Figure 15-17 shows a sample online book in policies and procedures style. Note the sample company logo appearing in the topic header.

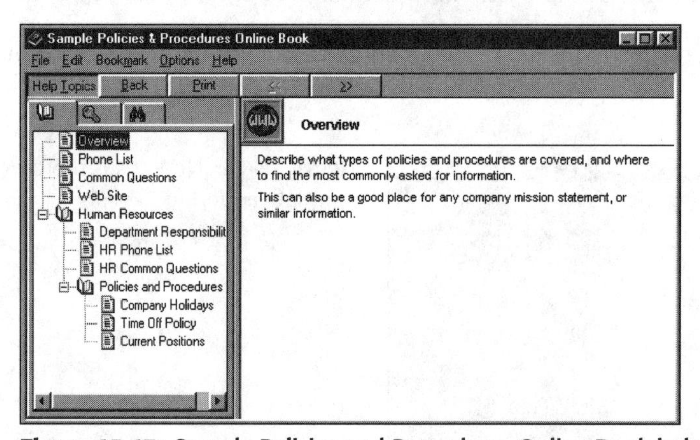

Figure 15-17: Sample Policies and Procedures Online Book help

As with the custom project templates, you can modify an existing online book to customize it for your company's specific needs. The template files for the online books are located in the \RoboHELP Office\RoboHELP\Template\OnlnBook\ folder. You can also add a new online book format using the same procedure for adding a new custom project template. Be sure to update the HPR file to reflect the name and description of the new online book template.

Modifying and creating other RoboHELP templates

You can modify any of the other RoboHELP templates or create new ones using the same procedures as described earlier for custom project templates. Always be sure to back up the existing templates before modifying them in case you want to revert to the original defaults.

Tracking Work with RoboHELP

RoboHELP provides several tools for tracking the work of each team member. You can track information on an online help project's status, topic priority, help authors, and the estimated hours for each topic. RoboHELP even provides a to-do list you can use to track tasks you need to do. These features are useful for identifying who's working on a given piece, providing an audit trail of work, and building performance statistics and metrics for estimating future projects.

Entering tracking information can be a valuable project management tool. For example, if you have metrics for estimating the time to completion for topics, you can enter estimate times for the outstanding topics and get a good idea of the resources needed to complete the project in a given time. Similarly, almost all RoboHELP reports will let you report on topics and tasks assigned to a specific author. You can use such reports for tracking the progress of specific writers and reapportion tasks to balance the workload.

Setting Topic Status Defaults

You may find it helpful to first set defaults for the help author, priority, or time, as follows:

1. Select the RoboHELP ⇨ Options command, and then select the Topic Defaults tab. Figure 15-18 shows the Topic Defaults tab with sample default information in the fields.
2. Enter information in the fields as follows:
   - **Topic ID Prefix:** Enter the default topic ID. The text you enter here will precede each of the topic context strings. Check the associated Prefix Topic ID with File Name box to include the file name in the topic ID.

The recommended default for this field is IDH_. The WinHelp compiler checks topics that begin with IDH_ to make sure that they have map numbers assigned.

   - **Author:** Enter the default author or select a name from the drop-down list. All topics created after this will have the entry in this field listed as the default author.

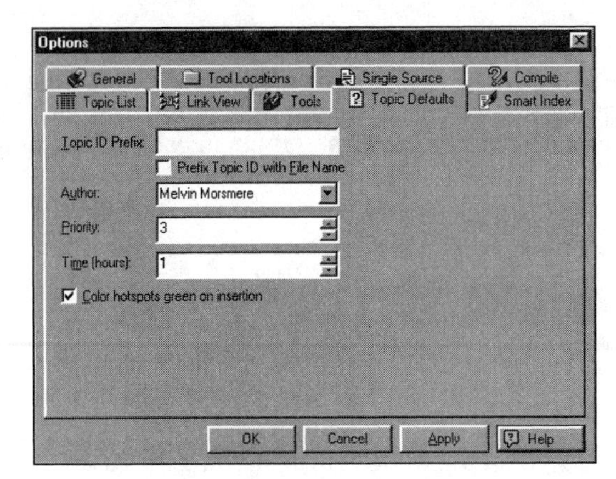

Figure 15-18: The Topic Defaults tab of the RoboHELP Options screen

Entering an author name in this field also stores the author's name in the drop-down list (which is initially empty). If you have RoboHELP installed on several different workstations in your group, you'll need to add the author names for each individual copy of RoboHELP.

- **Priority:** Enter the default priority or scroll to select the priority. All topics created after this will have the entry in this field listed as the default priority. (Multiple topics can have the same priority.)
- **Time (hours):** Enter the default estimated time to complete this topic or scroll to select the time in hours. All topics created after this will have the entry in this field listed as the default time. (Multiple topics can have the same estimated time.)
- **Color hotspots green on insertion:** Check this box (the default) to color hotspots green as the default.

3. When you are satisfied with your entries, click OK.

Once you have entered the default options on this screen, any new topics will have the default attributes you've entered.

Changing Topic Status Information for Individual Topics

However, you can also view and adjust the status, author, and properties for individual topics as follows:

1. In the RoboHELP Explorer Project Manager, right-click the topic you want to assign and select Properties from the right-click menu. (You can also position the cursor in a topic and select the Edit ➪ Topic Properties command in Word.) When the Topic Properties screen appears, select the Status tab, as shown in Figure 15-19.

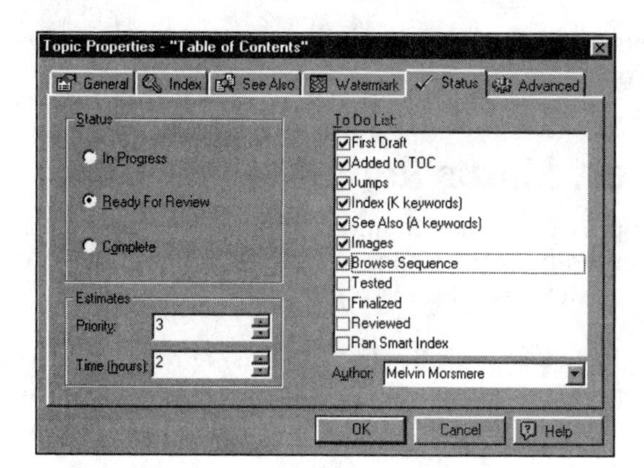

Figure 15-19: The Status tab on the Topic Properties screen

2. Enter information in the fields as follows:
   - **Status:** Select a status for the topic. You can change the topic status as needed. This status appears on the Project Status report (described later in this chapter).
   - **Priority:** Enter a priority for the topic or select a priority from the drop-down list.
   - **Time:** Enter the estimated time to completion for the topic.
   - **To Do List:** Check the boxes for the tasks that have been completed for this topic. The task completion information is reported on the Project Status report (described later in this chapter).

When you run the Smart Index Wizard, RoboHELP automatically checks the Smart Index Wizard box in the To Do list for you.

   - **Author:** Enter the name or initials for the author assigned for this topic or select an author's name from the drop-down list.

3. When you are satisfied with your entries, click OK.

You can assign a help author or change the status or priority (but not the estimated time to completion) for a group of topics as follows:

1. Highlight the topics in the RoboHELP Explorer Topic List.
2. Right-click the selected topics and select Status, Author, or Priority from the right-click menu. Enter the appropriate information in the small screen that appears for that option.
3. When you are satisfied with your entries, click OK. RoboHELP will update the highlighted topics. (This may take a while if you have selected a large number of topics.)

You can change the various options on the Status tab as necessary at any time. They are simply for external reporting and status checking.

Printing the Project Status Report

The Project Status report provides you with information about the topic status and priority information entered for the topics, as well as the overall status of the WinHelp project. To generate a Project Status report, do the following:

✦ In the RoboHELP Explorer, select the Tools ➪ Reports ➪ Project Status command. The Project Status report is displayed on the screen. Figure 15-20 shows part of a report for a single help author, Melvin Morsmere.

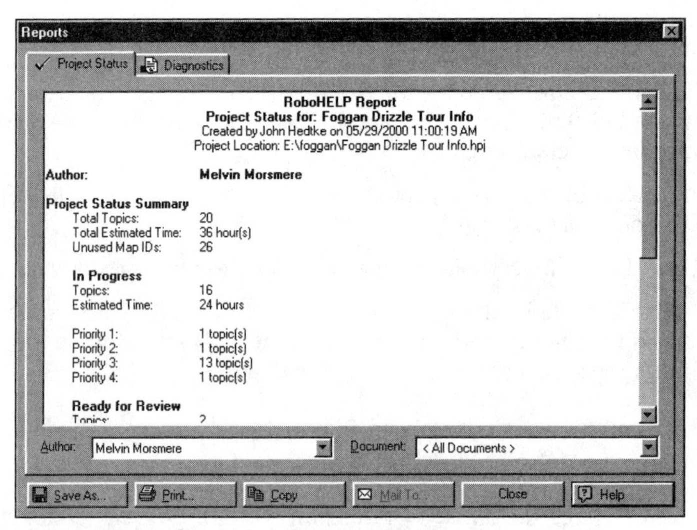

Figure 15-20: The Project Status report

Depending on the number of authors you have assigned to a project, you may want to run individual Project Status reports for each author on a regular basis for progress tracking. You can also run a Project Status report for all authors and for the unassigned topics.

Using Build Tags

Many large online help projects are released in multiple versions. For example, you may want to release an online help project for the main product release, and then several different versions for product versions with modules, and maybe even a custom version for a large corporate client.

There are several ways to accomplish this. The most common is to maintain separate online help projects for each version. Although this requires little planning, you must spend a lot of extra time maintaining parallel projects. You can also assemble each version out of separate project modules, but this may be impractical if the changes require your swapping many different modules in and out. In a case like this, the best solution may be to use build tags.

You can use a footnote with the @ symbol to enter comment text about a topic. This can be particularly useful for tracking changes to a specific topic or entering information about topics that should be included or excluded to create a specific version of the online help file.

Build tags are an internal code assigned to each topic using an asterisk (*) footnote symbol. When you compile the online help project, you can specify the build tags to include in the compile. The WinHelp compiler then looks for the specified build tags and then uses only those topics in the finished help file. With judicious assignment of build tags to topics, you can maintain one set of source files but use them to compile a wide variety of different help files.

Using build tags to include selected modules in the finished help file is also known as *conditional compiling.*

For example, you may want to use build tags to create a stripped-down version of the help file as a demo. You might also use build tags to provide minimal help for all but one or two modules of a file. This would have applications for creating module-level help that shows the relationship to the main product as well as for testing; a stripped-down version of the help file could be tested in pieces.

Build tags can also be used to create online help for different levels of users. The basic version of the help file might be aimed at the end-user while another version would also have system-level information on configuring and maintaining the product. Finally, you can use build tags to exclude portions of the help file for parts of a product that aren't currently enabled.

Setting Default Build Tags

When you use build tags, you'll usually have one main build tag for most of the topics in an online help project, after which you can add additional build tags for topics in specific modules.

To set a default build tag, do the following:

1. In the RoboHELP Explorer Project Manager, open the Topics tab. Right-click on the document in the list for which you want to set a default build tag and select Properties from the right-click menu. The Document Properties screen appears (shown in Figure 15-21).

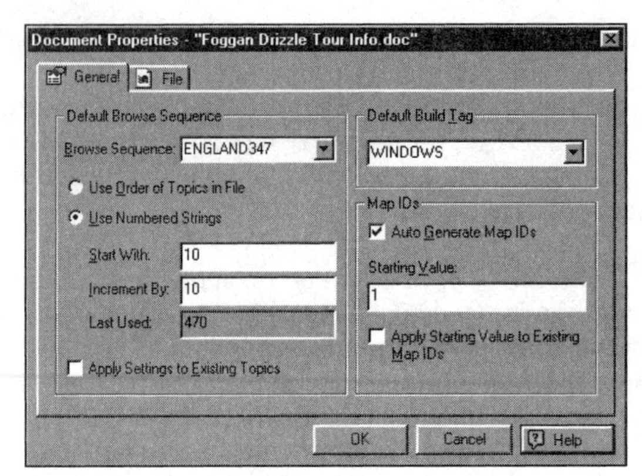

Figure 15-21: The Document Properties screen

2. Enter the build tag in Default Build Tag or select an entry from the drop-down list. Build tags can be up to 32 characters. They are not case sensitive. (The system default build tag is WINDOWS, but you can use any default build tag you wish.)

3. When you are satisfied with your entries, click OK.

All new topics created from this point on will use this build tag as the default.

Adding Build Tags to Topics

Use this procedure to create a new build tag. You can create build tags from RoboHELP Explorer's Project Manager (Project tab) or from the Topic Properties dialog. Once you create a build tag, you can select the build tag as the default for new topics in a Help document or add it to specific topics.

To assign a build tag to a topic, do the following:

1. In the RoboHELP Explorer Project Manager, right-click the topic you want to assign and select Properties from the right-click menu. (You can also position the cursor in a topic and select the Edit ➪ Topic Properties command in Word.) When the Topic Properties screen appears, select the Advanced tab, as shown in Figure 15-22.

2. Check the boxes for the build tags you want to assign to the topic in the Build Tag list. You can add new build tags on the fly by entering the new build tag in the field below the Build Tags list and clicking Add.

You can assign more than one build tag to a topic. This lets you include topics in multiple versions.

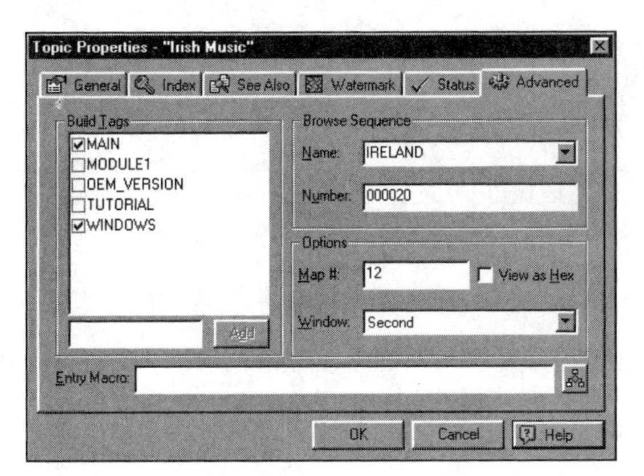

Figure 15-22: The Advanced tab on the Topic Properties screen

3. When you are satisfied with your entries, click OK.

If you need a new build tag but don't want to associate it with a topic right away, you can also create it as follows:

✦ In the RoboHELP Explorer Project Manager, right-click the Build Tags folder (within the Project folder) and select New Build Tag from the right-click menu. Enter the new build tag in single field on the New Build Tags screen that appears (not shown) and click OK.

The new build tag will appear on the list of build tags in the Advanced tab of the Topic Properties screen. You can also delete build tags from the project by right-clicking the build tag in the Build Tags folder and selecting Delete from the right-click menu.

You can assign one or more build tags to a group of topics as follows:

1. Highlight the topics in the RoboHELP Explorer Topic List.
2. Right-click the selected topics and select Build Tag from the right-click menu. The Build Tags screen appears (shown in Figure 15-23).

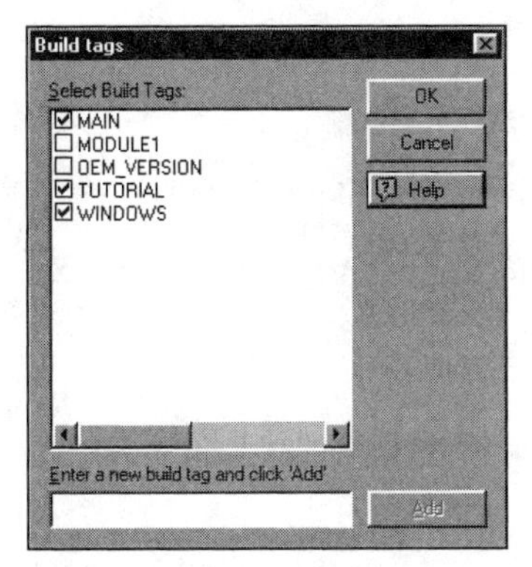

Figure 15-23: The Build Tags screen

3. Check the boxes for the build tags you want to assign to the topics. You can add new build tags by entering the build tag in the field at the bottom of the screen and clicking Add.
4. When you are satisfied with your entries, click OK. RoboHELP will update the highlighted topics with the build tag information you've specified. (This may take a while if you have selected a large number of topics.)

Once you've set build tags, you can choose which tags to compile as follows:

1. In the RoboHELP Explorer, select the File ➪ Project Settings command. (You can also select the RoboHELP ➪ Project Settings command in Word.) Click the Advanced tab. Figure 15-24 shows the Advanced tab.

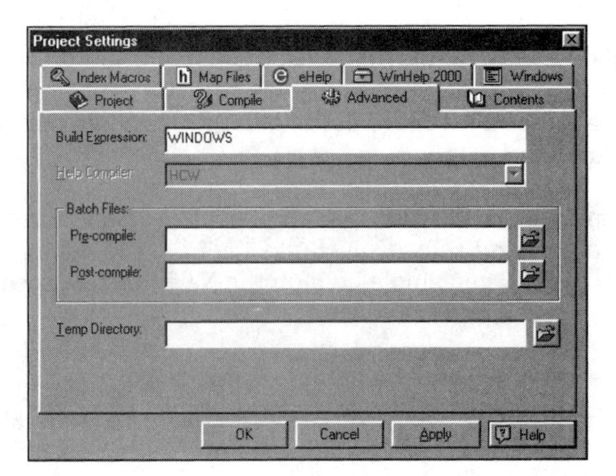

Figure 15-24: The Advanced tab on the Project Settings screen

2. Enter information in the fields as follows:
   - **Build Expression:** Enter the build expression (one or more build tags you want to compile). Any topics without build tags are automatically included. You can enter a build expression containing a single build tag or a combination of build tags using standard Boolean operators, as shown in Table 15-2.
   - **Help Compiler:** This display-only field shows you the WinHelp compiler that will be used to compile the project.
   - **Batch Files:** Enter the name of the DOS batch files you want to run before or after compiling the file. You might use these fields for copying specific modules to the project folder and then resetting them after the compile.

- **Temp Directory:** Enter the name of the folder to use for the temporary files for the compile process. (If you leave this blank, the compiler will use the standard Windows\TEMP folder.)

3. When you are satisfied with your entries, click OK. RoboHELP updates the `[BUILDTAGS]` section of the HPJ file with the build tags you've entered.

Table 15-2
Build Expressions

Build Expression You Want to Create	***Sample Build Expression***	***Effect***
<build tag>	WINDOW	Compiles all topics with the build tag WINDOWS, as well as any topics without build tags.
<build tag> OR <build tag>	WINDOW | MAIN	Compiles all topics with the build tag WINDOWS or the build tag MAIN, as well as any topics without build tags. (This is an inclusive `OR` rather than an exclusive `OR`.)
<build tag> AND <build tag>	WINDOW & MAIN	Compiles all topics that have *both* the WINDOWS and MAIN build tags, as well as any topics without build tags.
NOT <build tag>	~WINDOW	Excludes all topics that have the WINDOWS build tag and compiles all other topics.

You can also create more complex build expressions (WINDOW ! MAIN ! MODULE1 or WINDOW & MAIN | MODULE1) but these will require careful testing to make sure that you're including the build tag combinations you're after.

It's important to remember that using build tags requires additional testing. For example, jumps, popups, macros, context-sensitive help links, buttons, and table of contents entries that refer to topics that aren't in the finished help file will display a "Topic Not Found" error like any other broken link. However, you won't see the topic in the Broken Links folder in the RoboHELP Explorer Project Manager because the link still exists in the source files. You can display the build tags associated with topics on the RoboHELP Explorer Topic List by adding the Build Tags column to the list of displayed columns.

Releasing WinHelp Files

Many of the final tasks for releasing WinHelp files are similar to those having to do with any other documentation release. The online help must be checked for spelling and grammar as well as compliance with the company style for layout and presentation. The project must also be tested to the limits and standards normally applied to documentation.

However, online help also has some specific requirements for preparing it for release. This section will show you how to prepare and release your online help project.

Fixing Broken Links

The first step in preparing a project for release is to check for broken links. You can do this by opening the Broken Links folder in the RoboHELP Explorer Project Manager. Resolve any outstanding problems.

If you have a lot of broken links, you can also generate the Broken Links report, as follows:

✦ In the RoboHELP Explorer, select the Tools ➪ Reports ➪ Broken Links command. The Broken Links report appears. Figure 15-26 shows a sample Broken Links report.

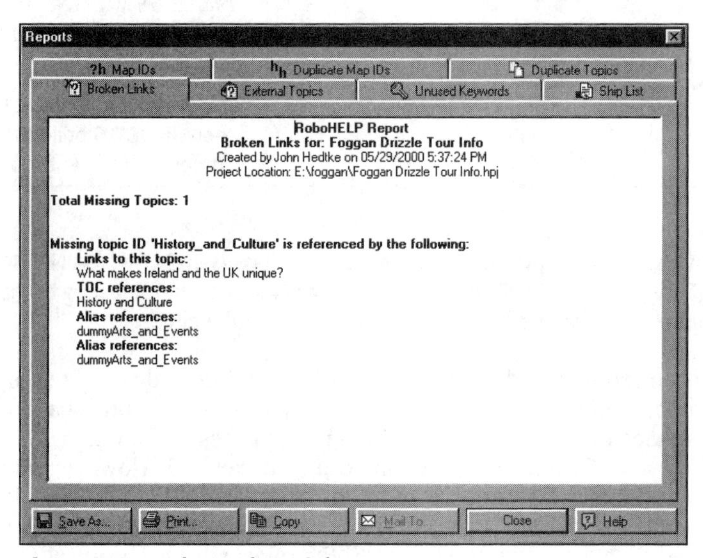

Figure 15-25: The Broken Links report

Fixing Unreferenced Topics

Once you've resolved any outstanding broken links, you need to make sure that all the topics can be reached by the user. The Unreferenced Topics report displays information on any topics that aren't accessible with the standard jumps, popups, table of contents and index entries, A-links, aliases, or context-sensitive help.

To generate an Unreferenced Topics report, do the following:

✦ In the RoboHELP Explorer, select the Tools ➪ Reports ➪ Unreferenced Topics command. The Unreferenced Topics report appears. Figure 15-26 shows a sample Unreferenced Topics report.

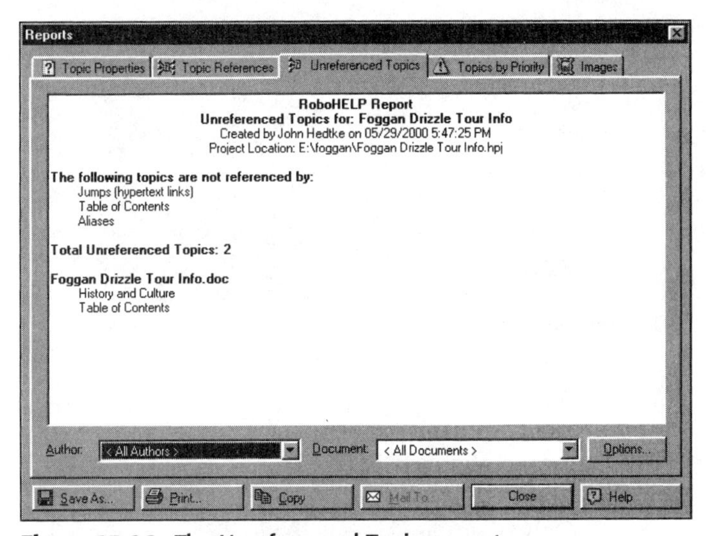

Figure 15-26: The Unreferenced Topics report

You may not want for some topics to be easily accessible by the users. For example, you may want to imbed a change log in a beta version of a help file that isn't directly accessible by the users but can be triggered by entering a specific map ID or by using the full-text search feature to find a key phrase.

Printing the Diagnostics Report

The Diagnostics report is used for reporting on a wide variety of possible error conditions such as missing files, documents, or images, unused or duplicate map IDs, and so on.

To generate a Diagnostics report, do the following:

1. In the RoboHELP Explorer, select the Tools ➪ Reports ➪ Diagnostics command. The Diagnostics report appears. Figure 15-27 shows a sample Diagnostics report.

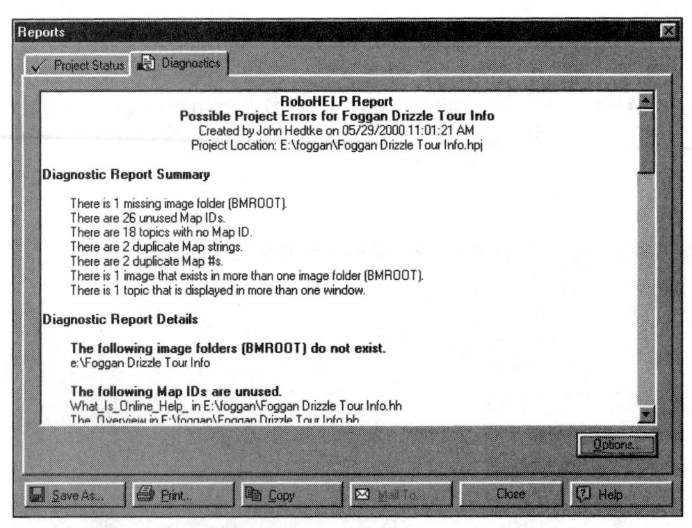

Figure 15-27: The Diagnostics report

2. You can set the options that the Diagnostics report displays by clicking Options at the lower right of the report screen. The Diagnostic Report Options screen appears (shown in Figure 15-28).

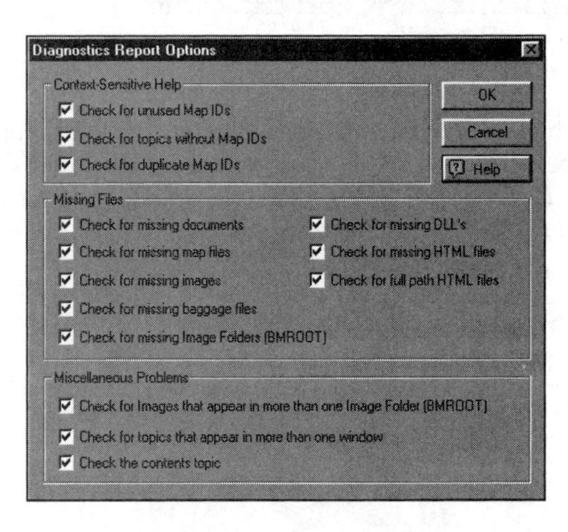

Figure 15-28: The Diagnostics Report Options screen

3. Check the options you want to include on the Diagnostics report. (The default is for all options to be selected.) When you are satisfied with your selections, click OK.

Using RoboHELP Testing Options

RoboHELP has several testing options you can add as part of the compile process. This section will show you how to use ActiveEdit and Help Author Mode.

Using ActiveEdit with WinHelp files

You've already seen how to use ActiveEdit with What's This? help. ActiveEdit works similarly with WinHelp files.

To turn on ActiveEdit, do the following:

1. In the RoboHELP Explorer, select the File ➪ Project Settings command. (You can also select the RoboHELP ➪ Project Settings command in Word.) Click the Compile tab. The Compile tab appears, as shown in Figure 15-29.

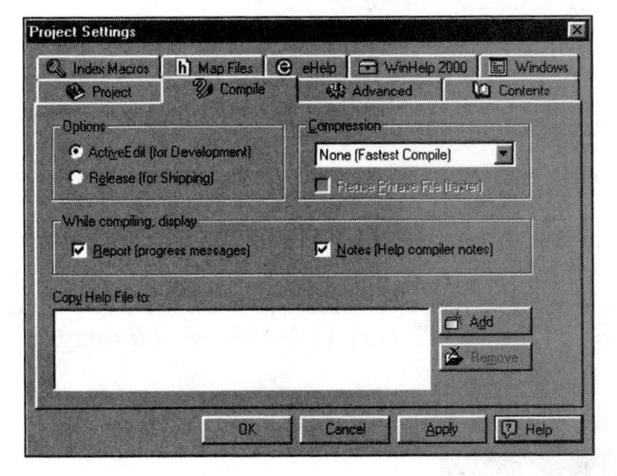

Figure 15-29: The Compile tab on the Project Settings screen

2. Select the ActiveEdit (for Development) option and click OK.
3. Compile the WinHelp file as normal.

When you have the ActiveEdit option selected, an ActiveEdit button appears on the WinHelp button bar. At any time, you can click the ActiveEdit button in the compiled WinHelp file and jump directly to the topic in the source file.

Using Help Author mode

Whereas ActiveEdit lets you quickly navigate to the topic entry in the source file, Help Author mode lets you get additional information about the construction of the WinHelp file itself.

To turn on Help Author mode, do the following:

1. In the RoboHELP Explorer, select the Tools ➪ Option command. (You can also select the RoboHELP ➪ Options command in Word.) Click the Compile tab. The Compile tab appears, as shown in Figure 15-30.

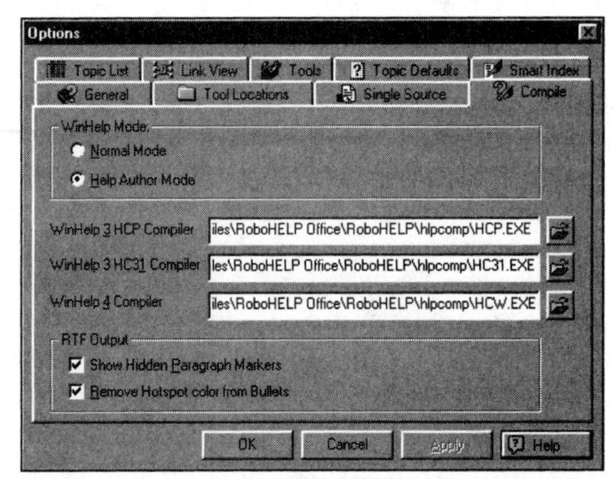

Figure 15-30: The Compile tab on the Options screen

2. Select the Help Author Mode option and click OK.
3. Compile the WinHelp file as normal.

When you have the Help Author mode option selected, the topic ID of the topic being displayed appears in the title bar. You can display information about the topic by right-clicking and selecting Topic Information from the right-click menu. The Topic Information screen (shown in Figure 15-31) shows information about the topic.

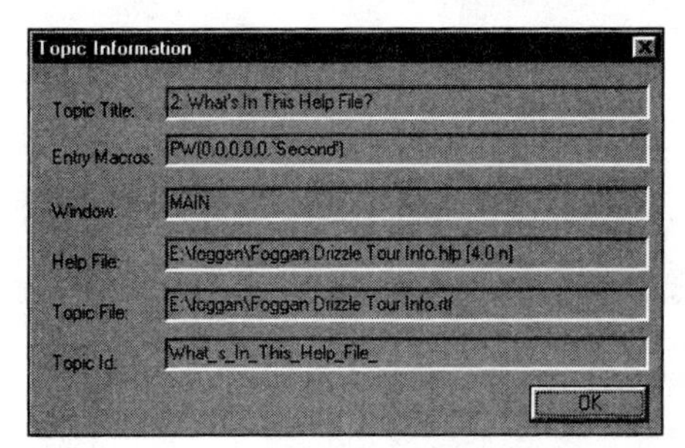

Figure 15-31: The Topic Information screen

Another feature of Help Author mode is the ability to prompt you before taking action when you click a hotspot. Right-click in a topic and select Ask on Hotspots in the right-click menu. Subsequently, when you click a hotspot, RoboHELP will display a small screen, such as the one shown in Figure 15-32, that shows information about the hotspot.

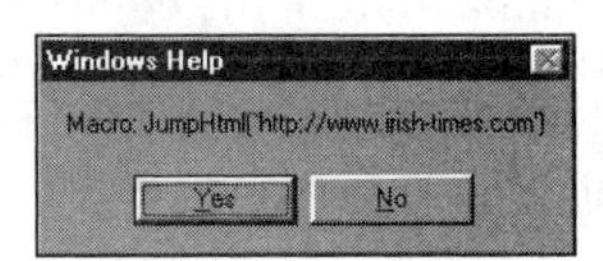

Figure 15-32: The Windows Help screen showing jump information

You can complete the hotspot action by clicking Yes.

ActiveEdit and Help Author mode can be used together or separately. You can also turn them on and off as needed.

Setting Final Compile Options

When you are in the final testing phase for your online help, you need to set your online help compile options for a released version of the project.

To set the final compiler options, do the following:

1. In the RoboHELP Explorer, select the File ➪ Project Settings command. (You can also select the RoboHELP ➪ Project Settings command in Word.) Click the Project tab. Figure 15-33 shows the Project tab.

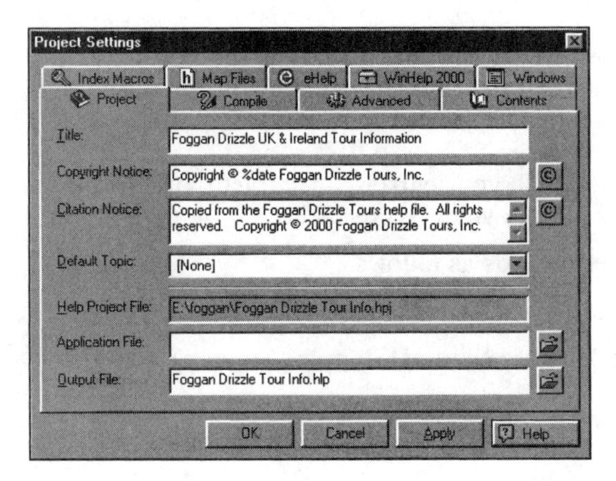

Figure 15-33: The Project tab on the Project Settings screen

2. Enter information in the fields as follows:

   - **Title:** Enter the title for the released WinHelp file in this field. (This title is used only if you haven't entered a title in the Contents tab of the Project Settings screen.)
   - **Copyright Notice:** Enter the copyright information that will appear when the users select the Help ⇨ Version command from the compiled WinHelp file. Copyright notices can be up to 255 characters in length. Click the button to the right of this field to insert the copyright symbol ((c)). You can include the date the WinHelp file was compiled by inserting %date as shown in Figure 15-29.
   - **Citation Notice:** Enter the text to append to selections that are copied from the WinHelp file or printed from the WinHelp file. You can use this option to add copyright notices, version information, and so on. The text in the citation can be up to 2000 characters or 1000 characters if you are using a DBCS language. Click the button to the right of this field to insert the copyright symbol ((c)).

The citation notice text not appended to text copied from a context-sensitive popup window.

   - **Default Topic:** Enter the topic ID for the default topic to be displayed if the CNT file cannot be found or opened.
   - **Help Project File:** This display-only field shows the HPJ file for the project.
   - **Application File:** Enter the path for the associated program file if this is a context-sensitive help file. RoboHELP uses this as a shortcut for running the program. Click the button to the right of the field to browse your folders.
   - **Output File:** Enter the name of the WinHelp file. The default is the name of the WinHelp file for the project. Click the button to the right of the field to browse your folders and specify a different location.

3. When you are satisfied with your entries, click the Compile tab. The Compile tab appears, as shown in Figure 15-34.

4. Enter information in the fields as follows:

   - **Options:** Select Release (for Shipping).
   - **Compression:** Select Maximum (Shipping Version) from the drop-down list.

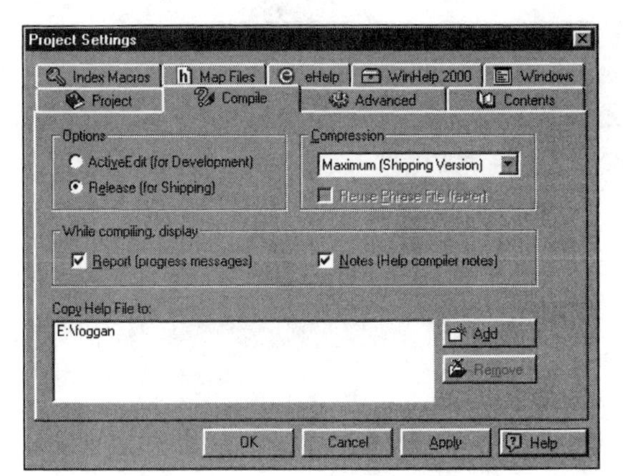

Figure 15-34: The Compile tab on the Project Settings screen

For more information on compression, see Chapter 3, "Creating Your First WinHelp Project."

- **When compiling, display:** Check the boxes for reports and notes. When selected, the report option displays progress messages during the compile and the notes option displays notes from the help compiler. (It's a good idea to display as much information as you can during the compile.)
- **Copy Help File to:** Click Add to enter a folder to copy the compiled WinHelp file to. You can use this option to compile the WinHelp and automatically distribute it to other locations (such as a shared drive) on the network.

5. When you are satisfied with your entries, click OK.

Printing a Ship List

When the final version of the WinHelp file has been produced, you'll probably need to hand it off to the production group in your company. You can generate a ship list report that identifies all the files that must accompany the final WinHelp file.

To generate a Ship List report, do the following:

✦ In the RoboHELP Explorer, select the Tools ➪ Reports ➪ Ship List command. The Ship List report appears. Figure 15-35 shows a sample Ship List report.

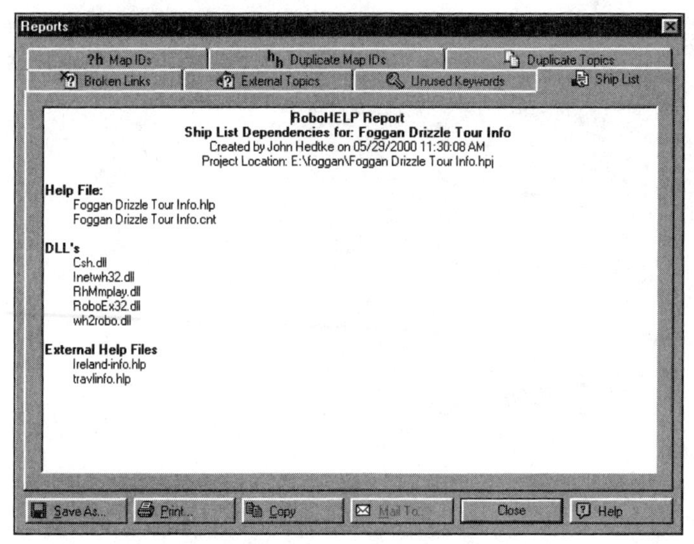

Figure 15-35: The Ship List report

As you can see, the Ship List report lists the files that must accompany the WinHelp file. You may also want to keep a copy of this report to create an audit trail for the project.

Wrapping Up

Once the final files are handed off for production, you should do some final wrapping up for the project:

✦ Back up all the source files and supporting files — including HPJs, internal RoboHELP files, images, DLLs, AVIs, and related programs used specifically by the online help — in a release folder on your network. Also burn a CD for archival purposes of these files.

✦ Generate and print any reports that may be necessary for subsequent auditing and tracking purposes.

✦ Schedule a postmortem analysis meeting with the team members. Discuss successes and problems encountered during the project. Identify ways in which the next online help project can be more efficient and effective.

Summary

This chapter has shown you how to manage large online help projects. You first saw how to back up your online help projects and use source control to track the progress on a project. The chapter then showed you how to convert and import existing documents and projects into your WinHelp project. You next saw how to use style sheets and custom project templates to make your online help more consistent. The chapter then discussed ways to enter and track topic status information. After this, you learned how to use build tags. The chapter concluded with a section on how to perform final testing of your WinHelp project and release it to production.

Congratulations! With this chapter, you've completed the section of the book that focuses on creating WinHelp with RoboHELP 2000. The following chapters introduce you to the basics of creating HTML Help.

✦ ✦ ✦

Creating HTML Help

PART

IV

✦ ✦ ✦ ✦

In This Part

✦ ✦ ✦ ✦

CHAPTER 16

What Is HTML Help?

In This Chapter

What is HTML Help?

HTML Help versus WinHelp

How HTML creates HTML Help

Anatomy of a project file

The HTML Help window

Steps for creating successful HTML Help

This chapter introduces you to the world of HTML Help. You'll learn about the history of HTML Help, as well as the likely future. You'll learn how and when to use HTML Help instead of WinHelp. After being introduced to the basics of HTML and the other Web-based languages that make up HTML Help, you'll also learn how to create HTML Help.

This section is about creating HTML Help only. For information about creating WinHelp, see Part II, "Creating WinHelp."

Introducing HTML Help

HTML Help is a help system created by Microsoft based on the Hypertext Markup Language (HTML). HTML's growing popularity led to its eventual status as the *lingua franca* of the World Wide Web. Information in HTML format can be displayed on any computer, regardless of platform.

HTML was developed in the early 1980s by a group called CERN as they tried to find a quick and simple way to display text on a computer far away, independent of the type of operating system it is running. This independence led to the massive growth of the Internet, because it no longer mattered what type of computer you were viewing the information from.

HTML also became very popular because it is simple. HTML is a subset of a very powerful and complicated language called Standard Generalized Markup Language (SGML); however, HTML retained the powerful independence that SGML is famous for while employing a simpler set of codes specifically designed for displaying text and images.

The power of HTML has been retained in the new help system, HTML Help. HTML Help allows you to create help with all of the most popular HTML functions, enabling you to get your point across with the power of HTML.

During the development of Windows 98, Microsoft decided to use HTML as a standard for online help. The versatility of HTML far surpassed anything available with the standard WinHelp online help systems, and many help developers already had some familiarity with the basic theory of HTML. Thus, Microsoft HTML Help was born, and this is the basis for the HTML Help we create today.

Because HTML Help is based in large part on HTML, HTML Help also becomes *platform independent*. Platform independence means that you can create an HTML Help system and use it on any computer that has an HTML browser. The RoboHELP HTML engine adds to the platform independence allowing you to create not only Microsoft HTML Help, but also to create it for different types of help using the same information.

RoboHELP HTML quickly became a front-runner in creating the new HTML Help online help standard. RoboHELP HTML allows you to create HTML Help out of documents you already process, as well as documents you can create on the fly. RoboHELP HTML inserts HTML codes into your work when it compiles data into a help project, thereby completing the process quickly and painlessly.

To learn how to install RoboHELP HTML, see Appendix E, "Installing RoboHELP 2000."

The New World of HTML Help

By harnessing the power of HTML for online help systems, Microsoft made a decision that is radically changing online help. The WinHelp engines still exist in the Microsoft operating system, but HTML Help is the current standard in online help.

WinHelp was the standard for years, and has been used successfully by thousands of help developers, so the new online help standard, HTML Help, had to as easy to use and provide more features to become the new standard. Since its debut during the development of Microsoft Windows 98, HTML-based Help has taken over more than 50 percent of online help development and is still growing.

The differences between HTML Help and WinHelp are numerous, but not cumbersome. The RoboHELP HTML development space is much like the one you got used to in RoboHELP Classic, and much of the organization topics are the same. The greatest difference is that all HTML Help development takes place in RoboHELP HTML. Because of its WYSIWYG (What You See Is What You Get) interface, there is no need to develop your online help in Microsoft Word and then use RoboHELP to compile the files.

For an outline of how to organize and plan your HTML Help project, see Chapter 2, "What Makes Help 'Help'?"

Table 16-1 describes some of the major differences between WinHelp and HTML Help.

Table 16-1
HTML Help versus WinHelp

RoboHELP HTML	***WinHelp***
Developed in RoboHELP HTML using a WYSIWYG editor	Developed in Microsoft Word
Uses HTML tags to identify text	Uses footnotes to identify text
A new system used for Windows 98 and 2000	An older system developed for Windows 3.1 and 95
Uses Web scripting languages for advanced features	Uses word Macro language for advanced features
Preview as you edit, and compiled files look exactly like the preview	No on-the-fly preview and compiled files may look different than the preview

How HTML Creates HTML Help

HTML Help uses the combined talents of a cast of languages to get its job done. HTML-based help uses HTML as the base to create the files and format for the topic pages. Scripting languages such as Java and Visual Basic are added to this base to create extra functions such as popup windows, special effects, a table of contents, and other added features. Microsoft HTML Help uses HTML and Active X controls to create HTML Help.

The beauty of this technique is that HTML Help can take advantage of new features in both HTML and scripting. This upgradeability has already been harnessed. When HTML Help was first developed, the HTML standard was at 2.0. The HTML standard at this writing is 4.0, and RoboHELP HTML takes advantage of all the latest and greatest in the HTML standard.

HTML creates and formats the topic pages, the pages where all the text content of your topics goes. Scripting creates the help objects that we've all gotten used to using in WinHelp (the popup windows, the table of contents, and so on) as well as new features that make HTML Help so much more (favorites, dynamically updating lists, graphics special effects, and so on).

The way it works is straightforward: The HTML sets the form for the page, much as a style sheet sets the form for the way a word processing page looks. This formatting is accomplished using the standard HTML tags you would use for any HTML page. After the formatting has been set, the scripting you need is added to the page. For example, when you add a popup window, the scripting for that action is added to the HTML tags on the page. For the table of contents, a series of scripts and pages are built when you compile your HTML Help project, providing your users with a fully functional table of contents. It is important to remember that the HTML defines how the page looks, whereas the scripting defines special actions that happen on the page.

Cross-
Reference

For more information about HTML, see Appendix F, "HTML Quick List."

The HTML Help Viewer

Not only has the background of how help works changed with HTML Help. What your user sees has changed as well. WinHelp provided two windows, one containing topic information and one containing table of contents and index information. In HTML Help, all the help information can be found in just one window, the HTML Help Viewer window. Figure 16-1 shows a compiled HTML Help file as the help user sees it.

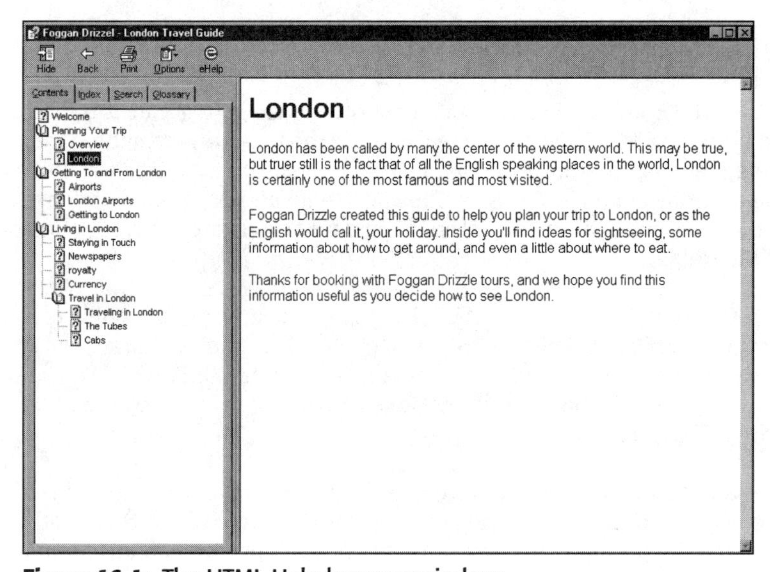
Foggan Drizzel - London Travel Guide
Hide
Back
Print
Options
eHelp
Contents
Index
Search
Glossary
Welcome
Planning Your Trip
Overview
London
Getting To and From London
Airports
London Airports
Getting to London
Living in London
Staying in Touch
Newspapers
royalty
Currency
Travel in London
Traveling in London
The Tubes
Cabs
London
London has been called by many the center of the western world. This may be true, but truer still is the fact that of all the English speaking places in the world, London is certainly one of the most famous and most visited.
Foggan Drizzle created this guide to help you plan your trip to London, or as the English would call it, your holiday. Inside you'll find ideas for sightseeing, some information about how to get around, and even a little about where to eat.
Thanks for booking with Foggan Drizzle tours, and we hope you find this information useful as you decide how to see London.

Figure 16-1: The HTML Help browser window

When you install RoboHELP HTML, the current version of Internet Explorer is installed at the same time. The Internet browser is the basis for your HTML Help system, since Internet Explorer includes the HTML Help Viewer by default. It is only logical that because your help information is now contained inside HTML tags and scripting languages, your information is now displayed using the Internet viewing tool, the browser.

Your users must have either HTML Help Viewer or Internet Explorer version 4.0 or later installed to run HTML Help. They do not need to use IE as their default browser. HTML Help just needs the viewer information in order for HTML Help to work. You can give your users the HTML Help Viewer with your HTML Help system if they do not have Internet Explorer installed.

As you can see from Figure 16-1, the browser contains all the parts of online help, the left side holds the table of contents, the index, the Search tab, and, if you choose, a Favorites tab. The right tab has the topic information your users need to get. On the top of the browser are the standard Internet navigation buttons. Table 16-2 lists all the buttons on the help browser.

Table 16-2
RoboHELP HTML Browser Buttons

Button	***Function***
Hide	Hide: Allows users to remove the left pane. When this is clicked, a Show button appears, allowing them to replace it.
Back	Back: Moves users back to the last topic page they accessed.
Print	Print: Prints the current topic.
Options	Options: Opens the options window allowing the user to set how the HTML Help topics display.
eHelp	eHelp: This is an optional button you can add that allows your users to get help online.

The advantage of using the browser as the basis for your help is twofold. First, you can be assured that most business users today are familiar with the Internet browser and comfortable working with it. Second, with the Internet browser as a basis, you can do many more things with your online help that you could not have accomplished before, using the power of scripting and HTML to create more interesting and interactive content.

Creating RoboHELP HTML Help

Now that you are familiar with the final product your users will see, you are ready to start planning your own RoboHELP HTML project.

For more information about planning your online help system, see Chapter 2, "What makes Help 'Help'?"

Single-sourcing of documentation has become a much sought-after ideal in the past several years, and RoboHELP HTML is fully functional as the sole creation environment for your help, regardless of the distribution method. You can choose to export any and all topic information out of RoboHELP HTML by using the options in the File menu. You can generate Microsoft Help, Web Help, Java Help and printed documentation using RoboHELP HTML.

Creating HTML Help is significantly different from creating WinHelp, in terms of both process and tools. Creating WinHelp was done with the combined talents of RoboHELP and Word. HTML Help creation happens with just one program: RoboHELP HTML. All of your information can be entered, or imported, into RoboHELP HTML, and then the remainder of your HTML Help project can be completed using the editors and tools in RoboHELP HTML itself.

For information about using these tools to create your first HTML Help project, see Chapter 18, "Creating Your First HTML Help Project."

This major difference between WinHelp and HTML Help is the steps you save with HTML Help. No longer do you need to work with two programs at once; now all you need to do is create your HTML Help project and it is ready to go without the translation step required with WinHelp.

Creating your HTML Help project in RoboHELP HTML also means you have total access to previews of your project without compiling, as any topic can be viewed at any time. Figure 16-2 shows you an HTML Help project in progress using the standard RoboHELP HTML window.

As you can see in Figure 16-2, there at least two major parts to the RoboHELP HTML window. The separation may look familiar to those who have created online help using WinHelp. The left side holds the project information, including the table of contents, the index, and the Project folder. The right side contains the topic text, as well as tools to help you find broken links and to edit the HTML code of your topics. Using each of these parts, you create your HTML Help project inside the window.

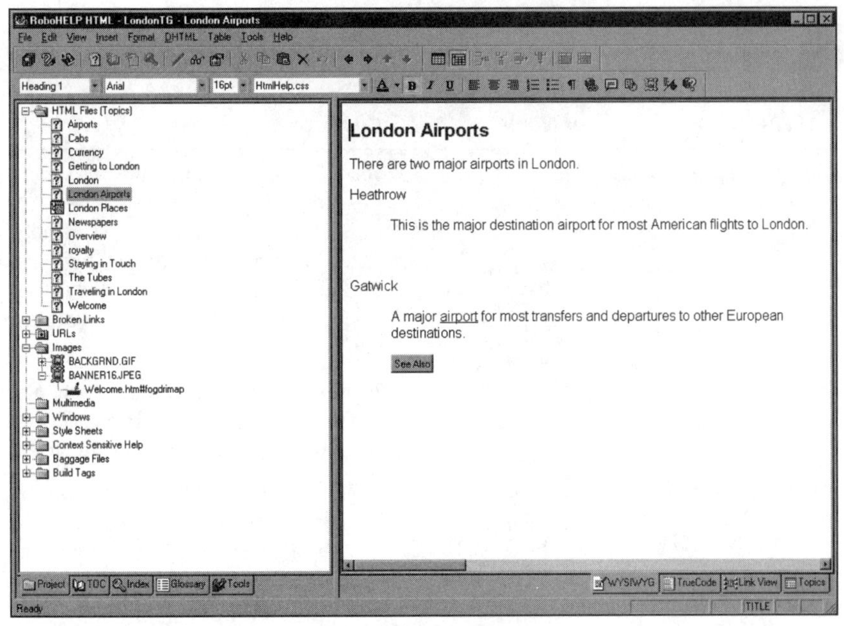

Figure 16-2: The main RoboHELP HTML window

Chapter 18, "Creating Your First HTML Help Project" explains each part of the RoboHELP HTML main window in detail.

Anatomy of a New Project File

When you create a new topic, RoboHELP HTML generates files for each of the different parts of your project, which you complete as you create your HTML Help project. Table 16-3 lists all the file types and their extensions.

Table 16-3
Contents of a New HTML Help Project

Type of File	*File Extension or Name*	*Contains*
eHelp's JavaScript File	BSSCDHTM.JS	Dynamic HTML Information. The default values for all the DHTML settings are kept in this file, as well as any new settings you enter when you use a DHTML object. If you add DHTML information to RoboHELP HTML, it is added to this file as well.

Continued

Table 16-3 *(continued)*

Type of File	*File Extension or Name*	*Contains*
Cascading Style Sheets	CSS	Topic Format Information. Four standard Cascading Style Sheets come with RoboHELP HTML: Default.CSS, HtmlHelp. CSSs, MS_Help.CSS, and w95help.CSS. These style sheets are included in every project, and you can also add your own if you like.
HTML	HTM	Text and formatting for each topic page. These are the individual HTML files that work together to make up your HHP.
HTML Help project	HHP	HTML Help Workshop information. This file allows your HTML Help project created in RoboHELP HTML to be compatible with the files created by HTML Help Workshop; and your HTML Help project can be opened by HTML Help Workshop.
Index	HHK	Index information. As with the TOC file, this is blank when you start your project; it fills as you create an index for your project and then compile it.
Project File	MPJ	Project settings, compiling settings, new window designs, context-sensitive help information, a complete list of all files for your HTML Help projects, and settings for special features
Table of Contents	HHC	Table of contents information. When you create a new project, this file is blank, but as you create the TOC and compile the project, this file becomes populated with your project information.

For more information about creating your own style sheets, see Chapter 22, "Using Styles."

Creating Successful HTML Help

As with WinHelp, following standard steps ensures that the creation of your HTML Help goes smoothly. The overall process for creating HTML Help is fairly simple. To create HTML Help, follow these steps:

1. Create a new help project in RoboHELP HTML. This will create the basic files listed in Table 16-3. It also sets properties and options for the project, and identifies the online help project to RoboHELP so that it can manage the files.
2. Create the topics in the HTML Help project. Enter in RoboHELP HTML the topics, the text, graphics, multimedia, and so on, that will communicate the information to the users. Format the topics using the WYSIWYG tab.
3. Add hyperlinks. Insert jumps, popups, and other hyperlinks to link the topics and provide navigation methods between topics in the HTML Help file.
4. Create the table of contents. The table of contents is a powerful navigational tool that provides a fast way for users to find information. The table of contents also provides an effective hierarchical order to the information in the HTML Help file.
5. Create the index. Many of the basic keywords are created with the creation of the topics, but you'll need to index the project when the topics have been written and organized, adding words and phrases.
6. Compile the HTML Help project. Check any warnings and errors that may be reported, correct them, and then recompile. Repeat this step as necessary.
7. Test the compiled HTML Help project. Evaluate the style for the headings, the formatting, the fonts, the colors for the topic text, and the overall content and organization. Also make sure that any context-sensitive links in the HTML Help project work correctly with the associated program. When you make changes or find errors that need correction, recompile and test again.
8. Hand off the completed HTML Help project. Distribute the HTML Help project as appropriate. Archive all the source files that went into creating this version of the HTML Help project.

For more information about planning your online help system, see Chapter 2, "What Makes Help 'Help'?"

Summary

This chapter introduced you to the world of HTML Help. You learned about the history of HTML Help. You learned how and when to use HTML Help instead of WinHelp. You were shown the basics of HTML and the other Web-based languages that make up HTML Help. You also learned the steps involved in creating HTML Help.

✦ ✦ ✦

Using RoboHELP HTML

17

CHAPTER

✦ ✦ ✦ ✦

In This Chapter

The RoboHELP HTML window

Using the menus and buttons

Special toolbars

Navigating the tabs

Using the right and left screens

The Output pane

✦ ✦ ✦ ✦

In this chapter, you learn your way around the RoboHELP HTML window. First you'll learn how to open RoboHELP HTML and look at a sample project. After examining the RoboHELP HTML window, you'll learn about the many menu options, as well as the button options. Eleven different screens come with RoboHELP HTML, and you'll learn how to make the most of them. You'll also learn how to use the standard views to see the progression of a project. Finally, you'll learn about the special toolbars that you will use in the course of your project, and you'll learn how to use the compiling screens.

Starting RoboHELP HTML

Before you can begin to investigate the RoboHELP HTML main window, you need to launch the RoboHELP HTML program.

To start RoboHELP HTML:

1. From the Windows taskbar, select Start ➪ Programs ➪ RoboHELP Office ➪ RoboHELP HTML. This opens the RoboHELP HTML window shown in Figure 17-1.
2. When you want to create your first project, choose to create a new project by selecting the appropriate radio button. For now, simply open one of the sample projects that come with RoboHELP HTML by selecting it from the list.
3. Click OK. This opens the RoboHELP HTML main window, with the tip of the day, as shown in Figure 17-2.

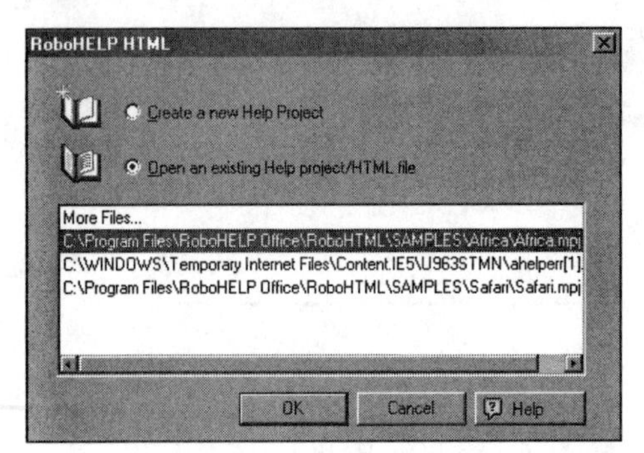

Figure 17-1: The RoboHELP HTML opening window

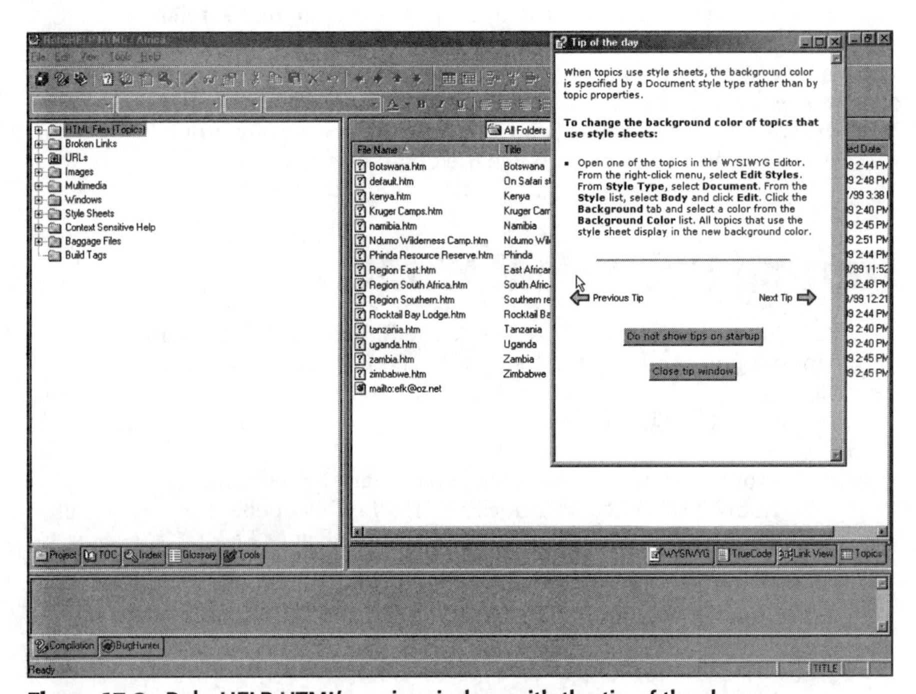

Figure 17-2: RoboHELP HTML's main window with the tip of the day

You can read as many tips as you like by using the Next and Previous buttons. You can also request that tips not be displayed again by choosing the button supplied.

4. After reading the tip of the day, use the Close button to dismiss the window.

Congratulations, you have successfully launched RoboHELP HTML!

The RoboHELP HTML Window

Once you have launched RoboHELP HTML, you are ready to start investigating the main RoboHELP HTML window. The RoboHELP HTML main window is shown in Figure 17-3, with the major features identified.

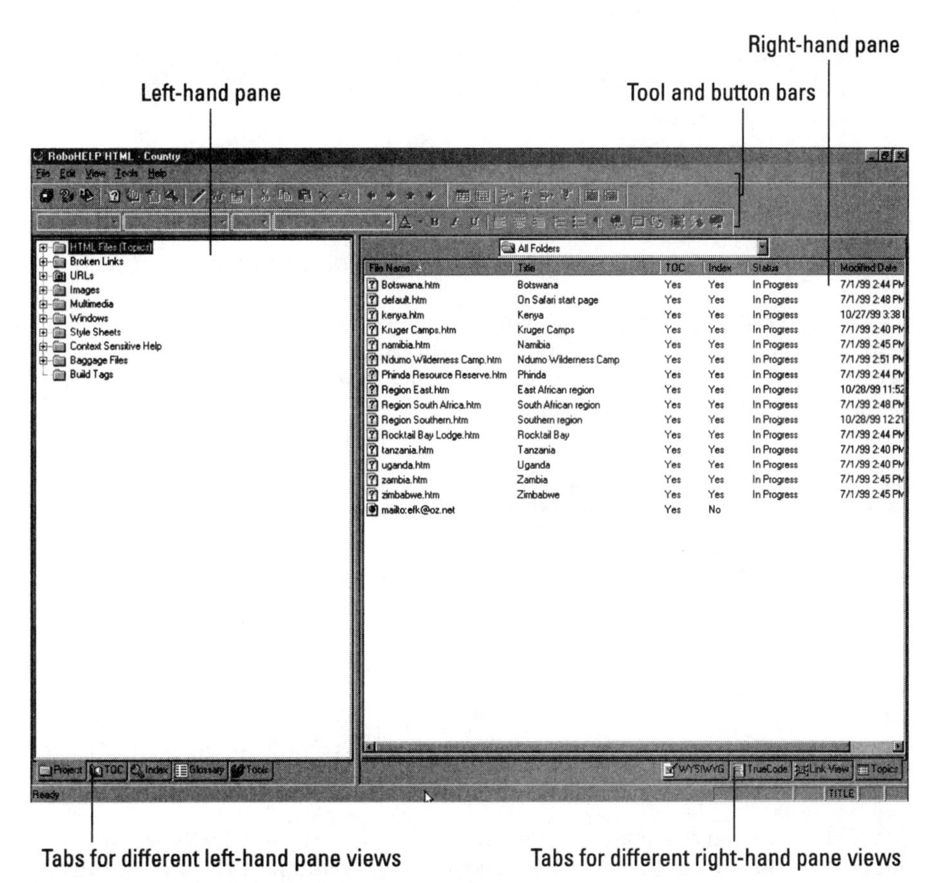

Figure 17-3: RoboHELP HTML's main window

The RoboHELP HTML main window is comprised of a row of menus; two rows of buttons; and two panes, both of which have several tabs. As you work on your project, another pane is displayed, showing you the status of your project as RoboHELP HTML compiles.

The major elements of the RoboHELP HTML main window are as follows:

- **Menu bar:** You select menu options from the menu bar, as in most Windows programs. The menu bar enables you to close, open, and alter your project.
- **Button bars:** Selecting a button launches a given menu item with just one click. Many menu options that are hidden or nested in the menus are easily available with the buttons.
- **Left pane:** Listed in the left pane are all the files and organizational settings for your project. The file structures, TOC, index, and glossary are all controlled from here.
- **Right pane:** Your HTML Help project is displayed in the right pane, as both HTML code and WYSIWYG images. Also in the right pane are the link and topic views, enabling you to see broken and missing links to your topics.
- **Tabs:** Tabs enable you to move between the different options in each pane.

All of these buttons, menus, and panes can become distracting if you don't know how to use them. This section walks you thorough each element of the RoboHELP HTML main window, and helps you understand how to make the most out of your HTML Help creation environment.

Using RoboHELP HTML Menus

The menu in the main RoboHELP HTML window varies depending on the task you are performing. When you are creating and editing new topics, the menu is larger than it is when you are simply navigating inside your file system.

Table 17-1 lists all the menu items, and briefly describes what is located under each one.

Selecting menu options, making selections from lists, and so on, are much the same in RoboHELP HTML as in most other Windows applications.

Several options underneath each menu heading are available only when you need them. Most of the Table menu, for example, is grayed out until you need to work with a table. If you would like to select a menu option that is grayed out, first make sure you are in the appropriate pane for that action. Many menu options work only when the WYSIWYG pane is displayed.

For more information about panes, see the "Understanding the RoboHELP HTML Panes" section later in this chapter.

Table 17-1
RoboHELP HTML Menu Items

Menu Item	*What It Does*
File	Creates, opens, closes, saves, and renames projects; generates and runs HTML Help code; displays and changes project settings; imports topic data from another source; and closes RoboHELP HTML.
Edit	Cuts, copies, and pastes text; allows undo and redo of actions; moves and deletes text and images; finds topics and text; clears text and hyperlinks; accesses the properties, Map ID, and What's This? dialogs.
View	Turns toolbars on and off; and enables you to view panes and display file folders and file extensions. Also shows the Preview view of your help project.
Tools	Generates reports; displays the links and references to a topic; launches wizards for the index, glossary, and topic keywords; alters the sequence of books; checks spelling; and helps resolve broken links and references.
Help	Provides online and Internet help for RoboHELP HTML.
Insert	Includes hyperlinks, text, images, bookmarks, multimedia files, script, or form into the current topic. This option is displayed only when editing in the WYSIWYG editor.
Format	Sets the way a character, paragraph, topic, or project is displayed for you and your user. This option is displayed only when editing in the WYSIWYG editor.
DHTML	Inserts DHTML scripts, allowing you to include special effects in the selected topic. This option is displayed only when editing in the WYSIWYG editor.
Table	Inserts and edits tables in the currently selected topic. This option is displayed only when editing in the WYSIWYG editor.

Understanding the RoboHELP HTML Buttons

Like the menus, the buttons on the RoboHELP HTML main window change as you move through the project creation process. Some buttons are grayed out when they are not necessary, becoming available when you can use them.

Tip

Both rows of buttons can be turned on and off using the Toolbars option in the View menu.

Table 17-2 describes each of the buttons.

Table 17-2
RoboHELP HTML Buttons

Button	***What It Does***
	Saves all parts of the current project
	Compiles the current project into the primary target
	Runs the primary target, launching your compiled project in the HTML Help window
	Opens a blank new topic
	Creates a new book
	Adds a new page
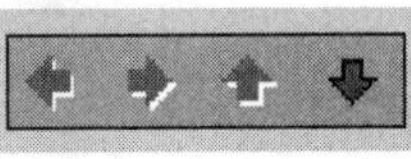	Adds a new keyword
	Edits images and scripts
	Opens a separate view window with the current topic
	Gives the properties for the current topic
	Cuts, copies, or pastes text and images
	Deletes the selected image or text
	Lets you undo the last action
	Moves an image left, right, up, or down.
	Inserts a table

Button	***What It Does***
	Indicates table gridlines
	Inserts or deletes a row
	Inserts or delete a column
	Merges selected table cells
	Splits selected table cell
Normal	Selects inline style for text
Arial 12pt	Sets text font and size
default.css	Sets style sheet for selected topic
A	Edits font color
B I U	Selects font style, including bold, italics and underline
	Sets font and image alignment, including left, center, and right
	Turns selected text into a numbered list
	Turns selected text into a bulleted list
¶	Toggles viewing paragraph and formatting markers
	Adds hyperlink to selected text or image
	Adds popup window to selected text or image
	Adds a link to selected text or image, including a-link, related topic control, and keyword link control

Continued

Table 17-2 (continued)

Button	*What It Does*
	Adds image
	Adds a bookmark to selected text or image
	Inserts HTML Help control from drop-down list

If you move your cursor over any of the buttons in RoboHELP HTML toolbar, the name of the button appears.

You use buttons in RoboHELP HTML as you would in most other Windows applications. Some buttons become active only when you are editing a particular section of the project. Generally, most buttons work only when the WYSIWYG pane is displayed.

Understanding the RoboHELP HTML Panes

Creating HTML Help can be complicated, with many steps and details to remember. All of these steps need to be readily accessible to you as you work your way through a project. RoboHELP HTML has included the use of *panes*, or nested work areas, each dedicated to a different task, to help you quickly and easily create stunning-looking HTML Help.

As you look at the RoboHELP HTML main window, under the menu and button bars, you'll notice two main areas, the left and right panes. They are separated by a gray line, and each pane has its own set of tabs in the lower fifth of the screen.

Each tab represents a different working area. The tabs allow you to move between different views of your project, and they provide you quick access to the varied work surfaces you need to create HTML Help. To move between the tabs, simply use your mouse to select each one.

Take some time now to take a quick look at each of the tabs. Move between them until you feel comfortable with how the look of the screen changes as you work your way around the RoboHELP HTML environment.

Once you are comfortable with how the tabs work, and how the different panes look, you are ready to examine the uses of each tab.

Using the Left Pane

The left pane contains all the system information about your project. It is the organizer, the tool holder, and the visual reference for the creation of your HTML Help project. Each tab on the left-hand pane contains information about the topic, keywords, and tools that make up your project.

As you might expect, some tabs are used more than others are, but all of the tabs change as you move through your HTML Help project. RoboHELP HTML is organized in an extremely logical fashion, and the layout of the tabs in the left-hand pane clearly shows that.

All the screenshots shown for the tabs illustrate how they look for a nearly completed sample project. Your tabs may look very different as you start your own project.

There are five tabs in the left-hand pane, each of which is covered in the following sections:

✦ Project

✦ TOC

✦ Index

✦ Glossary

✦ Tools

Project

The Project tab is the most frequently used tab in all of RoboHELP HTML. Most of the tasks you perform in the Project tab can be done in other places as well, but the Project tab enables you to perform basic tasks that make up your HTML Help creation while also providing invaluable visual information about the state of your project. The Project tab is shown in Figure 17-4.

From the Project tab, you can add topics and folders. You select a topic to view in the right-hand pane, and you can investigate the links for your topics. You can view the broken links and the URL references within your entire project.

The Project tab is where you are likely to start the organization of your project. From the Project tab, you add folders to contain your topics, you add topics to hold your information, and you verify that all the files needed are included with your project.

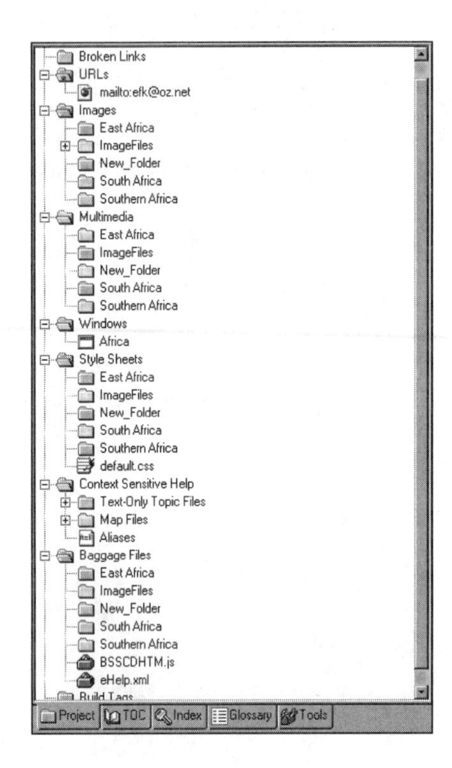

Figure 17-4: The left pane's Project tab's left pane

The folders listed in the Project tab are a representation of the actual file structure of your project. These folders have a corresponding directory in the place where you save your project. Following are the standard upper-level folders in the Project tab and what they contain:

✦ **HTML files (topics):** Lists all the topics and folders. Every individual HTML file is represented here as a topic.

✦ **Broken links:** Shows all the links that are broken because of deleted or moved files. If this file is empty, RoboHELP HTML is unaware of any missing links.

✦ **URLs:** Lists all the links made to external sources of any kind. You can use these links repeatedly by dragging them to the WYSIWYG tab.

✦ **Images:** Lists all the images contained in the project. Because all images used in a project are copied to the same directory, this is a list of image files.

✦ **Multimedia:** Lists all the sound and video files used in the project. Like image files, multimedia files are copied to the project directory.

✦ **Windows:** Lists all the created windows you include with the project. This allows you to launch and edit them by double-clicking the icon.

- **Style sheets:** Shows all the style sheets used in the entire project. Style sheets, like images, are copied to the project directory when you add them to the project.
- **Context-sensitive help:** All the aliases, links, and text files you create for context-sensitive help are shown in the folder. What's This? help can be saved here as well.
- **Baggage files:** A catch-all folder containing scripts, various bitmaps, and other assorted files that you include with your project.
- **Build tags:** Lists all the build tags you set for topics, allowing you to include or not include different topics for each of the builds of your project.

Always verify that View ⇨ Empty Folders is checked. If it isn't, some of the standard folders in the Project tab won't be visible until you add that type of file to your project.

Add a folder to your project in the Project tab as follows:

1. Make sure the Project tab is selected by clicking in the tab outside of any folder or topic. You will know when you have selected the Project tab by the blue line that surrounds it.
2. Select File ⇨ New ⇨ Folder. A new folder appears on the Project tab.
3. Type the name for your new folder. Once you have done this, you are ready to fill the folder with topics.

Follow these steps to add a topic in the Project tab:

1. Make sure the Project tab is selected.
2. Select File ⇨ New ⇨ Topic. A new topic appears on the Project tab.
3. Type the name of the new topic.
4. Move the topic to the appropriate folder.
5. Once you have added a topic, you can add content to the topic in the right-hand pane.

Contents are edited in the right-hand pane. For more information, see "Using the Right Pane" later in this chapter.

TOC

The table of contents for your project is a valuable asset for your users. They use it to navigate your HTML Help project, and the structure and look of your table of contents can make or break your project. The TOC tab helps you manage how your table of contents looks. The TOC tab is shown in Figure 17-5.

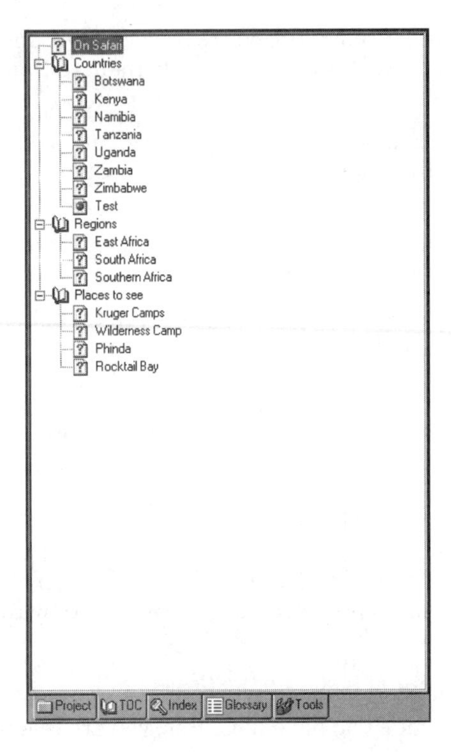

Figure 17-5: The left pane's Table of Contents tab

A table of contents is made up of books that contain topics or set of topics your users can use as a guide to your online help. You can create HTML Help without a table of contents, but you need to provide your users with some sense of your project, and a table of contents is the easiest way to do that.

From the TOC tab, you can organize your table of contents by including books and then organizing your topics within them. To add a book in the TOC tab:

1. Make sure you have selected the TOC tab. You will know when you have selected it by the blue box that surrounds the selected tab.
2. Select File ➪ New ➪ Book. You can also use the New Book button on the standard toolbar. This opens the New Book window.
3. Fill in the title for you new book in the New Book window and then click Ok. RoboHELP HTML closes the New book window and the book appears in the TOC tab.
4. Add topics, or pages, to your new book.

Pages make up the contents of books in your table of contents. Most of the pages in your table of contents are likely to be topics; however, you can include several other kinds of pages as well.

To add a new page to your table of contents in the TOC tab:

1. Make sure you have selected the TOC tab.
2. Select the File ➪ New ➪ Page command. You can also use the New Page button on the standard toolbar. This launches the new Page window discussed in the next chapter.
3. Once you have finished with the New Page window, click OK.
4. Move your page to the book in which you want it located.

Pages and books are discussed in detail in Chapter 23, "Creating a TOC and Index."

Index

The index is a searchable database of keywords and a-links your users need to move around your HTML Help project. The Index tab on the left-hand pane of the RoboHELP HTML main window contains the Index Designer, which helps you create and manage index entries. The Index tab is shown in Figure 17-6.

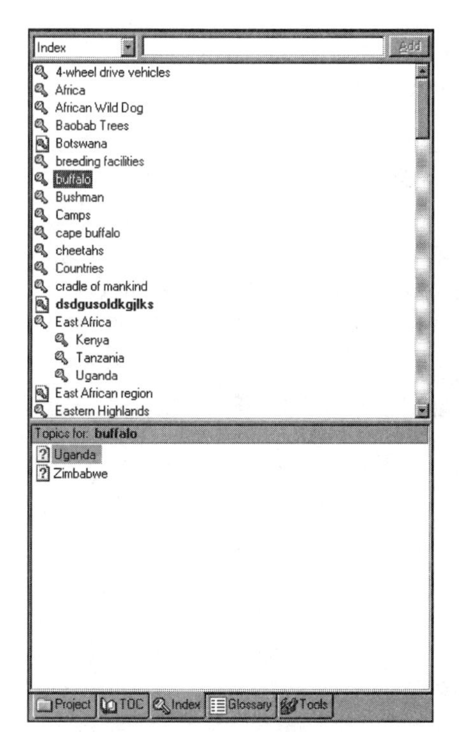

Figure 17-6: The left pane's Index tab

The Index tab looks very different from other tabs you have seen so far. It has three parts. The small upper portion, used to find and add entries to the list, contains two boxes and a button. The main portion contains a list, in alphabetical order, of all keywords or a-links in your project. The lower portion shows all topics currently referencing the keyword or a-link selected in the main portion.

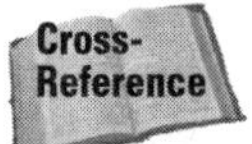

You need not create an index completely on your own. For more information about the index, see Chapter 23, "Creating a TOC and Index."

The Index tab allows you not only to view all the keywords in your project, but also to add them. To add a keyword on the Index tab:

1. Select the Index tab.
2. Make sure the drop-down list in the upper left-hand corner of the tab lists "Index."
3. Type the keyword in the blank to the right of the pull-down menu.
4. Click Add. This adds the keyword to the list.
5. Always relate keywords to a topic. To relate your new keyword, drag topics onto the keyword.

For more information about adding and using keywords, see Chapter 18, "Creating Your First HTML Help Project."

Glossary

The glossary, like the table of contents and the index, is a tool your users need to get the information they require from your HTML Help project. The Glossary tab in the left-hand pane of the RoboHELP HTML main window contains the Glossary Designer, which helps you add and manage glossary entries. The Glossary tab is shown in Figure 17-7.

Like the Index tab, the Glossary tab is broken into three portions. The upper portion contains a term box and a button to add glossary entries. The main portion lists all the glossary entries in alphabetical order. The lower portion displays the glossary text for the selected entry.

Terms listed in bold in the main portion of the Glossary tab do not have a definition.

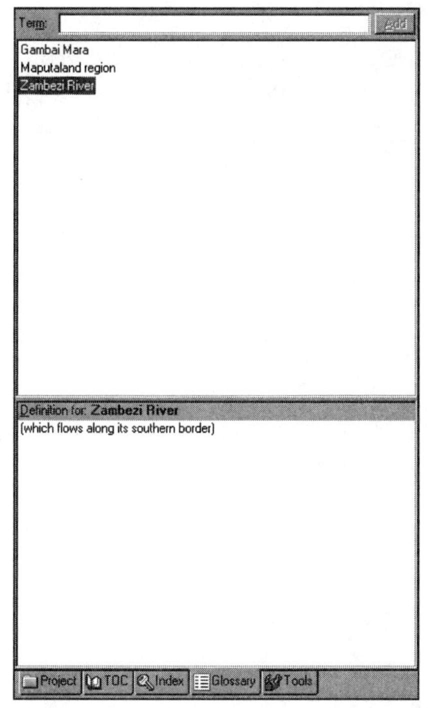

Figure 17-7: The left pane's Glossary tab

The Glossary tab allows you to see all the entries, as well as to add new entries into your glossary. Follow these steps to add a glossary entry on the Glossary tab:

1. Make sure the Glossary tab is selected.
2. Type the term you wish to add into the Term box in the upper portion of the screen.
3. Click Add. The term appears in the main portion of the tab.
4. In the lower portion of the tab, add a definition for the term by typing it in.

Your users can use glossary entries to search your HTML Help project. For more information about glossary entries, see Chapter 23, "Creating a TOC and Index."

Tools

The Tools tab in the left-hand pane of the RoboHELP HTML main window contains shortcuts to all the valuable tools that come with RoboHELP Office. The Tools tab is shown in Figure 17-8.

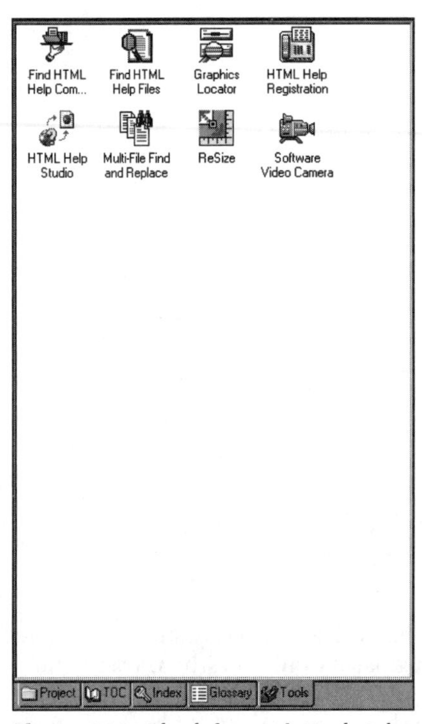

Figure 17-8: The left pane's Tools tab

Eight tools come with RoboHELP HTML:

- ✦ **Find HTML Help Components** helps you locate and manage all the pieces of your HTML Help project.
- ✦ **Find HTML Help Files** helps find and manage CHM files.
- ✦ **Graphic Locator** helps you find and manage image files.
- ✦ **HTML Help Registration** registers your CHM file so your developers can include it with their project.
- ✦ **HTML Help Studio** allows you to view and decompile HTML Help files.

✦ **Multi-File Find and Replace** allows you to quickly and easily replace several files defined by either type, file name, or location.

✦ **Resize** helps you manage the size and type of your image files.

✦ **Software Video Camera** helps you capture computer videos of your software in action to include with your HTML Help project.

Because the Tools tab contains shortcuts, you can include your own shortcut to a tool you often use as follows:

1. Make sure the Tools tab is selected.
2. Make a shortcut of the executable file for the program you wish to include. For example, if you want to include a shortcut to Notepad, navigate in your Windows directory until you find Notepad.EXE and make a shortcut to it. by selecting the New ⇨ Shortcut menu option.
3. Drag the shortcut onto the Tools tab in the RoboHELP HTML main window.

Once the tool has been added to the pane, you can add a short description of it, or change the location of the executable file, by right-clicking on it and selecting properties. This displays the properties window, in which you can make changes to the tool.

Using the Right Pane

While the left pane is where your project is organized, the right pane is where your project is constructed. This is where your project takes on a life of its own. Topics are constructed in this pane, and all the cross-checking of links and references that is so much a part of HTML Help creation happens here as well. The following sections describe the four tabs in the right pane:

✦ WYSIWYG

✦ True Code

✦ Link View

✦ Topics

WYSIWYG

You will spend most of your project creation time working on the WYSIWYG tab. It is where you add and modify text, where you seat links, and where you create the look of your HTML Help project. Figure 17-9 shows the WYSIWYG tab.

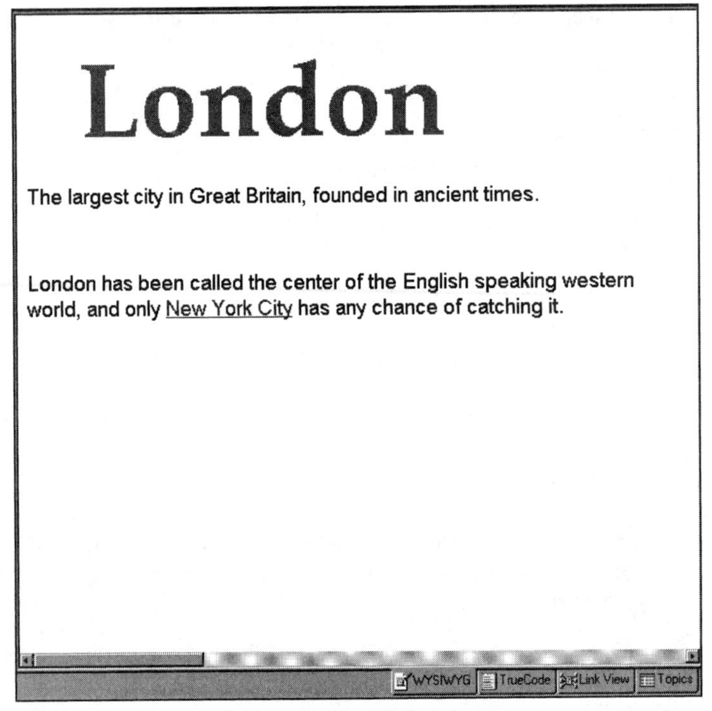

Figure 17-9: The right pane's WYSIWYG tab

The WYSIWYG tab acts like a window on your help project in action. RoboHELP HTML displays the HTML code behind your project as closely as possible to what your users will see in the WYSIWYG pane.

For WinHelp users, the WYSIWYG tab effectively reduces to zero the need for interim compiling to verify that your project looks like you want it to. You can still compile at any point, but you can do it a lot less often with the WYSIWYG editor showing you what your project looks like.

The WYSIWYG tab is also where you add and edit the text to your topics. You can type and edit text in the WYSIWYG tab just as you do in your favorite word processor, with the added advantage that as you create, you can see exactly how it will look to your user.

The majority of what you can do with the WYSIWYG tab becomes evident as you create a project. For numerous examples of the WYSIWYG tab in action, see Chapter 18, "Creating Your First HTML Help Project."

True code

The backbone of HTML Help is HTML. The True Code tab in the right-hand pane of the RoboHELP HTML main window contains all the HTML code for your topics. Although the color can't be seen in Figure 17-10, it displays the exact plain text of each page with color formatting of the code to help you understand what you are seeing. The True Code tab is shown in Figure 17-10.

```
<HTML>
 <HEAD>
  <!-- $MVD$:app("RoboHELP HTML Edition by Blue Sky Software, portions by
MicroVision Dev. Inc.","769") -->
  <!-- $MVD$:template("","0","0") -->
  <!-- $MVD$:fontset("Arial","Arial") -->
  <!-- $MVD$:fontset("Book Antiqua","Book Antiqua") -->
  <TITLE>London</TITLE>
  <SCRIPT LANGUAGE="JavaScript" TITLE="BSSC Special Effects"
SRC="BSSCDHTM.js"></SCRIPT><LINK
  REL="StyleSheet" HREF="default.css">
 <META NAME="generator" CONTENT="RoboHELP by Blue Sky Software www.blue-
sky.com HTML Edition"></HEAD>
  <BODY BGCOLOR="PURPLE" ONLOAD="BSSCOnLoad();" ONCLICK="BSSCOnClick();"
ONUNLOAD="BSSCOnUnload();">
  <BLOCKQUOTE>
   <BLOCKQUOTE>
    <H1 STYLE="text-align : left;" ALIGN=LEFT>
     <FONT FACE="Book Antiqua"><SPAN STYLE="font-size : 72.0pt;"><FONT
COLOR="GREEN">London</FONT></SPAN></FONT></H1>
    </BLOCKQUOTE>
   </BLOCKQUOTE>
  <P>
   <SPAN STYLE="font-size : 14.0pt;">The largest city in Great Britain,
   founded in ancient times.</SPAN></P>
  <P>
   <SPAN STYLE="font-size : 14.0pt;"><!-- $MVD$:spaceretainer() --
> </SPAN></P>
  <P>
   <SPAN STYLE="font-size : 14.0pt;">London has been called the center
   of the English speaking western world, and only <A
HREF="mailto:efk@oz.net">New
    York City</A> has any chance of catching it.</SPAN>
 </BODY>
</HTML>
```

WYSIWYG | TrueCode | Link View | Topics

Figure 17-10: The right pane's True Code tab

The True Code tab is not only for you to look at the code behind your HTML Help topic; if you wish, you can modify the code as well.

The True Code tab works like a simple text editor — for example, Notepad — allowing you to edit the text you see. RoboHELP HTML colors the text you add to help you follow the code. Table 17-3 lists the colors and what they mean.

For an overview of HTML, see Appendix F "HTML Quick List."

Table 17-3
True Code Colors

Color	*Meaning*
Red	File names, linked documents, exterior links
Blue	Standard HTML tags
Green	Any commented text or any text between two comment tags
Black	Plain text
Gray	Scripting text and scripting references
Purple	Special characters

Link view

Your HTML Help project is useful because content is linked together is a logical and helpful way. As you create your project, the number and location of links can get difficult to remember and manage. To help with this part of the creation process, RoboHELP HTML includes the Link View tab in the right-hand pane of the main RoboHELP HTML window, as shown in Figure 17-11.

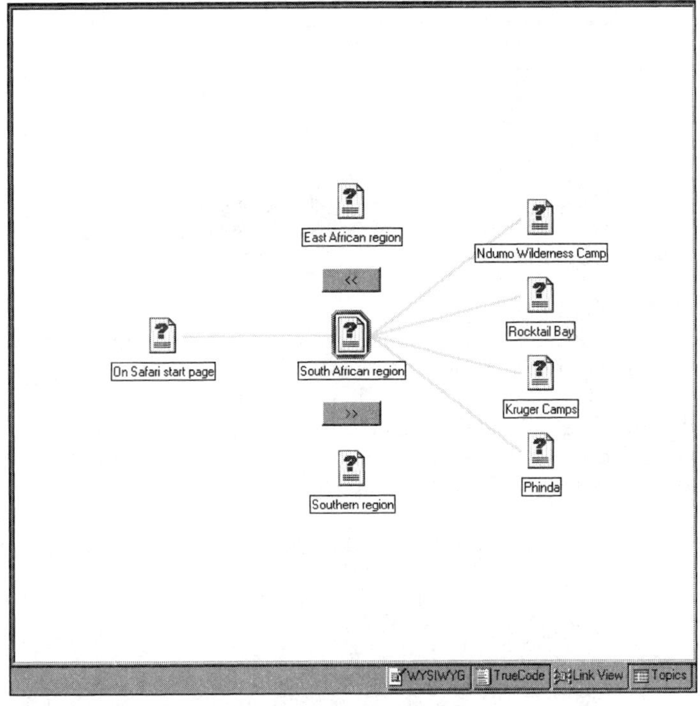

Figure 17-11: The right pane's Link View tab

The Link view changes as you click, giving you all the links to and from a particular topic. The selected topic is in the center and has a blue box around it. All the links to that topic from other topics are to the left. All topics that are linked to from the selected topic are to the right.

Above and below the selected topic are all the other topics in the same browse heading. This means that all the other topics of the same "level" are included above and below the selected topic. To browse though these topics, use the arrow buttons provided.

Not only does location on the Link view give you information, but information is also conveyed by the color of the lines connecting the topics. Valid and working links are shown in yellow, green, or blue; broken links are shown in red. You can even tell what type of link it is by the color. Links from image maps are yellow, links from popup windows are green, and links from a hotspot in the text are blue. For example, a yellow link indicates a valid link from an image map.

The topics themselves also convey information. They display as pieces of paper, and the icon on them gives you information about what kind of file it is. Topics with blue question marks are other topics in this project; those topics have their own HTML page and topic listed in the Project tab in the left pane. Topics with globes denote some external link, usually an URL to a remote site.

The Link view is most useful near the end of your project. Always check your links before you compile to test.

Topics

Topics are the backbone of your HTML Help project, and the Topics tab helps you identify each topic's state of completion. The Topics tab is shown in Figure 17-12.

The Topics tab, like the Index tab on the left-hand pane, has two parts: a drop-down list at the top and a list of files at the bottom. The Topics tab also has two views, accessible by the View menu: Detail view and List view.

The most commonly used view for the Topics tab is the Details view. The Details view shows the status of each topic and includes vital information about what has been accomplished with each topic. Figure 17-12 shows the Topics tab using the Details view.

In the Details view, you can sort topics by title, status, last modification date, or whether or not it has been added to the table of contents or index. Each category of information becomes the sorting criterion when you click on the button at the top of the window.

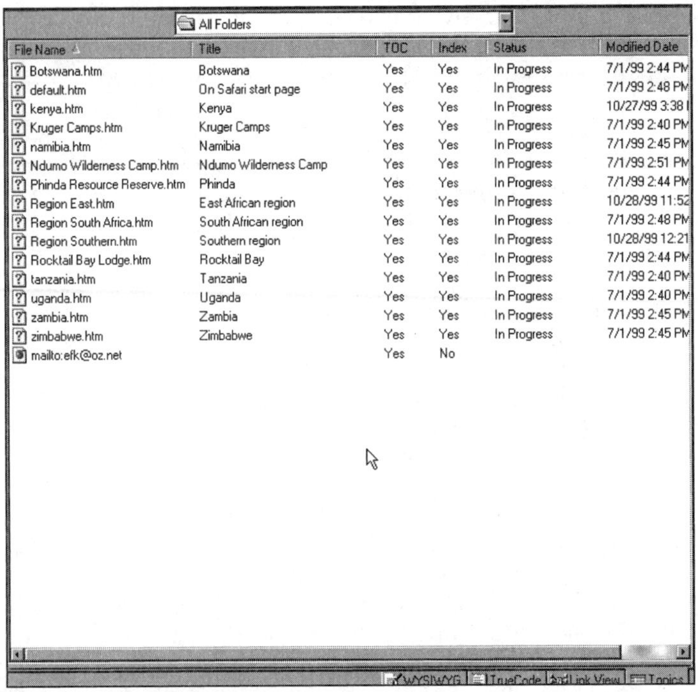

All Folders

File Name	Title	TOC	Index	Status	Modified Date
Botswana.htm	Botswana	Yes	Yes	In Progress	7/1/99 2:44 PM
default.htm	On Safari start page	Yes	Yes	In Progress	7/1/99 2:48 PM
kenya.htm	Kenya	Yes	Yes	In Progress	10/27/99 3:38
Kruger Camps.htm	Kruger Camps	Yes	Yes	In Progress	7/1/99 2:40 PM
namibia.htm	Namibia	Yes	Yes	In Progress	7/1/99 2:45 PM
Ndumo Wilderness Camp.htm	Ndumo Wilderness Camp	Yes	Yes	In Progress	7/1/99 2:51 PM
Phinda Resource Reserve.htm	Phinda	Yes	Yes	In Progress	7/1/99 2:44 PM
Region East.htm	East African region	Yes	Yes	In Progress	10/28/99 11:52
Region South Africa.htm	South African region	Yes	Yes	In Progress	7/1/99 2:48 PM
Region Southern.htm	Southern region	Yes	Yes	In Progress	10/28/99 12:21
Rocktail Bay Lodge.htm	Rocktail Bay	Yes	Yes	In Progress	7/1/99 2:44 PM
tanzania.htm	Tanzania	Yes	Yes	In Progress	7/1/99 2:40 PM
uganda.htm	Uganda	Yes	Yes	In Progress	7/1/99 2:40 PM
zambia.htm	Zambia	Yes	Yes	In Progress	7/1/99 2:45 PM
zimbabwe.htm	Zimbabwe	Yes	Yes	In Progress	7/1/99 2:45 PM
mailto:efk@oz.net		Yes	No		

WYSIWYG | TrueCode | Link View | Topics

Figure 17-12: The right pane's Topics tab

Each topic is listed separately, and as you use the drop-down list at the top of the Topics tab to navigate though the folders in the project, the files listed change. The drop-down list at the top of the screen lists all the folders, allowing you to choose what level you are looking at in the Topics tab. The top-level folder shows only those topics that do not reside in folders.

As you choose levels of topics, the information about them is displayed. The icon for each topic tells you something about the status of that topic. A standard topic icon is a page with a blue question mark, which indicates it is a topic included with the project. Icons with globes in them indicate a remote URL of some kind. A tag icon indicates that the item is a bookmark.

The status of each topic is provided, which is probably the most important thing about the Topics tab. Knowing the status of each topic can sometimes be difficult, especially as your topic grows. Making sure your topics have been added to the table of contents and index is often the hardest part of your project to remember. The Topics tab makes it easy by listing each separately as part of the information for the topic. Even better, the color of the icon changes to bright blue when each topic has been added to both the table of contents and the index.

To quickly make sure everything has been taken care of, use the Details view of the Topics tab. The colors and well-organized columns make it easy to see what needs to be done.

Using the Output Pane

When you are compiling your project, either at the end of the project or during the creation and testing process, RoboHELP HTML adds another pane to the main RoboHELP HTML window. The *Output pane* appears in the lower part of the main window, as shown in Figure 17-13.

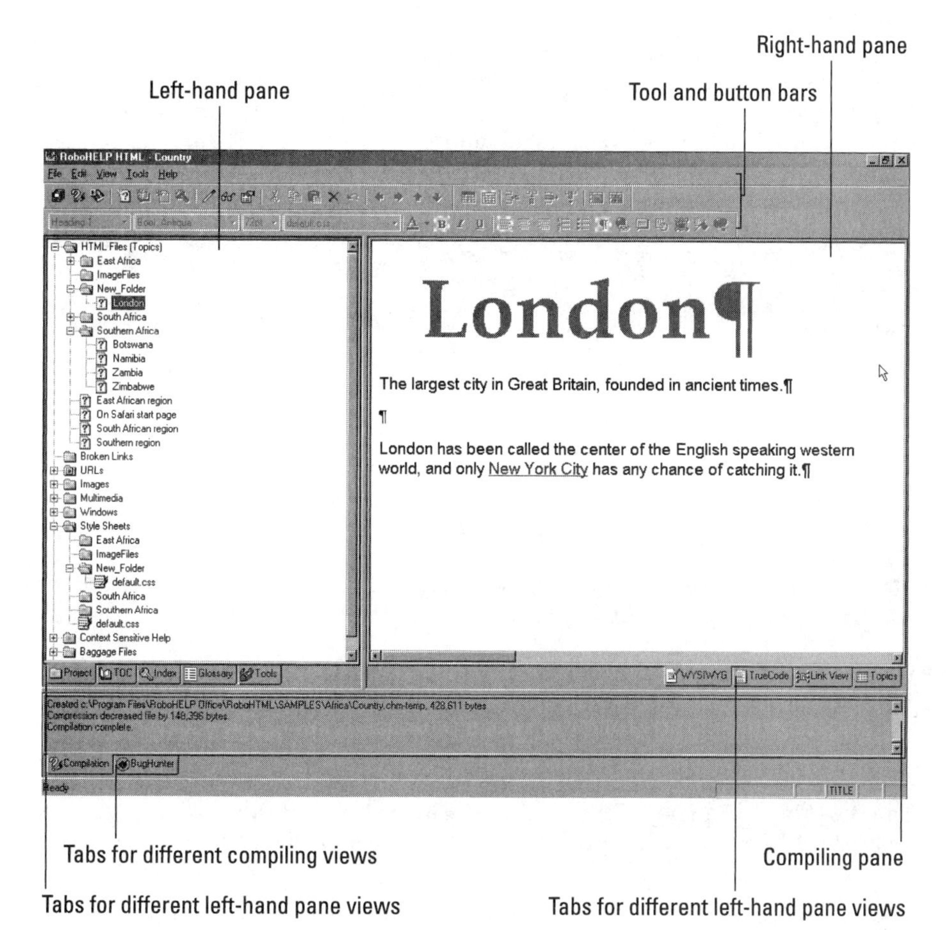

Figure 17-13: RoboHELP HTML's main window, showing the Output pane

The Output pane automatically appears when you start any compiling of the project. This means that any time you generate a target, the Output pane opens.

You can open the Output pane at any time by selecting View ➪ Pane ➪ Compiler or View ➪ Pane ➪ BugHunter

The Output pane has two tabs:

✦ Compiler

✦ BugHunter

Compiling

When you generate a primary target, what you are doing is compiling the HTML Help code into a file that can be called by a program or script. This compiling process has several steps, and has to access several files. The Compilation tab allows you to monitor the process and glean information from the HTML Help compiler in action. The Compilation tab is shown in Figure 17-14.

Figure 17-14: The Output pane's Compilation tab

As your project compiles, the Compilation tab shows you the progress and provides a readout of what is happening. It lists information about errors in the content or links of topics, it tells you about missing topics, and it even gives you feedback about the validity of your index file.

At the end of the text for each compiling session, RoboHELP HTML lists the total number of topics, links, and graphics for your HTML Help project.

For more information about compiling, see Chapter 24, "Using Reports and Compiling."

BugHunter

The BugHunter is a special tool included with RoboHELP Office to help you test context-sensitive help. The BugHunter tab is shown in Figure 17-15.

BugHunter Enabled...

Compilation | BugHunter

Figure 17-15: The Output pane's BugHunter tab

By default, the BugHunter is turned off. To turn it on, select Tools ⇨ Enable BugHunter. The BugHunter makes a note in the BugHunter tab as to whether or not it is enabled.

The BugHunter tab lists all the reference numbers, called *Map IDs,* for each topic. These numbers are used by the software developers to call the topics from within the software program.

BugHunter enables you to see just what number is used for each topic, helping you troubleshoot when some of the context-sensitive help is not working, and giving you the information you need to fix it.

For more information about context-sensitive help, see Chapter 25, "Creating Context-Sensitive HTML Help."

Summary

In this chapter, you learned how to use RoboHELP HTML. Easily launched from the Start menu, RoboHELP HTML's main screen shows you the basic layout. From here, you learned how to use the standard menus as well as the standard buttons that come with RoboHELP HTML. You now know what each menu contains and what each button on the standard tool bars does. After being introduced to RoboHELP HTML's pane layout, you learned how to use the left-hand pane to organize your work, and how to use the right-hand pane to add text and edit the topics, as well as manage links and follow the status of each topic. Finally, you learned about the Output pane and how to use the BugHunter.

✦ ✦ ✦

CHAPTER 18

Creating Your First HTML Help Project

✦ ✦ ✦ ✦

In This Chapter

Starting a project

Creating topics

Adding text

Organizing your project

Basic compiling

✦ ✦ ✦ ✦

In this chapter, you create your very first project. After learning how to start, name, and save your project, you learn what a new project looks like, and what each part of a new project contains. Once you are familiar with the look of a new project, you will learn how to add topics and organize your topics into folders. You also learn how to add text to your topics, and how to logically place information on your HTML Help topic pages. Finally, you learn how to initialize a RoboHELP HTML compiling session to see the results of your efforts.

Planning Before You Start

HTML Help is built out of topics and links that you create to give your user assistance with something. How you do this, and how your project is organized, should always be the first task of any project.

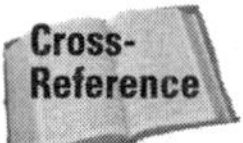

See Chapter 2, "What Makes Help 'Help'?" for an in-depth review of how to plan and outline a new Help project.

The best way to ensure that your HTML Help project goes smoothly is to create a *document plan*. A document plan is an outline of what you will include in your HTML Help project, how it will be written, by whom, and how long it will take. As you start your project, you should ask yourself some simple questions:

- ✦ What do you want to write?
- ✦ For whom do you want to write it?
- ✦ Why do you want to write it?

✦ How do you want to write it?

✦ Where will the document be written and produced?

✦ Who will do the work?

✦ When will they do it?

Once you feel you have a handle on the who, why, and how of your project, you are ready to start your first HTML Help project.

Starting Your First Project

In earlier chapters, you learned how to launch RoboHELP HTML and navigate around the RoboHELP HTML main screen. You also learned how to use the buttons and menus that form the foundation of the creation process. Now you are going to use all of your knowledge to create a real project.

The first step to creating a project is launching RoboHELP HTML. To do so, choose RoboHELP HTML from the Start menu, as detailed in the first section of Chapter 17, "Using RoboHELP HTML."

Creating the New Project

Once RoboHELP HTML has been started, choose Create a New Help Project. Choosing to create a new project opens the New Project screen, shown in Figure 18-1.

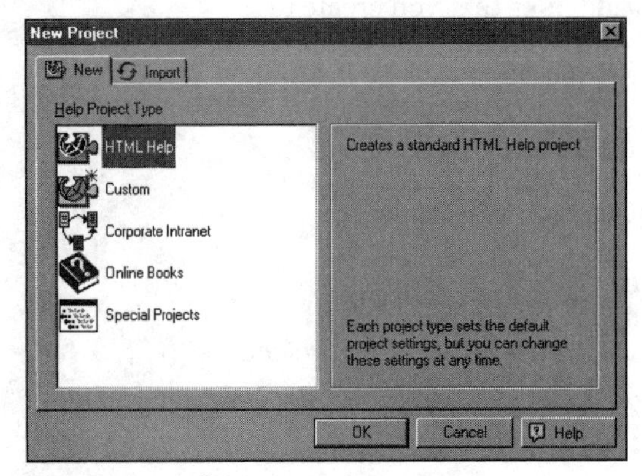

Figure 18-1: The New Project screen

The new project can be of many types, but for now choose to create an HTML Help project, and then click OK.

The file names, locations, and first topic define the RoboHELP HTML file. Once you decide to create a new HTML Help project, the New Project Wizard appears, asking for file information (as shown in Figure 18-2).

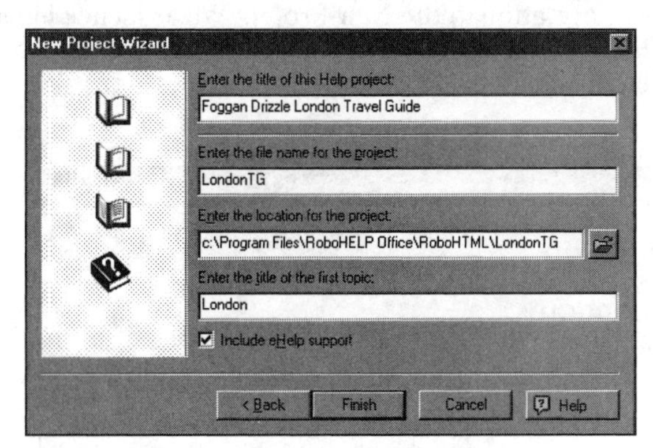

Figure 18-2: The New Project Wizard

The New Project Wizard walks you through all the information RoboHELP HTML needs to create a new project. Four pieces of information are vital:

✦ **Title of the Project:** This sets the title of the project as it will appear on the HTML Help viewer when you have compiled your project. Make sure you have a complete and informative name for your project title.

✦ **File Name:** All the files associated with your HTML Help project will have file names derived from this file name. This means that you will need to define only one file name for your entire project, saving you time and energy. Furthermore, the file name is what the RoboHELP HTML main screen shows as you edit your project.

✦ **File Location:** Just as with the file name, the file location is important because your entire project is based on the information you enter here. All the files and folders normally created in the standard project creation process are saved here as well. By starting a new project, you are creating a complete file set in this location.

Make sure the location you choose has more than enough room to hold your entire finished project. A good rule of thumb is to have at least three times the space you expect your HTML Help project to need when it's finished.

✦ **Title of the First Topic:** An HTML Help project is defined by its topics, and it is impossible to create a new project without at least one topic. Because you created a basic outline of your project earlier in this chapter, you should know which topic will be the highest-level topic in your HTML Help project. If you know the title of this topic, enter it here. If for some reason you do not know the exact title of the highest-level topic, enter something as close as you can and then remember to alter it later when you have more information.

Be sure to check Include eHelp Support if you want your project to have eHelp. For more information about eHelp, see Chapter 28, " Examining WebHelp, JavaHelp, and other Help systems"

Once you are satisfied with the information in the New Project Wizard, click Finish. This opens the main RoboHELP HTML window and opens your first topic in the WYSIWYG editor, as shown in Figure 18-3.

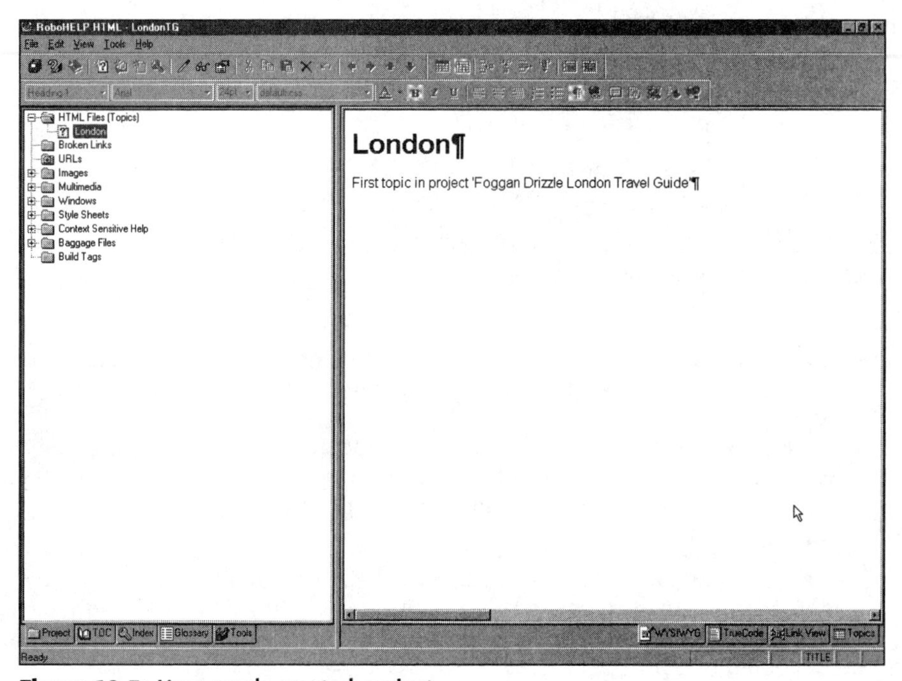

Figure 18-3: Your newly created project

Once you have created the project, you are ready to start editing your first topic.

Editing Your First Topic

RoboHELP HTML was created to make your work easier. It takes many of the repetitive tasks that go into making a help system out of your hands so you can concentrate on making outstanding help. Nowhere is the usefulness of RoboHELP HTML more evident than at the start of the project.

Chapter 17, "Using RoboHelp HTML," identifies all the folders in the new project.

You start your project with one topic already defined. This should be your highest-level topic, but it can be any of the topics you've planed to include. As a general rule starting with the topic you plan to have at the top level of your project helps the progression of topics happen in a more logical manner, but it is not necessary. The new topic is displayed with the title as a header and a placeholding text block, as shown in Figure 18-3.

To edit your first topic:

1. Select the topic from the list in the Project tab.
2. Select the WYSIWYG tab on the right-hand side of the RoboHELP HTML main window.
3. Select the placeholder text on the WYSIWYG tab.
4. Replace the placeholder text with content text.

Once you have replaced the placeholder text with content, your RoboHELP HTML main window should look like the one shown in Figure 18-4.

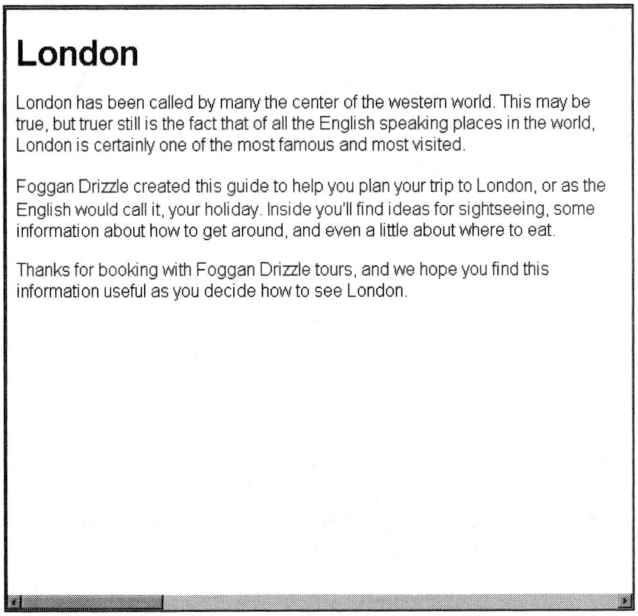

London
London has been called by many the center of the western world. This may be true, but truer still is the fact that of all the English speaking places in the world, London is certainly one of the most famous and most visited.
Foggan Drizzle created this guide to help you plan your trip to London, or as the English would call it, your holiday. Inside you'll find ideas for sightseeing, some information about how to get around, and even a little about where to eat.
Thanks for booking with Foggan Drizzle tours, and we hope you find this information useful as you decide how to see London.

Figure 18-4: First topic with content text

Now that you have edited your first topic, you are ready to start adding more topics to your HTML Help project.

Creating Topics

All HTML Help systems are based on topics. Topics are the foundation of your entire help system, and adding topics is the first major task of creating your new project. Topics are the single most important part of your HTML Help project. Your users are going to use the table of contents and index to access help, but that help takes the form of topics containing information.

Topics are HTML documents, and each separate topic is its own independent HTML page. As you add and change topics, you are creating and changing HTML code. RoboHELP HTML makes this easy by giving you wizards and WYSIWYG views to add and modify your topics.

See Appendix F, "HTML Quick List," for a quick introduction to HTML tags.

Topics are viewed differently by you, the HTML Help creator, and the HTML Help user. You see them as individual HTML files, made up of text and images you add to the WYSIWYG editor in RoboHELP HTML. In the RoboHELP HTML main window, the fact that topics are HTML files is clearly illustrated by the name of the topics folder in the Project tab, "HTML Files (Topics)."

Your users see topics very differently. They see topics as pages of a book, the leaflets that together make up the body of your help system. To the HTML Help user, topics do not appear to be independent, as they do to you, the HTML Help creator. The conception of individual topics as pages is reinforced by the images displayed in the compiled HTML Help system. Figure 18-5 shows a compiled HTML Help project with topics displayed as pages, and folders displayed as books.

In order to use topics as "pages" in your "book," you need to outline them just as you would for any other book. Ideally, you use the help information you have created for another source to create your HTML Help project, but even if all the content for your project is new and singular to this HTML Help project, it needs to be sectioned in a logical way into "pages" or topics.

The sectioning of information into topics by logical headings not only helps your users find the information they are looking for, it also helps them use what they find. If your topic pages are not organized logically into a "section-by-section" format, your users will find it difficult to use the information once they do find it.

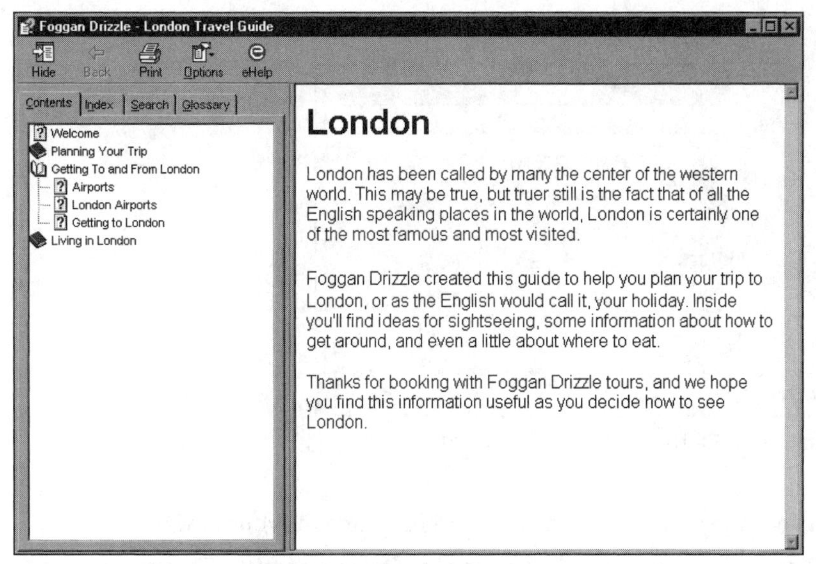
Foggan Drizzle - London Travel Guide
Hide
Back
Print
Options
eHelp
Contents
Index
Search
Glossary
Welcome
Planning Your Trip
Getting To and From London
Airports
London Airports
Getting to London
Living in London
London
London has been called by many the center of the western world. This may be true, but truer still is the fact that of all the English speaking places in the world, London is certainly one of the most famous and most visited.
Foggan Drizzle created this guide to help you plan your trip to London, or as the English would call it, your holiday. Inside you'll find ideas for sightseeing, some information about how to get around, and even a little about where to eat.
Thanks for booking with Foggan Drizzle tours, and we hope you find this information useful as you decide how to see London.

Figure 18-5: Compiled help, with topics as pages

Tip

Make an outline of your HTML Help project as you would for a printed resource, creating a heading for every topic. This should be just about the right amount of information for every topic page.

Adding New Topics

Once you know what topics you need in your project, creating topics in RoboHELP HTML is quick and easy.

New topics in RoboHELP HTML are created using the New Topic Wizard. The wizard is launched any time you choose to add a new topic, and it displays the Topic Properties window.

You can add a new topic in two ways: by using the File menu, or by using the right-click menu.

To add a new topic with the File menu:

1. In your new HTML Help project, select the Project tab.
2. Open the HTML Files (Topics) folder using the plus sign directly to its left.
3. With the HTML Files (Topics) folder selected, choose File ➪ New ➪ Topic. This displays the Create Topic Wizard, as shown in Figure 18-6.

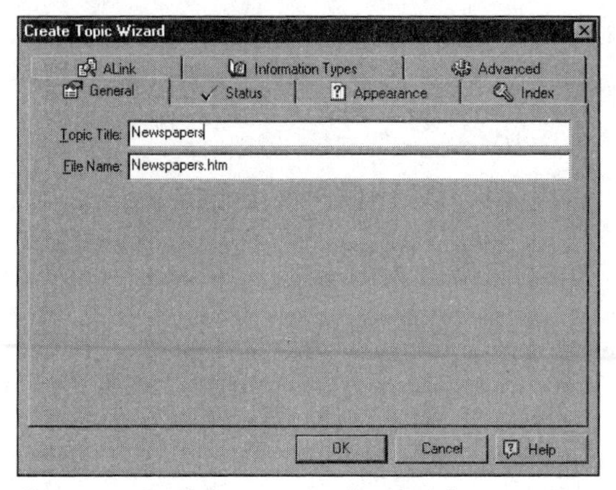

Figure 18-6: The Create Topic Wizard

4. Fill out the screen with the title and file name for your new topic.
5. Click OK when you have finished entering information. This closes the Create Topic Wizard and returns you to the RoboHELP HTML main window.

You can create a new topic from anywhere by selecting File ➪ New ➪ Topic, and then later place it in the correct folder.

Now you have finished adding your new topic. The new topic displays on the Project tab, giving you two topics, as shown in Figure 18-7.

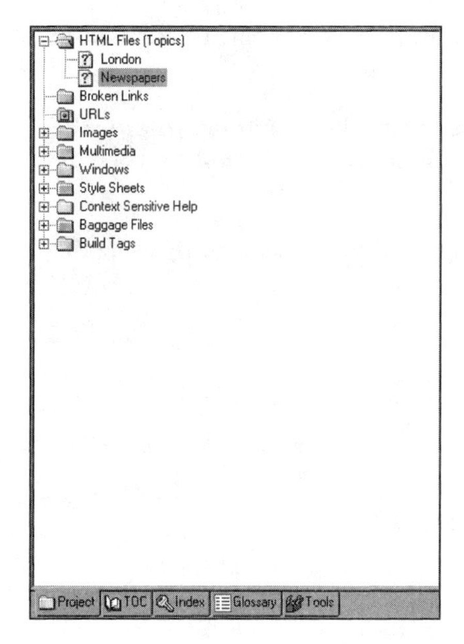

Figure 18-7: Project tab with an added topic

To add more topics, you can either repeat the process of adding them with the File menu or use the right-click procedure described next.

To add a topic with the right-click menu:

1. Open the HTML Help project in which you'd like to add the new topic.
2. Right-click on the Topics tab in the right hand pane or on any topic icon in the Project tab in the left-hand pane of the RoboHELP HTML main window. A context-sensitive right-click menu is displayed (see Figure 18-8).

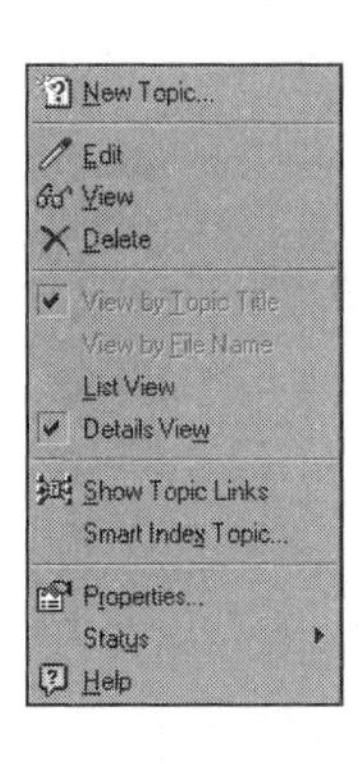

Figure 18-8: Topic right-click menu

3. Choose New Topic. This opens the Create Topic Wizard (refer to Figure 18-6).
4. Fill out the information in the Create Topic Wizard.
5. When you are done, click OK. This adds the topic to the HTML Files (Topics) folder.

You can use the right-click menu from anywhere in the RoboHELP HTML main window.

Adding Content to Topics

Once you have added topics, you need to add content to them. Topics with no content are not very useful, so most of your time spent creating HTML Help will be adding text, images, and links to your HTML Help project.

The following sections describe each type of content and how to add it to your HTML Help project.

Adding text

Text is the most common way for information to make its way from your project to your user. If the text content of your HTML Help project does not exist before you start your project, you need to add it in the WYSIWYG editor in the RoboHELP HTML main window.

To add text in the main RoboHELP HTML window:

1. Select the topic you want to add text to and then the WYSIWYG tab on the right-hand pane.
2. Place the cursor where you want the text to appear by clicking on the WYSIWYG tab.
3. Type content text.
4. Format the text as you would in a word processor. You can use either the Formatting Menu or the Formatting Toolbar.
5. Once you are pleased with the look of the text in your topic, select another topic page to add text to.

The WYSIWYG editor works and acts like a cross between a word processing program and a desktop publishing program, making it quick and easy to add and edit text.

Adding images

Graphics make your HTML Help look professional. HTML Help projects that don't include images can be boring, which increases the risk of losing your audience. Not only do many people learn more easily from looking at pictures than from reading text, but pictures support your text, allowing users to not only read information, but also see what you are talking about.

RoboHELP HTML has a fully functional system for adding images. Add all images through the WYSIWYG editor, just as you add text.

For an in-depth discussion of creating, adding, placing, and using images, see Chapter 20, "Creating and Adding Graphics."

Adding links

While text and images convey information inside your HTML Help project, it is the *links* that hold everything together. The beauty of HTML Help is that information takes on a whole new dimension when topics can be linked together.

Links can be added to text or images that already exist on the topic page; and just like text and images, they need to be planned out before you start. Links can also be added to your page by adding buttons or other link controls.

For an in-depth discussion of adding links to your HTML Help project, see Chapter 19, "Creating Outstanding Topics."

Topic Properties

No matter what your topic looks like, each topic still has a topic properties page. The content included for each page has little or nothing to do with the properties for each page.

You already have some experience with the properties of each topic; the Topic Properties window is the same screen displayed by the Create Topic Wizard. This section goes though the Topic Properties screen in detail, familiarizing you with each tab and section of this very important window.

Use these steps to view the topic property for any topic:

1. Open the HTML Files (Topics) folder.
2. Select the topic from the list.
3. Select Edit ➪ Properties. The Topic Properties window will be displayed, as shown in Figure 18-9.

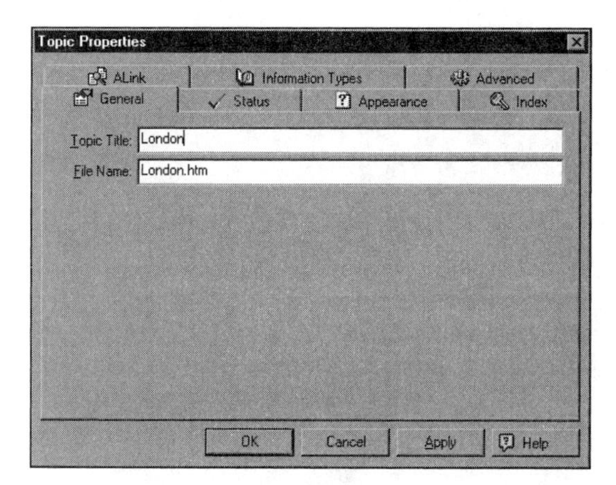

Figure 18-9: The Topic Properties window of the General tab

The Topic Properties window contains all the information about a specific topic. The seven tabs in the screen identify all the available attributes for your topic, including style sheet, file name, build information, index keywords, and dozens of other pieces of information.

General tab

The General tab, shown in Figure 18-8, is the most frequently used tab in the Topic Properties window.

This tab contains the title and file information for your topic. Information on this tab is the first thing added to any new topic; in fact, a topic cannot exist without the information on the General tab. The two fields of information on the General tab are Topic Title and File Name.

- ✦ **Topic Title** should be illustrative, both for you and for your users, because this is the title that RoboHelp HTML displays when you compile the HTML Help project.
- ✦ **File Name** should have no spaces in it, and should always end with an htm extension. If your file name has spaces in it, RoboHelp HTML replaces them with underscores.

Status tab

As you create your HTML Help system, your topics will progress at different rates. The Status tab enables you to keep track of what stage of development each topic is in at any time. The Status tab on the Topic Properties window is shown in Figure 18-10.

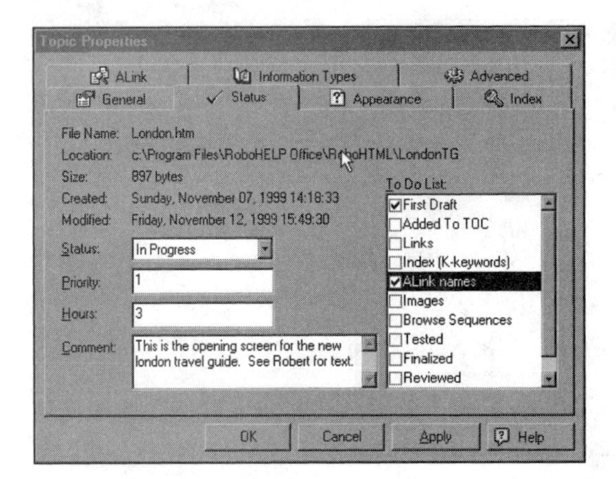

Figure 18-10: The Topic Properties window's Status tab

Information from the Status tab doesn't generally make its way to the WYSIWYG tab for the page, but it is important information for your topic. The contents of the Status tab are used to generate reports to help you track the topic, and the status information is displayed on the Topics tab on the right-hand side of the RoboHELP HTML main window.

The top of the Status tab simply displays information about the topic:

- ✦ **File Name** lists the file name as set in the General tab.
- ✦ **Location** lists the file path for your topic HTML file. This can be a remote or local file path.

- **Size** shows the size (in bytes) of the HTML file for your topic.
- **Created** lists the creation date for the topic.
- **Modified** shows the last time the topic was modified. If you change anything in the Topic Properties window, the new modified date will be the current date.

The bottom half of the Status tab shows the status and planning information for the topic, and gives you a place to comment.

- **Status** allows you to edit the status of the topic. The current status is displayed, and you can use the drop-down list to select a different status for the topic. You can choose from Complete, In Progress, and Ready for Review. For all new topics, the default is In Progress.
- **Priority** lets you set a priority for the topic; by default, it is set to zero. Priority is set by numerical values, and the values can be anything. To set a priority for a topic, enter a value in this box. Priority is a value used for reports.
- **Hours** allows you to estimate the amount of time you expect it to take to complete this topic. Indicate the number of hours by entering a value into this box. Use hours to track topic development. Hours is a value used for reports and planning.
- **Comment** helps you keep your help system development under control, even if the project involves more than one online help author. This box for is for writing comments about the topic, helping everyone keep straight which topic contains which information.
- **To Do List** shows all the tasks involved in completing an HTML Help topic. This is an itemized list of work tasks you should perform to complete your topics. By selecting these items as you complete tasks, you can keep track of the progression of a topic in a more detailed way than available from the Priority list.

For more information on reports in RoboHELP HTML, see Chapter 24, "Using Reports and Compiling."

Appearance tab

HTML Help is more than simply plain black text on a white background. The look and feel of your HTML Help project is based on an overall set of colors, backgrounds, and page layout settings.

This look and feel is set in the Appearance tab. The general settings for each topic page is set in the Appearance tab. The Appearance tab for the Topic Properties window is shown in Figure 18-11.

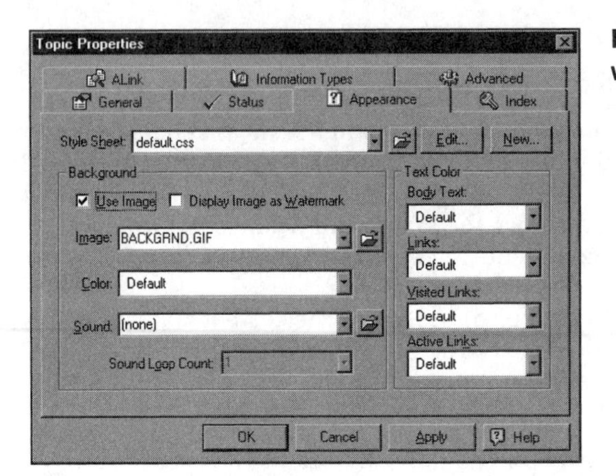

Figure 18-11: The Topic Properties window's Appearance tab

Formatting selections you make in the WYSIWYG tab can override settings in the Appearance tab.

The Appearance tab concerns itself mostly with the overall settings for your topic. The style sheet, the background texture, and the background sound are all set on this tab. You can also set the text color and the color of the links.

The upper row of boxes and buttons on the Appearance tab deals with the style sheet.

✦ **Style Sheet** sets the style sheet attached to the topic. Style sheets are collections of formatting information. Use the open folder button next to the box to browse for other style sheets to use with your topic.

✦ **Edit** allows you to change the styles for the current style sheet, and it also allows you to add new styles or remove styles.

✦ **New** helps you create an entirely new style sheet. The new style sheet becomes the default for all new topics until another one is selected or created.

For more information about style sheets, see Chapter 22, "Using Styles."

The next set of boxes, contained in the Background section, deals primarily with the look and feel of the background.

✦ Selecting **Use Image** allows you to use a jpg or gif image as a wallpaper or background for your topic. Selecting this enables the **Image** box below it.

✦ **Image** sets a GIF or JPEG file to use as the background image for your topic. Background images display behind the text and images on a topic page. They are usually kept plain and simple so they don't distract the user or interfere with the user's understanding of the topic content. By default, backgrounds scroll with the topic as the user moves up and down the page.

✦ **Display Image as Watermark** forces the background image to remain stationary relative to the HTML Help browsing window. The image does not move as the user moves up and down the topic page.

✦ **Color** sets the background color for the topic. If you decide not to use a background image, RoboHELP HTML sets a color for the background of your pages. By default, the color is set to white, but you can choose other colors from the list if you like.

✦ **Sound** allows you to set a sound clip to be played when your user opens the topic. Sound clips can be AU, MIDI, RMI, and WAV sound files. Use the open folder button to browse for your sound clips.

✦ **Sound loop count** sets the number of times the sound clip will be repeated when the user opens the topic By default, the sound clip is played only once. You can select to play it infinite times, which causes the sound to play continuously while the topic is open.

The last part of the Appearance tab, contained in the Text Color section, deals with the color of standard text, as well as the color of links.

✦ **Body text** sets the color for all normal topic text, including paragraph text, headings, lists, and tables.

✦ **Links** sets the color for all the links in the topic when the topic first opens.

✦ **Visited links** sets the color for links the user has already visited or has selected at any time earlier in this session.

✦ **Active links** sets the color for links currently being used, or currently activated, by the user.

It is best practice to set all the color settings for text in the style sheet, rather than in the Appearance tab. That way, you can use the same color setting for other topics.

Index tab

The index may well be the most frequently used part of HTML Help. The index is a quick way to access information, and to find topics that pertain directly to what the user needs to know.

The Index tab on the Topic Properties window is one place you can add index keywords for your topics. The Index tab is shown in Figure 18-12.

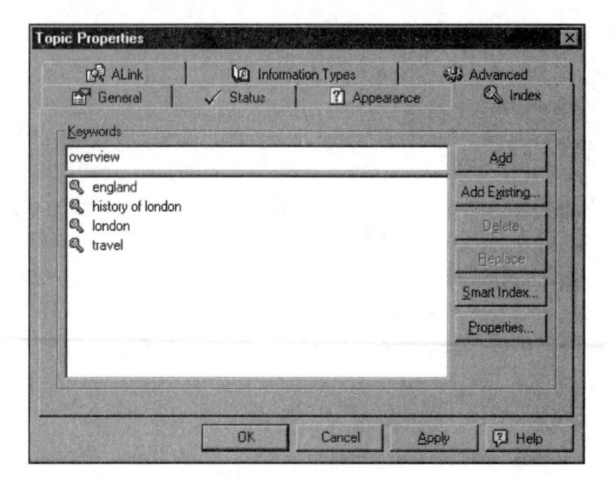

Figure 18-12: The Topic Properties window's Index tab

The Index tab allows you to work with keywords for both your specific topic and the index as a whole at once. Use the Index tab to create keywords for both your topic and the entire project. You can also use the Index tab to add keywords and other index information.

For more information about creating and maintaining the index, see Chapter 23, "Creating a TOC and Index."

The Index tab contains three sections. The first section is the keywords box.

✦ **Keywords** allows you to add keywords or edit existing keywords for the current topic. To add a keyword, type it into the box. To edit a keyword, select it from the list.

The list, located beneath the keywords, shows all keywords assigned to the current topic.

After you have added or edited keywords, use the buttons on the right side of the window to finish the job.

✦ **Add** includes in the index the keyword you entered in the keywords box. The keyword will be displayed in the list after you add it.

✦ **Add Existing** allows you to copy keywords from other topics into the current topic.

✦ **Delete** enables you to remove from the list box a keyword you have selected.

✦ **Replace** allows you to replace the keyword you have selected from the list box with the keyword you have entered into the Keywords box.

✦ **Smart Index** opens the Smart Index Wizard.

✦ **Properties** opens the Project Settings Window in which you can set a custom frame or window for the current topic. When users choose the keyword selected in the list box, the current topic opens using the settings in this window.

You have five ways to enter keywords into your index: by using the Index tab in the main window, by using the Index tab in the Topic Properties window, by dragging the keywords from the WYSIWYG tab, by right-clicking on text in the WYSIWYG tab, and by using the Smart Index window to auto-generate them.

A-link tab

The interconnectedness of online help is what makes it useful to your users. A-links, or the See Also links, help you connect your topics by providing pathways to related topics.

For a complete discussion of links, see Chapter 19, "Creating Outstanding Topics."

A-links can be added in several ways, but the A-link tab in the Topic Properties window is a handy way to add A-link keywords to the current topic. The A-link tab is shown in Figure 18-13.

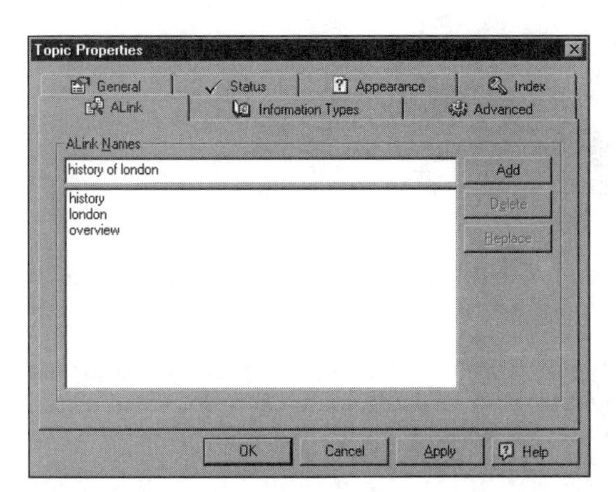

Figure 18-13: The Topic Properties window's A-link tab

✦ The **ALink Names** text box enables you to add new Alink names to your list, and to edit existing names from the list.

  The list box, beneath the Alink Names box, shows all the Alink names for the current topic. All names listed are the ALink names assigned to the current topic.

  The buttons on the left allow you to manipulate the Alink names.

✦ **Add** enables you to include the ALink name you entered in the ALink Names text box. The name is displayed in a list below the text box after it's added.

✦ **Delete** enables you to remove the ALink name selected from the list.

✦ **Replace** enables you to replace the Alink names selected from the list with the Alink text entered in the ALink Names text box.

You can also enter Alinks from the WYSIWYG tab in the RoboHELP HTML main window.

Information Types tab

Information types are a way for you to organize which users see which information. For anything to display in the Information Types tab, you must have added information types to your project. The Information Types tab is shown in Figure 18-14.

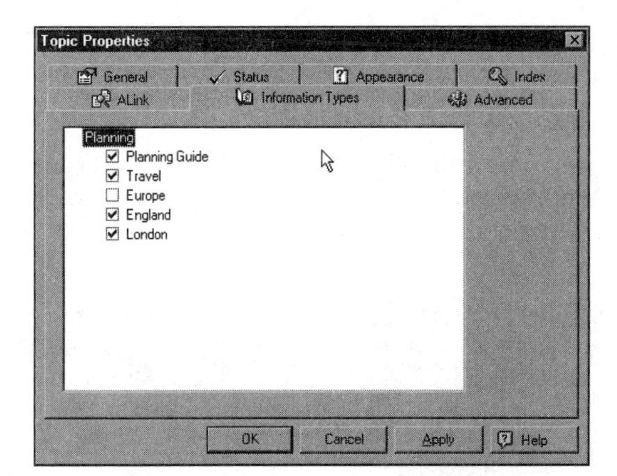

Figure 18-14: The Topic Properties window's Information Types tab

Once you have added information types to your project, RoboHELP HTML lists them in the list box on the Information Types tab.

If you have added information types to your project, you can assign one or more to the current topic by selecting it from the list. You can also remove information types from the topic in this window.

This entire tab is blank if you have not added information types to your project.

Advanced tab

As you create and distribute help materials, be they in printed or online format, you need to select different information for different audiences. The Advanced tab helps you do that by allowing you to select which level of information the current topic includes and when it will be compiled into your HTML Help project.

For more information about compiling, see Chapter 24, "Using Reports and Compiling."

The Advanced tab allows you to add build tags to your topic. You can also use this tab to view the browse sequences. The Advanced tab is shown in Figure 18-15.

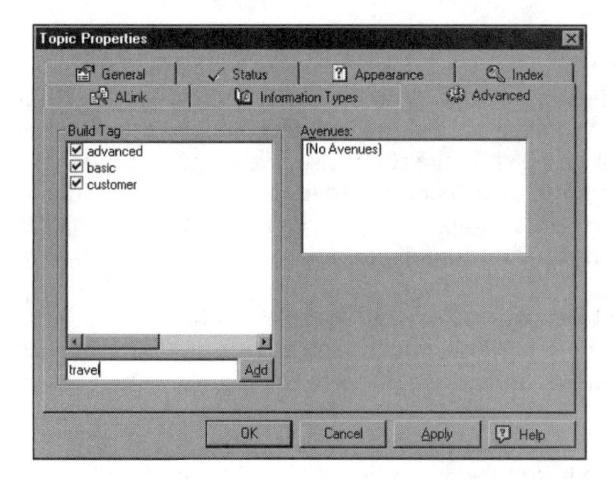

Figure 18-15: The Topic Properties window's Advanced tab

The Advanced tab contains two parts. The left side handles the build tags.

✦ **Build Tag** shows all the build tags available in your project. You can assign and remove build tags from the current topic, and the check box shows the build tag currently set for the topic.

✦ **Add,** and the text box next to it, allow you to create new build tags for the project that are automatically assigned to the current topic.

The right side of the window handles browse sequences.

✦ **Browse sequences** lists the browse sequence for the current topic. More than one browse sequence can be assigned to each topic.

Both build tags and browse sequences should be planned out and added before topics.

Organizing Your Topics

Your topics appear as pages of a book to your users. To you they are separate HTML documents organized into folders. The difference in these two perspectives of topics can create an unusable HTML Help system if you are not careful about how you organize your topics.

The folders that contain topics as you go about creating the HTML Help project become the books that contain the topic pages when RoboHELP HTML compiles them into online help. How these folders are organized is crucial to how your user sees and uses your HTML Help. Good topic organization should always be foremost in your mind as you create your HTML Help project.

Using Folders

HTML Help consists of HTML files linked together with images, text, and scripts. All of this requires numerous files and folders to organize them. Incorrect organization not only leads to confusion, but can also make the HTML Help system unusable. RoboHELP HTML helps you avoid this problem by creating an easy-to-use file set with which you can build your HTML Help project. You can add to this file set by creating your own folder to hold topic and information.

Topics are organized by subject for your users, and folders can help you organize them logical for yourself. Creating a folder for each logical information group helps you keep track of your topics, an organizational system that can be mimicked in your table of contents.

The titles of folders do not make it into the complied HTML Help project, so use whatever names make the most sense to you. Also, note that folders you create in RoboHELP HTML are only accessible through the RoboHELP HTML main window.

Follow these steps to add a folder to a RoboHELP HTML project:

1. Open the HTML Help project.
2. Select the folder you would like to hold the new folder.
3. Choose File ➪ New ➪ Folder. The new folder appears, ready to have you enter its name.
4. Type the name for the folder.
5. When you are done adding the name, press Enter. This deselects the folder and sets the name.

Congratulations, you have just created your first RoboHELP HTML folder!

Compiling

Once you have finished adding topics to your first project, and have included those topics into a folder, you are ready to compile your project.

At its most basic, compiling just requires that you click one button on the main toolbar, but compiling can involve much more than that. Here we will just handle the most basic compiling, but for a more in-depth discussion of compiling your RoboHELP HTML project, see Chapter 24, "Using Reports and Compiling."

Using the Output Screen

When you are ready to compile your project, click the Generate Primary Target button on the RoboHELP HTML main toolbar. This opens the Output screen, as shown in Figure 18-16.

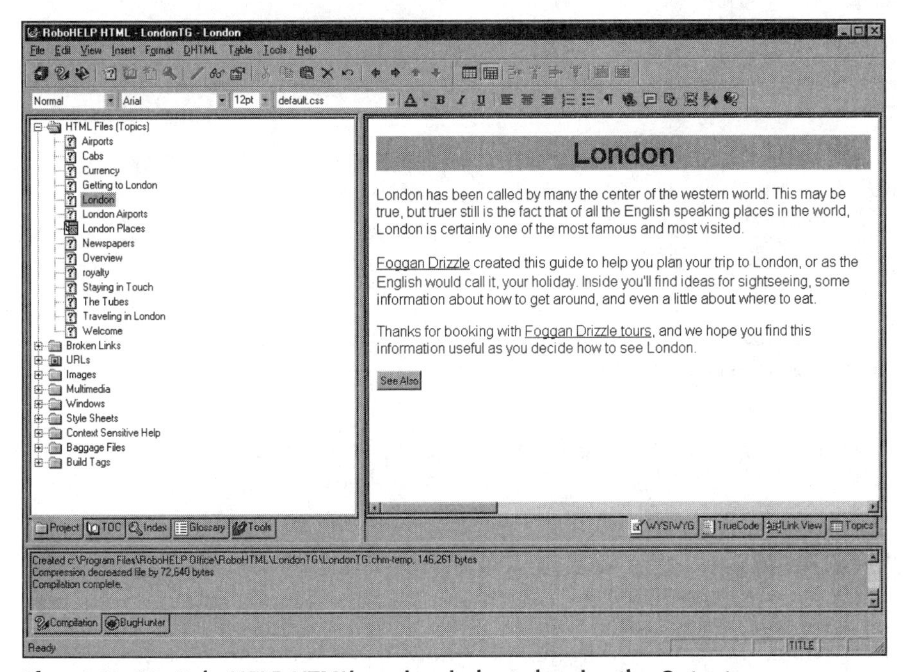
RoboHELP HTML - LondonTG - London
File Edit View Insert Format DHTML Table Tools Help
Normal
Arial
12pt
default.css
HTML Files (Topics)
Airports
Cabs
Currency
Getting to London
London
London Airports
London Places
Newspapers
Overview
royalty
Staying in Touch
The Tubes
Traveling in London
Welcome
Broken Links
URLs
Images
Multimedia
Windows
Style Sheets
Context Sensitive Help
Baggage Files
Build Tags
London
London has been called by many the center of the western world. This may be true, but truer still is the fact that of all the English speaking places in the world, London is certainly one of the most famous and most visited.
Foggan Drizzle created this guide to help you plan your trip to London, or as the English would call it, your holiday. Inside you'll find ideas for sightseeing, some information about how to get around, and even a little about where to eat.
Thanks for booking with Foggan Drizzle tours, and we hope you find this information useful as you decide how to see London.
See Also
Project
TOC
Index
Glossary
Tools
WYSIWYG
TrueCode
Link View
Topics
Compression decreased file by 72,640 bytes
Compilation complete.
Compilation
BugHunter
Ready
TITLE

Figure 18-16: RoboHELP HTML's main window, showing the Output screen

Cross-Reference

The Output screen has two tabs. For more information about these tabs, see Chapter 17, "Using RoboHELP HTML."

The Output screen shows you the progress of your compiling, and lists all the parts of your project as they are compiled into the primary target. The primary target is the file that runs your HTML Help project. It is the chm file you know as the main help file.

Running Your Project

Once the Output screen indicates "Compilation complete," you are ready to run your HTML Help project as a true help project. To do so, click the Run Primary Target button or select File ➪ Run - Microsoft HTML Help file. This opens as HTML Help project like the one shown in Figure 18-17.

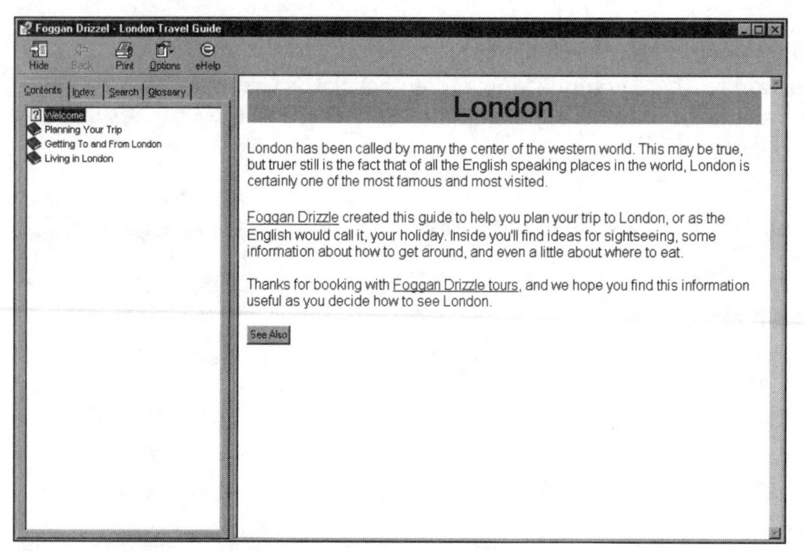
Foggan Drizzel - London Travel Guide
Hide
Back
Print
Options
eHelp
Contents
Index
Search
Glossary
Welcome
Planning Your Trip
Getting To and From London
Living in London
London
London has been called by many the center of the western world. This may be true, but truer still is the fact that of all the English speaking places in the world, London is certainly one of the most famous and most visited.
Foggan Drizzle created this guide to help you plan your trip to London, or as the English would call it, your holiday. Inside you'll find ideas for sightseeing, some information about how to get around, and even a little about where to eat.
Thanks for booking with Foggan Drizzle tours, and we hope you find this information useful as you decide how to see London.
See Also

Figure 18-17: A completed HTML Help project

Congratulations, you have just completed your first HTML Help project!

Summary

In this chapter, you created your very first HTML Help project. You learned how to start, name, and save your project, and how to add topics to your new project. You learned how to set the properties for your new topics. You also learned how to organize your topics into folders. You learned how to add text, graphics, and links to your topics, and how to logically place information on your HTML Help topic pages. Finally, you learned how to initialize a RoboHELP HTML compiling session to view the results of your efforts.

✦ ✦ ✦

CHAPTER 19

Creating Outstanding Topics

✦ ✦ ✦ ✦

In This Chapter

Page layout for topics

Formatting the topic page

Using color

Adding lists

Using tables

✦ ✦ ✦ ✦

In this chapter you'll learn how to create outstanding topics to keep your users interested and to help them learn from the content you create. You'll learn how to use formatting to help convey information, and you'll learn how to lay out topics in ways that increase interest in the subject matter. You'll learn how to use color to get your point across, and you'll learn when to stick with black and white. Once you've covered all the basics of topic layout, you'll learn how to add lists to your topics, both bulleted and numbered. Then you'll learn how to add tables to organize and display information. At the end of the chapter you'll feel confident that you can create interesting and dynamic topics that will interest and excite your users.

Laying Out Your Topic Pages

The look of your topic pages sets the look for your entire project. The way you lay out your topics has a huge effect on how the user perceives the information you are trying to convey. Therefore, layout is one of the most important early planning decisions you can make about your topics.

There are several ways you can lay out your topics. You can make many choices about fonts, colors, and images that have huge ramifications for the look and feel of your HTML Help project. RoboHELP HTML makes many of these choices easy to implement and helps you create just the look you want. But you must know what kind of look you want.

Deciding Layout Basics

There are four basic layout parts you need to determine before you begin creating topics in your HTML Help project, each of which is discussed in detail in this section.

Font

The text on the screen conveys the bulk of the information in any HTML Help project. Both style and size are important considerations. Here are some questions to help you narrow down your font choices:

- Does your organization have a preferred font style for printed and online material?
- What fonts are your users likely to have installed on their system already?
- At what resolution are you users likely to view your HTML Help project?
- Do you want a title font that is different from the body text font?

As a general rule, sans serif fonts (like Arial) are easier to read on a computer screen, so most online help uses this font.

Never use more than three different fonts on any given topic, and try to use less than five fonts for your entire project, title fonts included. This guideline ensures that your project looks well thought out, because too many fonts gives the reader a "ransom note" effect with different fonts starting to do battle on the page. Even within this guideline, make sure that all the fonts on a given page look good together, which means they look like they were meant to go together and not like they were developed in different universes.

Once you have decided on both the size and style of your font, you are ready to proceed to deciding on colors.

Colors

One of the best parts of online help over printed documentation is that in the online format you have the option of making your point with color. You can choose colors for text, background, and links on each and every topic page. However, too many colors can be confusing instead of allowing you to convey information better.

It is best to choose a small number of colors, called the *color set*, for your entire HTML Help project. A color set is a small number of related colors that you use in your HTML Help project; color sets help guarantee that your project looks like it was planned and that it goes together. Using the same set of colors throughout your project helps you create an overall look and theme for the project and not only helps you by making the inclusion of color organized, but it helps the users by inspiring confidence because your HTML Help project looks well planned.

You need to decide the color set for three parts of your HTML Help project:

- ✦ Font Color
- ✦ Background Color
- ✦ Hyperlink Color

The "Formatting Your Topics" section later in this chapter discusses in-depth how to include these colors in your HTML Help project.

Images

They say a picture is worth a thousand words. Whether or not that is true, pictures in your HTML Help project certainly are the most eye-catching part of the project. Images are important not only because they catch the interest of your users, but also because they convey information and help establish a cohesive theme for the entire online help system.

When you begin to think about images, there are three types that you are likely to want to include in your HTML Help project:

- ✦ Screen shots
- ✦ Conceptual art
- ✦ Flavor images

Screen shots are images that you take out of the computer program or other systems for which you are creating the HTML Help project. You may or may not need them, but if you are creating an online help system for some piece of software, you are going to need at least a few screen shots.

Conceptual art illustrates something that cannot be conveyed in any other way. Usually, it is supported by text explaining something. Conceptual art can be anything from a process flowchart to a simple arrow diagram. Include conceptual art when you need to communicate information that cannot be done with text, or when you need an image to do the speaking for you.

Flavor images include all art that you include for the "look and feel" effect. This means all images of people, places, or things, which don't convey information, are flavor text. Images, for their own sake, are very important in your HTML Help project. In addition to giving the impression of a very thoughtfully produced and executed project, they increase interest in your topics by giving the user something to look at.

See Chapter 20, "Creating and Adding Graphics," for a complete discussion of including graphics in you HTML Help project.

Page layout

Once you have decided on all the other parts of your HTML Help project, you are ready to start thinking about page layout within the topics. How your pages are laid out effects how the information is conveyed to the user. When users read a page of your online help project, they should never notice the page layout; it should be totally transparent to them. If your users are noticing the layout of pages, you haven't done the best job you could.

To achieve the concept of transparent page layout, you should create *layout templates* during the planning stage of your HTML Help project. Layout templates are standardized ways to lay out topics. They show the ways each type of topic will look to the user, and they show whoever is going to produce the pages how to do the work.

To create a layout template, make small sketches of how you would like the pages to appear to the user. Show the location of images, the flow of text, and the location of buttons. Figure 19-1 shows one example of the many layout templates in RoboHelp HTML.

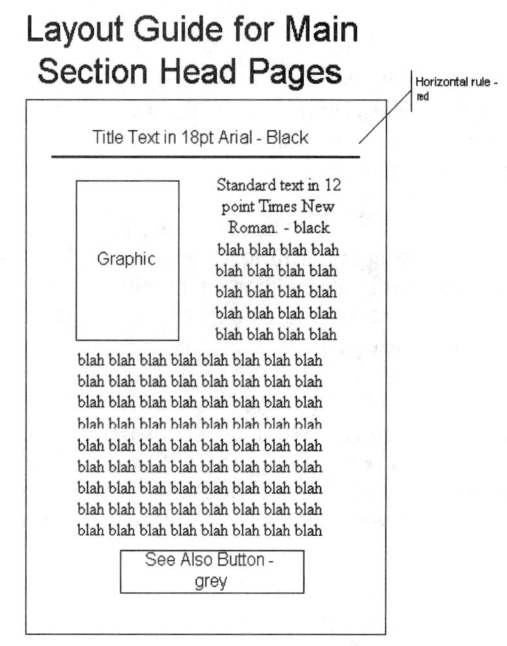

Figure 19-1: An example layout template

Most HTML Help projects of any size need at least three layout templates to complete the project because there are usually at least three different levels, or kinds, of topics. Take a look at all the topics you have proposed and start to organize them according to topic level and content, if you haven't already, and think about a layout template for each type of topic. The templates should all work together, but should be separate and fit the needs of the topics that will use them.

Last, include the layout templates, along with detailed information about font size and style, colors sets, and other formatting decisions, with your HTML Help project planning information. This ensures that your HTML Help project looks professional and that all information about the layout of your topics is quick and easy to find for those doing the work.

Make sure that your documentation plan includes some information about the layout of your topics. Otherwise you'll have to handle the situation later when it is much more cumbersome.

Using Your Layout Templates

Once you have set up the layout templates, including font and color information, you are ready to start creating topic pages. Here are some steps to help you use your layout information:

1. Make sure that you have created style sheets to correspond to your layout templates.

For more information about style sheets, see Chapter 22, "Using Styles."

2. Make sure that the selected fonts are installed on all the computers that will produce topics.
3. Finally, verify that all members of your team have the layout information and the documentation plan.

Formatting Your Topics

RoboHELP HTML starts all of your topics out as simple black text on a white background. This simple and elegant layout can be useful for communicating your topics to your users, but you will probably want to change the layout of at least some of your pages.

Choosing Fonts

You convey information from your online help using text. Just like this book, online help speaks to your users with words made up of letters. The forms of those letters are set by the font choice.

RoboHELP HTML has two different procedures for helping you choose a font. You can either change the font on the page, usually by selecting it and then altering its settings, or you can choose a font set.

Changing the font

By default all new topics in RoboHELP HTML start out with Arial (a standard Windows font) as the only font on the page. Headings are done in 24 point Arial and body text is done in 12 point Arial. Depending on your documentation plan and your layout templates, you may want to change this default.

The quickest and easiest way to alter the font is to use the toolbars. Here's how:

1. Open the topic you want to alter.
2. Choose the WYSIWYG tab in the right pane.
3. Using the text pointer, select the text you'd like to alter.
4. Using the text toolbars (shown in Figure 19-2), use the drop-down lists to change the font or the font size.

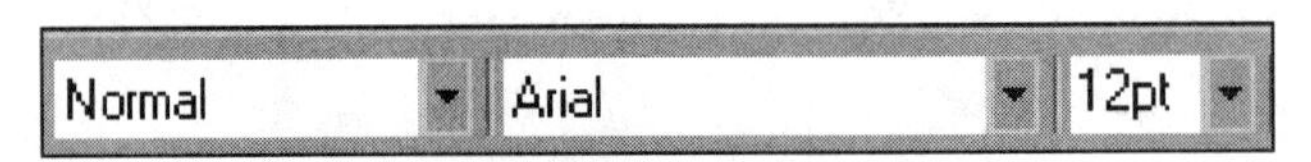

Figure 19-2: Text Formatting toolbars

5. Select somewhere else on the WYSIWYG tab to deselect the text.

Figure 19-3 shows a portion of a default topic (the second paragraph) that has had its text changed to Times New Roman, 14 point.

You can also alter the font settings for text by using the Character formatting window. The process for doing this is very much like the process for changing a font setting in a word processing program. Here's how:

1. Open the topic you want to alter.
2. Choose the WYSIWYG tab in the right pane.
3. Using the text pointer, select the text you'd like to alter.

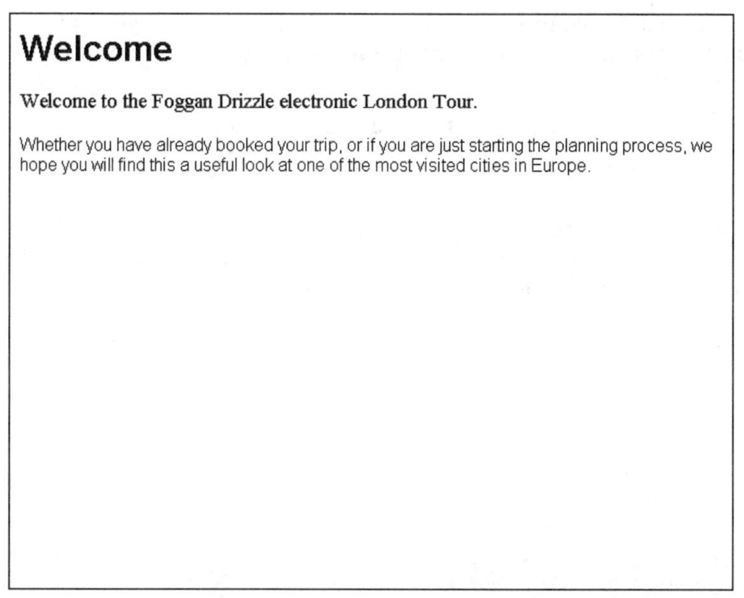

Figure 19-3: Topic with text changed to 14 point, Times New Roman

4. Select Format ➪ Character. This opens the Character window shown in Figure 19-4.

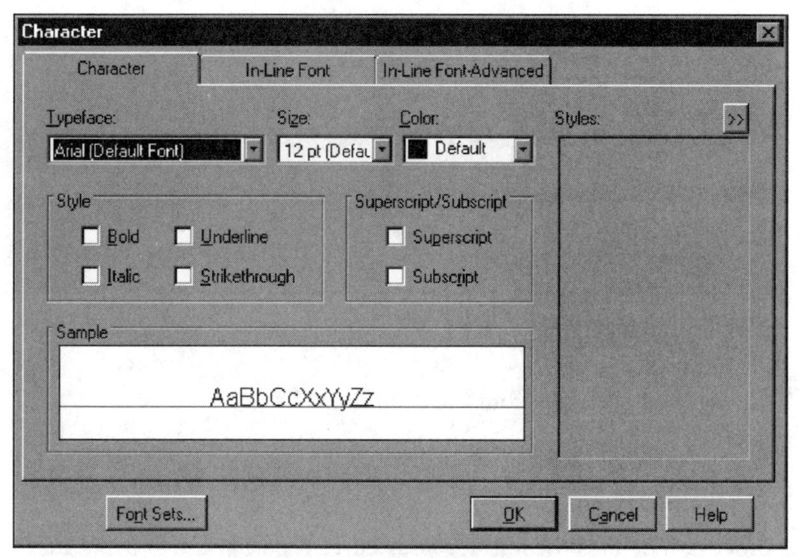

Figure 19-4: Character window — Character tab

5. Select the font name and font size you want for the text you are altering. As you choose changes from the list, the sample text shows how it will look on the screen.
6. Once you are satisfied with the changes, click OK.
7. Select somewhere else on the WYSIWYG tab to deselect the text.

Make sure you know which fonts your users are likely to have installed, or your font choices may be overridden by their system settings. Instead of choosing an exact font, you may want to choose a font set.

You can also alter the font when you alter the paragraph style, by using the Paragraph Style window like this:

1. Select the text you want to alter.
2. Choose Format ⇨ Paragraph. This displays the window shown in Figure 19-5.

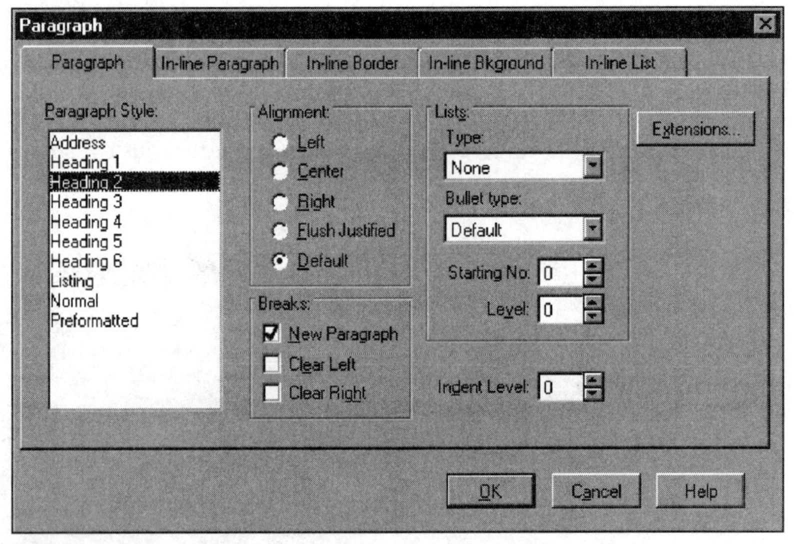

Figure 19-5: Paragraph window

3. Chose the font name from the drop-down list.
4. Choose the font size from the drop-down list.
5. When you are finished making choices about your font, click OK.

This process redefines the font for your current paragraph and all other paragraphs that use that style.

Creating font sets

You can choose fonts for all your topics and you can be judicious about using your layout templates and their corresponding style sheets. However, what if your users don't have that font installed on their system? HTML and HTML Help let you define fonts, but they don't guarantee that they will be there waiting for you to use by default. Any font that is called for that does not exist on the system is ignored, and the default system font is substituted instead. This means all your hard work could be for naught if the user does not already have your font installed.

There are two ways out of this common HTML dilemma.

- ✦ Use a font you can guarantee is installed, such as one of the standard fonts that ship with Windows.
- ✦ Choose a font family.

Using a font that you can be sure is installed is a reasonable solution, but it severely limits your choices of fonts, and it can become impossible as you start to cross platforms.

Choosing a font family, or a font set, is reasonable way out of the predicament. A font set is a defined group of fonts, and when HTML Help sees a font set definition, it uses any of the fonts in that set to display the topic. For example, Arial is part of the sans serif font set, and if you choose sans serif as your font set, then Arial is one of the fonts the system would choose if it were available. This means you need not worry about how your topics look to the your users because even if they don't have the font you wanted, they should have something similar.

The fonts that make up a font set are listed in a particular order, and the order is very important. This is the same order in which the HTML Help browser attempts to display the fonts. First it tries the first font on the list; if it is not installed, then it tries the second, and so on, before it reaches the end of the list. If your users have any of the fonts installed, HTML Help displays the topic using one of the fonts you chose. Font sets give you a much greater chance of finding and using a font your user has than a single font name does, and it also helps you feel secure that your topics will display as you choose.

Font sets are used in RoboHELP HTML the same way fonts are. In fact, once you create a font set, it displays on the formatting toolbar the same as any other named font loaded into your system, or at least it does in RoboHELP HTML.

Defining a font set should always be done in the HTML Help project in which you expect to use it, because font sets are saved with the project. Here' s how to define a font set:

1. Open the HTML Help project.
2. Select Format ➪ Font Sets. This opens the font sets window as shown in Figure 19-6.

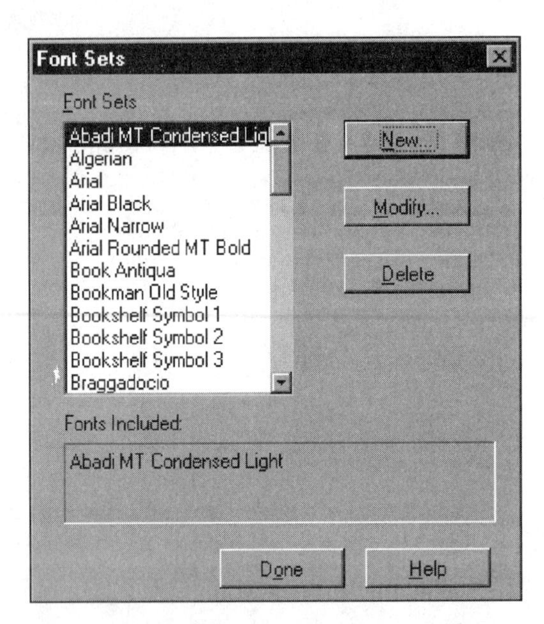

Figure 19-6: Font Sets window

3. Select to create a new font set by clicking New. This opens the Edit Font Sets window, as shown in Figure 19-7.

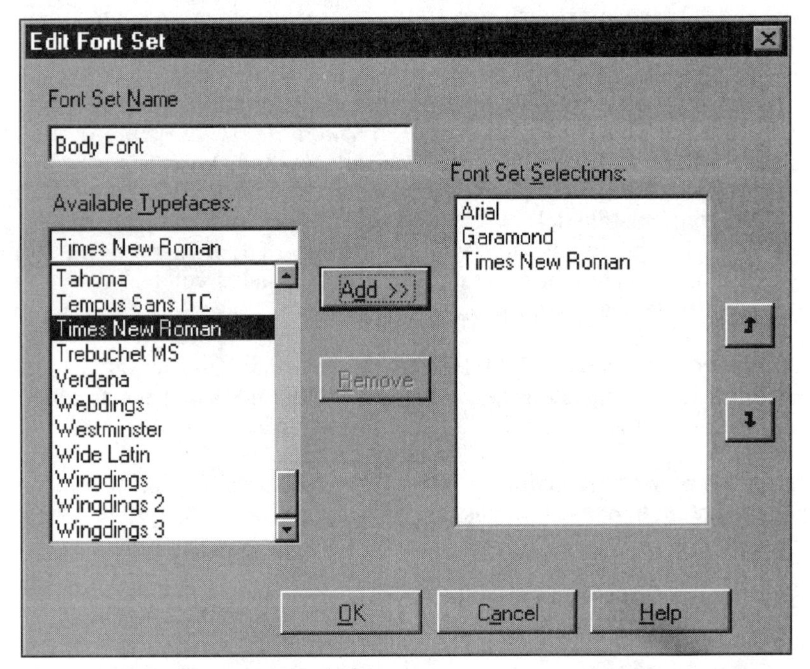

Figure 19-7: Edit Font Sets window

4. Type a name for your new font set into the Font Set Name box. Do not use the name of a font that already exists. You can distinguish font sets by adding "set" to the end of the name, if you like.
5. Select the font you want to be the primary font in the font set list.
6. Click Add. This moves the font to the right-hand box, which lists all the fonts included in the font set.
7. Continue adding fonts to the font set by selecting them and then clicking Add. Always use the default system font as the last font in your font set because the user's computer will choose it anyway. You can also add fonts that are not currently on your computer by typing their names into the font set box.
8. Sort the fonts in the right-hand box by selecting them and then using the up and down arrows.
9. Once all the fonts are included and in the correct order, save your new font set by clicking OK. Don't forget to close the Font Sets window as well as the New Font Set window.

Edit a font set by selecting the font set from the list, on the Format ⇨ Font Sets window, and then clicking Edit. The Edit Font Set window looks and behaves almost exactly like the new Font Sets window.

To use your new font set, select the text you wish to alter, and then choose the font set from the Formatting toolbar (shown in Figure 19-8).

Figure 19-8: Font set box on the Formatting toolbar

Font sets are treated like normal fonts in the RoboHELP HTML WYSISWG tab; however, if you look at the code created on the True Code tab, you'll see that RoboHELP HTML makes the font change a font set instead of just a font name.

Best practice is always to use font sets instead of only font names.

Using Color

Without color, your topics look no different on the screen than they would on paper—white background with black text. Color helps you communicate with your users, not only by helping you get their attention, but also by helping them see the most important information quickly and easily.

Judicious use of color brings attention to text and can liven up pages that might otherwise be boring. Use color as you would any other attention-drawing, page layout technique. Make sure that color is used carefully by applying some of the same rules that apply to fonts: no more than three colors per page and a limited color set for the entire project. Too many colors in a topic create the opposite of the desired effect by creating confusion and by not allowing your users to concentrate on the information they need.

There are three places you can make changes to the color in your RoboHELP HTML project:

✦ Text

✦ Background

✦ Hyperlink

This section outlines the how and why of each type of color change, as well as how to create your own custom colors.

Just as with fonts, the best practice is to create a "color set" for your project during the planning stages. Color sets help you make sure you don't over-stimulate the user with too many colors, and they help make sure your project has a consistent look throughout.

Coloring text

You can change the color of any text on the topic page. All plain text is set to be black by default for every newly created topic based on the default templates that come with RoboHELP HTML.

Not all colors are created the same. Some special colors do not transfer well to your users' systems. For more information, see the "Creating Custom Colors" section later in this chapter.

There are three ways to change the font color:

✦ Inline color change using toolbar buttons

✦ Using the Font window

✦ As a change to the Style Sheet

The way in which you alter the color of your font depends on the type of change you are making and how often you expect to make the change. Single word changes that you expect to be done only once can be inline changes made using the toolbar. If you want more control and are changing more than just the color of the font, use the Font window. For color changes you expect to affect more than just one topic, or for color changes that you need to do several times, use the style sheet.

For more information about style sheets, see Chapter 22 "Using Styles."

Here's how to make an inline color change using the toolbar buttons:

1. Select the word or words you want to change.
2. Open the drop-down menu using the text color button (shown in Figure 19-9).

Figure 19-9: Text color button

3. Select a color from the list. Once you select a color, the drop-down list disappears.
4. Deselect the word or words by clicking somewhere else on the topic page.

Take a look at your words now, to confirm that you've chosen the right color. If you need a different color, redo all the steps or use the next procedure for the font window.

If you want to try more than one color to see how it looks, or if you want to alter the color of more than one block of text on one topic page, use the Character window. Here's how:

1. Select the words or paragraph you wish to alter.
2. Choose Format ➪ Character. RoboHELP HTML opens the Character window shown in Figure 19-10.

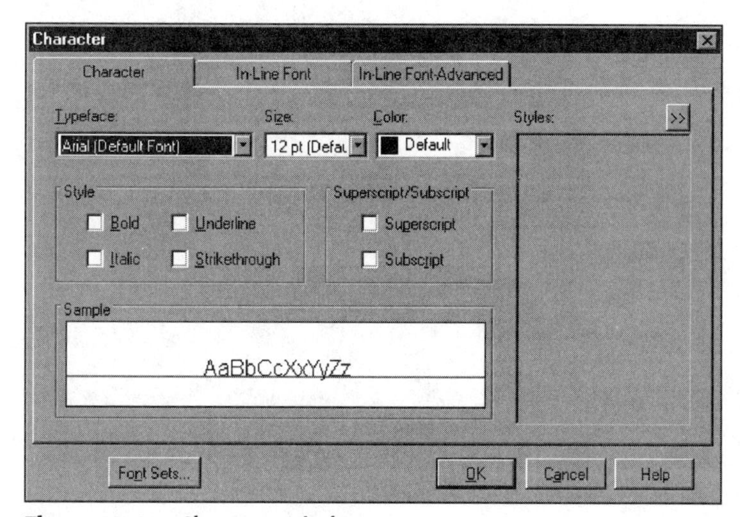

Figure 19-10: Character window

3. Use the drop-down Color list to choose a color.
4. Use the Sample window to preview the color choice.
5. Once you are pleased with the color, make all other font changes.
6. When you are finished altering the font, click OK. RoboHELP HTML closes the Character window.

Once the Character window closes, take a look at your changes and make sure they match the rest of your topics. The style and format of the rest of your topic may not be what you want with the color changes you made in the Character window.

The best and most consistent way to make sure all parts of your topics coordinate with the colors and fonts you select is to make these changes in the style sheet. Style sheets allow you to make all the changes to the default styles that come with Robo-HELP HTML at once, and then allow you to save them together to use over and over.

Altering the font color, or any other font information, on a style sheet requires that you alter the default style information. If you do not want to do so in the default templates that come with RoboHELP HTML, you need to create a new template to use. For information on how to do this, see Chapter 22, "Using Styles."

Here's how you use a style sheet to make changes to font color:

1. Select the topic you wish to change.
2. Choose Format ➪ Style Sheets. The Edit Style Sheet window appears, as shown in Figure 19-11.

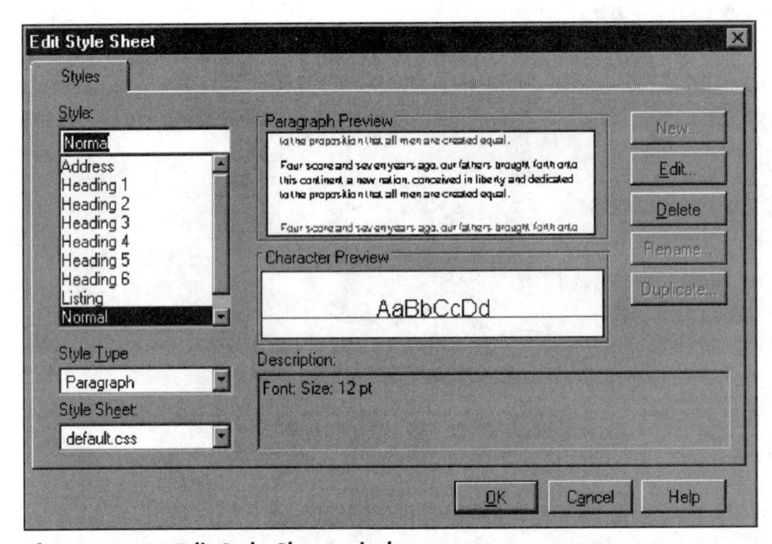

Figure 19-11: Edit Style Sheet window

3. Select the style you wish to change from the left-hand list.

4. Click Edit. This opens the Edit window for that paragraph style, as shown in Figure 19-12.

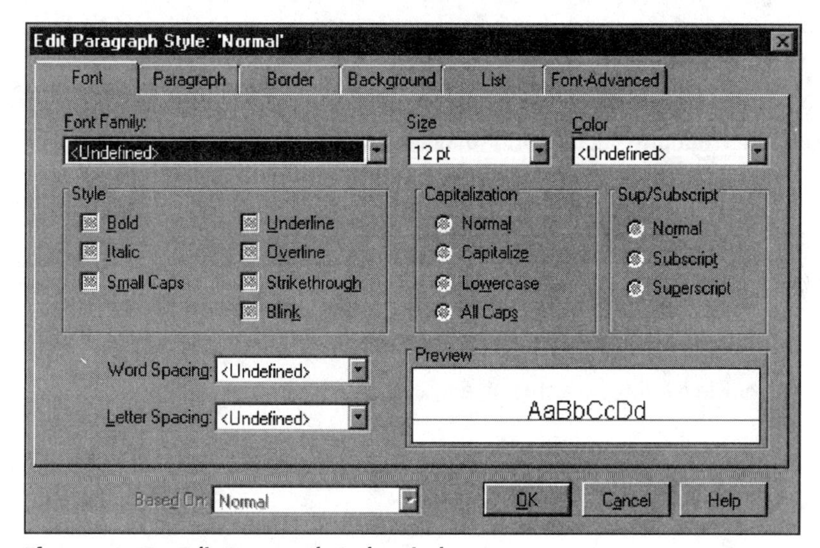

Figure 19-12: Edit Paragraph Style window

5. Make the change to the font color using the right-most drop-down list, labeled Color.

6. Use the Preview box to verify the color change is correct.

7. Make all other changes to the font style using the drop-down lists.

8. When you are satisfied with the font color and style, click OK. RoboHELP HTML closes the Edit Paragraph Style window.

9. If you want to edit another style, choose it from the list and click Edit. Repeat steps 4–8 to edit the style information.

10. When you are done editing the font colors for styles in this style sheet, Click OK on the Edit Style Sheet window.

RoboHELP HTML closes the window and returns you to the main RoboHELP HTML window. Take a few moments to look at your topic and make sure that all the colors and font styles you have chosen work well together.

Coloring the background

The color of your text is not the only thing your users see. By default, the background of every topic page is white. When the text is black, the white background gives the impression of a printed page, like one in your printed help materials. If you decide to change the text color, and maybe even if you don't, the white background may not go well with the color or style theme you've decided to use for your HTML Help project.

Altering the white background for your topics adds zest to your information. Subtle changes can give a quiet and interesting change to your HTML Help window. Bolder changes, on the other hand, can make a statement. Changing the background should be something you decide to do in the planning stages of your project, using the same general themes as for font color and font styles. Also, it is important to remember that any background images will hide the background color.

As a general rule, the background color should be consistent for your entire project, with only one or two colors used.

There are two ways to change your background:

✦ Change the white background to another color.

✦ Include a subtle graphic as a background.

This section covers changing your background to another color. If you wish to add a background image to your topics, please see Chapter 20, "Creating and Adding Graphics."

Changing the background color is something you should do only once or twice in a project, and not something you should do individually for every topic. Individually, different colors for every topic can be confusing and can lead to a very unprofessional looking HTML Help project. To avoid this problem, RoboHELP HTML forces you to change the background color for a style sheet, and consequently all the topics based on that style sheet, instead of one topic at a time.

If you attempt to change the background color in the Topic Properties window without first changing it on the style sheet, the change will not work.

Here's how you change the background color:

1. Select a topic with the style sheet you want to change attached to it.
2. Choose Format ➪ Style Sheet. RoboHELP HTML opens the Edit Style Sheet window shown in Figure 19-11.
3. Choose Document in the Style Type window. The Edit Style Sheet window changes to look like the one shown in Figure 19-13.
4. Verify that Body is selected in the Style box.

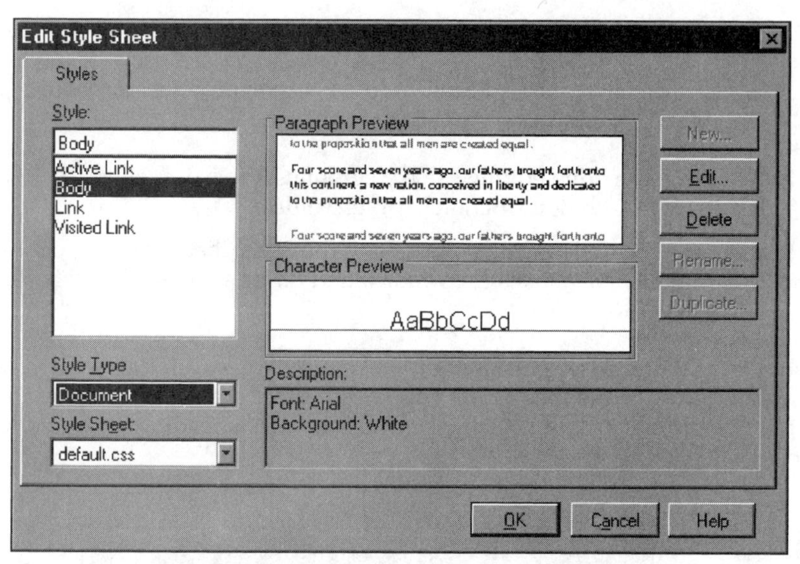

Figure 19-13: Edit Style Sheet Window – Document Style Type

5. Click Edit. RoboHELP HTML opens the Edit Document Style window.
6. Choose the Background tab. The Edit Documents Style window looks like the one shown in Figure 19-14.

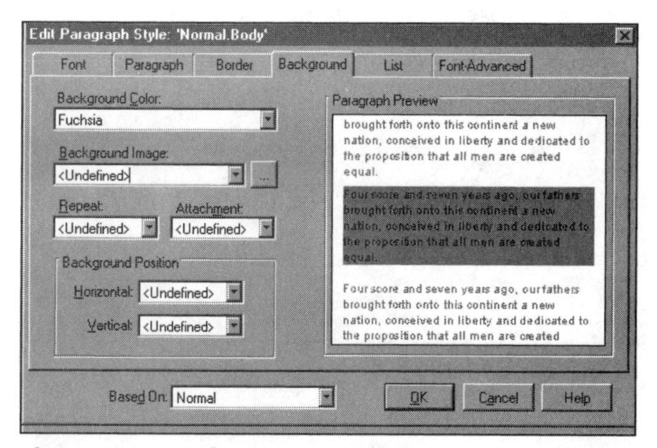

Figure 19-14: Edit Document Style window – Background tab

7. Use the Background Color drop-down list to select a background color.

If you change the color to transparent, the color displays as gray because it is the HTML default. Choose a color instead, unless you are using a graphic. If you choose undefined, then you can choose background colors individually for each topic in the Topic Properties window, which is usually not a good idea.

8. When you are done editing the background properties, click OK. RoboHELP HTML closes the Edit Document Style window.
9. After you are done making changes to the Style Sheet window, click OK. RoboHELP HTML closes the window and returns you to the main RoboHELP HTML window.

Also, you can alter all or part of your background color. Altering all of your background color is the most common choice, but there are occasions when you may want to color only part of your background, behind a heading for example, as shown in Figure 19-15.

London

London has been called by many the center of the western world. This may be true, but truer still is the fact that of all the English speaking places in the world, London is certainly one of the most famous and most visited.

Foggan Drizzle **created** this guide to help you plan your trip to London, or as the English would call it, your holiday. Inside you'll find ideas for sightseeing, some information about how to get around, and even a little about where to eat.

Thanks for booking with Foggan Drizzle tours, and we hope you find this information useful as you decide how to see London.

Figure 19-15: Example of HTML Help topic with the background altered behind a heading

Here's how to change just part of your background to another color:

1. Select the topic you want to change.
2. In the WYSIWYG tab, choose the paragraph you want to alter.
3. Choose Format ➪ Paragraph. RoboHELP HTML opens the paragraph window.
4. Choose the In-line Bkground tab as shown in Figure 19-16.

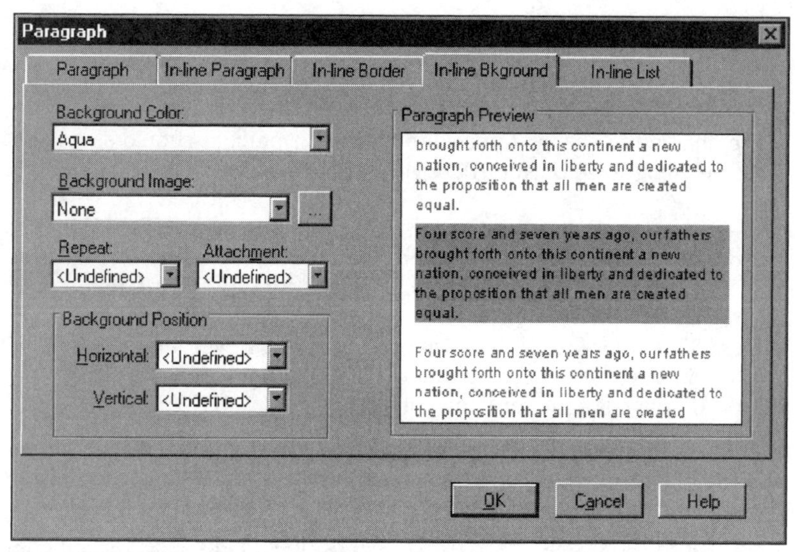

Figure 19-16: Paragraph window — In-line Bkground tab

5. Choose a background color from the drop-down list.
6. Use the Paragraph Preview box to verify your color choice.
7. When you are done editing the background information, click OK.

Once you are back to the RoboHELP HTML main window, verify that your color choices work well together.

You can permanently alter the background behind a style in the style sheet so that every time you use that heading level the background is different. See Chapter 28, "Using Styles."

Coloring the hyperlinks

HTML has, by default, set every hyperlink to be blue underlined text. As more and more people use the Internet and other hyperlinked information sources, they are getting used to this default. RoboHELP HTML allows you to change the color of your hyperlinks, but be very careful about doing so. Here are a few guidelines:

✦ Hyperlink colors should be changed only for your entire HTML Help project because when you change the color your users will need to relearn what hyperlinked text looks like; users should have to do that only once in your entire HTML Help project.

✦ Make sure you have colors for all the parts of a hyperlinks, both unvisited and visited, that work with your entire color scheme. A common mistake is to change the background color so that visited hyperlinks become almost or completely invisible.

✦ Be very careful about removing the underline or other visual cues that a piece of text is a hyperlink. Users expect highlighted underlined text to be hyperlinks and can get easily confused if it changes.

The decision to change the color or style of hyperlinks should always be made at the planning stage of your HTML Help project.

Also, there is more than just one type of hyperlink in your HTML Help project. The standard link, made of blue underlined text by default, is just one of three link types. They are referred to in RoboHELP HTML by their HTML names as follows:

✦ **Link:** This refers to any link that the user has never visited, or hasn't visited in the interval set in the browser (usually a few days to a month). By default, links display as blue text underlined.

✦ **Active Link:** This is a currently selected link. By default, it is red and underlined, and in newer browsers it may have a dashed box around it. Only one link can be active at a time.

✦ **Visited Link:** Any link that the user has clicked recently should show up as a visited link. Also red and underlined, you can have more than one visited link on a page.

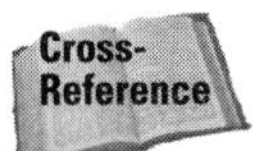

For information about including links to other topics and other documents in your HTML Help project, see Chapter 27, "Adding Links, Windows, and Popups."

Once you have dealt with the issue surrounding changing the link colors, and you understand the different types of links, you are ready to start editing your hyperlink colors. Editing hyperlink colors, like editing text colors, can be done a couple of ways. How you edit the hyperlink colors depends a great deal on how many times you plan to make the change, and in how many topics you plan to make the change.

You can edit the hyperlink color for just one topic in the Topic Properties window. This is a very bad idea and should be done only with serious consideration.

A better idea is to edit the hyperlink color on the style sheet, so that no matter which topic uses the style sheet, the hyperlinks are always formatted the same way.

Here's how you edit the hyperlink color for a style sheet:

1. Select a topic with the style sheet you want to edit attached to it.
2. Choose Format ➪ Style Sheets. This opens the Edit Style Sheet window as shown in Figure 19-17.
3. Make sure Document is selected in the Style Type drop-down list. RoboHELP HTML displays the three link types and body in the style list.

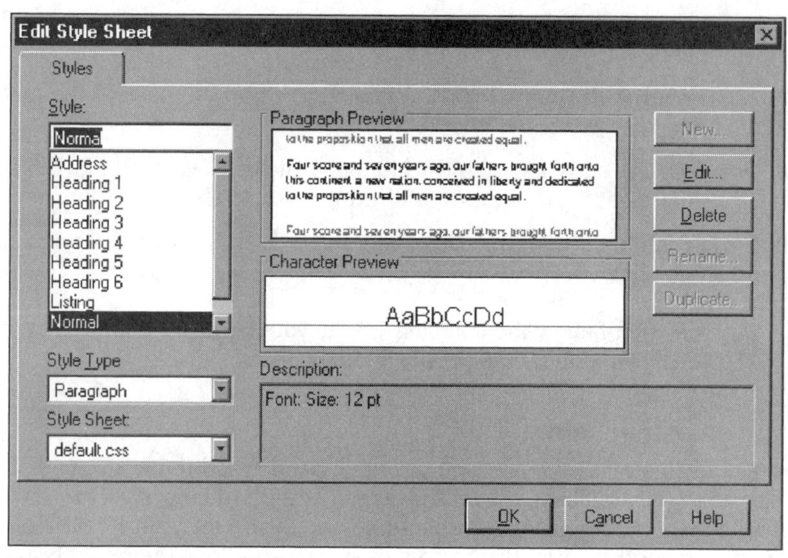

Figure 19-17: Edit Style Sheet window

4. Select a link type from the style list.
5. Click Edit. RoboHELP HTML displays the Edit Style Sheet window as shown in Figure 19-18.

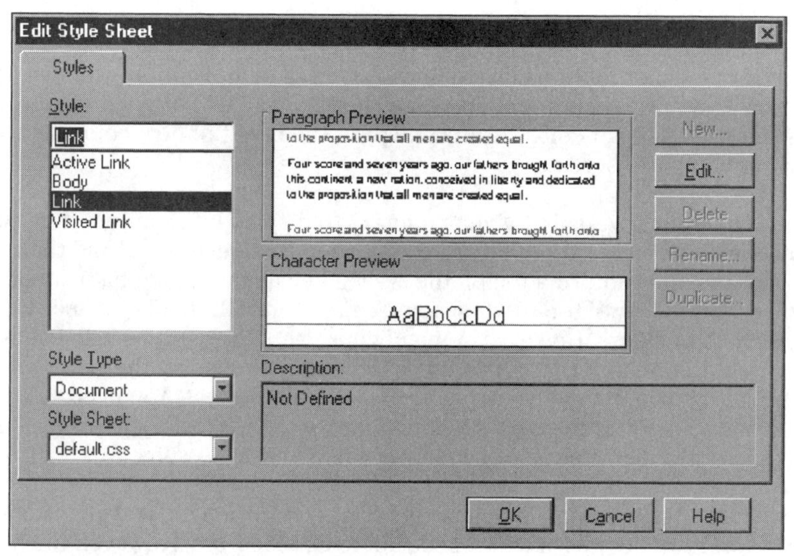

Figure 19-18: Edit Style Sheet window

6. Use the color drop-down list to select a color for your link and use the sample window to verify your color choice.
7. Use the other drop-down lists to make any other changes to the font and style of your hyperlinks.
8. Once you are satisfied with the changes, click OK. RoboHELP HTML closes the Edit Document Style window and returns you to the Edit Style Sheet window.
9. If you wish to edit another link type, select it and return to step 5. If you are finished, click OK.

For more information about adding links to your HTML Help project, see Chapter 21, "Adding Windows, Popups, and Special Effects."

Creating custom colors

Throughout this section on colors, you have been asked to choose your colors from the drop-down lists. These colors are default, standard colors, and often they are too limited to give you the true range of colors you desire for your HTML Help project. You may have noticed that the bottom of every drop-down color list is an entry for you to define your own colors. This section details how and why you would want to define a custom color for you HTML Help project.

First and foremost, before you can begin defining colors for your project, you need to understand the issues with colors and online help.

Understanding the issues with colors

Color is a simple concept, so simple that most people have mastered the basics before they are out of diapers. However, when it comes to electronic display of information, color takes on several new layers of complication — the most important being that your choice of color may not be available on your user's computer. This unavailability of colors is, in large part, the result of how colors are displayed on your computer screen.

When computers were first given monitors to display information, they could show only one color, either green or white. As computers developed, and their ability to display and show information on the screen became more sophisticated, more colors were added, until today when some computers can display as many as several dozen million colors. However, some of your users may still be using older computers or older monitors that do not have the ability to display the same colors as the computer on which you develop your HTML Help project. You need to be very careful to make sure that the colors you choose for your HTML Help project are supported by all the computers to which you're planning to ship.

Because the largest boon in computers happened when most systems could display 256 colors, you do have a wide spectrum to choose from. However, the list is not infinite and custom colors can lead to unsupported colors if you are not careful.

You can always be sure that the 16 colors in the drop-down list are supported; they are basic system colors. Other than that, you need to test any custom colors you choose.

Creating new colors

Once you understand how your color choices can affect your users, you are ready to start making custom colors for use in your HTML Help project.

Color choices are centrally controlled in RoboHELP HTML. This means when you create a custom color in one place it is available to you from every other color list in the entire project. Here's how you create a custom color:

1. Open any topic in the HTML Help project.
2. Choose Format ➪ Colors. RoboHELP HTML opens the Define Color window, as shown in Figure 19-19.

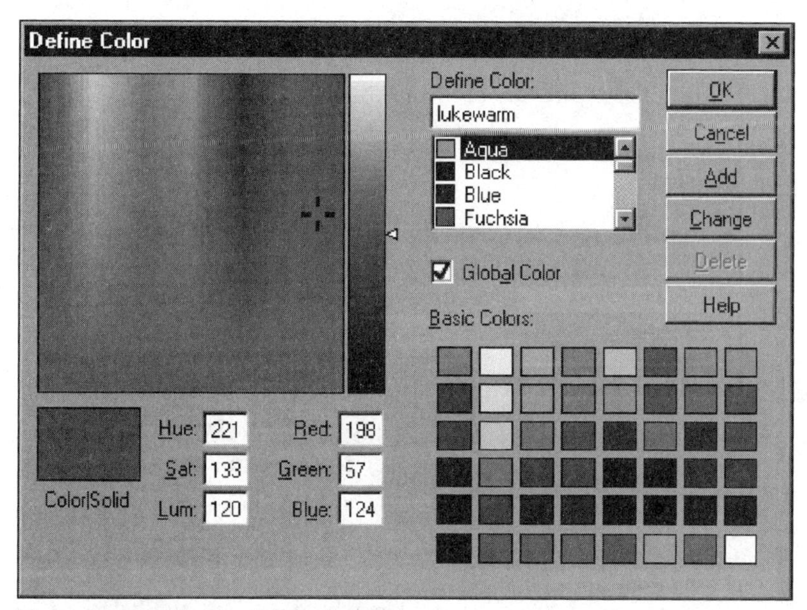

Figure 19-19: Define Color window

3. Type the name for your new color in the Define Color box.
4. Use the preselected colors, called the basic colors, to choose a color close to your new color.
5. Use the spectrum box and color density box to change the color until it is very close to your desired color. Use the sample box in the lower left corner as an aid to choosing your color.

6. Alter the numbers in the Hue-Saturation-Luminosity and Red-Green-Blue boxes to refine your color to the exact color you desire.
7. When you are satisfied with your color, click Add.
8. If you are finished adding colors, click OK.

Now your color is available from every drop-down list in RoboHELP HTML. If, for some reason, you need to define a color that you want available in only one topic, repeat the above directions, first by choosing the specific topic, and then by making sure the Global Color box is unchecked in the Define Color window.

If you ever need to change a color, select it from the Define Color list and click Change. You can also remove a color by selecting it and clicking Delete.

Adding Lists

The formatting of your topics is about more than just font and color choices. The layout of the pages is also very dependent on how you choose to format the text, and lists are an important way of formatting your information.

Lists in RoboHELP HTML work much like lists do in your favorite word processing program.

This section shows you how to include lists in your HTML Help project. There are three types of lists in RoboHELP HTML: bulleted lists, numbered lists, and definition lists.

Using Basic Lists

The simplest of the lists that come with RoboHELP HTML is the bulleted list. Bulleted lists are usually added when you need to highlight single pieces of information about a topic.

Here's how to add a bulleted list to your HTML Help project:

1. Select the topic where you want to include the bulleted list.
2. Type at least the first line of the list as plain text on the WYSIWYG tab.
3. Select the entire line, including the paragraph mark.

4. Choose Format ➪ Paragraph. RoboHELP HTML opens the Paragraph window as shown in Figure 19-20.
5. In the Lists section, choose Bulleted from the Type drop-down list.
6. Click OK.

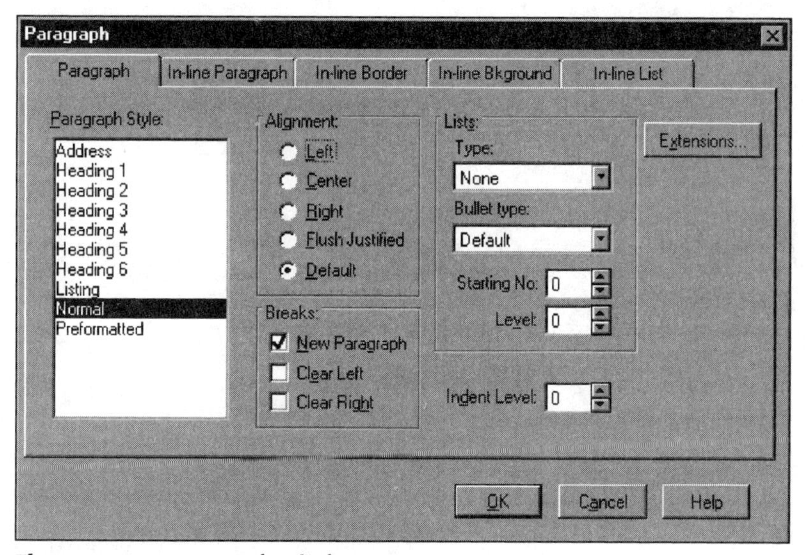

Figure 19-20: Paragraph window

Now you have at least one line of bulleted list. To add other lines to your list, you can move the end of the line and press Return.

Numbered lists are not much more complicated than bulleted lists and the procedure to add them to your topics is identical with one small difference: choose Numbered from the Type drop-down list in step 5.

Creating Nested Lists

RoboHELP HTML allows you to create more complicated lists by nesting lists inside other lists. Nesting implies that the first list is indented and the list inside it is nested even farther. A nested list in RoboHELP HTML looks like the one shown in Figure 19-21.

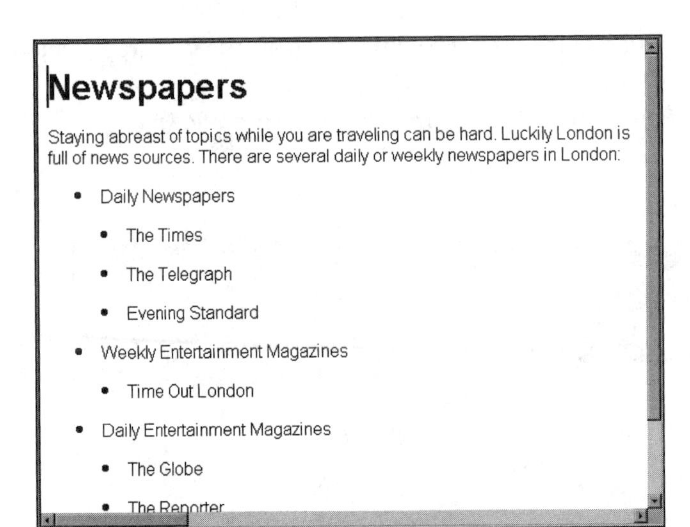

Figure 19-21: An example of a nested list

Here's how you create a nested list:

1. Follow the step to create a basic list, including adding all the list items.
2. Add the text you want to be indented.
3. Select the text to be indented.
4. Choose Format ⇨ Paragraph. This opens the Paragraph window shown in Figure 19-20.
5. Choose the type of list you want the indented lists to become.
6. Use the Indented Level box to indent your nested lists at least one level.
7. When you are done, click OK.

Adding Advanced Lists

So far you have seen how to create only various types of bulleted and numbered lists. Several other kinds of lists are available in RoboHELP HTML.

Using definition lists

Definition lists are those that have two types of indents. Figure 19-22 shows an example of topic using a definition list.

London Airports

There are two major airports in London.

Heathrow

This is the major destination airport for most American flights to London.

Gatwick

A major airport for most transfers and departures to other European destinations.

Figure 19-22: An example of a definition list

The most complicated part about a definition lists is that each part of the list needs to be formatted separately. Every definition needs to be selected and formatted separately from its definition. Use the drop-down list on the Paragraph window to add definition lists. The term is called the Definition Term, and the definition is called the Definition Data.

Adding menu and directory lists

The last two types of lists available in RoboHELP HTML are the Menu and Directory lists. These are both nonbulleted lists. They are described as follows:

✦ **Menu Lists:** These are used for short lists of items, as you would expect for a restaurant menu.

✦ **Directory Lists:** These are used for slightly longer items. These are lists of types of information or lists of other topics.

Changing list options

Beyond the different types of lists available in RoboHELP HTML, you can also alter the format of the bullets and numbers that directly proceed the list items.

In the Paragraph window, shown in Figure 19-20, there are two drop-down lists allowing you change the default bullets or numbers. Figure 19-23 shows each type of bullet and numbering scheme available in RoboHELP HTML.

It is best to change all the bullets or numbers in your entire project instead of just one paragraph at a time. Use the style sheet setting to change them for the entire project.

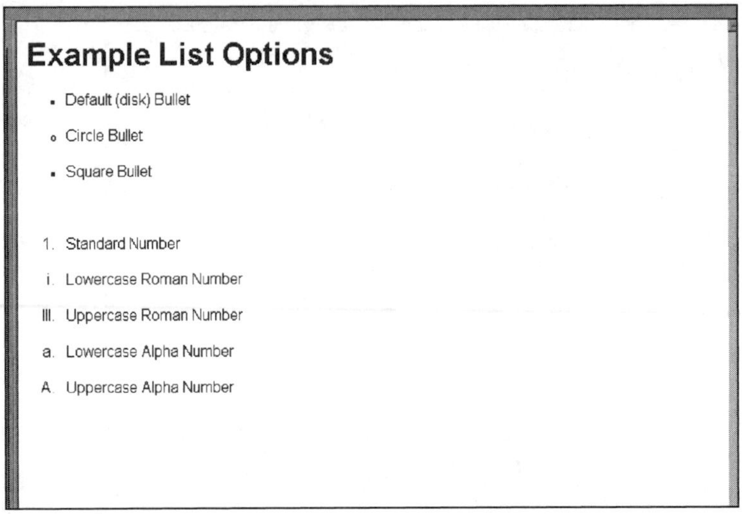

Example List Options

- Default (disk) Bullet
- Circle Bullet
- Square Bullet

1. Standard Number

i. Lowercase Roman Number

III. Uppercase Roman Number

a. Lowercase Alpha Number

A. Uppercase Alpha Number

Figure 19-23: Alternative numbering schemes and bullets for lists

Using Tables

Tables are a mainstay of layout for all types of publishing, and there is no reason they can't be the same for your HTML Help project. Just as with your printed and other help sources, your HTML Help project will benefit from tables as a way to organize information into rows and columns, helping your users find what they are looking for more quickly and easily. Figure 19-24 shows a table in an HTML Help project.

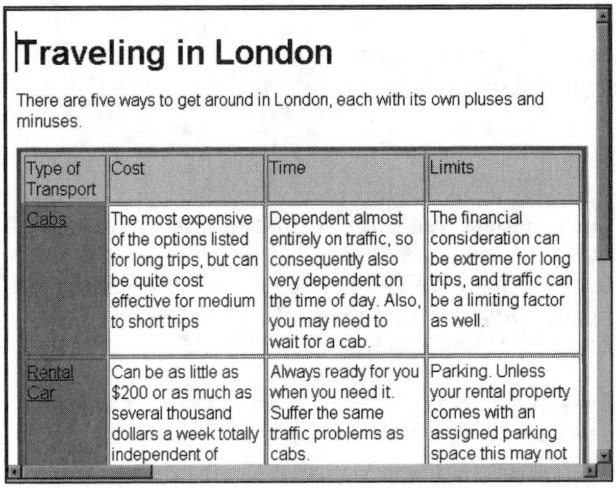

Traveling in London

There are five ways to get around in London, each with its own pluses and minuses.

Type of Transport	Cost	Time	Limits
Cabs	The most expensive of the options listed for long trips, but can be quite cost effective for medium to short trips	Dependent almost entirely on traffic, so consequently also very dependent on the time of day. Also, you may need to wait for a cab.	The financial consideration can be extreme for long trips, and traffic can be a limiting factor as well.
Rental Car	Can be as little as $200 or as much as several thousand dollars a week totally independent of	Always ready for you when you need it. Suffer the same traffic problems as cabs.	Parking. Unless your rental property comes with an assigned parking space this may not

Figure 19-24: A table in an HTML Help project

There are no tables at all in WinHelp. This is an exciting new feature in RoboHELP HTML.

Planning Your Tables

As with all other parts of your HTML Help project, planning your tables will make the creation process quicker and easier. Here are some questions to consider when you decide to add a table to your HTML Help project:

- How many rows and columns do you expect your table to have?
- How will the information be organized? Will it be alphabetically or in some logical order based on context?
- How will users use the information in the table?
- Will users want to print the information?
- How much of the screen do you want the table to take up?
- Where do you want the table to be placed on the topic page both horizontally and vertically?
- Do you want your table to have color or a border?

A table can contain no more than 1,000 cells total. More than that and your table won't be saved, but you won't be notified.

Once you have decided what your table will include, create a quick sketch of your table for reference. This drawing becomes a reference document for you while you go through the creation process.

For more information about planning your HTML Help project, see Chapter 2, "What makes Help 'Help'?."

Creating a Table

Creating a table in RoboHELP HTML is much the same as creating a table in your favorite word processor. There are two ways to go about it: with menus or with the toolbar button. The toolbar button is interactive and the easier way to create a basic table, so this section covers that method.

Here's how to add a table to your HTML Help project:

1. Open the topic you want to add the table to in the WYSIWYG tab.
2. Place the cursor where you want the table to be.
3. Select the table button (Figure 19-25) from the toolbar. A special drop-down menu appears with a grid as shown in Figure 19-26.

Figure 19-25: The table button

Figure 19-26: The table button drop-down menu

4. While holding down the mouse button, drag on the window until you have highlighted the correct number of rows and columns for your table.
5. Release the mouse button. RoboHELP HTML removes the window and places your table in the topic.
6. Add text to each table cell.

Congratulations! You have just created your first RoboHELP HTML table.

You can use the Insert, Delete, and Select options in the Table menu to change the layout of your table after you have created it.

Formatting Tables

Once you have created your table, you are ready to alter the formatting and add text. Formatting your tables is done in two parts: table formatting and cell formatting. Because tables in RoboHELP HTML are made up of HTML tags, they don't behave exactly as you might expect, and so the formatting process has to be a little different.

Using table formatting

At the table level you can control the overall look of your table. To change the overall format of your table, make sure your cursor is in the middle of the table and select Table ➪ Table Properties. RoboHELP HTML displays the Table Properties window shown in Figure 19-27.

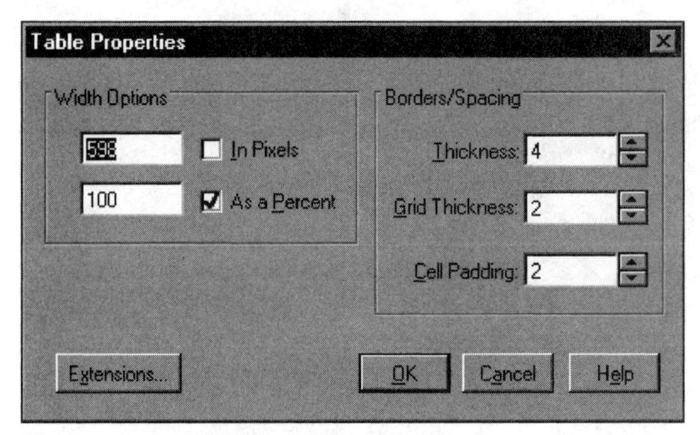

Figure 19-27: Table Properties window

The Table Properties window gives you options for altering the overall look of your table:

- ✦ **Width Options:** Contains the settings for the total width of the table. You can set them as either a total number of pixels or as a total width of the HTML Help window. Make sure to check the box for the option you want as well as fill the value in the box.
- ✦ **Thickness:** Sets the width of all the gridlines, both interior and exterior, for your table. If this is set to zero, your table will have no gridlines. The setting is listed in pixels.
- ✦ **Grid Thickness:** Sets the blank space between all columns and rows in your table. The setting is listed in pixels.
- ✦ **Cell Padding:** Sets the blank space between any text in your cells and the edge of the cell. This affects how crowded your tables look. The setting is listed in pixels.

As a general rule, you won't want to set any of the last three options to be more than five pixels.

Using cell formatting

In HTML, cells define tables. Because rows and columns cannot be defined, cells control all the formatting, including font and color choices. You need to make most changes that your users will notice about your table at the cell formatting stage.

To alter the formatting of a cell, place your cursor in the cell you wish to change and select Table ➪ Cell Properties. RoboHELP HTML opens the Cell Properties window, as shown in Figure 19-28.

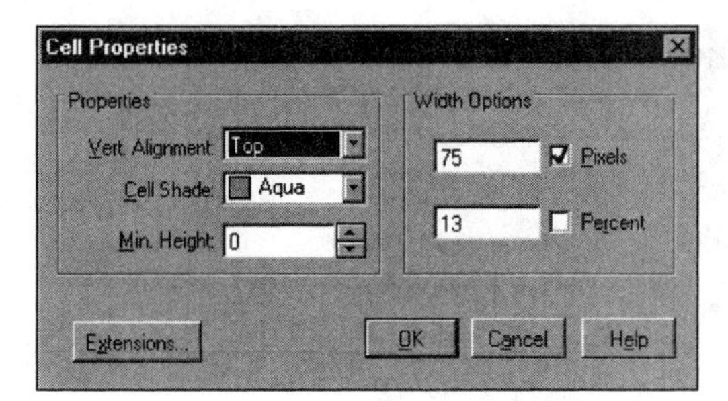

Figure 19-28: Cell Properties window

The Cell Properties window gives you several options for the look of this single cell:

✦ **Vert. Alignment:** Displays and sets how the text behaves inside the cell. The vertical alignment can be set to top, center, and bottom.

✦ **Cell Shade:** Sets the color of the background for the cell. By default this is set the same as the background color for the topic. Usually, you'll want to change this for just a few cells in your table.

✦ **Min. Height:** Sets the absolute minimum height of the cell in pixels.

✦ **Width Options:** Contains the setting for the width of your cell, like width options in the Table Properties window. Unlike the settings in the Table Properties window, this setting can be affected by other cells in the same column. HTML columns always expand to be the widest setting listed for any cell in the column.

You can change the format of more than one cell at a time by selecting more than one before you choose Cell Properties; however if the format of those cells differ at all the options, where they differ will be set to default for all of them.

Summary

In this chapter you learned how to create outstanding topics by formatting your topics. You learned how to change the font in a topic and how to create a font set. You learned how to alter the color of text, backgrounds, and hyperlinks. You even learned how to create your own colors. Once you covered all the basics of topic layout, you learned how to add lists to your topics. Finally, you learned how to create and use tables in your HTML Help project.

✦ ✦ ✦

CHAPTER 20

Creating and Adding Graphics

In This Chapter

Using RoboHELP HTML's image formats

Using the graphics locator

Adding graphics to your topics

Setting image formatting

Adding a splash screen

Creating image maps

Animated GIFs

In this chapter you'll learn how to add graphics to your topics. You'll learn how to insert images, how to set how the image displays on the topic page, and how to make text flow around the graphics you place. Next, you'll learn how to include a splash screen, how to create an image map, and then how to add animated GIFs to your HTML Help project. You'll also learn how to use the RoboHELP HTML tools to create image maps and how to enable them for your users.

Using Graphics in Your HTML Help Project

As anyone using or producing online help knows, text may be the center and body of the work, but images make your topic page come alive. Text alone can get very boring in your topics, and users enjoy the "eye candy" that images provide. Beyond this simple reason, images provide not only interest, but valuable content as well. The adage that a picture is worth a thousand words applies nowhere more than with online help. Not only can images help you get your point across much quicker, but also there are times when the only way to express your point is with a picture.

RoboHELP HTML does not include a tool for you to create images, allowing you to use what you are most familiar with to create the images you want to include in your HTML Help project. If you do not already have a favorite image-generating program, there are literally dozens of image creation programs available that you can use to generate images to include in your HTML Help project. Appendix D, "Resources," lists some of the more popular packages and gives you a Web link to find out more about them.

As a general rule, use the smallest, least complicated image creation program that does everything you need to create your images. It is easy to find an image creation program that is too complicated for the images you are creating, resulting in confusion and frustration.

Understanding Graphics Types

Before you can add a graphic to your topic page you need to create that image. You can save your newly created image in literally hundreds of different types of file formats, however RoboHELP HTML accepts only a few of these file types.

No matter which image format you choose to import into RoboHELP HTML, all images must be translated to either JPG or GIF format to run as an HTML Help project. RoboHELP HTML translates them automatically to the type you specify when it compiles your HTML Help project.

You can include five basic types of images in your HTML Help project, all of which are standard image formats to which any image creation program should be able to save. This section outlines each type in detail, giving you the pluses and minuses of each type, and the best circumstances in which to use each format.

Try saving your first couple of graphics to several different types of formats when you create them; that way you can try a couple of different types to see which one looks the best on your topic page.

GIF

Graphics Interchange Format (GIF) is one of the two most common image formats used in computers today.

GIFs contain information about an image, stored as a series of small pieces of information describing the pixels on each line of your image. This information is kept as a set of numbers for each pixel in relation to a standard color set of 256 colors. This standard color set means that a GIF can display a maximum of only 256 colors.

GIFs work well with images that have very few colors, like any text you want to include as an image, for example, a heading with a stylized font in a large size.

The bonus to the limited color set is that the file size of GIF can be very small, making them especially useful for any help systems that may be accessed through a network. GIFs are also very familiar to all computer systems (meaning they are platform independent), and thereby you can be assured they will always work with any computer your HTML Help project is viewed on.

The 256 colors for GIFs can be both a bonus and a drawback. With only the 256 standard colors in your image you can always be assured your image will display for your users just as it displays for you. Unfortunately, 256 colors can also seem to be too few for complicated images, such as photographs or very detailed large images.

GIFs also have the ability to have one color in the image set as transparent. This means that one color is replaced by the background color for your topic page, giving the image a more pleasing appearance than it would have if users could see the outline of the "box" containing the image. Figure 20-1 illustrates the difference between a GIF with a transparent background and one with a standard gray background.

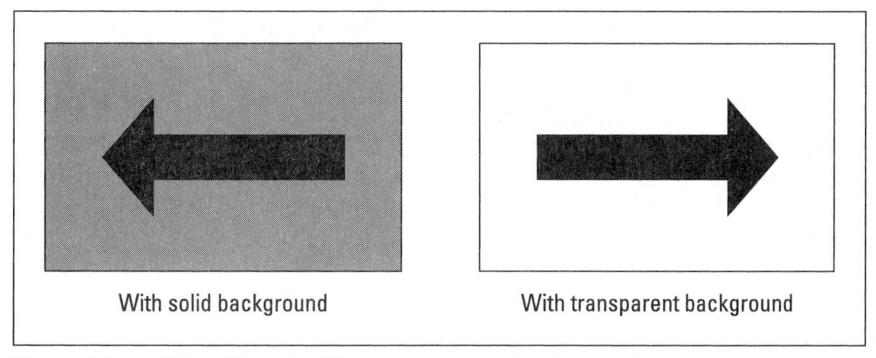

Figure 20-1: GIFs with and without transparent backgrounds

Choosing a color in an image sets the transparency. To make sure you don't choose a color you want to keep somewhere in the image, set the background color for your GIF to some very fluorescent color, such as neon pink or green. That way you are sure to notice if the transparency doesn't take, and you are assured that you won't lose a color you wanted to keep.

All of this makes GIFs ideal for the smaller images in your HTML Help project, such as icons, buttons, screen shots, small images, and even bullets.

JPEG or JPG

Joint Photographic Expert Group (JPEG or JPG) is the other standard format for images transferred between computers today.

JPGs contain two pieces of information that a computer compiles to display an image. First, they contain a database of every color in the image, and second, they contain a pixel-by-pixel list of the colors that create the image. In advanced JPGs, some information is condensed, and areas of large color are condensed so that instead of pixel-by-pixel information, the data or several pixels are listed together.

Because JPGs contain an extra piece of information above and beyond the GIFs, a database of colors specific to the image, this file type can be much larger in file size than the relatively small GIFs. The bonus of this added information allows you much greater color depth than GIFs can achieve because even if you have only 256 colors (an option you can set in most graphics creation programs), those are 256 colors specific to the image. This added color depth makes them ideal for full-color photos, large detailed images, and any complicated image containing lots of colors outside the 256 color set. You can include as many as 16 million colors in your JPG, allowing amazing resolution. In advanced graphics-creation programs, you can even set the number of pixels across and down. Doing this effectively sets the resolution for the image and allows you to make sure the image is always seen at its best resolution as opposed to when you alter it by changing screen and window sizes.

As a general rule, it's best to stay with 256 colors total for your JPG images. This helps ensure that your users will see the same image on their computers as you do on yours.

The balance between more and richer colors and file size can be a difficult one to achieve, and graphics developers have wrestled with it since computer graphics became a part of our lives. Whether or not the added colors in your JPGs justify the added bytes is something you need to decide as you start to include images on your topic pages.

BMP

Windows Bitmap (BMP) format is a standard Microsoft Windows format that is used widely in the Windows platform for images.

BMPs contain color and graphic information in 24-bit format, which gives you limited resolution but ensures that every Windows computer will display the image exactly as you see it. However, they cannot be used in HTML, so they must be converted to either JPGs or GIFs.

BMPs are best for standard Windows objects because you can screen capture directly to BMP from Windows. They can also be useful for icons, bullets, or other small screen objects.

MRB

Multi-Resolution Bitmap (MRB) format is another Microsoft Windows format. More advanced than BMP format, it includes the same image at several different screen resolutions in one file. These images can be very large, but like all Windows-specific formats, they cannot be used with HTML and are translated when you compile your HTML Help project.

WMF

Windows Metafile (WMF) format is a Microsoft Windows format that stores the information for your image as vectors instead of pixel information as all previous image file formats do. This means you can resize a WMF without losing any resolution because it redraws the vectors instead of trying to interpolate pixels. Normally, WMF format is used for images, which may be used at a different size than they are created, such as clipart or heading text saved as an image. Like all Windows standard images, WMFs are translated into either JPGs or GIFs when you compile your HTML Help project.

When you import WMF files from Winhelp, RoboHELP HTML automatically translates them into GIF format.

Adding Graphics to Your Topics

The first step in adding graphics to your HTML Help project is always to create the graphics by assembling them in a graphics creation program, by taking screen shots and collecting them, or even by purchasing images from a third party. Once you have the images you are ready to add them to your topic.

In RoboHELP HTML, adding graphics is a two-step process. First, you need to locate the graphic and copy it to your project folder. Then you need to place the graphic on the topic page. The first step is accomplished using the Graphics Locator, which is discussed in the next section.

Using the Graphics Locator

The Graphics Locator is a tool that helps you find and manage image files you want to include in your HTML Help project. Located on the Tool tab in the left-hand pane of the RoboHELP HTML main window, Graphics Locator significantly eases the trail of finding and copying images to your project folder.

To start the Graphics Locator, double-click the Graphics Locator icon on the Tools tab. This opens the Graphics Locator main window, as shown in Figure 20-2.

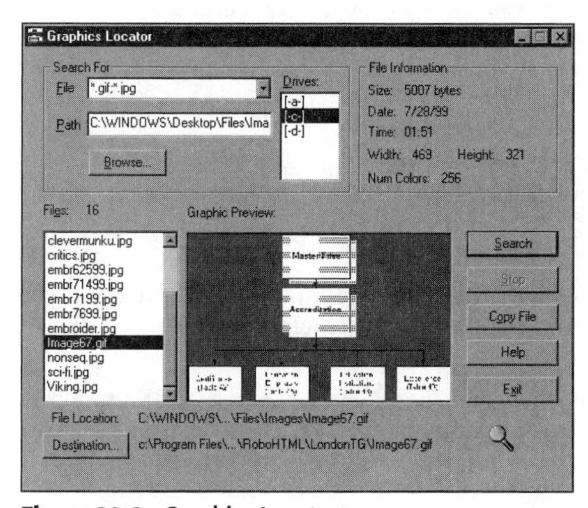

Figure 20-2: Graphics Locator

There are several parts to the Graphics Locator main window. This section outlines each part in detail.

✦ **Search For:** Graphics Locator is essentially a specialized version of the standard Find program that comes with all versions of Microsoft Windows 9*x* and later. The information in the Search For area sets where Graphics Locator looks for the image files and it sets what type of image file it is looking for.

- **File:** sets the type of image file Graphics Locator looks for. Use the drop-down list to select a file type or a set of file types.

Graphics Locator can find two image types that are not supported by RoboHELP HTML. Make sure not to import PCX or SHG files into your project by mistake.

- **Drive:** sets the general location where Graphics Locator is to look for the image files. This can be on any drive mapped to your computer, anywhere locally, or on a network. Select a drive by clicking on the corresponding letter in the window.
- **Path:** tells Graphics Locator where exactly to look for the image files. By default, Graphics Locator searches the entire drive indicated in the Drive box. Narrow the search by selecting a directory inside of a drive. You can select a directory graphically by using the Browse button. A Browse for Folder window appears as shown in Figure 20-3.

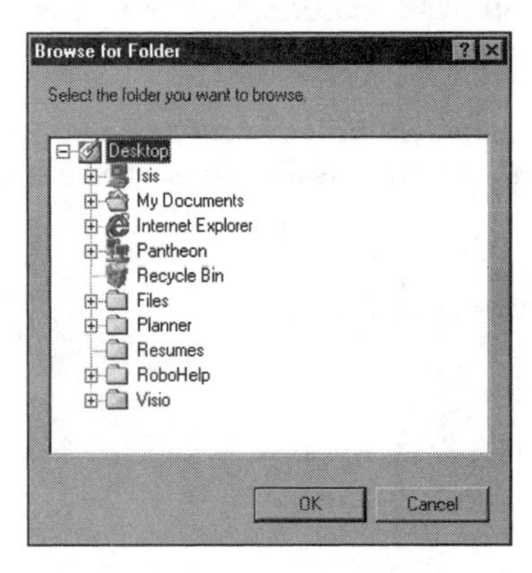

Figure 20-3: Browse for Folder window in Graphics Locator

When you are satisfied with the path information and the correct image type is set, click the Search button to find all the image files of that type in the path you indicated.

✦ **Selecting the Image:** After you have conducted a search, the bottom half of the Graphics Locator window lists all the images in the directory on the far left-hand side. In the center is a preview window for the image you currently have selected. On the right-hand side are buttons to help you deal with the image.

- **List of Image Files:** lists, by name, all of the image files in the path you indicate of the correct file type. Directly above this list is a file count of exactly how many files were found in that folder. Select an image file by clicking on its name in the list.
- **Preview of Image File:** shows a small, low resolution of the image selected in the List of Image Files. The image file is forced to fit into the rectangle given and, therefore, may be distorted.

✦ **Buttons in the Graphics Locator Window:** There are seven buttons on the Graphics Locator window, and you need them all to get your graphics where you want them to be.

- **Browse:** brings up the Browse for Folder window shown in Figure 20-3, allowing you to select graphically a path and all folders or directories within that path.
- **Search:** starts the search for image files based on the parameters set in the path and file windows.
- **Stop:** ends any search in progress immediately.
- **Copy File:** places a copy of the currently selected image in the destination identified at the bottom of the Graphics Locator window.
- **Help:** access the online help for Graphics Locator.
- **Exit:** closes Graphics Locator.
- **Destination:** sets where the image files copy to when you click the Copy File button. By default this is set as the project folder for the HTML Help project currently open. Click Destination to launch the Browse for Folder window shown in Figure 20-3.

✦ **File Information:** Each graphics file has a size and other information that are useful to know when you are trying to manage several different image files at once. The File Information section of the Graphics Locator main window gives you data about the image file currently selected in the List of Image Files.

- **Size:** displays the size of the image file, in bytes.
- **Date:** shows the last date the file was altered.
- **Time:** shows the last time the file was altered.
- **Width:** displays the width of the image file, in pixels
- **Height:** displays the height of the image file, in pixels.
- **Num. Colors:** shows the total number of colors in the image. For GIFs, this is always 256.

Because Graphics Locator is a separate program from RoboHELP HTML, you can launch it from RoboHELP HTML and then close RoboHELP HTML and keep Graphics Locator running in the background as you create images. That way you can move the images as they are created, making them ready to add to your topics next time you open RoboHELP HTML.

Placing Graphics on the Topic Page

After you have made sure the image you want on your topic page is in your project folder, you are ready to add it to the topic page.

To add an image to a topic:

1. Open the topic by selecting it from the Project list.
2. Make sure it displays in the WYSIWYG tab. Adding graphics to your topic page is done on the WYSIWYG tab.
3. Place your cursor where you want the upper left and corner of your image to be.
4. Click Insert Image on the toolbar to open the Image window shown in Figure 20-4. For a detailed explanation of the Image window, see the "Using the Image Window" section later in this chapter.

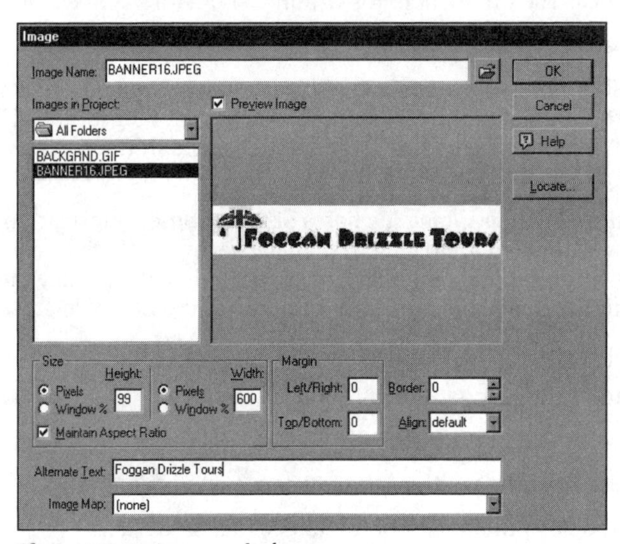

Figure 20-4: Image window

5. Select an image from the list. A thumbnail of the image appears in the preview window.
6. Once you are pleased with all the settings, click OK and RoboHELP HTML inserts the image into the topic.

Using the Image window

As you've seen in the procedure for inserting an image, and as shown in Figure 20-4, the Image window is very important. You use it to both insert images into topics and to alter the properties of images already residing on topic pages. This section outlines each part of the Image window in detail.

Many settings on the image window are available to you, but try not to worry at first about too many of them. The defaults for most of them are logical and unless you have a specific reason to change them, it is not usually necessary to alter them too much.

✦ **Image Name:** displays the file name of the selected image file.

✦ **Browse button:** allows you to browse to find a file name or path by displaying the Open window.

If you browse to an image not already in the project folder, you are prompted to allow RoboHELP HTML to copy the image. As a general rule, say yes to these questions because all the images you use for topics must be included in your project folder for your online help to compile correctly.

✦ **Images in Project:** lists all the image files saved in your project folder.

✦ **Drop Down Folder List:** allows you to select which images are displayed in the Images in Project window by selecting different types of folders in your project. If you have many images already in your project, viewing by folder can shorten the list and makes it easier to find the image you're looking for. All Folders is the default and displays a list of all images in all folders in your project.

✦ **Preview Image:** Shows a thumbnail (a small, low-resolution version) of the image when this is checked.

✦ **Size:** Sets the size of your image. Both the height and width of the image are set in Size by the same principle. You can indicate the size of your image either by pixels or percent. Pixels are the individual dots that make up your image on the computer screen and setting the number of pixels for height and width gives an absolute size for the image so that the image takes up the same number of pixels regardless of the size of the help viewer. Window % sets the size of your image relative to the total size of the window it's in, and the image automatically resizes if the window size changes.

You can also set RoboHELP HTML to make sure that no matter which settings you choose, it will not distort the image by checking Maintain Aspect Ratio. This means you define only one of the two settings, and RoboHELP HTML calculates what the other dimension should be based on the original size of the image. As a general rule, it's best to make sure Maintain Aspect Ratio is checked so that you do not accidentally distort your image by setting its size.

Maintain Aspect Ratio works only when both the height and width are set using one type of measurement. This means they are either both set by pixels or by percentage, but it will not work if you have one of each.

✦ **Margin:** sets the amount of space left between the image and the surrounding text. You can set both the left/right and top/bottom clearances for each image. These settings are entered as numbers and they represent the number of pixel spaces that RoboHELP HTML will leave between your image and any text wrapping around it. By default this is set to zero.

✦ **Border:** allows you to add a border around the image and sets the width of the border in pixels.

✦ **Align:** sets how RoboHELP HTML aligns the image in relation to the text around it. By default, the image is set to align the bottom of the image with the bottom of the text. For more information about setting image alignment, see the "Setting the relationship between Image and Text" section later in this chapter.

✦ **Alternate Text:** sets a small piece of text to display instead of the image in case your users turn off the graphics feature in their browsers. Also, for images that do not have hyperlinks or other special features, this text displays when the user holds the cursor over the image for longer than five seconds. This can be useful to provide extra information about an image, or instructions about how to use the image.

✦ **Image Map:** shows the name of the image map, if the image has one.

You can access the Image window anytime by right-clicking an image and selecting Insert/Edit Image from the drop-down list.

Dragging and dropping images

Once you get a feeling for how images are placed and what settings they need, you can place images quickly and easily by simply dragging and dropping them in from the project lists. Every image you have used already in your project is listed under the Images folder on the Project tab in the left-hand pane.

Select the Project tab on the right-hand pane, expand the Image folder, and then select the WYSIWYG tab on the left-hand pane to displace the topic to which you want to add an image. Then, simply drag the image from the list and drop it where you would like it to be included in your topic page. This places the image where the cursor was, at its maximum size and with all the settings at default.

If you need to edit settings for the image, you can access the Image window for your dropped image by right-clicking and choosing Insert/Edit Image from the drop-down list.

When you drag an image to the end of a line and it doesn't fit, RoboHELP HTML automatically wraps it to the next line.

Formatting Graphics

Placing images on your topic page is only the first part of making the most of your graphics. For images to play the important part they should in your topic pages, you need to make sure all the formatting of each graphic makes the most of the visual information.

Following are several layout questions to answer to guarantee that your images and text look great on the topic page:

- Are the images correctly placed on the topic page?
- Is the size of the image in relation to the page and text the best it could be?
- Do the text and image flow around each other naturally?

The answers to these questions, and the solutions to fix any layout issues with your graphics, are discussed in detail in this section.

It's always best to save your project before you start doing a lot of work on your graphics. That way you can work with confidence, knowing you can't mess anything up too bad to go back.

Moving the Image

There are two ways to answer the first question. Occasionally, after you have placed an image on your topic page, you realize that its placement could be better. Moving an image in RoboHELP HTML is simple to help you handle this situation.

To move an image you've already placed:

1. Open the topic with the image in the WYSIWYG tab.
2. Click the image until a red border appears.
3. Select Edit ➪ Cut. This removes the image from the topic page and places it on the clipboard.
4. Move your cursor on the topic page until it is where you want to put the image.
5. Select Edit ➪ Paste. This inserts the image from the clipboard to your topic page.

Setting the Justification

The second way your image relates to the topic page, after its placement, is which side of the page it is justified to.

To set the justification of an image:

1. Open the topic with the image in the WYSIWYG tab.
2. Click the image until a red border appears. You now have the image selected.
3. Use the justification buttons to set the image either to the right, center, or left of the page.

Any text sharing the line with an image affects how close to the sides of the topic page the image can get.

Changing the Size of the Image

Not every image is the correct size or shape when you first add it to your project folder, and sometimes you don't realize it needs to be a different size until you place it on your topic page. RoboHELP HTML has included ways for you to change an image's size or shape to handle just this problem.

There are two ways to change the size of an image you have already placed on a topic page:

✦ Use the Image window to change the size settings.

✦ Click the image until you see a red border and then drag the corner of the border to resize the image on the topic page. Hold down the Shift key while you drag the corner of the border to make sure the image is not distorted.

Changing the size of the image on the topic page by dragging the border forces your image to be defined by pixels and not by percentages. This means your image will no longer resize when the topic page is resized.

Be careful because you can change the shape as well as the size of the image with either of these methods, which can dramatically change the look of your image by resetting its proportions.

As a general rule, use the Image window for fine and precise adjustments. Drag the image border on the drawing page for quicker and easier changes that don't need to be as precise.

Setting the Relationship between Image and Text

The last question about layout concerns how the image and text relate to each other on the topic page. When you place an image inside a line of text, that text needs to wrap around the image in some way. HTML definitions are full of ways you can set image and text to relate to each other on one line, and RoboHELP HTML gives you access to all of them through the Image window (shown in Figure 20-4.).

Figure 20-5 shows some of the more common alignments for text and images on the topic page.

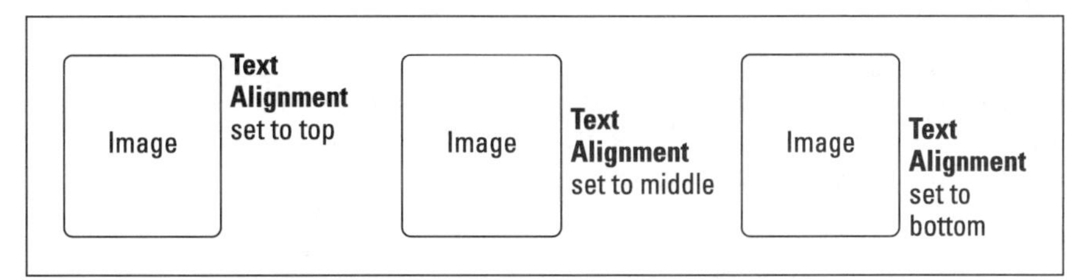

Figure 20-5: Text and image alignment

Only one line of text can be on the same line as an image.

The Align box on the Image sets how the text wraps around the image and where the image is placed in relationship to the text. There are ten settings for alignment, explained in detail here.

- **Default:** is the standard setting for all newly placed images and it sets the alignment to zero.
- **Left:** sets the picture on the left, and places the text on the right.
- **Right:** aligns the image to the right margin and wraps the text before it to the left side.
- **Top:** sets the top of the image equal with the average top of the text around it.
- **Middle:** aligns the middle of the image with the average middle of the text.
- **Bottom:** sets the bottom of the image equal with the average bottom of the text around it.
- **Text-top:** forces the image to align with the top of the tallest letter on the same line.
- **Abs-middle:** aligns the image with the mathematical middle of the current line.

✦ **Baseline:** sets the image equal with the bottom of the capital letters (baseline) on the same line as the image.

✦ **Abs-bottom:** forces the image to be equal to the absolute bottom of the current line.

Because the image can be with only one line of text at a time, try to make sure images of any size are situated on their own line. This way you cannot worry about one line of text wrapping on the same line as your image and looking weird.

Getting Fancy

After you have set all the basic formatting on your image, you are ready to start getting fancy. There are literally hundreds of things you can do to your images that give them a special flair and get the attention of your user. This section outlines some of the most common additions to images.

As with any special formatting, these fancy settings can be overused. Make sure you plan and execute these settings with a thought to ease of use.

Adding a Hyperlink to Your Image

The quickest and easiest extra to add to your images is to add a hyperlink. The hyperlinks enable your users to use the image as they would any text with a hyperlink. It also helps you get more mileage out of the image, using it not only for visual interest, but also as a link to another topic or piece of information.

Like all other links you add to your text, adding links to your images requires that you place the image inside your topic page before you add the hyperlink.

To add a hyperlink to your image:

1. In the WYSIWYG tab, open the topic to which you want to add the hyperlink.
2. Click the image until you see a red border appear.
3. Click the Insert Hyperlink button on the toolbar. The Hyperlink window appears as shown in Figure 20-6.
4. Verify the information in the top boxes in the Hyperlink window, including the name of the image.
5. Fill in the information for which topic or page to link to, either by choosing it form the list or by typing it into the box.

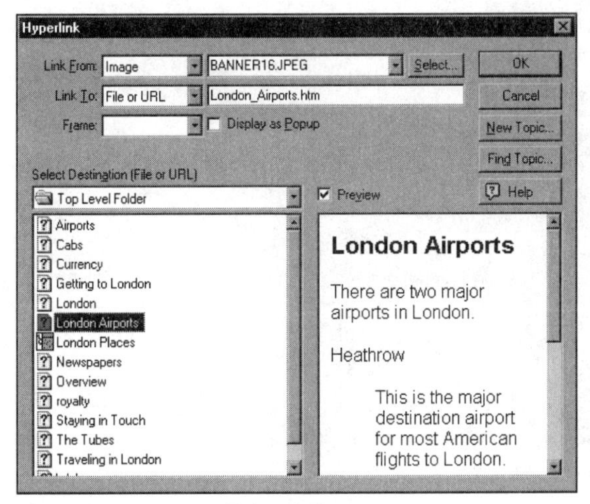

Figure 20-6: Hyperlink window

6. When you are satisfied with the hyperlink settings, click OK.
7. RoboHELP HTML sets the image to a hyperlinked image and closes the Hyperlink window.

For more information about hyperlinks, see Chapter 19, "Creating Outstanding Topics."

Making a Splash Screen

Once you have added hyperlinks to your images, you are ready to take the next step and create a page that is only an image, or a splash screen.

A splash screen displays an image just for a few moments as a new topic or page opens. Usually, they are used to display company or other information when your users start your HTML Help project.

Only BMP or GIF files can be splash screens.

To add a splash screen to a topic:

1. Open the topic you want to be the trigger for the splash screen. For a splash screen that opens when your users start your HTML Help project, open the topic you have set as default.
2. Click the Insert HTML Control button on the toolbar.

3. Choose Splash Screen from the drop-down list. This displays the Splash Screen Wizard shown in Figure 20-7.

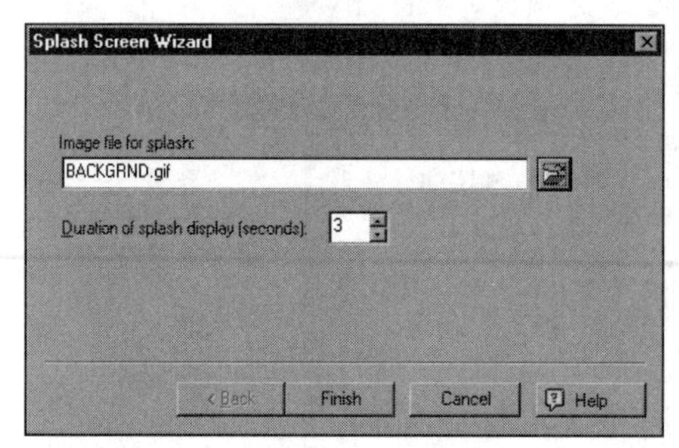

Figure 20-7: Splash Screen Wizard

4. Enter the file name for the Splash Screen, or use the browse button to locate the image. If you are navigating to an image not already in your project folder RoboHELP HTML will prompt you to copy it to your project folder.
5. Set the number of seconds the image will be visible with the Duration of Splash Display setting. After that number of seconds, the splash image disappears and the topic behaves normally.

Setting a splash screen to vanish automatically does not work in Internet Explorer version 5.0, and the user needs to click the image to make it vanish.

6. When you are satisfied with the settings for your splash screen, click OK.

The splash screen will not appear anywhere on your topic page or on your WYSIWYG tab. Only an icon indicating that the topic has a splash screen appears in the corner of your topic. To preview the topic with the splash screen, either run the whole HTML Help project and navigate to the topic, or use the preview feature for the topic. The icon is removed when the HTML Help project is compiled.

Image Maps

Earlier in this chapter you added a single hyperlink to your image. But how do you add more than one hyperlink to your image? Image Maps are the only way to include more than one hyperlink for your image. They allow each part of an image to contain its own hyperlink.

Image Maps are called hotspot graphics in WinHelp.

Image maps are GIFs or JPGs with clickable hotspots that take the user, via a hyperlink, to another topic or page. They act just like any other hyperlinked image, except they have different hotspots that take users to different pages.

An image map requires two files to work—first the image file you've already copied to the project folder, and second a Map file that tells the browser where each of the hotspots are on the image.

To create the map file, you need to edit the image you've already placed on the topic page in the RoboHELP HTML image map editor, HotSpot Studio. Here's how:

1. Open the topic where you've placed the image you want to turn into an image map.
2. Right-click the image and select Image Map from the list. This opens the Select Image map window, shown in Figure 20-8.

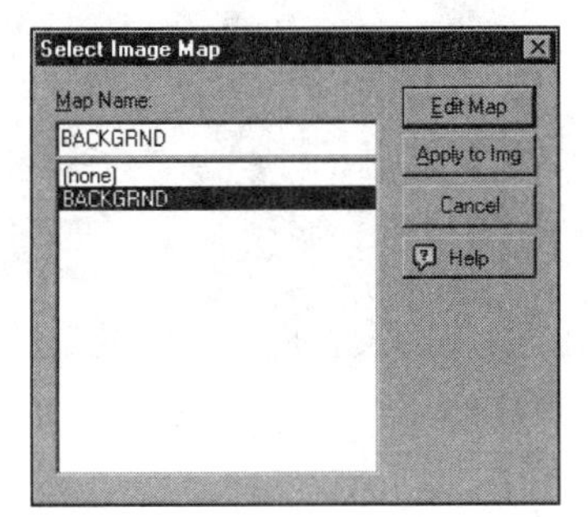

Figure 20-8: Select Image Map window

3. Click Edit map to create a new image. This opens a window, shown in Figure 20-9, telling you that RoboHELP HTML needs to alter your topic in order to create the image map.

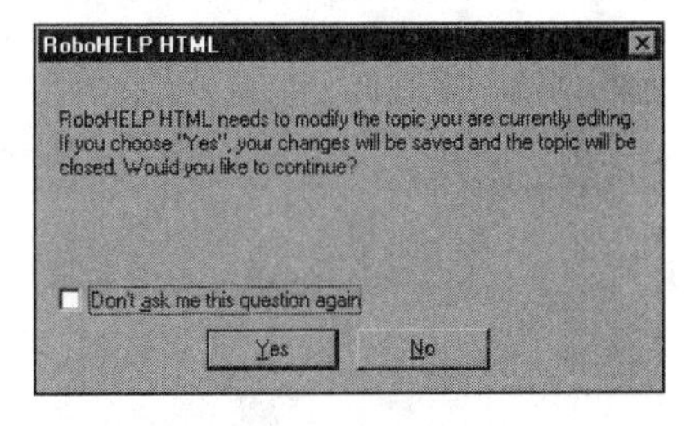

Figure 20-9: RoboHELP HTML confirmation window

If you have already created an image map for an image, select it from the list and click OK. This closes the Select Image Map window and applies the image map to your image.

4. Click OK on the RoboHELP HTML confirmation window. This opens the HotSpot Studio main window, shown in Figure 20-10.

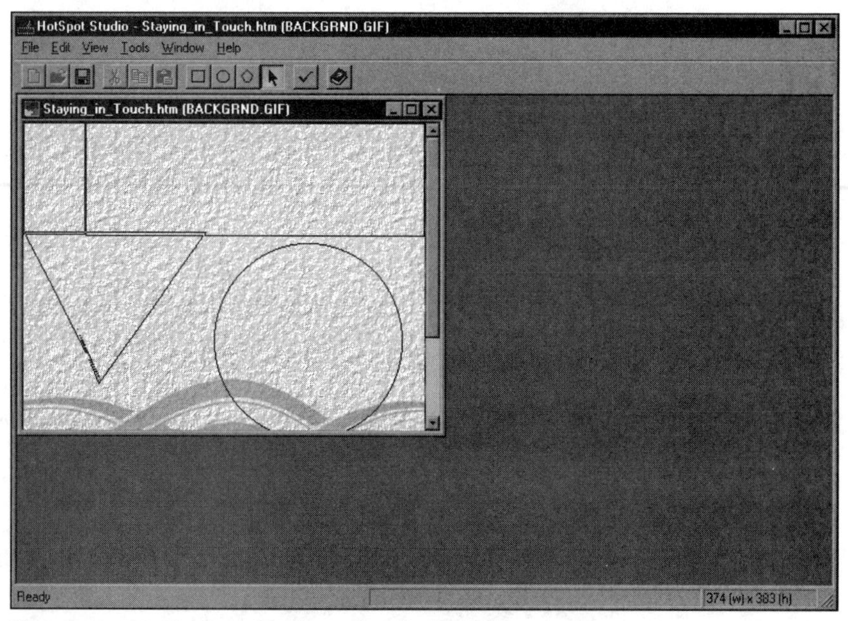

Figure 20-10: HotSpot Studio main window

5. Use the several geometric buttons in HotSpot Studio to help you divide your image into hotspot parts.
6. As you set each new hotspot region with the geometric shapes, the Set HotSpot Target window opens, shown in Figure 20-11.
7. Set the topic the hotspot hyperlinks to using the Set Hotspot Target window, choosing to display the target as a popup by clicking the Display as Popup box. You can also set the frame designation for the hotspot and any alternative text you want to display.
8. Once you are satisfied with the Hotspot Target settings, click OK. The Hotspot Target window disappears.
9. Repeat setting Hotspot targets for all the different hotspot sections in your image map.
10. When you are finished editing your image map, select File ➪ Save Image Map As. This opens a save as window, automatically pointed at your project folder.
11. Save the image map and then exit by choosing File ➪ Exit. When RoboHELP HTML prompts you to save your topic, choose yes.

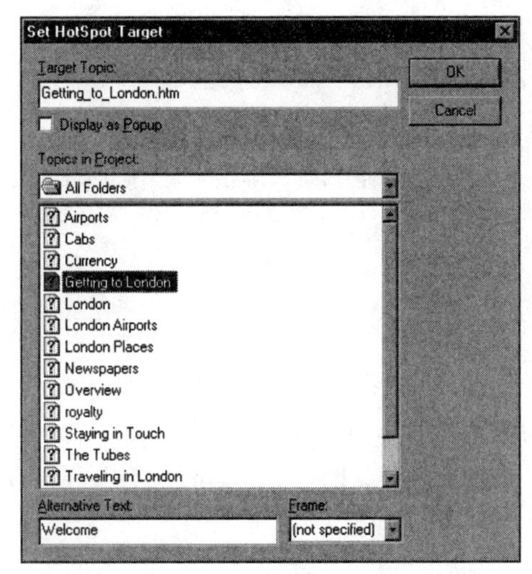

Figure 20-11: Set HotSpot Target window

Images with image maps display with icons different than standard images in the Project tab. They have a plus sign to the left of the image name indicating they include a list of all the image maps that you have applied to that image throughout your HTML Help project.

Adding Movement, Sounds, and Special Effects

Once you have mastered the topics of hyperlinks, splash screens, and image maps, there are still hundreds of different things you can do with HTML in your HTML Help project to add special interest. Here is an overview of different ways to use images and other HTML tricks to add pizzazz to your topics.

Animated GIFs

Most images are static and do not change as they reside on your topic page. With the small exception of splash screens, so far you have not included any images with movement. Animated GIFs are a way to add movement to you images.

Animated GIFs are compiled GIF files that contain more than one image and, when run together, give the illusion of motion, much like a cartoon.

As you may imagine, animated GIFs have to be created in a special program designed just for that purpose. They can be included like any simple GIF in your topics once you have developed them in another program.

See a list of graphics creation programs in Appendix D "Resources," including programs to help you create Animated GIFs.

Multimedia

Movies and sounds can add a great deal of excitement to a topic page. Luckily they are easy to include in your topics.

All video and sound files must be created before you add them to your topic page. See Chapter 5, "Adding Color, Formatting, and Special Effects," for information about creating video and sound files.

To add a video or sound file to your topic page:

1. In the WYSIWYG tab, open the topic to which you want to add the file.
2. Place the cursor where you want the sound or video to reside.
3. Choose Insert ⇨ Multimedia. This opens the Multimedia window, shown in Figure 20-12.

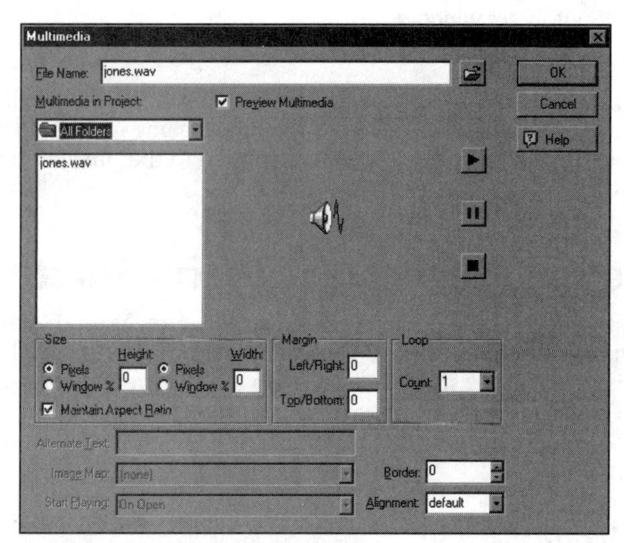

Figure 20-12: Multimedia window

4. Use the browse button to locate your multimedia file, remembering to allow RoboHELP HTML to copy the file to your project folder if it isn't already there.
5. Set all the properties for the multimedia file, including when to start playing it, and how to align it to the page.
6. Once you are satisfied with the settings, click OK. RoboHELP HTML closes the window and places the file in your topic.

You can drag-and-drop multimedia files that have already been added the project into a new topic, just like you can image files, by using the Project tab on the left-hand pane and the WYSIWYG tab on the right-hand pane.

Special effects with DHTML

Dynamic HTML (DHTML) is a special set of HTML instructions developed by Microsoft to add interest to HTML pages with minimum effort.

DHTML works only with Internet Explorer version 4.0 and later. Earlier versions of IE and all versions of Netscape do not support DHTML.

RoboHELP HTML comes with more than ten DHTML programs all ready for you to use. This section lists the DHTML programs that affect your images. For more information about other types of DHTML programs, see Chapter 21, "Adding Windows and Popups."

Add any of the image special effects by clicking the image and then choosing the effect from the DHTML menu. Once RoboHELP HTML has added the special effect, you can right-click the image, select Special Effect Properties, and change the settings for the special effect.

The image special effects are much easier to see than to read. Take a few moments to try them out before you decide how and where to use them.

- **Zoom In:** slowly creates the image out of blank space when the user opens the topic. It is useful when you have a small image and you want to give it more interest; the fading in effect guarantees that users will notice the image, no matter how small.
- **Transition:** fades in your image in one of 24 different ways. You can set the timing, the type of fade in, the rate of fade in, and when the image is revealed.

For more information about DHTML, see Chapter 27, "Adding Windows and Popups," which includes information about all the text DHTML effects.

Summary

In this chapter, you learned how to add graphics to your topics. You learned about the types of images you can use in RoboHELP HTML. You learned how to insert images, how to set how the image displays on the topic page, and how to make text flow around the graphics you place. Then you learned how to get fancy and include a splash screen, how to create an image map, and then how to add animated GIFs to your HTML Help project. You also learned how to use the RoboHELP HTML tools to create image maps and you'll learn how to enable them for your users.

✦ ✦ ✦

CHAPTER 21

Adding Windows, Popups, and Special Effects

✦ ✦ ✦ ✦

In This Chapter

Adding links

Types of windows

Opening links in popup windows

Adding text effects

✦ ✦ ✦ ✦

In this chapter, you learn how to add links to your RoboHELP HTML topics. After examining the different types of links and the different ways you can open topics in the RoboHELP HTML windows, you'll learn how to point links at both interior and exterior information, and how to add popup definition links. Finally, you'll learn how to add text special effects to your topics, including flying and fading text that launch from a link you set.

Linking in RoboHELP HTML

So far, you have created topics with outstanding layout by formatting your text and adding graphics. These important steps help your users understand information; however, it rarely helps them find the information. Linking, or connecting one or more pieces of information via a hyperlink, enables you to help your users find information by giving them a pathway between different ideas.

Hyperlinks are directional information available in HTML that allow your users to select some text or an image with the mouse and have another topic or web page open up in the browser window. Linking is the essence of HTML Help, and it is the main difference between it and standard printed documentation.

As helpful as links can be, excessive links can be distracting to users. In the planning stages, make sure you are using the least number of links that can do the job without using too few. As a general rule, use no more than four of five hyperlinks in the text of a topic.

You have already included hyperlinks in your topics. When you created links with your images, and when you created image maps, those were both ways of creating hyperlinks on your topics page. There are several other types of linking, only some of which are covered in this chapter. There are also several different actions a link can launch, such as opening a new window with a topic inside, launching a browser window and opening a web page, or even displaying a popup or hotspot text. This chapter covers all these different actions.

Adding a link to your topic page is a three-part process:

1. Decide how the link will display on the topic page
2. Decide what the link will do when clicked
3. Decide in which window you want the information to display

You can also think of settings links as a What, How, and Where process: first decide What the link looks like on the page, second decided How the list displays, and finally decide Where the link takes the userThis following sections takes you through each part of the process.

Setting How a Link Displays

First and foremost, you need to know what type of link you are setting before you can do anything else. This means you need to know how your link will appear on the topic page before you start to set it. Different types of links are set in different ways, so the procedure dictates that you know what type you are setting before you begin. This section outlines the major ways links can appear on your topic page.

Setting a link requires knowing the *how* and *what* of a link, but not the *where*. Where you are linking to is incidental, but how the link is displayed on the topic page and what the link does are very important.

Text links

Text links are hyperlinks placed in the text of your topics that open a link when the text is clicked. Unless you change the default, text links are underlined and display in a standard blue (in HTML Help) or green (in WinHelp). As with all links, when the user holds the mouse over the hyperlinked text, the cursor changes from the standard arrow into a hand icon. When users click on the hyperlinked text, the link is activated, and whatever you have set to launch is initiated in the HTML Help browser.

Image links

Image links are hyperlinks placed on images in your topic page. They open a hyperlink when clicked, just as text links do, and result in the same change to the cursor that text links do. As a general rule, image links are more of a navigational control than an information source, but they can be used in either way. As with text links, a hyperlink set on an image can do many different things, but generally they are not used to launch popups or other types of windows that might obscure the picture.

Image maps

Image maps are image links with an extra layer of complication. Instead of just one hyperlink on an image, an image map enables you to set several links on an image. Each link is defined by an area, and each area can contain only one link. Image maps must be created in a special image-map creation program, such as HotSpot Studio, which comes with RoboHELP HTML. These special programs enable you to set the *hotspots,* or different locations, for each link; and to set the link itself. Other than setting hotspots, links on image maps act the same as links anywhere else; when the user clicks on them, they launch whatever you have set them to launch.

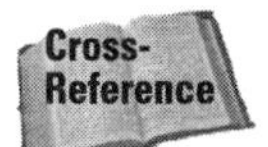

For more information about images in your topics or about image maps, see Chapter 20, "Creating and Adding Graphics."

Index and TOC links

Index and TOC use the entries into the table of contents and index to enable the user to move between topics. They are links because clicking on them changes the HTML Help project window in some way.

For a complete description of index and table of contents linking, see Chapter 23, "Creating a TOC and Index."

Selecting What a Link Does

All these link types are set based on how you want them to display for your user, not where they are going. The following sections examine each type of link and provide examples of common places in which you might use each type.

Expanding and drop-down hotspots

Expanding and drop-down hotspots are specially formatted text that expands in line with other text on the topic page to display information when clicked. They are valuable design tools because you can create fewer topics and provide more information for less effort, usually to your users' benefit. They don't have to sort through page after page because you have incorporated more information into a single topic (and have still managed to make it look neat and clean). You can create an expanding or drop-down hotspot by highlighting the text that will be the link to the information, and then selecting to create a Hotspot from the DHTML menu.

As useful as expanding or drop-down hotspots can be, don't overuse this tool. Having to click on every other word to get the required information out of the topic can be very annoying to your users.

Popups

Popups are text-only ways to link. A text-only popup is specially formatted topic text that displays information in a popup window when clicked. This is not a true link because the popup window displays only text — not topics or Web pages. Text-only popups are useful if you want to provide users with a little extra detail about information in a topic without displaying it in the content. Users who want to know more can click the hotspot to read the text, but those who do not need to know more about the specific topic can ignore the link and simply keep reading.

Link controls

Link controls are clickable objects (usually a button) that provide users with a list of alternative or related topics. This helps users find additional information in case the topic they are reading doesn't give them the exact help they need. Link controls also allow you to cross-reference information, so users realize that other information about the topic is available. There are three different kinds of link controls: related topic links, keyword links, and Alinks. Related topic links are links between topics. Keyword and Alinks are set in the glossary or index.

Bookmarks

A bookmark is a setting for other hyperlinks. Like anchors in HTML documents, they allow jumps from other topics. In WinHelp, bookmarks are called mid-topic jumps and they provide a way for users to link directly to the information they need without first going to the top of a topic.

WinHelp topic controls

WinHelp topic controls are a clickable objects (usually a button) that open a WinHelp system (HLP file) and display a WinHelp topic. Users can navigate to any topics in the WinHelp system once it's opened. This control provides a way for you to link to WinHelp topics from HTML topics.

Browse sequences

Browse sequences help users move forward and backward through a set of topics arranged in a specific order. You select the topics you want to use with a browse sequence and define the order. Browse sequences are very useful for online tutorials because you can take users through a sequence of topics in a specific order.

Understanding Different Windows

Not only can a link have a special action, but clicking on a link can open a window all its own, or alter your standard HTML Help project window to incorporate a different type of link. The following sections describe the different types of windows you can open with a link.

HTML Help Viewer

HTML Help Viewer is the standard viewer for your HTML Help project. It was designed by Microsoft to display compiled Microsoft HTML Help. By default, the viewer is a tri-pane window: Index, Contents and Search tabs are on the left, topic content is displayed on the right, and buttons are displayed across the top of the window. A link can change how any or all of these sections display. You can also set links that hide or show parts of the window, or make it behave in even more amazing ways.

Browser windows

Browser windows can display your HTML Help project. Internet Explorer and Netscape Navigator are the two most common, and both were developed to display HTML information. The standard viewer for a Microsoft HTML Help project is based on Internet Explorer 4.0, but has many additional features. You can use customization to create a tri-pane design similar to the one used with the Microsoft HTML Help Viewer. It can include navigation panes on the left with Index, Contents and Search tabs, topic content displayed on the right, and buttons displayed across the top.

JavaHelp Viewer

JavaHelp Viewer displays JavaHelp. Sun Microsystems designed this viewer to display JavaHelp systems. Like the HTML Help Viewer, its tri-pane window offers navigation panes on the left with Index, Contents and Search tabs, topic content displayed on the right, and buttons displayed across the top.

Framesets

Framesets are essentially small windows you can create inside your standard HTML viewer. They section off part or all of your topic pages to allow several different topics to be displayed at once, much like frames on standard web pages. This gives you more options, but they can be very distracting to your users and should be used with an eye to usability.

For more information about including frames and creating framesets, see "Adding Frames," later in this chapter.

Custom windows

Custom windows are secondary windows you can design for your HTML Help project. Links can cause them to open, and they can include any part of your HTML Help project content, including TOCs, keywords, Alinks, or topic controls.

Currently, Microsoft HTML Help does not support links to secondary windows from within topics, which are generally used for context-sensitive help purposes.

Selecting Where a Link Goes

The last step in the link process is actually the easiest: setting where the link goes.

A link can connect to any of several different types of information, both internal information from the current HTML Help project and external information in the form or a website, intranet, or other HTML information source.

Internal links and external links are treated the same way, but it is important you know which of the two types you are linking to. External links need to be verified to make sure that your users can access them from their systems. Internal links need to be checked to ensure that all necessary information is shipped with your help system. No matter which type of link you choose, always make sure that they are tested on several systems with various configurations. Shipping a bad link is very bad form.

Link view, accessible by the Link View tab in the right-hand pane of the RoboHelp window, can be a lifesaver when it comes to testing your links. Use it toward the end of your project to make sure all your links work.

Using Links

Now that you know all the details that go into creating links in your topics, you are ready to start setting those links on the topic page.

Your HTML Help project is linked together in many different ways. The table of contents, index, and Find features all help create links between topics to help your users find the information they need. Links that exist on the topic page also help your users find information, but they are substantially different from the interlinking of the TOC, index, and Find features.

For more information about using the table of contents and index to link your project together, see Chapter 23, "Creating a TOC and Index."

Links on the topic page are set by you, individually. They are called hyperlinks to identify them as a feature of HTML. Once you have decided where a link needs to go, you open the topic page you are linking from and set the link. The following sections describe the basics of setting a hyperlink, the hyperlink window, and how to set hyperlinks for both standard and text-only popup windows.

Adding Hyperlinks

After you have decided the what, how, and where of your links, you are ready to create the actual link. Here's how to add a basic link on a topic page:

1. Open the topic in which you want to include the link. Make sure it is showing in the WYSIWYG tab in the left-hand pane.
2. Highlight the text, image, or multimedia element you want to include the hyperlink, or place the cursor where you want the hyperlink to appear.

If you choose to link from an image or multimedia element, RoboHELP HTML displays a Select button so you can locate the element.

3. Select the Insert Hyperlink button from the toolbar. This opens the Hyperlink window shown in Figure 21-1.

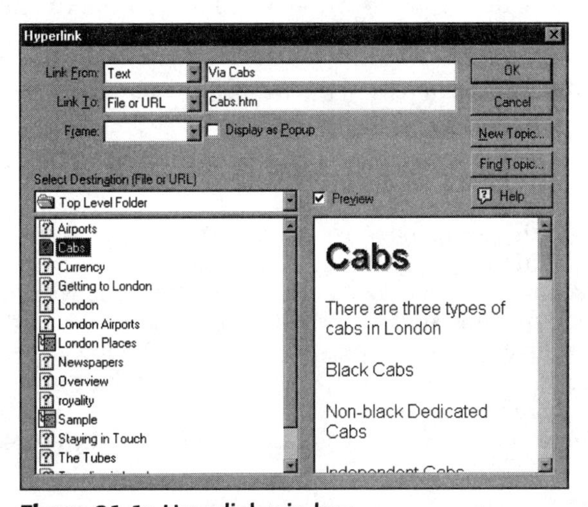

Figure 21-1: Hyperlink window

4. Enter link information into the Hyperlink window, including the text for the link and its designation. For more information about the Hyperlink window, see the next section.
5. Once you are satisfied with the information in the Hyperlink window, click OK. RoboHELP HTML closes the window and adds your hyperlink to the topic page.

Using the Hyperlink Window

The Hyperlink window, shown in Figure 21-1, is where almost all of your standard hyperlinks are set. Use the Hyperlink window to set links to jump between topics, to create popups of topics, to add an e-mail link, or even to move the user to some exterior information.

The Insert Hyperlink button and the Insert Popup button launch the same window; the only difference is the title. Everything described here also applies to the Popup window.

Because the Hyperlink window is so important, the following sections describe all the options available to you, and how to make the most of them.

As you can see in Figure 21-1, the Hyperlink window is divided into two major parts. The top part sets what type of link it is, how it is displayed, and where it goes. Every hyperlink you set requires this information to be added to the top of the Hyperlink window.

The bottom of the window lists all the topics in your project and helps you quickly and easily create hyperlinks to other topics in your project. On the right, it gives you the option of previewing the hyperlink before you add it so you can make sure you are linking to the right topic.

The following sections describe each part of the Hyperlink window and the options that can be set for it:

Link From

Link From sets how the link is viewed by the user on the topic page. It offers three options: Text, Image, or Multimedia. If you choose a text link, fill in the text you want to appear in the text box directly to the right of the list. (If you had highlighted text before you launched the Hyperlink window, it would automatically be filled into this box.) If you choose either Image or Multimedia, a Select button appears next to the text box, allowing you to navigate to the element you want to include in your topic. Don't forget to include it in the project folder if it is not already there. If either of the elements is already included in the project, you can select it from the drop-down list provided.

Link To

Link To sets where the link connects. You can select any of the seven options: File, URL. E-Mail, FTP, News, Multimedia, or Remote Topic, each of which is discussed in the following list.

- **File or URL** points the link at another topic in your HTML Help project, intranet Web page, or Internet Web page. Use the lower part of the Link To window to select a topic from your project or to select a remote web site you have already referenced in your project. Once you select the file from the list, RoboHELP HTML automatically copies its name into the text box directly to the right of the drop-down list. If you have not selected text to include for the link, the name in the text box becomes the text on the page for the link.
- **E-Mail** sets the link to open your user's default e-mail program with a new message addressed to the address you provide. When you select E-Mail from the list, RoboHELP HTML adds mailto: to the text box. Fill in the address you'd like to set the link to after the colons in mailto: (for example, mailto: username@bogusdomain.com).

Do not alter any of the text with colons that RoboHELP HTML adds automatically to the text box, such as mailto:, ftp://, or news:. Doing so causes the link to fail.

- **FTP** sets a link that takes your users to an FTP site from which they can download files to their computer. When you select FTP from the list, RoboHELP HTML automatically adds ftp:// to the text box. Fill in the Internet address of the FTP site after the colon, including the file name if you want your user to download a specific file when they click the link. Use only the main folder for the FTP site if you want users to be able to choose which file they are going to download.
- **News** points the link at a Usenet newsgroup. A newsgroup collects messages on a specified topic; you may want to use a newsgroup specific to the topic your help system discusses. When you choose News from the list, RoboHELP HTML automatically adds news: to the text box on the right. Add the address of the newsgroup after the colon.
- **Multimedia** points the link to a multimedia file. When you select Multimedia, RoboHELP HTML adds a Select button to the right of the text box. Use the Select button to navigate to the desired Multimedia file, making sure to include it in your project folder if it has not already been copied there.
- **Remote Topic** allows you to add a link to a topic not included in the current HTML Help project. You can choose CHM files to link to with this option. When you choose Remote Topic from the list, RoboHELP HTML adds a Select button to the right of the text box. Use the Select button to navigate to the remote topic. Make sure to include it in your project folder if it is not already part of this project.

Frame

Frame sets the link to open in part of a frameset. The drop-down list shows all the default frames. If the file you are linking from does not already have a frameset designated, this setting is ignored. If the file you are linking from has a frameset designated, you must include this setting or the link removes the frameset and opens as a standard window.

For more information about frames and framesets, see Chapter 26, "Using Forms and Frames."

Display as Popup

Display as Popup sets the link to open in a popup window. Popup windows are fairly small, so this option should really be applied only to links that are set to display a small amount of text. Usually this option is used for definitions in the text of a topic.

Select Destination (File or URL)

Select Destination (File or URL) shows all the topics in the current HTML Help project. You can choose which topics are displayed in this list by choosing different folders from the drop-down list. All Folders displays every topic in every folder in your project. Remote URLs shows all the web pages already referenced in the project that are not part of the HTML Help project. Top-Level Folders shows the topics in your HTML Files folder.

Preview

Preview shows a small version of the currently selected topic. This small version is called a *thumbnail*. Only local HTML topics in the current project, bookmarks, and frames are displayed when you select Preview. No remote web pages are displayed.

New Topic

New Topic allows you to create a new topic and a link to it simultaneously. When you choose New Topic, the Create Topic Wizard window opens allowing you to set the options for a new topic.

For more information about creating new topics, see Chapter 18 "Creating your First HTMLHelp Project."

Find Topic

Find Topic helps you find a topic you don't see listed by opening the Find Topic window. Find Topic works much like the standard Windows Find feature on the taskbar's Start button.

Inserting a Link That Opens in a Popup Window

Setting a link to open as just a part of a window can be useful when you don't want the new information to remove the old information from the screen. Popups were developed for just this scenario. They are fully functional windows that open on top of your project, and close when the user clicks outside the popup window on the topic page.

WinHelp allows only one type of popup window, called text-only popups in RoboHELP HTML. Popup windows in RoboHELP HTML are far more functional, with the capability to include anything a standard topic can. Text-only popups are discussed in the next section.

Popups are particularly useful when you have a relevant page you want your users to access, but you dont want them to close the current topic. Popups open up over an HTML Help project topic page as a smaller version of the standard window, as shown in Figure 21-2.

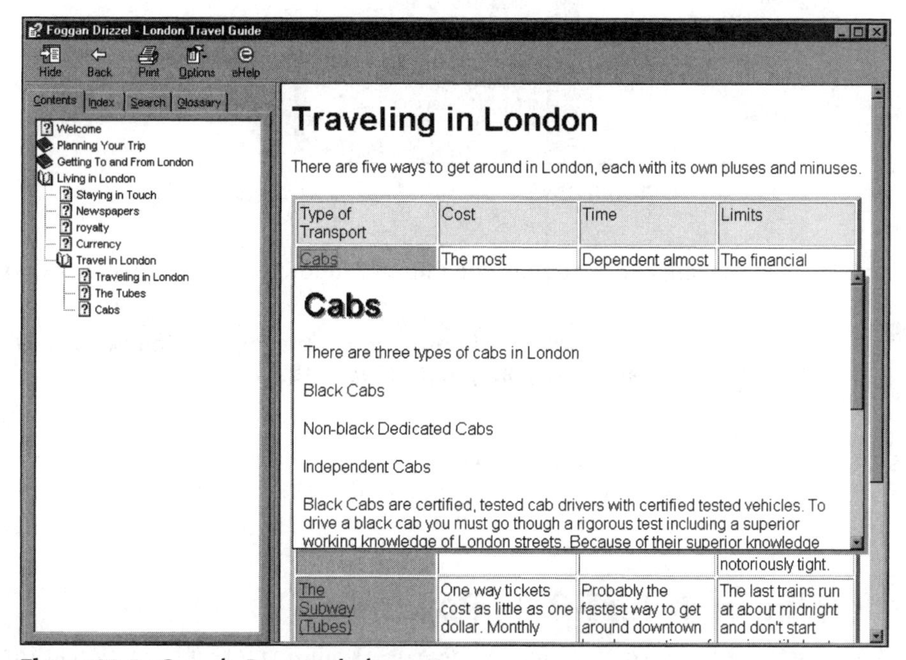

Figure 21-2: Sample Popup window

Here's how you add a popup link to a topic:

1. Open the topic in which you want to add the popup. Make sure the topic is visible in the WYSIWYG tab in the right-hand pane.
2. Place the cursor where you want the popup link to be. If you want the link to include text that is already on the topic page, highlight the text. If you want the link to include an image that is already on the topic page, select it.
3. Click the Insert Popup button on the toolbar. This opens the Popup window shown in Figure 21-3.

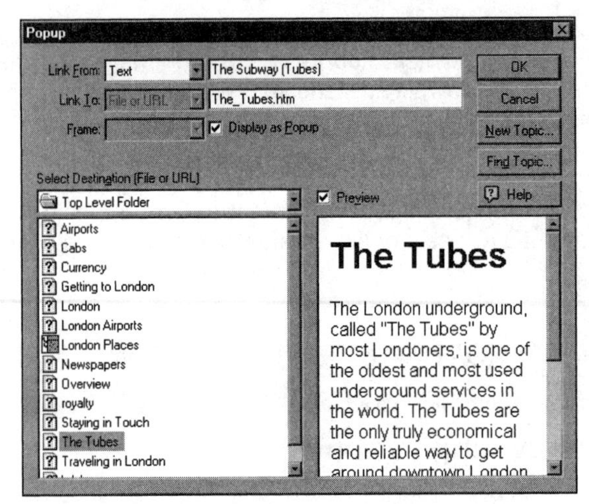

Figure 21-3: Popup window

4. Provide the link information in the Popup window. Leave the Display as Popup box checked.

5. When you are satisfied with the information in the Popup window, click OK. RoboHELP HTML adds the popup to the topic page and closes the Popup window.

The Popup window and the Hyperlink window are almost identical. For more information about using these windows, see "Using the Hyperlink Window," earlier in this chapter.

Working with Text-Only Popups

There are times when you just need to give users a little more information at their request, usually information that they do not need to use repeatedly. Text-only popups were created for this purpose. Like standard popups, text-only popups open when the user clicks on the link; and they close when the user clicks outside the text-only popup on the topic page. However, they cannot include images or links of their own.

Text-only popups are particularly useful for small amounts of information, such as a definition. Popups open up over your HTML Help project topic page as a small yellow window (shown in black-and-white in Figure 21-4).

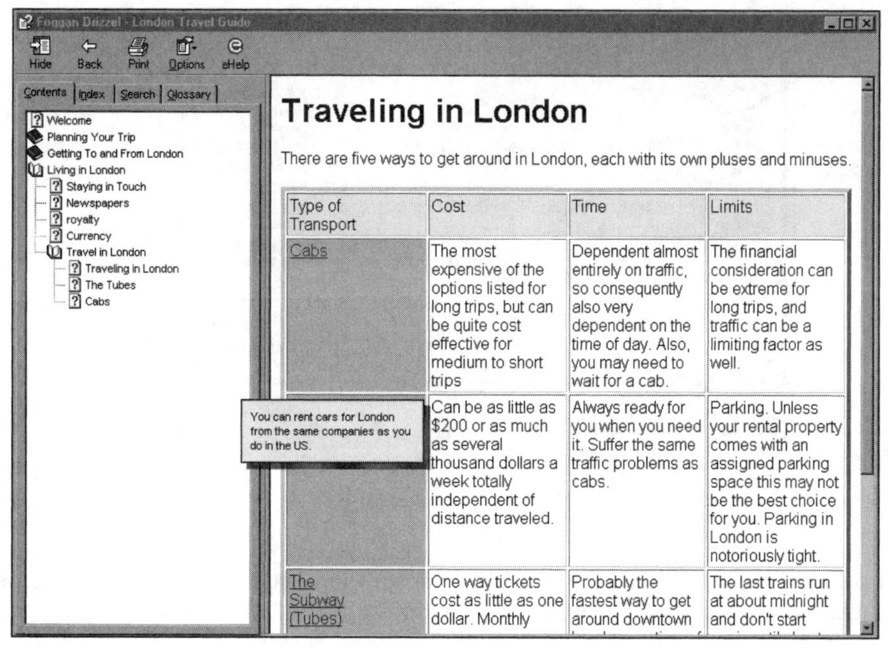

Figure 21-4: Sample text-only popup

Here's how to set a link for a text-only popup:

1. Open the topic in which you want to add the text popup. Make sure the topic is visible in the WYSIWYG tab in the right-hand pane.
2. Place the cursor where you want the text-only popup link to be. If you want the link to include text that is already on the topic page, highlight the text. If you want the link to include an image that is already on the topic page, select it.
3. Select Insert ⇨ Text-only Popup. RoboHELP HTML places an empty text popup on the topic page, as shown in Figure 21-5.
4. Fill in the text you want to include on the text-only popup.
5. When you have finished adding text, click on the topic page outside the text-only popup. This closes the editing of the text-only popup.

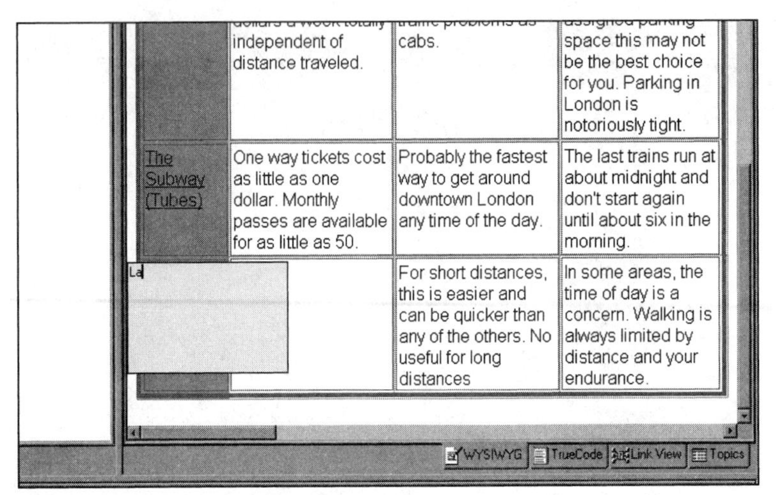

Figure 21-5: Inserting a text-only popup

Text-only popups can also have a color background and text formatting. A color background makes the popup interesting to users and text formatting can help you include them in the color and style schemes for your HTML Help project.

Here's how you alter the formatting of a text-only popup:

1. Open the topic that contains the text-only popup you want to edit. Make sure the topic is visible in the WYSIWYG tab in the right-hand pane, and that the link to the popup is visible in the window.
2. Right-click on the link to the text-only popup. Select Insert/Edit Hyperlink from the list. This opens the Text Popup Properties window, as shown in Figure 21-6.

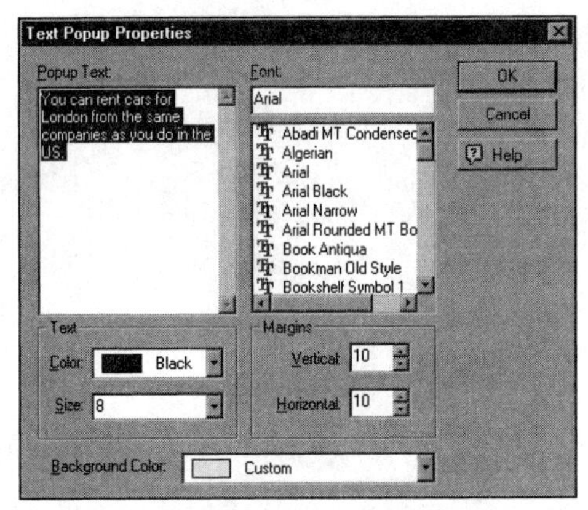

Figure 21-6: Text Popup Properties window

3. Alter the text, the formatting, the margins, and text and background colors of the text-only popup using the Text Popup Properties window.
4. When you have finished editing the text-only popup, click OK. RoboHELP HTML closes the window and reformats the text-only popup.

Any settings you choose for the text-only popup become the new default for all new popups. They do not, however, affect the properties of existing popups.

Creating Text Effects with Dynamic HTML

When your users click on a link and RoboHELP HTML opens a new page, you can make sure it does more than simply display plain text on a white background. You can make your topics do amazing things as they open, all with the help of Dynamic HTML (DHTML).

Dynamic HTML effects require Internet Explorer 4.0 or later.

Special effects were discussed in relation to images in Chapter 20, "Creating and Adding Graphics," but there are ways to add interesting effects to your topics without adding images that fade in and out. You can achieve exciting special effects with text alone using DHTML.

As you may guess, text special effects are easy to overuse because they are so much fun. Use them sparingly, as overuse can quickly change them from an amusing diversion to an extreme annoyance.

RoboHELP HTML comes with scripts for ten different DHTML features, all explained in the following sections.

Drop Shadow

Drop shadow is the simplest of the DHTML effects. It adds a static shadow to the background of the selected text. Here's how to add a drop-shadow effect:

1. Open the topic containing the text you want to add the drop shadow to in the WYSIWYG tab.
2. Highlight the text.
3. Select DHTML ⇨ Drop Shadow.

RoboHELP adds a green dashed box around the selected text to let you know the drop shadow's been added.

You can control the distance and substance of the shadow by setting the special-effect properties:

1. Open the topic with the special-effect text.
2. Right-click on text that has had a drop shadow added and select Special Effect Properties. This displays the Special Effects (Dynamic HTML) window, shown in Figure 21-7.

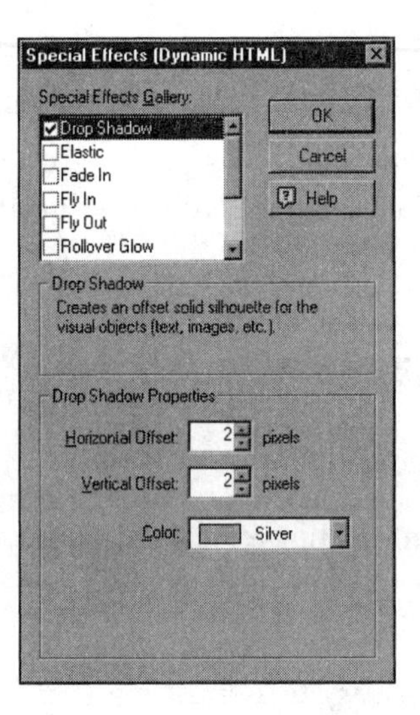

Figure 21-7: Special Effects (Dynamic HTML) – Drop Shadow window

3. Set the horizontal and vertical distance from the text to the shadow.
4. Set the color of the shadow.
5. When you are satisfied with the settings, click OK.

RoboHELP HTML closes the window and makes the changes to the text.

Elastic

Elastic brings in the text you select from off the topic page after the page has loaded. The text appears to spring into place. You can choose where the text flies in from off the page. Here's how to add elastic text that comes in from the bottom of the page:

1. On the WYSIWYG tab, open the topic containing the text you want spring onto the page.
2. Highlight the text.
3. Select DHTML ➪ Elastic ➪ From Bottom.

You choose DHTML ➪ Elastic ➪ From Right in step three if you want the text to fly in from the right of the screen instead.

RoboHELP HTML adds the effect to the text and adds a green dashed box around the selected text to let you know the effect has been added.

You can set the fly in directions, the rate, and when it happens by altering the special-effect properties:

1. Open the topic with the special-effect text.
2. Right-click on text that has had elastic added and choose Special Effect Properties. This displays the Special Effects (Dynamic HTML) window, as shown in Figure 21-8.

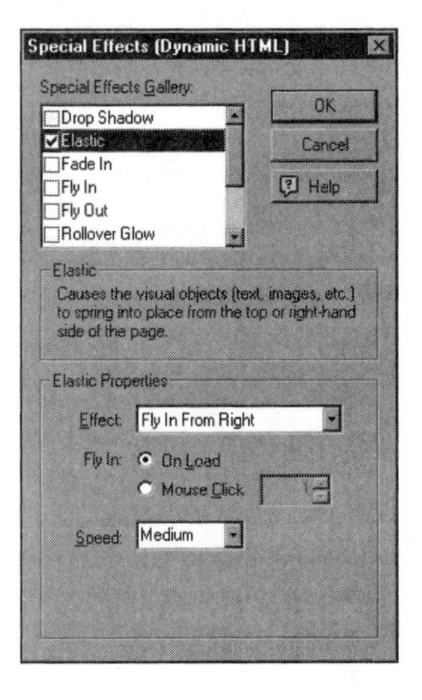

Figure 21-8: Special Effects (Dynamic HTML) – Elastic window

3. Set the fly-in direction using the drop-down list.
4. Set when the fly in should occur.
5. Set the speed for the fly in.
6. When you are satisfied with the settings, click OK.

RoboHELP HTML closes the window and makes the changes to the text.

Fade In

Fade in is a more complicated effect. Text selected with fade in appears gradually after the topic has been loaded. At first, it is simply a shadow, emerging gradually into fully black text. Here's how to add it to your text:

1. Open the topic containing the text you want fade onto the page on the WYSIWYG tab.
2. Highlight the text.
3. Select DHTML ➪ Fade In.

RoboHELP HTML adds the effect to the text and adds a green dashed box around the selected text, indicating that the effect has been added.

You can set the fade in rate and when it happens by altering the special-effect properties:

1. Open the topic with the special-effect text.
2. Right-click on text that has had fade in added and choose Special Effect Properties. This displays the Special Effects (Dynamic HTML) window, as shown in Figure 21-9.

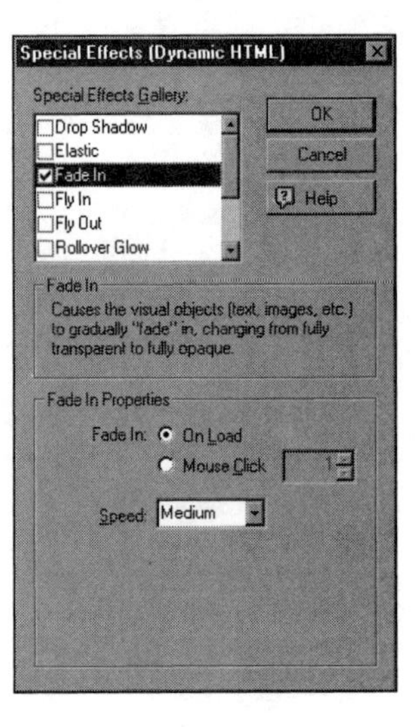

Figure 21-9: Special Effects (Dynamic HTML) - Fade In window

3. Set when the fade in should occur, either on loading the topic or when the user clicks.
4. Set the speed for the fade in.
5. When you are satisfied with the settings, click OK.

RoboHELP HTML closes the window and makes the changes to the text.

Fly In

Fly in is like a complicated elastic effect, without the bounce at the end. You can choose to have your text fly in from every imaginable part of your topic page. You can even choose to have text fly in from more than one direction. Here's how to add a fly in from the bottom of your topic:

1. Open the topic containing the text you want to spring onto the page on the WYSIWYG tab.
2. Highlight the text.
3. Select DHTML ➪ Fly In ➪ From Bottom.

You would choose DHTML ➪ Fly In ➪ (Direction) in step three if you want the text to fly in from other directions.

RoboHELP HTML adds the effect to the text and adds a green dashed box around the selected text, indicating that the effect has been added.

You can set the fly in directions, the rate, and when it happens by altering the special-effect properties:

1. Open the topic with the special-effect text.
2. Right-click on text that has had fly in added and choose Special Effect Properties. This displays the Special Effects (Dynamic HTML) window, as shown in Figure 21-10.

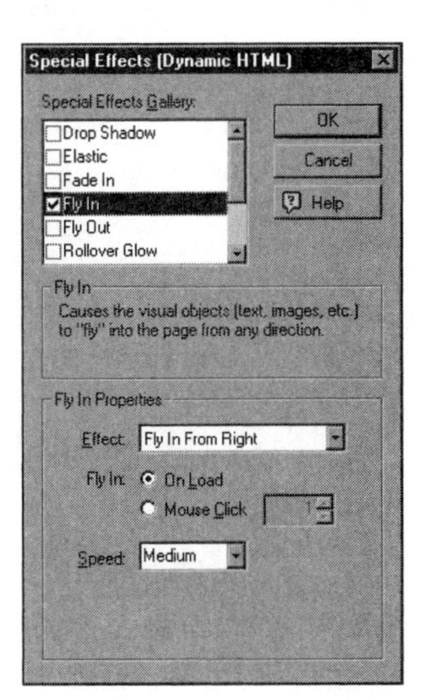

Figure 21-10: Special Effects (Dynamic HTML) – Fly In window

3. Set the fly-in direction using the drop-down list.
4. Set when the fly in should occur.
5. Set the speed for the fly in.
6. When you are satisfied with the settings, click OK.

RoboHELP HTML closes the window and makes the changes to the text.

Fly Out

Fly out is the reverse of text flying in. Fly out text removes the text from the topic page by flying it out of the page in any direction you choose. Here's how to add text that flies out:

1. Open the topic containing the text you want to fly off the page on the WYSIWYG tab.
2. Highlight the text.
3. For example, select DHTML ➪ Fly Out ➪ To Bottom.

RoboHELP HTML adds the effect to the text and adds a green dashed box around the selected text, indicating that the effect has been added.

You can set the fly out directions, the rate, and when it happens by altering the special-effect properties:

1. Open the topic with the special-effect text.
2. Right-click on text that has had fly out added and choose Special Effect Properties. This displays the Special Effects (Dynamic HTML) window, as shown in Figure 21-11.
3. Set the fly out direction using the drop-down list.
4. Set when the fly out should occur.
5. Set the speed for the fly out.
6. When you are satisfied with the settings, click OK.

RoboHELP HTML closes the window and makes the changes to the text.

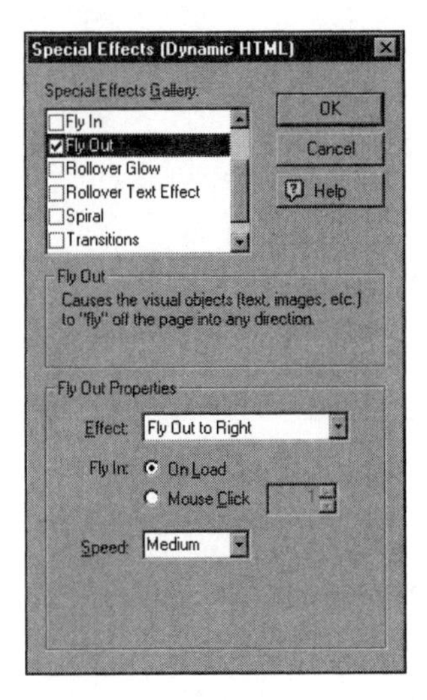

Figure 21-11: Special Effects (Dynamic HTML) - Fly Out window

Rollover Glow

Rollover glow is a totally different effect than the movement effects you have seen so far. Rollover glow alters your text so that when the mouse cursor is passed over the text, it appears to glow. It is an especially useful special effect for links or other text you want to make sure your user notices. Here's how to add a rollover glow to your text:

1. Open the topic containing the text you want to glow on the WYSIWYG tab.
2. Highlight the text.
3. Select DHTML ➪ Rollover Glow.

RoboHELP HTML adds the effect to the text and adds a green dashed box around the selected text, indicating that the effect has been added.

You can set the glow color and size by altering the special-effect properties:

1. Open the topic with the special-effect text.
2. Right-click on text that has had Rollover Glow added and choose Special Effect Properties. This displays the Special Effects (Dynamic HTML) window, as shown in Figure 21-12.

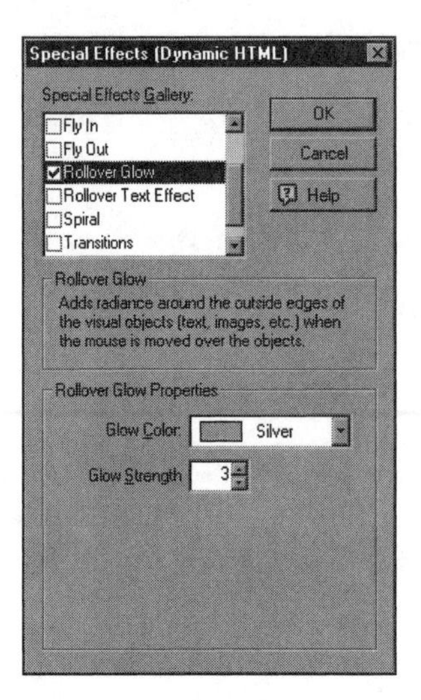

Figure 21-12: Special Effects (Dynamic HTML) – Rollover Glow window

3. Set the glow color using the drop-down list.
4. Set the depth of the glow, in pixels.
5. When you are satisfied with the settings, click OK.

RoboHELP HTML closes the window and makes the changes to the text.

Rollover Text Effect

Like Rollover Glow, Rollover Text Effect occurs when the mouse cursor is moved over the text. The Rollover Text Effect changes the formatting of the text when the cursor passes over it. Here's how to add Rollover text effect to your text:

1. Open the topic you want to have a rollover effect on the WYSIWYG tab.
2. Highlight the text.
3. Select DHTML ⇨ Rollover Text Effect. This opens the Special Effects (Dynamic HTML) window, as shown in Figure 21-13.
4. Select the new font set and size.
5. Select the new font style and color.
6. Use the preview box to make sure the formatting is what you wanted, and then click OK.

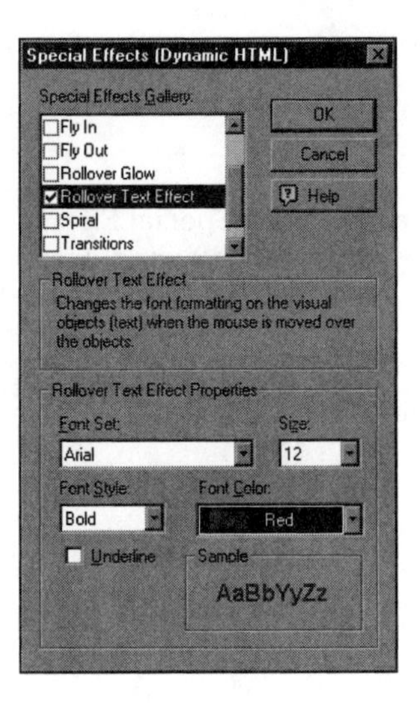

Figure 21-13: Special Effects (Dynamic HTML) – Rollover Text Effect window

It's best not to underline text because it will likely be confused with text that is hyperlinked.

RoboHELP HTML adds the effect to the text and adds a green dashed box around the selected text, indicating that the effect has been added.

You can alter all the same settings you used to set the effect by right-clicking on the text and choosing Special Effect Properties. This opens the Special Effects (Dynamic HTML) window shown in Figure 21-13.

Spiral

Spiral is a more advanced version of the fly in and fly out options discussed earlier. This effect causes text to spiral into the page from the top. Follow these steps to make your text spiral onto the page:

1. Open the topic containing the text you want to spiral onto the page on the WYSIWYG tab.
2. Highlight the text.
3. Select DHTML ➪ Spiral.

RoboHELP HTML adds the effect to the text and adds a green dashed box around the selected text, indicating that the effect has been added.

You can set the spiral rate and when it should occur by altering the special-effect properties:

1. Open the topic with the special-effect text.
2. Right-click on text that has had a spiral added and choose Special Effect Properties. This displays the Special Effects (Dynamic HTML) window, as shown in Figure 21-14.

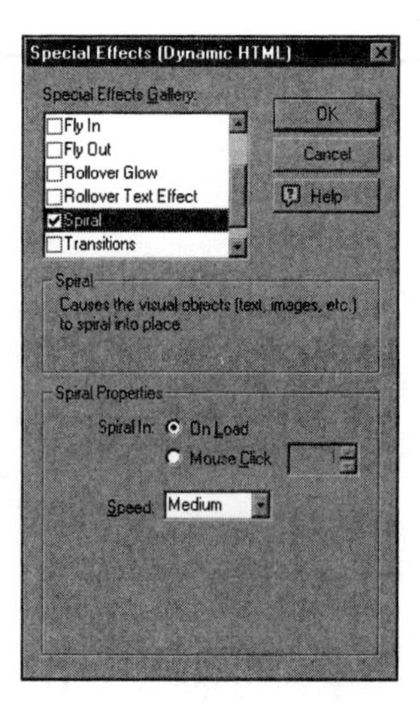

Figure 21-14: Special Effects (Dynamic HTML) – Spiral window

3. Set when the spiral should occur.
4. Set the speed for the spiral.
5. When you are satisfied with the settings, click OK.

RoboHELP HTML closes the window and makes the changes to the text.

Transition

Transition is like a super-advanced fade in effect. Transition allows you to fade in your text according to one of 23 different patterns. Here's how to use transition on your text:

1. Open the topic containing the text you want to fade onto the page on the WYSIWYG tab.
2. Highlight the text.
3. For example, select DHTML ➪ Transition ➪ Random.

RoboHELP HTML adds the effect to the text and adds a green dashed box around the selected text, indicating that the effect has been added.

You can set the fly out directions, the rate, and when it should occur by altering the special-effect properties:

1. Open the topic with the special-effect text.
2. Right-click on text that has had transition added and choose Special Effect Properties. This displays the Special Effects (Dynamic HTML) window, as shown in Figure 21-15.

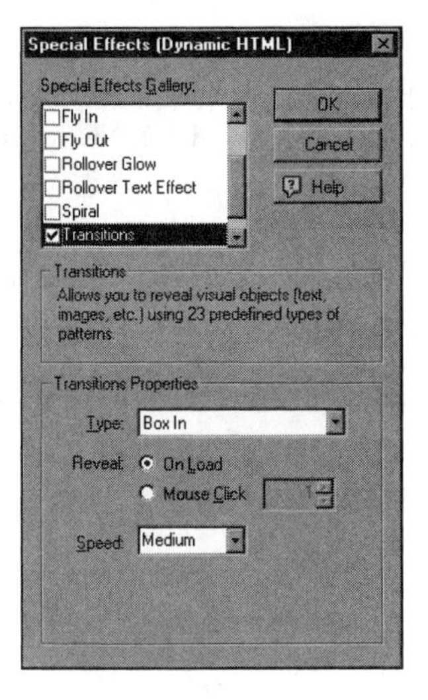

Figure 21-15: Special Effects (Dynamic HTML) – Transition window

3. Set the transition pattern type using the drop-down list.
4. Set when to reveal the text.
5. Set the speed for revelation.
6. When you are satisfied with the settings, click OK.

RoboHELP HTML closes the window and makes the changes to the text.

Zoom

Zoom keeps the text totally invisible and then zooms it in either by zooming up from small to normal size or by zooming down from huge to normal size. Here's how to zoom in your text:

1. Open the topic containing the text you want to zoom in onto the page on the WYSIWYG tab.

2. Highlight the text.
3. Select DHTML ➪ Zoom ➪ In.

Choose DHTML ➪ Zoom ➪ Out if you want the text to zoom from huge to normal size instead.

RoboHELP HTML adds the effect to the text and adds a green dashed box around the selected text, indicating that the effect has been added.

You can set the zoom type, the rate, and when it should occur by altering the special-effect properties:

1. Open the topic with the special-effect text.
2. Right-click on text that has had zoom added and choose Special Effect Properties. This displays the Special Effects (Dynamic HTML) window, as shown in Figure 21-16.

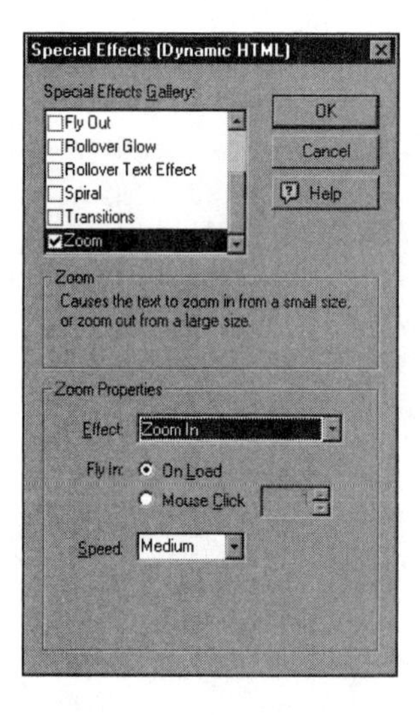

Figure 21-16: Special Effects (Dynamic HTML) – Zoom window

3. Set the zoom type using the drop-down list.
4. Set when the zoom should occur.
5. Set the speed for the zoom.
6. When you are satisfied with the settings, click OK.

RoboHELP HTML closes the window and makes the changes to the text.

Mixing DHTML Effects

You can mix and match Dynamic HTML elements to create stunning effects. First add one using the DHTML list, right-click, choose Special Effects Properties, and choose another effect by using the check boxes.

Because of how they are executed, some effects will not work with others. This sections describes which effects work well with others.

- Drop Shadow: Elastic, Fly In, Fly Out, Rollover Text, Spiral, Zoom
- Elastic: Drop Shadow, Rollover Text, Rollover Glow
- Fade In: Rollover Text
- Fly In: Drop Shadow, Rollover Text, Rollover Glow
- Rollover Glow: Elastic, Fly In, Fly Out, Rollover Text, Spiral, Zoom
- Rollover Text: Drop Shadow, Elastic, Fade In, Fly In, Fly Out, Rollover Glow, Transitions, Spiral
- Transitions: Rollover Text
- Spiral: Drop Shadow, Rollover Text, Rollover Glow
- Zoom: Drop Shadow, Rollover Glow

Summary

In this chapter, you learned how to add links to your RoboHELP HTML topics. You should now understand the different types of links, as well as the different ways you can open topics in the RoboHELP HTML windows. You learned how to point links at both interior and exterior information, and how to add popup definition links. Finally, you learned how to add text special effects to your topics, including flying and fading text that can be launched from a link you set.

✦ ✦ ✦

CHAPTER 22

Using Styles

This chapter shows you how to use styles in RoboHELP HTML. You learn about the different types of styles in RoboHELP HTML, including inline styles, embedded styles, and linked styles. You learn how to add style sheets to your project, and how the HTML of style sheets works. Finally, you learn how to both edit a style sheet and create an entirely new style sheet.

✦ ✦ ✦ ✦

In This Chapter

Styles in RoboHELP HTML

Adding inline styles

Using embedded styles

Modifying existing style sheets

Creating a new style sheet

✦ ✦ ✦ ✦

Styles in RoboHELP HTML

The options for styles in RoboHELP HTML are similar to those in any word processing program. You can change the formatting of text and the layout of a page. You can change the color and function of some text, especially links. You can change the background color and even add a background graphic. All of these changes are considered changes to the *style* of all or part of a topic.

Style can apply to three different areas:

- **Character Style** defines how individual words look and is usually altered using the WYSIWYG buttons.
- **Paragraph Style** defines how text wraps and how text is displayed. Common paragraph styles are Heading 1 or Normal. Boxes around text are also defined in the paragraph style.
- **Document Style** defines the look of your entire topic. Backgrounds, margins, body text fonts, and link fonts are all defined by the document style.

Each of these styles uses HTML code to change how the text or background looks on the screen. When your topic is displayed in the HTML Help screen, these styles define how the user sees it.

It's easy to get confused about the different types of styles. Just remember that if you can highlight a little text and make a change, it's probably a character style change. If you alter a paragraph marker or more than one line at a time, you've probably made a paragraph style change. If you change the look of a whole page, you've probably made a document style change.

You cannot define a set of styles for your whole project at once. Because each topic is a separate HTML document, you need to define the same document style for several different topics in order for them all to be displayed in the same way for your user.

Altering a Style

You have several ways to change a style in RoboHELP HTML, depending on what you are attempting to change. Here are the three ways to change a style in RoboHELP HTML:

- **Inline:** Inline styles alter one section of text within your topic, usually by using the WYSIWYG buttons on the toolbar; they are within the HTML codes for the text they alter. Inline styles always override all other styles that apply to a block of text.
- **Embedded:** Embedded styles alter one or more paragraphs, and may alter part of an entire topic or HTML document. They are saved with the topic page, and override all linked styles.
- **Linked:** Linked styles alter the look of all or part of your document. The information for a linked style is saved in a separate HTML document, and the topic links to the HTML document (called a *style sheet*).

Linked styles are accomplished using Cascading Style Sheets. For more information, see the subsection "How the HTML Works" under "Using Linked Style Changes."

Choosing Style Types

How you change the way the text is displayed on the screen depends on two main questions:

- What are you changing?
- How many times will it need to be done?

The way you create a change depends in large part on what you are changing. Some changes can be accomplished using a number of methods, and some things can only be changed in one way. Figure 22-1 gives you a rough outline of the types of changes and the most appropriate methods used with them.

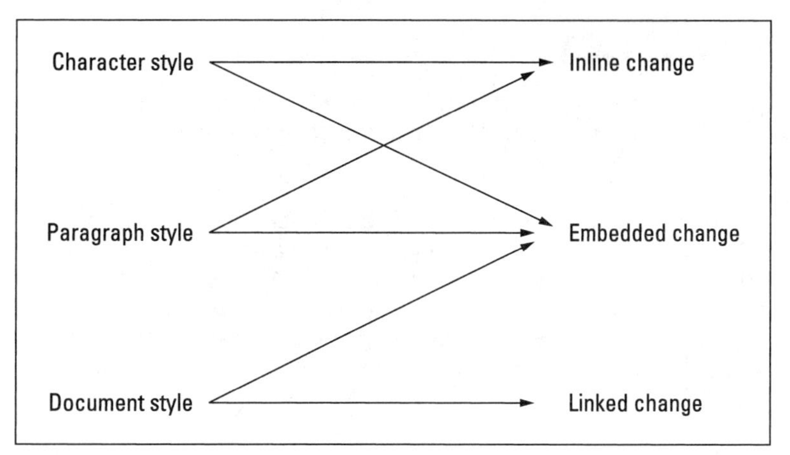

Figure 22-1: Methods of changing styles

As you can see in Figure 22-1, not all methods of altering a style are appropriate for all types of style changes. For example, it would be nearly impossible to make a change on the document level using inline styles. It would also be difficult to change document styles using an embedded change, but it is possible. However, character changes are performed perfectly well with embedded styles, and even better with inline styles. Understanding this difference in change styles needs to be your first step in deciding how to make the change you want.

Once you have decided what you are changing, you have only narrowed the types of changes down to two types. For example, if you decide your change is a paragraph change, you have eliminated using a linked change, but you still have two other options from which to choose. In order to choose between them, you need to answer the next question, How many times will it need to be done?" Because every type of style change uses a different method to accomplish the change, how many times you will need the style change is an important factor.

For changes that will be used only once, inline styles are best. For changes that you will use several times in the same topic, embedded styles are best. For changes that will need to be used in more than one topic, linked styles are best.

Therefore, most character changes are inline, most paragraph changes are embedded, and most document changes are linked.

Note

All changes can be made using a linked change. However, this can get very cumbersome and is only necessary when you are using the same change repeatedly or if consistency across pages is necessary.

Using Inline Styles

Inline changes are the most common type of style change. Every time you alter a style using the buttons on the toolbar, you have most likely created an inline change.

Remember that inline changes always override any other style that may be attributed to a bit of text. It is not uncommon to make a change in a linked or embedded way without it taking effect because you forget there is an inline change attributed to that bit of text. This is one of the major differences between how RoboHELP HTML functions and how a word processor functions. You cannot assume that a global change will override a character-level change, because inline changes always have precedence.

Changing Character Style Using the WYSIWYG Toolbar

The WYSIWYG (What You See Is What You Get) nature of the RoboHELP HTML editing screen is a powerful way to create your online help project. It enables you to alter your text quickly and easily so that your project looks the way you want it to, and the HTML Help you compile will look almost exactly like what you see on the screen.

Every time you make a change on your WYSIWYG editor, you are making an inline change, a change that's reflected in the HTML of your topic.

Table 22-1 lists the most frequently used toolbar buttons that affect the inline style of characters.

Table 22-1
WYSIWYG Buttons for Changing Inline Styles

Buttons	*Style Effect*
A	Changes the color of the font
B	Changes the style of the font to bold
I	Changes the style of the font to italic
U	Changes the style of the font to underscored
	Changes the alignment of the highlighted text to flush left

Buttons	Style Effect
	Changes the alignment of the highlighted text to centered
	Changes the alignment of the highlighted text to flush right
	Turns the highlighted text into a numbered list
	Turns the highlighted text into a bulleted list

For a complete discussion of the WYSIWYG tab, see Chapter 17, "Using RoboHELP HTML."

Changing Character Style Using the Character Window

Sometimes the buttons on the toolbar do not fulfill all your editing needs. If you need to make a change to the character style of text and you want to change more than one thing at a time, you need to do so by using the character window.

To make an inline change using the Character window:

1. Open the topic with the text you'd like to change and highlight the text.
2. Select Format ➪ Character. The Character Window displays as shown in Figure 22-2, with the Character tab selected.

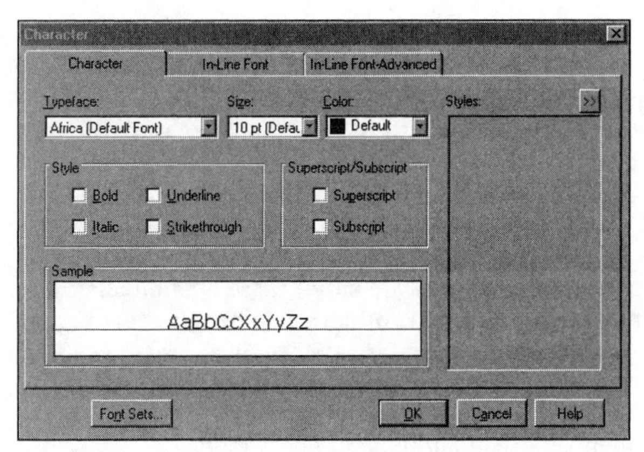

Figure 22-2: The Character window – Character tab

The Character tab allows you to set basic font styles and colors, much as you would with the WYSIWYG buttons. However, more options are available from this window.

3. Use the drop-down menu to select the typeface, size, and color for the selected text.
4. Use the checkboxes to select special attributes for your text, including Bold, Underline, Italics, Strikethrough, Superscripts, and Subscript. As you make these selections, the Styles box on the right lists the added styles.
5. Click the double right arrows next to the Styles box. This turns the box into a series of checkboxes, allowing you to choose from several dozen text-formatting options. Choose any of these you need by selecting the checkbox, but remember that not all of them are supported in all browsers.
6. Use the sample at the bottom of the window to verify that the text has the correct formatting. When you are happy with the settings on this tab, click OK.

If you ever want an inline setting to revert back to the setting for the whole document, choose <Undefined> for the value in any drop-down menu.

Once you have set the basic formatting with the Character window, you have set an inline style. You can set many other inline styles, most of which you have already done without knowing so. Most of the formatting changes in Chapter 19, "Creating Outstanding Topics," are inline formatting changes. The other tabs on the Character window are described there.

How the HTML Works

When you make an inline change, you are adding a special HTML tag to your code. This HTML tag includes information about how text is to be displayed. As the browser reads the text and begins to display the document, it reads the formatting changes you have set in the body with the text. It alters only the text that is displayed between the on and off tags of the formatting change, called the start and end tags.

Each separate change you make, either with the WYSIWYG buttons or on the Character window, is reflected as a separate set of tags. This means that every drop-down menu or checkbox you alter produces two tags, a start tag and an end tag.

Figure 22-3 shows how different the code can be for text formatted by the "normal" setting after the text has been given an inline style change.

```
  <TITLE>East African region</TITLE>
  <META NAME="generator" CONTENT="RoboHELP by Blue Sky Software www.blue-
sky.com HTML Edition">
  <SCRIPT LANGUAGE="javascript" TITLE="BSSC Special Effects"
SRC="BSSCDHTM.js">
</SCRIPT><LINK
  REL="StyleSheet" HREF="default.css">
 <META NAME="MS-HKWD" CONTENT="East African region"></HEAD>
  <BODY ONLOAD="BSSCOnLoad();" ONCLICK="BSSCOnClick();"
ONUNLOAD="BSSCOnUnload();">
  <H1>
   On S<FONT COLOR="BLACK">afar</FONT>i</H1>
  <P STYLE="text-align : center;" ALIGN=CENTER>
   <IMG SRC="ImageFiles\bar2.gif" ALIGN=BOTTOM WIDTH="500" HEIGHT="6"
VSPACE="0" HSPACE="0" BORDER="0"></P>
  <P STYLE="text-align : center;" ALIGN=CENTER>
   <IMG SRC="ImageFiles\eastaf.jpg" VSPACE="0" HSPACE="0" BORDER="0"
USEMAP="#east_africa"></P>
  <P STYLE="text-align : center;" ALIGN=CENTER>
   <IMG SRC="ImageFiles\bar2.gif" ALIGN=BOTTOM WIDTH="500" HEIGHT="6"
VSPACE="0" HSPACE="0" BORDER="0"></P>
  <P STYLE="text-align : right;" CLASS="region" ALIGN=RIGHT>
   East Africa</P>
  <P STYLE="text-align : right;" CLASS="region-drop" ALIGN=RIGHT>
   region
```

Figure 22-3: HTML code with inline style changes

The most immediate difference is the addition of HTML tags around the text you modified. Only the text between the tags has been changed, and all other formatting for that text is overridden by the inline style changes.

This type of HTML tag is called a *formatting tag* because it goes in the body of the document and changes only the text between the on and off settings.

Inline formatting has benefits: Because the tag is right next to the text, you can copy and paste the code in and out of the document without losing your formatting. Unlike other types of formatting, which usually are applied at the top of the document or in a separate reference document, inline formatting lives in the text and is part of the body tags.

The danger of inline formatting is that you can spend a lot of time and energy trying to figure out why a section of text is displaying incorrectly, forgetting that there were inline tags with the text. Also, remember to comment out why you changed the text in this one location so that later you'll remember why you decided to make the inline change.

Understanding Embedded Styles

Embedded styles operate much like inline styles do, usually affecting only part of the text in the document. However, unlike inline style changes, you can use embedded style changes repeatedly within the document. You don't need to copy and paste the changes over and over again. They affect the layout of paragraphs and how the text displays, usually for a whole document or a large part of the document.

Embedded styles are styles that you define for just one topic page. The information for an embedded style is included in the heading information for your topic, and not with the text it modifies, as it is with inline style changes. Embedded styles also differ by being included with the topic, setting them apart from linked styles, where the information is kept in another HTML page.

Usually, using embedded styles ends up being less efficient than doing the same thing with a linked style. Because an embedded style is used only once, including more than one or two of them in your project can be slow and cumbersome.

You create embedded styles by defining and using a totally new style. Most of the styles that come with RoboHELP HTML are not embedded styles, as the information about them is kept in a linked document. Whenever you create a new style that you do not add to a style sheet, you are creating and using an embedded style.

Changing an Inline Style

Several dozen styles come with RoboHELP HTML; however, you may need to change a style to suite your needs. You can only alter the style for the current topic; however if you plan to make the same text changes over and over again within a topic, it saves you time and energy to change the style.

You need to use a base style for the style you change. Take a quick tour of the styles before you decide which base style to use.

To change an embedded style for just the current topic, follow these steps:

1. Open the topic you in which you wish to change a style.
2. Select Format ⇨ Paragraph to open the Styles window, as shown in Figure 22-4.

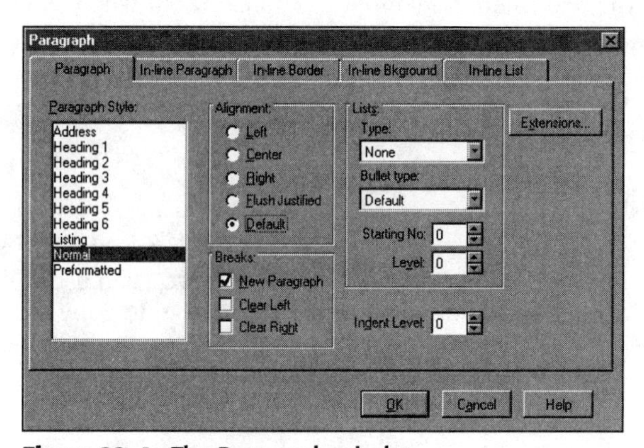

Figure 22-4: The Paragraph window

3. Select the style you wish to use as a base style for your changed style.
4. Using the radio buttons in the center of the Paragraph window, you can make changes to your selected style.
5. When you are satisfied with the style changes, click OK.

When you finish editing the style, RoboHELP changes the current paragraph and all new paragraphs for that topic with that style to reflect your style changes. To add the change to text you already created in the topic, select the text you want to apply the style to and then select the style from the list. This creates an embedded style in your document.

How the HTML Works

Embedded styles work like a hybrid of inline styles and linked styles. They are included with the HTML document, as inline styles are. They are kept in a separate document from the text they modify, as linked styles are. This difference can make them either useless or incredibly useful, depending on what you are trying to do.

Inline styles supersede embedded styles, and embedded styles supersede linked styles.

All of the information for your embedded style is included in the <HEAD> portion of your HTML document. At the top of the code for your topic page is a definition of each type of embedded style used on that page. The reference looks much like the inline style reference, only it is set at the top of the page.

Using Linked Style Changes

Linked style changes differ from the other two types of style changes by the addition of a separate file. Linked style changes create a notation in your topic file at the beginning of the text that is to be displayed differently, and then refer the help display engine to a separate file called a *style sheet* for detailed directions on how that change is to be interpreted.

Linked styles and style sheets are RoboHELP HTML's implementation of Cascading Style Sheets. To learn about the HTML behind Cascading Style Sheets, see "How the HTML Works."

Introducing Style Sheets

As you created your first several projects, you may have noticed a folder in the Project Manager that you haven't been introduced to: the Style Sheets folder. This folder lists all the style sheets used for your project. All of your topics automatically have a style sheet listed, default.css. This style sheet defines the normal and heading styles that come with RoboHELP HTML.

Style sheets can be complicated. You may want to create a few text topics and then experiment with their style sheets before you begin to do it on topics you plan to keep.

A style sheet is a collection of formatting and layout directions that you can apply to your topics. Every topic, because it is a separate HTML document, can have a separate style; however, if you add a different style sheet to each topic, your users can get very confused, as the formatting and layout change for every topic. A better, and more common, use for style sheets is to create one or two to use for your entire project.

Style sheets are a different name for a special kind of HTML page called a *Cascading Style Sheet* or .CSS. Microsoft developed Cascading Style Sheets to help manage large sites. Because all the style information is kept in a separate document, and you can refer to this document in as many different HTML documents as you want, you can keep all the style information for an entire site on one page. This consolidation of style information means you can make changes in just one place and they will be reflected in pages all over the site; hence, the name "cascading." The style sheet is an HTML text file, listing formatting for all parts of your topic, including font choices and colors, background colors, or images. Style sheets contain all the information about the styles you set up, as well as all the default styles.

Choosing a style sheet

Because style sheets define the look of your topics, and judicious use of style sheets can help your project look more professional, choosing the right style sheet is very important. This section walks you through that decision.

You always choose the style sheet for a topic through the Topic Properties screen. First you need to know how to change the style sheet assigned to a topic.

1. Open the topic for which you want to change the style sheet.
2. Right-click in the WYSIWYG screen, and select Topic Properties from the list. This opens the Topic Properties screen to the Appearance tab, as shown in Figure 22-5.
3. To change the style sheet, use the drop-down list to select one.
4. Use the Folder icon next to the Style Sheet field to search for a style sheet that is not listed.

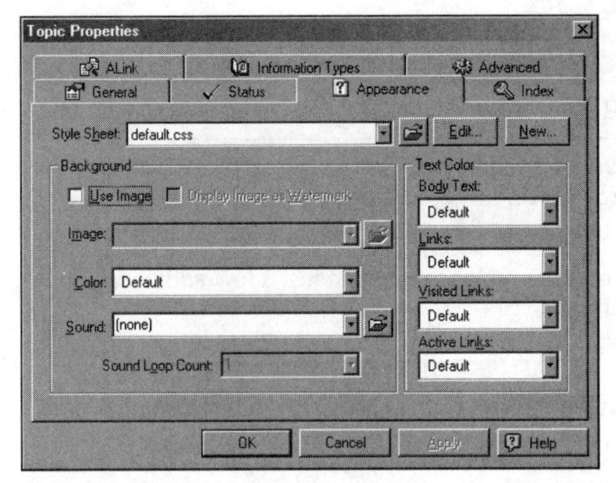

Figure 22-5: Topic Properties screen — Appearance tab

5. When you are done, click OK.

If you choose a style sheet that isn't listed, RoboHELP HTML displays a message telling you it is copying it to your project folder. This ensures that it compiles the style sheet when it compiles the rest of your project.

By default, four style sheets are attached to any new RoboHELP HTML project: DEFAULT.CSS, HTMLHELP.CSS, MS_HELP.CSS, and W95HELP.CSS. DEFAULT.CSS is automatically assigned to any new topic.

RoboHELP HTML also includes several other style sheets, in the RoboHELP Office\ RoboHTML directory under Templates. These other samples include modern.css, classic.css, colorful.css, and several other style sheets designed for various other help projects.

Table 22-2 briefly outlines the most useful style sheets and their intended use.

Table 22-2
Commonly Used Style Sheets

Style Sheet	***Uses***
Default.css	The default style sheet for every new topic. It includes several standard Web fonts, including Arial as the normal font.
HTMLHELP.css	A slightly more complicated version of the default style sheet, with some additions to title fonts and such.
MS_HELP.CSS	A style sheet meant to adhere very strictly to the look of Microsoft Corporations HTML Help.

Continued

Table 22-2 *(continued)*

Style Sheet	***Uses***
W95HELP.CSS	A style sheet meant for use with help projects to be deployed on Microsoft Windows 95. If you plan to ship to the older platform, it is best to use this style sheet.
modern.css	A dressed-up style sheet, with just a few additions over a very plain text layout.
classic.css	A very simple style sheet, with standard fonts and simple layout.
colorful.css	|A bright and colorful style sheet, with colored titles and interesting text.

The best way to choose a style sheet is to try it on a completed help topic and see what you think. Like much of help production, creating good-looking online help requires some sense of design, and designers created the default style sheet to look the best across all platforms.

If you decide to use another one of the standard style sheets, look at it on several computers to make sure it looks the best. All of the style sheets that come with RoboHELP HTML have been tested and are well designed, but it is always best to check.

Altering a style sheet

Sometimes the style sheets that come with RoboHELP HTML are *almost* perfect. They may need just one small change to work perfectly for your help project. It is possible to alter a style sheet that already exists:

1. Open the project containing the style sheet you want to alter.
2. Select the style sheet by double-clicking on it in the Style Sheets folder.
3. Verify that the Style Sheet box in the lower left corner of the window shows the style sheet you would like to alter.
4. Select the style type you would like to change from the list.
5. Click Edit. This opens the Edit Paragraph Style window. .
6. Make changes to the style using the Font tab and other tabs.
7. When you are satisfied with the changes to that style, click OK. This closes the Edit Paragraph Style screen.
8. If you want to edit another style, choose it from the list in the Style Window and start over with Step 5. If not, click OK.

When you click OK on the Style window, RoboHELP HTML saves the changes to the copy of the style sheet you have saved with your project.

How the HTML Works

A style sheet is a separate document listing styles that differ from standard fonts and headings; when you include it with an HTML page, it gives the browser all information it needs to display artfully created topics. To point a browser at the style information (also called *referencing* the information), the name and location of the file is listed in the HEAD portion of every HTML document that needs it. When the browser sees the reference to a style sheet, it loads all the information before it loads any of the text on the page; and when it does load the text, it follows the rules outlined in the style sheet.

Because style sheets, or cascading style sheets, can be so powerful, it is important to remember that one small change can alter the look of your online help radically. It is best to start with very small changes to the style sheets that come with RoboHELP HTML and then test them thoroughly before you embark on any advanced work with style sheets.

Creating a Style Sheet

Once you have mastered the techniques of choosing and altering style sheets, you may want to create your own style sheet. You can create style sheets in two ways:

- In RoboHELP HTML, using the Style Sheet window
- By creating a CCS file using a text editor, such as Notepad

The method you choose depends on how comfortable you feel with HTML and what kind of styles you would like to include.

If you would like to include styles as they are listed in RoboHELP HTML, and if you want to use RoboHELP HTML to create the style sheet, use the Style Sheet window, described in the next section.

If you would like to include a significant amount of VBscript or JavaScript code, or if you would like a look that is very different than the styles that come with RoboHELP HTML, you can create the style sheet from scratch. See "Creating a CCS File Using Notepad" later in this chapter for a description of this process.

Using the Style Sheet window in RoboHELP HTML is by far the simpler of the two ways. It can be very difficult to create the perfect format for a new style sheet by doing it freehand with a text editor.

Using the Style Sheet Window

If you have looked at all the style sheets that come with RoboHELP HTML and still feel you need to create your own, RoboHELP HTML enables you to create a new style sheet.

Creating new style sheets always happens from the same window, the Topic Properties window, on the Appearance tab. You can access this tab in two ways:

- ✦ When creating a new topic, the Topic Properties window opens by default.
- ✦ You can select one or more topics and then choose Edit ➪ Properties.

Always make sure you have selected at least one topic you wish to assign to the new style sheet before you begin this process.

Whichever way you open the Topic Properties window, choose the Appearance tab, shown in Figure 22-6.

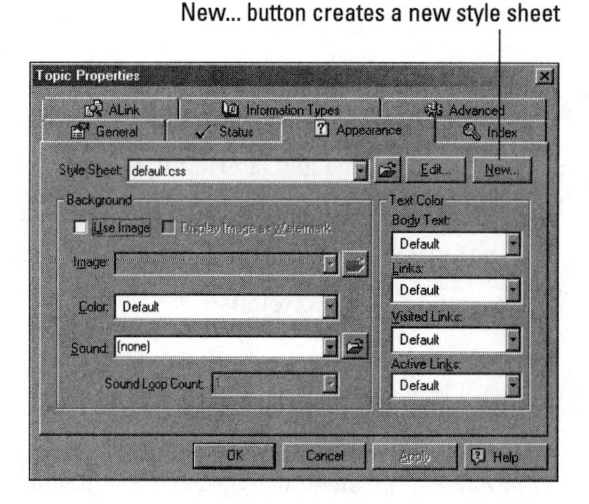

Figure 22-6: Topic Properties window – Appearance tab

From the Appearance tab on the Topic Properties window, here's how you create a new style sheet:

1. Click the New button. This opens a Save As window, shown in Figure 22-7.
2. Choose to save the new style sheet in the project folder containing all the other style sheets for your project. This is the default folder to which RoboHELP HTML prompts you.
3. When you have entered the name and location of your new style sheet, click Save. This opens the Styles tab of the Edit Style window, as shown

in Figure 22-8. All of the styles listed are currently in your style sheet, as they would have been in the default.css file.

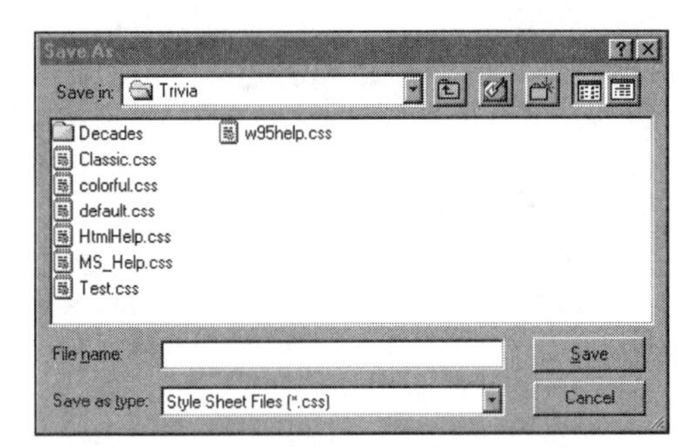

Figure 22-7: Save As window from the Appearance tab

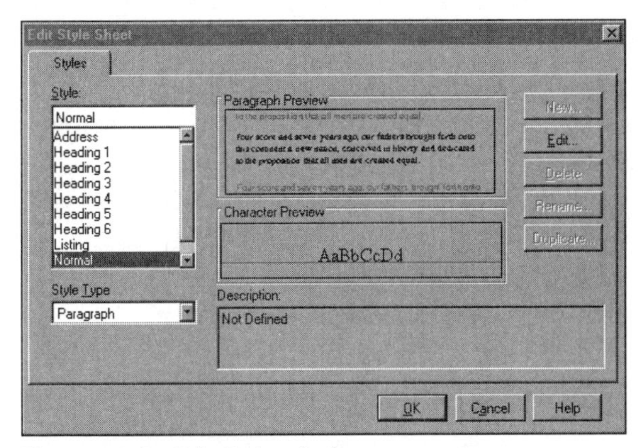

Figure 22-8: Edit Style window

4. Choose and alter the styles as outlined earlier in "Altering a Style Sheet."
5. When you are satisfied with the changes to your styles, click OK. This closes the Edit Style window.
6. Choose background, sound, and text color information from the Appearance tab in the Topic Properties window.

Remember that embedded and inline text formatting always supersedes text information from the style sheet.

7. When you are satisfied with the changes you have made to your new style sheet, click OK.

Once you have finished creating the new style sheet, you can add it to all the topics you please. If you want to use this style sheet again in another project, make sure that you have saved it in the RoboHELP HTML folder outside of your project folder as well as inside of it.

You can change the style sheet for more than one topic at a time. Choose all of the topics using Shift or CTRL, and then choose Edit ➪ Properties.

Creating a CSS File Using Notepad

Style sheets are just special kinds of HTML documents, and as such are just text document formatted in a particular way. You can create your own style sheets using Notepad (or any other text editor you choose), and they will work perfectly in RoboHELP HTML, as long as you follow the format.

You can get the best education about RoboHELP HTML CSS formats in the CSS files that RoboHELP HTML produces itself. Before you start creating your own files, take a look at the files already in your project folder.

In order to work in RoboHELP HTML, the format of your CSS file must be perfect. You may want to investigate Cascading Style Sheets with other sources before you begin this process.

Outline of a RoboHELP HTML CSS file

The following sections describe the basic outline of a RoboHELP HTML CSS document.

First lines

The first line needs to describe the font families in your topic and must use the following format:

```
/* $MVD$:fontset("Arial","Arial") */
```

You must leave the `/* $MUD$:fontset(` and the `) */` parts intact because RoboHELP HTML searches for these when it compiles your documents.

Each font family gets one line, and each needs to have its own `/* $MUD$:fontset(` and `) */` tags. You must list all the font families you wish to include with your style.

Body Description

The next line after the font families can be about the body element. This is where you set the font family of basic text and the color for the background. Its format is as follows:

```
BODY { font-family : "Arial";
        background-color : white;}
```

Style Elements

The majority of your style sheet describes styles. These generally follow standard CSS format, although it is best to follow RoboHELP HTML's indented tab settings.

Two types of style elements are listed in the style sheet: modifications and classes. Modifications are style changes that modify a standard HTML tag. Here's an example of a modification to the H1 tag:

```
H1 { font-family : "Verdana";
       font-weight : bold;
       font-size : 12.0pt;
       color : black;}
```

Classes are used in conjunction with the tag on a text to change how it looks, but not the tag used. In RoboHELP HTML, they are usually subsets of standard tags, and the class for a particular tag should be listed right after the modification of the tag. Here's an example of a class for the H1 listed above:

```
.mvd-H1 { font-family : "Verdana";
            font-weight : normal;
            font-size : 12.0pt;
            color : black;}
```

This produces a font identical to the H1 listed earlier, but lacks the bold, as the font weight is set to normal here.

Other Elements

If you are creating a style sheet of your own, it is likely because you could not make enough changes to the RoboHELP HTML standard CSS file format inside RoboHELP HTML and you need to add other CSS elements to your style sheet.

You can add other legitimate CSS elements into your style sheet, but be sure to test them. Some style elements may not work as you expect, and some formats can cause compiling problems. As long as you stay with the basic CSS elements, you should be fine.

Placing the New CSS File

Once you have created your style sheet, you need to place it so it can be included in your project. It is also a good idea to save a copy of your style sheet in the RoboHELP HTML directory structure so you can use it again with other projects.

Save a copy of your new CSS file in both of the following places:

✦ In your project folder, in the root directory with your project file

✦ In the RoboHELP HTML directory, under Templates\Custom

Summary

In this chapter, you learned about style sheets in RoboHELP HTML. You learned about the different types of styles as well as the different ways to modify them. After learning how to add style sheets to your project, and how the HTML of style sheets works, you learned how to edit a style sheet and how to create an entirely new style sheet using both RoboHELP HTML and a text editor.

✦ ✦ ✦

CHAPTER 23

Creating a TOC and Index

In This Chapter

Creating Tables of Contents

Customizing Tables of Contents

Adding External Contents Files to a Table of Contents

Troubleshooting tables of contents

Understanding Binary indexes

Understanding index files

Adding keywords to the index

Using the Index Designer

Using the Smart Index Wizard

Troubleshooting indexes

This chapter shows you how to enhance your help files by adding tables of contents and expanding your indexes. The chapter starts with a comparison of HTML Help and WinHelp indexes, and then discusses creating tables of contents in TOC Composer using drag-and-drop. Next you learn how to create a table of contents using the Auto Create TOC feature. After that, you learn how to create Master Contents files and add external files to a table of contents. Finally, you learn how to troubleshoot the table of contents you create and how to print a Table of Contents report. In the second half of the chapter, you learn the differences between HTML Help and WinHelp indexes. You then learn how to use the Index Designer to create and maintain keywords. Next, the chapter discusses the Smart Index Wizard and how to use it to automatically create and maintain comprehensive indexes. As with the Table of Contents section, this half of the chapter concludes with a discussion of ways to test your indexes and print an Index (K-Keywords) report.

Comparing Tables of Contents in Microsoft HTML Help and WinHelp

The table of contents shares the same function in WinHelp and HTML Help — it provides a hierarchical view of the contents of the help file and a point of reference for finding more information. WinHelp 4 (or WinHelp 2000) even shares the same look as HTML Help. As you'll see, however, HTML Help has some additional features and functions somewhat differently.

Like WinHelp, HTML Help's table of contents is on the left side of the window, along with the Index and Search tabs. The Table of Contents tab "tracks" where the user is in the help project, while displaying the topic on the right side of the window. You can see from Figure 23-1 that it looks very similar to the WinHelp 2000 table of contents, with books and pages to provide structure. Creating a table of contents by adding books and pages is also very similar to WinHelp.

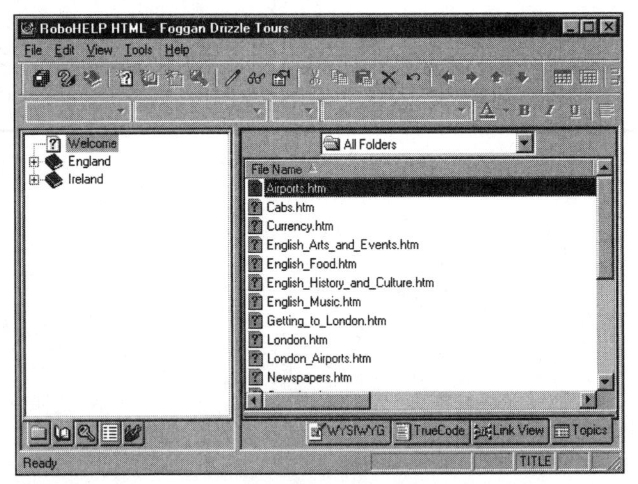

Figure 23-1: Microsoft HTML Help table of contents

Besides the table of contents file itself, many of the differences in HTML Help involve ease of use and customization. In WinHelp, you use macros to provide jumps to remote topics, URLs, files, and so on. In RoboHELP HTML, you use hyperlinks.

Unlike WinHelp, you can create a link from a book. You can also have an unlimited number of sublevels below a top-level book, although for better usability it's best to keep these at a reasonable number.

You can customize the table of contents in HTML Help, changing the icons for the books and pages, adjusting the appearance of the TOC pane and the fonts, and adding sound and video clips when books and pages are selected.

Building Tables of Contents

The table of contents is just as important to users in online help as it is in printed books, maybe even more so. Not only does a table of contents provide an outline, or hierarchical view, of the contents of the HTML Help file, it also shows users where they are in the help file and provides quick navigation. Users can rapidly skim books in the TOC to find the area they're interested in, and then expand a section to look for specific topics of interest. When they double-click on a topic in the table of contents, the corresponding topic is displayed.

Creating Tables of Contents

Figure 23-2 shows how the table of contents (HHC file) is organized hierarchically, like an outline. There are two kinds of entries in the table of contents: books and pages. Books are heading entries that let you group the various topics and subheadings (also shown as books) into a logical order. Below a book at the top level, you can create unlimited sublevels of books, each of which will have a different group of topics and books.

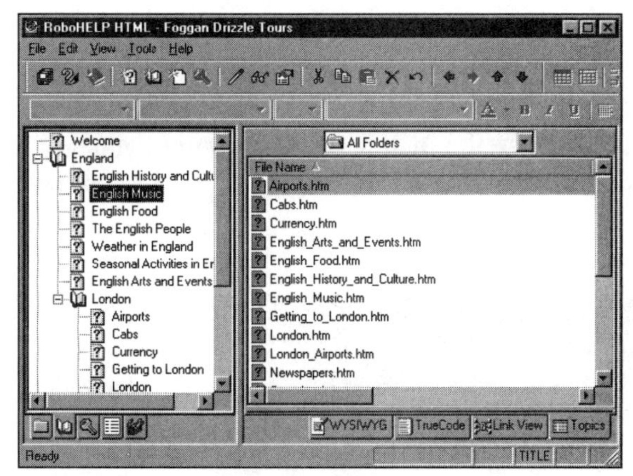

Figure 23-2: Sample table of contents in the Contents tab

Avoid using too many levels, however, or users may get lost.

When you click a book, the book "opens," as shown in Figure 23-2, and the next level of books and topics appears. You can have multiple levels of books open simultaneously.

Books in HTML Help can be connected to a specific topic or hyperlink; however, if you do this, make sure you are consistent by creating a link for all top-level books. The first book auto-expands when you open the CHM file. Pages are the entries for specific topics. When you click a page, the associated topic is displayed.

Following are two ways to create tables of contents:

✦ Use drag-and-drop to add each book and page to the table of contents in the TOC Composer and modify or create new entries as necessary.

✦ Use the Auto Create TOC function in the TOC tab to create a table of contents automatically from the folders you set up in Project view.

The following sections describe how to create a table of contents using both of these techniques.

Both of these techniques for creating and maintaining tables of contents has specific advantages. Try each one out to see which technique to use when.

Creating a Table of Contents Using Drag-and-Drop

When you create a table of contents using drag-and-drop, you select the topics you want to add to your table of contents from the Topic List on the left side of the window. You can select which topics to add and in which order. You can also add individual books or pages in the table of contents and even create a new HTML topic when you enter a new page in the table of contents.

To create a table of contents using drag-and-drop, do the following:

1. Select the TOC Composer in the TOC tab. It will be empty until you add books and pages. Select the Topics tab to display the Topic List in the right pane, as shown in Figure 23-3.

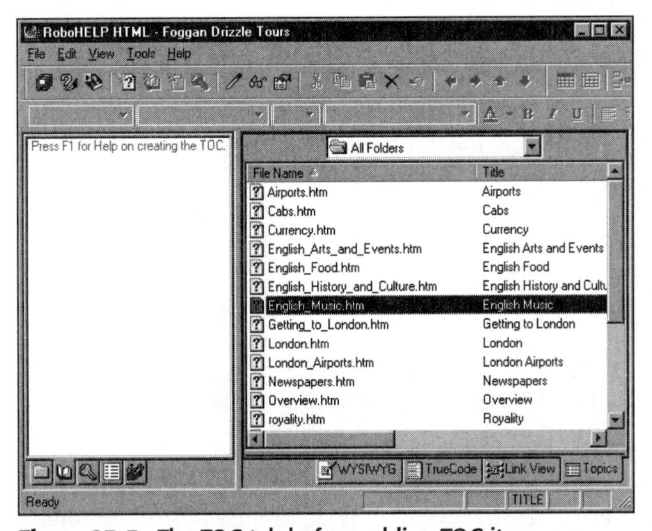

Figure 23-3: The TOC tab before adding TOC items

2. Create the first book in the table of contents by clicking the open book icon on the RoboHELP HTML toolbar. You can also just right-click in the TOC tab and then select the New ➪ Book command from the right-click menu. The Book Properties window appears, shown in Figure 23-4.

3. Enter the name of the first book in the Title field. If you want to link to a topic from the book, select Link to Single Topic. The previously grayed-out areas become active.

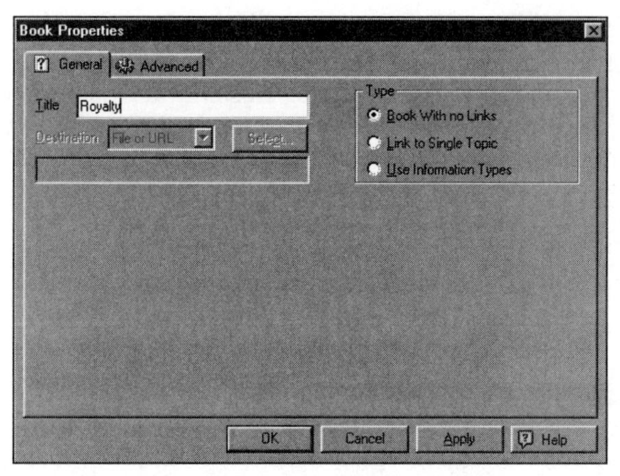

Figure 23-4: The Book Properties window

4. Select the destination type. If the destination is a file or URL, select it from the Topics list. You can also type in an URL if it's not listed. If the destination is multimedia or a remote topic, use the Select button. It opens a window for finding the correct file to use as the destination.

5. Once you are satisfied with the entry, click OK. RoboHELP HTML adds the book entry to the table of contents in the left pane, as shown in Figure 23-5.

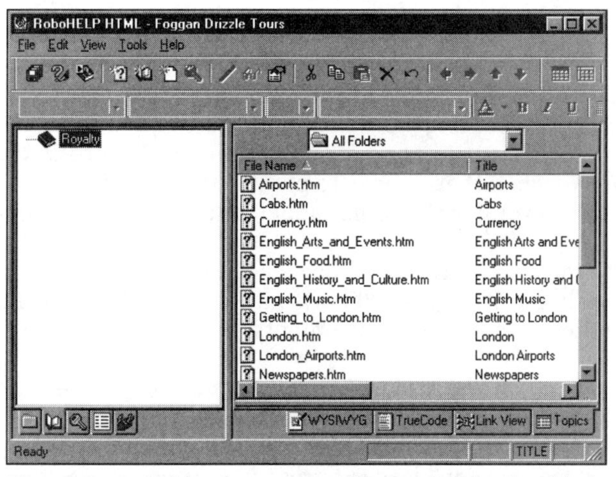

Figure 23-5: Table of contents with the first book added

6. Now add the first page in the table of contents by dragging "Overview" from the Topics list and dropping it below the book. As you do so, you'll notice that a large yellow arrow appears in the TOC tab. This shows where the entry will appear when you drop it. When you have multiple entries in the table of contents, you can shift the insertion point by moving the mouse pointer. When you drop the entry beneath the book you just created, RoboHELP HTML creates a page for the topic, as shown in Figure 23-6.

You can also add pages by dragging topics from the Link view.

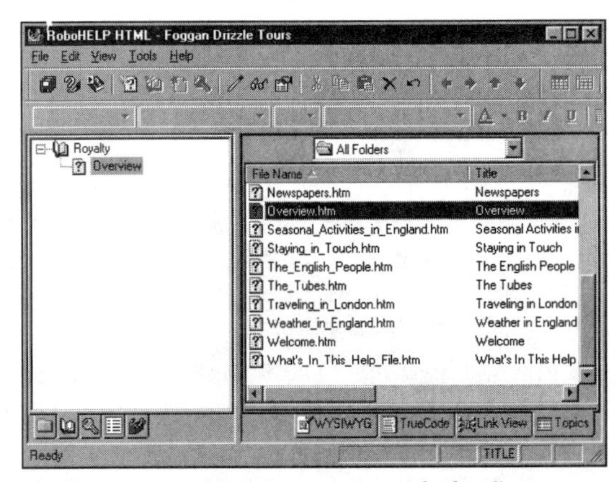

Figure 23-6: Table of contents with the first page added

7. Now you need to add some books as subheadings for each of the major headings. These topics are nothing more than topics with a submenu, so you can create books with these names and not link to the topics here. You can then add pages under each of these books to parallel the structure of your help file. Figure 23-7 shows several of the topics added to the table of contents.

When you drag-and-drop a topic from the Topics list, RoboHELP HTML changes the color of the page icon in the Topic List. This visual cue is helpful for making sure you've added all the topics to the table of contents.

You can drag a topic to the table of contents more than once if you wish. RoboHELP HTML adds a page each time you do this. This is helpful if you're creating a table of contents with several different groups that point to overlapping topics, but be careful that you don't inadvertently add a duplicate page for a topic.

6. Continue adding the books and pages to the table of contents. As you build up the books and pages in your table of contents, you can expand and collapse books to make it easier to work on a specific section. You can select multiple topics in the Topics list and drag them to the table of contents as a group. Figure 23-8 shows the completed table of contents. When you are satisfied with your entries, select the File ➪ Save All command.

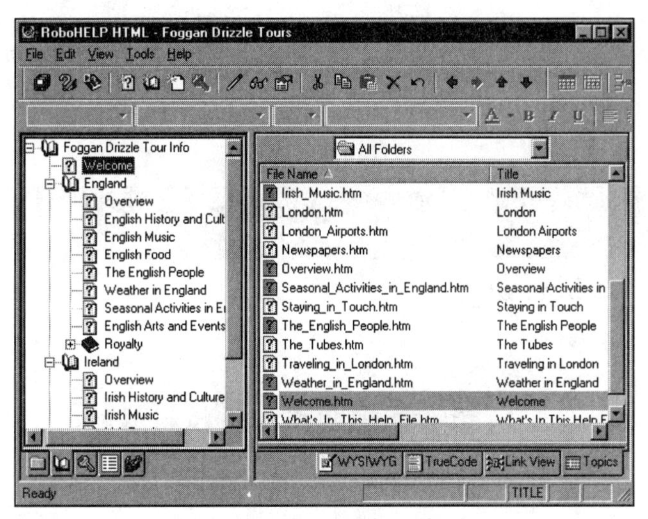

Figure 23-7: Table of contents with multiple entries

Note

Remember that you can provide different books that each point to an overlapping group of topics. Group by topic, such as country; and also by interests, such as food, music, weather, and so on. Your table of contents can be structured in the same way, although with a slight difference: The table of contents is linear, like an outline. The interconnectedness of hypertext is lost in the table of contents, but you gain the advantage of seeing more groups of topics.

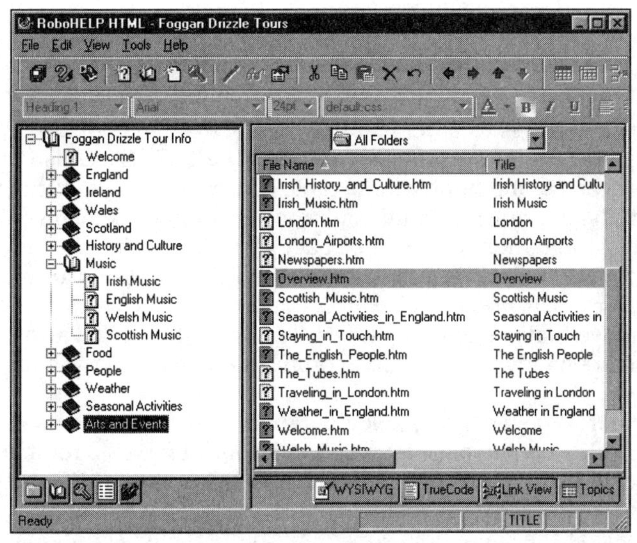

Figure 23-8: Completed table of contents

7. Once you've saved your table of contents, RoboHELP HTML will add the table of contents to the HTML Help project when you compile it. After compiling, you see the Contents tab on the left and the default topic on the right, as shown in Figure 23-9.

Figure 23-9: Contents tab for the help file

You can expand the table of contents in the Contents tab by double-clicking books. The books and pages appear in the table of contents in the same order as they appear in the table of contents as it was assembled in the TOC Composer. As with any other table of contents, click the appropriate page to go to a topic.

If you set the books in your table of contents to open with a single topic, you can set it to both open the book and jump to the topic with a single click.

You can move books or pages to other locations in the table of contents by clicking and dragging the page or book you want to move. RoboHELP HTML also lets you cut, copy, and paste pages and books in the table of contents: Right-click on the page or book and select the appropriate command from the right-click menu. In addition, you can change the indentation of a book or page by right-clicking the item and then selecting Move from the right-click menu. You're then given options for moving the item left, right, up, or down. You can also click the arrow icons on the RoboHELP HTML toolbar to move table of contents items. The right-click menu also has some other features that are handy when creating or maintaining a table of contents.

You can quickly create a new page by selecting the New ➪ Page command from the popup menu, or by clicking the page icon on the RoboHELP HTML toolbar. The Page Properties window will appear. Pages can also link to files or Web sites, FTP, e-mail, newsgroups, multimedia, or remote topics. Adding pages here is a good way to create a new topic at the same time you add it to the table of contents. Select the

New Topic button to access the Create Topic Wizard. The topic is added to your project and to the table of contents.

When you double-click a page in the table of contents in the TOC tab, RoboHELP HTML displays the associated HTML topic for viewing or editing.

Remember that editing the topic heading or topic ID is not automatically reflected in the table of contents.

You can preview how a page will appear to your users by compiling and running the help file. RoboHELP HTML displays the associated topic from the HTML Help file. You can modify the page information by right-clicking the entry and selecting Properties from the right-click menu. If the topic is incorrect, you can use the Find Topic command on the right-click menu to locate a topic and assign it to the page.

Setting the Default Topic for Your Table of Contents

Whenever you use a table of contents, it's a good idea to set a default topic for your HTML Help file. The default topic will appear if there is no table of contents. If you don't set a default topic, HTML Help uses the first topic in the HTML Help file.

To set the default topic for your HTML Help project, do the following:

1. Select the File ➪ Project Settings command and click the Compile tab.
2. Click the Select button to find the topic you want as the default and click OK.

Creating Effective Tables of Contents

Here are some tips for creating effective tables of contents in HTML Help. For more general tips on creating tables of contents, see Chapter 8, "Using Tables of Contents and Indexes."

✦ To use custom book icons and page icons, right-click on the book or page you want to change and select Properties from the right-click menu. Click the Advanced tab and an icon number under Image Index. You can see what each icon looks like at the right. You can't see the new icon in your help project; you need to compile and run the help file to see how it looks.

These icons will work with Microsoft HTML Help, and WebHelp, but not WinHelp, WinHelp 2000, or JavaHelp.

✦ Don't use an equals sign (=), an at sign (@), a semicolon (;), or a colon (:) in the titles for books or pages. These characters are reserved for use in the CNT file and can cause unpredictable results if they appear in book or pages.

✦ To print the Table of Contents report from your project, select File ➪ Print TOC. In the Print window, you can select to print an overview or a detailed view. The overview includes books and page titles and the topics that are linked to them; the detailed view includes book and page titles, topic titles that are linked to them, and the path for the files.

✦ If you're creating an extremely large HTML Help project, consider using a Binary Contents File. A Binary Contents File is a compressed form of an index that is faster and easier for your HTML Help project to access once it is compiled and is required for merged projects. However, Binary Contents Files do not work with external table of contents files (merged tables of contents) and don't support many of the customizable features available with HTML Help tables of contents.

✦ In order for books and pages to automatically adjust to the topic content displayed on the right, the topic file name must use underscores rather than spaces. To rename existing files, select Tools ➪ Convert Spaces to Underscores. RoboHELP HTML will also automatically insert underscores when you create new topics. Select Tools ➪ Options, click the General tab, and select Use Underscores with File Names.

✦ To save time when you're restructuring your table of contents, you can create books from existing pages. The book becomes a sub-entry of the book above it and uses the name of the page. In the TOC Composer, right-click on the page and select Create Book from Page from the right-click menu.

✦ You can create books and pages that link to a topic in a secondary window, allowing users to see two help windows simultaneously. First, make sure you've set up a secondary window for your project. Then, from the TOC tab, right-click on the page or book and select Properties from the right-click menu. Select the Advanced tab. Select the secondary window name from the drop-down menu. Click OK. When users close the main help window, the secondary window also closes.

See Chapter 27, "Adding Links, Windows, and Frames," for more information on adding secondary windows.

Creating a Table of Contents Using Auto Create TOC

The previous section showed you how to create and modify a table of contents using drag-and-drop and other manual techniques. Although these techniques are valuable when maintaining your table of contents, you can see that creating a table of contents from scratch this way could be time consuming and tedious.

If you've created your project using folders in the Project Manager to organize your topics, you can create your contents automatically. RoboHELP HTML creates books based on the folders, and corresponding pages based on the topics in each folder. Any topics you haven't saved in folders appear as pages at the top of the table of contents. You can move them where they need to go using drag-and-drop.

1. Open your project and select the TOC tab.
2. Select the Tools ➪ Auto Create TOC command. RoboHELP HTML creates a quick table of contents by creating a single top-level book for each of the folders in the HTML Help project, and then makes pages for each of the topics in the order that they appear in the folders.

Once you have created the entries in the table of contents, you can then use the techniques you learned in the previous section to modify, delete, and reorganize them.

Customizing the Table of Contents

One aspect of HTML Help that distinguishes it from WinHelp is its ability to customize the table of contents. You can change the appearance, such as the font or book icons; and the behavior, such as how the TOC adjusts to the right window and single-clicking to open books. You can change these characteristics easily by changing the TOC properties. Some features, such as displaying plus and minus signs beside books and pages, are not set by default, so it's worthwhile to take a look at these options when you set up your TOC.

These settings don't affect the Index and Search tabs.

To customize the table of contents, select the File ➪ Project Settings command and click the TOC Styles tab (see Figure 23-10). Under Styles, you'll find options for changing the appearance of the TOC pane. Experiment to find the look you like.

Before selecting the Binary TOC option, make sure you will not be creating external TOC files or information types. You also cannot customize some aspects of the TOC when you use a binary TOC.

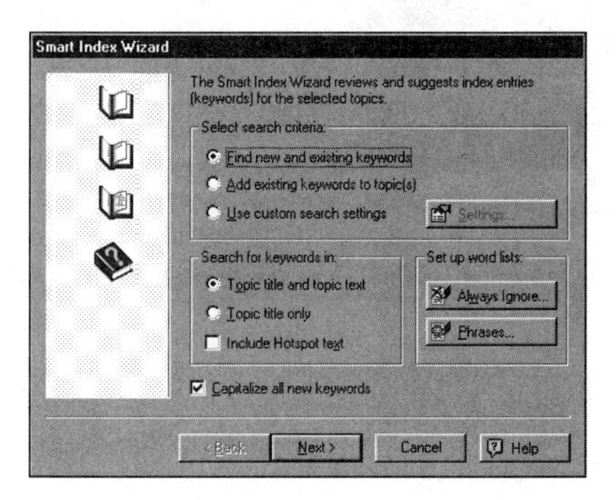

Figure 23-10: The TOC Styles window

Adding External Contents Files to a Table of Contents

HTML Help provides an easy way to combine several different Contents (HHC) files into your Master project. Using a Master Contents file, you can combine these individual files into one seamless whole: When users click on a topic in the table of contents, they see the associated topic regardless of which HTML Help project it's in.

Master Contents files are helpful when managing large HTML Help projects that have multiple authors. Each author can work on her or his own part of the file, and then the separate pieces can be integrated with a Master Contents file. Changes to an individual piece don't require changes to the entire project and the concomitant regression testing that may be required.

Creating a Master Contents file uses all the techniques for creating tables of contents you have seen so far. You must first create tables of contents for all the individual HTML Help projects you want to include. You can create tables of contents using any of the techniques shown earlier in this chapter.

Add external contents files to a table of contents as follows:

1. Open the Master HTML Help project you want to modify.
2. Click the TOC tab.
3. Select in the TOC Composer where you'd like to insert the external Contents file. You can add it as a top-level book or within an existing book. Right-click and select New ➪ External TOC from the right-click menu. The External TOC window displays, as shown in Figure 23-11.

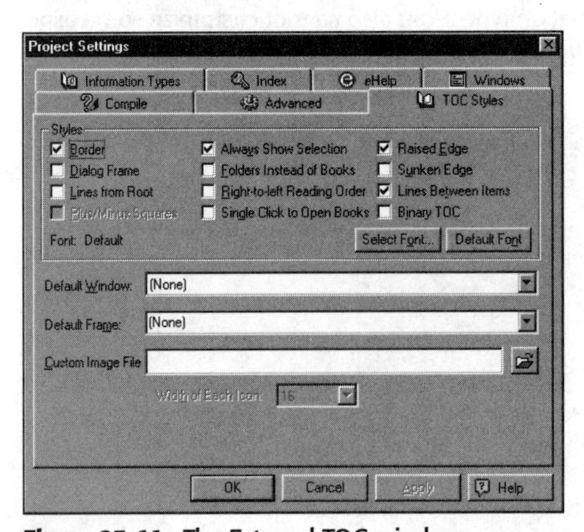

Figure 23-11: The External TOC window

4. Select the CHM file that contains the Contents file you want to add. You can select a project already in your project folder or navigate to a CHM file located in another folder. If you select a CHM file that is in a different project folder, a message is displayed indicating that the CHM file will be copied to your Master project folder. Click OK to continue.

5. If there is more than one Contents file, select it. If there is only one, it's automatically selected. Click OK to add the file to your Master Contents file. The external Contents file appears in the table of contents, as shown in Figure 23-12. Repeat the process for each HHC file to add additional external files to the Master Contents file.

When you compile and run the HTML Help project, the table of contents will show each of the included tables of contents as a seamless part of the whole.

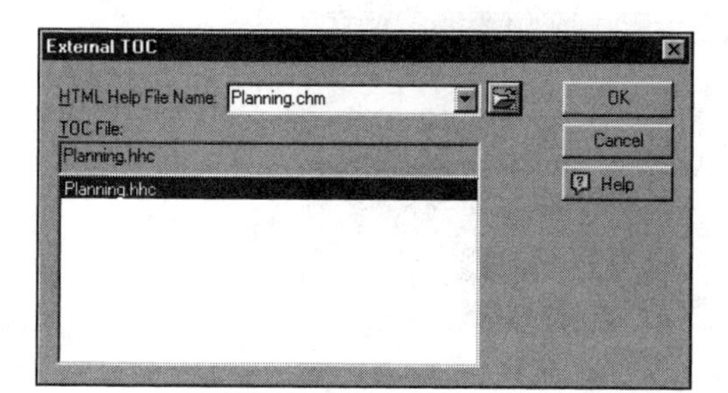

Figure 23-12: Table of contents with an external Contents file added

Troubleshooting Tables of Contents

You will probably not find many problems when working with tables of contents in HTML Help. Most of the reports available can help you fix broken links and find the solution you need. However, here are a few common problems you may encounter and suggested solutions:

✦ If the Contents, Index, and Search tabs don't appear in your compiled file and you've selected them using the Project Settings ➪ Windows ➪ Properties window, make sure you selected a default window. To do this, select File ➪ Project Settings ➪ Compile. Under Default Window, select a window that will display as the default and click OK.

✦ If all the settings are grayed out in the Project Settings ➪ TOC Styles window, the Binary TOC option is selected. Binary tables of contents do not support the customization features in this window.

✦ If an individual topic appears in the wrong display window when you select the page in the table of contents, you will need to change the properties for the page. The Table of Contents Detailed Report lists the windows for each page in the table of contents.

Printing the Table of Contents Report

The Table of Contents report provides you with information about the table of contents for your HTML Help project. You can use this report to check the topic titles and HTML file names against the entries in the table of contents. You can also use this report to easily edit the table of contents entries for spelling, grammar, and consistency.

To generate a Table of Contents report, do the following:

✦ Select Tools ⇨ Reports ⇨ Table of Contents. The Table of Contents report is displayed on the window, as shown in Figure 23-13. The table of contents entries appear on the report in the order they appear in the table of contents.

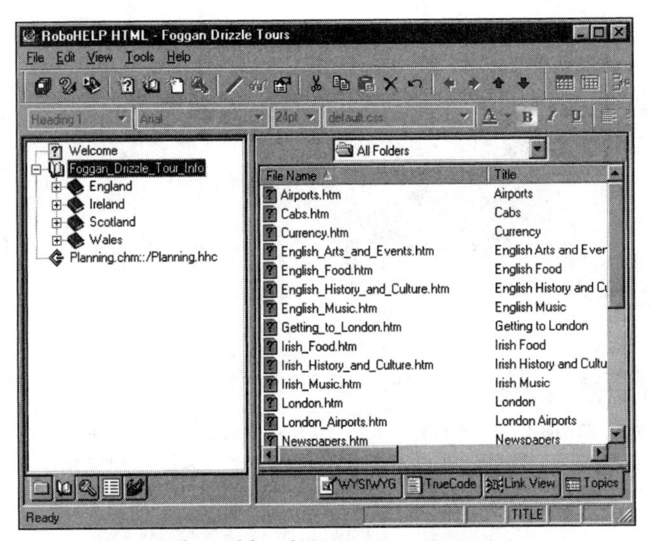

Figure 23-13: The Table of Contents report

As with many of the other reports you've seen in previous chapters, you can filter the information in the Table of Contents report in several ways. You can show the table of contents entries created by each author or all authors, or those that aren't assigned to specific authors, depending on your selection in the drop-down list in the Author field. You can also view the table of contents entries in all the documents in the project or in individual documents with the drop-down list in the Folder field. As with other reports in earlier chapters, you can switch the topic display between Topic Title and File Name by selecting View ⇨ By Topic Title or View ⇨ By File Name.

The sample Table of Contents report shown in Figure 23-13 is an overview report, displaying book and page titles and the related topics. Selecting the Report: Detailed option in the lower right corner of the window adds information about the documents containing the topics used by the individual page entries, the windows used to display the topics, and the names of any external HTML files.

You can print the Table of Contents report quickly by selecting the File ⇨ Print TOC command.

As with other RoboHELP HTML reports, you can run the Table of Contents report at any time.

Building Indexes

RoboHELP HTML offers several powerful features to create indexes for an entire project. This section shows you ways to use the Index Designer and the Smart Index Wizard, how to auto-create indexes, and the differences between adding keywords to topics and entering keywords into the index file (HHK).

To save time, be sure to consider style issues and platform issues before starting your index. You should settle on matters like keyword and subkeyword format and case, while keeping consistency and usability as your primary goals. For general tips on indexing, see Chapter 8, "Using Tables of Contents and Indexes."

Comparing Indexes in Microsoft HTML Help and WinHelp

You can create a powerful index in both HTML Help and WinHelp using the same indexing tools (Index Designer and Smart Index Wizard) as shown in Figure 23-14. The biggest difference between HTML Help and WinHelp indexes is the way in which they store keywords. As you'll see in the following sections, with HTML Help you can choose between two types of keywords, depending on your requirements.

There are two basic approaches to indexing in RoboHELP HTML, and which one you choose depends on what you plan to do with your project. The processes for creating a binary index or an index file (HHK) are almost identical, but if you want to customize your index, you need to know which type you plan to use. The following sections describe both.

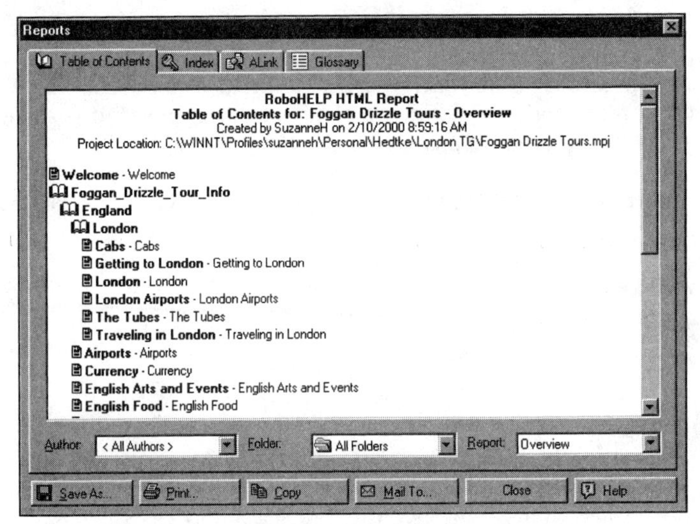

Figure 23-14: Microsoft HTML Help index

Understanding Binary Indexes

Binary indexes are created inside the Microsoft HTML Help file when it's compiled (CHM file). Therefore, you can use binary indexes only with compiled help formats such as HTML Help and WinHelp. You should use a binary index in the following situations:

- ✦ You will be merging keywords from multiple CHM files.
- ✦ The index is very large.
- ✦ You don't plan to sort your index manually. (In binary indexes, keywords are automatically arranged in alphabetical and numeric order.)
- ✦ You don't need to link to external topics, e-mail addresses, URLs, bookmarks, or FTP sites.
- ✦ You want to be able to keep specific keywords with each topic, and plan to copy or import topics between projects. Binary indexes use topic keywords. When you remove a topic keyword from the project, all its keywords are also removed, eliminating unused keywords from the index.

Topic keywords are stored within each HTML file, instead of in the index file, and are automatically compiled in a binary index. Although topic keywords are not compiled into the index file (HHK), they are merged with it when the HTML Help file is run and are displayed in the Index tab.

Understanding Index Files (HHK)

If you don't need to use a binary index, index files (the default) are sufficient for creating most HTML Help projects. Index files (HHKs) store all keywords (called *index file keywords*) in one file that is compiled into the HTML Help file (CHM). Using index files is useful in the following situations:

- ✦ You will be merging multiple indexes (HHK files) from other HTML Help projects.
- ✦ You want to cross-reference index file keywords to other index file keywords.
- ✦ You want to custom-sort your index, such as arranging it by subject instead of alphabetically. You can do this by right-clicking on the keyword and selecting the Sort command from the right-click menu, or by manually dragging and dropping keywords where you want them to appear in the Index Designer. However, if you have any topic keywords in your project, you can't sort keywords.
- ✦ You want to generate indexes for uncompiled formats such as WebHelp or JavaHelp.
- ✦ You want to be able to remove keywords regardless of which topics they're associated with. Removing keywords from the index removes the link to them from all topics.
- ✦ You want to link to local HTML topics, bookmarks, or URLs, or you want the topic to be displayed in custom windows and frames.

From the Index window you specify whether you want to use index file keywords or topic keywords To do so, select Project Settings ➪ Index and the Project Settings window opens as shown in Figure 23-15. Under Add New Keywords To, select Index File (HHK) or Topics. You can use a binary index with either the index file or topic keywords, but if you have topic keywords in your project, the binary index setting will stay selected. You can change this setting at any time while developing your project. If you selected the index file setting and have topic keywords in your project, the topic keywords will be combined with the HHK file when you compile.

Figure 23-15: Project Settings window – Index tab

Adding Keywords to the Index

After you've specified which type of keywords you'll be working with, you can start adding them. There are numerous ways to add keywords, including the following:

- ✦ Enter words or phrases in the Index Designer and drag-and-drop to add topics to keywords and subkeywords.
- ✦ Add entries to topics by selecting Topic Properties ➪ Index.
- ✦ Select a word or phrase in the WYSIWIG Editor, right-click it, and select Add Index Entry from the right-click menu.

Using the Index Designer

The Index Designer in RoboHELP HTML is similar to the TOC Composer. It provides you with an easy-to-use, effective interface for creating indexes in HTML Help projects.

To enter a new keyword using the Index Designer, do the following:

1. Select the Index tab, shown in Figure 23-16, also called the *Index Designer*.

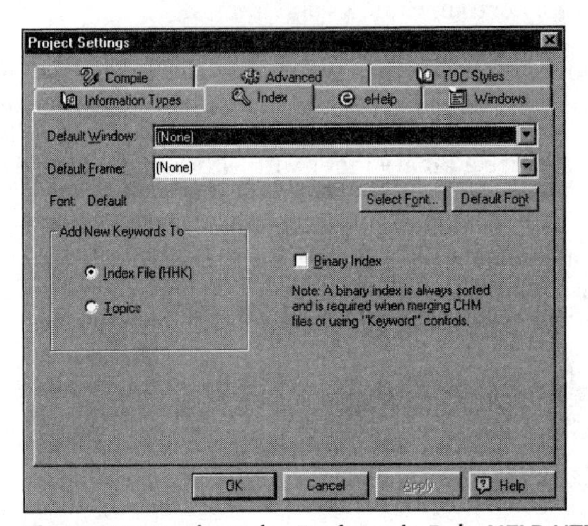

Figure 23-16: The Index Designer in RoboHELP HTML

As you can see from Figure 23-16, the keywords already entered in the HTML Help file appear in alphabetical order in the Index Designer in the upper window. The topic or topics associated with the highlighted keyword appear in the lower half of the Index Designer.

The Index Designer can be used to add standard keywords (also known as *K-Keywords*) and See Also keywords (also known as A-Link Names). This chapter describes how to add standard keywords. For information about adding See Also keywords, see Chapter 8, "Using Tables of Contents and Indexes."

2. Type the keyword you want to add in the Keyword field in the upper right corner of the Index Designer. If you wish, you can add several separate keywords at once by typing the keywords and separating them with semicolons. When you are satisfied with your entries, click Add. RoboHELP HTML adds the new keyword or keywords to the list. As you can see from Figure 23-17, the new keyword is displayed in bold, indicating that no topics are associated with the keyword yet.

Figure 23-17: Index Designer showing new keyword

With the new keyword added to the list, you now need to associate topics with the keyword. You can add topics to a keyword by dragging and dropping topics from the Topics list in the right pane of the HTML Help viewer to the Topics list in the lower half of the Index Designer. (This is very similar to dragging and dropping items in the TOC Composer, as described in the first part of this chapter.) Topics that are referenced in the index are color-coded blue in the Topics list, making it easy to spot topics that still need to have keywords added.

You can add subkeywords to a keyword by right-clicking the keyword and then selecting the New ➪ Subkeyword command from the right-click menu. RoboHELP HTML positions the subkeyword immediately below the highlighted index entry, as shown in Figure 23-18. You can move subkeywords to the left using the Move Left command on the right-click menu or the left arrow on the RoboHELP HTML toolbar.

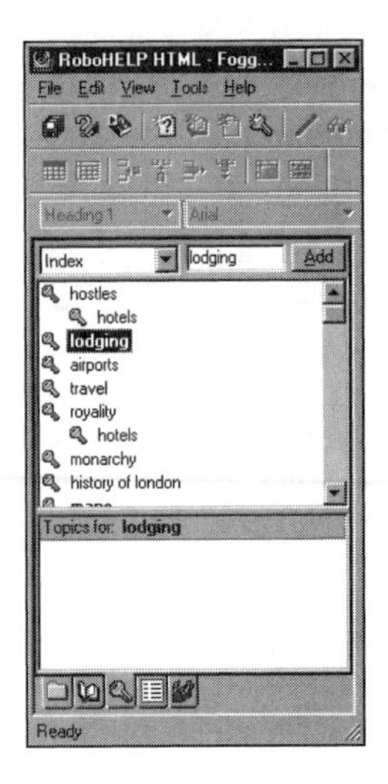

Figure 23-18: Index Designer showing new subkeyword

The right-click menu has some other features that are handy when creating or maintaining keywords.

Using the Smart Index Wizard

The Smart Index Wizard is a RoboHELP HTML tool for automating the creation and maintenance of indexes and keywords. It searches the topics in your HTML Help project based on criteria that you enter to assign keywords. You can create an index all at once or topic by topic. In addition, the Smart Index Wizard can suggest new and existing keywords based on the contents of topics. It also lets you copy keywords from one topic to another to speed up the indexing process and to make your indexes more consistent.

To create an index with the Smart Index Wizard, do the following:

1. Select the Tools ➪ Smart Index Wizard command on the RoboHELP HTML toolbar. The Smart Index Wizard main window appears, as shown in Figure 23-19.
2. Enter information on the window as follows:
   - **Find new and existing keywords:** Select this option to add keywords based on the contents of the topics using the search criteria you specify. Use this option when creating a new index or expanding an existing index to add entries for new topics.
   - **Add existing keywords to topic(s):** Select this option to search the topics for existing keywords. When the Smart Index Wizard finds one of the keywords in a topic, it adds the topic to that keyword. Use this option to index a collection of new or expanded topics on a subject that has already been indexed, or to make sure that all existing topics have been indexed completely.

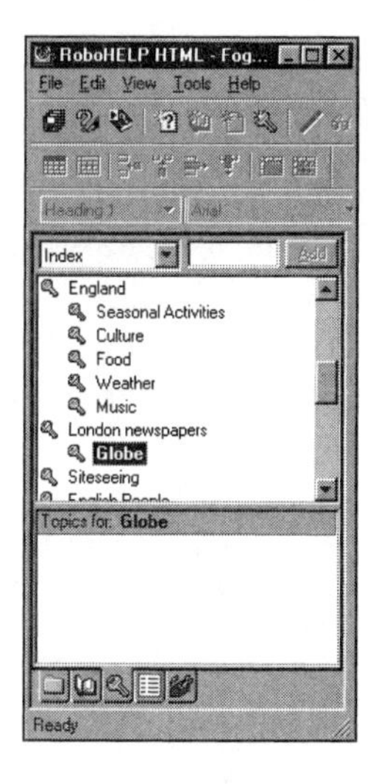

Figure 23-19: The main Smart Index Wizard window

- **Use custom search settings:** Select this option to create an index using the search criteria you specify through the Smart Index Settings window.
- **Search for keywords in:** Select Topic Title and Topic Text to have the Smart Index Wizard search for keywords in topic titles and topic content, or select Topic Title Only if you want the Smart Index Wizard to look only in topic titles.
- **Include Hotspot text:** Check this to have the Smart Index Wizard search for keywords in hotspot text as well as in general body text.
- **Capitalize all new keywords:** Check this to capitalize the initial letter of any keywords or phrases created by the Smart Index Wizard. (This is usually a style decision.)

3. If you wish to search for keywords based on custom settings, click Settings to display the Smart Index Settings window, shown in Figure 23-20.

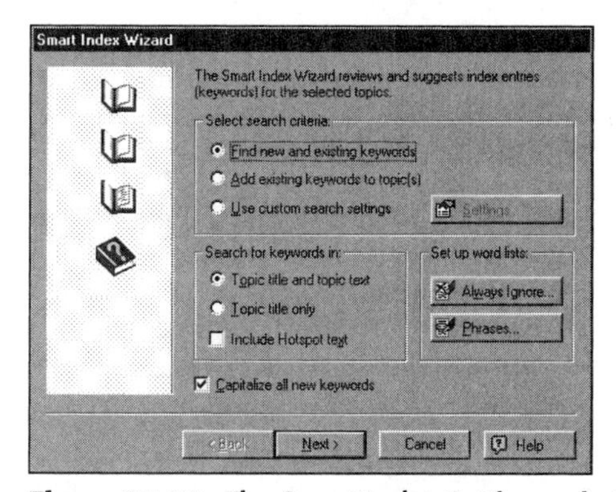

Figure 23-20: The Smart Index Settings window

4. Select the desired criteria on the Smart Index Settings window to tell the Smart Index Wizard what potential keywords and keyword phrases to include and exclude. In general, if an option is not checked, the Smart Index Wizard will not look for that keyword or phrase.

   - **Uppercase WORDS:** Check this to include words in capitals, such as ENGLAND.
   - **Mixed CaSe words:** Check this to include mixed-case words, such as BritRail. (Words with initial capital letters are not considered to be of mixed case.)
   - **Words with punctuation:** Check this to include words containing punctuation, such as periods (foggandrizzletours.com), hyphens (Newcastle-on-Tyne), the ampersand symbol (info@foggandrizzletours.com), the solidus (and/or), and so on.
   - **Words not in the dictionary:** Check this to include words that may not be found in a standard dictionary. The Smart Index Wizard uses a dictionary program installed as part of RoboHELP Office 2000.
   - **All words longer than *X* chars:** Check this to include all words longer than a certain number of characters you set in the associated field.
   - **Exclude all recognizable:** Check the parts of speech you want the Smart Index Wizard to ignore: verbs, adverbs, adjectives, and/or nouns.
   - **Multiple words:** Check this to have the Smart Index Wizard suggest phrases, such as *illuminated manuscript.*
   - **Single words in a phrase:** Check this to have the Smart Index Wizard suggest the words used in identifiable phrases separately, such as suggesting both *illuminated* and *manuscript* from the phrase *illuminated manuscript.*
   - **Include Verb phrases:** Check this to have the Smart Index Wizard suggest verb phrases, such as *examining an illuminated manuscript.*
   - **Subkeyword:** Check this to have the Smart Index Wizard create subkeywords when there's a relationship between words, such as *illuminated, manuscript.*
   - **Reversed Subkeyword:** Check this to have the Smart Index Wizard create subkeywords when there's a relationship between words, such as manuscript, illuminated.
   - **Subkeyword phrase:** Check this to have the Smart Index Wizard create a subkeyword from a phrase or set of verb phrases, such as *traveling by car, or shopping for shoes.*

   Clicking the Default button will clear any selections and restore the defaults. When you are satisfied with your selections, click OK.

5. To set up an optional list of words and phrases to ignore, click Always Ignore. During indexing, the Smart Index Wizard looks in the Always Ignore list for words or phrases that don't need to be indexed. The word or phrase must be an exact match; depending on the indexing criteria you specify, some suggested phrases may contain words that when found alone are ignored. For example, you may want to ignore all instances of your product name. The second Smart Index Settings window appears with the "Always Ignore" Words tab displayed, as shown in Figure 23-21.

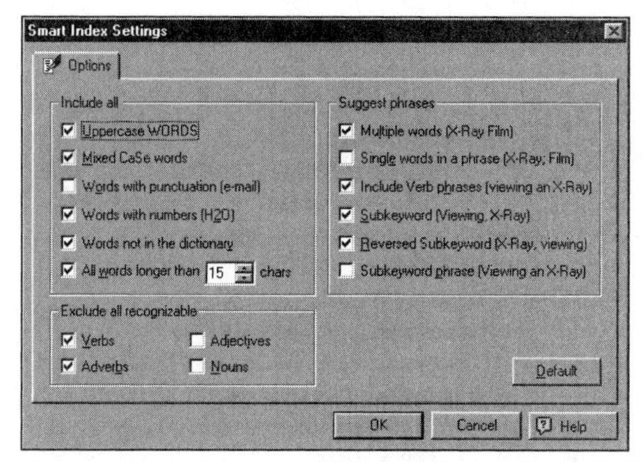

Figure 23-21: The second Smart Index Settings window, showing the "Always Ignore" Words tab

6. Edit the list of words or phrases to ignore. (RoboHELP HTML ships with a standard list of words and phrases that are commonly ignored during indexing.) When you are satisfied with your changes, click OK.

Note

The information for the Always Ignore list is stored in a text file named ALWYSIGN.WLF. You can edit this file directly with a text editor or word processor, and you can share the file with other HTML Help authors. To use a different Always Ignore file, entering the drive and directory in the Phrase File field at the bottom of the window or browse for it by clicking Browse.

7. To set up an optional list of specific phrases to search for, click Phrases. The second Smart Index Settings window appears with the Phrases tab displayed, as shown in Figure 23-22. Phrases entered in lowercase letters are not case sensitive, but mixed-case or all uppercase entries in the phrase list are case sensitive.

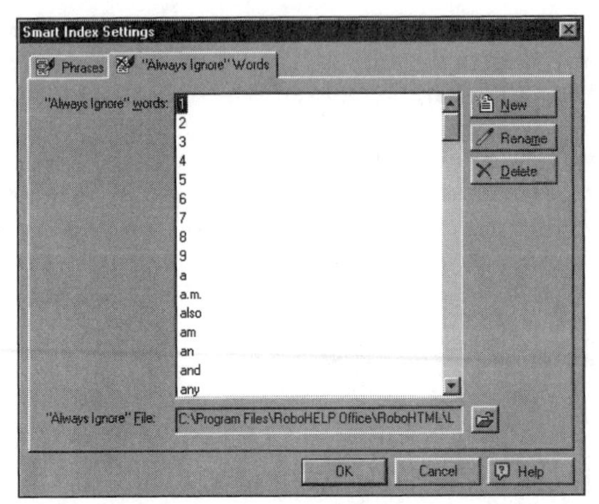

Figure 23-22: The second Smart Index Settings window, showing the Phrases tab

8. Edit the list of phrases to search for. (RoboHELP HTML ships with the phrase "html help" in the list.) When you are satisfied with your changes, click OK.

The information for the phrase list is stored in a text file named PHRASE.WLF. As with the Always Ignore list, you can edit this file directly with a text editor or word processor, and you can share the file with other HTML Help authors. You can use a different phrase file by entering the drive and directory in the Phrase File field at the bottom of the window or by browsing for it.

9. Click Next to continue with the indexing process. The second Smart Index Wizard window, shown in Figure 23-23, appears.

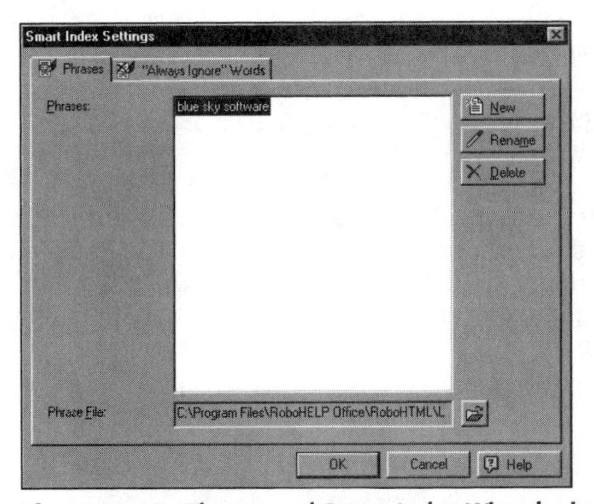

Figure 23-23: The second Smart Index Wizard window

10. Select information on the window as follows:

   - **How do you want to add keywords?:** You can choose to confirm the addition of each keyword or to have the Smart Index Wizard add keywords automatically.

You may want to confirm keywords the first few times you use the Smart Index Wizard.

   - **Set the filter to limit the topics reviewed:** As with many other windows and reports, you can filter the topics to be indexed based on a specific author, document, or project status. Select the options from the drop-down lists.

For more information about assigning authors and setting status, priority, time estimates, and to-do items, see Chapter 15, "Managing Large Projects."

   - **Check only new topics (that have not been Smart Indexed):** Leave this unchecked to search for keywords in all topics, or check this to search for keywords in topics that haven't already been indexed by the Smart Index Wizard. (When the Smart Index Wizard searches a topic, it updates the topic status, in the To Do list on the Status tab of the Topic Properties window, by checking the Ran Smart Index check box. If you want to exclude a topic manually, you can check Ran Smart Index box.)

11. When you are satisfied with your entries, click Next to start the indexing process. The Smart Index Wizard starts working through the topics in the project, checking for keywords. If you chose to have the Smart Index Wizard automatically add keywords, you will see a status bar and the name of the topic being indexed. (This process can take some time if you have a large HTML Help project.) If you chose to confirm each entry, you'll see a message displayed for each topic, something like the Smart Index Window shown in Figure 23-24.

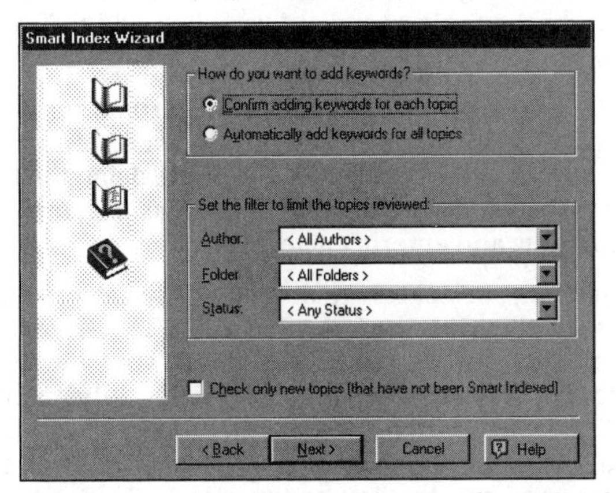

Figure 23-24: The Smart Index Wizard – Topic window

12. Check the boxes for any of the keywords you want to include for the topic. Any keywords already associated with this topic will be checked. Existing keywords appear on the list in normal type; keywords that have not been added appear in bold. When you highlight the keyword, sentences containing the keyword appear in the lower portion of the window. To select all the suggested keywords, click Select All Suggestions. Click Next to associate the topic with the keywords you've selected, or click Skip to skip this topic and continue processing the next topic.

    You'll find a number of helpful indexing options on the Smart Index Wizard—Topic window. You can rename a keyword by selecting the keyword and then clicking Rename. To remove the highlighted keyword from the list, click Remove. (This won't remove the keyword from any other topics or from the index. To delete a keyword completely, you must delete it in the Index Designer.) You can add a keyword or phrase to the Ignore list by clicking the Always Ignore button.

    The Options button provides you with a variety of options for adding and selecting keywords and suggestions:

    - **New Keyword:** Enters a new keyword in the Topic lists.
    - **New Subkeyword:** Enters a new subkeyword in the Topics list.
    - **Add Existing Keyword:** Displays the Add Existing Keyword window (described in Chapter 3) so you can add to the list a keyword that already exists in the index.
    - **View Topic:** Displays the topic in the preview window.
    - **Synonyms:** Displays the Synonyms window (shown in Figure 23-25). From this window, you can look up synonyms and antonyms for the word or phrase so that your index can be as complete as possible. You can also enter another word or phrase in the Word field and click Look Up to check for synonyms or antonyms for additional words and phrases. (To look for antonyms as well as synonyms, check Antonyms.) To add a new word to the topic's keyword list, click Add to Topic. Click Close to return to the Smart Index Wizard confirmation window.
    - **Verbs:** Displays the Add Verbs window. The Add Verbs window lets you add verbs (usually in the form of gerunds) to the list of common verb subkeywords. As you can see from Figure 23-26, the default list is aimed at software, but you can add other verbs, such as *visiting*, *traveling*, and *playing*, by clicking New and entering a new verb.
    - **Auto-Select Suggestions:** Select this to automatically select all the keyword suggestions starting with the following topic. This is very useful if you've looked at the first few lists of suggested keywords and are comfortable with automatically selecting the rest quickly. When you display the next topic, all the suggested keywords will be selected. You need only to click Next for each topic to accept all the keywords, but you can stop at any time and edit the lists appropriately. This option stays in effect until you deselect it.

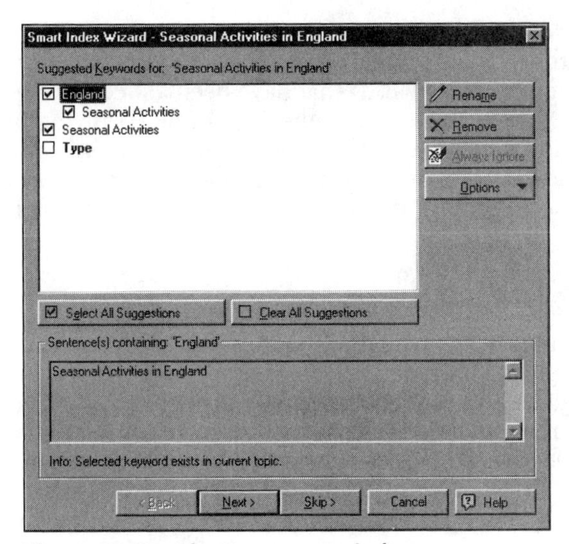

Figure 23-25: The Synonyms window

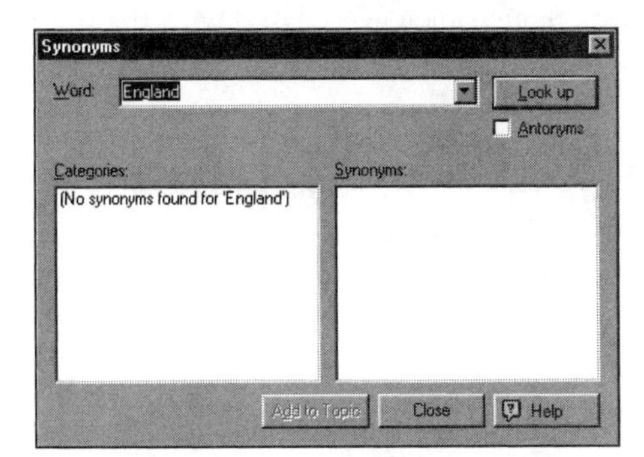

Figure 23-26: The Add Verbs window

- **Delete all suggestions:** This option deletes all the suggested keywords in the list for this topic.
- **Reload suggestions:** Select this to reload the original list of suggested keywords. This option is useful if you've made a number of changes to the list and want to start over.
- **Add Phrase:** This option displays the second Smart Index Settings window showing the Phrases tab, shown earlier in Figure 23-22.
- **Add "Always Ignore" Words:** This option displays the second Smart Index Settings window showing the "Always Ignore" Words tab, shown earlier in Figure 23-21.

13. When the Smart Index Wizard has completed indexing the HTML Help project, it will display a status window showing the number of topics reviewed and updated, and the number of keywords that have been added. It's a good idea to select the File ➪ Save All command on the RoboHELP HTML toolbar to save the new keywords and topic information. Then compile the project and test the index. You can always return to the Index Designer or the Smart Index Wizard to re-index some or all of the topics or to make other modifications.

Troubleshooting Indexes

Most of the problems you are likely to have with indexes will be easy to fix, such as similar entries that duplicate information, topics associated with the wrong keywords, and so on. You will be able to identify many of these problems using the Index (K-Keywords) report, described in the next section. Following are two common problems you may encounter:

✦ You need to sort your index but you've already added topic keywords to your project.

✦ You've added keywords with subkeywords but they aren't showing up in the index, make sure the keywords have topics associated with them. All keywords must have topics associated with them, even if they have subkeywords.

Generating the Index (K-Keywords) Report

The Index (K-Keywords) report provides you with information about the index keywords for your HTML Help project. You can use this report to check the keywords and associated topics. You can also use this report to easily edit the keywords for spelling, grammar, and consistency.

To generate an Index (K-Keywords) report, do the following:

✦ From the RoboHELP HTML toolbar, select the Tools ➪ Reports ➪ Index (K-Keywords) command. The Index report is displayed on the window, as shown in Figure 23-27. The keywords appear on the report in the order in which they appear in the index.

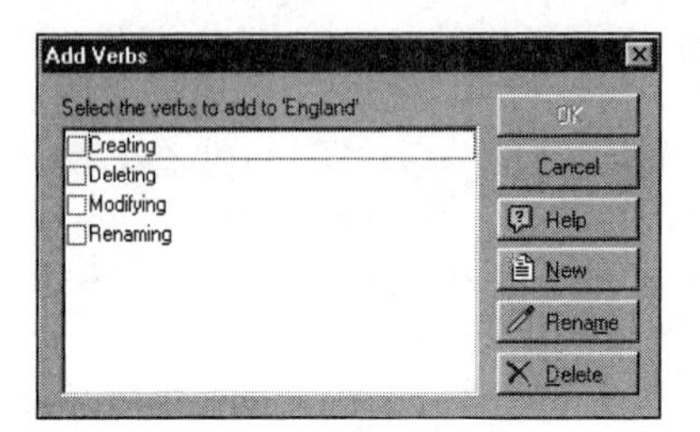

Figure 23-27: The Index (K-Keywords) report

You can filter the information on the Index (K-Keywords) report in several ways. You can show the keywords created by each author or all authors, or those that aren't assigned to specific authors, depending on your selection in the drop-down list in the Author field. You can also view the keywords in all the documents in the project or in individual documents with the drop-down list in the Folder field. As with other reports, you can switch between Topic Title and Topic ID by selecting View ➪ By Topic Title or View ➪ By Topic ID on the RoboHELP HTML toolbar.

There are three different versions of the Index (K-Keywords) report.

- The Keywords Only report simply lists the keywords in the index. This report is useful for editing your keywords and phrases for spelling, grammar, and consistency.
- The Keywords and Topics report (the version shown in Figure 23-27) lists the keywords in alphabetical order and the topics that are associated with the keywords. This report is useful for identifying keywords that may require additional topics, as well as for spotting keywords that have no topics associated with them.
- The Topics and Keywords report lists the topics in alphabetical order and the keywords that are associated with the topics. This report is useful for comparing similar topics for consistent indexing and for identifying keywords to remove from specific topics.

✦ You can select the report type from the drop-down list in the lower right corner of the window.

You can print this report quickly by selecting the File ➪ Print Index command on the RoboHELP HTML toolbar or by clicking the Print button from the Report window.

As with other RoboHELP HTML reports, you can run the Index (K-Keywords) report at any time.

Summary

In this chapter, you've learned how to add tables of contents and expand your indexes. In the first part of the chapter, you learned the differences between HTML Help and WinHelp tables of contents. You learned how to add a table of contents to an HTML Help file, how to use drag-and-drop with the TOC Composer, and how to use the Auto-Create TOC feature to create a table of contents. After learning how to use RoboHELP HTML to customize the TOC's appearance and behavior, you learned how to add external Contents files to a table of contents. The first part of the chapter concluded with information on troubleshooting tables of contents, and showed you the Tables of Contents report. In the second part of the chapter, you learned how to expand and enhance your indexes using RoboHELP's indexing tools.

Following an introduction to the two different types of index files and their associated keywords, you learned how you can use the Index Designer to create and maintain keywords using drag-and-drop techniques. You then learned how to use the Smart Index Wizard to automatically create and maintain comprehensive indexes; and how to troubleshoot your indexes and print an Index (K-Keywords) report.

✦ ✦ ✦

Creating Advanced HTML Help

P A R T

V

✦ ✦ ✦ ✦

In This Part

✦ ✦ ✦ ✦

CHAPTER 24

Using Reports and Compiling

In This Chapter

Using RoboHELP HTML Reports

Getting detailed report information

Using Reports to organize your project

Compiling your HTML Help project

Reading compiler codes

Shipping your HTML Help project

In this chapter, you learn about the final stages of HTML Help project creation: reports, compiling, and shipping. You'll learn how reports can help you with your HTML Help project, including a detailed description of what each report consist of, and how to use the report to complete your project. Then you'll learn how to compile your project by learning the compiler codes and what to look for in the compiling log. Finally, you'll learn what files you need to include with your HTML Help project when you send it off to your users.

Using RoboHELP HTML Reports

Reports are a vital tool for you when you are close to the end of your development cycle. They help you make sure that every topic has been referenced, that every link is still good, and that all your topics include the images they are supposed to. Reports also help you keep track of the status of each topic, the broken and unbroken links, and even the Map IDs you used in context-sensitive help.

Each report includes information about your current project, and most reports are generated using some version of the Reports window shown in Figure 24-1.

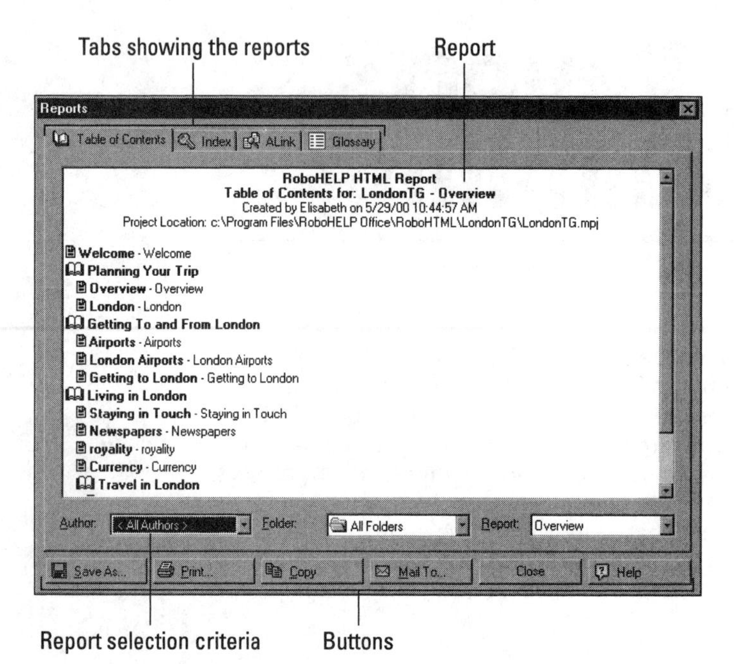

Figure 24-1: The Report Window

The Reports window has two basic parts: tabs that indicate the report and specific buttons or lists for that report, and the buttons at the bottom of the page. The buttons at the bottom of the page are the same for all reports:

- ✦ **Save As:** Exports the data shown in the report into a file in either rich text format (RTF) or text format (TXT), and opens a browse window so you can specify the location.
- ✦ **Print:** Sends the data to your default printer.
- ✦ **Copy:** Copies the data you've selected to the Windows clipboard. You can later paste the data into another file, such as a Word document or an independent HTML file.
- ✦ **Mail To:** Opens your default e-mail program and includes the data so you can send it to someone via electronic mail.
- ✦ **Close:** Closes the Reports window.
- ✦ **Help:** Launches RoboHELP HTML online help for the current set of reports.

You can generate 18 reports in RoboHELP HTML. The reports are grouped logically, and you can access other reports in a group by using tabs. This section outlines the different logical groups, and a later section outlines each individual report.

Every report includes a drop-down list that allows you to select report criteria based on author. Unfortunately, this feature does not in fact work. Perhaps the next version of RoboHELP HTML will include this feature.

The Project Status Report

The Project Status report displays a summary of your project's status, including the number of topics in the In Progress, Ready for Review, and Complete categories, and the outstanding to-do items. An example Project Status report is shown in Figure 24-2.

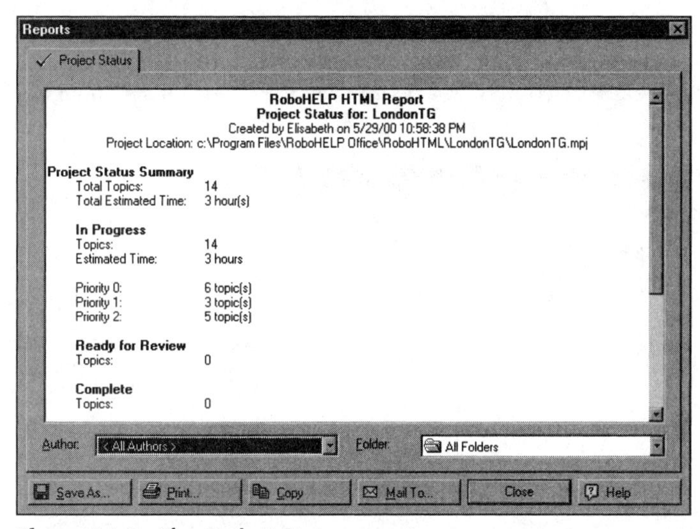

Figure 24-2: The Project Status report

You can use the Project Status report often throughout your project to monitor the progression of the topics. The Project Status report shows you the following:

✦ The total number of topics in your project, and the status of each

✦ The estimated time you entered to develop all the topics

RoboHELP HTML allows you to select subsets of your entire topic set. You can select the folder containing topics and the report will be based on the topics in that folder only. By default, the report is run with every topic in your HTML Help project.

While you are viewing a report, you cannot access any other part of RoboHELP HTML. You must close the report to access your project in any other way.

Reference Reports

As you work your way to the end of developing topics in your HTML Help project, you'll want to create a Table of Contents, Index and other linking features that add significant value to the online help for your users. As you create these features, you'll also want to make sure that every topic is referenced, and that all the links go where you want them to go. The Reference reports help you keep track of how topics are linked together, and ensure that each is referenced in the TOC and Index.

For more information about creating a Table of Contents and Index for your HTML Help project, see Chapter 23, "Creating a TOC and Index."

Table of Contents

The Table of Contents report contains both an overview and detailed information about the table of contents for your HTML Help project, as you can see in Figure 24-3.

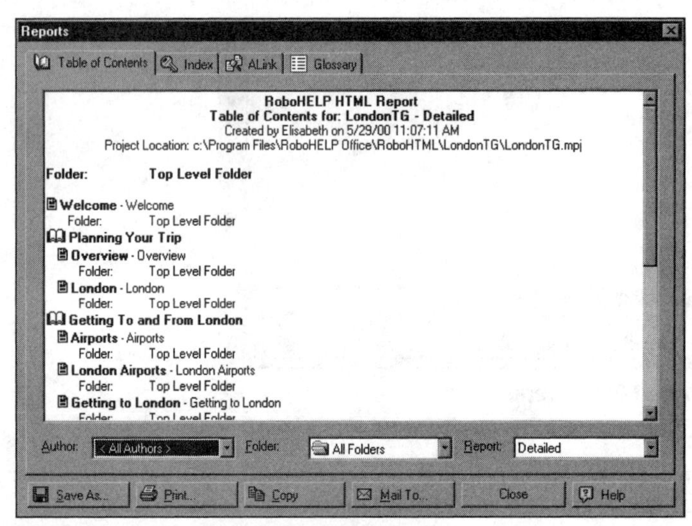

Figure 24-3: The Table of Contents Report

You can use this report to check the topic titles and HTML Help file names against the table of contents entries, and to edit the table of contents entries for spelling, grammar, and consistency. The report displays all of the books and pages of your table of contents. It also lists the topic, macro, or hyperlink that will be performed when the page is selected. If you select the Detail version of this report, you also see the document(s) in which the topics appear.

ALink

The ALink report provides information about the See Also (ALink) keywords for your HTML Help project, as shown in Figure 24-4.

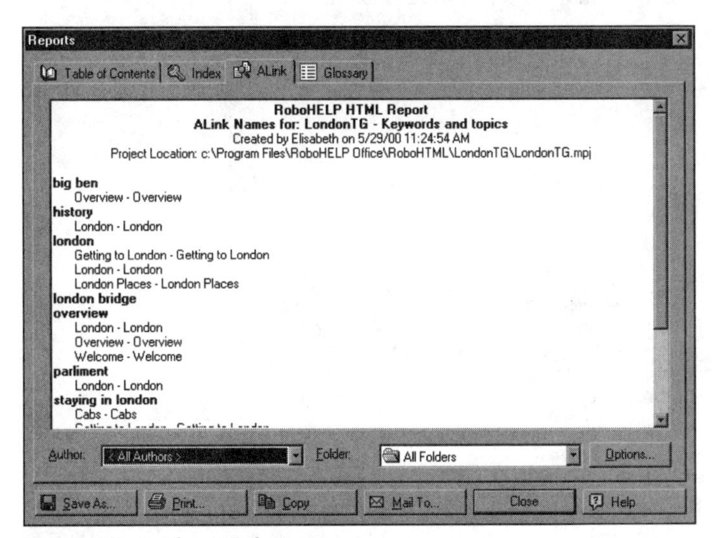

Figure 24-4: The ALink Report

You can use this report to check ALinks and their associated topics. You can also use this report to easily edit the keywords for spelling, grammar, and consistency.

The ALink report has an Options buttons that enables you to change what it does. It can be set to display one of three options:

- ✦ ALink keywords only
- ✦ All ALink keywords and their associated topics
- ✦ All topics and the ALink keywords that are linked to each topic

Index

The Index report provides information about the index keywords for your HTML Help project, as shown in Figure 24-5.

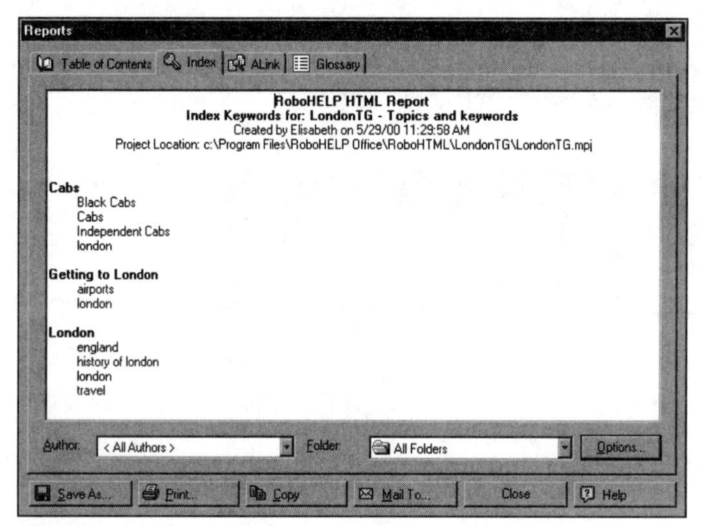

Figure 24-5: The Index report

You can use this report to check the keywords and their associated topics. You can also use this report to easily edit the keywords for spelling, grammar, and consistency.

The Index report also has an Options button that enables you to set the way the report will be displayed. You can set it to be displayed in one of three ways:

- ✦ Keywords only
- ✦ All keywords and their associated topics
- ✦ All topics and the keywords that are linked to each topic

You can also set the options to show the results in three ways:

- ✦ Index file keywords only
- ✦ Topic keywords only
- ✦ All topic keywords and all index file keywords

Glossary

The Glossary report displays the terms and definitions for glossary items in your HTML Help project, as shown in Figure 24-6.

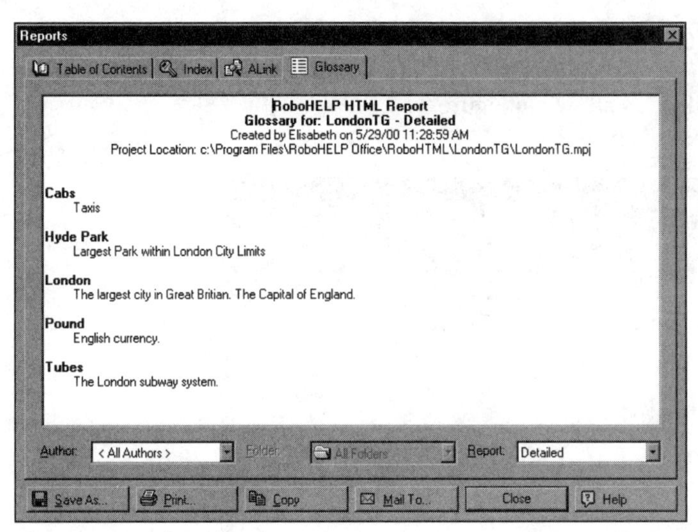

Figure 24-6: The Glossary report

Use this report to verify all the glossary entries in your HTML Help project, including spelling, grammar, and relevance.

You can view the Glossary report in two ways: The overview version lists the glossary terms without definitions; the detail version lists the terms as well as their definitions.

You do not have to include a glossary with your HTML Help project; and if you don't, the Glossary report will be empty. RoboHELP HTML does not automatically generate a glossary; you must do so manually.

Topic Reports

The Project Status report gives you the status of each of your topics, but that only scratches the surface of information about the topics. You can use this report at any stage in your development cycle. At the beginning, you can use the project status report for reviewing your list of topics and TOC entries. As you near the end of your development, you may need more detailed information about the topics, including the actual information they include. The Topic reports are a collection of reports that focus on the individual topics and their content.

For more information about creating topics, see Chapter 19 "Creating Outstanding Topics."

Topic Properties

The Topic Properties report lists all your topics and allows you to select the included information, as shown in Figure 24-7.

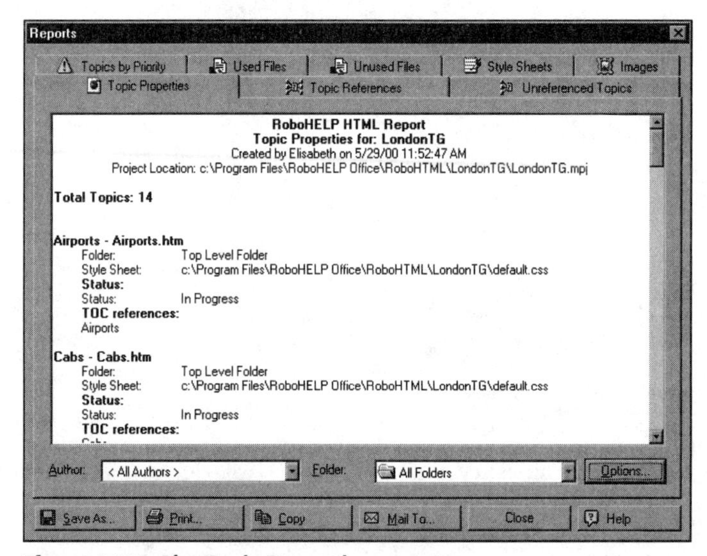

Figure 24-7: The Topic Properties report

Using the Options button on the Reports screen, you can set the Topic Properties report to display any selection of these topics properties:

✦ General information, including the following:
   • Folders
   • Bookmarks

✦ Topic status information, including the following:
   • Status
   • Priority
   • Time
   • Completed to-do items
   • Comments

✦ Reference information, including the following:
   • Links to the topic
   • Links from the topic
   • Aliases

- Table of contents
- Index keywords
- ALink names
- Topic keywords

✦ Additional advanced information, including the following:

- Info types
- Build tags
- Style sheets

Topic References

The Topic References report lists all the references to each topic in your HTML Help project, as shown in Figure 24-8.

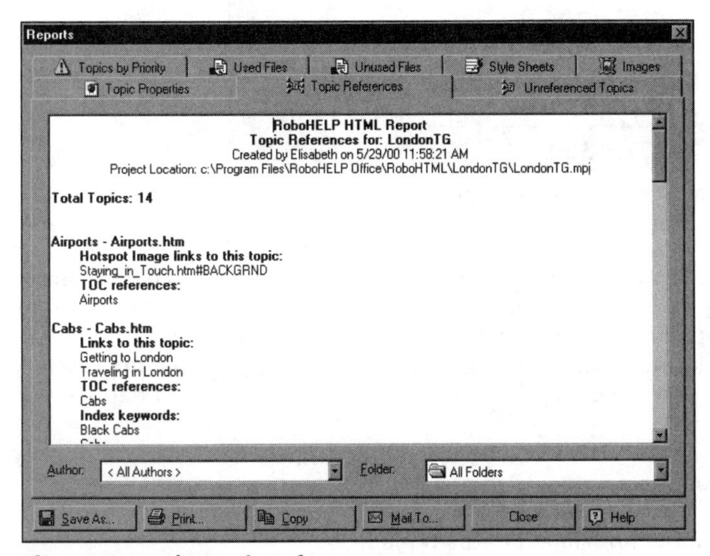

Figure 24-8: The Topic References report

The Topic References report lists the following:

✦ Hyperlinks to the topic, both standard and image links

✦ Table of contents entries

✦ Index entries

✦ ALink names assigned to the topic

Unreferenced Topics

The Unreferenced Topics report lists any topics for which there are no links anywhere in the HTML Help project, as shown in Figure 24-9.

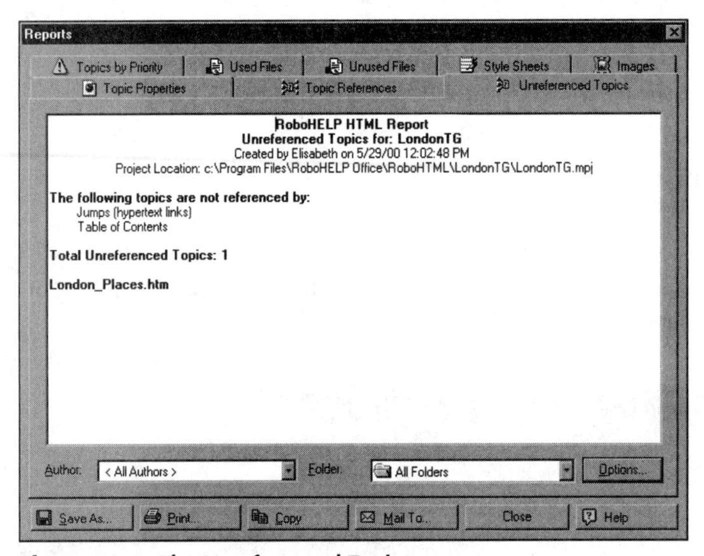

Figure 24-9: The Unreferenced Topics report

The Unreferenced Topics reports is a very important report to do before you send your HTML Help project to your users. Broken links (those that go nowhere) or topics that cannot be navigated to are sure signs to your users that your HTML Help project has not been skillfully done. No one wants to give that impression, and the Unreferenced Topics report helps you make sure it doesn't happen.

Using the Options button, the Unreferenced Topics report can look for a variety of unreferenced topics:

- ✦ Topics without jumps (links) to the topic
- ✦ Topics without table of contents entries
- ✦ Topics without index entries (K-keywords)

Topics by Priority

The Topics by Priority report lists topics by their topic priority, as shown in Figure 24-10.

Using the Options button on the report, you can choose to display all priorities or set a range of priorities for the report.

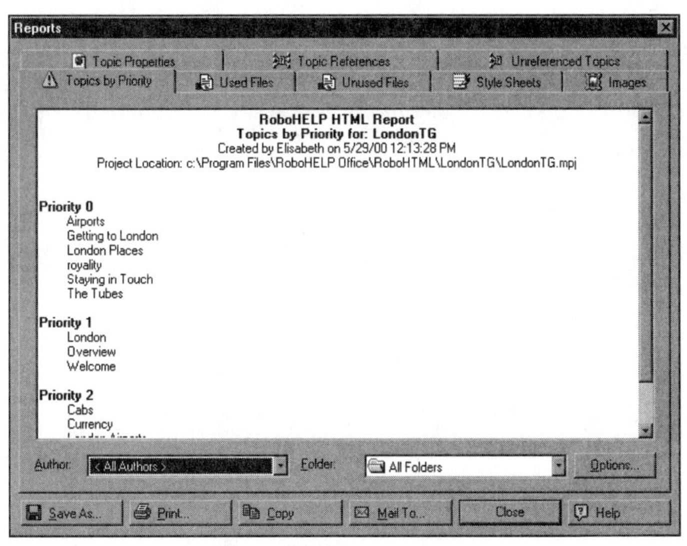

Figure 24-10: The Topics by Priority report

Priorities must be set manually for each topic; they are not automatically generated.

Used Files

The Used Files report lists the files that make up your HTML Help project, as shown in Figure 24-11.

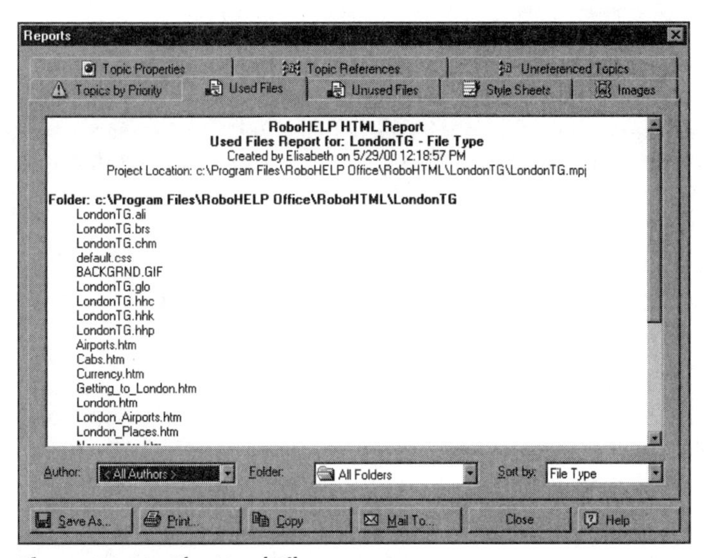

Figure 24-11: The Used Files report

You can choose to sort the files either by file name or file type by using the drop-down list in the lower right corner of the screen.

As with all the reports, you can choose to list files in the entire project or just in specified folders by using the Folder drop-down list.

Unused Files

The Unused Files report lists the files in your project folder and custom directories that are not currently included in the project, as shown in Figure 24-12.

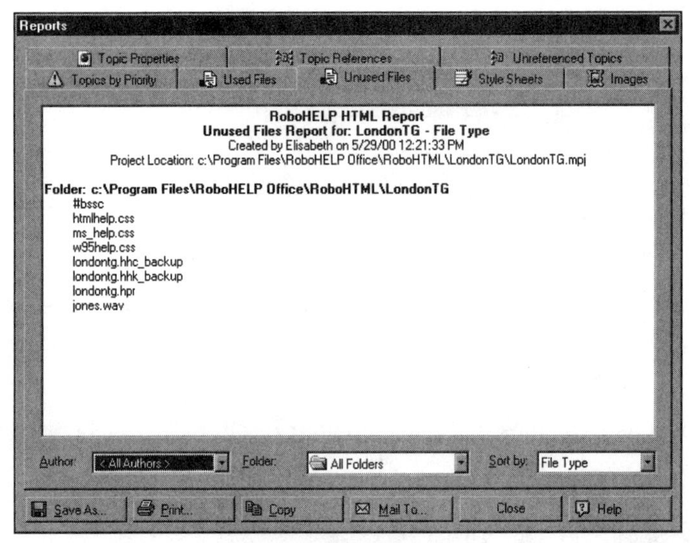

Figure 24-12: The Unused Files report

Because the files are unused, they don't appear in the RoboHELP Project Manager. Once you have identified the unused files with the Unused Files report, you must use the Windows Explorer to delete them.

Style Sheets

The Style Sheets report shows all the style sheets used in your HTML Help project, as shown in Figure 24-13.

The Style Sheet report is useful for verifying and fixing any style issues. Because it lists all the style sheets and topics, you can use it to make sure each topic has the correct style.

Using the drop-down list in the lower right-hand corner of the report, you can choose to display an alphabetical list of the style sheets in the HTML Help project and their associated topics, or an alphabetical list of topics and their associated style sheets.

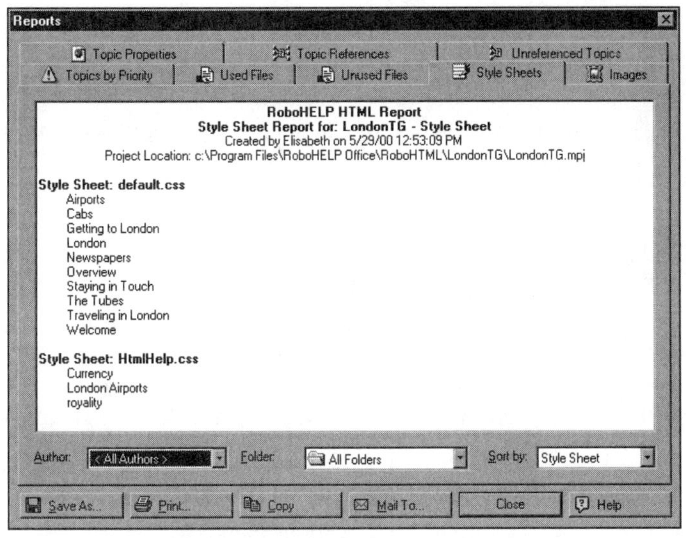

Figure 24-13: The Style Sheets report

Images

The Images report lists all the images in all the topics in your HTML Help project, as shown in Figure 24-14.

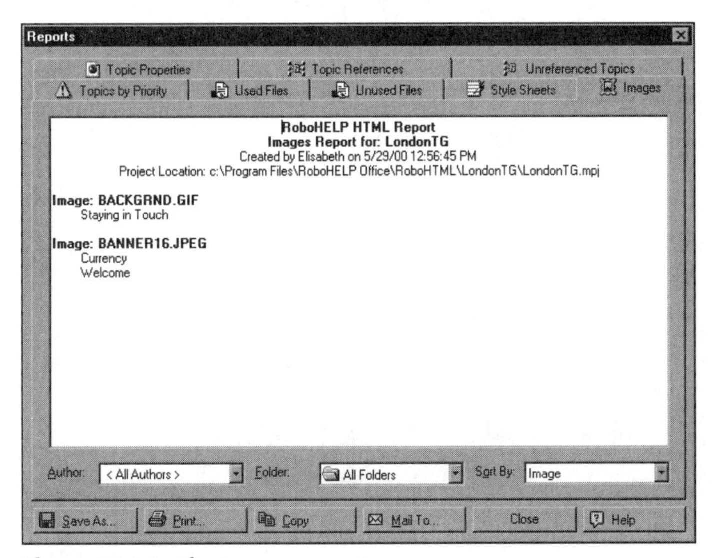

Figure 24-14: The Images report

Using the drop-down list in the lower right-hand corner of the report, you can choose to display an alphabetical list of the images in the HTML Help project and their associated topics, or an alphabetical list of topics and their associated images.

For more information about including graphics in your topics, see Chapter 20, "Creating and Adding Graphics."

Advanced Reports

Once you have verified the references, and made sure your topics are all in order, you are ready to deal with the stickier issues of context-sensitive help, map IDs, broken links, external references, and unused index entries. These are collected together in the Advanced reports. There are reports that handle something other than the references, such as the glossary and TOC, and do not directly handle topic information.

If you have done everything right, some of these reports may be blank. That is normal, and in the case of some reports it is even desirable.

Map IDs

The Map ID report provides you with general information about the map IDs, as shown in Figure 24-15.

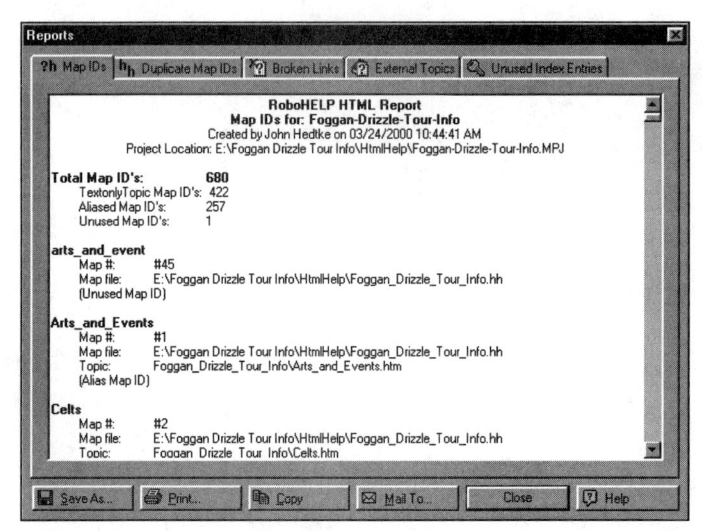

Figure 24-15: The Map IDs report

First the report displays a summary of the map IDs and unused map IDs in your HTML Help project. Then it lists topic IDs and displays the associated map ID, map file, topic title, and document.

Duplicate Map IDs

The Duplicate Map IDs report shows all the duplicate map IDs, as shown in Figure 24-16.

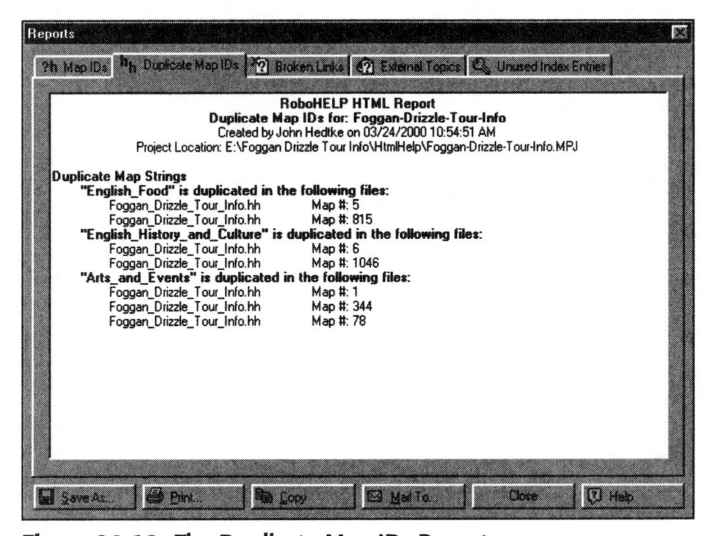

Figure 24-16: The Duplicate Map IDs Report

This is a diagnostic report that lists all duplicate entries for topic IDs and topic numbers. Use this report as you finish creating your context-sensitive help to make sure you have a clean Map ID list.

For more information on creating context-sensitive help, see Chapter 25, "Creating Context-Sensitive HTML Help."

Broken Links

The Broken Links report (see Figure 24-17) shows all the missing links in your topics.

This report displays any links that jump to topics RoboHELP cannot locate anywhere in your project. It is very useful for finding those links that you have moved or changed and forgotten to change in the topics themselves.

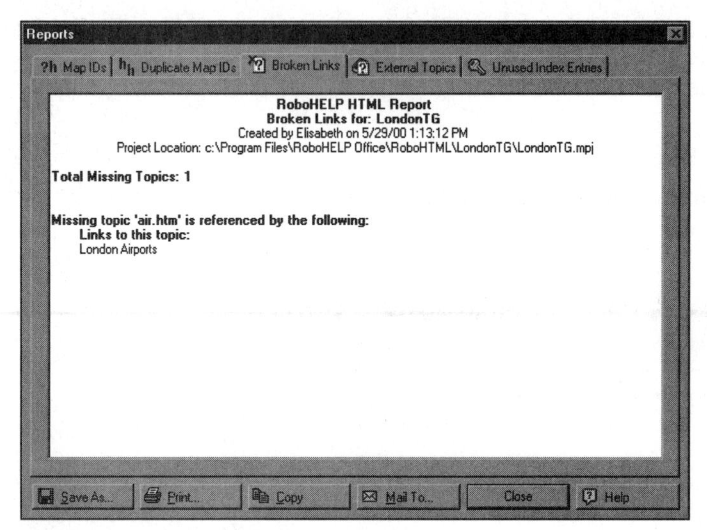

Figure 24-17: The Broken Links report

You can also locate broken links using the Link view in the right-hand pane of the RoboHELP HTML main window.

External Topic References

The External Topic References report displays links to any external material, as shown in Figure 24-18.

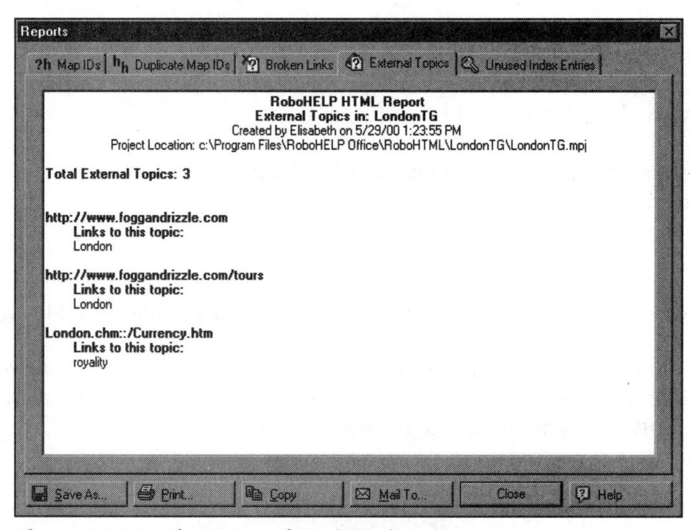

Figure 24-18: The External Topic References report

This report shows links to any external CHM topics, to any external Web sites, or to anything that is not contained within your HTML Help project. If any exist, this report lists links to the following:

- ✦ URLs that are intranet addresses and Web pages
- ✦ Links to HTML topics in other compiled Microsoft HTML Help projects, referenced by their CHM files
- ✦ FTP site addresses
- ✦ Newsgroup addresses
- ✦ E-mail addresses

Unused index keywords

The Unused Index Keywords report (see Figure 24-19) lists the index entries that do not reference topics.

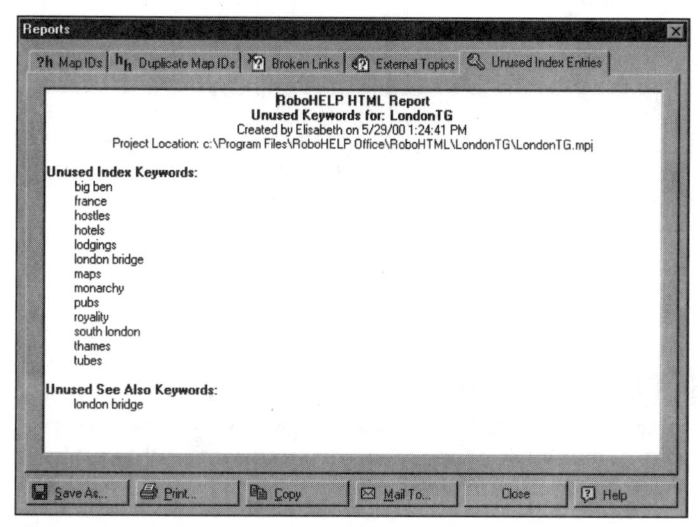

Figure 24-19: The Unused Index Keywords report

The Unused Index Keywords report shows you the index keywords that are not currently associated with topics.

These keywords will also appear in bold in the RoboHELP Explorer Index Designer.

Generating Your HTML Help Project

The last, and possibly most important, step in your HTML Help project is compiling. After you've created the topics, added a TOC and index, and run all the reports, you are not done until you've compiled your HTML Help project and turned it into online help.

As you saw in Chapter 18, "Creating Your First HTML Help Project," compiling is as simple as using the compiling button on the RoboHELP HTML toolbar. However, compiling can also be more complicated. For example, you may need to add build tags, or you may need to understand the compiler codes generated by RoboHELP HTML.

Especially as you get closer to the end of your project, your compiling may get increasingly complicated. Earlier in your project, you were compiling to simply see how the topics looked. As you get closer to finishing, you get closer to the final compiling run that will complete your project, and consequently your needs are more complicated.

This section helps you through the process of compiling, showing you how to change compiling settings, and how to make the most of build tags, the compiler codes, and the log.

Early in your project, you may not compile at all, because HTML Help, unlike WinHelp, can show you the look of your topics without compiling. As you reach the end of your development process, you'll want to compile often to make sure your HTML Help project has the overall look you want, and that all your links and features work.

Changing Compiling Settings

As you begin compiling at the end of your development process, you'll want to make sure that you are compiling the type of project you want, with the settings you require.

Your compiling settings control several different parts of the finished look and feel of your HTML Help project, including the file name and which topics are included. The compiling settings enable you to include full-text searches in your HTML Help project, and to select the first topic to open when users launch your online help. This section walks you through the necessary steps to change your compiling settings, set your default topic, and use build tags.

Of all the aspects of compiling that you will want to change, the most common ones are the file name and compiling error settings. These and all other compiling settings can be changed in the Project Settings window.

Here's how you change your basic compiling settings:

1. Open the project in which you want to change the compiling settings.
2. Select File ➪ Project Settings. This opens the Project Settings window.
3. Choose the Compile tab, shown in Figure 24-20.

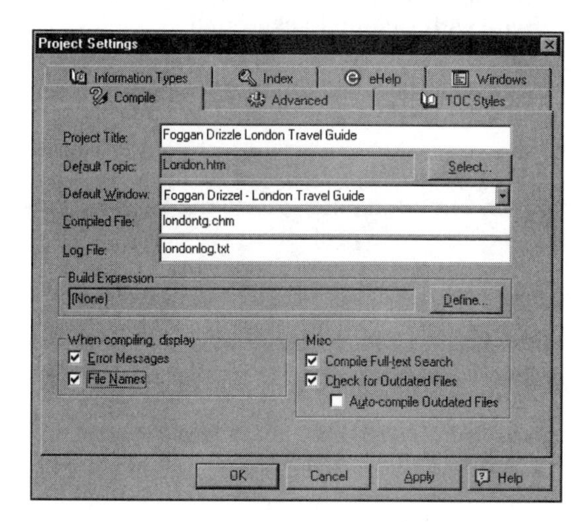

Figure 24-20: Project Settings - Compiling Settings Tab

4. Use the Project Title field to set the title displayed for your project.
5. Use the Default Window drop-down list to set the window in which your help project opens.
6. Set the file name for the compiled online help in the Compiled File field.

Note

By default, the file name is taken from the project name you selected when you started your HTML Help project. You can override that default here if you want.

7. Set the file name for the compiling log file in the Log File field. Remember to end it with a TXT extension so you can read it using standard text editing tools.
8. Select what you would like the compiler to display using the When Compiling, Display checkboxes.
9. Use the Misc checkboxes to add full-text searching or to have RoboHELP HTML check and compile outdated files.
10. When you are satisfied with the settings on the Compile tab, click OK.

    RoboHELP HTML updates the project settings and closes the Project Settings window.

Setting a default topic

Once you have almost completed your HTML Help project, and you have set the basic compiling settings, you are ready to select a *default topic.*

The default topic is the topic that opens first when your users launch your online help. This topic opens in the right-hand pane of your compiled online help. You'll notice that the default topic for RoboHELP HTML's online help is a topic containing the contact information for eHelp, with a cloud background.

By default, the default topic is set as the first topic listed in your project.

Choosing which topic should open your online help is usually done in the planning stages of your HTML Help project, but often not set until the last steps. Here's how you set the default topic for you HTML Help project:

1. Open the project in which you want to set the default topic.
2. Select File ➪ Project Settings. This opens the Project Settings window.
3. Choose the Compile tag, which displays as shown in Figure 31-20.
4. Choose the Select button to the right of the Default Topic text box. This opens the Select Topic window shown in Figure 24-21.

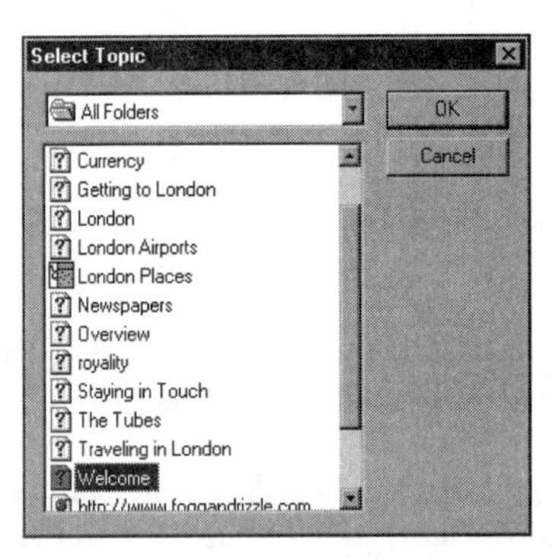

Figure 24-21: Select Topic window

5. Select the topic you want as the default from the list. You can narrow the list of topics by selecting a folder from the drop-down list.
6. When you are done, click OK.

RoboHELP HTML closes the window and enters the file name for the topic in the Default Topic text box.

Using build tags

Build tags allow you to create several different versions of your online help from one HTML Help project. They give you a way to identify each topic by its content and where it should be used. No matter what format you are exporting too, build tags give you a way to make sure that one set of topics compiles for one set of users. For example, you may want to include different parts of your HTML Help project for different platforms. You could have build tags for each platform, and compile only those topics that apply to each platform.

Of course, the first step to using build tags is to create them:

1. Open the HTML Help project in which you want to include a new build tag.
2. Make sure the Project tab is showing in the left-hand pane.
3. Right-click on Build Tags.
4. Select New Build Tag from the list. This displays the New Build Tag window, as shown in Figure 24-22.

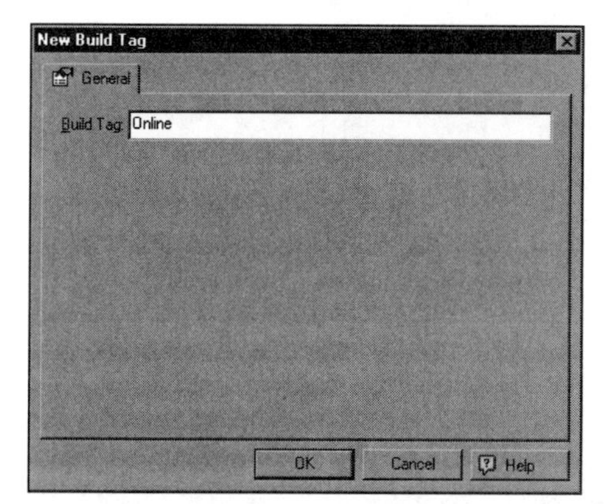

Figure 24-22: New Build Tag window

5. Enter the name for the tag into the Build Tag text box.
6. Click OK.

RoboHELP HTML closes the Build Tag window and adds the new build tag to the list.

Once you have defined a build tag, you are ready to start using it with your topics.

Here's how you add a build tag to your topics:

1. Open the HTML Help project with the topic to which you want to add build tags.
2. Right-click on the topic.
3. Select Topic Properties from the list.
4. Choose the Advanced tab, shown in Figure 24-23.

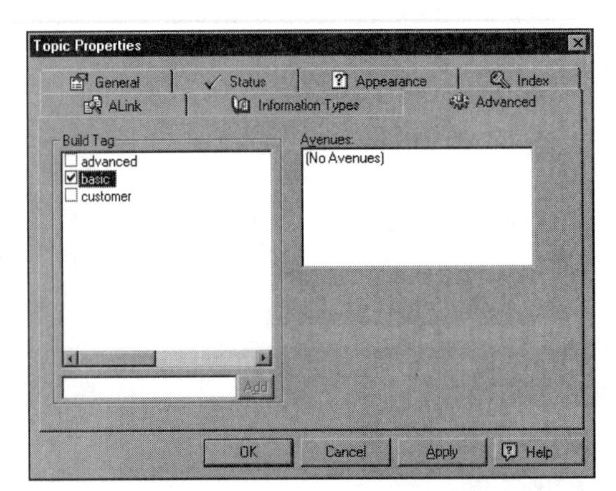

Figure 24-23: Topic Properties window – Advanced tab

5. Using the checkboxes, select all the build tags you want to apply to this topic.
6. When you are satisfied with your build tag selections, click OK.

Now when you choose those build tags to compile, RoboHELP HTML includes the topic. The build tag information is saved with all the topic property information.

The other tabs in the Topic Properties window are covered in Chapter 19, "Creating Outstanding Topics."

Here's how you compile with specific build tags:

1. Open the project you want to compile.
2. Select File ⇨ Project Settings.
3. Choose the Compile tag, shown previously in Figure 24-20.
4. Click the Define button next to the Build Expressions text box. The Define Build Tag Expression window displays as shown in Figure 24-24.

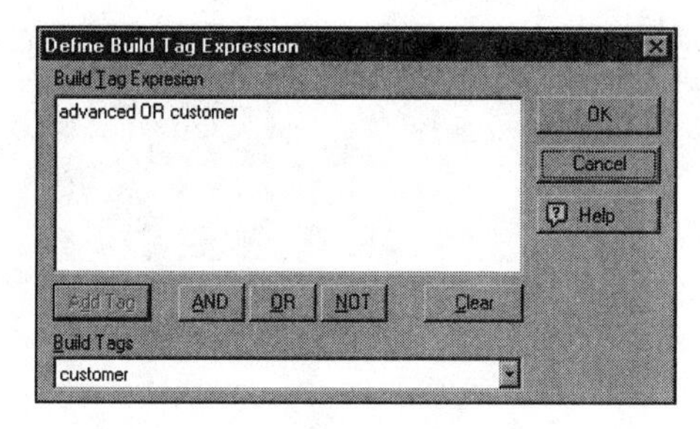

Figure 24-24: Define Build Tag Expression window

5. Choose build tags by using the drop-down list at the bottom of the window.
6. Click Add Tag to add the tag to the Define Build Tag Expression window.
7. Use the Boolean Expression buttons (AND, OR, and NOT) to add simple logic to your build tag expression.

NOT only works at the very start of your build tag expression, and RoboHELP HTML will not let you include it anywhere else in the expression.

7. When you are done defining your build tag expression, click OK.

   RoboHELP HTML closes the Define Build Tag Expression window and displays the build tag expression in the Build Tag text box on the Project Properties window.

Build tags are a very powerful too, but they may take a little while to get used to. Understanding how they work and planning how to use them are the keys to making them work for you

Understanding the Compiler

The compiler that creates your online help in RoboHELP HTML is the compiler developed by Microsoft. Microsoft created the original compiler, called the Windows Help Compiler, when they developed the idea of HTML Help. A version of this same compiler is still in use by almost everyone that creates online help for Windows. RoboHELP HTML lets you see the compiler in action by using the Output pane, shown in Figure 24-25.

As with many compilers, the Windows Help compiler has codes that give you information about what is happening as it compiles your HTML Help project. Understanding what the compiler is doing, and what it all means, is a two-step process. First you must understand how to read the compiler, and then you need to know what the compiler codes mean. The next two sections walk you through these steps.

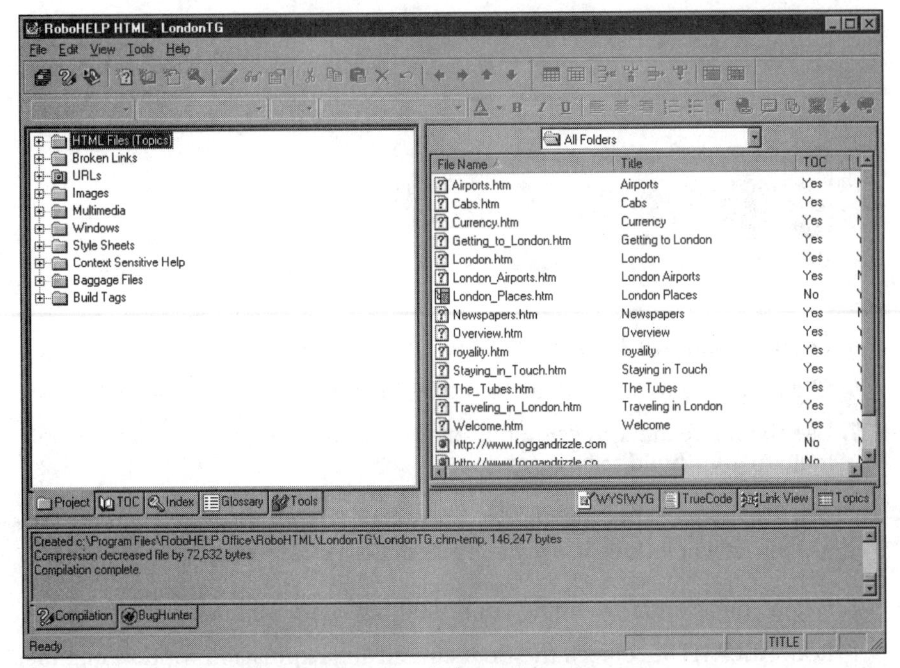

Figure 24-25: RoboHelp HTML main window with Output Pane

It is not necessary to understand the compiler to create great online help, but it can be useful when you are attempting tricky feats of HTML or scripting.

Reading the compiler

The compiler writes text to the Output pane as it creates your compiled online help from your HTML Help project. The text written to the Output pane is also written in the log file, described later in this chapter.

The text in the Output pane is a blow-by-blow listing of the compiler's actions when it creates the online help file. The results in the Output tab window look something like the following:

```
Starting compilation...
Microsoft HTML Help Compiler 4.73.8198

Compiling c:\Program Files\RoboHELP
Office\RoboHTML\LondonTG\LondonTG.chm-temp

HHC3001: Warning: The file "c:\Program Files\RoboHELP
Office\RoboHTML\LondonTG\London_Airports.htm" has a link to a
non-existent file: "c:\Program Files\RoboHELP
Office\RoboHTML\LondonTG\air.htm".
```

```
Compile time: 0 minutes, 1 second
16    Topics
54    Local links
2    Internet links
2    Graphics

Created c:\Program Files\RoboHELP
Office\RoboHTML\LondonTG\LondonTG.chm-temp, 146,251 bytes
Compression decreased file by 72,628 bytes.
Compilation complete.
```

As you can see, the information in the compiler can be quite dense, but it can also be very useful if you take the time to understand it.

First, the compiler tells you it is starting, and which version of the Microsoft HTML Help Compiler it is using. Then, it shows you which file it is compiling.

The next line, or it could be the next several lines in your project, list problems the compiler has had as it attempts to create your online help file. In the example above, the compiler found that there is a missing file linked to in the topic London_Airports. The file is supposed to be located in the project folder (c:\Program Files\RoboHELP Office\RoboHTML\LondonTG\), and is called air.htm. Broken links are always listed by the compiler.

Tip: Broken links can also be found by using the Link view in the right-hand pane of the RoboHELP HTML main window, or by using the Broken Links report.

After the compiler has listed all the errors it found, it indicates the total time it took to create the compiled online help, and lists all the topics, links, and graphics in the HTML Help project.

Finally, the compiler tells you the file name for the finished online help, gives you the file size, and indicates how much the final file reduces the file size in comparison to your entire HTML Help project.

The last line of your compiler code is always Compilation Complete when your online help file has been created successfully.

Understanding compiler codes

As you may have noticed in the previous section, the compiler gives you a lot of information if you know how to read it. Chief among the compiler's information is a set of codes that tell you exactly what kinds of compiler errors there were when your online help was created. Understanding and using these compiler codes is called *debugging,* and you'll usually have to do it at least once in the development of your HTML Help project.

You'll never get compiler codes because of incorrect HTML codes, because the compiler doesn't read your topics, it just links them with their jumps.

About 50 possible error messages are available to the compiler. All of the messages have the same format; they start with HHC and are followed by a four-digit number. The numbers are described in Table 24-1.

Table 24-1
Help Compiler Error Messages

Error Message Number	*Meaning*
1000	The compiler encountered an HTML tag with no text, meaning a <> with no text between it.
3000-3015	These error messages indicate something affecting how your online help works, usually incorrect tags or broken links.
4000-4016	These error messages indicate something affecting how your online help system works, usually missing augments in tags or too many augments. RoboHELP HTML always tells you which of the augments it has used when compiling.
5000-5013	These error messages indicate a failed compile of your HTML Help project. These occur when some miscoding or mis-scripting has made it impossible for RoboHELP HTML to compile your online help.
6000-6003	These are error messages indicating a corrupted file problem or a disk space problem. RoboHELP HTML lists the disk or file that caused the problem.

For a completely detailed list of compiler error codes, see the Keytools software listed in Appendix D, "Resources."

Getting Ready to Ship

After you have run all your reports, debugged your compiler, and proofed your final online help project, you are ready to send your HTML Help project to your users.

This section assumes you are compiling and shipping Microsoft HTML Help. If you are sending any of the other types of help, see Chapter 28, "Examining WebHelp, JavaHelp, and other Help Systems."

The most important part of shipping your project is making sure your users have all the tools they need to view your online help. The following components must either be present on the users' systems or ship with your online help:

✦ Microsoft Internet Explorer 4.0 or later

✦ The .chm file built by the compiler

✦ Microsoft HTML Help system files, which can be created by using the HHUPD.EXE that comes with RoboHELP HTML

If you have created help for a software application, you need to include a reference in your software to the .chm file your compiler built.

Work with your software developer to ensure that they have everything that needs to be installed on the user's system when they install the software.

If you added any ActiveX features to your online help, such as automatically updating the TOC, online glossary, or topic browse sequences, you need to include the ActiveX files as well. The ActiveX capabilities are in the HHActiveX.DLL file, which you need to install when you deliver your .chm file.

Once you have found all these files and included them, you can ship your online help to your users.

Summary

In this chapter, you learned about the final stages of HTML Help project creation: reports, compiling, and shipping. After being introduced to each of the reports that comes with RoboHELP HTML you learned how they can help you with your HTML Help project, beginning with a detailed outline of what each report includes, and ending with how to use the report to complete your project. Then you learned how to compile your project by examining the compiler codes and what to look for in the compiling log. Finally, you learned what files you need to include with your HTML Help project when you send it off to your users.

✦ ✦ ✦

Creating Context-Sensitive HTML Help

In This Chapter

Understanding context-sensitive help

Making a plan for creating context-sensitive help

Creating context-sensitive links manually

Associating multiple map IDs with a topic

Importing map files

Creating context-sensitive links automatically

Testing and debugging context-sensitive help

Understanding the strengths and weaknesses of What's This? help

Creating, compiling, and testing a What's This? help project

Releasing What's This? help for shipping

This chapter shows you how to create context-sensitive and What's This? help. It starts by describing the basics of context-sensitive help and how programs and HTML Help files interact. Next, the chapter discusses issues to consider with the developers when planning your efforts. You then learn how to add context-sensitive links manually and create them automatically. The first section of the chapter concludes with information on test context-sensitive help using the HTML Help BugHunter.

The second half of the chapter teaches you how to use What's This? help. You first learn basic What's This? help concepts and its advantages and disadvantages. Next, you are shown how to create and edit a basic What's This? help file using What's This? Help Composer. The chapter continues with information on configuring What's This? Help Composer, compiling What's This? help, and testing the result. You see several methods for automating parts of the What's This? help process. The chapter ends by discussing various maintenance and release issues.

What Is Context-Sensitive Help?

So far in this book, you've seen how to create stand-alone HTML Help files: files that are not linked to a specific program as the associated online documentation. Now you're going to see how to create *context-sensitive help*. Context-sensitive help is help that is directly linked to a program. When a user presses F1 or clicks on the help button in a window or dialog box, the context-sensitive link between the program and the help file identifies the topic to display and then displays it.

Two basic kinds of context-sensitive help are discussed in this chapter: window-level and text-only help. Window-level context-sensitive help is used to display a standard HTML Help topic. A single "window" of information — a single topic — is displayed that describes a window, a field, a command, a button, or a combination thereof. Text-only help (known more commonly as What's This? help) provides simple text-based popup help to describe a window item such as a field or a button. The first part of this chapter addresses context-sensitive help; What's This? help is described in the second part.

Figure 25-1 shows a diagram of the interaction between the program and the online help.

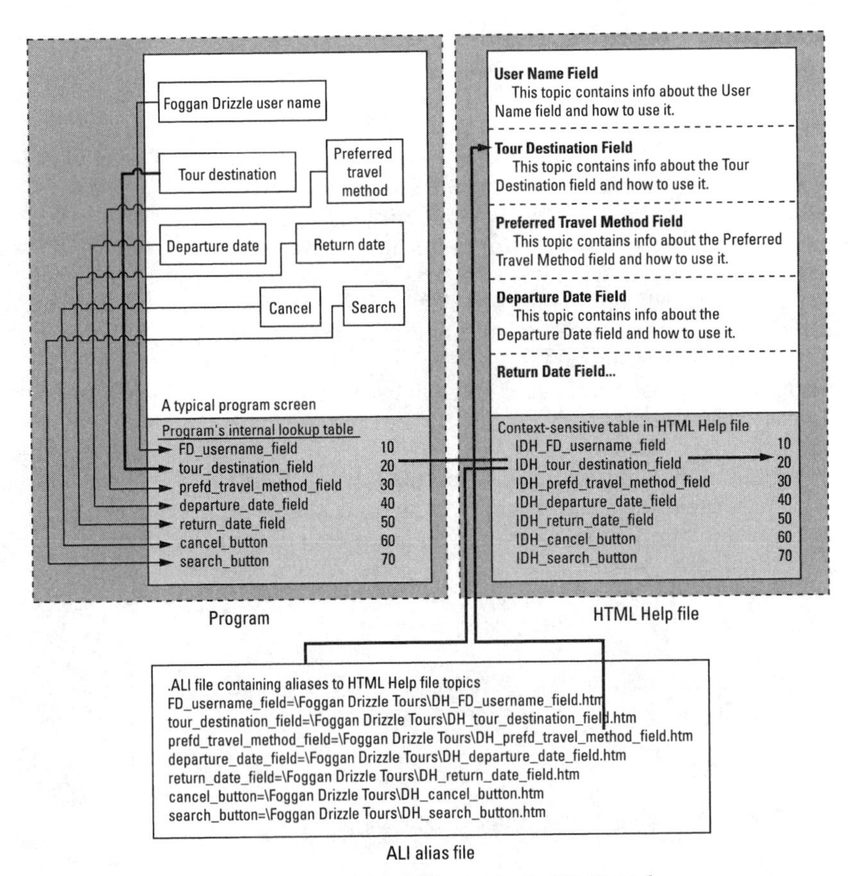

Figure 25-1: How context-sensitive help works in HTML Help

As Figure 25-1 shows, when the user requests help for the Tour Destination field in the application, the program looks up the map ID associated with the field in an internal table that is part of the program. (This topic is usually identified by a map

ID, also known as *map number* or a *help hook*, which you and the developer specify for each topic you want to create context-sensitive help for.) The program then issues a *call*—a request for information or action from one program to another—to the HTML Help API (application program interface), which is part of Windows, to look in the appropriate HTML Help file for the topic associated with the map ID. The specified HTML Help file is opened, and the HTML Help API looks in the HTML Help file's lookup table for the map ID and then finds the topic that's associated with the map ID. The HTML Help topic is then displayed on the user's window.

This may sound a little daunting, but most of the mechanisms for context-sensitive help actually work behind the scenes. All the communication between the programs and HTML Help files is done with the HTML Help API. The developers are in charge of implementing the calls to the HTML Help files using the HTML Help API from within the program. Most of what you and the developer need to do to create context-sensitive help is to agree on the map IDs for the various topics and link them.

Any HTML Help file can be turned into a context-sensitive file. Furthermore, the users can run a context-sensitive HTML Help file as a stand-alone file and access topics with keywords, tables of contents, and jumps; you just won't be able to display individual topics programmatically.

Planning Context-Sensitive Help

Creating context-sensitive help requires that you interact with the software developers. Here are some typical questions for which you should determine the answers:

✦ What programming language is the program being developed in (and are there any restrictions for developing context-sensitive help in the development environment)?

✦ What kinds and levels of context-sensitive help are required? For example, you can create context-sensitive help that provides help at the window level (a single overarching topic comes up when the user selects context-sensitive help anywhere on the window) or at the field level (individual topics come up for each of the fields). You can provide context-sensitive help for entire menus or for individual menus and commands.

✦ How will the users access context-sensitive help topics? Typical options include pressing F1, clicking a button on a window that says "Help" or displays a question mark, right-clicking the field and selecting a help option, or selecting a Help menu toggle and then clicking on the field or area that they want help on. The development team will program all of these options, but the choices for accessing HTML Help can affect the phrasing you use in the HTML Help file.

✦ Who will create the link in the HTML Help file? Although this is usually best managed by the HTML Help authors, it is sometimes handled by the development team. Some development environments also dictate the type of help link you use in the HTML Help file.

✦ What are the development schedule benchmarks? This should include such things as creation of functional specification, alpha and beta releases of the software, feature freeze, visual freeze, and product release.

✦ Is there a functional specification for the project? Will it be followed? What is the process for informing the writers of changes to the user interface? (The answers will determine when the context-sensitive help topics will be created.)

✦ When will the application's user interface freeze (no additional changes will be made to the user interface)? When will the functions being developed freeze? (The freezes will determine when you can schedule final testing of the HTML Help file against the application.)

✦ What naming conventions are the developers using for the unique names of the program controls? (*Controls* are anything in the program that you can request context-sensitive help for: windows, fields, menus, commands, and so on.) What naming conventions are you using for the topics and the aliases?

✦ How will you be structuring the HTML Help files? Will there be a single HTML Help file or many help files? What name(s) will you use for the HTML Help file(s)? The name of the HTML Help file needs to be coded into the software.

✦ What windows do you want to display HTML Help topics in? Will you be using multiple window types (such as procedure windows, reference windows, and popup windows) in the online help? This information is something that needs to be coded into the application.

✦ How will the context-sensitive help be tested, and who will test it? Is this being tested exclusively by the help developers, or will the developers also test this? Is there a testing group for the project that will be doing verification of the online help as well?

✦ How will changes be communicated from the developers to the writers, and vice versa? You may want to distribute a regular report to the developers you are working with to make sure that everyone is kept in the loop.

By answering these questions, you and the developer will have a much better idea of what to expect and what you each need to create. You can also set the expectations of the developers and the testers for the tasks related to creating the context-sensitive help that they'll need to schedule. Having a clear understanding of the way in which the developers are creating their context-sensitive help links and how the writers and developers can support each other is an essential part of the context-sensitive help development process.

Working with Developers

Producing great context-sensitive help requires that you be up-to-date on the features of, look-and-feel of, and any changes to the software. Developers in many companies are frequently resistant to extensive planning, specs, or information about the changes contained in internal alpha and beta releases, which can make writing the context-sensitive help more challenging than it needs to be. Wherever possible, develop informal lines of communication with the developers to find out what's really happening with a project. For example, many writers will get the official pronouncements on the schedule and the feature set from the development manager or team leader and will then talk to the individual developers and ask them the same questions.

You should also beware of any situation where the development manager says, "The developers are too busy to talk to the writers," as this is a clear sign that the project has not been planned. (The metric for budgeting time for the developers working on documentation issues is that writers require roughly 10 percent of the developers' time over the course of a project. Good development managers are aware of this.) In such cases, most of your interaction with the developers will be through informal rather than formal channels. Plan on taking a lot of developers to lunch to get information from them away from the office. It won't be a one-sided relationship; you'll learn a great deal about how your company develops products and will be able to anticipate needs and problems much more effectively.

Creating Context-Sensitive Help

The basic steps for creating context-sensitive help are:

1. Work with the developers to identify the windows, fields, commands, and other items in the program for which you want to create context-sensitive help.
2. Create a skeleton of topics for the various controls. (You don't need to have the content written to get the overall structure working, although you may have topics already written for some of the features.)
3. Assign aliases and map IDs for each of the HTML Help topics and the associated controls.
4. Compile and test the online help file with the program to see that the links work.
5. Develop the content for the topics.
6. Recompile and test the online help file with the program.

The most effective way to identify the items that need to have context-sensitive help topics is to get printouts of the various windows, menus, and objects. If the developers are working from an up-to-date spec, these will be readily available; however, it is more likely that you will have to take screen shots of the latest version of the software to get this information. Highlight all the items that need individual topics.

Developing help for applications that have not frozen can be tricky and is frequently one of the most unpleasant parts of the context-sensitive help development process. Identifying the field, windows, and features in a timely fashion that need to be documented is critical to creating complete and correct context-sensitive help.

If you are adapting an existing online help file to a program, you probably do not need to create many new topics, but when you are creating online help from scratch for a program, it's best to create an online help file with empty topics at first. This will let you test the layout and interaction between the program and the online help file before you spend too much time writing content for the individual topics. (For convenience when building browse sequences in the online help file, it's a good idea to create topics in the order they appear on the various windows and menus.)

Once you have a set of topics ready to be linked, you need to establish the links between the program and the online help file. Much of the work may already be done for you: depending on the programming language the program is being written in, the developer may already have a set of map IDs generated for the various controls. If not, however, you can work with the developer to create a simple system for assigning map IDs to the controls. Write the map IDs for each control on the printouts of the windows, fields, and menus. You'll use these for entering map IDs and for reference when testing the context-sensitive help.

If you're used to creating context-sensitive help with WinHelp, be aware that there are some differences in terminology between WinHelp and HTML Help. When you create context-sensitive help in WinHelp, you associate map IDs with topic IDs, the unique identifiers of the topics in the source file. In HTML Help, there are no topic IDs because each topic is considered a page and is stored in individual files, and thus has its own URL. The programmers can call individual pages (topics) directly, as long as you give them the list of URLs.

Aliases in WinHelp files are a method of redirecting map IDs to different topics and associating multiple map IDs with a single help topic. In HTML Help, you can create an HTML Help *alias*. Aliases take the place of topic IDs in HTML Help (and are frequently referred to as topic IDs), but they are also used for associating multiple map IDs with a single help topic.

The three basic scenarios for creating context-sensitive help are as follows:

✦ You create the aliases manually and let RoboHELP create the map IDs automatically. You then give the resulting map file to the developer for incorporation in the software.

✦ You create the aliases and map IDs manually. You give the map file to the developer if necessary.

✦ You import an existing map file given to you by the developer and use this to assign aliases and map IDs.

It's likely that you'll use a combination of these scenarios to create your context-sensitive help. For example, you'll import an existing map file for the bulk of the topics in your online help project, but you'll then add individual topics manually. The following sections will show you how to add aliases and map IDs for each of these scenarios.

Adding Aliases and Map IDs

To enter aliases manually, do the following:

1. In the RoboHELP HTML main window, double-click Aliases in the Context Sensitive Help folder. The Edit Map IDs window appears (shown in Figure 25-2).

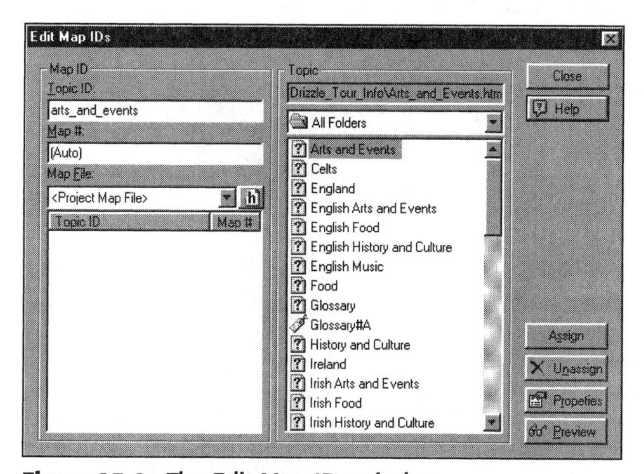

Figure 25-2: The Edit Map IDs window

2. Enter information in the fields as follows:

   - **Topic ID:** Enter an alias (the topic ID) to uniquely identify the topic. Aliases are not visible to the users. Aliases can't have embedded spaces, special characters, or punctuation except for underscores. As you enter the alias in Topic ID, RoboHELP automatically changes spaces, special characters, and punctuation that isn't allowed into underscores. For example, "arts and events" would be changed to "arts_and_events" (as shown in Figure 25-2).

- **Map #:** When you enter the alias in Topic ID, RoboHELP automatically enters <Auto> in the Map # field. If you leave this entry in the field, RoboHELP will generate the map ID for the topic automatically. You can enter a map ID if you prefer to associate a specific number with this topic.

Tip

It's a good idea to create map IDs with room between them for convenient expansion. For example, all map IDs between 100 and 199 are associated with the program's main window, all map IDs between 200 and 299 are associated with the next window in the program, and so on. By grouping the values logically, you can save time when testing and debugging later on. The main contents topic is usually given the value of 0. RoboHELP supports map IDs from 0 to 4,294,967,295 (2^{32}-1), but it's a good idea from a maintenance standpoint to keep the map IDs in a much smaller range. Most online help writers traditionally use the range from 0 to 32,767 or 0 to 65,535.

3. Highlight the topic in the topic list that you want to associate the mapping information with and click Assign. RoboHELP will assign the alias and the map ID to the highlighted topic. The mapping information will also appear in the lower left part of the window, as shown in Figure 25-3.

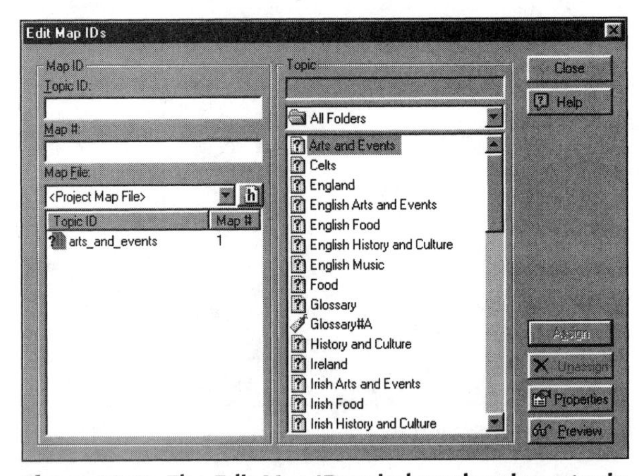

Figure 25-3: The Edit Map IDs window showing a topic associated with context-sensitive mapping information

Note

Depending on the development environment, you may receive the map IDs from the developers in hexadecimal (base 16) rather than decimal. Hexadecimal numbers are preceded with 0x as an identifier. For example, the hexadecimal equivalent of 10 is 0xa and the hexadecimal equivalent of 1000 is 0x3e8. The format for the number is not important; RoboHELP accepts map IDs in either format, although they are displayed on the lower left portion of the window in decimal format exclusively.

Once you've entered the mapping information, you can enter the next alias and map ID by repeating the process. After you enter all the aliases and map IDs, you can compile the help project as usual and then try it out with the program to see if it works. (Detailed information on testing context-sensitive help appears later in this chapter.)

You break a link between an alias and map ID by doing the following:

1. In the lower left corner of the Edit Map IDs window, highlight the topic ID you want to dissociate from a topic.
2. Click Unassign.

RoboHELP dissociates the mapping information from the topic with which it was associated. The topic icon in the list will change from blue to yellow (blue shows that mapping information is linked to a topic; yellow shows that the mapping information is not associated with any topic).

Linking Multiple Map IDs to a Single Topic

The previous section showed you how to create direct links between a single map ID in a program and a single topic. But you will frequently need to link several controls to the same topic; for example, you may have several buttons or fields in a section of a window that are all described in a single topic. Each of the buttons will have a separate map ID, but they all need to go to the same topic. Rather than create multiple identical topics, you can use aliases to aim each of the separate map IDs at a single topic.

For example, suppose that you've made some changes to the way online help is displayed for the Foggan Drizzle program window described in Figure 25-1. Where there was previously one topic for each control, the window's fields are now all covered in a single topic, and the buttons are covered in another topic. You need to link multiple map IDs to a single topic.

To associate multiple map IDs with a topic, do the following:

1. In the Edit Map IDs window, create dummy alias entries for each map ID you want to alias using the same procedure you saw earlier for adding aliases and map IDs manually. (It's a good idea to use a name for the dummy alias that is easy to remember and is clearly not an actual alias such as DUMMY_ALIAS_1.)
2. Associate the dummy aliases to the topic as before. Repeat this process as necessary to associate additional alias entries.

It's worth noting that the aliases in this scenario are just placeholders. They merely provide the other half of the entry so the map IDs have some place to go. The only requirement for HTML Help is that it can accept an initial map ID from the program that then resolves through the various aliases and map IDs to identify a valid topic in the HTML Help project that can be displayed.

You can see which topic IDs and map IDs are associated with any topic at any time by doing the following:

1. Highlight the topic in the Topic List and click Properties. The Alias Properties for Topic window appears (shown in Figure 25-4).

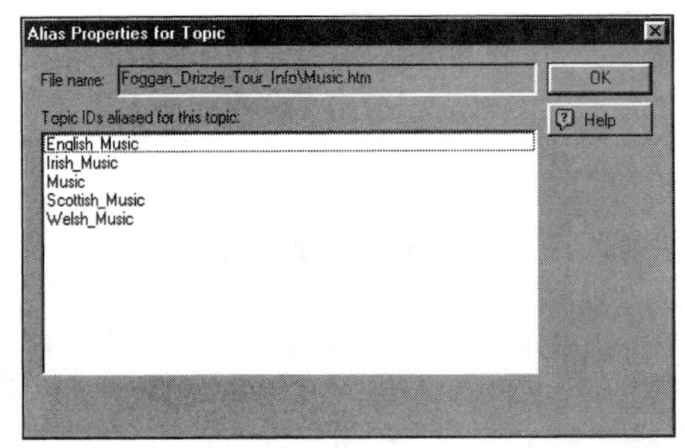

Figure 25-4: The Alias Properties for Topic window

Importing Map Files

Entering aliases and map IDs manually is effective, but it could be slow and cumbersome, particularly if you need to enter several hundred or even several thousand context-sensitive entries. Fortunately, RoboHELP has a way to make this process fast and easy.

Most development projects automatically generate the map IDs as part of the coding process and store the map IDs in a *map file* (also known as a *header file*), usually identified by the extension HH, H, or HM. The map file contains entries for the topics and the map IDs that you can then import into the HTML Help project.

There are several advantages to using map files for adding aliases and map IDs to your HTML Help project. First, you don't have to enter hundreds or even thousands of aliases and map IDs manually through the Edit Map IDs window. In addition, the files will contain all the aliases and map IDs referenced by the program. Perhaps most important, because the developers have created the map file, you can be sure that the map IDs are correct, cutting down on testing and debugging time.

To import a map file to your HTML Help project, do the following:

1. Obtain the map file from the developer and copy it into the project folder, or into the project's map file subfolder if you're using one.
2. Select File ➪ Import ➪ Map File and open the map file in the standard File Open window.

RoboHELP will open the map file and add the aliases and map IDs to the HTML Help project. The map file you've just added will appear in the list of map files appearing in the Context Sensitive Help folder. Once you've imported the map file, you can link the topics in the HTML Help project to the map information, as follows:

1. In the RoboHELP HTML main window, double-click Aliases in the Context Sensitive Help folder. The Edit Map IDs window appears.
2. Select the name of the map file you've just imported from the drop-down list in the Map File field. You can also choose <All Map Files> from the drop-down list to display the mapping information from all the map files in the project, or <Project Map File> to display the mapping information you've entered manually. (Manually entered information is stored in a special map file created by RoboHELP called BSSCDefault.h.) The list of topic IDs and map IDs appears in the lower left corner of the window, as shown in Figure 25-5.

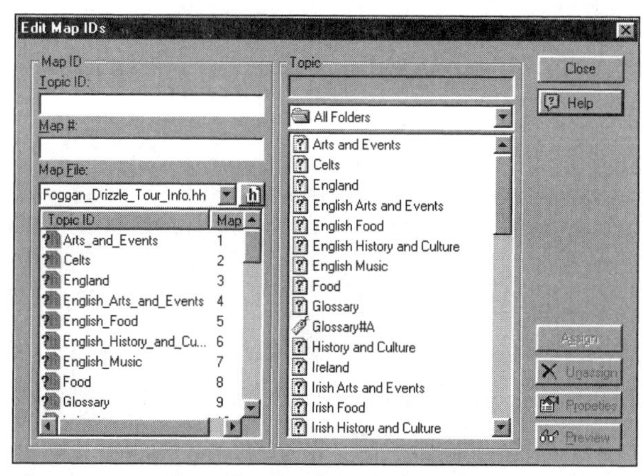

Figure 25-5: The Edit Map IDs window showing map file contents

3. Double-click a topic ID in the map file display. The mapping information will appear in the Topic ID and Map # fields.
4. Highlight a topic in the topic list and click Assign to associate the topic with the mapping information.

You can also import a map file directly from the Edit Map IDs window by doing the following:

1. Click the button to the right of the Map File field on the Edit Map IDs window. The New Map File window appears (shown in Figure 25-6).

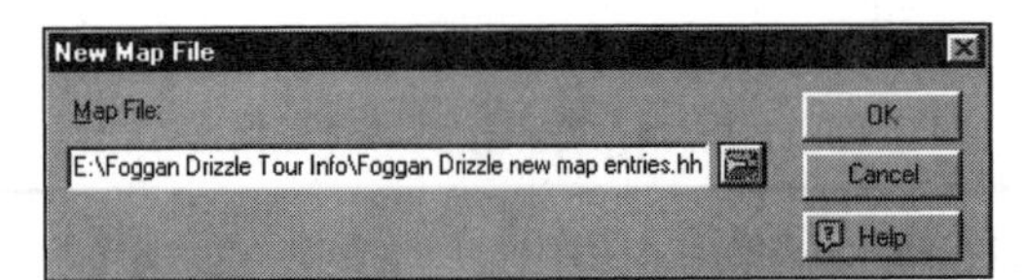

Figure 25-6: The New Map File window

2. Enter the name of the file to import or click the button to the right of the Map File field to browse for a specific file. (You can also create a new map file by entering the name of the file. This is useful if you are creating the CHM file from different modules and want to modularize the map entries to correspond with the help modules.)

Small numbers of changes can be handled manually as described earlier, but large numbers of changes are best handled by re-importing the map file whenever there are significant changes to the map IDs or aliases. If the aliases and map IDs are still in a state of change, you may want to hold off on creating the context-sensitive help.

Removing Unused Aliases

If you have made significant changes to the map files used in a project, you can sometimes end up with unused or "stray" aliases that have no map IDs and no associations. To remove unused aliases from the aliases list, do the following:

1. In the Edit Map IDs window, select <Aliases> from the drop-down list in the Map File field. The list of topic IDs and map IDs appears in the lower left corner of the window. Figure 25-7 shows an unassigned alias, test_id, in the list.
2. Highlight the unused alias (which has a gray icon in the list) and click Unassign. RoboHELP deletes them from the HTML Help project.

The automatic map ID numbering always starts at 1 and increments by one (it's not possible to change this setting), but your choices for map IDs may be dictated by other factors. For example, some development environments automatically establish the map IDs used by the various controls. You also might be adding a new or revamped HTML Help system to an existing program that already has numbers for all the controls. Even if the developers have already assigned map IDs for the controls or you're importing a project into RoboHELP, you can still create a map file to speed up the map IDing process, as follows:

1. Create the map file as described earlier in this section.

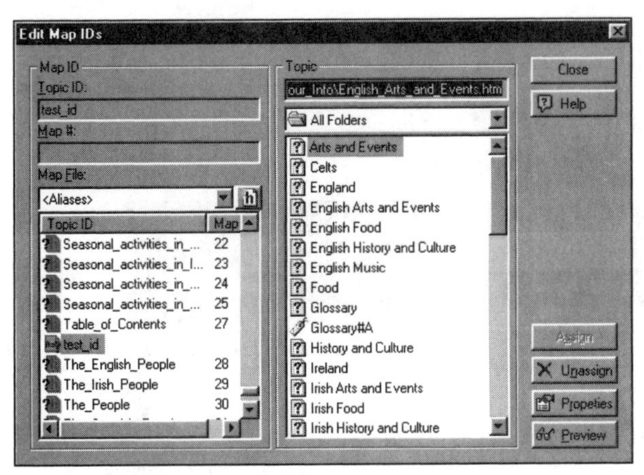

Figure 25-7: A sample unassigned alias

2. Open the .HH file with an editor such as Notepad or WordPad.
3. Change the map IDs as appropriate.

If you're using hexadecimal rather than decimal numbers, be sure that you're entering numbers in the right format.

4. When you are satisfied with your changes, click OK.

By starting with an automatically generated map file, you can be sure that you'll have all the aliases correctly entered in a file. All you need to do is change the map IDs to fit the program.

Generating an Automatic Map ID List

RoboHELP doesn't have a feature for generating map IDs automatically. This can be a nuisance if you're trying to enter mapping information for several hundred topics, but you can work around this by creating your own map file that contains the topics and map IDs in the online help project.

To generate an automatic map ID list, do the following:

1. Select Tools ⇨ Reports ⇨ Topics by Priority to display the Topics by Priority report (not shown). This report lists the names of all the topics in the HTML Help project.

For more information on the Topics by Priority report, see Chapter 24, "Using Reports and Compiling."

2. Save the report to a text file.

3. Open the text file in a text editor (such as Notepad) and delete the report headers, priority categories, and so on, leaving just the topic names. Globally replace spaces with underscores and save the file in text format with an extension of HH, as shown in Figure 25-8.

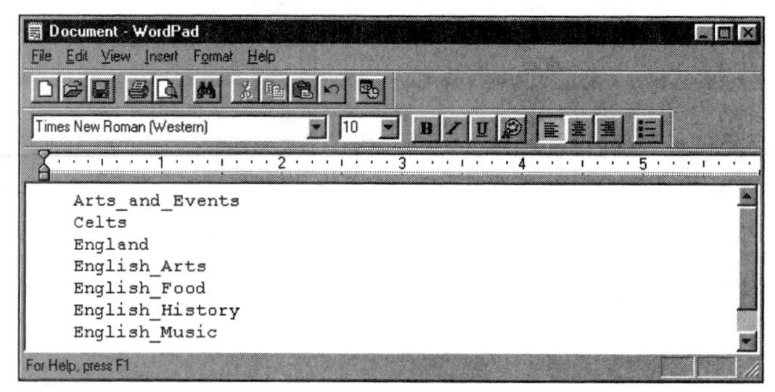

Figure 25-8: Creating a map file manually

4. Edit the HH file to create the map IDs for each different topic. Add #define to the front of each entry and the map ID after the topic ID, as shown in Figure 25-9. (The `#define` that precedes each map ID is a programming language convention that's included in the HH file. This makes it easier for you to use the map file with a number of common programming languages.) Save the HH file in text format.

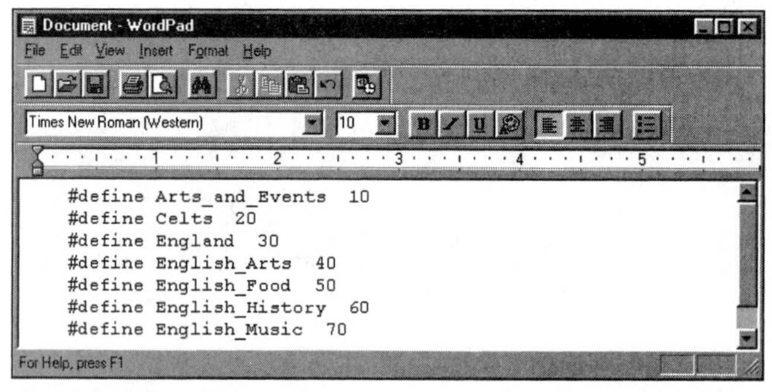

Figure 25-9: Adding #defines and map IDs to the map file

You can also use `#include` statements in the map file to include other files of mapping information in the map file, as shown in Figure 25-10. When the map file is imported, RoboHELP opens the file referenced by the `#include` statement and adds it to the mapping information. You can use `#includes` to modularize the mapping information in a given map file. For example, in Figure 25-10, the map IDs for the basic Foggan Drizzle help info are in one file, the map IDs for the Foggan Drizzle add-on help section are in a second file, and map IDs for common elements (such as Cancel and OK buttons and other standard features of the help) have been broken out into a third file.

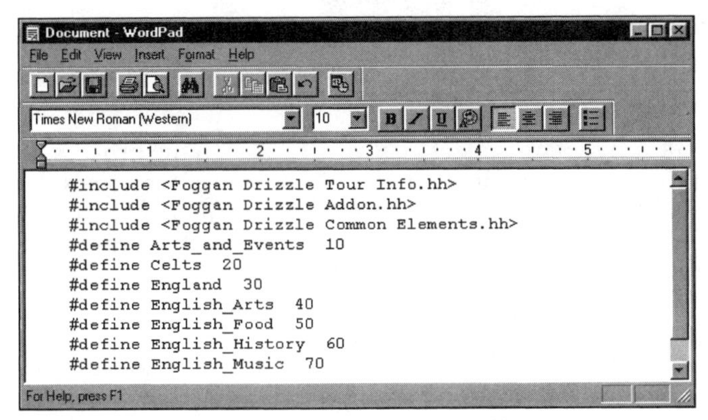

Figure 25-10: Using #includes in the map file

Even when you import a map file, you still have to associate the aliases with the topics in the HTML Help project. Fortunately, you can also create an automatic list to create a list of aliases and associated topics, which can significantly speed up the mapping process.

To create an automatic alias file, you need to first understand a little about aliases. Aliases are stored in the ALI file that accompanies the HTML Help project. RoboHELP creates an alias file for each HTML Help project. The ALI file will have the same name as the CHM file; for example, the Foggan Drizzle files would be Foggan Drizzle Tour Info.CHM and Foggan Drizzle Tour Info.ALI.

You use aliases to associate an alias with a new alias. Alias entries have the form:

```
alias=project directory\new-topic-ID.htm
```

The entry provides a link between the alias that appears on the Edit Map IDs window in the topic ID field and lists and the specific topic file in the HTML Help project. As you associate mapping information with specific topics, RoboHELP adds entries to the ALI file. For example, Figure 25-11 shows a portion of the ALI file for the Foggan Drizzle HTML Help.

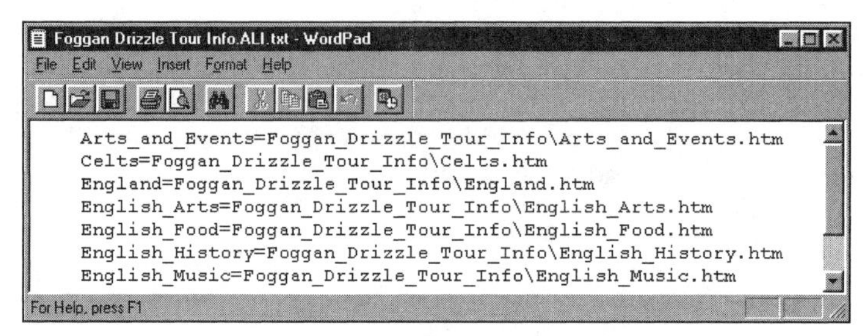

Figure 25-11: Alias entries in the Foggan Drizzle alias file

You can manually edit a copy of the project's ALI file (similar to the process for creating a map ID list) to build a complete set of alias entries for the topics in a file. Then, with the HTML Help project closed, replace the existing ALI file with the modified ALI file. (It's a good idea to make a backup copy of the original ALI file both as a precaution and so you can re-create your original aliases.) The next time you open the project in RoboHELP, you'll see the new aliases.

There are a few caveats to this procedure. Whenever you create automatic map ID lists or alias lists, take care that you use the correct file names and links. Make sure that alias entries in the list have a corresponding map ID number in the map ID list and, for convenience, that the aliases have the same names as the topic files. Finally, creating map IDs and aliases this way requires that you also do extensive checking and testing to verify each link. You can save time, but there are no safeguards on the process.

Testing Context-Sensitive Help

An essential part of creating context-sensitive help is testing the links you've created. The basic testing technique is simply to compile the online help file with the map IDs and then trigger each context-sensitive link in the program in turn. If the links are correct, you'll see the appropriate topic appear each time. This type of testing can be handled easily by a member of the testing team.

However, it's likely that the testers will find *broken links*: controls requesting context-sensitive help in the program that do not display a topic or that display the wrong topic. These broken links will be reported to you by the testers for identification and resolution. The types of broken link you will generally encounter are as follows:

✦ **No topic is found.** In this case, the program is using the wrong map ID. For example, the map ID being called by the program is 2500 but the online help file doesn't have a map ID 2500. You can fix this by changing the online help file and recompiling or by having the developer change the HTML Help call in the program and recompiling.

✦ **The wrong topic is displayed.** This is similar to the previous error: the map ID the program is calling exists in the online help file, but, in this case, the map ID is assigned to the wrong topic. The solution for this is the same: change the information in the online help file or in the program and recompile.

✦ **The help file is not found.** This is caused by having the wrong file name or path being used by the program, having the online help file in the wrong folder, or otherwise not having the online help file available. Change the name or path of the online help file being called by the program or change the name or location of the compiled online help file.

The challenge when identifying problems with context-sensitive help is to determine where the error is happening. To determine if the error is happening in the program or in the online help file, you need to find out what the program is actually telling the online help file to display and also to simulate the program's calls for specific topics. To do this, you'll use a handy tool that's part of RoboHELP called the HTML Help BugHunter.

It's a good idea for bugs reported about the online help to first be reported to the writers. Although many of them will probably be reassigned to the development team, documentation issues tend to get overlooked by the developers when they're fixing bugs; as a result, you may not hear about bugs that aren't fixes for development until it's too late. In addition, you'll probably be able to quickly identify the specific problem and solution for the developer in charge of fixing it.

Using the HTML Help BugHunter

The HTML Help BugHunter is a diagnostic tool that lets you monitor the behind-the-scenes activities of the program and the online help file when you are testing context-sensitive help. With the HTML Help BugHunter, you can monitor the calls from the program to the online help file to see which file and map ID are being called by the program. You can also use the HTML Help BugHunter as if it were the program to call a topic in a file using a map ID you enter.

You can use the HTML Help BugHunter for such tasks as testing the various help buttons in your HTML Help project, displaying a specific topic associated with a map ID, checking aliases, and determining the cause of various context-sensitive errors.

To start the HTML Help BugHunter and monitor the interaction of a program and the associated HTML Help file, do the following:

1. In the RoboHELP HTML main window, select View ➪ Output View to display the output pane at the bottom of the window.

2. Select Tools ➪ Enable BugHunter to start the HTML Help BugHunter. Click the BugHunter tab on the output pane to see the HTML Help BugHunter messages. Figure 25-12 shows the HTML Help main window immediately after starting the HTML Help BugHunter.

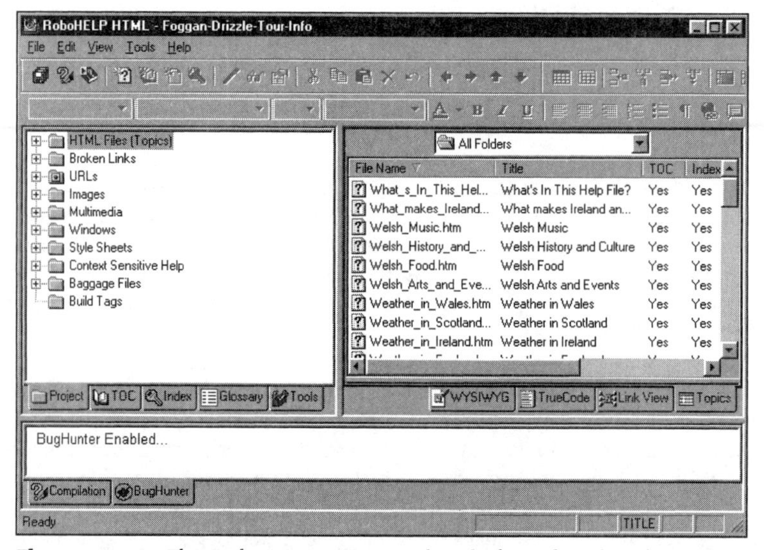

Figure 25-12: The RoboHELP HTML main window showing the HTML Help BugHunter started

3. Run the application and trigger context-sensitive help for a topic you want to check. The HTML Help BugHunter will display the calls from the program to the HTML Help file on the window as well as routines that the HTML Help viewer will process as it opens the file and runs macros. (The information may scroll by quickly, but you can scroll down through it and examine it.) Figure 25-13 shows typical information from the HTML Help BugHunter window for a sample application linked to an HTML Help file. As you can see, HTML Help BugHunter captures the following information for a help call:

   - **CHM File Name:** The name of the HTML Help file being called by the application.
   - **Topic:** The topic called by the application. (This is the topic referred to by the alias in the HTML Help project and the associated map ID. This may not be the correct topic but simply the topic associated with the map ID.)
   - **Command:** The HTML Help API command sent to the HTML Help file.
   - **Map number:** The map ID issued by the application.

- **Result:** The result of the call to the HTML Help file. The message shown in Figure 25-13 ("Topic launched") shows that an alias was associated with the map ID and that the help topic associated with the alias has been displayed. (This doesn't mean that the topic displayed is necessarily the correct topic, simply that there was an associated HTML Help topic that could be displayed.)

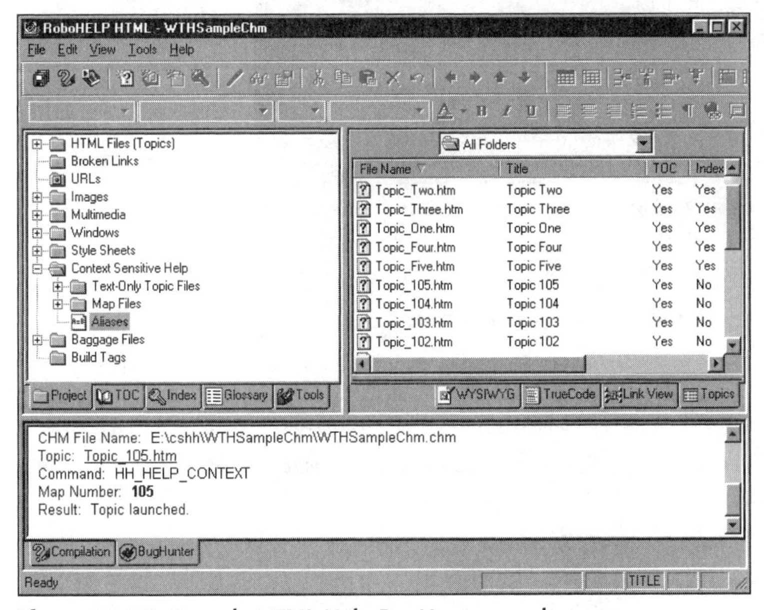

Figure 25-13: Sample HTML Help BugHunter results

4. As you access the HTML Help file from the program or within the HTML Help file itself, the HTML Help BugHunter logs the HTML Help activity. You can save the results in the HTML Help BugHunter window to a text file at any time by selecting File ➪ Save BugHunter Output. If you want to add comments on the conditions you were testing, position the cursor where you want the text to appear and right-click, and then select Annotation from the popup menu. You can also clear the window with Edit ➪ Clear All.

5. When you're done, you can stop monitoring HTML Help activity by selecting Tools ➪ Enable BugHunter again.

You can set several options in the HTML Help BugHunter, as follows:

1. Select Tools ➪ Options. The Options window appears. Select the BugHunter tab. Figure 25-14 shows the BugHunter tab on the Options window. (You can also display the BugHunter tab on the Options window by right-clicking in the BugHunter window and selecting Options from the popup menu.)

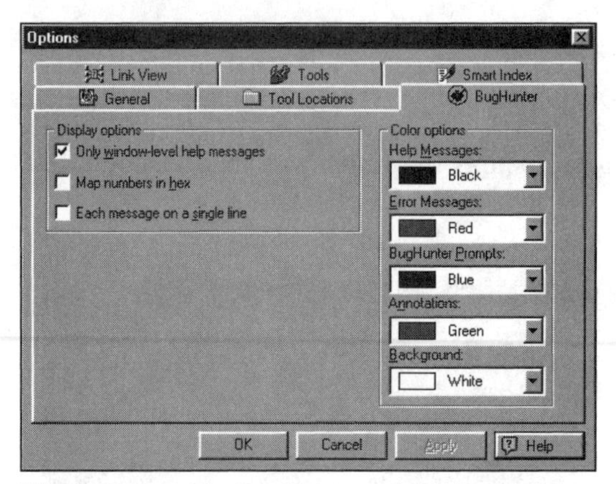

Figure 25-14: The BugHunter tab in the Options window

2. Enter information in the fields as follows:
   - **Only window-level help messages:** Check this box (the default) to display information about window-level messages. (Uncheck this box if you are testing What's This? help.)
   - **Map numbers in hex:** Check this box to view map IDs in hexadecimal rather than in decimal notation.
   - **Each message on a single line:** Check this box to display the information on a single line, which is more compact if you are testing a number of HTML Help calls. Clearing this box (the default) will display information on multiple lines with prompts, which is easier to read if you're not familiar with the HTML Help BugHunter or you are just testing a few items.
   - **Color options:** Use these fields to change the colors used for help messages, error messages, BugHunter prompts, annotations, and the message background.
3. When you are satisfied with your changes, click OK.

The Map IDs and Duplicate Map IDs reports are extremely useful debugging tools. The Map IDs report shows the map IDs and associated information for each topic in the HTML Help project. The Duplicate Map IDs report identifies any duplicate map IDs (duplicate map IDs will happen most frequently when you import map files). For more information on generating both reports, see Chapter 24, "Using Reports and Compiling."

Debugging broken and incorrect links in context-sensitive help can be complex, frustrating, and laborious. By using the HTML Help BugHunter, you can quickly isolate problems and determine if the program is calling the wrong topic or if the HTML Help file is mismapped.

Understanding What's This? Help

In the first part of this chapter, you saw how to create context-sensitive help at the window level for the various controls in a program using context-sensitive IDs. As you saw, the process for creating context-sensitive help can be complex.

There's another, faster way to create basic context-sensitive help for many of the controls on your program's windows and dialog boxes. RoboHELP provides What's This? Help Composer to create context-sensitive What's This? help.

What's This? help provides quick popup help for individual options and controls in an application. Figure 25-15 shows a sample of What's This? help for an application.

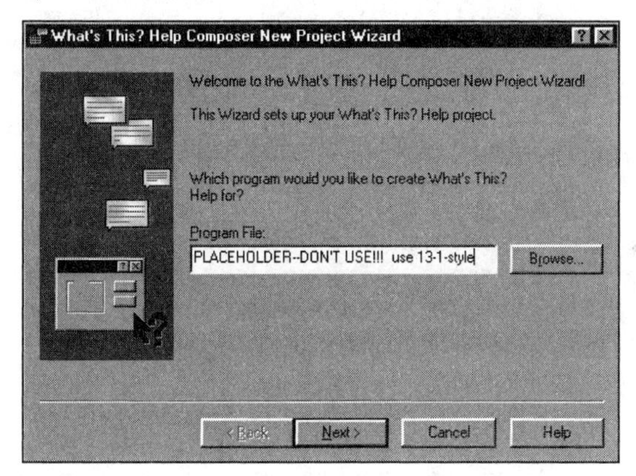

Figure 25-15: Sample of What's This? help

Users can start What's This? help in several different ways:

✦ Click the question mark in the upper right corner of a window to change the mouse pointer to a question mark pointer, and then click an item on the window.

✦ Position the mouse pointer on an item on the window and press F1 on the keyboard.

✦ Right-click an item on the window and then select What's This? from the popup menu.

The options for starting What's This? help in a program will depend on the way the program has been designed and which options are enabled. You'll need to talk to the developers to find out what will start What's This? help in the program with which you're working.

How What's This? Help Composer Works

You can use What's This? Help Composer to create help for the following file types:

- C or C++ program files (EXE)
- Dynamic Link Libraries (DLL)
- ActiveX Controls (OCX)

When you start a new What's This? help project, What's This? Help Composer examines the program file for dialog box controls and uses this information to generate a text file of information, with a topic with suggested text for each control in the dialog boxes. It then creates the TXT file each time you compile the project. You can create What's This? help projects that are stand-alone, with only the What's This? help, or you can link What's This? help to an existing HTML Help project in RoboHELP.

The general process for creating What's This? help is as follows:

1. The developers create a program.
2. The help author accesses the developer's source control system and checks out the program files, uses What's This? Help Composer to create the initial What's This? help files, and then checks the program files back in so that they can be incorporated. (The developers need to pause working on the files while the What's This? help files are being created.)
3. The help author works on the help files, testing and compiling the What's This? help and refining the text for the various controls.
4. The help author sends the completed help files back to the developers for incorporation into the program.

Coordinating Your Efforts

As with other types of context-sensitive help, it's important that the help author and the developers work together to create effective What's This? help. The timing for handoffs of files is important; for example, if the developers change the program files while the help author is working on the initial What's This? help before they've been checked back in and incorporated into the program code, any changes to the program will cause What's This? Help Composer to treat the revised program as new, and it will wipe out the changes and start over.

During the program development process, the developers should provide frequent program updates to the help author. (If the developers store the program files on a shared network drive that you also use as the program source for the What's This? help project, then What's This? Help Composer will automatically update the What's This? help project every time you open it.) The developers can also make the What's This? help development process easier by letting you know if the program contains any dynamic dialog boxes, custom class dialog boxes, unused dialog boxes, or dynamic controls in the application and, if so, where they can be found. In addition, the programmers can set a tab order for the controls in the dialog boxes and link controls where appropriate.

Advantages and Disadvantages of What's This? Help

The biggest advantage of using What's This? Help Composer is that it creates online help for you with minimum effort: you don't need to worry about matching aliases and map IDs with HTML topics. What's This? Help Composer lets you work directly with the program's dialog boxes in a dialog box editor, which makes it unnecessary to take screen shots when writing text for the various topics. It also provides a variety of tools for examining the dialog box controls, testing and editing the What's This? help, and printing help status reports. In addition to the advantages to the help author, using What's This? Help Composer can save time for the developers as well. They can call the What's This? Help Composer DLL to generate context-sensitive help instead of having to add code for the controls in the dialog box.

However, despite its simplicity, there are a few disadvantages to What's This? help. One of the biggest disadvantages is that, unlike standard online help, What's This? help is usually a brief description of the feature displayed in a popup window. Also, because it is directly linked to controls in the program, you can't have What's This? help topics that are background or descriptive topics. What's This? help topics are also stand-alone; they don't link to other topics. Furthermore, the What's This? help requires a certain amount of standardization on the part of the developers. The program's source code must use any of a wide range of standard dialog box features, as What's This? Help Composer may not be able to see or identify certain types of custom-coded windows. Finally, you can create What's This? help only for windows that are based on the Cdialog class. If you want to create What's This? help for other windows or for applications that are not written in C or C++, you'll need to use the HTML Help API to directly access and display the What's This? help information.

You can create What's This? help as a stand-alone online help system for quick context-sensitive help for dialog boxes, or you can add What's This? help to an existing RoboHELP HTML Help file and use the two forms of online help in conjunction.

Starting a What's This? Help Project

Creating What's This? help is fairly simple. To create What's This? help, do the following:

1. Open an HTML Help project.

Although What's This? help must be linked to an open HTML Help project, you can create a stand-alone What's This? help file by creating an empty HTML Help project, creating the What's This? help, and compiling the HTML Help project.

2. Select File ➪ New ➪ What's This? Help Project. The first time you do this, What's This? Help Composer starts a project wizard to set up the new project. The first What's This? Help Composer project wizard window is shown in Figure 25-16.

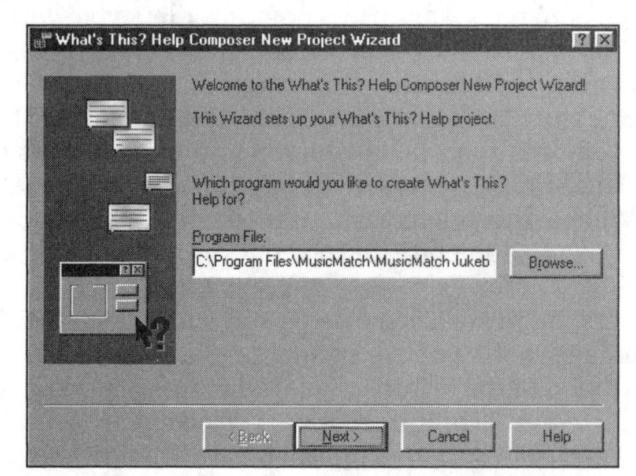

Figure 25-16: The first What's This? Help Composer project wizard window

3. Enter the name of the program for which you want to create What's This? help. You can browse for a program by clicking the button to the right of the Program File field. When you are satisfied with your entries, click Next. The second What's This? Help Composer project wizard window appears (as shown in Figure 25-17).

This example demonstrates creating What's This? help for MusicMatch Jukebox, an excellent all-in-one MP3 player and recorder available at `www.musicmatch.com`.

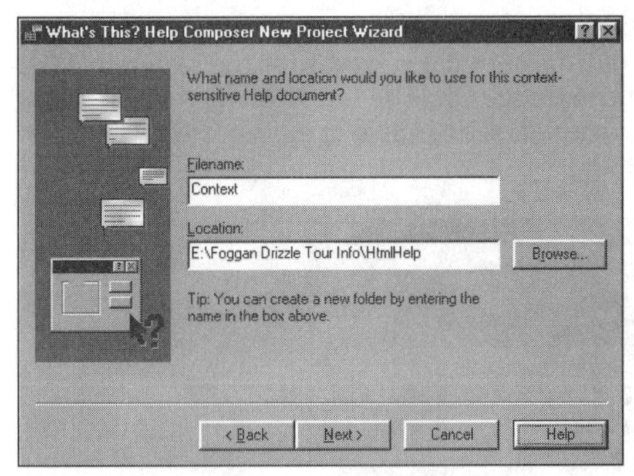

Figure 25-17: The second What's This? Help Composer project wizard window

4. Enter information in the fields as follows:
   - **Filename:** Enter the file name for the What's This? help file. (The default entry is Context.)
   - **Location:** Enter the folder to use for the What's This? help.
5. When you are satisfied with your entries, click OK. The third What's This? Help Composer project wizard window appears (shown in Figure 25-18).

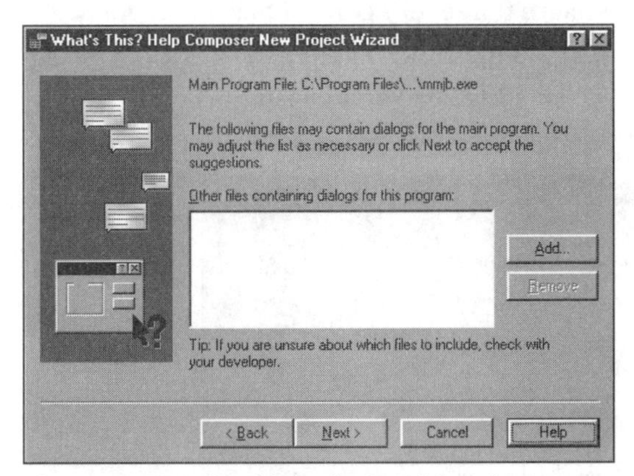

Figure 25-18: The third What's This? Help Composer project wizard window

6. Add or remove the names of any additional files (subprograms, DLLs, and so on) that contain controls and dialog boxes for the program. When you are satisfied with your entries, click OK. The fourth What's This? Help Composer project wizard window appears, as shown in Figure 25-19.

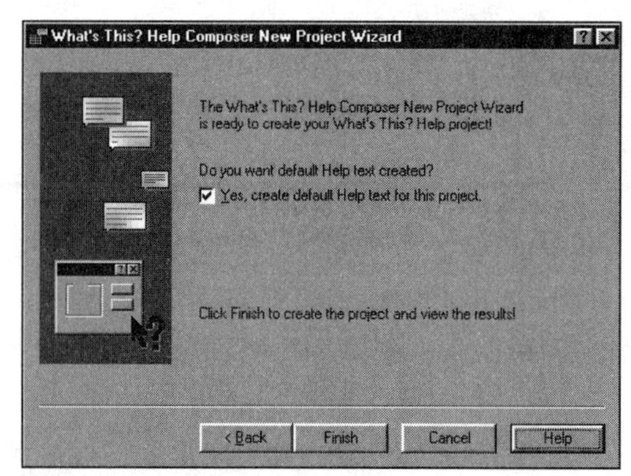

Figure 25-19: The fourth What's This? Help Composer project wizard window

7. Check the box if you want What's This? Help Composer to create default help text for the project. Although the box is not checked as the default option, it's a good idea to check this. Even if you're going to create custom entries for all the controls, this will ensure that every control has a text entry.

8. Click Finish to generate the What's This? help files. Figure 25-20 shows What's This? Help Composer Project Results summary report.

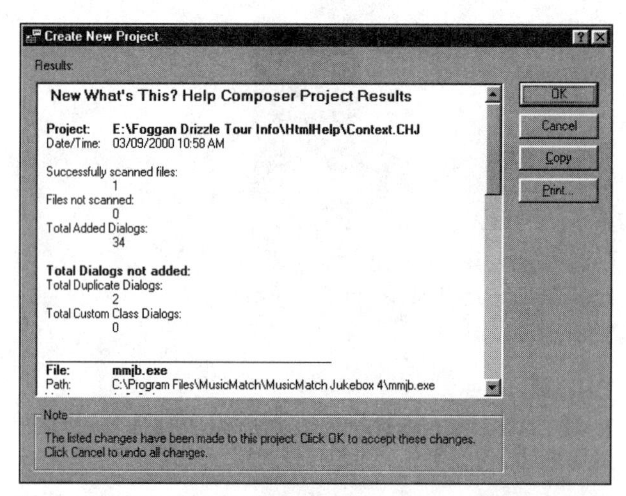

Figure 25-20: What's This? Help Composer Project Results summary report

The Project Results summary report lists extensive information about the What's This? help you're creating, including such things as:

- ✦ The path and name of the project file (CHJ)
- ✦ The number of files What's This? Help Composer scanned and did not scan (Note that 16-bit files and files with dialog boxes will not be scanned.)
- ✦ The number of dialog boxes that have changed and the number of dialog boxes added to and removed from the What's This? help project
- ✦ The number of dialog boxes that were not added to the What's This? help project because they are duplicates or because they are coded as a custom class (You'll need to create What's This? help manually for dialog boxes coded with a custom class.)

The report also shows information for each that file you've selected to scan, including:

- ✦ The path and name of the file
- ✦ The version number (if applicable)
- ✦ The file date and time
- ✦ Any comments about the file
- ✦ The dialog boxes that have been added, changed, or removed since the last time you scanned the file
- ✦ Any dialog boxes that weren't added because they're duplicates or coded as a custom class

Note

What's This? Help Composer generates a report when you create the What's This? help project and when you update and recompile the files. It's a good idea to print a copy of this report each time it's generated and save it for an audit trail and for subsequent maintenance.

At this point, What's This? Help Composer has created context-sensitive entries for each of the controls in the dialog boxes. The new What's This? help project contents appear in What's This? Help Composer (shown in Figure 25-21).

As you can see from Figure 25-21, What's This? Help Composer lists the program (in this case, MMJB.EXE) and any additional files and all the dialog boxes in the program along with the additional files by their assigned names. In the sample dialog box shown, What's This? Help Composer has identified each of the buttons, fields, and controls on the dialog box and assigned a brief default text description to each of them. The OK button highlighted in Figure 25-21 has a default text entry of "Closes this dialog and saves any changes you have made."

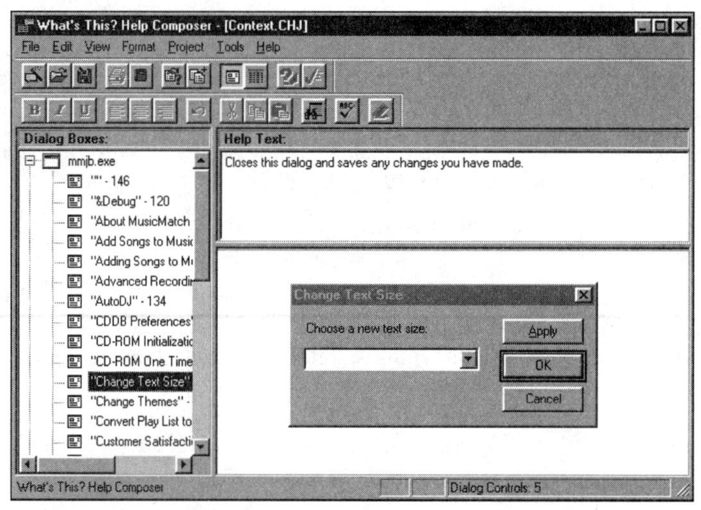

Figure 25-21: What's This? Help Composer with a new project

You can examine each of the controls and areas on the dialog box by clicking the area on the dialog box in the dialog box editor window. (The display in the status bar shows that What's This? Help Composer has identified five controls.) By highlighting the various areas on the window, you can see the default text. For example, the Cancel button has a default text entry of "Closes this dialog without saving any changes you have made" and the Apply button has a default text entry of "Click this button to make your choice." Similarly, when you highlight the field with the drop-down list, the default text is "Choose an item from the list."

When What's This? Help Composer creates a new What's This? help project, it creates a number of project files, as described in Table 25-1.

Table 25-1
What's This? Help Project Files

Extension	*Description*
CDX	One of the What's This? help database indexing files.
CHJ	The What's This? help project file, which contains project settings and other information.
CID	The context-sensitive ID file. This contains the links for the dialog box controls and the topic IDs in the What's This? help file. When you compile the What's This? help project file, it is stored as baggage in the compiled help file.

Extension	*Description*
CSS	The cascading style sheet for the What's This? help files.
DBF	The What's This? help database file.
DTO	The default topic information. This information appears in the default topic if you open the What's This? help file as a standard WinHelp file.
FPT	One of the What's This? help database indexing files.
H	The What's This? help map file. (The What's This? help HH file is maintained by What's This? Help Composer. It is not the same as a standard WinHelp HH file.)
TXT	The source file for the What's This? help. The RTF file is created when you compile the What's This? help project.

When you compile the What's This? help project, the information in the TXT file is included in the HTML Help project's CHM file. As with window-level context-sensitive help, the program issues a call to the HTML Help API, which in turn looks up the What's This? help topic in an internal look-up table and then displays the topic. You can have one TXT file for each map file in the HTML Help project.

Modifying the Default Text Entries

The default text entries in What's This? Help Composer are pretty useful and will fit most of the generic controls for programs. However, if you have specific application requirements, you can modify the default text entries for each category of control through the Windows Registry, as follows.

Editing the Registry can damage your computer to the point where you need to reinstall Windows and your applications. It is strongly advisable to make a backup copy of your Registry before making any changes to the Registry.

1. Start the Registry Editor (REGEDIT.EXE, located in your system's Windows folder).
2. Go to the \Hkey_Current_User\Software\Blue Sky Software\What's This? Help Composer\1.00\Default Text registry key. Figure 25-22 shows the Registry Editor with the information for this registry key displayed.
3. Double-click the entry that you want to change. Edit the text for the entry and click OK.
4. Select Registry ⇨ Exit. The Registry Editor saves your changes. (You may need to restart your computer for the changes to take effect.)

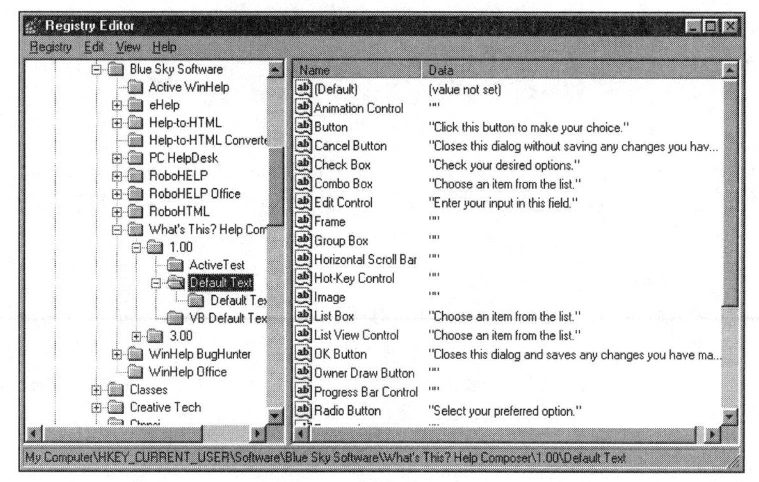

Figure 25-22: The Registry Editor displaying the default text entries

Modifying Individual Text Entries

In many cases, the default text entries for items such as OK and Cancel buttons will be just fine for your program. However, the default entries for individual items that are more complex or specific to the application (such as radio buttons and drop-down lists) will require editing to make them apply to the specific control on the dialog box.

To edit the text for a single context-sensitive help entry, do the following:

1. Select the dialog box you want to edit from the list on the left side of What's This? Help Composer window.
2. In the dialog box editor window, highlight the control you want to edit.
3. Edit the text in the Help Text window. The standard text editing commands are available on the Edit menu. You can also use the buttons on the formatting toolbar to add character attributes such as bold, italic, and underline, and paragraph attributes such as text justification, and so on.

You can change the font for all entries in the What's This? help file by selecting Format ➪ Project Help Text Font. This is a global change.

4. If the dialog box has a More button or is otherwise expandable, you can display the expanded version of the dialog box by selecting View ➪ Expand Dialog.
5. You can optionally add a graphic by clicking the Graphics button (shown in Figure 25-23) and selecting a graphic to insert from a standard graphic window.

Figure 25-23: Graphics button

6. You can spell check the text by clicking the Spell check button shown in Figure 25-24. The Project Spell Check window appears (as shown in Figure 25-25). You can check the spelling for this control, all the controls in the dialog box, or throughout the entire What's This? help file (the default selection). Click OK to start spell-checking.

Figure 25-24: Spell check button

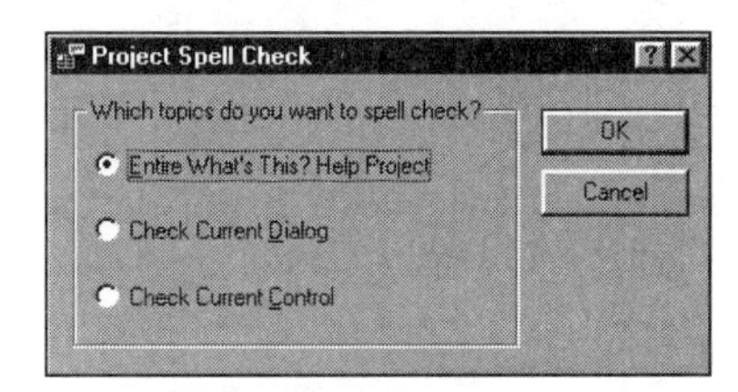

Figure 25-25: The Project Spell Check window

7. When you are satisfied with your changes, click OK. You can continue making changes to specific What's This? help entries. To save your changes, select File ➪ Save. You can compile the file by clicking the Generate Files button (shown in Figure 25-26) on the standard toolbar.

Figure 25-26: Generate Files button

Here are some tips for editing topic text:

✦ You can use the graphic insertion feature to create bulleted lists by inserting a bullet bitmap from the standard RoboHELP Clipart files, as described in Chapter 20, "Creating and Adding Graphics."

✦ To create a numbered list, just type the numbers into the list where you want them to appear.

✦ If you delete all the topic text, What's This? Help Composer will delete the topic from the file and will not display a What's This? help topic. (Users trying to display What's This? help will see a message that says "No Help topic associated with this item.")

Using Control View

If you're editing several entries, you may prefer to switch from Dialog View (the default display mode) to Control View, as follows:

✦ Select View ➪ Control View, or simply click the Control View button (shown in Figure 25-27) on the standard toolbar. Figure 25-28 shows What's This? Help Composer window shown in Figure 25-21 in Control View.

Figure 25-27: Control View button

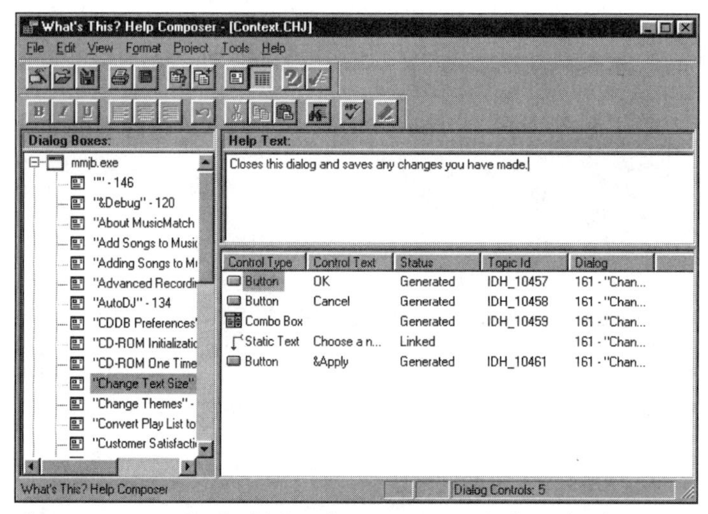

Figure 25-28: What's This? Help Composer window displaying Control View

Control View has a number of advantages. You can view all the controls for the dialog box, the topic status, and the topic ID.

The topic status is very useful when tracking changes. When What's This? Help Composer first generates the topic, the default status for topics is "Generated." Once you edit a topic, the status changes to "In Progress." There are two other status conditions that you can set manually: For Review and Complete.

You can change the status of a topic between any of these three conditions as follows:

✦ Highlight the control that you want to change the status of and select the appropriate status option from the Edit menu. You can also press Ctrl+1, Ctrl+2, or Ctrl+3 as keyboard shortcuts for In Progress, For Review, and Complete, respectively. As an alternative, you can right-click the control you want to change the status of and then select the status from the popup menu.

To change the status for all the topics in a dialog box, do the following:

✦ Right-click the dialog box you want to change and select Set Dialog Status from the popup menu.

By changing the status to reflect the editing status of the controls, you can track the status of the controls using the What's This? help reports described later in this chapter. As an interim technique, if all the controls in a dialog box have a status of "Completed," the dialog box icon in the Dialog Box list turns blue, making it easy to identify dialog boxes that have not been completely edited.

Linked controls always have a status of Linked. In Figure 25-28, the static information is also coded as a control and has a status of "Linked." The arrow in the example shows the control to which the static information is linked. You don't need to write text for linked controls as What's This Help Composer will display the text for the control to which it is linked. (You can suppress the display of linked controls by selecting View ➪ Linked Controls.)

Press Ctrl+Up and Ctrl+Dn to navigate to the previous and next controls in the dialog box. When you highlight a control on the Control View, the associated text appears in the Help Text display. You can also press Ctrl+PgUp and Ctrl+PgDn to navigate to the previous and next dialog boxes. To change the sort order for the displayed items, click the column header.

Another thing that's visible in the Control View display is the type of control. Table 25-2 shows the icons for each of the controls and the descriptions. Knowing the type of control can be helpful when testing and debugging What's This? help and also when interacting with the developers.

Table 25-2
Control View Icons

Icon	*Type*	*Description*
	Button	A button is a control that does something when clicked, such as OK and Cancel buttons.
	Check box	A check box lets the users select an option. If there is a group of check boxes, the users can select multiple options.
	Combo box	A combo box is similar to a list box in that it contains a drop-down list of selectable items; however, the users can select from the drop-down list or type in an entry.

Continued

Table 25-2 (continued)

Icon	Type	Description
ab|	Edit control	An edit control is a box in which the user can enter multiple lines of text (such as a comment). Edit controls will frequently also have scroll bars and other features.
	Frame	A frame is a box that encloses two or more related controls, such as check boxes or radio buttons, to show a relationship. As with group boxes, frames are frequently linked to the first control in the group they contain and, as a consequence, do not need to have their own descriptive text.
XYZ	Group box	A group box contains two or more related controls, such as check boxes or radio buttons. Group boxes are frequently linked to the first control in the group they contain and, as a consequence, do not need to have their own descriptive text.
	Horizontal scroll bar	A horizontal scroll bar is a control that lets the users move the contents of the window horizontally (left and right).
	Image	An image is a type of graphical control that displays a picture.
	List box	A list box contains a drop-down list of selectable items. Items can be selected from the list, but the user cannot type a selection.
	List view control	A list view control is a display window that displays a list of items the users can select. Items can be selected from the list but the user cannot type a selection.
	Owner draw button	An owner draw button is a type of button that the program creates on the fly when the program runs.
	Progress bar control	A progress bar control is a control in the status bar that shows the progress of an operation.
	Radio button	A radio button is a control that lets the users to select an option to use. If there is a group of radio buttons, the users can select only one option.
	Rectangle	A rectangle is a type of control that specifies an area of a dialog box. Common examples of rectangles are scrolling or formatting areas.

Icon	Type	Description
	Slider control	A slider control is a control that is moved left and right or up and down to change the value being controlled. The most common example of a slider control are the sliders used to change the sound volume on the Window Play Control window.
Aa	Static text	Static text is descriptive text that appears on the dialog box, usually as a description or label for a field or button. Static text is frequently linked to the control it describes. Static text cannot be changed by the user.
	Tab control	A tab control is a control with two or more tabs. When a tab is selected, the corresponding folder appears.
	Tree view control	A tree view control is a control that lists information in a tree view (such as the list of dialog boxes in What's This? Help Composer).
	Vertical scroll bar	A vertical scroll bar is a control that lets the users move the contents of the window vertically (up and down).

Deleting a What's This? Help Project

To remove What's This? help from an HTML Help project, do the following:

1. In the RoboHELP HTML main window, double-click Text-Only Topic Files in the Context Sensitive Help folder.
2. Right-click the CONTEXT.TXT file (or the TXT file if you're using a different name) and select Delete from the popup menu. (This also deletes the DIALOG.CID file from the Baggage Files section.)

You can't undo this kind of deletion. If you delete a What's This? Help project from your HTML Help project and then change your mind, you'll have to re-add the What's This? Help project.

You may want to delete What's This? help from the HTML Help project and then add it again later. For example, when you're testing your help, the What's This? help file can increase the compile time. By separating the What's This? help from the HTML Help project, you can also test the two types of help separately.

Importing What's This? Help Projects

If you already have a What's This? Help project, you can import it to an existing HTML Help project, as follows:

1. Open the HTML Help project in RoboHELP HTML. (You can have only one What's This? Help project associated with an HTML Help project, so this HTML Help project can't already have What's This? help.)
2. Select File ➪ Import ➪ What's This? Help Project.
3. Open the CHJ file for the What's This? Help that you want to import from the standard file dialog box.

One way in which you could use this feature is during HTML Help testing. You could move or rename the various What's This? help files and DIALOG.CID file so that they aren't visible to the HTML Help project, and then import the What's This? help later to add the What's This? help to the HTML Help project at a later time. This would let you test just the HTML Help before the What's This? help is completed or before the What's This? Help code has been added to the software.

Creating and Editing What's This? Help Manually

You can create What's This? help topic files manually, as follows:

1. In the RoboHELP HTML main window, right-click Text-Only Topic Files in the Context Sensitive Help folder, and then select Create/Import Text-Only Topic File from the popup menu.
2. Enter the name for the new TXT file in the standard file creation dialog box and click OK. The Context-Sensitive Text-Only Topics window appears (shown in Figure 25-29).

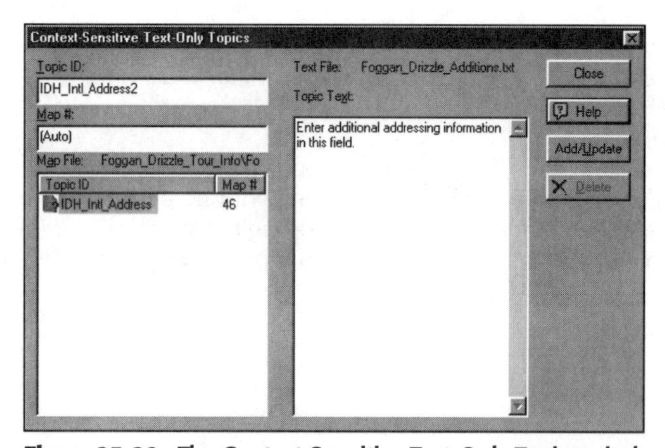

Figure 25-29: The Context-Sensitive Text-Only Topics window

3. Enter information a topic ID and map # as you did before on the Edit Map IDs window shown in Figure 25-1 and enter the topic text for the item in the Topic Text field on the right side of the window.
4. When you are satisfied with your entries, click Add/Update. The new entry appears in the list on the lower left portion of the window.

You can also use the Context-Sensitive Text-Only Topics window to directly edit What's This? help entries in TXT files, as follows:

1. In the RoboHELP HTML main window, double-click Text-Only Topic Files in the Context Sensitive Help folder, and then right-click the TXT file you want to edit and select Edit from the popup menu. The Context-Sensitive Text-Only Topics window appears.
2. You can add new information as before. You can also edit existing entries by highlighting an entry in the list, editing the text as desired, and then clicking Add/Update.

The What's This? help topics and the HTML Help topics are stored separately. As a result, you may need to maintain duplicate information in both sets of topics.

If you have a lot of entries, you can speed up the entry of topic IDs and map IDs by opening the CONTEXT.H file in an editor such as Notepad and then copying and pasting the appropriate information from the map file you received from the developer. You'll then need to enter the topic text, either through the Context-Sensitive Text-Only Topics window or by editing the TXT file directly. (This will also let you make a global change or addition to the topic text quickly and easily.)

To edit the What's This? help TXT file, do the following:

1. Open the What's This? help TXT file in an editor such as Notepad. (Make sure the What's This? help project is closed.) Figure 25-30 shows a portion of a sample CONTEXT.TXT file.

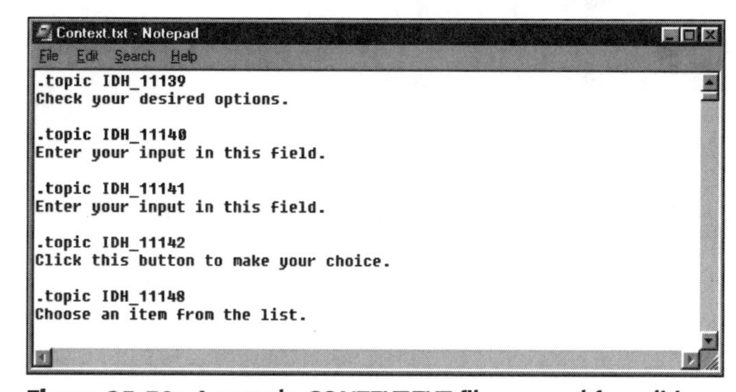

Figure 25-30: A sample CONTEXT.TXT file opened for editing

2. Make any changes to the text you wish. You can add topics to the list by adding a .topic line followed by a line of text for the What's This? help item. You can also delete a topic by deleting the .topic line and the associated help text.

3. When you are satisfied with your changes, click OK.

Compiling and Testing What's This? Help

When you have made all your changes, you're ready to compile and test the What's This? help file.

Configuring What's This? Help Composer

The first time you compile a What's This? help project, you'll need to make sure that your configuration and compiler options are correct, as follows:

1. Select Project ➪ Configuration. The Configuration window appears (shown in Figure 25-31).

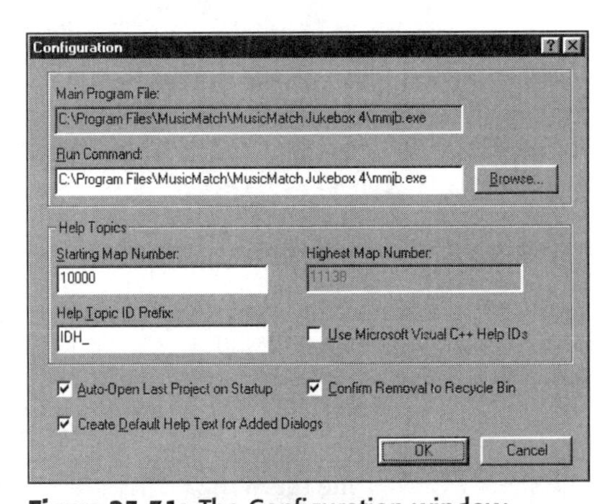

Figure 25-31: The Configuration window

2. Enter information in the fields as follows:

   - **Main Program File:** This display-only field shows the path and filename for the main program file for which you're creating What's This? help.
   - **Run Command:** Enter the path and filename for the command to run the program file for which you're creating What's This? help. This is usually the same as the entry in Main Program File, but you might also add parameters for specific files or runtime options.

- **Starting Map Number:** If you're creating What's This? help for a C or C++ program, you can enter the starting map number (context-sensitive ID) that What's This? Help Composer assigns to the topics. The map numbers are maintained internally (although you can change them if you need to), so all you have to do is make sure that the map numbers used in What's This? Help Composer don't conflict with the map numbers used when you're creating context-sensitive help in the main RoboHELP project. The highest map number used appears in the display-only Highest Map Number field to the right of this field.
- **Help Topic ID Prefix:** Enter the help topic prefix for What's This? Help Composer to use when creating help topics. The default is IDH_.
- **Use Microsoft Visual C++ Help IDs:** Check this box to use the existing Microsoft Visual C++ help IDs instead of the map IDs created by What's This Help Composer.

This option may cause duplicate ID errors because the IDs in the Visual C++ help file aren't verified.

- **Auto-Open Last Project on Startup:** Check this box to automatically open the last What's This? help project you were working. (This box is checked by default.)
- **Create Default Help Text for Added Dialogs:** Check this box to have What's This? Help Composer automatically generate default help text when you're creating or updating the What's This? help project. (This box is checked by default.)
- **Confirm Removal to Recycle Bin:** Check this box to confirm removal of a dialog box or control to What's This? Help Composer recycle bin.

3. When you are satisfied with your entries, click OK.

Compiling the What's This? Help Project

Once you've configured What's This? Help Composer and set the compiler options you need for this project, you're ready to compile the What's This? help project.

To compile a What's This? help project, do the following:

✦ In What's This? Help Composer, select File ➪ Generate HTML Files or simply click the Generate Files button on the toolbar. What's This? Help Composer will generate the HTML files.

It's not necessary to save the What's This? help project as you must when you are compiling standard WinHelp projects in RoboHELP. What's This? Help Composer automatically saves the information as you work on the file in What's This? Help Composer and creates the RTF file each time you compile the What's This? help project.

Testing the What's This? Help Project

You can use the HTML Help BugHunter (described earlier in this chapter) to test the What's This? help. Start the HTML Help BugHunter as normal and run the associated application. When testing What's This? help, be sure to uncheck the Only window-level help messages box in the BugHunter tab in the Options window shown earlier in Figure 25-14.

Updating a What's This? Help Project

If you're creating What's This? help for a program that is being developed at the same time, you will periodically need to update the What's This? help to add the new controls and dialog boxes. For example, suppose that you've just received a new copy of the program from the developers. To update the information in the What's This? help project, do the following:

1. Install the new version of the program in the same folder on your system (making sure to completely replace the previous version of the program files) and open the What's This? help project in What's This? Help Composer. What's This? Help Composer examines the program when it loads the What's This? help project's database. When What's This? Help Composer sees changes to the file, it displays the message shown in Figure 25-32.

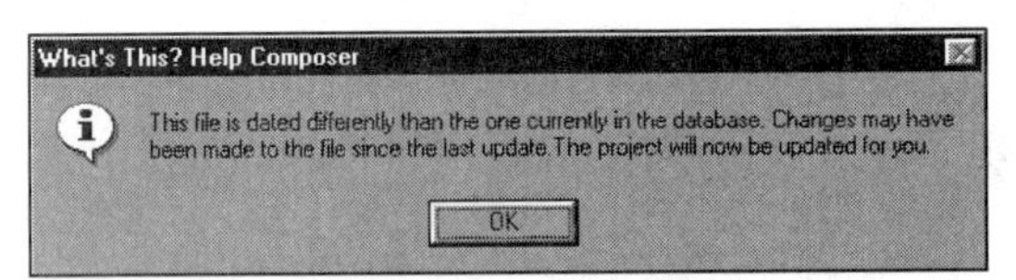

Figure 25-32: Message showing that the program files have changed

2. When you click OK on the message, What's This? Help Composer displays the Update Project window, shown in Figure 25-33.
3. Select the file or files to scan for updated dialog boxes. (You can click Select All on the right side of the windowto select all the files.) When you are satisfied with your entries, click Update to start updating the What's This? help project. What's This? Help Composer scans the selected files for new or updated dialog boxes and then generates a report of the changes, as shown in Figure 25-34.

Note

If you want to work with a specific version of the files, unchecking the box at the bottom of the Update Project window will prevent What's This? Help Composer from reminding you to update the What's This? help project for the remainder of the session. (What's This? Help Composer will reset this option when you start it the next time.)

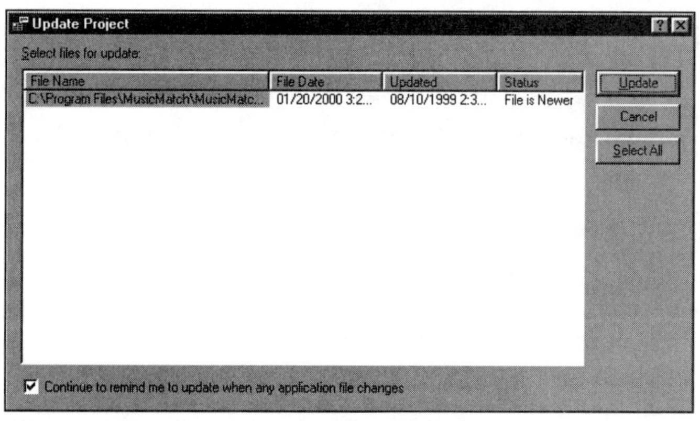

Figure 25-33: The Update Project window

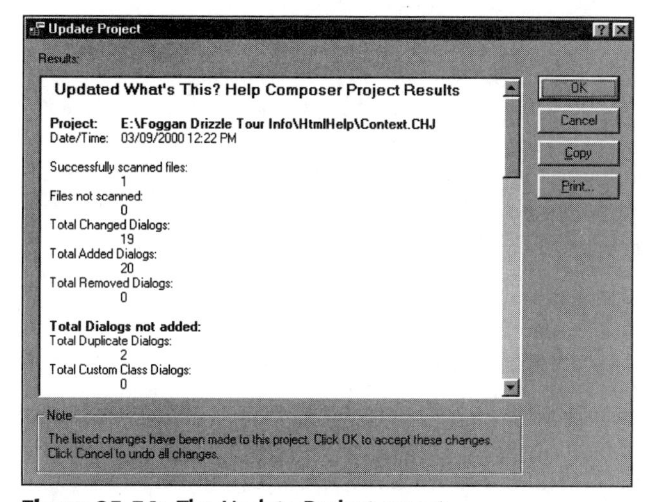

Figure 25-34: The Update Project report

4. Click OK to accept the changes and incorporate them into your What's This? help project. What's This? Help Composer will update the database of information for the project. You can now recompile the WinHelp project and test it against the program as described earlier.

You can also manually update a What's This? help project. This is a good idea if you want to check the entries in the project or if you are using a new program file. To start a manual update, do the following:

✦ Select Project ➪ Update Project , or just click the Update button on the standard toolbar (shown in Figure 25-35).

Figure 25-35: Update button

You can then continue updating the What's This? help project as before.

Removing and Replacing Dialog Boxes

You may need to delete the entry for a control or a dialog box. For example, the program may have several internal dialog boxes that are for debugging or internal program options for use only by the developers. There may also be unused dialog boxes that are still in the program files but are not used in the program. Documenting dialog boxes such as these is usually unnecessary and may even present security problems if the users become aware of them. Removing extraneous or unused dialog boxes also makes it easier to maintain the active dialog boxes.

To remove a dialog box in the What's This? help, do the following:

1. Highlight the dialog box you want to delete in the Dialog Box list on the left side of What's This? Help Composer window and press Delete. (You can also right-click the dialog box and select Remove from the popup menu.) What's This? Help Composer displays a message asking you to confirm the deletion.
2. Click OK to remove the dialog box to What's This? Help Composer's recycle bin. All deleted dialog boxes appear in the recycle bin at the bottom of the dialog box list.

When you update a What's This? help project and What's This? Help Composer finds a control or dialog box that's no longer used, it automatically removes the entry and puts it into the recycle bin.

As with files deleted but still in the Windows Recycle Bin, you can view the dialog box information by highlighting the entry. You can even "undelete" dialog box entries in the recycle bin, as follows:

✦ Right-click on the dialog box entry you want to restore and select Restore Recycled from the popup menu. (You can also click and drag the dialog box entry to the active part of the dialog box list.)

If you prefer, you can restore all the entries in the recycle bin by selecting Edit ➪ Restore Recycled.

You can delete an entry from the recycle bin by right-clicking and selecting Delete from the popup menu, and then confirming the deletion. As with the Windows recycle bin, removing something from What's This Help Composer recycle bin removes it completely from the What's This? help project. You can delete all the entries in the recycle bin by selecting Project ➪ Empty Recycle Bin.

It's a good idea to keep all the entries in the recycle bin until you're ready to create the final version of the What's This? help project.

Changing, Adding, and Removing Program Files

It's not unusual as part of the development cycle for the program to change its name or for the installation program to add the program to another folder. When this happens, you need to tell the What's This? help project where to look for the program, as follows:

1. Select File ➪ Relocate Main Program File. The Locate File window appears (shown in Figure 25-36).

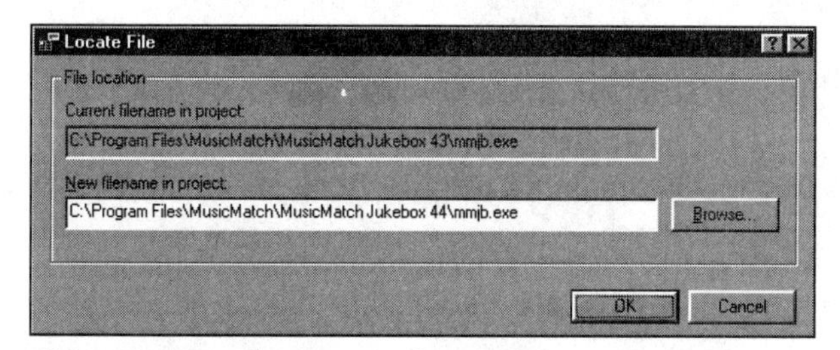

Figure 25-36: The Locate File window

2. Enter the new path and filename in New file name in project. You can browse for the file using the browse button to the right of the field. When you are satisfied with your entry, click OK. What's This? Help Composer will then use the new program for the What's This? help project.

Occasionally, you may also need to add program files to a What's This? help project. Normally, any DLL or other program files called by the program from within the program's EXE file will be found and examined automatically by What's This? Help Composer when it does an update. However, you may need to specify an additional file — for example, if the program requires that you use a different DLL file from the one called in the program. To add a program file to the What's This? help project, do the following:

1. Select Project ➪ Add File, or just click the Add File button on the standard toolbar, shown in Figure 25-37. A standard Open File window appears.

Figure 25-37: Add File button

2. Select the program or file you want to add to the project from the list and click OK. What's This? Help Composer will scan the program or file, add the information for the dialog boxes, and generate the standard update report like the one shown earlier in Figure 25-20.

You can also remove a program or file from a What's This? help project as follows:

✦ Highlight the name of the program or file in the Dialog Box list on the left side of What's This? Help Composer window and select Edit ➪ Remove File. You can also right-click the file and select Remove from the popup menu.

When you remove a program or file, What's This? Help Composer puts it in What's This Help Composer's recycle bin. You can restore a program or file from the recycle bin in the same way as restoring a dialog box.

Renaming a What's This? Help Project

It's possible that you will need to rename a What's This? help project after you've created it. Although there is not a command that renames a What's This? help project, you can edit the CHJ file to change the names, as follows:

1. Close What's This? Help Composer.
2. With the Windows Explorer, rename the What's This? help files to the new project name.

Be sure to rename *all* the files in the project. It's a good idea to use the file extensions in Table 25-1 as a checklist. If you miss a file, What's This? Help Composer may update the project with new information and overwrite any edits you've made.

3. Open the project's CHJ file in a text editor such as Notepad.
4. In the [PROJECT] section of the CHJ file, change the file names for the component files. The following code shows a portion of the CHJ file for a program file of FDTOURS.EXE and a What's This? help project named Travel.

```
[PROJECT]
Primary File=fdtours.exe
Help File To Build=travel.HLP
Database File=travel.DBF
Run Command=fdtours.exe
Help Project File=travel.HPJ
DefaultTopicFile=travel.DTO
```

```
HelpMapFile=travel.H
ExeTime=1094354176, 29320094
```

5. When you are satisfied with your changes, save your changes and close the CHJ file.

After you've renamed the project, the automatic file open option won't know where to find the project. Open the project using File ➪ Open in What's This? Help Composer the first time after you've renamed it.

You can move the What's This? help project from one folder to another by moving all the files in the folder. You don't need to change any of the information in the project files, although you'll have to open the What's This? help project manually in What's This? Help Composer after you've moved it.

Using Programmer-Generated Topic IDs

What's This? Help Composer automatically creates your What's This? help topics and topic IDs. However, the programmer may already have generated the topic IDs. In the likely event that you won't be able to get these changed, you'll need to edit the What's This? help to use these topics IDs, as follows:

1. Create a stand-alone What's This? help project for the program. Compile and test the What's This? help.
2. If the program doesn't have an associated HTML Help project in RoboHELP, create a "dummy" HTML Help project. (This project is only for the purpose of importing the What's This? help project into RoboHELP for editing, so it doesn't need anything other than the default topic.)
3. Close the project in What's This? Help Composer.
4. Edit the CONTEXT.H file (using any text editor, such as Notepad), changing the topic IDs to those provided by the programmer.
5. Save the CONTEXT.H file, and then open the What's This? help project and recompile.

Supporting Other Applications

You can use What's This? help only for windows that are based on the Cdialog class in C or C++ applications. If you want to create What's This? help for other types of windows or for applications that are not written in C or C++, you'll need to use the HTML Help API to directly access and display the What's This? help information.

Notes for Programmers

If you are a programmer developing a C or C++ program, there are some things you need to do to enable What's This? help in the program:

- ✦ You must set the tab order for the controls in each dialog box. The tab order should move the focus logically from one control to the next and from one group of controls to the next. Controls that have an ID of –1 are not included in the tab order and will not have a What's This? help topic. It's a good idea to set static text to –1 and to have the control the static text is describing as the next item in the tab order. For group boxes, use either a unique ID or set the group box to –1 so the next control will have the same What's This? help text as the group box.
- ✦ If you are developing with a C or C++ program, you need to use the calls in the CSHUSER.H file. These calls are documented in detail in What's This? Help Composer documentation. The CSHTML.DLL and CSHUSER.H files appear in the \RoboHELP Office\RoboHELP\WhatsThs\ProgDlls folder along with the LIB files for the various supported C/C++ compilers.
- ✦ If the program is being developed with the C++ AppWizard, enabling the context-sensitive help in the AppWizard duplicates the What's This? help project's topic information.
- ✦ As noted earlier, What's This? help works only for the Cdialog class of dialog boxes in C++ programs.

Specific examples of the code you need to add appear in the What's This? help online documentation and through `www.ehelp.com`.

Shipping What's This? Help

As part of the release to shipping, you need to do a final verification that the What's This? help code has been added to a program, as follows:

1. Get the final version of the program and any related files from the developer.
2. Update the What's This? help in What's This? Help Composer to make sure that any late changes to the program have been incorporated in the What's This? help.
3. Test the program together with the What's This? help independent of What's This? Help Composer. Verify each of the What's This? help links.

If the What's This? help passes the tests, you can optionally make any final edits to the TXT file as described earlier in this chapter and then ship the What's This? help HTML files. If the program is a C/C++ file, you must also provide the CSH.DLL file, which should be installed in the user's \Windows\System folder. This DLL file contains the code the program requires to call the What's This? help.

Summary

In this chapter, you've learned how to create context-sensitive and What's This? help. You first learned the basics of context-sensitive HTML Help. The chapter then identified concerns for planning the context-sensitive help and provided information on working with developers. The chapter taught you several ways to add and maintain context-sensitive links, followed by ways to test and debug context-sensitive help. The chapter continued with basics on What's This? help. You saw how to use What's This? Help Composer to create and edit a basic What's This? help file. The chapter continued with information on configuring What's This? Help Composer, compiling What's This? help, and testing the result. You learned about ways to automate the What's This? help creation and maintenance process. In conclusion, the chapter discussed issues for maintaining and releasing What's This? help.

✦ ✦ ✦

CHAPTER 26

Using Forms and Frames

✦ ✦ ✦ ✦

In This Chapter

Frames and framesets

Creating your framesets

Forms and CGI scripts

Working with CGI scripts

✦ ✦ ✦ ✦

In this chapter, you learn about working with frames and forms in RoboHELP HTML. First you'll learn what frames and framesets are, and why they're used. You'll learn how to add, customize and, if necessary, delete your frameset. The section on frames ends with information about how to link your frames to the topics they'll display.

The second part of the chapter discusses the basics of forms. You'll learn what forms are used for, as well as what elements you can use to create forms in your help system. You'll then learn how to add, modify, and delete those elements. Because working with forms means also working with CGI (Common Gateway Interface) scripting, you'll discover where CGI scripts come from, what they can do, and what your role as an author is in associating a CGI script with the form you've designed.

Frames and Framesets

Frames, a common feature used in HTML, are a great way to help your users find their way through your content. They're often used in instances when clicking a hyperlink in one frame results in contents appearing in another frame. They help organize content and give users a constant, reliable interface that's easy to navigate.

Although frames are being discussed in the advanced section of this book, they're simple features to use. As a matter of fact, you're already using them. The HTML Help browser configuration you've seen most includes a basic frameset: The Contents, Index, and Search tabs are in the left pane, while the actual help topics are displayed in the right pane (shown in Figure 26-1).

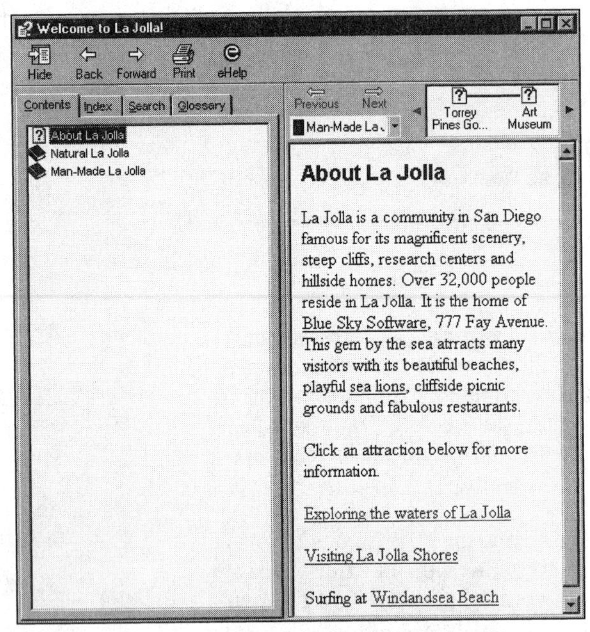

Figure 26-1: The default HTML Help window

The simple division between two frames is sufficient for many help systems. If you have a lot of content, however, or content that is very complex, you may want to configure your own frames for optimum navigation. This can assist your users in reaching the help they need more efficiently.

Defining Frames and Framesets

You should first understand the difference between frames and framesets.

Frames are windows that divide the HTML Help viewer or browser into several areas so that multiple topics can be displayed at once. A frame (shown in Figure 26-2) is part of a frameset.

A frameset (shown in Figure 26-3) is made up of two or more of the aforementioned frames. Framesets provide a way for some topics to remain static while others change. The frameset design dictates how frames are displayed and what topic(s) are available in each frame.

Figure 26-2: A single frame

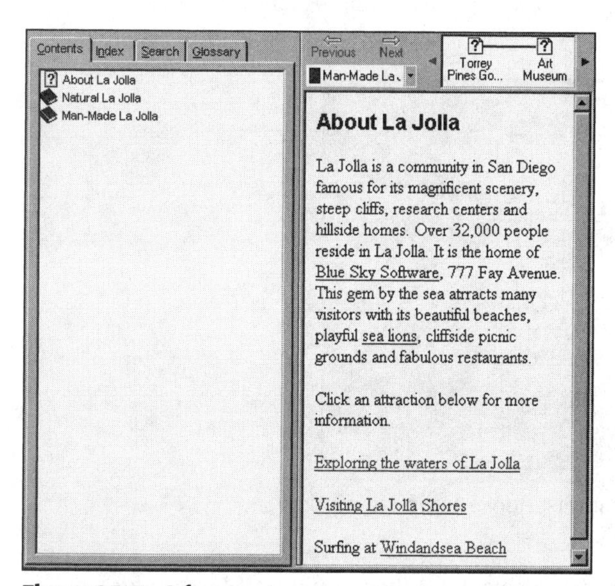

Figure 26-3: A frameset

For example, in this frameset, the left pane is used for navigation. The contents in this pane remains static so that the user will always have access to it. The contents on the right, however, changes depending on what the user clicks in the left (static) pane.

You may have reasons other than navigation for having frames that contain static images. For example, you may wish to display a banner or a corporate logo that identifies your help system.

Creating Your Framesets

There are several steps to adding frames to your Help system, the first of which is choosing a frameset. Luckily, you don't have to design it from scratch — RoboHELP HTML provides several preset framesets from which you can choose. These framesets are customizable, too.

Here's how you add a frameset:

1. Click the Project tab.
2. Select File ➪ New ➪ Frameset. The Frameset-Choose Template window opens. Figure 26-4 displays previews of the available framesets.

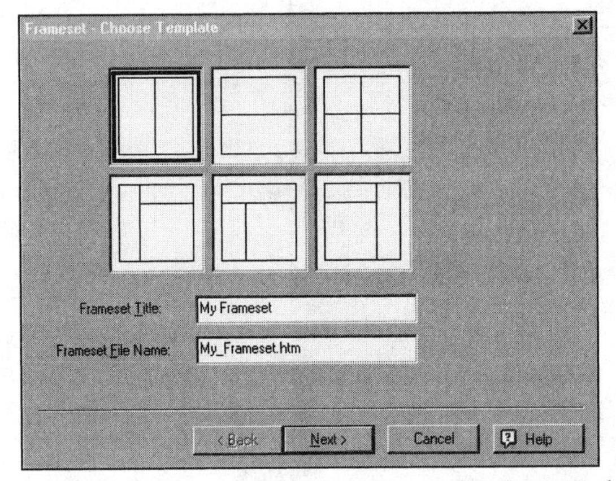

Figure 26-4: The Frameset-Choose Template window

3. Click a frameset preview to select it. When you do, a blue border will appear around the frameset preview.
4. Enter a name for the frameset in the Frameset Title text box. As you enter a name for the frameset, the Frameset File Name will automatically be entered for you. For example, if you call the frameset "My Frameset," the frameset file will be named My_Frameset.htm. If you want to call the frameset file something else, delete what was automatically entered and enter a new name.

5. Click Next. This opens the Frameset-Frame Attributes window, shown in Figure 26-5. Use this window to define each frame in the frameset. Click a frame to select it. Selected frames are blue.
6. In the Name text box, enter a name for the selected frame. The name should imply a purpose or location. For instance, you could name a frame "Left" or "Navigation."
7. Select a topic or URL from the list on the right. As you do, the topic file name will appear in the Initial File text box.

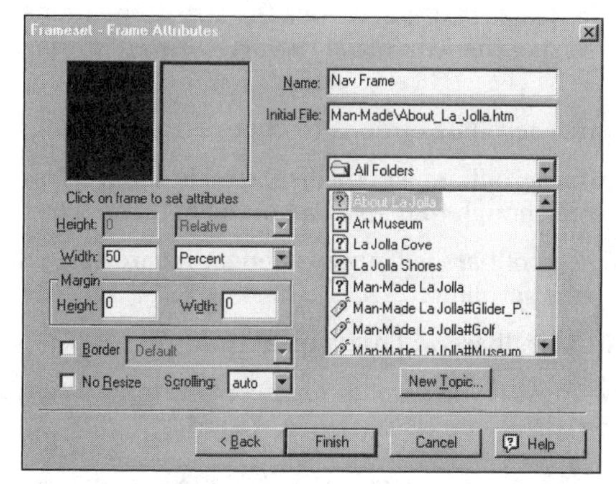

Figure 26-5: The Frameset-Frame Attributes window

8. Repeat Steps 6 and 7 for each frame in your frameset.
9. Click Finish. The specified frameset appears in the topic list with a frameset icon before it.

If you want to change any of your frame settings in the future, double-click your frameset file to open the Frameset-Frame Attributes window.

Customizing Frames

The framesets provided by RoboHELP HTML are customizable. You can customize the frame you've chosen by setting the attributes of the frame:

✦ **Height:** Enter a value to set the height of the frame. Height can be entered in pixels, percent, and relative to other frames in the frameset. If you don't require exact measurements, you can adjust the height of a frame with your mouse by dragging the border that divides the frame.

✦ **Width:** Enter a value to set the width of the frame. Width can be entered in pixels, percent, and relative to other frames in the frameset. As with height, if you don't require exact measurements, you can also adjust the width of a frame by dragging the border that divides the frame.

✦ **Margin:** Enter values to set the height and width of the frame margins. Margin height and width can be entered in pixels and percent.

✦ **Border:** Click the Border text box to add a border around the frame. You can also select the border color from the drop-down menu to the right of the Border text box.

✦ **No Resize:** Click the No Resize text box to lock the size of the frame. This prevents users from resizing the window in their HTML Help or browser window.

✦ **Scrolling:** You have three scrolling options to choose from:

- If you choose **Auto**, scrollbars will be displayed in the window if the window is not large enough to display all of the content.
- If you choose **Yes**, scrollbars will always appear regardless of whether the content requires scrolling.
- If you choose **No**, scrollbars will not appear.

✦ **New Topic:** Click New Topic if you want to create a new topic to assign to the frame. This will launch the Create a New Topic Wizard.

After you set the attributes you want, click Finish. Be sure to set all of these attributes for each frame in your frameset. Your new frameset will be listed as an HTM file in the Topics list (shown in Figure 26-6).

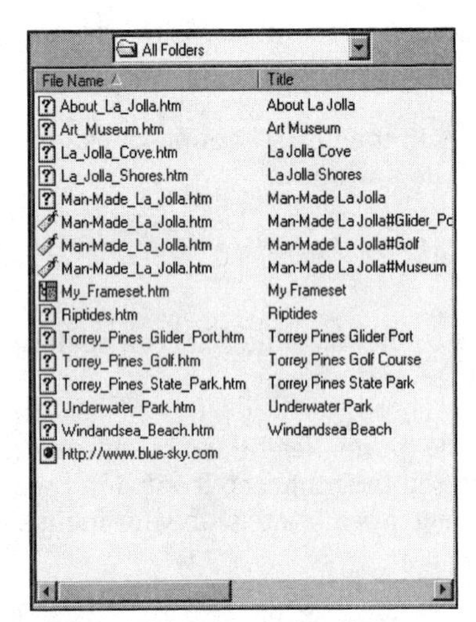

Figure 26-6: The Topics list, including My_Frameset.htm

To change your frameset attributes after this point, simply double-click the frameset file. This will open the Frameset-Frame Attributes window.

Linking to a Frameset

There are three ways to link frames or framesets. The method you choose should be dictated by which topics you want to open in which frames, as well as how you want your users to navigate them. The three methods are as follows:

✦ Linking a frameset to a TOC book or page

✦ Linking a hyperlink to a frame

✦ Linking a hyperlink to a frameset

Linking a frameset to a TOC book or page

By linking a frameset to a TOC book or page, you enable the frameset to display the contents of that book or page in the HTML Help browser. Moreover, the whole frameset can open in a secondary window if you wish. To link a frameset to a TOC book or page, follow these steps:

1. Click the TOC tab to select it. You'll know the tab is selected by the blue border that surrounds it.
2. Select File ➪ New ➪ Book, or File ➪ New ➪ Page.
3. Enter the title of the book or page in the Title text box.
4. Under Type, select Link to Single Topic.
5. Under Topic, click the frameset file.
6. If you want the frameset to open in a secondary window, click the Advanced tab and specify which secondary window you want to use.
7. Click OK or Apply.

You must have already created a secondary window type for your help project to accomplish this. For more information, see Chapter 21, "Adding Windows and Popups."

Linking a hyperlink to a frame

By linking a hyperlink to a frame, you can jump from the contents of a topic to a frame. To link a topic to a frame, follow these steps:

1. Double-click the topic you want to link from in the WYSIWYG Editor to open it.
2. Highlight the text you want to use as the hyperlink.
3. Select Insert ➪ Hyperlink.

4. In the Frame text box, choose the frame you wish to serve as the target for the link.
5. Under Select Destination (File or URL), select the topic or URL to link to the frame.
6. Click OK or Apply.

Linking a hyperlink to a frameset

By linking a hyperlink to a frameset, you can jump from the contents of a topic to a frameset. To link a topic to a frameset, follow these steps:

1. Open the topic you want to link from in the WYSIWYG Editor.
2. Highlight the text you want to use as the Hyperlink.
3. Click Insert ➪ Hyperlink.
4. Under Select Destination (File or URL), select the frameset file to serve as the link.
5. When you are satisfied with the link you've set, click OK.

You need to repeat this procedure for each of the topics you want to link to your frameset. Every single link needs to be set individually. After you have set the links you can view them using the Link View in the right-hand pane.

Deleting a Frameset

The best-laid plans for a Help file sometimes change, and you may decide to remove a frameset you had planned to use. Here's how you delete a frameset:

1. Click the Project tab.
2. Open the HTML files folder.
3. Right-click the frameset file you want to delete.
4. Click Delete.
5. When asked to confirm that you want to delete the frameset, click Yes.

If the deleted frameset was part of your TOC or linked to a hyperlink, the frameset will be moved to the Broken Links folder so you can fix the links. This gives you the opportunity to restore the frameset if you change your mind; simply right-click the frameset file and click Include Topic.

Forms and CGI Scripts

There are many types of forms. You may have encountered forms on the Internet as a guest book or a counter on a Web site. Perhaps you've voted in an online poll or entered your address and credit card information to purchase something on the Web. In all those cases, you were using forms and probably, in turn, CGI scripts.

Forms are another of HTML's advanced features. Forms enable you to gather information from the users of your help system, and in turn do something with that data. The information is gathered via a series of form elements, including text boxes, check boxes, drop-down menus, radio buttons, and push buttons. The gathered information is sent as data values to a CGI script, which in turns executes a task with that data. Examples of such tasks might include processing a purchase request or updating a database.

Before you proceed, understand the difference between the HTML forms and the CGI script, for they are two very different things. The HTML form itself is an entry point for data that you as a Help author create. The CGI script, on the other hand, performs a function with that data.

Using Forms in a Help System

Before you start designing your form, you should ask yourself, What do I want to accomplish with this form? You must have a clearly defined purpose for it. What needs could a form fill in a help system? For one, you could use forms to collect a user's name, address, and serial number to register his or her product. You could also have a form that allows users to send orders for related software or peripheral devices. Whatever the task, make sure it is clearly defined.

Once you've settled on the task, you need to determine what information the CGI script will need to execute the task. The form must gather this information. For instance, if you collect information for product registration, you'll want the following information:

- Name
- Company name
- Street address
- E-mail address
- City, state and zip code
- Product serial number

When your intent and information needs are clearly defined, it's time to add your form.

Here's how you add the container that will house your form:

1. Open the topic you want to add a form to in the WYSIWYG Editor.
2. Click in the topic where you want to insert the form.
3. Select Insert ➪ Form. A rectangular box that serves as the container for the form appears (shown in Figure 26-7).

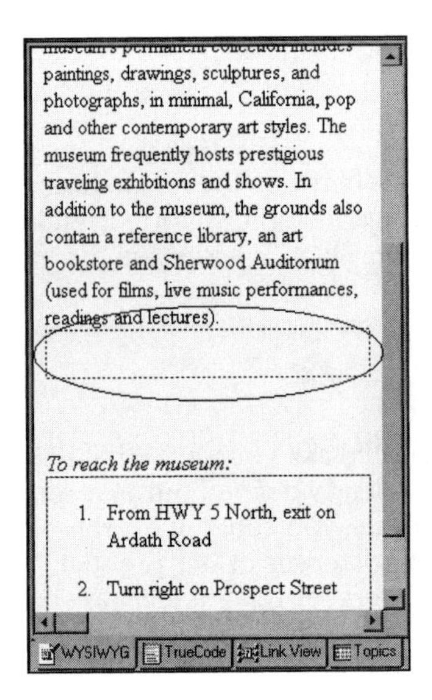

Figure 26-7: The Form container is inserted

Adding Form Elements

A blank form container won't do anything for you. You need to add form elements. Form elements allow users to enter and submit their data.

As you add your form elements, you'll give each of them names and values. Here are two important guidelines to follow:

✦ Each form element must have a unique name and a unique value. Remember that each form element will represent a single, unique piece of information to the CGI script. If you give the same name and/or value to two form elements, the CGI script may not run correctly. Even if it does, your data will be inaccurate.

✦ While maintaining their uniqueness, keep the names and values as simple as possible. This will make it easier for anyone who has to deal with the code of the CGI script.

You can use five different types of elements to compose your form:

✦ **Text boxes:** Text boxes enable users to enter text in your form.

Here's how you add a text box to a form:

1. Click inside the form container you've already inserted in the topic.
2. Select Insert ⇨ Form Element ⇨ Text Box.
3. In the Text Box Properties window (shown in Figure 26-8), enter the name of the text box in the Name text box. This name identifies the text box to the CGI script.
4. If you want the text box to contain default text (such as "type your text here"), enter that text in the Value box.
5. Enter the width you want in the Width in Characters text box.
6. Enter the maximum numbers of characters you want to allow in the Maximum Characters text box.
7. Enter the number of lines of text you want in the Number of Lines text box. If you want a single-line text box, enter 1; this forces the height of the text box to one line.
8. Click the Password Field text box if you want to have password protection for the text box. Any text entered in the text box will appear as asterisks (*).
9. Select Scrolling Text Box if you want the text box to have both vertical and horizontal scrollbars.
10. Click OK.

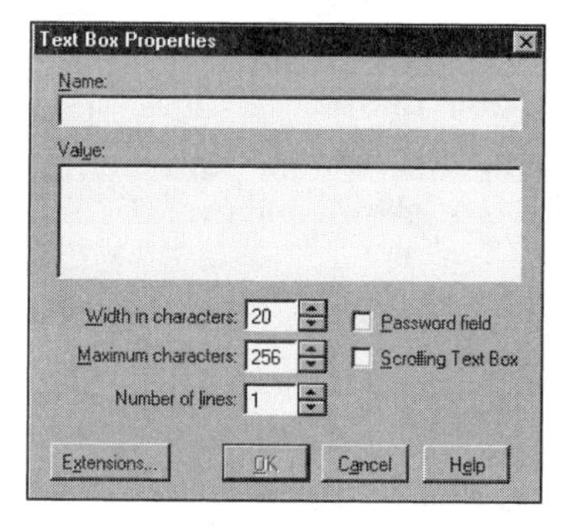

Figure 26-8: The Text Box Properties window

✦ **Check boxes:** Check boxes enable users to make a series of selections.

Here's how you add a check box to a form:

1. Click where you want to place the check box inside the form container.
2. Select Insert ➪ Form Element ➪ Check Box.
3. In the Check Box/Radio Button Properties window (shown in Figure 26-9), enter the name of the check box in the Name text box. This name identifies the check box to the CGI script.
4. Enter a Value. This value will be recognized and processed by the CGI script.
5. Click the Checked box if you want the check box to appear checked sby default.
6. Click OK.

Figure 26-9: The Check Box/Radio Button Properties window for adding a check box

This same window is for both check boxes and radio buttons; in this instance, the Check Box radio button is selected under Type.

✦ **Radio buttons:** Radio buttons enable users to make a single selection from a group of options.

Here's how you add a radio button to a form:

1. Click where you want to place the radio button inside the form container.
2. Select Insert ➪ Form Element ➪ Radio Button.
3. In the Check Box/Radio Button Properties window, enter the name of the radio button in the Name text box (shown in Figure 26-10). The name identifies the radio button to the CGI script.
4. Enter a Value. This value will be recognized and processed by the CGI script.

5. Click the Checked box if you want the radio button to be selected by default.
6. Click OK.

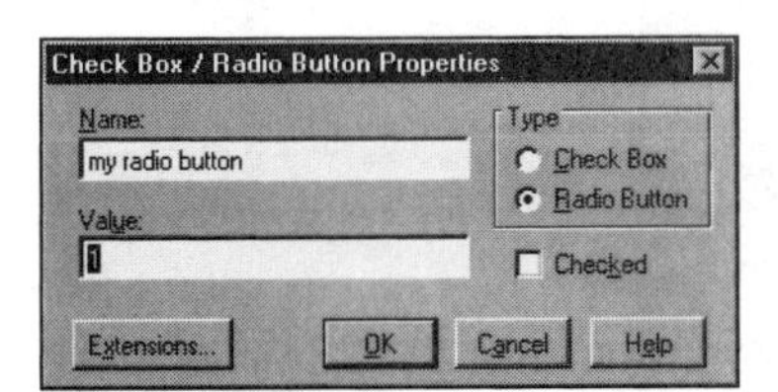

Figure 26-10: The Check Box/Radio Button Properties window for adding a radio button

This window is the same for both check boxes and radio buttons; but in this instance, Radio Button is selected under Type.

✦ **Drop-down menus:** Drop-down menus enable users to make selections from a list.

Here's how you add a drop-down menu to a form:

1. Click where you want to place the drop-down form inside the form container.
2. Select Insert ➪ Form Element ➪ Drop-Down Menu.
3. In the Drop Down Menu Properties window (shown in Figure 26-11), enter the name of the drop-down menu in the Name text box. The name identifies the drop-down menu to the CGI script.

   Because a drop-down menu provides a list of options, you have to enter the options for the list and give each one a unique value.
4. Enter an option you want listed in the Choice text box.
5. Enter a value for that choice in the Value text box.
6. If you want to the choice to be selected by default, click the Selected text box.
7. Specify a height, either by entering it in the Height text box or by clicking the arrows. Note that if you enter 1, the drop-down menu will be displayed as a drop-down menu. If you enter a number greater than 1, it will appear as a scrollable list.
8. If you want to allow users to choose more than one item on the list, click the Allow Multiple Selections text box.
9. Click OK.

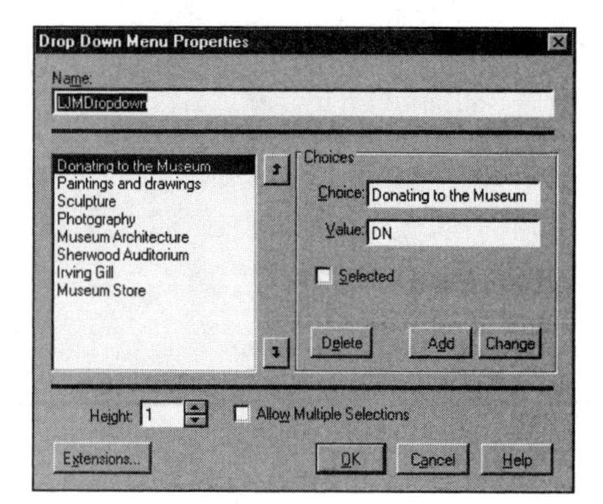

Figure 26-11: The Drop Down Menu Properties window

To add, delete or change items in a drop-down menu you've created:

1. Open the topic with the drop-down menu in the WYSIWYG Editor.
2. Double-click the drop-down menu.
3. To add a menu item, enter the Choice and Value, and then click Add.
4. To change a menu item, click the item to select it, change the Choice and/or Value as desired, and then click Change.
5. To delete a menu item, click the item to select it, and then click Delete.
6. Click OK.

✦ **Push buttons:** Push buttons enable users to either submit their information or reset the form. You can also create image push buttons.

Here's how you add push buttons to a form:

1. Click where you want to place the push button inside the form container. It is best to place Submit and Reset push buttons at the bottom of a form.
2. Select Insert ➪ Form Element ➪ Push Button.
3. In the Push Button Properties window (shown in Figure 26-12), click the General tab.
4. Enter the name of the button in the Name text box. The name identifies the push button to the CGI script.
5. Enter the value of the button in the Value text box.

6. Under Type, click the type of push button you want. A Submit button will send information from the form to the CGI script. A Reset button will clear any information currently entered in the form and return the form elements to their default state. A Script button will execute a command contained in the CGI script. An Image button will perform an action when clicked, and uses an image as a button.
7. If you're creating an Image button (shown in Figure 26-13), click the "..." button next to Image URL.
8. Browse to the image you want to use as a button, and then click OK.
9. Click OK.

If you want to have both a Submit and a Reset button, you'll have to follow this procedure twice, once for each type of button.

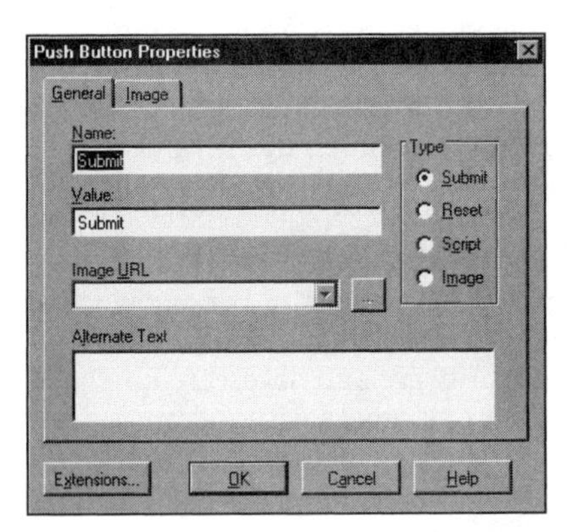

Figure 26-12: The Push Button Properties window

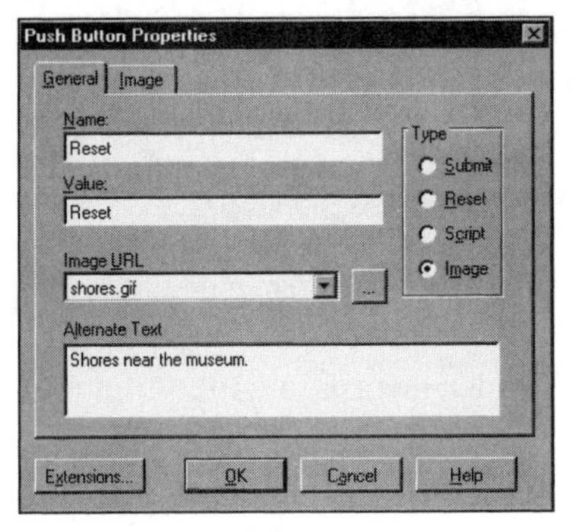

Figure 26-13: The Push Button Properties window when creating an Image button

CGI Scripts

As a help author or help authoring coordinator, you don't necessarily need to know how to create CGI scripts yourself. You should, however, know what they are, how they work, and where to get them.

CGI scripts act as the go-between for the information your form collects and the server that processes it. When a Submit button is clicked, the data collected by each form element is sent to its CGI script. The CGI script performs some sort of operation relative to the data. The type of operation executed is up to the creator of the script.

RoboHELP HTML does not include any CGI scripts, nor does eHelp Corporation provide CGI scripts for use with the product. So where do you find someone to write or otherwise provide these scripts? There are three general sources for CGI:

✦ **You:** You can write your own, if you know how. Perl is the most common language used for creating CGI, but other languages such as Java and C/C++ can be used as well. People who have both the need for a CGI script and the expertise to create one, however, are very much in the minority.

✦ **A developer:** You may already be working with a developer on the help system you're creating. Approach them about CGI scripts.

✦ **Your Internet Service Provider (ISP):** CGI scripts of various kinds are widely used on the Internet. Because of this, most ISPs maintain a library of CGI scripts that they know will work with their software and hardware configurations. They usually share these scripts with their customers without any fee. This may be the easiest and least expensive route for you, providing that your ISP has a script that meets your needs.

Ensuring that the CGI Script Works with Your Form

There is no need for you to become proficient in authoring your own CGI scripts, unless it's something you want to invest the time in learning. You should, however, understand the process by which you associate the forms in your help system to their respective scripts. Here's a quick overview of the steps:

1. Design your forms with clear intent, with each form element having a unique and intuitive name and value.
2. With guidance from the script provider, incorporate the script into the topic that contains your form.
3. Work with the provider of the script to ensure that the script is inserted correctly into the HTML, and that it executes as expected with the desired results.

Reading CGI Scripts

Just so you know what CGI scripting looks like, here's an example:

```
<html><head><body>
Register my product.
<form method="post" action=http://yourispserver.com/cgi-
bin/email.pl>
Name: <input type=text name="name" size=32><br>
Company Name: <input type=text name="coname" size=32><br>
Company Address: <input type=text name="coadd" size=32><br>
Email Address: <input type=text name="email" size=32><br>
Serial Number: <input type=text name="sernum" size=32><br>
Comments: <br>textarea wrap=virtual name="body" rows=5
cols=45</textarea><br>
<input type=submit value="send mail">
</form>
</body></html>
```

If you don't know how to write CGI scripts, at first glance this scripting probably seems like Sanskrit to you. If you look at it line by line, however, it starts to make sense. "Form method="post"," for instance, indicates what the script will do; post your information. Name, Company Name, and so on, dictate the information to be gathered and handled by the script. The script ends with the line that indicates the data will be sent via e-mail:

```
<input type=submit value="send mail">
```

For more information on CGI scripting, consult with your developer, your ISP, or your local library. There is also an enormous amount of free information on forms and CGI scripting on the Internet, so start surfing.

Summary

In this chapter, you learned how to use frames and forms. After learning how to create and modify framesets, you learned how to link those framesets to the topics you want them to display. You also learned about forms and CGI scripts. You learned what forms do versus what CGI scripts do. You learned to add form elements to a topic. Lastly, you learned what your role is in ensuring that a CGI script works with your form.

✦ ✦ ✦

CHAPTER 27

Programming for HTML Help

✦ ✦ ✦ ✦

In This Chapter

✦ ✦ ✦ ✦

In this chapter, you'll be introduced to ActiveX and JavaScript. You'll learn about scripting hosts and engines, server-side and client-side scripts, and how they work with HTML pages. You'll learn about all the HTML Help controls and how to insert a third-party control, and then you'll learn the difference between Java and JavaScript. Finally, you'll learn how to insert a piece of JavaScript using the TrueCode editor and all the essential keys to adding great interactivity to your help systems.

Introduction to ActiveX

Active X is a scripting language, which simply means it is a programming language meant to work with HTML. Because your HTML Help project is based on the technology of HTML, you can take advantage of Active X to add special features and actions to your topics.

This chapter introduces you to ActiveX, including the basics of ActiveX, its origin, and how to use it in your HTML Help project. The chapter focuses on the use of ActiveX within RoboHELP HTML for creating HTML Help and WebHelp projects.

The Origin of ActiveX

ActiveX, formerly known as OLE (Object Linking and Embedding), was developed by Microsoft in 1991. Originally developed for the purpose of making developing easier, OLE technology allows one application to use a feature that is part of another application. The most common examples of OLE technology is in Microsoft Office. There, a user can embed a feature from one application into another; for example, an Excel spreadsheet into a Word document.

With the emergence of the Internet, Microsoft turned their focus to the Web and expanded the development focus of OLE to include Internet development. To highlight this change, Microsoft renamed OLE to ActiveX, based on Microsoft's new objective to "activate the Internet." This transformation allowed developers to take a web site that presented material simply and recreate it into an interactive site.

ActiveX is one of the big contributors to today's e-commerce movement, allowing development of web-based applications, such as Internet shopping sites. The reusability of the controls, and their broad areas of application, attract developers because they can be used for anything from simple calendars to complex parts of an online application, and they can be used repeatedly as the site changes.

Always check with your developers to make sure they know you are thinking of using ActiveX controls in your HTML Help project.

What Is ActiveX Scripting?

ActiveX is composed of two main pieces: ActiveX controls and Active scripts. ActiveX scripting, which encompasses both client and server-side scripting, is an essential key to adding interactivity to a Web page. You will learn about Active X controls later in this chapter. This section discusses Active scripts.

A script can be just a section of code, an executable file, or even a DOS batch file. Client scripting resides on the Web page itself and consists of different types of script; for instance, VBScript and JScript. Client scripts are inserted directly into the HTML of pages, which are then processed by the user's local machine. Examples of server-side scripts are ISAPI and CGI. These scripts are more robust than their client-side counterparts, and require a Web page manager in order to work with the server's files.

Scripting Engines and Hosts

The two main components of ActiveX scripting are *scripting engines* and *scripting hosts*. A scripting host is essentially your user's link to the server and the information it contains; it is usually a browser such as Microsoft's Internet Explorer. Scripting hosts contain scripting engines that process the scripts on a Web page. A scripting engine is one or more DLLs containing the information necessary to process the scripts on any given HTML page. Another great feature of ActiveX is the design of the scripting engine. A scripting host can contain several scripting engines, allowing developers to code a Web page with whatever scripting language they prefer.

Dangers of ActiveX

There are things you must be aware of when add ActiveX controls to your HTML Help project. ActiveX is very versatile and it has the ability to modify your user's system. It can delete files, read data from the computer, and transfer it to the Web server of any sites the user visits. It also has the capability to use e-mail address lists in order to send offensive and possibly destructive e-mails, forwarding them in your name to your friends and coworkers. You must make sure you protect yourself and your users by updating your virus software regularly and scheduling regular system scans, as well as scanning any ActiveX controls before your computer processes them, and before they are shipped with your HTML Help project.

The dangers of Active X are real, and you may want to include a note about scanning for viruses with your HTML Help project.

Inserting ActiveX into Your Topics

RoboHELP HTML contains several samples of ActiveX controls, ready to be inserted into your topics. Many of these controls are designed by Microsoft to be used as HTML versions of WinHelp macros.

If you are trying to create a RoboHELP HTML project to work on both Netscape and Internet Explorer, you should avoid Active X. While it is possible to develop with Active X in both, it is complicated and annoying. Try using JavaScript instead.

Inserting an ActiveX control into your RoboHELP HTML Help project follows the same basic outline, no matter how you do it:

1. Place your cursor where you want the control (usually a button) to appear in the topic.
2. Launch the Wizard for the control by selecting it from the Insert menu.
3. Follow the Wizard to add the text and information to the button.

Some ActiveX controls require more information than others; however, all follow this simple process. This chapter includes a complete outline of the most complicated ActiveX controls to include in your topics: the ALink and Related topics controls, as well as an overview of all the other ActiveX controls that come with RoboHELP HTML.

You can edit any control once it has been inserted by double-clicking the control in the WYSIWYG Editor. Its properties will be displayed, allowing you to make any changes you require.

ALink Control

By using the ALink control, you can add See Also buttons quickly and easily. The ALink control is almost identical to the Related Topics and Keyword Link controls, except the ALink control allows you to specify an ALink name, which can be linked to several of your topics.

1. First, load the topic you want to add the button to into the WYSIWYG Editor, and then place the cursor at your desired location for the button.
2. Select Insert ➪ ALink. The Button Options window will be displayed, as shown in Figure 27-1.

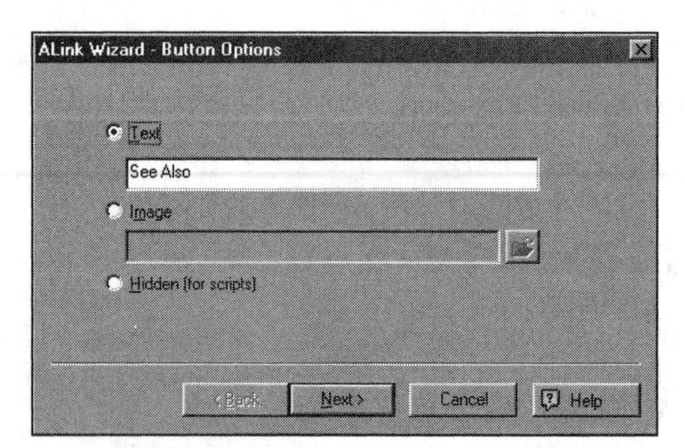

Figure 27-1: ALink Wizard Button Options window

3. Use the ALink Wizard to choose the options for the buttons. The default is a text button, with the sample text "See Also." You can select the Image radio button to browse to the image you would like to display on the button. The Hidden option allows you to add your own scripts to the control.
4. When you have finished selecting the options, click Next. The ALink Names Selection window appears, as shown in Figure 27-2.

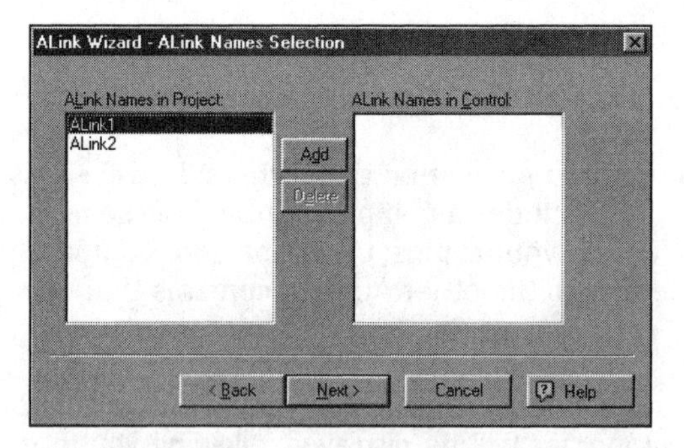

Figure 27-2: ALink Wizard ALink Names Selection window

5. Use the ALink Names Selection window to select the topics you would like your See Also button to reference by using the ALink names listed.

Associations of ALinks and topics are created in the Topic Properties window.

6. Once you have selected the ALinks you want, click Next. The ALink Display Options window opens, as shown in Figure 27-3.

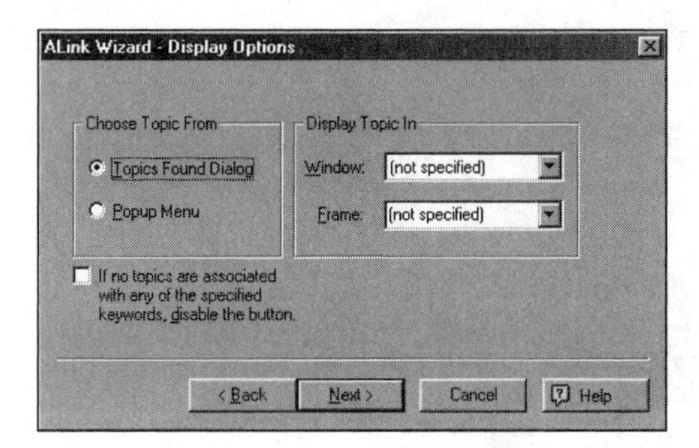

Figure 27-3: ALink Wizard Display Options

7. Set the Choose Topics From option. This sets the type of window that displays when your users click the button. The Topics Found Dialog window is larger and has more information than the Popup Menu window.
8. Set the Display Topic In option. Choose whether you would like the topic to be displayed in one of the windows in your project, or in a particular frame in a frameset. By default, the topics selected from the ALink control will display in the current window.

The topic with the button must be in a frameset in order for the linked topic to display in a frameset.

9. Select to disable the button if there are no topics available with the same ALink names. Then click Next. The ALink Wizard Font Options window appears, as shown in Figure 27-4.

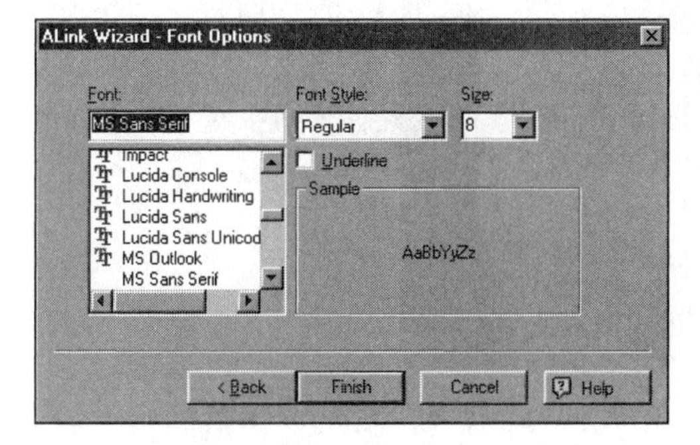

Figure 27-4: ALink Wizard Font Options

10. Choose the font and style options for the text of your Active X button and then click Finish.

Related Topic Control

The Related Topic control is very similar to the ALink and Keyword Link controls; however, this control requires you to select each topic the button displays.

1. Open your topic in the WYSIWYG Editor and place your cursor where you would like the button to be displayed.
2. Select Insert ➪ Related Topics. The Related Topic Wizard appears, as shown in Figure 27-5.

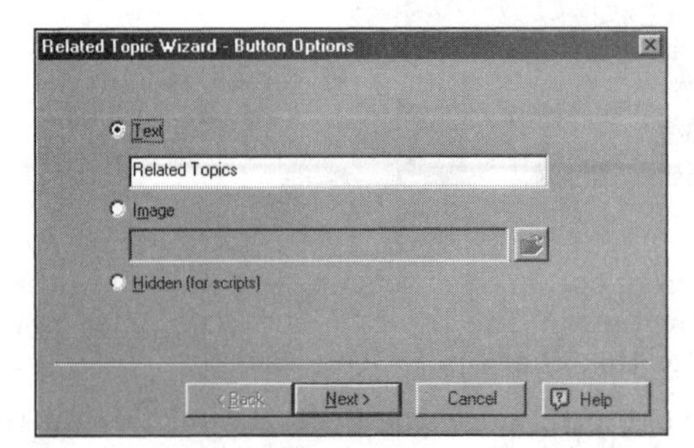

Figure 27-5: Related Topic Wizard - Button Options window

3. Use the radio buttons to choose the options for the button. The default is a text button, with the sample text "Related Topics." You can select the Image radio button to browse to the image you would like to display on the button. The Hidden option allows you to add your own scripts to the control.
4. Once you have selected your desired options, click Next. The Related Topic Selection menu, opens, as shown in Figure 27-6.

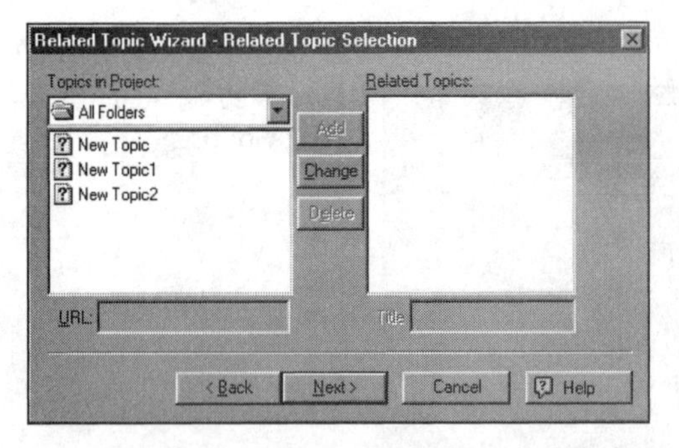

Figure 27-6: Related Topic Wizard - Related Topic Selection window

5. Use the Related Topic Selection window to choose which topics are included when your users click the Related Topics button. After adding the topics to the list, click Next. The Display Options window opens, as shown in Figure 27-7.
6. Use the radio buttons on the left side of the window to specify the type of selection dialog box your end users will see when they select the Related Topics button. The Topics Found Dialog box is larger and has more information than the Popup Menu.

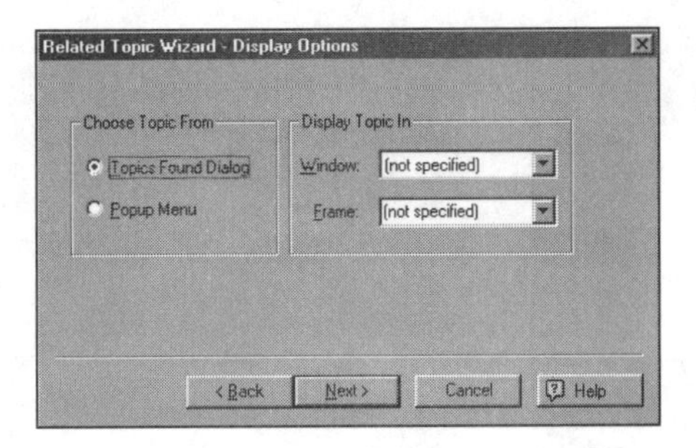

Figure 27-7: Related Topic Wizard - Display Options window

7. Use the drop-down lists on the right side of the window to specify the destination of the topic the user selects, whether it be one of the windows in your project or a frame in a previously create frameset. By default, topics selected from the Related Topic control are displayed in the current window.

The topic displaying the Related Topic control must be loaded in a frameset in order for any of the topics selected to appear in one of the frames of that frameset.

8. Once you finish setting the display options, click Next. The last window of the Wizard, the Font Options window appears (shown in Figure 27-8).

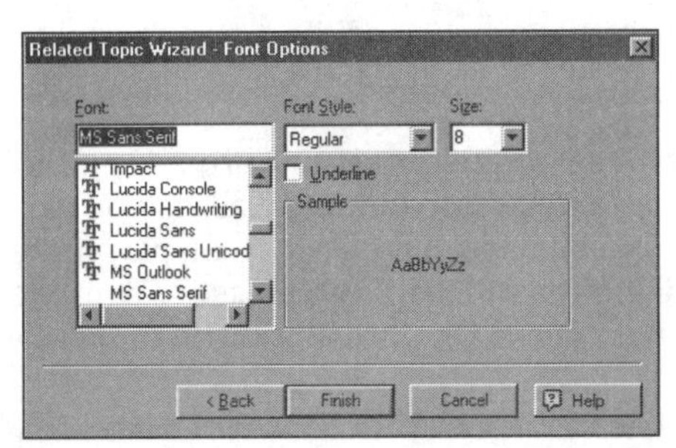

Figure 27-8: Related Topic Wizard - Font Options window

9. Use the Font Options window to select the font family, size, and formatting of the caption on your Related Topic control.

Keyword Link Control

Keyword Link controls are very much like Related Topic and ALink controls; they create links that easily allow your users to jump to similar topics. Keyword Link controls are very similar to Related Topic controls, except instead of specifying an ALink or a Topic in your control, you can select keywords from your index and use their predetermined topic links.

The only difference between the procedures to insert a Keyword control and either of the controls listed above is the second window, which is shown in Figure 27-9.

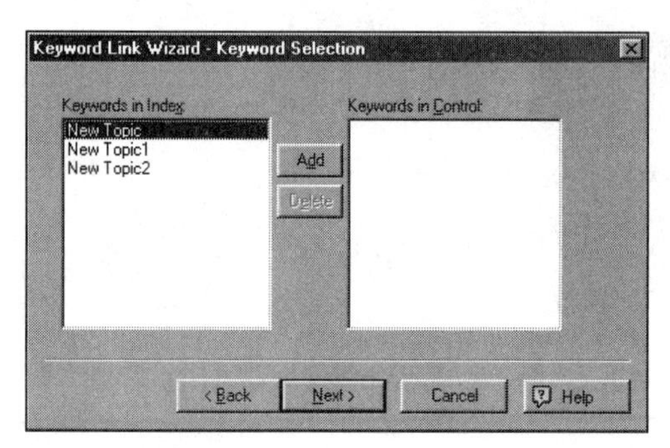

Figure 27-9: Keyword Link Wizard - Keyword Selection window

Use the Keyword Selection window to choose which keywords are displayed when your users click the Keyword button. Once you have finished choosing keywords, click Next and proceed with the Wizard.

Shortcut Control

The Shortcut control is the best way to insert a link to an executable program or a file. Inserting a Shortcut control is nearly the same as inserting any other ActiveX control, except it is one step easier. There are only three windows in the Wizard for the Shortcut control.

Only the second window is new, as shown in Figure 27-10.

Use the Shortcut Selection window to select the program to run when the button is selected. You can also specify any parameters or window classes you would like to pass to the application. In addition, you can select a topic to display if the file does not exist, although the HTML HELP viewer will display a message stating that the file does not exist. Then, once the user clicks OK, it displays the topic selected as the alternative.

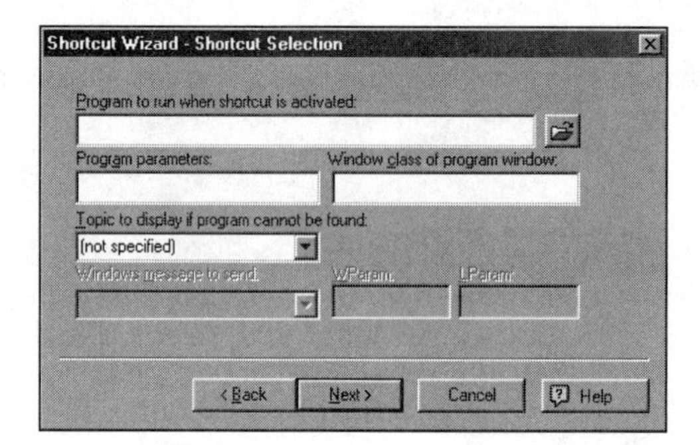

Figure 27-10: Shortcut Wizard - Shortcut Selection window

Be careful when inserting paths into this field; any paths specified will need to exist on your user's PC. It is recommend that you not enter a path; rather, enter only the file name and then simply ship the file in the same directory as your Help system.

WinHelp Topic Control

The WinHelp Topic control allows you to link to any topic within an HLP file, by topic title, topic id, or map number. Inserting a WinHelp Topic control is almost identical to inserting a Shortcut control, with the exception that the second window is different, as shown in Figure 27-11.

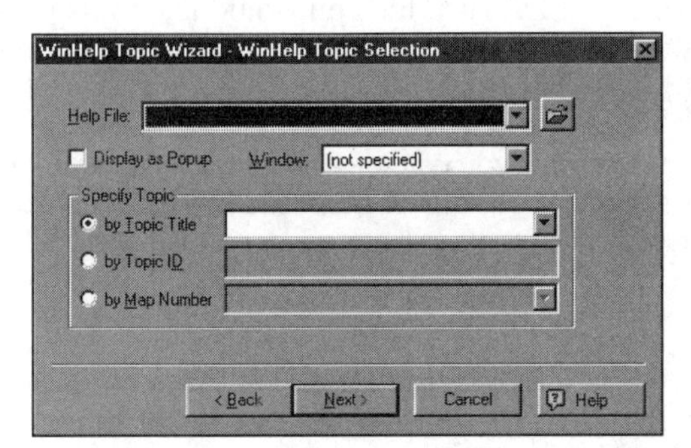

Figure 27-11: WinHelp Topic Wizard - WinHelp Topic Selection window

Use the WinHelp Topic Selection window to select another WinHelp topic to open. Here, you need to select the Help file. If you have an HLP file in the same directory as your RoboHELP HTML project, you can use the drop-down list to select the file. Otherwise, you will need to click the Folder icon to browse to the file. It will then prompt you to copy the file to the same directory as your project; make sure you click OK here. RoboHELP HTML will not allow the link unless the HLP file is in the same directory.

Various platforms may act differently with Active X controls. Make sure to test your HTMLHelp Project and any Active X controls on all systems where your users will run it.

Table of Contents Control

The Table of Contents control enables you to embed the navigation window of the Table of Contents tab inside of one of your topics. To insert this control you must have already created an HHC file, the file in which the table of contents is stored.

Inserting a Table of Contents control is very simple. The Wizard has only one window, as shown in Figure 27-12.

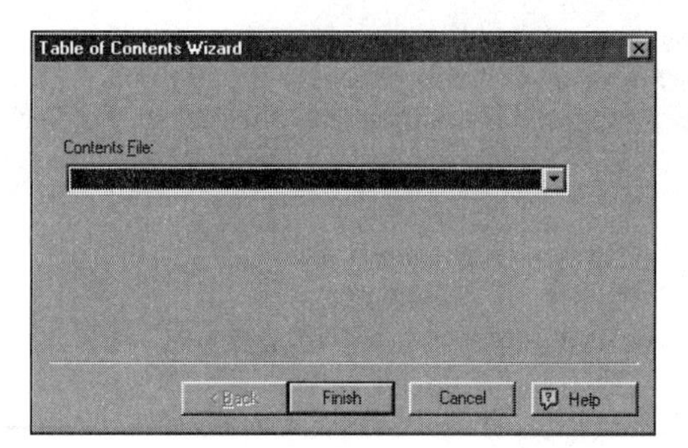

Figure 27-12: Table of Contents Wizard

Use the Table of Contents window to select the HHC file you would like to use and click Finish. By default, your project's HHC file will have the same name as your project or MPJ file.

After inserting the Table of Contents control, you will see a small rectangle with the text "Contents." You must enlarge this area in order to make the control accessible to your users. Otherwise, your Table of Contents will appear as a small, gray dot.

Index Control

The Index control is very similar to the Table of Contents control. It allows you to embed the navigation frame of the Index tab into one of your topics. As with inserting a Table of Contents control, inserting an Index Control is simple and involves only one window, shown in Figure 27-13.

The Index Wizard allows you to select an HHK file from your project directory using a drop-down list. Click Finish once you have selected your desired file. By default, RoboHELP HTML will store your Index in an HHK file, with the same name as your project or MPJ.

After inserting the Index control, you will see a rectangle with the text "Index." You may want to enlarge this area to make is easier for your users to see the control.

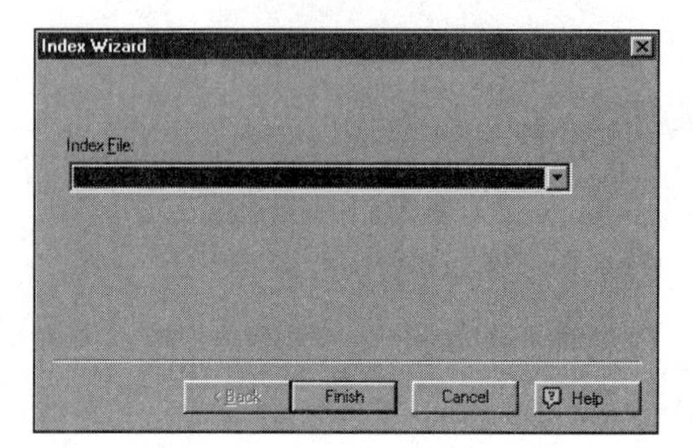

Figure 27-13: Index Wizard for the Index control

Splash Screen Control

A *splash screen* is a graphic that appears on the user's screen, either in BMP or GIF format. Typically, the graphic is set to be displayed for a few seconds and then automatically disappear; they are predominantly used at the start of applications. Splash screens can be set on a per topic basis, meaning you can set a splash screen to display before any given topic.

Inserting a splash screen is very simple. There is only one screen in the Splash Screen Wizard, shown in Figure 27-14.

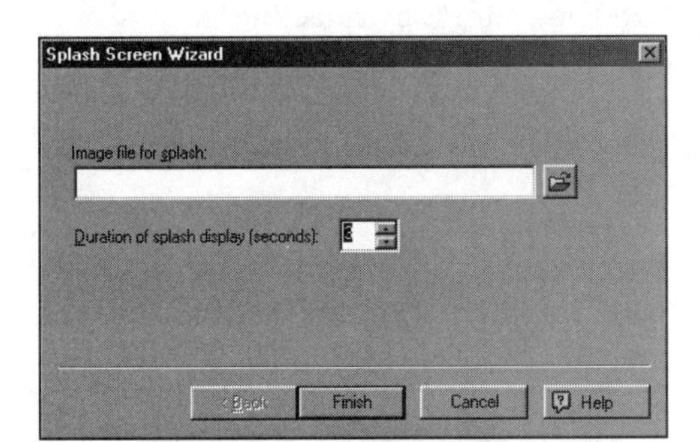

Figure 27-14: Splash Screen Wizard

In the Image File for Splash text box, either enter the path of the image you would like to display or click the Folder icon to start the Graphics locator and select an image. You can also set the number of seconds the splash screen should be displayed.

For more information about using graphics with RoboHELP HTML, see Chapter 20, "Creating and Adding Graphics."

Close Window Control

The Close Window control performs the task you would expect; it closes the current window.

Inserting a Close Window Control requires a wizard with two windows. The first window is the simple Display Control window used previously for the ALink and Related Topics controls. The second window is the Font Options window, also used previously for the ALink and Related Topics controls.

HHCTRL Version Control

The HHCTRL Version control is designed to inform users of which version of the HTML Help control they have. This is a nice feature to use so your users can easily determine if they have the latest version from Microsoft.

Like the Close Window control, the HHCTRL Version control has only two windows: the Display Options control and the Font Options control, both of which you have seen in the sections on ALink controls and Related Topics controls.

Inserting ActiveX from Other Sources

You are not limited to the HTML Help ActiveX controls; however, the HTML Help controls are designed to be used with the HTML Help viewers. Make sure you test any controls from other sources before you begin planning their use. You can insert any ActiveX control registered on your PC by selecting Insert ⇨ ActiveX from the RoboHELP HTML menu bar. You can also see any controls that are already registered.

Registering an ActiveX control

In order to register an ActiveX control, do the following:

1. Copy the OCX file (the Active X control) to C:\Windows\System (if your are using Windows) or C:\Winnt\System32 (if you are using Windows NT).
2. From the Windows taskbar, select Start ⇨ Run.
3. In the resulting dialog box, enter the text regsvr32 followed by the file name of the OCX, for example: regsvr32 hhctrl.ocx.
4. Click the OK button and you should see the message "Regsvr32-DllRegisterServer in hhcrtl.ocx succeeded."

Introduction to JavaScript

The following sections focus on JavaScript pertaining to RoboHELP HTML in conjunction with creating HTML Help and WebHelp systems. Beginning with its origin, the chapter will then explain the basics of JavaScript and continue with some informative examples.

For a comprehensive reference on JavaScript and all its varied uses, see *JavaScript(tm) Bible, 3rd Edition*, by Danny Goodman (ISBN: 0-7645-3188-3).

What Is JavaScript?

JavaScript is a scripting language that is embedded within the HTML files for your Web pages. JavaScript can be written as sections of code within your HTML content or it can be coded into an external file, which is then referenced in the <HEAD> section of your HTML topic. This allows developers to keep their HTML pages free from complex functions, and they can simply include a brief call to the external file.

JavaScript was originally a project developed by Netscape called LiveScript. The idea behind it was to use two types of scripts, client and server-side, in order to automate a Web site. The server-side script handles the communication with databases and other similar tasks, whereas the client side is focused on increasing the interactivity of the HTML page.

JavaScript and Java

Many first impressions of JavaScript are misleading, and many people presume it is somehow related to Java. In reality, JavaScript and Java do have some similarities, but at their core they are very different.

Sun Microsystems was developing Java around the same time as Netscape was working on LiveScript, leading to the joint decision to make some of the basic components of Java and JavaScript similar. This is where the similarities end. JavaScript is a scripting language that is coded into an HTML file that is processed by the end user's PC. Java works from the format of creating Java Applets. Java Applets are distributed in compiled form, and are referenced by an HTML file. When the compiled Java Applet is executed, it accesses the server, which in turn sends the end user's PC the instructions to perform various tasks.

One of JavaScript's advantages is that it is considered a secure language, which means that the end user's PC is less likely to be damaged or to contract a virus from using JavaScript. JavaScript is not completely impervious to hackers, however. It is still suggested that virus software be run on any Web content before it is processed.

Inserting JavaScript into Your Topics

JavaScript can be added to both WebHelp and HTML Help systems. If your target help system is WebHelp, you need to make sure that the script you are inserting is compatible with the browsers your users have installed on their systems. Your first step in considering what types of JavaScript to insert is to research the browsers your target audience is using. Your developers should have the best idea of what types of systems your product supports.

Testing Your JavaScript

If you are going to add JavaScript to your HTML Help project, you need to make sure that the Microsoft HTML Help viewer can interpret the JavaScript you insert. This viewer uses many of the same components as Microsoft's Internet Explorer, so by testing your script on Internet Explorer version 4.0 or later, you will have a good idea how the JavaScript will function in the compiled CHM.

You can also use the Preview feature of RoboHELP HTML, which uses the Internet Explorer display engine, to accurately test your files.

A JavaScript Example

The following steps describe in detail how to properly insert JavaScript into your Help project, whether it is a WebHelp or HTML Help system. The JavaScript code used as an example here will create a button on your topic that will call a secondary window and display one of your other topics.

Using the TrueCode Editor

First, you must load one of your topics into the TrueCode editor. Once you have your RoboHELP project open, do the following:

1. Click on the Project tab of the RoboHELP HTML navigation window.
2. Expand the HTML Files (Topics) folder.
3. Double-click the topic into which you would like to insert the JavaScript example.

The topic you selected will load in the right-hand frame. Along the bottom of that frame, you will see a series of tabs. Double-click the TrueCode tab to see the code that comprises your HTML file. You will insert the code of this sample JavaScript using the TrueCode editor.

The first step is to insert the code for the function of this JavaScript example. This function is the main piece of code that defines the secondary window and the topic to which you are linking. The function is a commonly used method of programming; it allows the developer to reference the same piece of code several times in one HTML file.

Place your cursor just before the text </HEAD> and enter the following lines of code:

```
<SCRIPT LANGUAGE="javascript">
function SecondaryWindow()
{
window.open('New_Topic.htm','SecondaryWindow','toolbar=no,statu
s=no,scrollbars=no,location=no,menubar=no,directories=no,width=
350,height=250,top=300,left=300')
}
</SCRIPT>
```

The function inserted is called `SecondaryWindow( )`, and it can be called any number of times, using several different methods. The method we will use is a simple button with the label "Click Here." In this section of code, I have referenced an HTML file called New_Topic.htm; replace the file name with any topic in your project.

In the TrueCode editor, insert the cursor where you would like your button to appear. Unfortunately, there is no easy way to remove the existing tags in the TrueCode editor, so you will need to scroll through the code until you find the location you would like.

Tip If there is a word you are inserting the button after, you may want to use the Find feature to locate that area of the HTML file.

Once you have placed your cursor where you would like to insert the button, enter the following code:

```
<FORM>
<Input Type="Button" Value="Click Here"
onClick"SecondaryWindow()">
</FORM>
<P>
```

This code creates a button with the label "Click Here," and sets the button's onClick event to perform the function `SecondaryWindow( )`. The onClick event is the process that occurs when the button is selected. Once all your code has been entered, your window should look similar to Figure DP40.

Make sure you insert a <P> after the </FORM>. This is done because if you switch over to the WYSIWYG editor, you will see a dashed line that corresponds to the <FORM> and </FORM> tags. Without the <P>, you will not be able to click in the space following this area.

Take particular care to confirm that your JavaScript code has been color-coded properly by the TrueCode editor after you insert it. Your code should match the example shown in Figure 27-15 and should be the color green. This is a quick identifier of areas of code that have been inserted improperly. For instance, an area that appears all one color after a certain point is most likely missing a parameter such as </FORM> or </SCRIPT>.

Running Your JavaScript

After you have double-checked your code to make sure your spelling and syntax are correct, right-click the window and select Preview Topic. Your topic should load without errors and you should see your topic in a small browser window, with the button we have created. Click the button to make sure your code functions properly. If the button does not work or you see extraneous HTML code such as <E> or <S>, you may have mis-typed a section of code. Reload your topic in the TrueCode editor and check your work.

Congratulations, you have just inserted your first piece of JavaScript!

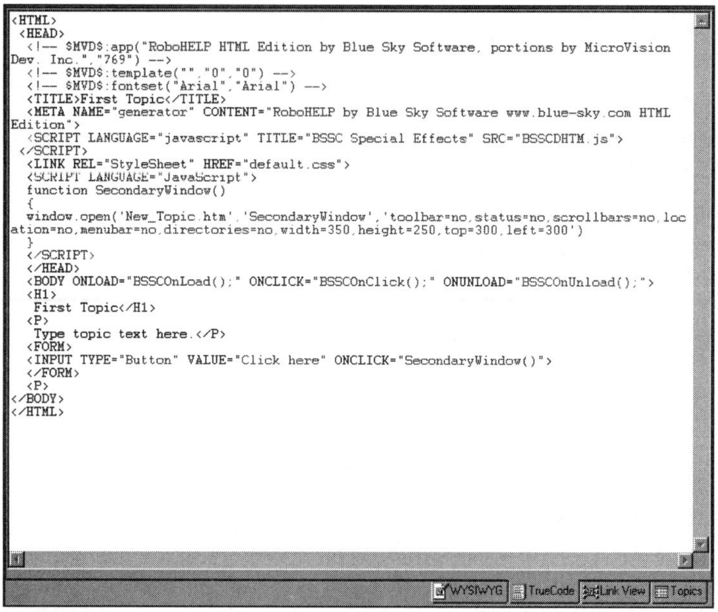

```
<HTML>
 <HEAD>
  <!-- $MVD$:app("RoboHELP HTML Edition by Blue Sky Software, portions by MicroVision
Dev. Inc.","769") -->
  <!-- $MVD$:template("","0","0") -->
  <!-- $MVD$:fontset("Arial","Arial") -->
  <TITLE>First Topic</TITLE>
  <META NAME="generator" CONTENT="RoboHELP by Blue Sky Software www.blue-sky.com HTML
Edition">
  <SCRIPT LANGUAGE="javascript" TITLE="BSSC Special Effects" SRC="BSSCDHTM.js">
 </SCRIPT>
  <LINK REL="StyleSheet" HREF="default.css">
  <SCRIPT LANGUAGE="JavaScript">
  function SecondaryWindow()
  {
  window.open('New_Topic.htm','SecondaryWindow','toolbar=no,status=no,scrollbars=no,loc
ation=no,menubar=no,directories=no,width=350,height=250,top=300,left=300')
  }
  </SCRIPT>
  </HEAD>
  <BODY ONLOAD="BSSCOnLoad();" ONCLICK="BSSCOnClick();" ONUNLOAD="BSSCOnUnload();">
  <H1>
   First Topic</H1>
  <P>
   Type topic text here.</P>
  <FORM>
  <INPUT TYPE="Button" VALUE="Click here" ONCLICK="SecondaryWindow()">
  </FORM>
  <P>
</BODY>
</HTML>
```

WYSIWYG | TrueCode | Link View | Topics

Figure 27-15: TrueCode editor with JavaScript example

Summary

In this chapter, you received an introduction to ActiveX and JavaScript. You learned about scripting hosts and engines, and server-side and client-side scripts and how they work with HTML pages. After learning about all the HTML Help controls and how to insert a third-party control, you learned the difference between Java and JavaScript. Finally, you learned how to insert a piece of JavaScript, using the TrueCode editor, all the essential keys to adding great interactivity to your help systems.

✦ ✦ ✦

CHAPTER 28

Examining WebHelp, JavaHelp, and Other Help Systems

In This Chapter

WebHelp

JavaHelp

NetHelp

This chapter introduces additional help systems and illustrates how they can benefit you and your users. You will learn about the differences between the various help systems and what platforms and browsers are best suited for them. You will learn how to create WebHelp and JavaHelp from existing project files, as well as the benefits and limitations of NetHelp2.

Understanding Online Help Format Options

A variety of options are available to you when it comes to designing your help system. You may need to provide your help system to an audience whose requirements are very diverse. The operating systems on which they work may be other than Microsoft Windows, such as Macintosh, Unix, or Linux.

The discussion of help formats in this chapter provides you with the highlights of each system, the platforms on which they work, the browsers with which they operate, and details about each system, enough information for you to make an informed choice about which one is best for you and your audience. RoboHELP HTML provides an environment in which you can generate WebHelp and JavaHelp from the help files you create in RoboHELP. NetHelp is available directly from Netscape.

Comparing Help Format Features

Each help system has the same basic objective: to present your information in the most productive manner possible. Variations in the use of platforms and browsers makes each help system unique in its approach. The following lists illustrate the basic elements of the help systems and what they can accomplish for you. You then need to consider what your readers will be using to read your information and the nature of your application.

Here is a list of the principal help systems:

- Microsoft HTML Help
- WinHelp
- WinHelp 2000
- WebHelp
- JavaHelp
- NetHelp2

Many of these help systems contain some or all of the following features:

Expandable and collapsible table of contents
Multilevel index
Merged indexes
Merged tables of contents
Custom TOC icons
Full-text search
Online glossary
Related topics (See also)
ALinks
Microsoft HTML Help controls
Browse sequences
Cross-platform compatibility
Browser independence
Compilation and compression
Tri-pane window
Custom windows
Popup windows
Information types
ActiveX controls
Dynamic HTML
Display images
Multimedia
Forms
Scripts
Context-sensitive help

Each help system is different and supports different features, and the list of supported features is growing everyday. Read the section for the system you are interested in to make sure that it supports the features you and your users need. If you plan to use these formats often, make it a point to keep up on the new developments.

WebHelp

WebHelp is a tool that allows you to deliver HTML help files, and enables your readers to view them regardless of platform or browser. You first create your project as you would in RoboHELP HTML; and after you complete your project, select WebHelp as the help format and begin to generate the compiled help files.

WebHelp is flexible enough to work with a variety of browsers (Netscape and Microsoft Internet Explorer) and on different platforms (Unix, Windows, and Macintosh). WebHelp makes it possible for any combination of platform and browser to access the information through the use of specific, hidden routines at startup.

Differences between WebHelp and Microsoft HTML Help

Standard HTML Help is a compiled help format that is designed to operate on Windows operating systems. The Standard HTML Help engine supports specific features of the program. It also uses components of Microsoft Internet Explorer to display the compiled help in a special HTML Help viewer. Standard HTML Help is derived by compiling the project files into a single file (CHM), and it is supported on 32-bit Windows systems.

WebHelp is not compiled and uses Dynamic HTML (DHTML), Java applets, and HTML lists to provide functionality. Older browsers that do not have complete Java or DHTML support use the HTML lists.

WebHelp supports all the primary Microsoft HTML Help features, such as a table of contents, multi-level indexes, related topics, and full-text search.

Recommended WebHelp browsers and platforms

WebHelp works on all common platforms and browsers, including the following: Microsoft Windows 3.1, 95, and 98; Windows NT 4; Macintosh; and Unix. The list of browsers includes Microsoft Internet Explorer 4.0 or later and Netscape Navigator 4.01 or later.

Browser Limitations

The following list details current limitations that develop when a WebHelp project is viewed on a particular browser as of this publication. Make sure you verify this information before you publish to your users.

- **Internet Explorer 2.0:** This does not support cascading style sheets (CSS), DHTML, Java, or frames.
- **Internet Explorer 3.0*x*:** This does not support cascading style sheets (CSS), DHTML, Java applets resizing when the browser is resized, or FONT FACE.

In Internet Explorer 3.00 and 3.01, Java applets cannot read or write to local or network media. WebHelp must be accessed through a Web server.

✦ **Netscape Navigator (all versions):** Navigator cannot load Java applets from locations specified by UNC file names on local area networks. Map a drive letter to solve this problem.

✦ **Netscape Navigator 3.0x:** Java applets do not resize when the browser is resized.

✦ **Netscape Navigator 3.04 or earlier:** This version does not support cascading style sheets (CSS), DHTML, ActiveX, or margin settings.

✦ **Netscape Navigator 4.6:** Java applets do not resize when the browser is resized.

Generating, Viewing, and Distributing WebHelp

RoboHELP HTML generates the source files for WebHelp through the WebHelp Wizard. The Wizard generates and saves the HTML files in your project folder within a subfolder named WebHelp. Then you distribute the source files, and other project-related files, to your Web Help users.

You can create WebHelp for use as application help, standalone projects, or online documents.

Generating WebHelp

To generate WebHelp:

1. Open the completed HTML Help project you wish to convert to WebHelp.
2. Choose File ➪ Generate ➪ WebHelp 3. The WebHelp Options wizard appears, as shown in Figure 28-1.

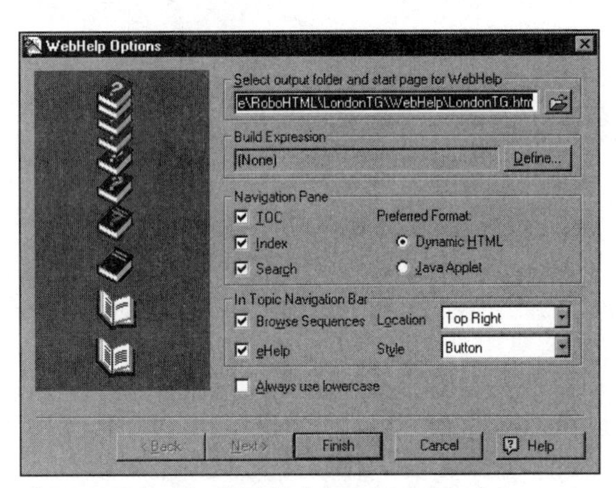

Figure 28-1: The WebHelp Options window

3. A location is suggested for the output folder. To select a different location for the output folder, click the Folder icon and navigate to a different location.
4. Select the options you want to include in the Navigation Pane and the In Topic Navigation Bar.
5. If you want to use build tags, click Define and select build tag options. RoboHELP HTML opens the Define Build Tag Expression window as shown in Figure 28-2.

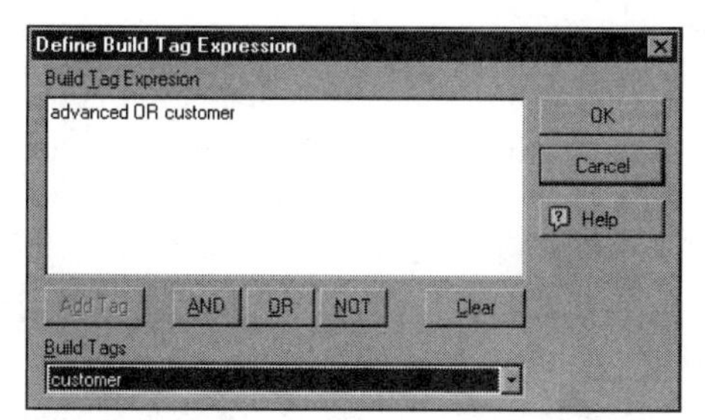

Figure 28-2: Define Build Tag Expression window

For more information about build tags, see Chapter 24, "Using Reports and Compiling."

6. Select a preferred format for your WebHelp files. DHTML uses a mix of DHTML and Java applets to create your help system. Java Applet uses Java applets to create your help system. Your choice of formats will be invisible to users of your compiled help system.
7. If you are creating files for Unix users, be sure to check Always Use Lowercase. This is highly recommended for Unix users because case sensitivity is important with Unix.
8. When you are done selecting options for your compiled WebHelp files, click Finish.

RoboHELP HTML compiles your WebHelp and displays a message, shown in Figure 28-3, telling you it was completed successfully and asking if you wish to view your files.

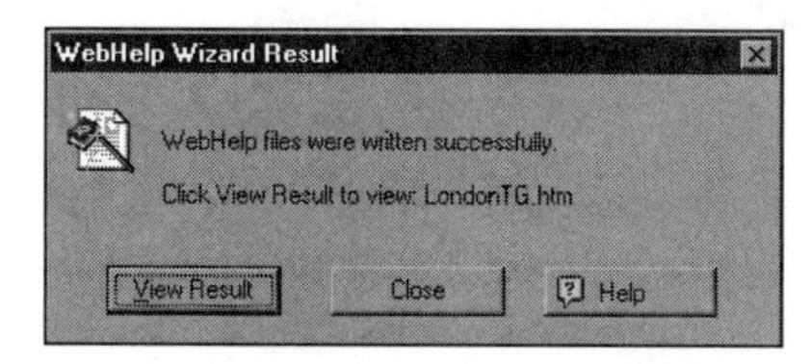

Figure 28-3: WebHelp Wizard Result window

Note

By default, WebHelp has eHelp capabilities turned on.

Viewing WebHelp

After generating WebHelp, you need to see what it looks like. Unless you specify otherwise, when you open the WebHelp files, the help system opens in your default Web browser.

1. Open the project you wish to preview.
2. Select File ⇨ Run WebHelp 3 with Internet Explorer, or select File ⇨ Run WebHelp 3 with Netscape Navigator. The WebHelp displays in your browser as shown in Figure 28-4.

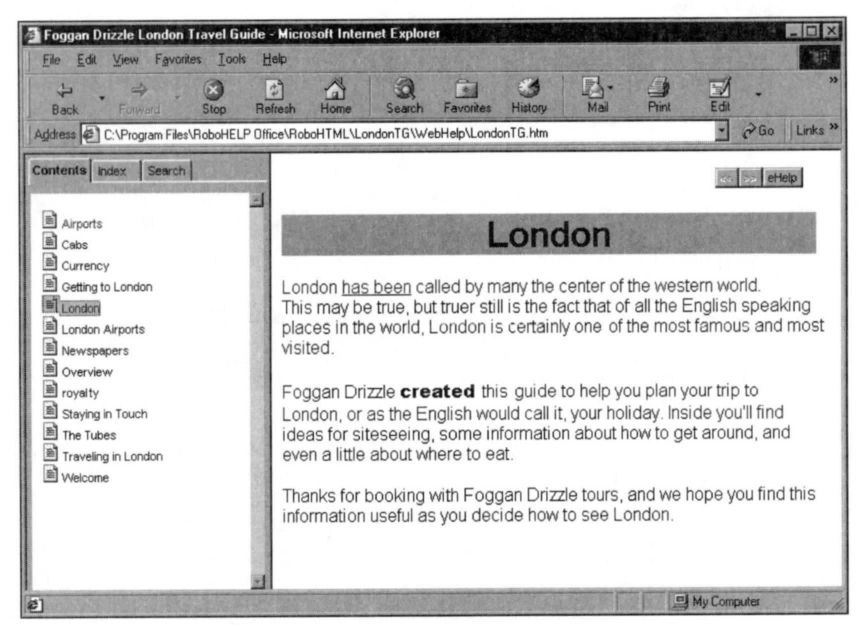
Foggan Drizzle London Travel Guide - Microsoft Internet Explorer
File Edit View Favorites Tools Help
Back Forward Stop Refresh Home Search Favorites History Mail Print Edit
Address C:\Program Files\RoboHELP Office\RoboHTML\LondonTG\WebHelp\LondonTG.htm
Go Links
Contents Index Search
Airports
Cabs
Currency
Getting to London
London
London Airports
Newspapers
Overview
royalty
Staying in Touch
The Tubes
Traveling in London
Welcome
eHelp
London
London has been called by many the center of the western world. This may be true, but truer still is the fact that of all the English speaking places in the world, London is certainly one of the most famous and most visited.
Foggan Drizzle created this guide to help you plan your trip to London, or as the English would call it, your holiday. Inside you'll find ideas for siteseeing, some information about how to get around, and even a little about where to eat.
Thanks for booking with Foggan Drizzle tours, and we hope you find this information useful as you decide how to see London.
My Computer

Figure 28-4: WebHelp Project opened in Internet Explorer

Caution

To keep everything current, make sure you generate your WebHelp again every time you change your HTML Help project files.

Distributing WebHelp

WebHelp is used as cross-platform help for applications as well as standalone help for books and other electronic documents not shipped with software programs. The freedom to distribute WinHelp alone gives you maximum flexibility with your HTML Help project information.

Distributing WebHelp with an Application

Adding WebHelp to an application is a process that involves not only you, the help creator, but the combined efforts of you and your software developers working as a team. Your developers will need to work with you to make sure the WebHelp files meet the needs of the program.

They will also need to tell you where to copy the WebHelp folder and its contents once you are ready to start including them in the development process. Always make sure to let the developer know the name of the start page (the HTM file) for your help project.

Distributing WebHelp as Separate Files

There are three ways to distribute WebHelp independent of an application:

- ✦ Copy the WebHelp folder and its contents to a disk or CD-ROM.
- ✦ Copy these files to any location on the end user's system.
- ✦ Set up WebHelp so that the users of the system select the start page (HTM file) when they run the system.

Using a Web Server with WebHelp

WebHelp is well suited for the development of intranet materials and Web pages. To make your project functional, you need to deploy it on a Web server. Once it is posted to the server, it is available for everyone to use, regardless of the user's platform (Windows, Macintosh, Unix, and Linux) or browser (Internet Explorer or Netscape Navigator).

Contact the Web master or network system administrator for the specific procedures you need to follow. This person will let you know where you need to store the files so that they can be loaded onto the server.

Using Context-Sensitive WebHelp

WebHelp gives you the capability to create full-featured help systems that include context-sensitive help. WebHelp files are supported by applications created in C and C++, Java applets, Visual Basic forms, and Web pages. Creating context-sensitive help is always a cooperative effort combining the talents of the developers and the help author.

The author creates the topics and text within the editor. Each context-sensitive help topic is a separate HTML file that describes the use of the application at that dialog box or window level.

The application developer programs the help topics in the application so that the correct ones are displayed when the user requests help. As the help author, all you need to do is specify for the application developer which .htm files goes with each page of the program.

WebHelp does not support individual topics for each field or control.

JavaHelp

JavaHelp, developed by Sun Microsystems, is a compressed help format designed to work with applications written in the Java programming language. JavaHelp and Java applications run on a variety of platforms (Windows, Unix, Macintosh, Linux, etc.). JavaHelp is an online help-delivery system, not a help-authoring tool.

RoboHELP provides rich support for the emerging JavaHelp format, and automatically creates all the Java-based help features, such as tables of contents, full-text search, dynamic indexes, navigation controls, and popup windows, along with HTML-based features such as HTML content, hyperlinks, images, etc.

Supporting JavaHelp

A copy of the Java Development Kit (version 1.2 or later) and the JavaHelp 1.0 components are necessary in order to properly generate and view JavaHelp files.

JavaHelp is the preferred help format for use with applications written in the Java programming language.

What Do Your Users Need?

Your users need the Java Runtime Environment (JRE) 1.2.1 and the JavaHelp 1.0 components in order to view your JavaHelp system.

The following components come packaged with JavaHelp 1.0:

- A set of file formats for the creation of help content files
- An API enabling Java developers to integrate JavaHelp with their applications. The APIs are standard extensions to the Java Development Kit (JDK).
- The JavaHelp viewer, an HTML-based help system viewer. It includes the components necessary to view a JavaHelp system.
- Documentation for help authors and developers
- Several example help systems

How JavaHelp Works

Behind the scenes, JavaHelp is a compressed file (JAR file) or a set of files used to run a help system for a particular Java application. You generate JavaHelp after you finish authoring help topics, creating a table of contents, and building the index in RoboHELP. All the files you need to distribute are copied into a single folder called "JavaHelp," or into a JAR file if you choose to compile the files.

JavaHelp Feature and Advantages

JavaHelp comes with many new parts that do not ship with HTML Help. The following list describes each new feature and the advantages it offers:

✦ **JavaHelp help viewer:** This viewer is HTML-based and has a toolbar, a content pane, and a navigation pane.

✦ **Table of contents:** The table of contents includes an unlimited number of levels, as well as collapsible and expandable topics.

✦ **Index:** The index is a complete tool that lists keywords and all of the topics that reference keywords.

✦ **Full-text search:** The search engine examines the complete text of the content as well as multi-word queries.

✦ **Display flexibility:** You can view JavaHelp in its own window or embedded in an application.

✦ **Context sensitivity:** Context-sensitive help and ID mapping are provided in the JavaHelp API through the use of the Swing toolkit of the Java Foundation Classes (JFC).

✦ **Popups:** JavaHelp supports two types of popups: text-only popups that open in a small window within the topic, and popup links that open in a special popup window.

✦ **Merging:** The JavaHelp API supports the merging of tables of contents, indexes, and search databases.

✦ **Compression:** You can compress a JavaHelp project into a single file in the Java Archive (JAR) format. Using this process significantly reduces the size of your JavaHelp project.

✦ **Bulleted and numbered lists:** JavaHelp supports both bulleted and numbered lists.

✦ **Internationalization:** JavaHelp coordinates with the Java Development Kit 1.2 to provide full I18N support.

Unsupported JavaHelp Features

The following list details some of the known limitations of JavaHelp 1.0. As of this writing, these features are not currently supported in JavaHelp, unless otherwise noted. This information is for reference only, and is not applicable to every JavaHelp project.

- Links to e-mail, FTP sites, and other external files
- Fonts (they are automatically set to the JavaHelp default font set)
- Text spacing and paragraph positioning
- Table widths, alignment, and border effects
- Multimedia
- Macros, DHTML, ActiveX controls, JavaScript, and VBScripts
- Lists (regular and numbered)
- Background images (watermarks) and colors
- Image maps
- Images (they do not display consistently in JavaHelp)
- Small caps
- All caps
- Popups
- Text animations and effects
- Some custom colors
- Framesets
- HTML files generated by Microsoft Word 2000

This list is sure to shrink as development of JavaHelp proceeds.

JavaHelp tips

As with any large help project, organization and planning are essential elements for success. The following pointers will help ensure success:

- Avoid the use of elements not supported by JavaHelp
- Use build tags

✦ Use care and precision in the creation of context-sensitive JavaHelp

Generating, Viewing, and Distributing JavaHelp

You create JavaHelp from within a completed RoboHELP HTML project. RoboHELP automates the generation of all source files and saves them in a specified subfolder in the project folder. These source files, along with all project-related files, should be shipped to the users of the project.

By default, your new JavaHelp files are saved in your RoboHELP HTML Help project directory in a folder called JavaHelp.

Generating JavaHelp

To generate JavaHelp:

1. Open the project you plan to use to generate JavaHelp.
2. Select File ➪ Generate ➪ JavaHelp. This opens the JavaHelp Options wizard as shown in Figure 28-5.

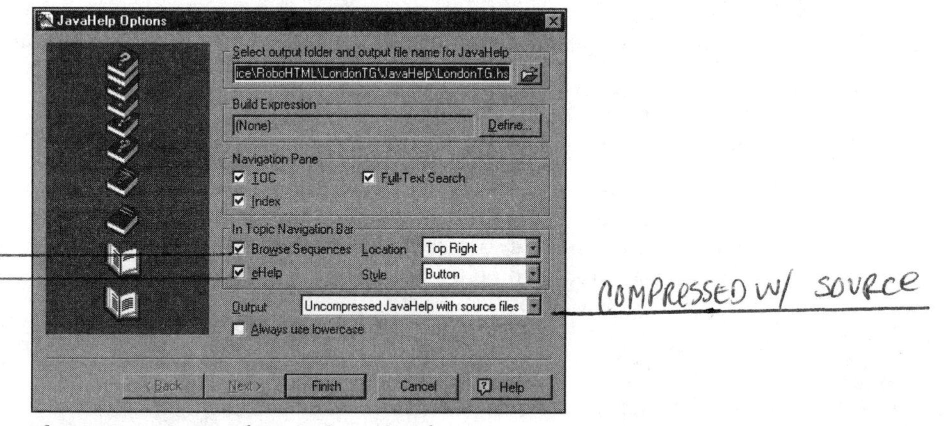

Figure 28-5: JavaHelp Creation wizard

3. Choose a place to save your JavaHelp files. RoboHELP HTML lists a default location. You can change the location by clicking the Folder icon and navigating to another folder.
4. If you want to use build tags, click Define and select Build Tag Options. Robo HELP HTML opens the Define Build Tag Expressions window as shown in Figure 28-6.

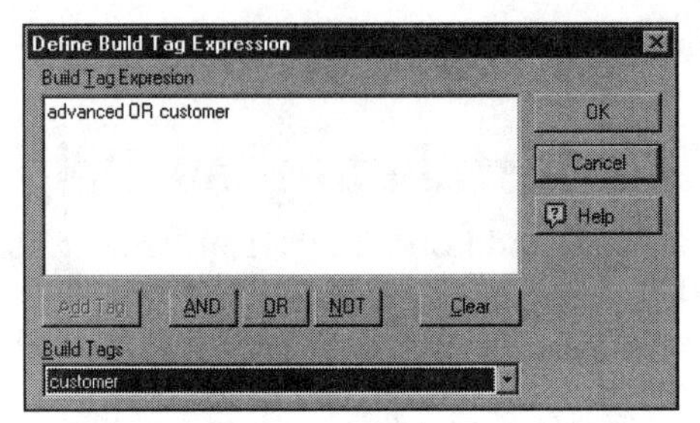

Figure 28-6: Define Build Tag Expression window

For more information about build tags, see Chapter 24, "Using Reports and Compiling."

5. Select the options to include in the JavaHelp navigation pane and the JavaHelp topic navigation bar.
6. From the drop-down menu, select the type of JavaHelp output to generate. For the smallest option (just a JAR file and an HS file) select Compressed JavaHelp. For a JAR file, an HS file, and individual source files, select Compressed JavaHelp with source files. For an HS file and individual source files, select Compressed JavaHelp without source files
7. If you are creating files for Unix users, be sure to check Always Use Lowercase. This is highly recommended for Unix users because case sensitivity is important with Unix.
8. To create file names with only lowercase letters, select Always Use Lowercase. Again, this option is strongly recommended for users of Unix operating systems, as all versions of Unix are case sensitive. Your choice of formats will be invisible to users of your compiled help system.
9. When you are done selecting options for your compiled WebHelp files, click Finish.

If you do not have JavaHelp 1.0 installed, when you click Finish, RoboHELP HTML asks you to choose to install it or not to generate Full Search Help.

RoboHELP HTML compiles your JavaHelp and displays the message shown in Figure 28-7, telling you it was completed successfully and asking if you wish to view your files.

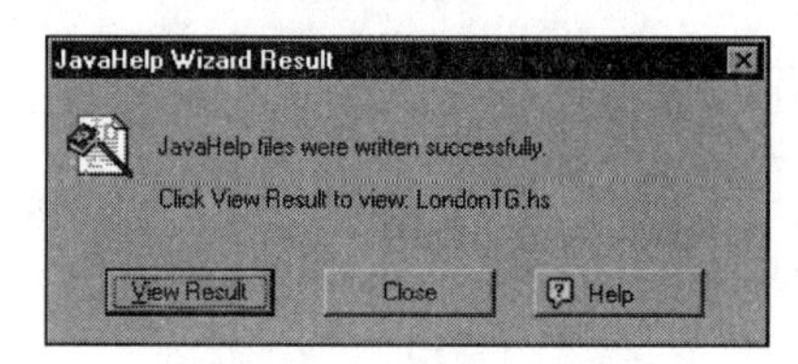

Figure 28-7: JavaHelp Wizard Results

Viewing JavaHelp

The JavaHelp user interface is very similar to the Standard HTML Help viewer, and includes the following features:

- Table of contents
- Index
- Full-text search
- Customizable display window
- Compressed project file (JAR file)
- Context-sensitive help

Distributing JavaHelp

JavaHelp operates on several platforms: Windows, Macintosh, Unix, Linux, and Sun Solaris. When JavaHelp is generated, all source files are saved in a subfolder within your project folder.

Your JavaHelp works properly and efficiently if you include the following:

- The JAR file, if the project is compressed
- If the project is not compressed, all the individual source files in the JavaHelp output folder
- The JavaHelp 1.0 components
- The Java Runtime Environment (JRE)

Context-Sensitive JavaHelp

Context-sensitive help provides information about what readers see inside an application — details about fields and controls, explanations of messages, and descriptions of windows and screen objects. Creating context-sensitive help is done with the assistance of the developer who does the custom programming.

The author creates the topics and text within the editor. Each context-sensitive help topic is a separate HTML file that describes the use of the application at that dialog box or window level.

The application developer programs the help topics in the application so that the correct ones are displayed when the user requests help.

JavaHelp does not support individual topics for each field or control.

NetHelp

NetHelp is an open standards-based platform for creating and viewing HTML-based online Help. Using Netscape Navigator 3.0 or later, NetHelp provides a context-sensitive online Help solution for any Web-based application or native Macintosh, Unix, or Windows program.

NetHelp2, the current version of NetHelp, was created during the Netscape Communicator project to provide a robust help platform for Communicator itself. It is based on technology built into Communicator, so users of NetHelp2 systems need to have Communicator installed in order to access NetHelp.

The main advantage of NetHelp is that online authors can use it to create a single help system capable of being deployed across an entire enterprise—PCs, Macs, and Unix. This is great for companies that have use a wide range of computing platforms and already have a Netscape Navigator or Communicator user-base.

Features Included in NetHelp

NetHelp is based on standard HTML and JavaScript. The navigation aids are all scripted, and they include the following:

- ✦ An expandable/collapsible table of contents
- ✦ A keyword index
- ✦ A simple Find feature
- ✦ Browse sequences

What Browsers Support NetHelp?

NetHelp2 works only with Navigator 4 and later, including the Navigator 4 component of Communicator. NetHelp2 was designed using advanced, new features of JavaScript not supported by Navigator 3.0.

A customer using Microsoft Internet Explorer 4.0 or later cannot view NetHelp. Net Help uses some new features of JavaScript 1.2 that are not yet available in Internet Explorer. The method used for providing context-sensitive help depends on the use of

NetHelp, but it is usually via URLs that are implemented only in the Netscape browser. NetHelp does work for standalone applications, but it requires the Netscape browser.

Summary

This chapter introduced help systems beyond HTML Help and illustrated how they might benefit you and your user. You learned about the differences between the various help systems and what platforms and browsers are best suited for them. You learned how to create WebHelp and JavaHelp from existing project files, and you learned about the benefits and limitations of NetHelp2.

✦ ✦ ✦

The WinHelp HPJ File

In This Appendix

Understanding the HPJ file

Understanding the HPJ file sections

Editing the HPJ file

In this appendix, you'll learn about the sections and options in the HPJ file. You'll also see how to edit the HPJ file manually and how to set some WinHelp options in the WIN.INI file.

The HPJ File

The HPJ file contains essential information about a WinHelp project. It tells the WinHelp compiler, which files to compile, how to compile them, and how the WinHelp project will appear when you run it. The HPJ file also sets a variety of options for such things as linking the WinHelp file to a program by context-sensitive help links and which external programs and DLLs to use with the WinHelp file. It contains all the necessary information for the WinHelp compiler to create and manage your help project.

When you start a WinHelp project in RoboHELP, RoboHELP creates a default HPJ file that contains many of the basic options. When you make changes to the project settings in RoboHELP, RoboHELP updates the settings in the HPJ file. It's a good idea to update the HPJ file exclusively through RoboHELP to avoid entering an incorrect setting or option.

Tip: Numeric values are described in decimal notation in this appendix; however, the default for the Microsoft Help Compiler Workshop is to enter many numeric values as hexadecimal numbers. If you are working with a project that was created in the Microsoft Help Compiler Workshop, you may need to convert values to hexadecimal notation for consistency.

The HPJ Sections

The HPJ file is composed of eleven separate sections. Each section has a specific function, as shown in Table A-1. The information in the sections is performed in the order it appears in the HPJ file.

They do not need to appear in any particular order in the HPJ file, although the [OPTIONS] section usually appears first because it contains the WinHelp project's file name and other basic information.

Table A-1
HPJ File Sections

HPJ File Section	*Description*
[OPTIONS]	Contains various options for naming, compiling, and reporting warnings and errors for a WinHelp project. This section is mandatory.
[ALIAS]	Associates topic IDs defined in the [MAP] section with other topic IDs.
[BAGGAGE]	Identifies the files that are stored within the compiled WinHelp file.
[BITMAPS]	Identifies the location of individual bitmaps. (This HPJ file section is no longer used in WinHelp 4, having been replaced by the BMROOT option in the [OPTIONS] section. You should use this only in WinHelp 3 projects or WinHelp 4 projects with WinHelp 3 compatibility.)
[BUILDTAGS]	Identifes the build tags you can use in the WinHelp project.
[CONFIG] [CONFIG-(Secondary Window)]	Contains any WinHelp macros that are to be performed when the WinHelp file is opened.
[FILES]	Contains a list of the RTF file(s) that will be compiled into the WinHelp project. This section is mandatory.
[MACROS]	Contains macros that run when you select a given keyword in the WinHelp file's index.
[MAP]	Lists topic IDs or aliases and the related context-sensitive hooks issued by the calling program.
[WINDOWS]	Defines the types of display windows that may appear in the WinHelp project.

The information in this appendix is intended as a quick reference only. For detailed information on using specific sections or options, please refer to the RoboHELP documentation and the online help files accompanying the Microsoft Help Compiler Workshop.

[OPTIONS] section

The [OPTIONS] section holds the majority of the settings for your project. You use the [OPTIONS] section to identify such things as the name of the project, where to find graphic files, what level of compression to use, and how to report errors and warnings during the compile. The [OPTIONS] section is mandatory and should appear as the first section in the HPJ file.

You can enter the following options in the [OPTIONS] section:

BMROOT	HLP
BUILD	INDEX_SEPARATORS
CHARSET	LCID
CITATION	MAPFONTSIZE
COMPRESS	MULTIKEY
CONTENTS	NOTES
CNT	OLDKEYPHRASE
COPYRIGHT	REPLACE
DBCS	REPORT
DEFFONT	ROOT
ERRORLOG	TITLE
FORCEFONT	TMPDIR
FTS	

BMROOT

The BMROOT option specifies a folder where you can keep all your graphic files. For example, the following BMROOT option would tell the WinHelp compiler to look in the Foggan Drizzle Tour Info directory on the E: drive as well as in the standard RoboHELP Clipart Letters directory for graphics:

```
BMROOT=e:\Foggan Drizzle Tour Info,C:\Program Files\RoboHELP
Office\RoboHELP\ClipArt\Letter
```

If you omit this option, the WinHelp compiler will look in the same directory as the source files for the project.

This setting replaces the [BITMAP] section used in WinHelp 3.

The BMROOT option is set through the RoboHELP Explorer Project Manager.

For more information on using different directories for graphics, see Chapter 6, "Adding Simple Graphics."

BUILD

The BUILD option identifies which build tags to use during the compile. The compiler will compile all the topics with the build tags as well as all topics that have no build tags assigned. You can also use standard boolean operators such as; ~, &, and | to set up conditions for build tags. The ~ operator is used to select topics that do not have the build tag specified. The & operator is used to select only topics that have those two build tags. The | operator is used when the topics selected can have either build tag. For example, the following BUILD option would tell the WinHelp compiler to compile all topics with the build tag MAIN or the build tag OEM_VER, as well as any topics without build tags:

```
BUILD=MAIN | OEM_VER
```

The BUILD option is set in the Advanced tab of the Project Settings screen.

For more information on using build tags for conditional compiles, see Chapter 15, "Managing Large Projects."

CHARSET

The CHARSET option identifies the default character set to be used for fonts in the WinHelp file. This lets you take advantage of specific character substitutions used in the language. (A list of common character sets appears in Table A-2.) For example, the following CHARSET option sets the default character set to Hebrew:

```
CHARSET=177
```

Table A-2
Character Set Values

Character Set Description	*Value*
ANSI	(no CHARSET option entry necessary)
ARABIC (simplified)	178
ARABIC (traditional)	179

Character Set Description	*Value*
BALTIC	186
CHINESEBIG5	136
DEFAULT	1
EASTEUROPE	238
GB2312	134
GREEK	161
HANGEUL	129
HEBREW	177
MAC	77
OEM	255
PC437	254
RUSSIAN	204
SHIFTJIS	128
SYMBOL	2
THAI	222
TURKISH	162

Depending on your application, there may also be other supported character sets you can use. Check with your development team to find out if you need to provide support for additional character sets.

Many programs, including Microsoft Word, will specify a character set as part of the RTF file creation process. The character set specified in the RTF file will override the character set identified with the `CHARSET` option.

The `CHARSET` option cannot be set directly in RoboHELP. To set this option, you must manually edit the HPJ file as shown later in this appendix.

CITATION

The `CITATION` option lets you specify text to append to text whenever text is copied to the Windows Clipboard or printed from the WinHelp file. You can use this option to add copyright notices, version information, and so on. The text in the citation can be up to 2000 characters or 1000 characters if you are using a DBCS language. For example, the following would append a copyright message for Foggan Drizzle Tours after each block of text is copied or printed from the WinHelp file:

```
CITATION=Copyright 2000, 2001  Foggan Drizzle Tours, Inc.
```

The CITATION text is not appended to text copied from a context-sensitive popup window.

The CITATION option is set in the Project tab of the Project Settings screen.

COMPRESS

The COMPRESS option lets you specify the desired compression level for the compiled WinHelp file. Table A-3 shows the various compression settings you can specify. For example, the following COMPRESS option sets maximum compression for the WinHelp file:

```
COMPRESS=18
```

Table A-3
Compression Values

Value in the COMPRESS Option	*Description*
0	No compression
1	Allows the compiler to determine the best compression level
2	Phrase compression on the text in the WinHelp file
4	Hall compression on the text in the WinHelp file
8	Zeck compression on the text in the WinHelp file
10	Both Zeck and Phrase compression on the text in the WinHelp file
12	Both Hall and Zeck compression on the text in the WinHelp file
16	RLE compression on the bitmaps in the WinHelp file
18	Maximum compression
32	Zeck compression on the bitmaps in the WinHelp file

The COMPRESS option is set in the Compile tab of the Project Settings screen.

For more information on the types of compression, see Chapter 13, "Creating What's This? and Training Card Help."

CONTENTS

The CONTENTS option identifies the default topic in the WinHelp file. Whenever you click the Contents button on the WinHelp file's button bar or you go to the Contents topic with a macro, WinHelp displays this topic. If you have no topic specified as the default Contents topic, WinHelp displays the first topic in the WinHelp file. For example, the following CONTENTS option would set the Welcome_to_Foggan_Drizzle topic as the default contents topic for the WinHelp file:

```
CONTENTS=Welcome_to_Foggan_Drizzle
```

The CONTENTS option is set in the Project tab of the Project Settings screen.

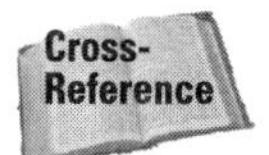

For more information on the types of compression, see Chapter 13, "Creating What's This? and Training Card Help."

CNT

The CNT option specifies the CNT file to use for the WinHelp file's table of contents. For example, the following CNT option would use Foggan Drizzle Tour Info.cnt for the WinHelp file's CNT file:

```
CNT=Foggan Drizzle Tour Info.cnt
```

The CNT option is set in the Master CNT screen accessible from the Contents folder of the Project Settings screen.

For more information on using and editing CNT files, see Chapter 8, "Using Tables of Contents and Indexes."

COPYRIGHT

The COPYRIGHT option lets you specify a copyright message that will appear in the Version Information screen displayed when you select the Help ⇨ Version command. For example, the following COPYRIGHT option would display copyright information for the Foggan Drizzle WinHelp file:

```
COPYRIGHT=Foggan Drizzle Tours, Inc., Copyright 2000-2001. All
rights reserved.
```

The COPYRIGHT option is set in the Project folder of the Project Settings screen.

For more information on setting copyright notices, see Chapter 15, "Managing Large Projects."

DBCS

The DBCS option specifies whether or not the language used in the WinHelp file is a double-byte character set so the WinHelp compiler can compile it appropriately. Enter 0 for no or 1 for yes.

Many languages will override the setting of this option. Check the documentation accompanying the Microsoft Help Compiler Workshop for a complete list of languages and DBCS characteristics.

For example, the following DBCS option would set double-byte support on for the WinHelp file:

```
DBCS=1
```

The DBCS option cannot be set directly in RoboHELP. To set this option, you must edit the HPJ file manually as shown later in this appendix.

DEFFONT

The DEFFONT option specifies the default font name, font size, and character set for the WinHelp Contents, Index, and Find folders and the Topics Found screen used for A-Links. This option has the form:

```
DEFFONT=fontname, font size, character set
```

Enter the name of the font, the font size in points, and the character set (see the list of character set values in Table A-2). For example, the following DEFFONT option would set the defaults for 12-point Arial in Greek:

```
DEFFONT=Arial,12,161
```

The DEFFONT option cannot be set directly in RoboHELP. To set this option, you must manually edit the HPJ file as shown later in this appendix.

ERRORLOG

The ERRORLOG option specifies the text file in which to store the compiler messages. This is useful when debugging large WinHelp projects and you want use a copy of the text file as a checklist of errors and warnings to correct. You can also break the text file up and assign groups of error messages to several different writers for resolution. For example, the following ERRORLOG option would specify an error log file of ERRORLOG.TXT in the Foggan Drizzle Tour Info in the E: drive:

```
ERRORLOG=e:\Foggan Drizzle Tour Info\errorlog.txt
```

The ERRORLOG option cannot be set directly in RoboHELP. To set this option, you must manually edit the HPJ file as shown later in this appendix.

FORCEFONT

The FORCEFONT option overrides all the fonts specified in the RTF files with the specified font. You can use any of the following fonts:

- Arial
- Athens
- Bookman
- Courier
- Courier New
- Geneva
- Helv
- Helvetica
- London
- Modern
- Monaco
- MS Sans Serif
- MS Serif
- Roman
- Times
- Times New Roman
- Tms Rmn

For example, the following FORCEFONT option would set the font to Times New Roman for all the fonts in the WinHelp file:

```
FORCEFONT=Times New Roman
```

The FORCEFONT option cannot be set directly in RoboHELP. To set this option, you must manually edit the HPJ file as shown later in this appendix.

FTS

The FTS option (short for "full-text search") specifies how much information appears in the Find tab. Normally when you run a WinHelp file for the first time and go to the Find tab, the Find wizard tells you that it needs to compile the full-text search file. You can do this automatically so that the Find wizard doesn't appear.

The FTS option's parameter works a little differently from other options. You figure out which full-text search options you want and then add the values together. As you can see from Table A-4, each of the full-text search options has a different value.

For example, the following FTS option would create the minimum search file and would also include searches by phrases for the WinHelp file:

```
FTS=5
```

Similarly, the following FTS option would provide the maximum full-text search capabilities in the WinHelp file (this is the same as the "maximum" option in the Find wizard):

```
FTS=31
```

Table A-4
FTS Values

Value	*Description*
1	Create the FTS file for the Find tab. (This is the "minimum search capabilities" option in the Find wizard.)
2	Include any topics that do not have a title (no $ footnote).
4	Allow support for searches by phrases
8	Include feedback from phrase searches
16	Include support for similarity searches

The FTS option cannot be set directly in RoboHELP. To set this option, you must manually edit the HPJ file as shown later in this appendix.

HLP

The HLP option identifies the name of the compiled WinHelp file. (If you omit this option, the compiled WinHelp file will take the same name as the HPJ file.) For example, the following HLP option would set "Foggan Drizzle Tours Info v2.0" as the name of the compiled WinHelp file:

```
HLP = "Foggan Drizzle Tours Info v2.0"
```

The HLP option is set in the Project folder of the Project Settings screen.

For more information on setting the project name, see Chapter 3, "Creating Your First WinHelp Project."

INDEX_SEPARATORS

The INDEX_SEPARATORS option specifies the separator to use between primary and secondary keywords. The default keyword separators are commas ("Ireland, lodgings in") and colons ("Ireland:music"). For example, the following INDEX_SEPARATORS option would set the keyword separators to comma and hyphen for the WinHelp file:

```
INDEX_SEPARATORS=",-"
```

The INDEX_SEPARATORS option cannot be set directly in RoboHELP. To set this option, you must manually edit the HPJ file as shown later in this appendix.

For more information on keywords, see Chapter 3, "Creating Your First WinHelp Project," and Chapter 8, "Using Tables of Contents and Indexes."

LCID

The `LCID` option specifies the language of the WinHelp file. WinHelp uses the language setting for sorting order for keywords and what character set to use for quotes and special characters. You can also set a variety of options for case-sensitive and case-insensitive spacing marks and symbols. The various languages and the values you enter in the `LCID` option appear in Table A-5.

Table A-5
LCID Values

Value	*Language*	*Value*	*Language*
1033	American	6153	Irish
3081	Australian	1037	Israeli
3079	Austrian	1040	Italian (Standard)
1069	Basque	1041	Japanese
2060	Belgian	11265	Jordan
2057	British	13313	Kuwait
1026	Bulgarian	1062	Latvia
4105	Canadian	12289	Lebanon
1050	Croatian	4097	Libya
1029	Czech	5127	Liechtenstein
1030	Danish	1063	Lithuania
1043	Dutch (Standard)	5132	Luxembourg (French)
3073	Egypt	4103	Luxembourg (German)
1035	Finnish	1071	Macedonian
1036	French (Standard)	2058	Mexican
3084	French Canadian	2073	Moldavian
1031	German (Standard)	2072	Moldavian
1070	Germany	6145	Morocco
1032	Greek	5129	New Zealand
3076	Hong Kong	1044	Norwegian (Bokmal)
1038	Hungarian	2068	Norwegian (Nynorsk)
1039	Icelandic	8193	Oman
2049	Iraqi	1045	Polish

Continued

Table A-5 (continued)

Value	*Language*	*Value*	*Language*
1046	Portuguese (Brazilian)	4108	Swiss (French)
2070	Portuguese (Standard)	2055	Swiss (German)
1048	Romania	2064	Swiss (Italian)
1049	Russian	10241	Syria
1025	Saudi Arabia	1028	Taiwan
2074	Serbian	1054	Thailand
4100	Singapore	1073	Tsonga
1051	Slovak	1055	Turkish
1060	Slovenia	14337	U.A.E.
3082	Spanish (Modern Sort)	1058	Ukraine
1034	Spanish (Traditional Sort)	1056	Urdu
1072	Sutu	1078	Zulu
1053	Swedish		

The case-sensitive and case-insensitive parameters for ignoring nonspacing marks and symbols are as follows:

- 2: Ignore nonspacing marks in the text.
- 4: Ignore punctuation in the text.
- 6: Ignore nonspacing marks and symbols in the text.

For example, the following `LCID` option would set the language to "British," ignore punctuation in case-sensitive text, and ignore nonspacing marks in case-insensitive text in your WinHelp file:

```
LCID=2057,4,2
```

The `LCID` option cannot be set directly in RoboHELP. To set this option, you must manually edit the HPJ file as shown later in this appendix.

MAPFONTSIZE

The `MAPFONTSIZE` option lets you change the specified font sizes from one size to another. You enter the font size to replace followed by the new font size. For example, the following MAPFONTSIZE options would change all 10-point fonts to 14 point for the WinHelp file and all fonts from 12 to 14 points to 16-point in your WinHelp file:

```
MAPFONTSIZE=10:14
MAPFONTSIZE=12-14:16
```

The `MAPFONTSIZE` option cannot be set directly in RoboHELP. To set this option, you must manually edit the HPJ file as shown later in this appendix.

MULTIKEY

The `MULTIKEY` option is used in conjunction with the WinHELP API command `Help_Multikey` (described in the Microsoft Help Compiler Workshop documentation). You need to first specify a new footnote character, then insert that footnote symbol into your topics' existing footnotes and add a keyword in that footnote. You can then pass the `Help_Multikey` call from your application with the keyword and it will call the topic that has that keyword in the Multikey footnote.

You cannot use the footnote characters that are already designated to other WinHelp functions (#,$,K+,@,!,>,A).

For example, the following `MULTIKEY` option would create a new footnote symbol of "M" in your WinHelp file:

```
MULTIKEY=M
```

The `MULTIKEY` option cannot be set directly in RoboHELP. To set this option, you must manually edit the HPJ file as shown later in this appendix.

OLDKEYPHRASE

The `OLDKEYPHRASE` option tells the WinHelp compiler to either use the existing phrase (PH) file when compressing the compiled file or to create a new phrase file. For example, the following `OLDKEYPHRASE` option creates a new phrase file for the WinHelp file:

```
OLDKEYPHRASE=1
```

The `OLDKEYPHRASE` option is set in the Compile folder of the Project Settings screen.

For more information on the types of compression, see Chapter 13, "Creating What's This? and Training Card Help."

REPLACE

The `REPLACE` option lets you identify a new drive and directory for files that have been moved. You usually will use this option when you have moved the files for part or all of a large WinHelp project and you have many references throughout the HPJ file that would be impractical to change. You can also use the REPLACE option to aim the WinHelp compilation process at a different set of files temporarily, which may be useful for creating similar WinHelp files that use slightly different file sets.

For example, the following REPLACE option would find all files referenced in the \RoboHELP\Samples directory and look for the same files in the \HelpProjects\ProjectA:

```
REPLACE= c:\RoboHELP\Samples\ = c:\HelpProjects\ProjectA\
```

The REPLACE option cannot be set directly in RoboHELP. To set this option, you must manually edit the HPJ file as shown later in this appendix.

REPORT

The REPORT option tells the WinHelp compiler if you want to display the compiler messages when compiling the WinHelp file. Enter 0 for No and 1 for Yes. For example, the following REPORT option would display messages during the compile process for the WinHelp file:

```
REPORT=1
```

The REPORT option is set in the Compile folder of the Project Settings screen.

ROOT

The ROOT option specifies the folder to look in for the files listed in the [FILES] section. If the ROOT option doesn't appear in the HPJ file, the WinHelp compiler looks for the RTF files in the same directory as the HPJ file. For example, the following ROOT option would aim the WinHelp compiler at the e:\Foggan Drizzle Source directory:

```
ROOT=e:\Foggan Drizzle Source
```

The ROOT option cannot be set directly in RoboHELP. To set this option, you must manually edit the HPJ file as shown later in this appendix.

TITLE

The TITLE option specifies the title, which appears in the title bar of the compiled WinHelp file. For example, the following TITLE option would set the title to "Foggan Drizzle Tour Online Help" for the WinHelp file:

The TITLE option is set in the Project folder of the Project Settings screen.

For more information on setting the title, see Chapter 3, "Creating Your First WinHelp Project."

TMPDIR

The TMPDIR option specifies which directory the WinHelp compiler should use to store temporary files during the compilation process. The default directory is the system default for temporary files, usually either c:\windows\temp for Windows 9*x* systems or c:\temp for Window NT systems. For example, the following TMPDIR option would set the temporary directory to e:\tempfile:

```
TMPDIR=e:\tempfile
```

The TMPDIR option cannot be set directly in RoboHELP. To set this option, you must manually edit the HPJ file as shown later in this appendix.

The [ALIAS] Section

The [ALIAS] section associates topic IDs defined in the [MAP] section with other topic IDs. Alias entries must have the format:

```
old-topic-ID = new-topic-ID
```

The old-topic-ID can be an existing topic ID defined in the [MAP] section or it can be another topic ID already defined elsewhere in the [ALIAS] section.

For more information on using aliases, see Chapter 11, "Creating Context-Sensitive Help."

The [BAGGAGE] Section

The [BAGGAGE] section is used to store files within your compiled help system. Files listed in the [BAGGAGE] section will be included in the WinHelp file, which can cause it to grow substantially. Entries in the [BAGGAGE] section are case-sensitive.

Entries in the [BAGGAGE] section are entered through the Baggage folder within the Project folder in the RoboHELP Explorer Project Manager.

For more information on using the [BAGGAGE] section, see Chapter 12, "Linking to the Internet and Adding Multimedia."

The [BUILDTAGS] Section

The [BUILDTAGS] section lets you define variables that you can assign to your topics to create different versions of your WinHelp file. It's a good idea to avoid using spaces and any characters other than A–Z and 0–9.

For more information on using build tags and the [BUILDTAGS] section, see Chapter 15, "Managing Large Projects."

The [CONFIG] Section

The [CONFIG] section contains macros that WinHelp will run when it opens the WinHelp file. The macros will run in the order they appear in the [CONFIG] section. Common examples of startup macros are register routines or WinHelp macros such as the CreateButton macro, which adds a button to the button bar across the top of your help window.

If you have secondary windows, you can create [CONFIG] sections for each of the secondary windows. For example, if you have a secondary window called "Tutor," the [CONFIG] section would look like this:

```
[CONFIG Tutor]
```

It's a good idea to have a [CONFIG] section for each secondary window, even if you have no startup macros associated with them. As with the main [CONFIG] section, these [CONFIG] sections run the macros in the order they appear the first time that type of window is opened.

For more information on startup macros, see Chapter 10, "Understanding Macros."

The [FILES] Section

The [FILES] section contains a list of all the RTF files in the WinHelp project. The files are compiled in the order they appear in the [FILES] section. The [FILES] section, along with the [OPTIONS] section, is mandatory. (All other HPJ file sections are optional.)

The [MACROS] Section

The [MACROS] section specifies macros that will run from the index when you select the associated keyword. Each keyword macro must have three separate lines.

1. The first line contains the name of the keyword as you would like it to appear in the compiled HLP file.
2. The second line contains the macro that WinHelp will run when the keyword is selected. Be careful that your macro includes all the necessary parameters. You must also use the abbreviated form of the macro.
3. The last line contains a title for the macro.

For example, the following entry will insert the keyword "Test" into your WinHelp index, which, when selected, will run the ExecFile macro and run the file, test.txt.

```
Test
EF(`test.txt',`',1,`')
Sample
```

The [MAP] Section

The [MAP] section identifies the context-sensitive help links. You can make manual entries or insert a file of entries by using the #Define or #Include statements.

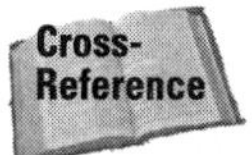

For more information on using the [MAP] section, see Chapter 11, "Creating Context-Sensitive Help."

The [WINDOWS] Section

The [WINDOWS] section specifies how the main window and any secondary windows will appear. The window entries take the form:

```
window-name="caption", (x-coord, y-coord, width, height),
initial_state, (scrolling-RGB), (nonscrolling-RGB),
window_options
```

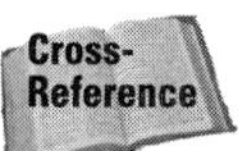

Many of these options are discussed in Chapter 9, "Using Help Windows and Browse Sequences."

The first parameter, window-name, specifies the title of the window "Tutor." Following that in quotations is the caption of the window "Sample Window," the caption that will appear in the title bar of the window. (Captions can be up to 50 characters long.)

In the first set of parentheses are the parameters that define the position of the help window. The first number is the x-coordinate, the horizontal position of the top of the window. The second number is the y-coordinate, the vertical position of the left side of the window. The third parameter is the width of the window. The last number is used to determine the height of the window. All four of these parameters are between 0 and 1023.

The initial_state parameter determines the initial display state and what buttons will appear on the window. The initial_state option is the sum of the various options that you want to appear in the window when it first opens. The initial_state values are described in Table A-6.

Table A-6
initial_state Values

Value	*Description*
1	Maximizes the help window (If you use this option, WinHelp will ignore the x-coord, y-coord, width, height, and state parameters for the window.)
4	Displays no buttons (Use this only with the Main window.)
256	Adds the Options button to the window's button bar
512	Adds the Browse buttons to the window's button bar
1024	Adds the Contents button to the window's button bar
2048	Adds the Index button to the window's button bar
4096	Adds the Help Topics button to the window's button bar
8192	Adds the Print button to the window's button bar
16384	Adds the Back button to the window's button bar
32768	Adds the Find button to the window's button bar

The colors for the scrolling and non-scrolling regions are identified in standard RGB format.

The `window_options` parameter sets the secondary window to stay on top of other windows as well as certain options, as described in Table A-7. (All but the first option are preceded with an "f.")

Table A-7
window_options Values

Value	*Description*
1	Sets the window to "Always On Top."
f2	Sets the window to "Auto-Size Height," a setting that makes the window's length shrink or grow based on the amount of the topic's text.
f3	Sets both "Always On Top" and "Auto Size Height" on.
f4	Sets the window to "Use Absolute," a setting in RoboHELP that lets you enter pixels instead of percentages for the definition of the window's position.
f5	Sets both "Use Absolute" and "Always On Top" on.
f6	Sets both "Use Absolute" and "Auto Size Height" on.
f7	Sets "Use Absolute," "Auto-Size Height," and "Always on top" on.

For example, the following entry will set the Tutor window with a caption of "Sample Window," sets the opening position for the window, adds the Options, Help Topics, and Back buttons to the window's button bar, establishes colors for the scrolling and non-scrolling regions, and sets the initial state of the window to "Always On Top" and "Auto Size Height:"

```
Tutor="Sample Window",(235,184,634,604),20736,(255,255,224),
(255,255,224),f3
```

Editing the HPJ File Manually

The HPJ file is actually a text file, which means that you can edit it with any text editor, such as Notepad or WordPad.

To edit the HPJ file from within RoboHELP, do the following:

1. In the RoboHELP Explorer, select the File ➪ Open File From Project command. (You can also press Ctrl+Shift+V.) The Open File from Project screen appears, as shown in Figure A-1.

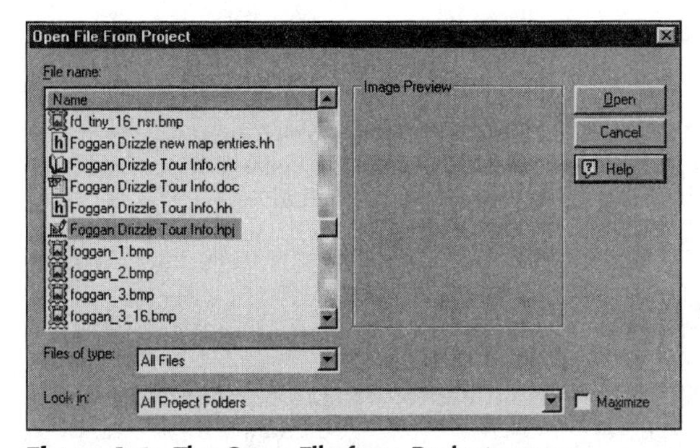

Figure A-1: The Open File from Project screen

2. Select the HPJ file you want to open from the file list on the left side of the screen and click Open. (You can change the setting in the Files of Type drop-down list to "Project File (*.hpj)" to make it easier to find the HPJ file.) RoboHELP displays the HPJ file in the default editor.
3. Make any changes necessary to the file and then save the file.

To change the default editor in RoboHELP, do the following:

1. In the RoboHELP Explorer, select the Tools ➪ Options command, and then click the Tool Locations tab. Figure A-2 shows the Options screen with the Tool Locations folder displayed.

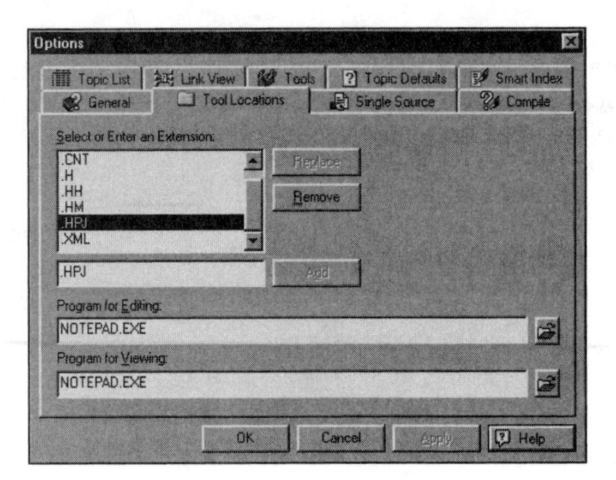

Figure A-2: The Options screen with the Tool Locations folder displayed

2. Select HPJ from the list on the left side of the screen. The default programs for editing and viewing the file appear in the fields at the bottom of the screen. Enter the new names of the programs to edit and view the HPJ file. You can click the icons to the right of the fields to browse for editing and viewing programs.

3. When you are satisfied with your entries, click OK.

You can enter comments in an HPJ file by entering a semicolon and then following it with a comment. The WinHelp compiler will ignore anything you enter after the semicolon until the next hard return. Examples of comments embedded in the HPJ file can be seen in any HPJ file created by RoboHELP.

The WIN.INI File

The standard WIN.INI file in the Windows folder contains a number of settings for WinHelp files in the `[Windows Help]` section. You can set any or all of the options shown in Table A-8.

Table A-8
WinHelp Settings in the WIN.INI file

Setting	*Description*
Backtrack=num	Determines the number of topics, from 1 to 500, that are saved in the WinHelp history list.
Help Author=1	Specifies whether or not Help Author mode is on. (This option is set automatically.)

Setting	*Description*
JumpColor=(R,G,B)	Sets the color, in RGB format, for jump hotspots. If this option is not set in the WIN.INI file, the default color is green.
IFJumpColor=(R,G,B)	Sets the color, in RGB format, for external jump hotspots. If this option is not set in the WIN.INI file, the default color is the same as the color for jump hotspots.
PopupColor=(R,G,B)	Sets the color, in RGB format, for popups. If this option is not set in the WIN.INI file, the default color is the same as the color for jump hotspots.
IFPopupColor=(R,G,B)	Sets the color, in RGB format, for external popups. If this option is not set in the WIN.INI file, the default color is the same as the color for jump hotspots.
MacroColor=(R,G,B)	Sets the color, in RGB format, for macro hotspots. If this option is not set in the WIN.INI file, the default color is the same as the color for jump hotspots.

✦ ✦ ✦

APPENDIX B

WinHelp Footnote Symbols

✦ ✦ ✦ ✦

In This Appendix

Understanding the footnote symbols

✦ ✦ ✦ ✦

In this appendix, you'll learn about the footnote symbols used in WinHelp files.

The WinHelp compiler uses information stored in standard Word footnotes in the source files for your project to identify and link the topics in your WinHelp file. The footnotes must be placed at the start of the line immediately after the start of the document or a hard page break with no intervening characters, spaces, paragraph marks, or symbols. You can view the footnotes by selecting the View ➪ Footnotes command in Word.

The standard footnote symbols are described in Table B-1.

You can create user-defined footnote symbols using the `MULTIKEY` option in conjunction with the WinHelp API command `Help_Multikey`. These are useful for creating additional search and classification criteria used with a programmatic interface. See the Microsoft Help Compiler Workshop documentation for additional information on the WinHelp API.

Table B-1
Footnote Symbols

Symbol	*Name*	*Description*
*	Build tag	Identifies the build tag(s) for the topic.
#	Topic ID	Specifies the topic ID. The topic ID is used within the WinHelp file to identify topics uniquely. This is a required footnote.
$	Topic title	Specifies the topic title.
K	Index keywords	Specifies the keywords associated with the topic. The default keyword separators are commas ("Ireland, lodgings in") and colons ("Ireland:music"). You can use the `INDEX_SEPARATORS` option described in Appendix A, "The WinHelp HPJ File," to change the default separators.
A	See Also ("A-Link") keywords	Specifies the A-Link keywords for See Also topics.
+	Browse string	Specifies the topic's order in a browse sequence.
!	Topic entry macro	Specifies a macro or macros that will be performed whenever the topic is displayed.
@	Comment text	Used by RoboHELP to hold topic property information such as status, author, and to do list information.
>	Window display	Specifies which help window is to be used to display the topic.

✦ ✦ ✦

Reports

In this appendix, you'll see a brief overview of each of the reports in RoboHELP Office 2000.

✦ ✦ ✦ ✦

In This Appendix

An overview of WinHelp reports

An overview of HTML Help reports

✦ ✦ ✦ ✦

WinHelp Reports

RoboHELP Office 2000 comes with an extensive variety of WinHelp reports:

- Broken Links
- Diagnostics
- Duplicate Map IDs
- Duplicate Topics
- External Topic References
- Images
- Index (K-Keywords)
- Map IDs
- Project Status
- See Also (A-Keywords)
- Ship List
- Table of Contents
- Topic Properties
- Topic References
- Topics by Priority
- Unreferenced Topics
- Unused Index and See Also Keywords

To generate any of the WinHelp reports, do the following:

1. With a WinHelp project open, select the Tools ⇨ Reports command from the RoboHELP Explorer, and then select the report you want to generate.

2. Select any report options. Most WinHelp reports can be filtered by Author or Document and many have additional filtering or sorting options.
3. When you are satisfied with your entries, click OK. The report will appear on the screen. You can print or save the report.

All the WinHelp reports may be generated at any time. They do not affect the status of the WinHelp project.

The Broken Links Report

The Broken Links report displays any links that jump to topics that RoboHELP cannot locate.

For more information on this report, see Chapter 15, "Managing Large Projects."

The Diagnostics Report

The Diagnostics report can be used to check for a variety of conditions:

- unused map IDs
- topics without map IDs
- duplicate map IDs
- missing documents
- missing map files
- missing images
- missing baggage files
- missing image folders (`BMROOT`)
- missing DLLs
- missing HTML files
- full path HTML files
- images that appear in more than on image folder (`BMROOT`)
- topics that appear in more than one window
- contents topic

For more information on this report, see Chapter 15, "Managing Large Projects."

The Duplicate Map ID Report

The Duplicate Map ID report is a diagnostic report that lists all duplicate entries for topic IDs and topic numbers.

For more information on this report, see Chapter 11, "Creating Context-Sensitive Help."

The Duplicate Topics Report

The Duplicate Topics report displays all the topics that have the same topic ID. (You cannot have duplicate topic IDs in the WinHelp project files unless you are using build tags.)

For more information on this report, see Chapter 11, "Creating Context-Sensitive Help."

The External Topic References Report

The External Topic References report displays links to any external WinHelp topics.

For more information on this report, see Chapter 15, "Managing Large Projects."

The Images Report

The Images report can be set to display either all the images and the topic they reside in or a list of your topics and the images that each one contains. This report can be run based on author or document.

For more information on this report, see Chapter 6, "Adding Simple Graphics."

The Index (K-Keywords) Report

The Index (K-Keywords) report provides information about the index keywords for your WinHelp project. You can use this report for checking the keywords and the associated topics. You can also use this report as an easy way to edit the keywords for spelling, grammar, and consistency.

The Index (K-Keywords) report can be set to display in one of three ways:

✦ Keywords only

✦ All keywords and the associated topics

✦ All topics and the keywords that are linked to each topic

For more information on this report, see Chapter 8, "Using Table of Contents and Indexes."

The Map ID Report

The Map ID report provides general information about the map IDs. The report will display a summary of the map IDs and unused map IDs in your WinHelp project. It also lists topic IDs and displays the associated map ID, map file, topic title, and document.

For more information on this report, see Chapter 11, "Creating Context-Sensitive Help."

The Project Status Report

The Project Status report displays a small summary of your project and then totals the number of topics in the categories In Progress, Ready for Review, and Complete. It also displays a list of the To Do items and a count of how many topics in each category are completed and how many are still on the To Do list.

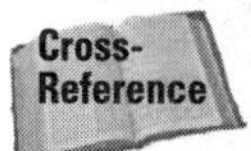

For more information on this report, see Chapter 15, "Managing Large Projects."

The See Also (A-Keywords) Report

The See Also (A-Keywords) report provides information about the See Also (A-Link) keywords for your WinHelp project. You can use this report for checking the keywords and the associated topics. You can also use this report as an easy way to edit the keywords for spelling, grammar, and consistency.

The See Also (A-Keywords) report can be set to display in one of three ways:

- A-Link keywords only
- All A-Link keywords and the associated topics
- All topics and the A-Link keywords that are linked to each topic

For more information on this report, see Chapter 8, "Using Table of Contents and Indexes."

The Ship List Report

The Ship List report lists any external files, such as associated HLP, CNT, HTML, URL, DLL, or EXE files, that must accompany the final WinHelp file.

For more information on this report, see Chapter 15, "Managing Large Projects."

The Table of Contents Report

The Table of Contents report contains overview and detail information about the table of contents for your WinHelp project. You can use this report for checking the topic titles and WinHelp file names against the table of contents entries and to edit the table of contents entries for spelling, grammar, and consistency. The report displays all the book and pages of your contents. It also lists the topic, macro, or hyperlink that will run when the page is selected by the users. If you select the Detail version of this report, you also see the document(s) in which the topics appear.

For more information on this report, see Chapter 8, "Using Table of Contents and Indexes."

The Topic Properties Report

The Topic Properties report lists all your topics and can be set to display any of the following topics properties:

- ✦ Document
- ✦ Mid-topic IDs
- ✦ Author
- ✦ Status
- ✦ Priority
- ✦ Time
- ✦ Completed To Do's
- ✦ Comment
- ✦ Jumps to the topic
- ✦ Jumps from the topic
- ✦ Table of Contents
- ✦ Index (K-Keywords)
- ✦ See Also (A-Keywords)
- ✦ Aliases
- ✦ Browse Sequence
- ✦ Window
- ✦ Map ID number
- ✦ Entry Macro
- ✦ Build Tags

For more information on this report, see Chapter 15, "Managing Large Projects."

The Topic References Report

The Topic References report shows the links, TOC and index (K-Keywords) entries, graphics, and macro references for each topic in the report.

For more information on this report, see Chapter 4, "Adding Jumps and Popups."

The Topics by Priority Report

The Topics by Priority report lists topics by their topic priority. You can display all priorities or set a range of priorities for the report to display.

For more information on this report, see Chapter 15, "Managing Large Projects."

The Unreferenced Topics Report

The Unreferenced Topics report lists any topics to which there are no links from anywhere in the WinHelp project. You can have the report look for a variety of unreferenced topics:

- Topics without jumps (links) to the topic
- Topics without table of contents entries
- Topics without index entries (K-Keywords)
- Topics without See Also (A-Keywords)
- Topics without aliases
- Topics without map IDs
- Topics that can't be navigated to

For more information on this report, see Chapter 15, "Managing Large Projects."

The Unused Index and See Also Keywords Report

The Unused Index and See Also Keywords report shows you both the index (K-Link) and A-Link keywords that are not currently associated with topics. (These keywords will also appear in bold in the RoboHELP Explorer Index Designer.)

For more information on this report, see Chapter 8, "Using Table of Contents and Indexes."

HTML Help Reports

RoboHELP Office 2000 contains an extensive variety of HTML Help reports:

✦ ALink
✦ Broken Links
✦ Duplicate Map IDs
✦ External Topic References
✦ Glossary
✦ Images
✦ Index
✦ Map IDs
✦ Project Status
✦ Style Sheets
✦ Table of Contents
✦ Topic Properties
✦ Topic References
✦ Topics by Priority
✦ Unreferenced Topics
✦ Unused Files
✦ Unused Index Entries
✦ Used Files

To generate any of the HTML Help reports, do the following:

1. With an HTML Help project open, from the RoboHELP HTML Help screen select the Tools ⇨ Reports command, and then select the report you want to generate.
2. Select any report options. Most HTML Help reports can be filtered by author or folder, and many have additional filtering or sorting options.
3. When you are satisfied with your entries, click OK. The report will appear on the screen. You can print or save the report.

All the HTML Help reports may be generated at any time. They do not affect the status of the HTML Help project.

For more information on any of the HTML Help reports, see Chapter 24, "Using Reports and Compiling."

The ALink Report

The See Also (A-Keywords) report provides information about the See Also (A-Link) keywords for your HTML Help project. You can use this report for checking the keywords and the associated topics. You can also use this report as an easy way to edit the keywords for spelling, grammar, and consistency.

The Also (A-Keywords) report can be set to display in one of three ways:

- A-Link keywords only
- All A-Link keywords and the associated topics
- All topics and the A-Link keywords that are linked to each topic.

The Broken Links Report

The Broken Links report displays any links that jump to topics that RoboHELP cannot locate.

The External Topic References Report

The External Topic References report displays links to any external CHM topics.

The Glossary Report

The Glossary report displays the terms and definitions for glossary items in your HTML Help project. The overview version lists the glossary terms without definitions; the detail version lists the terms and their definitions.

The Images Report

The Images report displays an alphabetical list of the images in the HTML Help project and their associated topics or an alphabetical list of topics and their associated images.

The Index Report

The Index report provides information about the index keywords for your HTML Help project. You can use this report for checking the keywords and the associated topics. You can also use this report as an easy way to edit the keywords for spelling, grammar, and consistency.

The Index report can be set to display in one of three ways:

- ✦ Keywords only
- ✦ All keywords and the associated topics
- ✦ All topics and the keywords that are linked to each topic

The Project Status Report

The Project Status report displays a summary of your project status, including the number of topics in the In Progress, Ready for Review, and Complete categories, and the outstanding To Do items.

The Style Sheets Report

The Style Sheets report displays an alphabetical list of the style sheets in the HTML Help project and their associated topics or an alphabetical list of topics and their associated style sheets.

The Table of Contents Report

The Table of Contents report contains overview and detail information about the table of contents for your HTML Help project. You can use this report for checking the topic titles and HTML Help file names against the table of contents entries and to edit the table of contents entries for spelling, grammar, and consistency. The report displays all the book and pages of your contents. It also lists the topic, macro, or hyperlink that will run when the page is selected by the users. If you select the Detail version of this report, you also see the document(s) in which the topics appear.

The Topic Properties Report

The Topic Properties report lists all your topics and can be set to display any of the following topic properties:

- ✦ Folder
- ✦ Bookmarks
- ✦ Status
- ✦ Priority
- ✦ Time
- ✦ Completed To Do's

- ✦ Comment
- ✦ Links to the Topic
- ✦ Links from the Topic
- ✦ Table of Contents
- ✦ Index Entries
- ✦ Info Types
- ✦ Style Sheet

The Topic References Report

The Topic References report lists the links, TOC and index entries, and hotspots for each topic in the report.

The Topics by Priority Report

The Topics by Priority report lists topics by their topic priority. You can display all priorities or set a range of priorities for the report to display.

The Unreferenced Topics Report

The Unreferenced Topics report lists any topics that there are no links to from anywhere in the HTML Help project. You can have the report look for a variety of unreferenced topics:

- ✦ Topics without jumps (links) to the topic
- ✦ Topics without table of contents entries
- ✦ Topics without index entries (K-Keywords)
- ✦ Topics that can't be navigated to

The Unused Files Report

The Unused Files report lists the files that exist in your project and custom directories that are not currently included in the project.

Because the files are unused, they don't appear in the RoboHELP Project Manager. Once you have identified the unused files with the Unused Files report, you must use the Windows Explorer to delete them.

The Unused Index Entries Report

The Unused Index report shows you the index keywords that are not currently associated with topics. (These keywords will also appear in bold in the RoboHELP Explorer Index Designer.)

The Used Files Report

The Used Files report lists the files that make up your HTML Help project.

✦ ✦ ✦

Resources

In this appendix, you'll learn about a number of Web sites that will be of use to the online help developer. The appendix lists Web sites for WinHelp and HTML Help resources, HTML tutorials and references, developing Web sites, utilities and tools, and sound and music software. The appendix continues with a list of newsgroups related to WinHelp, HTML Help, and HTML. The appendix concludes with a list of recommended books on online help, project management, and enhancing creativity.

✦ ✦ ✦ ✦

In This Appendix

Exploring Web sites for online help, HTML, and additional tools

Reading newsgroups

Learning about some recommended books

✦ ✦ ✦ ✦

Web Sites

There are a number of Web sites of interest to the online help developer.

WinHelp and HTML Help Resources

These Web sites provide additional tools, information, and resources on WinHelp and HTML Help.

✦ `http://www.eHelp.com`: The Web site for eHelp (formerly Blue Sky software), makers of RoboHELP. (You can still reach the company through their old URL, `http://www.blue-sky.com)` Look here for product support, information on new features, downloadable examples, and opportunities to interact with other RoboHELP users. **Recommended.**

✦ `http://www.helpmaster.com`: Josef Becker's first-rate Web site for help developers. The motto, "More stuff than you can find in an hour of searching," is a serious understatement. **Recommended.**

✦ `http://winwriters.com`: The WinWriters Web site. WinWriters is the premier organization for online help developers. It sponsors the WinWriters Online Help Conferences, publishes salary surveys for help developers, and has an enormous variety of resources online. You should make a point of looking at the WinWriters' Online Help Journal at `http://www.ohj.com`. **Recommended.**

- http://member.aol.com/LindaMoore/: Linda Moore's home page. Resources for WinHelp and HTML Help developers, including some exceptional links.
- http://www.tanstaafl-software.com/forums.html: Web-based BBSs (bulletin board systems) for WinHelp and HTML Help discussions.
- http://www.sol-sems.com: The Solutions Web site. Solutions sells and conducts training courses all over the world for online help, documentation, HTML, and related subjects.
- http://www.keyworks.net: The KeyWorks Software Web site. There's a variety of free software add-ons and stand-alone tools that are essential for help developers. **Recommended.**
- http://www.geocities.com/Area51/6793/helpsurv.htm: The WinHelp Survival Kit, a collection of tips, tools, and resources. The Web site is maintained by the Northern California STC WinHelp SIG.
- http://www.hypertexas.com: John Daigle's HyperTexas Web site.
- http://www.workwrite.com/: The Work Write Web site. Many resources for online help developers as well as Help Matters; a Web-based newsletter about online help.
- http://www.humberc.on.ca/~byrnes/winhelp.html: The WinHelp-l Home Page, a listserv for authors of WinHelp and other types of online help. **Recommended.**
- http://www.sky.net/~parnote/helpful.htm: Paul Arnote's WinHelp World Web site.
- http://www.freelancestoryteller.com/: The Story Teller Group. This Web site has a number of tools and templates for WinHelp developers.
- http://www.hedtke.com: John Vernon Hedtke's Web site. Check out the Links section for pages of links on WinHelp, HTML Help, HTML, graphics, MP3, and many other subjects.

HTML Tutorials and References

These Web sites provide tutorials, references, and forums on HTML.

- http://www.davesite.com/webstation/html: HTML: An Interactive Tutorial for Beginners. This tutorial is exceptional for anyone who's starting in HTML. If you don't look at any other beginning HTML Web sites, look at this one. **Recommended.**
- http://www.webpagesthatsuck.com: Web Pages That Suck, Vince Flanders's brilliant Web site, is an essential URL for every Web developer and HTML Help expert! This Web site shows how to avoid many of the more grievous offenses commonly made by Web developers. **Recommended.**

- `http://werbach.com/barebones/`: An easy-to-use Web site listing every HTML 4.0 tag.
- `http://www.htmlcompendium.org/`: A compendium of HTML elements.
- `http://webreview.com/wr/pub/guides/style/mastergrid.html`: A comprehensive table outlining the compatibility issues between browsers and versions of HTML. This page loads very slowly but it's worth the wait.
- `http://www.w3.org/`: The World Wide Web Consortium (W3C) home page. Contains specifications and information about HTML versions 2 through 4, DHTML, and XML (Extensible Markup Language).
- `http://www.xml.com/xml/pub`: XML reference and tutorial. Although it is not fully supported yet, XML is being used by an increasing number of organizations for Web-based help and Web applications.
- `http://www.htmlguru.com/`: Dynamic HTML Link. A very attractive Web site and a good example of some of the things you can use Dynamic HTML for.

Web Site Development Tools and Tips

These Web sites provide tools, tips, and resources for Web site development. Although some of the information may be slightly peripheral to HTML Help development, there are many valuable tips and techniques for making your HTML Help look and work better.

- `http://www.stars.com`: The Virtual Library. This is an extraordinarily comprehensive selection of links, files, and information for Web developers. **Recommended.**
- `http://msdn.microsoft.com/workshop/author/default.asp`: This is a collection of FAQs, tips, and tutorials on Web site development from Microsoft.
- `http://www.stc.org` and `http://www.stc-va.org`: The Society for Technical Communication, an international professional organization for technical communicators of all kinds. **Recommended.**

If you're a developer of online help, you are strongly encouraged to become a member of the Society for Technical Communication. You'll have opportunities to interact with thousands of other online help developers and get information on integrating online help development with other aspects of documentation development.

- `http://developer.netscape.com/one/index.html`: Netscape's Open Network Environment Pages. Netscape has a portion of their Web site for developer information (not surprisingly). Look for information on HTML and Java here.

- http://www.ncsa.uiuc.edu/Indices/Resources/html-resources.html.html: The National Center for Supercomputing Applications has a variety of HTML resources for beginning and intermediate HTML users.
- http://www.ology.org/tilt/cgh/: Composing Good HTML This site contains basic tips and techniques on composing good HTML.
- http://www.quadzilla.com: D. J. Quad's Ultimate HTML Site. This is another great site for all kinds of HTML resources. **Recommended.**
- http://www.devry-phx.edu/webresrc/webmstry/lrntutrl.htm: Beginning HTML Tutorials. More HTML tutorials for beginners.
- http://www.charm.net/~lejeune/tables.html: HTML Table Tutorial. It can be a nuisance to understand all the ins and outs of tables. Here's a tutorial specifically for information on creating tables in HTML.

Additional Software

These utilities and programs — some of the best of their respective classes — will help you at various stages of the online help development process.

- http://www.arachnoid.com: Arachnophilia HTML editor from Paul Lutus. Arachnophilia is the best Web editor I've ever used. (Be sure to check out the Table Wizard; it makes creating HTML tables a five-second operation!)
- http://www.forteinc.com: Free Agent newsreader from Forté, Inc. Free Agent is my favorite newsreader. You can register to get Agent, the full version.
- http://ourworld.compuserve.com/homepages/BobBerry/: CompuShow graphic viewer from Canyon Software, Inc. CompuShow is extraordinarily helpful for viewing graphics when you are sorting through backgrounds and pictures while building Web pages. (Hint: Use the "Slide Show" feature to scroll through a list of graphics, and then press M to move a graphic you like to another directory to set it aside.)
- http://www.eudoramail.com/: Eudora Lite mail reader (freeware) or a 30-day evaluation version of Eudora Pro from Qualcomm, Inc. (You can also download documentation in Adobe Acrobat format.)
- http://www.isbister.com/: Time & Chaos personal information manager from iSBiSTER International, Inc. A first-class PIM and contact manager.
- http://www.jasc.com: Paint Shop Pro graphic painting and editing program from JASC Software, Inc. Need a world-class graphics program? Try this one! JASC is also the home for other great graphics products such as Media Center Plus 3 and JASC Trajectory Pro. All of these are well worth examining.

Timed demo versions of Paint Shop Pro and Media Center Plus 3 appear on the CD accompanying this book.

- http://www.winzip.com: The home page for Nico Mak Computing, source for WinZip, one of the all-time best zipping and unzipping utilities for Windows. WinZip should be required for all Windows users.
- http://www.ipswitch.com/: WS_FTP file transfer program from Ipswitch, Inc. It's one of the best and most popular Windows FTP programs available. Use this to transfer files to and from the Internet.
- http://www.datafellows.com/: The home page for various antivirus products.
- http://www.mcafee.com/: The home page for McAfee VirusScan, an excellent virus scanner.
- http://www.mjs.u-net.com/mike.htm: MTU-Speed Home Page. The home page for MTUSpeed, a very useful utility from Mike Sutherland for speeding up your Internet access. **Recommended.**
- http://www.robertgraham.com/pubs/: Robert Graham's great FAQ on network security. If you're accessing the Internet at a company, you may have a firewall in place already; however, most home office users don't have firewalls set up. Find out the basics of what you might want to be concerned about and then check out the comp.security.firewalls newsgroup for additional information.

Multimedia

If you're including multimedia in your help project, you may need to get involved with editing WAV files, creating MP3 files, and so on. These resources and tools can help you explore some of the basics.

- http://members.xoom.com/snarfdude/iaf.html: Internet Audio Page. A really good Web site for links and information about MP3 and many other forms of audio from Scott Snailham.
- http://www.musicmatch.com/: The home page for MusicMatch Jukebox, the best all-in-one MP3 program. Download the latest version of MusicMatch Jukebox here. **Recommended.**
- http://www.syntrillium.com/: The home page for Cool Edit 96, a comprehensive sound-editing program.
- http://www.sonicfoundry.com/index.html: The home page for Sound Forge XP, another first-rate sound editing program.

Newsgroups

In addition to the many Web sites listed in this section, there are a number of Usenet newsgroups you may want to follow for current information and an opportunity to exchange ideas with other online help developers.

You will need a newsreader to read and post to newsgroups. If you don't already have a newsreader installed on your computer, consider downloading Free Agent from Forté (`http://www.forteinc.com`).

The following newsgroups will be of interest to people developing WinHelp, HTML Help, or working with HTML and other online technologies:

- `alt.discuss.programming.html`
- `alt.html`
- `alt.html.critique`
- `alt.html.dhtml`
- `alt.html.dynamic`
- `alt.html.editors`
- `alt.html.editors.enhanced-html`
- `alt.html.editors.webedit`
- `alt.html.server-side`
- `alt.html.tags`
- `alt.html.webedit`
- `alt.html.writers`
- `alt.html.writers.guild-list`
- `alt.hypertext`
- `bit.listserv.techwr-l`
- `comp.infosystems.www.authoring.html`
- `comp.os.ms-windows.programmer.winhelp`
- `microsoft.public.activex.authoring.html`
- `microsoft.public.htmlhelp`
- `microsoft.public.windows.inetexplorer.ie5.programming.components.dhtml-editing`

- microsoft.public.windows.inetexplorer.ie5.programming.dhtml.authoring
- microsoft.public.windows.inetexplorer.ie5.programming.dhtml.behaviors
- microsoft.public.windows.inetexplorer.ie5.programming.dhtml.scripting
- microsoft.public.windows.inetexplorer.ie5.programming.dhtml.scriptlets
- microsoft.public.windows.inetexplorer.ie5.programming.html+time
- microsoft.public.windows.inetexplorer.ie5.programming.xml
- netscape.public.dev.html

Books

The following books (listed in alphabetical order) should be in the libraries of anyone creating online help or software documentation.

- *The Chicago Manual of Style: The Essential Guide for Writers, Editors, and Publishers* (14th Edition), (University of Chicago Press, 1993). The bible of style for those who work in traditional book publishing, it will also be useful to technical communicators.
- *The Deluxe Transitive Vampire* (Pantheon Books, 1993) and *The Well-Tempered Sentence* (Ticknor & Fields, 1993) by Karen Elizabeth Gordon. Both of these books are short, snappy, and amazingly funny. Gordon's sample sentences are inspired and inspiring.
- *Designing and Writing Online Documentation (2nd Edition)* by William Horton (Wiley & Sons, 1994). A guide to designing and creating good online help. Also check out Horton's *Designing Web-Based Training* (Wiley & Sons, 2000).
- *Designing Online Help for Windows 95* by Scott Boggan, Dave Farkas, and Joe Welinske (Solutions, 1999). The basics of WinHelp 4 using Microsoft Help Compiler Workshop. Available directly from the Solutions online bookstore at http://www.sol-sems.com.
- *Managing Your Documentation Projects* by JoAnn T. Hackos (Wiley & Sons, 1994). An excellent book on how to plan, start, and manage documentation projects.
- *The Mythical Man-Month* by Frederick P. Brooks, Jr. (Addison-Wesley, 1995). An essential book for resource planning on any large project.

- *Peopleware* by Tom DeMarco and Tim Lister (Dorset House, 1999). A delightfully seditious book for dealing with the exigencies of project management in corporations with the premise that most software projects fail because of people problems, not technological problems. The "Furniture Police" chapter is essential reading for anyone who's been in an office cubicle.
- *RoboHELP 7 for Dummies*, by Jim Meade (IDG Books, 1999). A basic book that will introduce you to the previous version of RoboHELP.
- *The Secrets of Consulting* by Gerald M. Weinstein (Dorset House, 1986). Although written for consultants and freelancers, this book contains many helpful tools for everyone who is solving problems in business. This book's conversational style and delightful illustrative stories are a real pleasure to read. Also check out *The Psychology of Computer Programming* (Dorset House, 1998) for a better idea of the underlying motivations and thought processes of the people you have to work with.
- *A Whack on the Side of the Head* by Roger von Oech, (Warner Books, 1998). Not directly concerned with writing, this book shows how to be more creative in any venue by playing. For example, the chapter "That's Not the Right Answer" shows how there is usually more than one "right" answer to any problem, and that the "wrong" answer can lead to a new solution. The illustrations alone are worth the price of the book.
- *Word 97 Annoyances*, by Woody Leonhard, Lee Hudspeth, and T. J. Lee (O'Reilly, 1997). An essential book for making Microsoft Word 97 usable and avoiding all of its shortcomings. The book is worth it for information on how to turn off the annoying paperclip help alone. (There will probably be a *Word 2000 Annoyances* coming out, too.)
- *Writing Software Documentation: A Task-Oriented Approach* by Thomas T. Barker (Allyn & Bacon, 1997). A good basic textbook on writing software documentation.

✦ ✦ ✦

Installing RoboHELP 2000

✦ ✦ ✦ ✦

In This Appendix

Preparing to install RoboHELP Office 2000

Installing RoboHELP Office 2000

✦ ✦ ✦ ✦

In this appendix, you'll see how to prepare your system for installing RoboHELP Office 2000 and see some tips on how to install it with a minimum of problems.

Before You Begin

Before you begin installing RoboHELP Office 2000, you can do several things to ensure that the installation process will go as smoothly as possible:

- ✦ First, close any other applications you may have running. (Advanced users may also want to load the Task Manager and end some of the additional processes that are running.)
- ✦ Clear out your C:\Windows\Temp directory (C:\Temp if you're installing on Windows NT). These folders are the temporary areas where your computer stores files while installing and processing your applications. Although many of these files are erased at the end of an installation process or when you're done running an application, some files can remain if the installation program doesn't clean up after itself or Windows crashes. By deleting the files in the temp directory, you'll ensure that your computer will run with maximum efficiency.
- ✦ Turn off any antiviral software while you're installing RoboHELP Office 2000. (You can turn it back on immediately after the installation is done.) Antiviral software has been known to cause problems during installations of programs and files, particularly Word templates.

- ✦ Verify the location of your Word templates and the Word startup location. You can check your settings by starting Word, and then selecting the Tools ➪ Options command and choosing the File Locations tab. From this folder, you can see where the Template and Startup directories are located. If you're running on a network and you're saving files to a network drive, you should also make sure that you have read/write access to this directory.
- ✦ Make sure you have access to update your Windows Registry settings. If you're installing on a stand-alone computer, this probably won't be a problem, but if you're running on a network, you should discuss this with your IS staff. If necessary, you'll need to have them grant your user name full administrative rights during the installation. Once RoboHELP Office 2000 is installed, you can change your privileges back.
- ✦ You should have at least 100MB of free disk space on your C: drive and 30MB on your target directory (130MB total if the C: drive is your target directory). Also run Defrag and Scandisk to ensure that your hard drive space is being used optimally.
- ✦ Locate the RoboHELP Office 2000 serial number prior to the installation. (Several serial number labels are included with the product. Put one of these on the CD and another on the product box. You may want to write the serial number on the inside front cover of each of the product manuals in case you need to phone RoboHELP customer support.)

If you are updating from a previous version of RoboHELP, back up your old templates along with any RoboHELP templates that you've customized.

Installing RoboHELP Office 2000

The RoboHELP Office 2000 installation procedure is largely automatic, but there are a number of things that will make the process easier and trouble-free.

To install RoboHELP Office 2000, do the following:

1. Place the RoboHELP Office 2000 CD in your CD drive. If you have your computer set to autostart CDs, then the install routine will begin immediately; otherwise, you should display the CD's contents in the Windows Explorer and double-click the SETUP.EXE file on the CD. The RoboHELP splash screen will appear, and the setup process will begin. There will be a screen of legal information and a welcome screen. On each screen, click OK to progress to the next screen.
2. Enter your name, company name, and product serial number. When you are satisfied with your entries, click OK.

When you are asked to enter your serial number, be careful when entering the following commonly confused characters:the letter O and the number 0;the letters I and L and the number 1;the letter G and the number 6;the letter Z and the numbers 7 and 2;the letter S and the number 5.

3. The installation procedure will then ask you to select which version of Word is installed. Make sure you select the version of Word that is your current default. (You may have several versions of Word on your system, so make sure that you specify the version that runs when you double-click a DOC file.)

4. The installation process will ask you to select your installation directory. Unless you have a specific reason not to do so, install RoboHELP Office 2000 in the default directory.

5. The installation process will ask you what type of install to do. In general, it's probably a good idea to do a complete installation, but this can take a fair amount of time and may cost prohibitively in disk space. For the simplest installation, select Typical. If you are concerned about disk space or you don't want to install application components you know you may not be using, then select Custom to review the items to install.

Tip

If you do perform a custom install, you should be sure to select ODBC files, DAO files, and the HTML Help files.

6. The installation process will ask you if you want RoboHELP to appear in your Start menu. When you are satisfied with your selection, click Next to begin the installation process.

7. When the installation process is complete, you will be prompted to register RoboHELP online. This is a good idea: if you misplace your serial number, the RoboHELP support technicians can still look you up by your name and company name.

8. After you've registered the software, you will have an opportunity to review the release notes. Click Finish to end the installation process. Depending on your system and configuration, you may need to reboot your computer.

✦ ✦ ✦

HTML Quick Guide

✦ ✦ ✦ ✦

In This Appendix

Using HTML in RoboHELP HTML

An overview of commonly used HTML tags

Using nested Tags

Using cascading style sheets

✦ ✦ ✦ ✦

You can do a great deal with the WYSIWYG tab in RoboHELP HTML. However, there are times when you need to know more about the HTML code that makes up your topic pages. This appendix gives you a quick look at HTML and how it works.

Table F-1 provides the color key for the HTML code you see in the True Code Editor in RoboHELP HTML. Tables F-2, F-3, and F-4 provide a quick overview of the most common tags, what they do, and topics of which you should be aware. The "Basics of HTML" section provides more information about the tag, including syntax and their most common uses. The "Cascading Style Sheet" section shows you how to use the most common formatting changes in CSS.

This appendix is not meant to teach you HTML, only help you edit the HTML created by RoboHELP HTML. If you want to learn more about HTML, see Appendix E, "Resources," for additional information.

Modifying HTML in RoboHELP HTML

RoboHELP HTML provides a way for you to edit your HTML by including the True Code Editor as part of the RoboHELP HTML creation programs. The True Code Editor was created for manually entering nonstandard HTML code.

The True Code Editor has a special color code it uses to help you distinguish between the different types of HTML. Table F-1 shows the meaning of the text color codes.

Table F-1
True Code Editor Color Codes

Color	*Identifies*
BLUE	HTML tags
RED	Nested information set inside other tags, such as hyperlinks, file names, or reference text
GREEN	Comments (see the <!-- --> entry later in this appendix.)
BLACK	Standard text that displays on the topic page
GRAY	Scripting elements and object tags for ActiveX controls
PURPLE	All nonstandard characters

What Is HTML?

As discussed in Chapter 16, "What Is HTML Help," your topic pages are simply HTML documents, which are made up of standard text files. These files are saved using an .htm, or .html extension and then compiled into the finished product of your HTML Help project. Even after compiling, it is the HTML tag that gives the browser the information about how to display your topic pages.

HTML tags follow a standard format that starts with the angle brackets that enclose each tag. Most tags have a format such as the following, which centers text on the page:

```
<CENTER>This text is centered</CENTER>
```

You can identify the tag because it is surrounded by angle brackets. The first <CENTER> tag is the on tag and it tells the browser to center the text. The second tag, the </CENTER> tag, tells the browser it can go back to default and stop centering text; it is called the off tag. Most HTML tags have both and on and off tag. Some have only an on tag. Be sure you turn off HTML tags; otherwise their formatting may be carried throughout the rest of your document. Table F-2 lists the most common tags used in HTML.

All HTML tags in this appendix are listed in uppercase to make them easier to see. When you create HTML the tags are case insensitve, so they can be any case you want as long as they have the angle brackets before and after them.

Table F-2
Common Tags

Tag	*Title*	*Function*	*Where It Is in the HTML Document*	*Where It's Discussed in Detail in This Appendix*
`<!-- -->`	Comment	Text between the hyphens will not be displayed	Anywhere, but usually found in the HEAD	Other Tags
`<A HREF="# ">`	Anchor	Any word after the pound sign becomes an anchor	BODY	Links
`<A HREF="ftp: ">`	FTP	Creates a link to an FTP site	BODY	Links
`<A HREF="http: ">`	Link	Creates a link to another web page	BODY	Links
`<A HREF="mailto: ">`	Mail to	Calls the default browser or e-mail client to send mail	BODY	Links
`<A HREF>`	Basic Link	All clickable links start with this tag	BODY	Links
`<A NAME=" ">`	Anchor	Any word between the quotes becomes an anchor	BODY	Links
`<B>`	Bold	Displays text in bold	BODY	Text Tags
`<BACKGROUND>`	Background	Defines the background color or image	BODY	Other Tags

Continued

Table F-2 (continued)

Tag	Title	Function	Where It Is in the HTML Document	Where It's Discussed in Detail in This Appendix
<BODY>	Body	Defines the body, where the page is made	BODY	Basic Tags
 	Break	Inserts a hard Return without extra leading	BODY	Text Tags
<CENTER>	Center	Centers a line of text or an image	BODY	Text Tags
<DD>	Definition Element	Defines a list element	BODY	Lists
<DIR> and <MENU>	Directory and Menu List tags	Identifies a Directory or Menu list.	BODY	Lists
<DL>	Definition List	Defines a definition list; must be followed by :	BODY	Lists
<DT>	Definition Item	Identifies the word being defined	BODY	Lists
<FRAME>	Frame	Begins the frame definition tag	FRAME	Frames
<FRAMESET>	Frameset	Starts a frameset document instead of <BODY>	FRAME	Frames
<H1> - <H6>	Headings	Allows six heading levels	BODY	Heading Tags
<HEAD>	Header	Identifies the header for a document	HEAD	Basic Tags

Tag	*Title*	*Function*	*Where It Is in the HTML Document*	*Where It's Discussed in Detail in This Appendix*
<HR>	Hard Rule	Places a hard rule on the page	BODY	Other Tags
<HTML>	HTML	Identifies a text document as HTML	HTML	Basic Tags
<I>	Italics	Displays text in italics	BODY	Text Tags
<IMG SRC=" ">	Image Tag	Displays the image listed between the quotes	BODY	Links
<LI>	List Element	Identifies list elements for most list types	BODY	Lists
<LINK>	Link Element	Links to a cascading style sheet	HEAD	Other Tags
<META>	Meta Tag	Used in header to give meta information	HEAD	Other Tags
<OL>	Ordered List	Defines an ordered list	BODY	Lists
<P>	Paragraph	Hard Return with extra leading	BODY	Text Tags
<TABLE>	Table	Starts a Table	BODY	Tables
<TARGET>	Frame Target	Used in the document to point to a frame	FRAME	Frames
<TD>	Table Cell	Identifies an individual cell within a row	BODY	Tables

Continued

Table F-2 *(continued)*

Tag	*Title*	*Function*	*Where It Is in the HTML Document*	*Where It's Discussed in Detail in This Appendix*
<TITLE>	Title	Contains the title of the document Displayed in the window bar	HEAD	Basic Tags
<TR>	Table Row	Identifies an individual row within a table	BODY	Tables
<UL>	Unordered List	Defines an unordered, or bulleted, list	BODY	Lists

Regardless of the on and off tags mentioned previously, some HTML tags can be combined together, called *nesting*, to display text or images in different ways. Table F-3 lists the common nested tags, and Table F-4 lists HTML terms with which you should be familiar.

Table F-3
Nested Tags

Tag	*Nests Inside*	*Function*
ALIGN	<TABLE> and <IMG>	Sets alignment
ALT	<IMG>	Defines text to be displayed instead of image
BORDER	<IMG>	Defines width of border; Default is 0
COLS	<FRAMESET>	Defines layout
COLSPAN	<TD>	Defines layout of table
NAME	<FRAME>	Defines the name of a frame window
NORESIZE	<FRAME>	Defines frame resizing properties

Tag	*Nests Inside*	*Function*
`ROWS`	`<FRAMESET>`	Defines layout
`ROWSPAN`	`<TD>`	Defines layout of table
`SCROLLING`	`<FRAME>`	Defines frame scrolling properties
`SRC`	`<IMG>`	Defines the source for an image
`VALIGN`	`<TD>`	Defines vertical alignment of a cell
`WIDTH & HEIGHT`	`<IMG>`	Defines size of image

Table F-4
HTML Topics and Words You Should Know

Topics You Should Know	*Basic Information*
.htm, .html	Extensions used to identify HTML files
Anchors	Allow a link into the middle of an HTML document
Browsers	Utilities for viewing HTML pages
Cascading Style Sheets	Advanced HTML tool to add layout and design
Colors	All colors in HTML are in hexadecimal
Current standards	Current HTML standard is 3.0; 4.0 is in review
Frames	Layout tool in HTML
Headings	View-determined text formatting for HTML
HTML	Hypertext Markup Language
Images	Graphic Files that can be imbedded in HTML
Links	A connection created between HTML documents
Relative versus Absolute	The two types of path names for HTML
Scripting	Advanced HTML tools that allow dynamic pages
Special characters	A way to display special characters
Tables	Layout tool in HTML
Tags	HTML markup tools
Text Editors	Utilities for constructing HTML from scratch
Translators	Utilities for turning documents into HTML

Detailed Tag Information

There are only a few basic tags that exist in every HTML document. This section outlines them for you.

<HTML>

The <HTML> tag is the first and last tag in your document. It tells your browser this is an HTML document and not a graphic file or a program. It also helps distinguish it from a plain text file, which essentially it is. Consequently, <HTML> must be the first tag in your document, and its corresponding </HTML> tag must be the last tag in your document.

The <HTML> tag is extremely important and must not be forgotten. If you are creating Web pages in a word processor, you may want to set up a document template for all of your HTML documents that has some of the very basic tags like <HTML> and many of the other basic tags in this section.

<HEAD>

The <HEAD> tag tells the browser to expect a title in the document as well as commands that deal with the format or nature of the document. The title and formatting elements belong in the <HEAD> tag. For basic HTML, only the <TITLE> tag must be included. For all HTML documents, however, you must still have a <HEAD> tag.

<TITLE>

The <TITLE> tag contains the title of the document and is intended to tell your users what this HTML document is about. The text between <TITLE> and </TITLE> displays if the user opens the topic in its own window. The <TITLE> tag must be inside the <HEAD> and </HEAD> tags.

<BODY>

The <BODY> tag tells the browser to look for the bulk of the document. The <BODY> tags are the text and links that make up your Web page. The <BODY> tag comes right after the </HEAD> tag and informs the browser that is has finished the formatting and title information and will begin the bulk of the information that is to be displayed on the screen. Inside the <BODY> of your document you will place all of the text and graphics, as well as the links to be displayed in your topic pages.

The <BODY> tag is one of the HTML tags meant to enclose many other tags, called nested tags. The <BODY> tag often includes some sort of formatting information, such as the <BACKGROUND> tag.

The </BODY> tag will end the bulk of your document, with only the </HTML> tag following it.

Heading Tags

The heading tags go in the body of your HTML document and can be very useful in providing headings without the necessity of changing fonts.

<H1> through <H6>

Tags such as <H1> are called header tags. Header text is larger and bolder than standard text. Headers can go anywhere inside the <BODY> tag, but are usually used before the bulk of the text on your page. There are six levels of headers. Header 1 is defined by <H1>, header 2 by <H2>, header 3 by <H3>, and so on until header 6.

The <H1> tag defines the largest, boldest text on your page. You can also skip header numbers, so you don't need to use all six headings on any one page. You may want to investigate what each header level looks like in your own browser before you use them in your topic pages.

Text Tags

The majority of the text on your topic pages uses the paragraph and formatting tags described in this section.

<P> and <BR>: The paragraph tags

There are two commands used to tell the browser when you want to insert a hard return. The <P> tag is called the paragraph mark. You place <P> at the start of your new line, and </P> at the end of one.

The <P> tag tells a browser that you are starting a new paragraph. The </P> off tag tells the browser you have just ended one. When you are creating text for your topics, use <P> almost anywhere you would press the Enter key when you are word processing. The browser will line wrap the text between the on and off paragraph marks, thus making the length of a line dependent on the width of your customer's browser. It will create some extra space before a <P> tag and after a </P> tag to help distinguish a paragraph from surrounding text, images, or links.

If you do not want the extra space created by the <P>tag, or if you simply want to control when a line ends, you can use the <BR> tag.
 is referred to as Break. Break tells your browser that the line ends at that point, and it is one of the few tags that has no off feature; </BR> means nothing to your browser. It is a convention to make only limited use of the <br> feature. The most common use of <BR> is when you want several lines of space before or after text. Because <BR> does not create the extra space, you can also use it inside <P> to control line breaks within your paragraph. Either way, <BR> will give you a hard return without the extra white space before the tag as <P> will.

Only <P> and <BR> allow you to control the end of a line. All lines without these tags are formatted by line wrap, regardless of how they look on your word processor screen.

<B>, <I>, <U>, and <CENTER>: The text formatting tags

To change text to display in anyway other than standard text format, or left justified, you will need the Text Formatting Tags. All formatting tags work the same. The on tag starts directly before the text you want to format, and the off tag comes directly after it. You can also use more than one formatting tag on the same text. For example, this would place your company name centered, bolded, and in italics:

```
<P><CENTER><B><I>Foggan Drizzle</I></B></CENTER></P>
```

Notice how the tags are turned on and then turned off in reverse order. This convention has been developed to help you make sure all tags get turned off. Here is a list of what each of the four most common formatting tags do:

- The <CENTER> tag tells the browser to center a line and its corresponding </CENTER> off tag ends the line you want to center.
- The bold tag, <B>, tells the browser that should be darker and slightly larger than the surrounding text. </B> turns off the bold formatting.
- The italics tag, <I>, tells the browser that the text should be slanted in relation to the standard text format. </I> turns off the italics formatting.
- The underline tag, <U>, tells the browser to place a line under the text. </U> turns off the underline formatting. Underline should be used with great care because, by default, links are underlined and users could become very confused.

Lists

As a quick and easy formatting decision, lists can't be beat. The four types of lists are described in this section.

<UL>: The unordered list tag

To create a bulleted list in the body of your HTML document, you need to use this set of tags:

- <UL> defines text as an unnumbered, or bulleted, list
- <LI> indicates a list item
- </UL> turns off the listing tag

You combine the tags in the body of the HTML document like this:

```
<P>My Grocery List for this week is:</P>
<UL>
<LI>Eggs
<LI>Milk
```

```
<LI>Bread
<LI>Orange Juice
</UL>
```

This creates a list that looks like the following:

My Grocery List for this week is:

- Eggs
- Milk
- Bread
- Orange Juice

Bulleted lists can be any length, and are commonly used for making a set of points or arguments about a subject. You can include bulleted lists on your topic page anywhere as you would if you were desktop publishing the document. Remember, however, that the bulleted list will always appear flush with the left margin.

<OL>: The ordered list tag

To create a numbered list in the body of your HTML document, you need to use this set of tags:

- `<OL>` defines this as an ordered, or numbered, list
- `<LI>` indicates a list item
- `</OL>` turns off the listing tag

You combine the tags in the body of the HTML document like this:

```
<P>Here are our top three support questions.  The answers are
on the Questions and Answers page.</P>
<OL>
<LI>How do I create a list?
<LI>What can lists do for me?
<LI>Where does the list go in the HTML document?
</OL>
```

This creates a list that looks like the following (italicized to distinguish it from the normal text in this book, even though no italic tags were used in the example):

Here are our top three support questions. The answers are on the Questions and Answers page.

1. *How do I create a list?*

2. What can lists do for me?

3. Where does the list go in the HTML document?

Numbered lists can be any length, and are commonly used for listing items you would see in tables of contents or other informational listings. You can include numbered lists on your Web page anywhere you would include it is you were desktop publishing the document.

<DL>: Definition lists

To create a definition list, you need to use these list elements:

- `<DL>` defines text as a definition, or indented, list
- `<DT>` indicates the word being defined
- `<DD>` indicates the definition
- `</DL>` ends the definition list

You combine the tags in the body of the HTML document like this:

```
<P>Here are all the most common British words traveling
Americans have trouble with:</P>
<DL>
<DT>Lift (British)
<DD>Elevator (American)
<DT>Biscuit
<DD>Cookie
<DT>Bobbie
<DD>Policeman
</DL>
```

This creates a list that looks like the following (again, italicized to distinguish it from the normal text in this book, even though no italic tags were used in the example):

Here are all the most common British words traveling Americans have trouble with:

Lift (British)
Elevator (American)
Biscuit
Cookie
Bobbie
Policeman

Definition lists, as their name implies, are generally used to define terms. They can also be used any time you need to indent a paragraph under another, because the amount of text in the list element, <DD>, can be as large as you need it to be. You can even use the <BR> tag inside the <DD> tag.

<DIR> and <MENU>

Both <DIR> and <MENU> lists have fallen into disuse because there are very few reasons to use them instead of the other list tags. However, you may see them being used with the <LI> tag and they are simple enough to learn to spot.

Links

Links are the backbone of your HTML Help project. This section walks you through the standard link, its additions, and the image link.

<A HREF>: The standard link

To insert a link, you need to learn a new kind of HTML tag, the <A HREF=> tag.

Links to other pages use the URL for the page so page links have tags such as <A HREF= "basic.html">, where basic.html is the name of the page to which you are linking. It is turned off with a </A> tag. So the completed link looks like this:

```
<A HREF= "basic.html">basic document</A>
```

As you can see from the example, a link to a page has three parts: the URL, the text, and the </A>. The URL tells the browser which page to link to and is placed directly after the equal sign enclosed in quotes. Don't forget the final closing bracket or to enclose your URLs in quotes. Both are very common mistakes, and forgetting them will turn your pages into a mess. The text for a link always comes after the closing bracket (>) of the URL reference and before the opening bracket of the link closing signal. The </A> closes the entire link.

You need to include the absolute URL for pages that are not part of your HTML Help project. There are two kinds of URLs: absolute URLs and relative URLs. The URL http://www.londontravelword.com/london.html is an absolute URL because it includes everything your user's browser would need to find it anywhere on the entire Web. An example of a relative URL is london.html, which is used to reference a page or file included within your HTML Help project. When a browser sees a relative URL, it looks for that page or file in the set of files as the page that calls for it.

Unless the user changed the default, a link appears in blue before the user clicks it, and in red or purple after the user has clicked it. It has become standard practice to attempt to work links into text seamlessly. Therefore, you should avoid phrases such as "This link takes you to another interesting page."

<A HREF: mailto> and other additions to the standard link

You can make additions to the standard `<A HREF="">` link so the link does something other than link to another document.

- `<A HREF="# ">` sets an anchor wherein the name of the anchor is set after the # like this:

  `<A HREF="#LONDON">`

  where `LONDON` could be referenced later as a linking spot inside a topic page.
- `<A HREF="ftp: ">` sets a link that sends your user to and FTP site to download a document or file of some kind. If you want the user to download a file automatically, put the entire URL here and include a file name.
- `<A HREF="http: ">` isn't really an addition, but a different way to state an absolute reference inside a standard link.
- `<A HREF="mailto: ">` sets a link that opens up the default e-mail program on your users system and creates a new mail message to the address you include after the colon.

<IMG>: Image links

To add a graphic to your topic page use the `<IMG SCR="">` tag exactly as you used the `<A HREF="">` tag in the previous section.

Suppose you want to include an image of a duck, which you have called DUCK.GIF. You would insert a line of HTML text like this:

```
<IMG SCR="duck.gif">
```

When the customer loads this page, the browser looks at this HTML tag and displays the file DUCK.GIF.

As you can see, there is no closing tag for an image reference because it is simply a place holder that shows the browser where to display the image, and not like the on-off tags in most of HTML.

`<IMG SCR="">` does operate like `<A HREF="">` as far as the URL portion is concerned. You can have relative and absolute URLs between the quotes, but for most images, you will want to place that image within the directory for the page that calls it. This rule of thumb is usually broken only when an image is carried throughout the entire site, for instance, your company logo.

Tables

Although rarely used in your HTML Help project, tables are a useful tool for defining space on your topic page. As a general rule, it is best to define your tables in RoboHELP HTML using the WYSIWYG tools, and then only edit them if necessary.

There are three tags for defining your tables in HTML:

✦ <TABLE> tells the browser that you are creating a table

✦ <TR> defines a row of the table

✦ <TD> defines a cell within a row

The tags for tables are combined as in the following example, which shows how to create a three-row, three-column table with each cell labeled:

```
<TABLE>
<TR>
<TD>This the upper left cell</TD>
<TD>This the middle upper cell</TD>
<TD>This the upper right cell</TD>
</TR>
<TR>
<TD>This the middle left cell</TD>
<TD>This the middle middle cell</TD>
<TD>This the middle right cell</TD>
</TR>
<TR>
<TD>This the lower left cell</TD>
<TD>This the lower middle cell</TD>
<TD>This the lower right cell</TD>
</TR>
</TABLE>
```

Frames

Frames are discussed in Chapter 26, "Using Forms and Frames". This section shows you the format of HTML that makes frames possible.

Frames combine several different HTML documents into what appears to be one topic page to your users. This is accomplished by an entirely new document, different from the standard HTML document, called a Frameset document. The Frameset document contains information about the layout of the frames, and uses these tags to do it:

✦ <FRAME SET> is placed where the body tag is in a standard HTML document. This tag tells the browser that it is defining a frameset and not displaying text information of it's own.

✦ <FRAME> defines the height and width, name, and options of each frame as well as which HTML document it displays.

The only change to a standard HTML document that frames might make is in the links. When you are linking from a frame window to another document, and you want the new document to open up in part of the frameset, you need to use the <TARGET> tag.

<TARGET> defines which of the frames in a frameset a linked to document is supposed to open up in.

Other Tags

There are literally hundreds of other possible tags in HTML even without the option of cascading style sheets. This section outlines the most commonly used ones and gives you some idea of what the tags do.

<BACKGROUND>

If you want something other than a standard gray HTML background for your topic pages you need to use the <BACKGROUND> tag. The <BACKGROUND> tag is usually nested inside <BODY> tag and defines a background for the entire topic page.

<BACKGROUND> can define either a color (by name or number) or a file containing an image to be tiled.

<HR>

A Horizontal Rule is a line that crosses your topic page horizontally. Use <HR> to create horizontal lines. By default the hard rule covers the entire window, from one side to the other. You can have less of a hard rule by setting a percentage like this:

```
<HR 80%>
```

which gives a hard rule that is only 80 percent of the screen width.

<LINK>

Used to point the browser at the cascading style sheet for an HTML document, <LINK> is always found in the <HEAD> of an HTML page. The type of document is defined by REL (usually STYLE SHEET) and the path to the style sheet is provided by HREF.

<META>

Used primarily for creation information, the <META> tag is an informational tag that appears in the <HEAD> of your HTML page. Almost every topic page has a <META> tag to point the browser at the style sheet that you have applied to the document. As a general rule, the <META> tags in your topics look like this:

```
<META NAME="generator" CONTENT="RoboHELP by eHelp www.ehelp.com
HTML Edition">
```

The NAME indicates what type of document it is. The CONTENT tag tells where the topic was created and how.

<!-- -->: The comment tag

Nothing inside a comment tag is displayed on your user's screen. This unique attribute displays text for anyone looking at the HTML code and is very useful for later developments. Comments are used in both the HEAD and BODY of your topic, but they always use this format:

```
<!--This text will not display-->
```

Comments are unique in that the open tag, <!-- , and the close tag, -->, do not follow the standard format of most tags.

Usually seen in the HEAD part of your basic topic page, these useful HTML tags are read by the browser, but never displayed for the user. Topics use the comment tag to set format parameters, to reference style information, and to set scripting options.

Cascading Style Sheets

RoboHELP HTML makes large use of cascading style sheets to create new tags and format elements on topic pages. Most of the cascading style sheet information used for topic page formatting is contained in a separate style sheet, though inline style changes also have cascading style sheet tags.

Table F-5 briefly lists the most common properties and values for cascading style sheets.

Table F-5
Common Properties and Values for Cascading Style Sheets

<table>
<tr><th>Property</th><th>Value</th><th>Default Setting</th><th>Applies to</th><th>Inherited?</th><th>Comment</th></tr>
<tr><td>font-size</td><td>xx-small |
x-small |
small |
medium |
large |
x-large |
xx-large |
<number> |
<length> |
<percentage></td><td>medium</td><td>all elements</td><td>yes</td><td>Percentage values refer to size relative to parent's font size.</td></tr>
<tr><td>font-style</td><td>normal |
italic ||
small-caps |
oblique ||
small-caps |
small-caps</td><td>normal</td><td>all elements</td><td>yes</td><td>The keyword values can be combined. Legal combinations of the values are: one of the four values (normal, italic', oblique, small-caps) italic or oblique, combined with small-caps.</td></tr>
<tr><td>font-family</td><td>[<family-name>]</td><td>UA specific</td><td>all elements</td><td>yes</td><td>This can be a list of fonts separated by commas, allowing you to define the font even if the user does not have your first choice installed. A generic-family may also be included after the family-name and a comma. Valid generic-family names are:serif (e.g. Times) sans-serif (e.g. Helvetica) cursive (e.g. Zapf-Chancery) fantasy (e.g. Western) monospace (e.g. Courier). Font names containing white space should be quoted: BODY { font-family: "new century schoolbook", serif }.</td></tr>
</table>

<table>
<tr><th>Property</th><th>Value</th><th>Default Setting</th><th>Applies to</th><th>Inherited?</th><th>Comment</th></tr>
<tr><td>color</td><td><color></td><td>UA specific</td><td>all elements</td><td>yes</td><td>This property describes the text color of an element, that is, the "foreground" color. There are several different ways to define color. For instance, here are two ways to specify red: EM { color: red } EM { color: rgb(255,0,0) }.</td></tr>
<tr><td>text-decoration</td><td>none |
[underline |
overline |
line-through |
blink]+</td><td>none</td><td>all elements</td><td>no, but see clarification</td><td>This property can be used to decorate text blocks. Any colors required for the decoration are inherited from any color property value settings. For example: A:link, A:visited, A:active { text-decoration: underline }would underline all links within the document. A:link, A:visited, A:active { text-decoration: none}would remove the underline from all links within the document.</td></tr>
<tr><td>text-align</td><td>left |
right |
center |
justify</td><td>UA specific</td><td>block-level elements</td><td>yes</td><td>This property describes how text is aligned within the element. The actual justification algorithm used is UA and human-language dependent. As above, implementation of this property is browser dependent and may differ for different languages.</td></tr>
</table>

✦ ✦ ✦

APPENDIX G

What's on the CD-ROM?

This appendix provides you with information on the programs that are included on the CD that's included with this book.

There are three programs included on this CD:

- RoboHELP Office 2000
- Paint Shop Pro 6.02
- Media Center Plus 3

Each of the programs on the CD is a timed demo version of the full program. You can order the complete version of each program from the manufacturer. You should also check the manufacturer's web site for program updates, add-ons, and additional information.

RoboHELP Office 2000

RoboHELP Office 2000 is a 30-day timed demo version of the full program described in this book. You can use this program to do everything you've seen in the chapters, including creating complete WinHelp and HTML Help systems of your own.

Paint Shop Pro 6.02

Paint Shop Pro 6.02 from JASC Software, Inc., is the best shareware graphics editing program currently available. With Paint Shop Pro, you can open files in virtually any graphic file format, perform a wide variety of edits, and save the files in any graphic format of your choosing. Paint Shop Pro not only lets you view and edit standalone graphics, you can also use it to do graphic animation, capture and edit screen images, design Web graphics, acquire and enhance photos from digital cameras and scanners, and print proof sheets of thumbnails.

There is a wide selection of third-party tutorials available online (a list appears on the JASC web site at `http://www.jasc.com`). There are a dozen books on Paint Shop Pro as well, including *Paint Shop Pro for Dummies* by David Kay.

The timed demo version of Paint Shop Pro 6.02 is good for 30 days, after which you must register the program for $99 with JASC Software, Inc.

Media Center Plus 3

Media Center Plus 3 from JASC Software, Inc., is a graphics and multimedia file organizing and cataloging program. Media Center Plus 3 scans directories on your computer for graphics, MP3 files, AVI and MPEG video files, then creates an album of thumbnail images for quick reference. When you view the thumbnails in an album, you can click a thumbnail to access the graphics or multimedia file. This is exceptionally useful when you have hundreds or even thousands of images to catalog.

Media Center Plus 3 is a good visual source control system for your graphics and multimedia files as well. You can save and edit the contents of albums, then share them with other users. Online help developers will find this feature particularly useful for keeping track of groups of files for a specific product or online help system.

There are basic editing features for graphics and multimedia files built into Media Center Plus 3, so you can edit the file associated with a thumbnail without having to leave the program. In addition, you can acquire images from scanners and digital cameras, create slideshows, and export graphics to HTML formats.

The timed demo version of Media Center Plus 3 is good for 30 days, after which you must register the program for $29 with JASC Software, Inc.

✦ ✦ ✦

Glossary

absolute path The fully qualified location of a file, including the drive letter and folder names, such as E:\Foggan Drizzle\WinHelp\Foggan Drizzle.rtf. See also *relative path*.

absolute positioning The size and position of a window based on a specific position using pixel coordinates. See also *relative positioning*.

absolute URL The fully qualified Internet address of a Web site; for example, `http://www.hedtke.com`. See also *URL*.

accelerator keys See *automatic button accelerators*.

active link The currently selected link.

ActiveEdit Displays the text and other information for a control in What's This? Help Composer so you can edit the help easily (WinHelp only). When you enable ActiveEdit, RoboHELP adds the ActiveEdit button to the button bar in the compiled WinHelp file. You can jump from a compiled WinHelp topic to the source topic and make changes or corrections instantly.

ActiveTest Lets you test the What's This? help against the program before the developers have enabled the What's This? help links and calls in the program by displaying an uncompiled WinHelp topic as it would appear in a compiled WinHelp file.

ActiveX A Windows protocol that uses the Windows Component Object Model, or COM. ActiveX lets one application use a feature that is part of another application. Primarily used in HTML Help and other HTML-based help files.

ActiveX controls A section of code, an executable file, or even a DOS batch file that adds interactivity to a Web page. Primarily used in HTML Help and other HTML-based help files.

A-Keywords A-Keywords (also known as *A-Link keywords* or *See Also keywords*) let you create See Also links that display related topics.

AKW file An internal file created and maintained by RoboHELP that contains information on "See Also" keywords that aren't currently used in the WinHelp project.

ALI file The file that stores the aliases that accompany an HTML Help project. RoboHELP creates an alias file for each HTML Help project. The ALI file will have the same name as the CHM file.

alias In WinHelp, aliases are pseudonymous entries that can be used to fix links to topic IDs that have changed or been deleted, and also to link multiple map IDs to a single topic. In HTML Help, aliases provide the link from the program to the HTML Help file by providing an artificial topic ID. Aliases in HTML Help link the map ID to an alias and the alias to the topics HTM file. In addition, you can use aliases in HTML Help files to link multiple map IDs to a single topic.

ALink A WinHelp macro that looks for A-Keywords (See Also keywords) and will then list the topics that contain the See Also keywords that meet the criteria you've set. See also *A-Keywords* and *KLink*.

A-Link control In HTML Help files, the A-Link control lets you specify an A-Link name that can be linked to several of your topics.

animated GIFs In HTML Help, compiled GIF files that contain more than one image. When run in sequence, they give the illusion of motion. See also *GIF*.

API Abbreviation for application program interface.

application help An online help project that will provide context-sensitive help specific to a development environment.

array In a program or script, an arrangement of data elements that can be accessed with an array index, a counter that describes which slot in the array to examine.

ASCII Acronym for American Standard Code for Information Interchange, pronounced "ask-key." Frequently used to describe a standard text file (such as a README.TXT) created or read with an editor such as Windows Notepad.

authorable buttons Three-dimensional push buttons in a WinHelp project that can contain custom text.

auto size In WinHelp files, an option that automatically adjusts the size of a secondary help window based on the length of the topic being displayed.

AUTOCORR.TLX file A dictionary file that contains words to correct automatically.

automatic button accelerators Characters you can specify that activate menu or button functions. (Also known as *accelerator keys*.) For example, you can use X to specify that the C character activates the Contents function.

AVI file Abbreviation for Audio-Video Interleave. The standard file format for video files (with or without sound) in Windows. AVI files use the Microsoft RIFF (Resource Interchange File Format) specification.

back A button that displays the prior topic in a help file.

background region In WinHelp, the area of a window below the titlebar and (optionally) the *non-scrolling region* that contains the body of the topic.

baggage A way to store graphics, multimedia files, and other information in the body of a compiled help file.

Base A statement used in CNT files for WinHelp projects to identify the base WinHelp file. The Base statement can also identify the default window used to display topics in the WinHelp file.

binary index An index file created inside the Microsoft HTML Help file when it's compiled.

bitmap A standard and popular graphics format that breaks an image into pixels, equal-sized graphic elements. Bitmap graphics are edited by working with individual pixels in the bitmap. Also known as BMP files.

boilerplate Common text that is repeated frequently, such as the topic text for OK and Cancel buttons or standard license agreements.

book A category or group of topics in a table of contents. Books in tables of contents let you group related topics and sort items hierarchically.

bookmark In WinHelp, a placeholder for specific topics so the user can quickly find a topic. In HTML Help, a named area that you can use to jump to sections of that or other HTML Help topics. (HTML Help bookmarks are the same as midtopic IDs in WinHelp files.)

bounding box Sets the dimensions and locations of a hotspot.

broken link Any link that doesn't correctly point to a topic or link destination. Broken links usually indicate a missing topic or a changed topic ID.

Broken Links report Used to identify and locate broken links in a project.

browse buttons Buttons on the toolbar that display the previous and next topics in the browse sequence in the help file.

browse sequence A link that lets the user moves forward and backward through a set of topics arranged in a specific order. Browse sequences let the users step through groups of topics very much like paging through a book. Each topic in a browse sequence has a browse sequence string, which is composed of a browse sequence string name that identifies the browse sequence group and a browse sequence number that uniquely identifies that topic with the group.

browser window A program that displays an displays an HTML file of any kind, including HTML Help and WebHelp. Internet Explorer and Netscape Navigator are the two most common browsers.

BugHunter A diagnostic tool included with RoboHELP Office 2000 that lets you monitor the behind-the-scenes activities of the program and the online help file when you are testing context-sensitive help.

build tag A way to conditionally include or exclude topics for compilation in WinHelp and HTML Help projects.

bulleted list A list used to highlight single pieces of information about a topic. Each item in the list is preceded by a "bullet," which is usually a small solid dot.

button macros Let you create, modify, and delete the buttons that appear on the WinHelp window button bars.

call A request for information or action from one program to another.

cascading style sheet See *style sheet.*

CBT Abbreviation for computer-based training.

CDX files One of the What's This? help database indexing files.

CGA Monitors that display a maximum of four colors at 200 × 320.

character style In HTML Help, defines how individual words look; is usually altered using the WYSIWYG buttons.

character window In HTML Help, lets you set basic font styles and colors, much as you would with the WYSIWYG buttons. However, more options are available from this window.

CHJ file The What's This? help project file, which contains project settings and other information.

CHM file A compiled HTML Help file.

chunking Presenting the optimal number of concepts for the user in a section, usually seven concepts, plus or minus two, depending on the complexity and depth of the material.

CID file The context-sensitive ID file, which contains the links for the dialog box controls and the topic IDs in the What's This? help file.

client area Another name for background region.

client scripting In HTML Help, scripting that resides on the Web page itself and consists of different types of scripts.

Close Window control In HTML Help, closes the active window.

CNT file A text file containing the raw data for the table of contents for the WinHelp file. CNT files also can combine topics, keywords, and See Also keywords from several WinHelp files into a single master help file.

compile Combining and processing the various source files for an online help project into the compiled help system.

compiler The software that compiles an online help project into a completed help.

compiling tab In HTML Help, allows you to monitor the compiling process and glean information from the HTML Help compiler in action.

compression A way to decrease the size of a compiled WinHelp file. See also *Hall compression*, *phrase compression*, and *Zeck compression*.

conceptual art Art that illustrates something that cannot be conveyed easily with words alone (such as goatees and spiral staircases). Usually it is supported by text explaining the concept or process being illustrated. Conceptual art can be anything from a process flowchart to a simple arrow diagram.

CONDCORR.TLX file A dictionary file that contains words to correct conditionally.

conditional compiling Using build tags to include selected modules in the finished help file.

contents database file See *GID file*.

contents file See *CNT file*.

Contents tab One of the tabs in a compiled WinHelp file containing the table of contents for the WinHelp file.

contents topic The default topic displayed when a WinHelp file is first opened or when the user presses the Contents button within the WinHelp file.

Contents() macro A macro that displays the Contents tab of the Help Topics screen or the default topic in the WinHelp file.

context ID See *map ID*.

context number See *map number.*

context string See *map string.*

context string mapping file See *map file.*

context-sensitive access Pressing F1 or Shift+F1, or using help buttons in the product itself, to trigger a context-sensitive link to a help topic.

context-sensitive help Help that is directly linked to a program.

Control menu A window menu containing commands that can be used to restore, move, size, minimize, maximize, or close the window. The Control menu is accessible by clicking the Control menu button in the upper left corner of the window or by pressing Alt+Spacebar.

Control View In What's This? Help Composer, a view option for viewing all the controls for the dialog box, the topic status, and the topic ID.

controls Any element in the program for which you can request context-sensitive help, such as screens, fields, menus, buttons, and commands.

CreateButton macro A macro for creating custom buttons on a WinHelp window's button bar.

CSS file In HTML Help, a style sheet file created for a DOC file.

custom class dialog boxes Any dialog boxes that have been defined as belonging to a nonstandard class by the programmer.

custom controls In What's This? Help Composer, controls that do not appear on the dialog box in Dialog View but are listed in Control View.

Custom tabs Programmatic extensions to the Help Topics screen. You must use a DLL (dynamic link library) to create a Custom tab.

custom window A secondary window designed for an HTML Help project.

DBF file The What's This? help database file.

debugging Finding and removing errors from an online help project.

definition list In HTML Help, lists that have two types of indents.

Details view In HTML Help, shows the status of each topic and includes vital information about what has been accomplished with each one.

DHTML Abbreviation for *dynamic HTML.*

Diagnostics report Used for reporting on a wide variety of possible error conditions such as missing files, documents, or images, unused or duplicate map IDs, and so on.

dialog box A small screen in the program, such as the standard File Open dialog box, that contains command buttons and, optionally, various kinds of options for performing a particular command or task.

Directory list In HTML Help, lists of types of information or lists of other topics. Directory lists are slightly longer than Menu lists.

DLL file Abbreviation for *dynamic link library*. DLLs are files containing programs, macros, images, or other information that you can use to extend the features or options of an online help project.

DOC file A standard Word for Windows DOC file. The default file extension for Microsoft Word document files.

Document style In HTML Help, defines the look of your entire topic, including such things as backgrounds, margins, body text fonts, and link fonts.

document template A special type of Microsoft Word document that contains styles, macros, AutoText entries, and custom toolbar, menu, and shortcut key settings. RoboHELP uses a default template of ROBOHELP.DOT for WinHelp projects; it contains RoboHELP commands, toolbars, menus, and shortcut keys for RoboHELP.

documentation plan A document that identifies what you're going to do to create your help project and how you're going to do it.

drag-and-drop Dragging a topic, file, or item from one location to another (usually within a program) to open or incorporate the dragged object in the new program, usually at the location where the object was dropped.

drop-down hotspots See *expanding hotspots*.

DTO file The default topic information file.

duplicate dialog boxes Dialog boxes that appear in the program more than once but look the same and are coded identically.

Duplicate Map ID report A diagnostic report that lists all duplicate entries for topic IDs and topic numbers.

Dynamic HTML A special set of HTML instructions developed by Microsoft to add interest to HTML pages with a minimum of effort. Also known as DHTML.

dynamic link library See *DLL file*.

Dynamic WYSIWYG Displays the actual graphics when you're developing a WinHelp file (as opposed to True Code, which shows the code that will display the graphic). WYSIWYG is an acronym for What You See Is What You Get.

EGA Monitors that display up to 16 colors at 640 × 350.

eHelp A feature for searching the Web for answers to specific questions. Also the new company name for Blue Sky Software.

embedded graphics A graphic stored in a document as a graphic file instead of being included by reference and displayed from another file location.

embedded styles Styles that can be used over and over again within the document without your needing to copy and paste them repeatedly. See also *inline styles*.

Exit() macro Exits the WinHelp file.

expanding hotspots Specially formatted text that expands in line with other text on the topic page to display information when clicked. (Also known as drop-down hotspots.)

Explorer View Help See *WinHelp 2000*.

external topic Any topic that is not part of the current online help project. External topics can be topics in other WinHelp files (for WinHelp projects) or in HTML Help files (for WinHelp or HTML Help projects).

External Topic hotspot A jump to an external topic.

Favorites tab In WinHelp, a tab used for quick navigation to previous or frequently referenced help topics.

Find tab In WinHelp, a tab for doing a full-text search in the WinHelp file.

Find() macro In WinHelp, displays the Find tab of the Help Topics screen.

flavor images Graphics and images that you include to add to the "look and feel."

font set In HTML Help, a defined group of fonts. When HTML Help sees a font set definition, it uses any of the fonts in that set to display the topic.

footnote symbols Any of the characters that appear at the beginning of each topic in a WinHelp file, such as #, $, K, and so on. The WinHelp compiler uses the footnotes to identify the attributes of the topics when compiling the files.

formatting tag In HTML Help, a marker that goes in the body of a document and changes only the text between the on and off settings.

FPT files One of the What's This? help database indexing files.

frameset In HTML Help, a small window you can create inside your standard HTML viewer.

FRM files The Visual Basic form files (which contain the dialog boxes) with additional information added for the What's This? help calls. (Visual Basic projects only.)

FTG file The file (FTG file) generated by WinHelp 4 containing the full-text search by group information.

full-text search The ability to search an online help system for a particular word, phrase, or keyword.

full-text search index file The file (FTS file) generated by WinHelp 4 containing the full-text search by keyword information.

gerunds Words that describe actions, such as "adding," "changing," "printing."

GHC file A map file for creating context-sensitive help with a Visual Basic application.

GID file A hidden file created by the WinHelp viewer when a WinHelp file is run for the first time or when you update the file.

GIF Acronym for Graphics Interchange Format. GIFs contain information about an image stored as a series of small pieces of information describing the pixels on each line of the image.

Glossary Designer In HTML Help, a tool for helping you manage and add glossary entries.

gold master The final release candidate for a help system or program that, if approved, can be sent out for duplication and distribution.

graphical buttons Three-dimensional topic buttons that use a macro and can contain two different images, one that is normally visible and one that appears when the button is clicked.

Graphics Interchange Format See *GIF*.

Graphics Locator A tool to help you find and manage image files you want to include in your online help project.

Hall compression A compression method used for compressing WinHelp files that are over 100K. See also *compression*, *phrase compression*, and *Zeck compression*.

hash codes Internal codes created by the compiler that tell the WinHelp viewer where to find topics in the WinHelp file.

HCRTF.EXE The WinHelp 4 compiler.

HCW.EXE The Microsoft Help Compiler Workshop.

header file See *map file.*

help author The person(s) creating an online help project.

Help Author report A report showing priority and status of the help project and topics.

help authoring The complete life cycle for creating an online help system, including planning, organizing information, testing, and debugging.

help file The compiled file or files that constitute an online help system.

help hook See *topic number.*

Help menu The item on a program's menu bar that contains the Help commands.

help project See *online help project.*

help project file See *HPJ file.*

help topic The basic unit of information in an online help project. These blocks of text constitute the written content of an online help system. In HTML Help, each separate topic has its own independent HTML file.

help window The frames in which topics are displayed. Help windows contain settings for such things as colors, size, and buttons. Also known as display windows or windows.

help windows Let you customize the appearance of the topics in your WinHelp files. Also known as display windows or just windows.

Help-to-Source A decompiler that opens a WinHelp file and turns it back into its component source files and graphics.

HH file A file containing map IDs, which are used to create context-sensitive links between a WinHelp file and its associated application.

HHC file In HTML Help, a table of contents file.

HHCTRL Version control In HTML Help, tells you which version of the HTML Help Control you are using.

HHK file In HTML Help, an index file.

History() macro In WinHelp, displays the history of the last 40 topics viewed in the WinHelp file.

History button A button on the WinHelp button bar that shows the last 50 topics that were displayed in the WinHelp file.

HLP file The compiled WinHelp file.

hotspot A link in an online help project that provides a method of moving directly from one topic to another. (Also known as hyperlinks). See also *external topic hotspot*, *HTML jump, jump*, *macro*, *popup*, and *see also hotspot.*

hotspot image A graphic that the user can click and thereby trigger a hotspot. Hotspot images (also known as hotspot graphics) can also be SHED graphics with multiple hotspots.

hotspot macros A hotspot with an associated macro.

hotspot text The text associated with a hotspot that the user clicks on to perform the action for the hotspot.

HPJ file In WinHelp, a set of instructions in a text file that describe how to compile the online help project and what source files to use. The HPJ file has the same name as the associated WinHelp project but with an extension of HPJ. (Also known as a help project file.)

HPT file In WinHelp, an internal file created and maintained by RoboHELP that contains a list of the topics in the DOC files and is used to identify topics for hyperlinks.

HTML Abbreviation for hypertext markup language. A set of tags used to mark up text files for formatting, to create hyperlinks, include graphics, and perform other functions.

HTML Help An HTML-based online help format developed by Microsoft and first released in 1997. HTML Help is compiled into a single CHM file.

HTML Help BugHunter A diagnostic tool included with RoboHELP Office 2000 for debugging context-sensitive HTML Help. See also *BugHunter* and *WinHelp BugHunter.*

HTML Help Studio A tool used for creating and maintaining HTML Help.

HTML Help Viewer The standard viewer for an HTML Help project.

HTML hotspot In WinHelp, a hotspot that takes the user to intranet sites, Internet Web sites, e-mail, or topics in HTML Help files. Also known as an HTML jump.

HTML macros In WinHelp, macros that permit the user to access URLs on the Internet and jump to HTML Help topics.

HTTP Abbreviation for hypertext transfer protocol. HTTP defines how information is exchanged on the Internet between a server and your browser.

hypergraphic See *hotspot image.*

hyperlink See *hotspot.*

hypermedia A term for an online document that contains hotspots or other navigation methods that allow for nonsequential access to the information in the file.

hypertext markup language See *HTML.*

hypertext transfer protocol See *HTTP.*

icon A small picture or symbol representing a program, task, command, or option.

image links In HTML Help, hyperlinks placed on images in your topic page. See also *hotspot image.*

image maps In HTML Help, image links that allow you to set several links on an image.

Image Window In HTML Help, used to insert images into topics and to alter the properties of images already residing on topic pages.

Image Workshop An image manager and editor that is part of RoboHELP Office 2000.

INC file A map file created and maintained by RoboHELP for creating context-sensitive help with a Turbo Pascal Include application.

index A list of keywords or phrases for finding topics in an online help system.

Index control Allows you to embed the navigation frame of the Index tab into one of your topics.

Index Designer An easy-to-use, effective interface for adding, changing, or deleting keywords while creating indexes in online help files.

Index file In WinHelp, the file (FTS file) generated by WinHelp 4 that contains the full-text search by keyword information. See also *full-text search index file.* In HTML Help, a file that stores all keywords (called index file keywords) in one file that is compiled into the HTML Help file.

index keyword See *keyword.*

Index Links Uses the entries in the index to let the user link to topics.

Index report Provides you with information about the index keywords for your HTML Help project.

Inline styles In HTML Help, alters one section of text within your topic, usually by using the WYSIWYG buttons on the toolbar.

intranet A local Web resource network used within a company.

Java A language designed for the creation of Java Applets, which are distributed in compiled form and referenced from an HTML file. Different from JavaScript.

JavaHelp A compressed online help format developed by Sun Microsystems that works with Java applications.

JavaHelp viewer A viewer designed to display JavaHelp systems.

JavaScript A scripting language that is embedded within the HTML files of Web pages. JavaScript can be written as sections of code within HTML content or can be coded into an external file, which is then referenced in the `<HEAD>` section of the HTML topic. Different from Java.

JPEG Acronym for Joint Photographic Expert Group. Picture files that contain a database of every color in the image and a pixel-by-pixel list of the colors to use. When JPG files are displayed, the two items are combined to form the image. (Also known as JPG.)

jump A hotspot that moves the user from one topic to another. See also *hyperlink.*

JumpID macro A specific type of macro hotspot that tells WinHelp to jump to a specific topic in the same or another WinHelp file.

justification How text or images are positioned (left, right, or centered) on a page.

K footnote In WinHelp, used to list the index keywords for a topic.

Keyboard macros In WinHelp, macros used to add or remove accelerator keys for custom macros.

keyword Words or phrases associated with topics that are used to define the online help system's index. Also known as index keywords or K-Keywords.

Keyword link control In HTML Help, allows the user to select keywords from the index and use their predetermined topic links.

keyword search Searching an online help file by entering a keyword.

K-Keywords See *keyword.*

K-Keywords report See *Index report.*

KKW file In WinHelp, an internal file created and maintained by RoboHELP that contains information on index keywords ("K-Keywords") that aren't currently used in the WinHelp project.

KLink A WinHelp macro that looks for K-Keywords (also known as index keywords and keywords) and displays resultant index entries. See also *keywords* and *ALink.*

knowledge base A collection of online resources, FAQs, tips, technical support information, bug reports, notes, and comments that is used to augment the primary documentation.

link See *hotspot.*

Link control A clickable object (usually a button) that gives users a list of alternate or related topics.

Link View The pane on the right side of the RoboHELP Explorer that graphically displays the links between topics as well as the browse sequences.

Linked styles In HTML Help, styles that alter the look of all or part of your document.

Linking macros In WinHelp, macros that let you create internal and external jumps, popups, See Also, and keyword links.

macro A collection of embedded commands and features that let you create "behind-the-scenes" features and functions and extend the capabilities of your WinHelp files.

Macro Editor A tool that lets you edit WinHelp macros.

Macro hotspot A standard hotspot — text, a graphic, or both — that runs a macro when the user clicks on it.

Macro Wizard A tool that steps you through the macro creation process and checks the syntax of parameters for a macro.

Mailing List command Displays a screen of mailing lists (listservs) to which the user can subscribe.

Main window In WinHelp, the default window for help windows.

map file A file containing entries for the topics and the topic numbers that is imported into your online help project.

map ID The mapping information for a context-sensitive link. Map IDs contain the map string (also known as the topic ID or the context string) and the map number (also known as the help hook or topic number). *Map ID* is also used to refer to the map number itself.

Map ID report A report that provides general information about the map IDs.

map number A unique integer sent by the program to the associated help system that is linked to a specific topic with a map ID. An identifying number specified for each topic for which you want to create context-sensitive help.

map string The topic ID or other identifier used in the map ID.

master CNT A CNT file that concatenates several separate online help files into a single online help system using a contents (CNT) file.

MCI commands In WinHelp, used to control multimedia devices.

menu list In HTML Help, lists used for short lists of items.

Menu macros In WinHelp, macros that let you create, modify, and delete WinHelp menus and add, check, change, delete, disable, enable, and uncheck submenus and menu items.

mid-topic ID In WinHelp, a jump that takes the user to the middle of a topic. (The same function is referred to as a bookmark in HTML Help.)

mini buttons In WinHelp, small gray 12 pixel × 12 pixel buttons that have no text on them.

MRB file Abbreviation for multiresolution bitmap. Graphic files that contain the same image in several different screen resolutions.

Multi-File Find and Replace In WinHelp, a tool that finds and optionally replaces text in multiple text or RTF files in a single operation. (Multi-File Find and Replace doesn't work on DOC files because of the proprietary Word file format.)

multimedia Embedded sounds, video, or combined video and sound.

Nested list In HTML Help, a list where the first list is indented and the lists inside it are nested (indented to a greater degree).

NET act See *No Electronic Theft Act.*

NetHelp An open standard development platform for creating and viewing HTML-based online help.

Netscape NetHelp An uncompiled HTML-based help format that runs on Netscape Navigator.

New Project wizard In HTML Help, a tool that walks you through all the information RoboHelp HTML needs to create a new project.

No Electronic Theft Act A federal act, passed in 1997, that makes it a federal felony to digitize music from a CD without the expressed permission of the copyright owners.

non-scrolling region In WinHelp, an area at the top of a help window that stays visible while the remainder of the topic information scrolls. Non-scrolling regions are traditionally used to keep topic headings visible.

OEM Abbreviation for original equipment manufacturer. Typically refers to a manufacturer that makes a product that is then licensed to other companies for resale under their brand name.

online help project The suite of files containing topic text, graphics, formatting instructions, tables of contents, indexes, and so on that, when compiled, create an online help system.

OLE Acronym for object linking and embedding. See also *ActiveX*.

OLE controls A type of control that appears as a border when you view a dialog box in Dialog View in What's This? Help Composer.

online books In WinHelp, a type of custom project template used to create WinHelp with contents, index, and search tabs displayed in a WinHelp 2000 format.

page A single topic in a table of contents. Pages can also be used to display Web pages and run macros.

palette A collection of the colors Windows can display.

palette shift A flash on the screen and a change in the colors that are being displayed when a topic is displayed in a WinHelp file that requires colors not currently on the Windows palette.

pane In the RoboHELP Explorer, a frame that displays one of the RoboHELP components, such as the RoboHELP Explorer Project Manager or Topic List. Can also refer to nested work areas in an online help system that are dedicated to different tasks.

paragraph style In HTML Help, defines how text wraps and how text is displayed.

parameter list A list of parameters (also known as "parms") that a macro uses.

PAS file An internal map file created and maintained by RoboHELP for creating context-sensitive help with a Delphi application.

PC HelpDesk A tool for creating knowledge bases. A knowledge base is a collection of online resources, FAQs, tips, technical support information, bug reports, notes, and comments that is used to augment the primary documentation.

phrase compression In WinHelp, used to compile files that are under 100K in size. See also *compression*, *Hall compression*, and *Zeck compression*.

popup A hotspot that displays a topic temporarily in a small, self-sizing window.

popup link Specially formatted topic text that displays information in a popup window when clicked.

popup window A help window for popups whose size and general appearance are defined automatically. Popup windows stay as long as the user doesn't do anything on the screen, such as clicking the mouse or pressing a key, after which, they disappear.

Program macros In WinHelp, let you access external programs and files.

Project Manager A tool for managing the specific elements of your help files using a standard folder style.

Project Status report A summary report that shows the number of topics with each status classification such as "In Progress" or "Complete."

RBH file In WinHelp, an internal file created and maintained by RoboHELP for tracking information about the DOC and RTF files used in a project.

Related topic control In HTML Help, a type of control that displays a list of related topics. See also See Also links. each topic the button displays.

Related Topics link A hotspot that checks for See Also keywords (A-Keywords). Also known as a See Also hotspot.

relative path A reference to a file that implies the location of the file. For example, if the current project directory is E:\Foggan Drizzle, referring to a file simply as FDLOGO.GIF implies that the file will be found in E:\Foggan Drizzle as well. See also *absolute path*.

relative positioning The size and position of a window based on a percentage of the display screen. See also *absolute positioning*.

relative URL A form of relative addressing for URLs that omits some of the directory names and relies on the implicit location of the files. For example, if a Web page is based on `http://www.hedtke.com`, one could refer to the `http://www.hedtke.com/logo.gif` file simply as logo.gif. See also *URL*.

ReSize A tool that lets you resize images and change the depth of colors in the graphic.

RHB file In WinHelp, an internal file that tracks document properties and other information for a DOC or RTF file.

RHMMPLAY.DLL The RoboHELP multimedia DLL that provides extended multimedia features for WinHelp files.

rich text format See *RTF*.

ricochets Multiple levels of aliasing that occur when you are fixing broken links with aliases. (Ricochets are very hard to trace and debug.)

RoboHELP Explorer RoboHELP Explorer is a program for managing online help source files and projects, starting various help tools, and performing a wide range of maintenance and testing operations.

RoboHELP extension macros A set of macros that are not part of the standard WinHelp macro set. Instead, they are included as part of the RoboHELP redistributable DLLs.

ROBOHELP.DOT template A template that contains the styles used by RoboHELP as well as a number of internal macros necessary for RoboHELP to work in Word.

RTF A document exchange format that is recognized by many different word processors and applications; with this format, much formatting (such as bold, italic, font size, and the like) can be retained. These files containing the actual topic content that will appear in the online help. Also known as rich text format.

RTF file A file in RTF format. RTF files are the source documents for WinHelp files.

script A section of code, an executable file, or even a DOS batch file.

scripting engine In HTML Help, one or more DLLs that contain the information necessary to process the ActiveX Scripts on any given HTML page.

scripting host In HTML Help, a user's link to the server and the information it contains, usually a browser such as Netscape or Internet Explorer.

scroll limits A way of setting the smallest size, a table in an online help file can be before the horizontal scroll bar appears to minimize the amount of scrolling your users will need to do within a table.

Search dialog box Accessed from the Help menu to search for specific topics.

Search() macro Displays the Index tab of the Help Topics screen.

secondary window One of several other windows, in addition to the Main window, that you can use for displaying topics. Unlike popups, secondary windows remain up when the primary window has been closed. (For example, many of the "wizard" windows in programs like Word and Excel are secondary windows.)

See Also hotspot A hotspot that checks for See Also keywords (A-Keywords). Also known as a Related Topics link.

See Also keyword See *A-Keywords*.

See Also links Links that point the user to related topics that may be of interest.

segmented hypergraphic See *SHED graphic*.

self-sizing popups for Dynamic HTML Popup windows that do not need to use ActiveX or Java controls.

server side scripts Scripts that are more robust than client-side scripts. Server side scripts require a Web page manager in order to work with the server's files.

SHED graphic A bitmap graphic with embedded hotspots.

SHG file See *SHED graphic*.

shortcut buttons Simple button graphics that have been formatted as hotspots.

Shortcut control In HTML Help, a type of control that lets you insert a link to an executable program or a file.

Smart Index Wizard A tool in RoboHELP Explorer for automating the creation and maintenance of indexes and keywords.

Smart See Also button Automatically displays the topics for the A-Link keywords associated with the current topic without your having to specify them.

Software Video Camera A tool for creating video files of screen actions for tutorials or training purposes.

source control system A system that tracks the component files of a project.

source files Files containing the content that will appear in a compiled WinHelp file.

splash screen The image that appears when a new file, topic, or page is opened. Splash screens are usually used to display company or other information.

Splash Screen control In HTML Help, allows you to insert a graphic that is set to display for a few seconds and then automatically disappear. Used primarily at the start of applications.

standalone help An online help file that is not connected by context-sensitive links with an application.

startup macro In WinHelp, a macro that is run when the WinHelp file is opened.

static graphics Simple graphics; graphics that don't do anything when a user clicks on them.

style sheet An HTML text file listing formatting for all parts of your topic, including font choices and colors, background colors, or images.

subkeywords Keywords that are linked to other keywords so they appear as indented items beneath the associated keyword.

SVGA Monitors that can display from 256 colors or more and have a resolution of at least 800 × 600.

system menu See *Control menu.*

table of contents A hierarchical or outline view of the topics in the online help, usually organized into books containing topics or sets of topics and pages that refer to individual topics, external topics, and macros.

Table of contents control In HTML Help, allows you to embed the navigation window of the Table of Contents tab inside one of your topics.

table of contents links In HTML Help, a way of using the entries in the Table of Contents to let the user link to topics.

table of contents macros In WinHelp, used to provide links to multimedia files or external programs such as demos and program wizards.

text links In HTML Help, hyperlinks placed in the text of your topics that open a link when the user clicks on the associated text.

text-marker macros In WinHelp, macros that let you set text markers when a topic is displayed.

text-only context-sensitive help In HTML Help, provides simple text-based popup help to describe a screen item such as a field or a button. Also known as What's This? Help.

thumbnail A small image of a graphic for quick reference.

title Can be the project title, which appears in the title bar of the Contents window of the WinHelp file, or the topic title, which appears in the $ footnote and is used to reference the topic in the index.

TOC Abbreviation for table of contents.

TOC Composer A tool for reorganizing a help project, creating new entries in a TOC, and creating new topic headers. Also useful for creating a TOC for a help file.

topic See *help topic.*

topic entry macros In WinHelp, a macro that runs when the topic is displayed.

topic ID In WinHelp, a unique identifier for a topic. Topic IDs are entered with the # footnote. Each topic must have a topic ID.

Topic List A list of the topics and their attributes displayed in the RoboHELP Explorer.

topic number See *map number.*

Topic Properties report A report of information about your help topics and their properties.

Topic References report Shows the links, TOC and index (K-Keywords) entries, graphics, and macro references for each topic in the report.

training cards A set of WinHelp topics that appear in secondary windows. They are most typically used for intensive online tutorials and demonstrating specific procedures on a step-by-step basis.

transparent graphic When a topic is displayed containing a transparent graphic, WinHelp replaces the white pixels in the graphic with the background color of the window so that the graphic blends smoothly into the surrounding topic.

True Code Displays the reference to a graphic as a command statement. See also *Dynamic WYSIWYG.*

UIGNORE.TLX file A dictionary file that contains words to ignore when doing the spell check.

Uniform Resource Locator See *URL.*

Unreferenced Topics report Displays information on any topics that aren't accessible with the standard jumps, popups, table of contents and index entries, A-Lnks, aliases, or context-sensitive help.

URL Abbreviation for Uniform Resource Locator. An Internet address. URLs identify where to get information on the Internet or an intranet as well as how to get it (such as http for a Web page and ftp for an FTP site).

VAR Acronym for value-added reseller. VARs take a product, add other products or services, and resell the package.

VBP files The Visual Basic project file containing the files and resources in the project. (Visual Basic projects only.)

VGA Monitors that display up to 256 colors at 640 × 480.

visited link Any link that the user has clicked recently.

watermarks Graphics that appear as formatting for the topic background and the non-scrolling region.

WAV files The standard file format for sound files in Windows.

WebHelp A RoboHELP tool that allows you to deliver HTML help files and have your readers view them without regard to platform or browser.

What's This? help Provides quick popup help for individual options and controls in an application. Also known as text-only context-sensitive help.

What's This? Help Composer A tool for creating What's This? help.

WIN.INI file A file in the Windows folder that contains a number of settings for Windows and Windows programs, including WinHelp files and how they are displayed.

Window macros In WinHelp, macros that close and position windows, set size and position, toggle whether the help is on top of the other windows, and set the background color for the popup window.

window-level context-sensitive help In HTML Help, the standard context-sensitive help (as opposed to text-only context-sensitive help).

Windows bitmap See *bitmap*.

Windows CE Help An abbreviated version of HTML Help that runs on products using Windows CE, which is a version of Windows designed to run on handheld computers.

Windows Metafile See *WMF*.

WinHelp An online help file format for use exclusively on Windows computers.

WinHelp 2000 A three-paned WinHelp display that looks much like the standard HTML Help window. Also known as Explorer View Help.

WinHelp 3 The original 16-bit Windows help format. WinHelp 3 files will work on any Windows computer.

WinHelp 4 The 32-bit Windows help format introduced with Windows 95. WinHelp 4 files will work only on computers running Windows 9*x* or later.

WinHelp API The WinHelp Application Programming Interface, which communicates between programs and WinHelp files.

WinHelp Compatibility Wizard A tool for adding basic WinHelp 4 features — specifically, the standard Contents, Index, and Find tabs — to WinHelp 3 files.

WinHelp Find+ A full-text search in WinHelp that finds the topics that a word or phrase appears in and shows the number of occurrences of the search item in the text.

WinHelp Graphics Locator A tool used for viewing, locating, and copying graphics files.

WinHelp HyperViewer A tool that automatically creates a table of contents the user can expand and collapse headings in for the WinHelp 3 file using the links and structure of the help topics in the file.

WinHelp Inspector An older tool from eHelp (formerly Blue Sky) for analyzing WinHelp files that are already compiled. It works on WinHelp 3 files and some WinHelp 4 files that are not overly complex.

WinHelp topic control In HTML Help, allows you to link to any topic within a HLP file by topic title, topic ID, or map number. In WinHelp, a clickable object (usually a button) that opens a WinHelp system (.HLP file) and displays a WinHelp topic.

WMF Abbreviation for Windows metafile. A Microsoft Windows format that stores the information for an image as vectors instead of pixel information as most other image file formats do.

WYSIWYG Acronym for What You See Is What You Get. In HTML Help, acts like a window on your help project in action. It displays the HTML code behind your project as closely as possible like what your users will actually see.

Zeck compression Use Zeck compression with Phrase compression for greater compression of files under 100K. Use Zeck with Hall compression to maximize the compression for files over 100K. See also *compression*, *Hall compression*, and *phrase compression*.

Index

B

C

Continued

E

F

Continued

Continued

N

Continued

S

Continued

Continued

T

Continued

Continued

Continued

X

Z

IDG Books Worldwide, Inc.
End-User License Agreement

license agreements recorded on the Software Media. These limitations may include a requirement that after using the program for a specified period of time, the user must pay a registration fee or discontinue use. By opening the Software packet(s), you will be agreeing to abide by the licenses and restrictions for these individual programs that are detailed in Appendix G and on the Software Media. None of the material on this Software Media or listed in this Book may ever be redistributed, in original or modified form, for commercial purposes.

5. **Limited Warranty**.

   (a) IDGB warrants that the Software and Software Media are free from defects in materials and workmanship under normal use for a period of sixty (60) days from the date of purchase of this Book. If IDGB receives notification within the warranty period of defects in materials or workmanship, IDGB will replace the defective Software Media.

   (b) **IDGB AND THE AUTHORS OF THE BOOK DISCLAIM ALL OTHER WARRANTIES, EXPRESS OR IMPLIED, INCLUDING WITHOUT LIMITATION IMPLIED WARRANTIES OF MERCHANTABILITY AND FITNESS FOR A PARTICULAR PURPOSE, WITH RESPECT TO THE SOFTWARE, THE PROGRAMS, THE SOURCE CODE CONTAINED THEREIN, AND/OR THE TECHNIQUES DESCRIBED IN THIS BOOK. IDGB DOES NOT WARRANT THAT THE FUNCTIONS CONTAINED IN THE SOFTWARE WILL MEET YOUR REQUIREMENTS OR THAT THE OPERATION OF THE SOFTWARE WILL BE ERROR FREE.**

   (c) This limited warranty gives you specific legal rights, and you may have other rights that vary from jurisdiction to jurisdiction.

6. **Remedies**.

   (a) IDGB's entire liability and your exclusive remedy for defects in materials and workmanship shall be limited to replacement of the Software Media, which may be returned to IDGB with a copy of your receipt at the following address: Software Media Fulfillment Department, Attn.: *RoboHELP® 2000 Bible*, IDG Books Worldwide, Inc., 10475 Crosspoint Blvd., Indianapolis, IN 46256, or call 1-800-762-2974. Please allow three to four weeks for delivery. This Limited Warranty is void if failure of the Software Media has resulted from accident, abuse, or misapplication. Any replacement Software Media will be warranted for the remainder of the original warranty period or thirty (30) days, whichever is longer.

   (b) In no event shall IDGB or the authors be liable for any damages whatsoever (including without limitation damages for loss of business profits, business interruption, loss of business information, or any other pecuniary loss) arising from the use of or inability to use the Book or the Software, even if IDGB has been advised of the possibility of such damages.

(c) Because some jurisdictions do not allow the exclusion or limitation of liability for consequential or incidental damages, the above limitation or exclusion may not apply to you.

7. **U.S. Government Restricted Rights.** Use, duplication, or disclosure of the Software by the U.S. Government is subject to restrictions stated in paragraph (c)(1)(ii) of the Rights in Technical Data and Computer Software clause of DFARS 252.227-7013, and in subparagraphs (a) through (d) of the Commercial Computer—Restricted Rights clause at FAR 52.227-19, and in similar clauses in the NASA FAR supplement, when applicable.

8. **General.** This Agreement constitutes the entire understanding of the parties and revokes and supersedes all prior agreements, oral or written, between them and may not be modified or amended except in a writing signed by both parties hereto that specifically refers to this Agreement. This Agreement shall take precedence over any other documents that may be in conflict herewith. If any one or more provisions contained in this Agreement are held by any court or tribunal to be invalid, illegal, or otherwise unenforceable, each and every other provision shall remain in full force and effect.

CD-ROM Installation Instructions

There are three programs included on the CD-ROM:

- RoboHELP Office 2000 Test Drive
- Paint Shop Pro 6.02
- Media Center Plus 3

Each of the programs on the CD is a timed demo version of the full program. You can order the complete version of each program from the manufacturer. You should also check the manufacturer's Web sites for program updates, add-ons, and additional information.

For a brief overview of each of these programs and what they do, see Appendix G, "What's on the CD-ROM?"

Installing RoboHELP Office 2000 Test Drive

To install the 30-day timed demo version of RoboHELP Office 2000 Test Drive, do the following:

1. Insert the CD accompanying this book into your computer's CD-ROM drive.
2. Using Windows Explorer, open the \RoboHELP folder on the CD.
3. Double-click SETUP.EXE in the folder. The RoboHELP Office 2000 setup program will step you through the setup process. (This will be almost identical to the RoboHELP setup process described in Appendix E, "Installing RoboHELP Office 2000.")

Installing Paint Shop Pro 6.02

To install the 30-day timed demo version of Paint Shop Pro 6.02, do the following:

1. Insert the CD accompanying this book into your computer's CD-ROM drive.
2. Using Windows Explorer, open the \Paint Shop Pro folder on the CD.
3. Double-click SETUP.EXE in the folder. The Paint Shop Pro setup program will step you through the setup process.

Installing Media Center Plus 3

To install the 30-day timed demo version of Media Center Plus 3, do the following:

1. Insert the CD accompanying this book into your computer's CD-ROM drive.